ENGLISH HISTORICAL DOCUMENTS

General Editor

DAVID C. DOUGLAS

M.A., F.B.A.

ENGLISH HISTORICAL DOCUMENTS

General Editor: DAVID C. DOUGLAS, M.A., F.B.A.

The following is a complete list of volumes in preparation; those marked★ are already published, and those marked† are expected shortly.

GENERAL PREFACE

ENGLISH HISTORICAL DOCUMENTS is a work designed to meet a present need. Its purpose is to make generally accessible a wide selection of the fundamental sources of English history.

During the past half-century there has been an immense accumulation of historical material, but only a fraction of this has been made readily available to the majority of those who teach or who study history. The transcendent importance of the original authorities is recognized, but direct approach to them remains difficult, and even some of the basic texts (which are frequently quoted) are hard to consult. A gulf has thus opened between the work of the specialist scholar and those students, both at schools and universities, who best can profit by his labours. Historical studies tend too often today to consist of a commentary on documents which are not included in the available books; and, in the absence of any representative and accessible collection of the sources, the formation of opinion proceeds without that direct study of the evidence which alone can give validity to historical judgment.

The editors of these volumes consider that this situation calls for a remedy. They have striven to supply one by providing what they hope can be regarded as an authoritative work of primary reference.

An enterprise of this nature could be effective only if planned on a large scale. In scope and content, therefore, these volumes differ materially from the conventional 'source-books' which usually contain only a restricted number of selected extracts. Here, within much wider limits, the editors have sought to produce a comprehensive *corpus* of evidence relating generally to the period with which they deal. Their aim, in each case, has been to present the material with scholarly accuracy, and without bias. Editorial comment has thus been directed, in the main, towards making the evidence intelligible, and not to drawing conclusions from it. Full account has been taken of modern textual criticism to compile a reliable collection of authentic testimony, but the reader has in general been left to pass his own judgment upon it, and to appraise for himself the value of current historical verdicts. Critical bibliographies have been added to assist further investigation.

The material to be included in each volume naturally varies in accordance with the needs of each period as assessed by the editors. In the more modern periods the problem of selection inevitably becomes more acute, but, by way of compensation, it becomes possible, as in the present volume, to include a larger proportionate number of texts which have never before been printed.

Furthermore, in view of the existence of authoritative collections dealing more specifically with foreign policy, it has been deemed advisable, in the case of the nineteenth century, to concentrate rather more directly upon home affairs, and on the changes in the political, social and economic structure of England which occurred during that dynamic age. Special attention has been paid to the documentation of constitutional development, to social and economic statistics, and to public finance. The scope of the present volume, the unity of the period with which it deals, and the principles upon which the documents have been selected are explained by the editors in their general introduction.

All concerned in this Series are fully aware of the magnitude of the under-taking to which they have addressed themselves. They are conscious of the hazards of selecting from the inexhaustible store of historical material. They realize also the difficulties involved in editing so large a mass of very varied texts in accordance with the exigent demands of modern scholarship. They believe, however, that the essential prerequisite for the healthy development of English historical studies is wider acquaintance with the original authorities for English history. And they are content that their work should be judged by the degree to which they have succeeded in promoting this object.

DAVID DOUGLAS

VOLUME XI

ENGLISH HISTORICAL DOCUMENTS
1783 – 1832

ENGLISH
HISTORICAL DOCUMENTS

1783 – 1832

Edited by

A. ASPINALL

M.A., D.Litt.

Professor of Modern History in the University of Reading

and

E. ANTHONY SMITH

M.A.

Lecturer in Modern History in the University of Reading

New York

OXFORD UNIVERSITY PRESS

1959

EDITORS' PREFACE
AND ACKNOWLEDGEMENTS

THE problems of selection and compression inseparable from editorial work in a comparatively recent period of English history are so notoriously baffling and indeed insoluble that we propose to waste no time in making an elaborate apology for the omission of either topics or specific kinds of documents which our readers might have expected to see illustrated in the following pages. Whatever its shortcomings in these respects, this volume, we feel, has one substantial merit. It is something more than a compilation of easily accessible printed materials; it embodies the fruits of research extending over many years, and prints for the first time important documents from many private archives as well as from the great MS. collections in the Public Record Offices in London, Edinburgh, Belfast and Dublin, the British Museum, and elsewhere. It is therefore our pleasant duty to express our gratitude to the following owners of private MSS. for permission to quote from their papers: Her Majesty the Queen, Her Royal Highness the Princess Royal and the earl of Harewood, His late Royal Highness the duke of Brunswick and Lunebourg, Captain C. K. Adam, R.N., Lord Annaly, the marquess of Anglesey, Miss Madeline Arbuthnot, Mr. Robin Bagot, Mr. R. Bankes, his grace the duke of Buccleuch, Earl Camden, Earl Fitzwilliam and the trustees of the Fitzwilliam Settled Estates, Mr. George Fortescue, Earl Grey, the earl of Harrowby, Lord Hatherton, Mr. R. S. Herries, the late Mr. Henry Hobhouse, Mr. George Howard, the marquess of Lansdowne, the marquess of Londonderry, the earl of Lonsdale, the late Brigadier-General Madocks, the Countess Mountbatten, Sir John Murray, and Mr. J. Blackett-Ord (for a typescript copy of No. 242), his grace the duke of Northumberland, Sir Ernest Scott, Earl Spencer, the representatives of the Vyvyan family, and his grace the duke of Wellington. In addition, the owners, or former owners, of many MS. collections which have been either donated to or deposited in public institutions, including local Record Offices: some of these collections were studied whilst they were still in private hands.

Permission has been generously granted to include excerpts from works still under copyright. Our grateful thanks are therefore due to the Comptroller of H.M. Stationery Office and to the following owners of copyright: the Royal Historical Society (*The Formation of Canning's Ministry* and the *Correspondence of Charles Arbuthnot*, and *Parliamentary Papers of John Robinson*); the Navy Records Society (*Naval Miscellany*, vol. II); the duke of Wellington (*Journal of*

Mrs. Arbuthnot); Ernest Benn Ltd. (*Diary of Henry Hobhouse*); Cambridge University Press (J. H. Clapham: *Economic History of Modern Britain*, E. & A. G. Porritt: *The Unreformed House of Commons* and *The Letters of George IV*); Cassell & Co. Ltd. and Curtis Brown Ltd. (*Letters of George III*); J. M. Dent & Sons Ltd. and E. P. Dutton & Co. Inc. (*John Wesley's Journal*); Herbert Jenkins Ltd. (*Wellesley Papers*); John Lane, The Bodley Head Ltd. (*Letters of Hannah More*); John Murray Ltd. (Lord Broughton, *Recollections of a Long Life*); Oxford University Press (Harlow & Madden, *British Colonial Developments, 1774–1834*, and Pressnell, *Country Banking in the Industrial Revolution*).

The editors would also wish to thank Professor David Douglas for his encouragement and advice, given at every stage in the preparation of this volume; the publishers, who have been most helpful with questions of copyright; and, last but not least, the staffs of the Public Record Offices and County Record Offices, the British Museum and the other great libraries both in Great Britain and abroad, whose assistance in innumerable ways has been invaluable.

One or two small points remain to be explained. A few excerpts from Stanhope's *Pitt* have been corrected from the original MSS. in the Public Record Office and are therefore cited as *Chatham Papers*. To save space, the Treaties and Statutes (the reproduction of which is almost inevitable, though some are admittedly available in other source-books) have necessarily been drastically cut down (though we believe that these eliminations have not involved the omission of any point of importance); and phrases like 'His Majesty' have generally been shortened. In all the Bibliographies the place of publication is London, unless otherwise specified.

A. ASPINALL
E. ANTHONY SMITH

CONTENTS

C. THE ROYAL PREROGATIVE

(a) Choice of Ministers

(b) The right of dissolution

(c) The veto

(d) The Royal influence over the framing of policy

(e) The Royal control of patronage

Part II. PARLIAMENT PAGE

Part III. THE ADMINISTRATION OF JUSTICE

D. THE ADMINISTRATION AND REFORM OF THE CRIMINAL LAW

PART IV. LOCAL GOVERNMENT AND POOR LAW ADMINISTRATION

A. THE ORGANIZATION OF LOCAL GOVERNMENT

B. THE POOR LAWS AND THEIR ADMINISTRATION

B. INDUSTRY AND COMMUNICATIONS

(a) The Textile Industries

(b) The Industries of the Midlands

(c) The Coal Industry

(d) The Luddites

(e) The Restrictions on the Emigration of Artisans and the Export of Machinery

(f) Communications

(a) Road Transport

(b) Canals

(c) Railways

D. FACTORY LEGISLATION

(a) The Factory Children

(b) The Chimney Sweepers

E. TRADE UNIONS, CO-OPERATIVE SOCIETIES, FRIENDLY SOCIETIES AND SAVINGS BANKS

(a) Trade Unions

PART VII. THE EMPIRE

C. THE CANADIAN PROVINCES   PAGE

D. INDIA AND THE FAR EAST

E. CAPE COLONY

PART VIII. WARS AND FOREIGN POLICY

A. THE ARMY AS AN INSTRUMENT OF WAR AND POLICY
(a) Recruitment

(b) Conditions of Service

MAPS

TABLES

GENERAL INTRODUCTION

IT was the proud boast of educated eighteenth-century Englishmen that, under their Constitution, which was believed to be the envy and pride of the world, the model of all others, they had attained a greater measure of happiness and civil liberty than any other people had ever before enjoyed. It guaranteed a large measure of freedom–freedom of speech and of publication, freedom of the person, security of property. England had taught Europe that liberty was the foundation of true greatness, and so long as she retained her freedom she would never fail to dazzle her neighbours by her exploits. After 1789 England rather than France seemed to be the beacon of the civilized world, for Frenchmen had destroyed their aristocracy and their monarchy, and had overturned their other historic institutions, and their country consequently had forfeited its proud reputation as the model of civilization. England had become the foremost country in the world, surpassing all others in wealth, commerce, manufactures, naval and colonial power; and that astonishing progress was attributed not only to the wealth of her mineral resources, her progressive agriculture, her freedom from internal trade barriers, but also to peculiarly favourable social and political conditions. As was often pointed out, too, there were no privileged orders, as in pre-Revolutionary France, possessing a monopoly of the honours and dignities of the State. Said Canning, "It is one of the peculiar boasts of this country, one of the prime fruits of its free Constitution, and one main security for its continuing free, that men as humble as myself [his mother was an actress] with no pretensions of wealth or title or high family or wide-spreading connexions, may yet find their way into the Cabinet of their Sovereign, through the fair road of public service, and stand there upon a footing of equality with the proudest aristocracy of the land."

According to its eighteenth-century panegyrists the English Constitution was neither monarchical nor aristocratic nor democratic, but a mixed Constitution in which all three elements shared power, its movements being made regular and safe by an elaborate system of checks and balances, preserving the country from the evils of absolute monarchy, aristocratic oligarchy and democratic upheaval. The Revolution of 1688 had destroyed the absolutism of the Crown and had made it impossible for the king to govern without the consent and co-operation of Parliament.

Montesquieu had praised the English Constitution as providing without excessive friction a balance of power between King, Lords and Commons. The power of the purse possessed by the House of Commons was an effective check on the sovereign. The right of the Crown to create peers was an effective check on the House of Lords. The right of the Crown to dissolve Parliament and to veto Bills was an effective check on the Legislature as a whole. But it was felt that the operation of such severe checks, involving a head-on collision between powerful rival forces, would give a severe shock to the whole machinery of government and impair its efficiency and security. The Fox-North majority in the Commons at the beginning of 1784 shrank from such an extreme step as the withholding supplies from the Crown as a means of enforcing the resignation of the minister clinging to power without the confidence of the House. George III preferred to influence the votes of the peers in December 1783 rather than to exercise his veto, when he sought to procure the rejection of Fox's odious India Bill. If the sovereign were to veto a series of popular Bills sent up by the Commons, or if the Lords rejected them, a constitutional crisis of the first magnitude would ensue (as actually happened during the struggle for the Reform Bill in 1831–1832). If, on the other hand, the sovereign were to accept as a matter of course every Bill which had passed the Commons, whilst he and his servants had no effective influence over their deliberations, the power of the Crown would be gone and the government would become virtually a republic.

The House of Lords, it was felt, would be an even less formidable barrier than the Crown to popular legislation. The balance of the Constitution had been endangered since 1688 by the growing power and influence of the House of Commons, exercised through its exclusive control of supplies, the dependence of the king's ministers on the support of a majority in the House, and its connexion with the physical force of the nation. If the lower House were to be composed entirely of the representatives of the people, it would inevitably transform the government into a pure democracy, sweeping away the power of the Crown and of the aristocracy. Checks on the power of the Commons had to be devised which would operate smoothly, without the risk of disturbance. If either the Crown or the peers were hostile to a Bill which was being discussed in the Commons, opposition to the measure must be directed against it whilst it was still there, so as to avoid the shock of rejection either by the peers or by the sovereign. Conflict between Crown and Commons, or between the two Houses, could best be avoided if the Crown and the peers could influence the deliberations of the Commons by securing representation there. Through the 'influence' of the Crown, the king's ministers and a substantial phalanx of placemen secured seats in the Commons. More than half the members of the House were connected with the peerage by birth or marriage, or else owed their seats to individual peers. So the House of Commons represented not the people but the aristocracy, the people and the Crown—and in that order of importance. And the Crown and the aristocracy exercised their restrictive functions, not *against* the House of Commons, but *in* it; not directly but indirectly, through their ability to secure representation in the House. And so the 'balance' of the Constitution existed in the Commons, and the representation of the Crown and the House of Lords in the House of Commons was seen to be essential to the preservation of our 'mixed' government.

Before the end of the eighteenth century, parliamentary reformers had discovered, or rather rediscovered, a danger to the balance of the Constitution and to the independence of the Commons: the royal influence in the House was now *over*-represented. Hence Dunning's famous motion (which echoed Bolingbroke's views in the 1730s) that "the influence of the Crown has increased, is increasing and ought to be diminished". The number of placemen must be cut down, and the enormous patronage at the Crown's disposal must be reduced. On the question whether the aristocracy too was over-represented in the Commons, the reformers were divided. Many of them would be content to reduce the influence of the Crown and to disfranchise the 'rotten' boroughs where bribery and corruption had been proved to exist, leaving the aristocracy in possession of the 'nomination' boroughs, and increasing the number of county members–a change which, in the absence of secret voting, was calculated actually to *increase* the representation of the aristocracy. These reformers considered that, with the rapid expansion of trade and industry, the whole landed interest, of which the peerage formed only part, had become scarcely a match for the moneyed interest, either in Parliament or in society.

Only the less discerning of the reformers wished to *destroy* the influence of the Crown by ejecting all placemen from the Legislature. That solution had been seen to be impracticable as long ago as Anne's reign. And the later remedy for the excessive 'influence' of the Crown arising from control of patronage –the creation of an independent civil service, recruited impartially by public competitive examination–was beyond the imagination of most of the early parliamentary reformers, and was in any case impracticable until the emergence of political parties of the modern type made possible the development of the idea of party loyalty replacing patronage as the 'cement' of politics.

George III had been king for twenty-three years when the period covered by this volume opens. With a very modest intellectual endowment, he was, nevertheless, as superior to his two immediate predecessors as his granddaughter was to hers. His court, like Victoria's, was a model of decorum. He was unswervingly faithful to his prim, austere, unattractive wife, Charlotte of Mecklenburg-Strelitz, who bore him fifteen children. No evidence has come to light that he ever sought improper relations with any other woman until he became insane. His simple tastes, his frugality, his love of country life and of farming, his courage (displayed during the terrible Lord George Gordon riots of 1780 and on every occasion when attempts were made on his life) and his quite remarkable devotion to duty, were qualities which endeared him to his people. Thus it was that the monarchy remained firmly rooted in the loyalty and affection of its subjects at a time when crowned heads were everywhere else threatened, either by the forces of revolution or by the armies of Napoleon, from Lisbon to Vienna, from Stockholm to Naples. The Radical journalist Cobbett, who referred to the House of Brunswick as "a set of beggarly Germans put upon the throne and kept there by a band of boroughmongers as mere tools in their hands", acknowledged that it was "quite impossible for any writer to be more unpopular than I am".

It must be admitted that George III's outlook was narrow (he himself regretted his want of education); that he was a man with strong prejudices, obstinate, tenacious of his resentments. He never visited the Continent: he merely contemplated a non-return journey to his electorate in 1783 and again in 1809 when abdication seemed preferable to surrender to the Whigs. He never set foot in Scotland or Ireland (nor did George IV except for a few days in 1821, his coronation year; nor did William IV when king). On rare occasions he had a seaside holiday–at Weymouth–and once he actually went as far from London as Lord Boringdon's home near Plymouth. More frequently he inspected the fleet at Chatham and Portsmouth, and the troops at Maidstone or elsewhere in the Home Counties. But he knew nothing of the great new centres of industry that were springing up in the Midlands and the North, or of the grave social problems arising from these changes.

The king governed on the advice of a body of ministers whose collective existence was unknown to the law. The old confusion about the composition of the Cabinet now came to an end. In spite of the extraordinary series of errors in the lists of Cabinet ministers in such works as the *Annual Register*, Cobbett's *Parliamentary Debates*, and all the textbooks, there is no longer any doubt about the composition of the Cabinets of this period. And there was but one instance of an ex-Cabinet minister claiming the right to retain membership of the new Cabinet: in 1801 Loughborough, the outgoing Lord Chancellor, attended several meetings of Addington's Cabinet after his successor had received the Great Seal. Addington soon put an end to a disagreeable and embarrassing situation by informing him politely but firmly that his presence was not desired. Henceforth, privy councillors who were not 'confidential servants' of the king attended the Cabinet to give advice only when invited to do so; and these occasions were not frequent. With few exceptions membership of the Cabinet was confined to ministers holding the great offices of State and in charge of the most important Departments.

The second most important difference between the Cabinets of this period and earlier ones lies in the fact that the 'Departmental' system was giving way to that of joint Cabinet advice: the Cabinet was growing in cohesion and solidarity. Hitherto, ministers had generally been considered as individually

GENERAL INTRODUCTION 5

responsible to king and Parliament for their actions and advice, and George III
had therefore been, in a real sense, his own Prime Minister, the effective as well
as the nominal head of the executive. When Fox and North planned their
coalition in 1783, they considered the question whether the king should still be
allowed to be "his own Minister". Fox urged the "necessity of governing
independent of the King", whereupon North replied,

> "If you mean by that, that there should not be a Government of Depart-
> ments, I agree with you. I think it a very bad thing. In this country some
> one man or some body of men like a Cabinet should govern the whole and
> direct every measure. However, the Government of Departments was not
> brought about by me when I came into His Majesty's Government. I found
> it so, and I am ready to confess that I had not sufficient vigour and resolution
> to put an end to it. But I am clearly of opinion that the King should be
> treated with all sort of respect and attention–and indeed, the appearance of
> power is all that a King of this country can have, for though the Government
> in my time was a Government of Departments, yet the whole was done by
> the Ministers except in a few instances."

The alternative theory of joint Cabinet responsibility, which implies unanimity of political opinion, at any rate on questions affecting the honour and
credit of the government, common responsibility to Parliament, and submission
to a Prime Minister enjoying the largest share of the king's confidence, was
gradually to be worked out during the next half-century, but it could not
become fully translated into practice until the king had ceased to govern and
merely reigned, his place as head of the government being taken by the Prime
Minister. Fox and the Whigs professed to believe in the virtues of joint Cabinet
responsibility, but in 1806, when defending the appointment of Lord Chief
Justice Ellenborough to the Cabinet, Fox seemed to repudiate his own doctrine.
He was, however, taking a narrow, legalistic view, which meant not joint
Cabinet responsibility to Parliament involving loss of office if the Cabinet failed
to retain the confidence of the Commons, but the legal responsibility and
liability to impeachment of a single member of the Cabinet for his illegal
actions. The parliamentary debates on this question show that the Tories had
come to accept this idea of collective responsibility as an article of their creed.

The documents, however, illustrate not merely the progress of this doctrine
but the incomplete acceptance of it in practice. It was still possible for a minister
to retain office though disagreeing with his colleagues on questions of first-rate
importance, and for the king to be informed of such differences. Cabinet
disunity was further revealed whenever he demanded individual opinions, and
when, in the absence of a formal dissenting minute, the names of the minority
were sent to him. In theory, individual consultation and the recording of

minority views (as well as the presence of "King's friends" such as Thurlow in the Cabinet) were calculated to afford useful opportunities for intrigue on the king's part, but there is little evidence that they did so. George IV knew in Sept. 1822 that several members of the Cabinet shared his hostility to the appointment of Canning as Foreign Secretary, but all of them had to acquiesce in the Prime Minister's determination to enforce the views of the majority; the alternative would probably have been the dissolution of the government. The loyalty of Liverpool's colleagues was always proof against the undermining tactics of George IV, who in 1824 tried to get rid of Canning (being thoroughly dissatisfied with the proposal to recognize the independence of the former Spanish-American colonies) by typically eighteenth-century methods of back-stairs intrigue; but Canning received effective support from the Prime Minister and the Cabinet majority. The non-existence of a genuine two-party system – the fact that parties still consisted of assortments of 'connexions' and 'interests' – accounts for differences of opinion in the Cabinet as in the House of Commons on such important questions as Catholic emancipation, parliamentary reform, the repeal of the Test and Corporation Acts, and the abolition of the slave trade. On these 'open' questions ministers agreed to disagree.

The development of the office of Prime Minister has been touched upon in the previous volume of this series. All that need be said here is that this development was a necessary consequence of the destruction of royal absolutism in 1688 and the establishment of parliamentary supremacy. The king had to govern through ministers, and, he himself having withdrawn from the Cabinet (or, more correctly, the Cabinet having withdrawn from him), it was necessary that one of their number should replace him at the head, so that conflicting opinions could be reconciled and decisions taken. There could be no real collective responsibility of the Cabinet either to king or Parliament without the primacy of one of its members, and the First Lord of the Treasury, who had the largest amount of political patronage to dispose of, was normally that person. "In critical times", Lord North had written, "it is necessary that there should be one directing Minister who should plan the whole of the operations of Government and control all the other Departments of Administration, so as to make them co-operate zealously and actively with his designs even though contrary to their own." The disasters which overtook the country during the remaining years of the American war convinced most people of the necessity of a Prime Minister, and the perilous situation during the struggle against revolutionary and Napoleonic France taught the same lesson. Pitt's controlling influence was everywhere felt, and his career is an important landmark in the development of the premiership. Controlling finance and the armed forces, the Commons had long since become the more important of the two Houses of Parliament. Recognizing this, Pitt never wished for a peerage, and most of his eminent followers shared his view that the Prime Minister should be in the Commons. Personal rivalries frequently dictated another solution so long as the Tories remained in power. As for the Whigs, who returned to office after nearly half a century of opposition (apart from the brief interlude of 1806–1807), the great families had always regarded power as something to be shared amongst themselves rather than monopolized by an individual, and Grey, disapproving of the alleged dictatorship of Wellington (1828–1830), had no wish to follow the duke's example. He left to each of his Cabinet colleagues "full latitude to manage his Department in accordance with his own judgment". "Counsel of the Cabinet will then be a veritable counsel, and the dictatorship is abolished."

Peel, not Pitt, was the first Prime Minister of the modern type. His predecessors were different in these ways. First, the Prime Minister was not necessarily the person chosen by the sovereign to form the government. Second, whenever two or more exceptionally able men competed for the premiership, their claims, if irreconcilable, had to be passed over in favour of a nominal, or 'dummy' Prime Minister (*e.g.* Portland in 1783 and in 1807–1809). Third, the Prime Minister's resignation was not necessarily considered as dissolving his ministry. Fourth, he was not always free to choose his Cabinet colleagues. Fifth, he was not necessarily the minister who enjoyed the largest share of the king's confidence. Sixth, the Prime Minister was not the leader of a homogeneous party which comprised a majority of the members of the House of Commons.

Even Pitt did not feel strong enough to insist that the king must receive advice only from the Cabinet. Portland, though an opponent of Catholic emancipation, was clearly perturbed on hearing (March 1795) that George III had been shown letters from Lord Fitzgibbon, the Lord Chancellor of Ireland, calculated to "prejudice his mind and to alarm his conscience" against further concessions to the Catholics. "If this is to be the practice", commented the duke, who, as Home Secretary, was responsible for the government of Ireland, "no Government can go on in Ireland, and I believe there are not two opinions in the *greater part* of the Cabinet respecting it."

George III (and his sons) ruled as well as reigned.

The power of the Crown had never been precisely defined, and, consequently, was a matter of controversy. Since 1688 the king had been statutorily disabled from ruling without the co-operation of Parliament, whose consent was necessary for the imposition of taxation, the making of laws, and maintaining an army in time of peace. His power rested on his right to choose the Prime Minister, and he retained that right until the development after 1832 of a real two-party system, based on an enlarged electorate, in effect transferred that right to the House of Commons. Pitt was not "the choice of the people". He was the choice of the king, and he remained the king's minister only so long as he retained the king's confidence. Addington did not become Prime

Minister in 1801 because he was a party leader commanding the votes of a substantial portion of the House of Commons. As Speaker he had had no following of any sort; he became a party leader when he became Prime Minister, and he was chosen because his anti-Catholic views were acceptable to the king, and because he was popular with the country gentlemen in the House.

Everyone recognized that a new sovereign was perfectly at liberty to change his ministers as well as to 'choose' another House of Commons (until 1867 a general election had to follow a demise of the Crown). Pitt would have been dismissed in 1789 had the Prince of Wales become regent; nothing but the king's timely recovery of his senses saved him. More than forty years later no one would have raised an eyebrow had William IV, on his accession, chosen a Prime Minister other than Wellington.

In March 1807 as in Dec. 1783 George III showed in no uncertain fashion that no government could long survive which did not possess his confidence.

Nor was the king's right to choose his servants restricted to his choice of First Minister. George III's veto against Fox, his personal as well as political enemy, endured from 1783 to 1806. Similarly, George IV's veto against Grey lasted throughout his reign, though it might have been overcome whilst Wellington was Prime Minister (1828–1830), for the king's hostility to Grey was no stronger than his hostility to Canning in 1821–1822, but the duke, reluctant to share power with so able a man, did not really want him in the Cabinet. Wellington did insist on the appointment of the Whig Lord Rosslyn as Privy Seal in May 1829, and he doubtless made known at Windsor the Cabinet's determination to resign if its advice was rejected.

The continued existence of the power of the Crown (though that power was tending to decline) is further seen in (a) the extent to which the sovereign had an effective share in the framing of policy and an effective veto on measures which he strongly disapproved; (b) the right which he still possessed to seek and to act on advice from persons other than his responsible ministers; and (c) the extent to which he still controlled patronage.

(a) George III's direct and continuous supervision of administration and policy after 1783, though less than it had been, was not negligible. He was the most conscientious of monarchs; none has ever taken his duties more seriously. Always an early riser, he often started to answer letters at seven in the morning, and, when business pressed, he would still be writing late at night. He read all important dispatches before they were sent abroad. He saw several times a week those ministers whose duties brought them into personal contact with him. In the exercise of the prerogative of mercy he carefully examined the case of every convict capitally convicted at the Old Bailey Sessions. No important appointments to offices, civil, military or ecclesiastical, were made without his consent.

His activities came, indeed, to be limited by increasing bodily and mental infirmities, and, after the recovery of his sanity in Feb. 1789, he wrote to Pitt: "I must decline entering into a pressure of business, and indeed for the rest of my life shall expect others to fulfil the duties of their employments, and only keep that superintending eye which can be effected without labour or fatigue." Failing sight compelled him in 1805 to employ a private secretary (Colonel, afterwards Sir, Herbert Taylor) to whom he dictated his letters; he continued to sign them in an increasingly shaky hand until, in 1810, he became permanently insane as well as blind. His son, the prince regent, never sought to exercise that same continuous and conscientious control. Absorbed in the pursuit of sensual pleasures, his interventions in matters of State were spasmodic and unpredictable, and, during the last years of the reign, his own physical and mental condition greatly deteriorated, necessitating the employment of a private secretary, though ministerial objections on constitutional grounds withheld from Sir William Knighton the actual title after the dismissal of his predecessor, Sir Benjamin Bloomfield, in 1822. George IV certainly never scrutinized Foreign Office documents with half that care and attention given them either by his father or by his brother William IV. Wellington, indeed, alleged in 1823 that George IV had never before corrected a dispatch. By 1825 his indolence was becoming painfully embarrassing to his ministers. He was apt to stay in bed for most of the day. Cabinet boxes containing papers requiring his signature if not his perusal, sometimes lay for weeks unopened.

Yet in spite of the lamentable shortcomings of George IV and his successor, there was little republican feeling in England; its absence illustrates the essential conservatism of the nation so far as its ancient institutions were concerned. George III's sons were criticized in the Press with that freedom of comment which goes with acceptance of the monarchy.

By the Constitution, ministers were responsible both to king and Parliament for the measures they proposed. As the sovereign possessed, by his prerogative, the power to change his ministers if they proposed something to which he strongly objected, the Constitution presumed that every act or measure of the administration had, by the fact of their continuance in office, the sovereign's sanction. Very exceptional circumstances, therefore, created the necessity to exercise the royal veto. Though it had not, in fact, been used since Anne's reign, George III was advised in March 1807 that it was not obsolete, and that he might properly have recourse to it, if the necessity arose, in order to prevent the passage into law of the Catholic Relief Bill sponsored by the 'Talents'. Moreover, the veto was customarily exercised in a preliminary form: no ministers could even introduce a Bill into Parliament which had not received the king's previous consent. Thus George III would never have allowed them to introduce a comprehensive Catholic Relief Bill, and William IV said in 1831 that he would never agree to a Bill embodying either secret voting at parliamentary elections, or universal suffrage, or annually elected Parliaments.

(b) Every sovereign, especially when he was planning a change of government, was ready to accept advice from persons other than his ministers, though the practice was beginning to be considered improper. It was indulged in much less frequently by George III after 1783 than by his successor, and Canning remarked in 1825 that all parties agreed in taking the former as "the model of an English King". Pitt avoided all direct communication with George III during the years (1801–1804) when he was out of office.

(c) The principle had not yet become fully established that patronage must be dispensed only on the advice of ministers. All sovereigns continued to control it to some extent; all Prime Ministers tried to keep a close hold on it, weak ones like Goderich being less successful than determined men like Liverpool and Wellington.

"I fear that the true kingly authority of this country is fast passing away", George IV wrote to Wellington in 1828. To this state of affairs he himself had powerfully contributed. The factors which were tending to diminish the power of the Crown even before 1835 when, as a result of the Reform Act, William IV realized that he was no longer in a position to nominate his Prime Minister, will be briefly touched upon presently.

The prevailing political thought believed that that country is the happiest in which the aristocracy is in effective political control. Rank, wealth and official position constituted important sources of influence over individuals, and it seemed right and proper that, whilst every class should be represented in the Legislature, rank, wealth and office should be predominant.

The composition and character of the House of Lords underwent significant changes between 1783 and 1832: changes reflecting, first, the immense social and economic transformation of the country, and, second, the increasing difficulty, after the 'economical' reforms of the Rockingham Whigs had deprived the Crown of some of its means of reward by the abolition of pensions and sinecures, of forming and maintaining an administration without frequent recourse to the granting of hereditary honours for political services.

In 1783 the Upper House consisted of 238 members, including the 16 Scottish representative peers and 26 bishops. The Union of 1801 added 28 Irish representative peers and 4 bishops. To strengthen his position in both Houses, Pitt, who, like his father, was unfettered by aristocratic prejudice, increased the number of peers by nearly 50 per cent (apart from a large number of new Irish peerages which did not affect the composition of the House of Lords); and his successors added many more. Lord Liverpool alone, during his premiership of nearly 15 years, was responsible for 56 new members of the House and for 30 promotions; and Lord Grey, Premier from 1830 to 1834, was no less backward with his recommendations, which were designed to redress in favour of the Whigs the balance of Tory creations during the preceding 40 years. The 9 new peers created between 1784 and 1792 controlled, directly or indirectly, 24 seats in the Commons. Pitt's policy has often been severely criticized as corrupting the House of Lords, degrading it morally and intellectually, demeaning the peerage by introducing into its ranks the *nouveaux riches*, the representatives of commercial and banking interests, and transforming it from a predominantly progressive into a reactionary body which, by rejecting the Reform Bill in 1831, brought the country near to revolution. The practice of granting peerages to proprietors of boroughs in return for seats for ministerial nominees did not originate with Pitt. With no veneration for the great families which had dominated English politics since 1714, Pitt swamped the Whig oligarchs by his numerous creations, and in so doing brought much-needed new blood into the peerage, including the ablest soldiers, sailors and diplomatists of the period. In accordance with the classical eighteenth-century doctrine that the peerage must always represent property, it was time that forms of capital other than land were represented. And, among the peers whose titles were derived from Pitt, a majority voted for the second reading of the Reform Bill on 14 April 1832. Pitt, said Turberville, was "ultimately responsible for the rapid transformation of the House from a small and highly exclusive assemblage into a large body, rather more representative of the body politic than it had been, though still standing essentially for the interests of property". This transformation was in any case inevitable, and was largely the work of his successors. A peerage irremovable and hereditary, having co-ordinate jurisdiction with the other estates of the realm, would have become master of the country but for the sovereign's right to add to its numbers.

Whilst this considerable infusion of popular feeling into the deliberations of the House of Lords was in progress, the representation of the Church of England remained stationary, with the result that the Establishment, which had always been considered capable of turning most questions according to the scale into which it threw its weight, suffered a sensible diminution of its influence. Reformers indeed calculated in 1831 that whilst the influence of the aristocracy *had* increased, it had done so only in proportion to the influence of the other classes in the community, but the bishops were only one-seventh as dangerous as they had been at the beginning of George III's reign.

Both George III and Pitt became somewhat uneasy about the 'inconvenient' size of the peerage after some years of the vigorous exercise of the prerogative. Pitt's "uncommon share of good nature", said his colleague, George Rose, caused him to give way to solicitations which he should have resisted. "So far from gaining political strength thereby . . . he suffered by them, for it frequently happened that an enemy was chosen in the room of the newly-created peer."

The aristocracy remained the chief depository of executive power; down to 1834 at least half the Cabinet ministers sat in the House of Lords, and the proportion was often two or three to one.

The wealthy peer with a seat in the Lords either for life or for the duration of a Parliament, and a rich commoner who bought his seat in the Lower House, had substantially identical interests, lived in the same society, were educated at the same public schools and universities, and were often enough connected by family attachments. So long as the aristocracy preserved its ascendancy in the Commons, the danger of serious constitutional conflict between the two Houses was negligible; but even before the passing of the Reform Bill there were indications of impending trouble. The increased representation of commercial and manufacturing interests, and the impact of the new ideas of *laissez-faire* on the minds of the liberal Tories after 1820, were reflected, for example, in the legislation affecting the corn trade. The Corn Bill of 1827 which was a compromise between the views of the agricultural interests and those of free traders, easily passed the Commons but was rejected by the peers in the form of Wellington's wrecking amendment; and the Bill of 1828 had to embody more concessions to the protectionists than their opponents could have wished, in order to facilitate its acceptance by the peers.

At the beginning of George III's reign the House of Commons comprised three groups: the politicians (themselves divided between the 'ins' and the 'outs'); the placemen (the king's personal representatives); and the Independents, the members unconnected with party. To what extent does this classification hold good during the first three decades of the nineteenth century?

Writing in 1812 Charles Wynn, M.P. for Montgomeryshire, said that since he had been in Parliament (since 1797) there had usually been only three parties in the House–the 'ins', the 'outs' and the Independents. He admitted that there were more in 1812–that the 'ins' and the 'outs' had split into various groups because of the want of distinguished men "to two of whom we all should naturally look up as leaders, and in whose ranks all the minor squads would unite".

The essential difference between the situation in 1760 and that in 1812 was that these two parties, the 'ins' and the 'outs' *were* parties, not factions; united not merely by the desire, in the one case, to retain power and in the other to gain it, but also to an appreciable extent by common political ideas on major points of domestic and foreign policy. Moreover, Wynn drew no distinction between the placemen and the 'ins', because by 1812 the rule had become established that the placemen were politicians, who would naturally resign with ministers when there was a complete change.

So long as the sovereign retained the right to choose his ministers and was able freely to exercise it, opposition could plausibly be stigmatized almost as disloyalty to the throne. Politicians in opposition could be represented to be the king's personal enemies–and George III certainly considered Fox in that light. Systematic or 'formed' opposition made it appear as if "men, not measures" was the criterion of praise or blame. The 'ins' could denounce the 'outs' as a mere factious league of place-hunters: a view which seemed to be strengthened by a contemplation of the ease with which men, long and inveterately opposed to each other, like Fox and North during the American war, could suddenly lay aside their hostility and unite in an apparently factious scramble for power. Such coalitions seemed to mark the profligate abandonment of public principle for private gain.

'Systematic' opposition, then, was generally deprecated because it challenged the right of the Crown to choose the ministers; moreover, during the greater part of this period, when the country was engaged in the most formidable war in its long history, 'formed' opposition seemed almost unpatriotic. The view that all party feelings should be laid aside (and also, incidentally, that the last years of an aged and beloved sovereign should be entirely peaceful, unpunctuated by factious and party bickerings) was constantly expressed. Systematic opposition could be justified only when ministers, by their conduct, clearly proved themselves unfit for their situations. Wilberforce was certain that very great misfortune had resulted from the progress of party. "I am more of a patriot, I flatter myself, than a party man", another member declared in 1789. "To be of a party", remarked Lord Sheffield in 1784, "may be necessary in some respects, but it is attended with obloquy." Shelburne went so far as to say that it was unconstitutional, for it tended to restrict the king's power and might on occasion "force the Closet". In 1809 Robert Dundas entered Perceval's Cabinet. A year later, at the time of the second regency crisis, his father, Lord Melville, warned him that although, as a Cabinet minister, it was his duty to act in co-operation with his colleagues, he must not embark with them "on the footing of a party man". Wellington would not go so far as that when *he* joined the government in 1818, but he agreed to do so only on the understanding that, in the event of ministers being turned out, he should not be considered as pledged to follow them as a party in opposition to the sovereign.

Ideally, therefore, the government should consist of men unconnected with party, men chosen from all parts of the House for their ability to serve their king. George III was false to his own ideal of non-party government in May 1804, when his hostility to Fox prevented the formation of a truly national government. The necessity of a non-party ministry in war-time was widely recognized. Lord Grenville then said that the aim should be to unite in the public service "as large a proportion as possible of the weight, talents and character to be found in public men of all descriptions, and without any exception".

In the 1780s the Whigs acted as their predecessors had done during the reigns of the first two Georges: they attempted to remove the taint of faction by connecting themselves with the heir-apparent, who used the 'reversionary' influence of the Crown to build up his own party. During the last years of Lord Liverpool's ministry the ultra Tories looked to George IV's brother and heir-presumptive, the duke of York, as their hope and their leader, and, after his death in Jan. 1827, to the duke of Cumberland, though he spent most of his time in Hanover, the kingdom to which he succeeded in 1837. Neither of these brothers, however, sought to act against the king; they wished merely to fortify his anti-Catholic prejudices, and, in Cumberland's case, to prevent him from falling completely under the domination of 'Duke Arthur'. Ironically enough, though every sovereign disliked party as restrictive of the royal authority, Cumberland in 1829 was profoundly thankful that there *were* political parties in existence which could keep ministers in check. "If that was not the case, they would certainly be *paramount* to the Sovereign", he said. His party of ultra Tories called themselves "the King's friends".

After the renewal of the war in 1803, Pitt became increasingly dissatisfied with Addington as Prime Minister, but he remained decidedly of opinion that the king ought not to be *forced* to change the government, and that the only proper way to achieve that result was to expose in the House the incapacity of ministers, thereby opening the king's eyes to the reality of the situation, and making it impossible for him to suppose that they were doing very well because little criticism of their measures had been voiced. Before Pitt ventured to go into open opposition, he wrote to the king on 21 April 1804, through the Lord Chancellor, explaining why he reluctantly proposed to do so, and making it clear that he would not join with Fox and Grenville in a binding engagement which might cause the king "dissatisfaction or uneasiness".

The events of 1806 further illustrate the unpopularity of the idea of a 'formed' opposition. Pitt's colleagues felt unable to carry on the government after his death, and the king was necessarily compelled to fall back on the Whigs, the Grenvilles and the Addingtons who had been in opposition. They could hardly be said to have "stormed the Closet", as Fox and North had done in 1783, and Pitt's friends felt that it would be improper to organize an opposition. The king in fact made known to the nation his support of the new ministers by creating peers, and that circumstance helps to account for the government's comfortable majority in the Commons. No opposition was formed until the Catholic question came into the foreground and occasioned the famous quarrel between the king and his ministers. Even as late as the middle of March 1807 Canning, one of the leading 'outs', was negotiating with Grenville to be brought in with some of his friends.

The forty ministers and placemen who resigned in April 1827 rather than acquiesce in George IV's choice of Canning as Prime Minister were in a similarly embarrassing position; they and their friends could not, with any consistency, go into opposition to the minister of the king's own choice. Toryism was a creed which suited only men in power. Then, four years later, those Tories who opposed the Reform Bill (which seemed to have the enthusiastic support of the king–for he agreed to dissolve Parliament after the Bill had been defeated in the Commons) were again in a quandary, from which they tried to escape by suggesting that this poor, weak, deluded monarch was half-mad.

One of the benefits which, it was believed, would result from the Reform Bill was a lessening of the importance of party and an increase in the independence of members. A reformed Parliament would be far less under the domination of party spirit, far less a prey to faction than the old House of Commons. Ironically enough, the creation of a mass electorate after a further instalment of parliamentary reform in 1867, by developing the party machine, destroyed the independence of members far more effectually than did the "influence of the Crown" in the eighteenth century.

The mid-eighteenth-century politicians had called themselves Whigs and Tories, meaningless though those labels had become; nevertheless they survived, and at the end of the century, as at the beginning, they did mean something. That was the result, partly of the sharp division of opinion on the issues of the French Revolution and the ensuing war. Under the leadership of Fox and Pitt the politicians were again acting together because they had certain political opinions in common which they considered sufficiently important to be a bond of union. That is why they were no longer little more than factions, as they had been in 1760. Fox's friends after 1792 opposed the French war as an unjustifiable interference by the reactionary European Powers with the right of an independent country to choose its own form of government. Those members who supported Pitt's war policy did so because they believed that the aggressive conduct of the revolutionary dictatorship in Paris threatened the independence of every other State in Europe. Similarly, for example, the party which supported ministers after March 1807 was united in opposition to the Whig-Grenville policy of forcing the Catholic question on a king who honestly, though mistakenly, believed that to consent to the proposed Relief Bill would be to violate his coronation oath.

So the scramble for place among the great families was again to be dignified and made respectable with the title of party differences. The Grenvilles were often denounced as mere place-hunters, loaded with sinecures and pensions, but even at their worst, under the nominal leadership of the second marquess of Buckingham, Lord Grenville's ambitious nephew, they were not without public virtue: they hesitated long before joining a government (in 1822) which merely tolerated disunity on the Catholic question. Charles Wynn, their leading man in the Commons, refused to enter the Cabinet until Liverpool had assured him that he was to be at liberty to initiate a discussion on that question either in the Cabinet or in Parliament. And Grenville himself, from 1807 until his retirement from active politics, went much further than his nephew in resolving never again to take office without the power to make the Catholic question a government question. Grey's devotion to principle similarly kept him (and his friends) out of office for more than twenty years.

Their opponents, the 'ins', were similarly united on this question of principle –not, indeed, in opposition to Catholic emancipation (for Canning, Castlereagh and the other 'liberal' Tories were all in favour of it) but in opposition to the Whig policy of forcing it on the sovereign. Here, then, is another reasonably clear-cut distinction between the two groups of politicians. Those who stood for "the advancement of kingly power"–who upheld the right of the sovereign to choose his ministers, to veto legislation which the country did not desire, to dissolve Parliament at will, and to have an effective voice in the framing of policy–were Tories (their opponents often referred to them as the court party). And these men were the supporters of the Established Church, with all its privileges. Croker called the Tory party the "Church and King" party. Those who upheld the supremacy of Parliament and sought, in effect, to deprive the king of his choice of ministers (though, for the sake of appearance, acknowledging his theoretical right to choose whom he pleased) were Whigs. Fox, referring to the dismissal of the duke of Norfolk from the Lord Lieutenancy of the West Riding of Yorkshire, wrote: "I hope that . . . the dismissal is grounded upon the toast relative to the sovereignty of the people, for there cannot be a better or a more advantageous line of demarcation for us, to distinguish the two parties in the country; for it is impossible to support the Revolution [of 1688] and the Brunswick succession upon any other principle." And these men stood for the cause of "civil and religious liberty all over the world". This, said Fox in 1790, was the distinction that characterized Whigs. The younger Pitt, though a member of Brooks's Club from 1781 onwards, never labelled himself either a Whig or a Tory (he had written in 1779, "I do not wish to be thought enlisted in any party or to call myself anything but an independent Whig, which in words is hardly a distinction, as everyone alike pretends to it"), nor did most of his followers during his lifetime; they were generally content to describe themselves as "the friends of Mr. Pitt". Croker said of them in 1831: "We talk of them in common parlance as Tories, as they all opposed the Whigs and formed the Conservative party." They united and acted, he said, "on the principles of an enlightened Toryism". The magic of Pitt's personality kept them more or less united until 1801, but subsequently they came to be divided into six groups, led by Addington, Grenville, Canning, Perceval, Wellesley and Castlereagh. Their attachment to the king helped to keep some

of them together, though Grenville and his friends fell back into the Whig
connexion during the years 1804–1817, and though personal rivalries and
jealousies at times got the upper hand, as in 1809 when Canning and Castlereagh
fought a famous duel, and again in 1812, after the assassination of Perceval,
when Wellesley startled his fellow peers with his reference to those "dreadful
personal animosities" which prevented the formation of a national government
for the more vigorous prosecution of the war.

Whilst paying lip-service to the acknowledged right of the Crown to choose
its servants, the Foxite Whigs, from their study of English history since 1688,
developed the opposing theory that the House of Commons had the right to
demand the dismissal of ministers who did not possess its confidence. They
pointed to the enforced resignation of Walpole and to the appointment of
Henry Pelham and the elder Pitt, and they alleged that their doctrine (which
had only a flimsy historical basis) had been completely overturned by
George III during the first ten years of his reign. In the end, the disasters which
overtook the country during the war of the American Revolution gave the
Whigs the opportunity of enforcing their constitutional principles. So, in 1784,
with two recent precedents to bolster up their case (the defeat of the North
and Shelburne ministries in 1782 and 1783) they demanded the resignation of
Pitt following his repeated defeats in the Commons, and denounced his clinging
to power without a majority as flagrantly unconstitutional. Later, the Whig
theorists suggested that, in the selection of ministers, the wisdom of many was
preferable to the bias and partiality of one. "We are sensible, however, that a
contrary sentiment is very prevalent in the country . . . and the difference of
opinion upon this point constitutes one of the chief distinctions between the
Whigs and Tories of the present day."

Too clear-cut a distinction between them should not, however, be drawn.
The *Edinburgh Review* declared in Jan. 1807: "The names . . . of Tory and
Whig are sometimes, idly enough, kept up, but the former denomination is
hardly acknowledged by any political disputant." Even the Foxites were ready
to act on Tory principles in 1789 when their friend the Prince of Wales, during
his father's mental illness, was expected to put them in power by an act of the
prerogative on assuming the regency. Hitherto there had been no question of
Pitt losing the confidence of the Commons, but the Whigs would have come in
had George III not recovered his senses, and, like any other government, they
would have secured a parliamentary majority had they found it necessary to
advise a dissolution. George Rose, the Pittite, suggested to the king in 1804
that Fox, if given office, would, like any Tory, "maintain the just power of
the Crown", while Wraxall wrote of Fox as minister in 1783 that "all his
original principles were monarchical" and questioned "whether a more complying Minister, or one more disposed to have gratified his master in every

legitimate object of royal desire, could have been found among his Majesty's subjects". The Whigs again planned a ministry in 1810 and 1811, after the king's final relapse into insanity, but they were disappointed when the regent, as the prince became, fearing his father's extreme displeasure in the event of his recovery, decided to retain the Tory ministers. On the other hand, the action of more than forty ministers and placemen in resigning office in April 1827 when George IV chose Canning as Liverpool's successor, had the unusual, even extraordinary, appearance of Tories seeking to dictate to the Crown the choice of the Prime Minister. It was remarked at the time that the Tory aristocracy, of which the duke of Rutland was the self-appointed organ, then tried to do to George IV what the great Whig families had tried to do to his father, who had gained so much popularity by defeating that combination.

The "friends of Mr. Pitt", then, were united by a common attachment to their royal master and a detestation of 'Jacobinical' principles associated with the English reformers such as Burdett and Whitbread, but on many points, which today would be regarded as great party questions, they agreed to differ. Ministers in every government down to 1829 differed on the Catholic question. Pitt was prepared to find a government seat for his young admirer, Canning, in Aug. 1792, though they differed on the question of the repeal of the Test and Corporation Acts. Pitt required of him not agreement on what he called "speculative subjects" but merely "a general good disposition towards Government". Similarly, the opposition, led in the Commons successively by Fox, Grey, Ponsonby, Tierney and Althorp, differed on the question of parliamentary reform. When new and important questions arose, parties easily broke into fragments, as in 1794 when the Portland Whigs separated from Fox and his friends on the issue of the French Revolution; and again in 1817 when the Grenvilles and Foxite Whigs parted company on the question whether popular agitation for reform should be suppressed by 'Gagging' Acts. The Pittites split on the Catholic question after Pitt's resignation in 1801, and, later, on the question whether the Addington ministry should continue to be supported after the renewal of the French war; and still later, after Pitt's death in Jan. 1806, for lack of a successor whom all would recognize as leader. Each of these various splinter groups was held together, partly by common political ideas, partly by patronage or hopes of patronage, partly by ties of friendship dating back to school and college days, and partly by family connexion (it was said that about twenty great families would have to go into mourning in 1809 on the death of the duke of Portland). Thus, during this period there were the followers of Fox, Pitt, Portland, Grenville, Addington, Canning, Castlereagh, Wellesley, the Prince of Wales, Grey and Lansdowne, together with three 'ideological' groups–the 'Saints', the Radicals and the High Tories.

By 1822 Lord Liverpool had succeeded in reuniting all the surviving "friends of Mr. Pitt", and he derived considerable satisfaction from this achievement, but it is possible to exaggerate the effects of this process of consolidation, and the extent to which a two-party system operated during the remaining years of his premiership. For the government side of the House, as in Walpole's time, really provided an opposition as well as a government party. Palmerston, the Secretary at War, himself remarked that the real opposition sat behind the Treasury Bench.

> "It is by the stupid old Tory party, who bawl out the memory and praises of Pitt while they are opposing all the measures and principles which he held most important; it is by these that the progress of the Government in every improvement which they are attempting is thwarted and impeded. On the Catholic question, on the principles of commerce, on the corn laws, on the settlement of the currency, on the laws regulating the trade in money, on colonial slavery, on the game laws ... the Government find support from the Whigs, and resistance from their self-denominated friends."

Palmerston might have added that the main features of Canning's foreign policy–his recognition of the independence of the former Spanish colonies in America, his plans to liberate the Greeks in co-operation with Russia, and his support of the constitutional party in Portugal, received support from the opposition benches, and opposition from those behind the Treasury bench. And these latter were the very gentlemen who soon brought about the downfall of the Wellington ministry after the 'great betrayal' of 1829. For the second time, the Whig opposition, in 1829 and 1830, gave general support to the government which had earned the gratitude of all liberal-minded men by conceding Catholic emancipation. Some of them, indeed, took office in this Tory administration, with the full approval of their friends, and one reason why the Whigs finally went into opposition in the summer of 1830 was the fact that they were not invited to join the government as a party. Moreover, some members expressed regret in Nov. 1830 that some of the outgoing ministers had not been invited to serve under Lord Grey. His ministry was only nominally a Whig ministry. It was a coalition of Whigs, Tories, ultra Tories, Canningites and near-Radicals, formed for the specific purpose of satisfying the popular demand for an effective measure of parliamentary reform, and, once the Reform Bill had been carried, the government soon shed all its non-Whig elements except the Canningites, who became completely identified with the Whig party. The question of parliamentary reform, then, which completely dominated the political scene in 1831–1832, was not at all a party question. Most of the Tories in opposition had become reconciled to the idea of some measure of constitutional change, and the struggle was not between reformers and anti-reformers but between the supporters and opponents of the ministerial plan, which was too far-reaching for many of the Tories to accept. John Cam Hobhouse remarked that "the old appellations of Whig and Tory should be forgotten. . . . The only distinguishing title of parties now should be reformers and anti-reformers." There never was a time, said the ultra Tory Sir Robert Inglis in March 1831, when the influence of party was so slight. It was "one of the many misfortunes of the times that there are now no leading men under whose banners gentlemen might range themselves". "Every man on every side acts for himself, and there is no struggle of factions by which the interests of the people are sacrificed." So there was more independence in the House than at any former period. Had there been organized parties in the House, said Inglis, there would have been a case for constitutional change, for organized parties meant corruption and the destruction of the independence of members.

When out of office the various Tory groups existing after 1801 went by the name of 'floating' parties or 'flying squads'. It was from these shifting formations that the sovereign selected his ministers. The ranks of the 'thick-and-thin' men, whether on the government or the opposition side, were always swollen by numbers of hangers-on; men who, for the most part, being loosely attached to the party, possibly for what they could get out of it, were, as William Eden said in 1784, neither useful nor creditable to anybody. Men of this description survived the great upheaval of 1832. In April 1835 Palmerston was confident that thirty or forty members who had supported the short-lived Peel ministry (1834–1835) would support Melbourne: "people who are for the Government in the abstract"; and twenty or thirty more, he added, would stay away. "Thus we shall have a much larger majority in office than we had in opposition." And as late as 1858 it was said that the House of Commons always contained a group of about forty members who inclined to *any* government–'men who dislike opposition, or whose family connexions are interested in contracts or in certain objects". The allegiance of such people was readily transferred when the power to reward it passed into other hands. Lord North's party rapidly dwindled from about 120 in 1783 to a mere 17 five years later. The Addington group fell away from about 68 in 1804 to about 43 in 1805 and to less than a dozen some years later, when it was merely a rather unattractive assortment of relations and personal friends. As early as Oct. 1804 (only a few months after his resignation of the premiership), Addington, realizing, no doubt, that he would never again be in that commanding situation, made it known that he had no wish to keep together any party of his own. Canning and Wellesley, having failed to force Lord Liverpool's government to capitulate, disbanded their troops in 1813 when they could no longer hope to be in a position to reward their followers. Their combined strength had never exceeded thirty, but, under the multiple-party system, it was always possible that effective power would be wielded by very small minorities. The Grenville party had shrunk to seven in 1830, with the fat and rather odious duke of Buckingham and Chandos its sole representative in the Lords; and its value is indicated by the remark of Ellenborough, the President of the Board of Control: "We all feel as if an alliance with the Grenville party would bring us ill luck." The Carlton House party practically disintegrated in 1812 even though the prince then *was* in a position to reward his friends. Some of them broke away from disinterested motives; valuing political consistency, they would not countenance his abandonment of his old political friends and his decision to retain his father's Tory ministers.

It was Radical propaganda that created the legend about the universal sordidness of politics: that Parliament was nothing more than a sink of corruption, an assemblage of unprincipled place-hunters, ribbon-fanciers and job-mongers; that the 'ins' and the 'outs' were equally determined to defend corruption and peculation, that the people were reduced, politically, to a condition of slavery by a junto of boroughmongers. But even Cobbett (in his less prejudiced days) admitted that not all placemen were sordid office-seekers: "Though present experience teaches us that some men certainly wish for office to gratify their own covetousness and vanity, there are others, and I trust a far greater number, who, in their pursuit of power, are actuated by the noble motive of advancing the power and happiness of their Sovereign and their country." This Radical propaganda, scattered broadside over the country after 1807, and aimed indiscriminately at boroughmongers, sinecurists and pensioners as well as placemen, seemed to imply that all politicians were worthy of the contempt of honest men, that all were equally possessed by the devil of self-interest, all engaged in an unceasing scramble for place and emolument. The popular hatred of sinecurists and pensioners grew to such an extent that by 1830 politicians who had spent a long life in the service of their country, had in some cases developed an extraordinary guilt-consciousness about accepting public money in the form of a retirement pension. It was not realized that the right of the Crown to reward political services in ways apparently so indefensible, at a time when official salaries, especially in the highest ranks, were notoriously inadequate to the expenditure which the situation required, tended to prevent the government from being monopolized by the rich, and to enable persons not born to a large estate, to render political service to their country.

This universal condemnation of public men was unjustified even at the beginning of George III's reign, and very much more so at the end of the century when devotion to principle, attachment to party, disinterestedness, and the readiness to sacrifice prospects of place and power, did mean something. The Whig opposition led by Fox and Grey would have shed most of its members if rooted ambition and habitual love of place had been their sole guiding motive. Devotion to principle did, after all, contribute to the Whigs being in the wilderness for more than twenty years after 1807. It would be quite fantastic to argue that men like Wilberforce were in politics for personal gain. This can be said too of the great majority of independent country gentlemen, even though some of them *were* ready to accept a peerage after long service in the Commons. J. C. Curwen, after his retirement from active politics in 1812, looked back on twenty-eight years of public life, with their "unavailing mortifications and unprofitable expense". None but the violently prejudiced could justly denounce as unprincipled even the class of borough proprietors. In general, it is true, they bought or held this species of patronage, like any other property, to make the most they could out of it. But not all of them thought of making their parliamentary interest a paying proposition by ranging themselves on the side of ministers. There were those who exercised this power of nomination from the noblest motives, choosing persons merely from the high opinion they entertained of their principles and their abilities.

No one made a fortune out of electioneering. The first Lord Eliot, looking back in 1797 over nearly half a century of borough patronage during much of which time he had had seven seats at his disposal, and for which in 1790 he was asking £3,000 per seat, wrote: "In election transactions I have never received what in the one town or the other I had not previously laid out. Such receipts were matters of necessity–I have never submitted to them without a feeling of reluctance. Often I have received nothing, and not infrequently have thereby suffered very considerable personal inconvenience."

On the whole, politicians, even those not burdened with extensive electoral interests, retired from public life poorer than when they went into it. Pitt, though he had had the valuable sinecure office of Lord Warden of the Cinque Ports and had been without family responsibilities and expensive habits, left debts exceeding £40,000: debts which a grateful country discharged as an act not merely of generosity but of justice. Lord Liverpool's fortune was much reduced during his long career (he was in office for nearly thirty-three years). Canning spent more than £60,000 of his wife's fortune in a quarter of a century (less than £40,000 remained at his death). Perceval sacrificed a highly lucrative practice at the Bar and impoverished his large family by taking office in 1807, and Parliament had to come to the rescue of his widow and children five years later. So, as Wellington said, a Prime Minister (and, indeed, his Cabinet colleagues) must be ruined in consequence of the heavy expenses necessarily incurred whilst in office, unless he possessed a large private fortune. A comparatively poor man could hardly afford to accept office without the reasonable prospect of retirement provision in the form either of pension or sinecure.

Less than half the members of the House of Commons were firmly connected with party. At the beginning of 1783, when the Shelburne ministry was about to be overthrown by the coalition, out of 558 members fewer than 350 were professed party men, and these included the placemen. It was calculated that the government could count on 140 votes, Lord North on 120 and Fox on 90, the remaining 208 being uncertain. This figure is not strikingly different from John Robinson's at the end of the year: there were then 178 'hopefuls' or 'doubtfuls' (from Pitt's point of view), and after the expected general election he believed that there would be 182. In 1788 it was stated that "the party attached to Mr. Pitt" numbered only 52, and the total number of professed party men was only 250 out of 558.

The extent to which the House consisted of men unconnected with party is further illustrated by the fact that, during the half-century from 1780 onwards, the four governments which resigned through forfeiture of the confidence of the House (North's, 1782; Shelburne's, 1783; Addington's, 1804; Wellington's, 1830) were in effect defeated by an opposition which, even when reinforced by the votes of some of the independent members, in every case consisted of much less than half the House. Before 1831 there never had been an opposition 250 strong. Against such an opposition, in a House numbering, after the Irish Union of 1801, 658, no government, in the ordinary course of events, could have lasted a month. In 1818 it was stated, no doubt correctly, that an opposition numbering 173, if well managed and supported by public opinion (in other words, by the votes of the independent country gentlemen) was strong enough to turn out any government. This meant that the ministerial party, including the placemen, numbered less than one-third of the House. In Jan. 1817 the opposition numbered 161, but only 140 were capable of attending, the rest being either abroad or ill. Yet, said Lord Grey: "That we are a party sufficiently powerful to form an Administration, if called to the government by the voice of the public and the acquiescence of the Crown . . . is not, I think, likely to become a subject of doubt." Speaker Abbot said in 1805 that "the standing strength of the Government" was about 230–a figure which obviously included the placemen and the "King's friends". A government upheld by the certain votes of about 200 members in a House of 658 could normally survive when supported by the Crown; it fell only when either the king or the 'independents' abandoned it. An opposition rarely had an effective strength of 170. When many members owed their seats, not to the nomination of a party nor to a numerous electorate, but to the friendship of a borough proprietor or to the length of their own purses, they could not be induced to attend regularly. Grey said in 1804, after an opposition vote of 181 against the Additional Forces Bill (8 June) that if only some of his followers could have been persuaded to leave their claret half an hour earlier, Pitt's government would have been decisively defeated instead of having a majority of 40. Moreover, it was almost impossible to keep a large body of members in town after the middle of June. And the 'shabby' ones ('trading' or 'speculating' politicians, they were sometimes called) were always ready to change sides when it seemed advantageous to 'rat', and Burke thought that these men always formed "a very large part of those who belong to the men in power". The Fox-North majority perceptibly crumbled during the opening weeks of the 1784 session when it became increasingly evident that Pitt, with the king's support, would be able to stand his ground. On the other hand, Pitt's parliamentary position was immediately threatened in 1788–1789 when a regency seemed imminent, and so was Perceval's for a similar reason in 1810. About forty of his usual supporters turned against him in that year when the inquiry into the Walcheren expedition produced a secondary disturbance to his security. The same House of Commons which had supported Pitt's last ministry (1804–1806) supported the Grenville ministry. The parliamentary position remained substantially the same after the general election of Nov. 1806. Then, in March 1807, the king dismissed the Grenville ministry and recalled the "friends of Mr. Pitt", who could have retained power without again dissolving the Parliament.

In 1829 Sir Richard Vyvyan said that if George IV could pluck up courage to dismiss Wellington and form an ultra Tory ministry, it would be supported by at least 278 certain votes (this number must have included the placemen and the "King's friends" because only about 200 members voted against the Wellington administration on the Catholic Relief Bill). Such a government would be opposed by 175 certain votes. That meant that 205 votes (204 without the Speaker) in the existing House were an unknown quantity.

Even though the general election of 1831 was fought on a single issue – the Reform Bill (the nearest approach there had been to a referendum in this country) – it was calculated that whilst the government had about 360 sure votes for the Bill and the opposition about 240, there were still about 60 'loose' members.

No eighteenth-century government could have done the king's business in Parliament without the support of those 'men of business' in the Commons who were generally referred to as the placemen. Their function was not so much to explain and defend the government's executive actions or legislative proposals (except when the head of the department concerned was in the Lords) as to provide ministers with indispensable votes, and, in general, to facilitate the progress of business in the House.

In 1782 the placemen in the Commons numbered 112. As 32 held their places for life (9 being actually in opposition) the votes of only 80 could be relied upon. George III once complained to Pitt that he had too often found offices for life a ground of not supporting administration. The Union of 1801 added about a score of Irish placemen and pensioners, but one or two of these also were in opposition–notably George Ponsonby, who, as an ex-Lord Chancellor in Ireland (1806–1807), enjoyed a retiring pension of £4,000 a year (by 6 Anne, c. 7, no one could sit in the Commons who held a pension during pleasure; members were not ineligible if they held one for life. They, of course, were quite independent, except from the ties of gratitude). The traditional jealousy of placemen is revealed by the clause of 41 Geo. III, c. 52, which said that not more than twenty Irish members might hold places of profit under the Crown. Thus the proportion of placemen to members, in Ireland and Great Britain, was approximately the same.

In 1808 there were about 84 placemen and pensioners in the House, and 89 in 1822. Of these, 4 usually voted with opposition, 6 held military commissions, 5 held offices for life in the gift of the Chancellor, and to 3 others no salary was attached. The placemen always included some naval or military men holding service posts such as a military governorship. In this period no service man was deprived of his commission on account of his votes in either House of Parliament, but the prospects of promotion for a confirmed opposition man might have been sensibly affected. It was said that the impartiality of the duke of York, the Commander-in-Chief, was such that it was a matter of indifference to him which way an officer voted. But the Whigs disputed this, and J. C. Hobhouse said in 1826:

"We have officers on our side of the House, it is true, but where is the great majority of those holding commissions in the army and navy? Certainly ranged with Ministers, and certainly amongst their most faithful adherents. . . . Even those with whom I have the honour to be associated do not feel themselves perfectly free agents when questions touching their profession come before the House; they cannot help recognising the influence to which they are to look up for promotion, and they are, besides, bound together by that *esprit de corps* which prevents them from merging the officer in the member of Parliament."

In Oct. 1831 Lord Hill, then Commander-in-Chief, found himself in considerable difficulty as to the line he should take when the Reform Bill came up to the Lords. Though he had never considered his office a political one, he did not feel free to vote against the Bill. He stayed away. When the revised Bill came before the peers in 1832 he decided to resign if he was required to vote for it. The Prime Minister reluctantly allowed him to absent himself from both the debate and the division.

During this period such essentially administrative posts as the Secretaryships of the Treasury and of the various boards were transformed into political offices, vacated whenever there was a 'total' change of government, as in 1807 and 1830. In Nov. 1830 there was no question of any placeman being invited to stay under Lord Grey, whereas in 1783 George Rose, for example, could have kept his office of Joint Secretary of the Treasury when the Fox-North coalition ousted Shelburne. That situation, however, was already exceptional, and very few later illustrations of continuity of tenure on a 'total' change can be cited.

Placemen, then, had to support ministers or resign. On rare occasions the penalty was not exacted. Two of the official members of the Irish Parliament who opposed the Union in 1799 were not dismissed. In 1829, of the four placemen who voted against the Catholic Relief Bill only Wetherell, the Attorney-General, was dismissed – he having given additional offence by his rudeness and insubordination. Wellington was then only too anxious to reunite his party, which had been shattered by the political upheavals of the previous twelve months, and he had no wish to exacerbate feeling by calling for or accepting the resignations of Lord Lowther (Chief Commissioner of Woods and Forests), George Bankes (Secretary to the Board of Control) and Sir John Beckett (Judge Advocate-General).

In 1807 the parliamentary position of the Portland ministry was considered to be shaky, and the rule was adopted that everyone holding an office tenable with Parliament must provide himself with a seat, and at his own expense. On rare occasions a man was brought in without cost to himself.

The members of the Royal Household with seats in either House were placemen – with a difference. Not until 1830 was the principle definitely established that these officials went out on a change of government. Neither George III nor his successor habitually allowed the Prime Minister a free choice of his personal servants; William IV was the first sovereign to give him *carte blanche*. The extent to which preceding Premiers were able to nominate the Household depended on the extent to which they enjoyed the king's confidence. In the spring of 1783 George III made great efforts to keep them, but, as he told Lord North, "the number I have saved is incredibly few". Even Pitt, on forming his government in May 1804, was unable to prevent the dismissal of his friend Lord Amherst, a Lord of the Bedchamber: the king resented the fact that Amherst had refused to support Addington with his vote during the last few months of Addington's Premiership. The king declared that he had insisted on appointing to Household offices persons with whom he could live comfortably. Grenville had even less choice in Jan. 1806: the king evidently refused to part with the Lord Chamberlain, the Lord Steward, the Comptroller, the Vice-Chamberlain and the Captain of the Yeomen of the Guard. Elliot, the Irish Secretary, thought that his friends ought to resign rather than submit to such want of confidence. He told a Cabinet minister: "Nothing, surely, can be so injurious to your own characters as to hold your offices subject to a vexatious opposition from *the Crown* to the measures which you consider . . . as essential to the strength and security of the Empire."

In 1789 there were 7 Household officials in the Commons, 18 in the Lords. These numbers were not so insignificant as might at first sight appear. Lord

North thought it not unimportant that 18 peers voting on one side made a difference of 36 on a division; and Mr. Marsham said that if the Queen's Household too was taken into account, the total number in Parliament would be nearer 60 than 30. But the really important point was that if these votes were withheld, the king's hostility to his ministers was revealed to the world–and that meant that "the King's friends" in both Houses would probably withhold their support too. Consequently, after 1783 the Whigs elaborated the theory that the Household must change with the ministry and in 1812 they made this point a *sine qua non* of their taking office–a thing which they had not ventured to do in Jan. 1806. In their view, the alternative theory–that the Household were merely the king's personal servants who remained with him during pleasure–gave rise to the evil of government by two Cabinets, the one responsible to Parliament, the other, in the palace, irresponsible, ready, as in Dec. 1783, with Lord Temple's co-operation to strangle any government by the exercise of secret influence. Grey and Grenville, therefore, when opening negotiations with Moira in a preliminary way, inquired whether the principal Household offices were to be placed at their disposal–whether, in short, they were to receive from the prince those marks of confidence without which an efficient government could not be formed. But Moira replied that the prince should part with nobody, and the negotiations ended forthwith. The two Whig lords were then unaware that the regent was in fact prepared to part with his servants who, it was revealed later, had already determined to resign if the Whigs came in. William IV remembered this episode eighteen years later, in Nov. 1830, and, much to the disgust of his servants, placed their offices at Grey's disposal.

One further difficulty remained. The dissolution of Parliament in 1831 enabled the government to carry the Reform Bill through the Commons without undue trouble, but the issue in the Lords was so doubtful that Grey was compelled to put forward the unprecedented demand that the members of the Queen's Household, too, who were in Parliament, must support ministers on pain of dismissal. Lord Howe, her Lord Chamberlain, was consequently removed, and she never forgave the Whigs for compelling her to part with her favourite servant. She used her influence to undermine their position at court, and she refused to appoint a successor.

The clearest evidence in support of the Whig notion of secret influence is to be found in the events of Dec. 1783, when George III's unofficial advisers and Household servants planned the dismissal of the hated coalition. The Household troops, said Fox bitterly, were always ready, like the Praetorian bands of ancient Rome, to execute the secret mandates of the court; and he quoted George Grenville, the Prime Minister, who, twenty years earlier, had said, "I will never again be at the head of a string of Janissaries who are always ready to strangle or dispatch me on the least signal." Pitt did not deny that what Fox called secret influence had destroyed the coalition government; he merely declared, with the utmost stoutness, that he himself would never tolerate it, and one of the reasons for his resignation in 1801 was the fact that the king received advice on the Catholic question from persons other than the Prime Minister.

During the regency debates in 1789 Lord North argued that the parliamentary support of the Household was essential to the stability of the government. He spoke of "that general influence which the Constitution had deemed necessary to be given to the Crown and to the executive power of the country – that general influence without which the Crown could not exercise its duties". Similarly, Lord Grey, referring to the people at court in 1831 who were either hostile to the Reform Bill or lukewarm in support of ministers, puzzled the king with the remark that the government found a considerable portion of "what may be considered as its natural strength, turned against it". Grey was making two points: first, that the Parliament had been 'chosen' by the late ministers, and all the seats usually at the command of the ministers were now filled by their bitterest opponents, and second, that "the active and avowed hostility of persons connected by official situations with your Majesty's Court has undoubtedly the effect of diminishing the strength of your Majesty's Government in the House of Lords". Whenever, in fact, the independent members of either House doubted the warmth or sincerity of the sovereign's attachment to his ministers (and in 1831 they had good reason to doubt whether William IV would go all lengths to secure the passage of the Reform Bill through the Lords) those members who considered themselves "King's men" tended to withhold their support from his ministers. Pitt owed his victory over the coalition in 1784 to the king's firm support, publicly revealed in unmistakable fashion when the dissolution of Parliament was announced. Then, said Wraxall, "the King's friends were found in every part of the House of Commons". "The great strength of ministerial support rests on the King's favour", said Lord Lowther in Nov. 1803, "and I think *that* fortress will not easily be shaken." "The principle upon which we must most rely to keep us together, and to give us the assistance of floating strength", wrote Perceval in 1809, "is the public sentiment of loyalty and attachment to the King." George Rose thus referred to "the King's friends" on 10 May 1804: "All those who consider themselves as his friends will be *hearty*, *uniform* and *steady* in their support, which will make a most essential difference in any computation of strength." After the assassination of Perceval (May 1812) his colleagues saw little chance of receiving adequate parliamentary support, yet they said that the prospect was not hopeless "if the Administration is known to possess the entire confidence of the Prince Regent". When, in Feb. 1812 Lord Percy, M.P. for Northumberland, was given a peerage, his father the duke of Northumberland, wrote: "It is Carlton House and not the Minister whose wishes I am anxious he should follow." A year earlier the duke of Norfolk announced his determination to give full support to the regent's ministers, "it being clearly understood . . . that it was the Regent alone who supplied them with such support, and not their own merits". His allegiance to the Whigs, he said, had been broken by the death of Fox. In 1827 it was stated that the duke of Buckingham had offered his parliamentary interest to the king personally, not to Canning, the new Prime Minister. The duke of Rutland wrote at the same time: "My attachment is to the Crown rather than to any set of men." Lord Seaforth deeply regretted that George III had come to be so completely dominated by anti-Catholic advisers that he regarded the preservation of the Protestant Constitution of England as his prime preoccupation: "But since it is so", he said, "I must give my vote to save the King from annoyance and disturbance on the subject." He added, "Whatever turn things take, I am resolute for one to adhere to the King and to lend my feeble voice for the support of his prerogatives and rights, believing their support to be necessary for the welfare of his people." Attachment to the sovereign was stronger during George III's reign than was the case with either of his successors; his influence was far greater because of the universal respect for his character and the affection which he inspired in his people. As late as 1837 the personal influence of the sovereign was a political factor to be reckoned with. At the general election of that year some candidates called upon the electors to support reform, not because ministers were reformers but because the young queen was for it. "It is now well known to all that the Queen is with us", wrote Palmerston. "That is a great point, and will have its effect on many men." "Many of those put down in the list as Tories will begin by staying away and will end by voting with us."

Both supporters and opponents of Catholic emancipation believed that the attitude of the sovereign was likely to be the decisive factor whenever a Relief Bill was before Parliament. On 9 March 1827, a few days after Burdett's motion on the Catholic question had been defeated in the Commons by 276 to 272, a member remarked: "Even as it stands now, a favourable Crown would carry the measure by above 70." Another member correctly remarked that the anti-Catholic M.P.s were for the most part men who, if the king said a word, would vote for the Bill. Consequently the situation was transformed in Feb. 1829 when the king apparently allowed his ministers to introduce a Relief Bill. Those placemen, Household troops and king's friends who had previously supported 'No Popery' now called for emancipation–and with decisive effect, the numbers being 353 v. 173 and 320 v. 142 on the second and third readings of the Bill. And in the Lords, where the question had hitherto been uniformly defeated by two to one, the Bill was now carried by a similar proportion of votes (217 v. 112, and 213 v. 109 on the second and third readings). Lord Durham had remarked that the bishops would go whichever way the king wished them to go (the numbers, however, were 10 for and 20 against the third reading). George IV never really forgave Wellington for forcing him to surrender at discretion on this all-important issue, and, referring to the duke's continuing unpopularity at court, Mrs. Arbuthnot wrote: "All those Tories who consider themselves *King's men* are unwilling to support a man they believe to be so obnoxious."

During this period every government of a definitely different complexion from that of its predecessor found it expedient to dissolve the Parliament 'chosen' by the late ministers, in order to consolidate its own power (Pitt's in 1784, Grenville's in 1806, Portland's in 1807, Grey's in 1831). Great as was the electoral influence of the Crown, at no time was it sufficiently extensive of itself to give ministers a working majority in Parliament. Had it been so, the House would have been a packed House. To say that "the King and the Treasury could always carry a Government through" was to over-simplify the situation – otherwise the king would never have been compelled to part with his ministers in March 1783, in May 1804, or again in Jan. 1806. The support, therefore, not merely of the placemen and the king's friends but also of the independent members who, as Perceval said, constituted "the floating strength of the House of Commons", was necessary for the continued survival of an administration. It was amongst these, "the independent part of the House, the country gentlemen, and the representatives of the popular boroughs", he remarked in 1809, that "we must find our saving strength or our destruction". As Wellington once remarked, no government was ever beaten by its enemies, but some were by their friends.

Although some of the representatives of trading and industrial interests, too, were unconnected with party, most of the independent members were country gentlemen, whom Wilberforce described as "the very nerves and ligatures of the body politic", "the very cement of our society". They claimed that, from their character and connexions, they were best able to voice public opinion in Parliament. The Tory Prime Ministers of the period were, then, kept in office not merely by the king's favour and by the "influence of the Crown", but also by the weight of public opinion. Pitt and his successors were the men whom the country not only needed, but wanted.

One of the characteristics of English society which struck observers was the absence of rigid class divisions such as predominated on the Continent. The English aristocracy was never a caste. The eldest son of a duke, though styled (by courtesy) a marquess, was as much a commoner as the untitled country gentleman. It is impossible to define a country gentleman in a phrase. Obviously he was a substantial landed proprietor. He might even be a peer, for Lord Mulgrave referred in 1803 to the existence of a "strong body of country gentlemen in both Houses of Parliament". Earl Bathurst spoke of himself as such; the eldest son of a peer so regarded himself. Lord Milton, Lord Fitzwilliam's heir, drew a distinction between peers and heirs to peerages on the one hand, and the gentry on the other, by describing the latter as 'pure' country gentlemen.

They were being constantly recruited from the ranks of the lawyers, country attorneys, merchants, bankers and manufacturers; men who invested their money in a large landed estate, partly, no doubt, because of the social prestige which had traditionally gone with ownership of the soil. So the Barings, the London bankers, became country gentlemen, and, later, peers; and Peel, the cotton spinner, became a baronet and Lord of the Manor of Drayton. Ricardo protested that he was not "a mercantile man"–he was a landed proprietor. After his death his family, having become "people of fortune and of some consequence, and landed gentry", tried hard to draw a veil over their Jewish and mercantile origin. Cobbett reviled the stock-jobbers who were buying out the old families. A 'City' man transformed into a landed proprietor, like one risen from yeoman stock, had much prejudice to encounter if he aspired to represent his county in Parliament. Lord Malmesbury had little respect for G. P. Jervoise, M.P. for Hampshire, 1820–1826 ("so strange a person"), but he did after all come from an old-established local family, and as such was much to be preferred to the upstart Barings who, said Malmesbury, would eventually monopolize the county (unless, indeed, their establishment in the City went bankrupt). However, by that time, he added, "they will have become country gentlemen like Hulse, Heathcote and many others who began exactly in the same line".

The father of Lord Eldon, the Lord Chancellor, was a Newcastle coal merchant who was said to have invested his savings in a public house. Eldon invested *his* in a landed estate (Encombe) in Dorsetshire. Earlier in the century Lord Chancellor Hardwicke had become a Cambridgeshire landed proprietor, and his family came to dispute with the duke of Rutland for the political control of the county.

The old-established country gentlemen were proud of their ancestry. Sir Robert Heron claimed that his forbears came over with William the Conqueror. Sir John Sebright's thirteenth-century ancestor was one of the king's tenants-in-chief. Sir Thomas Acland traced his line back to the middle of the twelfth century. The *Radical* country gentleman, Sir Francis Burdett (who, in old age, was converted to Toryism) boasted that one of his ancestors had been of sufficient importance to be executed for high treason by Edward IV.

Living on their property (unlike a great many of the Irish landed proprietors who rarely set eyes on their estates), dispensing a lavish hospitality, diffusing "comfort and order and decorum and moral improvement", providing the labouring classes with employment, and exercising the laborious duties of the magistracy, the country gentlemen were the leaders of their society. They rejoiced that their lot was cast at a distance from factories and populous towns and amongst "an orderly and quiet race of people". They took upon themselves the arduous duties of parliamentary representation much as they carried out the multifarious administrative and judicial duties of the county magistracy. Because of their wealth and social importance they were largely independent of court and Treasury influence.

The more enthusiastic of them hardly missed a day's shooting during the autumn months (autumn sessions of Parliament were so unpopular because they interfered with it). Littleton, M.P. for Staffordshire, considered that his wife's brothers were "lost to all the pleasures of life" because they never handled a gun or even lived in the country. At the beginning of the hunting season, when he was approaching the age of sixty, he wrote: "I felt all my youthful ardour revive, and believed fox-hunting to be a necessary part of the English Constitution." In 1823 Sir James Graham of Netherby, the father of the statesman, drew up instructions for the guidance of his executors. He wrote:

"My first and the last wish for my son may best be expressed in my prayer that he may be brought up an English country gentleman; that he may live on his paternal property, adorn it by his virtues and be beloved by his tenantry. All other ambition is vain. Success in public life does not compensate for the heart-burnings of the conflict, the loss of friends, the sacrifice of domestic peace, and the many unforeseen disappointments which attend even the possession of power, much less the loss of it."

They entered Parliament, not for personal advantage but from a sense of duty to the country. As a rule their ambition was satisfied when they were chosen to represent their county or a neighbouring populous borough. Addressing the electors, one of them declared: "I would not exchange my character of an independent English gentleman for that of the proudest monarch upon earth." Lord Hardwicke said that the situation of a county member was the first to which an English gentleman could aspire. William Morton Pitt, M.P. for Dorsetshire, believed that the representation of a county was hardly less creditable than that of a university. Some, indeed, aspired to a peerage, but, generally, only after long service in the House. One of them said that he would not dream of accepting a peerage until he had earned it–by service to his constituents and his country. "Aristocratic paste is good for nothing until it has been well kneaded and pressed under the rolling-pin of a constituency."

Some country gentlemen, like Sir James Graham, were men of great ability, but for the most part they were plain unpretentious squires with a modest opinion of their intellectual capacity. Lord John Russell thought that they were always kind and humane in performing their magisterial duties, but they were "ignorant, prejudiced and narrow-minded". Wraxall remarked that Pitt, "who well knew how large a part of his audience, especially among the country gentlemen, were little conversant in the writings of the Augustan Age, or familiar with Horace, always displayed great caution in borrowing from those classic sources" in his parliamentary speeches, whilst Colonel Barré "usually condescended, whenever he quoted them, to translate for the benefit of the County members". Brougham used to say, with his customary exaggeration, that they could hardly count ten on their fingers, that they were little better than dolts and blockheads. Sir Thomas Gooch, Member for Suffolk, explaining why he had never once opened his mouth on the question of Catholic emancipation, humbly admitted that the subject was too great for him to grapple with; he thought it would be presumption in a person of his calibre to intrude himself upon the House when so many abler and more eloquent Members were anxious to address it. Sir Robert Heron, at his first election, modestly said that the utmost he could hope for was that he might occasionally succeed in delivering his opinions "in a plain and manly manner, without becoming ridiculous". And another wrote: "I always told you I was not fit to represent the County.... You say... you wish I had the courage to speak–but you must first give me the ability. I wished much to have said something, but I had not two words to put together, so I sat like a log of wood . . . I cannot help it if they turn me out for it." 'Orator' Hunt once said of the member for Wiltshire that this fox-hunting squire was completely destitute of the qualifications of a House of Commons man, except that he came of an ancient family: he was remarkable only for his stupidity; though a sportsman he scarcely knew how to address his tenants when his health was drunk on a rent day. But Lord Milton remarked in 1830: "Pure country gentlemen are not always very wise or well-informed legislators, but, taking them *as a mass*, I come to the conclusion that power and authority cannot be deposited in safer hands."

Their independence meant three things. First, independence of ministers. Rarely was a county member a placeman: there were less than a dozen in the forty years preceding the passing of the Reform Bill (they usually found other constituencies on taking office). Often, indeed, they asked ministers for favours for their constituents, but they considered that in so doing they were not sacrificing their political independence, for they regarded the local county patronage as theirs by right, and this ministers grudgingly admitted. Some of them, nevertheless, felt that they could go too far in seeking favours of this sort. One, replying to an applicant who was also a constituent: said, "You are well aware of the impossibility of my pressing an affair of ministerial favour as I could have done had I been more my own master in the House of Commons. No vote is more severely scrutinised than that of a County member, and the man who represents a small borough may talk with more decision to a Government about the support he gives them, and the return he expects." Wilberforce declared in 1820: "It has for many years been an invariable rule with me not to ask favours of Government. Not being an official man I could not do it without laying myself under obligations which would interfere with my parliamentary independence." It was remarked that they were more dependent on government in bad times than in good, because, to repair their damaged fortunes they tended to ask for places for their sons and connexions. The asking of favours was always considered to be the most disagreeable part of a county member's task. If these requests were not attended to, the member lost the support of some of the electors, and it was for this reason that one of them said in 1789 that he would not again stand for the county.

Independence meant, second, independence in their own financial position. Financial insecurity meant more dependence on the Treasury. There was a feeling that the revival of the medieval practice of paying for their attendance would increase their independence. And, too, how *could* a member be independent if he had to pay a large sum for his election? He would seek to recoup himself at the expense of the public. That, of course, applied to all members. A candidate for a county constituency was apt to stress the importance of having a fortune honestly acquired by the industry of his ancestors. William Pole Tylney Long Wellesley (Wellington's nephew) qualified himself as a county member by marrying a wealthy heiress. When Lord Herbert, Lord Pembroke's son, was elected to Parliament, a friend wrote to him: "Do, for God's sake, marry a woman with half a million of money, and be an independent man at once!"

Independence meant, third, independence of party. Yet some of the county members *were* attached to party. In the summer of 1818 the regular members of the Whig opposition included 19 English and Welsh county members. A great cry was raised in Devonshire in 1820 against Lord Ebrington because he was an opposition man–unlike all the rest of his family. The Treasury list of opposition members in the summer of 1830 contained the names of 41 English and Welsh county members, including one or two radicals like Joseph Hume, Member for Middlesex (which was not a typical county). The Whigs claimed 47 (out of 94), and said that only 28 supported ministers; 7 were neutral, "not leaning much towards the Government". Among the 41 was Lord Morpeth, member for Yorkshire. Referring to the newly formed Reform ministry, in which his father, Lord Carlisle, had Cabinet rank, Morpeth told the House on 23 Nov. that any support which he could give the government must necessarily be independent, conscientious and conditional.

Attached as the country gentlemen were to the sovereign rather than to any set of ministers, they considered it their duty to support the ministers of the king's own choice until measures were proposed which proved the government to be no longer worthy of confidence. The House of Commons 'chosen' by

Lord North supported three very differently constituted governments—Rockingham's, Shelburne's, and the Fox-North coalition. That which was elected in 1802 similarly supported Addington, Pitt and Grenville. But in 1806 the situation was confused. Whereas 49 county members were said to be supporting Grenville, as many as 45 supported the 'outs', 8 others being 'doubtful unfavourable' (to the government) and 17 more 'altogether doubtful'. So many independents were non-supporters of administration at that time, partly, no doubt, because their views on the Catholic question differed from those of the majority of the Cabinet, and partly because the 'Talents' could hardly be described as a ministry of the king's own choice. But still less was the Fox-North coalition of 1783 which, according to John Robinson's calculations, was supported by 42 out of the 80 English county members. The habit of supporting the government of the day had evidently become ingrained.

Especially among the parliamentary reformers there was a feeling that county members should be independent not only of the Treasury, not only of party, but also of aristocratic influence: a feeling that a county ought not to be represented by the son or connexion of a peer. There was opposition to the election of Richard Neville for Berkshire in 1812 not merely because his father was a placeman but because he was Lord Braybrooke. Such a man, it was felt, should sit for a rotten borough. There was a feeling that in some counties the great families had converted the representation into a species of pocket borough: the Lowthers, the Russells, the Cavendishes, etc. Of the 92 (94 from 1826 to 1832) English and Welsh county members, there were never fewer than 20 who were the sons of peers, and in the Parliament of 1812–1818 the number exceeded 30. Many of the county members who *were* professed party men, supporting administration, were the sons or nominees of peers, elected in defiance of the wishes of the independent freeholders.

Some county members carried their independence still further: they must be independent even of their constituents. Charles Western said in 1812 that if he was elected for Essex he would be most happy to profit by their advice, but he would never receive instructions from anyone. No gentleman with any independence of feeling, said Lord Chandos in 1830, would submit to dictation in the shape of pledges. But county members in general were considered as standing in some awe of their constituents; whenever public opinion was strongly expressed, as in 1830–1831 on the subject of parliamentary reform, many members felt they had to swim with the stream, and it was well known that they paid particular attention to the supposed wishes of the electors when a dissolution of Parliament was believed to be imminent.

Only on rare occasions, when their feelings were strongly aroused on political issues, did the independent members act as a group—as during the first few weeks of 1784 when they made really strenuous efforts to reconcile Pitt and

Fox: strenuous because failure meant the certainty of the hazards and expense of a general election. They did so again in 1822, forcing the government drastically to cut down taxation as a means of relieving the unparalleled distress of the agricultural interest caused by the sensational fall in the price of corn. "What I complain of", wrote Wellington, "is their acting in concert, and as a party independent of, and without consultation with, the Government which they profess to support but really oppose." They acted as a party, with decisive effect in 1829 and 1830. In 1829 they gravely weakened the Wellington ministry by opposing the Catholic Relief Bill, and in Nov. 1830 these seceding ultra Tories contributed to his overthrow. In 1831 the opposition of most of them to the excessively drastic Whig Reform Bill, again drove them into party courses.

The things that most of the country gentlemen, whether 'independents' or party men, really cared about were, first, the preservation of the Protestant Constitution of England (until the passing of the Catholic Relief Act, most of them were hostile to parliamentary reform). Second, the preservation of the ascendancy of the landed interest in its privileged position, protected economically by the corn laws (Lord Liverpool's government was most seriously threatened in Parliament when the price of corn was abnormally low). And third, the preservation of the Church of England in its privileged position. They also demanded reasonably low taxation, which, apart from its obvious direct advantages, tended to keep up the price of the funds, and therefore to keep down the interest charges on a mortgaged estate; and, finally, they stood for a policy of peace and non-intervention in continental affairs, so long as the honour and interests of the country were not adversely affected–again, in the interests of economy. Thus in 1791 they defeated Pitt's policy of restraining Russia in the Oczakoff crisis; in 1796, after supporting him for three years in carrying on an unsuccessful war against Revolutionary France, they compelled him to open peace negotiations; and they defeated his proposal to levy succession duties on real estate. In 1821–1822, as has been noticed, they forced the Liverpool ministry drastically to reduce expenditure. It was largely because the independent country gentlemen were opposed both to Catholic emancipation and to the Whig view of the French war that the Whigs were kept out of office for a generation after 1807. Liberal Tories like Canning and Castlereagh did not share the unpopularity of the Whigs on the Catholic question because they were not prepared to coerce either the king or the country into accepting a Relief Bill; they were ready to leave the question in abeyance until king and public opinion were prepared to promote its progress. Fox, too, had openly rejoiced at French victories; later, Grey and his friends were convinced, in spite of Wellington's successes in the peninsula and the failure of the Moscow campaign, that peace with victory was out of the question, and that ministers should end the war on the best terms that could be obtained, even though it meant leaving the Continent at Napoleon's mercy. This defeatist attitude found little favour with the independent part of the House.

The Whigs rightly considered the independents, who always professed to weigh measures, not men, as acting on a Tory principle–in supporting the king's prerogative right to choose and sustain his ministers. That, too, helps to account for the Whigs being so long in opposition. The independents were often ready enough to support them in an agitation for a reduction of government expenditure, but when questions arose which ministers chose to treat as questions of confidence, the independents always came forward to protect the sovereign and prevent the opposition from storming the Closet. As the independents held the key position in the House of Commons, their votes had a value altogether disproportionate to the mere number. When in Dec. 1794 four of them voted with the opposition, ministers at once took the alarm. Parliament, incidentally, was always dissolved at a time convenient to the country gentlemen–never at the harvesting season, and ministers always considered their prospects particularly bright if the harvest was a good one.

The country gentlemen, who were so powerfully represented in the House of Commons, almost monopolized the county representation, and sat for a great number of both 'open' and 'close' boroughs. In 1831 it was estimated that of the 168 members who were to lose their seats by the Reform Bill 110 were either country gentlemen or the near connexions of the aristocracy.

The defects of the old representative system are sufficiently notorious. Its merits tend to be overlooked, and are worth remembering. In the first place such public opinion as there was in England was represented in Parliament. The varieties of the franchise in the English boroughs ensured the representation of all sorts of opinion. The land, which was still the most important form of property, was obviously over-represented, but all the other great 'interests'– the Services, the Law, commerce, banking, shipping, industry and the colonies –had members in the Commons; and the agricultural labourers alone were without direct representation. The rotten and nomination boroughs provided a means of entry for those politicians who were needed both by the government and by the opposition–especially young careerists of exceptional ability, without the advantages of extensive landed possessions, a large fortune, or influence in a large commercial or manufacturing town. Amongst the representatives of these boroughs were some of the most independent members of the House: having bought their seats, they were the nominees neither of the Treasury nor of a patron nor of electors. The fact that there were many such boroughs indicates that both the government and the aristocracy lacked the financial resources requisite for packing the House. The representation of interests other than that of the land would have been even more extensive if there had been more rotten boroughs; and, paradoxically, the necessity for parliamentary reform would, in a sense, have been reduced, since these boroughs were the means whereby men of wealth, who had accumulated their fortunes in commerce and industry, obtained seats—and in the cheapest way, for the most modest contest in a county or an open borough generally cost far more than the £5,000 needed for the purchase of a seat for the duration of one Parliament. As the growing wealth of the country made it easier for the moneyed interest to get into Parliament, it constituted an increasingly formidable challenge to the political supremacy of the landed interest; politically it was a levelling factor which prevented either the Crown or the aristocracy from acquiring excessive power. Even parliamentary reformers perceived a possible danger from the triumph of their cause: the abolition of the rotten boroughs might narrow too much the access of the moneyed interest to Parliament. The progress of currency inflation was, politically, another levelling factor. In this period prices were perhaps fifteen times higher than in Henry VI's time, when the right of voting in the counties was restricted to the 40 shilling freeholders; the depreciation of money had most effectually defeated the object of that disqualification statute. In some measure the rotten boroughs enabled the Constitution insensibly to adapt itself to changing social conditions, and, like the works of Nature, to perpetuate itself by constant change.

The events of 1831–1832 were to show in most convincing fashion that a House elected under this theoretically indefensible system already represented public opinion very considerably, and was subject to the pressure of outdoor opinion. A House of Commons differently constituted would not have prevented the war of the French Revolution, which was opposed by the Whigs as unjust and impolitic (Fox's motion condemning the war was supported by only 45 members, of whom 6 were county members and 13 representatives of populous places). On at least one question—that of Catholic emancipation—the unreformed House was definitely in advance of public opinion and without the rotten boroughs the Relief Bill could not have been carried in 1829. And it would be a mistake to assume that public opinion could not express itself even in a nomination borough. Lisburne was under the control of the marquess of Hertford, so much so that there was never a contest in all the twelve elections to the Imperial Parliament before 1832. But of the electors (75 in 1818) all but about four were staunch Orangemen, and Lord Hertford would never have ventured to recommend to the electors anyone favouring Catholic emancipation. Nor would the electors at Saltash, a pocket borough owned by the Russell family, return Sheil, a papist, in 1831. It would also be a mistake to suppose that all the electors in a rotten borough were corrupt. When the second Viscount Palmerston heard that a 'Nabob' was to oppose him at Southampton and to bring down "such loads of rupees with him as shall buy the town", he remarked that the number of persons there who were not to be bought with money was very great. The situation there could doubtless be paralleled in many other boroughs.

Speaking on 13 March 1784, Pitt rightly maintained that no government could be formed which would be united in support of parliamentary reform: there were so many different opinions, and a free vote of the House had necessarily to be allowed—and also a free vote of his Cabinet colleagues and the placemen. As the majority of them, like the king and the peers, were hostile, it seems extraordinary that when, in 1785, Pitt again brought the subject before the House, he should believe "the success of the measure by no means improbable". He proposed a voluntary disfranchisement of thirty-six rotten boroughs (he did not name them, but they can in some degree be discovered because he said that the number of houses they contained was to be the criterion of decay), and their seventy-two members were to be added to the representation of London and the counties or given to large unrepresented towns like Birmingham, Manchester, Sheffield and Leeds. A sum of over £1,000,000 was to be set aside as a compensation fund. On the application of two-thirds of the voters, each borough to be disfranchised was to be entitled to one-thirty-sixth part of the total sum. If the amount was not large enough to tempt the voters to sell their rights, it was to accumulate at compound interest until the temptation to sell became irresistible. And the franchise was to be extended to the 40s. copyholders in the counties. The plan was opposed by most of the followers of Lord North, by Whigs like Burke who believed only in 'economical' reform, and by some of the independent country gentlemen.

Pitt has often been criticized for his virtual abandonment of the cause after the defeat of his plan by 248 v. 174 votes. But his majority was never a stable one; it included anti-reformers (king's friends and former supporters of Lord North) and many country gentlemen who generally but not invariably supported him. And as the Cabinet itself was deeply divided, it was impossible for Pitt to stake the government's existence on the issue. The reformers themselves never censured him for failing to make it a government question. Fox himself frankly admitted that no Cabinet of men could be found who would agree to sponsor a Reform Bill. It was left to nineteenth-century historians, ignorant of the nature of party in the pre-1832 House of Commons, to censure Pitt for failing to do what none of his Whig opponents could have done. Right down to 1830 Grey, the titular leader of the opposition Whigs, always maintained that parliamentary reform could never be made a party question because of the extraordinary diversity of opinion in their ranks; any attempt to make it such would quickly have broken up the Whig party, and Grey never dreamed of criticizing his friends who, to his dismay, joined Canning's ministry in 1827, for failing to make the question of parliamentary reform a *sine qua non* of their taking office. Some of the reformers had criticized the Fox-North coalition precisely because Fox had taken office with a determined enemy of parliamentary reform. Fox replied to this charge as Pitt did: that it was impossible to form a government united in favour of the question. Pitt, he said, had not sacrificed his opinion in forming a Cabinet consisting mainly of anti-reformers, nor did he, Fox, give up his when he coalesced with Lord North. Nor did Wilberforce criticize his friend for not making the questions of the slave trade and Catholic emancipation, too, Cabinet questions. Fundamentally, it was Pitt's failure to unite with Fox's party of reformers in 1784 that caused his failure to carry a Reform Bill. The king's opposition could doubtless have been overcome (it was not a question of conscience, like that of Catholic emancipation), and so, consequently, could the opposition of the peers. Pitt found an excuse for shelving the question after 1785 in the apathy of public opinion. With the return of prosperity after the dislocation of trade caused by the American war, and with the accession to office of a popular minister, the agitation in the country for a Reform Bill gradually subsided. Not until 1830 was national enthusiasm sufficiently roused to overcome the hostility of vested interests and the fears of timid anti-reformers. Then, in 1789, the outbreak of revolution in France roused the reformist societies to new activity and enthusiasm. The leaders of this second movement for reform were philosophic dissenters like the scientist and Unitarian Joseph Priestley and Dr. Richard Price, whose famous sermon in 1789, in which he compared the French Revolution with that of 1688, and declared that in 1688 the English people had acquired the right to choose their governors and to cashier them for misconduct, provoked Burke to write his celebrated *Reflections*. The Birmingham riots of July 1791 crushed this movement; Priestley's house was set on fire by the 'Church and King' mob, and his scientific instruments were destroyed.

Parliamentary Reform did not become a really popular movement until after 1815. The reformers of 1780–chiefly middle-class men–had been much more anxious for retrenchment of expenditure than desirous of far-reaching constitutional change. The movement inaugurated by Thomas Paine, who published his *Rights of Man* in two parts (1791-1792), was a minority movement and made little impression on the masses. The French Revolution had disastrous repercussions on English politics and blighted the Liberal cause for a generation. Fox wrote in 1801: "Till I see that the public has some dislike . . . to absolute power, I see no use in stating in the House of Commons the principles of liberty and justice." Paine's republicanism was an invaluable asset to the government, which chose to identify moderate reformers like Fox and Grey with the thorough-going democratic and 'treasonable' doctrines of the extreme Radicals. The unwise demonstrations of these agitators (they sent congratulatory addresses to the revolutionaries in France and expressed the hope that the French would soon reciprocate with addresses to a National Convention in London) thoroughly discredited the cause of reform. It made little headway because the progress of events in France–the September massacres in the Paris prisons, the downfall of the monarchy, the spoliation of the Church and the persecution of the aristocracy–alienated and horrified most decent English people. Pitt lost all interest in reform: it was no time for hazardous experiments. These issues split the Whig party in 1792, when the reformers, such as Grey, Sheridan, Mackintosh, Whitbread, Lambton (the father of the famous Lord Durham) and Lord John Russell (the father of the Prime Minister) founded the Society of the Friends of the People to further the cause of parliamentary reform. The anti-reforming Whigs, headed by Portland and Windham and indoctrinated by Burke, decided, after the outbreak of war in 1793, that the government must be supported at all costs against the danger from France and from the Jacobins at home; and they actually joined the ministry in July 1794. The leading agitators, like Thomas Muir and Thomas Palmer, were tried on charges of sedition and savagely punished, though Erskine secured the acquittal of Thomas Hardy and other London reformers charged with high treason, in 1794. The 'Gag' Acts of 1795 were carried through both Houses of Parliament by overwhelming majorities, and Francis Place admitted that they were popular measures. Two years later, Grey's last motion for parliamentary reform (26 May 1797) was defeated by 256 to 91. His proposals were nearer the Act of 1867 than that of 1832: triennial parliaments, household suffrage in the boroughs, the extension of the county franchise to certain leaseholders and copyholders, an increase in the number of English and Welsh county members from 92 to 113, the counties to be divided into single-member constituencies to put an end to compromises among the great families; and the rearrangement of the borough constituencies in proportion to population (about 1,500 constituents per member). Disgusted with politics the Foxite Whigs now more or less seceded from Parliament as a protest against government 'tyranny'–but Parliament was the only place where ministers could be criticized with impunity; debate could not be silenced, and the Press was completely free to report the speeches. Later, Grey admitted that the secession was a mistake: he was in effect disfranchising his constituents, and he should have resigned his seat. The Whigs returned three years later to register their protests against the Union Bill.

Curwen's Act (1809) to prevent the sale of seats in the Commons for money was the first substantial measure of parliamentary reform to be carried, though anti-reformers denied it the title. But for the carrying of a government amendment which did away with the possibility of preventing Crown patronage being used for the purchase of seats, the Bill would have been a more effective measure. As it was, no Prime Minister subsequently recommended a man for a peerage solely on account of his borough influence.

The distress resulting from the dislocation of trade and industry during the last years of the Napoleonic war–a dislocation largely due to the intensification of Napoleon's economic blockade of the British Isles–produced the Luddite riots which, in turn, gave rise to renewed agitation for a radical reform of Parliament as well as for cheap food and lower taxation. That agitation was intensified during the first post-war years by the unexampled depression of both agriculture and industry. But the repressive legislation of 1817 and 1819 drove discontent underground, and the return of prosperity in 1820 (except for agriculture), together with large tax remissions, further contributed to the decline of popular agitation.

This agitation damaged the prospects of the reformers in Parliament, as the previous one had done during the French Revolutionary era. Considering that parliamentary reform had become a Radical cry, the Whigs, who had no desire again to be confounded with the Radicals, thought it should be dropped. They believed in 1816 that it had fewer supporters of weight and consequence than at any former period. Many of the great Whig borough proprietors were in any case reluctant to countenance an agitation which, if successful, would deprive them of some of their property and political influence. But the events of 1819, culminating in the Manchester 'Massacre' and the passing of the 'Six Acts', convinced the Whigs that the question should be taken out of Radical hands, and the young Lord John Russell made it his own. The proceedings in the Lords against Queen Caroline again seemed to show that the House of Commons was no longer in touch with public opinion (the people had little or no notion of the essential worthlessness of her character, and conceived her to be a deeply wronged woman). The government's 'persecution' of her caused the anti-reforming Whigs like Pascoe Grenfell and Alexander Baring to become converts to parliamentary reform.

The earlier agitation had not been entirely fruitless. Throughout the eighteenth century attempts had been made to put down direct bribery, but the various statutes directed against it had produced little effect because of the difficulty of drawing a clear distinction between legitimate and illegitimate influence, and, too, most members had a vested interest in preserving the old practices. Particularly flagrant cases were, however, punished: New Shoreham (1770), Cricklade (1782), Aylesbury (1804), where the franchise was thrown open to the 40s. freeholders in the adjacent 'Hundreds' in which the borough was situated; whilst in the case of Grampound (1821) the electors were entirely disfranchised and the right to return two members was transferred to Yorkshire, the Tory peers defeating Russell's purpose of creating a precedent to give the seats of a disfranchised rotten borough to a large unrepresented town (Leeds). Even the reformers admitted that the Act of Union (1801), by depriving eighty-four cities and boroughs of the right of parliamentary representation, and permitting only the thirty-three most important of them to return members to Westminster, was in itself a substantial measure of reform, and they thought that little more was needed in that direction except the removal of the disqualification of Catholics from membership of the House. Burdett went so far as to say that Ireland's representation formed a model of an efficient reform for England. Even anti-reformers admitted that Yorkshire's additional members would represent manufacturing interests, and that the change in 1821 introduced the new principle of increasing the county members in proportion to population.

By this time the question was entering upon a new stage, for, as a new convert to the cause (Lord Milton) declared, the demand for reform was now coming from the middle class as well as from the lower orders. Russell subsequently raised the question in the House on several occasions during the next few years—advocating the disfranchisement of 100 of the smallest boroughs to the extent of one member each, and the enfranchisement of large towns together with additional representation for the counties. But he never secured the support either of the country gentlemen or of the Liberal Tories, the Canningites, and one of the conditions of the Whig-Canning coalition of 1827 was that parliamentary reform was not to be a government question.

Various factors contributed to the extraordinary progress of the demand for parliamentary reform in 1829–1830: first, the renewed onset of trade depression; second, the ill-calculated refusal of the House of Commons to transfer the right of representation from the corrupt borough of East Retford to Birmingham helped to destroy the people's confidence in the wisdom and justice of the House, and convinced them that no concession would be made without the stimulation provided by an agitation similar to that by which O'Connell had recently extorted Catholic emancipation. And third, when in 1829 Wellington surrendered to the threat of revolution and civil war in Ireland, and passed the Relief Bill, he prepared the ground for the Reform Bill of 1831. The Relief Act converted many reactionary Tories into Radical parliamentary reformers. When they, the High Church party, found their opinions suddenly disregarded on the question which they had always considered the most important in the whole range of politics, they began to think that a Parliament which could bring about such a disastrous result was not entirely faultless. They dreaded the consequences of emancipation upon the representation. They were afraid that wealthy Catholics might buy up the rotten boroughs and secure a substantial representation in the House of Commons, thus exposing to mortal danger the Established Church, the Union, and the Protestant Constitution of England. Moreover, some of them had for years been dissatisfied with the government's free trade policy—diminishing the protection which Parliament had afforded not merely to manufacturers but also to farmers and landlords. But for the rotten boroughs, they alleged, the government would have been unable to change its fiscal policy, nor would it have had such a large majority during the progress through the Commons of the Relief Bill which had overthrown the Constitution. Recent events seemed to have shown how completely the House could be separated from the feelings, wishes and opinions of the people, and all the rights and liberties of the country would remain in jeopardy so long as majorities were to be obtained by trafficking in seats. Nothing but the abolition of the rotten boroughs and additional representation for towns and counties (the latter proposal being calculated to increase the strength of the landed interest) would afford statutory protection for agriculture, trade and manufactures, and especially for the Protestant community, against the influx and increase of the Catholic party. By a masterpiece of irony the ultra-Tory Lord Blandford's motion in favour of a Radical reform of Parliament was seconded by O'Connell himself (5 Feb. 1830). Ultra-Tory votes contributed to the defeat and downfall of the Wellington ministry in Nov. 1830, and prepared the way for the Whig Reform Bill.

By sweeping away nearly all the rotten and nomination boroughs and extending the franchise, the Reform Act destroyed the greater part of the elaborate system of patronage which had enabled the king to change his ministers and to secure for them adequate parliamentary support. Other factors, however, were contributing to curtail the power of the Crown. The personal character of George IV deprived it of that moral influence which his father had possessed, and which the monarchy was not to recover until some time after the accession of Victoria. "We are a people strangely fond of royalty," Lord Holland once remarked. George IV sometimes put that fondness to a severe test. Devotedly attached to the monarchy as an institution, the Tories had little respect for the monarch after 1811 when the dissolute Prince of Wales was installed as regent; and before the close of his reign he had ceased to have any personal weight with either of the two main parties. William IV put himself in a somewhat similar position with the Tories in 1831 when, having reluctantly accepted the Whig Reform Bill as a measure loudly demanded by the country, he forfeited the confidence of the Tories in opposition. Their anger reached its height in April when he agreed to dissolve Parliament, for then they, in effect, lost the battle against the Bill. One of them remarked during the elections: "The King is as much alarmed as an idiot can be. He avows to one or two persons his anxiety to get rid of his Ministers, but this is folly after having done all the evil, and having made it impossible for any men of any party to govern the country." "All sentiment of respect is gone from him for ever," it was said of him in 1834.

The steadily growing political consciousness of the people, fostered by the more general diffusion of knowledge among the agricultural and industrial workers as well as the middle class, by the astonishing progress of the newspaper and periodical Press with the consequential publicity speedily and effectively given to all that passed within the walls of Parliament (the publication of the parliamentary debates introduced a greater change into the government than was ever brought about by statute), and by the well-established practice of discussing public affairs at public meetings and through the medium of parliamentary petitions: all these developments made for political change. As the anti-reformers admitted: "The voice of the people, especially when it speaks with reason, is irresistible." The Press had acquired a range and intensity of power unparalleled in history. In 1783 the average circulation of newspapers daily was only about one for every 300 inhabitants; in 1831 one for 150, in spite of punitive stamp duties. The number of circulating libraries in London rose from four in 1782 to over 100 in 1821, and there were then about 900 others in the provinces. Book clubs and reading societies, which were unknown in 1783, numbered over 1,500 in 1821. A single firm of booksellers in London sold over five million books a year in the 1820s, and gave more than 250 printers and bookbinders continuous employment. Nothing now passed in Parliament which was not submitted to the tribunal of public opinion. No one in authority, whether in high station or low, could exercise power oppressively or corruptly, unchecked by the apprehension of having his conduct called in question either in Parliament or in the newspapers. Many members of Parliament were now effectively subjected to the influence of public opinion, and it was felt that this new and unwelcome factor had appreciably advanced the cause of reform. Without the irresistible pressure which public opinion brought to bear on parliamentary deliberations, the Reform Bill could hardly have been carried in 1832. Herein lies the revolution silently in progress during the preceding half-century. Brougham told his fellow peers in 1831 that the Press had come to rival the House of Commons, and that it was the only organ of public opinion capable of dictating to the government, since at that time nothing else could speak the sense of the people.

Moreover, the gradual diminution of the 'influence of the Crown' during this period marked the decline of the old system of government by 'influence'. That influence was derived from patronage in connexion with appointments to civil, military, diplomatic, colonial and ecclesiastical offices, and it included a portion of the East India Company's patronage.

The process of disintegration originated with the 'economical' reforms of the Rockingham ministry in 1782, which were designed both to diminish the 'influence' of the Crown and to promote economy and administrative efficiency. Many useless offices were abolished and the number of placemen in Parliament reduced. Contractors, whose votes had generally been given to ministers, were disqualified from membership of the Commons. The amount of public money which could lawfully be spent by the Treasury on elections was

sharply reduced by the reduction to £10,000 a year of the amount of home
secret service money available for purposes other than the detection of treasonable conspiracies. As pensions continued to absorb much of this sum, little was
available either for bribing the Press or to meet the election expenses of government supporters. The amount of secret service money which could be spent by
the Foreign Secretary was not cut down, but he had to swear that his money
had been *bona fide* applied. In 1783 this principle of limitation was applied to
Ireland and a mere £5,000 a year was all that the Irish Executive could spend
for purposes other than the detection of treason. So the Dublin Castle authorities
had to apply to ministers in London for financial assistance at election times, and
the evidence shows that very little was forthcoming.

The Foxite Whigs abandoned 'economical reform' as an article of their
coalition with Lord North's party in 1783, and they made no attempt to reduce
Treasury patronage when they came into office with the Grenville and Addington groups in 1806, but the process was taken up by Pitt at the beginning of his
first ministry, not now in order to reduce the royal 'influence' over the Commons, nor in response to the pressure of a parliamentary opposition, but simply
from a desire to promote economy and efficiency in government. A series of
ten reports on the several departmental offices, issued between 1786 and 1788
by the Commissioners appointed in 1785 to inquire into the "Fees, Gratuities,
Perquisites and Emoluments . . . received in the . . . Public Offices" recommended a far-reaching reorganization of governmental machinery, the abolition
of many sinecures, and the payment of regular civil service salaries to replace
remuneration by fees and perquisites of office. A further series of reports
followed in 1797, and the Irish departments were the subject of investigation
between 1806 and 1814. There were more inquiries into governmental finances
and sinecure offices at intervals until 1834, when the abolition of the remaining
sinecures was recommended.

From the beginning of the Revolutionary war the influence which ministers
had derived from the negotiation of government contracts and the floating of
loans on specially favourable terms to friendly financial houses was more or less
destroyed by the introduction of open tender. And the granting of offices in
reversion (a system of mortgaging future patronage to pay for present support)
came to an end in the post-war period.

After 1782 the *droits* of the Admiralty and of the Crown were the only
important source of public money beyond the control of Parliament which
might be secretly spent on elections. Very large sums came into the Treasury
in war-time in the form of prize-money from the sale of captured enemy ships
and their cargoes, but in practice little was available for electioneering, because
such money had first of all, in order to become secret money, to be made over
to the king's privy purse which, as the sovereign's 'pocket money', was always

beyond Parliament's control; and there would have been a great outcry from the opposition if large sums had been siphoned off in this way.

William Eden, later Lord Auckland, wrote: "Burke's foolish Bill has made it a very difficult task for any set of men to form or maintain an Administration." John Robinson, surveying the parliamentary situation on the eve of the general election of 1784, lamented "how little the real substantive weight is which Government carries". Wraxall, the diarist M.P., thought that the diminution of the number of placemen effected by Burke's Act almost *compelled* Pitt and the king to counteract that loss of influence by increasing the peerage.

But these were exaggerated estimates of the effects of the reforms of 1782, which, indeed, proved disappointing to the reformers. The disfranchisement of the revenue officers did not, as Rockingham was reported (erroneously, no doubt) to have claimed, deprive the government of seventy boroughs; in actual fact this change affected the returns in only about fifteen constituencies where the electorate was minute. The Whig aim had been merely to *limit* the power of the executive to 'choose' the House of Commons–not to weaken the political influence of the great families who believed themselves to have almost a prescriptive right to govern the country (there was no proposal to abolish the nomination boroughs, which would have effectively accomplished both purposes), nor to strengthen the influence of the people. Moreover, the saving of money, and therefore the reduction of patronage, was less than had been expected. The Board of Trade, abolished in 1782, was revived as early as 1786, and so was the Third Secretaryship of State in 1793; and over-spending on the Civil List continued. Ministers admitted after 1815 that the patronage of the Crown had increased since pre-war days, the long struggle with France having greatly increased the public debt and the civil, military and colonial establishments. These, as Edward Cooke, the Under-Secretary of State for Foreign Affairs, remarked in 1817, "provide a sufficient support to the Crown under any reasonable system of management and conduct". He added: "If the direct influence in Parliament was much greater in Sir Robert Walpole's time, I have no doubt that the indirect influence is five times as great out of Parliament *now*." Charles Wynn, the Grenvillite M.P., said in 1812 that "the real grievance at present" was "the great increase of the mercantile men in the House of Commons above all former precedent, and their having become, from the circumstances of the war and the new commercial system, more entirely in the power of the Government than ever". Consequently, these men, together with those country gentlemen who, in order to obtain local patronage, supported every Prime Minister, constituted "a floating transferable body so powerful as to enable the Crown to give a majority to any Minister, however small may be the number of his adherents".

On the other hand, as Frederick Robinson, the President of the Board of

Trade, said in 1822, this increase in the amount of patronage was being power-fully counteracted by an increasing weight of public opinion, "a check far more effective upon the influence of the Crown than any which had existed when that influence . . . had been much greater than at present". The large-scale creation of peers by Pitt and his successors, by subtracting from the House of Commons a great weight of landed property, and placing a great weight of political influence at the government's disposal, had similar results. As early as 1797 Fox acknowledged the futility of the economical reforms of 1782, and said that Burke's prediction (that no House of Commons would hereafter be strong enough to oppose ministers) had been literally fulfilled. The opponents of Curwen's Bill (1809) maintained that if seats were no longer to be bought and sold like cattle at Smithfield, the market in them would contract, and the Treasury would monopolize the 'seat trade'; that unless dealings in this market could be effectively stopped (and nothing but parliamentary reform would bring this about) there would be only one set of jobbers. But the Act worked the other way: private dealings continued unimpeded, and it was the Treasury which had to put a stop to 'money transactions'.

On the other hand, the return of peace in 1815 brought about a large reduction of establishments and consequently of ministerial patronage; and it ushered in a period of deflationary finance, during which that patronage was appreciably reduced. The economy campaign of the early 1820s, stimulated by the agricultural depression and the consequential fall in the value of landed property and the income therefrom, made substantial progress, because on this issue the Whig opposition had the support of the independent country gentle-men; and taxation was reduced by impressive amounts. It was to public opinion, said Huskisson, that ministers must henceforth look "for any durably prevailing influence in Parliament itself". Canning declared in 1827 that he meant "to found his Government upon public opinion rather than borough interests", in which, remarked Palmerston, the Secretary at War, "I think he is as right as possible". His predecessor Lord Liverpool continued after 1820 to defend the existence of useless places as necessary to keep up the influence of the Crown. In 1822, however, the number of junior Lords of the Admiralty was reduced by two, both of whom could have been members of the House. At the same time a placeman disappeared from the Lords when the two Postmasters-General were reduced to one, and the consolidation of the British and Irish Treasuries in 1816 involved a net loss of three parliamentary offices. The economy cam-paign made further headway whilst Wellington was Prime Minister; so much so, indeed, that when the Whigs returned to power in Nov. 1830 they found that there was little scope for additional retrenchment, and they were quite unable to satisfy the extravagant notions popularly held as to the reductions they would be able to effect. Althorp, the new Leader of the House, admitted that the Wellington ministry had sacrificed more patronage than any preceding government. The duke himself remarked, in 1830 (with some exaggeration, however): "No Government can go on without some means of rewarding services. I have absolutely none!" Peel said, somewhat ruefully, that during the first two years of the duke's premiership he had never had at his disposal an office worth more than £100 a year. The retrenchments of his government, it was said, had been particularly exercised upon those offices which were given for patronage purposes.

In one respect George IV and his Prime Ministers were in a stronger position than their predecessors had been. He himself was never embarrassed, as he had so grievously embarrassed both his father after 1782 and his own ministers for some years after he became regent, by the political activities of an heir-apparent, seeking to build up a parliamentary connexion of his own by the lavish bestowal of 'post obits' (many of which were presented for redemption after 1812). This was the 'reversionary' influence of the Crown. He might well have been so embarrassed had his daughter, Princess Charlotte, survived (having married Prince Leopold, she died in childbed in 1817 at the age of twenty-one), for, although her grandmother warned her that for "any of the royal family taking a part against the Crown was lowering it most essentially", she was warmly attached to Whig principles in opposition to the court and the ministers, and she was in secret correspondence with Grey, the leader of the opposition. Neither the duke of York nor his brother William, who succeeded him as George IV's heir-presumptive in Jan. 1827, sought to set up a party of his own *in opposition to* the Crown.

A portion of the Crown patronage had at all times been diverted from the ministerial channel into which it necessarily flowed: Lord Lieutenancies, Garters and Ribbands were occasionally given to opposition peers who enjoyed the sovereign's personal friendship. Moreover, it would be a mistake to suppose that all civil servants tamely voted for the government candidate at an election; true, a tidewaiter was once dismissed for voting the wrong way, but many examples of downright insubordination and 'damn the consequences' could be cited. In 1822 Castlereagh denied that the Admiralty and the Horse Guards took political opinion into account in the distribution of patronage, and he said that colonial appointments were no longer a source of political influence (seven-eighths of all appointments there were in the hands of local officials and "In some islands there were only three or four, and in others six or seven appointments vested in the Crown"). Not one-third of appointments in the East India Company's service, he added, were at the disposal of ministers. And only 47 or 48 members of Parliament held offices under the Crown "in a sense to which influence could be fairly attached". Within a few years the agitation of O'Connell's Catholic Association succeeded in destroying a large proportion of the influence over the Irish county elections which the great families had possessed (and, therefore, indirectly, the government).

Ministers were not insensitive to the idea gaining ground in the country that political and ecclesiastical patronage as well as public money ought not to be used to purchase votes in Parliament. Peel said in 1817 that Lord Whitworth, the Lord Lieutenant of Ireland, had never "in any single instance recommended an elevation in the peerage for the purpose of securing a powerful interest at an election for a county member, as he does not think that it would be consistent with his duty to procure such influence by such means". No one, he declared in 1816, could justly accuse the Irish Government of using the pension list for the purchase of parliamentary support. "No member of Parliament has been assisted by it. No vote has been influenced by it." Apparently afraid of opposition criticism, the Treasury in 1822 took what was described as the "desperate and most destructive step" of relinquishing to the Commissioners of Customs (civil servants independent of all administrations) control of the departmental patronage, without having seriously considered, it was suggested, the consequences of this 'renunciation of power' whenever a general election occurred. Bootle Wilbraham, who sat for Dover, protesting against a decision which affected him personally (the local Customs patronage had always been given to the member supporting administration), declared: "The idea of carrying on the government in times like the present, without using that lawful influence which has always been exercised by Government, and even with the assistance of which, it has been found difficult to carry measures of importance at critical periods, and to stem the torrent of popular prejudice and feeling at general elections, is quite Utopian."

As early as 1814 ministers had repudiated the notion that Church preferments were "the proper fund for the requital of election services". "The Government", wrote Peel, "is not so weak or so contemptible in the eyes of the people as to make it necessary to err against principle for the purpose of securing a single vote." And Wellington boasted that whilst he was Prime Minister ecclesiastical patronage had been dispensed on a strictly non-political basis. Victorian statesmen have rightly been praised for rescuing public life from the evil traditions of corruption inherited from the eighteenth century, yet some credit should be given also to men like Liverpool, Peel and Wellington, who, even more than Pitt and Burke, set their faces against the grosser forms of aristocratic jobbery both in Church and State. In 1831 Peel proudly claimed that no government, during the previous forty years had been more pure than that which had just been defeated–and Lord John Russell admitted the justice of the claim. Peel was sure that no government could then go on without the support of popular opinion, and Althorp "thanked God the time was passed when the government . . . could be carried on by patronage". This process of constitutional change in itself amounted to a revolution, silently accomplished during the preceding half-century, and comparable in importance with the Act of 1832 itself.

The reaction that set in against the excesses of the French Revolution, and the avalanche of reformist legislation that followed the great Act of 1832, have tended to obscure the fact that the period here covered was itself an Age of Reform, and its achievements are all the more impressive when one remembers the opposing strength and variety of reactionary forces both inside and outside Parliament. The abolition of the slave trade (and the end of slavery itself was quite obviously in sight in 1832), the Catholic Relief Act, the humanizing of the penal code, the better treatment of pauper and criminal lunatics, the creation of the Metropolitan Police, the legalization of trade unions, the enlargement of the liberty of the working man by the removal of the statutory prohibition against emigration, the liberation of trade and industry from a great variety of injurious governmental restrictions, the encouragement given by Parliament to such voluntary 'self-help' organizations as friendly societies and savings banks, the progress of administrative reform in both Church and State, and the Reform Act of 1832 itself: these are impressive achievements, illustrating the impact on the Legislature of the ideas associated with the names of Adam Smith, Bentham and Ricardo, and of Pitt, Fox, Wilberforce and Huskisson. It is easy, then, to do less than justice to the unreformed Parliament and to accept unquestioningly the Radical view of a corrupt and worn-out body, riddled with selfish class interest. Its prestige, in fact, stood unassailably high; except for an insignificant number of physical-force extremists and hotheads, even the Radicals did not agitate for its abolition, but merely for its reformation; it was everywhere recognized to be the sovereign instrument of reform and improvement, and the Radicals had a touching faith in its ability to sweep away poverty and unemployment and to establish the social millenium. That their faith was not shared by the statesmen of the time is no proof that these men were indifferent to the grave social evils which the rapid progress of industry was producing. The willingness of the propertied classes to bear the heavy burden of poor rates, and the enormous sums voluntarily contributed by the rich for an extraordinary variety of philanthropic activities, are a sufficient answer to suggestions of heartlessness and selfish class feeling. Whenever an abuse of either political or economic power was pointed out, there were always, in both Houses, members ready to bring the matter to public discussion and to press for a remedy. In the unreformed Parliament men like Whitbread, Romilly and Henry Grey Bennet were as sensitive to cries of distress from the poor as, after 1832, men like Shaftesbury. It would be unrealistic to blame the Legislature for failing to soften the harsh impact of trade depressions on poor starving factory workers and agricultural labourers by the creation of a welfare state; Adam Smith had convinced the governing class that economic forces were infinitely stronger than governments and legislatures, and that the most effective way to increase the country's prosperity was to allow these economic forces free play. So the Prime Minister could write in 1816: "I have never known any period of internal distress arising from defective crops or stagnation in trade, in which the discussions of Parliament did not do more harm than the measures of relief proposed, afforded benefit." It was Perceval, the most reactionary Prime Minister of the century, who, supported by Wilberforce, introduced a Bill to compensate the poverty-stricken curates, who sometimes worked as cotton weavers to save themselves and their families from downright starvation, for the increased cost of living caused by currency inflation. Other 'reactionaries', believing that the condition of the West Indian slave was in some measure preferable to that of the English agricultural labourer, advocated State-sponsored schemes of employment on the grand scale in the form of railway construction "from one end of England to the other", and the apportionment of waste lands in small holdings, to relieve the workless and avert civil strife. But these were voices crying in the wilderness; ministers, irrespective of party labels, believed that the government could do little more to make the country prosperous than to maintain law and order and external security, and to keep taxation at the lowest possible level compatible with the discharge of its functions.

No one today believes that, during these years, everything was getting worse for the working man. The near-starvation condition of the agricultural worker in the south of England in 1830 was temporary and exceptional. The earlier trade cycles of a predominantly rural economy were, in the final analysis, caused chiefly by the vagaries of the weather; rapid industrial changes were now tending to increase the range of cyclical fluctuations, and consequently, the sufferings of the poor in bad times. It may be that an unusually large proportion of the country's production was taking the form of capital rather than consumer goods, but in the long run a rapidly expanding production (and the figures are beyond dispute) was incompatible with a falling standard of living for the workers as a whole. Clapham's general conclusion was that "whereas on the average the potential standard of comfort of an English (with Welsh) rural labouring family in 1824 was probably a trifle better than it had been in 1794, assuming equal regularity of work, there were important areas in which it was definitely worse, and many in which the change either way was imperceptible". "There were declining, improving and stagnant trades and districts: there were trades liable to sharp wage changes, and others in which standard rates were remarkably uniform; but an index number covering all, shows a curious stability. A great war-time rise; a post-war fall, less than the rise, often very much less; then comparative stability–is the general formula for the years 1790-1850." Bad though conditions in the factories remained (and in any case the number of factory workers using steam-driven machinery was still comparatively small in 1830), they were tending to improve, and on the whole the mill operatives were better off than the agricultural workers and those employed in their own homes. The handloom weavers were not the only employees who worked longer hours in their homes than the factory workers. Women employed in agriculture had always had a longer working day, and though the work might be healthier it could be at least as exhausting; and it would probably have been better to work in cotton mills than in such homes in the Midlands where the small metal trades were carried on. The industrial revolution introduced neither the capitalist nor the factory system of production, nor did it begin the evils of child labour. Defoe had long ago noted whilst travelling through the West Riding that hardly any children above the age of four were to be seen playing out-of-doors: they were helping their parents spinning yarn and weaving and finishing cloth; all were employed, "from the youngest to the oldest". Nevertheless it cannot be denied that the 'discipline' of the new factories was such that many people, men and women, preferred to work for a pittance in their homes, under the worst conditions, than in the mill, where wages were higher. The contrast is sufficiently glaring between the great and growing prosperity of the upper class, proud of its rank, achievements and intelligence, and of the Constitution under which it flourished, and the wretched state of the labouring poor, particularly in the new industrial areas. Yet the workers, whether in town or country, were very much better off than the Irish peasants, whose lives were completely unaffected by industrial change. Among them were many sub-tenants, paying £50 a year rent for their small holdings and living with their numerous children in two-roomed huts, littered down like a loose stall with straw; and it was said that the worst cottage of the most miserable English pauper was a mansion in comparison. There can be no doubt that one of the causes of the low standard of living in England was the annual influx of thousands of starving Irish labourers, whose presence enabled employers to depress wages. Yet the condition of the poor was in some respects improving. A wheat-bread diet had been largely substituted for rye bread; the consumption of meat was increasing by a higher percentage than the increase of population; in the 1820s most country cottages had brick or stone or wood floors, feather or flock beds with blankets and sheets, chairs and tables, earthenware plates and dishes: whereas half a century earlier cottages had usually an earth flooring, unplastered walls, no ceiling under the straw roof, doors and windows which did not keep out rain or snow, straw beds with a single rug for covering, benches instead of tables, wooden trenchers instead of earthenware plates. And the people were cleaner: three times as much soap was used in the 1820s as in the 1780s. Many working men were contriving to save money through the medium of savings banks and friendly societies. Of the latter, several thousand were in existence after the wars, with a membership of nearly a million (about one-eleventh of the population), who were thus enabled to live, in sickness and old age, without having to resort to parish funds. This affords proof of a spirit of independence such as could hardly be matched in any other European country.

At times, of course, especially when the harvest failed or when trade was unusually stagnant, fears of social revolution were widespread among the propertied classes; and it cannot be said that those fears were groundless, because history showed that popular insurrections were often successful, because the forces of law and order were relatively weak, and because the country seemed to exhibit the conditions that might be expected to produce revolt–spectacular contrasts between wealth and poverty, and strains inseparable from rapid industrialization. Those who disliked the progress of industrialization because, as they believed, it increased the misery and depravity of the poor were confident that revolution was inevitable. An industrial proletariat, concentrated in great conurbations of population, was always ripe for rioting; the terrible events in London in 1780 were never forgotten and the ugly temper of the mob was again displayed in the Birmingham riots of 1791 and after the assassination of Perceval in 1812.

Very different explanations of the avoidance of revolution have been offered, both by contemporaries and historians. Some have emphasized the immense strength of the great conservative force of religion. "We have a moral and religious people sensible of the blessings which they possess," and though reactionary Tories trusted to Divine Providence (and the effects of morning and evening prayers which they hoped to see introduced in the factories) to bring the country safely through the dangers that beset it, they saw in the increasing defection of the people from the Established Church an alarming symptom of national danger. Others stressed the essential conservatism of the English people: their attachment to their historic institutions, their dislike of sweeping Utopian theories and pen-made Constitutions (Tom Paine had never much of a following during his lifetime), their horror of bloodshed and violence, revealed by their attitude to the excesses of the French Jacobins. In England it was notorious that there was a real respect for rank and title. The aristocracy, which all but monopolized political power, was not unpopular, as was the French, and the successful merchant or manufacturer sought to marry his daughters into the peerage or himself aspired after its honours. The few who wanted to destroy the monarchy and 'start afresh' were, for the most part, half-crazy people like Thistlewood and Brandreth, and their handful of followers either criminals or poor, deluded, ignorant men driven by hunger and unemployment into desperate courses. The Radical reformers had no wish to end the parliamentary system; they attacked only what they considered to be its corrupt excrescences, repudiated the title of innovators, and professed to aim only at the restoration of the House of Commons to its pristine purity. And we have already noticed that, when reform was really seriously demanded by the people, the agitation eventually proved successful. Moreover, in 1829 on the question of Catholic emancipation, and in 1832 on the question of parliamentary reform, Peel and Wellington, the leaders of the Tory party, established the tradition that that which can no longer be defended except at the cost of civil strife, must be surrendered; that in political conflict the time comes when it is more injurious to the public interest to continue resistance to change than to accept change and make it as harmless as possible. So, as Peel said, "amid foreign wars, the shock of disputed successions, rebellion at home, extreme distress, the bitter contention of parties, the institutions of this country have stood uninjured". The Conservative party, then, showed itself capable of learning by experience that the way to avert revolution was to abandon opposition to inevitable change.

One factor of great importance remains to be mentioned. The most significant of the social changes of the period was not the pauperization of the agricultural labourers as a result of 'Speenhamland' (that deplorable phase soon passed), but the growth of a large and powerful middle class and the increasingly widespread ownership of property: a solid and powerful guarantee against social revolution. Thousands of people were dying every year leaving property attracting legacy duty, and the revenue arising therefrom was increasing rapidly. In 1823 the number of people with money invested in government securities exceeded 288,000; about 92,000 had dividends not exceeding £5 a year; more than 42,000 drawing dividends of between £5 and £10, and over 101,000 whose dividends were between £10 and £50 a year. The average holding of these 101,000 people must have been something not very far short of £1,000 each (? the equivalent of about £10,000 today). There were, then, about 53,000 people drawing dividends exceeding £50 a year–and, incidentally, just about the same number of people employing one or more male servants (a rather larger number–72,000–owned a carriage). More than 148,000 people kept a horse for pleasure, and more than 40,000 had more than one. All the available figures seem to indicate that the greater part of the increased wealth of the country was falling into the hands of the middle class, and the Act of 1832 made it certain that political power would be transferred to a middle-class electorate, proud of its wealth, its energy and its enterprise. The idea was gaining ground that, under middle-class leadership, the country was entering upon an era of rapid material and moral progress. The cyclical view of history was repudiated; in spite of periods of obscurantism and reaction, mankind was moving onward to a consummation of glory, and no advance that was made was ever lost. There was no lack of faith in the natural progress of society, no lack of contempt for 'reactionaries' who were convinced that industrialism bore within itself the seeds of its own destruction, that its downfall was being hastened by the competition of foreign manufacturers persuading their governments by the imposition of tariffs to destroy our export trade. The prosperity of nations was advancing, and all the arts of life were approaching nearer and nearer to perfection. In 1830 Macaulay was confident that by 1930 England would have achieved even more astonishing progress than the preceding century had witnessed.

> "A population of 50 millions, better fed, clad and lodged than the English of our time, will cover these islands . . . Sussex and Huntingdonshire will be wealthier than the wealthiest parts of the West Riding now are. . . . Machines, constructed on principles yet undiscovered, will be in every house. . . . There will be no highways but railroads, no travelling but by steam. . . . Our debt, vast as it seems to us, will appear to our great-grand-children a trifling encumbrance, which might easily be paid off in a year or two."

All that was necessary to ensure this progress was that government should be sufficiently enlightened to confine its activities within the narrowest limits, that its functions should continue to be largely negative: to maintain peace at home and abroad, to defend property, to observe the strictest economy in every department of the State (the individual citizen knowing how best to spend his money, rather than having it spent for him by gentlemen in Whitehall), to leave capital to find its most lucrative course, commodities their fair price, industry and intelligence their natural reward, idleness and folly their natural punishment.

And this material progress would be matched by the moral progress of the nation, a progress bound up with the advancement of knowledge. Knowledge, it was felt, begets prudence. To acquire habits of reflection, engendered by reading, will generally reclaim men from idleness and drunkenness. The possession of knowledge will produce the same effect upon the working classes that the possession of wealth produces among the rich: it gives them a direct interest in the peace and good order of society. They cannot learn much without discovering how inseparably their interests are connected with the preservation of order, and, above all, the inviolable security of property. And, the better informed the people are, the more they will know about the management of public affairs and be the more determined to correct abuses.

There had been no such breezy optimism in 1783. Few who then surveyed England's situation would have ventured to prophesy that the next half-century was to be one of the most glorious periods of her history. With the successful revolt of the American colonies the greater part of the empire had disappeared. Ireland, taking advantage of England's embarrassments, had just extorted

legislative independence and freedom of trade, and, until the Union, the Crown
was the sole remaining constitutional link between the two countries. The great
Whig families, having joined Lord North and his friends in what was widely
considered to be a peculiarly odious coalition, had successfully, as it seemed,
challenged the admitted right of the king to choose his ministers. Burdened
with a staggering debt of unparalleled dimensions, the nation, emerging from
unsuccessful war, was apparently destined to suffer all the evils of financial
collapse such as was hurrying France on to revolution and bankruptcy. Few,
moreover, would have thought that, within a few years of the conclusion of a
protracted war against the rebellious colonists and the combined strength of the
Bourbon Powers, England would again be engaged in a far greater struggle
with France which would last for nearly a quarter of a century. As a great
maritime Power, it was felt that we could never be led astray by specious views
of continental conquest. As a great commercial people we were peculiarly
interested in the preservation of European peace, by which alone markets
everywhere could be kept open to the products of British industry. During the
first years of Pitt's premiership the European Powers seemed on the whole to be
making progress in the direction of internal prosperity and external security.
Governments had apparently convinced themselves that more was to be gained
by cultivating the arts of peace than in the pursuit of aggressive designs on their
neighbours. The intelligentsia were coming to regard war as odious and unworthy of the enlightenment of the age. Four months after the meeting of the
States-General, Pitt declared that "everything seems to be going on very well
for us both at home and abroad". Even as late as Feb. 1792, when the Austro-
Prussian armies were preparing to restore Louis XVI, Pitt looked forward to
fifteen years of peace and prosperity as a reasonable expectation for the British
people. But this pleasing prospect quickly vanished, and, as in the days of
Louis XIV, Europe was soon confronted with the menace of universal monarchy.

The long wars were not, however, wholly disastrous to England. Her naval
supremacy, achieved by Jervis, Duncan and Nelson, enabled her to engross the
greater part of the carrying trade of Europe, the ships of her enemies being
more or less confined to their harbours. The superior skill and inventive power
of her workmen gave her pre-eminence in manufacture and enabled her to
emerge from war with greater wealth and resources than when she was driven
to embark on it. And, throughout these years, the rapid progress of science, the
arts and manufactures seemed to furnish proofs of the superior wisdom and
attainments of the age. As in preceding wars, those of the years 1793–1815
compelled a marked expansion of production and helped to push her commerce
into the markets of the world. And the enormous cost of these wars forced the
government drastically to overhaul the inefficient system of taxation: a change
which marks an important stage in the history of administrative reform.

In 1815 England emerged from the conflict the greatest naval, commercial, industrial and colonial Power in the world. Of the European countries she alone had never suffered invasion. She had set a glorious example of unconquerable fortitude and endurance; she could claim the proud distinction of having kept alive the sacred flame of liberty and the spirit of national independence. For all her privations and sacrifices she reaped a rich harvest of glory. Under the protection of her navy a new empire had arisen, and, until the rise of Germany and Japan as great naval Powers at the close of the century, the British fleet, equal in strength to the united fleets of the world, was unchallenged and unchallengeable.

The year 1783 saw the virtual end of the First British Empire, but, before the close of the decade, the foundations of the Second had been laid. The new beginnings, however, owed nothing to government inspiration or encouragement. Official opinion was marked by complete lack of enthusiasm for further colonial enterprises: the loss of the American colonies effectively damped enthusiasm for imperial expansion. The Third (Colonial) Secretaryship of State was abolished by the Rockingham ministry as an economy measure before the American war had reached its close, and for the next twelve years such colonial business as remained was divided between the Home and Foreign departments. Then (1794) the pressure of events under the stress of war necessitated the revival of the Third Secretaryship as a War Secretaryship; finally, in 1801, colonial business was transferred from the Home to the War Office, whose head thus became the Secretary of State for War and the Colonies.

Pitt's India Act (1784) gave legal sanction to the official view that territorial expansion in India was to be firmly deprecated. But even Pitt had to admit that the wars in which Wellesley embarked were essentially defensive, brought on by the determination of the French Government, working in co-operation with the Indian princes, to strike a fatal blow in the East against British trade and greatness. The court of directors, however, thoroughly alarmed at Wellesley's ambitious policy of annexation and subsidiary alliance, recalled him in 1805. One of the arguments put forward in support of the continuance of the East India Company's trade monopoly in 1793, when its charter was due to be renewed by Parliament for a further period of twenty years, was that if the trade was thrown open India would soon attract thousands of Englishmen in the pursuit of wealth, and they would presently imitate the example of the thirteen mainland colonies in North America. If, during the Revolutionary and Napoleonic wars, the territorial expansion of the East India Company made astonishing progress, that result was achieved despite the wishes of Leadenhall Street and of Governors-General like Sir John Shore (1793–1798) who made every attempt to carry out the non-interventionist orders from home, but who came to realize that such a policy was utterly impracticable, leading only to disaster and disgrace. Whereas in 1783 India could hardly be mentioned without filling the benches of both sides of the House of Commons (it was the question of the Company's future management which, for the first and last time in English history, produced a change of government at home) twenty years later any discussion about India was calculated to empty the chamber as effectively as Burke's 'dinner-bell' speeches had done. An influential body of opinion condemned the 'all-grasping system' which had too long guided our Indian administrators, consuming our resources in ruinous conquests and cutting off the flower of our army in wholly unnecessary wars.

During this long period of war, interest in overseas expansion was virtually non-existent. Almost at the beginning of the struggle, Pitt and Dundas confirmed the aversions of Englishmen from colonial ambitions by sending 40,000 men to die of disease in the West Indies: heavier casualties than were sustained by Wellington's army during the whole of the Peninsular campaigns. Most of our overseas conquests—even the rich Spice islands—were retroceded in 1815–1816 with a light-hearted generosity calculated to make our earlier empire-builders turn in their graves. A few, indeed, were retained, but, in the main, only for strategic reasons or to serve as naval stations. Malta, the British protectorate over the Ionian islands, and the Cape were considered to be of some use in guarding the long sea-routes to India and the Far East and providing British merchantmen with supplies of food and fresh water. Ceylon too was kept, largely because of the high value attached to the fine harbour of Trincomali—the only safe retreat for shipping on the west side of the Bay of Bengal during the period of the stormy south-west monsoon.

These, and the acquisitions of the East India Company, were regarded with extreme disfavour by the Whig opposition in Parliament and an important section of public opinion as adding to the cost of imperial defence and colonial administration (and therefore to the burdens of the British taxpayer) and as increasing the 'influence' of the Crown. In the view of these 'Little Englanders', as a later generation would have dubbed them, colonies were nothing but a source of embarrassment and expense. The convict settlement in Australia seemed to offer few advantages to free emigrants. Nor did the Cape, where the settlers, mostly Boer farmers, were in immediate contact with fierce and hostile tribes. Canada had a rigorous winter, and its productions were similar to those of Europe, so that the advantages to the mother country of sending out her sons and daughters seemed few and remote. "To save a halfpenny a lb. in sweetening our tea" we crowded our West Indian plantations with hundreds of thousands of wretched slaves, to the exclusion of white labour. On the one hand, emigration was calculated to raise wages at home, but on the other, higher wages were calculated to bring Irish paupers across St. George's Channel so much the faster. Whigs and Radicals alike maintained that colonies gave rise to war and corruption. They represented a vast system of outdoor relief for the younger sons of the aristocracy, a system needed because of the peculiarly British system of entailing landed property—a powerful instrument, indeed, for the maintenance of an aristocracy, but it had unfortunate repercussions on the lives of younger sons left without provision for their maintenance. Some of the Radicals wanted to make Canada independent. The Whigs, "like all men of sense", knew that Canada must, at no distant period, be merged in the American Republic; in the meantime it might have its uses as a dump for a million Irish paupers—and the government itself experimented in this direction in 1823 with the idea of ascertaining the cost. Far from deriving any benefit from the colonies, their possession involved us in heavy expense. The English consumer paid dearly for Canadian timber, which was very inferior to Baltic. And the virtual monopoly of the English market enjoyed by the West Indian planters meant that the Englishman spent more on sweetening his tea than he would have done under a system of unrestricted competition. The military cost alone, of defending our overseas possessions, exceeded one and a half millions a year. Most Whigs considered it a matter of indifference whether emigrants were established in the empire, or in the United States or anywhere else. A colony like Australia was in any case too distant to be governed long from home. We should breed up another set of Washingtons and Franklins who would wish to imitate their example, and we should have to add another hundred millions to the national debt in discovering their strength, for a spirited and commercial people would hardly be likely voluntarily to abandon their sovereignty over an important colony. Newgate in its colonial environment, would eventually evince a heroism worthy of the characters by whom it had been originally peopled. The Radical view was that if only England would emancipate her colonies and establish free trade, wars would cease, and the colonies would no longer be a burden to the taxpayer and would grow up into free and friendly nations. And the revolutions in Spanish America seemed to confirm the lesson of 1776, the truth of Turgot's doctrine that colonies were like fruit which falls from the tree as soon as it is ripe.

This 'cut the painter' attitude did not, however, appeal to most Tories, who took pride in the fact that England was carrying its arms, its commerce, its civilization into every corner of the habitable world; that already, upon the empire the sun never set. Whatever might be the ultimate fate of the British possessions beyond the sea, to have spread our laws, our language, our culture, our moral character over the most distant parts of the globe was a great and glorious achievement. A mistaken colonial policy had indeed lost us America, but we could derive consolation from the fact that whatever civilization there existed, whatever was ennobling, whatever was good and great, was of English origin. Her language, her laws, her free institutions, and her Bible: these gave

Britain pre-eminence amongst the nations, and it was her duty to send forth these, her blessings, to the remotest parts of the earth. And from a purely material point of view, colonies were of value as enlarging our trade; trade required ships, ships created seamen for manning the royal navy, and the whole contributed on the grand scale to individual and national wealth and national strength.

And the English people were beginning to take pride in the achievements of their countrymen in India. The impeachment of Warren Hastings had shown that they were no longer prepared to countenance injustice or oppression in the government of dependent oriental peoples. The days of ruthless exploitation had gone for ever, and, as Wellesley remarked, British power in India was henceforth to be "conducive to the happiness of the people as well as to our national advantage". The good effects produced by a beneficent government among a people who for centuries had lived under the shadow of a cruel despotism were becoming apparent. A permanent settlement of the revenues of Bengal put an end to the arbitrary exactions of the landholders. A better system of judicature was introduced by Cornwallis and improved by his successors. After centuries of intermittent war, the people were experiencing the blessing of peace. Famine was becoming a thing of the past. Missionary activity was seeking to improve the moral and religious condition of the depressed classes. Under the inspiration of some of the ablest and most devoted servants that British rule ever produced, a new and enlightened spirit entered into the Indian Civil Service. It was not enough to give the people of India the blessings of peace and prosperity; their gradual preparation for self-government should be the goal of British policy, and that aim the justification of the existing autocracy.

GENERAL BIBLIOGRAPHY

A. MANUSCRIPT SOURCES

Even more so for this than for earlier periods, the printed sources are a mere fragment of the unpublished materials available to the research student.

(1) The Public Record Office, London

For a description of the State Papers, see M. S. Guiseppi, *Guide to the Manuscripts Preserved in the Public Record Office* (2 vols., 1923–1924). In addition to the vast quantity of Departmental Records, there are some important collections formerly in private ownership. Until recently they were classified as 'Gifts and Deposits'; now they are described as 'P.R.O. 30'. The most valuable are the *Chatham Papers* (P.R.O. 30/8), the papers of the 1st and 2nd earls and of the Younger Pitt, the 2nd earl's brother; the *Colchester Papers* (P.R.O. 30/9), the diaries (in 7 large vols.) and correspondence of Charles Abbot, Speaker of the House of Commons, and 1st Baron Colchester. Some valuable portions of the diary and most of the correspondence are unpublished. Comprising part of this collection, too, are 10 vols. of the Journal of the 1st earl of Ellenborough, 1828–1832, most of it being published. Then there are the *Ellenborough Papers* proper (P.R.O. 30/120), the papers of the 1st earl, including his unpublished later Journal, and a small quantity of his father's correspondence; the *Granville Papers* (P.R.O. 30/29), especially those of Canning's friend, the 1st earl; the Papers of *Lord John Russell* (P.R.O. 30/22), mostly, however, comprising the years after 1832; and the Papers of *General Sir Galbraith Lowry Cole* (P.R.O. 30/43). The *Cornwallis Papers* (P.R.O. 30/11) are valuable both for Irish and Indian history.

(2) H.M. General Register House, Edinburgh (the Public Record Office of Scotland)

Recent acquisitions of MSS. are listed in the annual volumes of the *Scottish Historical Review*. Amongst the private collections deposited there are the Bught (Grant family), Dunglass, Eglinton, Hamilton of Pinmore, James Loch, Kinross House, Cunningham-Graham of Ardoch, Dalhousie, Seaforth, about ninety boxes of Melville Papers, including Indian, and the Records of the Carron Iron Company.

(3) The Public Record Office of Northern Ireland (Belfast)

For accessions of MSS., see the Annual Reports of the Deputy Keeper of the Public Records. Recent acquisitions are the MSS. of the marquess of Downshire, Sir George Fitzgerald Hill and of the marquess of Abercorn, additional Drennan MSS., and that portion of Lord Anglesey's MSS. (the remainder being at Plas Newydd) relating to the 1st marquess's Irish Viceroyalty. There is also a good collection of the MSS. of Earl Macartney (1736–1806).

(4) The Public Record Office, Dublin

Most of the records were destroyed during the 'troubles' of 1922, when the Four Courts were burnt to the ground. The MS. letter books of Lord Francis Leveson-Gower, whilst he was Irish Secretary (1828–1830), are here.

(5) The State Paper Office, Dublin Castle

Two Series of Official Papers, also the 'Rebellion' Papers and Secret Service Account Books, 1780–1833, survived the holocaust of 1922 because they were not then in the Four Courts; they are of great value for this period of Irish history.

(6) The British Museum

The reader is referred to J. P. Gilson's *Students Guide* to the MSS., to the admirably detailed Catalogues of MSS., and to the annual Bulletin of the National Register of Archives for acquisitions of MSS. since 1954 (earlier, to the Bulletin of the Institute of Historical Research). The great collections are those of Lords Hardwicke, Auckland, Liverpool and Wellesley; Pelham and Place. The most important are as follows (the numbers of the volumes are those of the Additional MSS., unless identified by Egerton): *Lord Wellesley*, 12564–13914 (mainly Indian), 29238–9, 36274–318, 37414–16; *John Reeves*, 16919–28; *Francis Place*, 27789–859, 35142–54, 36623–8, 37949–50; *Duke of Leeds*, 27918, 28040–95, 28570, Egerton, 3324–3508; *Sir Robert Wilson*, 30095–144; *Pelham* (1st and 2nd earls of Chichester), 33087–135; *Bentham*, 33537–64; *Auckland*, 34412–71, 45728–30, 46490–1, 46519; *Ricardo's letters to J. R. McCulloch*, 34545; *Nelson*, 18676, 34902–92, 35191–202, 37953, 43504, 46356, Egerton, 1614–23; *General Rowland Hill, 1st Baron Hill*, 35059–67; *Hardwicke*, 35349–36278, 45030–47; *John Cam Hobhouse, Lord Broughton*, 36455–83, 47222–35; *Windham*, 37842–935; *Lord John Russell*, 38080; *Liverpool*, 38190–489, 38564–81; *Huskisson*, 38734–70, 39948–9; *Canning's correspondence with J. H. Frere*, 38833; *Lord Grenville's letters to Starhemberg*, 39841–2; *Peel*, 40181–617; *Brougham's letters to Lord Murray*, 40687; *Sir Philip Francis*, 40756–65, 47781–3; *Charles Greville's diary*, 41095–123; *Clarkson*, 41262–6; *George Rose*, 42772–846; *Lord Aberdeen*, 43039–358; *Dukes of Cleveland*, 43507; *Thomas Wilde, 1st Baron Truro*, 43727–8; *Account book of a Liverpool slave trader* (1785–1787), 43841; *Establishment book of George IV as Prince of Wales* (1795), 44843; *Pretyman* (material for Bishop Tomline's Life of Pitt), 45107–8; *Letter book of Maj. Gen. A. M. A. Hamilton*, in the West Indies (1804), 45112; *Sir Stamford Raffles*, 45271–3; *David Anderson* (of the East India Company's service, and friend of Warren Hastings), 45417–41; *Private letters of Lord Melbourne's family*, 45546–56, 45911; *Vice-Admiral Sir T. Boulden Thompson*, 46119; *Knightley*, 46356–61; *Worsley*, 46501–4; *Sir G. Don* (Deputy Adjutant-General to the duke of York's army in the Netherlands), 46702–11, 46883–4; *Canning's letters to E. Bootle-Wilbraham*, 46841; *Lieven*, 47236–435; *Fry and Gurney family correspondence* (including Elizabeth Fry's diary (1796–1845), 47456–7, Egerton, 3672–5; *C. J. Fox*, 47559–601; *John Bellingham* (murderer of Perceval, the Prime Minister), 48216; *Earl of Morley*, 48218–301; *General Sir George Cockburn*, 48312–39; *Sir Arthur Paget*, 48383–416; *3rd Viscount Palmerston's* Letter-books (mainly official papers), 48417–589; *Maj. Gen. Thomas Grosvenor's Journal* relating to the English expedition to Copenhagen in 1807, 49059; *Napier*, 49086–172; *Spencer Perceval*, 49173–95; *Sir William Hamilton* (British Envoy at Naples), Egerton, 2634–41; *Hertford* (Seymour-Conway family), Egerton, 3257–65; *Burney family*, Egerton, 3690–3708; *Duke of Northumberland's MSS.* at Syon House, Isleworth (microfilm copy); *Abergavenny MSS.* (photostats).

(7) The National Library of Ireland (Dublin)

The duke of Richmond's MSS. covering the years of his Viceroyalty (1807–1813); miscellaneous MSS.

(8) The National Library of Wales (Aberystwyth)

Charles Wynn MSS.; Letter Books (1808–1810) and diary (1809) of C. C. Cope Jenkinson; papers of family of Sir Thomas Picton.

(9) The National Library of Scotland (Edinburgh)

Letters of Henry, Lord Cockburn; of Edward Ellice; of George Rose; of Thomas Graham, Baron Lynedoch; of Lord Stuart de Rothesay; and a large quantity of Melville MSS.

(10) The Bodleian Library

Letters from Lord Grenville to Sir John Newport (MS. English Letters, d. 80); Letters to S. L. Giffard, editor of the *Standard* (MS. English Letters, c. 56); Correspondence of Sir T. D. Acland (MS. English Letters, d. 81–82); General John Briggs, papers concerning Indian affairs, 1817–1834; Correspondence of Charles Philip Yorke (MS. English Letters, c. 60); Lord Arden's letters as Lord Lieutenant of Surrey, etc., 1812–1840; Barham MSS. (West Indian estates, and papers of Joseph Barham, M.P. for Stockbridge (MS. Clar. deposit, b. 33–38, c. 357–391).

(11) The Cambridge University Library

Copies of c. 4,000 letters received by Pitt, 1786–1805 (Add. 6958), and Pitt family (6959); MSS. of Sir Henry Hardinge, 1st Viscount Hardinge.

(12) Other Libraries

The John Rylands (Manchester): 60 letters from Dundas to Pitt; a catalogue of Pitt's correspondence, 1778–1806, compiled in 1834 by W. E. Tomline, son of Pitt's tutor and literary executor, 6 vols.; copies of George III's correspondence with Pitt, 1783–1787; correspondence of the 1st and 2nd Viscounts Melville respecting East India Company's affairs; Papers of Edward Davies Davenport; Sneyd MSS.; MSS. of Samuel Oldknow (d. 1828), a leading figure in the early history of the cotton industry; 600 letters and documents from the Pitt Papers about Indian and the East India Company's affairs.

University College, Bangor. For an account of the various collections containing material for the study of local economic history, see A. H. Dodd's *Industrial Revolution in North Wales* (Cardiff, 1933).

University College, London: Bentham MSS.; Brougham MSS.; Papers of the Society for the Diffusion of Useful Knowledge.

Aberdeen University: G. Kerr's journal on voyage to northern whale fishery on the *Christian* of Aberdeen, 1791.

Bristol University Library: The Pinney MSS. (for the history of the West Indies).

Brotherton Library, University of Leeds: Miscellaneous MSS.

Manchester City Library: Henry Hunt's correspondence and journal whilst in prison after 'Peterloo'.

Queen's University, Belfast: c. 300 letters, etc., concerning Sir John Newport and his family.

Nottingham University: Newcastle MSS.; Portland MSS.; Galway MSS.

The Co-operative Union, Holyoake House, Manchester: Robert Owen MSS.

The National Maritime Museum, Greenwich: MSS. of Lord St. Vincent and of Admiral Sir William Parker.

W. L. Clements Library, Ann Arbor, Michigan, U.S.A.: J. W. Croker Papers, c. 90 vols., occupying 17 feet; Thomas Townshend, 1st Viscount Sydney (4 ft.); Henry Goulburn (c. 200 items); George Canning (214 items); Melville MSS., c. 30 vols.; Pitt MSS. (1 ft.); Lord Sheffield's MSS. (1 ft.); Brougham MSS. (c. 1,000 letters); Sir Henry Clinton's MSS., 1750–1812 (80 ft.); George III correspondence, 1784–1810 (typescript of unpublished MSS. in the Royal Archives at Windsor, purchased 1929); and miscellaneous MSS.

Huntington Library, San Marino, California: A large quantity of miscellaneous MSS.

(13) MSS. in Local Record Offices, etc.

Many of these offices (lists of which are to be found in the annual *Bulletins of the National Register of Archives*, an offshoot of the Historical Manuscripts Commission, and published by H.M. Stationery Office) have issued guides to their collections.

Berkshire: The Braybrooke, Benyon, Pleydell-Bouverie, Mount, David Hartley MSS., and the parliamentary diaries, etc., of Richard Neville Aldworth Neville; Wallingford borough parliamentary election papers.

Buckinghamshire: Earl of Buckinghamshire MSS.; Tyrwhitt-Drake Papers.

Cornwall: Tremayne and Rashleigh MSS.; Saltash borough parliamentary election papers; Sir Christopher Hawkins MSS. in Royal Institution of Cornwall, Truro.

Devonshire: Sidmouth MSS.

Gloucestershire: Bragge-Bathurst MSS.

Grimsby Public Library: Tennyson MSS.

Hampshire: Sloane Stanley, Blachford, Bolton, T. Holt White, and Heathcote (of Hursley) MSS.

Hertfordshire: Wm. Baker MSS. (The Panshanger MSS. for a time deposited here are now in the Royal Archives at Windsor.)

Ipswich Borough Library: Henniker MSS.

Kent: Lord North's MSS. and papers of the 5th earl of Guilford, and of the 1st Viscount Hardinge.

Lincolnshire: Amcotts, and earl of Ancaster collections; Tennyson, Heron and Monson MSS.

Northamptonshire: Fitzwilliam (Milton); Diaries and Correspondence of George Agar-Ellis, 1st Baron Dover.

Rhodes House, Oxford: Anti-Slavery Society's MSS.

Spalding Gentlemen's Society: J. H. Stanhope MSS.

Staffordshire: Hatherton MSS.

East Suffolk: Barne MSS.; Pretyman-Tomline MSS.

Surrey: Goulburn MSS.

Worcestershire: Lechmere MSS.

Yorkshire (West Riding) [Sheffield]: Wharncliffe, Fitzwilliam, and Spencer-Stanhope MSS.

B. PRINTED SOURCES

(a) GENERAL WORKS

E. L. Woodward's *Age of Reform, 1815–70* (Oxford, 1954 edition) is the best short survey of the later part of this period; the preceding volume in the *Oxford History of England* by J. Steven Watson is still in preparation. Such older general histories as Sir Spencer Walpole's *History of England from the Conclusion of the Great War in 1815* (vols. I to III, 1890 edition), Sir John Marriott, *England since Waterloo* (1913), Wm. Hunt's volume in Longman's *Political History of England Series* (1905) and the succeeding vol. (XI) by G. C. Brodrick and J. K. Fotheringham (1906), covering the period 1760–1801 and 1801–1837 respectively, are still useful. Halévy's *History of the English People*, vols. I to III, covering the years 1815–1841, is a brilliantly suggestive survey; and his *Growth of Philosophical Radicalism* (1928, translated by M. Morris), though less well known, is of great value. Sir C. Grant Robertson's *England under the Hanoverians*, like Marriott's volume in the same (Methuen) series, has passed through many editions. Professor G. M. Trevelyan's *British History in the Nineteenth Century* (1938 edition) is equally well known. The non-political chapters of Lecky's *History of England in the Eighteenth Century*, which in any case stops at 1792, are still useful, and also his *History of Ireland in the Eighteenth Century*. On the economic side, Dr. J. H. Clapham's *Economic History of Modern Britain* (vol. I, *The Early Railway Age, 1820–50*, Cambridge, 1930 edition) and on the legal, Sir William Holdsworth's *History of English Law*, vols. X to XII (1938–1950) are exhaustive and indispensable. T. S. Ashton's

Economic History of England: The Eighteenth Century (1955) covers part of this period. *The Village Labourer* (1925), *The Town Labourer* (1925) and *The Skilled Labourer* (1920) by J. L. and B. Hammond are controversial books, written with rare gifts of imagination and insight, which portray the life of the English working man in this transitional age. The history of local government is covered by S. and B. Webb's classic volumes, *The Parish and the County* (1906), *The Manor and the Borough* (2 vols., 1908), *Statutory Authorities for Special Purposes* (1922), *The Story of the King's Highway* (1913) and *English Prisons under Local Government* (1922), together with *English Poor Law History* (3 vols., 1927–1929). Only 2 vols. (1929–1930), covering the years 1801–1810, of A. F. Fremantle's *England in the Nineteenth Century*, have appeared. *The Age of Improvement, 1783–1867* by Asa Briggs, has just been announced.

(b) BIOGRAPHIES, MEMOIRS, CORRESPONDENCE, AND SECONDARY WORKS

(i) *Prime Ministers of the Period*

Addington: G. Pellew, *Life of Henry Addington, Lord Sidmouth* (3 vols., 1847); **Canning**: A. G. Stapleton, *Political Life of George Canning 1822–7* (3 vols., 1831), and *George Canning and His Times* (1859); E. J. Stapleton, *Some Official Correspondence of George Canning* (2 vols., 1887); J. Bagot, *Canning and His Friends* (2 vols., 1909); D. Marshall, *The Rise of George Canning* (1938); *Speeches*, edited by R. Therry (6 vols., 1836 edition); Sir Robert Wilson, *Canning's Administration: Narrative of Formation*, edited by H. Randolph (1872); A. Aspinall, *The Formation of Canning's Ministry, 1827* (Camden 3rd Series, vol. LIX, 1937); Lives by H. Temperley (1905), J. A. R. Marriott (1903), Sir C. Petrie (1946 edition); H. Temperley, *Foreign Policy of Canning, 1822–7* (1925); A. B. Beaven, "Canning and the Addington Administration in 1801" (*English Historical Review*, Jan. 1913); H. Temperley, "Joan Canning on her husband's policy and ideas" (*ibid.*, July 1930); **Goderich**: "The Goderich Ministry" (article by A. Aspinall in *English Historical Review*, Oct. 1927); **Lord Grenville**: *Dropmore Papers* (Historical MSS. Commission, 10 vols., 1892–1927); duke of Buckingham and Chandos, *Court and Cabinets of George III* (4 vols., 1853–1855), *Court and Cabinets of the Regency* (2 vols., 1856), *Court and Cabinets of George IV* (2 vols., 1859), *Court and Cabinets of William IV and Victoria* (2 vols., 1861); **Lord Grey**: *Life and Opinions of Earl Grey* by C. Grey (1861); G. M. Trevelyan, *Lord Grey of the Reform Bill* (1920); *Correspondence of Earl Grey with William IV, 1830–32*, edited by Earl Grey (2 vols., 1867); Guy Le Strange, *Correspondence of Princess Lieven and Earl Grey* (2 vols., 1890); **Lord Liverpool**: Life by C. D. Yonge (3 vols., 1868); W. R. Brock, *Lord Liverpool and Liberal Toryism, 1820–27* (Cambridge, 1941); Sir C. Petrie, *Lord Liverpool* (1956); **Spencer Perceval**: Life by Sir Spencer Walpole (2 vols., 1874); **Pitt**: Lives by Bishop Tomline (3 vols., 1821), Earl Stanhope (4 vols., 1861–1862), Lord Rosebery (1891), P. W. Wilson (New York, 1930), Sir C. Petrie (1935); Lord Ashbourne, *Some Chapters of His Life and Times* (1898); J. H. Rose, *William Pitt and National Revival* (1911), *William Pitt and the Great War* (1912), *Pitt and Napoleon: Essays and Letters* (1912); and *Short Life* (1925); P. W. Wilson, *The Younger Pitt* (New York, 1930); *Correspondence of Pitt with the Duke of Rutland, 1781–7* (Edinburgh, 1890); *War Speeches*, edited by R. Coupland (Oxford, 1915); *Speeches* (4 vols., 1806); D. G. Barnes, *George III and Wm. Pitt, 1783–1806* (1939); *Secret Correspondence connected with Pitt's return to office, 1804*, edited by Lord Mahon (1852); **Wellington**: Col. Gurwood, *Wellington Despatches* (12 vols., 1837–1838); *Supplementary Despatches*, edited by 2nd duke (15 vols., 1858–1872), and *Despatches, Correspondence and Memoranda* [covering the years 1819–1832], edited by 2nd duke (8 vols., 1867–1880); Earl Stanhope, *Notes of Conversations with Wellington* (1938 edition); Sir C. Webster, "Some Wellington Letters, 1807–17" (*Camden Miscellany*, vol. XVIII, 1948); Lives by

G. R. Gleig (1873), Sir H. Maxwell (2 vols., 1900), O. Brett (1928), Sir J. Fortescue (1925), Muriel Wellesley (1937), P. Guedalla (1931), C. R. M. F. Cruttwell (1936), R. Aldington (1946), Sir C. Petrie (1956); Sir Wm. Fraser, *Words on Wellington* (n.d.); G. R. Gleig, *Personal Reminiscences of the Duke of Wellington* (1904).

(ii) *Other Cabinet Ministers*

Lives of Lord Aberdeen by Sir Arthur Gordon (Lord Stanmore) [1893] and Lady F. Balfour (2 vols., 1923); Lives of Lord Althorp by Sir D. Le Marchant (1876) and E. Myers (1890); Bathurst Papers (Historical MSS. Commission, 1923); Lives of Brougham by John, Lord Campbell, in *Lives of the Chancellors*, vol. VIII (1869), J. B. Atlay in *The Victorian Chancellors*, vol. I (1906), G. T. Garratt (1935), Frances Hawes (1957), and Chester New (in preparation); *Brougham and His Early Friends*, edited by R. H. M. B. Atkinson and G. N. Jackson (3 vols., 1908); *Speeches* (4 vols., Edinburgh, 1838); *Life and Times, written by himself* (3 vols., Edinburgh, 1871) [with corrections by A. Aspinall in *English Historical Review*, vol. LIX (1944)]; A. Aspinall, *Lord Brougham and the Whig Party* (Manchester, 1927); Lives of Castlereagh by Sir C. Alison (1861), A. Hassall (1908), Sir J. A. R. Marriott (1936); *Memoirs and Correspondence of Castlereagh*, edited by 3rd marquess of Londonderry (12 vols., 1848–1853); H. M. Hyde, *The Rise of Castlereagh* (1933); Sir C. K. Webster, *Foreign Policy of Castlereagh* (2 vols., 1925–1931); Life of Cornwallis by W. S. Seton-Karr (1890); *Cornwallis Correspondence*, edited by C. Ross (3 vols., 1859); Lives of Lord Derby by T. E. Kebbel (1893) and G. Saintsbury (1892); Lord Dudley's *Letters to the Bishop of Llandaff* (1841) and *Letters to 'Ivy'*, edited by S. H. Romilly (1905); Lives of Henry Dundas, 1st Viscount Melville by J. A. Lovat-Fraser (Cambridge, 1916), H. Furber (Oxford, 1931) and C. Matheson (1933); Lives of J. G. Lambton, 1st Earl of Durham by S. J. Reid (2 vols., 1906) and C. W. New (Oxford, 1929); H. Twiss, Life of Lord Eldon (3 vols., 1844); A. Farnsworth, "Lord Chancellor Eldon" (*Law Quarterly Review*, April 1956); Lord Ellenborough's *Political Diary, 1828–30*, edited by Lord Colchester (2 vols., 1881); Lives of Lord Erskine by J. A. Lovat-Fraser (Cambridge, 1932) and L. P. Stryker (1949); *Speeches* (4 vols., 1810); C. J. Fox, *Speeches* (6 vols., 1815); *Memorials and Correspondence*, edited by Lord John Russell (4 vols., 1853–1857); Lives by Lord John Russell (3 vols., 1859–1867), J. L. Hammond (1903), J. Drinkwater (1928), Lord David Cecil (1931), E. C. P. Lascelles (Oxford, 1936), C. Hobhouse (1947 edition); W. F. Rae, *Wilkes, Sheridan and Fox* (1874); Life of Sir James Graham by W. T. McCullagh Torrens (1863); C. S. Parker, *Life and Letters of* (2 vols., 1907); Life of Lord Moira, Marquess of Hastings by Ross-of-Bladensburg (1893); Lord Hastings *Private Journal*, edited by Lady Bute (2 vols., 1858); E. Herries, Life of J. C. Herries (2 vols., 1880); Lord Holland, *Memoirs of the Whig Party*, edited by his son (2 vols., 1852–1854), and *Further Memoirs of the Whig Party, 1807–21*, edited by Lord Stavordale (1905); Sir J. Barrow, Life of Earl Howe (1838); Huskisson's *Speeches*, edited by E. Leeves, with a biographical memoir (3 vols., 1831); A Brady, *Huskisson and Liberal Reform* (1928); *Huskisson Papers*, edited by L. Melville (1931); C. R. Fay, *Huskisson and His Age* (1951); G. S. Veitch, "Huskisson and Liverpool" (*Transactions of Historic Society of Lancashire and Cheshire*, 1929); *Political Memoranda* of the Duke of Leeds, edited by O. Browning (Camden Society, New Series, vol. XXXV, 1884); Private Correspondence of Lord Granville Leveson-Gower, 1781–1821, edited by Lady Granville (2 vols., 1916); Lives of Lord Lyndhurst by Sir T. Martin (1883), John, Lord Campbell, in *Lives of the Chancellors*, vol. VIII (1869); and J. B. Atlay in *The Victorian Chancellors* vol. I (1906); Lives of Lord Melbourne by H. Dunckley (1890), W. T. McCullagh Torrens (2 vols., 1890 edition), and B. Newman (1930); Lord D. Cecil, *The Young Melbourne* (1939) and *Lord M.* (1954); *Melbourne Papers*, edited by L. C. Sanders (1889); Lives of Palmerston by H. L. E. Bulwer (2 vols., 1871), P. Guedalla (1926), E. F. Malcolm-Smith (1935) and H. C. F.

Bell (2 vols., 1936); Sir C. Webster, *Foreign Policy of Palmerston, 1830–41* (2 vols., 1951); Lives of Sir Robert Peel by J. R. Thursfield (1891), Lord Rosebery (1899), A. A. W. Ramsay (1928), G. Kitson Clark (1936), Sir T. Lever (1942); Peel's *Correspondence*, edited by C. S. Parker (3 vols., 1891–1899) and Peel's *Private Letters*, edited by G. Peel (1920); Peel's *Memoirs*, edited by Earl Stanhope and E. Cardwell (2 vols., 1856–1857); Lives of Lord John Russell by Sir Spencer Walpole (2 vols., 1889), S. J. Reid (1895) and A. W. Tilby (1930); *Early Correspondence of Lord John Russell, 1805–40*, edited by R. Russell (2 vols., 1913); Russell, *Recollections and Suggestions, 1813–73* (1875); Lives of Lord St. Vincent by E. P. Brenton (2 vols., 1838), J. S. Tucker (1844), W. V. Anson (1913), O. A. Sherrard (1933), Sir W. James (1950); Memoir of Lord Thurlow by 'E.T.' (1869); H. K. Olphin, George Tierney (1934); Lives of the Marquess Wellesley by W. T. McCullagh Torrens (1880), G. B. Malleson (1889), W. H. Hutton (1893); R. R. Pearce, *Memoirs and Correspondence of Wellesley* (3 vols., 1846); *Wellesley Papers*, edited by L. Melville (2 vols., 1914); Windham, *Speeches*, edited by T. Amyot (3 vols., 1812); R. W. Ketton-Cremer, *Early Life and Diaries of Windham* (1930); *Windham's Diary*, edited by Mrs. H. Baring (1866); *Windham Papers*, edited by L. Melville (2 vols., 1913); *Correspondence of Burke and Windham*, edited by J. P. Gilson (1910); Lady Crewe, *The Crewe Papers* (Philobiblon Society, 1865–1866).

(iii) *Other Works*

Abergavenny MSS. (Historical MSS. Commission, 1887); Lady Airlie, *In Whig Society, 1775–1818* (1921); *Lady Palmerston and Her Times* (2 vols., 1922); earl of Albemarle, *Fifty Years of My Life* (2 vols., 1876); William Allen, *Life and Correspondence* (3 vols., 1846); Lord Amherst, *Life* by A. T. Ritchie and R. Evans (Oxford, 1894); C. B. Andrews (editor), *Clouds and Sunshine by an English Tourist of the Eighteenth Century* (Marlow, 1935); *The Anti-Gallican* (1804); Charles Arbuthnot, *Correspondence*, edited by A. Aspinall (Camden 3rd Series, vol. LXV, 1941); Mrs. Arbuthnot, *Journal, 1820–32*, edited by F. Bamford and the duke of Wellington (2 vols., 1950); A. Aspinall (editor), *Three Early Nineteenth Century Diaries* [E. J. Littleton, Sir D. Le Marchant and Lord Ellenborough] (1952); J. B. Atlay, *The Trial of Lord Cochrane before Lord Ellenborough* (1897); Lord Auckland, *Journal and Correspondence*, edited by bishop of Bath and Wells (4 vols., 1861–1862); C. Badham, *Life of James Deacon Hume* (1859); W. Bagehot, *Biographical Studies*, edited by R. H. Hutton (1895); Wm. Beckford, *Life and Letters*, edited by L. Melville (1910); *Life* by G. Chapman (1937); Jeremy Bentham, *Memoirs* by John Bowring (11 vols., Edinburgh, 1843); John Beresford, *Correspondence*, edited by Wm. Beresford (2 vols., 1854); Miss Berry, *Journals and Correspondence, 1783–1852*, edited by Lady Theresa Lewis (3 vols., 1865); Lady Bessborough, *A Regency Chapter: Lady Bessborough and Her Friendships* by E. C. Mayne (1939); earl of Bessborough, *Georgiana, Duchess of Devonshire* (1955); earl of Bessborough and A. Aspinall, *Lady Bessborough and Her Family Circle* (1940); G. F. A. Best, "The Protestant Constitution and its Supporters, 1800–1829" (*Trans. Royal Historical Society*, 5th Series, vol. VIII [1958]); *The Extraordinary Black Book* [edited by John Wade], 1832 edition (enumerating political abuses: a Radical publication); C. Black, *The Linleys of Bath* (1911); Lord Bloomfield, *Memoir of*, edited by Lady Bloomfield (2 vols., 1884); [J. Warren Boyle], *Letters on the State of Ireland* (Dublin, 1825); Lord Brougham, *Historical Sketches of Statesmen who flourished in the time of George III* (3 parts, 1839–1843); P. A. Brown, *The French Revolution in English History* (1918); Lady Brownlow, *Reminiscences of a Septuagenarian, 1802–15* (2nd edition, 1867); Arthur Bryant, *The Years of Endurance, 1793–1802* (1942), *Years of Victory, 1802–1812* (1944), and *The Age of Elegance, 1812–1822* (1950); J. K. Buckley, *Joseph Parkes of Birmingham* (1926); Sir Henry Lytton Bulwer (Lord Dalling), *Historical Characters* (1900); Sir J. Bland Burges, *Letters and Correspondence*, edited by J. Hutton (1885); Lady Burghersh, *Letters*, edited by Lady Rose Weigall (1893); *Correspondence with the Duke of Wellington*, edited by Lady Rose Weigall (1903); Lord Burghersh, *Correspondence*, edited by Lady Rose Weigall (1912); Edmund Burke, *Works and Correspondence*, edited by W. King and F. Laurence (8 vols., 1792–1827); *Correspondence*, edited by Earl Fitzwilliam and General Sir R. Bourke (4 vols., 1844); *Correspondence with Dr. F. Laurence* (1827); biographies or studies by J. Prior (1839); John Morley (1893); B. Newman (1927); A. A. Baumann (1929); A. Cobban (1929); R. H. Murray (Oxford, 1931); Sir Philip Magnus (1939) and also his *Character and Private Life of Burke* (1949); and G. M. Young (1946); J. H. Rose, "Burke, Windham and Pitt" (*English Historical Review*, Oct. 1912 and Jan. 1913); Sir T. F. Buxton, *Memoirs*, edited by C. Buxton (3rd edition, 1849); P. Byrne, *Lord Edward Fitzgerald* (1955); Lord John Campbell, *Life* by Mrs. Hardcastle (2 vols., 1881); Thomas Campbell, *Life and Letters*, edited by W. Beattie (3 vols., 1850); *The Capel Letters*, edited by Lord Anglesey (1955); *Carlisle MSS.* (Historical MSS. Commission, 1897); John Cartwright, *Life and Correspondence*, edited by F. D. Cartwright (2 vols., 1826); E. B. Chancellor, *Life in Regency and Early Victorian Times* (1933); *Charlemont MSS.* (Historical MSS. Commission, vol. II, 1894); P. W. Clayden, *Early Life of Samuel Rogers* (1887); *Rogers and His Contemporaries* (2 vols., 1889); Lord Cloncurry, *Personal Recollections* (Dublin, 1849); A. Cobban (editor), *The Debate on the French Revolution, 1789–1800* (1950); William Cobbett, Lives by E. I. Carlile (1904) and G. D. H. Cole (1925); Henry, Lord Cockburn, *Memorials of His Time* (Edinburgh, 1856); *Life of Lord Jeffrey* (2 vols., Edinburgh, 1852); *Journal, 1831–1854* (2 vols., Edinburgh, 1874); *Letters to T. F. Kennedy, 1818–1852, chiefly concerned with the affairs of Scotland* (1874); *Coke of Norfolk and His Friends*, edited by Mrs. A. M. D. W. Stirling (2 vols., 1912); Lord Colchester, *Diary and Correspondence*, edited by Lord Colchester (3 vols., 1861); G. D. H. Cole, *Robert Owen* (1925); *A Short History of the British Working Class Movement*, vol. I (1789–1848) [1925]; M. Cole, *Robert Owen of New Lanark* (1957); E. H. Coleridge, *Life of Thomas Coutts* (2 vols., 1920); Brian Connell, *Portrait of a Whig Peer* [2nd Viscount Palmerston] (1957); G. Costigan, *Sir Robert Wilson* (Wisconsin, 1932); R. Coupland, *Wilberforce* (Oxford, 1924); *Creevey Papers*, edited by Sir H. Maxwell (2 vols., 1904); *Creevey's Life and Times*, edited by J. Gore (1934); *Croker Papers*, edited by L. J. Jennings (3 vols., 1884); J. W. Croker, *Life* by M. F. Brightfield (1951); F. O. Darvall, *Popular Disturbances and Public Order in Regency England* (Oxford, 1934); Thomas, Lord Denman, *Memoir* by Sir J. Arnould (2 vols., 1908); Georgiana, duchess of Devonshire, "Selections from her letters", *Anglo-Saxon Review*, vol. I (1899); *The Two Duchesses: Georgiana, Duchess of Devonshire; Elizabeth, Duchess of Devonshire*, edited by V. Foster (1898 edition); C. Dickson, *The Wexford Rising in 1798* (Tralee, 1955); *Drennan Letters, 1776–1819*, edited by D. A. Chart (Belfast, 1931); 10th earl of Dundonald, *Autobiography of a Seaman* (1872); General Wm. Dyott, *Diary, 1781–1845*, edited by R. W. Jeffery (2 vols., 1907); L. Ellis and J. Turquan, *La Belle Pamela* [Lady Edward Fitzgerald] (1924); T. Evans, *The Background of Modern Welsh Politics, 1789–1846* (Cardiff, 1936); E. Eyck, *Pitt versus Fox, Father and Son, 1735–1806* (1950); *Farington Diary, 1793–1821*, edited by J. Greig (8 vols., 1922–1928); K. G. Feiling, *Sketches in Nineteenth Century Biography* (1930); *The Second Tory Party, 1714–1832* (1938); W. J. Fitzpatrick, *The 'Sham Squire' and the Informers of 1798* (Dublin, 1866); *Secret Service under Pitt* (1892); Lord E. Fitzmaurice, *Life of Shelburne* (3 vols., 1875–1876); *Fox's Martyrs; or A New Book of the Sufferings of the Faithful* (1784); Mary Frampton, *Journal, 1779–1846*, edited by H. G. Mundy (1886 edition); Philip Francis, *Memoirs, with Correspondence and Journals* by J. Parkes and H. Merivale (2 vols., 1867); *Letters*, edited by B. Francis and E. Keary (2 vols., 1901); *J. H. Frere and His Friends*, edited by G. Festing (1899); Elizabeth Fry, *Memoir of the Life of*, edited by her daughters (2 vols., 1847); J. G. Fyfe (editor), *Scottish Diaries and Memoirs, 1746–1843* (Stirling, 1942); N. Gash, *Politics in the Age of Peel* (1953); M. D. George, *Catalogue of Political and Personal Satires preserved in the Department of Prints and Drawings in the*

British Museum, vols. V–XI (1935–1954); Sir J. T. Gilbert, *Documents relating to Ireland, 1795–1804* (Dublin, 1893); James Gillray, *Works*, edited by T. Wright (1873); Lord Glenbervie, *Journals*, edited by W. Sichel (1910); *Diaries*, edited by F. Bickley (2 vols., 1928); William Godwin, *Life* by H. N. Brailsford (1934); 3rd duke of Grafton, *Autobiography and Correspondence*, edited by Sir W. R. Anson (1898); H. G. Graham, *Social Life in Scotland in the Eighteenth Century* (2 vols., 1899); Henry Grattan, *Memoirs of Life and Times* (5 vols., 1849); *Lives* by R. J. McHugh (1936) and R. J. McHugh (New York, 1937); Charlotte Grenville, *Correspondence with Lady Williams Wynn and her three sons* (1920); Lady Gregory (editor), *Mr. Gregory's Letter-Box, 1813–1830* (1898); Charles Greville, *Diary*, edited by L. Strachey and R. Fulford (8 vols., 1938); Robert Fulke Greville, *Diaries*, edited by F. McKno Bladon (1930); E. L. Griggs, *Thomas Clarkson* (1936); D. Gwynn, *The Struggle for Catholic Emancipation, 1750–1829* (1928); F. W. Hackwood, *William Hone, His Life and Times* (1912); E. Halévy, *Thomas Hodgskin* (1955); Mary Hamilton, *Letters and Diaries, 1756–1816*, edited by E. and F. Anson (1925); *Hamwood Papers of the Ladies of Llangollen*, edited by G. H. Bell (1930); *Hastings MSS.* (Historical MSS. Commission, 1934); F. J. C. Hearnshaw, *The Social and Political Ideas of some representative thinkers of the Revolutionary Era* (1931); *The Heber Letters, 1782–1832*, edited by R. H. Cholmondeley (1950); Sir Robert Heron, *Notes* (Grantham, 1851); John Cam Hobhouse, Lord Broughton, *Recollections of a Long Life*, edited by Lady Dorchester (6 vols., 1909–1911); *Life* by M. Joyce (1948); Henry Hobhouse, *Diary, 1820–1827*, edited by A. Aspinall (1947); Thomas Holcroft, *Memoirs* (3 vols., 1816); *Letters*, edited by E. Colby (2 vols., 1925); Elizabeth, Lady Holland, *Journal*, edited Lord Ilchester (2 vols., 1908); *Spanish Journal*, edited by Lord Ilchester (1910); *Letters to Her Son, 1821–45*, edited by Lord Ilchester (1946); The 4th Lord Holland, *Journal 1818–30*, edited by Lord Ilchester (1923); *Maria Josepha Holroyd, Girlhood of . . . Lady Stanley of Alderley*, edited by J. H. Adeane (1896); J. M. Holzman, *The Nabobs in England: A Study of the returned Anglo-Indians, 1760–85* (New York, 1927); *Hone's Reformists' Register, 1817* (2 vols.); Francis Horner, *Memoirs* (2 vols., 1843); Sir Wm. Hotham, *Private Papers*, edited by A. M. W. Stirling (2 vols., 1918); *Three Howard Sisters. Correspondence of Lady Caroline Lascelles, Lady Dover and Countess Gower*, edited by Lady Leconfield (1955); T. B. Howell, *A Complete Collection of State Trials* (vols. XXI–XXXIV, and New Series, vols. I–III, cover this period); E. M. Howse, *Saints in Politics: The 'Clapham Sect' and the Growth of Freedom* (1954); Henry Hunt, *Memoirs, written in Ilchester Gaol* (3 vols., 1820); Leigh Hunt, *Autobiography* (1855); *Correspondence*, edited by eldest son (2 vols., 1862); H. M. Hyde, *Princess Lieven* (1938); Lord Hylton, *The Paget Brothers, 1750–1840* (1918); Lord Ilchester, *The Home of the Hollands, 1605–1820* (1937); R. Jacob, *The Rise of the United Irishmen, 1791–4* (1937); *Edward J. Jerningham and his friends*, edited by L. Bettany (1919); *The Jerningham Letters, 1780–1843*, edited by E. Castle (2 vols., 1896); M. G. Jones, *Hannah More* (Cambridge, 1952); Sir Robert Murray Keith, *Memoirs and Correspondence, 1769–92* (2 vols., 1849); Betty Kemp, *King and Commons, 1660–1832* (1957); Lloyd Kenyon, *Sketch of the Life of Lord Kenyon* (1802); *Kenyon MSS.* (Historical MSS. Commission, 1894); Klingberg and Hustvedt, *The Warning Drum: Broadsides of 1803* (California, 1944); Sir William Knighton, *Memoirs*, edited by Lady Knighton (2 vols., 1838); *Laing MSS.* (Historical MSS. Commission, vol. II, 1925); Andrew Lang, *Life and Letters of J. G. Lockhart* (2 vols., 1897); E. Lascelles, *Granville Sharp* (Oxford, 1928); H. J. Laski, *Political Thought from Locke to Bentham* (1925); Lady Sarah Lennox, *Life and Letters, 1745–1826*, edited by Lady Ilchester and Lord Stavordale (2 vols., 1904); F. Leveson-Gower (editor), *Letters of Lady Granville, 1810–45* (2 vols., 1894); Sir G. Leveson-Gower (editor), *Haro-O. Letters of Lady Harriet Cavendish, 1796–1809* (1940); *Private Correspondence of Lord Granville, Leveson-Gower*, edited by Lady Granville (2 vols., 1916); Princess Lieven, *Letters during her residence in London, 1812–34*, edited by L. G. Robinson (1902); *Correspondence of Princess Lieven and Earl Grey*, edited by G. Le

Strange (2 vols., 1890); *Lieven-Palmerston Correspondence, 1828–56*, edited by Lord Sudley (1943); *Private Letters to Prince Metternich, 1820–26*, edited by P. Quennell (1937); C. Lloyd, *Fanny Burney* (1936) and *Lord Cochrane* (1947); Lady Londonderry (editor), *Life and Times of Frances Anne, Marchioness of Londonderry, and Charles, third Marquess of Londonderry* (1958); *Lonsdale MSS.* (Historical MSS. Commission, 1893); R. Lucas, *Lord North* (2 vols., 1913); Zachary Macaulay, *Life and Letters*, edited by Lady Knutsford (1900); *Life* by C. Booth (1934); S. Maccoby, *English Radicalism, 1786–1832* (1955); *The English Radical Tradition, 1763–1914* (1952); M. Macdonagh, *Daniel O'Connell and the Story of Catholic Emancipation* (1929); *Life of O'Connell* (1903); R. B. McDowell, *Irish Public Opinion, 1750–1800* (1944); *Public Opinion and Government Policy in Ireland, 1801–46* (1952); R. R. Madden, *The United Irishmen* (7 vols., Dublin, 1842–1846); Sir James Mackintosh, *Life* by R. J. Mackintosh (2 vols., Boston, 1853); *Miscellaneous Works* (1851); 1st earl of Malmesbury, *Diaries and Correspondence*, edited by 3rd earl (4 vols., 1844); *Letters, 1745–1820*, edited by 3rd earl (2 vols., 1870); *The Marlay Letters, 1778–1820*, edited by R. W. Bond (1937); W. L. Mathieson, *England in Transition: A Study of Movements* (1920); C. E. Maxwell, *Dublin under the Georges, 1714–1830* (1936); H. W. Meikle, *Scotland and the French Revolution* (Glasgow, 1912); L. Melville (editor), *The Berry Papers, 1763–1852* (1914); W. A. Miles, *Correspondence on the French Revolution, 1789–1817*, edited by C. P. Miles (2 vols., 1890); *Life and Letters of Sir Gilbert Eliot, 1st earl of Minto*, by Lady Minto (3 vols., 1874); *Notes from Minto MSS.* (privately printed, Edinburgh, 1862); Mrs. Montague, *Letters and Friendships, 1762–1800*, edited by R. Blunt (2 vols., 1923); Thomas Moore, *Memoirs, Journals and Correspondence*, edited by Lord John Russell (8 vols., 1853–1856); Mrs. Hannah More, *Life and Correspondence*, edited by W. Roberts (4 vols., 1834); *Letters*, edited by B. Johnson (1925); *Letters to Zachary Macaulay*, edited by A. Roberts (1860); *Lives* by T. Taylor (1838), H. Thompson (2 vols., Philadelphia, 1838), H. C. McKnight (New York, 1853), C. M. Yonge (Boston, 1888), A. M. B. Meakin (1911); Lady Morgan, *Memoirs* (2 vols., 1863 edition); R. H. Mottram, *Buxton the Liberator* (1946); Sir R. Musgrave, *Memoirs of the different Rebellions in Ireland* (2 vols., Dublin, 1802); Macvey Napier, *Correspondence*, edited by M. Napier (1879); C. G. Oakes, *Sir Samuel Romilly* (1935); Daniel O'Connell, *Correspondence*, edited by W. J. Fitzpatrick (2 vols., 1888); *Life* by R. Dunlop (New York, 1900); H. K. Olphin, *George Tierney* (1934); *The Paget Brothers, 1790–1840*, edited by Lord Hylton (1918); Thomas Paine, *Political and Miscellaneous Works* (2 vols., 1819); *Life* by F. J. Gould (1925), M. A. Best (1927), H. Pearson (1937), F. Smith (New York, 1938) and W. E. Woodward (1946); Lady Palmerston, *Letters*, edited by Tresham Lever (1957); M. W. Patterson, *Sir Francis Burdett and His Times, 1770–1844* (2 vols., 1931); A. Temple Patterson, *Radical Leicester, 1780–1850* (Leicester, 1954); M. L. Pearl, *William Cobbett: A Bibliographical Account of His Life and Times* (Oxford, 1953); *Pembroke Papers, 1780–94*, edited by Lord Herbert (1950); M. D. Petrie, *The Ninth Lord Petrie* (1928); F. Podmore, *Life of Robert Owen* (1923 edition); R. W. Postgate, *Robert Emmet* (1932); Mrs. P. L. Powys, *Passages from the Diaries of*, edited by E. J. Climenson (1899); *Public Characters* (10 vols., 1799–1809); C. Redding, *Fifty Years' Recollections* (3 vols., 1858 edition); J. A. Reynolds, *The Catholic Emancipation Crisis in Ireland, 1823–29* (Yale, 1954); David Ricardo, *Works and Correspondence*, edited by P. Sraffa and M. H. Dobb (10 vols., Cambridge, 1951–1955); M. Roberts, *The Whig Party, 1807–12* (1939); J. A. Roebuck, *History of the Whig Ministry of 1830* (2 vols., 1852); Henry Crabb Robinson, *Diary, Reminiscences and Correspondence*, edited by T. Sadler (2 vols., 1872); R. M. Robinson, *Coutts': The History of a Banking House* (1929); Samuel Rogers, *Table Talk*, edited by A. Dyce (1856); Sir Samuel Romilly, *Memoirs*, edited by his sons (3 vols., 1840); *The Romilly-Edgeworth Letters, 1813–18*, edited by S. H. Romilly (1936); William Roscoe, *Life* by H. Roscoe (2 vols., 1833); George Rose, *Diaries and Correspondence*, edited by L. V. Harcourt (2 vols., 1860); O. Rudney, *Thomas Spence and His Connections*

(1927); R. Rush, *Residence at the Court of London*, edited by B. Rush (2nd Series, 2 vols., 1845); *Rutland MSS.* (Historical MSS. Commission, vol. III, 1894); L. Sanders, *The Holland House Circle* (1908); L. J. Saunders, *Scottish Democracy, 1815–40: The Social and Intellectual Background* (Edinburgh, 1950); James Scarlett, Lord Abinger, *Life* by P. S. Scarlett (1877); Sir Walter Scott, *Life* by J. G. Lockhart (10 vols., Edinburgh, 1869); *Letters*, edited by Sir H. Grierson (12 vols., 1932–1937); Lady Seymour, *The 'Pope' of Holland House. Selections from the correspondence of John Whishaw and his friends* (1906); Granville Sharp, *Memoirs* by Prince Hoare (2 vols., 1828 edition); R. Lalor Sheil, *Sketches, Legal and Political*, edited by M. W. Strange (2 vols., 1855); Frances, Lady Shelley, *Diary*, edited by R. Edgcumbe (2 vols., 1913); R. B. Sheridan, *Lives* by Thomas Moore (1825), W. F. Rae (2 vols., 1896), W. S. Sichel (2 vols., 1909); E. M. Butler (1931), W. A. Darlington (1933), R. C. Rhodes (Oxford, 1933); J. Silvester, *William Wilberforce, Christian Liberator* (1934); Sir John Sinclair, *Correspondence* (2 vols., 1831); Samuel Smiles, *Memoirs of John Murray* (2 vols., 1891); Lieut.-Gen. Sir Harry Smith, *Autobiography*, edited by G. C. M. Smith (2 vols., 1902); Sydney Smith, *A Memoir* by Lady Holland (2 vols., 1855); *Letters*, edited by N. C. Smith (2 vols., Oxford, 1954); R. Southey, *Colloquies on the Progress and Prospects of Society* (2 vols., 1829); G. Stanhope and G. P. Gooch, *Life of 3rd Earl Stanhope* (1914); *Miscellanies* (1st Series, 1863); Lady Hester Stanhope, *Life* by Joan Haslip (1934); A. Stephens, *Memoirs of John Horne Tooke* (2 vols., 1813); James Stephen, *Letters*, edited by C. E. Stephen (1906); *Memoirs*, edited by M. M. Bevington (1954); A. M. W. Stirling, *The Hothams* (2 vols., 1917); *The Letter-Bag of Lady Elizabeth Spencer-Stanhope* (2 vols., 1913); D. M. Stuart, *Dearest Bess. The Life and Times of Lady Elizabeth Foster, Duchess of Devonshire* (1955); Lady Louisa Stuart, *Correspondence*, edited by Mrs. G. Clark (3 vols., Edinburgh, 1895–1898); *Letters*, edited by R. B. Johnson (1926); *ibid.*, edited by J. A. Home (2 vols., Edinburgh, 1901–1903); J. Summerson, *John Nash, Architect to George IV* (1935); W. Johnston Temple, *Diaries, 1780–96*, edited by L. Bettany (Oxford, 1929); *Marianne Thornton, 1797–1887* by E. M. Forster (1956); *Thraliana, the Diary of Mrs. Thrale, 1776–1809*, edited by K. C. Balderston (2 vols., Oxford, 1942); *Life* by J. L. Clifford (Oxford, 1941); Theobald Wolfe Tone, *Memoirs*, edited by his son (2 vols., 1827); *Torrington Diaries*, edited by C. B. Andrews (4 vols., 1934–1938); G. O. Trevelyan, *Life and Letters of Lord Macaulay* (1883); A. S. Turberville, *History of Welbeck Abbey and its Owners* (2 vols., 1939); R. E. Turner, *James Silk Buckingham, 1786–1855* (1934); E. G. Twitchett, *Thomas Cochrane, 10th Earl of Dundonald* (1931); Marjorie Villiers, *The Grand Whiggery* (1939); C. E. Vulliamy, *The Onslow Family, 1528–1874* (1953); Joan Wake, *The Brudenells of Deene* (1953); Graham Wallas, *Life of Francis Place* (1918); Horace Walpole, *Correspondence* (Yale edition, 1937+, superseding Mrs. Paget Toynbee's edition, 19 vols., Oxford, 1918–1925); R. Plumer Ward, *Memoirs*, by E. Phipps (2 vols., 1850); Miss Weeton, *Journal of a Governess, 1807–25*, edited by E. Hall (2 vols., 1936–1939); Wm. Wickham, *Correspondence*, edited by W. Wickham (2 vols., 1870); Wm. Wilberforce, *Life* by his sons (5 vols., 1838); *Correspondence*, edited by his sons (2 vols., 1840); *Private Papers*, edited by A. M. Wilberforce (1897); John Wilkes, *Letters to His Daughter, 1774–96* (4 vols., 1804); Mrs. E. Stuart-Wortley, *A Prime Minister and His Son, from the correspondence of the 3rd Earl of Bute and of Lieut. Gen. Sir Charles Stuart* (1925); Sir N. Wraxall, *Historical and Posthumous Memoirs*, edited by H. B. Wheatley (5 vols., 1884); H. Wyndham, *Correspondence of Sarah Spencer, Lady Lyttelton 1787–1870* (1912); C. Wyvill, *Political Papers* (6 vols., York, 1794–1802); T. Wyse, *Historical Sketch of the late Catholic Association of Ireland* (2 vols., 1829).

(iv) *Periodicals*

Agricultural History Review; American Historical Review; Analecta Hibernica; Annual Register; Anti-Jacobin Review; Army Quarterly; Blackwood's Magazine; Bodleian Quarterly

Record; British Museum Quarterly; Bulletin of the Institute of Historical Research; Bulletin of the Board of Celtic Studies; Bulletin of the John Rylands Library; Cambridge Historical Journal; Canadian Historical Review; Church Quarterly Review; Cornhill Magazine; Dublin Review; Economic History (a Supplement to the Economic Journal); Economic History Review; Economica; Edinburgh Review; Evangelical Magazine; Gentleman's Magazine; History; History Today; Huntington Library Bulletin; Irish Historical Studies; Journal of Economic and Business History; Journal of Modern History (Chicago); Journal of the Royal Statistical Society; Law Quarterly Review; Library; Mariner's Mirror; Notes and Queries; Politica; Political Science Quarterly; Proceedings of the British Academy; Proceedings of the Royal Irish Academy; Quarterly Review; Review of English Studies; Scottish Historical Review; Transactions of the Royal Historical Society; University of Birmingham Historical Journal; Westminster Review.

Part I

THE EXECUTIVE

Introduction

THE later nineteenth-century system of 'Cabinet Government', based on the collective responsibility of the chief ministers of the Crown to the majority of the elected representatives of the nation in Parliament, was unknown in 1832. Throughout our period the king remained the active, controlling head of the government, his ministers his individual servants, their policies subject to his preliminary approval, and, though the process of 'economical reform' was steadily diminishing the extent of ministerial influence over the House of Commons, the king remained a vital prop to every administration. Government was still based on the 'mixed' system established at the Revolution of 1688, control of the executive branch being placed in the hands of a hereditary monarch, but the exercise of its powers checked by a representative Legislature. In practice, the smooth working of the system depended on conventions which ensured the linking together of the two branches of government; the chief of these were the development of the Cabinet system, and the extension of the royal influence over the two Houses of Parliament. The working out of these factors makes this period important as a transitional stage between the 'mixed monarchy' of the eighteenth century and the parliamentary government of the later nineteenth.

The relationship between the king and his ministers was in many ways the central constitutional problem of the reign of George III. Therefore the composition and procedure of the Cabinet, and subsequently the relations between it, or its individual members, and the monarch are illustrated in the following documents.

The closet and the 'Efficient' Cabinet were now the centres of political action. The 'Grand' or 'Nominal' Cabinet, meeting always under the presidency of the king, had long ago given up its political functions:[1] advice was now tendered or decisions taken by the departmental minister in the closet, or by the collective opinions of the principal ministers who comprised the 'Efficient' Cabinet. This body, whose origins are to be found in the 'inner ring' of early eighteenth-century ministers, meeting informally to discuss business and to formulate a common attitude, had grown up independently of the Crown and consequently did not meet in the king's presence. By 1783 it had shed much of its earlier informality–though often much business was transacted round the dinner-table[2]–and was recognized, if not explicitly by the Constitution, in effect as the central institution of government. In 1801 Addington found it necessary to lay down the rule–already generally understood–that membership should be restricted to the persons whose responsible situations in office required their being members of it,[3] but its composition was never determined solely by the arrangement of offices in the administration; both membership of the

[1] No. 3.   [2] No. 8.   [3] No. 4.

Cabinet and the distribution of office were rather determined by the nature of the political groupings of the day.[1] It was necessary, not to secure in the structure of the Cabinet a proportionate reflexion of the party complexion of the House of Commons, but to ensure a sufficient degree of parliamentary support for the king's government, and every Cabinet formed during this period was consequently a coalition of various groups and interests. The Cabinet did not always, therefore, act together as a unit, and in particular, so long as Cabinets were so composed and ministers were regarded as individually the servants of the Crown, no conception of joint Cabinet responsibility could be enforced. Charles Fox was the champion of party, or, as his nephew Lord Holland called it, "well-concerted" government, and effective leader of the group which in 1782–1783 had sought to enforce the doctrine that the Cabinet should be a union of men agreed on principles and acting together if necessary to compel the king to accept their advice, but even he in 1806–the last year of his life–declared in Parliament that the responsibility of ministers was that of individual servants of the Crown rather than that of collective members of a Cabinet.[2] In the same debate Canning–then out of office–put forward arguments to support the principle of joint responsibility, but those arguments were rather a forecast of future developments than an analysis of present conditions, for joint responsibility in fact implied, to a greater degree than had yet been reached, the retirement of the Crown from the control of administration; it was incompatible, not merely with monarchical government but with the 'mixed' system of the time.

The extent of the limits to joint responsibility during the period are indicated in the succeeding documents. First, ministers might still transact their departmental business in the closet,[3] and occasionally, as when Wellesley, notoriously scornful of his colleagues, was Foreign Secretary in 1811, to a degree that led the Prime Minister to complain of lack of consultation.[4] Conversely, ministers in charge of important departments–the Admiralty and Ordnance especially–were not always expected to take part in general discussions of policy except when the business of their departments was in question. Lord Barham, First Lord of the Admiralty at the time of Trafalgar, could not have been left out of Pitt's Cabinet in the interests of the navy and of the country, but he was not a politician; he came from outside the social circles from which ministers were usually drawn, and as a professional sailor stood in the non-political tradition of Howe and St. Vincent.[5] Others might be brought into the Cabinet, not that the country might benefit from their professional knowledge or political experience, but in order to secure to the government the support of some political group or interest with which they were connected; the balancing of the claims of the various groups comprising the administration might lead to such unusual events as the summoning to the Cabinet of Lord Chief Justice Ellenborough[6] or the appointment of a Lord Privy Seal[7]–the office ranking second in order of precedence only to Lord President–or even of a prime minister,[8] whose presence at meetings was not regarded as indispensable for the transaction of business.

The Cabinet's advice to the king was not always unanimous. It was customary not only for the king to be informed, in the Cabinet Minute, if one was submitted, of the names of those present at the meeting,[9] but for those who dissented from the opinion of the majority to be allowed to record their disagreement in the minute,[10] or even, in certain circumstances, in a private letter to the king.[11] Sometimes ministers who were

[1] No. 6.   [2] No. 5.   [3] Nos. 6, 11.   [4] No. 20.   [5] No. 17.   [6] No. 5.
[7] No. 18.   [8] No. 7.   [9] Nos. 11, 25.   [10] No. 36.   [11] Nos. 37, 44, 45.

unable to be present at Cabinet discussions asked that their names be entered as agreeing with or dissenting from the decision taken.[1] George III seemed on occasion to expect to be informed of the tone and temper of Cabinet discussions,[2] and more than once both he and George IV required the submission of individual opinions.[3] It was inevitable that Cabinets composed of men not connected by membership of a single party[4] should be torn by differences of opinion even on quite fundamental questions. No Cabinet could have been formed before 1830 to agree on a measure of parliamentary reform as a condition of their taking office, nor was any Cabinet able to compel the king to give way on the Catholic question until Ireland was driven to the verge of rebellion in 1829. There were other questions–the abolition of the slave trade, or such questions of social policy as the reform of the poor law[5]–where disagreement amongst ministers or their political followers, quite apart from the king's views, was such that no Cabinet could, or thought it necessary to, make them 'Government questions'. Every Cabinet in this period had its 'open' questions[6] and (with the exception of the Catholic question until 1821) ministers were free to introduce measures into either House as private members of Parliament, as Pitt did with parliamentary reform in 1785 or the slave trade in 1788, without pledging the government or expecting support from their colleagues.[7] On one occasion in this period members of the same government are even found contesting an election against each other,[8] for the Catholic question in 1826 was not a 'bond of party' in the administration though it was a live political question with the electorate. On the whole, however, ministers agreed harmoniously to disagree on such questions,[9] for even the apparently most solid of eighteenth- and early nineteenth-century Cabinets were full of rifts and disagreements below the surface. Pitt's Cabinets were a mass of conflicting opinions even on the most urgent questions,[10] and a desperate or an unscrupulous king might be able to turn such divisions to his temporary (though rarely to his long-term) advantage.[11]

Nor did the king always consider himself bound to seek advice solely from his responsible servants. The legend of 'double Cabinets' fostered by Burke for party purposes during the American War was merely the exaggeration of the fact that George III, and still more his eldest son, did on occasion listen to advisers other than his ministers. George III did so after 1783 only on the rare occasions when he considered his principles or his conscience at stake, and after some experience of his son's practice the politicians came to regard his example as in this respect the model for a constitutional monarch.[12] But Pitt's resignation in 1801 was due not merely to the king's refusal to accept his advice on the Catholic question but to his lack of success in preventing the king from listening to others.[13] In 1806 Lord Hawkesbury, in 1807 the duke of Portland, both then out of office, went so far as to offer written advice encouraging the king to act contrary to the wishes of his servants,[14] and though it is not known whether George III countenanced their actions, Lord Grenville, who had then been prime minister, wrote five years later of " *Court intrigue* and *double government*" as factors that had done "so much evil" during the reign.[15] When he and Lord Grey were offered entry into the government by the prince regent, they tried to impose a condition that he would not consult his private friends on politics[16]–a demand that was considered hard and unreasonable. George IV, however, was soon

[1] Nos. 12, 14, 42. [2] Nos. 21, 22. [3] Nos. 24–28. [4] Nos. 48–50. [5] cf. No. 221. [6] No. 29.
[7] Nos. 31, 34. [8] No. 33. [9] Nos. 34, 35. [10] Nos. 39, 46. [11] No. 47. [12] No. 40.
[13] Nos. 51–52. [14] Nos. 54–56. [15] No. 58. [16] No. 57.

notorious for his intrigues, not only with disgruntled outsiders, but even with foreign ambassadors against his own Foreign Secretary.[1]

An illustration of the changing relationship between the king and the Cabinet may be found in the further development of the office of Prime Minister. Pitt's ministry marks an important stage in this process. It is no longer accepted that George III was saved from his enemies in 1783–1784 at the price of capitulation to his friends; Pitt was the minister of the king's choice, and his personal parliamentary following was so small that, had he ever tried to stand as a party leader against the king, he would have had even less success than Fox in "storming the Closet". He held, however, a high conception of his office, and the king was shrewd enough to understand how indispensable was Pitt's support to any administration, and that Pitt would never consent to accept a subordinate situation. As long as the alternative to Pitt was Fox, and as long as Pitt's colleagues paid such deference to his transcendent abilities,[2] he was able to some extent to impose his own terms, as when the king had to agree to the dismissal of Lord Thurlow, his personal representative in the Cabinet, in 1792.[3] When, however, king and Prime Minister failed to agree on Catholic Emancipation in 1801 it was Pitt who had to give way. So conscious nevertheless was Pitt of the necessity of the superintending role that in 1803, when the tottering Addington Government sought a coalition, he repudiated the suggestion that the two former Prime Ministers should serve under Pitt's brother as a 'dummy' head, and authorized Lord Melville to make the famous statement of his views to Addington.[4] Four years later recourse was had to a similar expedient, the aged duke of Portland being appointed as ostensible minister to prevent deadlock between the claims of colleagues whose services were equally necessary to the stability of the administration.[5] After two years' experience of this arrangement, Canning echoed Pitt's views of 1803,[6] and after the appointment of Perceval in 1809 and Liverpool in 1812 the office resumed its development on the old lines,[7] though it was still not yet inevitable that the result would be to consolidate the unity of the Cabinet as against the king.

The unity of the Cabinet was in some respects weakened by the emergence of the office of Prime Minister and by the accompanying tendency to the formation of 'inner rings', or small confidential cliques, to the exclusion of other ministers from full confidence.[8] This was notoriously true of Pitt's Cabinets; Lord Carmarthen and Lord Thurlow, respectively Foreign Secretary and Lord Chancellor in 1791, complained of lack of communication,[9] and after 1794 Pitt, Dundas and Grenville, by far the ablest in the Cabinet, formed almost a triumvirate for the prosecution of the war.[10] Since this arrangement made for greater security and efficiency in the dispatch of secret business, it was encouraged by the king.[11] In peace-time, too, however, later ministers complained of separation from their colleagues.[12]

Despite the tendency of the Cabinet in general to consolidate itself as against an individual relationship between king and ministers, it would be misleading to regard this period as witnessing a decline in all the powers of the Crown. George III in 1784 defined the remaining prerogatives of the Crown as the right to choose the ministers, and to veto legislation.[13] Both were maintained, in modified form, until the effects of the 1832 Reform Act made themselves felt. The right to nominate the ministers was conceded, in theory, by all; even Fox in 1784 claimed no more than that its exercise

[1] Nos. 40, 60. [2] No. 62. [3] No. 101. [4] No. 64. [5] No. 67.
[6] No. 120. [7] Nos. 70, 71. [8] Nos. 75, 78–87. [9] Nos. 78–79. [10] Nos. 83–85.
[11] Nos. 80–83. [12] No. 87. [13] No. 89.

should be subject to the approval or animadversion of Parliament,[1] while in the regency crisis of 1788–1789 he was quick to declare the prospective regent's right to change his ministers at will. In practice, however, Fox wished to restrict the king's freedom of choice, and the king's power to maintain it varied according to circumstances. It may have been true that to the end of this period the king's support was essential to any government,[2] but kings on the whole had to make the best of such governments as they could get. George III was able to veto Fox in 1804 only by flaunting his tendency to insanity at Pitt, who was peculiarly susceptible on this point;[3] in 1806 he made no serious objection to Fox's entering the Cabinet when it became plain that there was no alternative.[4] Experienced politicians like Liverpool knew that kings could always be forced to take or part with ministers, but that it was not always wise or expedient to coerce them too openly,[5] and that the king had a right to expect his personal prejudices to be considered, particularly when an office was closely connected with the royal person.[6] George IV even tried to insist—with varying success—that appointments to all Household offices were outside the concern of his ministers.[7] Liverpool's stoutness on this point, as on other questions of patronage, was not the least of his services to his country's political development.

The legislative veto as George III defined it was never exercised by the Hanoverian monarchs, though George III contemplated its use on several occasions. It was nevertheless a reality, for no government Bill could be introduced into Parliament without the king's previous consent. George III was particularly stubborn on the Catholic question:[8] the impressive array of Pitt's arguments for concession to Ireland in 1801 met the blank wall of the royal prejudice,[9] and the Talents' attempt to hoodwink the king as to the extent of their relief measure in 1807 merely removed any scruples he might have felt at playing a similar double game with them. Henceforth, George III and his son demanded from their Cabinets the pledge extracted from Pitt in 1801 and 1804[10] and refused by Grenville in 1807,[11] while as late as 1832 William IV placed a firm (if unnecessary) veto on manhood suffrage and secret ballot as part of a Reform Bill.[12]

George III might have added to his enumeration of the royal prerogatives the right to grant or to withhold from his ministers a dissolution of Parliament—a prerogative whose exercise might be so vital to a ministry unsure of its parliamentary position that Pitt contemplated its restriction in the Regency Bill of 1789, and Hawkesbury attempted to persuade George III not to grant it to the Grenville Ministry in 1806.[13] A year later it was used to strengthen the newly appointed Portland Ministry, but though there was bitter criticism of the step in Parliament no one denied that it was a legitimate part of the prerogative.[14] As late as 1831 William IV was driven to agree to his ministers' request for a dissolution only by their threat of resignation and the disturbed state of the country.[15]

Finally, the royal prerogative included the ultimate control of the distribution of patronage, and in no respect was royal interference with the minutiae of government so fruitful of discord during the Hanoverian period. The four Georges felt a particular concern for the control of army and navy promotions—which was not always to the disadvantage of those services—but in the Church too there was much 'interference' with the free-hand ministers were coming to expect. Pitt was so incensed by the

[1] No. 88.   [2] Nos. 91–92.   [3] Nos. 95–96.   [4] No. 98.   [5] No. 98.
[6] Nos. 100, 102. [7] No. 134.   [8] No. 110.   [9] Nos. 111–114. [10] Nos. 115–117.
[11] Nos. 119, 122. [12] No. 123.   [13] Nos. 54, 103. [14] No. 105.   [15] Nos. 106–109.

king's refusal to make his former tutor archbishop of Canterbury that he contemplated resignation, at one of the most desperate crises of the war with Napoleonic France,[1] while George IV's ministers were driven to despair by the royal obstinacy on the promotion of his favourite Dr. Sumner.[2] On the whole, weak ministers, like Addington[3] and Goderich,[4] indulged the royal appetite for control of patronage; stronger ones resisted stoutly.[5] In this as in other spheres where the royal prerogative was in question, the relationship between king and ministers was affected more by personalities and the clash of political circumstances than by the formulation of any fresh constitutional doctrine.

BIBLIOGRAPHY

I. WORKS ON CONSTITUTIONAL HISTORY

Sir William R. Anson, *Law and Custom of the Constitution*: vol. 1, *Parliament*, edited by Sir M. L. Gwyer (Oxford, 1922); vol. 11, *The Crown*, 4th edition, by A. B. Keith (1935), are still useful, though in need of revision. D. L. Keir's *Constitutional History of Modern Britain, 1485–1937* (1956 edition) has some fine chapters; M. A. Thomson's *Constitutional History of England, 1642–1801* (1938) and Sir William Holdsworth's *History of English Law*, vol. XIII (edited by A. L. Goodhart and H. G. Hanbury, 1952), are authoritative on a larger scale. D. L. Keir and F. H. Lawson, *Cases in Constitutional Law* (1948 edition), and W. C. Costin and J. Steven Watson, *The Law and Working of the Constitution: Documents*, vol. II, *1784–1914* (1952), are useful selections of documents illustrative of constitutional development during this period. See also, R. B. McDowell, "The Irish Executive in the Nineteenth Century" (*Irish Historical Studies*, March 1955); R. Pares, "Limited Monarchy in Great Britain in the Eighteenth Century" (*Historical Association Pamphlet*, 1957); and Sir Lewis Namier, "Monarchy and the Party System" (in *Personalities and Powers*, 1955).

II. THE ROYAL FAMILY

Sir John Fortescue's unsatisfactory edition of the *Correspondence of George III, 1760–83* (6 vols., 1927–1928) left the whole of the present period uncovered. In preparation, under the editorship of A. Aspinall, are (1) *The Later Correspondence of George III, 1783–1810*, in approximately 6 vols., based on the Windsor Archives and many other private collections of MSS.; and (2) *The Early Correspondence of George IV, c. 1770–1812* (Cambridge, 3 vols.), completing his *Letters of George IV, 1812–30* (3 vols., Cambridge, 1938). A very small selection of George III's letters, edited by Bonomy Dobrée, including some previously unpublished ones from the *Chatham Papers* in the P.R.O., was published in 1935. There are modern *Lives* of George III by J. D. G. Davies (1936), C. E. Vulliamy (1937) and G. M. Boustead (1940), but much more valuable are R. Pares's Ford Lectures, *King George III and the Politicians* (Oxford, 1953). There are modern studies of George IV by Shane Leslie (1926), R. Fulford (1935) and D. M. Stuart (1953). For William IV, see P. Fitzgerald, *Life and Times of William IV* (2 vols., 1884), and, for his connexion with the celebrated actress, *Mrs. Jordan and Her Family*, edited by A. Aspinall (1951). For George IV's only legitimate child, see *The Letters of Princess Charlotte, 1811–17*, edited by A. Aspinall (1949); G. J. Renier, *The Ill-fated Princess* (1932); D. M. Stuart, *Daughter of England* (1951); Sir Eardley Holland, "The Princess Charlotte . . . A Triple Obstetric Tragedy" (article in *Journal of Obstetrics and Gynaecology*, December 1951). For George IV's connexion with Mrs. Fitzherbert, see W. H. Wilkins, *Mrs. Fitzherbert and George IV* (2 vols., 1905); *Life and*

[1] No. 127.   [2] Nos. 133, 137–139.   [3] No. 128.   [4] No. 138.   [5] Nos. 132, 135, 140.

Letters of Mrs. Fitzherbert, edited by Shane Leslie (2 vols., 1939–1940), C. Langdale, *Memoirs of Mrs. Fitzherbert* (1856). For Queen Caroline, see Lady Charlotte Bury, *Diary of a Lady-in-Waiting*, edited by A. F. Stewart (2 vols., 1908); L. Melville, *An Injured Queen* (2 vols., 1912). For other members of the Royal Family, see R. Fulford, *The Royal Dukes* (1933); *Lives of Ernest, duke of Cumberland*, by H. van Thal (1936) and G. M. Willis (1954), the latter extravagantly royalist in outlook. Also, W. S. Childe-Pemberton, *The Romance of Princess Amelia* (1910); Mary Anne Clarke, *The Rival Princes* (2 vols., 1810); *The Book, or The Proceedings and Correspondence upon the subject of the Inquiry into the conduct of the Princess of Wales* (1813); *Evidence and Proceedings upon the Charges against the Duke of York* (1809). For the Court, see Fanny Burney's *Diary and Letters*, edited by A. Dobson (6 vols., 1904–1905). See also, *The Royal Pavilion*, by H. D. Roberts (1939). For the sovereign's relations with his ministers, see General Bibliography.

III. THE DEVELOPMENT OF CABINET GOVERNMENT

The Cabinet Council, 1783–1835, by A. Aspinall, the British Academy Raleigh Lecture for 1952 (*Proceedings of the British Academy*, vol. xxxviii and published separately by the Oxford University Press), based on a wide range of published and MS. material, will be found of some use as an introduction to a difficult and complicated subject. The same author's article, "The Grand Cabinet, 1800–1837" (*Politica*, December 1938), traces the history of that larger but less important body.

A. THE SOVEREIGN

1. George III refuses the Imperial Crown, 1800

(A. G. Stapleton, *Political Life of George Canning*, II (1831), pp. 361–362 n.)

Stapleton was Canning's private secretary and biographer, and his information was doubtless derived from Canning himself.

His late Majesty, George III, was advised, at the time of the Union with Ireland, in compensation for H.M.'s abandonment, then voluntarily made, of the title of King of France, which had been so long annexed to the Crown of England, to assume the title of Emperor of the British and Hanoverian Dominions; but his late Majesty felt that his true dignity consisted in his being known to Europe and the world by the appropriated and undisputed style belonging to the British Crown.

2. The Regency Act, 1811 (51 Geo. III. c.1.)

(*Statutes at Large*, LXV, pp. 1–14.)

In 1810 George III became permanently insane. The Regency Act appointed the Prince of Wales regent, while the personal care of the king was vested in Queen Charlotte and a council. It was still hoped that the king would recover his reason, consequently the regent's authority was restricted for one year: limitations were imposed upon the grant of peerages, places and pensions. Resolutions were agreed to by both Houses, authorizing the issue of letters patent under the Great Seal for giving the royal assent to the Bill by commission, and on 5 Feb. the Bill received the royal assent by virtue of that commission. The regent informed his Tory ministers that feelings of delicacy alone prevented him from removing them from office so long as any hope remained of his father's early recovery, and his Whig friends confidently expected a speedy invitation to form a government. On 13 Feb. 1812, however, five days before the restrictions expired, he informed them that Perceval was to remain Prime Minister. An invitation to Lords Grey and Grenville to join the existing Cabinet was rejected on the ground that the Whigs differed on too many points with the ministers.

... Whereas by reason of the severe indisposition with which it hath pleased God to afflict the King's most excellent Majesty, the personal exercise of the royal authority by H.M., is for the present, so far interrupted, that it becomes necessary to make provision for assisting H.M. in the administration and exercise of the royal authority, and also for the care of his royal person during the continuance of H.M.'s indisposition. and for the resumption of the exercise of the royal authority by H.M.; Be it therefore enacted ... That H.R.H. George Augustus Frederick, Prince of Wales shall have full power and authority, in the name and on the behalf of H.M., and under the style and title of "Regent of the United Kingdom of Great Britain and Ireland," to exercise and administer the royal power and authority to the Crown of the United Kingdom of Great Britain and Ireland belonging, and to use, execute and perform all authorities, prerogatives, acts of government and administration of the same, which lawfully belong to the King ... to use, execute and perform; subject to such limitation, exceptions, regulations and restrictions, as are hereinafter specified and contained; and all and every act and acts which shall be done by the said Regent, in the name and on the behalf of H.M., by virtue and in pursuance of this Act, and according to the powers and authorities hereby vested in him, shall have the same force and effect to all intents and purposes as the like acts would have if done by H.M. himself, and shall to all intents and purposes be full and sufficient warrant to all persons acting under the authority thereof; and all persons shall yield obedience thereto, and carry the same into effect, in the same manner and for the same purposes as the same persons ought to yield obedience to and carry into effect the like acts done by H.M. himself; any Law, course of office, or other matter or thing to the contrary notwithstanding.

II. [Lays down the form of Signature of the Regent.]

III. . . . When H.M. shall by the blessing of God be restored to such a state of health as to be capable of resuming the personal exercise of his royal authority, and shall have declared his royal will and pleasure thereupon, as hereinafter provided, all and every the powers and authorities given by this Act, for the exercise and administration of his royal power and authority, . . . or for the care of H.M.'s Royal Person, shall cease and determine; and no act, matter, or thing, . . . shall, if done after such declaration of H.M.'s royal will and pleasure, be thenceforth valid or effectual.

IV. Provided always, . . . That all persons holding any offices or places, or pensions during H.M.'s pleasure, at the time of such declaration, under any appointment or authority of the Regent, or her Majesty, under the provisions of this Act, shall continue to hold the same, and to use, exercise, and enjoy all the powers, authorities, privileges and emoluments thereof, notwithstanding such declaration of the resumption of the royal authority by H.M., unless and until H.M. shall declare his royal will and pleasure to the contrary; and all orders, acts of government or administration of H.M.'s royal authority, made, issued or done by the said Regent, before such declaration, shall be and remain in full force and effect, until the same shall be countermanded by H.M.

V. Provided also, . . . That no acts of regal power . . . which might lawfully be done or executed by the King's most excellent Majesty, personally exercising his royal authority, shall, during the continuance of the Regency by this Act established, be valid and effectual, unless done and executed in the name and on the behalf of H.M., by the authority of the said Regent, according to the provisions of this Act, and subject to the limitations, exceptions, regulations and restrictions hereinafter contained.

VI. [The Regent to take three oaths: (i) allegiance to the King; (ii) to execute duties according to this Act and for the welfare of King and people; (iii) to maintain the Presbyterian Church in Scotland.]

VII. [The Regent on taking the oaths to subscribe the declaration 30 Chas. II, c. 2, and produce a certificate of having taken the sacrament.]

VIII. Provided always, . . . That until after the 1st day of February 1812, if Parliament shall be then assembled, . . . for six weeks . . . or if Parliament shall be then assembled, but shall not have been so sitting for six weeks, then until the expiration of six weeks after Parliament shall have been so assembled . . . or if Parliament shall not then be assembled, then until the expiration of six weeks after Parliament shall have been assembled . . . the Regent shall not have or exercise any power or authority to grant, in the name or on the behalf of H.M. any rank, title or dignity of the peerage, by letters patent, writ of summons, or any other manner whatever, or to summon any person to the House of Lords by any title to which such person shall be the heir apparent, or to determine the abeyance of any rank, title or dignity of peerage, which now is or hereafter shall be in abeyance, in favour of any of the coheirs thereof by writ of summons or otherwise.

IX. Provided also, . . . That the said Regent shall not, until after the said 1st Feb. 1812, or the expiration of such six weeks as aforesaid, have power or authority to grant, in the name or on the behalf of H.M., any office or employment whatever, in reversion, or to grant for any longer term than during H.M.'s pleasure, any office, employment, salary or pension whatever, except such offices and employments in possession for the term of the natural life, or during the good behaviour of the grantee or grantees thereof respectively, as by law must be so granted: provided always, that nothing herein contained shall in any manner affect or extend to prevent or restrain the granting of any pensions under the provisions of . . . . [The Acts 39 Geo. III, c. 110, 48 Geo. III, c. 145, 40 Geo. III (Ireland), c. 69.]

X. [Exempts pensions under 41 Geo. III, c. 96, 43 Geo. III, c. 160, 45 Geo. III, c. 72.]

XI. . . . Nothing in this Act contained shall extend or be construed to extend to empower the said Regent, in the name and on the behalf of H.M., to give the royal assent to any Bill or Bills in Parliament, for repealing, changing, or in any respect varying the order and course of succession to the Crown of this realm, as the same stands now established. . . .

XII. Provided also, . . . That if his said R.H., George Augustus Frederick Prince of Wales shall not continue to be resident in the U.K. of Great Britain and Ireland, or shall at any time marry a Papist, then and in either of such cases, all the powers and authorities vested in his said R.H. by this Act, shall cease and determine.

XIII. . . . The care of H.M.'s royal person, and the disposing, ordering and managing of all matters and things relating thereto, shall be, and the same are hereby vested in the Queen's most excellent Majesty, during the continuance of H.M.'s indisposition. . . . [The section further provides for the King's Household being managed by the Queen, giving her the right to appoint to offices, except the Lord Chamberlain, the Gentlemen of the Bedchamber, the Equerries, the Captain of the Guard, and the Captain of the Band of Pensioners. She cannot dismiss those appointed by the King.]

XIV. [Officers of the Household may not make appointments for any longer term than during H.M.'s pleasure.]

XV. [Provides the Queen with a Council.]

XVI. [Members of Her Majesty's Council to take an oath.]

XVII, XVIII, XIX. [Prescribe the duties of the Council concerning the King's health and his recovery.]

XX. [Deals with the summoning of the Privy Council should the King recover.]

XXI. . . . If H.M., by the advice of six or more of such Privy Council so assembled, shall signify his royal pleasure to resume the personal exercise of his royal authority, and to issue a Proclamation declaring the same, such Proclamation shall be issued accordingly, countersigned by the said six or more of the said Privy Council, and all the powers and authorities given by this Act shall from thenceforth cease and determine, and the personal exercise of the royal authority by H.M. shall be and be deemed to be resumed by H.M., and shall be exercised by H.M., to all intents and purposes, as if this Act had never been made.

XXII. [On the death of the Regent, or on his ceasing to be Regent under the provisions of this Act, a Proclamation to be issued by the Privy Council in the King's name; on the Queen's death, the Regent to issue a Proclamation.] . . . And in case the Parliament in being at the time of the issuing of any Proclamation declaring the death of the Regent or of her Majesty, or at the time of the issuing of any Proclamation for the resumption of the personal exercise of the royal authority by H.M., shall then be separated, by any adjournment or prorogation, such Parliament shall forthwith meet and sit.

XXIII–XXX [Deal with the dissolution of Parliament; the death of the Queen; the issue of money from the Civil List to the Queen and Royal Family; the Keeper of the Queen's Privy Purse; the care of the King's estates; and authorizing the Regent to dispose of Droits of the Crown and of the Admiralty.]

B. THE CABINET

(a) THE 'NOMINAL' CABINET

3. List of Persons to attend the Recorder's Report on 7 Feb. 1810[1]

(Public Record Office, Home Office 42/100.)

Throughout this period the 'Nominal' Cabinet (now alternatively described as the 'Great' or 'Grand' or 'Honorary' Cabinet) continued in existence. It consisted of the king's confidential servants (the members of the 'Efficient' Cabinet), together with (a) the principal Household officials (who were sometimes referred to as 'the Black Cabinet'), and (b) the archbishop of Canterbury, the Speaker of the House of Commons, and the Lord Chief Justice. Meeting invariably in the sovereign's presence (which the 'Efficient' Cabinet never did), it performed two functions. It heard the Home Secretary or the Prime Minister read the speech which the sovereign was to deliver in the House of Lords at the opening and at the close of each parliamentary session. Usually the meeting was a formality, the speech having previously been approved by the 'Efficient' Cabinet, but last-minute alterations, especially in war-time, were occasionally made. Also, it considered the report submitted by the Recorder of London of all criminals capitally convicted at the City of London and County of Middlesex Sessions held at the Old Bailey, and advised the sovereign on the exercise of the prerogative of mercy. It was consequently referred to as the 'Hanging' Cabinet. The archbishop and the Speaker never, apparently, attended the Cabinet meetings for the report, which, incidentally, after 9 Feb. 1793, were to be held in the Great Council Chamber instead of in the Closet. (P.R.O., H.O. 43/4/185. Dundas [Home Secretary] to the Lord Chamberlain.)

Whitehall, Friday, 2 Feb. 1810.

The Archbishop of Canterbury
Lord President [Earl Camden]
Duke of Montrose [Master of the Horse]
Earl of Dartmouth [Lord Chamberlain]
Earl of Ashburnham[2]
Earl of Winchilsea [Groom of the Stole]

[1] The fact that this list came from the Home Office doubtless explains the omission of the Home Secretary, Richard Ryder, whose attendance was indispensable.

[2] The second earl of Ashburnham (1724–1812) was First Lord of the Bedchamber and Groom of the Stole, 1775–1782. His remaining on the lisit is distinctly curious.

Earl of Aylesford [Lord Steward]
Lord Ellenborough [Lord Chief Justice]
Mr. Perceval [First Lord of the Treasury, Chancellor of the Exchequer,
    and Chancellor of Duchy of Lancaster]
Lord Chancellor [Lord Eldon]
Lord Privy Seal [Earl of Westmorland]
Marquess Wellesley [Foreign Secretary]
Earl of Liverpool [Secretary for War & Colonies]
Earl of Harrowby [Cabinet Minister without portfolio]
Earl of Chatham [Master-General of the Ordnance]
Earl Bathurst [President of the Board of Trade & Master of the Mint]
Lord Mulgrave [First Lord of the Admiralty]
Mr. Robert Dundas [President of the Board of Control]
Notice to be given to the gentlemen ushers and keepers of the Council Chamber.
Notice to be given to the Recorder.

(b) THE 'EFFICIENT' CABINET

(i) *Composition*

4. Henry Addington to Lord Loughborough, 25 April 1801

(Campbell, *Lives of the Lord Chancellors*, VIII (1868), p. 197.)

To the astonishment of Addington, who succeeded Pitt as Prime Minister in 1801, Lord Loughborough, the ex-Lord Chancellor, retained his key of the Cabinet boxes, and even continued,
unsummoned, to attend Cabinet meetings, apparently on 10, 13, 19 and 21 April, until, on the
25th, eleven days after he had resigned the Great Seal, he received a formal dismissal.

A misconception appears to have taken place, in consequence of which I am led to
trouble your Lordship from various considerations, and particularly from a sense
of duty to the King. I have reason to believe that H.M. considered your Lordship's
attendance at the Cabinet as having naturally ceased upon the resignation of the Seals,
and supposed it to be so understood by your Lordship. Much as I should feel personally
gratified in having the benefit of your Lordship's counsel and assistance, I will fairly
acknowledge to you that I did not offer to H.M. any suggestion to the contrary; and,
indeed, I must have felt myself precluded from doing so by having previously, in
more instances than one, expressed and acted upon the opinion that the number of
the Cabinet should not exceed that of the persons whose responsible situations in
office require their being members of it. Under these circumstances, I feel that I have
perhaps given way to a mistaken delicacy in not having sooner made the communication to your Lordship; but I am persuaded you will see that I should be wanting in
duty to the King, and in what is due to yourself, if I delayed it beyond the time when
a Minute of Cabinet, with the names of the persons present, must be prepared in
order to be submitted to H.M.

    I hope your Lordship will give me full credit for the motives by which I can alone
be actuated upon this occasion, as well as for the sincere sentiments of esteem and
regard with which I am, my dear Lord, [&c.]

5. Debate in the House of Commons, 3 March 1806

(Cobbett's *Parliamentary Debates*, VI, 286–341.)

Like all other governments of the period, the 'Talents' Ministry of 1806–1807 was a coalition of party groups. Sidmouth demanded adequate representation in the Cabinet, and, as Lord Bucking-hamshire was objected to, he insisted that another friend, Lord Ellenborough, the Lord Chief Justice, should be substituted. The appointment was severely criticized in both Houses of Parliament on the ground that the judges should be independent of the executive. Ministers had majorities in the divisions, but it was the last appointment of its kind.

*M*r. *Spencer Stanhope* . . . moved, 1st. That it is the opinion of this House, that it is highly expedient that the functions of a Minister of State and of a confidential adviser of the executive measures of Government, should be kept distinct and separate from those of a Judge at common law.

2nd. That it is the opinion of this House that those members of H.M.'s most honourable Privy Council, whom H.M. is advised to direct to be habitually summoned, and who are so summoned to that Committee or selection of the said Council, which deliberates upon matters of State, and which is commonly known by the name of the Cabinet Council, are, and are deemed to be, the confidential Ministers and advisers of the executive measures of Government.

3rd. That the so summoning to the said Committee, or Cabinet Council, a Lord Chief Justice of England, to sit and deliberate as a member of the same, is a practice peculiarly inexpedient and unadvisable, tending to expose to suspicion, and bring into disrepute the independence and impartiality of the judicial character, and to render less satisfactory, if not less pure, the administration of public justice.

Mr. Canning . . . thought that the holding a situation which was in its nature precarious, and yet an object of ambition, had a tendency to destroy the confidence which resulted from the independence of the Judge. . . . It was well known there was no positive law existing at present which opposed this measure, and therefore it could not properly perhaps be called illegal, and it might not be correct to call it unconstitutional till the point was clearly established. But . . . it was extremely inconvenient, and contrary to the principles of reason and common sense, that the judicial and executive powers should be combined in the same person. . . . With regard to the Cabinet, the right hon. gent. [Mr. Bond] said that it was not recognised by the Constitution, and that, in fact, it was nothing else than a Select Committee of the Privy Council, called at the discretion of H.M. He never heard a more untenable proposition. In a free country such as this, where a control was necessary, and where responsibility must necessarily lodge somewhere, were we at this day to be turned round by being told that there was no such thing in the Constitution as a Cabinet? . . . It might be true, indeed, that the Constitution recognised nothing under the name of the Cabinet, but it was not the less certain that there was such an assembly with whom the responsibility for whatever advice they gave rested. Now, as to the question of responsibility: the right hon. gent. allowed that every individual who joined the Council in advising H.M. was responsible for the whole. Lord Ellenborough then might be responsible for the whole, and if this was the case, he would beg of gentlemen to consider whether, on the principles of reason and common sense, or those laid down by the best authorities, whether a Judge ought to be placed in a situation where it would be utterly impossible for him to divest himself entirely of the feelings of party, and which would naturally render him liable to suspicion? . . .

Lord Temple . . . Lord Ellenborough had assisted in the Cabinet at the examination of Governor Picton, and afterwards sat as Judge on his trial.[1] The Judges were often called to the House of Peers to give their advice to the Lords, and therefore might often give opinions which might afterwards lead to trials before themselves in their own Courts. Yet this was no objection to their giving their advice to the peers. The Lord Chancellor sat in the House of Lords and voted in appeals from his own decisions. He desired them to look at the case of the rebel peers,[2] in which, as well as in other instances, many peers sat in the Cabinet during the examination, and afterwards voted as Judges in the House of Peers. Chief Justice Eyre had sat in the Cabinet and examined offenders whom he afterwards tried in his own Court. . . . He could take upon him to say that Lord Mansfield attended every Council from 1760 to 1763. In 1763 he left off attending the Council, not from any sense of its incompatibility with his judicial situation, but, according to a letter of his own which was in existence, because he would not sit with the Duke of Bedford, whose measures he disapproved of. In 1765 he returned again, and was named as one of the Council of Regency. . . . In the riots of 1780 Lord Mansfield was present at the proceedings in the Council, and afterwards sat as Judge upon the rioters. . . . From the earliest periods of our history, the Chief Justice had been one of the King's Viceregents, one of the members of the Councils of Regency, and always summoned to give his advice on cases of great public delinquency. Thus the principle of constitutional law was in favour of the appointment.

Mr. Canning admitted that up to 1763 Lord Mansfield sat regularly in the Cabinet, but never after 1765; therefore, the latter part of his life was, in this respect, a condemnation of the first.

Mr. Secretary Fox. . . . In point of fact, there is nothing in our Constitution that recognises any such institution as a Cabinet Council. . . . That part of the Privy Council which H.M. thinks proper habitually to consult has, indeed, of late years, been denominated the Cabinet Council. But names are of small account upon this question. Call this Council what you will–either the Ministers of State or the Executive Committee, still the law can know nothing of its members but as Privy Councillors. . . . As the existence of a Cabinet Council has never been legally acknowledged, there is, of course, no legal record of the members comprising any Cabinet; and we have it not in our power to state anything of authority upon the subject, but what may have come within our own observation, or may have been communicated to us by our fathers. Therefore, when the hon. gent. ask us to produce precedents, applying to the case before the House, we must answer that we have it not in our power to produce many, and they appear to doubt even the few we can offer. . . . The right hon. gent. [Canning] has frequently spoken of the Cabinet as a responsible body; I wish that right hon. gent., or any gentleman who supports his opinion, to point out from what parts of our Statutes, or of the recorded proceedings of this House, he

[1] On 24 Feb. 1806 Picton was tried before the Lord Chief Justice on charges of cruelty whilst Governor of Trinidad, and he was found guilty.

[2] Balmerino, Kilmarnock and Lovat, executed after the '45.

has learned that the Cabinet, or any individual belonging it, has been, as such, held to be legally responsible. . . . When the right hon. gent. speaks of the responsibility of the Cabinet, I would recommend him to consider whether it would be expedient to insist upon the attachment of responsibility to the whole of such a body, for every ministerial act; and whether such a measure might not be apt to endanger, if not in most instances to defeat, the object of responsibility? For any act done in my office, I am directly responsible to Parliament and the country; and perhaps it is much better for any purpose of practical responsibility, that it should fall on one man than on a body; for this obvious reason, that the difficulty of producing conviction and punishment is the less in one case than in the other. I do not mean to say that it is not desirable to bring forward the charges of guilt against all the advisers as well as the agent, if it were practicable to prove the charge. The immediate actor can always be got at in a way that is very plain, direct and easy, compared to that by which you may be able to reach his advisers. . . . The Cabinet has never been deemed a responsible body. . . . If in any shape, you acknowledge the existence of a Cabinet Council, we must go on to make such a body not alone formally, but really known to the House and to the laws. . . . Some gentlemen may confound the functions of what is called the Cabinet Council, and therefore it may be necessary to state a distinction, of which the noble Lord (Castlereagh) must be aware. Councils frequently meet which are assembled solely for the purpose of affording to the members an opportunity of consulting with each other, and stating their ideas reciprocally on points connected with their several Departments, but with no intention of communicating the result to H.M. Indeed, upon many points it would not only be unnecessary, but improper to communicate with H.M. . . . On other occasions the Cabinet Council meet to advise H.M. in person. In the former case of meeting, it will not surely be pretended that any responsibility can attach to the proceedings of this Council, or that any individual Minister can incur censure for consulting them, the aid of whose counsels may be useful and necessary. And to whom should responsibility attach to the latter description of meetings? To the agent, to be sure, who executes the plan resolved on. This I maintain to be well founded. For if this Committee of the Privy Council should order any project which did not meet my approbation, and against which I should consequently protest, still, if the plan were exceptionable, my protest would not avail to acquit me of the responsibility that would arise from the execution of it. This I take to be the general rule with regard to ministerial responsibility; and everything that has occurred different from this rule, I consider in the light of an exception. . . .

Lord Castlereagh. . . . The right hon. gent. has argued as if, because a Chief Judge is usually a Privy Councillor, and because a seat at that Board is a situation which most men are desirous of obtaining, and which they are unwilling to be deprived of, it must therefore follow that the objection on the score of influence would not be strengthened by the introduction of a Judge from the Privy Council into the Cabinet. But surely it cannot be contended that the degrees of influence arising from the two situations are in any respect to be compared to each other. Can an ordinary seat at the Privy Council, which does not necessarily give, or in its consequences lead to, any political consequence, and from which no one is ever removed except for misconduct, bear any comparison with the situation of a person included among those members of the Council to whom H.M. entrusts the general administration of his affairs, and who, for the time, are collectively charged with the trust of advising him upon every act of his Government? . . .[1]

(ii) *Procedure*

6. Lord Holland on the Cabinet in 1806–1807

(Lord Holland, *Memoirs of the Whig Party*, II (1854), pp. 84–90.)

Lord Holland (1773–1840), nephew of Charles James Fox, was Lord Privy Seal in the Grenville Ministry of 1806–1807, and Chancellor of the Duchy of Lancaster in Grey's Reform Ministry (1830–1834) and under Melbourne.

When I came into office, I was curious to understand the course of proceeding or interior constitution of our Government. It is vague in the extreme, and often irregular and inconvenient. The Cabinet, which is legally only a Committee of the Privy Council appointed by the King on each distinct occasion, has gradually assumed the character and in some measure the reality of a permanent Council, through which advice on all matters of great importance is conveyed to the Crown. But though the necessity of a well-concerted or party Government in a limited Monarchy and popular Constitution has generally established the wholesome doctrine that each and every member of the Cabinet is in some degree responsible for the measures adopted by the Government while he is a member of it, yet there are no precise laws nor rules, nor even any well-established or understood usages which mark what measures in each Department are or are not to be communicated to the Cabinet. Measures of foreign policy seem indeed more emphatically designated by the history of the origin of this Committee in Charles II's time, by usage and by reason, as the objects of their deliberation. Yet there is nothing but private agreement or party feeling generally, or the directions of the King accidentally, which obliges even a Secretary for Foreign Affairs to consult his colleagues on any of the duties of his office before he takes the King's pleasure upon them. In all Administrations, I believe, and in ours I am sure, his Dispatches, his measures, and even his appointments were more generally submitted to the judgment of the Cabinet than those in any other Department. When a Cabinet is held at a Public Office, it is generally at the Foreign Office. The acts of that Office, however, are not invariably nor necessarily laid before the Cabinet, and the Secretary of State at his own discretion advises and completes many without any such consultation. In the other branches of Administration, such as the Treasury, the Home Secretaryship, the Chancery, the Admiralty, the discretion is yet larger as to the matters in their respective Departments on which the Ministers take the King's pleasure directly, or previously consult their colleagues before they advise him. Nomination to places is, for obvious reasons, seldom submitted to the consideration of the Cabinet. Yet by usage, arising out of the necessity of placing a large portion of that species of power in one Department, the patronage

---

[1] Ellenborough, defending his acceptance of a seat in the Cabinet in a letter to Wilberforce, added, "I have stipulated that I should not be expected to attend except on particularly important occasions" (*Private Papers of Wilberforce*, pp. 125–130).

does *not* always in practice or substance belong to those officers who are the legal channels, and consequently in a strict constitutional sense, the sole legal and ostensible advisers of the appointment. Thus, for instance, the First Lord of the Treasury actually and constantly takes the King's pleasure on the appointment to many dignities and places, to the warrant, patent, or instrument for which he neither affixes signature nor seal, but which are conferred by the Great Seal, the Privy Seal, and the Signet. Such an undefined distribution of authority and the want of a distinct line between the jurisdiction of the Cabinet and of the individual Ministers who compose it, as well as between the jurisdiction of their respective offices, is sometimes convenient to the public service, inasmuch as the person whose abilities qualify him for the largest share of power, may from other circumstances be incapacitated from holding the office which would technically render him responsible for the exercise of it. On the other hand, the looseness of the obligation of referring the measures of each Department to the Cabinet, and the undefined limits of the authority of many of the high offices, afford great scope for intrigue and cabal with the Crown. A favourite might by these means contrive insensibly to separate his interests from those of his colleagues, and at the secret suggestion of a King thwart the measures and defeat the views of a Council which, though not technically, is virtually responsible to the public for the whole conduct of affairs. These remarks are speculations resulting from reflection, not the fruit of experience. No such inconvenience was felt in Lord Grenville's Administration. There did indeed occur one embarrassment from the irregular manner in which, according to long usage and practice, the correspondence with the Irish Government had been conducted. The wishes, and even commands of the Government, had for many years been communicated to the Government of Ireland by private letters from the Secretary of the Home Department to the Lord Lieutenant or his Secretary. We could not, in honour or duty, proceed in discussing our project of a limited Catholic Bill with the Irish Government, much less with the Catholics in Ireland, without bringing the subject in some way before H.M.'s notice. The slovenly and irregular method of transacting business which I have described, prevented its coming, as a matter of course, before his eyes, and consequently compelled us to present it to him in the first instance as a measure of great importance connected with the subject on which his mind was morbidly predisposed to take alarm. . . .

The patronage of a Government is not submitted to the consideration of a Cabinet; and as my office, the Privy Seal, gave me none, I know little of the history of its distribution during the Administration to which I belonged.

7. The duke of Portland (Prime Minister) to Spencer Perceval (Chancellor of the Exchequer), Bulstrode, 27 Dec. 1807

(Perceval MSS.)

Summonses to Cabinet meetings often went astray or were received too late, and meetings occasionally took place in the absence even of the Prime Minister.

. . . I did not intend coming to town till tomorrow or Tuesday sevennight . . . Lord Castlereagh was so good as to inform me of the result of the last Cabinet. It has my entire concurrence, and I am very glad to find that you parted so well satisfied. Had I been apprised of Lord Castlereagh's intention of summoning a meeting so early as Friday I would have remained in town, but when he left me on *Thursday afternoon* I had not an idea of our being called together till the beginning of this week.

8. Lord Ellenborough's Diary, 3 June 1828

(*Lord Ellenborough's Political Diary, 1828–30*, ed. Lord Colchester (1881).)

Lord Ellenborough (1790–1871), the son of the Lord Chief Justice (No. 5), and afterwards (1841–1844) Governor-General of India, was at first Lord Privy Seal and then President of the Board of Control, in the Wellington Ministry (1828–1830). Lord Aberdeen, later Prime Minister, was Foreign Secretary, June 1828–Nov. 1830.

. . . Aberdeen asked me to write a dispatch to Madrid, which I did. Its object is to do everything short of threatening war in the event of Spain's interfering in the affairs of Portugal *by force*. I sent it to the Duke, and we are to have a Cabinet upon it to-morrow. The Duke goes to Ascot and will not be at the Cabinet. . . . [1, p. 136.]

[2 July 1828.] Cabinet dinner at Lord Bathurst's. The Chancellor not there. I suspect he thought we should have an angry discussion, and chose to be absent, and so clear of it. . . . [1, p. 155.]

. . . We had a great deal of useless talk, a large portion of which originated in Lord Bathurst's being rather drunk.[1] His wine was excellent, and he is a generous host. Peel was in better humour; but he is not the man for his station. . . . [1, p. 156.]

[3 April 1828.] . . . The Chancellor said to me, "We should have no Cabinets after dinner. We all drink too much wine and are not civil to each other." [1, p. 76.]

9. Sir George Shee to Colonel McMahon, *c.* 26 June 1804

(*Windsor Archives*, 40220.)

Shee was a civil servant. McMahon (*c.* 1754–1817), afterwards the prince regent's private secretary (baronetcy, 1817), was now Secretary and Keeper of the prince's Privy Seal and Auditor of the Duchy of Cornwall.

. . . A greater trust cannot be reposed in a messenger than the custody of an official box, and a higher offence cannot be committed by him than getting a false key made to it. The excuse that he only intended to *smuggle* appears to me to be quite frivolous, and the assertion that the offence is justified by usage quite unfounded.

The locks of all the Cabinet boxes are opened by the same key, the possession of one of which is only entrusted to Cabinet Ministers, Under-Secretaries of State, and perhaps two or three other confidential servants. The most secret Dispatches and other such papers are conveyed in these boxes without any seal, as the messengers are supposed to be of a description of persons quite above the treachery of opening them. Now, you know, the possession of a false key puts so much in a messenger's power that even the safety of the State may be risked by his making use of the information

---

[1] Cf. Lord Melville to Chas. Bragge-Bathurst, 26 Jan. 1825: "Lord Sidmouth, as you know, has left us. We were therefore quite orderly and abstemious." (*C. B. Bathurst MSS.*)

within his reach. The temptation to such conduct you may easily judge of in times when the stocks are high or low in proportion to the knowledge on the Exchange of continental transactions. If the offence were punishable by law, the necessity for dismission from office for it would not be quite so absolute as it now appears. . . .

It is singular that H. [the messenger] should acknowledge having kept an office box two years in his possession.

10. Lord Grenville to Earl Spencer, 11 Feb. 1807

(Althorp MSS.)

Grenville was First Lord of the Treasury, Spencer Home Secretary, and Bedford Lord Lieutenant of Ireland.

We framed a Minute last night which I sent to the King with a letter from myself of which I send you the copy because of the liberty I have taken in it with your name.

. . . We have a Cabinet dinner here today but I fear you are not well enough to be of our party.

It will, I think, be necessary that you should today send to the Duke of B[edford] in confidence copies of the last Minute, with its inclosure of the King's answer, and of this Minute. . . . It would also be right that in a matter of such importance the Cabinet Ministers should each of them also have copies—but this does not press for a day.

11. George III to William Pitt, 8 March 1795

(Public Record Office, Chatham Papers, 104.)

I cannot too strongly express my approbation to Mr. Pitt of his sentiments on the present situation of the west part of Germany, and his proposed Minute of Cabinet, with which I most entirely concur. As Mr. Pitt has not yet shewn the Minute finally to the Cabinet, I trust I am acting agreeable to his wish in returning it to him, and shall be glad to receive after the meeting this identical paper with only at the top of the first page the names of the Ministers present. . . .

12. Lord Mulgrave (First Lord of the Admiralty) to George III, 21 Sept. 1809

(Windsor Archives, 14655.)

Lord Mulgrave has just learned that his name does not appear upon the Minute of Cabinet which was transmitted to your Majesty, and humbly begs your Majesty's permission to have his name inserted in that instrument, having coincided with your Majesty's other servants in the opinions therein expressed. . . .

[The King's reply, 22 September.] The King acknowledges the receipt of Lord Mulgrave's letter of yesterday, and will not fail to have his name inserted in the Minute of Cabinet of the 18th inst. . . .

13. G. Aust (Senior Clerk in F.O.) to Lord Hardwicke, 21 Oct. 1784

(British Museum Additional MSS. 35623, f. 53)

Lord Sydney was Home Secretary, Richmond Master-General of the Ordnance, and Carmarthen (later, duke of Leeds) Foreign Secretary. Thurlow, who had a reputation for intrigue, and who was the king's personal representative in the Cabinet, was visiting the *Whig* duke of Devonshire. The letter illustrates the difficulty of assembling the Cabinet, especially during the parliamentary recess.

. . . There was a Cabinet meeting at Lord Sydney's Office today, attended only by his Lordship, the Duke of Richmond and Mr. Pitt. Lord Carmarthen was engaged with the Foreign Ministers. The other members were in the country, the Chancellor in particular on a visit to *Chatsworth.*

(iii) *Limits to collective responsibility*

14. Earl Fitzwilliam to Lord Grenville, 25 Jan. 1807

(Hist. MSS. Comm., Dropmore Papers, IX, p. 22.)

Fitzwilliam (minister without portfolio) refers to the 'Delicate Investigation'–the official inquiry into the conduct of the Princess of Wales. His opinion is not referred to in the Cabinet minute.

I am so unwell this evening as to be quite unable to attend Cabinet; but in the hope that the outline of the proposition chalked out by Lord Howick last night will be adopted, that H.M. will be advised to accompany his permission to the Princess to appear again before him with a clear and strong animadversion on the many parts of her conduct which are so justly liable to censure, I beg to be understood as giving my cordial assent to such advice, and earnestly beg to have my name recorded as doing so.

15. Letters from the duke of Richmond (Master-General of the Ordnance) to Pitt, 15 Dec. 1794 and 12 Jan. 1795

(Hist. MSS. Comm., Bathurst Papers, p. 706.)

The earlier eighteenth-century practice of a minister expressing dissent from his colleagues' policy by ceasing to attend Cabinet meetings persisted into the nineteenth century, but on rare occasions (No. 16). Richmond's situation was probably unprecedented: he had been attending the Cabinet dinners but had retired from the consultations that followed. His removal from office (Feb. 1795) did not end his friendship with Pitt.

. . . Hearing that some of the members of the Cabinet, who last came into office, had expressed dissatisfaction at my having of late discontinued attending the meetings, I called on Lord Spencer . . . in order to prevent an impression that might possibly have been conceived, that this conduct of mine had been caused by my feeling some coolness towards those gentlemen, which certainly is not the case . . . Lord Spencer . . . expressed his opinion that the situation was extraordinary for a member of a Cabinet, and as such, considered responsible amongst others for its measures, to absent himself from the consultations; and, feeling the force of this observation, I am sensible that it would have been a much more simple and direct course for me to have followed, formally to have asked H.M.'s permission to retire from the Cabinet. . . .

As to responsibility, although I have found myself unable to concur in several of the measures that have been adopted for carrying on this war, yet approving of the principles upon which it was undertaken, and trusting to improvement from experience in some of the modes of conducting it, I have had no objection to remain committed with those who have had the management of it, and who, I am persuaded, mean well.

I will not, however, deny to you that one of my principal motives for not attending the meetings, is the great reserve in respect to public matters which for some time past you have shown me, although in private concerns which have nearly interested me, I with pleasure acknowledge your attentions. But as my office is not one that would naturally give me a seat in the Cabinet, I in fact have no business there, and the only footing on which it could ever be pleasant to me was that of particular confidence and friendship from the leading Minister. . . . But deprived of these, I stand quite isolated in the Cabinet, unconnected with any party or individual, and in a situation I must think not very becoming for me. . . .

[12 January 1795.] . . . My former letter stated the grounds . . . on which I offered to return to the Cabinet. . . . You must . . . be sensible how very awkward it must be to me to attend the dinners, which I do to show that I have no dissatisfaction with individuals, and afterwards to retire from the consultations that follow. And I do trust that, feeling the regard for me which you profess, you will not leave me much longer in so very extraordinary and unpleasant a predicament. . . . [Ibid., p. 709.]

[Pitt to the Duke, 26 January 1795.] . . . Your Grace's ceasing to attend the Cabinet, and your breaking off the habits of familiar and friendly intercourse between us, proceeded entirely from yourself. In that situation (which naturally precluded your being previously consulted) the state of public affairs led to a new and extensive arrangement of Government. Many months afterwards elapsed without your taking any share in its deliberations. . . . I see that your resuming a seat in the Cabinet must prove equally unpleasant and embarrassing to public business. This consideration must decide my opinion. . . . The consequence does not stop here; . . . the execution of the important duties of your Department is incompatible with a state which precludes confidential intercourse on all the points of public business. . . . [Ibid., p. 711.]

16. Lord Ellenborough's Diary, 22 March 1828

(*Lord Ellenborough's Political Diary, 1828–30*, ed. Lord Colchester (1881).)

Grant is not yet brought to a point,[1] and his conduct is most contradictory. He never comes to a Cabinet, and yet he sits on the Treasury bench. . . . [I, p. 65.]

[2 April.] . . . Grant reappeared at the Cabinet dinner. I think the Duke is disappointed at his remaining, and heartily repents having ever brought him and the Canningites into his Cabinet. I wish they were out. [I, p. 76.]

[1] As to whether he, the President of the Board of Trade, will accept the Government's new Corn Bill.

[11 May.] . . . Grant is obstinate and useless. However, he is seldom there[1] and takes little part. . . . [I, p. 104.]

17. William Pitt to George III, 21 April 1805, and reply

(*Windsor Archives*, 11651; Earl Stanhope's *Life of Pitt*, IV (1862), App., p. xxiii.)

The seventy-eight-year-old admiral who succeeded Lord Melville as First Lord of the Admiralty, and who now became Baron Barham, was expected to attend Cabinet meetings only when matters affecting his own department were to be considered.

Mr. Pitt humbly begs leave to represent to your Majesty that, after the fullest reflection on the best mode of filling the vacancy in the office of First Lord of the Admiralty, he can submit no arrangement which appears to be so advantageous to your Majesty's service under all the present circumstances, as the appointment of Sir Charles Middleton. . . . In general politics he cannot be expected to take any share, but his strength and vigour of mind seem fully equal to the business of the Department for a time. . . . Should your Majesty be graciously pleased to approve of this proposal, Mr. Pitt trusts your Majesty will see no objection to conferring on Sir Charles Middleton the rank of a Baron, as it seems necessary that a person holding so high and responsible an office should have a seat in one of the Houses of Parliament, and his becoming a member of the House of Commons seems in this instance to be neither desirable nor practicable.

[The King's reply, 22 April.] The King, from the moment of the unfortunate necessity of Lord Melville's resigning his seat at the Board of Admiralty, had no object but that Mr. Pitt should recommend as successor the person best qualified to supply the vacancy. As Mr. Pitt, on the whole, thinks Sir Charles Middleton answers that description, H.M. will not object to it, nor to his being advanced to the rank of a Baron, but his attending Cabinet meetings ought to be confined to subjects regarding the Navy.[2] . . .

18. Mrs. Canning to the duke of Portland, *c.* 20 April 1827

(A. Aspinall, *The Formation of Canning's Ministry*, Camden Third Series, LIX (1937), p. 155.)

Mrs. Canning urges her brother-in-law, the fourth duke (son of the Prime Minister) to take office in order to give much-needed support to her husband's government.

. . . Will you consent to come into the Cabinet and lend your name as a *sleeping* partner in the firm? . . . The office proposed to you for your acceptance is that of Privy Seal, which in point of rank is second in the Government but has absolutely nothing in the way of business belonging to it, and you need not remain one hour longer in town from holding it, nor need you (if you do not feel disposed to do so) ever attend the Cabinet Councils while you are in town. . . .

[1] At Cabinet meetings.
[2] Charles Abbot, the Speaker commented (16 June 1805): "Lord Barham has been but once at the Cabinet since his appointment. He was wanted the other day between five and six, but, upon inquiry, the Cabinet messenger brought for answer that he was gone to drink tea somewhere in the City." (Colchester, *Diary*, II, p. 11.)

19. William Pitt to Lord Harrowby (Foreign Secretary), 18 Sept. 1804
(Harrowby MSS.)

The letter further illustrates the difficulty of assembling the Cabinet during the parliamentary recess; and a decision on a grave matter such as a declaration of war might have to be taken in the absence of the Foreign Secretary and without the king's authorization.

. . . It has appeared to all the members of the Cabinet who were within reach of town, that instructions should be immediately sent to our naval commanders to stop at all events the sailing of either Spanish or French ships from Ferrol, or any further reinforcements being collected there. . . . We have drawn a Minute of Cabinet on these ideas, and have thought it best to send it you [at Weymouth] that you may take the first convenient opportunity of laying it before the King. In the meantime, as every hour may be material to the execution of the instructions, they will be immediately forwarded to Admiral Cornwallis, and H.M. will, I am persuaded, not disapprove of this step being taken without waiting for his previous orders. . . .

20. Spencer Perceval (Prime Minister) to Lord Wellesley (Foreign Secretary), 9 Aug. 1811
(Perceval MSS.)

Wellesley, one of the greatest of eighteenth-century empire builders (he had been Governor-General of Bengal, 1798–1805), was temperamentally unfitted for Cabinet office not only because of his notorious inefficiency – he could scarcely be induced to answer dispatches – but on account of his autocratic habits and his ill-concealed contempt of his less able colleagues, whose opinions he seldom sought. Vice-Admiral Saumarez commanded the fleet operating in the Baltic.

. . . I should see no objection to your giving power to Sir James Saumarez to put an end to the war directly with Russia by signing Preliminary Articles of Peace, except that I doubt whether it might not, by betraying too great an eagerness and forwardness on our part, rather tend to defeat our object. . . .

But upon this point particularly I lament that we have not had a Cabinet, for I think our colleagues would be a little surprised to find such a measure taken without any previous communication with them – and indeed I think you will feel that if it would occasion too much delay now to have a Cabinet upon this paper, yet before it is dispatched (and we could not hope to have one assembled before Monday next) it will be very desirable that the paper should be circulated as soon as possible, for though I do not conceive that there is any point in it on which any of our colleagues can differ from us, yet it is not impossible, especially with those who are every week in town, that they might feel hurt at not having so much as the appearance of being consulted upon such important subjects. . . .

21. George III to Henry Dundas (Home Secretary), 18 March 1793
(British Museum Additional MSS. 40100, f. 73.)

George III evidently expected to receive not only a statement about Cabinet decisions but also an indication of the tone and temper of the discussion.

The Minute of Cabinet is correctly written agreeable to the idea stated yesterday to me by Lord Chatham, which I thoroughly approved, and therefore do so to the putting it into official form. By Mr. Dundas not having stated that anything unpleasant passed at the meeting, I trust that good humour prevailed, which is essential to carry on the public service with alacrity and indeed with comfort to the individual most concerned in transacting the business.

22. Lord Hawkesbury to George III, 28 May 1807

(British Museum Additional MSS. 38242, f. 80.)

Cabinet minutes sometimes contained a statement not merely of decisions reached, but also of the supporting arguments. Here, the Home Secretary offers to supply additional information verbally.

Lord Hawkesbury has the honour to send your Majesty a Minute of Cabinet on the subject of the letter of H.R.H. the Prince of Wales. The opinion contained in this Minute has been most seriously considered, and is the result of two Cabinet meetings. If your Majesty should be desirous of any explanation of the grounds on which this opinion has been formed, Lord Hawkesbury will do himself the honour of waiting upon your Majesty at any hour on Saturday which your Majesty may be pleased to appoint.

23. Lord Ellenborough's Diary, 26 March 1828

(Lord Ellenborough's Political Diary, 1828–30, ed. Lord Colchester (1881).)

Acute differences of opinion in the Cabinet on questions of both domestic and foreign policy resulted in the secession of Huskisson, Palmerston, Goderich and Charles Grant at the end of May. The convention laid down by Pitt that a Cabinet minister must communicate with the king only on matters concerning his own department, and that the Prime Minister must, in general, be the link between sovereign and Cabinet, was as yet imperfectly recognized.

. . . Dudley told the King to-day in what a state we were. This he had no right to do. To tell the King the Cabinet differences, which have not yet had any result is either *bétise* or treachery. . . . [I, p. 70.]

[27 March.] . . . The Duke had an audience, and told the King in what state we were, saying he should not have mentioned it unless he had known that Dudley had spoken of it to His Majesty, as he was unwilling to trouble him with a difference which might have no result. [I, p. 71.]

24. Lord Hawkesbury (Home Secretary) to his father, Lord Liverpool, 23 Jan. 1806

(C. D. Yonge, *Life and Administration of Robert Banks, 2nd Earl of Liverpool,* I (1868), p. 207.)

Both George III and George IV occasionally demanded of their ministers individual opinions, either verbal or in writing: a practice inconsistent with the idea of joint Cabinet advice. The letter was written on the day of Pitt's death. His colleagues decided that they lacked the strength to carry on the Government.

. . . I have had a very long and distressing conversation with the King. . . . He has desired that we would, each of us (after the subject has been thoroughly discussed) send him our opinion in writing of what is best to be done. I do not believe there will be any material difference of opinion, as far as I can judge at present. . . .

25. Cabinet Minute, 27 May 1812

(The Letters of George IV, 1812-1830, ed. A. Aspinall, I (1938), p. 90.)

Present:–The Lord Chancellor, the Lord President, the Lord Privy Seal, Earl of Buckinghamshire, Earl of Harrowby, the Viscount Melville, Lord Mulgrave, Mr. Secretary Ryder, Mr. Vansittart, Earl of Liverpool. Earl Camden and Viscount Castlereagh absent at their own desire.[1]

Your Royal Highness's confidential servants having received the communication made to them on the 25th inst. by your R.H.'s commands through the Lord Chancellor, the Earl of Liverpool and Viscount Melville, have taken that communication into their most serious consideration, and have most anxiously and repeatedly deliberated upon the same, and they beg leave most humbly to submit to your R.H. their decided conviction that no beneficial result is likely to arise to your R.H.'s service from any further attempt being made on their part, under the present circumstances, to bring about an union between your R.H.'s servants and Marquis Wellesley and Mr. Canning.

[The Prince Regent's Reply, communicated by his Private Secretary, 27 May 1812.] Colonel McMahon is commanded by H.R.H. the Prince Regent to state his commands to Lord Liverpool to attend himself, and to desire the attendance of his colleagues at Carlton House tomorrow morning at 12 o'clock, as the Prince is desirous to learn from each of his servants the grounds of the opinion which they have communicated to H.R.H. in the Minute of this day.[2] [*Ibid.*, I, p. 91n.]

26. Diary of Henry Hobhouse (Under-Secretary of State for Home Affairs), 9 Sept. 1822

(Diary of Henry Hobhouse, 1820-1827, ed. A. Aspinall (1947), pp. 95-97.)

Discussing the question who should succeed Castlereagh as Foreign Secretary and Leader of the House of Commons. The Cabinet's advice was not sought: in any case unanimity was out of the question.

... The King's first impression was to place Peel in the lead of the House of Commons, with the office of Chancellor of the Exchequer, to which he considers the situation to be accustomably attached, and he made a proposition on this head to Peel, who begged to decline saying a word on the subject. ... Lord Liverpool ... went to the King and declared his opinion to be that it was necessary to place Canning in Lord Londonderry's position, and that the Duke of Wellington, Lord Bathurst and Lord Westmorland (neither of them personally favourable to Canning) were of the

---

[1] Out of delicacy. With his usual generosity Castlereagh, who had fought a duel with Canning in Sept. 1809, did not wish to prejudice the chance of a successful negotiation with the two dissident Tory groups led by Canning and Wellesley by attending the Cabinet discussions.

[2] Each Cabinet minister received on the 28th instructions from the regent to state *in writing* the grounds of his concurrence in the recommendation contained in the Cabinet minute. Liverpool's reply is in Yonge's *Life of Lord Liverpool*, I, p. 393; Bathurst's in H.M.C., *Bathurst Papers*, p. 176, and those of Melville, Mulgrave, Sidmouth, Westmorland, Buckinghamshire, Eldon, Harrowby, Ryder and Vansittart, are in *Letters of George IV*, I, pp. 91-98.

same opinion. The King asked Lord Liverpool whether his continuance in office depended on his opinion prevailing in this instance. On this question his Lordship reserved himself. . . . The King sent for Lord Sidmouth. . . . His Lordship declared his opinion that H.M.'s service would be best promoted by placing Mr. Peel in the lead of the House of Commons and filling the Foreign Office otherwise than by Mr. Canning, who should be permitted to proceed to India.[1] . . . Peel had had an audience of the King before Lord Sidmouth, and professed . . . his acquiescence in whatever was deemed best. . . . The Lord Chancellor (who had never had any communication with Lord Liverpool since Lord Londonderry's death) probably did not abstain, as Lord Sidmouth did, from giving weight to the King's personal prejudice against Canning. . . .

The King was slow to decide between the conflicting opinions given to him. The Duke of Wellington, who was not able to have an audience till Saturday,[2] probably decided his wavering judgment. For he yesterday wrote to Lord Liverpool authorizing him to make an offer of the Foreign Office to Canning.

27. George Canning (Foreign Secretary) to Mrs. Canning, 19 Dec. 1824

(*Harewood MSS.*)

The Cabinet was deeply divided on the question of recognizing the independence of the South American Republics.

. . . It was impossible to say how far the King might be prepared to go. And I went to Windsor yesterday determined, if I found his temper in my audience like that which appeared to prevail in his letter, to tender my resignation. I even sent to Planta[3] in the morning for the seals of my office, that I might have them ready to put in H.M.'s hand, but by some accident they did not arrive . . . till after I had set out. Liverpool called to take me to Windsor and I could not propose to him to wait for such an object.

On our road Liverpool endeavoured to argue me into temperance. He did not pretend not to see all the inconveniences of our situation and of the Duke of Wellington's use of *his*. And he contended that when the King *did* what we desired, against his opinions, we ought to let him grumble a little for consolation. That if he refused to *do* it, that was a cause for resignation, but ungraciousness *in doing* so was not. He said that not once but twenty times the King had wished and intended to get rid of him, Liverpool, and had pledged himself to others to do so. That when he knew the King less, he used to feel, as I did now, a determination to bring the matter to a point, but that the King always saved him the trouble by stopping short, just when that point came near, and he then found that if he (Liverpool) had acted according to his first impulse, he should have given the King the very thing he wanted—a peg to hang his design upon, and courage to execute it. That just now he (Liverpool) was sufficiently well with the King, perhaps *because* I was his *bête noir* at the moment, but that all that might change any day, and that he conjured me at least to do nothing

[1] As Governor-General of Bengal. [2] Because of illness. [3] The Under-Secretary.

myself that should make my going out my own act—that if I did not, he would answer for it, the King would never have courage to displace me. I promised so far, and said I would be decided by what passed in our interview that day.

Liverpool went into the Closet first and had a pretty long audience. My turn came next, and as we passed each other (Liverpool coming out and I going in) in the ante-chamber, Liverpool had just time to whisper, "You will find him perfectly quiet and reasonable." And so, to my great surprise, I did. I do not remember to have had with him a more calm and amicable *chat*.

. . . He . . . said . . . that he really thought us all wrong, but that he had consented to the thing, since we said it must be, and was only now anxious that it should be executed in the manner least offensive to his allies. I told him how I intended to manage this part of the question, which he perfectly approved; and we parted in as good-humour as could be desired. Only we did not shake hands, which, however, is not necessarily a purposed omission.

After me, Lord Bathurst, Lord Westmorland and Peel had audiences. The *sôt*[1] did not tell us (Liverpool or me) a word of what passed. I have no doubt that he did all the mischief he could, and took abundance of merit to himself for having fought desperately against us. Bathurst did, and it was rather amusing. The King evidently took for granted that *he*, Bathurst, had been in the minority throughout, but when Bathurst in stating the opinions which he had held, came to say, *I* was *for* Mexico but against Colombia, he had hardly got the words '*for* Mexico' out when the King interrupted him, turned the conversation to quite another topic, and never reverted to the subject of the Cabinet discussions again. Peel I had no opportunity of seeing afterwards, as the Council followed immediately upon it. But he went in, determined to speak his mind freely, and his mind happens to be strongest on the very points to which the king feels most objection, and being as he is (and as he said he should tell the King he was) a *convert* since July (when Buenos Ayres was decided) he found it necessary (he said) to be the more explicit. And I have no doubt that he *was* so, for his conduct in the late discussions has been eminently honourable, and *de plus*, I have no doubt, highly useful. The Duke of Wellington's and *le sôt's* faces on the day on which he (P.) first declared himself, were *pictures*.

I cannot help hoping that this concurrence of all the active members of the Government—of the 3 Secretaries of State, the First Lord of the Treasury, and Chancellor of the Exchequer (for Robinson's opinions must be known to the King, though he did not give them with half the openness and manliness of Peel) will gradually reconcile the King's mind to a measure which (to be fair) I do not wonder at his feeling to be the most distasteful of his whole reign. It sanctions what he conceives to be a revolutionary principle. It cuts him off from his dearly-beloved Metternich and more effectually than any merely *European* difference of opinion would do, and it exposes him to the risk of having a cocoa-nut-coloured minister to receive at his Levée—a circumstance to which I, *liberale* that I am, do not look forward altogether with indifference. . . .

[1] Westmorland was Privy Seal—'le sot (sceau) privé'. Canning disliked him.

28. Peel's Endorsement on his Memorandum of 12 Jan. 1829

(Memoirs of Sir Robert Peel, I (1856), pp. 297–298.)

The memorandum ends, "My advice . . . to H.M. will be, not to grant the Catholic claims, or any part of them, precipitately and unadvisedly, but in the first instance to remove the barrier which prevents the consideration of the Catholic question by the Cabinet–to permit his confidential servants to consider it in all its relations on the same principles on which they consider any other great question of public policy, in the hope that some plan of adjustment can be proposed, on the authority and responsibility of a Government likely to command the assent of Parliament, and to unite in its support a powerful weight of Protestant opinion, from a conviction that it is a settlement equitable towards the Roman Catholics, and safe as it concerns the Protestant Establishment."

The paper . . . was communicated to the King by the Duke of Wellington. The day after its receipt by H.M., those of his Ministers who had voted uniformly against the Catholic claims had each a separate interview with H.M., and expressed opinions in general conformity with those expressed in this paper.

The Ministers were–the Duke of Wellington, the Chancellor, Lord Bathurst, Mr. Goulburn, Mr. Herries, Mr. Peel.

The King, after this interview, intimated his consent that the Cabinet should consider the whole state of Ireland, and submit their views to H.M., H.M. being by such consent in no degree pledged to the adoption of the views of his Government, even if it should concur unanimously in the course to be pursued.

29. Macaulay on 'open' questions: speech in the House of Commons, 18 June 1839

(Hansard's Parliamentary Debates, 3rd Series, XLVIII, 464.)

Nothing was more common than to hear it said that the first time a great question was left open, was when Lord Liverpool's Administration left the Catholic question open. Now there could not be a grosser error. Within the memory of many persons living, the general rule was this–that all questions whatever were open questions in a Cabinet, except those which came under two classes; namely, first, measures brought forward by the Government as a Government, which all the members of it were, of course, expected to support, and second, motions brought forward with the purpose of casting a censure, express or implied, on the Government, or any department of it, which all its members were, of course, expected to oppose. He believed that he laid down a rule to which it would be impossible to find an exception. He was sure he laid down a general rule when he said that, 50 years ago, all questions not falling under these heads were considered open. Let gent. run their minds over the history of Mr. Pitt's Administration. Mr. Pitt, of course, expected that every gentleman connected with him by the ties of office, should support him on the leading questions of his Government–the India Bill,–the resolutions respecting the commerce of Ireland–the French Commercial Treaty. Of course, also, he expected that no gentleman should remain in the Government who had voted for Mr. Bastard's motion of censure on the naval administration of Earl Howe, or for Mr. Whitbread's motion on the Spanish armament; but, excepting on such motions, brought forward as attacks on Government, perfect liberty was allowed to his colleagues, and that not merely on trifles but on constitutional questions of vital importance. The question of

Parliamentary Reform was left open; Mr. Pitt and Mr. Dundas were in favour of it, Lord Mulgrave and Lord Grenville against it. On the impeachment of Warren Hastings, likewise, the different members of Government were left to pursue their own course; that Governor was attacked by Mr. Pitt and defended by Lord Mulgrave. In 1790, the question whether the impeachment should be considered as having dropped, in consequence of the termination of the Parliament in which the proceedings were commenced, was left an open question; Mr. Pitt took one side, and was answered by his own Solicitor-General, Sir J. Scott, afterwards Lord Eldon. The important question respecting the powers of juries in cases of libel was left open; Mr. Pitt took a view favourable to granting them extensive powers; Lord Grenville and Lord Thurlow opposed him. The abolition of the slave trade was also an open question. Mr. Pitt and Lord Grenville were favourable to it; Mr. Dundas and Lord Thurlow were among the most conspicuous defenders of the slave trade. All these instances occurred in the space of about five years.

30. Lord Hawkesbury (Master of the Mint) to Pitt, 5 July 1800

(Public Record Office, *W. Dacres Adams MSS.*)

The debate (inaccurately given in Debrett's *Parliamentary Register* as taking place on the 5th) was a debate on the Bill to incorporate the London Company for the manufacture of flour, meal and bread. The third reading was carried by 48 (tellers, Lord Hawkesbury and George Rose) *v.* 44 (tellers, Perceval and Plumer).

After the extraordinary debate which took place last night in the House of Commons, I have felt very anxious to see you for a few minutes in private.–The situation in which I found myself placed, was more distressing than anything I could have conceived, the whole responsibility of the measure being thrown *upon me personally*, abandoned as I was, with three or four exceptions, by every person in office, and opposed by one person connected with Government with a degree of rancour, spleen, and vexation, which I should have thought very unwarranted in any person in opposition, upon a question of this nature. I can appeal to you, whether I have ever made myself *a party* to any measure or have ever introduced a motion or Bill into Parliament against your opinion or without your approbation. I am ready to admit that if any person in office entertains a very strong and decided opinion against a measure of this sort, introduced by a member of Government, he should be allowed to act according to that opinion, but it is not to be tolerated that he should for such purpose combine, and consult with Opposition, and make himself a party to every motion which can tend to impede the progress of a Bill, or throw a censure and reflection on those who support it. I feel concerned to be obliged to trouble you on such an occasion, but I know these feelings are not confined to myself, and if persons in my situation are to be exposed to such treatment, they will be very cautious how they engage themselves in any business for the good of the public. Disappointment in the issue of the business cannot be considered as the source of my feelings upon the present occasion, as, from the steady and honourable support I received from many members of the House, and amongst them, from Hawkins Browne and Buxton, the Opposition were frustrated in their endeavours to defeat the Bill.

31. Debate in the House of Commons, 26 March 1807

(Cobbett's *Parliamentary Debates*, IX, 268, 279.)

Lord Howick: ... A Minister may, as an individual member of Parliament, introduce measures for which the authority of Government is not at all pledged. I could adduce instances of this in the Administration of the late Mr. Pitt. The House will at once recollect the motion for a reform in Parliament, and that for the abolition of the slave trade: both these motions were introduced by him as an individual member of Parliament, without the responsibility of Government being attached to them. Sir, during the short period that I have had the honour of holding a situation under H.M., I and my noble colleagues have, in the same manner, brought forward success-fully the measure of the abolition of the slave trade. ... But, Sir, where a measure arising out of various causes which have engaged the attention of H.M.'s confidential servants is to be brought forward with the authority of Government, the measure itself, as well as the case to which it applies, ought undoubtedly to be first submitted to H.M. ...

Mr. Fuller rose to ask the noble Lord if the Slave Trade Abolition Bill had been introduced into that House by the persons composing the late Administration, in their individual capacities as members of Parliament or in their collective character of the Government.

Lord Howick replied that the Bill ... had been introduced by certain of his colleagues and himself, in their individual capacity of members of Parliament.

32. Diary of Henry Hobhouse, 19 July 1823

(*Diary of Henry Hobhouse, 1820–1827*, ed. A. Aspinall (1947), p. 103.)

Towards the end of the session a circumstance occurred which has occasioned Canning to remark on the inconvenience of Huskisson's not being in the Cabinet. ... He introduced a Bill for repealing all the laws for the regulation of the weaving trade in Spitalfields. The Bill was solicited by the masters, and Huskisson taught them to believe that it was approved by the Cabinet. Probably he had the authority of some of the Ministers, but it had never been sanctioned by the Cabinet, and other Ministers disapproved it. The Bill was so much cut down in the House of Lords that Huskisson tauntingly refused to propose a concurrence in their Amendments, and the Bill dropped, to the great joy of the journeymen by whom it was opposed.[1]

33. Lord Palmerston (Secretary at War) to Lord Liverpool, 19 Jan. 1826

(*Broadlands MSS.*)

I think I should not be doing justice to myself nor acting candidly towards you, if I were not to state to you frankly and explicitly the extreme embarrassment of the situation in which I am placed by the contest now carrying on for the University

[1] The Repeal Bill referred to revealed the differences that existed in the Cabinet on the question of State control of trade and industry. Harrowby, the Lord President of the Council, opposed the Bill; the Prime Minister supported it.

of Cambridge; a situation so extraordinary that I can scarcely imagine that any official man could ever before have stood in similar circumstances.

After having represented the University for fourteen years, during which period I have been three times re-elected without disturbance from any of my political opponents, I am now attacked by my political friends and my seat is endangered by the avowed competition of two members of the Government[1] to which I myself belong.

I apprehend that it is somewhat unusual for persons belonging even to the same political party to endeavour forcibly to dispossess each other from their seats, but such acts of mutual hostility among the members of the same Government appear not easily reconcilable with those principles of union by which alone a Government can be held together. But if an attack of colleague upon colleague is under any circumstances a novel course of proceeding, the turn which the attack has taken in any particular case and the ground upon which it rests more especially call for observation.

I have always conceived that the Government of which your Lordship is the head was formed and is maintained upon the distinct and unequivocal understanding that difference of opinion upon the Catholic question was not to be a reason for political division, and that the members of the Government were to be at full liberty to take in Parliament whatever course each might choose upon that question, and were to act by each other in all respects as if no such question depended, and no such difference of opinion existed.

Upon this principle, if I am rightly informed, the members of the Administration who oppose the Catholic claims have recently called upon some of their colleagues who support those claims to assist at the next election anti-Catholic candidates recommended by them, alleging that the only inquiry that ought to be made respecting a candidate is whether he supports the Government, and not how he votes on the Catholic question. But in my case the principle upon which the Government stands is violated. Two of the anti-Catholic members of the Government appeal to my constituents against me upon the Catholic question, and the course which I have taken in Parliament upon that question is to be made by my own colleagues the instrument to dispossess me of my seat.

It might not unnaturally have been supposed that when an individual holding office under the Crown communicated to the head of the Government his intention to stand for a place actually represented by two persons, the one[2] a member of the Government and the other[3] a supporter of the Administration, he might have been informed that however strong his desire to stand, or however high the quarter by which that desire might be stimulated, it was not expedient that a place so represented should be so disturbed. But if it was thought fitting that under such circumstances a contest should commence, at least it must be admitted that the official man in possession had a just and indisputable claim to the fullest and most effective support which the Government as a body could give him to protect him against danger from the permitted intervention of his colleague, and it might be imagined that if it so happened

[1] Sir John Copley (Attorney-General) and Goulburn (Irish Secretary).
[2] Palmerston himself.   [3] W. J. Bankes.

that the head of the Government himself, those persons connected with the Administration who possessed most influence in the scene of contest, and the intervening
candidate, were all opposed to the Catholic claims, while the member in possession
supported them, this circumstance might of itself furnish peculiar motives arising out
of the considerations already adverted to for giving such support in a prompt and
unequivocal manner, because in such a case the necessity would seem obvious of
placing beyond the reach of doubt the good faith of that arrangement by which
difference of opinion on that particular question was to be freely permitted without
altering in any respect the natural relations of the individual to the Government.

When, however, I applied to your Lordship as head of the Government for
support, you informed me that although your wishes were for the sitting members,
you intended to take no part in the contest; when I asked the Lord Chancellor for
his assistance, he replied in a note which I inclose, that if he had any influence in
Cambridge, though his Oxford prejudices against a change in representation and his
personal and official respect for me would incline him towards me, yet *the claims* of
my two competitors, and *an unlucky difference of opinion about the Catholic question,*
would be puzzling. When I wrote to Lord Bathurst for his aid he expressed, in a note
which I also inclose, his regret that he must limit his exertions to one of my competitors. A Lord of the Treasury[1] who votes against the Catholic claims has been
Chairman of the Committee of one of my opponents; and one of the Secretaries to
the Treasury,[2] officers who are generally considered by the public as the peculiar
organs of ministerial influence, has given to the same candidate all the advantage in
point of impression which may arise from transmitting under his official frank a
considerable number of canvassing letters.

I say nothing as to the refusal of assistance from some of the steady adherents of
the Government or the active opposition of others, because finding that your Lordship
took no apparent interest in my favour, those persons might naturally imagine that
it was at least a matter of indifference to you which of the candidates they might
support.

How, let me ask, can all this be reconciled with the avowed basis upon which the
Government is formed, or with the explanation of their situation with reference to
the Catholic question which members of the Administration who vote for that
question have repeatedly given in Parliament; or what new basis of union is to be
adopted by the Administration, if this uncalled-for excitement of feeling in the
University by anti-Catholic members of the Government against one of their Catholic
colleagues should be adduced in Parliament as a proof of the fallacy of that basis which
has hitherto been set forth.

Attacked by colleagues, unsupported by the head of the Administration, and
opposed by many of the anti-Catholic connexions of the Government, I have had no
resource left but to make a strong and general appeal to all those who agree with me
upon that question on which the election is made to turn; and if you find me in the
course of this contest in closer and more general communication with the parties who
are opposed to your Government than you may think suitable to the official situation

---

[1] Lord Lowther.   [2] S. R. Lushington.

in which I stand, I beg you will recollect that this is not of my own seeking, that it is entirely at variance with my wishes, and in many instances repugnant to my feelings, but that I am driven to it by a part of the Government itself as the only possible measure of self-defence.

I can assure you that among the various causes of regret necessarily growing out of this contest it is far from being the least to think that if I should succeed, as I by no means despair of doing, by making effectually to that part of my constituents who are favourable to the Catholic claims, an appeal as strong and as general as that of my opponents to that portion who are adverse to those claims, and by adding the support of the former to that of my own personal friends in the University, I shall find myself sitting in the House of Commons a servant of the Crown indebted for my seat to the unanimous support of the Opposition, against the efforts made by members of the Government to dispossess me–a position for a man in office not very creditable to the Government to which he belongs.

I am bound to say that from the Duke of Wellington and from Peel I have experienced the most cordial kindness, but their connections with Cambridge are not extensive. The sentiments which they, and others of your colleagues whom I have not mentioned in this letter entertain upon this matter you will best learn from themselves. But among the great mass of those with whom I have communicated in my canvass, whether friend or opponent, I have met with a general expression of a feeling to which I purposely abstain from applying a stronger expression than surprize.

34. Canning's Memorandum for Lord Lansdowne, 23 April 1827

(A. Aspinall, *The Formation of Canning's Ministry*, Camden Third Series, LIX (1937), p. 158.)

The refusal of more than forty ministers and placemen to serve under Canning compelled him to seek aid from the Whig party. It was impossible to form a Government united either in support of, or in opposition to, the Catholic question.

1. The Catholic question is to remain, as in Lord Liverpool's Government, an open question, upon which each member of the Cabinet is at perfect liberty to exercise his own judgment in supporting that question if brought forward by others, or in propounding it either in the Cabinet or to Parliament. But if any member of the Cabinet should deem it an indispensable duty to bring forward individually the Catholic question in Parliament, he is distinctly to state that he does so in his individual capacity.

2. The inconvenience (now unavoidable) of having *one* open question in the Cabinet, makes it the more necessary to agree that there should be no other. All the existing members of the Cabinet are united in opposing the question of Parliamentary Reform, and could not acquiesce in its being brought forward or supported by any member of the Cabinet.

3. The present members of the Cabinet are also united in opposition to the motion for the repeal of the Test Act, of which notice stands on the books of the House of Commons. They see great inexpediency in now stirring a question which has slept for upwards of 30 years, and they could not consent to a divided vote by the members of the Cabinet upon it.

35. Lord Ellenborough's Diary, 25 Feb. 1828 and 17 July 1830

(Lord Ellenborough's Political Diary, 1828–30, ed. Lord Colchester (1881).)

On 25 Feb. 1828 an 'open' question ceased to be so. But Russell's repeal motion was carried against the Government next day by 237 *v.* 193. In 1828–30 there was much acrimonious discussion in the Cabinet on the question whether the seats available for distribution upon the proposed disfranchisement of the corrupt boroughs of Penryn and East Retford should be bestowed upon the large unrepresented towns of Manchester and Birmingham, or whether these boroughs should be 'opened' by giving the franchise to the neighbouring 'Hundreds'.

Cabinet at 3. Decided that the repeal of the Test and Corporation Acts should be opposed by the Government on the ground that there was no practical inconvenience, that the thing worked well, and that it was unwise to change the relative position of persons who went on so well together. [I, p. 39.]

[17 July 1830.] Cabinet. . . . The East Retford question. . . . The Duke *thinks* it will be thrown out, and *I hope* it will. It will be very difficult to make a speech in favour of the Bill which will not commit us to a bad precedent. . . . The interfering with the existing franchise never was made a Cabinet question. The giving the franchise to Bassetlaw rather than to Birmingham was, and it was because after an agreement that we should all vote for Bassetlaw, Huskisson voted for Birmingham and then resigned, that the separation took place. These questions never were made Government questions before, and it is much better they should not be. [II, p. 315.]

36. Cabinet Minute, 8 April 1795 (in Pitt's handwriting)

(Public Record Office, Foreign Office 97/248.)

Present:–The Lord Chancellor, Earl of Mansfield, Earl of Chatham, Duke of Portland, Earl Spencer, Lord Grenville, Lord Hawkesbury, Mr. Secretary Dundas, Mr. Windham, Mr. Pitt.

It is humbly recommended to your Majesty that Lord Henry Spencer should be instructed to make an overture to the Court of Berlin for establishing a fresh concert for the prosecution of the war. . . .

Lord Grenville desires to express his dissent to the measure of making an overture of this nature to the Court of Berlin.

37. Lord Grenville to George III, 8 April 1795

(Hist. MSS. Comm., Dropmore Papers, III, p. 50.)

. . . Nothing could be more painful to Lord Grenville than the necessity of differing from the rest of your Majesty's servants at such a time as the present, but the importance of the subject itself, and its immediate relation to the whole business of that Department of your Majesty's Government in which your Majesty has been graciously pleased more particularly to require Lord Grenville's service and advice, make it his indispensable duty to act according to the best opinion which he has been able to form upon it, and to which, after repeated reconsideration, he finds it impossible for him not to adhere. He is at the same time very far from presuming to press that opinion upon your Majesty in opposition to the sentiments of those whose opinion ought on every account to have more weight than his. He trusts to that goodness of which he has had so many proofs, and which he will ever acknowledge with the deepest and most heartfelt gratitude, that your Majesty will put a favourable interpretation upon that line of conduct which, under such circumstances, a conscientious discharge of his duty seems to require from him.

38. George III to Lord Grenville, 9 April 1795

Lord Grenville will easily conceive that I must ever look on a difference of opinion between my Ministers on a material question with sorrow; but far be it from me to wish that any of them should ever for unanimity concur in appearance when not dictated by conviction. Lord Grenville may therefore rest assured that his dissent on the present occasion will not in the least diminish my opinion of him. . . . [*Ibid.*]

39. Henry Dundas's Memorandum on the state of the Cabinet, 22 Sept. 1800

(*British Museum Additional MSS.* 40102, ff. 79–81.)

Pitt's Cabinet was deeply divided not merely on the Catholic question, which was soon to cause his resignation, but also on foreign policy.

Some of us are of opinion that the repose of Europe and the security of Great Britain are only to be obtained by the restoration of the ancient royal family of France, and that every operation of war and every step to negotiation which does not keep that object in view is mischievous and will ultimately prove to be illusory. Some of us are of opinion that although we ought not to consider the restoration of the ancient royal family as a *sine quâ non*, we ought not to treat with a revolutionary Government, and that the present Government of France is of that description. Some of us are of opinion that whatever has been the foundation of the present Government, it has established within its power the whole authority, civil and military, of the country, and that we are not warranted to reject the negotiations with a Government so constituted and *de facto* existing. Some of us are of opinion that although we ought to negotiate with the present rulers of France, we ought only to do it in conjunction with our allies, particularly the Emperor of Germany, it being the interest of this country closely to connect our interests with his. Some of us are of opinion if ever it was practicable to influence by force of arms the interior Government of France, that time is past. That it is even problematical if the present revolutionary principles of that country are not maintained and supported in place of being weakened by the external pressure of its enemies; that we may lose much and can gain nothing by implicating our interests with Austria, and that we have nothing solid to depend upon, except what we may derive from our own vigour and energy, and that under these circumstances it is our duty neither to court nor to repudiate negotiations, but when we do enter upon it, to do it, not in a spirit of despondency but with a sense and

feeling of dignity, determined to insist on terms adequate to our successes and compatible with the permanent security of our national interests.

In this short statement I believe I have given a just analysis of the leading principles
which operate upon the opinions of the persons who at present compose the confidential Councils of H.M. If this difference of sentiment could be considered as so many
abstract theories it would be of no moment to examine them minutely, but they
daily enter into every separate discussion which occurs on the subject of either peace
or war. It is natural for every man to be partial to his own view of a subject, but
neither that partiality nor the sincere personal respect or reciprocal good opinion we
may entertain of each other can blind us so far as not to perceive that amidst such
jarring opinions the essential interests of the country must daily suffer.

It is earnestly hoped that Mr. Pitt will take these observations under his serious
consideration before it is too late.

40. George Canning to Mrs. Canning, 28 Jan. 1825

(Harewood MSS.)

The Cabinet is over, and . . . it has passed off in the most satisfactory manner.
Liverpool and I brought our two papers and read them successively; each contained a tender of resignation. I hardly know who in the Cabinet was *not* forward
to testify their dissent from such a proceeding and to insist upon making common
cause. But I must in justice to Peel say that *he* was *foremost*. The discussion has lasted
four or five hours, and has been upon the whole useful and satisfactory. The result
of it has been to place the South American question beyond the reach of shuffling
and change, and to determine upon exacting from our master a more unequivocal
acquiescence than he has ever yet given. . . . This Liverpool and I insisted upon as
absolutely necessary, and as that without which we would not give up our separate
papers, which the Cabinet proposed to exchange for *one* unanimous answer in the
name of all. Such an answer is to be drawn up by Liverpool and me against tomorrow.
I do not say that our master may not *still* recalcitrate, but he will at least see that if
he is bent upon having a new Government he cannot have for it *any* of the present
materials.

I shall talk to Lieven and Esterhazy[1] when next I see them, in a manner that will
check their meddling in future. I told the Cabinet that I knew the whole of this
tracasserie to be the work of foreign interference, of which (as Liverpool would vouch)
I had warned *him* six weeks ago that it was concocted at Vienna, and that the object
was to force the King to change his policy by changing part of his Government.

Will the Duke of Wellington tell all that has passed to Mad. Lieven tonight? If
this sort of work goes on I shall be obliged to remind H.M. that *constitutionally* he has
no right to see Foreign Ministers at all except in my presence, and that his father never
thought of such co-joberations. I really hope that we shall all go on the better for
this last attempt, and that the ultras among us will now see that they have nothing
for it but to submit.

[1] The Russian and Austrian Ambassadors.

41. Charles Arbuthnot (First Commissioner of Woods and Forests) to Lord Liverpool, 5 Sept. 1826

(C. D. Yonge, *Life and Administration of ... 2nd Earl of Liverpool*, III (1868), p. 395.)

... The Duke [of Wellington] has been dissatisfied with much of the management of our foreign relations ever since we lost Lord Londonderry. He is resolved to be no party to what he may think would involve this country in war; and if efforts are not made to prevent collision between Spain and Portugal, and if that collision should take place, he will, I am certain, write to you that he must withdraw from the Cabinet. If also in the management of our internal affairs measures of magnitude and importance should be brought forward in Parliament without having been previously settled in Cabinet, the Duke will feel himself at liberty to oppose such measures in every way that he can. I have the more deprecated anything like disagreement between you and him, because I have been aware that while you two are well together, he will look to the surmounting of difficulties, and not to separation from the Government.

42. E. G. G. S. Stanley to Earl Grey, 22 Nov. 1831

(*Howick MSS.*)

It was decided that Parliament should meet again on 6 Dec. (instead of in Jan.) in order to calm public opinion on the subject of the Reform Bill, and to be in a position to propose measures to curb, if necessary, the growing power of the political unions. Grey, Richmond and Palmerston were against calling Parliament before Jan., but felt bound to acquiesce in the decision of the majority. This minority view was communicated in the Cabinet minute.

Stanley was the first Irish Secretary to be in the Cabinet. He was necessarily in Ireland for many months in the year.

*D*ublin Castle. I have received yesterday from the Duke of Richmond, and today from Althorp, the decisions of the Cabinet upon the meeting of Parliament and the Reform Bill. I cannot say that I approve of all the resolutions upon the latter, but the first has filled me with *dismay*. I do not know whether, not having been present, such a course would be regular, but I understand that a Cabinet Minute was made upon the subject, and if not against rules, I should be anxious to record my opinion as amongst the dissentients. ...

43. Earl Grey to Lord Holland, 1 Jan. 1832

(*Howick MSS.*)

Grey refers to the proposed creation of peers to facilitate the passage of the Reform Bill through the House of Lords. Taylor was William IV's private secretary.

... There are two particular points to be settled–the concurrence of the Cabinet and the King. From Lansdowne's letter to me I am afraid he will positively oppose. The objections of Palmerston are, I fear, scarcely less strong. Melbourne will be adverse, but I should think more reconcilable, and so also the Duke of Richmond.

The King, you are aware, would dislike the thing to the greatest degree, and I have less hope of surmounting his repugnance, which will be confirmed by the concurrence in his opinion of some of the most important members of the Government, since a conversation which he had on this subject with Sir H[erbert] Taylor, has been repeated to me by the Duke of Richmond. . . .

44. Richard Ryder (Home Secretary) to Lord Harrowby (Minister without portfolio), 21 Dec. 1811

(Harrowby MSS.)

A private letter to the sovereign was considered stronger than a dissent in the Cabinet minute.

At the Council on Wednesday Perceval received back from Wellesley the paper upon the Regency which he had sent him . . . with a private letter from W. stating that he could not agree to the plan: that he thought the Prince ought to have £150,000 instead of £100,000 for Regency services. . . . He . . . wished Perceval to communicate that letter to the Prince.

Perceval . . . determined on receiving that, to summon the Cabinet next day, that we might understand what that meant, as it had been before taken for granted, from Wellesley making no objection, that he agreed to the plan and had waived his objection, and at all events, that if he dissented, the dissent should not be communicated in a manner so strong as a private letter. . . .

The next day I was in bed with a headache, but I find from Perceval, Bathurst and Liverpool that the private letter was withdrawn by Wellesley, and the word 'unanimous' struck out of Perceval's statement. . . .

45. W. Wellesley-Pole (Irish Secretary) to Perceval (Prime Minister), Phoenix Park, 31 Dec. 1811

(Perceval MSS.)

. . . I congratulate you upon having settled the financial part of the unrestricted Regency in so satisfactory a manner. . . . I hope the acquiescence of the Regent augurs well for our continuance in office, though I own I have little faith in the favourable sentiments of H.R.H. towards us. . . . I lament extremely that Lord Wellesley should have differed from the Cabinet, and I am still more sorry he thought it necessary the Regent should know it. Whatever any man's opinion might be upon the propriety of granting £50,000 more or less, I should have thought that, if all the Cabinet but one were agreed, that one had better have given way, and desired that the act should have been carried to the Regent as the unanimous decision of the Cabinet. . . .

46. Lord Hardwicke (Lord Lieutenant of Ireland) to Charles Yorke, 25 Jan. 1805

(British Museum Additional MSS. 35706, f. 160.)

. . . It is . . . reported . . . that the Cabinet is divided into two parties: with Pitt—Lord Melville, Duke of Montrose, Lord Mulgrave and Lord Camden; with Lord Sidmouth—

Lords Westmorland, Hawkesbury, Castlereagh and Buckinghamshire; and that the Chancellor, Lord Chatham and another are considered as the King's friends, and will probably incline to Lord Sidmouth. Possibly all this may be mere newspaper supposition, raised into more importance than it deserves, but I know the impression is that Pitt's weight with the King is diminishing, and that matters are in a very awkward state. What Lord Sidmouth can expect by encouraging such a schism I cannot imagine, for it is evident that if the King is alienated from Pitt, he must be given up to the enemy, I mean the Opposition. . . .

47. George Canning to Mrs. Canning, 7 March 1807

(Harewood MSS.)

Canning refers to his negotiations with Lord Grenville for the return to office of himself and some of the leading 'friends of Mr. Pitt'.

. . . Upon my again pressing Lord Eldon for the Cabinet without office, he said, more decidedly than before, "That cannot be. Situated as we are, we cannot venture to have any person about the King likely to intrigue against us; and when you are embarked with us . . . you will, I am sure, agree to the wisdom and necessity of this decision." . . .

48. Viscount Melville to his son, R. S. Dundas, 6 Nov. 1810

(Buccleuch MSS.)

The new regency crisis further weakened the position of Perceval's Ministry (see No. 2). Melville's view of the party responsibilities of a Cabinet minister should be compared with Wellington's (No. 49).

. . . Considering the present difficult state of the country contrasted with its calm, tranquil and prosperous situation in 1788, it is impossible to disguise from oneself that the crisis is most embarrassing, and the anxiety of the country for the attainment of a strong and vigorous Government will revive with multiplied force. I trust and pray that there may be found enough of honourable and independent men who will look solely to the safety and prosperity of the Empire without regard to the selfish objects or party views of any sort of men whatever. . . . Being in the King's Cabinet, it is your duty to concur with your colleagues in every measure which they may deem necessary for the quiet, safety, ease, happiness and security of the rights of the Monarch in whose service they are, but I must guard you against every idea of embarking with your colleagues on the footing of a party man. They have no claims of any kind upon you to form such a connection with them, and I think I know enough of the state of the country to know that if you were to place yourself in so unnatural a predicament, you would soon find yourself insulated, and destitute of that honourable and natural connection in politics which circumstances have prepared for you, and which seems to be almost within your grasp.

49. The duke of Wellington to the earl of Liverpool, 1 Nov. 1818

(*Supplementary Despatches, Correspondence and Memoranda of the Duke of Wellington,* ed. by his son, XII (1865), pp. 813 and 822.)

Now that the allied army of occupation had been withdrawn from northern France, Wellington, its commander, who was never a real party man, was free to enter the Cabinet as Master-General of the Ordnance.

. . . I don't doubt that the party of which the present Government are the head will give me credit for being sincerely attached to them and to their interests, but I hope that in case any circumstance should occur to remove them from power they will allow me to consider myself at liberty to take any line I may at the time think proper. The experience which I have acquired during my long service abroad has convinced me that a factious opposition to the Government is highly injurious to the interests of the country; and thinking as I do now I could not become a party to such an opposition, and I wish that this may be clearly understood by those persons with whom I am now about to engage as a colleague in Government.

I can easily conceive that this feeling of mine may in the opinion of some render me less eligible as a colleague, and I beg that, if this should be the case, the offer you have so kindly made to me may be considered as not made, and I can only assure you that you will ever find me equally disposed as you have always found me to render you every service and assistance in my power.

50. The earl of Liverpool to the duke of Wellington, 9 Nov. 1818

F[ife] H[ouse],

. . . I should certainly not think of proposing to any person to become a member of the Government upon any condition or understanding that he was necessarily to adopt the course of conduct which the party of which the Government was composed might be inclined to pursue in the event of their being removed from office; but, strongly as I should be impressed with this sentiment with respect to any other individual, I feel it more peculiarly in your case, as it is impossible not to be sensible that there are many special circumstances in your situation which render it of the utmost importance, in the event to which you refer, that you should be at full liberty to adopt that line of conduct which you may at that time judge most proper and advisable, with a view to the country and to yourself. [*Ibid.*, p. 822.]

(iv) *The Sovereign seeks advice from persons other than his confidential servants*

51. Lord Malmesbury's Diary, 8 Feb. 1801

(*Diaries and Correspondence of 1st Earl of Malmesbury,* ed. 3rd Earl, IV (1844), p. 4.)

Pitt's resignation was the outcome not merely of the king's rejection of his advice on the Catholic question, but also of the manner in which the king, under the influence of other advisers, had opposed him. Canning was Joint Paymaster of the Forces.

Canning . . . came to tell me of the resignation, and of the Speaker's being appointed First Lord of the Treasury. . . . He confessed he had been one of those who had strongly advised Pitt *not* to yield on this occasion in the Closet; that for several years (three years back) so many concessions (as he called them) had been made, and so many important measures overruled, from the King's opposition to them, that Government had been weakened exceedingly; and if on this particular occasion a stand was not made, Pitt would retain only a nominal power, while the real one would pass into the hands of those who influenced the King's mind and opinion out of sight. . . . He said he suspected those who had tainted the King's mind, but would not name them. He glanced at Lord Westmorland as being one.

52. Edward Cooke to Viscount Castlereagh, 27 Feb. 1801

(*Memoirs and Correspondence of Viscount Castlereagh*, ed. Marquess of Londonderry, IV (1849), p. 64.)

Cooke was Under-Secretary (Civil Dept.) in Ireland; Castlereagh was Irish Secretary.

. . . It appeared to me, when I was in England, that there was an unfair game playing against the Cabinet. There seems to be a little Court Windsor party that were always irritating the [King], always endeavouring to make him form opinions of his own, to make arrangements and appointments without the advice of his Cabinet, and who used every sinister artifice and low flattery for the purpose. This set must now highly plume themselves upon having fretted his mind at this crisis to take a decision against his Ministers. . . .

53. Earl Bathurst to Lord Harrowby, 2 June 1806

(*Harrowby MSS.*)

Ministers could never take it for granted that the king would accept their advice to dissolve Parliament. Here, Bathurst and Harrowby, now in opposition, were obviously hoping that the king would refuse his ministers (who were hardly the ministers of his own choice) a dissolution, and that they would soon be back in office. Windham's Bill providing for short-term service in the army on a voluntary basis became law.

. . . It appears to me there is but one point where it would be advisable for the King to make his stand, and that is, if a dissolution of Parliament were proposed to him, which I think he ought at all hazards to refuse–such a refusal would be no justifiable ground of resignation, and probably would not occasion one. And if it did, and the King were to have his new Government overturned, he would not be in a worse situation than he would be by agreeing to their dissolving Parliament, as the new Parliament would be composed more of Fox's friends than those of Lord Grenville who has no extended parliamentary acquaintance while he continues separate from his original connections. And after so recent a dissolution Lord Grenville could not have recourse to another, should he afterwards quarrel with Fox and form a Government against him. I do not think it possible that they can continue long together. . . . There is an idea of the Duke of Portland coming forward as the head of Administration, should this measure for enlisting for a limited time be rejected by the House of Lords, and the present Government resign in consequence. He is amazingly well after his operation. I called on him a few days ago, and took an opportunity of giving him my opinion on the impropriety of any extraordinary exertions being made against this measure, in which I am happy to say he entirely agreed with me: and he added that as he was to see the King this week to return him thanks for all his gracious enquiries, he should deliver his opinion to that effect, should H.M. enter on any political subjects with him. The Duke had not heard of this idea of rejecting the measure when I saw him, and you will take notice that I am by no means sure it is in the King's contemplation, but I have heard it is talked of by some who seem to think that the King might be brought to it. It will give me great satisfaction to find that you agree with me on this point. I need not tell you that I wish my conversation with the Duke of Portland not to be repeated to any person.

54. Lord Hawkesbury to George III, c. Oct. 1806

(C. D. Yonge, *Life and Administration of Lord Liverpool*, I, pp. 218–220.)

This letter may not have been sent, but it is a valuable indication of Hawkesbury's views.

... Since the change which took place in your Majesty's councils in the beginning of February last, an alteration has been produced in the relative state of parties much more rapid and extensive than could have been expected in so short a space of time. Your Majesty's present Ministers have disappointed the expectations of many persons who were in the first instance disposed to place confidence in them; their strength in Parliament has evidently diminished, has proved much less than could have been imagined, and they have been progressively losing ground in the opinion of the country. On the other hand, the party which constituted your Majesty's last Administration have become more united amongst themselves, and have confessedly acquired a great increase of strength and influence in Parliament and in the country, and more particularly in the House of Commons, where they were supposed, both by themselves and by their opponents, to be most weak some months ago. The result appears to be, upon the most accurate investigation, that, independent of that strength which belongs to Government as such, and which may be considered as transferable from one Administration to another, the number of persons attached to your Majesty's present servants in the House of Commons very little exceed the number of those who are attached to their opponents. The state of the county representation in Great Britain will furnish a reasonably fair test of the truth of this observation. The number of county members of Great Britain favourably disposed to the present Administration are 49; those favourably disposed to their opponents are 45; there are eight undecided, but more inclined to the latter than to the former; and 17 altogether doubtful.

Under these circumstances I cannot avoid most anxiously requesting your Majesty's attention to the effect of a dissolution of Parliament at the present time. Such a measure would have the inevitable effect of throwing the whole influence of Government in the borough elections into the hands of the present Administration.

It would secure to them the strength they would thereby acquire for the whole of a new Parliament. It would determine in their favour the opinions of many persons who are undecided at present, and, in the event of your Majesty's feeling it expedient to change your Administration, it would deprive their successors of the advantage of that measure which would be essential to the establishment of their power.

This measure, if it should be proposed, cannot fairly be pressed upon your Majesty on any public grounds. The present Parliament was chosen in the month of June 1802. Three years of its legal existence, then, are unexpired, and no pretence for a dissolution can be advanced either on the ground of any obstruction having been given in the House of Commons to the necessary business of Government, or on account of any material difference of opinion between the two Houses of Parliament. I feel the less difficulty in submitting these observations for your Majesty's consideration in consequence of knowing that, whatever shades of difference of opinion may exist on other points, there is an unusual agreement upon this subject amongst all those who are not connected with the present Administration whose opinion it has been judged practicable or prudent to ascertain.

There are several points connected with the subject of this letter which I could explain more fully to your Majesty in conversation; but, until I receive your Majesty's commands to attend you, I feel the impropriety there would be in my obtruding myself into your presence at this time.

55. George Canning to Mrs. Canning, 11 March 1807

(Harewood MSS.)

Canning is reporting an interview with the duke of Portland at Burlington House on the 9th.

. . . The King, he was confidently certain – he had the most undoubted authority for it – would not suffer the Bill now in the House of Commons for admitting the Roman Catholics and Dissenters to the army and navy, to pass into a law: he would rather resort to the last extremity and refuse his royal assent (however unusual such a step might be) than pass an Act against his conscience. . . . He added, "The King has declared his intention of opposing the Bill with all his influence. . . ." I answered the Duke that I was infinitely obliged to him for this communication, of which I felt the full importance; that my opinions upon the whole subject of the Catholic question . . . were the same that Mr. Pitt had gone out upon in 1801, but that I should certainly be prepared to act upon them as Mr. Pitt did in 1804 – that is, to keep back any discussion upon any part of the subject on which the King's conscience was really and painfully alive; that whatever advantage might result from such concessions to the Catholics as Mr. Pitt had had in view would, I thought, be dearly purchased by any violence offered to the King's feelings at his time of life, in his situation, &c &c. . . .

At the House of Commons Perceval began upon the same subject – of the Bill, I mean – and told me I should probably have some intimation of the King's feelings. . . .

Lord Eldon has been here to relate what passed about the Princess on Saturday[1]

---
[1] When he saw the king at Windsor.

... Lord Eldon said the King had talked to him upon other subjects,[1] but that, having given his honour to Lord G[renville] that he went upon *no other subject* than the Princess, he did not think it right to say what passed upon others. I did not combat this delicacy, but I shall try to ascertain whether he is the Duke of Portland's informer.

56. The duke of Portland to George III, 12 March 1807

(Windsor Archives, 12706.)

I am so sensible of my presumption in addressing your Majesty upon a subject of a public nature, that nothing but the confidence I have in the devotion and attachment I bear to your Majesty could induce me to take such a liberty; but those sentiments will not suffer me to be silent upon the present occasion, and the sense of the duty I owe to your Majesty impels me to expose myself to the risk of incurring your Majesty's displeasure rather than forfeit, as my feelings tell me I should deserve to do, what I am most ambitious to possess, the honour of being considered by your Majesty among the number of your most faithful subjects and servants.

... Should ... the belief I wish to entertain be well founded, and that your Majesty shall not have given your consent to the measure in its present shape, I have little apprehension of disappointing your Majesty when I venture to express my opinion that it may be ultimately defeated, though not sooner, I fear, than in the course of its progress through the House of Lords; but for that purpose I must take the liberty of saying that it will be absolutely necessary that your Majesty's wishes should be so distinctly intimated, that no doubt may exist respecting them, that your Majesty's Ministers must not have any pretext for equivocating upon the subject, or any ground left them for pretending ignorance of your Majesty's sentiments, or of your Majesty's determination not only to withhold your sanction from the measure, but if necessary, which God forbid, to put those means in force with which the Constitution has vested your Majesty, to prevent its becoming a law. The effects of such a proceeding as this on the part of your Majesty (though it may and is to be hoped that it will stop far short of the length to which I have pointed) may possibly prevent any material change among the persons who at present administer your Majesty's affairs, if it shall be your Majesty's pleasure to retain them in their present situations. But as it is more natural to expect that they will desire your Majesty's permission to quit your service, I cannot but suppose that your Majesty is prepared in case of such an event, and there seems no reason to apprehend that your Majesty can be seriously

---

[1] Cf. memorandum, written in 1838 by Sir Herbert Taylor, who had been George III's private secretary, and quoted in *Edin. Review* (Oct. 1838), p. 197: "When the change of Administration took place in 1807, H.M. took counsel from himself only in the communications with those with whom he differed; and I am warranted in saying that there existed not the slightest foundation for the reports which were then spread of advice secretly conveyed, or of influence behind the throne, or of communication, direct or indirect, with his previous Ministers, pending the discussion with 'the Talents', or before their removal from the Administration had been established. Nay, on that occasion, he placed in my hands, unopened, a letter addressed to him, before that event was positively fixed, by one of the leaders of the opposite party, and I have it to this day, with a minute to that effect." This may be compared with the duke of Portland's statement, in a letter to Lord Malmesbury, dated 13 March 1807, referring to the duke's letter to the king of the 12th (No. 56): "You will ... understand that the letter went, and I *know from* Taylor that he delivered it to the King, *and that is all I know.*" (Malmesbury, *Diaries & Correspondence*, IV, p. 364.)

at a loss to meet with persons of sufficient abilities and experience to undertake and perform the duties of the respective stations which your Majesty may think fit to assign to them in consequence of the event I have alluded to. In such a case it will be obvious to your Majesty of what importance it must be, and what advantages it must afford, to those to whom your Majesty shall think fit to intrust the management of your affairs, that the necessity you have been under to part with your present servants should be generally made known, and I cannot therefore but most humbly submit to your Majesty's superior wisdom the expediency of ordering Lord Grenville and such others of your Majesty's confidential servants as you may think proper to attend you for the purpose of stating to them distinctly the sentiments which your Majesty has uniformly professed respecting any concessions that have been proposed to be made to the Roman Catholics . . . and of observing to them how grossly your Majesty's conduct has been misrepresented, as your Majesty never had consented or would consent to such a measure, or could acquiesce in it in any manner whatever, consistently with the principles which your Majesty has uniformly professed. . . . Should this suggestion . . . be . . . adopted . . . it would probably tend to expose the fallacy and discover the real object of those professions which assume to be the dictates of a pure and genuine spirit of disinterested liberality, while in fact they are undermining and sapping the most venerable and sacred barriers of our Constitution. . . . Could these designs be disclosed, and could it be made [to] appear what the object of the present measure really was, that it could not operate to any good purpose and must necessarily tend to embarrass your Majesty by reducing you to the alternative of becoming a party to the measure in question, or of quarrelling with your Parliament, I cannot but believe that the nation in general as well as individuals would be anxious to come forward and testify its loyalty, its gratitude and its attachment to your Majesty; that your Majesty would have an abundant choice of persons capable of managing your Majesty's affairs, and that so circumstanced, those persons would receive the general support of the nation at large. . . .

And as for myself, incapable as *I know* I am, from age, infirmity and want of ability to render your Majesty any profitable service, should your Majesty be of opinion that I can be of any use to you, I will do the best I can to serve you to my life's end.

57. George Rose's Diary, 17 Jan. 1811

(*Diaries and Correspondence of George Rose*, ed. L. V. Harcourt, II (1860), p. 471.)

One reason why the Whig Lords were disappointed in their hopes of coming into office, once the regency was established, was that the prince was unwilling to dispense with the advice of his personal friends, Moira and Sheridan. He disliked the dictatorial tone assumed by Grey and Grenville.

. . . Lord Grey was with the Prince of Wales on the 15th, and agreed to accept the situation of First Lord of the Treasury on the express condition that H.R.H. should engage to consult only *his Ministers*, excluding thereby Lord Moira and Mr. Sheridan, even *from that time*, before he assumed the Regency. . . . Of these hard conditions made with the Prince, his intended Ministers speak without reserve, which seems to be unnecessary and somewhat indelicate, for although it might be fit, and perhaps indispensable, to impose, there could be no use in publishing them. . . .

58. Lord Grenville to Lord [addressee unknown], 22 Nov. 1812
(*Fortescue MSS.*)

. . . I am, on principle, . . . a warm friend to the union of public men in all cases where it can be done without the sacrifice of opinion and principle. By the contrary system I think the leading men of the country do all they can to deliver it over absolutely into the hands of the Court. But then I think it must be kept *prominently* in view that the principle on which our party acts is not that merely of agreement on particular public measures, but that of a determined resistance to favouritism, *Court intrigue* and *double government*, the very system which, in the King's hands, has done so much evil, and which is now pursued with increased activity and success by his sons. . . .

59. Earl Grey to Lord Holland, 18 Feb. 1820
(*Howick MSS.*)

Grey is discussing the attitude of the Whigs, in the event of their being called upon to form a Government, to the questions of the royal divorce and the limitation of the expenditure of the court–the two questions on which the new king and his ministers had come into conflict.

. . . One word, too, on the sort of compromise at which you hint, to obtain certain advantages for the public by some concessions. This might be a very good, and would I think be a very honest policy if it could be successful. But this appears to me impossible. The certain result of such an attempt would in my opinion be this–you would carry enough to excite the secret enmity of the Court, and you would concede enough to furnish ground for popular attack and to deprive you of all support from public opinion. In this situation you would be at the mercy of the secret Cabinet, which, under such circumstances, would not fail to have the ear of the King, and whose powers of intrigue and influence would be exerted to ruin you on the first occasion that might present itself. We have had some experience of this. . . .

60. Canning to Viscount Granville (Ambassador to France), 11 March 1825
(Public Record Office, *Granville Papers*, 8.)

English politicians out of office, and courtiers, were not the only people who sought to exercise 'unconstitutional' influence over the sovereign; at times, in George IV's reign, considerable influence was exerted by the Austrian and Russian Ambassadors, Esterhazy and Lieven, and by Mme Lieven.

. . . You ask me what you shall say to Metternich.

In the first place you shall know what I think of him. That he is the greatest rogue, and liar on the Continent, perhaps in the civilised world.

In the second place you shall learn that I have evidence, which I entirely believe, of his having been for the last twelvemonth at least, perhaps longer, at the bottom of an intrigue with the Court here, of which Madame de Lieven was the organ, to change the politics of the Government by changing *me*.

Recently, very recently, he is convinced that this intrigue has totally failed, and that there is no chance of renewing it to advantage. Prince Esterhazy had arrived at this conviction some time ago, but he could not so easily impress it upon his principal. Some incredibly unadvised expressions in a letter from *too high* a quarter to Prince Metternich himself, continued the delusion, which Prince Esterhazy tried to dissipate. Metternich's instructions to Prince Esterhazy were to keep himself safe, to let Madame Lieven do all; to watch the impression upon the King, but not to commit himself or his Government. So Esterhazy has told a person who has reported what Prince Esterhazy told him to me.

Now you shall know what I would have done if this intrigue had gone on, and if, fortunately, the intemperance or miscalculation of the King had not brought it to a premature *dénouement* and so been obliged to give in, I would have resigned upon the South American question, and I would have declared openly, in the House of Commons, taking care to keep safe my sources of intelligence, that I was driven from office by the Holy Alliance, and further, that the system which I found established of personal communication between the Sovereign and the Foreign Ministers, was one under which no *English* Minister could do his duty. If after such a denunciation and the debates which would have followed it, the Lievens and Esterhazy did not find London too hot for them, I know nothing of the present temper of the English nation.

Now, with this knowledge, what do *you* say to the question of what you shall say to Metternich? I am of opinion upon politics nothing, until he begins, and then as little as possible till you have reported to me what he has said. I have no sort of hope of any good being done with him by conciliation. But I should be glad that he should know that I *know* him, and am aware how much I am indebted to him for his good intentions, but that I am nevertheless disposed to be on good terms with him, and to act for the best with him on the points on which we agree. . . .

If he talks of coming to England, do not encourage him. . . . I trust that he has given up the notion of a visit to Windsor. He would have come, to triumph: I would not advise him to come to intrigue.

61. Sir Richard Vyvyan, M.P., to the duke of Cumberland, 13 July 1829
(*Vyvyan MSS.*)

. . . If, Sir, you quit England at present, the Protestant party will be left without that powerful support which you have afforded them; no avenue will be open between them and the throne; the preponderating influence of the present Ministry will be without a counterpoise; whatever projects may be in contemplation, your R.H. will not be at hand to convey the sentiments of the Tories, and I firmly believe of the nation at large, to that quarter which you alone can approach without a fear of undutiful intrusion. . . .

Even now I believe that a Ministry could be formed in which the staunch supporters of the Protestant interests in Church and State might be dominant, and that such a Government would be most powerfully supported by the country and a new Parliament. But a new Parliament convened by the present Administration would be doubly injurious to our cause, since the influence of the Treasury must always be paramount in a general election, and it would be ungracious to dissolve again in the event of any change which gave power to the Tories, yet a second dissolution would be more necessary if the first had taken place under the influence of the present Government. Your R.H.'s stay in this country would no doubt check an attempt to dissolve Parliament, and without such a change it is most probable that the Cabinet will not be able to maintain itself in another session. . . .

The party is now scattered, and the ministers have no longer any immediate reason for fearing our efforts in Parliament, but so long as the champion of the party is in England, they cannot close up all means of access to the throne. On the other hand I fear that his absence puts an end to all immediate communication between H.M. and the uncompromising Protestants of the United Kingdom.

(v) *The Prime Minister*

62. Henry Dundas to William Pitt, 9 July 1794

(Public Record Office, *Chatham Papers*, 157.)

Dundas's close connexion with Pitt and his long experience of Cabinet government make this comment on the relationship between Pitt and his colleagues valuable.

I take it for granted you will this day explain to the King the proposed arrangements in the Government, and you will of course state to him the accident which prevented the intended division of the Secretary of State Department. I therefore feel myself obliged to give you the trouble of a few lines to entreat that you will not mention, or more think of, the idea you entertain of my being still a Secretary of State with a War Department. Perceiving that you have an anxiety about it, it is with real pain I speak so decisively on the subject. I give you my honour I have for these two days endeavoured to argue myself into a compliance with your wishes, but the more I do so I find the ground hollow under me, and feeling as I do upon it, you are the last man to wish me to lend myself to an arrangement which I am perfectly convinced has not one public ground to support it, and must of course bring discredit and just animadversion on the person immediately the object of it. It would be gross affectation and adverse to the truth was I to state to you that, in the present state of the dependencies of the British Empire, to have been the Colonial Minister of this country was not the object of my predilection in every view I could take of it, but I can at the same time assure you with the most perfect sincerity that there is no hour of my life in which I ever felt more pride and satisfaction than when an opportunity offered of sacrificing that and every other sentiment of ambition to the accomplishment of an arrangement which you think of great national importance. I should be most insatiable indeed if I was capable of entertaining any other sentiments, for in the accidents of life it has so happened to me that in a ten years administration of India, and a three years administration at home, the general run of occurrences have been such as to leave me without reproach. . . .

. . . The idea of a War Minister as a separate Department you must on recollection be sensible cannot exist in this country. The operations of war are canvassed and adjusted in Cabinet and become the joint act of H.M.'s confidential servants, and the Secretary of State who holds the pen does no more than transmit their sentiments. I do not mean to say that there is not at all times in H.M.'s Councils some particular person who has and ought to have a leading and even an over-ruling ascendancy in the conduct of public affairs, and that ascendancy extends to war as it does to every other subject. Such you are at present as the Minister of the King; such your father was as Secretary of State; such you would be if you was Secretary of State, and such Mr. Fox would be if he was Secretary of State, and the Duke of Bedford First Lord of the Treasury. In short, it depends and ever must depend on other circumstances than the particular name by which a person is called, and if you was to have a Secretary of State for the War Department to-morrow, not a person living would ever look upon him or any other person but yourself as the War Minister. All modern wars are a contention of purse, and unless some very peculiar circumstance occurs to direct the lead into another channel the Minister of Finance must be the Minister of War. Your father for obvious reason was an exception from this rule.

It is impossible for any person to contravert the position I now state, and therefore when you talk of a War Minister, you must mean a person to superintend the detail of the execution of the operations which are determined upon. But do you think it possible to persuade the public that such a separate Department can be necessary? Yourself so far as a general superintendence is necessary must take that into your own hands. If it was in the hands of any other it would lead to a constant wrangling between him and the various Executive Boards which could only end in an appeal to yourself, and the decisions upon that appeal would give you just as much trouble as the original superintendence and direction. Besides, you must recollect that the Master-General of the Ordnance, the First Lord of the Admiralty, the Commander-in-Chief, and now the Secretary at War are all of the Cabinet. I enter not into the question whether that is a good or a bad system in the present frame of our Government, but so in fact it is, and to maintain with any chance of success in the opinion of the public that another Department was necessary for the conduct of the executive measures of war, would, you may depend upon it, be a fruitless attempt. The public would put another construction upon it very disgraceful to the puppet who held the Department. The very reverse will be the feeling of the public with regard to a person who, after having at the desire of his friend and for the accommodation of the public held a great and laborious situation for three years, has upon the same principle of public accommodation, returned exactly to the situation from which he was taken. . . .

63. Henry Dundas to William Pitt, 7 Feb. 1801

(Public Record Office, *Chatham Papers*, 157.)

Addington was the first Prime Minister to spring from the professional class. He was a lawyer and his father a physician.

I know not to what stage the Speaker's endeavours to form an arrangement have proceeded, but it is impossible for me not to whisper into your ear my conviction that no arrangement can be formed under him, as its head, that will not crumble to pieces almost as soon as formed. Our friends who, as an act of friendship and attachment to you, agree to remain in office, do it with the utmost chagrin and unwillingness, and among the other considerations which operate upon them, the feeling that they are embarking in an Administration under a head totally incapable to carry it on, and which must of course soon be an object of ridicule, is almost uppermost in all their minds. Add to this, that altho' they will not certainly enter into faction and oppose him, all the aristocracy of the country at present cordially connected with Government and part of it under you, feel a degradation in the First Minister of the country being selected from a person of the description of Mr. Addington, without the smallest pretensions to justify it and destitute of abilities to carry it on. . . .

64. Viscount Melville to Henry Addington, 22 March 1803

(Earl Stanhope's *Life of Pitt*, IV (1862), pp. 22-25.)

Melville's well-known statement of Pitt's views is often taken as the first real definition of the office of Prime Minister. It arose from Addington's attempt to strengthen his Government by the inclusion of Pitt. The problem of precedence between them was to be solved by the appointment of Pitt's elder brother, the earl of Chatham, as a 'dummy' Prime Minister. The rival claims of Perceval, Castlereagh and Canning in 1807 were solved by the appointment of the duke of Portland as a neutral figurehead (No. 67).

. . . I did not conceal from him[1] the idea you mentioned of his returning to a share of the Government, with a person of rank and consideration at the head of it perfectly agreeable to him, and I even specified the person[2] you had named. But there was no room for any discussion on that part of the subject, for he stated at once, without reserve or affectation, his feelings with regard to any proposition founded on such a basis. . . . He stated . . . his sentiments with regard to the absolute necessity there is in the conduct of the affairs of this country, that there should be an avowed and real Minister, possessing the chief weight in the Council, and the principal place in the confidence of the King. In that respect there can be no rivality [*sic*] or division of power. That power must rest in the person generally called the First Minister, and that Minister ought, he thinks, to be the person at the head of the finances. He knows, to his own comfortable experience, that notwithstanding the abstract truth of that general proposition, it is noways incompatible with the most cordial concert and mutual exchange of advice and intercourse amongst the different branches of Executive Departments; but still, if it should come unfortunately to such a radical difference of opinion that no spirit of conciliation or concession can reconcile, the sentiments of the Minister must be allowed and understood to prevail, leaving the other members of Administration to act as they may conceive themselves conscientiously called upon to act under such circumstances. During the last Administration such a collision of opinion I believe scarcely ever happened, or, at least, was not such as the parties felt themselves obliged to push to extremities; but still it is possible, and the only remedy applicable to it is the principle which I have explained. . . .

[1] Pitt.   [2] Pitt's brother, the earl of Chatham.

65. W. Dacres Adams to John Gifford, 11 Dec. 1808

(Public Record Office, *W. Dacres Adams MSS.*)

This sketch, by Pitt's former private secretary, confirms the well-known impressions of Wilberforce and Canning.

It would certainly gratify me very much could I hope to give you any information which might be of the least assistance to you in the very interesting work you have undertaken, and I only regret that the means which I possess of doing so are so very inadequate to my wishes. Indeed I cannot bring to my recollection any one fact with which the public is not already acquainted, that would be likely to throw a light on any of the transactions of the latter years of Mr. Pitt's life—nor can I furnish you with an account of the *test* which he had devised towards the close of his first Administration, as I had not the advantage of a personal connection with him, until the period of his accepting office for the last time.

The most striking traits in his public character are of course too well known to you, who have studied it, to make it necessary for me to trouble you with any observation upon them. The vast powers of his mind, and the extent and splendour of his talents are sufficiently felt and acknowledged. But it has always been a subject of serious regret to me to observe the little justice which the world has done to his private excellence—for he was as amiable as he was great. He was remarkable for a peculiar sweetness and equanimity of temper, which I never saw ruffled during the whole of that daily and hourly intercourse which it was my happiness to be permitted to hold with him, under all the varying circumstances of health and sickness, of good and adverse fortune. The victory of Trafalgar elated him to no unbecoming height —nor did the overthrow of his dearest hopes at Austerlitz sink him to an unmanly dejection—yet this calmness arose not from any apathy or coldness—on the contrary, the various expressions of his countenance and the fire of his eye shewed him to be, as he really was, exquisitely sensible to every feeling—but the ascendancy of a well regulated mind—the conscious rectitude and wisdom of his measures—together with that happy mildness of temper with which nature had endowed him—seemed to place him above the reach of being violently affected by events.

The same benevolence & simplicity of heart was strongly marked in his manners and deportment, which were in the highest degree prepossessing towards all classes of people. They evinced the total absence of any thing like moroseness in his nature. With the most playful vivacity, he assumed no superiority in conversation, nor oppressed any man with his sallies. The wonder was how so much fire could be mitigated and not enfeebled by so much gentleness—and how such power could be so delightful.

It is no great praise to him to say that "the low passion of avarice had no root in his mind"—or that he was above the vulgar temptation of being influenced by pecuniary considerations—but it may with truth be stated that this freedom from any interested or ignoble feeling was far from being the most conspicuous emanation of that perfect purity which actuated all his thoughts and actions. With all his knowledge and all his power, he was a modest man—attentive to the most humble opinions—and kindly patient to the weakest. No man I believe was ever more beloved by his friends – or inspired those who had the benefit of living in his society with a more sincere and affectionate attachment.

This is the sort of idea which my observation of Mr. Pitt's private character has led me to form of him – and which it appears to me has not been sufficiently impressed upon the world at large.

Respecting his last illness I can only state that it appeared to be a gradually increasing debility and decay, without any active disease or acute pain. I was with him during the last fortnight of his stay at Bath, and saw him once after his return to Putney – and every day seemed to add to his weakness of body, though not at all to alter the frame of his mind – And the closing scene of his life was I believe accurately represented by the newspapers of the day.

66. The 5th earl of Carlisle's character of Fox, 1806

(Castle Howard MSS.)

Though Fox was never Prime Minister in fact, he was virtually so in the Coalition Ministry of 1783, and it seems appropriate that Lord Carlisle's sketch should follow Adams's account of Pitt.

No character I believe was ever more mistaken. He has been generally considered as a man devoted to desperate ambition: another Rienzi, capable of seizing on power by any means, even to the excitement of revolutionary commotion. In truth ambition was not his ruling passion. Pleasure, in all its most extravagant gratifications, held a stronger dominion over him. For pleasure, ambition was perpetually sacrificed. For sensual indulgences, he himself helped to bar all the avenues to pre-eminence and to those high situations in the State, which his rare abilities had so widely opened to him, even on the first step of public life. For pleasure, he has cast aside the opinion of the world, and taken so little care to fling a veil over the incorrect habits of his general conduct, that the public felt itself affronted by his barefaced exhibition of failings, which, had he but attempted to have concealed, would have possibly met with pardon. Popular esteem, so indispensable to the part which his talents marked out for him to assume on the political stage, is only to be won by appearing to think it worth obtaining. A hypocrite would have stood better with the world, even with a more real practice of vice. He was incapable for a moment of assuming virtues he had not, and equally incapable of putting any restraint upon himself, where the gratification of his passions were [sic] concerned, nor even could be persuaded to use the smallest caution in yielding to them. At length, feeling that by gaming, wine, women, loss of fortune, and by that which oppressed him most, a subscription to supply him with an income, the respect and esteem of the public was difficult to retrieve, he became so callous to what was said or thought of him, that he almost seemed to take a puerile delight in outraging the world, rather than in conciliating it: and I know no other way of accounting for such wantonness of indiscretion which so unnaturally increased with age. He could have little valued the opinions of those who composed his audience at the Whig Club. But it being a theatre on which he could give a loose [sic] to any sentiment, however violent, without the pain of weighing the consequence of uttering it, he accepted an applause which he knew would be loud in proportion as it was desperately mischievous. He was well aware that the doctrines he promulgated would, the moment he retired from that wretched Senate, plunge him deeper in the public odium. But for Fox to have benefitted by any such prudential reflexion, would have marked a departure from the general tenor of his whole life, but more particularly so, when he saw the game of opposition becoming every day more hopeless, and Mr. Pitt's Government striking deeper roots.

When to a misjudging world he seemed to be hastening a course of most wild ambition, he was in fact more precipitated by those about him, than from himself, and he would willingly have forfeited all that Kings or nations had to bestow for the pleasure of lying on a bank in the sun at St. Ann's Hill, explaining Homer or Ariosto to the person he afterwards married. He had so little cunning or suspicion in his nature, that he was ever the prey to knaves, even to fools. In his distresses he would listen to any absurd scheme to obtain a temporary relief, and the story of the heiress from the West Indies proposed to him as a wife, and who turned out to be a blackamoor, had too much truth in it. Foote got hold of it, and brought it upon the Stage.

Having felt a painful obligation not to conceal his imperfections, and having reluctantly thus dwelt on his defects, let me turn to the reverse of the medal, which an early affection, and intimate friendship, make me contemplate with very different sensations from those which truth would not dispense with.

By temper and endowments of mind he was formed to be the charm and delight of society. Equal to soar to any height with the learned, he could hover near the ground with those of no literary pretensions, and betray no condescension in so doing. On the contrary he then seemed most in his element, and nothing could force him out of that stream of common talk, on trivial topics, which suits almost everybody, and makes no one feel his own inferiority. Often in the country have I seen strangers, alarmed to be in the same room with him, in half an hour forget they were in company with a new acquaintance.

On his public talents it is needless to expatiate. His strong and manly eloquence has never been excelled, and his fair and generous manner of grappling with the strongest points of his opponents' argument (sometimes almost to a neglect of language) ought to be a lesson to the many, who, won by the flowers of oratory, forget the irresistible force of simple logic.

This amiable and yielding disposition rendered him unfitted to be a leader of a party, and he maintained too little authority over those who ought to have been on many occasions governed by him, and he was unfortunately surrounded by those whose violent courses called for perpetual restraint. I speak of a period before he himself became desperate. I never abandoned an idea I had formed in the morning of our friendship, that he was ever in his heart more inclined to Tory, than what in these times are called Whig principles. His purse and his parents had done much in his infancy to make his relationship, through his mother, to the royal House of Stuart, by no means indifferent to him; and if an idle quarrel had not happened between him and Lord North, we might have seen him a supporter of the American War, a champion for the prerogatives of the Crown, and a favourite in the Closet.

Lord North I think used him ill. He consulted me upon his situation; and with every wish not to widen the breach, I could not deny but that he had fair cause of complaint. Lord North did nothing to heal the wound, and the consequence was the converting a most powerful and attached friend into a bitter enemy, and driving him into the arms of a faction, the principles of which he adopted not from inclination but resentment. Five days before that event he was held by the Opposition in execration, and in return those who composed that faction in contempt by him. Lord North at the onset of their connexion had placed an unbounded confidence in him, which he suddenly withdrew, at the suggestion of some, jealous of the intimacy, who persuaded [him] he risked too much in trusting one so young, and whose private life excited such severe and such general animadversion. Upon this hinge has turned what has been of such moment to Fox, during a long period of his political career, and equally to Lord North, as it raised an enemy more distressing and formidable in the House of Commons than the whole Opposition in their united forces together.

67. Spencer Perceval to William Huskisson, 21 Aug. 1809
(Perceval MSS.)

Perceval was Chancellor of the Exchequer, and Huskisson Joint-Secretary of the Treasury.

. . . Our Administration is so constituted that, let us change our head how we please, it is impossible or next to impossible that we should have such a controlling power as you have been used to see exist with advantage, and consequently wish for again; there never can be the sort of acquiescence amongst us in control as there naturally and necessarily was under Mr. Pitt. Mr. Pitt must have felt, and his colleagues must have felt also, that he had such comprehensive talents and powers, that he was himself essentially the Government in all its Departments–that he could form a Government almost of himself, and each of his colleagues must have felt that Mr. Pitt could do without him, though he could not do without Mr. Pitt. Yet even under these circumstances, I have understood from you that Mr. Pitt himself could not in all Departments control expenditure as he wished. But the present Government is so constituted, with so many of equal or nearly equal pretensions with respect to personal weight in the Government and importance to its continuance, by the share of public opinion for talent and character which attach on such an individual's belonging to it may contribute to the whole–that the Government, under whatever head, must to a great degree be and remain a Government of Departments. It is not because the Duke of Portland is at our head, that the Government is a Government of Departments: but it is because the Government is and must be essentially a Government of Departments that the Duke of Portland is at our head, and is the best head possibly that we could have. I very much doubt us continuing long under any other. There are more than one among us who might by saying, "If you will not do so and so, I will resign," bring the Government to very great difficulty if not nearly to an end–and while there is that power in several, provided there is a disposition to use it, it is impossible there can be in any one that sort of control, but this persuasion, conviction, and consent which you seem to require. This may be in your opinion a great defect in the Government and a great misfortune to the country–and it certainly is so, as compared with a Government under an acknowledged head who upon the best view and judgement would select the best system and insist upon its being followed, but we should not do fairly by the subject unless we look upon it in this light. It is a state of things certainly which makes the principal situation in Government, the place of Prime Minister, very far from desirable;[1] it makes it one in which I cannot conceive any man desirous of having it–nay I can hardly conceive him consenting to have it, except it was with the perfect conviction that his leading colleagues wished him there, upon the persuasion that it was the best for themselves, and for the whole. . . .

68. Viscount Castlereagh to George III, 1 Oct. 1809
(*Windsor Archives*, 14696.)

In the earlier part of the letter, Castlereagh, who had resigned a fortnight before, defended his conduct whilst Secretary of State for War and the Colonies. Pitt had established the convention that the Prime Minister was the normal channel of communication on non-departmental business between the king and the other members of the Cabinet.

. . . Lord Castlereagh . . . is fully aware that it is through the individual at the head of your Majesty's Councils that your Majesty's other confidential servants should alone humbly submit on matters not purely departmental their sentiments to your Majesty, but your Majesty will graciously be disposed to admit that it is impossible for Lord Castlereagh, wounded as his feelings decidedly are, to avail himself of a channel through which misrepresentations to the prejudice of his public conduct have been allowed to reach your Majesty, without any opportunity being allowed to him to meet and to refute them. . . .

69. Lord Liverpool (Prime Minister) to the earl of Wellington, 19 Aug. 1812
(*Wellington Supplementary Despatches*, ed. by his son, VII (1840), p. 402.)

[Because of the failure of the negotiations for Canning's return to office: –]

. . I have had . . . no resource but to bring forward the most promising of the young men, and the fate of the Government in the House of Commons in another session will depend very much on their exertions. I should be most happy if I could see a second Pitt arise amongst them, and would most willingly resign the Government into his hands, for I am fully aware of the importance of the Minister being, if possible, in the House of Commons. I can assure you I never sought the situation in which I find myself placed, but having accepted it from a sense of public duty, I am determined to do my utmost for the service of the Prince Regent as long as I have reason to believe that I possess his confidence, and at all events I will endeavour to keep that party together which affords the only security either to the Crown or to the people against the complete and uncontrolled dominion of the Opposition.

[1] Words scored through: "a situation of responsibility without power".

70. Charles Arbuthnot (First Commissioner of Woods and Forests) to the earl of Liverpool, c. 7 Oct. 1823

(*Corresp. of Charles Arbuthnot*, ed. A. Aspinall, Camden Third Series, LXV, pp. 46–58.)

Draft with changes [marked *] suggested by Wellington.

. . .* [The King is not out of temper with any act of his Government, but he is not satisfied with the existing state of things, and he is prepared to make a change upon the occurrence of any event which can afford an excuse for it, of which change you would be the sacrifice. . . . I don't think it is strictly true that the King harbours no ill-will against Lord Liverpool. He is in perfect good humour with the Government and its measures, and with Lord Liverpool. But he hates him and he is anxious to get rid of him . . . because he thinks him under the influence of Canning. Soreness and ill temper will always precede the explosion. That which excites at present is a desire to find cause for blame, and a successor for Lord Liverpool. . . .]

Putting aside, more perhaps than you were aware of, all his own personal objections against Canning, the King dreaded his admission into the Cabinet from the fear he had lest his influence should be great with you. The King now thinks that those fears have been realised. . . . He never did like Canning, and my belief is that he never will like him, but I am sure I am not going too far in saying that he would far rather make Canning his Prime Minister rather than continue to have the conviction that the real power is already vested in him, while the name alone remains with you. . . . For a long time he has been thinking of nothing else. . . . To put an end to what he is so convinced exists, he would most readily risk the very existence of his Government. Do not, however, imagine that he wants to get rid of you. He wants, on the contrary, to have you his Minister, as Mr. Pitt was at one time the Minister of his father; but if he cannot effect this, and if circumstances should still rivet him in the belief that from you he is always hearing Canning's sentiments and not your own, he would *faute de mieux* rather go to Canning and put himself entirely in his hands, than allow him . . . to have the reality of the power, tho' not the name of it. . . .

You may say that the King cannot detest him and yet be ready under certain circumstances to make him Prime Minister. Ask the Duke, and he will confirm all that I have told you. You could hear from the Duke that the King hates what he calls the *sarcastic* ways of Canning; that he abuses him for what he calls his sophistry and for his false policy in foreign affairs; and that he despises him for what he thinks political cowardice and for what he considers a contemptible seeking after popularity. . . . In one word, he will have you as his real Minister if he can, and with pleasure he will keep you as such, but he is wild with the idea, and you may call it insanity if you please, that Canning never leaves you for a moment at rest, and that by assiduity, by perseverance, by insinuation, and by every tool and weapon he can use, he continues to pervert your better judgment and to turn you in all things to his own purposes. . . .

How is all this to be remedied? How is the King to be brought to feel that Canning does not exercise over you more than his due influence? This I cannot undertake to point out, nor do I know what advice to give. I would only say that I know those of your colleagues who are devotedly attached to you, and who, I am grieved to say, do share this feeling of the King. It may not be difficult for you t o prove to your colleagues that while you listen to Canning with the deference whic h his talents merit, you are resolved to guide yourself by your own and not by his judgment. Let them see that this is the case, and soon will it be seen to be the case by the King also. It is not that your colleagues let the King know what is passing in their minds, but we all know full well that when ideas exist, they get abroad.

I should be acting unkindly and most unfairly by you if I attempted to conceal that in those who are the most attached to you, there is great uneasiness and great regret from the belief that Canning is the one of the Cabinet in whom you confide the most. . . .

[Lord Liverpool's reply, 8 October 1823.] . . . You say the King conceives Canning to have an unbounded influence over my mind and opinions. I know not on what he grounds this. As long as the Government is to be conducted on the system of the last twelve years, it cannot be conducted without a thorough good understanding and confidence between the First Minister and the Minister of the House of Commons. When the situations were reversed, Perceval felt this as to me; Londonderry and I always felt it, and I am quite sure the Government could not stand many months if the persons in my situation and Canning's were to look at each other with jealousy and suspicion; but I am not aware of Canning having *assumed* in a single instance authority or influence in matters which do not belong to him, and the whole (if it has any foundation) must be grounded upon the notion that Canning and I happen to have agreed more nearly than some of our other colleagues, not upon what was to be *done*, but upon our views of the possible result of the successful French invasion of Spain.

How can the King, however, think he can accomplish his object, if I was to resign, or if I was to put myself decidedly in the wrong in any difference with the King? There is no reason why any of my colleagues should follow me, but I think the King will find himself very much mistaken if he supposes that if he dismissed me because it was *his royal will and pleasure*, or if he created an obvious pretence for this purpose, that Canning, Peel or anyone of my colleagues would remain behind. . . . The King is mistaken if he supposes that I have any anxious desire to remain in his service. He cannot be too strongly apprized of this truth. If I see I cannot go on with honour and with credit, it will be for me to consider *when* I can most easily retire, but let the King take care that he does not make the close of a reign which has been hitherto most glorious and upon the whole most prosperous, stormy and miserable. . . .

71. Lord Ellenborough's Diary, 29 Nov. 1828

(*Lord Ellenborough's Political Diary, 1828–1830*, I (1881), p. 267.)

. . . The Duke manages to get from Lady [Jersey] all the secrets of Opposition, and while he does all his own business, all Aberdeen's, and overlooks the business of all the Departments, he finds time to call upon ladies and to secure them to his party. . . .

72. The duke of Portland to George III, 20 March 1807

(*Windsor Archives*, 12733.)

During this period the man who became Prime Minister did not necessarily form the Government. Portland's position was in some respects an unusual one (see No. 67). Very curiously, Lord Lowther was not even in the Cabinet, when formed.

As your Majesty is fully acquainted with my sense of the uneasiness under which I labour to do your Majesty that service which it is my duty to endeavour to render to your Majesty to the utmost of my power, and has, notwithstanding, been graciously pleased to order Lord Hawkesbury and Lord Eldon to signify your commands to me that I should occupy the most confidential situation in an Administration of which I am directed to form the plan of an arrangement in conjunction with the Earl of Chatham and the Viscount Lowther and submit it to your Majesty's consideration, it would ill become me to hesitate in obeying your Majesty's commands. . . .

73. Robert Peel (Home Secretary) to the duke of Wellington, 3 March 1826

(*Despatches, Correspondence and Memoranda of Duke of Wellington*, New Series, III (1868), p. 143.)

During this period the Prime Minister's resignation was not considered as necessarily dissolving the Government.

. . . We have been placed in a very unpleasant predicament on the . . . issue of Exchequer Bills by Government. The feeling of the City, of many of our friends, of some of the Opposition, was decidedly in favour of the issue of Exchequer Bills to relieve the merchants and manufacturers . . . Lord Liverpool said that he not only felt the issue of Exchequer Bills by the Government to be wrong, but he was personally pledged against such a measure, and observed in conversation with more persons than one, that the best mode of solving the difficulty was for him (Lord Liverpool) to retire from office, the rest of the members of the Government retaining their offices . . . I told him . . . that what he proposed to do–namely, to retire singly –should not take place; that I should feel it dishonourable to allow one member of the Government–and that member the head of it–to make himself a sacrifice; and if he retired (though I should feel deeply the necessity of throwing up my share of the Government at a moment of danger) yet I could not but consider that his retirement under such circumstances would be a dissolution of the Government. . . .

74. Lord Ellenborough's Diary, 1828

(*Lord Ellenborough's Political Diary, 1828–30*, ed. Lord Colchester (1881).)

The premiership, it was felt, should not be united with the office of Commander-in-Chief. The Cromwellian despotism had not been forgotten.

24 Jan. Went to the Cabinet for the first time. . . . The Duke [of Wellington] . . . addressed us on the subject of the separation of the army from the Treasury. His feelings were strongly excited, and he evidently would have been desirous of retaining the army. This we are to decide tomorrow, in his absence. [I, pp. 6–7.]

25 Jan. Cabinet at two. Decided unanimously that the Duke shall resign the army.[1] . . . [I, p. 7.]

11 Feb. Lord Clanricarde . . . read an extract from a letter of Canning's to the Duke in May last, in which Canning spoke of the impossibility of the Duke's being Minister, because he could not divest himself of influence over the army, and the union of military and civil patronage could not be borne. [I, p. 24.]

75. Lord Lowther to his father Lord Lonsdale, 1815

(Lonsdale MSS.)

The Prime Minister did not always consult his colleagues about new Cabinet appointments. The duke of Grafton had resigned from Shelburne's Cabinet in Feb. 1783 because the duke of Rutland had been brought into the Cabinet without the Cabinet's previous knowledge and consent.

I should say Lord Liverpool has no right to complain of Lord Bathurst or any of his colleagues not treating [him] with proper confidence, as it is known not one of the Cabinet were aware of W[ellesley] Pole having a seat amongst them till he was ushered in to take his seat, and I believe Castlereagh would have resigned upon it if he had not undertaken to go to Congress. . . .

76. The duke of Wellington to the earl of Westmorland, 18 Jan. 1828

(Despatches, Correspondence and Memoranda of Duke of Wellington, New Series, IV (1871), p. 201.)

The Prime Minister's choice of Cabinet colleagues was limited in 1828 by some of those first appointed. Peel (and doubtless others) would not have acquiesced in offers being made to the ultra Tories Eldon, Bexley and Westmorland, who had been in Liverpool's Cabinet less than a year earlier.

. . . [Since receiving the King's commission to form a government] I have not ceased to endeavour to be allowed to call to my assistance my old friend and colleague, but have found in all quarters the difficulties and objections insurmountable, and I have no doubt that if I had persisted I must have resigned the commission. You will tell me, perhaps, that the commission has been ill-executed, which is a matter of opinion, and that the best thing to be done would have been to form a Government consisting exclusively of those who would not have objected to your being a member; or that I ought to have declined the attempt to form a Government without you. I assure you that the first alternative was out of the question, as being impossible; and as to the last I am convinced that you would yourself be the person to tell me not to take such a line in the existing state of affairs. . . .

---

[1] Lord Dudley, the Foreign Secretary, wrote in *his* journal on the 25th: "Cabinet on the King's Speech till six. We began however by deciding the question left to us by the Duke as to his holding both offices. (Commander-in-Chief as well as First Lord.) The Chancellor spoke first–mildly–and shortly but against. Then the President–still more gently, but still against. I more strongly against–Ellenborough and Peel ably and manfully against–Nobody for–except Aberdeen, feebly, and with hesitation–he hates liberty–and despises the people overmuch." (*Hatherton MSS*. Quoted in Hatherton's own journal, 22 July 1838.)

77. Earl Grey to the marquess of Lansdowne, 18 Nov. 1830

(Bowood MSS.)

Lansdowne endorsed this letter: "The meeting took place the same evening at my house, and after a long deliberation it was determined to make Brougham Chancellor, all present considering it to be a dangerous experiment, but less so than Master of the Rolls."

... I think it necessary to submit the appointment of the Chancellor to the consideration of those whom we may now consider as forming the new Cabinet. Could you allow us to meet at your house this evening at 9, for this purpose? I propose this, your house being so much more convenient than mine. ...

(vi) *Unequal influence of individual Ministers, and indications of an inner Cabinet*

78. The duke of Leeds' Memorandum, March 1791

(Political Memoranda of 5th Duke of Leeds, ed. O. Browning, Camden New Series, XXXV (1884), pp. 148–149.)

The duke of Leeds was Foreign Secretary, 1783–1791. He resigned in April 1791 when Pitt and the Cabinet reversed his policy concerning the Russian attack on Oczakov. Thurlow's disagreements with Pitt ended in his dismissal in 1792 (No. 101).

On Friday, March 4th, Burges[1] called upon me in the evening, and mentioned a report which he had heard from Nepean, that besides Dundas being appointed Secretary of State for India it was supposed to be in contemplation to make Lord Auckland Secretary of State for the Home Department, Ld. Grenville to take that for Foreign Affairs, that Mr. Pitt, Lord Grenville, the D. of Montrose and Dundas were daily closetted together for hours at a time. Nothing had transpired respecting the mode in which the Foreign Department was to be vacated, whether I was to be dismissed, driven to resign, or any arrangement proposed to me.

Wednesday, March 9th, Burges wrote me word of a conversation he had had with Mr. Smith, Mr. Pitt's Private Secretary, in which the latter seemed much hurt at his mentioning how long it had been since I had been honoured with any conversation by Mr. Pitt. Mr. S. said there must be some mistake somewhere. ...

The next day ... not being able to get any private conversation with the Chancellor[2] I put down upon paper the report above mentioned, desiring to know if he had heard anything of it. ... On Friday 11th I went to the House of Lords. ... I had but little conversation with the Ch., as there was a cause before the House. He told me however that he had heard reports similar to those contained in my letter, but that the Duke of Montrose had been mentioned to him as likely to succeed to the Foreign Department. On my return home I found his letter, in which he observed that he himself was in a situation similar to if not worse than mine, as to want of communication on the part of other Ministers; that he hardly knew whom he could look upon as his colleagues, unless those who with him happened to attend the Hanging Cabinets.

[1] Under-Secretary of State in the Foreign Department.   [2] Thurlow.

March 12. . . . He (Thurlow) told me he was convinced they meant to get rid of him when their minds should be made up respecting his successor. He talked of a want of confidence between members of the same Administration as not only unpleasant to individuals but injurious to the general interests of the Govt. . . .

79. Lord Thurlow to Lord Hawkesbury (Docketed 10 Aug. 1791)

(British Museum Additional MSS. 38192, ff. 151–152.)

The manifest impossibility of my attending a Cabinet in the morning while the Court of Chancery continues to sit was apparently the reason of this day's appointment, after which hint, if any accident not to be foreseen had liberated me, I should certainly not have attended, nor is it indeed of any use, considering that I am not in the full circulation, and the few papers which are sent come to me in an order which, not to mention the impertinence of it, make all assistance impossible. I never see all nor the few which are sent till the time consulting on the matter of them is over. This happened in the case of the Spanish business[1] which I have thought of a great deal since, and formed upon it, not so much a judgement as an idea much more extensive and bearing upon many more subjects than occurred upon the moment. I have the less reason to be mortified at my own surprise when I find that you, who are much more used to such speculations, are in some degree of the same predicament. My notions are at best but formed on general history and reflections. They have need of much discussion to be corrected, which require more conversation than the Ministers are disposed to favour me with.

80. George III to Lord Grenville, the Foreign Secretary, 4 Sept. 1796

(Hist. MSS. Comm., Dropmore Papers, III, p. 242.)

Yesterday I received Lord Grenville's letter forwarding the written project of opening a negotiation of peace at Paris. . . . The avocations of the day prevented me from reading the paper in time to return it by the regular daily messenger, which I think rather advantageous, as it enabled me to put it into Mr. Pitt's hands and permit him to communicate it to the Chancellor and the Duke of Portland, both of who[m] approving of it, it has now been looked upon as equivalent to a Minute of Cabinet. I certainly do not object to the trial, but should have liked it better if the preparations for an active campaign had been first prepared and this been the subsequent step, as it would have come with more dignity, but as perhaps others think the refusal which most probably will ensue may rouse men's minds and make them more ready to grant supplies of men and money, I do not object to the mode proposed being adopted. . . .

[1] The Nootka Sound crisis of 1790.

81. Henry Dundas (Secretary for War) to George III, 23 Jan. 1797, and reply

(*Windsor Archives*, 8315.)

Mr. Dundas takes the liberty humbly to submit to your Majesty's perusal the accompanying papers. The subject of them is of the utmost importance, and the success of every part of the idea depends upon the secrecy with which it is planned and executed. Under these circumstances Mr. Dundas feels it essentially necessary to confine the subject to those only whose co-operation is necessary for the execution. Under that impression he is afraid he can scarcely venture to make the business the subject of a discussion in a general Council of your Majesty's confidential servants, and must therefore hope for your Majesty's approbation in conveying his instructions under such orders as your Majesty may be pleased to sanction with your approbation. Mr. Dundas is perfectly aware that in case of failure he is thereby exposed to additional responsibility, but that is a consideration which he is free to confess does not on such an occasion operate one moment on his mind in the decision of what is right to be done for the general service of the country.

[The King's reply, 24 January.] I have authorised Mr. Secretary Dundas to take the necessary steps for effecting an expedition from the Cape of Good Hope to the Spanish settlements in South America, the knowledge of which to be kept from all but the Duke of York,[1] Earl Spencer,[2] Mr. Pitt and Mr. Nepean.[3]

82. Canning (Under-Secretary of State for Foreign Affairs) to Lord Grenville, (Foreign Secretary), 31 July 1797

(*Hist. MSS. Comm., Dropmore Papers*, III, p. 337.)

Malmesbury had been sent to Lille to negotiate a peace with France.

. . Lord Malmesbury recommends so earnestly the keeping a profound secret the particulars of all that has passed at Lille upon this subject, that Mr. Pitt had thought it right that the enclosed bulletin (written under his direction) should be circulated among the members of the Cabinet, as containing all that was fit to be communicated of what Mr. Wesley brought with him.

But since seeing Mr. Pitt, a doubt has arisen in my mind (which I should state to him if he were still in town, and which I hope your Lordship will pardon me for suggesting to you) that the members of the Cabinet might feel some degree of displeasure at so professed a limitation of confidence in them, and that it might be better (if it is thought right not to communicate the whole) to withhold *everything* from them until a future opportunity. The ostensible Dispatch (no. 15) is as much as Wesley *need* have brought, considering the circumstances which occasioned and will account for his coming over. No. 16, in which *he* is referred to for details of great importance, must of course in this case be entirely suppressed. I have separated the Dispatches with this view, and with a view of leaving it open to your Lordship to send as much or as little as you may think right to the King. . . .

[1] The Commander-in-Chief.   [2] First Lord of the Admiralty.   [3] Under-Secretary of State for War.

83. George III to Lord Grenville, 5 Aug. 1797

(Hist. MSS. Comm., Dropmore Papers, III, p. 344.)

. . . I have read with attention the paper drawn up by Mr. Wesley, and perfectly coincide in opinion with Lord Grenville that it by no means holds out any view that can found an opinion that peace will be effected . . . I thoroughly approve of Lord Grenville's having only communicated this paper to Mr. Pitt, as it can be of no use in forming any opinion, and the less papers not necessary towards effecting that are circulated, the better.

84. William Pitt to Lord Grenville, 20 March 1800

(Hist. MSS. Comm., Dropmore Papers, VI, p. 170.)

A Cabinet has been summoned tomorrow, at the desire of several of our colleagues, to discuss further our military plans and prospects. It will be very desirable that you and Dundas and myself should have some previous conversation. . . .

85. Lord Grenville to William Pitt, 11 April 1800

(Public Record Office, Chatham Papers, 140.)

. . . If I can in no other way obtain an opinion on the subject, I must summon a Cabinet to consider of the answer to be given to Wickham and Lord Minto[1] about the Condé army—for I cannot take upon myself in such a business to guess at the opinions of my colleagues. But before we summon our numerous Cabinet, it is much better that those who are to execute should understand each other upon the subject. . . .

If we are to ask for co-operation from Austria we must explain our ideas to them at least in general, and how can I explain those ideas without knowing what they are? But with the present opinions, it is surely better to give the thing up, for sanguine as I was in the hope of brilliant and useful operations there, I am not such a novice as to expect that success, in opposition to the opinions of the Commander-in-Chief, the War Department and the War Office.

86. Lord Liverpool to Viscount Wellington, 20 Jan. 1812

(Wellington, Supplementary Despatches, VII, pp. 256–257.)

. . . Lord Wellesley has intimated to the Prince Regent his intention of resigning his situation in the Government. I am not aware of the existence of any distinct difference of opinion on any public question of importance which has led to this determination.

[1] Wickham was Under-Secretary of State for the Home Department. He and Minto (Minister Pleni-potentiary at Vienna) had been jointly given power to negotiate with the emperor.

He says generally that he has not the weight in the Government which he expected when he accepted office. I have never seen any want of attention to his opinions, nor do I recollect a single question (except one of comparatively little moment lately, respecting the King's and Regent's Establishments) to which he ever entered a dissent. The Government through a Cabinet is necessarily a Government *inter pares*, in which every man must expect to have his opinions and his despatches canvassed, and this previous friendly canvass of opinions and measures appears to be absolutely necessary under a Constitution where all public acts of Government will be ultimately hostilely debated in Parliament. I have always regretted that Lord Wellesley's habits of late have prevented him seeing as much of his colleagues and mixing as much in general business as is usual with persons in public office. I do not believe he has attended more than half the Cabinet meetings which have taken place since he has been in Government: this circumstance, combined with others, unavoidably prevents a man from having the same common feelings with his colleagues as exist amongst those who not only act but live together. Lord Wellesley declares it is not his intention to go into opposition, and that he does not even wish his son to resign his seat at the Treasury. . . .

87. Charles Wynn to the duke of Buckingham and Chandos, Nov. 1822

(*Duke of Buckingham and Chandos, Memoirs of Court of George IV*, I (1859), p. 398.)

. . . I continue most completely separated from the rest of the Cabinet. Whether they live at all together I know not, but believe they do. However, we have all been in town now for more than a week, and I never have seen anything of any of them except in Cabinet. No one dinner have I been asked to since the conclusion of the session, excepting one in the beginning of September at Robinson's. Now we all know that business can never be really settled in the meetings of so numerous a Cabinet, but that it must be *in fact* arranged at more private meetings and dinners.

Canning is certainly not cordial, though there is nothing I have a right to complain of. Still I see that he is disposed to discuss the business of his own office, &c. with Lord Bathurst, Peel or Robinson, but not with me. Peel is reserved in his natural manner, but I rather get on with him. . . .

[10 September 1823.] . . . My own belief is that the only real and efficient Cabinet upon *all* matters consists of Lords Liverpool and Bathurst, Duke of Wellington and Canning, and that the others are only more or less consulted upon different businesses by these four. Huskisson[1] will, I think, be equally in the confidence of Liverpool and Canning. . . . [*Ibid.*]

[1] President of the Board of Trade, who was about to be admitted to the Cabinet.

C. THE ROYAL PREROGATIVE

(a) CHOICE OF MINISTERS

88. Fox's speech in the House of Commons, 16 Jan. 1784

(Cobbett's *Parliamentary History*, XXIV, 364–369.)

George III's dismissal of the Fox-North coalition in Dec. 1783, and the appointment of Pitt in face of a hostile House of Commons, raised in an acute form the constitutional question of the Crown's right to appoint ministers, and the power of the Commons to criticize or reject that choice.

. . . In my conversations with the rankest Whigs, and in the whole course of my reading, I have never found the hardiest of them deny a right inherent in the prerogative to elect its own Ministers. On this point all are agreed. But though this be the admitted and established right of the Executive branch of the Constitution, is it not also the privilege of this House, and of Parliament, to decide on the conduct of Administration, on the peculiarity of their introduction into office, and on those circumstances which either entitle them to the confidence or the reprobation of the House? . . .

But although it is undoubtedly the prerogative of H.M. to appoint his Ministers, it may still be a point worthy of consideration how far it may be prudent, wise and politic in a Monarch to continue them in power and support them in office, when they are declared by that House to have been elevated to their station by means unconstitutional, and such as have rendered them unworthy of confidence. . . .

I readily agree . . . that the failure of any Bill proposed by Ministers is no cause for their dismission from office. This is a sound doctrine; let it be applied to the dissolution of the late Ministry. A Bill[1] received the sanction of one branch of the Legislature, and was submitted to the consideration of the other. Everything seemed to promise it at first a favourable reception in the other House: there was only one method, a method as new as unexpected, as secret as infamous, by which it could be overthrown. This dark design was accomplished by a member[2] of the present Administration, but who has since, for reasons best known to himself, resigned his charge. It was not therefore the failure of the India Bill in the other House which ejected the late Ministry from office, but the mode by which that failure was accomplished; a mode which, being new and extraordinary, this House has condemned. . . .

It has been asserted that the influence of the Crown in this House is diminished. Still, however, is it not great and extensive? Does not the dismission of the late Ministry, and the adoption of the present, exhibit its magnitude? Were not both these measures effectuated by the means of a dark and secret influence on the royal mind? Was it not in this way that Ministers, who had been emphatically styled the Keepers of H.M.'s conscience, were dismissed from the participation of his Councils and Government? . . .

. . . . Whilst I assert the privilege of this House to decide on the conduct of Ministers, and to consider the modes or artifices by which they have crept into office;

---

[1] One of Fox's two India Bills.   [2] Lord Temple.

whilst I exhibit and condemn their conspiracies against the Constitution of this country, let it not be understood that I wish to diminish those rights which are legally invested in Majesty. The prerogative of the negative is a maxim which I have always admitted, always asserted, always defended. . . . And had this prerogative on a late occasion been exerted, not in the dark and under the baleful shade of a secret influence, but in an honest, open and avowed manner, I should have applauded the measure. . . .

89. George III to Pitt, 4 Feb. 1784, 8 m.pt. 8 a.m.

(Public Record Office, *Chatham Papers*, 103.)

The whole conduct of Opposition confirms the opinion I gave very early of its dangerous intentions of going step by step as far as the House of Commons can be led, avoiding if possible any avowed illegality of conduct; but not looking to the spirit either of the Constitution or of justice. The directing the Resolution of Monday to be brought to me without having proved any charge against Administration or indeed pretending to any, must make every man of reflection grieve that the House can be carried such lengths. I trust the House of Lords will this day feel that the hour is come for which the wisdom of our ancestors established that respectable corps in the State, to prevent either the Crown or the Commons from encroaching on the rights of each other. Indeed, should not the Lords stand boldly forth, this Constitution must soon be changed; for, if the two only remaining privileges of the Crown are infringed–that of negativing Bills that have passed both Houses of Parliament, or that of naming the Ministers to be employed–I cannot but feel, as far as regards my person that I can be no longer of any utility to this country, nor can with honour continue in this island.

90. Debate in the House of Lords, 26 March 1807

(Cobbett's *Parliamentary Debates*, IX, 232–259.)

Lord Grenville: . . . On the present occasion . . . a change of Administration has taken place, not by resignation but in consequence of the exercise of the royal prerogative. . . .

I speak of the publication of the Minutes of advice given to H.M. by his late Ministers. That advice was given . . . in writing, and though it was proper that the paper should be transferred to the persons who succeeded to the Administration in order that they might know the grounds upon which their predecessors were dismissed, it was a very extraordinary proceeding in those persons to authorize its publication . . . I must ask them[1] whether they can refer to any instance in the history of the country in which any similar publication had, from party views or any other motive, ever been made . . . I was induced[2] to ask leave of H.M. to make the statement I am about to lay before your Lordships, for, without that permission, I should not, most

[1] The ministers.   [2] Because of newspaper misrepresentation.

anxiously as I desired to explain every circumstance connected with the important transactions that have taken place, have taken this opportunity of addressing your Lordships. . . .

Lord Hawkesbury. . . . Much had been said . . . of the publications that had taken place on this subject. Of these he knew nothing, and felt as much regret as any person that such statements should have found their way to the public. . . .

Lord Erskine. . . . Although a member of the late Government, he was decidedly adverse to the measure, and should not have advised it, because he did not see the political necessity for it which had induced the great majority of his colleagues to recommend it to H.M., yet he thought they were highly commendable and only doing their duty in giving H.M. such advice as they in their conscience thought just, as well as in declining to be bound by any pledge to refrain from giving to their Sovereign upon this, or any subject, such advice as they conceived to be just. The firmness with which H.M. had maintained his own conscientious opinions by resisting the Bill in the extent to which it went, had also his respectful approbation, but he must say that his colleagues did right in declining to be bound never again to advise the measure under any possible pressure of circumstances. . . . The right of H.M. to change his Ministers, no man could deny, but to have remained in power, or accept office upon any such condition as the pledge alluded to, was, in his opinion, contrary to every principle of ministerial duty, and directly in violation of the Constitution. . . .

91. Colonel J. W. Gordon (Quartermaster-General) to Colonel McMahon, 15 Nov. 1811

(*Windsor Archives*, 18839–18842.)

It was generally expected that the Prince of Wales, as regent, would replace his father's ministers by his own friends led by Grey and Grenville, who had been dismissed in March 1807 when the king refused to assent to a measure of Catholic relief. In the event, the Perceval Ministry was continued in office. (See Nos. 57 and 90.)

. . . The text of every conversation in every company is the question "What will the "Prince do when he has full power? Will he change the Government? Will he "abandon his old friends, and will he concede any thing to the Catholics?" This I need not tell you is the substance of every conference, at every table, & in every society at this moment in the metropolis, & probably in the Kingdom. Not being any politician myself, at least having no political expectation, but having a very general acquaintance & a business kind of communication with the several leading men of the day, and being known also to be honoured with the Prince's regard I am perhaps as much in the way of ascertaining the various bias and bearings of opinion as any man, and I thus endeavour to lay them before you.

You know that the present Ministers with Mr. Perceval at their head, owe their situations and power wholly and solely to the undivided support of the King, arising from His Majesty's conscientious opposition to the Catholic Petition. You know also that this Administration is the remains of the Pitt school, of which school, however, *two* most important members are schismatic, Canning and Castlereagh, each of whom have their supporters and followers, and may be considered as possessed of a large share of the confidence and respect of the House of Commons and also of the country: –the other party (of this school also) is the Sidmouth party, of which Mr. Bathurst is the usual organ, and they also have their share of power in the House.

This, I believe, may be considered as the main body of the Pitt school, orthodox, and heterodox, but all sprung from the tree of Pitt.

The opposite party, those hitherto distinguished by the appellation of the Prince's friends, are the remains of the Fox school, the head of which may be considered Earl Grey, uniting the whole Grenville family and followers, and having as their organs in the House of Commons, Messrs. Whitbread, Ponsonby and Tierney. There are many eminent young men on both sides, but certainly of no leading capacity, and it is therefore unnecessary to mention them in this disquisition.

As the Fox Administration in fact dissolved itself upon the Catholic question, it may be fairly considered as a great political party indisputably pledged and committed to carry it when in power, and if taken into power as a party, they would not have an alternative, but must effect it or resign their seats as ill-judging & incompetent men.

Upon a due consideration of these points, it appears to me that the Prince stands between these two parties, as the arbiter upon the Catholic question, that is, if he rejects it, he draws upon him at once the united hostility of his former friends, and also of the great mass of the people of Ireland, and he unites himself for ever as the head of the Pitt party, subjecting himself also to the violence of decided opposition upon a great public question, and which if ever carried, would be a sort of assault upon the Crown. If, on the other hand, he forms an Administration of which Catholic concession is the basis, he unites against him the Perceval part of the Pitt school (the remaining part of that school will be hollow supporters for the popularity of the moment) and he risks all the consequences attendant upon a failure, which in this Protestant, and I may add Protestantly bigoted Kingdom, I doubt whether any man can safely predict,–indeed if I may trust my own limited observation, I should certainly say that as an English question the Catholic Petition is decidedly unpopular, and unless the temper of the people is very much changed, there is nothing which would be more likely to create a popular ferment, if handled by designing knaves, (of which there is never a scarcity) than a Catholic concession.

In this state of political difficulty, let me appeal to your good sense whether it would not be practicable and easy for the Prince to avow himself wholly unfettered by any conscientious feelings upon the Catholic cause, and to be ready to do that which shall appear to be the true sense of the nation upon the case, but that he will not himself personally interfere in the discussion, seeing that his family is a Protestant family, and seated upon this Throne upon sound Protestant principles, and seeing also that his father was uniformly adverse to it–that he wishes the question to be decided as a great national question, unfettered by party, unbiassed by power, and that his fiat will be given when the decision of the Legislature shall be duly laid before him–in short, that he wishes it to be discussed as was the slave trade, where every individual spoke as his mind dictated.

If the Prince should see this matter in a point of view similar to this, he would be at perfect liberty to form an Administration as extended as he pleased, and by includ-ing in his Household Establishment the heads and heirs of the great families of this country, *viz.* the Devonshires, Bedfords, Northumberlands, Rutlands, Beauforts, Hertfords, Moira, he might then, aided by his old friends, dictate to any Administra-tion he chose to form, nor could any formidable power be raised against him. No reasonable objection could be made by the King's old friends, as it must be a natural proceeding for every new Monarch to surround himself with those who, from political & personal interests, he may consider most useful to his Government, and most satisfactory to himself. . . .

92. Lord Eldon to the duke of Cumberland, 23 July 1827

(Cumberland MSS.)

. . . We have, I believe, now an Administration formed for this country – an Adminis-tration, which from all accounts – they may be partial – that reach me from the country, is the least popular of any of which I have a recollection. But they have a support in that quarter without which no Administration can stand – with which, such is the attachment of this country to the royal family, even this Administration may long endure. . . .

93. Minute of Cabinet, 8 May 1832

(Correspondence of Earl Grey and William IV, ed. Earl Grey, II (1867), pp. 394–395.)

Present: the Lord Chancellor, the Lord President, the Lord Privy Seal, the Duke of Richmond, the Earl Grey, the Viscount Melbourne, the Viscount Goderich, the Viscount Palmerston, the Lord Holland, the Lord John Russell, the Viscount Althorp, Sir James Graham, the Rt. Hon. E. G. Stanley, the Rt. Hon. C. Grant.

Your Majesty's servants having been assembled to consider the situation in which they are placed by the vote of the Committee of the House of Lords last night, beg leave humbly to represent to your Majesty, that they find themselves deprived of all hope of being able to carry the Reform Bill through its further stages in a manner that would be for the advantage of your Majesty's Government, or satisfactory to the public.

So circumstanced, your Majesty's servants would naturally be led at once to tender to your Majesty, with every sentiment of respect and gratitude, the resignation of the offices which they hold from your Majesty's favour, if they did not feel it to be a paramount duty not to withdraw themselves from your Majesty's service in a moment of so much difficulty, so long as they can contemplate the possibility of remaining in it with advantage to your Majesty and to the public interests, and without dishonour to themselves.

They, therefore, feel themselves bound humbly to suggest to your Majesty the expediency of advancing to the honour of the peerage such a number of persons as might insure the success of the Bill in all its essential principles, and as might give to your Majesty's servants the strength which is necessary for conducting with effect the business of the country.

In the opinion thus humbly submitted to your Majesty the Duke of Richmond alone of your Majesty's servants does not coincide. [pp. 394–395.]

[William IV to Earl Grey, 9 May 1832.] It is not without the truest concern that the King acquaints his confidential servants that, after giving due consideration to the Minute of Cabinet which was brought to him yesterday afternoon by Earl Grey and the Lord Chancellor, and to the consequences of the alternative which it offers for his decision. . . . H.M. has come to the painful resolution of accepting their resignations. . . . [*Ibid.*, II, p. 395.]

[William IV to Earl Grey, 18 May 1832.] The King's mind has been too deeply engaged in the consideration of the circumstances in which this country is placed, and of his own position, to require that H.M. should hesitate to say, in reply to the Minute of Cabinet left with him this afternoon by Earl Grey and the Lord Chancellor, that it continues to be, as stated in his recent communications to his confidential servants, H.M.'s wish and desire that they remain in his Councils.

H.M. is, therefore, prepared to afford to them the security they require for passing the Reform Bill unimpaired in its principles and in its essential provisions, and as nearly as possible in its present form; and with this view H.M. authorises Earl Grey, if any obstacle should arise during the further progress of the Bill, to submit to him a creation of peers to such extent as shall be necessary to enable him to carry the Bill, always bearing in mind that it has been and still is H.M.'s object to avoid any permanent increase to the peerage, and therefore that this addition to the House of Peers, if unfortunately it should become necessary, shall comprehend as large a proportion of the eldest sons of peers and collateral heirs of childless peers as can possibly be brought forward. In short (to quote the Lord Chancellor's own words used in the interview between H.M., his Lordship, and Earl Grey), that the lists of eldest sons and collaterals who can be brought forward shall be completely exhausted before any list be resorted to which can entail a permanent addition to the peerage.

Subject to these conditions, which have been already stated verbally, and admitted by Earl Grey and the Lord Chancellor, H.M. assents to the proposal conveyed in the Minute of Cabinet of this day; and this main point being so disposed of, it is unnecessary that H.M. should notice any other part of the Minute. [*Ibid.*, II, p. 434.]

94. George IV's message to the Cabinet, 29 March 1827

(A. G. Stapleton, *George Canning and His Times* (1859), p. 586.)

In an effort to avoid the necessity of choosing between Canning, Wellington and Peel as Prime Minister, George IV tried, unsuccessfully, to throw the responsibility on to the Cabinet. Canning and Peel agreed that such procedure was unconstitutional, and the king abandoned it.

That H.M. is desirous of retaining all his present servants in the stations which they at present fill, placing at their head, in the station vacated by Lord Liverpool, some Peer professing opinions, upon whom H.M.'s confidential servants may agree, of the same principles as Lord Liverpool.

[Memorandum read by Canning to the Cabinet on 31 March.] Mr. Canning received on Thursday H.M.'s commands to communicate to the Cabinet a Memorandum (written in H.M.'s presence) of H.M.'s wishes in reference to the arrangement of the Administration. Mr. Canning in consequence summoned the Cabinet for today. Yesterday evening Mr. Canning received a verbal message from H.M., through Mr. Peel, leaving to Mr. Canning's *discretion* to make or to withhold the prescribed communication. In the exercise of this discretion Mr. Canning feels great difficulty, especially as he had taken the liberty of humbly stating to H.M. the objections which he individually felt both to the form and to the substance of the communication; and as he might be exposed to blame therefore alike, either for keeping it back, on the one hand, or for bringing it forward unnecessarily, on the other. In this state of things Mr. Canning can only decide to withhold the communication for the present, and humbly to request H.M.'s definitive pleasure thereupon.

Mr. Peel will state to the Cabinet that his opinion concurs with Mr. Canning's (and has been, like his, stated to H.M.) of the inexpediency of referring the point to which the Memorandum relates, to the collective opinion of the Cabinet.

95. William Pitt to Lord Chancellor Eldon, 2 May 1804

(Stanhope's *Life of Pitt*, IV, App., p. iv.)

Pitt's attempt to form an all-party Government in 1804 for the more vigorous prosecution of the war was defeated by the king's refusal to employ Fox. (No. 116.)

(To be laid before the King.)

York Place.

... It becomes my indispensable duty to entreat H.M.'s permission to lay before him distinctly and without reserve the best opinion which I can form respecting the nature and description of Administration which appears to me likely to be most conducive to H.M.'s service, together with the reasons for that opinion; but in doing so, I am anxious at the same time humbly to repeat the assurance that I do not presume to request more from H.M. than that he would condescend to give a full and deliberate consideration to the proposal which I feel it my duty to submit to him. If, after such consideration, and receiving such further explanation as the nature of the subject may require, H.M. should feel insuperable objections to any part of the proposal, much as I must in that case regret H.M.'s decision, I shall feel myself bound to acquiesce in it; and if I should in that case be honoured with H.M.'s further commands to endeavour to form a plan of Administration free from such objections, I shall be ready to obey them to the best of my power.

My opinion is founded on the strong conviction that the present critical situation of this country, connected with that of Europe in general, and with the state of political parties at home, renders it more important and essential than perhaps at any other period that ever existed, to endeavour to give the greatest possible strength and energy to H.M.'s Government, by endeavouring to unite in his service as large a proportion as possible of the weight of talents and connections, drawn without exception from parties of all descriptions, and without reference to former differences and divisions. There seems the greatest reason to hope that the circumstances of the present moment are peculiarly favourable to such an union, and that it might now be possible (with H.M.'s gracious approbation) to bring all persons of leading influence either in Parliament or in the country to concur heartily in a general system formed for the purpose of extricating this country from its present difficulties, and endeavouring, if possible, to rescue Europe from the state to which it is reduced. The consequences of the French Revolution, universally understood and acknowledged, its effects in France, and Europe, and the world, and the present conduct and character of the First Consul, seem to have produced a very general desire that all the abilities and resources of the country should be exerted in meeting its present danger; and in pursuit of this object, all the points of difference, however great and important, which at a former period prevailed in this country, seem, to all practical purpose, to be superseded.

The various advantages which may be derived from such a comprehensive system as I have pointed at are . . . obvious. . . . Zealous and united as the country appears to be at this moment in its efforts against the enemy, the present contest may probably be of very long duration, attended with great and heavy burdens. . . . It is impossible not to feel that a system of this nature would furnish a security that cannot otherwise be obtained for our being enabled to persevere in the struggle with unabated vigour till it can be really brought to a safe and honourable issue. The same considerations which apply to this country separately, will operate as powerfully, if not still more so, on our means and prospects abroad. A firm and stable Administration, not thwarted or embarrassed by any powerful opposition either in parliament or the country, must furnish the best and perhaps the only chance of attracting sufficiently the respect and confidence of Foreign Powers, and of improving any favourable opportunity to unite them once again in a great and combined effort for reducing the power of France within limits consistent with the safety of other states, or at least of rescuing from its yoke some of those countries in whose fate, both from inclination and policy, we ought to feel most deeply interested.

. . . The state of Ireland, and the delicate and difficult questions which may arise respecting the internal condition of that country, are scarcely less deserving of attention. I need not repeat to your Lordship what has long since been known to H.M., how fully my own determination has been formed to prevent H.M. being ever disquieted for a moment, as far as depends upon me, by a renewal of the proposition which was in question three years ago respecting the extension of privileges to the Catholics; but I cannot help seeing that, although my own conduct, under all circumstances, is fixed, there may arise moments of difficulty in which, if this country remains divided by powerful parties, the agitation of this question may be productive of great inconvenience and embarrassment. The formation of such a system as I have supposed would . . . effectually remove this source of anxiety, as I certainly can never suppose or wish it to be formed on any other ground but that of all those who might form part of the Administration joining in the same determination with myself to endeavour to prevent the renewal of any such discussion.

. . . Nothing is so likely to ensure H.M.'s personal repose and comfort, and the future prosperity and glory of his reign, as the plan which I have thus taken the liberty of submitting to H.M.'s consideration; and I am therefore most deeply anxious that, after full reflection, H.M. may deem it not unworthy of his approbation. In that event it would become my duty to entreat H.M.'s permission before I entered further on any details, to converse both with Lord Grenville and with Mr. Fox, in order to learn how it might be practicable to submit, for H.M.'s consideration, any arrangement which might include them, and a proportion of those who act with them, together with some of H.M.'s present servants, and other persons to whom I might wish to draw his majesty's favourable attention.

I have only now to request that your Lordship will have the goodness to take the first convenient opportunity of laying this representation of my sentiments before H.M., together with the humble assurances of my constant sentiments of respect, duty, and attachment towards H.M., and of my deep and grateful sense of H.M.'s condescension and goodness in the gracious communication which I had the honour of receiving through your Lordship. I have thought that this mode of submitting my opinion in the first instance for H.M.'s consideration at his most convenient leisure, was that of which H.M. would not disapprove. I trust I may be permitted to hope, before H.M.'s final decision on the subject, he will allow me to have the honour of personally submitting to H.M. any further explanation which any part of the subject may appear to require. . . .

96. George Rose to Bishop Tomline, 8 Aug. 1806

(*Pretyman MSS.*)

. . . Disliking, as you know I did *most thoroughly* the three Lords mentioned in the enclosed[1] (especially the two first, for their conduct in preventing the King from admitting Mr. Fox to his Councils when pressed to do so by Mr. Pitt) I could not now listen to any overture[2] without communication with those I have been acting with. . . .

97. Charles Arbuthnot's Memorandum, c. middle of June 1821

(*British Museum Additional MSS.* 38370, f. 57.)

Canning had resigned office in Dec. 1820, being unable to acquiesce in the Government's treatment of Queen Caroline after the withdrawal of the Bills of Pains and Penalties. This was the main cause of the king's hostility to him in 1821–1822. George IV seems, too, to have thought (erroneously, no doubt) that Canning had committed adultery with her when she was Princess of Wales.

. . . I related to Lord Liverpool . . . the conversation which Lord Sidmouth had had with the King. I mentioned in particular the very strong expressions which Lord Sidmouth had used in urging the King not to run the risk of breaking up his present Government; and I quoted the King's answer, which acknowledged that with new

[1] A 'most private' letter of the same date to the bishop. ". . . You know too as well as I do the feelings I had about Lord Eldon, Lord Castlereagh and Lord Hawkesbury, and the ground of those respecting at least the first and the last of them. . . ." [2] From Lord Grenville. (See No. 47.)

men he certainly should not occupy the same station abroad, nor be so likely to preserve his present system at home. I also mentioned what the King had said to Lord Sidmouth in respect to the malady of his father, and of his dread lest political worry should produce a similar effect upon himself. I went on to state that the King, as he had told Lord Sidmouth, did not mean to proscribe Mr. Canning, nor express his determination to exclude him for ever from the Cabinet: that he only begged not to have Mr. Canning pressed upon him at present, not being prepared on the sudden to give him that full confidence which a Cabinet Minister had a right to expect. . . .

I said that the Duke of Wellington felt strongly that as the King did not mean to proscribe Mr. Canning eternally . . . we could not with propriety force H.M.'s feelings: that if we were to attempt so to force them, we should have no case to stand upon, and that our conduct would be censured both by our party and by the country. . . .

98. Earl Bathurst and the earl of Liverpool: Correspondence, June 1821

(Wellington MSS.)

[Lord Bathurst's letter (undated)] . . . The question whether the Sovereign should be forced to accept any particular individual into his confidential service has more than once occurred in the course of my political life. I have on each of those occasions acted under the impression that he should not be so forced, and I own I see nothing in the existing circumstances which would justify me in a departure from that opinion. . . .

[Lord Liverpool's reply, 27 June.] . . . Upon the abstract question whether a King should be allowed to exclude an individual from his Cabinet, it is very difficult to give any general opinion. There are circumstances which might certainly justify such a decision: strong discordance of opinion on political events actually depending; belief of disloyalty; the moral character of a man materially tainted–may all sufficiently account for such exclusion.

There may likewise be many other cases which I do not at this moment contemplate, but I am quite sure a King should be most cautious in acting on such a principle, for the effect of it will generally be to exalt the individual and to lower the King.

I speak not without experience on this subject. I was the person in 1806 to advise the late King to waive his exclusion of Mr. Fox. I had then seen the evil effects of such exclusion. A few months before Mr. Pitt was sent for in 1805 [1804] by the King, no man could stand lower in reputation, character and credit than Mr. Fox. You will recollect that he had been termed by Windham the pander of all the base passions of the people, and yet the day after he had been proposed by Mr. Pitt as a colleague and personally excluded by the King, his character stood higher in the eyes of the country than it had ever stood at any former period of his political life.

In the present case it is to be observed that there is no pretence for any discordance of opinion between Mr. Canning and the King's Government on any material public question, foreign or domestic. He is known to agree on every point as much as we agree one with another; and since the termination of the discussion on the Queen's business, he has, when in England, regularly attended the House of Commons and supported the Government much more steadily than many of those who are considered as their decided friends. . . .

It is not *Mr. Canning out of office*, but Mr. Canning *out of office by the personal exclusion of the King, agreed to by his Government*, which is the question. Can anyone doubt that he would become an object of compassion in the first instance, and afterwards of popularity–that his case would be taken up by all who on any account oppose the Government, and that we should be accused of meanness and servility in abandoning a man to the personal resentment of the Sovereign, whom we had thought it right to propose as one of his Ministers? I feel this perhaps the more strongly because I have reason to know that there will remain after this a further stock of humiliations in store for us, and yet of humiliations of such a nature that I do not see how we can do otherwise than submit to them.

It is said that the exclusion is only temporary. Ought we not to know what is meant by temporary? Kings may have said that they never would admit particular individuals into their Cabinet. Public men may have said that they never would sit in a Cabinet with this or that individual, but such declarations have always been justly considered as ebullitions of passion. No man can be proscribed for ever, and the temporary exclusion may operate therefore with exactly the same effect as a professed permanent one. . . .

I am quite ready to admit that whatever my own ultimate determination may be, I have no desire to influence the decision of others or to give the least obstruction to the formation of a Government by my colleagues even upon the principle of excluding Mr. Canning. [*Hist. MSS. Comm., Bathurst Papers*, p. 499]

[Lord Bathurst replied, 28 June.] . . . You deceive yourself if you think that your resignation will not be followed by a complete change. [*Ibid.*, p. 501.]

99. Charles Arbuthnot's memorandum of a conversation between Wellington and Sir Benjamin Bloomfield (George IV's private secretary), 21 July 1821

(British Museum Additional MSS. 38370, f. 25.)

[The Duke said] . . . "The King is proving by various of his acts that we have not his confidence, and is proving it also by the unwillingness he has manifested to allow us to strengthen ourselves. H.M. cannot suppose that we are not sensible that Mr. Canning's conduct was not very advantageous to us. But viewing the state of the Government, we were convinced that he was the person most likely from his parliamentary talents to assist the Government *if in office*, and on the other hand to be elevated to a station in which he would have the power of being most mischievous if *left out*. That *being left out*, he would immediately be surrounded by the discontented of all descriptions, and by the young philosophers who would look to him as their rallying point, and that in short he would have the means of collecting around him such numbers as would put the Government really in his hands. The only mode, therefore, of preventing him from attaining this power and of rendering him really useful was to bring him into the Cabinet. ... H.M. refused to act upon our advice. ... If we had not his permission to gain the strength which is within our reach, we must sooner or later be broken down. It is true that Lord Londonderry has in this last session done wonders. He has achieved more than could have been expected from any single man, but it is to be recollected that the intermediate parties[1] were expecting to be received among us, and when they find that this is not to happen, their conduct towards the Government will be very different."

It was the Duke's strong conviction ... that no other party could continue a Government for six months without dissolving the Parliament, and that if Parliament should be dissolved by the Whigs, a Radical House of Commons would be the inevitable consequence. Careless therefore as he was about official situation, it would nevertheless be his earnest endeavour to prevent the Government from breaking up, for he could not contemplate without horror and dread such a state of things as must ensue if the Whigs should have to conduct the affairs of the country with a House of Commons elected under such circumstances as he had represented. ...

100. The duke of Wellington to Peel, 9 Jan. 1828

(*Wellington Despatches, Correspondence and Memoranda*, New Series, IV (1871), p. 184.)

... This morning ... H.M. told me that he wished me to form a Government for him, of which I should be the head. I told H.M. that I was so situated professionally[2] that I could not say that I would form a Government of which I should be the head, without consulting with others; that I would not say I could form a Government at all without such previous consultation, but that, if he would give me a little time and leave to go to town to consult with others, I would inquire and see what could be done and report to him the result.

I then inquired what he desired: whether he had any wishes for particular persons, or objections to any. He said that he thought the Government must be composed of persons of both opinions in respect to the Roman Catholic question; that he approved of all his late and former servants; and that he had no objection to anybody excepting to Lord Grey.

He afterwards expressed a wish to retain the Duke of Devonshire[3] and Lord Carlisle in his service, and he spoke highly of Lord Lansdowne and Lord Dudley; but upon the whole he left me *carte blanche*, with the single exception above-mentioned; and he repeatedly desired that I would form for him a strong Government. The Chancellor was present. ... Excepting Lord Lyndhurst, who, it must be understood is in office, everything else is open to all mankind, excepting to one person. ...

The King said that it was to be understood that the Roman Catholic question was not to be made a Cabinet question; that there was to be a Protestant Lord Chancellor, a Protestant Lord-Lieutenant, and a Protestant Lord Chancellor in Ireland.

[1] First, the Grenville group, which had severed its connexion with the Whig Opposition in 1817; second, Canning. [2] He was Commander-in-Chief of the Army. [3] Lord Chamberlain since May 1827.

101. George III to Henry Dundas (Home Secretary), 16 May 1792, 42 m.pt.
6 p.m.

(*Windsor Archives*, 6953.)

From the sorrow I feel at taking up my pen to direct Mr. Dundas to wait on the
Lord Chancellor I can easily conceive how unpleasant the conveying the following
message must be. Mr. Dundas is to acquaint the Lord Chancellor that Mr. Pitt has
this day stated the impossibility of his sitting any longer in Council with him, it
remains therefore for my decision which of the two shall retire from my service. The
Chancellor's own penetration must convince him that however strong my personal
regard, nay affection, is for him, that I must feel the removal of Mr. Pitt impossible
with the good of my service. I wish therefore that the Great Seal may be delivered
to me at the time most agreeable to the Lord Chancellor and least inconvenient to
either the business of the House of Lords or Court of Chancery. Perhaps the Long
Vacation might be the time every way most proper, but of this the Lord Chancellor
must be the best judge.

102. George IV to George Canning, 1 May 1827

(*Harewood MSS.*)

Lord Carlisle became First Commissioner of Woods and Forests on 30 May, Lord Lowther, who
was Lord Lonsdale's elder son, having refused an offer of it. For the negotiations with Lowther,
who had resigned his seat at the Treasury Board on Canning's appointment as Prime Minister, see
A. Aspinall, *The Formation of Canning's Ministry*, pp. 106, 107, 125, 127, 143, 218.

In regard to the office of Woods and Forests I have no particular objection that
Mr. Charles Grant, although I do not know him, should *temporarily* hold it until
Lord Lowther can take it. The Lonsdale interest is too great an object to be put aside.
The more you can strengthen yourself by the Tory party, the greater security I feel
in the stability and permanency of my present Government. You see that I am all
sincerity towards you.

One word more on the subject of the Woods and Forests. My comfort and
tranquillity are so intimately mix'd up in this office that I must consider myself, and
myself only, in whatever arrangements are made. . . .

(b) THE RIGHT OF DISSOLUTION

103. Mr. Speaker Abbot's diary, 29 and 30 April 1804

(Public Record Office, P.R.O. 30/9/33.)

The King dreads a defeat of the Ministry in Parliament as the forerunner of a
Regency. To keep his health safe is the cause of the country. At present, if necessary
he may still change his Minister without being driven to it by a forced junction of
the three Oppositions.[1] Mr. Pitt is not now pledged to any man. But the King is ready
to avert this by the utmost exercise of his authority, if that can, all things considered,
succeed; and Parliament would be dissolved now if the state of business and public

[1] The groups led by Pitt, Fox and Grenville.

affairs did not preclude that measure. . . . The King is earnest to do for Mr. Addington everything and more than he can desire or may choose to accept, but to belong to any new arrangement, Mr. Addington is resolved not to consent.

[30 April.] Mr. Addington . . . said . . . that the King dreaded his Closet being forced: there was no want of zeal or honourable attachment or fidelity to the support of his present Ministers, but a want of confidence in the success of the contest, according to the King's view of the state of affairs, and therefore a communication had been made (not through Mr. Addington) which would, for the present, suspend all proceedings upon contested measures, and I should not see him upon the Treasury Bench for more than a very few days. . . .

104. Lord Bathurst to Lord Harrowby, 2 June 1806
(Harrowby MSS.)

. . . The pressing the measure of enlisting for a term of years has irritated very much, it is understood, both the Duke of York[1] and the King. There is, I think, no doubt but that in the House of Lords it *might* be rejected, but I am one of those who deprecate the *exertions* which must be made to produce such a majority, from being persuaded that no Government could be formed (fit for this country in its present situation) without any acknowledged leader, and with Lord Grenville and Mr. Fox united against it.

It appears to me there is but one point where it would be advisable for the King to make his stand, and that is, if a dissolution of Parliament were proposed to him, which I think he ought at all hazards to refuse.[2] Such a refusal would be no justifiable ground of resignation, and probably would not occasion one. And if it did, and the King were to have his new Government overturned, he would not be in a worse situation than he would be by agreeing to their dissolving Parliament, as the new Parliament would be composed more of Fox's friends than those of Lord Grenville, who has no extended parliamentary acquaintance while he continues separate from his original connections. And after so recent a dissolution, Lord Grenville could not have recourse to another, should he afterwards quarrel with Fox and form a Government against him.

105. Debate in the House of Commons, 26 June 1807
(Cobbett's *Parliamentary Debates*, IX, 615–619.)

The Parliament elected in Nov. 1806 was dissolved, after the dismissal of the 'Talents' and the return to office of the Pittites, on 29 April 1807. Howick, later Earl Grey, was one of the dismissed ministers.

Lord Howick:– . . . The power of dissolving Parliament was an indisputable prerogative of the Crown, given for the advantage of the subjects, but . . . this, like every other prerogative, was subject in its exercise to be considered by Parliament. . . . Not a long time had elapsed since Parliament was before dissolved. On that occasion

---

[1] Commander-in-Chief. [2] Cf. No. 54. The king agreed to a dissolution, which took place on 24 Oct.

the House had heard a great number of observations from the gentlemen opposite. If human imagination had been tortured to devise a combination of circumstances which should expose this prerogative of the Crown to all the objections that had been then urged against it, it could not have been more successful than in the present instance. The hon. gent. reprehended the dissolution of Parliament after it had been sitting four years; they themselves dissolved a Parliament after it had been assembled only four months. The hon. gent. opposite censured the dissolution which took place at the end of a session; they themselves dissolved Parliament in the middle of a session. The hon. gent. opposite had complained of undue influence having been exerted against them; they themselves had exercised an influence not in the detail but in wholesale, and such as they ought to have been ashamed of. Unless Parliament were to say at once that the prerogatives of the Crown ought to be curtailed, and that Parliament should be rendered permanent, it could never be contended that any dissolution was better timed than that which took place under H.M.'s late Minister's. At the end of a negotiation which left little hope of a peace, it was surely advisable to show the enemy and the allies of the country that the King, the Parliament and the people were determined to unite in withstanding all the efforts of an unrelenting enemy. . . .

In the interesting debate on this subject which took place in the year 1784, an opinion was quoted of Lord Somers, that H.M. during a session of Parliament, had no power to dissolve the Parliament. With all the deference which was due to the abilities of so able a lawyer and so great a statesman, he confessed that he differed greatly from Lord Somers on this point. The strongest necessity might, in his opinion, exist for a dissolution during a session of Parliament, namely, such a difference between the two Houses as should impede the progress of public business. . . . Now, what necessity existed in the present instance? The hon. seconder declared that the late Ministers had proposed measures replete with danger to the Protestant Establishment. What then? Those Ministers had been turned out: the hon. gent. had himself stated they had lost the confidence of Parliament. What interruption therefore was expedient? What necessity was there for a dissolution? . . .

Mr. Windham:–. . . Ministers seemed to have adopted the doctrine that it was necessary to form a Parliament that was likely to support them, and for this purpose they had taken a moment when they thought the people would be rendered furious by religious zeal. . . . [c. 640.]

106. William IV to Earl Grey, 21 March 1831

(*Correspondence of Earl Grey with William IV*, ed. Earl Grey, I (1867), pp. 179–180.)

The Reform Bill was read a second time in the Commons by a majority of one (302 v. 301) on the 22nd. The king's opposition to a dissolution was overcome a month later after the Bill had been defeated in committee by 299 v. 291 on 19 April. He then felt that the resignation of his ministers would produce a revolutionary agitation in the country which would be a greater evil than a general election.

. . . [The King] has already, in his letter to Earl Grey of yesterday, stated generally his ground of objection, and that he considers as imposing upon him, as a sacred duty, the obligation of resisting any proposal for the dissolution of Parliament at this period; but upon this occasion, and with reference to the general nature of Earl Grey's communication, H.M. is induced to remark further, that it is his firm conviction, that if a general election were to take place at this moment, in consequence of his Government being defeated in the attempt to carry the Bill of Reform, thereby throwing back, upon an excited population, a measure which is considered by that population to have been brought forward in deference to the expression of its opinion; if what is called an appeal to the people be now made upon a popular question so strenuously advocated by those who have been supported by popular clamour, when a spirit of agitation which has been so long in progress has been so much increased by the introduction of the Bill and the discussion upon it, this country would be thrown into convulsion from the Land's End to John O'Groat's house: miners, manufacturers, colliers, labourers, all who have recently formed Unions for the furtherance of illegal purposes, would assemble on every point in support of a *popular* question, with the declared object of carrying the measure by intimidation. It would be in vain to hope to be able to resist their course, or to check disturbances of every kind, amounting possibly to open rebellion, while the few troops which might be brought forward in support of a civil power, often timid and inefficient (as recently shown in Lancashire), would probably have been assembled in the neighbourhood of London, for the preservation of tranquillity in the metropolis, or embarked for Ireland. Here again the effects of dissolution at this period would probably be still more serious. . . .

107. Earl Grey to Sir H. Taylor (William IV's private secretary), 23 March 1831

(*Correspondence of Earl Grey with William IV*, ed. Earl Grey, 1 (1867), p. 201.)

. . . You will see a printed list of the Division, an examination of which will afford no bad ground for estimating the state of public opinion. The activity, the intrigue, the falsehood that was used to influence votes is not to be described. What hurt us most was the report so industriously propagated, that the King had put a positive veto on a proposal to dissolve the Parliament. Several members, representing popular constituencies, who had before declared their intention of voting, changed on this assurance. . . .

108. William IV to Earl Grey, 21 April 1831

(*Correspondence of Earl Grey with William IV*, ed. Earl Grey, 1 (1867), pp. 228–231.)

. . . Although it has not been presented to him in words in the Minute of Cabinet, H.M. could not expect that his refusal to dissolve Parliament, when he had been so strongly urged to do so by his confidential servants, would not be followed by their resignation. With this view of the question–with a mind happily unbiassed by any predilection for this or that party, and wholly free from political prejudice–with a deep sense of the obligations which the duties of the station in which Providence has placed him impose upon him to divest himself of every feeling, except that which is directed to the interests, the welfare, and the prosperity of the country entrusted to his charge, and to consider calmly and dispassionately the various contingencies under which his decision was to be made, and the consequences which might result from it–H.M. has endeavoured, upon this occasion, to discharge correctly the duty which he owes to his God and to his subjects; and, although he may have erred in judgment, his conscience assures him that his intentions are pure and honest.

H.M.'s objections to a dissolution of Parliament at this period have been so fully stated in repeated communications to Earl Grey, that it would be quite superfluous to recapitulate them in this letter; but he cannot forget that, upon the first occasion in which the possibility of such a measure was brought before him, he stated that he had made up his mind not to sanction it; and in his letter of the 19th instant, as well as in the former part of this letter, H.M. has declared that his objections have not been removed, nor weakened, although his confidential servants have assured him that they have not come to the determination of offering this advice to H.M. without having anxiously deliberated on the state of every part of the United Kingdom, and particularly of Ireland, and without having convinced themselves, from the best information they could collect, that the measures which they recommend would be perfectly consistent with the public safety. To which statement, recorded in their Minute, Earl Grey has added the verbal assurance, that Lord Anglesey has pledged himself for the maintenance of the tranquillity of Ireland during a general election.

The apprehensions which H.M. entertains must be strong indeed not to be removed, as indeed they have not been removed, by these assurances and opinions, submitted by individuals whose conduct, under the pressure of the difficulties in which they undertook and have continued to discharge the duties of their responsible situations, has so well merited H.M.'s confidence. He therefore owes it to his own character, he owes it to his claim to consistency, to state, fairly and without reserve, the considerations which have, upon due reflection, led him to waive his objections to a dissolution, or rather to subscribe to it, as the lesser of two evils.

The King does not deny that, in his general view of the situation and of the interests of this country, of its foreign relations, and of the influence of the state of the Continent, by reaction, upon the tranquillity and the prosperity of this country, he attaches the greatest and an almost paramount importance to the stability of his Government, and to the maintenance of a fixed system of policy, which shall inspire confidence at home and abroad. He feels deeply the mischiefs which must result, the danger which may arise, from the frequent change of men and measures; and these considerations have induced him to abandon his objections to much which, in less perilous times, might, in his opinion, have justified his adopting and pursuing a different course. Upon this principle H.M. had, upon his accession to the throne, made no change in his Councils; he gave his strenuous support to the Duke of Wellington's Administration, and he sincerely regretted its dissolution. Upon the same principle, he determined to give his utmost support to the Administration which Earl Grey was then called upon to form, and he cannot be said to have departed from that determination. . . .

The King does not disguise from Earl Grey and his confidential servants, that this apprehension of a frequent change of Government, so detrimental to the general interests of the country, has had a principal share in producing his determination to yield to the proposed measure of a dissolution of Parliament; and that, upon this occasion, he had considered very seriously whether the state of parties and the feeling of the country offered a fair prospect of making any permanent arrangement which might relieve him from the necessity of conceding that which is so repugnant to his feelings; and that he is satisfied, from the best attention he has been able to give to the subject, that he would not be justified in resorting to an alternative which, in his opinion, would not have secured him for many months against an event, the dread of which could alone have induced him to contemplate an arrangement so much at variance with the feelings he entertains towards his present Government, nor indeed have secured him against the recurrence of the alternative. . . .

109. Debate in the House of Lords, 21 June 1831

(*Mirror of Parliament*, June 1831, I, p. 20.)

The debate illustrates the continuing importance of the king's personal influence both in Parliament and with the electorate.

Lord Wharncliffe:–. . . Before the dissolution of Parliament, and even previous to any proceeding on the Reform Bill, complaints were made, and with reason, that the King's name had been most improperly used in connexion with the measure introduced by the Government. So completely, indeed, was the King's name identified with the Reform Bill, that it was generally asserted that a dissolution would inevitably follow if it were rejected. . . . Can they [Ministers] deny that the assumption that the King was favourable to Reform has been one of the principal means by which they carried the elections? In fact, when the friends of the Constitution, or, I will plainly say, the high Tories, presented themselves to the electors, requesting their support, they generally answered by a refusal couched in some such terms as these:–"We're for the King and the Reform Bill. He has shown us that he wishes to have it carried, and we shall, therefore, support it." . . .

The Marquess of Lansdowne:–. . . I . . . positively deny that the feelings of H.M. were engaged on this occasion, otherwise than that he was anxious to rebut the false and unconstitutional assertions which were on all sides made, to the effect that he entertained a want of confidence in, and was hostile to, the course pursued by his responsible advisers. It became essential that a contradiction should be put forth to this unfounded assertion, and that it should be clearly proved that the opinions and feelings of H.M. had gone along hand in hand, as they ought to do, with those of his accredited and constitutional advisers. . . .

The Earl of Mansfield:–. . . The Reform Bill is popular because it is said to be approved by the King. . . . This statement . . . had great effect in places which had long been represented by men of worth and talent. . . . A refusal was given to the candidates in plain terms–"We cannot vote against the King, we never did, we never will. . . . This is the King's Bill, and we must return members who will vote for it. . . ."

The Lord Chancellor (Brougham):–. . . It seems to me most strange that H.M.'s

Ministers should be accused of the abuse of the King's name by the very persons who have largely resorted to it against the measure of Reform. . . . Now, my Lords, I will appeal to you, if, when the people were told over and over again that H.M. would not dissolve Parliament, it was not a much more unjustifiable use of the King's name than that which is charged to have been made by his Ministers? . . . At the corner of every street the King has been the object of prints, conversations and songs. It was said of his Ministers, "You talk of dissolving Parliament. You cannot dissolve it. H.M. will not allow you." . . . It is ridiculous to speak of there having been recently an improper use made of the name of the Monarch; surely in 1784 and in 1806 [1807] the extent to which that liberty was taken was a thousand-fold greater. At this time the 'No Popery' cry was at its summit, and both in and out of the House the King's name was in constant use. . . .

(c) THE VETO

110. George III to William Pitt, 6 Feb. 1795

(Public Record Office, *Chatham Papers*, 103.)

This, and succeeding documents, illustrate the exercise of the royal veto over legislation in a preliminary form. No Government could initiate legislation without the sovereign's previous consent. George III, referring to the Catholic question, once said that he might be driven to live in a cottage, but he could not be driven to consent to that from which his conscience revolted.

Having yesterday, after the Drawing Room, seen the Duke of Portland, who mentioned the receipt of letters from the Lord Lieutenant of Ireland,[1] which to my greatest astonishment propose the total change of the principles of government which have been followed by every Administration in that Kingdom since the abdication of King James II, and consequently overturning the fabric that the wisdom of our forefathers esteemed necessary, and which the laws of this country have directed—and thus after no longer stay than three weeks in Ireland, venturing to condemn the labours of ages, and wanting an immediate adoption of ideas which every man of property in Ireland and every friend to the Protestant religion must feel diametrically contrary to those he has imbibed from his earliest youth.

Undoubtedly the Duke of Portland made this communication to sound my sentiments previous to the Cabinet meeting to be held tomorrow on this weighty subject. I expressed my surprise at the idea of admitting Roman Catholics to vote in Parliament, but chose to avoid entering farther into the subject, and only heard the substance of the propositions without giving my sentiments. But the more I reflect on this subject the more I feel the danger of the proposal, and therefore should not think myself free from blame if I did not put my thoughts on paper even in the present coarse shape, the moment being so pressing, and not sufficient time to arrange them in a more digested shape previous to the Duke of Portland's laying the subject before the Cabinet.

[1] Lord Fitzwilliam, one of the Portland Whigs, became Lord Lieutenant at the beginning of 1795, but he was recalled a few weeks later for, among other things, allowing a Catholic Relief Bill to be introduced into the Irish Parliament.

The above proposal is contrary to the conduct of every European Government, and I believe to that of every State on the globe . . . Ireland varies from most other countries by property residing almost entirely in the hands of the Protestants, whilst the lower classes of the people are chiefly Roman Catholics. The change proposed, therefore, must disoblige the greater number to benefit a few, the inferior orders not being of rank to gain personally by the change. That they may also be gainers, it is proposed that an army be kept constantly in Ireland, and also a kind of yeomanry, which in reality would be a Roman Catholic police corps, established, which would keep the Protestant interest under awe. . . .

English Government ought well to consider before it gives any encouragement to a proposition which cannot fail sooner or later to separate the two Kingdoms, or by way of establishing a similar line of conduct in this Kingdom adopt measures to prevent which my family was invited to mount the throne of this Kingdom in preference to the House of Savoy.[1] . . .

Besides the discontent and changes which must be occasioned by the dereliction of all the principles that have been held as wise by our ancestors, it is impossible to foresee how far it may alienate the minds of this Kingdom; for though I fear religion is but little attended to by persons of rank, and that the word toleration, or rather indifference to that sacred subject, has been too much admitted by them, yet the bulk of the nation has not been spoilt by foreign travels and manners, and still feels the blessing of having a fixed principle from whence the source of every tie to society and government must trace its origin.

I cannot conclude without expressing that the business is beyond the decision of any Cabinet of Ministers. . . .

111. William Pitt to George III, 31 Jan. 1801

(*Windsor MSS.* and Stanhope's *Life of Pitt*, III, App., p. xxiii.)

Mr. Pitt would have felt it, at all events, his duty, previous to the meeting of Parliament, to submit to your Majesty the result of the best consideration which your confidential servants could give to the important questions respecting the Catholics and Dissenters, which must naturally be agitated in consequence of the Union. The knowledge of your Majesty's general indisposition to any change of the laws on this subject would have made this a painful task to him, and it is become much more so by learning from some of his colleagues, and from other quarters, within these few days, the extent to which your Majesty entertains, and has declared, that sentiment.

He trusts your Majesty will believe that every principle of duty, gratitude, and attachment must make him look to your Majesty's ease and satisfaction, in preference to all considerations but those arising from a sense of what in his honest opinion is due to the real interest of your Majesty and your dominions. Under the impression of that opinion, he has concurred in what appeared to be the prevailing sentiments of

[1] In accordance with the terms of the Act of Settlement, 1701.

the majority of the Cabinet–that the admission of the Catholics to Parliament (from which latter the Dissenters are not now excluded) would, under certain conditions to be specified, be highly advisable, with a view to the tranquillity and improvement of Ireland, and to the general interest of the United Kingdom.

For himself, he is on full consideration convinced that the measure would be attended with no danger to the Established Church or to the Protestant interest in Great Britain or Ireland–that now the Union has taken place, and with the new provisions which would make part of the plan, it could never give any such weight in office, or in Parliament, either to Catholics or Dissenters, as could give them any new means (if they were so disposed) of attacking the Establishment: that the grounds on which the laws of exclusion now remaining were founded, have long been narrowed, and are since the Union removed: that those principles, formerly held by the Catholics, which made them considered as politically dangerous, have been for a course of time gradually declining, and, among the higher orders particularly, have ceased to prevail: that the obnoxious tenets are disclaimed in the most positive manner by the oaths which have been required in Great Britain, and still more by one of those required in Ireland, as the condition of the indulgences already granted, and which might equally be made the condition of any new ones: that if such an oath, containing (among other provisions) a denial of the power of absolution from its obligations, is not a security from Catholics, the sacramental test is not more so: that the political circumstances under which the exclusive laws originated, arising either from the conflicting power of hostile and nearly balanced sects, from the apprehension of a popish Queen or successor, a disputed succession and a foreign pretender, and a division in Europe between Catholic and Protestant powers, are no longer applicable to the present state of things: that with respect to those of the Dissenters who, it is feared, entertain principles dangerous to the Constitution, a distinct political test, pointed against the doctrine of modern Jacobinism, would be a much more just and more effectual security than that which now exists, which may operate to the exclusion of conscientious persons well affected to the State, and is no guard against those of an opposite description.

That, with respect to the Catholics of Ireland, another most important additional security, and one of which the effect would continually increase, might be provided by gradually attaching the Popish clergy to the Government, and, for this purpose, making them dependent for a part of their provision (under proper regulations) on the State, and by also subjecting them to superintendence and control.

That, besides these provisions, the general interests of the Established Church, and the security of the Constitution and Government, might be effectually strengthened by requiring the political test, before referred to, from the preachers of all Catholic or Dissenting congregations, and from the teachers of schools of every denomination.

It is on these principles Mr. Pitt humbly conceives a new security might be obtained for the civil and ecclesiastical Constitution of this country, more applicable to the present circumstances, more free from objection, and more effectual in itself, than any which now exists, and which would at the same time admit of extending such indulgences as must conciliate the higher orders of the Catholics, and by furnishing to a large class of your Majesty's Irish subjects a proof of the good will of the United Parliament, afford the best chance of giving full effect to the great object of the Union–that of tranquillising Ireland, and attaching it to this country.

It is with inexpressible regret, after all he now knows of your Majesty's sentiments, that Mr. Pitt troubles your Majesty thus at large with the general grounds of his opinion, and finds himself obliged to add that this opinion is unalterably fixed in his mind. It must, therefore, ultimately guide his political conduct, if it should be your Majesty's pleasure that, after thus presuming to open himself fully to your Majesty, he should remain in that responsible situation in which your Majesty has so long condescended graciously and favourably to accept his services. It will afford him, indeed, a great relief and satisfaction if he may be allowed to hope that your Majesty will deign maturely to weigh what he has now humbly submitted, and to call for any explanation which any parts of it may appear to require.

In the interval which your Majesty may wish for consideration, he will not, on his part, importune your Majesty with any unnecessary reference to the subject; and will feel it his duty to abstain himself from all agitation of this subject in Parliament, and to prevent it, as far as depends on him, on the part of others. If, on the result of such consideration, your Majesty's objections to the measure proposed should not be removed or sufficiently diminished to admit of its being brought forward with your Majesty's full concurrence, and with the whole weight of Government, it must be personally Mr. Pitt's first wish to be released from a situation which he is conscious that, under such circumstances, he could not continue to fill but with the greatest disadvantage.

At the same time, after the gracious intimation which has been recently conveyed to him of your Majesty's sentiments on this point, he will be acquitted of presumption in adding, that if the chief difficulties of the present crisis should not then be surmounted or very materially diminished, and if your Majesty should continue to think that his humble exertions could in any degree contribute to conducting them to a favourable issue, there is no personal difficulty to which he will not rather submit than withdraw himself at such a moment from your Majesty's service. He would even, in such case, continue for such a short further interval as might be necessary to oppose the agitation or discussion of the question, as far as he can consistently with the line to which he feels bound uniformly to adhere, of reserving to himself a full latitude on the principle itself, and to the temper and circumstances of the moment. But he must entreat that, on this supposition, it may be distinctly understood that he can remain in office no longer than till the issue (which he trusts on every account will be a speedy one) of the crisis now depending shall admit of your Majesty's more easily forming a new arrangement, and that he will then receive your Majesty's permission to carry with him into a private station that affectionate and grateful attachment which your Majesty's goodness for a long course of years has impressed on his mind–and that unabated zeal for the ease and honour of your Majesty's Government and for the public service which he trusts will always govern his conduct.

He has only to entreat your Majesty's pardon for troubling you on one other point, and taking the liberty of most respectfully, but explicitly submitting to your Majesty the indispensable necessity of effectually discountenancing, in the whole of the interval, all attempts to make use of your Majesty's name, or to influence the opinion of any individual or descriptions of men, on any part of this subject.

112. George III to William Pitt, 1 Feb. 1801

(Public Record Office, *Chatham Papers*, 104.)

I should not do justice to the warm impulse of my heart if I entered on the most unpleasant subject to [my] mind without first expressing that the cordial affection I have for Mr. Pitt, as well as high opinion of his talents and integrity, greatly add to my uneasiness on this occasion; but a sense of religious as well as political duty has made me, from the moment I mounted the throne, consider the oath that the wisdom of our forefathers have enjoined the Kings of this Kingdom to take at their coronation, and enforced by the obligation of instantly following it in the course of that ceremony with taking the holy sacrament, as so binding a religious obligation on me to maintain the fundamental maxims on which our Constitution are placed, namely, the Church of England being the established one, and that those who hold employments in the State must be members of it, and consequently obliged not only to take oaths against Popery, but to receive the holy communion agreeably to the rites of the Church of England.

This principle of duty must therefore prevent me from discussing any proposition tending to destroy this groundwork of our happy Constitution, and much more so that now mentioned by Mr. Pitt which is no less than the complete overthrow of the whole fabric.

... My opinions are not those formed on the moment, but such as I have imbibed for forty years, and from which I never can depart; but, Mr. Pitt once acquainted with my sentiments, his assuring me he will stave off the only question whereon I fear from his letter we can never agree–for the advantage and comfort of continuing to have his advice and exertions in public affairs I will certainly abstain from talking on this subject, which is the one nearest my heart. I cannot help if others pretend to guess at my opinions, which as yet I have never disguised; but if those who unfortunately differ with me will keep this subject at rest, I will on my part most correctly be silent also, but this restraint I shall put on myself alone from affection for Mr. Pitt, but farther I cannot go, for I cannot sacrifice my duty to any consideration.

Though I do not pretend to have the power of changing Mr. Pitt's opinion, when thus unfortunately fixed, yet I shall still hope his sense of duty will prevent his retiring from his present situation to the end of my life, for I can with great truth assert that I shall, from public as well as private considerations, feel great regret if I shall ever find myself obliged at any time, from a sense of religious and political duty, to yield to his entreaties of retiring from his seat at the Board of Treasury.

113. William Pitt to George III, 3 Feb. 1801

(Stanhope, *Life of Pitt*, III, App. p. xxx.)

Mr. Pitt cannot help entreating your Majesty's permission to express how very sincerely he is penetrated with the affecting expressions of your Majesty's kindness and goodness to himself on the occasion of the communication with which he has been under the necessity of troubling your Majesty. It is therefore with additional pain he feels himself bound to state that the final decision which your Majesty has formed on the great subject in question (the motives to which he respects and honours) and his own unalterable sense of the line which public duty requires from him, must make him consider the moment as now arrived when, on the principles which he has already explained, it must be his first wish to be released as soon as possible from his present situation. He certainly retains the same anxious desire, in the time and mode of quitting it, to consult as much as possible your Majesty's ease and convenience, and to avoid embarrassment. But he must frankly confess to your Majesty that the difficulty even of his temporary continuance must necessarily be increased, and may very shortly become insuperable, from what he conceives to be the import of one passage in your Majesty's note, which hardly leaves him room to hope that your Majesty thinks those steps can be taken for effectually discountenancing all attempts to make use of your Majesty's name, or to influence opinions on this subject, which he has ventured to represent as indispensably necessary during any interval in which he might remain in office. He has, however, the less anxiety in laying this sentiment before your Majesty because, independent of it, he is more and more convinced that your Majesty's final decision being once taken, the sooner he is allowed to act upon it the better it will be for your Majesty's service. He trusts, and sincerely believes that your Majesty cannot find any long delay necessary for forming an arrangement for conducting your service with credit and advantage, and that, on the other hand, the feebleness and uncertainty which is almost inseparable from a temporary Government must soon produce an effect both at home and abroad which might lead to serious inconvenience. Mr. Pitt trusts your Majesty will believe that a sincere anxiety for the future ease and strength of your Government is one strong motive for his presuming thus to press this consideration.

114. W. Huskisson (Under-Secretary for War) to Lord Carlisle, 12 Feb. 1801

(*Castle Howard MSS.*)

. . . You may implicitly rely upon what I mentioned to you yesterday respecting the light in which the King views the question. Had his objection rested solely on his sense of the inexpediency of the measure, it would (as on many other occasions) have been overcome; but on the other ground he is prepared for any extremity rather than yield up the point—and I leave to your Lordship and every well-meaning friend to the Catholic claim, and indeed to every honest Catholic himself, to decide whether, in the present state of the country and with this impression on the King's mind, the question ought to be pressed to a decision in Parliament with a certainty of its being defeated in the last stage, if not by the King of England residing in England, by the King of England exercising his constitutional right from his palace in Hanover. This (though too delicate to meet the public ear) I have very good reason to believe was the final determination; and unless a man can doubt the Minister's firmness, in a case where the preservation of his office, joined to so many important public considerations, called upon him to be firm, or his discernment as to what would be the issue of pressing the question in Parliament, I think he will agree that the line Mr. Pitt means to adopt, holding out on the one hand the strongest pledge of his future intentions and calling upon his friends to give the same pledge to the Catholics; but on the other deprecating immediate discussion, is one in which he ought to be supported.

115. George Rose to Mrs. Rose, 25 Feb. 1801

(*Pretyman MSS.*)

Rose was Joint Secretary of the Treasury, 1783–1801. He is here reporting a conversation with Pitt the previous night on the Catholic question.

... He said that he had intended to pledge himself never to come into office without full permission to propose that measure upon the ground of thinking that by so doing he should keep the Catholics of Ireland more quiet from the hope that they might succeed in their wishes at some future time. I argued warmly and strongly upon this point, and Mr. Pitt owned that even what had now happened to the King in some sort shook his determination. I endeavoured to persuade him on public grounds that he ought to leave himself at liberty, and indeed, in the very beginning of our conversation, we both declared that no *personal* or *private* considerations ought to weigh in such a situation as the present of the country. I told him that Opposition would endeavour to draw such a pledge from him; that in thinking of the Catholic interest he was not to forget the Protestants of England; that there was still, and ought to be, a great prejudice in this country against Popery; and that the state of things might become such as to leave only the alternative of his taking office without proposing that measure or of abandoning the country to be ruined by a Jacobin Government. In such a case, surely the higher duty of saving his country was to prevail over his wish to grant this indulgence, or if he pleased, this right, to the Catholics and Dissenters.

He would not absolutely promise not to pledge himself, but I am satisfied that he will not ... I hope ... that I strengthened his doubts, which had begun to rise in his own mind, concerning the prudence of pledging himself upon the Catholic question, or indeed any other. I entreated him to leave himself at liberty to act as the situation of the country should demand; that this was true patriotism, and that nothing else could secure to him the confidence of the people or give a chance of our being extricated from our present difficulties ... I mentioned to him my opinion that if he had proposed the measure, he could not have carried it in the House of Lords; that I believed all the Bishops would have been against it, and that their number was considerable; besides, that in a question where religion was concerned,

I thought that the unanimous opinion of the Bishops ought to have weight, and that it probably would influence many persons in the House of Lords. All this he admitted. I think I made some impression upon him as to this great point. The decision upon it in the Cabinet seems to have been hasty and not well considered. The Ministers perhaps found themselves under the necessity of bringing the matter to a point by the open declarations of his Majesty concerning it. . . .[1]

116. George III to William Pitt, 5 May 1804

(Public Record Office, *Chatham Papers*, 104.)

Addington's falling majority in the Commons (51 on 23 April, 37 on the 25th) convinced him that he could not go on, and on the 26th he informed the king of his intention to resign. On the 30th the king, through Eldon, the Lord Chancellor, called on Pitt to plan a new ministry. On 2 May, Pitt expressed his wish to form an all-Party Government, including Fox and Grenville.

The King has through the channel of the Lord Chancellor expressed to Mr. Pitt his approbation of that gentleman's sentiments of personal attachment to H.M., and his ardent desire to support any measure that may be conducive to the real interest of the King or of his royal family; but at the same time it cannot but be lamented that Mr. Pitt should have taken so rooted a dislike to a gentleman[2] who has the greatest claim to approbation from his King and country for his most diligent and able discharge of the duties of Speaker of the House of Commons for twelve years, and of his still more handsomely coming forward (when Mr. Pitt and some of his colleagues resigned their employments) to support his King and country when the most ill-digested and dangerous proposition was brought forward by the enemies of the Established Church. H.M. has too good an opinion of Mr. Pitt to think he could have given his countenance to such a measure, had he weighed its tendency with that attention which a man of his judgment should call forth when the subject under consideration is of so serious a nature; but the King knows how strongly the then two secretaries of state[3] who resigned at that period had allied themselves to the Roman Catholics: the former, by his private correspondence with a former lord lieutenant of Ireland,[4] shewed that he was become the follower of all the wild ideas of Mr. Burke, and the other, from obstinacy, his usual director.

The King can never forget the wound that was intended at the palladium of our Church Establishment, the Test Act, and the indelicacy, not to call it worse, of wanting H.M. to forego his solemn coronation oath. He therefore here avows that he shall not be satisfied unless Mr. Pitt makes as strong assurances of his determination to support that wise law, as Mr. Pitt in so clear a manner stated in 1796 in the House of Commons, *viz.* that the smallest alteration of that law would be a death wound to the British Constitution.

The whole tenor of Mr. Fox's conduct since he quitted his seat at the Board of

[1] Rose wrote to Bishop Tomline on 21 July 1801: "I was not aware that Mr. Pitt had made up his mind not to bring forward the Catholic question during H.M.'s life, either in or out of office." (*Pretyman Ms.*)
[2] Addington, Prime Minister 1801–1804; cr. Viscount Sidmouth 1805.
[3] The duke of Portland and Lord Grenville.   [4] Lord Fitzwilliam (1795).

Treasury,[1] when under age, and more particularly at the Whig Club and other factious meetings, rendered his expulsion from the Privy Council indispensable,[2] and obliges the King to express his astonishment that Mr. Pitt should one moment harbour the thought of bringing such a man before his royal notice. To prevent the repetition of it, the King declares [that] if Mr. Pitt persists in such an idea, or in proposing to consult Lord Grenville, H.M. will have to deplore that he cannot avail himself of the ability of Mr. Pitt with necessary restrictions. These points being understood, H.M. does not object to Mr. Pitt's forming such a plan for conducting the public business as may under all circumstances appear to be eligible; but should Mr. Pitt, unfortunately, find himself unable to undertake what is here proposed, the King will in that case call for the assistance of such men as are truly attached to our happy Constitution, and not seekers of improvements which, to all dispassionate men, must appear to tend to the destruction of that noble fabric which is the pride of all thinking minds and the envy of all foreign nations.

The King thinks it but just to his present servants to express his trust that as far as the public service will permit, he may have the benefit of their farther services.

117. William Pitt to George III, 6 May 1804

(Stanhope, *Life of Pitt*, IV, App. pp. x–xii.)

I had yesterday the honour of receiving from the Lord Chancellor your Majesty's letter, and am very sensible of your Majesty's condescension and goodness in deigning to renew the assurances of your approbation of the sentiments of duty and attachment which it has been my wish to manifest towards your Majesty. At the same time I cannot refrain from expressing the deep concern with which I observe the manner in which my sentiments appear in some respects to have been misunderstood, and the unfavourable impression which your Majesty seems to entertain respecting parts of my conduct. Your Majesty will, I trust, permit me in the first place to assure you that the opinions I have expressed respecting the person now holding the chief place in your Majesty's Government have not arisen from any sentiments of personal dislike to that gentleman; they have been formed wholly on the view of his public conduct, and rest on grounds which I have already taken the liberty of laying distinctly before your Majesty.

On the subject of the proposal made in 1801 respecting the Catholics, it has been far from my desire to renew any detailed discussion; but I feel it due to two of my former colleagues to express my persuasion that they were guided on that important occasion by very different motives from those which your Majesty has been led to impute to them; and in justice to myself I must beg leave to declare that my opinion on that subject was formed on the fullest deliberation, and that the measure then suggested appeared to me, for the reasons which I have submitted at large to your Majesty, to be as much calculated to confirm the security of the Established Church

[1] Fox was dismissed on 24 Feb. 1774.
[2] Fox's name was erased from the Privy Council in May 1798 for giving the toast "Our sovereign the people" at a Whig banquet.

as to promote the general interest of the Empire. My opinion of the propriety and rectitude of the measure at the time it was proposed remains unaltered; but other considerations, and sentiments of deference to your Majesty have led me since to feel it both a personal and public duty to abstain from again pressing that measure on your Majesty's consideration. The humble assurance of this determinaton on my part has been long since conveyed to your Majesty, and recently renewed; and to that assurance, without any addition or alteration, I must humbly beg leave to adhere.

It now remains for me to express the extreme regret with which I learn your Majesty's strong disapprobation of the proposal which, on a view of the present state of affairs and of political parties, I thought it my duty to submit to your Majesty, for forming at the present difficult crisis a strong and comprehensive Government, uniting the principal weight and talents of public men of all descriptions. I have already stated that if, on full consideration, your Majesty should object to any part of that proposal, I am ready to acquiesce in that decision, and submit myself to your Majesty's commands; but I, at the same time, expressed my hope that before your Majesty's final decision, I might be permitted to offer such farther explanation as the case may appear to require. On a point, therefore, of this high importance, I cannot but feel it an indispensable duty again to request that you would condescend personally to hear from me the explanation of those reasons which satisfy me that such a plan of Government is best calculated to promote the only objects which I have at heart on this occasion—the lasting ease and honour of your Majesty's Government, the security and prosperity of the country, and the general interest of Europe. Unless your Majesty should so far honour me with your confidence as to admit me into your presence for this purpose, I am grieved to say that I cannot retain any hope that my feeble services can be employed in any manner advantageous to your Majesty's affairs, or satisfactory to my own mind.

118. Spencer Perceval to Viscount Sidmouth (Lord President), 11 March 1807

(Perceval MSS.)

Perceval, who was at this time on the Opposition side of the House, had been Pitt's Attorney-General; in the Portland Ministry he was Chancellor of the Exchequer and Leader of the House of Commons.

I have received from my brother a communication of your Lordship's sentiments upon the subject of the Roman Catholic Officers Bill which is now before the House, and it has given me unfeigned pleasure to find that you mean to take so distinct and so decided a part in opposition to it. It is a measure which in my judgment is as ruinous as any which can be proposed upon the subject with which it is concerned. And I need not say, after this, how happy I shall be to concert with you and your friends upon the best mode of giving it the most effectual opposition. But I incline strongly to think that the advantage, which conversation certainly has over written communications upon such subjects, is by no means equal to the inconvenience which for our common object might be experienced, if our personal communications should be known to have taken place by the public, before some distinct and overt acts known to the public (such as your friends in the House of Commons, concurring with me in opposition to this Bill) should account for our so coming together. There might be a degree of jealousy excited, which it would require more explanation to allay, than could possibly be given beyond a few persons, and therefore, unless you have some very decided reason for wishing it to be otherwise, I would rather that you should communicate (till after Friday next) anything which you may wish me to know, by letter.

I cannot close this, without suggesting to you, what occurs to me, and has occurred to others of my friends. It appears to me of infinite importance to the cause, that the King should take care to set himself quite right with his Ministers–that previous to their committing themselves on the second reading of the Bill in the House of Commons, he should distinctly tell them, (Lord Grenville at least if not others) in the manner however the most conciliatory, and least offensive, that whatever might be their conclusions from anything which had passed from him before, he must tell them that he never could give his consent to the Bill–that he would do nothing underhand upon the subject, but that he should make no secret of his opinion, but would communicate it to every one whom he met with without the least injunction of secrecy, but on the contrary with an expression of a wish that his opinion should be known; and that it should be known, that that opinion neither had changed nor could change upon this subject.

This communication may perhaps bring the Ministers, if they are not as mad as I fear they will make the King, to reconsider this absurd measure of theirs–and possibly give the King a chance of retaining them in his Councils, without being forced upon this great question–and though it may have this effect yet, I most decidedly wish that it may be made. It is obvious if it has not that effect, and the King should be driven to the extremity of either disposing of the measure by his friends in your House, or by his own negative, it will make his case complete with the country, leave no possible charge of duplicity, or underhand dealing, no complaint of political intrigue. It will shew a plain case of an honest mind, feeling sensibly and sincerely, and acting honestly and openly upon a great question upon which his conscience will not enable him to surrender his opinion, and with such a case the country will be and must be with him; and he under any circumstances which may then occur will be able to find inclination and power to support him. Now it appears to me that nobody can suggest this line to the King so advantageously as yourself; and as he does not leave town, I understand, till after the Drawing Room to morrow, if you should agree with me perhaps you may have the opportunity of communicating it.

I place much reliance upon the distinct explanation with Ministers; but it is material that they should be deprived of the means of saying that he had not so explained himself, and also that they should know that it was his purpose to express his mind fully and openly to every one.

I would wish the thing to be done if possible in such a manner that even if he and his Ministers should part upon the subject they should part with as little irritation, and mutual ill will as possible.

119. Viscount Howick to Earl Fitzwilliam, 17 March 1807

(Howick and Fitzwilliam MSS.)

The papers will have informed you that things had taken a very unfavourable turn with respect to the Bill which I had introduced into Parliament for the admission of Dissenters from the Church of England into the army and navy. I should not have left you to collect your information from these uncertain sources of intelligence, or under the suspense and anxiety which they must necessarily occasion, if a great pressure, both of parliamentary and official business, very much increased by this new embarrassment, had not made it absolutely impossible for me to enter into the detailed explanation which I wished to give you. The Bill was introduced with the acquiescence of the King, after a strong objection in the first instance. Between the first proposal and its introduction into Parliament, a doubt had arisen as to the under-standing which the King might have of the extent of the measure. It was apprehended, and this point was particularly urged by Lord Sidmouth, who declared that to be the ground on which he had himself given his consent, that the King might have con-ceived that it was to be strictly modelled after the Irish Act of 1793; that therefore the omission of the exceptions contained in that Act gave an extension to the measure beyond what the King might consider himself as having consented to. Lord Sidmouth at the same time declared his objection to any concession beyond what had been granted by the Irish Parliament. To set the matter quite clear, it was determined that I should write, in Lord Spencer's absence, a Despatch to the Lord Lieutenant, enclosing the new clauses (it being at that time intended to carry this measure into effect by enactments in the Mutiny Bill) and referring to the original Despatch which was written to Ireland, after the King's consent had been obtained, in such a manner as to make it impossible that the whole bearing and extent of the intended concession should escape his observation. This was accordingly done; the Despatch came back from Windsor without comment or objection, and was of course sent to the Lord Lieutenant. The day after it went the King came to town, and when I saw him in the Closet he said that he understood the new Bill to be the same as the Irish Act. I expressed my surprise at this misapprehension after the Despatch which the King had seen and authorised me to send on the preceding day, explained to him the difference, with the reasons of it, and ended by expressing my hope that, upon the whole, this change would not produce any further objection from him. He said he was sorry for it; he was no Catholic; that, if his opinion was asked, he must say that he disapproved of it; that he had consented to its being brought into Parliament and nothing more. I left him with general expressions of regret for the difference of our opinions, but certainly under an impression that he had not withdrawn the reluctant consent which he had originally given.

From this time, however, the measures of active opposition commenced. Lord Sidmouth tendered his resignation (it since appears that he had had communication with Perceval) and the King on Wednesday last signified to Lord Grenville his positive objection to the Bill.

Since that period, we have necessarily been taken up in considering what we should do. The Bill of course was suspended, and at last we came to a determination, in which my opinion yielded to that of others, to abandon the Bill; reserving to ourselves the liberty, both on that occasion, and on the Catholic Petition, if it should be presented, to declare openly the sentiments we entertain, and also to propose such measures in future as the state of Ireland might render necessary. To this, which was communicated in a regular Minute, on Sunday, an answer is come this morning requiring an absolute abandonment of the last condition, and that our acquiescence should be conveyed in writing. In other words, that we should bind ourselves by a written engagement not to propose, in any case, any further concessions to the Catholics. To this there can of course be only one answer. We are to meet (that is we who agree on this question, our late meetings having been so restricted) tonight, to prepare an answer, and the Government must be considered as broke up.

Of the situation in which we are now placed I am sure you will approve; probably more than of our previously yielding to the opposition of the Court. When that measure was discussed, Lord Holland, Windham, and myself alone were for immediate resignation, and it was left so much personally to me, that I could not venture to incur the responsibility of dissolving the Government, with a view to all the consequences which may ensue. Lord Spencer, however, who was not in town, upon hearing of our having determined to yield as to the Bill, expressed so strong a disapprobation of that resolution, and so positive a determination to resign himself, that, even if the King had not determined the matter for us, I think we should at all events have found ourselves compelled to come to that resolution at last.

. . . I do not mean to impute anything dishonourable to Lord Sidmouth, though I certainly consider him as having broke up the Government.

120. Spencer Perceval to Lord Liverpool (Home Secretary), 19 Sept. 1809
(Perceval MSS.)

As you desired me to give you a line upon my return from Windsor, I sit down for that purpose. But in the first place I must state that not arriving here till past 4 oclock, I found the summons to the Cabinet at ½ past 3 which as I could not possibly attend till past 5 oclock, I am obliged to neglect. As the King kept me for full an hour and half, and as his conversation was very precise, distinct and continued, it is impossible to attempt giving you any full idea of it. . . . He told me he must give me an account of Canning's conversation, which he called the most extraordinary he ever heard. He went through it with wonderful accuracy. I will endeavour at another time to give you the particulars. All that is now important, is that in the King's impression, and in mine also from his relation of it, it was very little different from his letter except that it was more explicit and more strong—and except that he distinctly stated to the King as his opinion that the Duke of Portland's health was such that it was not possible he should retain his situation. The points in which he was more precise were that the Minister who must in these times be necessarily in the House of Commons, must also necessarily have *complete authority* over all other *Departments*—that at the present time he and I were the only persons that *could* be this

Minister, not only in the present Administration, *but in any part of the House*–That he should not be surprised or displeased in the least if the King preferred me, that it would be the most rational thing of the two, it would hardly require a new patent, only the insertion of a new name in the old one–But that if H.M. honoured him with his commands *he would readily undertake it*–"Not," said the King, "that he would consider of it, that he would advise with others, as you or any other person would have said, but he was fully prepared to undertake it." "Now," continued H.M., "I do not believe, if he was to be the Minister, that there is any one of you who would continue with him, and he does not seem at all to think of that." I told him I had no authority to say or means of knowing that none of his present servants would continue; I thought some certainly would not, but I could not pretend to speak for any one but myself. I told him that when I had penned the passage in the Minute in which it was said that H.M. might collect from Mr. Canning's letter that he would undertake it, I had been almost afraid that I might have drawn an inference beyond what might have been intended. "Oh no," he said, "he stated it to me most distinctly, and said that the Ministers who retired when Mr. Pitt died, had done in his opinion very unwisely; that he was not then in the Cabinet, but that he should [have] advised otherwise." I said I had never heard before that he had thought so, but I could not pretend to say what his opinion was at that time, but if he had not said that he would have advised their continuance, I should rather have suspected the contrary to be his opinion. These are I think the most material points in the King's narrative of Canning's conversation. The comment and observation upon it I have no time for now, nor for many other particulars which I could state but for want of time. The account of this narrative and the observations upon it being over, he then proceeded to the subject of the Minute of Cabinet. He said he would consider of it very maturely, could not deliver any opinion then; I assured him I had not expected one, I only thought he might wish to see me, and converse upon various points of it. He was very glad I had come, he said, was glad to talk to me upon it, that he should talk to the Lord Chancellor and Lord Liverpool and others upon it tomorrow. He knew indeed that they could not represent it in any other view than had been done in the paper, but it was a decision *for life*, every thing was at stake, and he must not come to that decision without the maturest consideration–that he did not know how to make up his mind to it–He seemed disappointed at the [   ] leading to a communication both with Lord Grey and *Lord Grenville*; the latter evidently formed, as we anticipated, the great objection. He could do nothing towards it he said till he was satisfied upon one point (the Catholic question). When he was advised last to send to Mr. Pitt, by the Lord Chancellor, he had required to know expressly from Mr. Pitt that he would not bring forward that question–that he had the most direct assurance from Mr. Pitt in writing; he knew he had his letter, he had been looking for it–(he then digressed into an account of his papers. He was arranging them all regularly–that up to 1802 they were quite perfect–and from the commence-ment of the late Administration to August last, and that from that period he could turn to any paper in a minute)–but he said he should find Mr. Pitt's paper–it was an express assurance–and further he said when he saw Mr. Pitt, he not only confirmed the assurance but added that he would not only not bring it forward, but that for private reasons of his own, he would oppose it, whoever brought it forward. This he says he voluntarily said to him; it was more than he expected, it surprised him, it appeared to be an expression of his own opinion, that he might have paid him (the King) the compliment of supposing that the determination was taken out of compliment to him, but he stated it to be for private reasons of his own. He must he said have a similar assurance now; that this was a point he could not give up in honour, nor more he said could I–that I as well as he had both given our opinions upon that point solemnly to the country, that we could not give them up. I agreed that we could not give them up, that his servants were unanimous in their opinion that he must be protected against that question–that it was with that view and upon that principle that they had humbly given H.M. the opinion which that paper contained –that they thought under the circumstances of the times, that it was the most effectual, if not the only effectual means of protecting him–that if Lord Grey and Lord Grenville consented to form a Government with us, who were known to have such decided opinions upon that subject, they must come into that Government with a perfect knowledge that that measure could never be a measure of that Government, that this would necessarily be *implied* from the very formation of the Government. It must be *expressed*, he said, or he could not be satisfied. I stated that it did not appear to me possible to expect that Lords Grey and Grenville could, as men of honour, consent, after all that had been said upon this subject, to have even the question put to them to require an express declaration upon this. "Then," said he, "I am driven to the wall, and would be deserted." I assured H.M. again that the object of his present servants was to protect him, they would not desert him–that the opinion we had submitted to H.M., was, as we thought, the best mode of protecting him–that if we made an ineffectual attempt to form an Administration alone, we should be overthrown and would not be able to stand between him and the wall. Then, said he (rather hastily but very collectedly and firmly), they should take the Government to themselves, he would have nothing to do with it, they should not have his name. "Oh, Sir," said I, "what an extremity your Majesty is contemplating! what would become of your Majesty's country?" No country had a right to expect a man should give up his own honour–his honour was in his own keeping; if his country deserted him he could not help it. I again assured H.M. that deserting him was the last they ever thought of–but we conceived that the combined Government which we had an idea of forming was to be formed by H.M.'s present servants and with such a proportion of them that, having a full share in the efficient offices, we should, by refusing at any time, as we should refuse to concur in any measure of that description, be enabled to put a stop to it by bringing the Government to an end–that they would feel this, and that they therefore would naturally not think of attempting it. He then asked what reason we had for thinking they would form such a Government. I said that we could not fully without making an overture to them, have found their real sentiments, but that we had reason from various conversations of their friends to think it probable they would not generally object, though undoubtedly we could not tell in what manner they would expect it to be made. He asked what these conversations were; I told him–Lord Henry Petty's to Lord Euston–Lord Grey to Colonel Gordon, Lord G. Cavendish to Lord W. Bentinck. But then, he said, what is to be done if they refuse? I said we had not omitted to think of that, but that the manner of their refusing, and the grounds on which they refused might be so various, and it would depend so much upon them, that there was no possibility beforehand of distinctly saying what would in that event be to be done till the event occurred. Then he asked how it was to be done. I suggested the letter to both at once, stating H.M.'s commands that they should communicate with us and that we should jointly consider on the formation of a Government, and that we had his command also to acquaint them that if they wished to see H.M. first, that H.M. would see them. That would be very hard upon him, he said; he had no means of letting the world know what might pass, they might tell their own story. The last time he had the good fortune to have it in writing; that would not do, he could not see them, but he knew from us what they were prepared to do; that he was the worst person in the whole world to settle any point with them; he was sure he should quarrel with them at the first setting out. I said that certainly would not answer any purpose; that it was certainly an important consideration that H.M. might think of, but that we had considered that it would be better to offer them the alternative. Then he asked whether I thought I alone should communicate with them, or I and any one else. I said that as there were to be two of them, I thought it preferable that there should be some one joined with me. He agreed in this and suggested the Chancellor as the person. I explained the Chancellor's objection from the various instances of personal conflict in which he had been engaged with them. "What," says he impatiently, "do you think I could be advised to form a Government without the Chancellor?" By no means, I said. I thought that the present Chancellor must be one of the Government–that your Lordship must form another, that I considered this as indispensable. He then seemed to be satisfied as to the reason for not joining the Chancellor with me, and canvassed the question whether it should be you or Lord Bathurst, or who else, and this as well as other questions were left open for our further consideration. . . . He concluded however with saying that he could not yet form any opinion–that he must take time to think of it. He thanked me for coming down to him, and for giving him, as he expressed it, that opportunity of *thinking aloud* upon it.

Upon the whole I never knew him in any conversation which I have had the honour of having with him, so collected, so distinct, or any thing like so methodical in the view which he took of the different parts of the subjects on which he conversed. . . .

121. George IV's Memorandum for the Cabinet, 8 Aug. 1827

(*Letters of George IV*, ed. A. Aspinall, III (1938), p. 275.)

This was the day of Canning's death.

The King recommends the Cabinet to reorganise the Government.
The King has no desire to dissolve the present Government, provided they can agree in those principles of governing the country upon which the King has acted

from the time the King undertook the Regency, up to the period of the King's coming to the Crown, and from that hour to the present.

The King distinctly stated to poor Mr. Canning (on his becoming Minister) that the King had no desire of forming what is termed an exclusive Tory Government, as in that case it would have deprived the King of the distinguished talents of many members of the present Cabinet. Nevertheless there was a distinct understanding between the King and his late lamented Minister (Mr. Canning) on many very important points.

The King will begin, for example, by mentioning the question of parliamentary reform. The King joined with Mr. Canning in giving his decided negative to that destructive project.

The King could not of course require of Mr. Canning to abjure his strong and settled opinions upon the subject of Catholic emancipation: but there was a distinct understanding that the King's conscientious feelings should not be disturbed upon that painful question, upon which the King's opinions are unalterably fixed: and moreover, if at any time this question was to be forced upon Mr. Canning, from that moment the Cabinet was to be considered as dissolved.

If the present Government therefore chose to proceed upon the basis thus framed by Mr. Canning, the King would then place Lord Goderich at the head of the Treasury.

The King desires to have the decision of the Cabinet with as little delay as the pressing circumstances of the case will admit of.

122. Lord Ellenborough's Diary, Jan.–March 1829

(*Lord Ellenborough's Political Diary, 1828–30*, ed. Colchester, I.)

17 Jan. Cabinet. The Duke gave a detail of all he had been doing during the summer on the subject of the Catholic question. On Thursday last, the 15th, the King relieved the Government from the sort of understanding which prevailed when it was formed, and the Catholic question may now be considered as a Government question, the King only desiring that he may know what is the opinion of the Cabinet as to the details of the intended measure, and be enabled to exercise his judgment upon them. . . . [I, pp. 297–8.]

22 Feb. Cabinet at 2. The Duke said his conversation with the King had been very disagreeable. The King begged he would not speak to the Household and seemed to intimate that they were to vote against the Government. . . . [p. 361.]

An Oxford voter, who had promised to vote for Peel, wrote to him to say that, as he understood the King was hostile, he must retract his promise. This letter the Duke to-day sent to the King, to show him the evil effects of unguarded conversation. . . . [p. 362.]

26 Feb. Cabinet at 4. The Duke said he had an interview of $5\frac{1}{4}$ hours with the King. The King ultimately yielded all points, even to the extent of desiring the Duke of Cumberland to leave England. The King declared himself more satisfied with the Bill than with anything he had seen. He had great unwillingness to write *himself* to the Household, desiring their attendance in the House of Lords during the Catholic measures, but he had no objection to the Duke of Wellington writing to them in his name. That is, he acquiesced in this, but he did not much like it.

Accordingly the Duke read to the Cabinet a letter which he proposed to submit to the King before he sent it, in which, referring to his general request that they would attend the House, made to them at the beginning of the session, he informed them, that it being the intention of H.M.'s Ministers to introduce measures in conformity with the gracious recommendation in H.M.'s Speech, he had H.M.'s commands to desire their attendance in their places during the progress of those measures. . . . [pp. 366-367.]

The Duke represents his interview with the King to have been very painful indeed. The King was in a very agitated state, and even spoke of abdicating. The Duke said it was the more painful in consequence of the very peremptory language he was obliged to hold to him. However, the King was very kind, and kissed him when he left him. . . . [I, p. 368.]

2 March. . . . The Duke called at Windsor on his return to town. . . . The King confessed he had looked round, and could find no Minister but himself. He then spoke of abdicating, and said he should retire to Hanover with his present income. He had thought of desiring Lord Bexley to take a message to that effect to the House of Lords. The Duke told him any person bearing such a message must advise it, and he would find no one willing to make himself responsible. . . . [I, p. 372.]

4 March. . . . Cabinet dinner at Lord Bathurst's. The Duke having gone down to Windsor with the Chancellor and Peel, they joined us at a quarter before 10. The Duke told us that the result of the interview was that Peel would to-morrow declare in the House of Commons that he could not bring on the Relief Bill because he was no longer Minister. The King talked for six hours. The Duke says he never witnessed a more painful scene. He was so evidently insane. He had taken some brandy-and-water before he joined them, and sent for some more, which he continued to drink during the conference. During six hours they did not speak 15 minutes. The King objected to every part of the Bill. He would not hear it. The Duke most earnestly entreated him to avoid all reference to his Coronation oath. The King at one moment talked of postponing the consideration of the Bill till he had seen the Archbishop of Canterbury and the Bishop of London—but he gave up that idea of himself. It seems that he really does not know what his Coronation oath is. He has confused it with the oath of Supremacy. . . . [I, pp. 376-377.]

4 March. . . . It is impossible not to feel the most perfect contempt for the King's conduct. We should be justified in declaring we will have no further intercourse with one who has not treated us like a gentleman. [I, p. 377.]

5 March: At a quarter past 12 received a message from the Duke to go to him immediately. I went, thinking he had to announce the King's insanity. He, however, had to announce a complete victory. A quarter of an hour after he got home last night he received a letter from the King declaring that to avoid the *mischief of having no Administration* he consented to the Bill proceeding as a measure of Government, but with infinite pain. The Duke immediately wrote an answer, in which he stated clearly and strongly his understanding of the King's letter. The King replied that his understanding of it was correct. . . . [1, pp. 378–379.]

6 *March*. . . . Lord Bathurst said to-day he believed the King to be quite capable of *pretending* to be mad in order to carry his point. His yielding only two hours after he had dismissed the Duke looks a little like it. . . . [1, p. 381.]

123. William IV to Earl Grey, 4 Feb. 1831

(*Correspondence of Earl Grey with William IV*, ed. Earl Grey, 1 (1867), pp. 96–97.)

The Cabinet committee's plan of Parliamentary Reform is on pp. 461–463 of the above volume. Among the proposals was the adoption of secret voting, which the Cabinet rejected.

. . . The King does not deny that he hails that rejection as removing an insuperable bar from his assent to the proposed measure; and he is induced thus pointedly to notice the proposal of introducing *election by ballot*, in order to declare that nothing should ever induce him to yield to it, or to sanction a practice which would, in his opinion, be a protection to concealment, would abolish the influence of fear and shame, and would be inconsistent with the manly spirit and the free avowal of opinion which distinguish the people of England. H.M. need scarcely add that his opposition to the introduction of another, yet more objectionable, proposal,–the adoption of *universal suffrage*, one of the wild projects which have sprung from revolutionary speculation,–would have been still more decided. . . .

(d) THE ROYAL INFLUENCE OVER THE FRAMING OF POLICY

124. George III to William Pitt, 28 June 1800, 6.20 a.m.

(Public Record Office, *Chatham Papers*, 104.)

. . . I own not approving of the Minute of Cabinet of Thursday, as it will encourage Austria in treating with the enemy instead of in making exertions to recover the mischief that may have arisen, but of which we do not at present know the true extent. No disaster can make me think the treating for peace either wise or safe whilst the French principles subsist. An armed neutrality is the only thing that can be obtained, and that I look up[on] as most fatal, for no confidence can be placed in the present French Government. My opinion is formed on principle, not on events, and therefore is not open to change.

125. William Pitt to Henry Dundas (Secretary for War), 25 July 1800

(*Clements Library MSS., Ann Arbor*.)

On the 24th the king rejected the Cabinet's advice that a combined operation should be attempted either against the enemy's fleet and arsenals at Ferrol or, alternatively, against Cadiz. Sir Ralph Abercromby was to command the troops. Subsequently the king abandoned his opposition.

I am as much astonished and hurt as you can be at the note you have sent me. But I am persuaded the difficulty cannot be persisted in; and I cannot help thinking that, to save time, it would be much best if instead of waiting for any Cabinet, you were either to write immediately to the King or go tomorrow to Windsor, to lay before him a temperate statement of the various considerations to which he cannot be insensible. These seem shortly to be, first, that if he means that all the army which it has cost so much expense and unusual exertion to form, is to be kept inactive during the remainder of the campaign, he must expect to see the spirit of the country let down, the Government justly censured, and the impatience and clamour for peace *on any terms*, increasing every hour. Secondly (what you state in your note) that the expedition to Belleisle would have taken away as large a force, and would still have left sufficient here. Thirdly, that the data for thinking of the expedition, and the importance of striking *some* blow, and the opinion of a reputable officer that *this* is likely to be practicable, which are surely grounds sufficient for doing all that is proposed–*viz.* to refer it for decision on consultation between your Admiral and General, when they have acquired all the information they can. These topics calmly stated must I trust have their effect. If not there is only one left in which I must most decidedly join, that of begging H.M. to find servants whose judgment he can trust more than ours.

126. George III to Lord Hawkesbury (Foreign Secretary), 30 Sept. 1801, 1.55 p.m.

(British Museum Additional MSS. 38190, f. 2.)

The King has received the Minute of Cabinet on the proposed peace with France. To repeat his doubts whether any confidence can be placed in any agreement to be made with that country till it has a settled Government would be in reality a stop to all negotiation. He will not oppose the concluding peace, though he cannot place any reliance on its duration, but trusts such a peace establishment will be kept up as may keep this country on a respectable footing, without which our situation would be most deplorable.

(e) THE ROYAL CONTROL OF PATRONAGE

127. William Pitt to George III, 22 Jan. 1805

(Windsor Archives, 11546.)

The bishop of Norwich, Dr. Manners-Sutton, now succeeded Dr. Moore as archbishop.

It is with great reluctance that Mr. Pitt at any time reverts to any proposal which does not appear to meet your Majesty's wishes, but he considers it on every account his duty not to disguise from your Majesty how much his feelings are wounded and his hopes of contributing to your Majesty's service impaired by your Majesty's apparent disregard of his recommendation of the Bishop of Lincoln to succeed to the Archbishopric of Canterbury. . . . Your Majesty's refusal to comply with his request can hardly be understood by himself, and will certainly not be understood by the public in any other light than as a decisive mark of your Majesty's not honouring him with that degree of weight and confidence which his predecessors have enjoyed, and without which your Majesty must be sensible how impossible it is, especially under the present circumstances, that he can conduct your Majesty's affairs with advantage.

Mr. Pitt still flatters himself that if your Majesty condescends to weigh these considerations, it cannot be your Majesty's intention to reduce him to so mortifying and distressing a situation. . . .

128. Lord Bathurst to Lord Harrowby, 2 Feb. 1805

(Harrowby MSS.)

Bathurst was Master of the Mint, Harrowby in the Cabinet without portfolio. Addington had recently been given a peerage (title, Viscount Sidmouth).

. . . I entirely agree with you in all the observations you make respecting the bad effects which the constant interference of the King in the distribution of patronage must produce to any Government. All this was to be foreseen. He has, as all Kings must have, a natural inclination for it. During Addington's Administration he became accustomed to it, and illness has left him more eager to oblige, and more impatient of resistance. It requires great management to oppose this, and management of this sort is what Pitt's virtues and infirmities peculiarly disqualify him. . . .

From what I hear, the King has been alarmed by what has passed, and sees the difficulty of forming a Government, since Addington's advancement, if Pitt were to resign. A person very near him lamented to me a few days ago the embarrassments which the King's desire of obliging those he was in the habit of seeing must soon produce. But still I am afraid it will always be a battle. . . .

129. Lord Grenville to George III, 31 Jan. 1806

(Hist. MSS. Comm., Dropmore Papers, VIII, p. 2.)

The 'persons above-named' were the Cabinet ministers. Several new peerages and baronetcies were created in February, and there were promotions in the peerage. Fitzwilliam refused a marquessate.

. . . It would at all times be the earnest wish of the persons above-named to avoid to the utmost of their power submitting to your Majesty proposals for extending the peerage. But, in the first formation of a new Government, they trust that your Majesty would not be disinclined to honour with that dignity a very few persons, not exceeding four or five at the utmost, all of them of such rank and station in life as seem to point them out as unexceptionable objects for your Majesty's favour in that respect.

130. William Windham (Secretary for War) to Lord Grenville, 15 May 1806

Sir J. C. Hippisley, M.P., was not appointed a member of the Board of Trade.

. . . As to the King, after the many *gulps* that he has taken, the peerages, the earldoms, the baronetcies, the jobs without number that he has swallowed, it will be very odd if he should be choked at last by appointing a person who is a baronet, a member of

Parliament, a man of nine or ten thousand a year honourably acquired, and of marked qualifications for the situation in question, to a seat in the Committee of Council. [*Ibid.*, p. 140.]

131. Lord Grenville to Viscount Howick, 24 Sept. 1806

... I am persuaded there can be no difficulty about Lord Fitzwilliam's being made a Marquis. Baronets are more difficult. We have made two batches since we came in, and I have a list of I know not how many more to make whenever it can decently be done. [*Ibid.*, p. 354.]

132. Sir Henry Torrens to Lord Liverpool, 16 July 1817

(*British Museum Additional MSS.* 38573, f. 136.)

Torrens was Military Secretary to the Prince Regent.

Your Lordship will remember my having taken the liberty at the earnest desire of my friend and kinsman Lieut. General Orr, to mention to you his wish and ambition to be created a Baronet about a year ago. I then apprised your Lordship of the probability that this object would be brought under your consideration through another and more weighty channel. And I was happy to find from Colonel McMahon that in compliance with a message through him from the Prince Regent, your Lordship had been pleased to hold out the prospect of General Orr's success, with other candidates whose views to a similar promotion was intended to take effect at the period when you might think it expedient to submit the measure to H.R.H. ... Seeing that my friend is labouring under great anxiety upon a point which he has many reasons for being anxious to attain, I am induced to take the liberty of addressing you. ...

[Lord Liverpool's reply, 16 July 1817.] ... I perfectly recollect Colonel McMahon giving me a memorandum of several names for consideration, of which his was one – but I never held out the most remote expectation that this application could be complied with; and though I have every personal goodwill to General Orr, I cannot find in his case any of those special grounds on which alone I feel I am warranted, after the great augmentation which has taken place in the baronetage, to recommend a further increase in his instance. ...

I will further confess to you that I never can approve applications being made in the manner in which the one in question has been made. I think on every principle the Ministers are the proper channel to Carlton House, and not Carlton House to the Ministers. If the Prince Regent has very strong personal wishes, he has constant opportunities of expressing them to me or to my colleagues. It is very natural that those who are about his family or have been personally connected with him should occasionally make direct applications to H.R.H., but I have felt it a public duty to discountenance such applications when the individuals applying can have no special claim to address themselves immediately to him instead of to his public and responsible servants. ... [*Ibid.*, f. 138.]

133. George IV to the earl of Liverpool, 13 April 1821

(British Museum Additional MSS. 38190, f. 37.)

It is with considerable regret that the King has receiv'd Lord Liverpool's letter of yesterday, and the more, as the King feels that ever since the appointment of Lord Liverpool as his First Minister he has not merely shewn an uniform desire not to thwart any views of Lord Liverpool or of his friends in the disposal of the patronage of the Crown, but on the contrary, to oblige Lord Liverpool and to give every support in his power to an Administration created by himself, the King has yielded every personal feeling.

In illustration of which the King need only draw Lord Liverpool's attention to two very recent events amongst numberless others, namely, the removal of Lord Fife[1] (a measure certainly painful to the King's private feelings) and the disregard of the King's desire (convey'd to Lord Liverpool through Sir Benjamin Bloomfield) "that Mr. B. Paget should succeed to the office of Receiver-General." Notwithstanding which, the appointment of another individual (however eligible) took place *without further reference to the King*.

Under so extraordinary a proceeding, did the King withhold his signature to the warrant of appointment? Or did the King call upon Lord Liverpool *to forfeit his promise or his word*? The King might also add the instance in which he sacrific'd the most painful personal feelings and opinions to the advice and earnest desire of Lord Liverpool "that the King should not accept the resignation of Mr. Canning, but suffer him to remain in his Councils," in spite of the very unwarrantable conduct of that gentleman (as a member of the Cabinet) in his place in Parliament.[2]

The question of this nomination to the vacant canonry of Windsor does not rest upon *the* selection which the King has made for that appointment; nor does the King doubt the sincerity of Lord Liverpool's desire to make a suitable provision in lieu of *that* destin'd by the King for Mr. Sumner. But there are principles paramount to all other considerations which will ever guide the King in his course through life. Lord Liverpool, in his desire to relieve the King from any embarrassment which the present case may occasion, appears solely to have directed his view to the policy or the impolicy of this nomination, and wholly to have disregarded that *vital part* of the transaction which involves *the good faith and honour of his Sovereign*.

The King therefore sees no reason to alter his determination of appointing Mr. Sumner to the vacant canonry of Windsor; and, however willing the King might be to give up his own opinions to Lord Liverpool's wishes, *it is no longer a question* of the propriety of this little appointment (as the King has already stated), but whether the King's word *is to be held sacred or is to be of no avail*.

The King acquainted Lord Liverpool that the appointment was given by *himself*

[1] Lord Fife, a Lord of the Bedchamber, was dismissed for voting against the Government for the repeal of the malt tax.

[2] On 7 June 1820 Canning declared in the House of Commons that he felt an unaltered regard and affection for Queen Caroline, who was about to be charged with adultery with her Italian courier, Pergami; that if there had been any injustice meditated towards her, no consideration on earth would have induced him to be a party to it, and he would take no part in the proceedings against her. He tendered his resignation, but he was required to remain in office. He resigned in December.

alone, unsolicited by Mr. Sumner, or at the instance of any private friend of the King's or of Mr. Sumner. His merit and his character were his *only* recommendations, and the King thinks such recommendations more calculated to do honour and to give satisfaction than to give 'umbrage' to the Church.[1]

134. The earl of Liverpool to George IV, 24 July 1821, and reply

(*Letters of George IV, 1812–30*, ed. A. Aspinall, II, p. 448.)

Because of Lady Conyngham's intrigues with the Opposition and of her interference with ecclesiastical patronage, Lord Liverpool refused to acquiesce in the appointment of her husband either as Lord Chamberlain (in succession to Lord Hertford) or as Master of the Horse. Eventually he was given the office of Lord Steward.

Lord Liverpool is anxious to receive H.M.'s pleasure on the vacancy occasioned by the resignation of the Marquis of Hertford. Lord Liverpool has no personal nor political wishes on the subject, and he is earnestly desirous upon this occasion, as upon all others of a similar nature, to meet the personal feelings of the King as far as he can do so consistently with the responsibility which necessarily belongs to his situation as H.M.'s First Minister.

[The King's reply, 25 July.] . . . The King desires Lord Liverpool distinctly to understand that whatever appointments the King may think proper to make in his own family, they are to be considered as quite independent of the control of any Minister whatever; and Lord Liverpool must be aware that the present Government was framed on that basis alone under him. The King will always take care that such persons as it may be his pleasure to appoint, to fill the offices about his person, shall steadily support his Government. [*Ibid.*, II, p. 449.]

135. George IV to the duke of Wellington, 17 July 1823

(*Wellington MSS.*)

The king was complaining that the Prime Minister refused to make his confidential friend and adviser Sir William Knighton, who was Keeper of the Privy Purse, a Privy Councillor.

. . . It is right I should say something on your very kind conduct relative to my friend Sir Wm. No man ever deserved more from the Government or from myself in providing him for their use; and the return is Lord Liverpool's *usual* absurd, weak and disgusting conduct. Depend upon it, that Lord Liverpool, if he lives till doomsday, will never be corrected, or made fit for the high office to which I raised him, and I should consider it a mercy to be spared the irritations to which he continually subjects me. I value Sir Wm.'s feelings as I ought, more than I can express, and I therefore desire him to take no further step in this measure. He will continue to

---

[1] Lord Liverpool refused to acquiesce in the king's nomination of Dr. Sumner, then a mere curate at Highclere, to a canonry of Windsor. Sumner had been tutor to the two sons of Lady Conyngham, George IV's reputed mistress, and had become a favourite at court. He was afterwards (1826) bishop of Llandaff and (1827) bishop of Winchester. (See No. 138.)

manage my private affairs, which are beginning, thank God, to be most prosperous, but as to Lord Liverpool, he must manage *his* interests and the Government business as he can.

136. Sir William Knighton to Lord Graves, 16 Dec. 1823

(Letters of George IV, ed. A. Aspinall, III, p. 53.)

... I am ... commanded to state that, from the Constitution of this country, it is always inconvenient for the King to name particular individuals to his Ministers for lucrative situations, because it is an interference with that patronage which enables the Minister, or at least assists, in carrying on the Government for the benefit of the country. ...

137. George IV to George Canning, 6 May 1827

(Harewood MSS.)

For the final arrangements, see *Letters of George IV*, III, p. 251.

In the ecclesiastic promotions & arrangements that you will now have to settle, there are one or two matters that I am particularly desirous about. Dr. Wellesley, in consequence of his great living being situated in the north, had better have his Stall at Durham, & then I think that the Duke of Wellington must feel that good care has been taken of him. Now it is very intimately connected with my own domestic comfort, that my friend the Bishop of Chichester should have the Stall at St. Paul's vacated by Dr. Wellesley, & the Deanery of Hereford will then, of course, be at your disposal. I mention this in detail because I am sorry on this occasion to interfere with your wishes respecting Lord Harrowby's brother, the Bishop of Lichfield & Coventry, but Dr. Hughes is an old man, & as I am inform'd, not in very good health, so that another opportunity will in all probability soon offer itself. You will take care to make a vacancy for me in my Canons at Windsor; I believe poor Bagot has the greatest number of children. That excellent man Dr. Sumner, who is now Prebend of Durham, will I hope be mov'd into the Bishop of St. David's Stall in that Cathedral, upon the Bishop's being nominated the Dean, by which means Dr. Wellesley goes into Dr. Sumner's Stall.

138. George IV to Viscount Goderich (Prime Minister), 16 Nov. 1827

(Buckinghamshire Record Office, Aylesbury.)

I think it right before I leave town, to write you first on the subject of the Church preferments, and next, relative to the peerages.

My settled determination is that the Bishop of Llandaff goes to Winchester. This arrangement is not new, for it was understood by Lord Liverpool and myself at the time that I raised him to the Bench. You will not be surprised that I should so distinguish him, for I have made him *one of my executors to my Will*; you may judge therefore of my feelings, and my opinion of him. I think you would do well to take the new Bishop from Oxford. If you can, therefore, get from Copleston under *his own hand* that he is *thoroughly Protestant upon the Catholic question*, I will appoint him as the new Bishop. I think it will do *your* character *good*. If this takes place, then I recommend Dr. Phillpotts to be Dean of Chester. Now, if you do not understand the policy of this, I shall indeed be much surprized. The next Bishopric that may be vacant, I completely agree with you that we must devote to Dr. Sumner, the new Bishop of Winchester's brother.[1]

With respect to the peers, rely upon it, the *political part* had better wait until the end or the close of the ensuing session of Parliament. I know *what* it is, I recommend, by this proposition; the diplomatic part may stand as we before settled. I will send you the list of Baronets tomorrow.[2]

139. Dr. Charles Lloyd (bishop of Oxford) to Robert Peel, 28 Dec. 1827

(British Museum Additional MSS. 40343, f. 96.)

The objections to Sumner's appointment are chiefly two. First and greatest that which you mention–it gives to the public the most unquestionable evidence of an absolute authority in the Crown, and, which is of still more importance, of an irresponsible authority behind the Crown. It is not a thing done in secret, nor an arrangement between the King and his Minister which may sometimes be necessary, and which, if the Minister should yield improperly to the King, may at least be concealed from the public. I hold the publicity of this transaction to be a point of the last importance, for it teaches the clergy to fix their minds on the wrong point: instead of endeavouring to approve themselves to a Minister who is responsible for his appointments, it will necessarily lead them to truckle to the Crown. It leads, besides, to the idea that a Minister, who surrenders the ecclesiastical preferment to the King, can care very little about the Church, or the principles or qualifications of its members. I confine myself to the Church, but I suppose it will have the same effect in other professions, *mutatis mutandis*. Now the *publicity* of this transaction arises in this case out of the unquestionable certainty of the following facts. Sumner went thro' Eton and Trinity College Cambridge without gaining any single honour or distinction, tho' he was always an industrious young man. He married early the daughter of a Genevese lawyer and took the curacy of Highclere, on which he expected to live and die. Before, however, he accepted this curacy, he had been private tutor to Lady Conyngham's sons and travelled with them on the continent, so that his connection with her is certified. She introduced him to the King and the rest followed. Now these facts being certain and public, it is no matter of doubt that S. owes his promotion to the Lady C.

[1] See *Letters of George IV*, III, pp. 327, 333–336.
[2] For the peers and baronets, see *ibid.*, III, pp. 330–332.

Second, it is a promotion perfectly unprecedented in the Church of England. Van Mildert told me that he had examined it and found that there was not a single instance of a man of the age of 37 being raised to one of the higher Sees either with or without blood. What no Minister, therefore, has dared to do the King has done at once. The reasons on which the imprudence and impropriety of such an appointment rests, are evident at once. The two Archbishops and the Bishops with rank, London, Durham and Winchester, ought to be men who, from their learning or their birth or their experience and age, are entitled to be looked up to by their brethren with deference and attention. Sumner will of course be listened to by nobody. On this ground, the difference between the appointment of Sumner and Van Mildert is very remarkable.

In regard to Sumner himself, I would observe, that he is a man neither with or without learning, neither with or without ability. He is unexceptionable as a moral man, and a bit of a Methodist, and will, consequently, have the support of all the Evangelical party in England. He is a man of great activity and very fond of preaching, which I am told he does, if not well, at least acceptably, so that I should not wonder if one day or other he made a noise as Bishop of Winchester. So that it will be advisable for anybody who takes the subject in hand to speak of Sumner himself with great discretion, and to separate him altogether from the principles of his appointment.

In regard to the case of Codrington[1] I consider it a very strong fact, but, as the Ministers will of course conceal the fact of the honours having been sent from the Cottage without any consultation with them, and will assume the distribution of these honours to themselves, it will be difficult to make a charge of it, although I cannot see, how they can get out of the dilemma; if they approve of the honours, they cannot throw the blame on Codrington, if they disapprove of Codrington why did they grant the honours?

On the woman living in adultery,[2] I should be as silent as most of the manuscripts in the N[ew] T[estament]. Of the *unfitness* of the man appointed to one of the first places in the Church nothing must be said for the reasons above given, but with great discretion. But if anything be said it should be in this form. If a man of 37 was to be named Bp. of W. on the ground of learning, it should clearly be on the ground of learning distinguished and notorious beyond the ordinary limits. But Sumner, tho' a very good man, has not this learning—ergo etc.

As for Herries's appointment, I should confine myself to the threats and submission, without any mention of the appointment itself, especially as H. was recommended to the King by the Minister.[3]

As for the proscription of individuals, is not the King permitted to object to the admission of such or such an individual into the Ministry? And would not the argument tell eventually very much in favour of the Whigs and tend very much to strengthen their hands in case they should come into office? . . .

---

[1] Admiral Codrington commanded the allied fleet which destroyed the Turkish fleet at Navarino on 20 Oct. 1827. His G.C.B. was gazetted on 13 Nov. The [King's] Cottage was in Windsor Forest.
[2] Lady Conyngham.
[3] The Whig ministers had threatened to resign in Aug. 1827 when Herries, an ultra Tory, was appointed Chancellor of the Exchequer in succession to Canning. It was in effect a court appointment.

140. G. R. Dawson (Joint Secretary of the Treasury) to Sir George Hill, M.P.
7 Nov. 1829

(Public Record Office, Northern Ireland, D.O.D. 642/239 A.)

Dawson, Joint Secretary of the Treasury and Peel's brother-in-law, refers to the strained relations
between the king and Wellington.

. . . There is no cordiality between him and the Duke, and H.M. has done a thing
which may be the cause of quarrel. The present Lord Barrington sent in his resignation as a Lord of the Bedchamber to the Groom of the Stole, who laid before H.M.
without any reference to the Prime Minister. The King, without any reference also,
has appointed Lord Amherst, and the first intimation which the Premier will have of
the vacancy will be the notification from the King that he has filled it up. The Duke
is not a likely man to bear such conduct . . . Lord Goderich allowed the King to
appoint a Bishop of Winchester in this way, but whether the Duke will follow the
same example is another question. . . .

141. Letters from George IV to the duke of Wellington, 11 and 17 Feb. 1828

(*Wellington MSS.*)

The Grenvillite Charles Wynn had been President of the Board of Control, 1822–1828, in the
Liverpool, Canning and Goderich ministries. Wellington invited neither him nor Goderich to
remain in the Cabinet in Jan. 1828.

11 Feb. I do not quite understand your letter respecting Mr. Wynn. When Lord
Goderich made the application in favour of that gentleman, I stated that I did not
disapprove his having done so, but that it must remain open for future consideration.
Now, if *you* choose to give this gentleman, his £3000 pr. *an.*, well and good, but
I shall certainly not permit Lord Goderich to consider that he has a right to do so,
and as King of this country I hold it very objectionable that every man who has the
good luck to become a Cabinet Minister, with or without talent, is to be rewarded
by a parliamentary pension. But alas! I fear that the true Kingly authority of this
country is fast passing away. . . .

17 Feb. . . . When in the hurry of our talk in our short interview before the
Council on Wednesday last, you ask'd my consent to the Dean of St. Patrick being
appointed to the vacant Bishopric in Ireland, and which, without giving it a moment's
thought, I then hastily gave you, it did not in the least occur to me either who the
Dean [of] St. Patrick is, nor who his family and connexions are, and it is only just
now, before I receiv'd the inclos'd warrant, that the whole of the circumstances
relating to him flash'd suddenly across my mind, and have given rise to those powerful
feelings within me, which must make me demur and refuse the affixing my name to
a warrant nominating him to a seat on the Irish Bench of Bishops until I can know
somewhat of his principles, and that [I] am quite secure as to his being steadfastly
orthodox in his attachment to the Establish'd Church and religion of my Dominions.
It is *utterly impossible for me* (and I should think for you also) *ever* to give *my* consent
to the elevation of *any individual, be he who or what he may* (or whatever other meritorious qualifications he may be suppos'd to possess, which might make him otherwise

possibly not unworthy of being considered) to the Bench of Bishops either in England or Ireland, and without I first ascertain beyond the reach of all question or doubt, and that I am quite sure and secure that the individual to be nominated or recommended to be made a Bishop *does now and will forever* from *his heart* strenuously uphold and support *throughout*, our Protestant faith and religion as *now* existing, and establish'd in Church and State. I must after this *positive* and *final declaration* on *my* part, therefore, trouble you to make further enquiries, to satisfy me before I can allow the matter to proceed any further. I have no individual of any sort of my own to recommend in case Dr. Ponsonby should (according to my principles) ultimately turn out to be ineligible, and I am only actuated on the present occasion by those *unalterable principles* of paramount *duty* which *I owe* to the *exalted situation* in which it has pleas'd Providence by my birth to place me as Sovereign of these Realms.

141A. Henry Hobhouse's Diary, 1 Aug. 1821
(*Diary of Henry Hobhouse, 1820–1827*, ed. A. Aspinall, p. 69.)

... Lord Liverpool ... received another slight in regard to the creation of four extra Knights of the Thistle, which the King resolved on without any communication with Lord Liverpool, and first imparted his resolution to Lord Melville, telling him that he was to be one, Lord Lauderdale another, and Lord Cassillis a third of the new Knights, and that he should leave the fourth for Lord Liverpool. This measure was accordingly executed. ...

Part II

PARLIAMENT

Introduction

THE Act of Union with Ireland[1] increased the size of both Houses of Parliament at Westminster, the Upper House by the addition of 4 Irish bishops serving in rotation and 28 representative peers elected for life, the Lower House by 100 members from the counties, boroughs and Trinity College, thus increasing the membership to 658. The House of Lords, including the 16 Scottish representative peers who were elected by their fellow peers at the beginning of each new Parliament, was already growing in size owing to Pitt's creations; by 1830 the English peerage, excluding the royal dukes and peeresses, numbered 310 as against 193 in 1783: the total size of the House of Lords had increased from 238 to 388. Men like Wilberforce, Lord Grosvenor and Lord Camden[2] deplored this increase, which reflected not only the increasing inability of governments, in a period of 'economical reform', to find rewards other than peerages acceptable to their supporters, but also the growing wealth and social aspirations of the upper ranks of the gentry and the commercial classes. George III and IV kept as firm a hand on the process of growth as they could:[3] except for Wellington and Buckingham, no dukes were made outside the royal family in this period,[4] and George III made a condition that no individual actively engaged in trade, however respectable his fortune, could be admitted to the British peerage. Only in the case of Pitt's friend (and banker) Robert Smith, Lord Carrington, was an exception allowed. It was indeed generally agreed, not only that an active commercial man ought not to be ennobled, but that a peerage, or even a courtesy title,[5] disqualified its holder from taking part in business and following a learned profession. The British peerage was saved from being a closed caste, however, by intermarriage with the wealthy commercial classes, by the facility with which younger, untitled, sons were accepted into the professions, by the rise to the peerage of retired commercial men or their descendants,[6] and by the extensive social obligations that, by and large, the peerage was responsible enough to accept. It was the Irish peerage, until the Union placed restrictions on its growth, that was the resource of the commercial families and the political adventurer,[7] and even some of its older families lacked the means to keep up the dignity of what was then very much a second-rate honour.[8] Yet none were so avaricious of honours as the Irish: Liverpool, who bore the brunt of their solicitations for many years, could only suggest that it was a national trait.[9] After the Union it was at least stipulated that only residents in Ireland should be raised to its peerage,[10] but the correspondence of English ministers was full of claims for appointment to the peerage,[11] for promotion within it,[12] or for election as representative peers,[13] from men pressing their electoral services to

[1] No. 142. [2] Nos. 144–146. [3] No. 147. [4] No. 148. [5] No. 166.
[6] No. 154. [7] Nos. 153–154. [8] Nos. 164–165. [9] No. 166. [10] No. 151.
[11] Nos. 154, 159. [12] Nos. 155, 161. [13] Nos. 156–157, 160.

187

188   PARLIAMENT

government: Irish peers tried, not always successfully, to buy British peerages with borough influence.[1]

Though the existence of the Upper Chamber was held to guarantee the "proper poise of the Constitution",[2] holding the balance between the monarchical and democratic elements which were fused into it, in practice the government of the day could expect a safe majority in the Lords as long as it was known to possess the royal favour: support came from the numerous peers attached to the Royal Household, the bishops who looked to the Crown for preferment, and the representative peers whose elections were subject to ministerial management,[3] added to the Lords who served as ministers and those whose feelings of loyalty to the throne swayed their votes. A defeat in the Lords could, however, shake a government severely if its majority in the Commons was uncertain; Liverpool suggested in 1809 that it might even be brought down.[4]

Though many of the political groups of the time were led from the Lords, and all were based upon the territorial influence of the aristocracy, it was in the House of Commons that the great battles were fought. Extracts from the Report of the Committee of the Society of the Friends of the People,[5] issued in 1793, show how the Lower House was recruited, and the committee's table of parliamentary patronage, here combined for the first time with three similar tables published by the reformer T. H. B. Oldfield between 1794 and 1816,[6] reveals the extent of private and government patronage in England and Wales. Croker's calculations[7] suggest that the picture was substantially the same in 1827. Finally, a "Sketch of the Political Interest in Scotland"[8] drawn up in 1810 throws light on the intricacies of Scottish electoral management as practised by Henry Dundas and his successors.

These documents suggest that about four-fifths of the members for Great Britain were returned by 'influence', though the figures need some interpretation; many 'interests' apparently firmly rooted depended in fact on the goodwill rather than on the coercion of even small electorates. They show too how small the direct influence of the government was in the constituencies.[9] That influence was commonly exercised, not by direct pressure, but through the services of patrons; thus in December 1783 when John Robinson was making his calculations for the management of a general election, he expected the government's gains to come principally from the 'close' boroughs and from Scotland, where the electorate was peculiarly susceptible to management, rather than from the English and Welsh counties and 'open' boroughs where public opinion could make itself felt.[10] But this did not mean that men returned for 'close' constituencies were necessarily corrupted or corruptible. Lord North pointed out in 1785 that many of these seats were occupied by country gentlemen,[11] while the evidence of such respectable members as Henry Beaufoy[12] and Sir Samuel Romilly[13] shows that the purchase of a seat was often the sole resource of a man of independent principles who wished to enter Parliament. None could act so independently as he who represented only his own purse, and though there were still men who sought to capitalize their borough influence, or to recoup their election expenses by seeking government favours,[14] by no means all patrons or their nominees were open to the blandishments of a Treasury which was becoming increasingly short of offices or pensions for rewarding long service in the House.

[1] No. 158.   [2] No. 143.   [3] Nos. 149–150, 152.   [4] No. 163.   [5] No. 167.
[6] No. 168.   [7] No. 169.   [8] No. 170.
[9] It should be noted that Oldfield made no distinction between the power of nomination and mere 'influence' in his table of Government patronage in 1816.
[10] No. 183 (and see No. 208 for Ireland).   [11] No. 274.   [12] No. 173.   [13] No. 174.   [14] No. 175.

The social structure of the House so recruited showed little radical change from the Commons of Walpole's day. The majority of members were still men of landed property, but the growing importance of commercial, financial and industrial interests was now changing the balance of membership.[1] Professional men–with the exception of the clergy, whose ambiguous position was cleared up in 1801[2]–completed the structure of the House.[3] The lawyers contributed most of the leading politicians of the day, and some Prime Ministers. It was this class, according to Jenkinson, that was most dependent on the 'close' boroughs for entry into the House and that would accordingly suffer most from parliamentary reform.[4]

Membership of these groups did not coincide with the division of the House into parties. 'Party' connexion was still deplored by some as destructive of the proper independence both of individuals and of Parliament; to others, such as Fox, membership of a party was matter for pride and a guarantee of liberty and independence.[5] Under the stress of the American and French revolutions, the terms 'Whig' and 'Tory' were beginning to focus, as they had not done since Queen Anne's day, on the political issues of the time, but it remains true throughout this period that parties were formed and led in the House on narrower, more personal bases than such vague, inchoate sentiments. In practice, less than half the House was organized, even loosely, into party groups.[6] It followed that no government during this period could be a party government, though oppositions could be party oppositions; but every minister from Pitt to Grey was dependent on the support of the 'Court and Administration' party and needed also to cultivate the good opinion of the unattached independents.[7] Thus during the long exclusion of the Whig party from office after 1807 Tierney calculated that its strength–about 200 in 1811, 170 in 1818–would be sufficient to carry on the government.[8] The difficulty was that neither as regent nor as king was George IV prepared to give it his confidence, and so reinforce its numbers from the court party and the independents.

Finally, the size of a party, as earlier in the eighteenth century, tended to fluctuate according to its prospects of office. Pitt's personal following in 1788 would, it was said, lose over half its members if its leader were no longer minister.[9] George Rose, Pitt's Secretary of the Treasury, correctly foretold in 1804 that a large part of Addington's party would desert him if he went into opposition,[10] and in 1809 Tierney pointed out to Lord Grey that any party leaving office must expect to drop a large part of its members.[11] Liverpool in 1811 found that the uncertainty as to the regent's intentions respecting the government seriously weakened Perceval's position in both Houses.[12]

The 'Court party' was therefore the largest and in some ways the most important of the party groups in the Commons. Its structure is investigated in the succeeding documents.

The 'Influence of the Crown' in the Lower House was maintained in three ways: by the exertion of government influence at elections,[13] securing the return of a number of members committed to the support of ministers who had been granted the use of the prerogative of dissolution;[14] by the return as members, not necessarily through government influence in the constituencies, of men in office–the placemen[15]–and by reason of the deference many otherwise independent members paid to the known

[1] Nos. 178–180. [2] No. 177. [3] No. 181. [4] No. 176. [5] No. 182. [6] Nos. 184, 187. [7] No. 186. [8] Nos. 192, 194. [9] No. 184. [10] No. 186. [11] No. 190. [12] Nos. 191, 193. [13] Nos. 202–208, 212–219. [14] Nos. 197–199. [15] Nos. 200, 221–247.

wishes of the monarch. Some objected to the Irish Union on the grounds that, since the 100 Irish members who were to enter the House would be largely unconnected with British political issues, they would be peculiarly susceptible to government influence and become "a . . . regular band of ministerial adherents".[1] Lord Redesdale, Lord Chancellor of Ireland in 1805, declared that this was the natural tendency of the Irish if well managed,[2] and extracts from Sir Arthur Wellesley's papers as Chief Secretary in 1807[3] and the Lord Lieutenant's correspondence in 1831[4] show how this was done. Despite this reinforcement, however, the influence of the Crown in this respect continued to decline owing to the progress of administrative reform and the corresponding difficulty in finding money to finance election expenditure[5] or to provide rewards for the steady attachment of aspiring supporters.[6]

Once elected, a placeman was not necessarily at the complete disposal of the ministers, who were not entitled to expect his vote except on political questions which involved the stability or existence of the government;[7] at the outset of Pitt's career as Prime Minister, George III on this ground refused to place the votes of his servants at the disposal of Pitt for a private motion on parliamentary reform.[8] In carrying its necessary business through the House every administration counted on the service of a group of regular attendants,[9] but it could not always discipline the placemen—it might be inexpedient to do so—for voting against its measures,[10] nor was it 'correct' for newly appointed ministers to require placemen appointed by their predecessors to vacate seats to which they had been returned by government influence.[11]

The influence of the Royal Household, though considerable in the Commons, was greater in the Lords. Here too, however, ministers might have difficulty in securing majorities for a 'non-political' measure,[12] especially when they lacked the full confidence of the king.[13] Such a situation fostered suspicions of court intrigue and 'double Cabinets',[14] and intriguing or desperate kings might be tempted to use their personal influence in the Upper House as George III used it in 1783 to thwart ministerial policies they found distasteful.[15] The extent of this personal influence was greater than the number of peers holding office; loyalty to the throne was never more widespread than during the long wars with revolutionary and Napoleonic France, and the diminution in the power of ministers to reward support with government patronage[16] had therefore one unexpected result: it was less easy for ministers to stand against the wishes of the Crown unless public opinion was firmly behind them.

The influence of the Crown was not, for the whole of this period, used as a single *bloc*. With the coming of age of the Prince of Wales in 1783 there reappeared that intermittent phenomenon of eighteenth-century politics, the 'reversionary interest' of the Crown. Hanoverian heirs-apparent naturally quarrelled with their fathers or grandfathers—partly owing to political frustration in an age of monarchical government, partly owing to squabbles over income, and in this case owing to personal friendship between the prince and Charles Fox. Carlton House therefore became a focal-point for the discontented—men who, baulked of employment or income under the Crown, sought either the prospect of office or of pension in the next reign, or the immediate enjoyment of the patronage of the prince's Household. Until the virtual break-up of the Carlton House party in 1812,[17] therefore, there existed two

[1] No. 201.   [2] No. 220.   [3] No. 208.   [4] No. 219.   [5] Nos. 213–218.
[6] Nos. 259–266.   [7] Nos. 221–222.   [8] Nos. 228–229.   [9] No. 225.   [10] No. 226.
[11] No. 223.   [12] Nos. 230, 235–236. [13] No. 234.   [14] Nos. 236–239. [15] Nos. 242–244, 277.
[16] Nos. 258–266. [17] No. 271.

royal nuclei for government and opposition parties, each attracting support by the magnetism of its patronage or by personal loyalty and affection for the king or his son.[1] After 1812 the 'reversionary interest' transferred itself, in a weaker form, to the person of Princess Charlotte; with her death in 1817[2] it finally disappeared from English politics.

The remainder of this section illustrates the relationship between the House of Commons and the electorate. The structure of the electoral system was such as to minimize the impact on the House of 'public opinion' in any large sense, but at times of political crisis it made itself felt by petition, address, or direct pressure on members.[3] The 'influence' or coercion[4] that could be applied to electors in many constituencies has already been indicated;[5] it needs to be added that it was not always the 'close' constituency that was the most corrupt, and that very often the larger the electorate the more violent and disorderly was the election.[6] The Whig campaign for parliamentary reform was intended not to introduce universal suffrage and so extend mob violence to every borough, but to place political power firmly in the hands of the propertied middle classes; Russell later earned the name of 'Finality Jack' on that issue.

The long history of the movement for parliamentary reform is briefly followed in the last part of the section. Vol. X of this series has shown that the reform movement of 1780–1785 was essentially a movement of the middling ranks of gentry, anxious not to widen the franchise generally so much as to consolidate the power of their own class and diminish that of the Crown. The failure of Pitt's motion in 1785 marks the end of this stage of the movement: Pitt was not prepared to sacrifice his career and the king's good opinion for the sake of a reform which few of the public seemed to want now that a stable and popular administration was formed and the American War ended. The impact of the French Revolution changed the situation in two ways: it introduced more far-reaching democratic ideas, and inspired with enthusiasm for reform the more educated sections of the working class, whose political interests had formerly been intermittent and ineffective. The Birmingham riots of 1791,[7] directed against the Dissenters, originated as much in that religious prejudice that lay close to the surface of Hanoverian England as in opposition to schemes of reform, but they encouraged the propertied classes in the hope that, in resisting and repressing the reformers, they had the people on their side. During 1792 reform became further tainted with Jacobinism, and the contacts of the popular societies with French reform clubs and their encouragement of eccentric speculations on government, founded on the ideas of Thomas Paine,[8] provoked much alarm. Most of the societies were harmless enough, and such discontent as they expressed was due rather to difficult economic and social problems than to revolutionary unrest, but such savage reactions as the brutal sentences imposed on the Scottish reformers by Braxfield in 1793[9] and the panic report of the Committee of Secrecy in 1794[10] set the tone for Pitt's repressive measures of 1795.[11] Under such discouragement, the reform agitation almost died out except in the House of Commons until an accentuation of economic difficulties in 1812 helped to revive it. In the meantime, J. C. Curwen's Act[12] had prohibited one open scandal–the sale of seats in the House; its effectiveness was such that the government was unable for the future to buy

[1] Nos. 267–270.   [2] No. 273.   [3] No. 276, 279.   [4] Nos. 278, 281, 282.
[5] Nos. 167–168.   [6] No. 283.   [7] No. 286.   [8] No. 287.
[9] No. 288.   [10] No. 289.   [11] Nos. 290–291.   [12] No. 292.

seats from the borough patrons and its nominees had to find their own way into Parliament.[1]

The revival of the reform agitation after 1812 was met by a renewal of Pitt's repressive legislation. The report of a secret committee[2] was used to secure the suspension of Habeas Corpus[3] and an Act against seditious meetings.[4] Not all the governing class shared in this panic; Earl Fitzwilliam, a devoted disciple of Burke and Lord Lieutenant of the West Riding, remarked on the absence of any real revolutionary spirit among the people in this particularly troubled area, and suggested to the Home Secretary that the more ominous activities of otherwise peaceable citizens were provoked by his own spies and *agents-provocateurs*–notably the notorious Oliver.[5] At the time of the "Peterloo massacre" Liverpool thought that "the great body of the population is still sound"[6] but he excepted certain disturbed areas where public opinion was inflamed. It was to prevent a spread of this discontent that the "Six Acts"[7]–neither so novel nor so unreasonably repressive in their provisions as has sometimes been suggested–were passed in 1819 and the popular agitation was damped down by this discouragement and by the slow recovery from the worst of the post-war economic depression. Not until the united opposition of the Tories to reform had been shattered by the grant of Catholic emancipation and the death of George IV had removed the royal veto on the introduction of a government measure was there any real prospect of legislation: the Reform Bills[8] then proposed by Lord Grey's Government and passed after a prolonged political crisis proved to be so drastic in their implications that the relationship between executive and legislature, and the whole constitutional development of the country, were to be profoundly modified in the next generation.

BIBLIOGRAPHY

Reference should also be made to the general works on constitutional history in the sectional bibliography on the Executive, and to the General Bibliography.

I. MEMBERSHIP, PROCEDURE AND DEBATES

On membership, the official "Return of Members of Parliament" (*Parliamentary Papers, House of Commons*, 1878, vol. LXII, part ii) is substantially accurate. For a picture of the House of Commons at the beginning of this period, see *The Parliamentary Papers of John Robinson, 1774–84*, edited by W. T. Laprade (Royal Historical Society, Camden 3rd Series, vol. XXXIII, 1922), and an article arising from a study of these Papers (I. R. Christie, "The Political Allegiance of John Robinson, 1770–84" in *Bulletin of the Institute of Historical Research*, 1956). G. P. Judd, *Members of Parliament, 1734–1832* (1955) analyses the social status and occupation of M.P.s, but is unreliable–inevitably so, since the official *History of Parliament* is still only in the preparatory stage. For the legislation of this period, see vols. 34 to 87 of *The Statutes at Large*. For the Debates, see *The Parliamentary Register* (54 vols. covering the years 1783–1803); Cobbett's *Parliamentary History of England*, vols. 24 to 36 (the last) is, on the whole, less full; and, for the years after 1803, Cobbett's *Parliamentary Debates* (subsequently known as *Hansard's Parliamentary*

[1] Nos. 293–295. [2] No. 296. [3] No. 297. [4] No. 298.
[5] No. 299. [6] Nos. 300–301. [7] No. 302. [8] Nos. 303–305.

Debates), in 80 vols. to 1832. Also valuable is *The Mirror of Parliament*, which, under the editorship of J. H. Barrow, started in 1828 (20 vols. cover the years 1828–1832). The *Mirror* has many speeches corrected by members themselves. For an account of the differences between these various collections, and a detailed description of methods of parliamentary reporting at this time, see A. Aspinall, "The Reporting and Publishing of the House of Commons' Debates, 1771–1834", in *Essays Presented to Sir Lewis Namier* (1956). For a somewhat less complete bibliography of collections of Debates, see *A Bibliography of Parliamentary Debates of Great Britain* (House of Commons Library, Document No. 2, 1956) and *Bulletin of the Institute of Historical Research*, vol. x. For the debates in the Irish House of Commons during the last few years of its existence, see the *Irish Parliamentary Register*; also M. W. Jernegan's description of the contents of 37 vols. of MS. Debates, together with a supplementary set of 45 vols. of shorthand reports covering the years 1776–1789, in *English Historical Review*, January 1909.

The proceedings, as distinct from the debates, are recorded in the *Journals* of both Houses (*House of Commons*, vols. 39 to 87; *House of Lords*, vols. 37 to 64). Throughout this period the two sets of *Journals* are swollen to the extent of many thousands of pages in the aggregate by vast quantities of information not only about Government expenditure in the minutest detail, but also about the state of the country; Reports of Select Committees on the state of Ireland, on the coal trade, the slave trade, the collection and payment of tithes, evidence supporting Divorce Bills, foreign relations, and so on, the whole showing in quite a remarkable manner the increasing attention which Parliament was paying to the economic, religious and social welfare of the nation, and, indeed, of the Empire. Later, this extraneous matter was removed from the *Journals* and published in the form of White Papers and Blue Books. But even before 1832 the House of Commons' *Parliamentary Papers* (consisting of Accounts and Papers, Public Bills, Reports, etc.) are very considerable; they furnish information on an extraordinary range of subjects, and illustrate the growing complexity of the machinery of government. For this period the British Museum's collection of *Parliamentary Papers* is almost complete, and the bound volumes occupy about 108 feet of shelving. In addition to these House of Commons' Papers there are the House of Lords' *Sessional Papers*, the bulk of which start only in 1802. The British Museum's set fills about 54 feet of shelving, but this collection is much less complete than that in the Library of the House of Lords. For an account of these two sets of Papers, see *Hansard's Catalogue and Breviate of Parliamentary Papers, 1696–1834*, edited by P. and G. Ford (Oxford, 1953). See also H. H. Bellot and E. S. de Beer, "Parliamentary Printing, 1660–1837" in *Bulletin of the Institute of Historical Research*, vol. xi (1933–1934), and C. G. Parsloe and W. G. Bassett, "British Parliamentary Papers: Catalogues and Indexes" (*Ibid.*, vol. xi).

There is as yet no article about the division lists of this period. Like the debates, they were compiled from the newspapers, and most of them were copied by Debrett, Cobbett and Hansard. Occasionally, important ones were published in pamphlet form. The number of Lords' divisions is very small, and so is that of Commons' divisions before 1812 (less than 10 per year on an average). There is a striking increase after 1820 (an annual average of over 40), and the total number for the period is well over 900. As a rule, lists of the minority alone are given, except on a great popular issue like the Catholic question. The Whigs, who were in opposition almost uninterruptedly from 1783 to 1830, professed to be the popular party, and those who sat for 'open' constituencies, in particular, wished to keep their constituents informed about their votes on popular questions. It was often remarked, incidentally, that their speeches too seemed to be addressed, not to the House but to the electorate. On important occasions, lists of those who went out into the Lobby on a division were compiled by the opposition whips and sent to the newspapers, especially, during the early part of the period, to the *Morning Chronicle*. The provincial papers sometimes copied them, or, alternatively, made a point of informing their readers how the local members had voted.

This unofficial, *ad hoc* method of compilation inevitably resulted in inaccuracies, but the newspapers themselves often printed *corrigenda* following pained protests from members whose votes had been inadvertently misrepresented.

For the composition of the Irish House of Commons during the last years of its existence, of the party affiliations of its members, and of the controlling 'interests' in each constituency, see (1) *Proceedings of the Royal Irish Academy*, vol. LVI, Section C, No. 3, March 1954: "Contemporary Sketches of the Members of the Irish Parliament in 1782", printed from the Stowe MSS. in the Huntington Library, San Marino, California; (2) *Ibid.*, vol. LIX, Section C, No. 1, March 1957: "The State of the Irish House of Commons in 1791", from a MS. in the possession of the duke of Abercorn at Barons Court, County Tyrone; and (3) an unpublished MS. at Belvoir Castle, undated, but written whilst the duke of Rutland was Lord Lieutenant of Ireland (1784–1787). For a list of the boroughs disfranchised at the Union, the names of the patrons and their respective shares of the compensation money (£1,260,000), see C. Ross, *Cornwallis Correspondence*, III, pp. 321–324. Among the Melville MSS. in the National Library of Scotland is a *State* of the Irish House of Commons in 1793. Among the Fane MSS. in the Record Office, Dublin Castle, is a list of Government supporters in the Irish House of Commons, with the names of those who influenced their votes; a copy of the document was given to Lord Fitzwilliam, presumably at the beginning of 1795, when he was appointed Lord Lieutenant of Ireland.

Complementary to Sir Arthur Wellesley's *State* of the Irish representation in 1807–1808 (No. 208) are the following: (1) Edward Wakefield's analysis in vol. II of his *Ireland, Statistical and Political* (1812); (2) the *State* written for the information of Lord Hardwicke, the Lord Lieutenant, in June 1802, in British Museum Additional MSS. 35735, ff. 76–82; (3) a *State*, compiled for the duke of Bedford, the Lord Lieutenant, in May 1806, for use in the event of a general election (copy in the Althorp MSS.); (4) an analysis of the situation in 1818 and 1820 in the Peel MSS. (British Museum Additional MSS. 40298), together with the Lord Lieutenant's Application Books, 1801–1805, containing particulars of applications made at audiences with the Lord Lieutenant, or by letter, for posts under Government, titles, pensions, etc., in the Hardwicke MSS. (*Ibid.*, 35781–35787), and, Oct. 1820, with additions to the end of 1821 (*Ibid.*, Peel MSS. 40296–40297 [duplicates]).

II. VARIOUS WORKS

C. E. Adam, *The Political State of Scotland* (Edinburgh, 1887); W. W. Bean, *The Parliamentary Representation of the six northern counties of England and their cities and boroughs* (Hull, 1890); R. Beatson, *A Chronological Register of both Houses . . . of Parliament, 1708–1807* (3 vols., 1807); W. P. Courtney, *The Parliamentary Representation of Cornwall to 1832* (1889); R. S. Ferguson, *Cumberland and Westmorland Members of Parliament* (1871); E. G. Forrester, *Northamptonshire County Elections and Electioneering, 1695–1832* (Oxford, 1941); [James Grant] *Random Recollections of the House of Commons* (1836) and *Random Recollections of the House of Lords* (1836); J. Grego, *History of Parliamentary Elections* (1892); F. B. Hamilton, *The Picture of Parliament* (1831); J. Hatsell, *Precedents of Proceedings in the House of Commons* (1818 edition); T. H. B. Oldfield, *Representative History of Great Britain and Ireland* (6 vols., 1816, incorporating the substance of his *History of the Boroughs of Great Britain*, 3 vols., 1792); R. H. Peckwell, *Cases of Controverted Elections, 1802–6* (2 vols., 1805–1806); L. O. Pike, *A Constitutional History of the House of Lords* (1894); E. and A. G. Porritt, *The Unreformed House of Commons* (2 vols., Cambridge, 1909: the standard work); H. Stooks Smith, *The Parliaments of England* (3 vols., Leeds, 1844–1850: useful but inaccurate); J. Stockdale, *Parliamentary Guide, or, Members' and Electors' Complete Companion* (1784); A. S. Turberville, *The House of Lords in the Eighteenth Century* (Oxford, 1927) and *The House of Lords in the Age of Reform, 1784–1837* (1958); A. Aspinall, "The Canningite Party" (*Transactions of the Royal Historical Society*, 4th Series, vol. XVII, 1934) and "The Last of the Canningites" (*English Historical Review*, 1935); Ian Christie, "Private Patronage versus Government Influence: John Buller and the contest for control of parliamentary elections at Saltash, 1780–90" (*English Historical Review*, 1956); H. Butterfield, "Charles James Fox and the Whig Opposition in 1792" (*Cambridge Historical Journal*, vol. IX, 1949); D. Cook, "The Representative History of the County, Town and University of Cambridge, 1698–1832" (*Bulletin of the*

Institute of Historical Research, vol. xv, 1937–1938); A. S. Foord, "The Waning of 'The Influence of the Crown'" (*English Historical Review*, 1947); C. E. Fryer, "The General Election of 1784" (*History*, vol. IX, 1924); M. D. George, "Fox's Martyrs: The General Election of 1784" (*Transactions of the Royal Historical Society*, 4th Series, vol. XXI, 1939); R. W. Greaves, "Roman Catholic Relief and the Leicester Election of 1826" (*Transactions of the Royal Historical Society*, 4th Series, vol. XXII, 1940); R. C. Jasper, "Edward Eliot and the Acquisition of Grampound" (*English Historical Review*, vol. LVIII, 1943); D. L. Keir, "Economical Reform, 1779–1787" (*Law Quarterly Review*, vol. L, 1934); Betty Kemp, "Crewe's Act, 1782" (*English Historical Review*, vol. LXVIII, 1953); "The Stewardship of the Chiltern Hundreds" in *Essays presented to Sir Lewis Namier* (1956); W. T. Laprade, "Public Opinion and the General Election of 1784" (*English Historical Review*, 1916); "William Pitt and Westminster Elections" (*American Historical Review*, vol. XVIII); R. Pares, "George III and the Politicians" (*Transactions of the Royal Historical Society*, 5th Series, vol. I, 1951); C. H. Phillips, "The East India Company 'Interest' and the English Government, 1783–4" (*Transactions of the Royal Historical Society*, 4th Series, vol. XX, 1937); G. C. Richards, "Peers created by the younger Pitt" (*American Historical Review*, vol. XXXIV); A. S. Turberville, "The House of Lords as a Court of Law, 1784–1837" (*Law Quarterly Review*, 1936); "The younger Pitt and the House of Lords" (*History*, vol. XXI, 1937); "Aristocracy and Revolution. The British Peerage, 1789–1832" (*Ibid.*, vol. XXVI, 1942); "The Episcopal Bench, 1783–1837" (*Church Quarterly Review*, CXXIII, 1937); G. S. Veitch, "William Huskisson and the Controverted Elections at Liskeard in 1802 and 1804" (*Transactions of the Royal Historical Society*, 4th Series, vol. XIII, 1930); C. K. Webster and H. Temperley, "The duel between Castlereagh and Canning in 1809" (*Cambridge Historical Journal*, vol. III, 1929).

III. THE MOVEMENT FOR PARLIAMENTARY REFORM

A. Bain, *Life of James Mill* (1882); Samuel Bamford, *Passages in the Life of a Radical* (2 vols., 1903); R. Birley, *The English Jacobins from 1789 to 1802* (1924); F. A. Bruton, *Three Accounts of Peterloo* (Manchester, 1921); J. R. M. Butler, *The Passing of the Great Reform Bill* (1914); William Godwin, *Political Justice* (1793); H. Jephson, *The Platform* (2 vols., 1892); C. B. R. Kent, *The English Radicals* (1899); Freda Knight, *The Strange Case of Thomas Walker* (1957); Sir James Mackintosh, *Vindiciae Gallicae* (1791); L. S. Marshall, *The Development of Public Opinion in Manchester, 1780–1820* (1946); H. W. Meikle, *Scotland and the French Revolution* (Glasgow, 1912); Thomas Paine, *The Rights of Man* (1791–1792); *Life* by M. D. Conway (2 vols., New York, 1892); A. Prentice, *Historical Sketches and Personal Recollections of Manchester* (1851); D. Read, *Peterloo: The 'Massacre' and its Background* (Manchester, 1958); J. Rutt, *Life of Joseph Priestley* (2 vols., 1831); Leslie Stephen, *The English Utilitarians* (3 vols., 1900); Mrs. Thelwall, *Life of John Thelwall* (1837); G. S. Veitch, *The Genesis of Parliamentary Reform* (1913); C. M. Wakefield, *Life of Attwood* (1885); Christopher Wyvill, *Political Papers* (6 vols., 1794–1802); W. H. Yate, *Political and Historical Argument proving the necessity of a Parliamentary Reform* (2 vols., 1812); H. W. C. Davis, *The Age of Grey and Peel* (Oxford, 1929).

Articles

Asa Briggs, "Thomas Attwood and the Economic Background of the Birmingham Political Union" (*Cambridge Historical Journal*, vol. IX, 1948) and "The Background of the Parliamentary Reform Movement in Three English Cities, 1830–32" (*Ibid.*, vol. X, 1952); H. W. C. Davis, "Lancashire Reformers, 1816–17" (*Bulletin John Rylands Library*, vol. X); N. Gash, "English Reform and French Revolution in the General Election of 1830" in *Essays presented to Sir Lewis Namier* (1956) and "Brougham and the Yorkshire Election of 1830" (*Proceedings of Leeds Philosophical Society*, vol. VIII, Part I, 1956); G. P. Jones, "The Reform Movement in Sheffield" (*Hunter Archæological Society*, vol. IV); J. Taylor, "The Sheffield Constitutional Society, 1791–95" (*Ibid.*, vol. V); G. M. Trevelyan, "The Casualties at Peterloo" (*History*, vol. VII, 1922);

A. S. Turberville and F. Beckwith, "Leeds and Parliamentary Reform" (*Thoresby Society Miscellany*, vol. XLI, 1943); G. Whale, "The Influence of the Industrial Revolution (1760–90) on the demand for Parliamentary Reform" (*Transactions of the Royal Historical Society*, 4th Series, vol. V, 1922).

The following are useful for the history of **The Press**:

A. Aspinall, *Politics and the Press, c. 1780–1850* (1949); R. H. D. Barham, *Life of Theodore Hook* (1877); F. Beckwith, *Account of the Leeds Intelligencer, 1754–1866* (Thoresby Society, 1954); K. G. Burton, *The Early Newspaper Press in Berkshire, 1723–1855* (Reading, 1954); Cobbett's *Weekly Political Register*; biographies of Cobbett by E. I. Carlile (1904) and G. D. H. Cole (1925); and M. L. Pearl, *A Bibliographical Account of Cobbett's Life and Times* (Oxford, 1953); W. J. Couper, *The Edinburgh Periodical Press . . . to 1800* (2 vols., Stirling, 1908); M. E. Craig, *The Scottish Periodical Press, 1750–89* (Edinburgh, 1931); R. S. Crane and F. B. Kaye, *A Census of British Newspapers and Periodicals, 1620–1800* (Chapel Hill, 1927); *Drennan Letters*, edited by D. A. Chart (Belfast, 1931); H. R. Fox-Bourne, *English Newspapers* (2 vols., 1887); J. Grant, *The Newspaper Press* (3 vols., 1871–1872); W. Hindle, *The Morning Post, 1772–1937* (1937); D. Hudson, *Thomas Barnes of 'The Times'* (Cambridge, 1943); F. K. Hunt, *The Fourth Estate* (2 vols., 1850); B. Inglis, *The Freedom of the Press in Ireland, 1784–1841* (1954); W. Jerdan, *Autobiography* (4 vols., 1852–1853); C. Knight, *Passages from a Working Life* (3 vols., 1864–1865); A. Lang, *Life and Letters of J. G. Lockhart* (2 vols., 1897); Wm. Lovett, *Life and Struggles* (2 vols., 1920 edition); W. A. Miles, *Correspondence on the French Revolution, 1789–1817*, edited by C. P. Miles (2 vols., 1890); Stanley Morison, *The English Newspaper, 1622–1932* (Cambridge, 1932), and *John Bell* (Cambridge, 1930) and *The History of The Times*, vol. I, 1785–1841 (1935); [J. G. Muddiman] *Tercentenary Handlist of English and Welsh Newspapers* (1933 edition); C. Pollitt, *De Quincey's Editorship of the Westmorland Gazette* (Kendal, 1890); *Proceedings of the Catholic Association in Dublin, 1823–25* (1825); J. Savage, *An Account of the London Daily Newspapers* (1811); S. Smiles, *A Publisher and his friends: Memoir of John Murray* (2 vols., 1891); John Taylor, *Records of My Life* (2 vols., 1832); Rev. Dr. Trusler, *The London Adviser and Guide* (1790); R. K. Webb, *The British Working Class Reader, 1790–1848* (1955); W. H. Wickwar, *The Struggle for the Freedom of the Press, 1819–32* (1928); and the newspapers themselves. The London newspapers to 1800 are filed in the British Museum; those after 1800, together with Scottish, Irish and English provincial newspapers (many of which were destroyed by enemy action during the war of 1939–45) are stored in the British Museum's Depository at Colindale. The best collections of Irish newspapers are in the National Library of Ireland, Dublin, and the Linen Hall Library, Belfast.

Articles

A. Aspinall, "The Irish 'Proclamation' Fund, 1800–46" (*English Historical Review*, vol. LVI, 1941); "The Use of Irish Secret Service Money in subsidizing the Irish Press" (*Ibid.*, vol. LVI, 1941); "Statistical Accounts of London Newspapers" (*Ibid.*, vol. LXIII, 1948, and vol. LXV, 1950); "The Social Status of Journalists in the early nineteenth century" (*Review of English Studies*, July 1945); "The Circulation of Newspapers in the early nineteenth century (*Ibid.*, 1946); R. Boucher, "Eighteenth century Irish newspapers" (*Genealogical Magazine*, December 1936); J. H. Rose, "The Unstamped Press, 1815–36" (*English Historical Review*, vol. XII, 1897); Mrs. M. D. George, "Pictorial Propaganda, 1793–1815: Gillray and Canning" (*History*, vol. XXXI, 1946); A. P. Wadsworth, "Newspaper Circulations, 1800–1954" (*Manchester Statistical Society*, 1955).

142. An Act for the Union of Great Britain and Ireland, 2 July 1800 (40 George III, c. 67)

(*Statutes at Large*, XLII, Part II, pp. 648–679.)

Whereas in pursuance of H.M.'s most gracious recommendation to the two Houses of Parliament in Great Britain and Ireland respectively, to consider of such measures as might best tend to strengthen and consolidate the connection between the two Kingdoms, the two Houses of the Parliament of Great Britain and the two Houses of the Parliament of Ireland have severally agreed and resolved that, in order to promote and secure the essential interests of Great Britain and Ireland, and to consolidate the strength, power and resources of the British Empire, it will be advisable to concur in such measures as may best tend to unite the two Kingdoms of Great Britain and Ireland into one Kingdom, in such manner, and on such terms and conditions, as may be established by the Acts of the respective Parliaments of Great Britain and Ireland.

And whereas, in furtherance of the said Resolution, both Houses of the said two Parliaments respectively have likewise agreed upon certain Articles for effectuating and establishing the said purposes, in the tenor following:

Article First. That it be the first Article of the Union of the Kingdoms of Great Britain and Ireland, that the said Kingdoms of Great Britain and Ireland shall, upon the 1st day of January which shall be in the year of our Lord 1801, and for ever after, be united into one Kingdom, by the name of *The United Kingdom of Great Britain and Ireland*; and that the royal style and titles appertaining to the Imperial Crown of the said United Kingdom and its dependencies; and also the ensigns, armorial flags and banners thereof shall be such as H.M., by his royal Proclamation under the Great Seal of the United Kingdom, shall be pleased to appoint.

Article Second. That it be the second Article of Union, that the succession to the Imperial Crown of the said United Kingdom, and of the dominions thereunto belonging, shall continue limited and settled . . . according to the existing laws, and to the terms of union between England and Scotland.

Article Third. That it be the third Article of Union that the said United Kingdom be represented in one and the same Parliament, to be styled *The Parliament of the United Kingdom of Great Britain and Ireland*.

Article Fourth. That it be the fourth Article of Union that four Lords Spiritual of Ireland by rotation of sessions, and 28 Lords Temporal of Ireland elected for life by the peers of Ireland, shall be the number to sit and vote on the part of Ireland in the House of Lords of the Parliament of the United Kingdom; and 100 commoners (two for each County of Ireland, two for the City of Dublin, two for the City of Cork, one for the University of Trinity College, and one for each of the 31 most considerable Cities, Towns and Boroughs) be the number to sit and vote on the part of Ireland in the House of Commons of the Parliament of the United Kingdom:

That such Act as shall be passed in the Parliament of Ireland previous to the

Union, to regulate the mode by which the Lords Spiritual and Temporal, and the Commons, to serve in the Parliament of the United Kingdom on the part of Ireland, shall be summoned and returned to the said Parliament, shall be considered as forming part of the Treaty of Union, and shall be incorporated in the Acts of the respective Parliaments by which the said Union shall be ratified and established:

That all questions touching the rotation or election of Lords Spiritual or Temporal of Ireland to sit in the Parliament of the United Kingdom, shall be decided by the House of Lords thereof; and whenever, by reason of an equality of votes in the election of any such Lords Temporal, a complete election shall not be made according to the true intent of this Article, the names of those peers for whom such equality of votes shall be so given, shall be written on pieces of paper of a similar form, and shall be put into a glass, by the Clerk of the Parliaments at the table of the House of Lords whilst the House is sitting; and the peer or peers whose name or names shall be first drawn out by the Clerk of the Parliaments, shall be deemed the peer or peers elected, as the case may be:

That any person holding any peerage in Ireland now subsisting, or hereafter to be created, shall not thereby be disqualified from being elected to serve, if he shall so think fit . . . for any county, city or borough of Great Britain, in the House of Commons of the United Kingdom, unless he shall have been previously elected as above, to sit in the House of Lords of the United Kingdom; but that so long as such peer of Ireland shall so continue to be a member of the House of Commons, he shall not be entitled to the privilege of peerage, nor be capable of being elected to serve as a peer on the part of Ireland, or of voting at any such election; and that he shall be liable to be sued, indicted, proceeded against, and tried as a commoner, for any offence with which he may be charged:

That it shall be lawful for H.M., his heirs and successors, to create peers of that part of the United Kingdom called Ireland, and to make promotions in the peerage thereof, after the Union; provided that no new creation of any such peers shall take place after the Union until three of the peerages of Ireland which shall have been existing at the time of the Union, shall have become extinct; and upon such extinction of three peerages, that it shall be lawful for H.M., his heirs and successors, to create one peer of that part of the United Kingdom called Ireland; and in like manner so often as three peerages of that part of the United Kingdom called Ireland shall become extinct, it shall be lawful for H.M., his heirs and successors, to create one other peer of the said part of the United Kingdom; and if it shall happen that the peers of that part of the United Kingdom called Ireland, shall, by extinction of peerages, or other-wise, be reduced to the number of 100, exclusive of all such peers of that part of the United Kingdom called Ireland, as shall hold any peerage of Great Britain subsisting at the time of the Union, or of the United Kingdom created since the Union, by which such peers shall be entitled to an hereditary seat in the House of Lords of the United Kingdom, then and in that case it shall and may be lawful for H.M., his heirs and successors, to create one peer of that part of the United Kingdom called Ireland as often as any one of such 100 peerages shall fail by extinction, or as often as any one peer of that part of the United Kingdom called Ireland shall become entitled, by descent or creation, to an hereditary seat in the House of Lords of the United Kingdom; it being the true intent and meaning of this Article, that at all times after the Union it shall and may be lawful for H.M., his heirs and successors, to keep up the peerage of that part of the United Kingdom called Ireland to the number of 100, over and above the number of such of the said peers as shall be entitled, by descent or creation, to an hereditary seat in the House of Lords of the United Kingdom:

That if any peerage shall at any time be in abeyance, such peerage shall be deemed and taken as an existing peerage; and no peerage shall be deemed extinct unless on default of claimants to the inheritance of such peerage for the space of one year from the death of the person who shall have been last possessed thereof; and if no claim shall be made to the inheritance of such peerage, in such form and manner as may from time to time be prescribed by the House of Lords of the United Kingdom, before the expiration of the said period of a year, then and in that case such peerage shall be deemed extinct; provided that nothing herein shall exclude any person from afterwards putting in a claim to the peerage so deemed extinct; and if such claim shall be allowed as valid, by judgement of the House of Lords of the United Kingdom, reported to H.M., such peerage shall be considered as revived; and in case any new creation of a peerage of that part of the United Kingdom called Ireland, shall have taken place in the interval, in consequence of the supposed extinction of such peerage, then no new right of creation shall accrue to H.M., his heirs or successors, in consequence of the next extinction which shall take place of any peerage of that part of the United Kingdom called Ireland:

That all questions touching the election of members to sit on the part of Ireland in the House of Commons of the United Kingdom shall be heard and decided in the same manner as questions touching such elections in Great Britain now are, or at any time hereafter shall by law be heard and decided, subject nevertheless to such particular regulations in respect of Ireland as, from local circumstances, the Parliament of the United Kingdom may from time to time deem expedient:

That the qualifications in respect of property of the members elected on the part of Ireland to sit in the House of Commons of the United Kingdom, shall be respectively the same as are now provided by law in the cases of elections for counties and cities and boroughs respectively in that part of the United Kingdom called England, unless any other provision shall hereafter be made in that respect by Act of Parliament of the United Kingdom:

That when H.M., his heirs or successors, shall declare his, her, or their pleasure for holding the first or any subsequent Parliament of the United Kingdom, a Proclamation shall issue, under the Great Seal of the United Kingdom, to cause the Lords Spiritual and Temporal, and Commons, who are to serve in the Parliament thereof on the part of Ireland, to be returned in such manner as by any Act of this present Session of the Parliament of Ireland shall be provided; and that the Lords Spiritual and Temporal and Commons of Great Britain shall together with the Lords Spiritual and Temporal and Commons so returned as aforesaid on the part of Ireland, constitute the two Houses of the Parliament of the United Kingdom:

That if H.M., on or before the first day of Jan. 1801, on which day the Union is to take place, shall declare, under the Great Seal of Great Britain, that it is expedient that the Lords and Commons of the present Parliament of Great Britain should be the members of the respective House of the first Parliament of the United Kingdom on the part of Great Britain, then the said Lords and Commons of the present Parliament of Great Britain shall accordingly be the members of the respective Houses of the first Parliament of the United Kingdom on the part of Great Britain; and they, together with the Lords Spiritual and Temporal and Commons, so summoned and returned as above on the part of Ireland, shall be the Lords Spiritual and Temporal and Commons of the first Parliament of the United Kingdom; and such first Parliament may (in that case) if not sooner dissolved, continue to sit so long as the present Parliament of Great Britain may now by law continue to sit, if not sooner dissolved; provided always, that until an Act shall have passed in the Parliament of the United Kingdom, providing in what cases persons holding offices or places of profit under the crown in Ireland, shall be incapable of being members of the House of Commons of the United Kingdom, no greater number of members than 20, holding such offices or places, as aforesaid, shall be capable of sitting in the said House of Commons of the Parliament of the United Kingdom; and if such a number of members shall be returned to serve in the said House as to make the whole number of members of the said House holding such offices or places as aforesaid more than 20, then and in such cases the seat or places of such members as shall have last accepted such offices or places shall be vacated at the option of such members, so as to reduce the number of members holding such offices or places to the number of 20; and no person holding such office or place shall be capable of being elected or of sitting in the said House, while there are 20 persons holding such offices or places sitting in the said House; and that every one of the Lords of Parliament of the United Kingdom, and every member of the House of Commons of the United Kingdom, in the first and all succeeding Parliaments, shall, until the Parliament of the United Kingdom shall otherwise provide, take the oaths, and make and subscribe the declaration, and take and subscribe the oath now by law enjoined to be taken, made, and subscribed by the Lords and Commons of the Parliament of Great Britain:

That the Lords of Parliament on the part of Ireland, in the House of Lords of the United Kingdom, shall at all times have the same privileges of Parliament which shall belong to the Lords of Parliament on the part of Great Britain; and the Lords Spiritual and Temporal respectively on the part of Ireland shall at all times have the same rights in respect of their sitting and voting upon the trial of peers, as the Lords Spiritual and Temporal respectively on the part of Great Britain; and that all Lords Spiritual of Ireland shall have rank and precedency next and immediately after the Lords Spiritual of the same rank and degree of Great Britain, and shall enjoy all privileges as fully as the Lords Spiritual of Great Britain do now or may hereafter enjoy the same (the right and privilege of sitting in the House of Lords, and the privileges depending thereon, and particularly the right of sitting on the trial of peers, excepted); and that the persons holding any temporal peerages of Ireland, existing at the time of the Union, shall, from and after the Union, have rank and precedency next and immediately after all the persons holding peerages of the like orders and degrees in Great Britain subsisting at the time of the Union; and that all peerages of Ireland created after the Union shall have rank and precedency with the peerages of the United Kingdom, so created, according to the dates of their creations, and that all peerages both of Great Britain and Ireland, now subsisting or hereafter to be created, shall in all other respects, from the date of the Union, be considered as peerages of the United Kingdom; and that the peers of Ireland shall, as peers of the United Kingdom, be sued and tried as peers, except as aforesaid, and shall enjoy all privileges of peers as fully as the peers of Great Britain; the right and privilege of sitting in the House of Lords, and the privileges depending thereon, and the right of sitting on the trial of peers, only excepted.

Article Fifth. That it be the fifth Article of Union, that the Churches of England and Ireland, as now by law established, be united into one Protestant Episcopal Church, to be called, *The United Church of England and Ireland*; and that the doctrine, worship, discipline and government of the said United Church shall be, and shall remain in full force for ever, as the same are now by law established for the Church of England; and that the continuance and preservation of the said united Church, as the Established Church of England and Ireland, shall be deemed and taken to be an essential and fundamental part of the Union; and that in like manner the doctrine, worship, discipline and government of the Church of Scotland shall remain and be preserved as the same are now established by law, and by the Acts for the Union of the two kingdoms of England and Scotland.

Article Sixth. That it be the sixth Article of Union, that H.M.'s subjects of Great Britain and Ireland shall, from and after the first day of Jan. 1801 be entitled to the same privileges, and be on the same footing, as to encouragements and bounties on the like articles being the growth, produce or manufacture of either country respectively, and generally in respect of trade and navigation in all ports and places in the United Kingdom and its dependencies; and that in all treaties made by H.M., his heirs and successors with any foreign Power, H.M.'s subjects of Ireland shall have the same privileges and be on the same footing as H.M.'s subjects of Great Britain. . . .

[From 1 Jan. 1801 all prohibitions and bounties on the export of articles the produce or manufacture of either country to the other shall cease. All articles the produce or manufacture of either country, not hereinafter enumerated as subject to specific duties, shall be imported into each country from the other, duty free, other than the countervailing duties in Schedule 1, or to such as shall hereafter be imposed by the United Parliament; and for 20 years from the Union, the articles in Schedule 2 shall be subject, on importation into each country, to the duties in the said Schedule. Calicoes and muslins on importation into either country shall be subject to the duties now payable on the importation thereof from Great Britain into Ireland till 5 Jan. 1808, which shall then be annually reduced so as to stand at 10% from 5 Jan. 1816 until 5 Jan. 1821. Cotton yarn and twist shall, on importation into either country, be subject to the duties now payable on importation from Great Britain into Ireland, until 5 Jan. 1808, and shall then be annually reduced, so that all duties shall cease from 5 Jan. 1816. Articles of the produce or manufacture of either country, subject to internal duty, or to duty on the materials, may be subjected on importation into each country to countervailing duties, and upon their export a drawback of the duty shall be allowed.

Schedule 1 contains a long list of articles subject to countervailing duties upon importation from Ireland into Great Britain, and from Great Britain into Ireland. Schedule 2 charges the following articles with a 10% duty upon importation into Great Britain and Ireland respectively: apparel, wrought brass, cabinet ware, coaches and carriages, wrought copper, cottons, other than calicoes and muslins, glass, haberdashery, hats, tin plates, wrought iron, hardware, gold and silver lace, gold and silver thread, millinery, stained paper, pottery, manufactured leather, silk manufactures and stockings.][1]

Article Seventh. That it be the seventh Article of Union, that the charge arising from the payment of interest, and the sinking fund for the reduction of the principal, of the debt incurred in either kingdom before the Union, shall continue to be separately defrayed by Great Britain and Ireland respectively, except as herein-after provided: that for the space of 20 years after the Union shall take place, the contribution of Great Britain and Ireland respectively towards the expenditure of the United Kingdom in each year shall be defrayed in the proportion of fifteen parts for Great Britain, and two parts for Ireland; and that at the expiration of the said 20 years, the future expenditure of the United Kingdom (other than the interest and charges of the debt to which either country shall be separately liable) shall be defrayed in such proportion as the Parliament of the United Kingdom shall deem just and reasonable upon a comparison of the real value of the exports and imports of the respective countries, upon an average of the three years next preceding the period of revision; or on a comparison of the value of the quantities of the following articles consumed within the respective countries, on a similar average; *videlicet*, beer, spirits, sugar, wine, tea, tobacco and malt; or according to the aggregate proportion resulting from both these considerations combined; or on a comparison of the amount of income in each country, estimated from the produce for the same period of a general tax, if such shall have been imposed on the same descriptions of income in both countries; and that the Parliament of the United Kingdom shall afterwards proceed in like manner to revise and fix the said proportions according to the same rules, or any of them, at periods not more distant than 20 years, nor less than seven years from each other; unless, previous to any such period, the Parliament of the United Kingdom shall have declared, as hereinafter provided, that the expenditure of the United Kingdom shall be defrayed indiscriminately, by equal taxes imposed on the like articles in both countries. . . .

Article Eighth. That it be the eighth Article of Union, that all laws in force at the time of the Union, and all the courts of civil and ecclesiastical jurisdiction within the respective kingdoms, shall remain as now by law established within the same, subject only to such alterations and regulations from time to time as circumstances may appear to the Parliament of the United Kingdom to require; provided that all writs of error and appeals, depending at the time of the Union or hereafter to be

---

[1] The importance of these restrictions on complete freedom of trade is brought out in *Parl. Deb.*, New Series, I, 1066 *sqq.* (14 June 1820).

brought, and which might now be finally decided by the House of Lords of either kingdom, shall, from and after the Union, be finally decided by the House of Lords of the United Kingdom; and provided, that, from and after the Union, there shall remain in Ireland an Instance Court of Admiralty, for the determination of causes, civil and maritime only, and that the appeal from sentences of the said Court shall be to H.M.'s delegates in his Court of Chancery in that part of the United Kingdom called Ireland; and that all laws at present in force in either kingdom, which shall be contrary to any of the provisions which may be enacted by any Act for carrying these Articles into effect, be from and after the Union repealed.

And whereas the said Articles having, by Address of the respective Houses of Parliament in Great Britain and Ireland, been humbly laid before H.M., H.M. has been graciously pleased to approve the same; and to recommend it to his two Houses of Parliament in Great Britain and Ireland to consider of such measures as may be necessary for giving effect to the said Articles: in order, therefore, to give full effect and validity to the same, be it enacted . . . that the said foregoing recited Articles, each and every one of them, according to the true import and tenor thereof, be ratified, confirmed and approved, and be and they are hereby declared to be the Articles of the Union of Great Britain and Ireland, and the same shall be in force and have effect for ever, from the first day of Jan. . . . 1801; provided that before that period an Act shall have been passed by the Parliament of Ireland, for carrying into effect, in the like manner, the said foregoing recited Articles.

II. [Recital of an Act of the Irish Parliament to regulate the mode by which the Lords and the Commons, to serve in the Parliament of the United Kingdom on the part of Ireland, shall be summoned and returned.][1]

III. And be it enacted, that the Great Seal of Ireland may, if his Majesty shall so think fit, after the Union, be used in like manner as before the Union, except where it is otherwise provided by the foregoing Articles, within that part of the United Kingdom called Ireland; and that his Majesty may, so long as he shall think fit, continue the Privy Council of Ireland to be his Privy Council for that part of the United Kingdom called Ireland.

A. THE HOUSE OF LORDS

143. C. J. Fox's speech in the House of Commons, 11 May 1791
(Cobbett's *Parliamentary History*, XXIX, 409.)

. . . He laid it down as a principle never to be departed from, that every part of the British dominions ought to possess a Government, in the constitution of which monarchy, aristocracy and democracy were mutually blended and united; nor could any Government be a fit one for British subjects to live under, which did not contain

---

[1] The members for the 31 boroughs, etc., referred to in Article 4, being now reduced in number from 62 to 31, were to be balloted for. The draw took place in Dublin on 1 Dec. 1800, but none was required in Clonmel and Dundalk, both members having resigned their seats, nor in the following boroughs, etc., where one member withdrew before the ballot: Belfast, Cashel, Coleraine, Drogheda, Dungannon, Enniskillen, Galway, Lisburne, Londonderry, Mallow, Portarlington, Ross, and the University.

its due weight of aristocracy, because that, he considered to be the proper poise of the Constitution, the balance that equalised and meliorated the powers of the two other extreme branches, and gave stability and firmness to the whole. It became necessary to look what were the principles on which aristocracy was founded, and he believed it would be admitted to him, that they were two-fold, namely, rank and property, or both united. In this country the House of Lords formed the aristocracy, and that consisted of hereditary titles, in noble families of ancient origin, or possessed by peers newly created on account of their extended landed property. He said that prejudice for ancient families, and that sort of pride which belonged to nobility, was right to be encouraged in a country like this; otherwise one great incentive to virtue would be abolished and the national dignity as well as its domestic interest would be diminished and weakened. There was also such a thing to be remembered, which gave additional honour to our House of Lords, as long established respect for the persons and families of those who, in consequence either of their own superior talents and eminent services, or of one or both in their ancestors, constituted the peerage. This he observed, was by no means peculiar to pure aristocracies such as Venice and Genoa, nor even to despotic or to mixed Governments. It was to be found in democracies, and was there considered as an essential part of the Constitution; affection to those whose families had best served the public being always entertained with the warmest sincerity and gratitude. . . .

144. Wilberforce on the change in the character of the House of Lords brought about by Pitt

(*Life of Wilberforce*, by his sons, 1 (1838), p. 391.)

It appeared to me that no little injury had been done to the credit and character of the House of Commons by the numerous peerages that were granted to men who had no public claims to such a distinction, and whose circumstances clearly manifested that borough or parliamentary interest was the basis of their elevation: hence the inference formerly to be drawn from the support of commoners of large landed property, that the Ministers who enjoyed it enjoyed also the esteem and confidence of the public, was no longer to be drawn; nor were such men entitled to more credit for the independence and purity of their political support than the representatives of the most ordinary boroughs. Various were the instances of country gentlemen of family and fortune, who appeared for a time to be honouring Government by their support, sometimes in opposition to their family habits or political connections, when at length out came the *Gazette*, proclaiming the explanation of their conduct, or at least bringing it into doubt with those who were disposed to suspect the purity of politicians.

145. Lord Grosvenor to William Pitt, 14 May 1804

(Public Record Office, *Chatham Papers*, 140.)

. . . It has long been a matter of regret with many, and myself among others, that the peerage should have been so much increased within the last half century, as it is certainly a prime object to maintain its dignity unimpaired, and thence preserve its due weight in the balance of the Constitution. By an increase of its numbers alone its *consequence* is lessened, but there are other circumstances that have also weakened its independence, namely, the practice that had prevailed of bestowing peerages on persons in all high legal situations, and on naval and military officers. In regard to the former, from their advanced age when created peers, the increase of Law Lords becomes obviously much too rapid, and in both cases their heirs, from the inadequacy of their fortunes, being seldom possessed of much landed property, become naturally too dependent on the crown. As to those who have distinguished themselves in the service of their country, there are other methods of rewarding them, equally gratifying and honourable when once the precedent is established, and less objectionable in a constitutional point of view. . . .

146. Lady Spencer to her husband, Lord Spencer, 28 Jan. 1811

(*Althorp MSS.*)

. . . [Lord Camden] said the worst thing Mr. Pitt had ever done was increasing the House of Lords to so over-grown and ungovernable a size, and that from henceforward whoever was Minister would find his greatest difficulty lie there. I told him that for a very long time that had been your opinion. . . .

147. The earl of Liverpool to E. Wilbraham Bootle, 5 Nov. 1814

(*British Museum Additional MSS.*, 38260, ff. 95–98.)

. . . It is now eight years since any peers have been created except for professional reasons. The King, previous to his illness, had allowed the Duke of Portland to make some eventual promises. The Prince Regent came to the Regency with some personal engagements of his own. There are some other official claims of a very peculiar nature, into which it is not necessary now to enter, but which, when combined with the two former, will make the number of peers to be created upon the first occasion of such creation really not unalarming.

I have had, as you may suppose, many conversations with the Prince Regent on this subject, and the result has been that we have found it necessary for the present, in order to keep the number within very reasonable bounds, explicitly to refuse the application of every country gentleman, whatever his fortune or pretensions may have been for the new honour, and to confine the expectations which may have been held out (with I think one only exception) either to persons who had claims on the ground of some public service, official or in the field, or to those who were already Scotch or Irish peers.

I have been obliged in consequence to refuse several of my oldest friends, and I can say with truth that there is not one person in the list to which I have referred, who will feel that he owes the honour personally to me. He may owe it in some degree to me as a Minister, but he will consider it as a claim which he would be equally entitled to urge on any other Minister whom he happened to have supported. The state of the Scotch and Irish peerage has made a very great difficulty in this question. For, as some of them say with much reason, "If we were commoners of old family and large property we might doubt whether it was our interest to be created peers, but our anomalous situation with half the privileges of the peerage, places us in an ambiguous and awkward situation, and makes us of course anxious to be invested with all the privileges which are considered belonging to our rank." Notwithstanding this, many more must be refused than can be gratified.

. . . In addition to what I have already said, I cannot avoid observing that a considerable creation of peers is a great evil to the Constitution. The character of the House of Lords as a legislative and judicial body is essentially altered by the number of peers Mr. Pitt created during his Administration; and it is likewise a greater evil to withdraw any considerable number of the natural landed aristocracy of the country from the House of Commons. For it is this body that makes the House of Commons what it is in the British Constitution, and it is the want of such a body that is the principal reason why the British Constitution is inapplicable to every other country in Europe. . . .

148. The earl of Liverpool to Robert Peel, 14 Aug. 1815

(British Museum Additional MSS. 40190, f. 244.)

The suggestions referred to in this letter to the Irish Secretary came from Lord Whitworth, the Lord Lieutenant of Ireland. Lord Darlington was refused a dukedom in 1793 (Chatham Papers, 128) and the marquess of Buckingham in 1789. The marquess's son was created duke of Buckingham and Chandos in 1822.

. . . I adopt every material suggestion which he has made except as to the creation of an Irish Duke. This would inevitably launch us into a sea of troubles. Irish Dukes could not be made without at the same time making English Dukes. The King has not made an English Duke (except the Princes of the Blood and the Duke of Wellington) for near fifty years. All claims of this nature are at rest, but I know they would all start up if a dukedom was conferred on any person of either part of the United Kingdom. . . .

149. Henry Dundas to the duke of Buccleuch, 22 Nov. 1787

(Buccleuch MSS.)

Respecting the election of Scottish Representative Peers by their fellow Peers. Cf. Canning's letter of 2 Aug. 1790 to his friend Lord Granville Leveson-Gower: ". . . Were you . . . at Holyrood House during the election of Scotch Peers? And if so, can you account for the Treasury list having been of so little weight with that truly respectable body of men, the Scotch nobility?" (P.R.O., Granville MSS.)

I have been led from Lord Dalhousie's death to think very seriously of the election of the Scotch Peers, and, independent of Mr. Pitt's wishes for Lord Cathcart personally, it appears to me that the whole train of that business is got into a very odd system. They have certainly no reason to complain now of any indecent or offensive interference of the King's Ministers in their elections, neither can it be condoned as hostile to Government, although particular Peers otherwise well disposed to Government should, from personal friendships or predilections on particular occasions, differ from the wishes of Government. But nothing of that kind at present operates in the election of a Scotch Peer: the whole of it proceeds on this ground. Those who, from principle or connexions, are adverse to the present Administration, of course vote in a body for any person to whom Government does not wish well, and they have the address to persuade great numbers, the real well-wishers of the present Administration, to join them in an association to vote against any man who has the good wishes of Government, and this they call supporting the independence of the peerage of Scotland. Surely it becomes your Grace and others who conceive that the present Government deserves every support that independent or honourable men or a grateful country can give them, to set themselves avowedly against such a combination. I confess it has been always my opinion that Government should not take part in the election of the individual Peers, but surely they are interested to set their faces in the most direct manner against combinations actuated by no principle but hostility to them . . . I think I can venture to say that in military promotion and everything else the King will be advised that there is a difference to be made between a young nobleman who associates himself with such a combination as I have alluded to, and another who is not ashamed to avow that a person being a friend to the Administration of which he himself is a friend, is a motive for him to vote with him in place of a motive to vote against him. I wish you would take a look at the list of the Peers of Scotland in the army, and daily soliciting promotion as matter of favour, and then you will be able to judge how childishly Government permits itself to be treated by them.

150. Henry Addington to Lord Liverpool, 31 Aug. 1802

(*British Museum Additional MSS.* 40358, f. 87.)

Some circumstances which attended the late election of the 16 Peers for Scotland render it material that Government should not be committed in consequence of the vacancy which has just occurred, till we know the sentiments & wishes of some leading interests in that quarter, & particularly those of the Duke of Buccleuch. Indeed I have understood that, for some years past, there has been no positive interference on the part of Government: but that its principal friends on the spot, of great authority & influence & well acquainted with the sentiments of the elective body, have been chiefly instrumental in forming those arrangements by which the Administration of the country has been strengthened during the whole of H.M.'s reign, & particularly within the last twenty years. Of late the Duke of Buccleuch has, I believe, taken the lead & I doubt whether any one could be so acceptable to the nobility of Scotland. Till his opinions are known, we should not, I think, act prudently in giving encouragement to any candidate. . . .

151. Robert Peel to the earl of Normanton, 23 Aug. 1823
(British Museum Additional MSS. 40358, f. 87.)

Most certainly the opposition to the Government of the elder branches of your family would not influence me in the slightest degree, and I think it would not influence Lord Liverpool, in throwing an obstacle in the way of your success as a candidate for the representative peerage. A much more formidable difficulty with which you have to contend is non-residence, and I will frankly avow to you that it is a difficulty which I think you will find insuperable. It has been assigned to others, to Lord Clonmell for instance, and very recently to a near connection of the present Lord Lieutenant, as a reason for withholding the countenance of Government.

I do assure you that there is no individual in the peerage of Ireland whose accession to the House of Lords would give me more pleasure . . . as yours, but I feel confident that you will not attribute it to any indifference or want of friendship on my part, if I cannot, after having *invariably* recommended that Irish honours should be conferred exclusively on Irish residents, now propose a special exception from a practice which has always appeared to me founded in justice and good policy.

152. Lord Liverpool to Lord Wellesley, 31 Dec. 1825
(British Museum Additional MSS. 38301, f. 62.)

Wellesley was Lord Lieutenant of Ireland. Lord Farnham had just defeated the Government candidate for the Irish Representative Peerage, Lord Mount Cashell: a most unusual event.

. . . I quite agree with you that it would be neither dignified nor expedient to visit those Peers actually in office, or those who are in the constant habit of receiving favours and countenance from Government, with any punishment for having voted for Lord Farnham. But I think it cannot be unfitting to take a proper opportunity of explaining at least to some of them that it has always been hitherto considered as an honourable obligation on the part of those who are officially connected with the Government that as long as they choose to retain their situations they should support the candidate recommended by the Government.

153. Sir William Manners to William Pitt, 26 Oct. 1793
(Public Record Office, Chatham Papers, 155.)

See *Letters of George IV, passim,* for the outcome of his various applications.

. . . If any Member in the interest of Government was likely to resign his seat in Parliament, I should think myself . . . obliged if I could be recommended as a purchaser, as I have been some time endeavouring to procure a seat, tho' hitherto without success. Understanding that a new creation of Irish peerages is now in agitation, I beg leave to mention the following particulars. In the year 1784, the Prince of Wales was so good as to give my father a promise in his own handwriting to this effect. "That when opportunity offered, John Manners Esq. or his eldest son should be created an Irish Peer." This promise I have in my possession, a circumstance which, if known in Ireland, might at this critical period be attended with unpleasant consequences, as it might be suspected that such promise was given in consideration of a sum of money, & thus occasion an enquiry to be made into the transaction. As a promise of this sort amounts to a recommendation, & as a recommendation from the Prince of Wales would without doubt at this time be attended to, I flatter myself I shall not be thought culpable in thus stating my claim on the present occasion. My father some years ago, on the strength of the Prince's promise, applied to the late Duke of Rutland, then Lord Lieut. of Ireland, to recommend him for an Irish peerage, but was answered that Ministry intended making no more Englishmen Irish Peers. . . .

154. P.I. Thellusson to William Windham (Secretary at War), 12 Nov. 1796

(Public Record Office, *Chatham Papers*, 182.)

Thellusson (1761–1808) was M.P. for Malmesbury; afterwards (1806) Lord Rendlesham. His brother Charles (1770–1815) was M.P. for Evesham. His brother George Woodford Thellusson (1764–1811), who had been returned at the general election of 1796 for Southwark, was deprived of his seat by order of the House of Commons, 12 Nov. He was elected for Tregony in 1804.

I am infinitely obliged to you for the kind concern you have expressed at the decision of the Committee on my brother's election. It is certainly a most unpleasant business, to say no more of it, but as it carries with it nothing degrading or dishonourable, it is (to use the language of Opposition) a general, not an individual battle; we have only to regret an immense expense and a yet more excessive labour.

Before, however, we again embark on this troubled ocean, it behoves our family well to consider its own private situation, its public duties, and those future prospects of honour and advancement which are laudable objects in us all, and which by blending the general with the individual interest gives to the one dignity and to the other zeal.

My father's fortune is certainly very large, our own not inconsiderable and is increasing. But great as they may be, they will not bear unperceived frequent contested borough elections. Our public duties I trust we have hitherto fulfilled towards the State to the very utmost limits of that which even exaggerated expectations could require, compatible with our profession and situation in life.

You are acquainted with the future prospects of honour and advancement we have formed, and have had the goodness in some degree to interest yourself in them, and to think that if it is judged advisable to confer such distinctions on mercantile men, we have at least as good pretensions as those who have obtained them.

The claims of parliamentary influence and exertions to insure to the country persons of property and character, well affected to its laws and Constitution, as its representatives, seem one of the acknowledged claims to the honours of the peerage. We are already possessed of two more yesterday, and may be tomorrow of three seats in our own family. We have also another seat offered us, which we are willing to fill by any person of consideration whom Administration wish to recommend. But surely these exertions and enormous expenses go beyond the duty imposed upon us towards the State, and must be looked upon as a bold and volunteering spirit in its defence. To look forward to some end and fruit of such exertions, to obtain some reasonable assurance that they are attainable, cannot, I trust, be called trafficking by bargain or sale. Our good wishes to Government are well known. We shall not be more or less attached to it, whether we obtain or not our ends. But we may reasonably confine ourselves to zealous duty, not encounter unreasonable difficulties. If therefore any *reasonable* assurance of the object of our wishes is given to us we are again willing to strain every nerve on the election. If not, Mr. Tierney must walk over the course, and my brother will take a quiet seat for a borough in the Isle of Wight.

Without comparing our pretensions to the honour we solicit with those of Lord Eardley or of the two last persons in our line who have lately obtained it I deem you will not deem it vain here to say that our family was ennobled above 400 years ago, was driven from France by the Edict of Nantes, and has ever since filled in Switzerland the very first offices in the Magistracy, the Army, and the Diplomatic line. My father, being a younger son, settled with a handsome fortune in this country. By his industry and his abilities he has increased it, and has proved himself a worthy member of the community. Since the year '90 he has completely left trade, and resides the greatest part of the year on his estates in the country. My continuing in business is uncertain. I am daily vesting my fortune in land, and certainly my eldest son will not be brought up to trade.

If you think that the favour I ask is not unreasonable and that the moment is not an improper one for obtaining a firm assurance that within some *reasonable* period I may look forward to it, I shall feel myself under new and greater obligations if you will forward this letter to Mr. Pitt and obtain his decision on it, as on that must depend the conduct we have now to hold. I flatter myself that even in the City, barring that envy which always follows the successful, it would not be an unpopular measure. I will not judge of popularity by the reports of designing and malevolent men. I will take its criterion from effects and will ask whether an election for the Borough by a large majority, one for the East India Direction carried against every effort of Ministerial and Presbyterian influence, a preponderating influence in the City, of which Mr. Lushington and Mr. Curtis can give proof, is evidence or not of popularity?

On reading over my letter I do not think that I have sufficiently explained that it is for my father that we are anxious to obtain this favour. Unless it should be deemed improper to grant it him from his peculiar situation. . . . I trust it will not be refused.

155. Lord Clanmorris to Lord Hardwicke, 20 July 1805

(*British Museum Additional MSS.* 35761, f. 36.)

Lord Clanmorris asks the Lord Lieutenant of Ireland for promotion in the Peerage.

. . . If I am not trespassing too much on your Excellency's time, I believe it will be right to state my pretensions to this honour in point of property; mine at present consists of about £12,000 a year in money and estates, and will rise considerably before my son is of age. I have therefore nothing to look to from Goverment but honours, to ensure which I mean immediately to purchase a seat in Parliament. . . .

156. W. Elliot (Irish Secretary) to Lord Grenville, 4 Nov. 1806

(Historical Manuscripts Comm., *Dropmore Papers*, VIII, p. 422.)

The borough referred to was Portarlington. Irish money was worth rather less than British.

Parnell states that he believes Lord Portarlington will let us have his seat for £4000 British, provided he is given to understand that he is to have the support of Government for the representative peerage on the *second* vacancy after Lord Charlemont's election. . . .

157. Sir Arthur Wellesley to Lord Liverpool, 27 Dec. 1808

(*Wellington Civil Correspondence & Memoranda* [Ireland] (1860), p. 515.)

Wellesley was Irish Secretary in the Portland Ministry, 1807–1809; Liverpool was Home Secretary. Lord Rosse returned one member for King's County and one for County Longford.

. . . It is . . . most desirable that you should come to an early determination who is to be the next representative peer. . . .

I must again take this opportunity of pressing Lord Rosse upon your attention. The attendance and support of three members in the House of Commons depend upon his goodwill, and I think that in these times Government cannot afford to be without them. . . .

158. Lord Liverpool to Robert Peel, 10 Oct. 1812

(*British Museum Additional MSS.* 40181, f. 15.)

The four seats were those at Newport and Yarmouth (Isle of Wight); the three were at Ilchester and Grantham.

I have received your letter respecting the borough of Carlow, but I do not see how it is possible for me to hold out the expectations suggested to Lord Charleville.

I could have had *four seats* from Sir L. Holmes, and *three* from Sir William Manners if I would have promised that they should have been made peers upon the first creation. I have *lost* them, but I would rather lose them [than] make such an engagement, and, though it has been intimated to me that without an engagement I might hold out the expectation that it might be a consequence, I have always felt that such a course of proceeding was either a virtual engagement in itself, or an act of deception on the party. I would rather lose a few votes than involve myself in any such dilemma. In addition to this, *entre nous*, the proprietor of the borough is a *very poor lord*. He is not much respected in Ireland, and his having such an advantage would offend many of our best and most respectable friends.

I know that there are engagements not more creditable and less advantageous, but these were not made by me, and I am particularly solicitous to avoid adding to engagements of this description. You must therefore do the best you can about the borough of Carlow without the promise of an English peerage either actually or virtually. . . .

Do not suppose me too romantic from the first part of my letter, but (independent of my indifference to office unless I can hold it creditably) I am satisfied that a disposition to contract engagements of this description will in the end rather weaken than strengthen any Government.

159. Robert Peel to Col. Crosbie, M.P. for County Kerry, 18 July 1817

(British Museum Additional MSS. 40293, f. 153.)

. . . Lord Whitworth never has in any single instance recommended an elevation in the peerage for the purpose of securing a powerful interest at an election for a County member, as he does not think that it would be consistent with his duty to procure such influence by such means. . . .

160. H. R. Westenra, M.P., to Lord Liverpool, 23 Feb. 1820, and reply

(British Museum Additional MSS. 38574, f. 161.)

Having received applications from candidates in this country who have conceived me to be favourably disposed towards the present Government for my vote and interest at the ensuing election, which in one county *is allowed to be indispensable*, I am in hopes your Lordship will excuse my intruding myself on your notice at this moment, and honour me with an immediate answer, mentioning the determination of H.M.'s Ministers on my father's (Lord Rossmore's) late application to your Lordship on the subject of his eligibility to the first vacancy in the Representative Peerage of Ireland. . . .

[Lord Liverpool's reply, 28 February.] . . . It will be quite impossible for me to hold out any expectation to Lord Rossmore that he will have the support of Government on the next vacancy in the Irish Representative Peerage.

You must of course decide as you think proper as to the use you will make of any interest which you may possess in the approaching Scotch elections. I will only add that considerations of this nature cannot influence my conduct upon the other point, more especially when they are brought forward in any degree as matters of condition. [*Ibid.*, f. 163.]

161. Earl Talbot (Lord Lieutenant of Ireland) to Lord Liverpool, 11 March 1820

(British Museum Additional MSS. 38574, f. 166.)

Lord Castlemaine has sent me word that he does not intend to sell his borough of Athlone as he has hitherto done, but that he will place it at the disposal of Government for this Parliament upon obtaining a step in the peerage, and receiving an assurance of a provision for his two nephews. I have informed Lord Castlemaine that the proposal was of too delicate a nature to be immediately decided upon, but that I would send him an answer shortly. . . . I imagine Lord Castlemaine would be satisfied with the promise of £400 or £500 a year for each of his nephews. . . .

162. Peel (Home Secretary) to Lord Aberdeen, 23 Aug. 1829

(*British Museum Additional MSS.* 40312, f. 65.)

Peel resigned his seat for the University of Oxford after the Government had announced its intention to concede Catholic emancipation. He took refuge in the pocket borough of Westbury. Aberdeen, the Foreign Secretary, appointed Henry Cowper, a relative of Lopes, to the Consulship of Pernambuco in October.

I had very little communication with Sir M. Lopes on the subject of my return, but considering the peculiar circumstances under which I was placed–the loss of Oxford–the notice given of the introduction of the Roman Catholic Relief Bill–the great difficulty of procuring a return for me, I really believe that the old Jew rendered essential service by consenting to vacate at the time he did. He also had not a very popular candidate to propose for Westbury–injured his interest there I believe in some degree, and had his own head very nearly broken by the missiles with which he was assailed. I understand that his own estimate of the damage done and service rendered was an *English peerage.* I think a foreign consulship much nearer the mark. I really believe he deserves that, and I shall be much obliged to you if you can accede to his wishes. . . .

163. Lord Liverpool to the Duke of Richmond, 23 Dec. 1809

(National Library of Ireland, *Richmond MSS.* 71, f. 1379.)

Rarely is an opinion expressed that a defeat in the House of Lords will bring down a Government. It did so in Dec. 1783 on the India Bill only because of the hostility of George III to the Coalition.

I must beg of you to use your best endeavours to secure us a good attendance on the first day of the Session. No excuses ought to be admitted on that day, as we know there will be an amendment to the Address, and we can not have the benefit of proxies which are not allowed to be entered till the day after. I should be obliged to you therefore if you would take the trouble to have personal applications made to all the Peers in Ireland, and if you would let me know how far they are successful. Under the circumstances in which we are placed, the strength and perhaps even the existence of the Government will depend upon a good majority and a favourable impression upon the first debate. No efforts should therefore be omitted which can lead to the attainment of this object.

164. S. Hamilton to the duke of Rutland, 18 Nov. 1785

(Historical Manuscripts Comm., *Rutland MSS.*, III, p. 260.)

This, and succeeding documents, throw light on the social position of the aristocracy. Strangford himself was an Irish peer.

Lord Luttrell desires me to solicit your Grace for a *concordatum* warrant of £130 for the use of Mr. Smythe, Lord Strangford's eldest son, who is in very great distress with a wife and five children, and for want of such a sum would be arrested and hindered of a preferment in the Church. Lord Luttrell puts his request on the ground that the young man must soon be a peer; that such a charity to a man of rank is not unworthy as a public matter of the consideration of Government; that if he misses the preferment he expects he must, when a peer, be thrown on the public for support, and that his preferment may save a future pension. If your Grace be disposed to order it, secret service is the only fund out of which it can, with propriety, be issued, for if it were *known* to be granted thousands of such applications would be poured upon you.

165. The duke of Richmond to Lord Shannon, 27 Nov. 1808

(National Library of Ireland, *Richmond MSS.* 74, f. 1928.)

The difficulty of doing any thing for your friend Mr. Peirce Butler is very great. There has been but one sinecure place to dispose of since I came to Ireland and that is not to remain so. Almost every situation has a great deal to do, which would not suit Mr. Butler's habits. As to pensions we are so hard pressed that I have with difficulty given an Earl £200 a year, which about doubles his income. I am sorry to say there are several other Peers and widows of Peers not much better off. Under these circumstances I dare not give hopes tho' you know how ready I am to attend to your wishes on all occasions.

166. Letters from Lord Liverpool to the earl of Bristol, 13 Oct. and 4 Nov. 1825

(*British Museum Additional MSS.* 38300, ff. 229–230.)

Lord Liverpool's first wife (d. 1821) was Lord Bristol's sister. Bristol was made a marquess in 1826. The third earl of Carhampton (d. 1829) was a Commissioner of the Excise, 1785–1826. Lord Barrington was a prebendary of Durham and rector of Sedgfield.

[13 October.] . . . I have heard no question of the sort more discussed than whether it was for the advantage of an Earl to obtain a marquisate, and unless the fortune and station of the individual was such as to lead to a dukedom, I have always heard it answered in the negative. The consequence is that it is the honour which has been most *refused.* . . .

The reason is this. An earldom is a *positive advantage* if a peer has a reasonable fortune to maintain it, as it gives title and rank to daughters, and does not give it to younger sons. To daughters the rank must in almost all cases be an advantage, but to younger sons, unless they have independent fortunes, it is the greatest possible disadvantage. It is of little or no use to them in the army or navy. It is supposed to prevent their following the law, or any mercantile concern, however unobjectionable, and it places them in a *false position* in the Church. The late Lord Stafford was so impressed with this that he never would take a marquisate till his son married Lady Sutherland, and he did not naturally choose that his English honours should merge in a Scotch title.

I might add to this that I myself refused a marquisate which the King offered to me and even pressed upon me at the coronation. It is true I have no family, but then the objection to which I have alluded did not in my case exist.

If you ask me why then do the Irish seek it, my answer must be because *they are*

Irish, and as such set a higher value on all distinctions of this sort than we do in this country. . . .

[4 November 1825.] . . . I have no difficulty on public grounds in recommending you to the King at a proper and early opportunity for a marquisate. . . . Having said thus much, my further observations may appear to be officious, but in the relation in which I stand to you, I do not feel that I should conscientiously discharge my duty to yourself and to your family if I did not state to you again that the step to which you look would be injurious to all your family, and probably ruinous to some of them. . . .

You have five younger sons—two of them may be said to be still in their infancy. You would either exclude some of these sons from situations and professions advantageous and not discreditable—or if they were not absolutely excluded, you would create an incongruity between rank and station really degrading as well as otherwise inconvenient.

1. I observed in my former letter that there was no example of a person with a title following the profession of the law in this country. . . .

2. Several sons of Earls and of peers of inferior rank are at this moment engaged in banking houses and other commercial establishments from which a title would appear to exclude them. This, though a possible, I admit to be in your instance, not a very probable case. But consider how many public and official situations there are to which a title, if not an exclusion, would form a very strong objection. I have at this moment before me three applications from Earls for seats at Customs, Excise etc. for younger sons or brothers—situations constituting permanent provisions, respectable in regard to the duties and creditable to the individuals holding them, providing they are industrious and have habits of business.

There is one and one only instance of a person with a title being appointed to any of these situations, and I have seen that person shrinks from his rank in society, as he has frankly expressed himself to me, in consequence of his own feeling of the incongruity of his two situations.

We have had sons and brothers of peers, even of Earls, clerks in the Treasury and in the Secretaries of State's offices, but *never* one with a title.

I come now to the Church, which is certainly open to all ranks.

It cannot be doubted, however, I think, that a parish clergyman with a title (and every clergyman ought to begin as a parish clergyman) is in a false position. I can quote here the opinion of the Bishop of Durham, a most munificent and liberal patron as to his preferment, as well as a man of the world. His nephew, Lord Barrington, holds one of the greatest livings in the kingdom. He was not Lord Barrington when he received it. The Bishop applied to me a few years ago to give his nephew some dignity in the Church, even though inferior in value to his living, in which case he would put the living at my disposal. The reason he gave for it was, the awkwardness of a person with a title officiating as a parish priest.

But independent of this consideration—observe only how it must affect the situation of a clergyman in other respects. Upon a question of marriage I heard it said not long ago, and I thought truly, that a clergyman with £1,500 a year was a richer man than a country gentleman with £3,000. I feel this so strongly that if I was to begin life again as a clergyman I would rather my father gave me £10,000 for my private fortune without a title, than £20,000 with one. This must be assumed upon the ground of a clergyman living as such, his establishment being regulated in all its details accordingly, and yet what must be the embarrassment of a person with a title, being obliged to place himself upon a lower line of life than those country neighbours with whom he is in daily intercourse.

With respect to the army and navy the objection does not apply professionally. But it is impossible to put many sons in the same profession without in some degree abridging the means of serving them and thereby unfavourably affecting the interest of all.

I beseech you, however, above all, to reflect on what is most material, the operation of such a promotion on the minds and feelings of your children. If they are formed according to the common principles of human nature, it must have the effect of raising their pretensions and expectations, and of filling their minds with notions which it would be very difficult for you afterwards to realise.

I am so impressed with this consideration, that though I am persuaded that the largest income you could leave to Hervey would not be more than he ought to have as Earl of Bristol, nor more than for the interest of his family as the head of it, it is desirable that he should possess, yet I should think it, nevertheless, more just that you should reduce his income than to give titles to your younger sons, with the provision which in your present situation you would probably think it sufficient to assign to them. . . . [*Ibid.*, f. 266.]

B. THE HOUSE OF COMMONS

(*a*) COMPOSITION, ETC.

167. Report of the Society of the Friends of the People on the state of the representation, 9 Feb. 1793

(*Wyvill Papers*, III, App. pp. 189–251.)

. . . Your committee have found it impracticable to obtain any accurate account of the total number of electors in England, but they conceive that the necessity for such an account is essentially obviated by the one which they are enabled to lay before you. The following statement . . . is conclusive to prove, that, by the partial and unequal manner in which the mass of electors is divided, such a proportion of the 513 representatives [of England and Wales] is returned to Parliament by a few, as renders it of little consequence by how many the remainder is elected. . . .

Your committee find that *256*[1] *members*, being a *majority* of the Commons of England, are elected by 11,075 voters; or in other words by little more than the 170th part of the people to be represented, even supposing them to be only two millions. . . .

___
[1] The report as printed gives the total as 257; but Higham Ferrers is wrongly classified as a 2-member constituency.

A statement of the proportions in which the elective franchise is distributed among that body of electors who return the majority of the 513 members for England and Wales.

Places where the right of voting is in burgage and other tenures of a similar description.

	Number of voters		Number of voters		Number of voters
Appleby	220	Downton	20	Richmond	270
Ashburton	200	East Grinstead	36	Ripon	186
Great Bedwin	80	Heytesbury	50	Reigate	200
Beeralston	100	Horsham	60	Saltash	38
Bletchingly	90	Knaresborough	110	Old Sarum	7
Boroughbridge	74	Malton[1]	200	Thirsk	50
Bramber	36	Midhurst	100	Weobley	45
Clitheroe	102	Northallerton	200	Westbury	50
Cockermouth	260	Petersfield	154		

Electors 2938
return 52 members.

Places where the number of voters does not exceed 50.

Aldeburgh (Suffolk)	35	Droitwich	14	St. Mawes	36
Andover	15	Dunwich	40	St. Michael	42
Banbury[2]	19	East Looe	20	Newport (I.o.W.)	24
Bath	32	Bury St. Edmunds	36	Newton (Lancs.)	50
Beaumaris	24	Gatton	10	Newtown (I.o.W.)	36
Bewdley	14	St. Germans	20	Orford	20
Bishop's Castle	50	Grampound	50	Romney	13
Bodmin	36	Harwich	31	Rye	15
Bossiney	20	Helston	36	Scarborough	44
Brackley	33	Hastings	12	Tavistock	50
Buckingham	13	Launceston	20	Thetford	31
Calne	34	Liskeard	50	Tiverton	26
Camelford	19	Lostwithiel	24	Truro	26
Castle Rising	50	Lyme Regis	31	Wilton	50
Christchurch	40	Lymington	18	Winchelsea	9
Corfe Castle	20	Malmesbury	13	Wycombe	48
Devizes	30	Marlborough	7	Yarmouth (I.o.W.)	13

Electors 1449
return 100 members.

[1] Oldfield (*History of the Boroughs* (1794), II, p. 280) also states that the right of election at Malton was restricted to the burgage holders, numbering about 100. But in fact the franchise was exercised by all householders paying the poor rate, and in 1807 there was an electorate of 500. The great majority of these were Lord Fitzwilliam's tenants. The absence of a contest for more than half a century may explain the uncertainty about the size of the electorate.

[2] Single-member constituencies are italicized.

Places where the number of voters does not exceed 100.

Amersham	70	*Higham Ferrers*	84	Salisbury	54
Aldborough (Yorks.)	57	Hythe	96	Seaford	82
Callington	62	*Montgomery*	80	Steyning	100
Dartmouth	98	Newport		Stockbridge [*sic*]	102
West Looe	70	(Cornwall)	62	Totnes	80
Fowey	63	Okehampton	96	Tregony	60
Great Grimsby	75	Poole	100	Wenlock	100
Haslemere	60	Portsmouth	60	Whitchurch	70

Electors 1781
return 44 members.

Places where the number of voters does not exceed 200.

Arundel	190	Huntingdon	200	Queenborough	131
Boston	200	Ilchester	150	Retford	112
Bridport	180	St. Ives	180	Wallingford	140
Chippenham	140	Ludgershall	110	Wareham	150
Cambridge	200	Minehead	160	Wendover	120
Dorchester	200	Milborne Port	114	Woodstock	200
Eye	200	Morpeth	200	Wootton Bassett	160
Guildford	120	Penryn	140	Winchester	110
Heydon	190	Plymouth	160	Electors 4461
Hindon	200	Plympton	104	return 56 members.

Places where the number of voters does not exceed 300:

Marlow 216   Bridgwater 230 [Electors] 446 return 4 members.
Abstract: 2,938 elect 52; 1,449 elect 100; 1,781 elect 44; 4,461 elect 56; 446 elect 4: [Total] 11,075 return 256.

Your committee will now call your attention to the various rights of voting which are exercised in the different places returning members to Parliament.

They find that the members for the 52 Counties are all elected by one uniform right. Every man throughout England, possessed of 40 shillings per annum freehold ... is entitled to a vote for the County in which such freehold is situated.

With respect to the different cities, towns, and boroughs, they exercise a variety of separate and distinct rights, scarcely capable of being classed in any methodical order, and still less of being ascertained by the application of any fixed principle. In the greater part of them indeed the right of voting appears to be vested in the freemen of bodies corporate, but, under this general description, an infinite diversity of peculiar customs is to be found. In some places the number of voters is limited to a select body not exceeding 30 or 40; in others it is extended to 8, or 10,000. In some places the freeman must be a resident inhabitant to entitle him to vote; in others his presence is only required at an election. The right to the freedom is also different in different boroughs, and may, according to the peculiar usage, be obtained by birth, servitude, marriage, redemption, &c. &c.

The remaining rights of voting are of a still more complicated description. Burgageholds, leaseholds, and freeholds,–scot and lot, inhabitants householders, inhabitants at large, potwallopers, and commonalty, each in different boroughs prevail, and create endless misunderstandings and litigation, from the difficulty which is daily found to arise in defining and settling the legal import of those numerous distinctions, which, in some places, commit the choice of two members to as many inhabitants as every house can contain; in others, to the possessor of a spot of ground where neither houses nor inhabitants have been seen for years. . . .

A man possessed of £1000 per annum, or any greater sum, arising from copyhold, leasehold for 99 years, trade, property in the national funds, or even freehold in the City of London, and many other cities and towns having peculiar jurisdictions, is not thereby entitled to vote.

Religious opinions create an incapacity to exercise the elective franchise. All Catholics are excluded generally, and by the operation of the Test laws, Protestant Dissenters are deprived of a voice in the election of representatives in about 30 boroughs, where the right of voting is confined to the corporate officers alone.

A man paying taxes to any amount, how great soever, for his domestic establishment, does not obtain a right to vote unless his residence is in some borough where that right is vested in the inhabitants.[1] . . .

On the mode of conducting elections.

. . . The first defect in the system . . . is, that the poll, whether the voters consist of 10, or 10,000 . . . is only taken in one fixed place. A freeholder of Cornwall, living in Northumberland, must forego the exercise of his franchise, or travel to Lostwithiel; and a freeman of Berwick, residing at Falmouth, can only be heard as an elector after a journey of 400 miles. . . .

In County elections, it frequently happens that the freeholder, living in the County itself, must go 40, 50, or 60 miles before he can be admitted to poll; but these are trifling journeys compared to what must be taken by those who, being freemen of one city or town, reside in another. Your committee have thought they could not furnish better information respecting this inconvenience, than by consulting and making extracts from a certain number of . . . poll books. . . . From these it appears that, at the following places, the proportion at the last contests stood thus:

					Residents	From London	From the Country	Total
Canterbury	-	-	-	-	832	153	354	1339
Coventry	-	-	-	-	1891	356	278	2525
Bedford	-	-	-	-	919	187	332	1438
Lincoln	-	-	-	-	428	126	406	960
Newcastle on Tyne	-	-	-	1148	208	889	2245	
Bristol	-	-	-	-	3957	663	1429	6049
Colchester	-	-	-	-	528	227	525	1280
Lancaster	-	-	-	-	657	144	1481	2182

[1] The Society's petition, presented to the House of Commons on 6 May 1793, added: "This exception operates in 60 places, of which 28 do not contain 300 voters each, and the number of householders in England and Wales . . . who pay all taxes is 714,911, and of householders who pay all taxes but the house and window taxes, is 284,459, as appears by a return made to your Hon. House in 1785; so that, even supposing the 60 places above-mentioned to contain, one with another, 1,000 voters in each, there will remain 939,370 householders who have no voice in the representation, unless they have obtained it by accident or by purchase."

Estimate of the least expense of conveying a voter from the place of his residence to the place of the poll.

  6d. per mile–cost of conveyance. 7s. 6d. per day–cost of maintenance. 10s. 6d. per day–for loss of time and trouble. . . .

According to this estimate it appears, that a voter taken 50 miles to poll, will cost, For conveyance out and home, £2 10 0; For three days maintenance, £1 2 6; For three days loss of time and trouble, £1 11 6 [total] £5 4 0.

A voter taken 250 miles to poll, will cost, For conveyance out and home, £12 10 0; For seven days maintenance, £2 12 6; For seven days loss of time and trouble, £3 13 6 [total] £18 16 0. . . .

At Colchester the voters resident in London, being 227, to be brought 50 miles to poll, must, if absent 3 days, cost at least £5. 4s. each, or all together, £1180. At Coventry the voters resident in London, being 356, to be brought 90 miles, supposing them only to be out 3 days, cost £7. 4s. each, or all together, £2563. At Newcastle-upon-Tyne the voters resident in London, being 208, to be brought 274 miles, must, supposing them to be absent from home 7 days, cost at least £20 each, or all together, £4160. At Bristol the voters resident in London being 663, to be brought 120 miles, even supposing them only to be out 4 days, must cost at least £9. 12s. each, or all together, £6364. . . .

This evil of the voters residing at a place distant from the poll has also another effect, namely, the rendering nugatory an Act passed *to prevent giving meat and liquor at elections.* Custom has sanctioned the propriety of opening public houses for the reception of voters from the country, and it may easily be conceived how impossible it must be, during the tumult of an election, to distinguish one description of electors from another; the consequence is, that the resident freemen are equally with the non-residents admitted to participate in the distribution of liquor, and that the whole town is a scene of drunkenness and confusion, to the great inconvenience of the inhabitants, and the intolerable expense of the candidates. . . .

Of Private Patronage, and the Influence possessed by Peers and Commoners.

  . . . Your committee report, that the gross defects and abuses which . . . they have proved to exist in the present mode of representation, have established a system of private patronage, which renders the condition of the House of Commons practically as follows.

71 Peers and the Treasury nominate – – –	92
Procure the return of – – – – –	77
	—
Patronage of 71 peers and the Treasury – –	169
91 Commoners nominate – – – – –	82
Procure the return of – – – – –	57
	—
Patronage of 91 commoners – – – –	139
162 return – – – – 308 out of 513 Members.[1] . . .	

[1] The report states the total as 306, and the number nominated by peers and the Treasury as 90. This is merely an arithmetical error; the totals have here been corrected.

The patronage your committee have divided under two heads—*nomination*, and *influence*; and attributed it to distinct persons, under the description of *Peers* and *Commoners*.

. . . Your committee desire to have it understood that, by a *nomination*, they would describe that *absolute authority in a borough which enables the patron to command the return.* The number of places set down in this class might, your committee have every reason to believe, be with strict propriety considerably increased, but from a wish to avoid all cavil, they have confined themselves to such boroughs as are under un-doubted control. These, in general, are the private property of the patrons, or have the right of voting vested in a small corporate body, the majority of whom are his immediate dependents.

By *influence*, your committee would describe *that degree of weight acquired in a particular county, city, or borough, which accustoms the electors on all vacancies to expect the recommendation of a candidate by the patron, and induces them, either from fear, from private interest, or from incapacity to oppose, because he is so recommended, to adopt him.* . . .

County elections may be said to be, in general, contested, either *by two political parties,* or *by two great families,* or *by a great family and the gentry.* In all these cases the expedient usually had recourse to, to prevent the consequences of a struggle, is *for each of the contending interests to name one member.* . . .

With respect to the influence of the Treasury, your committee apprehend that it will occasion much surprise to find it apparently so limited, but it must be observed, that this is not a species of influence subject to any direct proof, and therefore your committee have, wherever they could, avoided the mention of it, by inserting the name of the ostensible patron, even where he openly holds a place during pleasure under Government. . . .

The following boroughs, *viz.* Stockbridge, Hedon and Barnstaple, though under the management of no particular patron, must not however be passed over in silence. The number of voters in them all does not amount to 500; and though your Commit-tee do not think it prudent to state the sort of influence which they are informed has most weight in these places, they conceive it right to mention their names separately, and others may determine how far the Members they contribute, might with propriety be added to the list of those, with whose return to Parliament the unbiassed suffrages of the people have little or no concern. . . .

The following is a list of the places compromised by political parties: Newcastle upon Tyne–Bristol–Cheshire–Essex–York–Westminster–Leicester–Maldon–Lan-cashire–Gloucester–Preston–Cumberland–Herefordshire, and Sussex.

Scotland

Table of the Number of Electors in the Counties.

					1788 Real	1788 Nominal	1790 Real and Nominal	Valued rent of each Shire, in Scots money [shillings and pence omitted]
Aberdeen	-	-	-	-	82	96	158	235,665
Argyll				-	23	21	43	149,595
Ayr	-			-	86	119	220	191,605
Banff	-			-	19	103	108	79,200
Berwick				-	66	87	150	178,365
Dumbarton	-			-	15	51	65	33,327
Dumfries				-	34	11	49	237,941
Edinburgh, or Mid Lothian			-	83	10	96	191,054
Fife				-	153	32	188	362,584
Forfar, or Angus	-			71	24	92	171,519
Haddington, or East Lothian	-	61	13	76	168,878
Inverness	-			-	20	83	103	73,188
Kincardine	-			-	46	6	55	74,921
Kirkcudbright	-			-	80	72	155	114,571
Lanark	-			-	55	69	148	160,000
Linlithgow, or West Lothian	-	29	18	64	74,931
Moray, or Elgin	-			23	53	77	65,603
Orkney	-			-	18	21	40	56,551
Peebles	-			-	32	5	37	51,937
Perth	-			-	128	19	145	335,000
Renfrew	-			-	32	82	128	68,076
Ross	-			-	46	33	72	75,040
Roxburgh	-			-	56	49	81	315,594
Selkirk	-			-	27	13	40	80,307
Stirling	-			-	46	30	59	108,518
Sutherland	-			-	8	23	35	26,193
Wigton	-			-	29	34	53	65,338

.... At the last election in 1790:[1]

Caithness	-	-	-	-	10	11	22	37,256
Cromarty	-	-	-	-	3	6	6	12,897
Kinross	-	-	-	-	9	17	23	20,192
					1390	1201	2588	3,815,857

[1] Six Scottish counties elected members alternately, Caithness alternating with Bute, Kinross with Clackmannan, and Cromarty with Nairn. In 1790 Caithness, Cromarty, and Kinross were represented.

	1788 Real	Nominal	1790 Real and Nominal	Value drent of each Shire, in Scots money [shillings and pence omitted]
To return next election:				
Bute – – – – – –	3	9	12	15,022
Clackmannan – – –	5	11	16	26,482
Nairn – – – – –	6	14	20	15,162
	1404	1235	2636	3,872,526

Table of the Number of Electors in the Royal Burghs.

Number of Town-Council, who choose each one Delegate.

I.   Edinburgh City 33.
II.   Dinwall 15, Dornock 15, Wick 12, Kirkwall 23, Tain 17.
III.   Fortrose 15, Inverness 21, Nairn 19, Forres 17.
IV.   Elgin 17, Banff 17, Cullen 26, Kintore 9, Inverurie 15.
V.   Aberdeen 19, Montrose 21, Brechin 13, Aberbrothock 19, Inverbervie 15.
VI.   Perth 26, Dundee 20, St. Andrews 29, Cupar 31, Forfar 19.
VII.   Crail 21, Kilrenny 13, Anstruther, Wester 15, Anstruther, Easter 19, Pitten-
        weem 24.
VIII.   Kinghorn 22, Dysart 24, Kirkaldy 21, Burntisland 22.
IX.   Stirling 21, Inverkeithing 15, Dunfermline 26, Culross 19, Queensferry 21.
X.   Rutherglen 19, Glasgow 32, Renfrew 21, Dumbarton 15.
XI.   Jedburgh 25, Dunbar 20, North Berwick 12, Lauder 17, Haddington 25.
XII.   Peebles 17, Linlithgow 27, Selkirk 33, Lanark 17.
XIII.   Dumfries 25, Kirkcudbright 17, Annan 21, Lochmaben 15, Sanquehar 17.
XIV.   Whithorn 19, New Galloway 20, Stranraer 18, Wigton 18.
XV.   Irwine 17, Rothsay 19, Inverary 13, Cambelltown 17, Ayr 17.

Total–1220

In Edinburgh 33 persons elect one Member of Parliament. In each of the other 14 districts, the respective Town Councils nominate one Delegate each, and by the majority of those Delegates in each district, the Member of Parliament is elected. Thus in Edinburgh 33 persons elect 1 member. In the other districts 1220 choose 65 persons, who elect 14 members. So that ultimately in the Burghs 98 persons elect 15 members.

168. Table of Parliamentary Patronage, 1794–1816

This table is compiled from four lists of parliamentary patronage made during this period. The first is that drawn up by the Society of the Friends of the People and published in 1793 (*State of the Representation in England and Wales*). All the others were published by T. H. B. Oldfield–one in 1794 (*History of the Boroughs*, 2nd ed., II, pp. 477–484), compiled on the basis of the 1790 General

Election, another in 1797 (*History of the Original Constitution of Parliaments*, pp. 531–543) incorporating the results of the 1796 elections, and a final edition in 1816 (*Representative History of Great Britain and Ireland*, VI, pp. 285–296). The number of discrepancies in the lists illustrates both the difficulty of estimating the strength of electoral influence in the unreformed constituencies, and the fluctuating and insecure nature of much of that influence. All the lists agree in limiting the direct influence of Government in the English and Welsh constituencies to no more than 16 (and, before 1816, to less than 10). The actual influence of Government was greater, but it was largely made up of seats purchased from private patrons or placed at the Government's disposal by patrons holding offices or pensions. Such seats are invariably classified as under private patronage.

Scottish constituencies were not included in their lists by the "Friends of the People"; Oldfield's accounts of Scottish patronage are here given separately after the English and Welsh table. A number of misprints and minor errors–often in numerical addition–which may be found in the original versions has been corrected.

(*State of the Representation in England and Wales*, 1793; T. H. B. Oldfield, *History of the Boroughs* (1794), II, pp. 477–484, and *History of the Original Constitution of Parliaments* (1797), pp. 531–543, and *Representative History of Great Britain and Ireland*, VI (1816), pp. 285–296.)

Nominations are in roman type; seats under influence only are italicized.

PATRONAGE OF PEERS

Name	Friends of the People 1793	Oldfield 1794	Oldfield 1797	Oldfield 1816
Prince of Wales	—	—	—	2 *Plymouth*
Dukes				
Ancaster	—	2 *Boston*	1 *Boston*	—
Beaufort	1 *Gloucestershire*	1 *Gloucestershire*	1 *Gloucestershire*	1 *Gloucestershire*
	1 *Monmouthshire*	1 *Monmouthshire*	1 *Monmouthshire*	1 *Monmouthshire*
	1 *Monmouth*	1 *Monmouth*	1 *Monmouth*	1 *Monmouth*
			1 *Bristol*	
Bedford	2 *Tavistock*	2 *Tavistock*	2 *Tavistock*	2 *Tavistock*
	1 *Bedfordshire*	1 *Bedfordshire*	1 *Bedfordshire*	1 *Bedfordshire*
	1 *Okehampton*	2 *Bedford*	2 *Bedford*	1 *Bedford*
		1 *Okehampton*	1 *Surrey*	
Bolton	1 *Totness*	1 *Totness*	—	—
Bridgwater (1816 Earl of)	2 *Brackley*	2 *Brackley*	2 *Brackley*	1 *Brackley*
Devonshire	2 *Knaresborough*	2 *Knaresborough*	2 *Knaresborough*	2 *Knaresborough*
	1 *Derbyshire*	1 *Derbyshire*	1 *Derbyshire*	1 *Derbyshire*
	1 *Derby*	1 *Derby*	2 *Derby*	1 *Derby*
Dorset	2 *East Grinstead*	2 *East Grinstead*	2 *East Grinstead*	2 *East Grinstead*
Grafton	1 *Thetford*	1 *Thetford*	1 *Thetford*	1 Thetford
	1 *Bury St. Edmunds*	1 *Bury St. Edmunds*		1 *Bury St. Edmund*
Leeds	1 *Penryn*	2 *Helston*	2 *Helston*	2 Helston
		1 *Penryn*		
Manchester	1 *Huntingdonshire*	1 *Huntingdonshire*	1 *Huntingdonshire*	1 *Huntingdonshire*
Marlborough	2 *Woodstock*	2 *Woodstock*	2 *Woodstock*	2 *Woodstock*
	1 *Heytesbury*	1 *Heytesbury*	1 *Heytesbury*	1 *Oxfordshire*
	1 *Oxfordshire*	1 *Oxfordshire*	1 *Oxfordshire*	1 *Oxford*
	1 *Oxford*	1 *Oxford*	1 *Oxford*	
Newcastle	2 *Aldborough*	2 *Aldborough*	2 *Aldborough*	2 *Aldborough*
	2 *Boroughbridge*	2 *Boroughbridge*	2 *Boroughbridge*	2 *Boroughbridge*
	1 *East Retford*	1 *East Retford*	2 *East Retford*	2 *East Retford*
	1 *Newark*	1 *Newark*	2 *Newark*	1 *Newark*

Name	Friends of the People 1793	Oldfield 1794	Oldfield 1797	Oldfield 1816
Norfolk	1 *Arundel*[1]	2 *Carlisle*	1 *Steyning*	2 *Steyning*
		1 *Arundel*	2 *Hereford*	2 *Arundel*
		1 *Leominster*	2 *Carlisle*	2 *Horsham*
		1 *Hereford*	1 *Herefordshire*	2 *Hereford*
			1 *Gloucester*	1 *Gloucester*
			1 *Arundel*	1 *Carlisle*
			1 *Shoreham*	1 *Shoreham*
Northumberland	2 Launceston	2 Launceston	2 Launceston	2 Launceston
	2 Newport (Cornwall)	2 Newport	2 Newport	2 Newport
		1 *Northumberland*	1 *Northumberland*	1 *Northumberland*
Portland	1 *Nottinghamshire*	1 *Nottinghamshire*	1 *Nottinghamshire*	1 *Nottinghamshire*
		1 *Buckinghamshire*	1 *Buckinghamshire*	
		1 *Cumberland*	1 *Bristol*	
		1 *Wigan*		
Richmond	1 *Seaford*	1 *Seaford*	1 *Sussex*	1 *Sussex*
	1 *Chichester*	1 *Sussex*	1 *Chichester*	1 *Chichester*
		1 *Chichester*		
Rutland	1 *Bramber*	1 *Bramber*	1 *Bramber*	1 *Bramber*
	1 *Grantham*	1 *Grantham*	1 *Grantham*	1 *Scarborough*
	1 *Scarborough*	1 *Scarborough*	1 *Scarborough*	1 *Leicestershire*
	1 *Newark*	1 *Newark*	1 *Leicestershire*	1 *Cambridgeshire*
		1 *Leicestershire*	1 *Cambridgeshire*	2 *Cambridge*
			2 *Cambridge*	
Marquesses				
Bath	2 Weobley	2 Weobley	2 Weobley	2 Weobley
		1 *Bath*	1 *Bath*	1 *Bath*
Buckingham	2 Buckingham	2 Buckingham	2 Buckingham	2 Buckingham
	2 St. Mawes	2 St. Mawes	2 St. Mawes	2 St. Mawes
	1 *Buckinghamshire*	1 *Buckinghamshire*	1 *Buckinghamshire*	1 *Buckinghamshire*
	1 *Aylesbury*	1 *Aylesbury*	1 *Aylesbury*	1 *Aylesbury*
Cornwallis	2 Eye	2 Eye	2 Eye	2 Eye
			1 *Suffolk*	
Hertford	2 Orford	2 Orford	2 Orford	2 Orford
				1 *Totness*
Lansdowne	2 Calne	2 Calne	2 Calne	2 Calne
	2 *Wycombe*	2 *Wycombe*	1 *Wycombe*	
Stafford	2 Newcastle-u-Lyme[2]	2 *Newcastle-u-Lyme*	2 *Newcastle-u-Lyme*	2 *Newcastle-u-Lyme*
	1 *Staffordshire*	1 *Staffordshire*	1 *Staffordshire*	1 *Staffordshire*
	1 *Lichfield*	1 *Lichfield*	1 *Lichfield*	1 *Lichfield*
				1 *Brackley*
Townshend	1 Tamworth	1 *Tamworth*	1 *Tamworth*	1 Tamworth
				1 *Great Yarmouth*
Earls				
Abingdon	2 Westbury	2 Westbury	2 Westbury	—
			1 *Wallingford*	
Ailesbury	2 Great Bedwin	2 Great Bedwin	2 Great Bedwin	2 Great Bedwin
	2 Marlborough	2 Marlborough	2 *Marlborough*	2 Marlborough

[1] A slightly later edition (*Authentic Copy of a Petition praying for a reform of Parliament . . .* (1793)) adds 1 *Leominster* Norfolk's influence.   [2] The slightly later edition classifies these 2 seats as under influence.

Name	Friends of the People 1793	Oldfield 1794	Oldfield 1797	Oldfield 1816
Bathurst	1 *Cirencester*	1 *Cirencester*	1 *Cirencester*	2 *Cirencester*
Beauchamp	—	—	—	1 *Worcestershire*
Berkeley	1 *Gloucestershire*	1 *Gloucestershire*	1 *Gloucestershire*	—
Beverley	2 Beeralston	2 Beeralston	2 Beeralston	2 Beeralston
Bristol	—	—	1 *Bury St. Edmunds*	1 Bury St. Edmun•
Buckinghamshire	—	—	—	1 *Lincoln*
Caledon	—	—	—	2 Old Sarum
Camden (1816 Marquess)	1 *Bath*	1 *Bath*	1 *Bath*	1 *Brecknockshire*
Carlisle	2 *Morpeth*	2 Morpeth	2 *Morpeth*	1 *Morpeth*
Carnarvon	—	—	1 *Cricklade*	
Cholmondeley (1816 Marquess of)	—	—	1 Castle Rising	1 Castle Rising
Clarendon	1 *Wootton Bassett*	1 *Wootton Bassett*	1 Wootton Bassett	1 *Wootton Bassett*
Darlington	1 Winchelsea	1 Winchelsea	1 *Durham Co.*	2 Winchelsea
		1 *Durham Co.*		2 Tregoney
				2 Camelford
				1 *Durham Co.*
Derby	—	1 *Lancashire*	1 *Lancashire*	1 *Lancashire*
		1 *Preston*	1 *Preston*	1 *Preston*
Dorchester	—	1 *Dorchester*	1 Dorchester	
Egremont	2 Midhurst	2 Midhurst	—	1 *Sussex*
				1 *Chichester*
Exeter (1816 Marquess of)	2 *Stamford*	2 *Stamford*	2 *Stamford*	2 *Stamford*
Fitzwilliam	2 Malton	2 Malton	2 Malton	2 Malton
	1 Higham Ferrers	1 Higham Ferrers	1 Higham Ferrers	1 Higham Ferrers
	2 *Peterborough*	2 *Peterborough*	2 *Peterborough*	2 *Peterborough*
				1 *Yorkshire*
Grosvenor	2 *Chester*	2 *Chester*	2 *Chester*	1 *Chester*
Guilford	1 *Banbury*	1 *Banbury*	1 *Banbury*	1 *Banbury*
Hardwicke	1 *Reigate*	1 *Reigate*	1 *Reigate*	1 *Reigate*
	1 *Cambridgeshire*	1 *Cambridgeshire*	1 *Cambridgeshire*	1 *Cambridgeshire*
Lonsdale	2 *Haslemere*	2 Haslemere	2 Haslemere	2 Haslemere
	2 Cockermouth	2 Cockermouth	2 Cockermouth	2 Cockermouth
	1 Appleby	1 Appleby	1 *Cumberland*	1 Appleby
	2 *Westmorland*	2 *Westmorland*	2 *Westmorland*	1 *Cumberland*
		1 *Cumberland*	1 *Lancaster*	2 *Westmorland*
				1 *Carlisle*
Mount Edgcumbe	2 Plympton	2 Plympton	2 Plympton	1 Plympton
	2 Lostwithiel	2 Lostwithiel	2 Lostwithiel	2 Lostwithiel
	1 Bossiney	1 Bossiney	1 Bossiney	1 Bossiney
	1 *Fowey*	1 *Fowey*	1 *Fowey*	1 Fowey
Northampton (1816 Marquess of)	—	1 *Northampton*	1 *Northampton*	1 *Northampton*
Orford	1 Castle Rising	1 Castle Rising	—	1 *Lynn*
Oxford	1 *Radnorshire*	1 *Radnorshire*	1 *Radnorshire*	—
	1 *Radnor*	1 *Radnor*	1 *Radnor*	
		1 *Herefordshire*	1 *Herefordshire*	
Pembroke	2 Wilton	2 Wilton	2 Wilton	2 Wilton

Name	Friends of the People 1793	Oldfield 1794	Oldfield 1797	Oldfield 1816
Portsmouth	1 Andover	1 Andover	1 Andover	1 Andover
Poulet	2 Bridgwater	2 Bridgwater	1 Bridgwater	2 Bridgwater
Powis	1 Montgomery	1 Montgomeryshire 1 Montgomery	1 Montgomery	1 Montgomery 2 Bishop's Castle 2 Ludlow
Radnor	2 Downton 1 Salisbury	2 Downton 1 Salisbury	2 Downton 1 Salisbury	2 Downton 1 Salisbury
Sandwich	1 Huntingdonshire 2 Huntingdon	1 Huntingdonshire 2 Huntingdon	1 Huntingdonshire	1 Huntingdonshire 2 Huntingdon
Shaftesbury	1 Dorchester	1 Dorchester	1 Dorchester	1 Dorchester
Spencer	1 Okehampton 1 St. Albans	1 Okehampton 1 St. Albans	1 St. Albans	—
Thanet	1 Appleby	1 Appleby	2 Appleby	1 Appleby
Uxbridge (1816 Marquess of Anglesey)	1 Milborne Port 1 Anglesey 1 Carnarvon	1 Milborne Port 1 Anglesey 1 Carnarvon	1 Milborne Port 1 Anglesey 1 Carnarvon	2 Milborne Port 1 Anglesey 1 Carnarvon
Warwick	2 Warwick	2 Warwick	2 Warwick	1 Warwick
Westmorland	2 Lyme Regis	2 Lyme Regis	2 Lyme Regis	2 Lyme Regis
Viscounts				
Anson (1793-7 T. Anson)	—	—	—	1 Lichfield
Bolingbroke	1 Wootton Bassett	1 Wootton Bassett	1 Wootton Bassett	1 Wootton Bassett
Falmouth	2 Truro	2 Truro 1 Michael	2 Truro	1 Michael 2 Truro
Lady Irwin[1]	2 Horsham	2 Horsham	2 Horsham	—
Newark (1816 Earl Manvers)	—	—	1 Nottinghamshire	1 Nottinghamshire
Sydney	1 Whitchurch 2 Ludgershall	1 Whitchurch 1 Ludgershall	1 Whitchurch 1 Ludgershall	1 Whitchurch
Lords				
Berwick	—	—	1 Shrewsbury	—
Bradford (1793-4 Sir H. Bridgman, 1816 Earl of)	—	—	1 Wenlock 1 Wigan	1 Wenlock
Brodrick (1793-4, 1816 Visc. Midleton (I))	—	—	1 Whitchurch	1 Whitchurch
Brownlow (1816 Earl)	1 Grantham	1 Grantham	1 Grantham	1 Clitheroe
Bulkeley (1816 Viscount)	1 Beaumaris	1 Beaumaris 1 Carnarvonshire	1 Beaumaris 1 Carnarvonshire	1 Beaumaris 1 Carnarvonshire
Bute (1797 Marquess of)	1 Bossiney 1 Cardiff	1 Bossiney 1 Cardiff	1 Cardiff	1 Cardiff
Calthorpe (1793-4 Sir H. G. Calthorpe)	—	—	1 Bramber 1 Hindon	1 Bramber 1 Hindon
Camelford	2 Old Sarum	2 Old Sarum	2 Old Sarum	—
Carrington (1797 Irish Peer)	—	—	—	2 Midhurst 2 Wendover 1 Nottingham 1 Leicester

[1] Lady Irwin was classified by the 'Friends of the People' as a Commoner.

Name	Friends of the People 1793	Oldfield 1794	Oldfield 1797	Oldfield 1816
Cawdor	—	—	—	1 *Carmarthen*
Clinton (1793–4 R. G. W. Trefusis)	—	—	2 Callington / 1 Ashburton	2 Callington / 1 Ashburton
Clive (1793–4 Irish Peer)	—	—	2 Bishops Castle / 1 *Ludlow*	—
Craven	—	1 *Berkshire*	1 *Berkshire*	—
Curzon (1793–4 P. A. Curzon, 1816 Viscount)	—	—	1 *Clitheroe* / 1 *Leicestershire*	1 *Clitheroe*
De Dunstanville (1793–4 Sir F. Bassett)	—	—	2 *Penryn*	2 Bodmin / 1 *Penryn*
Delaval	—	1 *Berwick*	1 *Berwick*	—
Dundas (1793–4 Sir T. Dundas)	—	—	2 *Richmond*	2 Richmond
Dynevor	—	1 *Carmarthenshire*	—	1 *Carmarthenshire*
Eliot (1816 Earl of St. Germans)	2 Liskeard / 2 Grampound / 2 St. Germans	2 Liskeard / 2 Grampound / 2 St. Germans	2 Liskeard / 2 St. Germans	2 Liskeard / 2 St. Germans
Foley	2 Droitwich / 1 *Worcestershire*	2 Droitwich	2 Droitwich	2 Droitwich / 1 *Worcestershire* / 1 *Herefordshire*
Grantley	—	1 *Guildford*	1 *Guildford*	—
Grimston	1 *St. Albans*	1 *St. Albans*	1 *St. Albans*	—
Harewood (1793–4 E. Lascelles, 1816 Earl of)	—	—	1 *Northallerton* / 1 *Yorkshire*	1 Northallerton / 1 *Yorkshire* / 1 *Pontefract*
Harrowby (1816 Earl of)	2 Tiverton	2 Tiverton	2 *Tiverton*	2 *Tiverton*
Lyttelton (1793–4 Lord Westcote (I))	—	—	1 *Bewdley*	—
Malmesbury	1 Christchurch	1 Christchurch	—	—
Middleton	—	—	—	1 *Newark*
Monson	—	—	—	1 *Lincoln*
Mulgrave (1793–4 Irish Peer, 1816 Earl of)	—	—	1 *Scarborough*	1 Scarborough
Northwick (1793–7 Sir J. Rushout)	—	—	—	1 *Evesham*
Onslow (1816 Earl of)	1 *Guildford*	1 *Guildford*	1 *Guildford*	2 *Guildford*
Pelham	1 *Lewes*	1 *Lewes* / 1 *Sussex*	2 Seaford / 1 *Lewes* / 1 *Sussex*	—
Petre	1 *Thetford*	1 *Thetford*	1 *Thetford*	1 *Thetford*
Rivers	—	1 *Dorset*	1 *Dorchester*	—
Somers	1 *Reigate*	1 *Reigate*	1 *Reigate*	1 *Reigate*
Walpole	1 *Lynn*	1 *Lynn*	2 *Lynn*	—
Yarborough (1793–4 C. A. Pelham)	—	—	2 *Grimsby* / 1 *Beverley*	1 Newtown I.o.W. / 1 *Lincolnshire* / 2 *Grimsby*

Name	Friends of the People 1793	Oldfield 1794	Oldfield 1797	Oldfield 1816
Number of Peers	72	81	93	87
Members nominated	92	92	93	115
Seats under influence	72	103	124	103
Total returned by Peers	164	195	217	218

Patronage of Commoners

Name	Friends of the People 1793	Oldfield 1794	Oldfield 1797	Oldfield 1816
W. Drake (1816 T. T. Drake)	2 Amersham	2 Amersham	2 Amersham	2 Amersham
P. C. Crespigny (1797 T.C., 1816 Sir C. C. de Crespigny)	2 Aldeburgh	2 Aldeburgh / 2 Sudbury	2 Aldeburgh	2 Aldeburgh
J. Iremonger	1 Andover	1 Andover	1 Andover	—
R. Etwall	—	—	—	1 Andover
R. G. W. Trefusis (1794 cr. Lord Clinton)	2 Callington / 1 Ashburton	2 Callington / 1 Ashburton	—	—
Sir R. Palk (1816 Sir L.)	1 Ashburton	1 Ashburton	1 Ashburton	1 Ashburton
Sir G. Thomas	—	—	1 Arundel	
Lord G. Cavendish	—	—	—	1 Aylesbury
Earl of Lisburne (I)	—	1 Berwick	—	1 Cardigan
C. A. Pelham (1794 cr. Lord Yarborough)	2 Grimsby	2 Grimsby / 1 Beverley		
Lord Westcote (I) (1794 cr. Lord Lyttelton (GB))	1 Bewdley	1 Bewdley		
— Robarts	—	—	—	1 Bewdley
Lord Clive (I) (1794 Eng. Peer)	2 Bishop's Castle / 1 Ludlow	2 Bishop's Castle / 1 Ludlow	—	
Sir R. Clayton	2 Bletchingly	2 Bletchingly	2 Bletchingly	—
M. Russell	—	—	—	2 Bletchingly
C. Palmer	—	—	—	1 Bath
G. Hunt	1 Bodmin	1 Bodmin	—	—
Sir J. Morshead	—	—	2 Bodmin	—
J. Stuart Wortley	—	—	1 Bossiney	1 Bossiney
Sir P. Burrell	1 Boston	—	—	—
T. Fydell	—	—	1 Boston	
Sir H. G. Calthorpe (1796 cr. Lord Calthorpe)	1 Bramber / 1 Hindon	1 Bramber / 1 Hindon	—	
Sir C. Morgan	— / — / 1 Brecon	1 Monmouthshire / 1 Breconshire / 1 Brecon	1 Monmouthshire / 1 Breconshire / 1 Brecon	1 Monmouthshire / 1 Brecknock
T. Whitmore (1796 J. Whitmore)	—	1 Bridgnorth	2 Bridgnorth	2 Bridgnorth
C. Sturt	1 Bridport	1 Bridport	—	1 Bridport
J. Mortlock	2 Cambridge	2 Cambridge	—	—

Name	Friends of the People 1793	Oldfield 1794	Oldfield 1797	Oldfield 1816
Sir J. Phillips	2 Camelford	2 Camelford	2 *Camelford*	—
B. Howard	1 Castle Rising	1 Castle Rising	—	—
R. Howard	—	—	1 Castle Rising	1 Castle Rising
Sir S. Fludyer	1 *Chippenham*	1 *Chippenham*	1 Chippenham	—
J. Dawkins (1796 H. Dawkins)	1 *Chippenham*	1 *Chippenham*	1 Chippenham	—
J. Maitland	—	—	—	1 Chippenham
C. Brooke	—	—	—	1 Chippenham
G. Rose	1 Christchurch	1 Christchurch	2 Christchurch 2 *Southampton*	2 Christchurch 1 *Southampton*
T. Lister	1 Clitheroe	1 Clitheroe	1 Clitheroe	—
P. A. Curzon (1794 cr. Lord Curzon	1 Clitheroe	1 Clitheroe	—	—
J. Bond (1816 N. Bond)	1 Corfe Castle	1 Corfe Castle	1 Corfe Castle	1 Corfe Castle
H. Bankes	1 Corfe Castle	1 Corfe Castle	1 Corfe Castle	1 Corfe Castle
E. Bastard	2 *Dartmouth*	2 *Dartmouth*	2 *Dartmouth*	—
F. West	—	—	—	1 *Denbigh*
T. W. Coke	1 *Derby*	1 *Derby*	—	—
E. Coke	—	—	—	1 *Derby*
Sir W. W. Wynn	1 *Denbighshire*	1 *Denbighshire* 1 *Flint*	1 *Denbighshire* 1 *Flint*	1 *Denbighshire* 1 *Flint* 1 *Montgomeryshire*
R. Middleton	1 *Denbigh*	1 *Denbigh*	—	—
J. Sutton	2 *Devizes*	2 *Devizes*	2 *Devizes*	—
J. Smith	—	—	—	1 *Devizes*
T. G. Estcourt	—	—	—	1 *Devizes*
R. Williams	—	—	—	1 *Dorchester*
Sir J. Vanneck (1796 cr. Lord Huntingfield [I])	1 Dunwich	1 Dunwich	1 Dunwich	1 Dunwich
M. Barne (1793 B., 1816 S. Barne)	1 Dunwich	1 Dunwich	1 Dunwich	1 Dunwich
Sir H. V. Tempest	—	—	1 *Durham*	—
J. Lambton	—	—	1 *Durham*	—
Sir C. Davers	1 *Bury St. Edmunds*	1 *Bury St. Edmunds*	1 *Bury St. Edmunds*	—
Sir J. Rushout (1797 cr. Lord Northwick)	—	1 *Evesham*	—	—
Sir T. Mostyn	—	—	—	1 *Flintshire*
P. Rashleigh (1816 W. Rashleigh)	1 *Fowey*	1 *Fowey*	1 Fowey	1 Fowey
R. Ladbroke	1 Gatton	1 Gatton	—	—
W. Currie	1 Gatton	1 Gatton	—	—
J. Petrie	—	—	2 Gatton	—
Sir M. Wood	—	—	—	2 Gatton
J. Robinson	2 Harwich	2 Harwich	2 *Harwich*	—
E. Milward	2 Hastings	2 Hastings	2 *Hastings*	2 Hastings
Lord Milford [I]	1 *Haverfordwest*	1 *Haverfordwest*	1 *Haverfordwest*	—
Lord Kensington [I]	—	—	—	1 *Haverfordwest*
Baron Dimsdale	—	1 *Hertford*	—	—
B. Thompson	—	1 *Hedon*	—	—

Name	Friends of the People 1793	Oldfield 1794	Oldfield 1797	Oldfield 1816
L. Iveson	—	—	—	2 *Hedon*
Sir J. St. Aubyn	1 Helston	—	—	—
— Rogers	1 Helston	—	—	—
P. W. A. A'Court (Sir W. P. A.)	1 Heytesbury	1 Heytesbury	1 Heytesbury	2 Heytesbury
W. Beckford	1 *Hindon*	1 *Hindon*	1 *Hindon*	1 *Hindon*
Sir G. Yonge	1 *Honiton*	1 Honiton		—
— Flood				1 *Honiton*
— Townsend				1 *Honiton*
Sir C. F. Radcliffe	1 *Hythe*	1 *Hythe*	1 *Hythe*	
W. Evelyn	1 *Hythe*	1 *Hythe*	1 *Hythe*	
R. Troward (1797 J. Troward)	2 Ilchester	2 Ilchester	2 Ilchester	
Sir W. Manners	—	—	—	2 Ilchester
				1 *Grantham*
C. A. Crickett (1816 R.A.)	—	—	2 *Ipswich*	1 *Ipswich*
W. Praed	2 *St. Ives*	2 St. Ives	2 *St. Ives*	—
S. Stephens	—	—	—	1 St. Ives
T. Harley	1 *Leominster*[1]	1 *Leominster*	—	—
Lord Malden	—	—	2 *Leominster*	—
— Coleman				2 *Leominster*
T. Anson (1806 cr. Viscount Anson)	1 *Lichfield*	1 *Lichfield*	1 *Lichfield*	—
J. Buller	2 West Looe	2 East Looe	2 East Looe	2 West Looe
	2 Saltash	2 West Looe	2 West Looe	2 Saltash
		2 Saltash	2 Saltash	
— Buller	2 East Looe	—	—	—
Sir E. Buller	—	—	—	2 East Looe
T. Everett (1816 J. H.)	—	1 Ludgershall	1 Ludgershall	1 Ludgershall
Sir J. Graham	—	—	—	1 Ludgershall
Sir H. Burrard-Neale	2 Lymington	2 Lymington	2 Lymington	2 Lymington
Sir M. B. Folkes	—	—	—	1 *Lynn*
J. H. Strutt	—	1 Malden	1 *Malden*	1 *Malden*
C. C. Western	—	1 Malden	1 *Malden*	—
J. Wilkins	2 Malmesbury	2 Malmesbury	2 Malmesbury	—
J. Pitt				2 Malmesbury
				1 *Cricklade*
T. Williams (1816 O. Williams)	1 *Marlow*	1 Marlow	2 *Marlow*	2 Marlow
W. Lee Antonie	1 *Marlow*	1 Marlow	—	—
Lord Carrington [I] (1797 Eng. Peer)	—	—	2 Midhurst	—
			2 Wendover	
Sir C. Hawkins	1 *Michael*	—	2 *Michael*	1 Michael
			2 *Grampound*	1 St. Ives
				2 *Grampound*

[1] The slightly later edition attributes this influence to Lord Bateman.

Name	Friends of the People 1793	Oldfield 1794	Oldfield 1797	Oldfield 1816
Sir F. Bassett (1796 cr. Lord De Dunstanville)	1 *Michael* 1 *Penryn*	1 *Michael* 1 *Penryn*	—	—
W. C. Medlycott	1 Milborne Port	1 Milborne Port	1 Milborne Port	—
J. F. Luttrell	2 *Minehead*	2 Minehead	2 *Minehead*	2 Minehead
W. Ord				1 Morpeth
J. C. Jervoise	1 Yarmouth I.o.W.	1 Yarmouth I.o.W.	1 Yarmouth I.o.W.	
T. P. Legh	2 Newton (Lancs.)	2 Newton	2 Newton	2 Newton
Rev. L. T. Holmes (1816 Sir L.T.W.)	2 Newport I.o.W. 1 Yarmouth I.o.W.	2 Newport I.o.W. 1 Yarmouth I.o.W.	2 Newport I.o.W. 1 Yarmouth I.o.W.	2 Newport I.o.W. 2 Yarmouth I.o.W.
Sir J. Barrington	1 Newtown I.o.W.	1 Newtown I.o.W.	1 Newtown I.o.W.	1 Newtown I.o.W.
Sir R. Worsley	1 Newtown I.o.W.	1 Newtown I.o.W.	1 Newtown I.o.W.	
H. Peirse	1 Northallerton	1 Northallerton	1 Northallerton	1 Northallerton
E. Lascelles (1796 Lord, 1816 Earl of Harewood)	1 Northallerton	1 Northallerton		
T. Tyrwhitt	—	—	1 *Okehampton*	
R. B. Robson	—	—	1 *Okehampton*	
A. Savile	—	—		2 Okehampton
H. Barlow	—	1 *Pembroke*	1 *Pembroke*	
Sir J. Owen	—	—	—	1 *Pembrokeshire* 1 *Pembroke*
W. Jolliffe (1816 H. Jolliffe)	2 Petersfield	2 Petersfield	2 Petersfield	2 Petersfield
P. T. Treby	—			1 *Plympton*
B. Lester	—	1 *Poole*	1 *Poole*	1 *Poole*
J. Jeffery	—	1 *Poole*	1 *Poole*	1 *Poole*
Lord Galway [I]	—		1 *Pontefract*	
Sir J. Carter (1816 — Carter)	2 *Portsmouth*	2 Portsmouth	2 *Portsmouth*	2 *Portsmouth*
Sir H. P. Hoghton			1 *Preston*	
S. Horrocks	—		—	1 *Preston*
Sir T. Dundas (1796 Lord Dundas)	2 Richmond	2 Richmond		
Mrs. Allanson	2 Ripon	2 Ripon	2 Ripon	
Miss Lawrence	—	—	—	2 Ripon
Sir E. Dering (1816 Sir C.)	2 Romney	2 Romney	2 Romney	2 Romney
Sir G. N. Noel	—		—	1 *Rutlandshire*
T. Lamb	2 Rye	2 Rye	2 Rye	2 Rye
G. P. Jervoise	—	—	—	1 *Salisbury*
P. Stephens	1 *Sandwich*	2 *Sandwich*	1 *Sandwich*	
Lord Mulgrave [I] (1796 Eng. Peer)	1 *Scarborough*	1 Scarborough	—	
T. Pelham	—	1 Seaford	—	
C. Leach	—	—	—	1 Seaford
— R. Ellis	—	—	—	1 Seaford
J. Benfield	—	2 *Shaftesbury*	2 Shaftesbury	—
P. Whittaker	2 *Shaftesbury*	—	—	—
J. Dynley				2 Shaftesbury

Name	Friends of the People 1793	Oldfield 1794	Oldfield 1797	Oldfield 1816
Sir J. Honywood	2 Steyning	2 Steyning	1 Steyning	—
T. F. Barham (1797, 1816 J. F.)	—	2 Stockbridge	1 Stockbridge	1 Stockbridge
G. Porter	—	—	1 Stockbridge	1 Stockbridge
Sir J. C. Hippisley	—	—	—	1 Sudbury
R. Peel (1816 Sir R.)	1 Tamworth	1 Tamworth	1 Tamworth	1 Tamworth
Sir B. Hammett	—	2 Taunton	1 Taunton	—
Sir T. B. Lethbridge	—	—	—	1 Taunton
Sir T. Frankland	2 Thirsk	2 Thirsk	2 Thirsk	2 Thirsk
Sir F. Buller	1 Totness	1 Totness		
T. O. Powlett (1816 W. J. V.)	—		2 Totness	1 Totness
R. Barwell	2 Tregony 1 Winchelsea	2 Tregony 1 Winchelsea	2 Tregony 2 Winchelsea	—
Sir F. Sykes	2 Wallingford	2 Wallingford	1 Wallingford	—
J. Calcraft	2 Wareham	2 Wareham	2 Wareham	2 Wareham
C. Tudway (1816 J.P.)	1 Wells	1 Wells	2 Wells	1 Wells
J. B. Church	2 Wendover	2 Wendover	—	—
Sir H. Bridgman (1794 cr. Lord, 1815 Earl of, Bradford)	1 Wenlock 1 Wigan	1 Wenlock 1 Wigan	—	—
C. W. Forester	1 Wenlock	1 Wenlock	1 Wenlock	1 Wenlock
Sir M. M. Lopes	—	—	—	2 Westbury
W. Pulteney	4 Weymouth & Melcombe 1 Shrewsbury	4 Weymouth & Melcombe 1 Shrewsbury	4 Weymouth & Melcombe 1 Shrewsbury	—
Sir G. F. Johnstone	—	—	—	4 Weymouth & Melcombe
Viscount Midleton (I), (1796 cr. Ld. Brodrick (GB))	1 Whitchurch	1 Whitchurch	—	—
J. Cotes	—	—	1 Wigan	—
Sir R. Holt Leigh	—	—	—	1 Wigan
J. Hodson	—	—	—	1 Wigan
R. Gamon	1 Winchester	1 Winchester	—	—
H. Penton	1 Winchester	1 Winchester	1 Winchester	—
Earl Temple	—	—	1 Winchester	—
Sir H. C. S. Mildmay	—	—	—	2 Winchester
Sir T. Baring	—	—	—	1 Wycombe
Sir J. D. King	—	—	—	1 Wycombe
Number of Commoners	90	99	88	90
Members nominated	80	102	74	85
Seats under influence	57	54	70	52
Total returned by Commoners	137	156	144	137

Patronage of the Treasury

Name	Friends of the People 1793	Oldfield 1794	Oldfield 1797	Oldfield 1816
	2 Queenborough	2 Queenborough	2 Queenborough	2 Dartmouth
	1 Dover	1 Dover	1 Dover	1 Dover
	2 Windsor	2 Windsor	2 Windsor	2 Harwich
	1 Plymouth	2 Plymouth	2 Plymouth	2 Hythe
	1 Rochester	1 Rochester	1 Rochester	1 Windsor
			1 Sandwich	2 Hampshire
				1 Great Yarmouth
				1 Queenborough (Admiralty)
				1 Rochester (Admiralty)
				2 Sandwich (Admiralty)
				1 Queenborough (Ordnance)

Parliamentary Influence in Scotland

Peers	Oldfield 1794	1797	1816
Dukes:			
Argyll	1 Argyllshire	1 Argyllshire	1 Argyllshire
			1 Ayr Burghs
Athol	1 Forfarshire	1 Perthshire	1 Perthshire
	1 Perthshire		
	1 Perth Burghs		
Buccleuch	1 Berwickshire	1 Selkirkshire	1 Selkirkshire
			1 Selkirk Burghs
Duke of Buccleuch, Marquess of Queensberry and Earl of Hopetoun	—	—	1 Dumfriesshire
Duke of Buccleuch and Mr. Dundas of Arniston	—	—	1 Edinburghshire
			1 Edinburgh City
Gordon	1 Aberdeenshire	1 Aberdeenshire	1 Aberdeenshire
	1 Banffshire		
	1 Inverness Co.		
Hamilton	1 Lanarkshire	1 Lanarkshire	1 Lanarkshire
	1 Renfrewshire		
Montrose	—	1 Stirlingshire	1 Stirlingshire
			1 Dumbartonshire
Queensberry (1816 Marquess of)	1 Dumfriesshire	1 Dumfriesshire	1 Dumfries Burghs
	1 Roxburghshire	1 Peeblesshire	
	1 Dumfries Burghs	1 Dumfries Brughs	
Roxburgh	—	1 Roxburghshire	—
Marquesses:			
Tweeddale	—	1 Haddingtonshire	—

Earls:	Oldfield 1794	1797	1816
Bute (1797 Marquess of)	1 *Buteshire*	1 Buteshire	1 *Buteshire*
	1 *Ayr Burghs*		
Dundonald	1 *Stirling Burghs*	—	—
Eglinton	1 *Ayrshire*	1 *Ayrshire*	1 *Ayrshire*
	1 *Peeblesshire*		
Elgin	1 *Elginshire*	—	—
Fife	1 *Fifeshire*	1 *Banffshire*	—
Peers:			
Galloway	1 *Kirkudbright*	1 *Wigtownshire*	1 *Wigtownshire*
	1 *Orkney*		1 *Kirkudbright*
	1 *Wigtownshire*		1 *Stranraer Burghs*
	1 *Stranraer Burghs*		
Haddington	1 *Haddingtonshire*	—	—
Earl of Home and Mr. Home of Wedderburne	—	—	1 *Berwickshire*
Earl of Kintore and Earl of Fife	—	—	1 *Elgin Burghs*
Hopetoun	1 *Linlithgowshire*	1 *Linlithgowshire*	1 *Linlithgowshire*
	1 *Kinghorn Burghs*		1 *Haddingtonshire*
			1 *Stirling Burghs*
Lauderdale	1 *Jedburgh Burghs*	—	1 *Jedburgh Burghs*
Leven	1 *Kinross Co.*	—	—
Minto	—	—	1 *Roxburghshire*
Seafield	—	—	1 *Elginshire*
Countess of Sutherland (1816 Marchioness of Stafford)	1 *Sutherlandshire*	1 *Sutherlandshire*	1 *Sutherlandshire*
			1 *Tain Burghs*
Lords:			
Baroness Abercromby	—	—	1 *Clackmannanshire*
Cawdor	—	1 *Nairnshire*	1 *Nairnshire*
Dundas	—	1 *Orkney*	—
Lord Dundas and Sir W. Honyman	—	—	1 *Orkney*
Elphinstone	—	1 *Dumbartonshire*	—
Total Influence of Peers	30	20	31
Commoners:			
Sir G. Abercromby	—	—	1 *Banffshire*
—, Abercromby	—	1 *Clackmannanshire*	(see Baroness Abercromby)
Sir J. Anstruther	1 *Anstruther Burghs*	1 Anstruther Burghs	1 *Anstruther Burghs*
— Barclay of Urie	—	1 *Kincardineshire*	1 *Kincardineshire*
A. Brodie	1 *Elgin Burghs*	—	—
Lord F. Campbell	1 *Dumbartonshire*	—	—
— Davidson	—	1 *Cromartyshire*	—
H. Dundas	1 *Edinburghshire*	1 *Edinburghshire*	—
	1 *Edinburgh City.*	1 *Edinburgh City*	
Sir T. Dundas	1 *Stirlingshire*	—	—
	1 *Tain Burghs*		
J. Farquhar	—	—	1 *Aberdeen Burghs*
— Ferguson	—	—	1 *Kinghorn Burghs*

Commoners:	Oldfield 1794	1797	1816
— Fraser	—	1 *Inverness Co.*	
— Graham	—	1 *Kinross Co.*	
C. Grant	—	—	1 *Inverness Co.*
			1 *Inverness Burghs*
— Home	—	1 *Berwickshire*	(see Earl of Home)
— Mackenzie	—	1 *Ross Co.*	
R. Maule (1816 Wm.)	—	1 *Forfarshire*	1 *Forfarshire*
Sir J. Maxwell & A. Campbell	—	—	1 *Glasgow Burghs*
Sir J. Montgomery	—	—	1 *Peeblesshire*
J. Murray	—	1 *Kirkudbright*	—
W. Pulteney	1 *Cromartyshire*	—	—
late Lord Seaforth's heir[1]	—	—	1 *Ross Co.*
Sir J. Shaw Stewart (1816 Sir M.)	—	1 *Renfrewshire*	1 *Renfrewshire*
Sir J. Sinclair	1 *Caithness Co.*	1 *Caithness Co.*	
Sir D. Wedderburn	—	—	1 *Perth Burghs*
— Wemyss	—	1 *Fifeshire*	1 *Fifeshire*
Total returned by Commoners	9	15	14
Peers	30	20	31
Influence of the Treasury	—	13[2]	—
	39	48 [sic]	45

Totals, England and Wales

	1793	1794	1797	1816
Number of Members returned				
by Peers; by nomination	92	92	93	115
by influence	72	103	124	103
by Commoners; by nomination	80	102	74	85
by influence	57	54	70	52
by the Treasury, etc.	7	8	9	16
Total of the 513 Members for England and Wales said to be returned by patronage:	308	359	370	371

Scotland

Returned by Peers	—	30	20	31
Commoners	—	9	13[3]	14
the Treasury	—	—	12[4]	—
Total number of 558 Members for England, Wales and Scotland said to be returned by patronage:	—	398[5]	415	416

[1] Lord Seaforth d. 1815; the family estates passed to his eldest daughter, Mary Frederica Elizabeth, widow of Admiral Sir Samuel Hood. In 1817 she married James Alexander Stewart.

[2] Stated to be for 13 of the 14 Burgh districts; two of them, however, are also classified as under private patronage. Scotland was represented by 15 borough members and 30 county members; 27 counties were represented in every Parliament. The other six were grouped in three pairs, each pair electing one member in alternate Parliaments.

[3] 15 in the table, but three pairs of counties were represented only in alternate Parliaments.

[4] 13 in the table, but one also classified as under private patronage.

[5] "All the Members for Scotland are sent to Parliament under the influence of individuals, though the author has not been able to procure the names of all the patrons" (Oldfield's note). This increases the total to 404.

169. J. W. Croker to Canning, 3 and 6 April 1827

(*Correspondence and Diaries of John Wilson Croker*, ed. L. J. Jennings, I (1884), pp. 367–372.)

Croker was Secretary to the Admiralty; Canning was soon to be appointed Prime Minister in succession to Lord Liverpool, who had had a seizure on 17 Feb.

[3 April.] . . . I think it right to send you a memorandum which will show you, in one view, how impossible it is to do anything satisfactory towards a Government in this country without the help of the aristocracy. I know that you must be well aware of this, yet the following summary may not be useless to you, though I know that it is imperfect.

Number of members returned to the House of Commons by the influence of some of the peers:–

Tories–Lord Lonsdale 9, Lord Hertford 8, Duke of Rutland 6, Duke of Newcastle 5, Lord Yarborough (for W. Holmes) 5, Lord Powis 4, Lord Falmouth 4, Lord Anglesey 4, Lord Ailesbury 4, Lord Radnor 3, Duke of Northumberland 4, Duke of Buccleuch 4, Marquess of Stafford 3, Duke of Buckingham (2) 3 [*sic*], Lord Mount-Edgcumbe 4–[total] 70; besides at least 12 or 14 who have each two seats, say 26 –[total] 96.

Whigs–Lord Fitzwilliam 8, Lord Darlington 7, Duke of Devonshire 7, Duke of Norfolk 6, Lord Grosvenor 6, Duke of Bedford 4, Lord Carrington 4–[total] 42; with about half a dozen who have each a couple of seats, 12–[total] 54. . . . You will observe that I included the Whigs as well as the Tories, and I reckon Lord Seaford's and Lord Wharncliffe's interests as well as those of the older peers, and I arrive at this conclusion, and a very important one it is, that the *old Tory* and the *steady Whig* aristocracies have at least 150 members in the House of Commons, not by influence or connection but by direct nomination, and that no Government which did not divide them could stand for any length of time. I think the peers, &c., who are not either old Tories or old Whigs may have about a dozen members. . . .

[6 April.]–I send you a memorandum which I think will surprise you. The aristocracy, powerful as it is, does not enjoy any great share of political *office* in the House of Commons. So that, in fact, a Government has less to give to them or take from them than at first thoughts one would have supposed. Depend upon it, the aristocracy is the *unum necessarium*, or at least an *indispensable* ingredient, and that in order to conciliate and manage *it*, the union of the Duke [of Wellington], Peel and yourself is absolutely necessary.

I know very well that many of these grandees are very unreasonable, and I believe there has been too much indiscreet and even offensive talk (though I have not myself heard any), but indiscretions and offences are, I suppose, inseparable from the excitement which a state of things like the present naturally produces. If you, Peel and the Duke are once agreed, all the rest will soon subside into their accustomed channels, and flow along without even a murmur, which God grant.

Patrons	No. of members	Number of such members holding political office
Lord Lonsdale	9	2 (Beckett)
Lord Hertford	8	2 (Croker)
Duke of Rutland	6	0
Duke of Buckingham	6	1
Holmes's Trustees	5	2 (Canning, Phillimore)
Duke of Newcastle	5	0
Duke of Beaufort	3	1
Duke of Northumberland	4	0
Lord Powis	4	1 (Holmes)
Lord Ailesbury	4	1 (Nichol)
Lord Falmouth	3	0
Lord Anglesey	4	1
Lord Shaftesbury	3	0
Lord Bath	3	1 (Cockburn)
Lord St. Germans	4	1 (Arbuthnot)
Lord Somers	3	0
Lord Mount-Edgcumbe	3	0
The Bullers	4	0
Lord Stafford	3	0
Lord Sandwich	3	1 (Calvert)
Johnston Trustees	3	1 (Wallace)
Lord Huntingtower	3	0
Lord Beverley	3	0
Dorset Trustees	2	1 (Strathaven)
Lord Pembroke	2	0
Lord Westmorland	2	0
Lord Exeter	2	0
Lord Radnor	2	0
Duke of Leeds	2	0
Lord Londonderry	2	1 (Hardinge)
Lord Harrowby	2	0
Lord Donegal	2	0
Bridgewater Trustees	2	0
	116	18

So that of 116 members returned by the Tory aristocracy, only 18 hold political office, and of those 18 no less than 12 are persons on whom the patrons confer that favour at the request of the Government.

There are about 30 Tory peers who have each one seat. Two Tory commoners have each 4. Sixteen Tory commoners have each two seats, and about 17 Tory commoners who have one seat each. Total 203, in the hands of what may be called the Tory aristocracy. The Whig seats are about 73.

170. Sketch of the political interest in Scotland, Nov. 1810

(National Library of Scotland, *Melville MSS.*)

COUNTIES

Aberdeen: Duke of Gordon; Lord Aberdeen.

Argyll: Duke of Argyll.

Ayr: Earl of Eglinton.

Banff: Duke of Gordon; Earl Fife; Sir James Grant: Doubtful contest.

Berwick: Earl of Home; Marchmont; Mr. Baillie; Home of Wedderburn; Lord Lauderdale; Lord Melville: Doubtful contest.

Caithness: Sir John Sinclair.

Clackmannan: Mr. Abercromby.

Cromarty: Mr. Macleod of Cadboll.

Dumfries: Duke of Buccleuch; Earl of Hopetoun.

Dunbarton: Duke of Montrose; Sir Ilay Campbell; Sir Archd. Edmonstone.

Edinburgh: Lord Melville.

Fife: Earl of Kellie; General Wemyss; Sir John Hope; Lord Melville.

Forfar: Panmure Family; Earl of Strathmore; Lord Douglas: The Panmure the best in good hands, but much hurt by the present occupier.

Haddington: Marquis of Tweeddale; Earl of Haddington; Earl of Hopetoun; Baron Hepburn; Lord Melville: The present member safe while he stands, but on an opening by his retiring a *doubtful contest.*

Inverness: Duke of Gordon; Sir James Grant; Lord Macdonald; The Fraser Interest: Interests in the County much divided, and if not settled by compromise, a *doubtful contest.*

Kincardine: Sir Alex. Ramsay; Lord Keith; Lord Aberdeen; Mr. Harley Drummond: A *doubtful contest* if perfectly opened: but Harley Drummond the best at present.

Kinross: Mr. Adam; Mr. Graham of Kinross: Doubtful contest.

Kircudbright: Earl of Galloway; Earl of Selkirk: A *doubtful contest,* if Lord Melville does not take a warm part and interest the Anderson family.

Lanark: Duke of Hamilton; Lord Douglas; Sir Charles Ross; Sir Alex. Macdonald Lockhart: *Doubtful contest.* The Duke of Hamilton should be the best but not calculated to improve an interest.

Linlithgow: Earl of Hopetoun.

Moray and Elgin: Sir James Grant; Duke of Gordon; Mr. Brodie of Brodie; Earl of Moray: The Grant interest the best, but liable to be defeated by a coalition of other interests.

Nairn: Lord Cawdor; Mr. Gordon of Cluny.

Orkney: Lord Dundas; Lord Armadale: Lord Dundas should be the best, but neglected or mismanaged so as to make Lord Armadale's the best. It should perhaps be classed under the head of *doubtful contest*.

Peebles: Sir James Montgomery.

Perth: The Duke of Atholl; Lord Breadalbane: These are the most leading interests, but in a contested election, success will depend upon what line the majority of the unconnected interests in the County shall adopt.

Renfrew: Sir John Shaw Stuart; Mr. Campbell of Blytheswood; Earl of Glasgow; Earl of Eglinton; Lord Blantyre: doubtful contest.

Ross: Lord Seaforth.

Roxburgh: Duke of Buccleuch.

Selkirk: Duke of Buccleuch.

Stirling: Duke of Montrose.

Sutherland: Countess of Sutherland.

Wigtown: Earl of Galloway.

N.B. What are classed above under the head of *doubtful contest* would probably be carried by any respectable and resident candidate supported by the interest of Government.

BURGHS[1]

Aberdeen &c.: No decisive interest–doubtful contest.

Anstruther &c.: Sir John Anstruther.

Ayr &c.: Duke of Argyll; Earl of Eglinton.

Banff &c.: Lord Kintore; Lord Findlater; Sir James Grant: An union of any two interests secures it–otherwise a *doubtful contest*.

Dumfries &c.: Duke of Buccleuch; Earl of Hopetoun.

Edinburgh: Duke of Buccleuch; Lord Melville.

Glasgow &c.: Mr. Houston; Blytheswoode; Duke of Hamilton: Liable to great [expense?] and *doubtful contest*. The returning Burgh the best chance of success.

Inverness &c.: Sir James Grant; Lord Seaforth; Mr. Baillie: *doubtful contest* much depending on the returning Burgh.

Jedburgh &c.: The Earl of Lauderdale; Lord Tweeddale.

Kinghorn &c.: No decisive Interest. A *doubtful contest* much depending on the returning Burgh.

Perth &c.: The Duke of Atholl; Earl of Kellie; Sir David Wedderburn.

Selkirk &c.: The Duke of Buccleuch; Earl of Hopetoun.

Stirling &c.: Earl of Hopetoun; Lord Melville; General Campbell; Sir John Henderson: A doubtful contest.

Stranraer &c.: Earl of Galloway.

[1] The delegates met to hold the election at each burgh in turn, following the order of rotation laid down in 1707. In case of a tie (a frequent event in a 4-burgh district) the delegate representing the presiding burgh had the casting vote.

Tain &c.: Lady Sutherland; Lord Seaforth; Lord Dundas; Sir Charles Ross; Sir John
Sinclair: generally arranged by compromise, otherwise a *doubtful contest* depending
on the returning Burgh.

N.B. The Seats classed under the head of *doubtful contest* will generally be carried by
any candidate not sparing his purse, and supported by Government.

171. Extract from the will of George Venables Vernon, 2nd Baron Vernon (1735–1813), dated 18 Nov. 1809

(Somerset House Wills, P. C. C. Heathfield.)

Harbord (3rd Baron Suffield, 1821) was in Parliament, 1806–1812 and 1820–1821.

Codicil, dated 22 Aug. 1812: I hereby give and bequeath to my dear son-in-law, the
Hon. Edward Harbord, one sum not exceeding £5,000 towards the purchase of a
seat in Parliament. . . .

172. Advertisement in the *Star*, 18 May 1795

CORNWALL and DEVON. TO BE SOLD, THE FEE-SIMPLE and INHERITANCE of the MANOR
of POLAPIT-TAMER, in the Parishes of Worrington and North Petherwin, in the
County of Devon; the BARTON of NEWHOUSE, in the Parishes of Saint Stephens,
Saint Thomas, and Saint Mary Magdalen, by Launceston, in the County of Cornwall;
and the great and small Tythes of the said Parish of Saint Stephens.

The Manor and Barton contain in all upwards of 2000 acres of very fine arable
pasture, meadow and wood land, and are adjoining to the Town of Launceston.

Within the said Parish of Saint Stephens is THE BOROUGH OF NEWPORT, In which
Freeholders, as well of Tythes as of Land, have a right of Voting for Members of
Parliament.

There are many very desirable circumstances attending this property, which will
be explained to any Person who is willing to become a purchaser of it.

Apply on the 16th, 18th, 19th, and 20th inst. between the hours of twelve and
three, to Mr. J. Elford, at Mr. Aldridge's, No. 16, Red-lion-square; and afterwards
either to Mr. Aldridge, or Messrs. Elford and Foot, at Plymouth-Dock.

173. Henry Beaufoy's memoir of his entry into Parliament

(Hants. Record Office, 10 M57/63.)

Henry Beaufoy (*c.* 1751–1795) was a Member of Parliament from 1783 to 1795. He is best known
for his advocacy of the repeal of the Test and Corporation Acts in 1787 and 1789. The memoir
begins by explaining his renunciation of the Quaker doctrines about 1779, and continues:

I was now, for the first time in my life at liberty to attempt the execution of the
plans I had formed; and to avail myself of the earliest opportunity that should
offer of obtaining a seat in the House of Commons.

With this view I applied to those attorneys of whom there are always several in London, that consider a knowledge of the state of parties in boroughs, and a particular acquaintance with the commanding interest in each, as an important branch of their business. But these applications served only to convince me of the hazards to which a new man, who, without political connexions, endeavours to obtain an independent seat in Parliament, is unavoidably exposed: for, in the first place, he is generally excluded from all chance in such elections as are principally influenced by considerations of public good; the title to favour being naturally one of which he is not possessed, that of services performed and of patriotism already tried. If Wilberforce had not acquired a splendid reputation by his conduct in the former Parliament, he would not in the year 1783 [sc. 1784] have been chosen for the County of York.

In the next place, if he engages in a contest, he is exposed to the hazard of sacrificing his fortune, and with it his independence, to the acquisition of his seat in Parliament; by which means he loses in the pursuit, that which alone, if he has honest views, can give value to success. Or if, in order to avoid this risk, he attempts to procure for a specific sum, the possession of a quiet seat, he not only finds himself engaged in a competition with the several individuals who have the same object in view, and among whom those from the East are frequently indifferent to the price they give; but he is also obliged to outbid the Treasury itself, for the disposal of such seats is always of consequence to the Minister.

Such are the difficulties that occur in those negotiations for boroughs, in which there is no intention of fraud; but there are also hazards of a very different nature. Many were the offers I received from men who pretended to have such connexions in a borough, as for a small sum, immediately bestowed in bringing over a few persons of the opposite party, would insure the candidate's success: but perfectly well I knew, from the experience of others, that proposals of this sort for the payment of money to be secretly applied, are made with a view to fraud.

The late Alderman Hallifax, tho in general a most cautious man, was in this manner defrauded of £1,000, by an attorney whose services I had declined, and who seems to have owed his better success with Mr. Hallifax, to the Alderman's penurious solicitude to obtain a seat in Parliament for much less than the customary price. On some occasions misers are the easiest of dupes.

A second adventurer, who had also thrown away a visit upon me, defrauded a young man whom I afterwards knew, of no less a sum than £4,000, which he obtained under different pretences of money to establish an interest in a Cornish borough, and of more money to prevent the effect of the former from being wholly lost. Restricted to a line of cautious procedure by the smallness of my fortune, which, including the produce of my wife's estate, afforded but £1,600 a year; yet very desirous of representing a borough, in which the suffrages of honest men have at least a share, I resolved to ask the advice of some leader of a party, who might be willing to give me the assistance that is considered as due to a man, who will not indeed relinquish his independence, but from whom the sort of aid may be expected that similarity of principle affords. With this view I requested that my friend Dr. Shippis, to whose instructions in literature I had formerly been much indebted, and whose high character and proportionable influence among the Dissenters had given him consequence with the chiefs of the popular party, would introduce me to . . . Lord Shelburne. . . .

[After an interview] Lord Shelburne . . . wrote to a friend of his who had the commanding interest in a Cornish borough, to request that if the electors had not settled their terms with any other candidate, their proposals might be sent to me. This letter . . . arrived too late . . . and . . . I once more availed myself of Dr. Shippis's friendship, and solicited an introduction to [Charles Fox]. . . .

My endeavours . . . were fruitlessly continued till the general election [1780] was past. . . . The next two years were impatiently but ineffectually employed in searching for an opportunity of obtaining my object, when Lord Shelburne, who was now . . . in possession of the first office in the state, resolved to obtain for me, on my own terms of perfect independence, the offer of a seat in Parliament: and I accordingly received a message from Mr. Orde, who was much in his confidence, to say that for £3,000 the youngest Mr. Luttrell, one of the members for Minehead, would resign his seat, and would ensure my election in his room.

No arguments were necessary to prove, that this mode of obtaining a seat . . . however mortifying to my pride, or discordant to my ideas of the spirit of the constitution, was not only more consistent than any other plan I could possibly pursue, with that perfect independence which I had always determined should form the basis of my political character, but was in fact the only way in which, in my unconnected situation, an independent seat was likely to be obtained at all. Exorbitant therefore, considering the advanced period of the Sessions, as the price undoubtedly was, I deposited the money without hesitation, in the hands of Mr. Orde, who retained it, not only till the election was over, but till the 14 days immediately following were expired; after which as no petition against the validity of the election could be received by the House, and as of course my election was perfectly secure, he delivered the cash to Mr. Luttrell. . . .

174. Romilly on the sale of seats in the House of Commons

(*Memoirs of the Life of Sir Samuel Romilly*, ed. by his sons, II (1840), pp. 206 *sqq.*)

Diary, 27 April, 1807. . . . I shall procure myself a seat in the new Parliament unless I find that it will cost so large a sum, as, in the state of my family, it would be very imprudent for me to devote to such an object, which I find is very likely to be the case. Tierney, who manages this business for the friends of the late Administration, assures me that he can hear of no seats to be disposed of. After a Parliament which has lived little more than four months, one would naturally suppose that those seats which are regularly sold by the proprietors of them would be very cheap; they are, however, in fact, sold now at a higher price than was ever given for them before. Tierney tells me that he has offered £10,000 for the two seats of Westbury, the property of the late Lord Abingdon, and which are to be made the most of by trustees for creditors, and has met with a refusal. £6000 and £5500 have been given for seats with no stipulation as to time, or against the event of a speedy dissolution by the King's death, or by any change of Administration. The truth is, that the new Ministers have bought up all the seats that were to be disposed of, and at any prices. Amongst others, Sir C[?hristopher] H[?awkins], the great dealer in boroughs, has sold all he had to Ministers. With what money all this is done I know not, but it is supposed that the King, who has greatly at heart to preserve this new Administration, the favourite objects of his choice, has advanced a very large sum out of his Privy Purse.

This buying of seats is detestable; and yet it is almost the only way in which one in my situation, who is resolved to be an independent man, can get into Parliament. To come in by a popular election, in the present state of the representation, is quite impossible; to be placed there by some great Lord, and to vote as he shall direct, is to be in a state of complete dependence; and nothing hardly remains but to owe a seat to the sacrifice of a part of one's fortune. It is true that many men who buy seats, do it as a matter of pecuniary speculation, as a profitable way of employing their money: they carry on a political trade; they buy their seats and sell their votes. For myself I can truly say that, by giving money for a seat, I shall make a sacrifice of my private property merely that I may be enabled to serve the public. . . .

May 9. After almost despairing of being able to get any seat in Parliament, my friend Piggott has at last procured me one, and the Duke of Norfolk has consented to bring me in for Horsham. It is however but a precarious seat. I shall be returned, as I shall have a majority of votes, which the late Committee of the House of Commons decided to be good ones; but there will be a Petition against the return by the candidates who will stand on Lady Irwin's interest, and it is extremely doubtful what will be the event of the Petition. . . .

May 12. The terms upon which I have my seat at Horsham. . . . If I keep the seat, either by the decision of a committee upon a petition, or by a compromise (the Duke and Lady Irwin returning one member each, in which case it is understood that I am to be the member who continues), I am to pay £2000; if, upon a petition, I lose the seat, I am not to be at any expense. . . .

26 [February 1808.] The Committee on the Horsham Petition, which had decided all the questions raised by the counsel in favour of the sitting members, on this day finally decided against them, upon a question of law, which had never been insisted on by the counsel for the petition, and which was quite incapable of being supported. The effect of it, however, is to exclude me from Parliament, and to put an end, certainly for the present, and perhaps for ever, to my political existence.

26 March [1808]. My absence from Parliament is not likely to be of long duration. Lord Henry Petty has had some conversation with Calcraft about one of the seats at Wareham; and though Calcraft knows how little I was to have given for my seat at Horsham, he says that that circumstance does not afford an insuperable objection to my being returned for Wareham.

1 April [1808]. Piggott took occasion to speak to Calcraft on the subject of Wareham, and this morning informed me that I might have the seat for £2000, the sum which I was to have paid for Horsham; but that, though I was to pay no more, Calcraft would receive £3000; the remaining £1000 being paid out of a fund which, till now, I did not know existed, and which has been formed, as I understand, by the most distinguished persons in opposition, to answer extraordinary occasions. I was staggered

at the first mention of this, and stated my objections to Piggott. He told me that he did not see how I could consider it as in any respect objectionable; that the principal persons of Opposition were very anxious that I should be in Parliament, and only regretted that I should be at any expense at all. I cannot, however, persuade myself to accept a seat upon these terms; and accordingly, in the evening, I wrote Piggott a note in these words:–"... I feel a very great reluctance to consent to let the matter be arranged in the way that has been proposed. I am afraid that, after the matter is settled, I shall feel uncomfortable about it; and I had rather at once determine to be at all the expense myself. ..."

The matter has been settled with Mr. Calcraft accordingly, and I pay the whole £3000 myself. ...

20 [April 1808]. I was this day elected. Though Mr. Calcraft has the entire command of the borough, he wished me to go down, which I accordingly did. ...

175. Lord Liverpool to F. J. Robinson, 9 March 1818
(*British Museum Additional MSS.* 38270, f. 321.)

Lord Liverpool's statement may be compared with Stephen Lushington's remarks in the House of Commons (23 Feb. 1830) about "the hordes of needy adventurers, whom the power and influence of great men, from time to time, has sent into this House to prostitute the little talent which God had given them, and to make use of subserviency and corruption–from their inability, otherwise, to distinguish themselves" (*Mirror of Parliament* (1830), I, p. 366).

... If I had been consulted before Mr. Henry Ellis started for Boston, I should for his own personal interest have very much dissuaded *him* from it. I scarcely ever knew coming into Parliament answer to a person circumstanced altogether as he is, unless, indeed, the person came, and from first holding some office which is considered as connected with Parliament. The House of Commons is in sentiment much more a body of aristocrats than is commonly supposed. The members who have most influence upon opinion are very apt to ask themselves and each other why a person comes into Parliament. They have naturally a dislike to anything that can be termed a political adventurer, and I have seen some persons of the most splendid talents who have struggled for a considerable time before they have been able to bear up against this sort of imputation, even when it was not well founded. Besides, let us just consider to what sort of office Mr. Ellis can naturally aspire. He might like to be one of the Under-Secretaries of State. But these offices, as you know, are not in the patronage of Government generally. The Secretary of State for the time being chooses his own Under-Secretary, and the Minister never expects more from him than that he should communicate with him before the appointment takes place in order that he may say whether he has any objection. The same applies as to the Secretary to the Admiralty and to most of the offices in the Ordnance. I say nothing of the claims which there always are upon Government from persons who have been a long time in Parliament, but I am satisfied that the result of the whole is that Mr. Ellis will not promote his prospects in life by coming into Parliament, unless indeed he should show there a very great superiority as to talents in debate over other persons of the same time of life as himself. ...

176. Debate in the House of Commons on Grey's motion for Parliamentary Reform, 6 May 1793

(*Parliamentary Register*, xxxv, pp. 388–393.)

Jenkinson, afterwards second earl of Liverpool and Prime Minister, 1812–1827, was known by the courtesy title of Lord Hawkesbury from 1796 to 1803, when he was called up to the House of Lords as Baron Hawkesbury. In 1808 he succeeded to his father's earldom.

R. B. Jenkinson: . . . We must be all agreed that the House of Commons is meant to be a legislative body, representing all descriptions of men in this country. . . . He supposed every person would agree that the landed interest ought to have the preponderant weight. The landed interest was, in fact, the stamina of the country. In the second place, in a commercial country like this, the manufacturing and commercial interest ought to have a considerable weight, secondary to the landed interest, but secondary to the landed interest only. . . . There were other descriptions of people, which, to distinguish from those already mentioned, he should style *professional people*, and whom he considered as absolutely necessary to the composition of a House of Commons. By professional people, he did not mean to use that expression in the narrow and confined sense in which it was generally used; he meant those Members of the House of Commons who wished to raise themselves to the great offices of the State: those that were in the army; those that were in the navy; those that were in the law; and he maintained that these several descriptions of persons ought to be able to find some means of entering into that House. First, it is to be considered that by the practice of the Constitution the Ministers of the Crown are, in part, chosen out of the House of Commons. The landed interest, or country gentlemen, are, generally speaking, not ambitious of exercising those functions; and indeed it was not to be wondered that persons of considerable property and consequence in the country, should find themselves so much employed by the management of their property, by fulfilling the office of Magistrate in their different Counties, and by attending their duty as Members of Parliament, as not to be, in general, desirous of becoming members of the Administration of the country. Indeed, it may, perhaps, be more proper that such persons should be employed in watching over the conduct of those who exercise the functions of Executive Government, than that they should be employed in exercising those functions themselves. This applied still stronger to those gentlemen in the commercial line. They did not, generally speaking, come into Parliament till they were rather at an advanced period of life, and they were then so occupied with their commercial concerns, that even if they had the disposition, they could not have the leisure to become members of the Executive Government. Unless, then, the last description of persons whom he had mentioned; unless professional men could find their way into that House, you would strike at the root of this principle. . . . The principle itself was a very important one . . . it had been commonly observed, that whilst in other countries men could scarcely be found to discharge the offices of the State, in this country there were always more than were sufficient; but if the professional men he had mentioned were prevented from becoming Members of Parliament, we should lose one of the most important advantages of our Constitution. There was another reason why these persons were absolutely necessary: we were constantly in the habit of discussing in that House all the important concerns of the State; it was necessary, therefore, that there should be persons in the practice of debating such questions. . . . The very same reason which would, generally speaking, prevent either gentlemen in the landed interest, or in the commercial interest, from accepting the offices of the State, would likewise prevent them from exercising, in a considerable degree, their talents in the practice of debating. If, therefore . . . we were desirous that there should continue in that country a constant supply of men to form vigorous and effective Administrations; if we were desirous that there should continue in that House a constant supply of men to form vigorous and effective Oppositions for the purpose of watching over the conduct of such Ministers, the descriptions of persons he had mentioned were absolutely necessary to the composition of it. There was another reason; being constantly in the habit of debating in Parliament on all the different affairs of State, on the naval, on the military affairs, on the state of the law of the country, it was proper . . . that we should have within ourselves persons belonging to these different professions, to whom we might occasionally appeal on such subjects, and in whose opinion we might confide, if their character in their profession induced us so to do. There was a fourth reason, which was . . . stronger than all the rest. The professional persons he had mentioned . . . made that House the representation of the people. Suppose that in that House there were only country gentlemen; they would not then be the representatives of the nation, but the representatives of the landholders of the nation. Suppose there were in that House only commercial persons; they would not be the representatives of the nation, but the representatives of the commercial interest of the nation. See . . . from an example what would be the consequence of this. There cannot be a more important subject of legislation than the corn laws. It would be agreed by every one that Parliament should prevent corn from either becoming so dear as to distress the poor, or from its becoming so cheap as to affect agriculture. The landholders of the country have an interest that corn should be as dear as possible; persons in the commercial and manufacturing line have an interest that corn should be as cheap as possible: it must then inevitably follow that if one of these descriptions of persons only found their way into the House, the interest of that description of persons would be principally considered, and however respectable those persons might be, an *esprit de corps* would naturally be found in all their proceedings. Suppose the landed and commercial interests could both find their way into this House, the landed interest, it has been proved, ought to have the preponderant weight; it would consequently be able, if it had nothing but the commercial interest to combat with, to prevent that interest from having the weight in the Constitution which it ought to have; and all descriptions of persons in the country would, in fact, be at the mercy of the landholders of it. The professional persons, then . . . are what make this House the representatives of the people. They have collectively no *esprit de corps*, because they are composed of persons in very different professions. They mix themselves with the landed and commercial interest, and prevent any *esprit de corps* by this means from affecting our proceedings. Thus, whilst the landed interest has of any one description of persons the principal weight in this House, as it ought to have; whilst the commercial interest has of any one description of persons the secondary weight in this House, as it ought to have, neither the landed nor commercial interest can materially affect each other. The interests of the different professions of the country are fairly considered, and the House, by this means, become what it could not become by any other means, the representatives of the people at large.

What then . . . were the means of obtaining such a House of Commons? The Counties and many of the populous boroughs secured the election of country gentlemen; the commercial towns secured the election of certain persons in that line: but how were the last description of persons, the professional men, to find their way into that House? In the Counties, local connection would, in a great measure, decide the election. However great his property, or the property of any other gentleman, might be in a County, it would go a great way to decide between A and B, two considerable persons in that county; but it could never be made use of with effect for the purpose of bringing in a person who had no landed property in that County, and who could have no connection consequently with the various interests in it. In the populous boroughs, the same principle will in a great measure avail; and persons who, for the first time at least, are chosen for them, are generally chosen either on account of some local connection, or by means of the exertions which a very considerable property may enable them to make. Many gentlemen, after they have come into that House by other means, by the reputation they acquire from their exertions in it, are, at a subsequent period, frequently returned by the most populous places in the country; but if the names of the professional persons who had come into that House for a considerable number of years were examined, it would be found that far the greater part of them have come in, for the first time, by means of those boroughs which are called rotten boroughs; that having in general no strong local connection, and, comparatively speaking, no very considerable property, it is scarcely possible that they should come in by any other means; and if it was the object of the hon. gent. . . . to abolish those close boroughs, persons of the description he had mentioned would scarcely ever find means of obtaining a seat in that House; and those Members whom he considered himself to have proved absolutely necessary for creating that House the representatives of the people, would be entirely excluded.

He then considered himself to have shewn that the close boroughs, as being the means of introducing professional persons to that House, were absolutely necessary to its Constitution. Did any evil arise from them? It might be feared, that their influence collectively might be so great, as to prevent the landed and commercial interest from having that weight in the House which they certainly were entitled to. This objection had been answered before; for this description of individuals not being composed of any one sort of persons, but of persons of a variety of professions, not being returned by persons in one interest, but by persons in very different interests, possessed collectively no *esprit de corps*, and could consequently not affect the weight of either the landed or monied interest in that House. But it might be said, to a certain degree these persons may be necessary, but are not their numbers increasing? The reverse he asserted was the fact. Let any gentleman look at the various decisions on controverted elections since the passing of Mr. Grenville's Act, and he will find, that in almost every case, the decision has been in favour of the more open right of election; and that it is astonishing how many boroughs there are, which were believed to be close boroughs a very few years ago, and which have since been made as open as any boroughs in the country. . . .

177. Debates in the House of Commons on the Bill to prevent persons in Holy Orders from sitting in the House, 8 and 19 May 1801

(Cobbett's *Parliamentary History*, XXXV, 1402–1420.)

The election of the well-known Radical agitator, the Rev. John Horne Tooke, for the borough of Old Sarum raised the question of the capacity of the clergy to be elected to Parliament. The Act 41 George III, c. 63, disqualified clergy of the Established Church and ministers of the Established Church of Scotland. Clergy of the Roman Catholic Church were disqualified by the Roman Catholic Relief Act, 1829.

[8 May.] *Sir Francis Burdett* rose to express his decided opposition to the principle of the Bill, which went to stigmatize a large body of men, and to disfranchise them by a sweeping blow of their rights and privileges. He could see no fair reason why the clergy should be considered as more liable to sinister influence than any other order of persons; or why the man who wore a black coat should be more dependent on the Crown than the man who sported a red one. The arguments on which the Bill was founded were the offspring of superstition, a superstition more gross and flagrant than the tenets of Popery itself. It was pretended that such a degree of sacredness attached to the sacerdotal character that it would be a profanation to meddle and interfere in lay matters. This was a doctrine which he had hoped had been long since exploded. There were a variety of cases in which the clergy took an active part in lay offices, infinitely more discordant to their sacerdotal character than parliamentary duties. . . .

Mr. Horne Tooke . . . Had I either felt convinced in my own mind that my sitting in this House was productive of inconvenience, or had this been proved to be the case by others, I should have anticipated every attempt to expel me, and have been the first to quit the situation I hold, voluntarily, and from the impulse of my own feelings. But no inconveniences have or can result from my sitting in this House. The question is altogether personal. . . . For a century and a half there has not been a single Parliament in which some persons in holy orders did not sit. . . . No fears or apprehensions were expressed of there being any danger of the clergy rising *en masse* and rushing into this House, to come in for a share of the good things which are supposed to attach to a seat in Parliament. But, the moment I show my face in the House, the signal of alarm is given, and my presence is supposed to endanger the Constitution. . . .

[19 May.] *Mr. Joliffe* said that it was a Bill of disqualification and exclusion; for the eligibility of persons in holy orders was admitted by the very instance before us. Before, therefore, we went to disqualify so large a class of men, it became us to consider what were those qualities which rendered a man most eligible. Learning of all kinds, ancient and modern history, peculiarly fitted a man to make laws, and to judge of prudent policy. What description of persons was to be found so versed in general learning as the clergy? But it was said, they were liable to the influence of the

Crown. Who was not? The Crown had deaneries, canonries and livings to bestow; but had it no regiments, no Governments, no ships, and no naval commands? That it could bestow those Church preferments was true; but could it take them away? No; but the same hand which gave the others to-day could dispossess the enjoyers to-morrow. To talk therefore of influence was preposterous. The clergy are, says a learned gentleman, an indelible character; they are enveloped in holiness; they are so pure that they cannot mix in ordinary society. Were they so? How came the Bishops in the other House of Parliament? Were they one day too pure to be admitted here, and the next perfectly fit for legislation there?

Sir Francis Burdett . . . Was it not hard that Presbyterians, Anabaptists, Dissenters, jumping Methodists and fanatics of all descriptions should be eligible, and only the Clergy of the Established Church be disqualified? . . .

Mr. Grey denied that the characters of a priest and a legislator were incompatible. In the early periods of our history, the clergy, though they formed a distinct body, constantly mixed in temporal affairs, and held civil offices. He however wished to exclude the clergy, not because he thought that they were more liable to corruption than other men, but because their secular duties would interfere with their spiritual ones, and their sitting in that House would open a source of influence. He therefore wished that the Bill should render every person holding a benefice ineligible and, prohibit any clergyman having once a seat in that House from ever holding a benefice afterwards. . . .

178. George Canning to his uncle, the Rev. William Leigh, 23 Feb. 1795

(Harewood MSS.)

The reference is to the Budgetary restrictions on M.P.'s free postage facilities.

. . . As to the franks, it is a grand *shew* of sacrifice on *our* part, without in truth sacrificing much, while it will cut up by the roots the very flagrant abuses of the bankers and merchants who got into Parliament for no other purpose. . . .

179. Nathaniel Jefferys to the Prince of Wales, 9 April 1802

(Windsor Archives, 39795)

Jefferys was in Parliament from 1796 to 1803. He was a goldsmith and in 1793 was described as "jeweller to the Duke of York". The prince was one of his patrons, and Sheridan a close friend.

. . . The unfavourable state of my circumstances induced me some time since, publicly to decline offering myself again as a candidate [for Coventry], since which time, and particularly within these few days, the flattering opinion entertain'd by the leading people of both parties, with the principal members of the corporation, of my conduct in Parliament, has induc'd them to express a wish that I may be again their representative, accompanied with offers of support of the most liberal kind. . . .

One of my principal inducements for having declin'd to offer myself as a candidate arose from the idea I thought the world might entertain that the situation of retail trade in which I was engag'd was derogatory to a seat in Parliament. Such a prejudice, however, if it did prevail, no longer exists, as it is my intention in consequence of the impair'd state of my health and insufficiency of capital to carry on my business, to withdraw from my present line of business and engage in one of a more private nature and attended with less fatigue and anxiety.

180. Speech of Alderman Waithman on his election in 1818 for the City of London

(*Scotsman,* 4 July 1818.)

A merchant was a wholesaler. Waithman was a tradesman—a linen draper.

. . . Hitherto it had been the constant practice to elect members to the House of Commons from a body of men who, by their profession, were not obliged to be citizens, while, on the contrary, the respectable body of traders had been passed by. No interest, indeed, had a right to be overlooked, but the commercial interest had at all times a fair and full representation in Parliament, and could be a match to Ministers at any time, should any measure be proposed against it, whereas there was not one to defend the trader. He believed it was the first time now that any person had been elected from the profession he belonged to. If to be a merchant was a qualification for the House of Commons, he might long ago have had that by taking a small counting house at £50 a year, but he refused to sacrifice the principle he had laid down.

181. Charles Abbot's diary, 30 July 1796

(Public Record Office, *Colchester Papers,* P.R.O. 30/9/31.)

The MS. shows that the numbers were considerably altered, and the alterations are not very clear even under an ultra-violet lamp.

Upon an analysis of the new Parliament, the numbers of each component class seem to be nearly these:

Irish Peers		17
Eldest sons of British Peers		33
Other sons of Peers, English, Scotch and Irish		83
		133
Knights and Baronets		89
Professional: Law	31	
Merchants, &c.	55	
Military, &c.	58	
Diplomatists	7	
		151
Country gentlemen		172
Dead		2
Double election		11
		558

(b) THE PARTY COMPOSITION OF THE HOUSE

182. Wilberforce and C. J. Fox on Party, 18 April 1785

(*The Parliamentary Register*, XVIII, pp. 71, 73.)

Wilberforce:– . . . [Pitt's parliamentary reform plan] . . . would also tend, in his opinion, to diminish the progress of party and cohesion in this country, from which, he was well convinced, our greatest misfortunes arose. There were men and parties in this country which derive most of their power and influence from these burgage tenures, against which the operations of this Bill were to be directed. By destroying them, the freedom of opinion would be restored and party connections in a great measure vanish: for the consequence of coalitions and parties formed on one side of the House was that similar engagements were necessarily formed on the other; and for his part, he wished to see the time when he could come into the House and give his vote, divested of any sentiments of attachment, which should induce him to approve of measures from his connection with men. . . .

Fox:– . . . Much had been said of the merit of dissolving that cohesion which was said to subsist in the parties in that House. That cohesion did subsist, was a truth in which he took too much pride to think of denying, and from which this country derived too much advantage to be an enemy to; his connections were formed on liberal and systematic principles, and could not be dissolved by any regulations, while the same union in sentiment and principles continued to cement them. . . .

183. John Robinson's forecast of the result of the general election, Dec. 1783

The following calculations are compiled from his *Parliamentary Papers, 1774–1784*, published by the Royal Historical Society in 1922 [Camden 3rd Ser., XXXIII]. Robinson had an expert knowledge of the constituencies, for he had 'managed' the general elections of 1774 and 1780 for the Government. The figures in brackets are those for the Parliament elected in 1780. His calculations seem to have erred, if at all, on the side of caution; he was surprised at the result of the election: "It exceeds all expectation, the way in which all the contests turn out." And the king wrote (6 April 1784): "Undoubtedly as yet the elections have proved beyond the hopes of the most sanguine friends."

	ENGLAND			WALES	SCOTLAND	TOTAL
For Pitt	Counties	Close Boroughs	Open Boroughs			
pro	[18] 22	[49] 101	[70] 84	[5] 8	[7] 40	[149] 255
hopeful	[19] 18	[34] 32	[40] 54	[4] 10	[7] 2	[104] 116
						Total [253] 371
Against Pitt						
doubtful	[12] 11	[18] 13	[30] 36	[4] 2	[10] 2	[74] 64
hostile	[31] 29	[76] 31	[92] 58	[11] 4	[21] 1	[231] 123
						Total [305] 187

184. **A contemporary analysis of the House of Commons, 1 May 1788**

(Essex Record Office, D/DBy C9/44.)

1. Party of the Crown — 185[1]

This party includes all those who would probably support his Maj$^{ty's}$ Govern^t under any Minister not peculiarly unpopular

2. The Party attached to Mr. Pitt. — 52

Of this party were there a new Parliam^t, and Mr. P. no longer Minister, not above twenty would be returned

3. Detached Parties supporting the present Administration vizt
   1. Mr. Dundas — 10
   2. Marquis of Lansdowne — 9
   3. Earl of Lonsdale — 9
   4. East Indians — 15

4. The Independent or unconnected Members of the House. — [108]

Of this body of men about 40 have united together, in conjunction w^h some Members of the House of Peers in order to form a third party for the purpose of preventing the Crown from being too much in the power either of the two other parties who are contending for the government of the country, and who (were it really necessary) might with the assistance of the Crown, undertake to make up an Administration to the exclusion both of Mr. Pitt & Mr. Fox, and of their adherents.[2]

5. The Opposition to the present Adm^n.
   1. The Party attached to Mr Fox — 138
   2. Remnants of Ld North's Party — 17

6. Absentees and Neutrals — 14

—

[557]

"Third Party" Circular Letter, 1788.

It is proposed that such Members of the two Houses as hold themselves independent of, and unconnected with, the Parties that now exist, and are desirous of contributing their best endeavours to promote the general interests of the country, do assemble together as often as may be necessary for the purpose of taking into their consideration such important questions as are likely to be agitated in either House of Parliament. It is not intended that the Members of such a meeting should consider themselves under any restraint, or tied down to follow the sentiments of the majority; all that is required is this, that they should endeavour, as much as possible, on all great public occasions, to act in unison with each other, taking questions as they arise, opposing bad measures whoever may bring them forward, and supporting good ones, from whatever quarter they may be suggested. It is further proposed that such Members of the two Houses as may approve of this proposal should not consider themselves as merely politically united or connected for the purpose of acquiring that

---

[1] Elsewhere in this document this number is given as 186.   [2] See below.

public consequence, which without connexions and the certainty of support, the ablest and most independent characters will in vain endeavour to obtain; but it is also intended that it should be the means of establishing society and intercourse, and of promoting the pleasures of private friendship and connexion, amongst those to whom an idea of this kind may be agreeable. The following is an alphabetical list of those who have already acceded to the proposal:

Sir Ed. Astley	Mr. Hawkins	Capt. Macbride	Sir John Sinclair
Mr. Bastard	Mr. Heneage	Lord Middleton	Mr. Skene
Lord Breadalbane	Lord Hereford	Genl. Norton	Mr. Stanley of
Mr. Parker Coke	Capt. Kingsmill	Mr. Philipps	Hastings
Mr. Noel Edwards	Lord Kinnaird	Col. Popham	Mr. Trotman
Mr. Gipps	Mr. Loveden	Lord Shaftesbury	Genl. Vaughan.
Lord Hawke	Mr. Lygon	Sir Geo. Shuckburgh	

185. Analysis of the voting in the House of Commons on 36 important questions in 1821 and 1822

(Hansard's *Parliamentary Debates*, New Series, xv, 698.)

From	Members who vote	For Ministers	Against	Both	Not at all	Total
40	English Counties	25	37	10	8	80
12	Counties, and 12 towns, in Wales	13	9	1	1	24
89	Cities & Boroughs where election is open	57	107	5	11	180
114	Cities & Boroughs where election is close	151	41	5	28	225
2	Universities	4	0	0	0	4
33	Counties, & 66 Royal Burghs, in Scotland	25	11	0	9	45
32	Counties of Ireland	24	14	2	24	64
33	Cities & Boroughs of Ireland	21	7	0	8	36
		320	226	23	89	658

186. George Rose to the bishop of Lincoln, 18 Dec. 1804 and 8 Aug. 1806

(*Pretyman MSS.*)

[18 December 1804.] . . . I stated to Mr. Pitt, with the names of the members, the strength he would have to encounter before he took office. . . . Experience has shown the state of parties more favourable to him than I foretold, because a very considerable number of Mr. Addington's friends would not follow him into opposition. Of those who acted with him on the Defence Bill, few would be with him on any other question. Sir Theophilus Metcalfe, who he made a baronet, told me he could name 61 who would not, himself one of them, though he deeply regretted

Mr. Addington could not go on with the government. It is under *a strong impression* that Mr. Addington could not have carried 10 friends with him to Mr. Fox that I so deeply regret the intended arrangement, for that he would join any party in oppositon to Mr. Pitt I have not the slightest doubt, believing, however, that on account of the King he would not have done so *hastily*. . . .

[8 August 1806.] . . . There are at least 200 members who did not vote last session, most of them from an unwillingness to oppose Government, and in the hope of a stronger one being formed. I know Mr. Fox is not ignorant of that, but it is not *numbers* of which the Government stand in need so much as of men of business and debaters. . . .

187. C. J. Fox to Lord Lauderdale, 12 July 1805

(Lord John Russell, *Memorials & Corresp. of C. J. Fox*, IV, p. 97.)

. . . I *now* think . . . that Pitt will not make any proposal to Opposition . . . I know that nothing ought to be consented to unless he will consider the present Ministry as annihilated in all its parts, and consult about forming a new one. He will not, I think, bring his mind to this, and yet his weakness since the defection of the Doctor is extreme. . . . The House of Commons is evidently divided into four parties, nearly, upon a loose calculation, as follows:—supporters of the Chancellor of the Exchequer for the time being 180, Opposition 150, Pitt 60, Addington 60; [total] 450. There are besides, several members who vote whimsically, or, in such case as Melville's, from fear of their constituents, &c.; and many, of course, who never or very seldom attend. The first class, were it not for the very precarious state of the King, would, I fear, be much larger; and the second, for the same reason, and from the slowly increasing, but still increasing weight of Carlton House, will much more likely gain ground than lose any. The third class seems very unlikely to increase at present; and the fourth will either gain or lose, first, according to the notions that will be entertained of the Doctor's being more or less well regarded at Windsor; next, according to their success in setting themselves up (which they will endeavour to do) as opposers of corruption and guardians of the public purse, &c.

188. W. H. Fremantle to the marquess of Buckingham, 3 April 1807

(Duke of Buckingham and Chandos, *Court & Cabinets of George III*, IV, p. 155.)

Fremantle was Joint Secretary of the Treasury in the 'Talents' Ministry which the king had just dismissed. The newly established Portland Ministry, to whose views reference is made, found it expedient on 29 April 1807 to dissolve the Parliament which had been elected as recently as the previous November.

The principle upon which the Parliament was arranged is favourable to their views, for by not advancing one shilling of public money to any individual to assist him in his election we had nothing to depend upon but the opinion and promise of the person nominated to us. The present Government are aware of these terms, and you will see in all their papers the threat of a dissolution held out; I have no doubt of its having the proper effect upon many of them.

189. Thomas Grenville to the marquess of Buckingham, 20 April 1807

(Duke of Buckingham and Chandos, *Court & Cabinets of George III*, IV, p. 167.)

On 9 April the Portland Ministry unexpectedly had a majority of 32 (258 *v*. 226); on the 15th a majority of 46 (244 *v*. 198). Parliament was dissolved on the 29th, and in the new Parliament, which met on 22 June, ministers had a majority of 195 (350 *v*. 155) on 26 June.

... The numbers which the new Ministry have produced in their late divisions are not likely to change their original intention of dissolving the present Parliament, and Lord Grenville is persuaded that they are entirely occupied with this project, and that the dissolution will certainly take place in a fortnight or three weeks. Our friends are, therefore, beginning to consult together, and to take measures accordingly, without loss of time. There is an idea of endeavouring to make a stock-purse upon this occasion; but although it may be desirable, and I think is so, to communicate with some of our grandees upon that subject, I should be most decidedly against any minor subscriptions, as I know that in a great many instances such a course would produce subsequent claims that it would be very inconvenient to entertain, and utterly impossible to satisfy.

190. George Tierney to Lord Grey, ?12 or 13 Oct. 1809

(*Tierney MSS.*)

The quarrel between Canning and Castlereagh over their respective jurisdictions as Foreign Secretary and Secretary for War and the Colonies (and over personal matters) broke up the Portland Ministry. It was reconstructed by Perceval, who, however, conscious of the weakness of his parliamentary position, made unsuccessful overtures for a coalition to Lords Grey and Grenville, the leading members of Opposition.

... Notwithstanding your opinion on the probable stability of Perceval's Government, I as yet see no reason to alter mine, I still think it most likely that another communication will be made to you though perhaps in a different form, and so thinking I remain convinced of the necessity of your preparing to come to town.

... In what you say about coalitions you seem to write under an impression that I have a disposition that way. You are here quite wrong. I have, when that subject has been started, protested against giving any encouragement even to the show of negotiation, and maintained our policy to be to stand quite aloof for the present. But you ask what my opinions would be if no communication is made, whether the means exist of forming a regular Opposition and whether such a thing if practicable would be prudent, and you conclude by telling it me that should it be resolved upon you cannot make up your mind either to lead or serve.

As to the means of forming a regular Opposition they do undoubtedly exist in very ample means too after allowing for a falling off of great numbers amongst those who were accustomed to act with us. The propriety of embarking in a regular opposition is a question much more difficult to answer, and is one of the many points which ought to be discussed fully with those leading friends who have gone on steadily in the same course with ourselves. The party which existed when we came out of office is in any view of things at an end, but a great number of those who belonged to it co-operated fairly and honourably with you and Lord Grenville and are entitled to the compliment of being consulted before any final determination is taken as to the course to be pursued at the meeting of Parliament.

My own individual opinion will be very much regulated by what shall be settled with respect to the Catholic question. If I am given to understand that my friends, after full serious deliberation, think it their duty not to take office unless Catholic emancipation be granted–that is, not take office during the present reign–so far from recommending the formation of a regular Opposition, I should, if it were formed, refuse to belong to it, not only because I should hold it to be madness to embark on a crusade against the power of the Crown and the sense of the country united, but because I should not think myself warranted systematically to oppose a Government which, if I overthrew, I know I could not replace. On the other hand, I am most deeply impressed with a sense of the difficulties in which our affairs are involved both from without and from within and I cannot but think that every man ought to work hard to remove such an Administration as we are cursed with if there be anything like a reasonable prospect of forming a better. What is the public opinion on this subject can only be matter of conjecture, but from all I have seen and heard I am quite satisfied that what little strength Perceval has arises entirely from the despair which is felt of being able to substitute a more efficient Government without the hazard of such distractions as would make the remedy as dangerous as the disease.

When you tell me that of the many points which you agree with me must be settled, that of Catholic emancipation is the most easy, as it is quite clear that neither you nor Grenville can ever take office without a full explanation on that head, you give me no means whatever of satisfying the enquiries I daily receive as to your determination respecting it. I am not justified in saying you will not come in without the claims of the Catholics are acceded to and when I cannot affirm that broad proposition, it is necessary to be much more distinctly informed of your intentions than I am, to answer the sort of questions which are put to me. Now let me beg of you not to imagine I am asking you to write to me on this head, because it is the very thing I wish you not to do. The resolution you must come to, relative to this most delicate and important subject is one which ought not to be taken at Howick and still less committed to writing either to me or to anybody. To make your determination eminently satisfactory to yourself it must be the result of full discussion and concert with others, the circumstances of the times being taken into consideration.

191. The earl of Liverpool to Viscount Wellington, 17 Jan. 1811

(*Supplementary Despatches, Correspondence and Memoranda of the Duke of Wellington,* VII (1840), p. 46.)

... I am not able to give you any satisfactory information as to the Prince's intentions respecting his Government, if he should be invested with the Regency. WE have no share whatever of his confidence. He is in the constant habit of seeing some of the Opposition, and there can be no doubt of his consulting them. On the other hand, they are certainly much divided amongst themselves; and if the Prince is of opinion, at the time when the Regency Bill passes, that the King will speedily recover, he may hesitate before he changes the Administration. Such a measure, under such circumstances, would be very unpopular; and, notwithstanding all you may hear, be assured that we have a considerable majority of the well-disposed and respectable part of the community on our side. The Prince's ranks are thickened by ALL the JACOBINS without exception, who dread the return of the King to power, well knowing that his personal character has ever been and will be the greatest obstacle to all their designs. I am sorry to inform you that your Irish friends have, in general, behaved very ill; the Scotch universally well–scarcely one Scotchman has deserted us. Upon the whole, we have no right to complain, considering the host of influence exerted against us. We have, besides, had to contend upon our most difficult questions with all the floating parties in Parliament, with the exception of Lord Sidmouth's. In three weeks from this time the fate of the Administration for this session will probably be determined.

192. Lavinia, Lady Spencer to her husband, Lord Spencer, 21 Jan. 1811

(Althorp MSS.)

Tierney's calculations may be compared with those which he and his friends made in 1810. The 'thick-and-thin' men in opposition numbered 214; the Opposition were 'hopeful' of the support of 53 others, and 'doubtful' of the support of 117. On the other side were 81 or 82 Government members, exclusive of Perceval's following of 12; and 143 'against Opposition'; also Sidmouth's party of 8, Canning's 12, Castlereagh's 6 and Wellesley's 4. Then there were 5 'no Party' men (Radicals or near-Radicals).

... Tierney, to my astonishment, is the most sanguine man I have seen; that's to say, he thinks we could carry on the government under all the public exigencies, as far as the House of Commons is concerned, if we were in. This is an opinion almost everybody else differs from, they conceiving it impossible if Perceval maintains his ground, as he has done lately, when he is at the head of the Opposition; but this is Tierney's calculation: he says that Perceval has never divided lately stronger than 250, that his greatest majority has been 27; that therefore there must have been near 300 members who have never voted, lookers-on, ready to fall into whichever scale gets uppermost; that of these 250 members voting with Perceval now, a very large proportion possess places or are otherwise so connected that they must vote with whoever compose the Government, and that if you take all these data as true, which they are, you must conclude that we in Government might carry on business very well. ...

193. J. W. Ward to 'Ivy', Saturday [June 1811]

(Letters to 'Ivy' from the first Earl of Dudley, ed. S. H. Romilly (1905), pp. 140–141.)

... H.R.H. is certainly at this moment more courted and powerful than he ever will be again. Both parties are vying with each other in submission to him. But the choice must soon be made, and the mask will fall from the countenances of the unsuccessful candidates for his favour. I am inclined to think–though I well know how uncertain all conjectures upon such a subject must necessarily be–that he will try a partial change, and the new arrangement will not include Lords Grey and Grenville. At least, if that is his wish, he will easily be able to accomplish it. The bonds of party connection are becoming every day looser and looser, and people naturally and fairly consider themselves at liberty to follow their own individual inclination and convenience. Indeed, for some time past, all attempt at regular concerted opposition in the House of Commons seems to have been abandoned. . . .

194. W. H. Fremantle to the marquess of Buckingham, 15 July 1818

(Duke of Buckingham and Chandos, *Memoirs of . . . the Regency*, II, pp. 267–268.)

. . . I saw Tierney in the morning, and had much conversation with him. He told me he had actually gone over the list of the House of Commons, as far as the returns are now completed or known, and he calculates on those who were decided Opposition in the last Parliament; that is, those who always desired notes to be sent them, and who were ready to vote on any question. Of these, he considered there were 140, in the last, and 172 or 173, in this; and he did not take into consideration, on either side, the doubtfuls or uncertains, which might operate both ways, and make a calculation questionable. This, therefore, with the activity of new members, and the state of public opinion, must make it an Opposition which, if well managed, must break up any Government. . . .

195. Lord Londonderry to Sir Henry Hardinge, 6 July 1829

(*Londonderry MSS.*)

The third marquess of Londonderry, Castlereagh's half-brother, to whose title he succeeded in 1822, is referring to Wellington. The 'Brunswickers' were the ultra Tories alienated from the Government by the Catholic Relief Act.

. . . Suppose the Duke meets Parliament as he at present stands. To my own knowledge there are malcontents in his very camp. . . . The Brunswickers keep aloof from the Government. The Canningites and Whigs keep in position, and the Treasury Bench is not occupied by any Household troops, which are indispensably necessary in carrying on the Government in the contested debates and divisions of a Parliament. We never yet have seen a Minister without a commanding party who has successfully struggled through the difficulties which will ever surround the man who is called upon to rule the destinies of England; nor have we ever yet seen a Minister who could keep so many parties as now present themselves, in check, without coming to an understanding with one or the other of them. . . .

196. E. J. Littleton, M.P., to Ralph Sneyd, 24 Feb. 1830

(*Sneyd MSS.*)

. . . I found the House of Commons in a singular state. There are four parties in it. Putting the House at the scale of 300 (the average attendance in town) you may reckon about 120 to the Administration, Whigs about 70, old Canningites about 15, old Tories about 40, and the rest loose and perfectly independent of all party, so that the Government is clearly in a minority. The old Whigs, Tories and Canningites are generally a majority in the House, *if they could agree*; but this is the security of the Government. . . .

In the Whig party there is a schism. Brougham, Althorp, the Russells and the Mountain[1] are very Wellingtonian, so that they paralyze any hostile movement in the rest of the body. Sir James Graham had concerted with all parties a motion about the Treasurership of the Navy. He was obliged to abandon it at the moment he was about to rise, by a defection on the part of these gentry. . . .

(c) THE 'INFLUENCE OF THE CROWN'

197. Lord Althorp to his father, Earl Spencer, 24 Aug. 1811

(Althorp MSS.)

. . . I am sorry to hear that it is the intention to dissolve Parliament in case of a change of Administration without the King's death, for I think our friends would do very well without it, and it is so gross an avowal of the corrupt state of the representation to say that a Minister must always form his own Parliament in order to carry on the business of the country, that it does not at all accord with my political feelings. . . .

198. Earl Grey to Lord Holland, 20 Feb. 1820

(Howick MSS.)

Castlereagh had said on 13 Feb. that the Government was virtually at an end, and that they were holding their places only until their successors were appointed. But George IV was really unable to change his ministers because the Whigs in opposition, like his ministers, were opposed to the idea of a royal divorce and to giving him a greatly enlarged Civil List; and there was no other body of men capable of forming a government. A general election was necessitated by George III's death on 29 Jan.

. . . The King must have submitted to his Ministers. I think it most likely the quarrel will break out again, and with the same result. But if these squabbles should lead to any communication with us, I must add to what I have already said, that if the present Ministers choose the new Parliament, it must make a material difference. It would then become, in my opinion, quite impossible for us to undertake the Government. . . .

199. Earl Grey to Sir H. Taylor, 22 March 1831

(Correspondence of Earl Grey with William IV, ed. Earl Grey, I (1867), pp. 186–187.)

. . . This Government is now without its natural support, the Parliament having been chosen by the late Ministers, and all the seats usually at the command of the Ministers being now filled by their bitterest opponents.

It is objected to the plan of Reform, that the Ministers will not be able to command seats for themselves and their supporters. It is now ten times worse, as they not only have not the seats but that they afford a power against them. . . .

[1] The left-wing of the Whig party: so called because of their supposed Jacobin principles (the French Jacobins had sat on the highest bench on the Left of the Assembly).

200. Debate in the House of Commons on the Regency Bill, 9 Feb. 1789

(Parliamentary Register, xxv, pp. 410–415.)

Mr. Pitt: . . . The whole amount of the salaries of the Household, from the great officers at the head of the different Departments, down to the most menial servants in any of the palaces, or the stables, was no more than £100,000 per annum, out of which sum there was no more than about £30,000 received for salaries by members of the two Houses of Parliament; there were seven in the House of Commons whose salaries amounted to about £4000 and 18 Lords in the other House, whose salaries amounted to about £26,000. . . .

Lord North asked which of the two evils was the greatest, . . . the separating of the Household, or the withholding from the Regent the source of that general influence which the Constitution had deemed necessary to be given to the Crown and to the executive power of the country: that general influence without which the Crown could not exercise its duties. In all general influence there was necessarily a degree of parliamentary and political influence, but he saw no harm in this, and yet this influence was treated as of very little consequence. The right hon. gent. had acknowledged that 18 Peers of Parliament belonged to the Household. Did gentlemen consider that 18 Peers voting on one side made the difference of 36 on a division; and was that nothing? He did not say that a bad use would be made of that influence, but the withholding it from the person exercising the Royal authority was contrary to the principles of the Constitution. . . .

Mr. Pitt: . . . The grounds of objection to the clause were now stated to be that of parliamentary influence; a ground which he would venture to say it was wholly unusual to take broadly and openly in that House; because, whatever might have been gentlemen's private opinions respecting that particular kind of influence, it never had been avowed to be necessary to Government till the Lords had thought proper to avow it that day. . . .

Lord North: . . . With regard to the right hon. gent.'s charge against him, on the ground of his having avowed that the Regent ought to have the patronage of the Household for the sake of the parliamentary influence which accompanied it, he declared he had avowed no such doctrine, but had said that the patronage of the Household certainly gave some general, and, of course, parliamentary influence.

Mr. Marsham: . . . would affirm that there were members of Parliament under influence. He reminded the Committee, how often they had attempted by various Bills to prevent persons holding places from having seats in that House; and it was no reflection on the persons so disqualified. He instanced the Excise and Customs, in which every person enjoying a salary of four or five hundred a year, was, by Act of Parliament, rendered incapable of a seat in that House. With regard to the influence resulting from the patronage of the King's Household, if the right hon. gent. would add to it the weight of influence arising from the members of the two Houses holding places in the Household of the Queen, and would put the parliamentary influence of the two Households together, he would find that the number would be nearer 60 than 30. . . .

201. Debates in the British House of Commons on the proposed union with Ireland, 1800

(Cobbett's *Parliamentary History*, xxxv.)

21 April 1800.

Mr. Grey : . . . The right hon. gent. [Pitt] says too, that the new members will not increase the influence of the Crown. They will consist chiefly of the County representatives and those for the more populous towns. Though three-fourths of the County members are now against the Union, I confess I should distrust them when they come over here as members of the United Parliament. I suspect that they will rarely be adverse to the measures of any Administration. We have an example of the uniform support which the members for Scotland have given to every set of Ministers. We have reason to apprehend that the Irish members will become a no less regular band of ministerial adherents. The expenses of contested elections will become so great that it will be impossible for any man to sustain them who is not supported by the Treasury. All the hopes, all the views, of the members will centre in the Minister, and they will naturally be led to add themselves to the ranks of his constant and unalterable supporters. . . . [c. 71.]

25 April 1800.

Mr. Grey : . . . The right hon. gent. says that by introducing 100 members into the House, without any other composition of the House [*sic*], the alteration upon the whole must be very small. This, however, is a point that admits of great dispute. The alteration may not be less important because it is only partial in its immediate operation. . . . The introduction of 100 Irish members must be attended with a certain change in the composition of the House of Commons; and I am afraid that their weight will be thrown into the increasing scale of the Crown. . . . [xxxv, 98.]

Lord Hawkesbury : . . . The religious feuds that have subsisted there for so many years, the state of the public mind in that country, the jealousies on the subject of property, the recollection of the past and the apprehensions for the future, make it impossible for Ireland to bear the collision of contending factions without ruin to her peace, and ultimate destruction to her Government. Let this Union take place – all Irish party will be extinguished; there will then be no parties but the parties of the British Empire. The strength of Great Britain, the constitution of her Parliament will, I am persuaded, enable her to keep all such parties in subjection, and to secure to every member of the Empire the possession of its religion, its property and its laws. Such a union will give integrity and harmony to our whole system, and will make Ireland, in any future contest, a source of incalculable energy, strength and support to this Kingdom. [*Ibid.*, c. 114.]

Mr. Wilberforce : said that by the important change of adding 100 members to that House, there could not fail to be a very considerable addition to the influence of the Crown. From the great increase of our national debt, our commerce, our army and navy, and various other causes, this influence was far greater than ever. He could not, therefore, but be of opinion that the admission of 100 members would greatly add to that influence. . . . He never felt his mind more tremulously uncertain than on the present occasion. In the early part of his life he had zealously supported the cause of a reform in Parliament, and particularly the plan of his righ hon. friend [Pitt]. Much undoubtedly had passed in the course of 16 years to justify his right hon. friend for any change which may have taken place in his opinion on that head. An alteration, however, it seemed must be made. Was it not possible that modifications might be made in it? He thought there might. He thought it might be done by lessening the machinery of Government–by lessening the number of places held under Government. These places must certainly have had less influence in a body of 300 than they would in 20, which formed a fifth of the whole number of members to be returned to the united Parliament from Ireland. He thought also that there would be a great difference between their voting in Dublin and in London: from the great distance, the expenses of travelling, and the difference in the price of all the necessaries of life in this country and in Ireland, he feared we should not have the same number of independent characters returned for Counties to the united Parliament, as we had been used to have in the Irish House of Commons. [*Ibid.*, c. 116–117.]

202. W. Pennefather to Alexander Marsden, 8 July 1802

(State Paper Office, Dublin Castle, 520/131/4.)

In consideration of Mr. Pennefather getting a place from Government of five hundred a year, upon the usual tenure by which offices are held, and a cornetcy for his son or an equivalent for such Commission, Mr. Pennefather will return a person recommended by Government for the City of Cashel on the ensuing election, and so long as the Parliament shall continue.[1]

203. Lord Hawkesbury to his father, Lord Liverpool, 13 Sept. 1802

(*British Museum Additional MSS.* 38473, f. 117.)

. . . The expenses of elections have been great beyond measure. The Treasury had but one seat to dispose of for nothing, and Mr. Addington's brother was, I know, obliged to give £1500 for his election.[2] . . .

204. T. Brooksbank (treasury clerk) to Lord Wellesley, 19 Dec. 1806

(*British Museum Additional MSS.* 37309, f. 152.)

Fremantle was Joint Secretary of the Treasury. Wellesley and Montgomery were returned for Michael (Cornwall) at by-elections on 15 Jan. 1807, and Lushington for Great Yarmouth on 4 Nov. 1806. Wellesley was Irish Secretary in the succeeding Portland Administration, 1807-1809.

. . . An opportunity has occurred which enables Mr. Fremantle to comply with your wishes in recommending Mr. Stephen Lushington and Colonel Montgomery for seats. . . . The price will be £5,000 each. I enclose the arrangement which has been made for Mr. Lushington. Sir Arthur Wellesley's seat is secured.

[1] Cf. Lord Hardwicke's Application Book: "Wm. Pennefather, 12 Jan. 1802. Commissioner [of] Accounts in exchange for a seat in Cashel next Parliament." [Reply] "Thanks, but no promise." And "Mr. Pennefather, 7 Sept. 1802. A place for his son." [Reply] "Promised as soon as one can be found." (*Add. MSS.* 35782, ff. 109, 127.)   [2] John Hiley Addington, M.P. for Bossiney.

205. The duke of Wellington to J. C. Herries (Secretary of the Treasury), 6 Sept. 1826

(Herries MSS.)

If you wish that Mr. Philip Stevens should be the Barrack Master at Harwich he shall be appointed. But I protest against the claim of the Corporation to name the person to fill this or any other office under the Ordnance. I likewise beg to remind you that the Master-General of the Ordnance has lost one of the seats at Queenborough by the opposition of the officers of the Gov^t., *viz.* of the Transport Office & Custom House. I likewise wish you to consider whether Mr. Stevens, coming as he does recommended by the Corporation, is a very fit person to be the Barrack Master *at Harwich*; whether he is likely to perform his duty as we require he should; and whether you will not lose more by his dismissal, which will certainly occur if he should not perform his duty, than you will gain by his appointment.

It would probably be best at all events to appoint Mr. Stevens to some place at a distance from Harwich.

206. George Canning to Lord Wellesley, 22 May 1827

(Wellesley Papers, ed. L. Melville, II (1914), p. 161.)

On 17 Feb. 1827 Lord Liverpool had an apoplectic seizure which ended his political life. Before the appointment of his successor, Canning, the Catholic question was debated in the Commons (5 and 6 March), and the anti-Catholics unexpectedly found themselves in a majority (276 *v.* 272).

. . . He [Lord Liverpool] was scrupulously impartial, I can bear witness for him, in parliamentary arrangements, so far as the distribution of seats in the power of the Government could go–for of ten seats placed at his disposal, half were given to Protestants and half to Catholics, friends of the Administration. I cannot answer for it that the like impartiality was observed by the persons acting under him. I believe otherwise, and I believe still more that after his seizure, and at the moment when the Catholic question was brought on for discussion, no effort was left unestablished by those into whose hands the power of the Treasury fell, to influence the decision in the way in which it actually turned. . . .

207. Lord Hardwicke to Lady Londonderry, 7 Nov. 1804

(British Museum Additional MSS. 35753, f. 182.)

The Lord Lieutenant of Ireland uses the Crown patronage to purchase votes in the House of Commons for the Government.

. . . The late contests in Parliament and those which are preparing have brought upon me claims for Church preferment which might not otherwise have been urged, but which nevertheless cannot be postponed from the support which I feel myself called upon to give to my friends at Westminster. This circumstance has even obliged me to resort to the patronage of some of the Bishops for such assistance as they may be able to afford. . . .

208. House of Commons' representation of Ireland in the Parliament of 1807–1812. By Sir Arthur Wellesley (Chief Secretary)

(*British Museum Additional MSS.* 40221, ff. 15–62.)

Antrim Co:–Mr. McNaghten. Is brought in principally by the influence of Lord Hertford. Attends well and is a steady friend. Government are under an engagement to give him an office for life of £300 per annum, which was made at the period of the Union, and has been admitted by the Duke of Richmond. Lord Cornwallis was to have given him an office of this description and value, and had made an arrangement for it which was defeated by a trick of the late Lord Avonmore. Lord Castlereagh knows the whole story. Mr. McNaghten has lately desired to have a pension for his life, of the value and instead of this office, but by Lord Hawkesbury's desire I have refused it.

The Hon. John O'Neill–is the brother of Lord O'Neill, supports Government and attends tolerably. I believe he is a Lieut-Colonel of Dragoons. The patronage of the County of Antrim should be distributed according to the recommendation of Lord Hertford and Lord o'Neill. It must be observed however that Lord Donegal will claim that of the town of Belfast.

Armagh Co:–William Brownlow, Esq. This gentleman supports Government. Did not attend last Session. Wishes to be made a Privy Councillor. He has no [other] objects that I know of.

William Richardson, Esq. Supports Government generally. Attended last Session. Has no objects that I know of. Lord Gosford has a large interest in this County, and by his means, principally, Lord Charlemont's brother was thrown out, and Mr. Richardson brought in. The patronage of this County is at the disposal of Government. Neither of the members will lay claim to it, and there is not much necessity for giving it to Lord Gosford.

Borough of Armagh:–P. Duigenan–supports Government and attends constantly. This support and attendance depend however, as I imagine, upon the goodwill of the Primate towards Government. Has no objects excepting to forward his son-in-law, Mr. Heppenstall, in the army, and to provide for a relation of his wife's in the police.

Athlone:–Mr. Turner. This borough belongs to Mr. Handcock, the brother-in-law of Lord Clancarty, who invariably sells it to Government. I know nothing of Mr. Turner, and must refer to the Treasury.

Bandon Bridge:–Mr. Tierney. This borough belongs alternately to the Duke of Devonshire and Lord Bandon, the brother-in-law of Lord Shannon. The Duke returned Mr. Tierney, who is in opposition.

Belfast:–Mr. May is returned by Lord Donegal. He has not attended in this Session. He is inclined to quarrel with Government because they will not attend to Lord Donegal's pretensions in the County of Antrim.

Carrickfergus:–James Craig, Esq. Lady Downshire has fought this borough twice against Lord Donegal, and has now the member, who is in opposition.

Co. of Carlow:–Mr. Latouche. Is not disinclined to support Government. Does not attend Parliament. May be depended upon for any object of Government in Ireland. Mr. Bagenal is in opposition, but is inclined to come over if certain objects of his can be gratified, of which I have not a very distinct knowledge. Mr. Kingston can state them. The patronage of this County rests with Government.

Carlow Borough:—Mr. Strahan—belongs to Lord Charleville who sells it to Government. Refer to the Treasury for Mr. Strahan.

Cavan County:—Mr. Sneyd—supports Government, is a cordial friend, and attends well when in London. He is a connection of Foster's.

Colonel Barry—a Lord of the Treasury, a nephew of Foster's. He is brought in by the means of Lord Farnham, whose pretensions he has stated to become a Representative Peer. Wants [to be a Privy Councillor][1] and promotion in the Church for his brother. See memorandum book of requests. The patronage of this County may be divided between the members, but the nomination of the Sheriffs in particular should be given to Mr. Sneyd.

Clare:—Colonel Fitzgerald is member for Clare instead of Mr. Burton, and supports.[2] The brother of Lord Conyngham supports Government and attends constantly. He is the Lieut. Govr of Canada, & will bring in a member in his place. Has two or three little objects—see the Memo. of Requests, such as the succession of Mr. Fitzgerald's son to the father at the Board of Stamps; a Barrack Master's place at Limerick. He assisted the other member, Sir Edward O'Brien, in coming into Parliament, who has also supported Government and attended in this Session. He wants to have an office of £300 or £400 per annum for his brother, who has been 3 or 4 years at the Bar ['this is done'], to have a good frigate for his brother, a Captain in the Navy, who has the Sea Fencibles in Galway; and the objects of two others of his brothers promoted. The two first ought to be done or we shall lose his support. The patronage of this County should be given to Lord Conyngham.

Clonmel:—Colonel Bagwell is Muster Master General. His father stood for the County of Tipperary and fought a hard battle which has given him some pretensions. His particular objects are to have the office of Collector of Excise and of Barrack Master vacated, and it is desirable to give him these offices if they can be vacated without great inconvenience. Colonel Bagwell also wants some provision in the Church for his younger brother. Bagwell acts in Parliament with Lord Westmorland. He has got the office of Barrack Master.

Coleraine:—Mr. Jones—brought in by Lord Waterford. Supports Government and attends well. The patronage of Coleraine should be given to Lord Waterford.

Cork Co:—Mr. Ponsonby is in opposition. Lord Bernard is Lord Shannon's nephew and generally supports. The patronage of the County of Cork should generally be given to Lord Shannon, but it must be recollected that Lord Kingston's family and Lord Longueville's will probably claim some share in it.

Cork City:—Colonel Longfield supports Government and attends well—brought in by Lord Longueville, who is offended because his relation was not made Bishop of Cork. Lord Longueville acts in Parliament with Lord Westmorland. He has a nephew a Commissioner of Excise. Mr. C. Hutchinson—Lord Donoughmore's brother,

---

[1] Deleted. [2] By-election, 9 Aug. 1808.

is in opposition, but seldom attends. The patronage of the City of Cork must be given to Lord Longueville, but an endeavour should be made to ascertain and settle with him what offices are in the County and what in the City.

Cashel:–Mr. Peel[1]–Belongs to Mr. Pennefather who always sells it to Government. Refer to the Treasury for the member.

Donegal Co:–Sir James Stewart–a friend of Government but never attends. Colonel Montgomery–lately[2] came in on the interest of Lord Conyngham. Supports Government but not zealously, and I think will oppose when he can. He says he is attached to Lord Wellesley.

This County is in an extraordinary situation. The influence lies between Lord Abercorn and Lord Conyngham. The latter, with the smaller property, has the greatest influence, and has uniformly lately made the returns. The patronage however must be given to Lord Abercorn, which at some period or other will occasion great difficulties with Lord Conyngham. In case of difficulty in any instance I should imagine from what Lord Abercorn says, he wont be inclined to give it up.

Down Co:–Colonel Meade is in opposition. Mr. Savage is in opposition. Both these members are brought in by Lady Downshire, but she must at some time or other lose one of them. The patronage of this County is at the disposal of Government, but Lord Castlereagh, Mr. Croker and General Needham may claim parts of it.

Downpatrick:–Mr. Croker supports Government; is a zealous friend and attends constantly. He gave up an office in the Revenue when he came into Parliament, and he then requested that the man who was his deputy might be the principal in the office in one of the ports of Wexford, Ross or Waterford, when the arrangements for the office should be made. The patronage of Downpatrick should be given to Mr. Croker. It must be observed that he comes in for Downpatrick upon the interest of Lord De Clifford, which was obtained for him by Mr. Rowley, who is a Commissioner of Customs. This gentleman has a claim for provision in the Church for his brother.

Drogheda:–Colonel Foster is a Lord of the Treasury, the son of Mr. Foster; attends well. He is very anxious to obtain the office of Surveyor of the Port held by Mr. Molesworth for Mr. McIntegart. Mr. McIntegart is Collector of the Port of Drogheda. The patronage of Drogheda should be given to Colonel Foster.

Dublin Co:–Mr. Hamilton wants to be an Irish peer by the name of Lord Clanbrassil, to which Lord Dufferin objects, as he has a claim to it. If Government should agree to make him a peer, this difference must be settled by arbitration. A promise has been made to Mr. Hamilton, of the first office of Assistant Barrister or the first legal office that should fall, for his brother, Counsellor Hamilton. (This brother has been provided for.) A promise was likewise made to Counsellor Alex. Hamilton, at the instance of Colonel Falkiner, of the office of Assistant Barrister in Armagh in consequence of the support he gave Colonel Falkiner & Mr. Hamilton at the general election.

Mr. Talbot is in opposition. The patronage of this County is at the disposal of Government.

[1] Elected 15 April 1809; Under-Secretary for War and the Colonies, 1810.   [2] 4 Feb. 1808.

Dublin City:–Mr. Grattan in opposition. Mr. Shaw supports Government, attends tolerably well, wishes to have an office in the Police for his brother-in-law, Counsellor Lees. (Has had the office.) The patronage, of course, with Government.
Dublin University:–Mr. Leslie Foster, Mr. Foster's nephew, supports Government, attends constantly, has some trifling objects for his constituents. See Memo. of Requests.
Dundalk:–Mr. Hughan supports Government. This borough belongs to Lord Roden, who now sells it to Government, [as Mr. Bruce vacates his seat].[1]
Dungannon:–Claud Scott supports Government. This borough belongs to Lord Northland.
Dungarvon:–Geo. Walpole is in opposition–brought in by the Duke of Devonshire. The patronage of this borough should be given to Lord Waterford.
Ennis:–Mr. Fitzgerald is in opposition.
Enniskillen:–Mr. Pochin. This seat belongs to Lord Enniskillen who sells it to Government. Refer to the Treasury.
Co. Fermanagh:–General Archdall supports Government but attends badly and is not very well satisfied. He wants a military government and a regiment, to both of which he has well founded claims, having lost an arm in the service. He has also made a request respecting Messrs. Hamilton and Gordon, attorneys in Dublin, in regard to an office in the police. (This has been done for him.)
   General Cole, Lord Enniskillen's brother, is abroad. The patronage of Fermanagh should be given to Lord Enniskillen generally–occasionally to General Archdall. Lord Ely has a large property and influence in this County, but this ought not to be supported against the existing members.
Galway Co:–Richard Martin and Denis Bowes Daly in opposition. The patronage of Galway is at the disposal of Government, but Lord Clancarty and Mr. James Daly ought to be attended to in some degree in the disposal of it.
Galway City:–James Daly supports Government and attends well. He has no object that I know of. The patronage of the town of Galway should generally be given to him.
Kerry Co:–Mr. Fitzgerald and Mr. Herbert in opposition. The patronage of the County of Kerry is at the disposal of Govt. Lord Glandore and Lord Kenmare have the leading interests and might be consulted respecting it. Mr. Blennerhasset of this County is to be a Baronet at the desire of Colonel Crosbie, who formerly represented it.
Kildare Co:–Lord Henry Fitzgerald and Robert Latouche in opposition. The patronage of Kildare is at the disposal of Government.
Kilkenny Co:–Hon. James Butler, the brother of Lord Ormonde, is in opposition, but has not attended much this year. Lord Ormonde is now in treaty for the sale of his Butlerage[2] to Government, but I don't believe that any arrangement could be made to obtain his support under this treaty. Hon. Fred. Ponsonby in opposition. The patronage of this County is at the disposal of Government.

[1] Scored through. Hughan was elected, *vice* Bruce, on 27 July 1808.
[2] He sold to the Crown in 1810 for £216,000 the grant of the prisage of the wines of Ireland made to the 4th Butler by Edward I.

City of Kilkenny:–Hon. **Charles Butler,** Lord Ormonde's brother, in opposition. The representation of this City belongs alternately to Lord Ormonde and Lord Desart's family. The family is connected with Lord Sligo.

King's Co:–Mr. **Bernard** supports Government and has attended latterly. **Mr. Lloyd** supports Government and has attended latterly. Mr. Bernard is brought in for this County principally by the influence of Lord Charleville. And Mr. Lloyd, Lord Rosse's brother-in-law, by Lord Rosse. He is the most powerful of the two. The patronage of the County should be disposed of at the recommendation of Lord Rosse principally, with a desire that he should consult Lord Charleville. There will be some difficulty soon in settling which of these noble lords is the Custos Rotulorum of the County when Lord Drogheda will die. Lord Charleville has asked for the office, but I believe it ought to be Lord Rosse. The members have no particular objects, excepting Mr. Lloyd that his brother, Captain Lloyd of the 43rd Regiment, be promoted to a majority. And Mr. Bernard wants two ensigncies which will be applied for for him.

Kinsale:–This borough belongs to Lord de Clifford. **Mr. Martin** in opposition. The patronage of Kinsale at the disposal of Government.

Leitrim Co:–Mr. **Clements** supports Government and attends regularly. Has no particular object. **Mr. Rob[er]t[1] Latouche** in opposition. The patronage of Leitrim should be given generally to Mr. Clements.

Limerick Co:–Colonel **Odell** supports Government and attends regularly. Colonel Odell's son is Commissioner of Excise. He is Lieut.-Colonel of the Limerick Militia, of which Regiment he wishes the Colonelcy, but this favour ought to be reserved for the young Lord Clare. **Mr. Quin** in opposition. The patronage of this County should be disposed of according to the wishes of Lady Clare and the Chief Baron o'Grady. The Chief Baron in particular ought to be consulted respecting the nomination of the Sheriff, as he understands the claims of the different parties in the County.

Limerick City:–Colonel **Vereker** is a Lord of the Treasury, supports, and attends regularly. [Wishes to be a Privy Councillor.[2]] The patronage of the City of Limerick should be given to Colonel Vereker.

Lisburne:–Lord **Yarmouth** supports Government and attends regularly. The patronage to Lord Hertford.

Londonderry County:–General **Stewart** and Lord **George Beresford** support Government and attend regularly. The patronage of this County should be divided between Lord George and General Stewart, and care must be taken that Lord George, from his connexion with Sir Geo. Hill, and the claims of the latter upon the patronage of the City of Derry, and that of Lord Waterford upon that of Coleraine in this County, does not run away with the whole of it. General Stewart ought to have a fair share of all the offices that fall vacant, excluding those at Coleraine.

Londonderry City:–Sir **Geo. Hill,** a Lord of the Treasury, attends well.

Co. of Longford:–Sir **Thomas Fetherston** supports Government and attends well. He is brought in by the influence of the late Lord Rosse and considers himself in some degree attached to the present Lord Rosse. He wants to have an office of

---

[1] Should be John.   [2] Scored through.

£500 or £600 per annum for his son, or something of greater value for himself, for which he would relinquish his seat in Parliament. **Lord Forbes** in opposition but has not attended lately. The patronage of this County at the disposal of Government, but Sir Thomas Fetherston should be attended to occasionally.

Louth Co:–Mr. Foster. He has made several requests and has several objects–all stated in the Book of Requests. **Mr. Jocelyn,** the brother of Lord Roden, supports Government and attends well. He is to vacate his seat at the end of the next Session of Parliament,[1] and is to be a Commissioner of Customs, instead of Mr. Knox. The patronage of Louth should be given to Mr. Foster.

Mallow:–Mr. Jephson supports Government and is connected with Lord Longueville, but has not attended lately, as a pension for which he has asked has not been given to Lady Strangford.

Mayo Co:–Hon. D. Browne supports Government, is a cordial friend and attends constantly. Has no particular object, but his brother, Lord Sligo, urges requests occasionally. In particular he wants a better Deanery for Dean Mahon, and has asked for an office of Surveyor General. **Colonel Dillon** in opposition, but has not attended lately. The patronage of this County should be given to Lord Sligo.

Meath Co:–Sir Marcus Somerville in opposition. **Thomas Bligh, Esq.** supports generally and votes with Opposition with reluctance. The patronage of Meath at the disposal of Government.

Monaghan Co:–Mr. Leslie supports Government. He has an object for a Councillor Stack [?] in the Police. (Has been done). **Mr. Corry** supports generally. The patronage of Monaghan at the disposal of Government.

Newry:–General Needham supports Government. All that he requires is the disposal of the patronage at Newry.

Portarlington:–Sir Oswald Mosley in opposition.

Queen's Co:–Mr. Pole, Sec^y. to the Admiralty. Mr. Pole has some objects which are stated in Book of Requests. **Mr Parnell** in opposition. The patronage of this County should be given to Mr. Pole.

Roscommon:–Mr. French supports Government. Wants a better Deanery or Church preferment for his brother, and other trifling objects. **General Mahon** supports Government. His object is promotion in the peerage for his father. This has been promised to him by former Governments, and he ought to have taken it when any promotion of Viscounts is made. The patronage of this County at the disposal of Government, but should be given very much at the recommendation of the members. Mr. Trench and Lord Lorton should have the nomination of the Sheriffs.

New Ross:–Mr. Wigram brought in by Lord Ely, supports Government.

Sligo Co:–Mr. O'Hara in opposition but does not attend. **Mr. Cooper** supports Government and attends well. The patronage of this County is at the disposal of Government, but Mr. Cooper should be attended to. The nomination of the Sheriff in particular should be given to him.

Sligo Borough:–Mr. Canning[2] supports Government. He wishes to be a Lord

---

[1] The by-election was on 10 Feb. 1810.
[2] The statesman's cousin; afterwards Lord Garvagh.

of the Treasury in Ireland. This borough belongs to Mr. Wynne who always sells it to Government.

Tipperary:–Colonel Mathew in opposition. **Mr. Prittie** in opposition. The patronage of this County is at the disposal of Government, but Colonel Bagwell, who had a desperate contest for the representation, ought to be attended to and ought to have that of the town of Clonmell, and Lord Norbury who ought to be attended to in Tipperary.

Tralee:–Mr. Steven supports Government. This borough belongs to Mr. Blenner-hasset, who always sells it to Government.

Tyrone Co:–Mr. Stewart in opposition generally, but supports Government upon all questions in which the Catholics are concerned. **Mr. Knox** in opposition. The patronage of this County must be given to Lord Abercorn.

Waterford Co:–Mr. Beresford supports Government and attends. He wishes to have some arrangement made for a Mr. Fitzpatrick who is his son's deputy in his office of Storekeeper. **Richard Power** in opposition, but seldom attends. The patronage of the County of Waterford to be given to Lord Waterford.

Waterford City:–Sir John Newport in opposition. The patronage of the City of Waterford is claimed by Mr. Alcock, member for the County of Wexford, on the ground that he has contested the City twice in his own person and by Mr. Bolton against Sir John Newport. This claim has now however been admitted by the Irish Government, and the patronage is at its disposal. Lord Waterford must be attended to in the disposal of it in some degree, and Mr. Alcock and Mr. Bolton.

Westmeath Co:–Mr. Rochfort supports Government and attends regularly. He has objects for his sons which are stated in the Memoranda of Requests. His eldest son who is Accountant-General of the Post Office, ought to be removed when there is an opportunity to an office of less labour. **Captain Pakenham** supports Government and attends. The patronage of this County at the disposal of Government. But Lord Longford and Mr. Rochfort ought to be attended to in the disposal of it. Mr. Smith, the late member, has a claim for an office of Assistant Barrister for Mr. Lyne, and for promotion for his brother, who is Paymaster for Newry.

Wexford Co:–Mr. Ram supports Government and attends. **Mr. Alcock** supports Government but has not attended. He wants the patronage of the City of Waterford. The patronage of the County of Wexford to be given to Lord Ely who has brought in Mr. Alcock.

Wexford City:–Mr. Nevill supports Government and attends regularly. Lord Ely has the alternate return of this City and ought to have the patronage.

Wicklow Co:–Mr. Hume in opposition but is inclined to support Government. **Mr. Tighe** in opposition but does not attend. The patronage of this County at the disposal of Government.

Youghall:–Sir John Keane brought in by Lord Shannon; supports Government but does not attend well. The patronage of Youghall to be given to Lord Shannon.

209. Robert Peel to Denis Browne, M.P. for Co. Mayo, 18 Sept. 1813

(British Museum Additional MSS. 40284, f. 182.)

Lord Liverpool was too good an Evangelical to allow Church patronage to be used for political purposes irrespective of the merits of the clergyman concerned.

I have received your letter of the 12th instant respecting the disposal of the prebend of Killibegs in the Co. Mayo. The Duke of Richmond never considered that preferment in the Church formed part of that local patronage which is usually disposed of at the recommendation of the friends of Government in the respective Counties or towns which they represent, and I may add that since I came to Ireland your letter of the 12th inst. was the first intimation which I have received that even the representative himself so considered it. I can I believe with truth assure you that not even an application for an appointment to any living or Church preferment of any kind has been made by any County member of Ireland, on the ground that such preferment was situated in the County which he represented. I am sure I can with truth assert that if made it has never been complied with on that ground. Neither will I conceal my opinion that it is most expedient in every point of view that Church patronage should be considered in a light entirely different from that in which revenue patronage is. I trust therefore that this explanation will entirely remove from your mind any unfavourable impression which the disposal of the prebend of Killibegs without reference to you as a member of the County in which that sinecure happens to be nominally situate may be occasioned. . . .

210. Sir Arthur Wellesley to Lord Hawkesbury, 8 Dec. 1807

(Wellington MSS.)

The purchasing of votes in the House of Commons.

[Some Irish pensions] . . . One of them, that to Mr. Knox,[1] was arranged (with £400 additional, to be given next year) by Lord Castlereagh; and the others were asked for in the moment of the greatest difficulty of the present Administration,[2] when every vote was important. . . . Neither the Duke of Richmond or I can have any object in these pensions, or in any other arrangement, excepting to forward the views and to provide for the support of the Government. . . .

211. Lord Durham to Lord Grey, 13 Aug. 1828

(Howick MSS.)

The reference is to the duke of Clarence's resignation of the office of Lord High Admiral.

. . . It appears that the reason was the Duke's refusal to give the patronage of the navy with a view to parliamentary influence . . . I had long thought that, constituted as the House of Commons is, no Ministry could carry on the government with such a diminution of their patronage. . . .

[1] The hon. George Knox, M.P. for Dungannon in the Irish and Imperial House of Commons, had a pension of £800 a year for life.
[2] Evidently before the dissolution of Parliament on 29 April 1807.

212. Excerpts from Pitt's Secret Service Accounts, 1784–1793
(Public Record Office, *Chatham Papers*, 229.)

The following documents illustrate the spending of public money on elections.

Nicholas Mill's expenses at a contested election for Saltash the 7th of April 1784, when the candidates were Charles Jenkinson, Charles Ambler, Lord Strathaven and John Curtis.

	£.	s.	d.
Chaise hire from London to Saltash on the dissolution of parliament -	16	5	0
Paid for bringing two expresses from Plymouth to Saltash, one from Mr. Masterman to Mr. Hickes and the other to the mayor, which was sent to Truro by mistake - - - - - - - -		10	0
Paid John Hoskin for horse hire and expenses to Liskeard, Trinity Bodmin and Duloe with letters to Mr. Masterman, Mr. Lyne and Mr. Cole, desiring their attendance at the election. - - -	1	2	6
Paid John Bayley, attorney at law, for his attendance at the election, inspecting deeds produced by the freeholders to prove themselves possessed of burgage tenure freeholds, and other assistance. - -	5	5	0
Paid the like to Mr. Hannibal Hawkins who took abstracts of the deeds, &c. - - - - - - - - - - -	5	5	0
Paid the like to Mr. Richard Rodd taking poll and minutes for the candidates - - - - - - - - - - -	5	5	0
Paid the like to Mr. William Harris who took minutes of the election.	5	5	0
Paid the like to Richard Berryman taking the poll for the mayor -	5	5	0
Paid John Hancock for dinner on the day of election as per bill -	40	15	0
Servants - - - - - - - - - - -	2	2	0
Paid John Hobling expense of the constables & boatmen per bill -	5	0	6
Paid Jacob Landick expense of the ringers per bill - - -	2	12	6
Paid chaise hire for two of the aldermen going to Plymouth & Dock to get the free burgesses to attend the election - - - -	1	2	0
Town Clerk's fee for indentures & all other attendance & trouble as usual at general elections - - - - - - - -	42	0	0
Town Serjeant's fee for the election as usual - - - -	2	2	0
Clerk's journey to Penryn with the return for the sheriff to execute counterpart–out 5 days - - - - - - - -	2	12	6
Horse hire & expenses - - - - - - - -	2	7	8
Fee to Under-Sheriff for delivering precepts. He was dissatisfied & said he ought to have 5 guineas more, which you will add if you think it right to do so. - - - - - - - -	5	5	0
Paid for express to you giving an account of return and what passed at the election - - - - - - - - -	3	3	6
Messenger to Plymouth with the same - - - - -		3	0
John Hancock's charge for an intended election ball as usual if you approve thereof - - - - - - - - -	40	0	0
	193	8	2

J. Mallard's Bill for the Hampshire election, 1790

	£.	s.	d.
Crown Inn, Lyndhurst, 9 April 1790:			
46 dinners	6	18	0
Beer	2	5	0
Port	11	4	0
Sherry & Lisbon	1	16	0
Punch	5	0	0
Servants' dinners, &c.	1	5	0
Glass broke, &c.		10	6
	28	18	6
	1	5	0
	30	3	6

	£.	s.	d.
Crown Inn, Lyndhurst, 22 June 1790:			
20 breakfasts	1	0	0
Cyder		3	0
23 June – 20 suppers	1	0	0
Beer		7	6
Wine & punch	1	8	8
	3	19	2

	£.	s.	d.
Horse hire:			
22 June 1790: one pair horses per day	1	5	0
chaise	1	5	0
one chaise two days	1	10	0
one chaise two days	1	10	0
9 saddle horses 2 days	4	10	0
	10	0	0

	£.	s.	d.
27 July. Mary Mallard, for entertaining and carrying to Winchester, the 22nd & 23rd of June 1790.	42	0	0

Receipts, &c. for secret service money.

	£.	s.	d.
1788. July 28. Lord Hood, £500; 29 July, £1500; 17 August £1000:	3000	0	0
1784. 27 June. Mr. Lloyd, for my trouble in the several attendances I had previous to the dissolution of the Parliament concerning divers election business's on you & at your request.	10	10	0
Paid Mr. Rawle of Kelstone his bill for chaise hire & expresses	19	11	6
	30	1	6
Former account delivered in January last	50	0	0
	80	1	6

	£.	s.	d.
[ ]28 July Lord Hood	500 –	0 –	0
1790. 2 December. F. Moor Slade, on the Rochester election	73 –	0 –	0
1791. 18 April. Edmund Estcourt in full for my journeys & expenses previous to the last general election & for other law business done for him [i.e. George Rose, Joint Secretary of the Treasury]	500 –	0 –	0
1790. 19 November. Robert Smith	5000 –	0 –	0
1790. 15 June. William Shirreff, which I had advanced as a subscription for Mr. Rolleston for Hampshire election.	300 –	0 –	0
1784. 9 May. Sir Bernard Turner	560 –	0 –	0
6 July. Sir Robert Smyth	1000 –	0 –	0
23 June. W. Masterman	3000 –	0 –	0
24 July. W. Masterman, received for Mr. Edward Hawkins, due, 25 March 1784.	50 –	0 –	0
10 July. W. Masterman	4000 –	0 –	0
1 & 21 April. W. Mainwaring, £500 [plus] £500	1000 –	0 –	0
19 August. Jervis	1000 –	0 –	0
13 July. Sir Robert Smyth	1000 –	0 –	0
1791. 17 March. Carpenter, for expenses respecting the Camelford election.	68 –	0 –	0
17 May. Dean of Canterbury[1] (in addition to £400 already paid) in further part of the expenses at East Looe for the whole parliament.	500 –	0 –	0
17 May. Captain Finch, the remainder of the expenses for Surrey.	1288 –	17 –	0
1793. 11 April. Pole for Grimsby, £329–19 [plus] £96	425 –	19 –	0
15 May. Vernon for Grimsby	1000 –	0 –	0
7 June. Estcourt, for Lord Hood	500 –	0 –	0
Mr. Estcourt for Stafford	500 –	0 –	0
1790. November 2. Col. Manners for Northampton	94 –	0 –	0
December 2. Mr. Slade for Rochester	73 –	0 –	0
1791. January 21. Mr. Luttrell for Lord Parker's seat at Minehead.	2000 –	0 –	0
February 3. Mr. Finch for Surrey	500 –	0 –	0
February 22. Mr. Pole for Grimsby	300 –	0 –	0
February 28. Mr. Townson for Okehampton Petition	500 –	0 –	0
March. 1. Lord Hood for the former Westminster election, in part of an arrear.	1500 –	0 –	0
Mr. Elford for law expenses in the west	300 –	0 –	0
March 7. Colonel Balfour: expenses at Wendover & Retford.	139 –	15 –	0
April 14. Mr. Slade in full for the expenses at Rochester.	378 –	6 –	4

[1] "There is still due to Mr. Pybus for Dover £1500, and a balance to the Dean of Canterbury, besides further pressing demands for Westminster in the course of the year."

	£.	s.	d.

April 18. Mr. Estcourt–law expenses   500 – 0 – 0

      Expenses in Hampshire, beyond the sum in the last
      accompt, and exclusive of my private subscription
      of £300 and various expenses incurred during the
      contest:–

      Paid the Sheriff's Counsel   £210
      Mr. Rolleston's subscription   300
      The Rev. Mr. Jackson's   ,,   30
      Paid bills amounting to   215 – 10 – 2

                                            755 – 10 – 2

Paid Mr. Chinnery for writs, &c. money paid by him at the
general election.   147 – 18 – 6

                                          7688 – 10 – 0

In addition to the above sum of £30,000, the sum of £5,000 was received for the Leicester election, the voucher for which is among the others herewith delivered.

There are immediate demands to fulfil engagements for Dover, Stafford and East Looe, and to complete the one for Surrey.

213. George III to Pitt, 23 Jan. 1798, 8.25 a.m.

(Public Record Office, *Chatham Papers*, 104.)

... My income is certainly, in proportion to the greatness of the country, inadequate to my station, for my Privy Purse at £60,000 and the expense of my Household is the only real income I possess. As to the former, I have some debts, of which the sum borrowed for the late elections make[s] the most considerable part, which I am by instalments paying off. ...

214. Lord Holland on George III's contributions to the Government's election fund

(Lord Holland, *Memoirs of the Whig Party*, I (1852), pp. 93-94.)

The general election was very ill managed by the Government. In many instances no ministerial candidates were found; in others, not sufficient preference was shown to tried friends over their sunshine supporters who professed attachment to *the Ministry*, but who never felt, and scarcely affected, adherence to our party under any other denomination. The King, who throughout his reign had furnished every Treasury with £12,000 to defray election expenses on a dissolution, withheld that unconstitutional assistance from the Administration of 1806. Yet, such is the infatuation bred by the atmosphere of a Court, some of our friends then flattered themselves that we were not obnoxious to the King, and have since persisted in the foolish opinion that nothing but our own conduct gave him an inclination to change his Government.

215. Lord Palmerston's journal, 30 Dec. 1806

(Bulwer's *Life of Palmerston*, I (1870), p. 53, and *Broadlands MSS.*)

. . . The method adopted by Ministers with regard to their borough seats was very politic and ingenious. They purchased seats from their friends at a low price, making up the deficiency probably by appointments and promotions. Those seats they afterwards sold out at the average market price to men who promised them support; and with the difference they carried on their contested elections. The sum raised in this manner was stated by a person who was in the secret to be inconceivably great, and accounts for an assertion afterwards made by Lord Grenville in the Lords that "not one guinea of the *public money* had been spent in elections." It may be imagined that if seats were bought for £2500 or even £2000, and sold again for £5000, a comparatively small number of such transactions would furnish a considerable fund; and they had so many seats passing through their hands that, at last, in one or two instances, they sold them to people who only professed themselves in general well disposed towards them, without exacting a pledge of unconditional support.

216. Lord Hawkesbury to Sir Arthur Wellesley, 15 May and 5 June 1807

(*Wellington MSS.*)

[15 May.] I have received your letter on the subject of the borough of Downpatrick. With respect to the funds applicable to election expenses, I do not consider the secret service money of that nature. The object of the *vote* for secret service is certainly *different*, and it is to all intents and purposes public money which (if inquiry should take place) it would be important to prove had been applied to *legitimate public purposes*, but there can be no doubt that the surplus or savings of the Civil List, which belong to the King's Privy Purse, are his *private property* and are applicable by *him* to any purposes he might think proper. This is, therefore, an available fund, and I have no difficulty whatever in saying that a sum to the amount you mention, that is, £1500 or £2000, may be very properly given in furtherance of Mr. Croker's election. With regard to the payment of the sum in the first instance, we will endeavour to arrange it as well as we can out of the funds in our possession. . . .

[5 June.] I have talked both to Long and Huskisson[1] on your proposal to accelerate the receipt of the savings of the Civil List, but I find from them that it is impossible to adopt it. The truth is, we are not justified in taking any steps to make use of that money *till it has got into the King's Privy Purse*. It is then only that it cannot be treated as public money, and that no enquiries respecting [it] can be made. A different course was by inadvertency on one occasion[2] followed by Lord Sidmouth, and this is the precedent which has been stated to you; but he was very much alarmed afterwards at what he had done, and measures were taken in the best way they could to correct the error. I should think that our friends would be satisfied if they receive what is

---

[1] Joint Paymaster-General and Joint Secretary of the Treasury respectively. Hawkesbury was Home Secretary, Wellesley Irish Secretary. Croker, who succeeded Wellesley's brother as Secretary to the Admiralty in 1809, defeated his opponent at Downpatrick.

[2] Doubtless at the general election in 1802.

promised to them a month or two hence. This is the case in this country, not only from want of the money, but for the purpose of avoiding the appearance of advancing it just at the time of the election. We will assist you, however, from hence as soon as we can. . . . [*Ibid.*]

217. Lord Hawkesbury to the duke of Richmond, 28 May and 4 June 1807

(National Library of Ireland, *Richmond MSS.* 70, f. 1323.)

[28 May.] . . . I have written to Wellesley on the subject of pecuniary assistance to Bolton;[1] the only difficulty about it is supplying the money *at present*. We are very hard pressed here upon the same subject, and under the circumstances under which Parliament was dissolved, our means of *immediate supply* are very scanty. The savings of the Civil List which go into the King's Privy Purse are certainly *his private property* and at his disposal, but it is very material that we should be able to say in Parliament if necessary that no public money has been expended in either country in the elections. . . .

[4 June.] . . . I have not heard anything of Falkiner.[2] With respect to a Government seat, if he means a seat without purchase there is no such thing. All the members of Administration here have paid for their seats, and some of them very high. . . .

218. Sir A. Wellesley to John Bagwell, M.P., 1 June 1807

(*Wellington MSS.*)

. . . I declare to you most solemnly that we have not in this country one shilling that we can use in that manner. I am aware that the fact is generally supposed to be otherwise, and that the Government is accused by its enemies of spending the public money on elections; but you may rely on the truth of my assertion, that there is no such thing, and that we cannot venture to touch a farthing. . . .

219. Lord Anglesey's correspondence as Lord Lieutenant of Ireland on the financing of Government Candidates at by-elections in 1831

(*Plas Newydd MSS.*)

(*a*) E. G. S. Stanley (Irish Secretary) to Lord Anglesey, *Irish Office*, 2 Feb.: . . . Lord Grey . . . would evidently greatly prefer bringing in the two Solicitors for Russell's two seats, rather than Sheil, as he would not wish, I think, to put it in Sheil's power to say that the Government *money* had been applied, from secret funds, to bring him in, though he would not mind it in Crampton's case. . . .[3]

---

[1] Cornelius Bolton was defeated at Waterford City by the Whig Sir John Newport.

[2] Falkiner, Member for Dublin County in the previous Parliament, lost his seat.

[3] Sir William Horne, the Solicitor-General, was returned for Bletchingly on 18 Feb., P.C. Crampton, Solicitor-General (Ireland), for Saltash on the 26th, and Richard Lalor Sheil for Milborne Port on 4 March,

(b) Lord Anglesey to Lord Grey, *Dublin*, 7 Feb.: . . . I will venture to be bound that Sheil will never take advantage of being assisted by Government money, and I anxiously wish to see him fairly seated. . . . [*Ibid.*]

(c) Lord Grey to Lord Anglesey, *Downing St.*, 8 Feb.: . . . You must not tell Sheil, if he is to have Tennyson's seat, that anything is to be paid by Government; and it will be necessary that his £800 should be forthcoming immediately. . . . [*Ibid.*]

(d) Lord Anglesey to Lord Grey, *Dublin*, 10 Feb.: . . . If I can get Cashel (which I have every reason to expect) and you agree . . . to furnish money for that seat for any excess beyond £1000, which Sheil is ready to give for it, then you will have three stout members in Crampton, who is to pay £800 for Tennyson's seat, and Sheil for Cashel, and Byng for Milborne Port . . . I will flatter myself . . . that you will have consented to make up any difference there may be at Cashel. I do hope so, for I almost fear (ruined as I am by the frightful calls upon me here) that I shall not resist doing so out of my own funds, if your Treasury fails me. . . . [*Ibid.*]

(e) Lord Grey to Lord Anglesey, *Downing St.*, 10 Feb.: . . . I will only now add a word with respect to the new proposition of Cashel: the £1500 we [are] to pay for Tennyson's two seats certainly exhausts our funds here for the present, and it is very doubtful whether Parliament may not cut them off for the session. But if these means are left at our disposal, and we live so long as Ministers, I should hope to be able to advance before the end of the year as much as, added to £1000, which I understand you to say Sheil would give, would make up the price of Cashel, supposing it not to exceed £1500. . . . [*Ibid.*]

220. Lord Redesdale to Lord Hawkesbury, 1 Oct. 1805

(*British Museum Additional MSS.* 38241, f. 241.)

Wickham was Irish Secretary, 1802–1804, and Charles Long, 1805–1806.

. . . One great and important object with the Lord Lieutenant ought to be to keep together, as much as possible, the Irish members of the House of Commons. In general they are pretty strongly impressed with the opinion, suggested by the late Lord Farnham, that it was for the interest of Ireland that they should, in a body, generally support the King's Ministers in Parliament: and by thus making themselves of importance to Government, obtain for Ireland what they might think necessary for the advantage of the country. Wickham was strongly impressed with the necessity of attending to the Irish members, and preventing their becoming like sheep without a shepherd, and whilst his health lasted he was diligent on this subject. His ill health prevented a continuance of his assiduity; and I am sorry to say that this important duty of the Irish Government, which necessarily principally devolves on the Secretary, has been greatly neglected. I hope Mr. Long will endeavour to regain what has been lost. I think it will be found of great importance. Government, in every part of the world, has become much more an act of influence than authority. The first and most beneficial influence is that of good opinion and confidence: a secondary influence arises from good will, produced by affability, condescension, and general civility: the third and grosser influence is that of private interest, which operates more or less on all men, and I am afraid in Ireland has been long used as almost the *sole* engine of Government; and it seems difficult to say which have been most profligate, the governors or governed. The late Lord Clare once told me that this had been, in his opinion, carried to such an excess that it must of itself compel an union with Great Britain; for that the means of governing Ireland by this grosser influence had been so wastefully distributed, and so gluttonously devoured, that it was impossible the Government should go on unless the more honourable influence of public opinion were restored, which he thought could only be by union with Great Britain. I am happy to say that I think the Union has had this effect; that public opinion has now influence in this country which it had almost entirely lost, and that an honourable administration of the Government will give H.M.'s Ministers in Ireland more influence than corruption ever gave them. . . .

(d) THE PLACEMEN

221. Wilberforce on the votes of the placemen, 1788

(*Life of Wilberforce, by his Sons*, I, p. 165.)

Although Pitt himself was in favour of the abolition of the slave trade, both the Cabinet and the placemen were divided on the subject. Wilberforce commented:

This has afforded to his enemies a plausible, though certainly no just, ground for doubting his sincerity. The charge springs in part from ignorance of the practices of Parliament. It is undoubtedly the established rule that all official men are to vote with their principal; but notwithstanding the systematic support of a Ministry which has resulted from systematic opposition, the Minister is not considered as entitled to require the votes of the inferior members of Government except on political questions. What shall, and what shall not be a Government question, is not an arbitrary arrangement dependent on the part of the Minister–it turns upon the question, is the credit or stability of the Ministry at stake? In the instance therefore of my motion, as on Pitt's own motion for the improvement of the poor laws, everyone was perfectly at liberty to vote as he saw fit. It was in no sense a party question.

222. Lord Liverpool to Henry Dundas, 11 Oct. 1800

(*British Museum Additional MSS.* 38193, f. 83.)

[The scarcity of corn] . . . It is absurd to talk of the meeting of the Privy Council for Trade at present on this business. There is in fact during the summer, from the prorogation of Parliament, no Committee of Council for Trade. There has not been a single member of it but myself at the Office since the last prorogation except on one occasion when I obtained a small meeting for a day or two with great difficulty and much dissatisfaction. If I could obtain a meeting and the majority should agree to any measure, I am not sure that the minority would attend in Parliament and vote for it, so much are people wedded to favourite abstract notions on this subject, as was the case at the end of the last Session, when my son, at the express desire of Mr. Pitt, as I understood, carried a Bill calculated to do some little good in this business, and very little injury to anyone, through the House of Commons; and I, who had no share in the concoction of the measure, and previously knew nothing of it, carried it through the House of Lords, when we were opposed in both Houses by several members of Government. . . .[1]

223. Lord Grenville to William Wickham, 24 Oct. 1805

(Public Record Office, P.R.O. 30/9/15.)

Wickham resigned the Irish Secretaryship in Jan. 1804 because of ill health. In the summer Pitt wanted his seat (Cashel) for another placeman, Lord Fitzharris, but Wickham refused to accommodate him.

. . . In above twenty years of political life I never knew an instance where a person chosen for a Government seat, or chosen for a private seat in consequence of any Government arrangement made under one Administration, was called upon to resign that seat under any succeeding Administration; much less where such a call was complied with. The present House of Commons affords plenty of cases in point, as well as the last. Those who were chosen by Pitt[2] did not make room in that way for Addington's friends, neither when Pitt supported Addington,[3] nor when he opposed him.[4] Those whom Addington chose on the dissolution[5] did not resign their Government seats when Pitt came into Government on the ruins of Addington's Administration,[6] nor again when Addington joined Pitt,[7] nor do I believe that any one of them entertains an idea of doing so when Addington is likely again to be more or less in opposition. Why then should yours be the single instance? Many of them had friendships and connections in each of the different parties into which the mass of strength which composed Pitt's old Government is now broken. Every one of them has been allowed without reproach to make his option between those different bodies of his friends. Why should you be the only person to whom this is refused? They all holding the seats they happened to hold, acted in Parliament according to that option. Why should not you do the same?

When we last talked on the subject, we felt that there might be *some* difficulty if the call were made upon you by Addington; not that such a call *ought* in our judgment to be made upon you even by him; but because if made, a man in such a case would always rather go beyond the mark than fall short of it. But Addington made no such call. He is now opposed to those who do make it, and he has expressly told you that he considers you at full liberty to follow your own opinions. What possible claim then can the Irish Secretary of the present day have upon you more than on any one other member of Parliament who sits for Ireland? Neither he nor his friends contributed at all to bring you in; they are not even acting with those who did; and if they were, the universal practice adhered to by themselves is against such a demand. . . .

[1] See No. 30.   [2] In 1796.   [3] From 1801 to 1803.   [4] In 1804.
[5] In 1802.   [6] In May 1804.   [7] In Jan. 1805.

224. Lord Hawkesbury to the duke of Richmond, 27 April 1807

(National Library of Ireland, *Richmond MSS.* 70, f. 1347.)

The Home Secretary considers whether civil servants as well as placemen should be dismissed on a 'total' change of Government. The members of the Revenue Board in Ireland were civil servants. Three members of the Latouche family were elected to Parliament in 1807, and they often voted against ministers.

The Parliament is at an end and the prorogation took place at three oclock today. . . . I now come to the arrangements which it is important should be completed as far as possible without further delay. They are as follows: The Earl of O'Neill and the Earl of Clancarty to be Joint Post Masters–the Earl of Westmeath to be Clerk of the Hanaper–Mr. Foster to be Chancellor of the Exchequer; Lords of the Treasury–Earl of Rosse–Mr. Bagwell–Sir George Hill–Mr. Barry–and Mr. Foster (the Chancellor of the Exchequer's son, provided he brings himself into Parliament). Mr. Neville to be Teller of the Exchequer–The Marquis of Drogheda to be one of the Muster-Masters and Lord Lecale to be the other on the same condition that he brings himself into Parliament. This is determined as a general condition as to all persons holding political situations. . . .

With respect to the Revenue Board we approve entirely of Mr. Longford being restored and Mr. E. Taylor being turned out. There will likewise be no objection to turn out Hely Hutchinson or George MacQuay and Peter Dundas in favour of more loyal and better friends. As to Thery the Catholic, if he is an honest man it would be right to keep him, if not, I think it is very desirable that his place should be filled up by a loyal Catholic. The sooner the letters of recommendation come over the better. If any reason should appear for an alteration I can easily return your letter and beg of you to write others–this will be rendered more easy by your writing separate letters as to the different departments.

. . . As to the Revenue Board I am instructed that George McQuay should go next after Taylor, and Peter Dundas should depend upon the disposition of the Latouches.

225. Romilly's Memoirs, 8 July 1813

(*Memoirs of Life of Sir Samuel Romilly*, ed. by his sons, III (1840), pp. 116–117.)

. . . The division,[1] however, both tonight and on a former night in the Committee, took place in a very thin House; and the Ministers had, considering the numbers present, very large majorities. It is, indeed, on these occasions, on Bills which, though important, do not excite any great public interest, and which are protracted to a late period of the Session, when the attendance of Members is much neglected, that Ministers derive from the present constitution of the House a very great advantage. There are 30 or 40 minor placemen, Lords of the Treasury and of the Admiralty, Paymasters, Treasurers of the Navy, &c. &c., who, having places only that they may vote in Parliament, are constant and regular in their attendance there; or who, if they happen to be absent, as they live very near to the House of Commons, may be

[1] The third reading of the Bill for regulating the office of Registrar of the Admiralty was carried by 45 *v.* 9.

collected together in a few minutes, while it requires as many hours to convene as large a number of independent members, or of adherents to the Opposition, from their distant abodes, scattered over a great part of the metropolis. . . .

226. Lord Ellenborough's diary, Feb.–March 1829

(*Lord Ellenborough's Political Diary, 1828–30*, ed. Lord Colchester (1881).)

Of the placemen in the Commons who voted against the Catholic Relief Bill, only Wetherell, the Attorney-General, was dismissed–not for his vote but for rudeness and insubordination. George Bankes (Secretary to the Board of Control) and Lord Lowther (First Commissioner of Woods and Forests) were persuaded to withdraw their resignations. Lord Eliot, a Lord of the Treasury, was not dismissed after writing to the duke on 7 Jan (*W.N.D.*, v, p. 424); and Lord Granville Somerset, another Lord of the Treasury, voted *for* the Bill. Lord O'Neill, Joint Postmaster-General [Ireland], retained his office, even though he signed a protest against the Bill. Beckett did not resign his office of Judge Advocate-General.

6 Feb.: . . . Bankes told me he had written a letter of resignation to the Duke. I said he should have waited till he was obliged to vote against the Government; that he did not object to the consideration of the question; that he would approve of all the securities, and only feel called upon to vote against the Bill if, on the third reading, it should not be satisfactory to him. I said a great deal more, all to no purpose.

I saw the Duke, who was much annoyed. He said he did not know what to do with Bankes's letter. That it put him into a situation of much difficulty. That if he resigned others would–that Lord Lowther, Lord G. Somerset might. That if Bankes thought it necessary to resign he should be obliged to turn out some man or other who voted against him, whose vote he might otherwise have overlooked. That it would oblige him to break with some of the first families. He wished to keep the Government together. He said with great warmth, "There is Bankes, like most other men, looking only to himself, and not caring about the public!" The Duke said Lord Eliot had written to him some six weeks ago saying he must resign if the Government did not take up the Catholic question. The Duke had a great mind to turn him out now. . . . [I, pp. 338–339.]

. . . I asked, "Suppose members holding offices should vote against us, what will you do with them?" This seems to be considered a very serious question. We are to hold very high language, but I suspect we should do little. If we do not punish those who go against us in the Commons there may be a majority against us in the Lords, and then it will be too late.

The Duke said, "Let me take the Bill to the King, get his approval, and then I will answer for his making the Household vote; but it will not do to hold a pistol to his head now." . . . [I, pp. 346–347.]

7 March: . . . We had some conversation [at the Cabinet meeting] respecting Wetherell and the others who voted against us last night. The Duke is for doing nothing yet. He thinks we are strong enough in the Lords, and may risk our chance of recovering our friends if we adopt any measure of severity. Lord Lowther voted against us, and has resigned. Lord O'Neill has intimated that he intends to vote against us, which is an intimation that he resigns. . . . [I, p. 382.]

9 March: . . . In the House I found Lord Harrowby, Camden, and Rosslyn shocked and alarmed at the non-acceptance of the resignations offered. Last night Sir J. Beckett resigned. Lord Lowther on Saturday. Wetherell is to make a violent speech against us to-night. The Chancellor agrees with me, and thinks that execution should be done, or at least the resignations accepted. . . . [I, pp. 385–386.]

20 March: Cabinet. Discussed the expediency of removing Wetherell. He betrayed official confidence by mentioning the time at which Peel first made a communication to him of the intentions of Government. He certainly kept us in ignorance of what he intended to do till the 23rd of February, and I know I feared he meant to support it. His dismissal is to be placed, not distinctly upon the Catholic question, but upon his conduct in abusing the Chancellor, betraying confidence, &c. I expect that the King will make no objection to displacing Wetherell, but he will wish to fill his place (with Scarlett) immediately. However, it is thought we had better defer that till the Bill is passed. If the King should resist we are not to go out upon it now, but sacrifice everything to the carrying of the Bill, and deal with Wetherell afterwards. It is thought that should the King refuse to turn out Wetherell we shall hardly stand worse than we should if we did not notice his conduct. The Duke, and indeed many, seem to think that the King will now go through the measure with us, and take his revenge by turning us out afterwards. I care very little about what happens afterwards. We must do all we can to carry the Bill, happen what may. [I, pp. 400–401.]

(e) THE HOUSEHOLD TROOPS AND THE 'KING'S FRIENDS'

227. C. J. Fox's speech in the House of Commons, 17 Dec. 1783

(Cobbett's *Parliamentary History*, XXIV, 205–224.)

Fox was here condemning the conduct of the Lords of the Bedchamber who, in obedience to the king's orders, voted against the India Bill earlier that day. Next day the Coalition was dismissed.

. . . The question before the House involves the rights of Parliament in all their consequences and extent. . . . The deliberations of this night must decide whether we are to be freemen or slaves; whether the House of Commons be the palladium of liberty or the organ of despotism; whether we are henceforth to possess a voice of our own or to be only the mere mechanical echo of secret influence. . . .

Rumours of a most extraordinary nature have been disseminated in no common way and by no inferior agents. A noble Earl is said to have used the name of Majesty with the obvious and express intention of affecting the decisions of the Legislature concerning a Bill of infinite consequence to 30 millions of people, pending in Parliament. . . . This letter . . . states that "H.M. allowed Earl Temple to say that whoever voted for the India Bill, were not only not his friends, but he should consider them as his enemies. And, if these words were not strong enough, Earl Temple might use whatever words he might deem stronger or more to the purpose." . . . A Parliament thus fettered and controlled, without spirit and without freedom, instead of limiting, extends, substantiates and establishes beyond all precedent, latitude or condition, the prerogatives of the Crown. . . . The Lords of the Bedchamber . . . cordially give in [their proxies] before a rumour of the King's displeasure reaches their ears; the moment this intimation is made, on the same day and within a few hours, matters appear to them in quite a different light, and the opinion which they embrace in the morning is renounced at noon. . . . The Lords of the Bedchamber . . . we all know are constantly at the back of whoever is Minister of the day. How often have they not been stigmatized with the name of the Household troops who, like the Praetorian bands of ancient Rome, are always prepared for the ready execution of every secret mandate! I remember a saying of . . . the late Mr. George Grenville, in experiencing a similar treachery—and would to God the same independent and manly sentiments had been inherited by all who bear the name—"I will never again", said he, "be at the head of a string of janissaries who are always ready to strangle or dispatch me on the least signal." . . .

Where, Sir, is that undue, that unconstitutional influence with which the hon. gent. upbraids me and those with whom I act? Are our measures supported by any other means than Ministers have usually employed? In what, then, am I the champion of influence? Of the influence of sound and substantial policy, of open, minute, and laborious discussion, of the most respectable Whig interest in the Kingdom, of an honourable majority in this House, of public confidence and public responsibility, I am proud to avail myself. . . . But every sort of influence unknown to the Constitution, as base in itself as it is treacherous in its consequences, which is always successful because incapable of opposition, nor ever successful but when exerted in the dark, which, like every other monster of factious breed, never stalks abroad but in the absence of public principle, never assumes any other shape than a whisper, and never frequents any more public place of resort than the backstairs or closet at St. James's—all this secret, intriguing and underhand influence I am willing and ready to forego. . . . Let those who have no other object than place, have it and hold it by the only tenure worthy of their acceptance—secret influence: but without the confidence of this House as well as that of the Sovereign, however necessary to my circumstances and desirable to my friends, the dignity and emoluments of office shall never be mine. . . .

For that influence which the Constitution has wisely assigned to the different branches of the Legislature, I ever have contended. . . . That of the Crown, kept within its legal boundaries, is essential to the practice of Government. . . . A great writer has said that the English Constitution will perish when the legislative becomes more corrupt than the executive power. Had he been as sound a judge of the practice as of the theory of government, he might have added, with still greater truth, that we shall certainly lose our liberty when the deliberations of Parliament are decided, not by the legal and usual, but by the illegal and extraordinary exertions of prerogative. . . .

The Lords are undoubtedly entitled to advise the throne collectively, but this does not surely entitle every noble individual to take H.M. aside, and, by a shocking farrago of fiction and fear, poison the royal mind with all their own monstrous chimeras. . . . The question is not whether H.M. shall avail himself of such advice as no one readily avows, but who is answerable for such advice. . . . The responsibility of Ministers is the only pledge and security the people of England possess against the infinite abuses so natural to the exercise of this power. Once remove this great bulwark of the Constitution, and we are, in every respect, the slaves and property of despotism. And is not this the necessary consequence of secret influence? . . .

Ministers . . . hold their several offices, not at the option of the Sovereign, but of the very reptiles who burrow under the throne; they act the part of puppets and are answerable for all the folly, the ignorance and the temerity or timidity of some unknown juggler behind the screen. . . . It is a public and crying grievance that we are not the first who have felt this secret influence. It seems to be a habit against which no change of men or measures can operate with success. It has overturned a more able and popular Minister (Lord Chatham) than the present, and bribed him with a peerage. . . . The scenes, the times, the politics and the system of the Court may shift with the party that predominates, but this dark mysterious engine is not only formed to control every Ministry, but to enslave the Constitution. To this infernal spirit of intrigue we owe that incessant fluctuation in H.M.'s Councils by which the spirit of Government is so much relaxed and all its minutest objects so fatally deranged. During the strange and ridiculous interregnum of last year, I had not a doubt in my own mind with whom it originated, and I looked to an hon. gent. (Mr. Jenkinson) opposite to me, the moment the grounds of objection to the East India Bill were stated. The same illiberal and plodding cabal who then invested the throne and darkened the royal mind with ignorance and misconception, have once more been employed to act the same part. . . .

228. George III to William Pitt, 20 March 1785, 54 m pt. 8 a.m.

(Public Record Office, *Chatham Papers*, 103.)

I have received Mr. Pitt's paper containing the heads of his plan for a parliamentary reform, which I look on as a mark of attention. I should have delayed acknowledging the receipt of it till I saw him on Monday, had not his letter expressed that there is but one issue of the business he could look upon as fatal: that is, the possibility of the measure being rejected by the weight of those who are supposed to be connected with Government. Mr. Pitt must recollect that though I have ever thought it unfortunate that he had early engaged himself in this measure, yet that I have ever said that as he was clear of the propriety of the measure, he ought to lay his thoughts before the House; that out of personal regard to him, I would avoid giving any opinion to any one on the opening of the door to parliamentary reform except to him: therefore I am certain Mr. Pitt cannot suspect my having influenced anyone on the occasion;[1] if others choose for base ends to impute such a conduct to me, I must bear it as former false suggestions. Indeed on a question of such magnitude, I should think very ill of any man who took a part on either side without the maturest consideration, and who would suffer his civility to anyone to make him vote contrary to his own opinion. The conduct of some of Mr. Pitt's most intimate friends on the West-

---

[1] At this time it was customary for household officials who were members of Parliament to vote with the ministers of the king's choice. On this occasion he refused to coerce them, promising his neutrality.

minster scrutiny[1] shew[s] there are questions men will not by friendship be biassed to adopt.

229. Edward Leeds to the earl of Hardwicke, 19 April 1785
(British Museum Additional MSS. 35623, f. 284.)

Charles Jenkinson and Howard were considered to be leading members of the group referred to as the 'king's friends'.

. . . On a division at $\frac{1}{2}$ p. 3 on Mr. Pitt's motion for leave to bring in a Bill to alter the representation of the people in Parliament, I had the satisfaction of finding myself in a majority of 74 *against* the motion . . . Mr. Grenville did not speak, but voted with us, as did Jenkinson, Sir G. Howard, and the corps who usually look to them for direction. . . .

230. Lord Spencer to his mother, 22 May 1792
(Althorp MSS.)

The debate was on Fox's Libel Bill.

. . . We had a very curious division in the House yesterday where he [the Lord Chancellor] and all the interior Household voted against a Bill supported very strenuously by Mr. Pitt and by Lord Grenville in our House, and likewise supported by the Opposition, in consequence of which it was carried by 57 to 32, but if this schism continues at all, and should extend itself to other points on which the Opposition could join the Household, Lord Grenville will very probably be harder run than Mr. Pitt will like. . . .

231. Thomas Grenville to Lady Spencer, 18 May 1804
(Althorp MSS.)

Lord Amherst has received a letter from the Groom of the Stole, Lord Winchilsea, to tell him that he has the King's commands to acquaint him that H.M. will dispense with his services as Lord of the Bedchamber!!! I suppose that you recollect that on the last question in the House of Lords, Lord Amherst, on account of great personal obligations to Pitt, did not attend to support Addington's tottering Administration, and it is in Pitt's Administration that he is visited for this offence with the loss of his office. . . .

232. Sir Evan Nepean to Lord Hardwicke, 17 June 1804
(British Museum Additional MSS. 35715, f. 82.)

Nepean was Irish Secretary, Hardwicke Lord Lieutenant of Ireland. Strachey was Master of the Household.

. . . Your Excellency can have hardly any idea of the exertions which are making by the contending parties for the attendance of their friends, and I have had reason to believe, from what passed yesterday between me and Mr. Pitt, in respect to one

[1] At the close of the Westminster election (1784) the high bailiff granted Fox's unsuccessful opponent a scrutiny, and a struggle on this matter was kept up in Parliament for two sessions.

or two who were playing what they conceived to be the safe game, that he will not be trifled with by those who hold employments under the Crown, or are expecting favours from Government. One of the instances I allude to is that of Sir H. Strachey, wherein he requested me to tell him that if he did not give a fair and full support to H.M.'s Government that he could no longer hold a place in H.M.'s Household. This circumstance however Your Excellency will keep to yourself; I mention it only to shew you the temper Mr. Pitt is in, and his determination to ascertain who are his friends and from whom he is likely to derive support. . . .

233. The bishop of Lincoln to his wife, Mrs. Tomline, c. 28 Jan. 1806

(Pretyman MSS.)

Referring to the debate in the House of Commons on the 27th respecting funeral honours to Pitt.

. . . The temper of the House was exactly what could be wished. Nothing even from the opponents disrespectful to Mr. Pitt, only that he left the country worse than he found it, and Fox said that he had lent his great talents and character to support the 'odious deformity' of the system of King's Friends. Was ever man so injudicious?—at such a moment too—just coming into power. . . .

234. William Elliot (Irish Secretary) to Lord Spencer (Home Secretary), 17 May 1806

(Althorp MSS.)

. . . You seem to have a formidable opposition in Parliament from *high* quarters, and if you are not able to accomplish your new military arrangements, it will be *very* disparaging to remain in office. . . .

Your division in the House of Lords . . . indicates a formidable hostility on the part of the Court, and I daily become more confirmed in my opinion that you will disparage yourselves if you attempt to carry on your Administration, in such a perilous period, with weak numbers and in conflict with the King. Nothing surely can be so injurious to your own characters as to hold your offices subject to a vexatious opposition from *the Crown* to the measures which you consider, and have always held out to the public, as essential to the strength and security of the Empire. . . .

235. Lord Hawkesbury to George III, 18 Feb. 1808, and reply

(Windsor Archives, 13397.)

Lord Hawkesbury begs leave most humbly to submit to Your Majesty the Minutes of the House of Lords. It is with considerable regret that Lord Hawkesbury is under the necessity of informing Your Majesty that at an early hour in the day Your Majesty's Government were outvoted on a question for the production of a paper[1] embarrassing to Your Majesty's Gov[t]. The great and persevering activity of the

---

[1] Containing information received by ministers "with respect to the increased rigour exercised by the French Government" in carrying on its economic warfare against England.

Opposition renders it necessary for Lord Hawkesbury in duty to Your Majesty most humbly to state to you that Your Majesty's Gov^t. is not adequately supported in the House of Lords either by Your Majesty's Household, or by the Bishops, and that it is of the utmost importance that Your Majesty should communicate your wishes and expectations on the subject to the Lord Chamberlain and to the Archbishop of Canterbury.

Lord Hawkesbury trusts to Your Majesty's goodness in excusing this humble representation on his part, but as a great part of the labour of conducting Your Majesty's Gov^t. in the House of Lords falls unavoidably upon Lord Hawkesbury, he hopes he may be allowed to say that he feels it of the greatest importance to the credit and ease of Your Majesty's Government that in times like the present he should appear to have the constant and active support in the House of Lords of all those persons who hold offices in Your Majesty's Household as well as of those who must be sensible how much the security of the Establishment in Church and State is connected with the support of Your Majesty's Govt.

[The King's reply, 19 February.] The King has learnt with much concern from Lord Hawkesbury's letter of yesterday that he has so much reason to complain of the inadequate attendance in the House of Lords of H. M.^{ys} Household and the Bishops, and His Majesty therefore readily authorizes Lord Hawkesbury to speak in his name to Lord Dartmouth and to the Archbishop of Canterbury & to point out to them the very great importance of their taking proper & immediate steps for ensuring a better attendance. The King will himself as soon as he shall have an opportunity urge them to give every possible attention to this object. [*Ibid.*]

236. Lord Camden to Lord Malmesbury, 11 March 1808
(Malmesbury MSS.)

We had another division upon the Reversion Bill[1] yesterday and it was of the same complexion as the last, vizt. "the Court against the Government", the Government conceiving they had *at least* the King's acquiescence in the line they took. . . .

P.S. This business will have given the Government a considerable shake.

237. Robert Ward to Viscount Lowther, 13 Feb. 1812
(Lonsdale MSS.)

Ward was Clerk of the Ordnance, and Charles Yorke First Lord of the Admiralty. The restrictions imposed for a period of twelve months upon the prince regent's powers by the Regency Act of 1811 expired on 18 Feb. 1812.

. . . It is whispered . . . that Mr. Perceval yields the whole Household to the Prince's sole nomination, which produces long faces from many even of our well-wishers, who say Ministers cannot stand who suffer this . . . Yorke was, I think, indiscreet in telling Dent yesterday that no one's place was in his opinion worth 24 hours' purchase. . . .

[1] A Bill to prevent the granting of offices in reversion. The numbers in the division in the Lords on the 10th were equal (84 *v*. 84). The Bill was thrown out by the Peers on 15 March by 128 *v*. 48.

238. Debate in the House of Commons, 11 June 1812

(Cobbett's *Parliamentary Debates*, XXIII, 397–465.)

Stuart-Wortley refers to the breakdown of the negotiations between Lord Moira, acting on the instructions of the regent, and Lords Grey and Grenville for the formation of a new Administration, the breakdown being caused by Moira's refusal to agree to the preliminary condition, the removal of the leading members of the royal household.

J. A. *Stuart-Wortley:*– . . . Their excuse . . . was their jealousy of the influence which they supposed existed somewhere, over which they could have no control. The conduct of the noble Lords seemed to him the very way to strengthen that influence, for, suppose the persons alluded to . . . were to be turned out, would they then be less able to exercise this supposed predominance, or would they, for being turned out, be less inclined to exert it? And was such conduct a proper or likely method of conciliating the mind of him whom it must be most wished to conciliate, especially when all their great leading principles of policy were allowed them in full discretion? . . .

Mr. George Vansittart:– . . . approved of the constitutional principle that the House of Commons were bound in duty to represent to the King the misconduct of any Minister and to ask for his removal; but if they went one step further, if they attempted to dictate to the Crown the choice of its servants, this best of Governments would soon be changed from a limited and tempered Monarchy to a turbulent democracy. . . .

Mr. Johnstone:– . . . With respect to secret influence . . . the idea had long been exploded. . . . The cry had been found to originate in the voices of those who, having been turned out of office, complained that it was not accomplished by the mere volition of the Sovereign. It has been maintained that Lord Bute for many years exercised this secret influence, but the fact was now fully contradicted. And did Mr. Pitt and Lord Grenville when in power feel its effect? It was an empty cry, at all times destitute of foundation. . . . In the present times he deemed it his duty to support any Government. The representatives of large commercial bodies must and would support Government. . . .

Mr. Grattan:– . . . If the two noble Lords . . . were of opinion that the appointment of the Household was necessary to the strength of the Government–if they thought that the existence of two Cabinets, the one responsible, and the other not responsible, was not consistent with the well-being of the State, then they had acted wisely, honourably and disinterestedly in not taking power without the confidence necessary to enforce it. . . .

Mr. Elliot:– . . . well recollected that in the course of the discussions on the question of the Regency, enough was said of the importance of the Household, and the necessity of securing to the Government the influence of that Department. If it was thus mighty in the support of Government, must it not be equally formidable when arrayed against it, and, in conjunction with another Household, waging war against the responsible advisers of the Crown? . . .

239. Robert Peel (Irish Secretary) to Earl Whitworth (Lord Lieutenant of Ireland), 9 May 1816

(*British Museum Additional MSS.* 40291, f. 39.)

Colonel McMahon was the prince regent's private secretary, and Lord Yarmouth was Lord Warden of the Stannaries in Cornwall and Devon.

. . . There is . . . a domestic party at Carlton House that has separate interests from those of the Government. Lord Yarmouth has not voted this year on a single question except those in which the Prince Regent is involved as an individual, Civil List, &c., on the express ground that he is dissatisfied with the Government. The object in this particular application made by McMahon is to reward or to attach Sir M. Somerville, not to the Government but to Carlton House. Sir M. applies to you naturally and properly for his Government objects, but to McMahon for his Carlton House objects, and he dares not apply to you to let such a worthless fellow as Sir J. Barrington sell his office as a Judge, because he is half afraid that you would turn him out of the room. If I were Lord Liverpool and knew that McMahon made the propositions and attempts the objects which he makes and attempts in every quarter, I would certainly insist upon his removal. . . .

240. *The Scotsman,* on the dismissal of Lord Fife, a Lord of the Bedchamber, 1821

31 March: – Very few of the 72 placemen and pensioners who have seats in the House of Commons are so independent in their circumstances as Lord Fife, and his dismissal from office must be intended to convince them that *their means of existence depend on their supporting indiscriminately every measure of Ministers.* Mr. Pitt, when in the zenith of his power, would not have ventured upon such a step. It is, in fact, a distinct avowal that Ministers will tolerate no difference of opinion on the subject of taxation. Lord Fife might have voted any way he pleased on the great question of Catholic emancipation. . . . But a vote in favour of the reduction of that load of taxation which has entailed so much misery and distress on all classes of the community, is an unpardonable offence! . . . The number of placemen in the House of Commons renders it a matter of the greatest importance. A person who is not at liberty to vote according to the conviction of his conscience and his judgment, cannot possibly be a representative. But . . . placemen are in this situation . . . they ought to be excluded from the House.

7 April: – . . . We hope it [Fife's dismissal] will occasion some effort to be made with the view of diminishing the excessive number of placemen and pensioners in the House of Commons. Our Constitution . . . does not depend on our having a Parliament but on its being independent. The representatives of the people ought to decide according to the conviction of their conscience and their judgment. It is their duty to institute a severe examination of the measures of Ministers, and vigilantly to protect the rights and liberties of the people. But it would be worse than absurd to expect that a member who derives a considerable, perhaps the greatest, portion of his income from a place held at the discretion of Ministers, or from a pension granted by them, should act in this manner. . . . It is impossible for a member of the House of Commons to serve both his constituents and Ministers.

241. Lord Liverpool to Canning, 8 Sept. 1823

(British Museum Additional MSS. 38568, f. 122.)

Lord Maryborough, who had just been appointed Master of the Buckhounds after being Master of the Mint, was not to be allowed to retain his seat in the Cabinet.

. . . I quite agree with you that the *principle* that the King ought to be allowed to choose his own Household officers from *personal* considerations (subject only to the responsibility of Ministers that the appointments are not improper) decides the question that such officers ought not to be Cabinet Ministers, but I think further that allowing them to be so would be most inconvenient to King and Ministers. They would be suspected by each as spies upon the other. The Household officer would often be looked upon with jealousy by his colleagues, and would think he was so when he was not, and the King would feel a reserve upon him in the presence of that of his confidential servants, which we know it is very naturally the object of all Kings to extricate themselves from as much as possible. . . .

242. Earl Grey to Thomas Creevey, 1 May 1828

(Creevey MSS.)

On 26 Feb. Lord John Russell carried against the Government a motion for the repeal of the Test and Corporation Acts. Eldon led the opposition in the House of Lords to the Repeal Bill. Peel, anxious to avoid a conflict between the two Houses on a religious question, advised the bishops to substitute a formal declaration for the test hitherto in force, to be taken by the members of every corporation, and, at the pleasure of the Crown, by every office holder.

. . . On the affair of the Test Act the Duke and the Government have behaved as well as possible. Nothing but his authority could have overcome the violent opposition of the King, which on Sunday was inflamed to the highest possible of fury by Eldon's speeches in the House of Lords and by the instigation of the Duke of Cumberland. . . . The duke [of Wellington] must have had the thing fairly out with the King, and the Household for the first time came down to vote, and many of the Bishops, all of whom, with the exception of those who voted with us, and two who went behind the throne, had voted on the former division for Eldon's Amendment, changed sides, and when it was moved again, as the third reading, voted against it. . . .

243. William Lamb to Lord Anglesey, 11 June 1828

(Plas Newydd MSS.)

. . . The Duke of Wellington's speech last night was exceedingly conciliatory and is considered by some as a surrender of the [Catholic] question upon his part. His master, however, is more violent than ever, and has exerted himself personally in canvassing votes, &c. &c. This is a decided infraction of the promise of neutrality upon the part of the Government, but it is one which the Ministers cannot help.

244. The duke of Cumberland to Lord Eldon, 30 June 1829

(Eldon MSS.)

Cumberland, one of George IV's brothers, and (1837) king of Hanover, was the self-appointed leader of the ultra Tory party.

I have already had some conversation with my brother, and he has desired me to inform you of the following circumstance which he leaves in your hands to consider over and to act upon as you may think advisable. From the present state of things it is pretty evident that the existing Government cannot last as it is now composed, and my brother, as you well know, only wishes to get out of the sort of thraldom he feels himself in. There is no doubt, were we strong enough, that it would be more agreeable for us to act alone, but I believe that the most sanguine of us all, and I certainly am, I believe, one of them, cannot but see that this wish is out of the question, at least for the present moment. Therefore, our Party, which I call 'the King's Friends', must try *some junction*. . . . My brother has assured me that *he knows* from very good *authority* that in a late conversation Lord Lansdowne had declared himself upon the *two* following points most *distinctly* and *unequivocally*, namely, first, that he should never consent to granting anything further to the Roman Catholics, and secondly, that *he for one should most strenuously oppose parliamentary reform*. . . .

245. Lord Winchester (Groom of the Stole) to Wellington, 14 March 1830

(Wellington MSS.)

On Thursday, 18 March, the ultra Tory duke of Richmond's motion on the state of the working classes was defeated by 141 *v.* 61.

. . . In obedience to the King's commands I have written to the Lords of H.M.'s Bedchamber to signify *his* pleasure that they should attend in their place in the House of Lords on Thursday next–or, in the event of their inability to do so, that they will assign their proxy to some attending peers–and this upon all occasions of debates of moment affecting H.M.'s Government. . . .

246. Earl Howe to the duke of Wellington, 24 Aug. 1832, and the reply

(Despatches, Correspondence and Memoranda of the Duke of Wellington, VIII (1880), pp. 393–395.)

. . . May I shortly say the points on which I require advice? 1st. Shall I not, by accepting office, allow Lord Grey's power to appoint and remove the Queen's servants according to *his* will and pleasure, and admit he was right in dismissing me before? 2nd. Am I at liberty to vote as I think proper on all political questions? Without which power nothing should induce me to return. . . .

[Wellington's reply, 26 August.] . . . You did not render yourself conspicuous in opposition to the King's Government. You had not done so even when the King wrote to you upon the subject in the month of May preceding your removal. You subsequently did no more than the King consented to your doing. You voted upon the second reading of the Reform Bill in opposition to the Government. You, besides, held the proxy of your father-in-law. Upon this the Minister insisted with the King that you should be removed from your office. . . .

It is my opinion that there is nothing so necessary as that the Minister should have the support of the officers of the King's Household. But those of the Queen have always been considered as on a different footing. The reasons are obvious. They are paid out of her Majesty's personal allowance. The public have nothing to say to that expenditure after the money has once passed from the Exchequer. Certain of them must be noblemen of high rank, and they must be endowed with qualities to render them agreeable to their Majesties and to the Court. They must hold their offices, which are of the highest honour and confidence, permanently. That necessity alone precludes the notion of their political dependence upon the Minister. Such men as ought to be appointed to these offices will not hold them through all political changes, if such a political course should be expected from them.

If such a course should be expected from those holding the high offices of the Queen's Household, what is expected from the husbands of the ladies of the Queen's Court? It appears difficult, if not impossible, to draw a distinction between the cases of the Lords and the husbands of the ladies.

I am certain that common sense and precedent are against the course pursued last October. However, there can be no doubt that it is desirable that the great officers of the Queen's Court should keep themselves in a state of prudent reserve; and that particularly in times of irritated party feeling (such as, I am afraid, we shall never be without hereafter) they should not put themselves prominently forward. My opinion is, that you have nothing to do with what passes between the King and his Minister. Your affair is with the King.

I think that you ought to explain to the King, first, what is the nature of the office in reference to its political relations with the Administration; secondly, what was your own conduct during the period you held it, particularly after the month of May 1831; thirdly, that in obedience to his commands you are ready to return to the Queen's service, and to hold your office on the same footing as the same office and the other offices of the Household of the Queens of England have been held by others.

You might assure the King that your disposition and habits do not lead you to take any prominent part in politics; that you hold your own opinions, and feel them strongly. But that whether in the office of honour proposed to you or not, you feel that, situated as you are, it does not become you to take a violent course; and that if it is now, as it was heretofore, clearly understood that you were to vote as you should think proper, you would take care that the course which you would pursue would not embarrass the King either in his family or with his Ministers. . . .

247. Sir Herbert Taylor to Earl Howe, 31 Aug. 1832

(*Despatches, Correspondence and Memoranda of the Duke of Wellington*, VIII (1880), pp. 400–402.)

... The King has never denied having stated to you when, upon the change of Administration in 1830, he desired you to retain the situation to which you had been appointed upon his accession to the throne, that he considered you at liberty to pursue the line of conduct which should be consistent with the principles and political opinions you had always maintained; and H.M. also admits that he stated that, aware as he was of the strong objection you entertained to the Reform question, he rejoiced that the circumstance of your holding a high situation in the Queen's Household, and not in his own, had relieved H.M., in your case, from the painful situation in which he had been placed with respect to many individuals of his own Household, who, being members of either House of Parliament, had been removed from their offices in consequence of their opposition to H.M.'s Government upon this occasion.

But H.M. also stated that he had flattered himself that the character of your opposition would not have been such as to have placed him under any embarrassment, and to have given a colour to the rumours and reports so unfoundedly raised and circulated, that the Queen was taking a decided and active part against the Government and against the measures H.M. had sanctioned; and he did not conceal from you his belief that the manner in which you had expressed yourself, and had otherwise shown your determined and active hostility to the government, had had that effect.

Such was then H.M.'s feeling, such it continues; and, while H.M. heartily concurs in the sentiment expressed by Lord Grey, that you should not and could not be expected to make an unworthy compromise of your principles and opinions, he does not think that it would be compatible with any situation in the royal Household that the person holding it should be distinguished in a marked degree by active and declared hostility to his Government, or by a vehement exhibition of party feeling and spirit, instead of confining himself to an unostentatious opposition to its measures, if they should be irreconcilable to his principles and opinions.

This has, as H.M. has more than once endeavoured to explain it, been the chief ground of his objection to your proceedings, and it was to this that H.M. pointedly adverted when he stated, in May 1831, that he hoped you would in future not object so to shape the course of your opposition as to free it from features which were calculated to commit the Queen and himself.

You have in your letter claimed for the situations held in the Queen's Household perfect political independence, and you have, in former communications, stated that such had always been the understanding, and have adverted to precedents in which individuals so circumstanced had taken a line hostile to the government of the day without becoming thereby liable to any question.

H.M. cannot subscribe to this doctrine in the broad sense in which you appear to wish to establish it as a rule of conduct, nor does he believe that *any* Government would tolerate it, or that any precedent can be adduced by which it can possibly be maintained. It appears to him quite inconsistent with reason, or with the regard due by the Sovereign to the credit and security of his Government, that the individuals forming the Establishments of the King and the Queen respectively, who may be in Parliament, should be authorized to take a course decidedly opposite; that the King's Household should be required to support H.M.'s Government, while the Queen Consort's should be declared at liberty to place themselves in avowed, active, and determined hostility to it; that their Majesties' House should set the example of *being divided against itself.*

H.M. is so satisfied that the consequence of admitting such a principle and doctrine must be, as indeed it has proved on this occasion, an impression in the country (happily unfounded) that the Queen Consort is, while living under the same roof, encouraging opposition to the King's Government, and that the Sovereign himself is conniving at proceedings tending seriously to injure that Government in which he declares that he places his confidence, and does place his confidence.

There may be exceptions under peculiar circumstances, and such H.M. was pleased to admit your case to be, but the exception was subject to qualifications which a reasonable and guarded consideration and use of the privilege given might be supposed to suggest. . . .

248. The duke of Wellington to Earl Howe, 9 Nov. 1832

(*Despatches, Correspondence and Memoranda of the Duke of Wellington*, VIII (1880), p. 436.)

As I had not heard from you, I concluded that there was some difficulty in the appointment of yourself to be Lord Chamberlain to the Queen. . . . I conclude that the Minister objected to the Queen's Household being considered as holding their appointments independent of politics, with the understanding that there should be no unnecessary display of party sentiment; and that the King has found himself again under the necessity of adopting a course which, I will answer for it, is inconsistent with precedent and with the nature of the appointments, the duties of the officers, the mode in which they are paid, their station in society, &c. I am sorry for it, for the King's sake.

I think that you could not have acted otherwise than you have done. You manifested a readiness to serve your Sovereign. When you found that all reasonable concessions which you could make would not satisfy his Minister, and that you were required to sacrifice your opinion upon all subjects, and in fact to lose the good opinion of the world and of your friends, and thus to render yourself unfit and unable to be of any service to anybody, you did quite right to decline to accept. . . .

(f) THE SOVEREIGN'S PERSONAL INFLUENCE

249. Thomas Grenville to the marquess of Buckingham, 14 March 1807

(Duke of Buckingham and Chandos, *Court & Cabinets of George III*, IV, pp. 135–136.)

The Catholic Relief Bill was never introduced into the House of Lords. Its progress through Parliament was stopped by the king's dismissal of the 'Talents'.

[The Catholic Relief Bill] . . . I believe it might have been carried in the House of Commons, but not so in the House of Lords, for on Wednesday last, the King told Lord Grenville that he regretted having given any consent upon the subject, and should certainly think it right to make it known that his sentiments were against the measure. This seems to Lord Grenville to make the success of the Bill in the House of Lords quite impracticable. . . . By this time we knew that, even if the Bill was carried, the King was ready to resort to his last powers to prevent its passing into a law.

250. Lord Auckland to Lord Grenville, 3 April 1807

(Fortescue MSS.)

Auckland refers to the attitude of the Peers to the Portland Administration which had just replaced the 'Talents'.

I shall be content if we divide 80 in the House of Lords, proxies included. So many of our body are unwilling to come forward against what they call the King's Government, that I expect we shall see some uncreditable 'versatilities'. Even my old friend Lord Hood will, I suspect, be desirous to withdraw from giving any vote whatever, and I know others who say that they will stand aloof and watch the result of the struggle. . . .

251. General Craufurd's speech in the House of Commons, 26 June 1807

(Cobbett's *Parliamentary Debates*, IX, 641.)

Spoke in justification of the change of Ministers. The late Ministers had brought H.M. before his late Parliament to answer for that change, and a great portion of that Parliament, though very far from a majority, having taken part against H.M., an appeal to the people to decide between H.M. and his late Ministers was rendered absolutely necessary. . . . He had supported the late Ministers from a high opinion of their talents; he however condemned them for attempting to force themselves on the Crown by compelling the Crown to dismiss them. . . .

252. Lord Grenville to Earl Temple, 15 Dec. 1808

(Duke of Buckingham and Chandos, *Court & Cabinets of George III*, IV, p. 289.)

. . . My own impressions . . . are very much against any very active exertion. It can do no good–for I am satisfied these people, or any people, may command under the King's influence a majority in Parliament, and it would have the appearance of a struggle for power at a time when a man must, indeed, be of a most depraved ambition to wish for the appearance and responsibility of governing the country, with the certainty that a Court intrigue would be incessantly at work with ample means of depriving him of all power to be of real use.

253. Diary of John Cam Hobhouse, M.P., 1827

(Lord Broughton, *Recollections of a Long Life,* ed. Lady Dorchester, III, p. 179.)

24 March:–. . . Holmes [the government whip] . . . told me that the anti-Catholic members were, in great part, men who, if the King said a word, would vote for the Catholics.

16 July:–. . . H. Stephenson told me that the Duke of Buckingham had offered his parliamentary influence to the King personally, saying, at the same time, that the offer was made to H.M. and not to Mr. Canning.[1] The King accepted the offer. [*Ibid.*, p. 210.]

254. The duke of Rutland to Mrs. Arbuthnot, 20 April 1827

(A. Aspinall, *Formation of Canning's Ministry,* Camden 3rd Series, LIX (1937), p. 137.)

. . . You are aware that if I am satisfied as to the principles and efficiency of an Administration, my attachment is to the Crown rather than to any set of men. I shewed this to be the impulse of my conduct when Mr. Pitt, of whom I had an admiration ten times exceeding in degree that which I entertained for any other person in the land, gave up the reins of government to Lord Sidmouth.

255. Lord Ellenborough's Diary, 10 March 1829

(*Lord Ellenborough's Political Diary, 1828–30,* ed. Lord Colchester, I (1881), p. 387.)

. . . House . . . The Duke [of Wellington] . . . took occasion to say that in introducing the Catholic Bills he had the *sanction and support* of H.M., and that he had no doubt the perseverance, the honest perseverance of the Government, would lead to a satisfactory conclusion. . . . The Duke's declaration has gained us 10 votes. . . .

256. The duke of Wellington to Peel, 30 Dec. 1829

(*British Museum Additional MSS.* 40308, f. 307.)

The reference is to Sir W. H. Fremantle, the Treasurer of the Household.

. . . I never encouraged him to hope that we would pay for a seat for him. The best answer to give him is that there is no prospect at present of a vacancy in any place for which the Government could recommend him with any prospect of success. This subject is one of those on which our relation with the King is most inconvenient to

---

[1] The duke had written to Wellington on 21 Feb., "I can bring you ten or eleven votes in the House of Commons at least who will follow me."

us. Nobody will come to an Administration to whom the King is not favourably disposed, with an offer of a seat in Parliament, excepting for money which we have not to give.

257. Mrs. Arbuthnot's journal, 17 Jan. 1830

(*Journal of Mrs. Arbuthnot, 1820–1832*, ed. F. Bamford and duke of Wellington, II, p. 326.)

... It will be impossible, I think, for the Duke [of Wellington] to go on much longer without having some explanation with the King about the Duke of Cumberland, for it is not to be tolerated that the Duke should be constantly at the King's ear and at the same time be inundating the country with assertions that the Ministers are dismissed. Few Governments could have stood such conduct for so many months, and if the Duke of Wellington was not felt by almost all parties to be the only man who can guide the helm, and by *all* parties to be the most honest man in the Kingdom, he must have felt the fatal effects of such perpetual poison instilled into the King's mind. As it is, it only makes his position odious to him, for the King treats him shamefully, and all those Tories who consider themselves *king's men* are unwilling to support a man they believe to be so obnoxious.

(g) ADMINISTRATIVE REFORM, AND THE DIMINUTION OF THE 'INFLUENCE OF THE CROWN'

258. Advertisement in *The Edinburgh Advertiser*, 18 Oct. 1808

WANTED

A SITUATION under GOVERNMENT.—From 200 to 500 guineas, according to the emolument arising from it, will be paid to any person who can procure a genteel and permanent situation under Government in any part of Scotland. Letters addressed to A.B. to be left at the Courant Office, mentioning the nature of the situation and emolument, will be duly attended to, and the greatest secrecy may be depended upon.

259. Lord Liverpool to Robert Peel, 9 Dec. 1814

(*British Museum Additional MSS.* 40181, f. 59.)

Sir Thomas Fetherston, M.P., wanted a writership for his son. Lord Buckinghamshire was President of the India Board, 1812–1816; Lord Liverpool was a member of the board, 1793–1799.

... The Government have nothing to do with the appointment of writers to India. ... They are all named by rotation, by the Directors of the East India Company (one half of whom, I am sorry to say, are at this moment hostile to Government); and the only influence that Government possess as to these appointments is through the Chairman and Deputy Chairman, who are disposed occasionally to oblige the President of the Board of Control. All I can do, therefore, is to desire Lord Buckinghamshire would use his influence with the Chairman to meet Lord Rosse's and

Sir Thomas Fetherston's wishes. It may appear to you singular that though I was myself six years a member of the Board of Control, I never have to this day appointed more than one person writer in India–and this person had the peculiar claim of his grandfather having been Governor-General in India. . . .

260. The duke of Wellington to Sir John Malcolm, 11 Aug. 1816

(Duke of Wellington, *Supplementary Despatches*, XI, p. 458.)

. . . You may be quite certain that great situations are not obtained in this country by personal exertions and interest. Let a man show that he has talents, integrity, and enlarged views, and he may depend upon it that if employment abroad is his object, he is more likely to obtain it without solicitation than by making the most active exertions.

261. Robert Peel (Irish Secretary) to Earl O'Neill, 19 July 1817

(*British Museum Additional MSS.* 40293, f. 155.)

I am sorry that you were disappointed in not procuring for Mr. Rawson an exchange of the collectorship of Trim for that of Naas. . . . Your Lordship observes that you have only to regret this addition to the numerous unsuccessful applications which you have made to his Excellency. I regret also that your applications are unsuccessful –but when I consider that in every department of the State (excepting those of the revenue) extensive reductions have taken place–that the patronage which remains to the Government has been in a great measure applied in providing for those servants of the public whose former employments have ceased–I cannot be surprised that here, as in England, the means of dispensing favour are very considerably curtailed. I am afraid, too, that your Lordship receives very incorrect information with respect to the extent of those means–for so far from there being numbers of inspectorships of hearths vacant at present–there is not only not one vacant, but there has only been one vacancy within the last six months, which occurred in the County of Tipperary....

262. Lord Liverpool to Lord Wellesley, 9 Dec. 1824

(*British Museum Additional MSS.* 38299, f. 217.)

. . . The object of all the parliamentary inquiries and commissions which have been instituted in the course of the last ten years has been to get rid of everything like sinecure offices, and in this they have effectually succeeded, not only at home but even in the Colonies. Many offices of the above description have been utterly abolished. As to those that were executed by deputies, the deputies, as vacancies allowed, have been converted into principals, and as to others, in which the duties were nominal or inconsiderable, but which did not admit of entire abolition, new and considerable duties have in almost every instance, been annexed to them. . . .

263. Sir Henry Hardinge to Mrs. Arbuthnot, 30 Sept. 1828

(Arbuthnot MSS.)

Hardinge, the Secretary at War, was writing just after the famous Co. Clare by-election, when the influence of the priests secured the return of the Catholic O'Connell and the defeat of Vesey Fitzgerald, the newly appointed President of the Board of Trade.

. . . The really formidable question is the power of the priests with the 40 shilling freeholders to take the representation out of the hands of the gentry and aristocracy. This democratic preponderance would, in short time, pervade all the other relations of society and drive the gentry from the country; and if 60 Irish agitators were seated in the House of Commons, no Government could be carried on. . . .

264. Lord Camden's Memorandum for the duke of Wellington, June 1830

(Camden MSS.)

. . . Since the period when Lord Grenville's Government ceased to exist in 1807, and the accession of the Duke of Portland to be the Minister, there have been times when the Government of his Grace, of Mr. Perceval and of Lord Liverpool experienced the greatest difficulties in carrying on the government in the House of Commons. The Opposition always knew that questions of economy and of abolition of offices were those on which they could command the largest division. They did not, therefore, fail to urge them, and the various Governments to which attention has been made have abolished so many offices both in England and Ireland as renders it scarcely possible at present for *any* description of men to carry on advantageously the King's service.

Anyone who declares that disappointed men will not frequently urge measures which they in their hearts and in their reason do not approve, speaks with as little experience and knowledge of the world as he who pretends to say that 668 [658] members of the House of Commons and 400 members of the House of Lords can be managed without influence. In the three Governments to which I have alluded, the old hereditary influence of the Crown has been abolished and cannot be restored. . . . With a decrease of influence and no increase of authority, the House of Commons will become quite unmanageable.

265. Sir Robert Peel to Lady Floyd, 8 Aug. 1830

(British Museum Additional MSS. 40401, f. 105.)

Sir Henry Floyd was Peel's brother-in-law.

I deeply regret Sir Henry Floyd's situation . . . but I lament to say that it is absolutely out of my power to procure him any appointment. At this very moment, the one only engagement which the Duke of Wellington made on his assuming the Government in January 1828 remains unfulfilled. Nothing is more common, but nothing is so totally unfounded as the impression that it is not very difficult to procure employment for a gentleman in some branch of the service of the Crown.

I have been seven years Secretary of State. I have many near relatives in circumstances which would make employment most desirable to them—many persons with strong political claims upon me. I have not procured and not been able to procure one single appointment of any kind for any one of them, with the exception of my brother to be Under-Secretary of State—a parliamentary office.

Every day brings a reduction in some office or other, and imposes on the Government the painful duty of turning persons out of their situations, instead of making new appointments. . . .

266. The duke of Wellington to Lieutenant-General Sir Herbert Taylor, 3 Oct. 1830

(Desp. Corresp. & Memo. of the Duke of Wellington, VII (1878), p. 286.)

. . . I have been in office for nearly three years; and excepting parliamentary offices, which must be conferred on those who do the King's business in Parliament, I have nominated to but one office above a clerkship; and that was to the office vacated by the promotion of Mr. Barton to be Treasurer of the Queen's Household; which office was conferred by his Majesty's desire upon another Mr. Barton. So much for the patronage of the First Lord of the Treasury!

I have already told you how I have stood in respect to offices. In respect to pensions there is now no sum disposable that I know of. I will to-morrow send you a list of those granted at my recommendation since I have been in office, with a little memorandum upon each, which will tend to show how little the Government have gained by any influence of that description. Yet I must say that no Government can go on without some means of rewarding services. I have absolutely none![1]

(h) THE CARLTON HOUSE PARTY AND 'REVERSIONARY' INFLUENCE OF THE CROWN

267. Sir Gilbert Elliot to Lady Elliot, 5 May 1787 and 25 Nov. 1788

(Life & Letters of Sir G. Elliot, ed. Lady Minto, I (1874).)

George, Prince of Wales, came of age in Aug. 1783 and, like his grandfather, Prince Frederick, quarrelled with his father over his income and associated himself with the opposition to the Government. In 1787 it was proposed that the House of Commons should address the king to increase the prince's income and pay his debts. The motion, which was to have been debated on 4 May, was withdrawn when Pitt announced the king's unwillingness to do this.

[5 May.] There were yesterday circular cards of invitation to Carlton House to a great part of the House of Commons. . . . The meeting was at 3 o'clock, and there were about 180 members of the House of Commons. The Prince made a short speech, gracefully and naturally delivered. . . . He expressed some regret at having been obliged to trouble his friends on an occasion of so unpleasant a nature, and repeated,

---

[1] This letter may be compared with Maurice Fitzgerald's (Vice-Treasurer of Ireland in the Wellington Ministry), dated 28 Jan. 1831: "The influence of the Crown is almost extinct in Ireland. It has died with patronage. The only real tie between the countries now is the real interest of the farmer and shopkeeper." *(Ibid., VII, p. 401.)*

with a great deal of natural grace, his thanks and gratitude for the support he had met with. He then expressed a wish that we would go down to the House, although no difference of opinion was to be expected that day, but he could not help feeling that such a show of support would reflect credit on his cause; and away we all went. . . . [pp. 162–164.]

[25 November 1788.] . . . The Prince is, I believe, as much determined at present as possible never to have anything to do with Pitt, who was very absurdly arrogant in his good fortune, and insulted the Prince in his manner and conduct whenever he could, even in public and in his presence. . . . He will, I am persuaded, be always a great name and a considerable person in England. . . . He will continue to couple the violent affection and compassion of the people for the King in his present affecting situation, with his own fortunes, and he will certainly make a very popular if not at first a very powerful Opposition. To this it will be necessary to oppose popular measures on the part of the Prince's new Government, which is, however, always more difficult in a Government than in an Opposition, for there are few measures strong enough to have any effect which do not clash with the private interests or prejudices of numbers [? members], or which may not be misrepresented – witness our India Bill. [pp. 238–239.]

268. George Rose's diary, 8 May 1804

(*Diaries & Correspondence of George Rose*, ed. V. Harcourt, II (1860), p. 128.)

On 7 May, following the resignation of Addington, the king agreed to admit Grenville and his friends to office, but, whilst ready to accept Fox's friends, he refused, on both personal and political grounds, to allow Pitt to offer Fox a seat in the Cabinet. Fox generously urged his followers to join Pitt, but they refused to serve without him, and went into opposition.

. . . The part the Prince of Wales so decidedly takes in the matter, renders the forming an Administration with little more than some of the late Ministers (whom we have been holding up to ridicule for a long time) a desperate undertaking, not only on account of the number of H.R.H.'s friends in either House, but that a regular standard being set up at Carlton House will have the effect of a rallying place for all discontented men to go to, and it will become a rival Court to that at St. James's. In the event of the King's death or permanent disability, the Government would certainly be put into Mr. Fox's hands, and the recent transaction and intercourse with him will have a considerable effect in lessening the prejudices in the public mind against him. . . .

269. Lord Carleton to Lord Hardwicke (Lord Lieutenant of Ireland), 28 June 1804

(*British Museum Additional MSS.* 35750, f. 242.)

. . . The Opposition, headed by the Prince, derives a great part of its strength from the King's advanced stage of life and the frequent aberrations of mind to which he has been subject. From such a state of things great influence is acquired over the fears of some and the hopes of others, and the expectation of the Prince's being speedily at the head of the Government either as Regent or Monarch takes greatly from the strength of the Administration, and will continue to do so. . . .

This country is now rent into parties, with their minds in a state of great exasperation against each other; and let any one of the parties get possession of the Government, it will be weak in numbers. . . .

270. Lord Melville to William Pitt, 11 Nov. 1804

(British Museum Additional MSS. 40102, ff. 135–137.)

Moira was the leading member of the Carlton House party.

. . . In former times, ten or a dozen of years ago, the King and the Prince being at variance together, was comparatively of little moment, but the case is now totally changed, and no practicable means ought to be omitted to put the royal family in a state of decorous behaviour to each other. Unless that can be done, there can be no stable or strong Government at home nor no feeling of confidence abroad. . . . I don't mean to say that we may not, while the King lives, and is in health, keep our majorities in both Houses of Parliament, and by having recourse to extra measures, even add considerably to it, but that is a very superficial way of considering the subject. Unless a large and powerful party of great property and talents acting under the heir apparent as their head, can be dissolved, it is in vain to look for a strong Government in any beneficial sense of the expression. There is more than one way in which you can with ease make room for Lord Moira in the Cabinet, even independent of the way we have sometimes talked of and which we must all deprecate as a real calamity to the public. If Lord Moira was speedily placed there, and known to be so with the concurrence of the Prince, the cabal is at an end; and you might at will pick up from the different ingredients in Opposition any parts you pleased. . . .

271. The earl of Darlington to the prince regent, 21 Feb. 1812

(Letters of George IV, ed. A. Aspinall, 1 (1938), p. 23.)

The letter explains why the Carlton House party was practically broken up in 1812.

. . . As the restrictions upon the exercise of the royal authority by your R.H. have now ceased, from which you are enabled to form such an Administration as you conceive to be best calculated for conducting the affairs of the Empire at this great and eventful epoch of our history, the present period of Parliament must be considered as the commencement of your R.H.'s reign. . . .

It has long been my glory and pride to be considered as an attached friend to your R.H. in my public as well as private life, and in both I have never scrupled to avow that my obligations were such from an early period as to bind me to support your political opinions and more especially your individual interest whenever it was concerned, in order to do which I have never ceased to endeavour to increase my parliamentary influence at considerable expense, and formerly at some personal inconvenience. . . . The very last time that I was honoured with a private audience of your R.H., you still continued to repose that confidence in me as to inform me and shew me a list of those whom you considered your private friends in Parliament, attached to yourself, independent of those great political characters who might be expected to fill the first offices of the State, in which list, most flattering to my feelings, I had the honour of being included.

It is now necessary, Sir, to come to the most distressing and painful part of my duty. Both public and private reports agree in stating that Mr. Perceval and the principal members of his Administration still continue to enjoy your R.H.'s confidence, and that you have allowed him to use his discretion in strengthening the hands of Government . . . I cannot . . . support such Ministers and abandon those opinions that I have long formed, and some political characters whom I have long respected and supported, in which I had the great happiness to believe that I was acting in strict unison with your R.H.'s wishes. Thus circumstanced, I feel peculiar and distressing difficulty, and shall suspend my trifling parliamentary support to *any party* until I know whether it is your R.H.'s fixed determination that the same men with a trifling variation are to be continued to rule the affairs of the State and to persevere in the same system of conduct. . . .

272. Lord Temple to the marquess of Buckingham, 25 April 1812

(Duke of Buckingham and Chandos, *Memoirs of the Regency*, I (1856), p. 281.)

. . . Nothing could exceed the vacillation of Carlton House. On the first day, contradictory orders to its members in the House of Commons succeeded each other with a most amusing rapidity. At one time they received directions to vote with us, if the debate was confined merely to the Catholic question, but to vote against us if we attacked the conduct of the Irish Government. These orders were, however, soon countermanded, and they all voted steadily against us under all circumstances. The division, however, is well calculated to bring *him* to his senses, as all *his friends* voted with us, and out of the 94 majority against us, more than half stand pledged to support the pure Catholic question when it comes on, backed by the Petitions which are coming over.

273. G. W. Chad to Lady Castlereagh, 7 Nov. 1817

(*Blickling Hall MSS.*)

Princess Charlotte of Wales, the regent's only child and the heiress-presumptive, who had married Prince Leopold in 1816, died in childbed on 5 Nov. 1817 at the age of twenty-one. She had been Whiggishly inclined and had greatly admired Lord Grey. Tierney was elected leader of the Whig Opposition in the Commons in the summer of 1818.

. . . The general opinion amongst the Opposition is that this event will strengthen the Ministry. Indeed, Tierney, with whom I dined on Sunday, said, "The best thing that could happen for your friends would be that the Princess should die in childbed, as there then would never be any chance for us." . . .

(i) THE COUNTRY GENTLEMEN

274. Lord North on the country gentlemen, 18 April 1785

(*Parliamentary Register*, XVIII, pp. 69–70.)

... With regard to the idea of the country gentlemen making a considerable part of that House, the idea was a very just one: he was ready to admit the bulk and weight of that House ought always to be in the hands of the country gentlemen, who were, undoubtedly, the best and most respectable objects of the confidence of the people. Their disinterestedness, their virtue, their public spirit, he admired: they were fitted by their education and their situation in life more peculiarly for members of Parliament than almost any other description of men in the kingdom; besides, they had the greatest stake in the country after all, and were the most deeply interested in its welfare; because, let what would happen, men of business and manufacturers could go and get their living elsewhere; but a country gentleman could not quit his native country, because he could not carry his estate away with him. But, for God's sake, had not the country gentlemen their share in the representative body at present? Was it merely the representatives of Counties that were now country gentlemen? Let any man look round the House at the moment, and then let him say whether he did not see many very respectable characters, who were country gentlemen, representatives of large boroughs! ...

275. Lord Moira to Colonel McMahon, 15 June 1797

(*Windsor Archives*, 39381.)

This was one of the rare occasions when the independent country gentlemen acted in concert. Another was at the beginning of 1784 when, at meetings at the St. Albans Tavern, they made really strenuous efforts to avert a head-on collision between Pitt and the dismissed Coalition, and sought a reconciliation of parties.

... It was before Easter that some members of the House of Commons (not those who used to meet at Sir John Sinclair's) sent to ask for an opportunity of conversing with me on political topics. When we met, they said that a considerable number of the independent members, who had hitherto voted with Administration, saw with excessive alarm the difficulties into which the country had been plunged and which could not but increase rapidly unless adequate remedy were immediately applied. They added that they had reflected on the nature of that remedy, and were convinced that a change of Ministry must be the first step towards it, in consequence of which, they had communed together and had determined to fix their confidence upon me. They then requested that I would endeavour, on the assurance of their support, to form an Administration on the principle of excluding persons who had on either side made themselves obnoxious to the public. As I saw the dangers of the country in the same light that they did, and believed that nothing could dispel them but the calling forth the general confidence of the nation, I could not dissent from the theory of their plan; the execution of it, however, I deemed impracticable. I stated to them the impossibility of their overpowering the adherents of both Mr. Pitt and Mr. Fox, on which account I strenuously recommended that they should attempt to form with Mr. Fox's party an alliance that might be satisfactory to themselves and to the country, by discussing and (when accepted) reducing to strict engagement the extent of measures which Mr. Fox, when brought into office by them, would propose. The gentlemen said that many of their friends had taken so strong a part against Mr. Fox, and others had such a prejudice against him, that they had not any hope of bringing my proposition to bear with them. I repeated my reasoning as earnestly as possible and prevailed upon those gentlemen to say they would recommend the suggestion to the consideration of their comrades. I pressed the counsel upon many of those individually afterwards, and I went out of town. Public matters growing more gloomy in their aspect every day, I received letters from some of those gentlemen containing such remonstrance on my absence that I returned directly to London. The persons with whom I had before conferred came to me as soon as they heard I was arrived. They told me that the repugnance of their party to Mr. Fox was invincible, but that a sense of the extreme peril to which the State was exposed had become so general as to make it clear that a majority of the House of Commons would be for a new Administration, and they produced a very long list indeed of members, containing men of the greatest weight in the country, who wished that I should stand at their head. I explained to the gentlemen that to make myself the chief of a party would no more suit me than it would become them to enrol themselves under me; that, though I must be flattered very highly at being thought by such personages equal to the guidance of affairs in so formidable a crisis, the situation to which they destined me was most ineligible for me; that I would, notwithstanding, not shrink from it if my acceptance of it would be regarded by H.M. as an act of duty and by the public as an act of zeal. . . .

C. THE ELECTORATE

276. Extracts from the address to the king from the freeholders of Yorkshire, 25 March 1784

(*Life of Wilberforce*, by his sons, I, pp. 388–389.)

The address supported the king's action in dismissing the Fox-North coalition, in appointing Pitt Prime Minister, and in dissolving Parliament.

We, your Majesty's most dutiful and loyal subjects, the freeholders of the County of York, alarmed at the present distracted state of public affairs, beg leave to approach your throne with assurances of an unfeigned and zealous attachment to your Majesty's person and Government.

Convinced that the very existence of our excellent Constitution depends on the preservation of the due balance of power wisely placed in the different branches of the Legislature, we declare ourselves equally solicitous to maintain the due prerogative of the Crown, and the just privileges of the two Houses of Parliament.

We cannot too strongly reprobate the late attempt to seize the property and violate all the chartered rights of the East India Company, the enormous patronage of which would have produced an influence equally destructive of the prerogative of the Crown and the liberties of the people.

To remove Ministers who made such an attempt we deem to be a just exertion of your Majesty's prerogative, and under the peculiar circumstances of the case, we think your Majesty acted with equal justice by retaining your present Ministers until an appeal to your people could be made. Imperfect as such an appeal to the constituent body must ever be under the manifold defects of our national representation, we still conceive the calling of a new Parliament to be the only true constitutional measure which your Majesty in your royal wisdom can adopt to settle the present differences between the several branches of the Legislature.

277. Private instructions for Lord Milton's agents, 1807

(*Fitzwilliam [Malton Estate] MSS.*)

At the famous Yorkshire election of 1807 Wilberforce (11,806 votes) and Lord Milton, Lord Fitzwilliam's son (11,177) defeated Lascelles (10,989).

1st. To request as many of his voters as can with convenience ride their own horses will do so as it is impossible to provide carriages or Hack horses for every one.
2nd. Those voters who can travel to York and back without having their expenses paid before hand are desired to do so and on their return or after the election will be reimbursed such reasonable expenses as they may have incurred during their necessary absence by their canvassing agent if they require it. Where a voter gives Lord Milton *a plumper* it is thought by the committee that from Malton or that neighbourhood 30/–d. wd. be a reasonable allowance (his bed in York being provided by the committee at no expense to him). If he *splits* his votes then 15/–d. only. Where carriages or horses are provided for the voters the committee think they wd not be justified in allowing them more than 6/–d. per day for their expenses. Where voters are not of ability or do not choose to set out without money sufficient to defray their expenses during their absence the agents may supply them with what is necessary for that purpose according to their condition in life. The person appointed to conduct the voters to York to keep an account of chaise hire, horses &c. at the different Inns on the road which will be discharged as soon as the election is over.

278. The Rev. John Forth to G. Parker, 8 Aug. 1807

(*Fitzwilliam MSS.*)

Parker, a surgeon of Malton, was Lord Carlisle's apothecary. He was a leader of the party which sought in 1807 to liberate the borough from Lord Fitzwilliam's control by promoting two opposition candidates at the general election.

In consequence of the strong hostility which you have manifested at Malton to Lord Fitzwilliam, my Lord Carlisle feels himself called upon in justice to his friend to mark his disapprobation of it. Under this impression I have his Lordship's directions to inform you he has no further occasion for your services at Castle Howard, and requests you will transmit to me at your convenience a statement of your bill to this date.

279. Anthony Hamond to William Windham, 30 June 1807

(British Museum Additional MSS. 37887, f. 55.)

By the solicitation of a friend, a freeholder of the County of Norfolk, I am induced to trouble you with this in behalf of James Williamson, who is represented to me as having exerting [*sic*] himself in canvassing for your interest and having obtained several votes: that he is now without employment and is desirous of a place in the Customs, Surveyor of the Assessed Tax, War Office, Stamp Office, East India, Admiralty, Navy or Secretary of State's Office. Should a situation in any of the above offices be vacant and in your gift, by conferring the same upon him you will much oblige [etc.].

280. John Bagwell to Robert Peel (Irish Secretary), 14 Oct. 1812

(British Museum Additional MSS. 40222, f. 135.)

One example of the partial freedom of civil servants to vote as they pleased.

My son, Colonel Bagwell, has informed me that you were so kind as to say you would render me every assistance your official situation enabled you to do in my present arduous contest for the County of Tipperary. I therefore beg leave to suggest that it would be of the greatest possible consequence to me to prevail upon Mr. Holmes, one of the best interests in this County, to give me his support. He is Secretary to the Stamps, and his brother is Distributor for Dublin. If he is not interfered with, he will support my adversary Mr. Prittie. Sir Hugh O'Reily holds some situation in the Barrack Department, and has a very strong interest, and getting him for me conjointly with his object General Mathew would answer my purpose well enough. Mr. Jephson, Collector of Excise in Clonmel, and Mr. Tidd, Artillery Barrack Master, are the most bitter enemies of the Government, and of course my decided opponents. When Lord Wellington held your situation, he said he would displace them if they made use of any improper interference, and every act of theirs from that day to the present has been of that description. I have the most sanguine hopes of good success, yet it is necessary that Government should exert their natural influence, and it is a great hardship on me, who have all my life been the firm supporter of Government, and at the present moment again engaged on the most arduous and expensive contest that perhaps ever was in Ireland, in support of that same Government, that its immediate and most dependent servants should give me every possible opposition in their power, subverting that very service from which they derive their consequence and power.

281. Lord Althorp, M.P., to his father, Earl Spencer, 28 Jan. 1814

(Althorp MSS.)

I have had an application from Mr. Knott for the living at Wormleighton, which he says is likely to become vacant . . . Mr. Knott is, as far as I have ever heard, a very respectable man, and you know he got turned out of a curacy for voting for me.

282. Lord Palmerston (Secretary at War) to Peel (Irish Secretary), 19 Aug. 1817

(British Museum Additional MSS. 40269, f. 210.)

Could you tell me generally whether you think that there is any probability of a contest for the County of Sligo at the next election? I could at the present moment make from 280 to 290 voters by giving leases to tenants who are now holding at will. If there is any chance of their being of use next year I will do so forthwith and register them in time. If not I should perhaps postpone giving 21 years' leases till matters look a little more propitious to the payment of rents.

283. John Parker to Lord Fitzwilliam, 23 May 1826

(Fitzwilliam MSS.)

The East Retford election of 1826 was so violent that the military had to be called in, and so corrupt that the House of Commons afterwards declared the election void. The borough was disfranchised in 1830 by being thrown into the adjacent 'Hundred' of Bassetlaw.

I have the unpleasant news to inform you that in consequence of the approaching election we have had, and fully expect, sad work at the day of election. The Riot Act has been twice read already and the civil power is quite set at defiance. The constables have been struck and their staffs taken from them. They have been bound over on their own recognizances but they are as bad as ever. Some men have been nearly killed, not by freemen but by a hired mob of the scum of the neighbourhood no doubt hired by our opponents. About a fortnight ago a drunken freeman came before the house of the senior bailiff (being Saturday market day) and abused him shamefully and struck the constable and created a large mob before his house, so that no person could go quietly on business to his shop, being a druggist. The fellow afterwards the same day came before my house and insulted me and abused me at the time I had some friends dining with me, although noways concerned about the election but private business. It is expected 20,000 persons will be as spectators at the election from the neighbourhood, and they not only threaten to block up the road to prevent the candidates coming into the hall, but murder the freemen that vote for Roman Catholics, it being industriously circulated by wicked persons in the neighbourhood that our candidates are Roman Catholics. . . . The freemen have every reason to expect their lives will be in danger if they go to vote; they cannot now walk the streets (even in day time) without insult. My windows have been broken, and unless some military horse are ordered from Mansfield or Lincoln to be at Tuxford, the nearest market town (7 miles from Retford), lives will be lost. . . . The principals in these riots are the most abandoned characters about Retford, (not freemen). . . . Had we only to contend with the freemen [it] would be nothing, as we could out-number them, but a hired mob is very alarming. At a general meeting of the freemen on Saturday last they all declared unless some soldiers are not [sic] ordered near the town to support the civil power, they dare not go to vote; neither will the out vote[r]s venture into Retford (who know of these outrages) unless they are protected. All this is occasioned by an infernal Blue Club, in number about 200, who pretend they are inimical to Popery and have tried to compel freemen to break their promises, but in vain. They have endeavoured to starve them by taking away their businesses from them–but all to no purpose. His grace the D. of N[ewcastle] has encouraged this Club in a dishonourable manner, for, after having been applied to by his tenants to know how they should vote, he told them he should not interfere and they might vote as they pleased; his steward Parkinson has since applied to them to vote for Sir H. W. Wilson, but several have refused to break their promises, particularly as he set them first at liberty. Have the goodness to use your interest to get us imme-diately some troops which might go out a little way on the day of election and to be near if occasion required, which would deter the rascals from coming in to Retford....

N.B. We are very confident of success. The D. of N. has little or no interest and many of his friends abandon him for his ungentlemanlike conduct. . . .

284. The Act 10 George IV, c.8, restricting the county franchise in Ireland, 1829

(*Statutes at Large*, LXXXIII, pp. 59–71.)

The Catholic Relief Bill of 1829 was accompanied by a Bill to disfranchise the Irish 40s. free holders and to raise the Irish electoral qualification in the counties to £10, the object being to free the elections from the absolute control which, it was felt, could be exercised over them by the influence of the Catholic priests over the Catholic voters.

Whereas by an Act of the Parliament of Ireland, passed in the 33rd year of the reign of King Henry VIII . . . it is amongst other things enacted . . . that every elector of the . . . Knights [of the Shire] shall dispend and have lands and tenements of estate of freehold within the . . . Counties at the least to the yearly value of 40s., over and above all charges: . . . and whereas it is expedient to increase the amount of the qualification necessary to entitle persons to vote at such elections, and to amend the laws now in force in Ireland relating to the registry of freeholds; be it therefore enacted . . . that . . . that part of the said Act . . . which relates to the amount or value of the freehold necessary to qualify persons to be electors of Knights of the Shire to serve in Parliament for Counties in Ireland, shall be . . . repealed.
II. . . . No person shall be admitted to vote at any election of any Knight of the Shire . . . for any County in Ireland (save as hereinafter is provided), unless such person shall have an estate of freehold, in lands, tenements, or hereditaments in such County, of the clear yearly value of £10 at the least, over and above all charges, except only public or parliamentary taxes, County, Church, or parish cesses or rates, and cesses on any townland or division of any parish or barony.
III. . . . No person shall be admitted to vote . . . in respect of any estate of freehold

of less annual value than £20 of the late currency of Ireland, unless such freehold shall be registered pursuant to the provisions of this Act, save only as hereinafter provided.

[IV. A session for registering freeholds to be held in each County, as and when the Lord Lieutenant shall appoint.

V–XLIII Lay down the procedure for registration, for adjudging objections, and for appeals against refusal by the assistant barrister to register, &c.]

D. THE MOVEMENT FOR PARLIAMENTARY REFORM

285. Henry Dundas to the duke of Buccleuch, 16 April 1785
(Buccleuch MSS.)

Lord Courtown was Treasurer of the Household and M.P. for Marlborough. Lady Courtown was the duchess of Buccleuch's cousin. Later (1791) Lady Courtown's son (who became the third earl) married the duchess's daughter. (See No. 228.)

[Parliamentary reform] . . . There have always existed three substantial grounds of prejudice against Mr. Pitt's wishes upon that subject: first, as it gave any countenance to the principle of universal representation; secondly, as it tended to disfranchise families of rights they had long possessed, contrary to their consent; and lastly, as it pointed at increasing the number of members of parliament. I have always told Mr. Pitt that unless he could remove these three objections he could not give satisfaction upon it. I really think that in the line he has now adopted he has obviated these objections, and however his plan may be still unsatisfactory to zealous reformers, to those who are adverse to a spirit of innovation he certainly has modelled his ideas to comprehend their feelings. . . .

. . . Much pains has been and will be used to impress Mr. Pitt with an idea that he is privately thwarted by the Closet in a plan which is with him a favourite one, and in which he feels his credit very considerably concerned. Mr. Pitt feels no such jealousies in his own mind after the unequivocal assurances the King has given to him that he does not take part against him, but it must readily occur to your Grace to be of much consequence to Mr. Pitt's credit and future strength in the conduct of public business, not only that he should so feel, but that the public should have some proofs of it. Lord Courtown has never pledged himself to any other opinion . . . and therefore upon the whole I leave your Grace to decide how far it is under all circumstances the most expedient line of conduct that Lord Courtown should support him with his vote on this occasion; and from what passed betwixt his Lordship and Mr. Pitt some time ago upon this subject, he rather felt that Lord Courtown had made up his mind to that line of conduct, and if, after having so felt, if he should act now upon impressions of a different nature, it would still more add to the disagreeable sensations Mr. Pitt naturally feels under the notion of being opposed in this particular business by any of the friends of Government near the person of the King. . . .

286. Rev. W. Jesse to the earl of Dartmouth, July 1791

(Historical Manuscripts Comm., *Dartmouth MSS.*, III, pp. 272–275.)

An account of the Birmingham Riots, July 1791.

Your lordship will soon hear of our doings; probably at first a vague report of them. All Birmingham is in an uproar. The meeting of the Revolutionists to celebrate the infamous revolution in France has given occasion to the most dreadful riotous proceedings. Previous to the meeting, the republican Dissenters circulated a paper, of which I obtained a copy last night and mean to enclose. This paper gave great offence, as did the toasts at the meeting, which were immediately known all over the town. Someone had written in large characters on the church, "To be let" or "This barn to be let, or pulled down"; for the report of this writing is various. So great was the offence taken at this writing, with the other proceedings, that the mob assembled and destroyed all the windows of the hotel where the Revolutionists met. They then burnt down the new meeting house, the old meeting house, Dr. Priestley's house at Fair Hill, with everything therein contained. Some say that very treasonable papers were found in his study. The Doctor had escaped into Shropshire, or he would certainly have made his last exit. The mob solemnly cut off his head in effigy. Mr. Ryland's, formerly Baskerville's house, was next burnt and about twelve of the mob drinking in the cellar, when the roof fell in, perished. Mr. Taylor's house was next burnt; and here too, some of the drunkards perished. Mr. Humphrey's house was bought off by a sum of money, but it was expected the mob would return to it again. Mr. Hatton's town house was spared in consideration of a quantity of gunpowder in the house adjoining, but his country house quite consumed. I ventured to go to Birmingham yesterday afternoon. On all the houses, window-shutters, and doors in the approach to Birmingham, and on every house there, was written "Church and King for ever." . . . Every shop shut. Many of the principal inhabitants fled out of town. The mob were, at the time I was in Birmingham, assaulting Mr. William Russell's house at Moseley Wake Green. Captain Keir at the great house, Hill Top, was chairman at the meeting of the Revolutionists. He expects the mob has provided arms, &c. and means to stand on his defence. The coachman of one of the gentlemen whose house was burnt, attempted to defend [*sic*]. He killed one of the mob and then lost his own life. I hear he was the son of one of my parishioners, a worthy man. I met Mr. Ingram who told me that he narrowly escaped by the interposition of a servant in the critical moment, that one of his men had an arm and another a leg broken. Many I was told have suffered. The military are sent for. There is a report, which I do not credit, that the Republican party have pulled down a church at Coventry. Though I smiled and was much pleased to read the old toast 'Church and King' on every house, I am very sorry for the occasion. I fear this opposition will give strength to the opposed. I cannot help feeling sad apprehensions in view of the spirit which is prevailing through Europe. . . .

287. Proceedings of the Society for Constitutional Information at a general
meeting held at the Freemasons Lodge in Paradise Square, Sheffield,
26 March 1792

(Fitzwilliam MSS.)

This report was sent to Lord Fitzwilliam, probably by an agent who attended the meeting.

A number of persons (about 40 or 50) being assembled, a member was desired to
take the chair. The chairman proceeded to read the occurrences and transactions
since the last meeting, that they (the committee) had written to Mr. Paine for his
assent to their publishing the *first part* of the Rights of Man, that they had received his
answer and concurrence to this request, provided they confined the publication to the
members of their Society (about 2,000).

They had likewise written to Mr. Horne Tooke desiring him to propose to the
London Association that 12 of their friends might be admitted members of the Society
in London, in order to establish a means of communication with that and all other
Societies of like tendency in the Kingdom. They had received an answer from
Mr. H. T. favourably acknowledging the receipt of theirs with a promise to comply
with their request, applauding their spirited conduct, and intreating them not to doubt
but that by these means the eyes of the *common people* would be opened, and all their
desires fulfilled:–they had in consequence of this letter written to Mr. Payne of
Newnham Grange, near Rotherham (a gentleman of property and an advocate for
the books of his namesake), for his permission that his name should be enrolled as
one of the 12 delegates:–they had received his answer and hearty concurrence with
this proposal. . . . The chairman also recited a letter written in Ireland (which appeared
in one of the newspapers) applauding the institution of such Societies, urging the
necessity of an equal representation, that the Government was defective and oppressive, and that the only resource of the common people for redress of such oppression
was in themselves.

A second member Mr. —— arose and read a hand-publication stating that they
had received more knowledge and information from the works of Mr. Paine (Part 1st
and 2nd) than from any other author on the subject of government. That they meant
to return him their thanks for the same, and for his paternal care in laying down
a plan for the support of the young and the infirm. Here another member arose,
proposing that a copy of this hand-publication should be inserted in the *Sheffield
Register* and other newspapers, which was agreed to. Another member —— was
desired to read a manuscript which had been read in the preceding meeting, stating
the causes of their first assembling together–*viz.*–the enormity of the taxes,–the
depravity and venality of the House of Commons, and the luxury and dissipation of
persons in power and ministerial offices:–that they meant in course of time (for this
was but the infancy of their growing consequence) to petition his Majesty &c. Here
a person in the company (a stranger) arose to urge the "mildness of our Government
–the equity of our laws, which (he insisted) offered a security from every infringement of rights". What though we did pay taxes? What country did not? and if we
did pay something extra, compared with other nations, was not our opulence adequate

to the taxation? He wished them to consider that they relied upon mere speculation, and whatever they advanced was not upon the grounds of experience but information, and whilst they were declaiming against one party, and expressing their detestation of a government established by the wisdom of ages, they were become the dupes of the other party, and with bandages before their eyes were declaiming against the blindness of others. This produced the utmost confusion and agitated the whole meeting. Order was repeatedly called for, and one of the members insisted in none of the mildest terms that the gentleman was a 'fool'. Upon the explanation however of a friend of this advocate of Government (who was a member of this Society) his sentiments were soon accounted for. And their pity held out to him because "he had not read the Rights of Man". Another member having made some observations on the Corn Bill as oppressive and unparalleled, and having compared the expenses of different Governments, according to Mr. Paine's 2nd part of the Rights of Man, the assembly was dismissed.

288. Lord Braxfield's summing-up in the trial of Thomas Muir for sedition before the High Court of Justiciary at Edinburgh, 30 and 31 Aug. 1793

(*State Trials*, XXIII, pp. 229–231.)

The Lord Justice Clerk, Braxfield, made himself notorious for the severity with which he punished the Scottish Reformers charged with sedition. Muir, who had been expelled from the Society of Advocates, was sentenced to fourteen years' transportation, and similar sentences were passed on three others. A motion for the revision of these sentences was negatived in the House of Commons by 171 to 32.

. . . There are two things which you should attend to, which require no proof. The first is, that the British Constitution is the best in the world; for the truth of this, gentlemen, I need only appeal to your own feelings. Is not every man secure in his life, liberty and property? Is not happiness in the power of every man, except those, perhaps, who, from disappointment in their schemes of advancement, are discontented? Does not every man enjoy unmolested the fruits of his industry? And does not every man sit safely under his own vine and his own fig-tree, and none shall make him afraid? The other circumstance, gentlemen, which you have to attend to, is the state of this country during last winter. There was a spirit of sedition and revolt going abroad which made every good subject seriously uneasy. I observed the reflection of the master of the Grammar School of Glasgow, who told Mr. Muir, he conceived that proposing reform then was very ill-timed. I coincide in that opinion, and I leave it for you to judge whether it was perfectly innocent or not in Mr. Muir, at such a time, to go about among ignorant country people, and among the lower classes of the people, making them leave off their work, and inducing them to believe that a reform was absolutely necessary to preserve their safety and their liberty, which had it not been for him they never would have suspected to have been in danger. You will keep this in remembrance, and judge whether it appears to you, as to me, to be sedition. . . .

With respect to circulating Paine's book, Mr. Muir has said that it has never been condemned. But, gentlemen, Mr. Muir should recollect, and you must be sensible that a judgement of a court of law is by no means necessary to make it seditious. It is in itself most seditious, treasonable and dangerous. Sedition in England, gentlemen, must be sedition here; and sedition here must be sedition in England; and it would be right in forming your opinion to have an eye upon the judgements of the English courts, who have condemned the publication of that work. . . .

As Mr. Muir has brought many witnesses to prove his general good behaviour, and his recommending peaceable measures and petitions to Parliament, it is your business to judge how far this should operate in his favour, in opposition to the evidence on the other side.

Mr. Muir might have known that no attention could be paid to such a rabble. What right had they to representation? He could have told them that the Parliament would never listen to their petition. How could they think of it? A government in every country should be just like a corporation; and, in this country, it is made up of the landed interest, which alone has a right to be represented; as for the rabble, who have nothing but personal property, what hold has the nation of them? What security for the payment of their taxes? They may pack up all their property on their backs, and leave the country in the twinkling of an eye, but landed property cannot be removed.

The tendency of such a conduct was certainly to promote a spirit of revolt; and if what was demanded should be refused, to take it by force.

Mr. Muir's plan of discouraging revolt, and all sort of tumult was certainly political: for until everything was ripe for a general insurrection, any tumult or disorder could only tend, as he himself said, to ruin his cause; he was in the meantime, however, evidently poisoning the minds of the common people, and preparing them for rebellion.

Gentlemen, you will take the whole into your consideration. I now leave it with you, and have no doubt of your returning such a verdict as will do you honour.

289. First report from the Committee of Secrecy of the House of Commons respecting seditious practices, 16 May 1794

(Cobbett's *Parliamentary History*, XXXI, 475–497.)

The Committee to whom the several papers referred to in H.M.'s Message of the 12th of May 1794, and which were presented (sealed up) to the House, by Mr. Secretary Dundas, upon the 12th and 13th days of the said month, by H.M.'s command, were referred; and who were directed to examine the matters thereof, and report the same, as they should appear to them, to the House; have proceeded, in obedience to the orders of the House, to the consideration of the matters referred to them.

They find, on the first inspection, that the books and papers which they are directed to examine, contain a full and authentic account of certain proceedings of two Societies, calling themselves the Society for Constitutional Information, and the London Corresponding Society, who appear to be closely connected with other

Societies in many parts of Great Britain and in Ireland; and the Committee also observe . . . that these proceedings appear to become every day more and more likely to affect the internal peace and security of these Kingdoms, and to require, in the most urgent manner, the immediate and vigilant attention of Parliament. The Committee have, therefore, thought it their indispensable duty . . . to submit to the House the general view which they have been enabled to form of these transactions, reserving a more particular statement for a subsequent Report.

In the book containing the proceedings of the Society for Constitutional Information, which was found in the custody of the person acting as Secretary to the Society, there are regular entries of what passed on each day of meeting, from the end of the year 1791 to the 9th of May in the present year. From these it appears that during almost the whole of that period, and with hardly any considerable interval except during part of the summer in 1792 and 1793, this Society has, by a series of resolutions, publications, and correspondence, been uniformly and systematically pursuing a settled design, which appears to your Committee to tend to the subversion of the established Constitution, and which has of late been more openly avowed, and attempted to be carried into full execution.

The principles on which this design is founded are strongly and unequivocally proved, from resolutions formed as early as the 18th of May 1792, in which the Society applaud the intention of publishing a cheap edition of the first and second parts of the *Rights of Man*; and resolve, "That a copy of Mr. Paine's Letter [informing them of this intention] together with these resolutions, be transmitted to all the associated Societies in town and country; and that this Society do congratulate them on the firm as well as orderly spirit and tranquil perseverance manifested in all their proceedings, and exhort them to a steady continuance therein"; and also, "That 3,000 copies of the Letter and Resolution should be printed for the use of the Society". This single circumstance would, in the judgment of your Committee, leave little doubt of the real nature of the designs entertained by this Society: their conduct in other respects has corresponded with it.

On the 11th of May in the same year they vote an Address, in terms of approbation and applause, to the Society of Jacobins at Paris. They adopt a similar measure, under circumstances still more striking, by sending, on the 9th of November following, an Address to the National Convention of France, full of panegyric on the French Revolution, and expressing the strongest wishes for its progress and success. This Address was actually presented at the bar of the Convention by two persons, of the name of Barlow and Frost; and the answer of the President was read at the meeting of the Society on the 7th of December 1792. On the 14th of the same month a letter is received from persons calling themselves the Friends of Liberty and Equality, at Laon, capital of the Department de l'Aisne; and referred by the Society to their Committee of Correspondence. On the 21st of the same month, certain members are expressly appointed a Committee for Foreign Correspondence. . . . On the 25th of January and on the 1st of February 1793 (at the eve of the commencement of the war, and after the repeated representations which had been made on the part of the British Government, complaining of the conduct of France) the citizens Barrère and Roland (then leading members of the French Convention) are admitted associated honorary members of the Society; and the speeches of Barrère and St. André (also an honorary member of the Society) as given in the *Moniteur* of the 4th, 6th and 7th of January, are directed to be inserted in the books of the Society. Subsequent to the declaration of war, which interrupted this system of direct correspondence and concert with France, and down to the present time, the Society have continued, on various occasions, to manifest their attachment to the cause of the French Revolution; and have affected to follow, in their proceedings and in their language, the forms and even the phrases which are adopted in that country.

The next leading circumstance which has engaged the attention of your Committee, is the unremitting activity and diligence with which this Society have attempted to disseminate their principles, both by publications and resolutions industriously and extensively circulated, and by endeavouring to establish a general correspondence and concert among the other seditious Societies in the metropolis, and in different parts of England and Scotland, as well as in Ireland. With many of these, this Society appears itself to have carried on an immediate correspondence, particularly with those at Sheffield, Norwich and Manchester, who have, on all occasions, taken the most forward and active part in these transactions. . . .

From a review of these transactions your Committee feel it impossible not to conclude that the measures which have been stated are directed to the object of assembling a meeting which, under the name of a general Convention, may take upon itself the character of a general representative of the people. However at different periods the term of parliamentary reform may have been employed, it is obvious that the present view of these Societies is not intended to be prosecuted by any application to Parliament, but, on the contrary, by an open attempt to supersede the House of Commons in its representative capacity, and to assume to itself all the functions and powers of a national Legislature. . . .

When, in addition to these considerations, the Committee reflect on the leading circumstances which they have already stated, of the declared approbation, at an early period, of the doctrine of the Rights of Man, as stated in Paine's publications; of the connection and intercourse with French Societies and with the National Convention: and of the subsequent approbation of the French system; and consider that these are the principles which the promoters of a Convention evidently make the foundation of all their proceedings; they are satisfied that the design now openly professed and acted upon, aims at nothing less than what is stated in H.M.'s Message, and must be considered as a traitorous conspiracy for the subversion of the established laws and Constitution, and the introduction of that system of anarchy and confusion which has fatally prevailed in France. . . .

It appears to your Committee that in some of the Societies referred to, proposals have been received, and that measures have recently been taken, for providing arms to be distributed among the members of the Societies. It also appears, from such information as your Committee have hitherto had the opportunity of receiving, that since the apprehension of the persons in whose custody the papers were found which have been referred to your Committee, there have been several meetings of the

Societies in different parts of the metropolis; that the designs which were before entertained have been by no means abandoned; and that on the contrary there have been some indications of a disposition to concert means for forcibly resisting such measures as may be taken for defeating their accomplishment, or for bringing the authors and abettors of them to justice.

290. The Treasonable and Seditious Practices Act, 1795 (36 Geo. III, c. 7)
(Statutes at Large, XL, pp. 561–564.)

We, your Majesty's most dutiful and loyal subjects . . . duly considering the daring outrages offered to your Majesty's most sacred person, in your passage to and from your Parliament at the opening of this present session, and also the continued attempts of wicked and evil disposed persons to disturb the tranquillity of this your Majesty's kingdom, particularly by the multitude of seditious pamphlets and speeches daily printed, published, and dispersed . . . tending to the overthrow of the laws, Government, and happy Constitution of these realms, have judged, that it is become necessary to provide a further remedy against all such treasonable and seditious practices and attempts . . . do most humbly beseech your Majesty that it may be enacted; be it enacted . . . That if any person or persons whatsoever, after the day of the passing of this Act, during the natural life of our most gracious sovereign lord the King . . . and until the end of the next session of Parliament after a demise of the Crown, shall within the Realm or without, compass, imagine, invent, devise, or intend death or destruction, or any bodily harm tending to death or destruction, maim, or wounding, imprisonment or restraint, of the person of the same our sovereign lord the King, his heirs and successors, or to deprive or depose him or them from the style, honour, or kingly name, of the imperial crown of this realm, or of any other of H.M.'s dominions or countries; or to levy war against H.M., his heirs and successors, within this realm, in order, by force or constraint, to compel him or them to change his or their measures or counsels, or in order to put any force or constraint upon, or to intimidate, or overawe, both Houses, or either House of Parliament; or to move or stir any foreigner or stranger with force to invade this realm, or any other H.M.'s dominions . . . and such compassing, imaginations, inventions, devices, or intentions, or any of them, shall express, utter, or declare, by publishing any printing or writing, or by any overt act or deed; being legally convicted thereof, upon the oaths of two lawful and credible witnesses, upon trial, or otherwise convicted or attainted by due course of law, then every such person and persons, so as aforesaid offending, shall be deemed declared, and adjudged, to be a traitor and traitors, and shall suffer pains of death, and also lose and forfeit as in cases of high treason.

II. . . . If any person within that part of Great Britain called England, at any time from and after the day of the passing of this Act, during three years from the day of passing this Act, and until the end of the then next session of parliament, shall maliciously and advisedly, by writing, printing, preaching, or other speaking, express, publish, utter, or declare, any words or sentences to excite or stir up the people to hatred or contempt of the person of H.M., his heirs or successors, of the Government and Constitution of this realm, as by law established, then every such person and persons, being thereof legally convicted, shall be liable to such punishment as may by law be inflicted in cases of high misdemeanors; and if any person or persons shall, after being so convicted, offend a second time, and be thereupon convicted . . . such person or persons may . . . be adjudged, at the discretion of the court, either to suffer such punishment as may now by law be inflicted in cases of high misdemeanors, or to be banished this realm, or to be transported . . . which banishment or transportation shall be for such term as the Court may appoint, not exceeding seven years.

III. [Persons banished or transported, found at large within Great Britain before the expiration of their term to suffer death.]

IV. [No person to be prosecuted under this Act unless prosecuted within six calendar months of the offence, and no person to be convicted but by the oath of two witnesses.]

V. [Persons accused of treason under this Act entitled to the benefit of 7 Will. III, c. 3, and 7 Anne, c. 11.]

VI. [Nothing in this Act to prevent prosecution at common law for these offences.]

291. The Seditious Meetings Act, 1795 (36 Geo. III, c. 8)

(*Statutes at Large*, XL, pp. 564–573.)

Whereas assemblies of divers persons, collected for the purpose of or under the pretext of deliberating on public grievances, and of agreeing on Petitions, complaints, remonstrances, declarations, or other addresses, to the King, or to both Houses, or either House of Parliament, have of late been made use of to serve the ends of factious and seditious persons, to the great danger of the public peace, and may become the means of producing confusion and calamities in the nation: be it enacted . . . that no meeting . . . exceeding the number of 50 persons (other than . . . any meeting of any County, Riding, or division, called by the Lord Lieutenant, Custos Rotulorum, or Sheriff . . . or . . . by the convener of any County or Stewartry in . . . Scotland; or . . . by two or more Justices of the Peace . . . or . . . by the major part of the Grand Jury of the county . . . or any meeting of any city, borough, or town corporate, called by the Mayor or other head officer . . .) shall be holden, for the purpose or on the pretext of considering or of preparing any Petition, complaint . . . or other address to the King, or to . . . parliament, for alteration of matters established in Church or state, unless notice of the intention to hold such meeting, and of the time and place when and where . . . and of the purpose for which the same shall be proposed to be holden, shall be given, in the names of seven persons at least, being householders resident within the county, city, or place . . . and which notice shall be given by public advertisement in some public newspaper usually circulated in the county . . . five days at least before such meeting shall be holden. . . .

II. [Such notice may alternatively be given to the Clerk of the Peace, who must send copies to at least three Justices of the Peace.]

III. [Meetings without notice to be deemed unlawful Assemblies.]

IV. . . . If any persons, exceeding the number of 50, being assembled contrary to the provisions herein-before contained, and being required . . . by one or more Justice or Justices of the Peace, or by the Sheriff . . . or his Under-Sheriff, or by the Mayor or other head officer or Justice of the Peace of any city or town corporate, where such assembly shall be, by Proclamation . . . in the form herein-after directed, to disperse themselves and peaceably to depart to their habitations, or to their lawful business, shall, to the number of 12 or more, . . . remain or continue together by the space of one hour after such . . . proclamation, shall be adjudged felony without benefit of clergy, and the offenders therein . . . shall suffer death. . . .

V. . . . The order and form of the proclamation . . . shall be as hereafter followeth; (that is to say), the justice of the peace, or other person authorised . . . to make the said proclamation, shall, among the said persons assembled, or as near to them as he can safely come, with a loud voice command . . . silence . . . and . . . shall openly and with loud voice make, or cause to be made, proclamation in these words . . . "Our Sovereign Lord the King chargeth and commandeth all persons being assembled immediately to disperse themselves, and peaceably to depart to their habitations or to their lawful business, upon the pains contained in the Act, made in the 36th year of King George the Third, for the more effectually preventing seditious meetings and assemblies. GOD save the KING."

VI. . . . That in case any meeting shall be holden, in pursuance of any such notice as aforesaid, and the purpose for which the same shall in such notice have been declared to be holden, or any matter which shall be in such notice proposed to be propounded or deliberated upon . . . shall purport that any matter or thing by law established may be altered otherwise than by the authority of the King, Lords, and Commons, in Parliament assembled, or shall tend to incite or stir up the people to hatred or contempt of the person of H.M. . . . or of the Government and Constitution . . . it shall be lawful for one or more Justice or Justices, or the Sheriff . . . or the Mayor or other head officer . . . by Proclamation, to . . . command the persons there assembled to disperse themselves; and if any persons . . . shall, to the number of twelve or more, notwithstanding such proclamation made, remain . . . by the space of one hour after such . . . proclamation, that then such continuing together . . . shall be adjudged felony without benefit of clergy, and the offenders therein . . . shall suffer death. . . .

VII. [Justices at meetings on notice may order persons propounding or maintaining propositions for altering anything by law established except by the authority of King, Lords and Commons &c., to be taken into custody; and in case of resistance may cause Proclamation to be made as aforesaid; and if 12 or more shall continue together an hour thereafter, they shall suffer death.]

VIII. [Magistrates are empowered to attend any such meeting in order to act, and to require the attendance of constables, &c.]

IX. [Persons not dispersing within an hour after proclamation are to be arrested, and if killed or maimed by reason of their resistance, the magistrates and constables are indemnified.]

X. [Persons obstructing magistrates attending or reading the Proclamation to suffer death; and if the Proclamation cannot for this reason be made, the same regulations and penalties to be applicable as if it had been read; and persons forcibly obstructing the arrest of offenders to suffer death.]

XI. [The Act to apply to Scotland.]

XII. And whereas certain houses, rooms, or places within the cities of London and Westminster, and in the neighbourhood thereof, and in other places, have of late been frequently used for the purpose of delivering lectures and discourses on and concerning supposed public grievances . . . tending to stir up hatred and contempt of H.M.'s royal person, and of the Government and Constitution . . . be it therefore enacted . . . that every house, room, field, or other place where lectures or discourses shall be delivered, or public debates shall be had on . . . any supposed public grievance, or any matters relating to the laws, Constitution, Government or policy of these Kingdoms, for the purpose of raising or collecting money . . . from the persons admitted . . . unless the opening or using of such house, room, field, or place, shall have been previously licensed in manner herein-after mentioned, shall be deemed a disorderly house or place, and the person by whom such house, room, field, or place shall be opened or used . . . shall forfeit . . . £100 for every day that such house [&c] shall be . . . used as aforesaid . . . and be otherwise punished as the law directs in cases of disorderly houses. . . .

XIV. . . . It shall be lawful for any Justice . . . or Chief Magistrate . . . who shall by information upon oath, have reason to suspect that any house [&c.] . . . is opened . . . contrary to the provisions of this Act, to . . . demand to be admitted therein; and in case such . . . Magistrate shall be refused admittance . . . the same shall be deemed a disorderly house or place, within the intent and meaning of this Act. . . .

XV. [Magistrates may demand admittance to any licensed place at the time of delivering lectures, &c. and if refused it shall be deemed a disorderly house, and the person refusing admittance shall forfeit £100.]

XVI. [Two or more justices of the peace may license persons to open places for delivering lectures &c.; such licences may be revoked at any Quarter Sessions.]

XVIII. . . . Nothing in this Act . . . shall be construed to extend to any lectures or discourses to be delivered in any of the Universities . . . by any members thereof or any person authorized by the . . . proper officers of such Universities. . . .

XIX. . . . No payment made to any schoolmaster or other person by law allowed to teach and instruct youth . . . shall be deemed a payment of money . . . within the intent and meaning of this Act.

XXII. [Prosecutions to be started within six months of the commission of the offence.]

XXIII. [The Act to continue in force for three years and until the end of the then next session of parliament.]

292. The Act (49 Geo. III. c. 118) to prohibit the sale of seats in the House of Commons, 1809

(*Statutes at Large*, LXIII, pp. 454–457.)

Whereas it is expedient to make further provision for preventing corrupt practices in the procuring of elections and returns of members to sit in the House of Commons; and whereas the giving, or procuring to be given, or promising to give or to procure to be given any sum of money, gift, or reward, or any office, place, employment, or gratuity, in order to procure the return of any member to serve in

Parliament, if not given to or for the use of some person having a right or claiming to have a right to act as returning officer, or to vote at such election, is not bribery within the meaning of an act passed in the second year of King George II . . . but such gifts or promises are contrary to the ancient usage, right, and freedom of elections, and contrary to the laws and Constitution of this realm; Be it . . . enacted . . . that if any person or persons shall, from and after the passing of this Act, either by himself, herself, or themselves, or by any other person or persons for or on his, her, or their behalf, give or cause to be given, directly or indirectly, or promise or agree to give any sum of money, gift, or reward, to any person or persons, upon any engagement, contract, or agreement, that such person or persons to whom, to whose use, or on whose behalf such gift or promise shall be made, shall, by himself, herself, or themselves, or by any other person or persons whatsoever at his, her, or their solicitation, request or command, procure or endeavour to procure the return of any person to serve in Parliament for any county [&c.] or place, every person so having given or promised to give, if not returned himself to Parliament for such county, . . . [&c.] shall for every such gift or promise forfeit the sum of £1000 . . .; and every such person so returned . . . shall be . . . disabled and incapacitated to serve in that Parliament for such county, [&c.], and that such person shall be . . . deemed and taken to be no Member of Parliament . . .; and any person or persons who shall receive or accept of, by himself, herself, or themselves, or by any other person or persons in trust . . . any such sum of money, gift, reward, or any such promise . . . shall forfeit to H.M. the value and amount of such sum . . . or reward, over and above the sum of £500, which said sum of £500 he, she, or they shall forfeit to any person who shall sue for the same. . . .

II. . . . Nothing in this Act contained shall extend, or be construed to extend, to any money paid or agreed to be paid to or by any person, for any legal expense *bona fide* incurred at or concerning any election.

III. . . . If any person or persons shall, from and after the passing of this Act, by himself, herself, or themselves, or by any other person or persons for or on his, her, or their behalf, give or procure to be given, or promise to give or procure to be given, any office, place, or employment, to any person or persons whatsoever, upon any express contract or agreement that such person or persons, to whom or to whose use or on whose behalf such gift or promise shall be made, shall by himself, herself, or themselves, or by any other person or persons at his, her, or their solicitation, request or command, procure or endeavour to procure the return of any person to serve in Parliament for any County, [&c.], such person so returned, and so having given or procured to be given, or so having promised to give or procure to be given, or knowing of and consenting to such gift or promise upon any such express contract or agreement, shall be . . . disabled and incapacitated to serve in Parliament for such County . . . or place . . .; and any person who shall receive or accept of, by himself, herself, or themselves, or by any other person or persons in trust . . . any such office, place, or employment, upon such express contract or agreement, shall forfeit such office, place, or employment . . . and shall forfeit the sum of £500 . . . and any person holding any office under H.M., who shall give such office, appointment, or place, upon any such express contract or agreement, that the person to whom or for whose use such office, [&c.] shall have been given, shall so procure or endeavour to procure the return of any person to serve in Parliament shall forfeit the sum of £1000. . . .

IV. . . . No person shall be made liable to any forfeiture or penalty by this Act created or imposed, unless some prosecution, action, or suit, for the offence committed, shall be actually and legally commenced against such person within the space of two years next after such offence against this Act shall be committed. . . .

293. Peel (Irish Secretary) to Arbuthnot (Joint-Secretary of the Treasury), 17 Sept. 1812

(British Museum Additional MSS. 40280, ff. 32–33.)

This and the following documents show the effect of 'Curwen's Act' on the electoral influence of the Government.

. . . Pray let me know what course you adopt in apprising the friends of Government in England of the probability of a dissolution, whether by verbal communication only, or whether you do it at all. I should like also to know in what way the Treasury will act between the holders of boroughs and the candidates for seats in Parliament. I presume you will have nothing whatever to do with the receipt of money, and that you will be very careful even in hinting to a person the mode in which he might secure his return where a pecuniary consideration is to be given for it. You cannot conceive how useful all information on this subject will be to me. . . .

294. Lord Liverpool to Sir William Scott, 25 Sept. 1812

(C. D. Yonge, Life of Liverpool, I (1868), p. 444.)

. . . I can assure you I feel all the importance of having the King's Advocate in parliament. I should hope that this may be accomplished if he can assist himself to a certain degree. You will, perhaps, be surprised when I tell you that the Treasury have only one seat free of expense, for which our friend Vansittart will be elected. I have two more which personal friends have put at my disposal: and this is the sum total of my powers free of expense.

Mr. Curwen's Bill has put an end to all money transactions between Government and the supposed proprietors of boroughs. Our friends, therefore, who look for the assistance of Government must be ready to start for open boroughs, where the general influence of Government, combined with a reasonable expense on their own part, may afford them a fair chance of success. I should hope the King's Advocate would have no difficulty in agreeing to what has been proposed to him; in doing which he will have the same advantage as many of our official supporters who have been in Parliament for years.

295. Lord Liverpool to Robert Peel, 1 Oct. 1812

(*British Museum Additional MSS.* 40181, f. 7.)

. . . As it may be material for you to know without delay who are the persons we should be desirous of bringing in free of expense, if any such seats should be offered or procured on your side of the water, I think it may be material first to state to you, that with respect to *all official persons*, it has been thought necessary, that they should be elected for places, to which no imputation can attach under Curwen's Act. This has been nearly effected, but the elections of Croker for Downpatrick and William Fitzgerald for Ennis are still doubtful. I wish therefore that you would undertake to provide for them or either of them in Ireland, if the opportunity should offer; if they or either of [them] should prove successful for the places for which they are standing, and you should have a seat at your disposal free of expense, I should recommend Holford as one of the persons who has the best claims upon us, and for whom we have not been able to provide.

Long[1] will write to you on the subject of your own election, which he believes he has secured for Chippenham. If you feel any doubt upon the subject, it might be as well that you should get yourself returned for an *unobjectionable* Irish seat, and you might afterwards make your option. . . .

296. Report of the Secret Committee of the House of Commons on the disturbed state of the country, 19 Feb. 1817

(*Parliamentary Debates*, XXXV, 438–447.)

The Committee of Secrecy, to whom the several papers, which were presented (sealed up) to the House, by Lord Viscount Castlereagh, on the 4th day of February, by command of H.R.H. the Prince Regent, were referred, and who were directed to examine the matters thereof, and report the same, as they should appear to them, to the House–have unanimously agreed to the following Report:

It appears to your Committee, from the most attentive consideration of the several documents referred to them, that attempts have been made, in various parts of the country, as well as in the metropolis, to take advantage of the distress in which the labouring and manufacturing classes of the community are at present involved, to induce them to look for immediate relief, not only in a reform of Parliament on the plan of universal suffrage and annual election, but in a total overthrow of all existing establishments, and in a division of the landed, and extinction of the funded property of the country.

This hope and prospect of spoliation have been actively and industriously propagated by several Societies, openly existing in the metropolis, distinguished by the name of Spenceans; a title which they have assumed in consequence of having revived the principles, with some variation, of a visionary writer of the name of Spence, which first appeared in a publication of his near 20 years ago.

---

[1] Charles Long, afterwards Lord Farnborough; Joint Paymaster of the Forces. G. P. Holford was returned for Dungannon on 17 Oct.

It appears that at some of these Societies, held during the last month, the question was discussed whether the meetings for parliamentary reform are calculated to mislead or enlighten the public. In the course of the debates upon which question, it was strongly urged "that parliamentary reform was only a half measure, that they must look to the land, for nothing short of that would ever avail them: that we had no Constitution, there being no book in which it could be found, nor any man that could tell them what it was". In another discussion upon the question, "whether the practical establishment of Spence's plan be an effectual remedy for the present distresses", one of the doctrines maintained was that "the landholder was a monster to be hunted down; but that they should not suffer themselves to be amused; that there was a greater evil, namely, the fundholder; that these were the rapacious wretches, that took 15 pence out of every quartern loaf".

It further appears that in these meetings, the most blasphemous expressions and doctrines are openly and repeatedly advanced; that as the meetings are professed to be of a convivial nature, the political debates and readings are usually followed by songs, in many of which the most inflammatory topics are introduced, some of a seditious and treasonable nature, and others under the form of profane and indecent parodies of the Liturgy and of the Holy Scriptures.

These Societies appear to have extended themselves: and there are traces of the existence of a committee called Conservative, directing the operations of the whole. The doctrines above mentioned have been systematically and industriously disseminated amongst mechanics and manufacturers, discharged soldiers and sailors, and labourers of all descriptions: they have been inculcated at frequent appointed meetings, and at various places, by speakers, who have made the distresses of the times topics of excitement and inflammation; and they have been circulated, with incredible activity and perseverance, in cheap and often gratuitous publications. It has been proved, to the entire satisfaction of your Committee that some members of these Societies, acting by delegated or assumed authority, as an executive Committee of the whole, conceived the project, and endeavoured to prepare the means of raising an insurrection, so formidable from numbers, as by dint of physical strength to overpower all resistance. . . .

The design was by a sudden rising in the dead of the night, to surprise and overpower the soldiers in their different barracks, which were to be set on fire; at the same time (plans having been arranged, and some steps taken with a view to the accomplishment of that object) to possess themselves of the artillery, to seize or destroy the bridges, and to take possession of the Tower and the Bank. In furtherance of this design, a machine was projected for clearing the streets of cavalry. A drawing of this machine, fully authenticated, and also a manuscript sketch or plan of various important parts of the Tower, found with the drawing of the machine, have been laid before your committee.

This design was however relinquished a short time before its intended execution. It was thought more prudent previously to ascertain what force the conspirators could actually call together, and this it was agreed could best be done by convening a public meeting, for the ostensible purpose of obtaining a redress of grievances in a legal way.

The map of London was inspected, and Spa Fields were selected as the most eligible spot, from their vicinity to the Bank and the Tower. Advertisements were accordingly prepared, and written placards circulated, of the most dangerous and inflammatory nature; of one of which the following is a copy:

"BRITONS TO ARMS."

"The whole country waits the signal from London to fly to arms! haste, break open gunsmiths and other likely places to find arms! run all constables who touch a man of us; no rise of bread; no Regent; no Castlereagh, off with their heads; no placemen, tithes or enclosures; no taxes, no bishops, only useless lumber! stand true, or be slaves for ever.

"N.B.–Five thousand of these bills are up in the town, and printed ones, with further particulars, will appear in due time."

At this time, if not before, the intended insurrection assumed the symbols of the French Revolution; a committee of public safety, consisting of 24, was agreed upon, including the names of several persons, extremely unlikely to lend themselves to such a cause. A tri-color flag and cockades were actually prepared; the flag was openly carried and displayed at the first meeting which took place in Spa Fields, on the 15th of November. No acts of violence were however encouraged on that day, though some few instances of plunder occurred after the assembly dispersed, but care was taken to adjourn the meeting to the 2d of December, by which time it was hoped that the preparations for insurrection would be fully matured. . . . Plans for the seduction of the soldiers were now adopted and pursued with unremitting activity; appeals were made to excite their sympathy and induce them not to act against the insurgents; attempts were made to inflame their hopes by promises of rank and reward, and to alarm their jealousy by the absurd fiction of the actual landing of a considerable foreign army for the purpose of controlling them. . . .

Your Committee are further convinced that notwithstanding the failure on the 2d of December, the same designs still continue to be prosecuted with sanguine hopes of success.

Your Committee . . . have now the . . . painful duty of calling the attention of the House to what has been passing . . . in different parts of the country. . . . The first thing which has here forced itself upon their observation, is the widely diffused ramification of a system of Clubs, associated professedly for the purpose of parliamentary reform, upon the most extended principle of universal suffrage and annual Parliaments. These Clubs in general designate themselves by the same name of Hampden Clubs. On the professed object of their institution, they appear to be in communication and connexion with the Club of that name in London.

It appears to be part of the system of these Clubs, to promote an extension of Clubs of the same name and nature, so widely as, if possible, to include every village in the kingdom. The leading members are active in the circulation of publications likely to promote their object. . . . Nothing short of a revolution is the object expected and avowed.

Your Committee find, from equally undoubted information, that the doctrines of the Spencean Clubs have been widely diffused through the country, either by the extension of similar Societies, or more frequently by the intervention of missionaries or delegates, whose business it is to propagate those doctrines throughout every Society to which they have access: it is the universal practice of these Societies to require from the members a small weekly subscription, which provides a fund for the expenses of these missionaries, and also for the purchase of seditious tracts, which are read and commented on at their meetings. Some of these tracts . . . inculcate in the most artful manner the necessity of overturning what they call "the privileged class", as distinguished from the people, who are described as consisting of labourers, artisans, tradesmen, and every profession useful to society. A new order is declared to be the will of the people; rebellion is justified by the assertion that a nation cannot be a rebel; and all religion is disavowed, as well as loyalty, by the assertion, in answer to the question, "would you live without gods or kings?", "we abjure tyranny of every kind".

It seems, indeed, to be a part of the system adopted by these Societies to prepare the minds of the people for the destruction of the present frame of society by undermining not only their habits of decent and regular subordination, but all the principles of morality and religion. . . . About Manchester and some other places, the greatest exultation was manifested previous to the meeting in Spa Fields on the 2nd of December; and the taking of the Tower and the ruin of the Bank were publicly and confidently predicted. The news of the result was impatiently expected, the roads were crowded during the night with a number of persons, many of them delegates from the different societies in the country, waiting for the arrival of the mail coach, and the disappointment was not concealed when it was ascertained that the riot had been quelled without much serious or extensive mischief. . . .

Your Committee find that a system of secret association has been extended to the manufacturing population of Glasgow and some other populous towns of Scotland: and although these Societies have availed themselves of the same pretext, of parliamentary reform on the broadest basis, your committee are firmly persuaded, from the information which has been laid before them, that their ultimate object is the overthrow by force of the existing form of government. . . .

On a review of the whole, it is a great satisfaction to your Committee to observe that, notwithstanding the alarming progress which has been made in the system of extending disaffection and secret Societies, its success has been confined to the principal manufacturing districts where the distress is more prevalent and numbers more easily collected; and that even in many of these districts, privations have been borne with exemplary patience and resignation, and the attempts of the disaffected have been disappointed; that few if any of the higher orders or even of the middle class of society, and scarcely any of the agricultural population, have lent themselves to the more violent of these projects. Great allowance must be made for those who, under the pressure of urgent distress, have been led to listen to plausible and confident demagogues, in the expectation of immediate relief. It is to be hoped that many of those who have engaged, to a certain extent, in the projects of the disaffected, but in whom the principles of moral and religious duty have not been extinguished or perverted by the most profane and miserable sophistry, would withdraw themselves before those projects were pushed to actual insurrection.

But, with all these allowances, your Committee cannot contemplate the activity and arts of the leaders in this conspiracy, and the numbers whom they have already seduced and may seduce; the oaths by which many of them are bound together; the means suggested and prepared for the forcible attainment of their objects; the nature of the objects themselves, which are not only the overthrow of all the political institutions of the Kingdom, but also such a subversion of the rights and principles of property, as must necessarily lead to general confusion, plunder and bloodshed, without submitting to the most serious attention of the House the dangers which exist, and which the utmost vigilance of Government, under the existing laws, has been found inadequate to prevent.

297. The Habeas Corpus Suspension Act, 1817 (57 Geo. III, c. 3)

(*Statutes at Large*, LXXI, pp. 3–4.)

Whereas a traitorous conspiracy has been formed for the purpose of overthrowing by means of a general insurrection the established Government, laws and Constitution of this Kingdom: and whereas designs and practices of a treasonable and highly dangerous nature are now carrying on in the metropolis and in many other parts of Great Britain: therefore, for the better preservation of H.M.'s sacred person, and the sacred person of H.R.H. the Prince Regent, and for securing the peace and laws and liberties of this kingdom, be it enacted . . . That all or any person or persons that are or shall be in prison within . . . Great Britain, at or upon the day on which this Act shall receive H.M.'s royal assent, or after, by warrant of his said Majesty's most honourable Privy Council, signed by six of the said Privy Council, for high treason, suspicion of high treason, or treasonable practices, or by warrant signed by any of H.M.'s Secretaries of State, for such causes as aforesaid, may be detained in safe custody, without bail or mainprize, until the first day of July 1817; and that no Judge or Justice of the Peace shall bail or try any such person or persons so committed, without order from H.M.'s Privy Council, signed by six of the said Privy Council, until the first day of July 1817; any Law or Statute to the contrary notwithstanding.

II. [The Act made in Scotland in 1701 (an Act for preventing wrongous imprisonment, and against undue delay in trials) so far as relates to treason and suspicion of treason, suspended until 1 July 1817. Persons committed there not to be tried, &c. without such Order as aforesaid.]

IV. [Nothing in this Act to extend to invalidate the ancient rights and privileges of Parliament, or to the imprisonment or detaining of any member of either House of Parliament during the sitting of such Parliament until the matter of which he stands suspected be first communicated to the House of which he is a member, and the consent of the said House obtained for his commitment or detaining.]

VII. [The Act to be in force until 1 July 1817.]

298. The Seditious Meetings Act, 1817 (57 Geo. III, c. 19)

(Statutes at Large, LXXI, pp. 34–50.)

This statute is substantially a re-enactment of the Act of 1795 (36 Geo. III, c. 8), with the addition of certain new clauses, the most important of which are those prohibiting public meetings within one mile of Westminster Hall and declaring illegal certain specific societies and clubs.

I. [Meetings of more than 50 persons (except County meetings, &c.) not to be held without notice being published in some newspaper at least five days before the meetings, and signed by seven householders.]

II. [Notice may alternatively be sent to the Clerk of the Peace, who must send copies to at least three magistrates.]

III. [Meetings of more than 50 persons held without such notice to be deemed unlawful assemblies.]

IV. [No meeting held under such notice may be adjourned to any other time or place.]

V. [If more than 50 persons assemble without such notice they must disperse within an hour of a Proclamation being read by a magistrate; if 12 or more persons shall remain together for one hour after the Proclamation they shall suffer death.]

VI. [Lays down the form of the proclamation: "Our Sovereign Lord the King chargeth and commandeth all persons here assembled immediately to disperse themselves and peaceably to depart to their habitations or to their lawful business upon pain of death. GOD SAVE THE KING".]

VII. [Meetings held in pursuance of proper notice, such notice expressing that anything by law established may be altered otherwise than by the authority of King and Parliament, or tending to incite the people to hatred or contempt of the King, Government or Constitution, to be deemed unlawful assemblies; and persons to the number of 12 or more not dispersing within one hour after the Proclamation, to suffer death.]

VIII. [Magistrates may order speakers to be arrested, and if they are obstructed in so doing, may make the aforesaid Proclamation.]

X. [Persons not dispersing after one hour to be arrested; and if such persons are killed or maimed by reason of their resistance, the Justices &c. are indemnified.]

XI. [Persons obstructing the Justices in attending meetings or making the Proclamation to suffer death.]

XIV. And whereas divers places have of late been used for delivering lectures or discourses, and holding debates, which lectures, discourses or debates have in many instances been of a seditious and immoral nature; be it further enacted, that every house, room field or place at or in which any lecture or discourse shall be publicly delivered, or any public debate shall be had, on any subject whatever, for the purpose of . . . collecting money . . . from the persons admitted . . . shall be deemed a disorderly house or place, unless the same shall have been previously licensed in manner hereinafter mentioned; [persons opening such places to forfeit £100, and persons conducting the proceedings, or speaking, or who shall pay or receive any money for admission, to forfeit £20.]

XVI. [Magistrates may demand admittance to suspected places: if refused, the house

&c., to be deemed a disorderly house, &c. and every person refusing admittance to forfeit £20.]

XVII. [Two or more J.P.s may license persons to open such houses, &c., on payment of one shilling fee, the licence to be in force for one year or less.]

XVIII. [Justices may inspect licensed premises, and, if they are refused admittance, the premises to be deemed a disorderly house, &c.]

XIX. [Two Justices may revoke the licence upon evidence on oath that the premises are commonly used for the delivery of lectures of a seditious or immoral tendency.]

XX. [The Act not to extend to the Universities, the Inns of Court, Gresham College, the Colleges for the education of the East India Company's civil servants, and military servants, or to any society or body of men established by Royal Charter or by Act of Parliament. Payments to schoolmasters &c., not to be deemed payment for admission to lectures within the meaning of the Act.]

XXI. [Prosecutions to be started within six months after the commission of the offence.]

XXII. [All clauses herein-before mentioned to remain in operation until 24 July 1818.]

XXIII. And whereas it is highly inexpedient that public meetings or assemblies should be held near the Houses of Parliament, or near H.M.'s Courts of Justice in Westminster Hall, on such days as are hereinafter mentioned; be it therefore enacted . . . that it shall not be lawful . . . to convene . . . any meeting of persons consisting of more than 50 persons, or for any number of persons exceeding 50 to meet in any street, square, or open place in the city or liberties of Westminster, or County of Middlesex, within . . . one mile from the gate of Westminster Hall . . . for the purpose or on the pretext of considering or preparing any petition, complaint . . . or other address to the King, or to . . . the Prince Regent, or to . . . Parliament, for alteration of matters in Church and State, on any day on which . . . Parliament shall meet and sit . . . nor on any day on which H.M.'s Courts . . . shall sit in Westminster Hall . . . and that if any meeting . . . shall be assembled . . . contrary to the intent and meaning of this enactment, such meeting . . . shall be deemed . . . an unlawful assembly. [This clause not to apply to meetings convened for the election of M.P.s.]

XXIV. And whereas divers Societies or Clubs have been instituted, in the metropolis and in various parts of this Kingdom, of a dangerous nature and tendency, inconsistent with the public tranquillity, and the existence of the established Government, laws or Constitution of the Kingdom; and the members of many of such Societies or clubs have taken unlawful oaths and engagements of fidelity and secrecy, and have taken or subscribed, or assented to, illegal tests and declarations; and many of the said Societies or Clubs elect, appoint or employ committees, delegates, representatives or missionaries . . . to meet, confer, communicate or correspond with other societies . . . and to induce and persuade other persons to become members thereof, and by such means maintain an influence over large bodies of men, and delude many ignorant and unwary persons into the commission of acts highly criminal: And whereas certain Societies or Clubs calling themselves *Spenceans* or *Spencean Philanthropists*, hold and profess for their object the confiscation and division of the land, and the extinction of the funded property of the Kingdom: and whereas it is expedient and necessary that all such Societies and Clubs as aforesaid should be utterly suppressed and prohibited as unlawful combinations and confederacies, highly dangerous to the peace and tranquillity of this Kingdom, and to the constitution of the Government thereof, as by law established; be it enacted, that from and after the passing of this Act, all Societies or Clubs calling themselves *Spenceans* or *Spencean Philanthropists*, and all other Societies or Clubs, by whatever name . . . the same are called or known, who hold and profess . . . the same objects and doctrines, shall be . . . utterly suppressed and prohibited, as being unlawful combinations and confederacies against the government of our sovereign Lord the King, and against the peace and security of H.M.'s liege subjects.

XXV. [Societies administering to their members unlawful oaths, or electing committees, delegates, etc., to be deemed unlawful combinations within the meaning of the Act 39 Geo. III, c. 79 for the suppression of seditious and treasonable practices.]

XXVI–XXVII. [This Act not to extend or apply to Freemasons' Lodges, Quaker meetings or Societies formed solely for religious or charitable purposes.]

XXVIII. [Any person knowingly permitting unlawful societies to meet in his house, &c., to be fined £5 for a first offence and, for any further offence, to be deemed guilty of unlawful combination, etc.]

XXIX. [Licences of public houses where unlawful meetings are held, to be forfeited.]

XXX–XL [deal with the recovery of forfeitures, the limitation of actions to within three months of the commission of the offence, form of conviction, stay of executions, compensation for damage done by riotous assemblies, and a proviso that the Act shall not extend to Ireland.]

299. Lord Fitzwilliam to Lord Sidmouth, 14 and 17 June 1817

(Public Record Office, Home Office, 42/167.)

The Lord Lieutenant of the West Riding of Yorkshire reports to the Home Secretary on the supposed disaffection of the people. Oliver was a notorious Government spy and *agent provocateur*.

14 June: . . . I cannot discover that in this Riding any one man above the rank of a very inferior mechanic or shopkeeper has been suspected of being a party in these plans of insurrection. Here it is considered as the war of No Property against Property, and on this ground all of the latter description show themselves eager and anxious to resist their assailants. . . .

17 June: . . . There certainly prevails very generally in the country a strong and decided opinion that most of the events that have recently occurred in the country are to be attributed to the presence and active agitation of Mr. Oliver. He is considered as the *main spring* from which every movement has taken its rise. All the mischievous in the country have considered themselves as subordinate members of a great leading body of revolutionists in London, as co-operating with that body for one general purpose, and in this view to be under its instructions and directions, communicated by some delegate appointed for the purpose. Had not then a person pretending to come from that body and for that purpose, made his appearance in the country, it is not assuming too much to say that probably no movement whatever would have occurred—it does not follow that a dangerous spirit could not have been found lurking in any breast, but that that spirit would not have found its way into action. . . .

I collect that the spirit of resistance to legitimate government is not spread wide even in these districts,[1] considered as the most disaffected of the Riding: on the contrary, that the number of revolutionists is very limited and confined, and that the mass of the people is still sound and well affected to the present [state] of things, and that everything above the very lowest orders feel and understand that their interests are at stake, and that they must be themselves active in preventing the success of the attempts they have witnessed.

Now with respect to the opinions which I have collected, I am quite assured that the general opinion is that the mass of the people are sound, that the disaffected are few in numbers, and contemptible in description and consideration. It is not that as long as there exists a spark of disaffection in the embers of sedition it should not be watched with vigilance and care and every pains taken to smother and extinguish it, but considering it, such as it exists actually, the task is not an arduous one: and if I may presume to offer an opinion of my own with respect to measures fit for the purpose, none can be resorted to that will prove so expeditious and permanently efficacious for putting an end to all seditious planning, and revolutionary machinations in the country, as to make it known, to have it loudly promulgated, that there is not in existence a revolutionary Committee in London. The erroneous assumption and creed that such a body is in existence and in activity, has kept alive in the *country* the hopes and spirits of the wicked. Extinguish that hope, and there will be an end of the revolutionary spirit in the country.

300. Lord Liverpool to Canning, 23 Sept. 1819

(C. D. Yonge, *Life of Lord Liverpool*, II, pp. 408–411.)

... If certain manufacturing districts are excepted, that is, Lancashire, part of Cheshire, the West Riding of Yorkshire, some parts of the central Counties which are contiguous, and likewise Glasgow and Paisley and their neighbourhood, I have never known the country in general, since the conclusion of the war, and I believe I might say since I have been in Parliament, in a more prosperous situation. I include in this statement the metropolis where the reformers have been able to do nothing because they have no distress nor practical grievance to work upon.

The harvest, taking in the produce of the earth of all descriptions, has been most productive; the great complaint has been the want of hands to get it in.

Poor rates in many parts of the country are falling; crimes diminishing. In the metropolis and its neighbourhood there has been a diminution of one-third in the number of offenders since last year. This favourable statement may be applied likewise to many of the manufacturing districts; to Warwickshire, to Staffordshire, and to the iron works in Wales.

But I must now reverse the picture, and I must say that nothing can be worse or more alarming than the state of those parts of the country which I first excepted.

You will naturally ask whether the proceedings of the magistrates at Manchester on the 16th were really justifiable. To this I answer, in the first instance, that all the

[1] That is, Sheffield and Huddersfield.

papers on which they proceeded were laid before the Chancellor, and the Attorney and Solicitor-General, and that they were fully satisfied that the meeting was of a character and description, and assembled under such circumstances, as justified the magistrates in dispersing it by force.

You will have seen in the public papers that the Grand Jury of Lancashire have in a degree sanctioned their opinion by throwing out the bills against the Yeomanry, and by finding the bill against Hunt and his accomplices. . . .

When I say that the proceedings of the magistrates at Manchester[1] on the 16th ult. were justifiable, you will understand me as not by any means deciding that the course which they pursued on that occasion was in all its parts prudent. A great deal might be said in their favour even on this head; but, whatever judgment might be formed in this respect, being satisfied that they were substantially right, there remained no alternative but to support them; and I am sorry to say that, notwithstanding the support which they have received, there prevails such a panic throughout that part of the country that it is difficult to get either magistrates to act or witnesses to come forward to give evidence, and that many of the lower orders who were supposed loyal have joined the disaffected, partly from fear, and partly from a conviction that some great change was near at hand.

Under these circumstances we thought it right to assemble such of our colleagues as were within reach, for the purpose of considering whether Parliament should now be called to meet early in November. We have decided against calling it at present, but we feel that events may occur in the course of the next three weeks which may render the calling of Parliament before Christmas an imperative duty. . . .

When Parliament does meet, it will be indispensably necessary to consider what measures can be adopted for averting those evils with which the country is so seriously threatened by the frequency of these seditious meetings, and still more perhaps by the outrageous licentiousness of the Press.

The remedies are undoubtedly full of difficulty. The question must be, is the country ripe for strong and effectual measures on these points; and, how long can we venture to wait, and go on without them. One very material reason for not calling Parliament at an unusual and inconvenient time of the year was, that we must have been prepared with our measures without having had the means of informing ourselves of the sentiments of those who must support them. . . .

301. Lord Liverpool to Lord Grenville, 14 November 1819

(C. D. Yonge, *Life of Lord Liverpool*, II, p. 431.)

. . . Though it cannot be denied that the great increase of our manufacturing population, the dependence of a great part of that population on foreign demand, and the refinements in machinery (which enables manufacturers to perform that work in weeks which formerly occupied months, and which lead consequently to extravagant wages at one time, and to low and inadequate ones at another) have recently subjected this country to evils with which in the same degree we were formerly unacquainted;

---

[1] The famous 'Peterloo' incident at St. Peter's Fields, Manchester, when the yeomanry and regulars broke up the mass meeting of Reformers. The casualties amounted to eleven killed and over 500 wounded.

yet all these circumstances would not have accounted for the present state of the public mind in certain parts of the country, if the events of the French Revolution had not directed the attention of the lower orders of the community, and those immediately above them, to political considerations; had not shaken all respect for established authority and ancient institutions; and had not familiarised mankind with a system of organisation which has been justly represented to be as ingenious and appropriate to its purpose as any invention in mechanics.

I am sanguine enough to believe that the great body of the population is still sound, but it is impossible to say how long it will remain so. I am inclined to hope that preventive measures may even now prove effectual in England without the necessity of coming to extremities. But I am very apprehensive, from all the accounts I have recently seen, that in the western parts of Scotland the evil is in a more advanced state, and will not be stopped without bloodshed. . . .

302. The 'Six Acts', 1819

(*Statutes at Large*, LXXIV, pp. 1–42.)

1. An Act to prevent the training of persons to the use of arms, and to the practice of military evolutions and exercise (60 Geo. III, c. 1.)

Whereas, in some parts of the U.K., men clandestinely and unlawfully assembled have practised military training and exercise, to the great terror and alarm of H.M.'s peaceable and loyal subjects, and the imminent danger of the public peace: be it therefore enacted . . . that all meetings and assemblies of persons for the purpose of training or drilling themselves, or of being trained or drilled to the use of arms, or of practising military exercise . . . without any lawful authority . . . are hereby prohibited . . . ; and every person who shall be present at . . . any such meeting . . . for the purpose of training or drilling any other person or persons to the use of arms . . . or who shall aid or assist therein, . . . shall be liable to be transported for any term not exceeding seven years, or to be punished by imprisonment not exceeding two years, at the discretion of the Court . . . ; and every person who shall attend . . . any such meeting . . . for the purpose of being . . . trained or drilled . . . shall be liable to . . . fine and imprisonment not exceeding two years, at the discretion of the Court. . . .

II. [Persons so assembled may be dispersed, or detained and required to give bail, and prosecuted.]

III–VIII [deal with the enforcement of the Act in Scotland, the prosecution of offenders under the existing laws, and the limitation of actions to within six months of the date of the offence.]

2. An Act to authorize Justices of the Peace, in certain disturbed Counties, to seize and detain arms collected or kept for purposes dangerous to the public peace; to continue in force until 25 March 1822. (60 Geo. III, c. 2.)

Whereas arms and weapons of various sorts have in many parts of this Kingdom been collected, and are kept for purposes dangerous to the public peace . . . be it therefore enacted . . . that it shall be lawful for any J.P., upon the information on oath of one or more credible witness or witnesses that he or they believe that any pike, pikehead or spear, . . . dirk, dagger, pistol, gun or other weapon is, for any purpose dangerous to the public peace, in the possession of any person, or in any house or place, to issue his warrant to any constable or other peace officer to search for and seize such . . . weapon . . . and in case admission into such house or place shall be refused . . . to enter by force, by day or by night, into every such house or place whatsoever, and to detain . . . in safe custody . . . the arms or weapons so found and seized as aforesaid, unless the owner thereof shall prove to the satisfaction of such Justice, that such arms or weapons were not kept for any purpose dangerous to the public peace.

III. [Persons found carrying arms under suspicious circumstances, may be detained and required to give bail.]

V–VII. [Concerning the enforcement of the Act in Scotland, and the limitation of actions under this Act to a period of six months after the offence is committed.]

VIII. . . . This Act . . . shall extend to the several Counties of Lancaster and Chester, and to the West Riding of the County of York, and to the Counties of Warwick, Stafford, Derby, Leicester, Nottingham, Cumberland, Westmorland, Northumberland, Durham, Renfrew, and Lanark, the Counties of the towns of Newcastle-upon-Tyne and Nottingham, and of the city of Coventry, and such other Counties or Ridings of Great Britain as H.M. shall from time to time, upon the representation made by the Justices assembled at any Quarter or General Session of the Peace, or by any general meeting of the Lieutenancy of the County or Riding, in consequence of any disturbance therein, by any Proclamation made by and with the advice of his Privy Council, declare to be so disturbed as to make it necessary that the provisions of this Act should be enforced therein. . . .

IX. [H.M. in Council may declare the Act to be no longer in force in any Counties, etc. specified in this Act or to which the Act is extended as in clause VIII.]

3. An Act to prevent delay in the Administration of Justice in cases of Misdemeanour. (60 Geo. III, c. 4.)

Whereas great delays have occurred in the administration of justice, in cases of persons prosecuted for misdemeanors by indictment or information in H.M.'s Courts of Justice, . . . by reason that the defendants in some of the said cases have, according to the present practice . . . an opportunity of postponing their trials to a distant period, by means of imparlances in the said several Courts of King's Bench, and by time being given to try in such respective Courts of Session; for remedy thereof be it enacted . . . that [persons prosecuted in the Court of King's Bench for any misdemeanor, shall not be permitted to imparle to a following Term, but shall be required to plead or demur thereto within four days from the time of his or her appearance; and in default of his or her pleading or demurring, judgment may be entered against the defendant for want of a plea.]

II. [The courts may, upon sufficient cause being shown, allow further time to plead, &c.]

III. [Persons in custody or held to bail within 20 days before the Sessions, shall plead to the indictment, unless a writ of *certiorari* for removing such indictment into the Court of King's Bench at Westminster or Dublin shall be delivered before the jury shall be sworn for such trial.]

IV–X. [Lay down the procedure for issuing writs of *certiorari*, for trying indictments at subsequent sessions, delivering copies of informations, &c.]

4. An Act for more effectually preventing Seditious Meetings and Assemblies. (60 Geo. III, c. 6.)

Whereas in divers parts of this Kingdom, assemblies of large numbers of persons collected from various parishes and districts under the pretext of deliberating upon public grievances, and of agreeing on petitions, complaints, remonstrances, declarations, resolutions or addresses upon the subject thereof, have of late been held, in disturbance of the public peace, to the great terror and danger of H.M.'s loyal and peaceable subjects, and in a manner manifestly tending to produce confusion and calamities in the nation: Be it enacted . . . that no meeting of any description of persons, exceeding the number of 50 . . . (other than . . . any meeting of any County, or division of any County, called by the Lord Lieutenant, Governor or Custos Rotulorum, or Sheriff, . . . or any meeting called by five or more acting Justices of the Peace, . . . or by the major part of the Grand Jury of the County . . . at the Assizes, . . . or any meeting of any city, borough or town corporate called by the Mayor or other Head Officer . . .) shall be holden for the purpose of deliberating upon any public grievance, or upon any matter or thing relating to any trade, manufacture business or profession, or upon any matter in Church or State, or of considering, proposing or agreeing to any petition, complaint . . . or address upon the subject thereof; unless in the parish . . . within which the persons calling any such meeting shall usually . . . dwell; nor unless notice in writing of the intention to hold such meeting and of the purpose for which the same shall be proposed to be holden, shall be delivered personally to a J.P. residing in or near to such parish, . . . six days at least before such meeting shall be proposed to be holden . . . nor unless such notice shall be subscribed by seven . . . householders usually resident within the parish. . . .

III. [No meeting shall be adjourned.]

IV. [. . . No person (except J.P.s, Sheriffs, Under-Sheriffs, constables or other peace officers or other persons acting under their authority) shall attend any meeting whatever exceeding the number of 50 persons, which shall be held for the purpose of deliberating upon any public grievance, or upon any matter or thing relating to any trade, manufacture, business or profession, or of considering . . . any complaint . . . upon the subject thereof, unless such person, in the case of a County meeting, shall be a freeholder, copyholder or householder, or an inhabitant usually residing in the County; or, in the case of a meeting in a city or borough, shall be a freeman or member of the Corporation, or a householder usually resident therein, or a freeholder or copyholder having an estate in lands of the annual value of £50 of which he shall have been in possession twelve months, in that city or borough.] Provided always, that nothing herein contained shall extend to any member of the Commons House of

Parliament attending any such meeting as aforesaid in any . . . place for which he shall be serving in Parliament; nor to any person having a right to vote for a member to serve in Parliament for any city, borough, town, or place, attending any meeting of such . . . place, which may be called by the Mayor or other Head Officer.

V. [Anyone attending meetings contrary to the Act shall be liable to be punished by fine and imprisonment not exceeding 12 calendar months, at the Court's discretion.]

VII. [In case any meeting shall be held in pursuance of notice as aforesaid, and such notice shall express that any matter or thing by law established may be altered otherwise than by Act of Parliament, or shall tend to stir up the people to hatred or contempt of H.M. or of the Government and Constitution; every such meeting shall be deemed an unlawful assembly.]

VIII. [Persons attending meetings contrary to the Act shall be required by Proclamation to depart, and, not departing within a quarter of an hour after such Proclamation made, shall, upon being lawfully convicted, be adjudged to be guilty of felony, and shall be liable to be transported for any period not exceeding seven years.]

IX. [Lays down the form of the Proclamation.]

X. [Any person lawfully attending such meeting empowered to apprehend any person not entitled to attend and to carry him before a J.P.]

XI. [Persons assembling for the purpose of holding any meeting contrary to the provisions of this Act, or where any persons not entitled to attend any meeting as aforesaid shall refuse to depart within a quarter of an hour after such Proclamation made as aforesaid, shall, if assembled to the number of 12 or more, be adjudged guilty of felony upon being legally convicted, and be liable to be transported for any term not exceeding seven years.]

XII–XIV. [Persons resisting the Justices, &c. in the course of their duty to be adjudged felons and be liable to be transported for a term not exceeding seven years.]

XV. [Justices &c. shall be indemnified in case of persons being killed or maimed whilst an unlawful meeting is being dispersed.]

XVI–XVII. [Nothing hereintofore contained shall extend to any meeting held in private houses or buildings, or to meetings for returning Members to Parliament.]

XVIII–XIX. [Attending meetings with arms or weapons, or with flags, banners and other emblems unlawful; persons convicted of such offence to be fined and imprisoned for any term not exceeding two years.]

XXIII. [It shall be lawful, notwithstanding the Act 57 Geo. III, c. 19 [No. 298] to hold any meeting in the parishes of St. John and St. Margaret, Westminster within the distance of one mile from Westminster Hall, provided that the same shall not be held in Old or New Palace Yard at any time during the sitting of Parliament.]

XXVI. . . . Every house, room, field, or other place, at or in which any person shall publicly read, or at or in which any lecture or discourse shall be publicly delivered, or any public debate shall be had, on any subject whatever, for the purpose of raising or collecting money . . . from the persons admitted, or to which any person shall be admitted by payment of money . . . shall be deemed a disorderly house or place, unless the same shall have been previously licensed in manner hereinafter mentioned; and the person by whom such house . . . shall be opened . . . shall forfeit . . . £100 . . . and be otherwise punished as the law directs in cases of disorderly houses; and every person managing or conducting the proceedings, . . . and also every person who shall pay, give, collect or receive, any money . . . as aforesaid, shall for every such offence forfeit . . . £20.

XXIX. [Two Justices may license places for lectures, &c., for a fee of one shilling, the licence to be in force for no longer than one year; the Justices may revoke the licence at any Sessions.]

XXXI. [The Act not to apply to the Universities, Inns of Court, Gresham College, &c., nor to payments to schoolmasters &c. in respect of lectures &c. for the instruction of their pupils.]

XXXII. [A licence to be forfeited in case of seditious or immoral lectures.]

XL. [The Act to continue in force for five years from the day of passing this Act, and until the end of the then next Session of Parliament.]

5. An Act for the more effectual prevention and punishment of Blasphemous and Seditious Libels. (60 Geo. III, c. 8.)

Be it enacted . . . that from and after the passing of this Act, in every case in which any verdict . . . shall be had against any person for composing, printing or publishing any blasphemous libel, or any seditious libel, tending to bring into hatred or contempt the person of H.M. . . . or the Regent, or the Government and Constitution, . . . or either House of Parliament, or to excite H.M.'s subjects to attempt the alteration of any matter in Church or State as by law established, otherwise than by lawful means, it shall be lawful for the Judge . . . to make an order for the seizure . . . [of] all copies of the libel which shall be in the possession of the [convicted] person, . . . or in the possession of any other person named in the order. . . . Evidence upon oath having been previously given . . . that a copy or copies of the said libel is or are in the possession of such other person for the use of the person [convicted] . . . and in any such case it shall be lawful for any Justice, . . . constable or other peace officer . . . to search for any copies of such libel in any house or other place whatsoever belonging to the person . . . so named . . . ; and in case admission shall be refused, . . . to enter by force by day into any such . . . place . . . and to carry away all copies of the libel there found. . . .

II. [Copies of libels seized to be restored without fee if the conviction shall subsequently be quashed; otherwise to be disposed of as the Court shall direct.]

IV. [The punishment for a second offence shall be, at the discretion of the Court, either such punishment as is now inflicted in cases of high misdemeanours, or banishment from the United Kingdom and all other parts of H.M.'s dominions, for such term of years as the Court shall order.]

VI. [Persons thus ordered to be banished, who shall, after the end of 40 days, be at large within H.M.'s dominions, shall be transported for any term not exceeding 14 years.]

X. [Nothing in this Act to be held to alter the law of libel in Scotland.]

6. An Act to subject certain publications to the duties of stamps upon newspapers, and to make other regulations for restraining the abuses arising from the publication of blasphemous and seditious libels. (60 Geo. III, c. 9.)

Whereas pamphlets and printed papers containing observations upon public events and occurrences, tending to excite hatred and contempt of the Government and Constitution of these realms as by law established, and also vilifying our holy religion, have lately been published in great numbers, and at very small prices; and it is expedient that the same should be restrained, . . . be it enacted . . . that . . . all pamphlets and papers containing any public news, intelligence or occurrences, or any remarks or observations thereon, or upon any matter in Church or State, printed in any part of the U.K. for sale, and published periodically, or in parts or numbers, at intervals not exceeding 26 days between the publication of any two such pamphlets or papers, parts or numbers, where any of the said pamphlets or papers shall not exceed two sheets, or shall be published for sale for a less sum than sixpence, exclusive of the duty by this Act imposed thereon, shall be deemed . . . newspapers, . . . and be subject to . . . the same duties of stamps . . . as newspapers printed in Great Britain and Ireland respectively now are subject unto . . . and shall be . . . subject to all . . . rules, regulations, restrictions . . . relating to newspapers. . . .

II. . . . No quantity of paper less than a quantity equal to 21 inches in length and 17 inches in breadth, in whatever way or form the same may be made or may be divided into leaves, or in whatever way the same may be printed, shall be deemed to be a sheet within the meaning of this Act.

IV. . . . All pamphlets and papers containing any public news, intelligence or occurrences, or any such remarks or observations as aforesaid, printed for sale, and published periodically, or in parts or numbers, at intervals exceeding 26 days between any two such pamphlets or papers . . . and which said pamphlets, papers . . . shall not exceed two sheets, or which shall be published for sale at a less price than sixpence, shall be first published on the first day of every calendar month, or within two days before or after that day, and at no other time . . . [under penalty of £20 for every such offence.]

VIII. [No persons shall print or publish newspapers &c. or pamphlets without entering into a recognisance or giving bond for securing fines upon conviction for libels. Every person printing or publishing any such newspaper &c. or pamphlet shall enter into a recognisance in the sum of £300, if such newspaper &c. or pamphlet shall be printed in or within 20 miles of London, and in the sum of £200 if printed elsewhere in the United Kingdom, and his or her sureties, two or three in number, in a like sum—under penalty of £20 for every such offence.]

IX. [If sureties pay any part of the money for which they are bound, or become bankrupt, new recognisance or bond with sureties shall be given—under penalty of £20 for every offence.]

XIII. [The printer or publisher of any pamphlet or paper for sale, containing any public news &c. or remarks thereon, shall, upon every day upon which the same shall be published, or within six days thereafter, deliver to the Commissioners of Stamps, one copy of such pamphlet &c., signed by the printer or publisher with his name and place of abode. For every instance of neglect he shall forfeit £100.]

XV. [If any person shall sell or expose to sale any pamphlet or other paper not being duly stamped, if required to be stamped, he shall, for every offence, forfeit £20.]

XVIII. [Two or more J.P.s may hear and determine any offence committed against this Act.]

XXVI. Nothing in this Act shall extend to Acts of Parliament, Proclamations, Orders of Council &c. ordered to be printed by H.M., or to any Votes or other matters by order of either House of Parliament, or to books commonly used in schools, or books containing only matters of devotion, piety or charity, or of any matter wholly of a commercial nature.

XXVII. Nothing in this Act shall extend to charge with stamp duties any work reprinted and republished in parts or numbers, whether such work shall be wholly reprinted or shall be republished in any abridged form; provided that the work shall have been first printed and published two years at the least previous to such reprinting and republication, and provided the said work was not first published in parts or numbers.

303. An Act (2 William IV, c. 45) to amend the representation of the people in England and Wales, 7 June 1832

(*Statutes of the United Kingdom of Great Britain and Ireland, 2 & 3 William IV* (1832), pp. 154–206.)

Whereas it is expedient to take effectual measures for correcting divers abuses that have long prevailed in the choice of members to serve in the Commons House of Parliament, to deprive many inconsiderable places of the right of returning members, to grant such privilege to large, populous and wealthy towns, to increase the number of Knights of the Shire, to extend the elective franchise to many of H.M.'s subjects who have not heretofore enjoyed the same, and to diminish the expense of elections; be it therefore enacted ... that each of the boroughs enumerated in the schedule marked (A.) to this Act annexed ... shall from and after the end of this present Parliament cease to return any member or members to serve in parliament.

II. ... Each of the boroughs enumerated in the schedule marked (B.) to this Act annexed ... shall from and after the end of this present Parliament return one member and no more to serve in Parliament.

III. ... Each of the places named in the schedule marked (C.) to this Act annexed ... shall for the purposes of this Act be a borough, and shall as such borough include the place or places respectively which shall be comprehended within the boundaries of such borough, as such boundaries shall be settled and described by an Act to be passed for that purpose in this present Parliament, which Act, when passed, shall be deemed and taken to be part of this Act as fully and effectually as if the same were incorporated herewith; and that each of the said boroughs named in the said schedule (C.) shall from and after the end of this present Parliament return two members to serve in Parliament.

IV. ... Each of the places named in the schedule marked (D.) to this Act annexed ... shall for the purposes of this Act be a borough ... and shall ... from and after the end of this present Parliament return one member to serve in parliament.

V. [The boroughs of Shoreham, Cricklade, Aylesbury and East Retford shall include certain adjacent districts.]

VI. [Weymouth and Melcombe Regis to return two members only. Penryn to include Falmouth; Sandwich to include Deal and Walmer.]

VII. [Boundaries of existing boroughs in England to be settled by an Act to be passed in this parliament.]

VIII. [Places in Wales to have a share in elections for shire-towns as enumerated in schedule E.]

IX. [Boundaries of shire-towns and places in Wales to be settled by an Act to be passed in this present parliament.]

X. [Swansea, Loughor, Neath, Aberavon, and Ken-fig to form one borough, and electors thereof not to vote for a member for Cardiff.]

XI. [Description of the returning officers for the new boroughs.]

XII. [Six Knights of the Shire for Yorkshire, two for each Riding.]

XIII. [Four Knights of the Shire for Lincolnshire.]

XIV. [Certain Counties (schedule F.) to be divided, and to return two Knights of the Shire for each division.]

XV. [Certain Counties to return three Knights of the Shire (schedule F. 2.)]

XVI. [Isle of Wight, severed from Hampshire, to return one member.]

XVII. [Towns which are Counties of themselves to be included in adjoining Counties for county elections (schedule G.)]

XVIII. [Limitation on the right of voting for Counties and for cities being Counties of themselves, in respect of freeholds for life.]

XIX. . . . Every male person of full age, and not subject to any legal incapacity, who shall be seised at law or in equity of any lands or tenements of copyhold or any other tenure whatever except freehold, for his own life, or for the life of another or for any lives whatsoever, or for any larger estate of the clear yearly value of not less than £10 over and above all rents and charges payable out of or in respect of the same, shall be entitled to vote in the election of a Knight or Knights of the Shire to serve in any future Parliament for the County, or for the Riding, parts, or division of the County, in which such lands or tenements shall be respectively situate.

XX. . . . Every male of full age, and not subject to any legal incapacity, who shall be entitled, either as lessee or assignee, to any lands or tenements, whether of freehold or of any other tenure whatever, for the unexpired residue, whatever it may be, of any term originally created for a period of not less than 60 years, (whether determinable on a life, or lives, or not) of the clear yearly value of not less than £10 over and above all rents and charges payable out of or in respect of the same, or for the unexpired residue, whatever it may be, of any term originally created for a period of not less than 20 years (whether determinable on a life or lives, or not) of the clear yearly value of not less than £50 over and above all rents and charges payable out of or in respect of the same, or who shall occupy as tenant any lands or tenements for which he shall be *bonâ fide* liable to a yearly rent of not less than £50, shall be entitled to vote in the election of a Knight or Knights of the Shire to serve in any future Parliament for the County, or for the Riding, parts or division of the County in which such lands or tenements shall be respectively situate; provided always, that no person, being only a sub-lessee, or the assignee of any under-lease, shall have a right to vote in such election in respect of any such term of 60 years or 20 years as aforesaid, unless he shall be in the actual occupation of the premises.

XXI. . . . No public or parliamentary tax, nor any Church rate, County rate, or parochial rate, shall be deemed to be any charge payable out of or in respect of any lands or tenements within the meaning of this Act.

XXII. . . . In order to entitle any person to vote in any election of a Knight of the Shire or other member to serve in any future Parliament, in respect of any messuages, lands or tenements, whether freehold or otherwise, it shall not be necessary that the same shall be assessed to the land tax; any Statute to the contrary notwith-standing.

XXIII. . . . No person shall be allowed to have any vote in the election of a Knight or Knights of the Shire for or by reason of any trust, estate or mortgage, unless such trustee or mortgagee be in actual possession or receipt of the rents and profits of the said estate, but that the mortgagor or cestuique trust in possession shall and may vote for the same estate notwithstanding such mortgage or trust.

XXIV. . . . Notwithstanding anything hereinbefore contained, no person shall be entitled to vote in the election of a Knight or Knights of the Shire to serve in any future Parliament in respect of his estate or interest as a freeholder in any house, warehouse, counting-house, shop or other building, occupied by himself, or in any land occupied by himself together with any house, warehouse, counting-house, shop or other building, such house, warehouse, counting-house, shop or other building being, either separately or jointly with the land so occupied therewith, of such value as would, according to the provisions hereinafter contained, confer on him the right of voting for any city or borough, whether he shall or shall not have actually acquired the right to vote for such city or borough in respect thereof.

XXV. . . . Notwithstanding anything hereinbefore contained, no person shall be entitled to vote in the election of a Knight or Knights of the Shire to serve in any future Parliament in respect of his estate or interest as a copyholder or customary tenant, or tenant in ancient demesne, holding by copy of court roll, or as such lessee or assignee, or as such tenant and occupier as aforesaid, in any house, warehouse, counting-house, shop or other building, or in any land occupied together with a house, warehouse, counting-house, shop or other building, such house, warehouse, counting-house, shop or other building being, either separately or jointly with the land so occupied therewith, of such value as would according to the provisions hereinafter contained confer on him or on any other person the right of voting for any city or borough, whether he or any other person shall or shall not have actually acquired the right to vote for any such city or borough in respect thereof.

XXVI. . . . Notwithstanding anything hereinbefore contained, no person shall be entitled to vote in the election of a Knight or Knights of the Shire to serve in any future Parliament unless he shall have been duly registered according to the provisions hereinafter contained; and that no person shall be so registered in any year in respect of his estate or interest in any lands or tenements, as a freeholder, copyholder, customary tenant, or tenant in ancient demesne, unless he shall have been in the actual possession thereof, or in the receipt of the rents and profits thereof for his own use, for six calendar months at least next previous to the last day of July in such year, which said period of six calendar months shall be sufficient, any statute to the contrary notwithstanding; and that no person shall be so registered in any year, in respect of any lands or tenements held by him as such lessee or assignee, or as such occupier and tenant as aforesaid, unless he shall have been in the actual possession thereof, or in the receipt of the rents and profits thereof for his own use, as the case may require, for twelve calendar months next previous to the last day of July in such year : provided always that where any lands or tenements, which would otherwise entitle the owner, holder or occupier thereof to vote in any such election, shall come to any person, at any time within such respective periods of six or twelve calendar months, by descent, succession, marriage, marriage settlement, devise or promotion to any benefice in a Church, or by promotion to any office, such person shall be entitled in respect thereof to have his name inserted as a voter in the election of a Knight or Knights of the Shire in the lists then next to be made by virtue of this Act as hereinafter mentioned, and, upon his being duly registered according to the provisions hereinafter contained, to vote in such election.

XXVII. . . . In every city or borough which shall return a member or members to serve in any future Parliament, every male person of full age, and not subject to any legal incapacity, who shall occupy, within such city or borough, or within any place sharing in the election for such city or borough, as owner or tenant, any house, warehouse, counting-house, shop or other building, being either separately or jointly with any land within such city, borough, or place occupied therewith by him as owner, or occupied therewith by him as tenant under the same landlord, of the clear yearly value of not less than £10, shall, if duly registered according to the provisions hereinafter contained, be entitled to vote in the election of a member or members to serve in any future Parliament for such city or borough : provided always that no such person shall be so registered in any year unless he shall have occupied such premises as aforesaid for twelve calendar months next previous to the last day of July in such year, nor unless such person, where such premises are situate in any parish or township in which there shall be a rate for the relief of the poor, shall have been rated in respect of such premises to all rates for the relief of the poor in such parish or township made during the time of such his occupation so required as aforesaid, nor unless such person shall have paid, on or before the 20th day of July in such year, all the poor's rates and assessed taxes which shall have become payable from him in respect of such premises previously to the 6th day of April then next preceding : provided also that no such person shall be so registered in any year unless he shall have resided for six calendar months next previous to the last day of July in such year within the city or borough, or within the place sharing in the election for the city or borough, in respect of which city, borough or place respectively he shall be entitled to vote, or within seven statute miles thereof or of any part thereof.

XXVIII. . . . The premises in respect of the occupation of which any person shall be entitled to be registered in any year, and to vote in the election for any city or borough as aforesaid, shall not be required to be the same premises, but may be different premises occupied in immediate succession by such person during the twelve calendar months next previous to the last day of July in such year, such person having paid, on or before the 20th day of July in such year, all the poor's rates and assessed taxes which shall previously to the 6th day of April then next preceding have become payable from him in respect of all such premises so occupied by him in succession.

XXIX. . . . Where any premises as aforesaid, in any such city or borough, or in any place sharing in the election therewith, shall be jointly occupied by more persons than one as owners or tenants, each of such joint occupiers shall, subject to the conditions hereinbefore contained as to persons occupying premises in any such city, borough or place, be entitled to vote in the election for such city or borough, in respect of the premises so jointly occupied, in case the clear yearly value of such premises shall be of an amount which, when divided by the number of such occupiers, shall give a sum of not less than £10 for each and every such occupier, but not otherwise.

XXX. [Occupiers may demand to be rated.]

XXXI. . . . In every city or town being a County of itself, in the election for which freeholders or burgage tenants, either with or without any superadded qualification, now have a right to vote, every such freeholder or burgage tenant shall be entitled to vote in the election of a member or members to serve in all future Parliaments for such city or town, provided he shall be duly registered according to the provisions hereinafter contained; but that no such person shall be so registered in any year in respect of any freehold or burgage tenement, unless he shall have been in the actual possession thereof, or in the receipt of the rents and profits thereof for his own use, for twelve calendar months next previous to the last day of July in such year (except where the same shall have come to him, at any time within such twelve months, by descent, succession, marriage, marriage settlement, devise, or promotion to any benefice in a Church, or to any office) nor unless he shall have resided for six calendar months next previous to the last day of July in such year within such city or town, or within seven statute miles thereof or of any part thereof: provided always, that nothing in this enactment contained shall be deemed to vary or abridge the provisions hereinbefore made relative to the right of voting for any city or town being a County of itself, in respect of any freehold for life or lives: provided also, that every freehold or burgage tenement which may be situate without the present limits of any such city or town being a County of itself, but within the limits of such city or town, as the same shall be settled and described by the Act to be passed for that purpose as hereinbefore mentioned, shall confer the right of voting in the election of a member or members to serve in any future parliament for such city or town in the same manner as if such freehold or burgage tenement were situate within the present limits thereof.

XXXII. [Freemen not to vote in boroughs, unless resident; exclusion of freemen created since 1 March 1831, with provisos as to the freemen of certain specified boroughs.]

XXXIII. . . . No person shall be entitled to vote . . . for any city or borough, save and except in respect of some right conferred by this Act, or as a burgess or freeman, or as . . . liveryman . . . or as a freeholder or burgage tenant, as hereinafter mentioned . . . but that no such person shall be registered . . . unless he . . . shall have resided for six calendar months . . . within such city or borough or within seven statute miles. . . .

XXXIV. [Provision as to persons now entitled to vote for New Shoreham, Cricklade, Aylesbury or East Retford in respect of freeholds.]

XXXV. Provided nevertheless . . . that notwithstanding anything hereinbefore contained, no person shall be entitled to vote in the election of a member or members to serve in any future Parliament for any city or borough (other than a city or town being a County of itself, in the election for which freeholders or burgage tenants have a right to vote as hereinbefore mentioned) in respect of any estate or interest in any burgage tenement or freehold which shall have been acquired by such person since the 1st day of March 1831, unless the same shall have come to or been acquired by such person, since that day, and previously to the passing of this Act, by descent, succession, marriage, marriage settlement, devise or promotion to any benefice in a church, or by promotion to any office.

XXXVI. . . . No person shall be entitled to be registered in any year as a voter in the election of a member or members to serve in any future Parliament for any city or borough who shall within twelve calendar months next previous to the last day of July in such year have received parochial relief or other alms which by the law of parliament now disqualify from voting in the election of members to serve in Parliament.

XXXVII. And whereas it is expedient to form a register of all persons entitled to vote in the election of a Knight or Knights of the Shire to serve in any future Parliament, and that for the purpose of forming such register the overseers of every parish and township should annually make out lists in the manner hereinafter mentioned; be it therefore enacted, that the overseers of the poor of every parish and township shall on the 20th day of June in the present and in every succeeding year cause to be fixed on or near the doors of all the churches and chapels within such parish or township, or if there be no church or chapel therein, then to be fixed in some public and conspicuous situation within the same respectively, a notice according to the form numbered 1, in the schedule (H.) to this Act annexed, requiring all persons who may be entitled to vote in the election of a Knight . . . of the Shire to serve in any future Parliament, in respect of any property situate wholly or in part in such parish or township, to deliver or transmit to the said overseers on or before the 20th day of July in the present and in every succeeding year a notice of their claim as such voters according to the form numbered 2, in the said schedule (H.) or to the like effect: provided always, that after the formation of the register to be made in each year, as hereinafter mentioned, no person whose name shall be upon such register for the time being shall be required thereafter to make any such claim as aforesaid, as long as he shall retain the same qualification, and continue in the same place of abode described in such register.

XXXVIII. . . . The overseer of the poor of every parish and township shall on or before the last day of July in the present year make out or cause to be made out, according to the form numbered 3, in the said schedule (H.) an alphabetical list of all persons who shall claim as aforesaid to be inserted in such list as voters in the election of a Knight or Knights of the Shire, to serve for the County, or for the Riding, parts, or division of the County wherein such parish or township lies, in respect of any lands or tenements situate wholly or in part within such parish or township; and that the said overseers shall on or before the last day of July in every succeeding year make out or cause to be made out a like list, containing the names of all persons who shall be upon the register for the time being as such voters, and also the names of all persons who shall claim as aforesaid to be inserted in such last-mentioned list as such voters: and in every list so to be made by the overseers as aforesaid the christian name and surname of every person shall be written at full length, together with the place of his abode, the nature of his qualification, and the local or other description of such lands or tenements, as the same are respectively set forth in his claim to vote, and the name of the occupying tenant, if stated in such claim: and the said overseers if they shall have reasonable cause to believe that any person so claiming as aforesaid, or whose name shall appear in the register for the time being, is not entitled to vote in the election of a Knight or Knights of the Shire for the County, or for the Riding, parts or division of the County in which their parish or township is situate, shall have power to add the words 'objected to' opposite the name of every such person on the margin of such list; and the said overseers shall sign such list, and shall cause a sufficient number of copies of such list to be written or printed, and to be fixed on or near the doors of all the churches and chapels within their parish or township, or if there be no church or chapel therein, then to be fixed up in some public and conspicuous situation, within the same respectively, on the two Sundays next after such list shall have been made; and the said overseers shall likewise keep a true copy of such list, to be perused by any person without payment of any fee, at all reasonable hours during the two first weeks after such list shall have been made: provided always, that every precinct or place, whether extra-parochial or otherwise, which shall have no overseers of the poor, shall for the purpose of making out such list as aforesaid be deemed to be within the parish or township adjoining thereto, such parish or township being situate within the same County, or the same riding, parts or division of a County, as such precinct or place; and if such precinct or place shall adjoin two or more parishes or townships, so situate as aforesaid, it shall be deemed to be within the least populous of such parishes or townships according to the last census for the time being; and the overseers of the poor of every such parish or township shall insert in the list for their respective parish or township the names of all persons who shall claim as aforesaid to be inserted therein as voters in the election of a Knight or Knights of the Shire to serve for the County, or for the Riding, parts or division of the County, in which such precinct or place as aforesaid lies, in respect of any lands or tenements situate wholly or in part within such precinct or place.

XXXIX. [Notice of objection by third parties to persons not entitled to be retained in the County lists. Lists of persons objected to by third parties to be published.]

XL. [Lists of County voters to be forwarded to the clerks of the peace.]

XLI. [Judges of Assize to name barristers who shall revise the lists of County voters.]

XLII. [Clerk of the peace and overseers to attend before the barristers, who shall retain on the County lists all names not objected to, and shall expunge those whose qualification, if objected to, shall not be proved.]

XLIII. [Barrister to have power to insert in the County lists the names of claimants omitted by the overseers on proof of claim and qualification.]

XLIV. [Overseers to prepare lists of persons (other than freemen) entitled to vote in boroughs, and to publish them.]

XLV. [Provision for places within boroughs having no overseers.]

XLVI. [Town clerks to prepare and publish the lists of freemen.]

XLVII. [Persons omitted in the borough lists to give notice of their claims. Any person included on the list may object to the inclusion of any other name; such objections to be published.]

XLVIII. [List of liverymen of London to be transmitted to the returning officer. Notices to be given of omissions and objections in list of liverymen. Poll of liverymen to be taken at the Guildhall.]

XLIX. [Judges of Assize to name barristers, who shall revise the lists of borough voters.]

L. [Barrister to revise lists of borough voters, and upon due proof to insert and expunge names.]

LI. [Overseers and barristers to have the power to inspect tax assessments and rate books.]

LII. [Barrister, on revising the lists, to have power of adjourning, of administering oaths, etc.]

LIII. [Judges to appoint additional barristers in cases of need.]

LIV. [County lists to be transmitted to clerk of the peace. Borough lists to be kept by returning officer, and handed to successor. Lists to be copied into books, with the names numbered; such books to be the register of electors. Register to be in force for one year from the last day of October.]

LV. [Copies of the lists and of the registers to be printed for sale.]

LVI. [Expenses of overseers, clerks of the peace, etc. to be defrayed.]

LVII. [Remuneration of the barristers for revising the lists.]

LVIII. [No inquiry at the time of election except as to the identity of the voter, the continuance of his qualification, and whether he has voted before at the same election. Oath to be administered if required. No scrutiny to be allowed by returning officer.]

LIX. [Persons excluded from the register by the barrister may tender their votes at elections; tender to be recorded.]

LX. . . . Upon petition to the House of Commons, complaining of an undue election or return of any member or members to serve in Parliament, any petitioner, or any person defending such election or return, shall be at liberty to impeach the correctness of the register of voters in force at the time of such election, by proving that in consequence of the decision of the barrister who shall have revised the lists of voters from which such register shall have been formed the name of any person who voted at such election was improperly inserted or retained in such register, or the name of any persons who tendered his vote at such election improperly omitted from such register; and the Select Committee appointed for the trial of such Petition shall alter the poll taken at such election according to the truth of the case, and shall report their determination thereupon to the House, and the House shall thereupon carry such determination into effect, and the return shall be amended, or the election declared void, as the case may be, and the register corrected accordingly, or such other order shall be made as to the House shall seem proper.

LXI. [Sheriffs of the divided Counties to fix the time of, and to preside at, the elections.]

LXII. . . . . At every contested election of a Knight or Knights to serve in any future Parliament for any County, or for any Riding, parts or division of a County, the polling shall commence at 9 o'clock in the forenoon of the next day but two after the day fixed for the election, unless such next day but two shall be Saturday or Sunday, and then on the Monday following, at the principal place of election, and also at the several places to be appointed as hereinafter directed for taking polls; and such polling shall continue for two days only, such two days being successive days; (that is to say) for seven hours on the first day of polling, and for eight hours on the second day of polling; and no poll shall be kept open later than 4 o'clock in the afternoon of the second day; any Statute to the contrary notwithstanding.

LXIII. . . . . The respective counties in England and Wales, and the respective ridings, parts and divisions of counties, shall be divided into convenient districts for polling, and in each district shall be appointed a convenient place for taking the poll at all elections of a knight or knights of the shire to serve in any future parliament, and such districts and places for taking the poll shall be settled and appointed by the act to be passed in this present parliament for the purpose of settling and describing the divisions of the counties . . . provided that no county, nor any riding, parts or division of a county, shall have more than 15 districts and respective places appointed for taking the poll for such county, riding, parts or division.

LXIV. . . . . At every contested election for any County or Riding, parts or division of a County, the Sheriff, Under-Sheriff, or Sheriff's Deputy shall, if required thereto by or on behalf of any candidate, on the day fixed for the election, and if not so required may, if it shall appear to him expedient, cause to be erected a reasonable number of booths for taking the poll at the principal place of election, and also at each of the polling places so to be appointed as aforesaid, and shall cause to be affixed on the most conspicuous part of each of the said booths the names of the several parishes, townships, and places for which such booth is respectively allotted; and no person shall be admitted to vote at any such election in respect of any property situate in any parish, township or place, except at the booth so allotted for such parish, township or place, and if no booth shall be so allotted for the same, then at any of the booths for the same district; and in case any parish, township or place shall happen not to be included in any of the districts to be appointed, the votes in respect of property situate in any parish, township or place so omitted shall be taken at the principal place of election for the County or Riding, parts or division of the County, as the case may be.

LXV. [Provision as to Sheriff's deputies, the custody of poll books, and final declaration of the poll for Counties.]

LXVI. [Sheriff in County elections may act in places of exclusive jurisdiction.]

LXVII. . . . At every contested election of a member or members to serve in any future Parliament for any city or borough in England, except the borough of Monmouth, the poll shall commence on the day fixed for the election, or on the day next following, or at the latest on the third day, unless any of the said days shall be Saturday or Sunday, and then on the Monday following, the particular day for the commencement of the poll to be fixed by the returning officer; and such polling shall continue for two days only, such two days being successive days (that is to say) for seven hours on the first day of polling, and for eight hours on the second day of polling; and that the poll shall on no account be kept open later than 4 o'clock in the afternoon of such second day; any Statute to the contrary notwithstanding.

LXVIII. . . . At every contested election of a member or members to serve in any future Parliament for any city or borough in England, except the borough of Monmouth, the returning officer shall, if required thereto by or on behalf of any candidate, on the day fixed for the election, and if not so required may, if it shall appear to him expedient, cause to be erected for taking the poll at such election different booths for different parishes, districts or parts of such city or borough, which booths may be situated either in one place or in several places, and shall be so divided and allotted into compartments as to the returning officer shall seem most convenient, so that no greater number than 600 shall be required to poll at any one compartment; and the returning officer shall appoint a clerk to take the poll at each compartment, and shall cause to be affixed on the most conspicuous part of each of the said booths the names of the several parishes, districts, and parts for which such booth is respectively allotted; and no person shall be admitted to vote at any such election, except at the booth allotted for the parish, district or part wherein the property may be situate in respect of which he claims to vote, or in case he does not claim to vote in respect of property, then wherein his place of abode as described in the register may be; but in case no booth shall happen to be provided for any particular parish, district or part as aforesaid, the votes of persons voting in respect of property situate in any parish, district or part so omitted, or having their place of abode therein, may be taken at any of the said booths, and the votes of freemen residing out of the limits of the city or borough may be taken at any of the said booths: and public notice of the situation, division and allotment of the different booths shall be given two days before the commencement of the poll by the returning officer; and in case the booths shall be situated in different places, the returning officer may appoint a deputy to preside at each place; and at every such election the poll clerks at the close of each day's poll shall enclose and seal their several poll books, and shall publicly deliver them, so enclosed and sealed . . . to the persons from whom he shall have received the same; and every deputy so receiving any such poll books, on the final close of the poll shall forthwith deliver or transmit the same; so enclosed and sealed, to the returning officer, who shall receive and keep all the poll books unopened until the following day, unless such day be Sunday, and then till the Monday following, when he shall openly break the seals thereon, and cast up the number of votes as they appear on the said several books, and shall openly declare the state of the poll, and make proclamation of the member or members chosen, not later than two o'clock in the afternoon of the said day: provided always, that the returning officer or his lawful deputy may, if he think fit, declare the final state of the poll, and proceed to make the return immediately after the poll shall have been lawfully closed: provided also that no nomination shall be made or election holden of any member for any city or borough in any church, chapel or other place of public worship.

LXIX. [Polling districts to be appointed for Shoreham, Cricklade, Aylesbury and East Retford.]

LXX. . . . Nothing in this Act contained shall prevent any Sheriff or other returning officer, or the lawful deputy of any returning officer, from closing the poll previous to the expiration of the time fixed by this Act, in any case where the same might have been lawfully closed before the passing of this Act; and that where the proceedings at any election shall be interrupted or obstructed by any riot or open violence, the Sheriff or other returning officer, or the lawful deputy of any returning officer, shall not for such cause finally close the poll, but, in case the proceedings shall be so interrupted or obstructed at any particular polling place or places, shall adjourn the poll at such place or places only until the following day, and if necessary shall further adjourn the same until such interruption or obstruction shall have ceased, when the returning officer or his deputy shall again proceed to take the poll at such place or places: and any day whereon the poll shall have been so adjourned shall not, as to such place or places, be reckoned one of the two days of polling at such election within the meaning of this Act: and wherever the poll shall have been so adjourned by any deputy of any sheriff or other returning officer, such deputy shall forthwith give notice of such adjournment to the Sheriff or returning officer, who shall not finally declare the state of the poll, or make proclamation of the member or members chosen, until the poll so adjourned at such place or places as aforesaid shall have been finally closed, and delivered or transmitted to such Sheriff or other returning officer; anything hereinbefore contained to the contrary notwithstanding.

LXXI. [Candidates or persons proposing a candidate without his consent, to be at the expense of booths and poll clerks. Houses may be hired for polling in, instead of booths.]

LXXII. [Certified copies of the register of voters for each booth to be made.]

LXXIII. [Powers of deputies of returning officers.]

LXXIV. [Regulations respecting polling, etc. for the borough of Monmouth, and for the contributory boroughs in Wales.]

LXXV. [All election laws to remain in force, except where superseded by this Act.]

LXXVI. [Penalties on officers for breach of duty.]

LXXVII. [Writs, etc. to be made conformable to this Act.]

LXXVIII. Provided always . . . that nothing in this Act . . . shall extend to or in anywise affect the election of members to serve in Parliament for the Universities of Oxford or Cambridge, or shall entitle any person to vote in the election of members to serve in Parliament for the city of Oxford or town of Cambridge in respect of the occupation of any chambers or premises in any of the Colleges or Halls of the Universities of Oxford or Cambridge.

LXXX. [In case the proposed Boundary Act shall not pass before the 20th of June 1832, the preparations for first registration to be deferred; but if the Boundary Act pass after that day, the periods preparatory to and connected with the first registration to be settled by an order in council.]

LXXXI. [In case of a dissolution of parliament after the passing of the proposed Boundary Act, and before registration, the rights of voting shall take effect without registration.]

LXXXII. [In case of a dissolution of parliament before the passing of the proposed Boundary Act, Counties not to be divided.]

Schedule A. [56 boroughs ceasing to return any members]

Amersham, Wendover, Bossiney, Callington, Camelford, East Looe, Fowey, Lostwithiel, Newport, St. Germans, St. Mawes, St. Michael (Midshall), Saltash, Tregony, West Looe, Beeralston, Okehampton, Plympton, Corfe Castle, Stockbridge, Whitchurch, Newtown, Yarmouth, Weobly, Queenborough, New Romney, Newton, Castle Rising, Higham Ferrers, Brackley, Bishop's Castle, Ilchester, Milborne Port, Minehead, Aldeburgh, Dunwich, Orford, Blechingley, Gatton, Haslemere, Bramber, East Grinstead, Seaford, Steyning, Winchelsea, Appleby, Great Bedwin, Downton, Heytesbury, Hindon, Ludgershall, Old Sarum, Wootton Bassett, Aldborough, Boroughbridge, Hedon.

Schedule B. [30 boroughs to return one member only]

Wallingford, Helston, Launceston, Liskeard, St. Ives, Ashburton, Dartmouth, Lyme Regis, Shaftesbury, Wareham, Christchurch, Petersfield, Hythe, Clitheroe, Great Grimsby, Morpeth, Woodstock, Eye, Reigate, Arundel, Horsham, Midhurst, Rye, Calne, Malmesbury, Westbury, Wilton, Droitwich, Northallerton, Thirsk.

Schedule C. [22 new boroughs to return two members each]

Macclesfield, Stockport, Devonport, Sunderland, Stroud, Greenwich, Bolton, Blackburn, Manchester, Oldham, Finsbury, Marylebone, Tower Hamlets, Stoke-upon-Trent, Wolverhampton, Lambeth, Brighton, Birmingham, Bradford, Halifax, Leeds, Sheffield.

Schedule D. [20 new boroughs to return one member each]

Whitehaven, Gateshead, South Shields, Merthyr Tydvil, Cheltenham, Chatham, Ashton-under-Lyne, Bury, Rochdale, Salford, Warrington, Tynemouth, Frome, Walsall, Kendal, Dudley, Kidderminster, Huddersfield, Wakefield, Whitby.

Schedule E. Places sharing in the election of members with Shire-towns or
principal boroughs

Amlwich, Holyhead, Llangefni, sharing with Beaumaris; Aberystwyth, Adpar, Lampeter, sharing with Cardigan; Llanelly, sharing with Caermarthen; Bangor, Conway, Criccieth, Nevin, Pwllheli, sharing with Carnarvon; Cowbridge, Llantrissent, sharing with Cardiff; Holt, Ruthin, Wrexham, sharing with Denbigh; Caergwrley, Caerwis, Holywell, Mold, Overton, Rhyddlan, St. Asaph, sharing with Flint; Fishguard, Narbeth, sharing with Haverfordwest; Llanfyllin, Llanidloes, Machynlleth, Newtown, Welshpool, sharing with Montgomery; Milford, Tenby, Wiston, sharing with Pembroke; Kevinleece, Knighton, Knucklas, Rhayader, Presteigne, sharing with Radnor.

Schedule F. (Counties to be divided)

Cheshire, Cornwall, Cumberland, Derbyshire, Devonshire, Durham, Essex, Gloucestershire, Kent, Hampshire, Lancashire, Leicestershire, Norfolk, Northumberland, Northamptonshire, Nottinghamshire, Shropshire, Somersetshire, Staffordshire, Suffolk, Surrey, Sussex, Warwickshire, Wiltshire, Worcestershire.

Schedule F.2. (Counties to return three members)

Berkshire, Buckinghamshire, Cambridgeshire, Dorsetshire, Herefordshire, Hertfordshire, Oxfordshire.

Schedule G.

Cities and Towns	Counties at large in which Cities and Towns and Counties thereof are to be included
Caermarthen	Caermarthenshire
Canterbury	Kent
Chester	Chester
Coventry	Warwickshire
Gloucester	Gloucestershire
Kingston-upon-Hull	East Riding of Yorkshire
Lincoln	The Parts of Lindsey, Lincolnshire
London	Middlesex
Newcastle-upon-Tyne	Northumberland
Poole	Dorsetshire
Southampton	Hampshire
Worcester	Worcestershire
York and Ainsty	North Riding of Yorkshire

304. An Act (2 and 3 William IV, c. 65) to amend the representation of the people in Scotland, 17 July 1832)

(Statutes of the United Kingdom of Great Britain and Ireland, 2 & 3 William IV (1832),
pp. 383-435.)

Whereas the laws which regulate the election of members to serve in the Commons House of Parliament for *Scotland* are defective, whereby great inconveniences and abuses have been occasioned: and whereas it is expedient, and would be for the evident utility of the subjects within Scotland, that those defects should be remedied, and especially that members should be provided for places hitherto unrepresented, and the right of election extended to persons of property and intelligence, and that the mode of conducting elections should be better regulated and ordered: be it therefore enacted . . . that from . . . the end of this present Parliament, and in all future Parliaments to be assembled, there shall be 53 representatives returned for *Scotland* to the Commons House of Parliament, of whom 30 shall be for the several or conjoined Shires or Stewartries hereinafter enumerated, and 23 for the several cities, burghs and towns, or districts of cities, burghs and towns, hereinafter enumerated. . . .

II. . . . After the end of this present Parliament the burghs of Peebles and Selkirk shall no longer form parts of the district to which they now belong, or be entitled to contribute with any other burghs in the election of any member of Parliament, but shall, in the matter of elections, be held to be parts of the Counties of Peebles and Selkirk respectively; and in like manner that the burgh of Rothsay in the County of Bute shall no longer form part of the district to which it now belongs, but be held, in the matter of elections, to be part of the County of Bute.

III. . . . Of the 30 members hereafter to be returned to Parliament by the separate or combined Shires of Scotland, one shall always be returned by each of the separate Shires or parts of Shires enumerated in the schedule (A) hereunto annexed, and one by each of the combined Shires or parts of Shires enumerated . . . in schedule (B). . . .

IV. And be it enacted, that of the 23 members to be returned for the several or combined cities, burghs and towns of Scotland, two shall always be returned by each of the separate cities burghs and towns enumerated . . . in schedule (C) . . ., one by each of the separate cities, burghs and towns enumerated . . . in schedule (D) . . ., and one by each of the districts or sets of cities, burghs and towns enumerated . . . in schedule (E). . . .

VI. . . . No person shall acquire, by succession, purchase, gift or otherwise, the right of voting for a member of Parliament . . . except by one or other of the qualifications hereinafter prescribed . . . provided always that all persons who at the passing of this Act shall be lawfully on the roll of freeholders of any Shire in *Scotland* . . . shall so long as they retain the necessary qualification . . . be entitled to be registered and to vote . . . in the election of a member for such Shire.

VII. . . . Every person, not subject to any legal incapacity, shall be entitled to be registered as hereinafter directed, and thereafter to vote at any election for a Shire in *Scotland*, who, when the sheriff proceeds to consider his claim for registration in the present or in any future year, shall have been, for a period of not less than six calendar months next previous to the last day of August in the present or the last day of July in any future year, the owner . . . of any lands, houses, feu duties, or other heritable subjects (except debts heritably secured) within the said Shire, provided the subject or subjects on which he so claims shall be of the yearly value of £10. . . .

VIII. [Rule as to life-renters and fiars and joint owners] . . . Husbands shall be entitled to vote in respect of property belonging to their wives, or owned . . . by such husbands after the death of their wives. . . .

IX. . . . Tenants in lands, houses or other heritable subjects shall also be entitled to be registered, and to vote at elections for the Shires . . . provided each tenant . . . shall, for a period of not less than 12 months next previous to the last day of August in the present or the last day of July in any future year, have held such subjects or tenements, whether in his personal possession or not, under a lease . . . missive of lease, or other written title, for a period of not less than 57 years (exclusive of breaks) at the option of the landlord, or for the lifetime of the said tenant, where the clear yearly value of such tenant's interest, after paying the rent . . . is not less than £10, or for a period of not less than 19 years where the clear yearly value of such tenant's interest is not less than £50, or where such tenant shall, for the foresaid period of 12 months, have been in the actual personal occupancy of any such subject, where the yearly rent is not less than £50, or where the tenant, whatever the rent may be, has truly paid for his interest in such subject a price, grassum, or consideration of not less than £300. . . .

X. [The right of voting for burghs and towns no longer to be in town councils and delegates, but in qualified inhabitants.]

XI. [Occupants of houses, warehouses, shops or other buildings worth £10 a year, to be entitled to vote in cities, burghs and towns.] Provided . . . that no such person shall be entitled to be registered or to vote . . . unless he shall have resided for six calendar months next previous to the last day of August in the present or the last day of July in any future year within such city, burgh or town, or within seven statute miles of some part thereof. . . . No person shall be entitled to be registered or to vote for any city, burgh or town, who shall have been in the receipt of parochial relief within 12 calendar months . . . next previous to the last day of July. . . .

XIV. [Sheriffs to hold courts to examine and decide upon the merits of all claims for registration within their Counties.]

XV. [Claims for votes in burghs, etc. to be given in to the town clerk.]

XVI. [Lists to be published by, and objections lodged with, the town clerks.]

XVII–XXI. [Procedure for the hearing of claims and objections, and the completion of registers.]

XXII. [Sheriffs shall annually revise and correct their registers.]

XXIII–XXV. [Procedure for appeals against the Sheriffs' decisions or claims and objections.]

XXVI. [Registered voters only, to be allowed to vote.]

XXVII. [Sheriffs shall divide their Counties into districts for polling, and appoint polling places–not more than 15 for any one County] . . . and shall be so arranged as that no more than 600 persons or thereabouts shall poll . . . at any one place. . . . [Each town clerk shall similarly appoint polling places in cities and burghs. Voters to poll in the district where the property which gives the qualification lies.]

XXVIII. [Writs to be addressed to Sheriffs, who shall fix and notify the day of election.]

XXIX–XXX. [Order of proceedings at elections for Counties, cities, burghs and towns.]

XXXII. [Polls to be kept open for only two days.]

XXXIII–XXXIV. [Returns of members elected for Counties and burghs to be made by the sheriff.]

XXXV. [Voters in burghs not to vote in the County where the burgh is situated, and vice versa.]

XXXVI. [No Sheriff or Deputy, nor Town Clerk or Deputy, to vote or be elected at any election for the County or burgh where he holds office; no Sheriff Substitute, Sheriff Clerk, or Town Clerk to act as agent for any candidate in the County or burgh in which he holds office.]

XXXVII. [Eldest sons of Scottish peers shall be entitled to be registered and to vote at elections, and shall also be entitled to serve as members for any County, city, burgh or town or district of burghs in Scotland.] . . . After the end of this present Parliament no member for any County in *Scotland* shall be required to be qualified as an elector or to hold any superiority within such County.

Schedule (A). *Counties to return one member each*

Aberdeen, Argyll, Ayr, Banff, Bute, Berwick, Caithness, Dumbarton, Dumfries, Edinburgh, Fife, Forfar, Haddington, Inverness, Kincardine, Kirkcudbright, Lanark, Linlithgow, Orkney and Shetland, Peebles, Perth, Renfrew, Roxburgh, Selkirk, Stirling, Sutherland, Wigton.

Schedule (B). *Combined counties, each two to return one member*

Elgin and Nairn; Ross and Cromarty; Clackmannan and Kinross.

Schedule (C). *Towns to return two members each*

Edinburgh, Glasgow.

Schedule (D). *Towns to return one member each*

Aberdeen, Paisley, Dundee, Greenock, Perth.

Schedule (E). *Combined burghs and towns, each set or district jointly to return one member*

1. Kirkwall, Wick, Dornock, Dingwall, Tain, Cromarty.
2. Fortrose, Inverness, Nairn, Forres.
3. Elgin, Cullen, Banff, Inverury, Kintore, Peterhead.
4. Inverbervie, Montrose, Aberbrothwick, Brechin, Forfar.
5. Cupar, St. Andrews, Anstruther Easter, Anstruther Wester, Crail, Kilrenny, Pittenweem.
6. Dysart, Kirkaldy, Kinghorn, Burntisland.
7. Inverkeithing, Dunfermline, Queensferry, Culross, Stirling.
8. Renfrew, Rutherglen, Dumbarton, Kilmarnock, Port Glasgow.
9. Haddington, Dunbar, North Berwick, Lauder, Jedburgh.
10. Leith, Portobello, Musselburgh.
11. Linlithgow, Lanark, Falkirk, Airdrie, Hamilton.

12. Ayr, Irvine, Campbelltown, Inverary, Oban.
13. Dumfries, Sanquhar, Annan, Lochmaben, Kirkcudbright.
14. Wigton, New Galloway, Stranraer, Whithorn.

305. An Act (2 and 3 William IV, c. 88) to amend the Representation of the People of Ireland, 7 Aug. 1832

(*Statutes of the United Kingdom of Great Britain and Ireland,* 2 & 3 *William IV* (1832), pp. 529–554.)

Whereas it is expedient to extend the elective franchise to many of his majesty's subjects in *Ireland* who have not heretofore enjoyed the same, and to increase the number of representatives for certain cities and boroughs in that part of the United Kingdom, and to diminish the expenses of elections therein; be it therefore enacted . . . that, in addition to the persons now by law qualified to vote at the election of Knights of the Shire . . . every male person of full age, and not subject to any legal incapacity, who shall be entitled, either as lessee or assignee, to any lands or tenements, whether of freehold or of any other tenure whatever, for the unexpired residue . . . of any term originally created for a period of not less than 60 years, whether determinable on a life . . . or not, and having a beneficial interest therein of the clear yearly value of not less than £10 . . . or for the unexpired residue . . . of any term originally created for a period of not less than 14 years . . . and having a beneficial interest therein of the clear yearly value of not less than £20 . . . or for the unexpired residue . . . of any term originally created for a period of not less than 20 years, and having a beneficial interest therein of the clear yearly value of not less than £10 . . . shall be entitled to vote in the election of a Knight or Knights of the Shire for the County in which such lands or tenements shall respectively be situate. . . .

II. . . . Every male person of full age, and not subject to any legal incapacity, who shall be seised at law or in equity of any lands or tenements of copyhold tenure, for his life, or for the life of another, or for any lives whatsoever, or for any larger estate, of the clear yearly value of not less than £10 . . . shall be entitled to vote in the election of a Knight . . . of the Shire . . . for the County in which such lands or tenements shall be respectively situate.

III. . . . Nothing in this Act contained shall take away . . . the rights of voting for Knights of the Shire at present enjoyed by . . . any person by virtue of any Law now in force, except so far as herein specially provided.

V. . . . In every city or town, being a County of a city or County of a town by itself, and which shall return a member or members to serve in any future Parliament, in addition to the persons now by law qualified to vote . . . every male person of full age, and not subject to any legal incapacity, who shall be seised at law or in equity of any freehold estate in any lands or tenements within such city or town, and shall be in the actual occupation thereof, and who shall have a beneficial interest therein of the clear yearly value of £10 . . . or who shall hold as lessee or assignee any lands or tenements within such city or town, for such term, of such value, and subject to such provisions as would under this Act, if such lands or tenements were situate in a County at large without the limits of such city or town, entitle such person to register his vote for such County, or who shall hold and occupy within such city or town, as tenant or owner, any house, warehouse, counting-house, or shop, which, either separately, or jointly with any land within such city or town occupied therewith by him as tenant under the same landlord, or occupied therewith by him as owner, shall be *bonâ-fide* of the clear yearly value of not less than £10, shall, if duly registered according to the provisions of this Act, be entitled to vote in the election of a member . . . to serve . . . for such city or town: provided always, that no such occupier . . . shall be admitted to be registered . . . unless he shall have occupied such premises . . . for six calendar months next previous to the time of his registry, nor unless such occupier shall have paid or discharged all such grand jury and municipal cesses, rates and taxes, if any, as shall have become legally due and payable by him in respect of such premises, over and above and except one half year's amount of such cesses, rates and taxes. . . .

VI. [No freehold of less than £10 yearly value to give a vote in a city or town, saving of registered 40s. freeholders now entitled to vote.]

VII. [Right of voting in boroughs to be enjoyed by occupiers of houses, etc. of the annual value of £10.]

IX. [Freemen now entitled to vote in borough elections, and persons who may in future be admitted to their freedom, to continue to exercise the franchise provided they reside within 7 miles and are registered; no person admitted as honorary freeman after 13 March 1831 to be entitled to vote.]

XI. . . . The city of Limerick, the city of Waterford, the borough of Belfast, the County of the town of Galway, and the University of Dublin shall each respectively return one member . . . in addition to the member which each of the said places is now by law entitled to return.

XII. [Boundaries of boroughs, etc. to be defined by an Act to be passed in the present parliament.]

XIII. [No unregistered persons to vote. Six months possession required before registry.]

XIV. [A special session for registering voters to be held for each County, city, town and borough, at such days and places as the lord lieutenant shall appoint.]

XV–XLVI. [Procedure for registration, hearing of claims and objections, etc.]

XLVIII. [Candidates, or any person proposing a candidate without his consent, to bear the expense of booths and poll clerks.]

LI. [Two or more polling places to be provided where the voters shall exceed 600.]

LII. . . . No poll shall continue more than five days . . . (*Sunday, Christmas Day,* and *Good Friday* always excepted). . . .

LIII. [Poll to close when no more than 20 persons have polled during the day.]

LX. [Right of voting in the University of Dublin continued to all Fellows and Scholars so long as their names are kept on the books of the University.]

LXIII. . . . No clergyman shall be permitted to vote as such at any election . . . unless his name shall have been duly registered as a freeholder under this Act.

Part III

THE ADMINISTRATION OF JUSTICE

Introduction

THE classical theory of the eighteenth-century Constitution postulated the existence of three independent branches of government; the separation of powers and the machinery of checks and balances was designed to ensure liberty by preventing the concentration of executive, legislative and judicial functions in any one hand. In fact, as the Introductions to Sections I and II have shown, the smooth working of this Constitution depended on the development of 'conventions' which linked together administration and Parliament so that, while retaining their separate identity, Executive and Legislature co-operated harmoniously. The third branch—the Judiciary—was separated from the control of the Crown by the Act of Settlement (1701), which laid down that the appointment of judges was to be terminable only by joint address of the two Houses with the concurrence of the sovereign. This prevented him from dismissing judges who gave decisions (as in the Wilkes cases of 1763–1765) which were distasteful to the government. But though judges were thus freed from the peril of disciplinary action for their verdicts, their appointment remained a royal prerogative and therefore subject to political interference. Jobbery was particularly rife in Ireland despite Pitt's efforts,[1] but Brougham complained in 1828 that appointments to the Bench in England and Wales were too often determined by political interest rather than by professional merit.[2] Brougham's great speech on the defects of the Common Law Courts emphasized also the petty tyranny that might be exercised by the justices of the peace, representatives of the propertied classes set to judge offences against property. Whig purists, maintaining that even in Blackstone's time the powers of the justices were greater than they should have been (and during the remaining decades of the century these powers were being enlarged) particularly objected to continued inroads on the privileges of Englishmen by statute. Various Acts of Parliament were empowering the magistrates to try offences summarily and to inflict prison sentences (with hard labour), thus denying the accused the right to trial by jury.

The punishment of offenders against the criminal laws was notoriously brutal. Hanging, transportation and various forms of corporal punishment were inflicted, even on women,[3] for petty offences, while the appalling state of the prisons[4] would have vitiated any attempt to use imprisonment as a means of reformation. As Peel recognized when Home Secretary,[5] living conditions were such for the criminal classes that it was difficult to inflict on a prisoner a worse standard than he had enjoyed as a free man without exposing him to almost certain death from starvation or disease. The most frequently inflicted punishment was transportation, for seven or fourteen years or for life,[6] but all too often the judges had no alternative but to

[1] No. 306. [2] No. 308. [3] No. 325. [4] Nos. 314–316. [5] No. 319. [6] See Section VII.

pronounce sentence of death for relatively trivial offences. This severity originated less in inhumanity than in insecurity; the lack of an efficient system of police had led to attempts at deterrence by capital punishment for almost all crimes against person or property.

Until Peel's creation of the Metropolitan Police for the London area, such police duties as were performed in and outside the capital were the responsibility of the parishes, loosely supervised by the justices.[1] In times of popular disturbance this had to be supplemented by voluntary associations of householders[2] or by the calling in of troops, who were needed even for the suppression of election riots.[3] Information was gathered and sent to the Home Office by the magistrates through a system of spies,[4] whose activities often made a bad situation worse, but whose use proved necessary even to the reforming Secretary Peel.[5] His reform of the police of London[6] proved so successful, however, that it became the model for imitation by provincial authorities during the next half-century.

In the meantime the result of the severity of the eighteenth century was to deter the injured from prosecuting, juries from convicting, or the Crown from confirming the sentence, and thus to encourage crime by holding out to the criminal a substantial hope of immunity. It was on the ground of this inefficacy that the law reformers presented their case.[7] None wished to abolish the death penalty entirely; their concern was to make it a real deterrent by limiting its application to offences where public opinion would permit it to be enforced.[8] The statistics for the last twenty-one years of the period show that, of every 13 criminals sentenced to death in England and Wales, only 1 was executed–a total of 1,690 executed out of 22,066 sentenced to death.[9] Mackintosh pointed out in 1819 that in 170 out of the 200 capital felonies on the statute book not one conviction had taken place in England and Wales for thirty years; the committee whose appointment he carried against the government recommended the abolition or modification of the punishment of a proportion of these offences,[10] but to little avail against the prejudices and fears of politicians, judges and propertied men who argued that the relaxation of the extreme penalties of the law would lead to uncontrollable violence. This was soon shown to be false by Peel's reform of the criminal code, a process unspectacular in execution, but dramatic in effect; it enabled crime to be more effectively controlled and punished in an age which lived on the edge of violence, and it brought the law more closely into accord with the state of public opinion as influenced by the reformers, so helping to restore that necessary respect without which the law, however severely enforced, must be ineffective. The work of Bentham, Romilly and Mackintosh showed but meagre results in the statute book but was of the most profound importance: it enabled England, through the exertions of the existing governing class rather than by violent revolution, to make the transition from the hard, often merciless, loosely organized eighteenth century to the more humanitarian and closely knit society of the later age: it helped to develop in England that Victorian phenomenon, a social conscience.

[1] No. 309.　　[2] No. 310.　　[3] Section II, No. 283.　　[4] No. 311.　　[5] No. 312.
[6] No. 313.　　[7] Nos. 323–326.　　[8] No. 321.　　　　　　　[9] No. 317.　　[10] No. 322.

BIBLIOGRAPHY

The most comprehensive bibliographical aids are *Sweet and Maxwell's Complete Law Book Catalogue*, edited by L. F. Maxwell, vols. II (1651–1800) and III (1801–1932) and supplements, Sir William Holdsworth, *The Sources and Literature of English Law* (Oxford, 1928), and P. H. Winfield, *The Chief Sources of English Legal History* (Cambridge, Mass., 1925).

The primary sources consist principally of Official Returns and Reports of Committees, the Parliamentary Debates, and the writings of contemporary law reformers. The most important of the numerous reports of the period are the inquiries into the Court of Chancery (*Parliamentary Papers*, 1810–1811, vol. III, and 1812, vol. II), into the Courts of Common Law (1829, vol. IX; 1830, vol. XI; 1831, vol. X; 1831–1832, vol. XXV; 1833, vol. XXII; and 1834, vol. XXVII), into Imprisonment for Debt in 1792 (*Journals of the House of Commons*, XLVII, p. 640) and Transportation (*ibid.*, XL (1785), pp. 954 and 1161, and *Parliamentary Papers*, 1812, vol. II). There were Committees on the Game Laws in 1816 (*Parliamentary Papers*, 1816, vol. IV), 1823 (*ibid.*, 1823, vol. IV) and 1828 (*ibid.*, 1828, vol. VIII), on the Administration of Justice in Wales in 1817 (*ibid.*, 1817, vol. V) and 1821 (*ibid.*, 1821, vol. IV). Valuable evidence on the causes of crime was presented by the Select Committees on the increase of Commitments and Convictions (*ibid.*, 1826–1827, vol. VI, and 1828, vol. VI), and there are reports on the jails of England and Wales (1819, vol. VII (including an account of the convict settlements in Australia), and 1819, vol. XVII), of Great Britain (1821, vol. XXI), and of the City of London (1813–1814, vol. IV, and 1814–1815, vol. IV). All the debates on the subject reported in the *Parliamentary History* and *Parliamentary Debates* between 1785 and 1832, and all references in the journals of the two Houses, are listed in L. Radzinowicz, *A History of English Criminal Law*, I (1948), pp. 753–760.

Bentham's influential writings on law and punishment are best studied in Sir John Bowring's edition of the *Works* (11 vols., 1838–1843). Sir Samuel Romilly's *Memoirs* (1840, 3 vols.) present a vivid picture of the state of the criminal law and the obstacles to reform. His most influential publication was *Observations on the Criminal Law of England* (2nd edition, 1811), reviewed by Brougham in *Edinburgh Review*, XIX (1811–1812), p. 389. Other valuable contemporary works are P. Colquhoun, *A Treatise on the Police of the Metropolis* (1795), Sir Thomas Fowell Buxton, *An Enquiry, whether Crime and Misery are produced or prevented, by our present System of Prison Discipline* (1818), and Mrs. E. G. Fry, *Observations on the Visiting, Superintendence, and Government of Female Prisoners* (1827).

The principal secondary works are Sir W. Holdsworth, *A History of English Law* (13 vols. 1923–1952), A. V. Dicey, *Law and Public Opinion in England* (2nd edition, 1930), Sir James Stephen, *History of Criminal Law* (3 vols., 1883), and the authoritative L. Radzinowicz, *A History of English Criminal Law* (3 vols., 1948–1956). Shorter sketches are R. S. E. Hind, *The British Penal System, 1773–1950* (1951), and E. Jenks, *A Short History of English Law* (1912). On police, see W. L. M. Lee, *A History of Police in England* (1901) and the standard works, C. Reith, *The Police Idea: its history and evolution in England in the eighteenth century* (Oxford, 1938), and *A Short History of the British Police* (Oxford, 1948).

Studies of the great legal figures and reformers include Campbell, *Lives of the Chief Justices of England* (3rd edition, 1874), C. G. Oakes, *Sir Samuel Romilly* (1935), lives of Jeremy Bentham by C. M. Atkinson (1905), C. K. Ogden (1932), and J. L. Stocks (1933), and C. Phillipson, *Three Criminal Law Reformers, Beccaria, Bentham, Romilly* (1923). There is a valuable symposium on *Jeremy Bentham and the Law*, edited by G. W. Keeton and G. Schwarzenberger (1948).

A. THE COURTS

306. Charles Long to Sir A. Wellesley (Irish Secretary), 24 Oct. 1807

(*Wellington MSS.*)

Long had been Irish Secretary, 1805–1806. As Sir Laurence Parsons and M.P. for the King's County, Lord Rosse had been a Lord of the Treasury in Ireland since 1805. In 1807 he returned three members to the House of Commons. Rosse's brother never became a judge of the High Court in Ireland.

. . . You showed me a letter from Lord Rosse when you was [*sic*] in town, upon the same subject on which he, Lord Rosse, had written to me relative to placing his brother, who is at the Bar, upon the Bench. Lord Rosse always supported zealously Mr. Pitt's Government, and his brother, I believe, from his standing and eminence at the Bar, has pretensions to what he aspires to, but when I went to Ireland I was particularly enjoined by Mr. Pitt not to make any promise either for the Bench of Bishops or of Judges, and he said of the latter particularly, he was determined that none in future should be made except those who should really have, not good pretensions but the best, and in which the Chancellor's opinion ought almost entirely to decide, and that whoever was raised to the Bench should be so raised totally independent of political interests. He said he felt this due to Ireland, and spoke most decidedly and emphatically upon the subject. . . .

307. Fox's Libel Act, 1792 (32 Geo. III, c. 60)

(*Statutes at Large*, XXXVII, pp. 627–628.)

This Act made an important change, not in the law of libel but in its administration, by allowing the jury to pronounce a general verdict. During the eighteenth century the jury had been empowered to decide only the fact of publication and the truth of the innuendo; whether the publication was libellous had been the province of the judge as being a matter of law, not of fact.

Whereas doubts have arisen whether on the trial of an indictment or information for the making or publishing any libel, where an issue or issues are joined between the King and the defendant or defendants, on the plea of not guilty pleaded, it be competent to the jury impanelled to try the same to give their verdict upon the whole matter in issue; be it therefore declared and enacted . . . that, on every such trial, the jury sworn to try the issue may give a general verdict of guilty or not guilty upon the whole matter put in issue upon such indictment or information; and shall not be required or directed, by the court or judge before whom such indictment or information shall be tried, to find the defendant or defendants guilty, merely on the proof of the publication by such defendant or defendants of the paper charged to be a libel, and of the sense ascribed to the same in such indictment or information.
II. Provided always, that, on every such trial, the Court or Judge before whom such indictment or information shall be tried, shall, according to their or his discretion,

give their or his opinion and directions to the jury on the matter in issue between the King and the defendant or defendants, in like manner as in other criminal cases.

III. Provided also, that nothing herein contained shall extend, or be construed to extend, to prevent the jury from finding a special verdict, in their discretion, as in other criminal cases.

IV. Provided also, that in case the jury shall find the defendant or defendants guilty, it shall and may be lawful for the said defendant or defendants to move in arrest of judgement, on such ground and in such manner as by law he or they might have done before the passing of this Act; any thing herein contained to the contrary notwithstanding.

308. Brougham's speech in the House of Commons on the state of the Courts of Common Law, 7 Feb. 1828

(Hansard's *Parliamentary Debates*, New Series, XVIII, 127–247.)

Brougham's great speech on the defects of the Common Law took six hours to deliver, and, according to *The Times*, was received throughout with "respectful silence and unbroken attention".

. . . I stand engaged to bring before you the whole state of the common law of this country; the common law I call it (in contradistinction to equity), with the view of pointing out those defects which may have existed in its original construction, or which time may have engendered, as well as of considering the remedies appropriate to correct them. . . .

The great object of every Government, in electing the Judges of the land, should be to obtain the most skilful and learned men in their profession, and at the same time, the men whose character gives the best security for the pure and impartial administration of justice. . . . Our system of judicial promotion sins in both these particulars. Government ought to fill the Bench with men taken from among the most learned lawyers and most accomplished advocates. . . . The office of Judge is one of so important and responsible a nature, that one should suppose the members of Government would naturally require that they should be at liberty to make their selection from the whole field of the profession. . . . There is a custom . . . that party as well as merit must be studied in these appointments. One half of the bar is thus excluded from the competition, for no man can be a Judge who is not of a particular party. . . . Unless his party happen to be the party connected with the Crown, or allied with the Ministry of the day, there is no chance for him. . . . No one may hope to fill that dignified office unless he belongs to the side on which courtly favour shines; his seat on the Bench must depend, generally speaking, on his supporting the leading principles of the existing Administration. In Scotland, it is true, a more liberal policy has been adopted, and the right hon. gent. opposite [Peel] has done himself great honour by recommending Mr. Gillies, Mr. Cranstoun (now Lords Gillies and Carrhouse) and Mr. Clerk (Lord Eldin) all as well known for party men there as Lord Eldon is here. Two other instances should be added–the Lord Chief Commissioner [Wm. Adam] who has had the signal happiness of presiding over the introduction of jury trial into his native country, and Mr. Cathcart and Lord Alloway; though, unfortunately, their party has been what is now termed, the wrong side. . . .

Let me not be supposed to blame one party more than another; I speak of the practice of all Governments in this country; and I believe, when the Whigs were in office, in 1806, they did not promote to the Bench any of their political opponents. They had no vacancies in Westminster Hall to fill up, but in the Welsh Judicature they pursued the accustomed course. . . .

Is it a fit thing, I ask, now, when popery is no longer cherished or even respected, indeed hardly tolerated, among us–that one of its worst practices should remain, the appointment of some of the most eminent Judges in the Civil Law Courts by prelates of the Church? . . . I speak of all those who preside in the Consistorial Courts–who determine the most grave and delicate questions of spiritual law, marriage and divorce, and may decide on the disposition by will of all the personalty in the kingdom. Is it a fit thing that the Judges in these most important matters should be appointed, not by the Crown, not by removable and responsible officers of the Crown–but by the Archbishop of Canterbury and Bishop of London? . . . So it is in the Province of York, where the Judges are appointed by the Archbishop; so in all other Consistorial Courts, where the Judges are appointed by the Bishops of the respective dioceses in which they are situated. . . .

I next come to speak of the Privy Council: a very important judicature, and of which the members discharge as momentous duties as any of the Judges of this country, having to determine not only upon questions of colonial law in plantation cases, but to sit also as Judges, in the last resort, of all prize causes. . . . They hear and decide upon all our plantation appeals. They are thus made the supreme Judges, in the last resort, over every one of our foreign settlements, whether situated in those immense territories which you possess in the east, where you and a trading Company together rule over not less than seventy millions of subjects; or are established among those rich and populous islands which stud the Indian ocean and form the great eastern archipelago. . . . It is obvious that, from the mere distance of those colonies, and the immense variety of matters arising in them, foreign to our habits, and beyond the scope of our knowledge, any judicial tribunal in this country must, of necessity, be an extremely inadequate court of review. But what adds incredibly to the difficulty is, that hardly any two of the colonies can be named which have the same law; and in the greater number the law is wholly unlike our own. . . . The Privy Council, which ought to be held more regularly than any other court, sits far less constantly than any, having neither a regular bench nor a regular bar. It only meets on certain extraordinary days–the 30th of January, the Feast of the Purification, some day in May, midsummer day, and a few others. I find, on an average of twelve years, ending 1826, it sat in each year nine days, to dispose of all the appeals from all the British subjects in India; from our own civil courts, to the jurisdiction of which all our subjects are locally amenable, throughout the wide extent of the several Presidencies of Calcutta, Bombay and Madras. . . . But in the same nine days are to be disposed of, all the appeals from Ceylon, the Mauritius, the Cape, and New Holland; from our colonies in the West Indies and in North America. . . .

I now, Sir, come to the administration of law in the country, by justices of peace. . . . I cannot help thinking it worth inquiry whether some amendment might not be made in our justice of peace system. The first doubt which strikes me is, if it be fit that they should be appointed as they are, merely by the Lords Lieutenant of Counties, without the interference of the Crown's responsible Ministers. It is true that the Lord Chancellor issues the commission, but it is the Lord Lieutenant who designates the persons to be comprehended in it. Such a thing is hardly ever known as any interference with respect to those individuals on the part of the Lord Chancellor. He looks to the Lord Lieutenant, or rather to the Custos Rotulorum, which the Lord Lieutenant most frequently is (indeed everywhere but in Counties Palatine) for the names of proper persons . . . I have very great doubts as to the expediency of making clergymen magistrates. . . . There are some Lords Lieutenant, I know, who make it a rule never to appoint a clergyman to the magistracy; and I entirely agree in the policy of that course, because the education and the habits of such gentlemen are seldom of a worldly description, and therefore, by no means qualify them to discharge the duties of such an office; but, generally speaking . . . through the country the practice is far otherwise. Again, some Lords Lieutenant appoint men for their political opinions–some for activity as partisans in local contests. . . . Appointed, then, by irresponsible advisers, and irremovable without a conviction, let us now see what is the authority of men so chosen and so secure.

In the first place, they have the privilege of granting or withholding licences. . . . It is in their absolute power to give a licence to one of the most unfit persons possible; and it is in their power to refuse a licence to one of the most fit persons possible. . . . Who does not know . . . that licences are granted, and refused, from election motives? . . . Nor is the licensing power of the magistracy that in which alone great abuses exist. They prevail wheresoever their authority is exercised: in the commitments for offences against the game-laws, in dealing with petty offences against property, in taking cognizance of little assaults, especially on officers, in summary convictions for non-payment of tithes, and a number of other matters affecting the liberties and property of the subject. . . .

There is not a worse constituted tribunal on the face of the earth, not before the Turkish Cadi, than that at which summary convictions on the game-laws take place; I mean a bench or a brace of sporting justices. I am far from saying that, on such subjects, they are actuated by corrupt motives, but they are undoubtedly instigated by their abhorrence of that *caput lupinum* . . . a poacher. From their decisions on those points, where their passions are the most likely to mislead them, no appeal in reality lies. . . . Equally supreme are they in cases where sitting in a body at Quarter Sessions, they decide upon the most important rights of liberty and property. Let it be remembered that they can sentence to almost unlimited imprisonment, to whipping, to fine, nay, to transportation for seven and fourteen years. I have shuddered to see the way in which these extensive powers are sometimes exercised by a jurisdiction not responsible for its acts. . . . We are told that we cannot visit them severely, or even watch them very strictly, because they volunteer their duty and receive no remuneration for their trouble. But although they have no money for it, they may have money's worth. Cheap justice, sir, is a very good thing, but costly justice is much better than cheap injustice. If I saw clearly the means by which the magistrates could be paid, and by which, therefore, a more correct discharge of the magisterial duties might be insured, I would certainly prefer paying them in money to allowing them to receive money's worth by jobs and other violations of their duty. . . . It is through the magistracy more than through any other agency–except, indeed, that of the tax-gatherer –that the people are brought directly into contact with the government of the country. . . .

. . . The first inquiry that meets us is, by what means unnecessary litigation may be prevented; in other words, suits unjustly and frivolously brought, and wrongfully defended, by oppressive or intemperate parties. . . . The first and most obvious step is to remove the encouragement given to rich and litigious suitors, by lessening the expense of all legal proceedings; and I would put an end to all harassing and unjust defences, by encouraging expedition. Next, I would not allow of any action or proceeding which only profits the Court and the practitioners, and the object of which is always granted as a mere matter of course; all things should be considered as done at once and for nothing, which may now be done on a simple application to the Court with some delay and expense. Thirdly, no party should be sent to two Courts where one is able to afford him his whole remedy; nor to a dear and bad Court, when he can elsewhere have a cheaper and a better remedy; nor should anyone be obliged to come twice over to the same Court for different portions of his remedy, which he might have all in one proceeding. Fourthly, whenever a strong presumption of right appears on the part of a plaintiff, the burden of disputing his claim should be thrown on the defendant. This I would extend to such cases as bills of exchange, bonds, mortgages and other such securities. In those cases I think the plaintiff should be allowed to have his judgment, upon due notice given, unless good cause be, in the first instance, shown to the contrary, and security given to prosecute a suit for setting the instrument aside. This is a mode well known in the law of Scotland, and would put an end to all those undefended causes which are now attended with such great and useless expense, as well as injurious delay to the parties. Fifthly, I would suggest that in all cases where future suits are to be apprehended, proceeding might be adopted immediately to raise the question, and quiet the title. . . . Sixthly, I would abolish all obsolete proceedings, which serve only as a trap to the unwary, or tools in the hands of litigious and dishonest parties, and lie hid or unheeded until, unexpectedly, they are brought forth to work injustice. . . .

. . . The County Courts ought to be diligently reformed–their process extended to matters of a larger amount, and of greater variety–their officers rendered more able and effective. This improvement of itself would greatly diminish the number of trifling suits brought into the higher judicatures. . . . An extension and improvement of arbitration is one of the remedies I have ventured to suggest, at least for further discussion. If arbitrators were publicly appointed before whom parties themselves might go in the first instance, state their grounds of contention, and hear the calm opinion of able and judicious men, upon their own statements, their anger would often be cooled, and their confidence abated, so as to do each other justice without any expense or delay. . . .

In pursuing the course which I now invite you to enter upon, I avow that I look for the co-operation of the King's Government. . . . Whether I have the support of the Ministers or no–to the House I look with confident expectation that it will control them and assist me; if I go too far, checking my progress–if too fast, abating my speed–but heartily and honestly helping me in the best and greatest work which the hands of the law-giver can undertake. The course is clear before us; the race is glorious to run. You have the power of sending your name down through all times, illustrated by deeds of higher fame and more useful import, than ever were done within these walls. . . . It was the boast of Augustus–it formed part of the lustre in which the perfidies of his earlier years were lost–that he found Rome of brick, and left it of marble; a praise not unworthy a great Prince, and to which the present reign is not without claims. But how much nobler will be our Sovereign's boast when he shall have it to say that he found law dear, and left it cheap; found it a sealed book–left it a living letter; found it the patrimony of the rich–left it the inheritance of the poor; found it the two-edged sword of craft and oppression–left it the staff of honesty and the shield of innocence. . . .

B. THE ORGANIZATION OF POLICE

309. Sir Nathaniel Conant, Chief Magistrate at Bow Street, on the state of the Police in London, 1816

(Minutes of evidence taken before a select committee of the House of Commons on the state of the Police of the Metropolis (1816), pp. 1–36.)

[The attendance of the three Bow Street magistrates] . . . There is an attendance, all night as well as all day, of certain police officers and constables, to be ready if any disturbance of the public peace occurs. . . . The office opens with the clerks and officers at ten in the morning, and earlier if circumstances require; the Magistrates make a point of being there about eleven, the clerks having prepared matters which are to come before them. . . . One [magistrate] engages himself to be there on each day, at the hours that are named.

How long do they sit? They sit much oftener till near four o'clock than any other hour; but three is the nominal time, if the business is entirely done. They return at seven; but if there is any pressing occasion, or any expectation of urgent business, the magistrates always go to the office without regard to the hour. . . . He leaves the office soon after eight, if there is no business expected: but before the magistrate leaves the office in the evening, enquiry is made at the public theatres and other places, whether everything is quiet; if not, he stays till twelve o'clock, or all night, if necessary. . . . There are three Justices, and we take two days a week each. In case of the illness of any one, the others take his turn; and during any short vacation, the two magistrates agree to accommodate the third by taking his duty during his absence. We are subject to no positive regulations; but take the attendance always with a view to the public exigency. I have been myself, in times of riot and disturbance, in constant attendance, both night and day, for a fortnight together, without ever seeing my own house. . . .

What number of regular police officers have you in your establishment? There are eighty-seven patrols attached to the office, and thirteen conductors of that patrol, making together one hundred patrols; and eight police officers besides, who have general duties.

Have these conductors any profits in the nature of a share of the rewards on convictions? Nothing from the establishment at all; but in common with other persons who are within the distribution of rewards upon conviction by Act of Parliament, they, for a person they may have apprehended in the course of their duty, would, from the Judges at the time of the trial, receive a certificate for the rewards which the Acts of Parliament give them. . . . We allow, in another way, all the patrol attached to the office, 5s. a day for their trouble in attending Courts of Justice to give evidence, and for special duty in the day; . . .

Have the police officers any profits arising from being employed by individuals for the detection of robberies committed? Yes. . . . They are paid by the parties themselves, subject, sometimes, to a reference to the Magistrates; but in general the parties themselves induce the officers to assist them in their objects, and they pay them according to their private dispositions. . . .

Is the establishment at Bow-street to be considered as a central establishment for the Metropolis, or a police establishment connected with all parts of the kingdom? . . . Our legal powers are confined to the county of Middlesex, and neighbourhood of the Metropolis, but we extend our endeavours towards the preservation of the public peace, and the apprehending of felons, to every part of the kingdom, whenever it is found desirable.

Do you keep a constant correspondence with the seven public offices, and with the City establishments of police, in respect of the police of the metropolis? We have communications upon all the pressing occasions, but not as to lesser offences, or by any regular system.

Does the Bow-street office act independently of those offices, and do they all act independently of each other? They all act independently of each other, except where special circumstances may call for general co-operation.

Your office communicates with the Secretary of State on any public matter? I personally do every day; and indeed all the police offices communicate to the Secretary of State all matters of deep public interest.

Do you not think that it would be a great improvement in the police establishment of the metropolis, to have one central head police establishment, which might be the organ to the Government, and under which all the other different establishments should be considered to be; by which means there would be formed a regular system of communication from all the different inferior police establishments in the metropolis directed to one object? If that was confined to objects of great atrocity or great importance, it would be well; but if you are to have every sort of offence that is committed and brought to the offices, sent over to a central point, the lesser offences (although perhaps, felonious) would be infinitely the greater number, and there could be no practical benefit from their being communicated from one end of the town to the other; and it would throw a cloud over the whole transaction, and the few important cases would be obscured by the number of indefinite communications. . . .

Does the office in Bow-street keep up a correspondence with magistrates in provincial towns, and in different parts of the country? . . . No regular communication; but where the country magistrates wish to describe an offender who has escaped, or to have any other aid, they write to the office in Bow-street, and we do all we can to promote the object.

Do you not think that if that correspondence was more extensive and more regular, it would be the means of preventing the necessity of the police officers being so often taken, as they now are, from their regular town duty, and sent into the country? Such a correspondence does now exist in important cases, and perhaps it could not, by any system, be beneficially extended; it does not very frequently happen, even among the offences in the metropolis, that such a communication could be useful, and in distant places the advantages of the communication would be less. . . .

Is there not a Gazette, in the nature of a Hue and Cry Gazette, which is sent to all the different magistrates? There is, it is sent to all the magistrates in the kingdom, who desire it, and to the Clerks of the Peace of the counties, and Mayors and Functionaries of the great towns: it describes offenders whose description has been sent, from all parts of the kingdom, by advertisement.

Under whose control and direction is that Gazette? There is an editor appointed by the Secretary of State; the present editor is the chief Clerk in Bow-street. . . .

Is not there some sort of pre-eminence in Bow-street; some sort of control that the magistrates at Bow-street have over the other offices? Not the least; nothing can be more distinct. Every magistrate aids and assists in the general object, without the least idea of superiority or importance in one more than the other. I am not quite sure that I did not feel my own importance as great when I was an individual magistrate at Marlborough-street, as now that I am entitled the Chief Magistrate in Bow street, excepting that it brings me more immediately within the confidence of H.M.'s Government. . . .

Are you aware that there are certain public houses within your district which are not frequented by respectable persons, but by thieves and prostitutes? Respectable persons are not those only for whom public-houses are provided: people may be reduced to their last penny, who may want refreshment; they are open for the poor more than the rich, and laborious persons more than any other description.

Are there not houses which are solely opened for thieves and prostitutes, in which they live; not that they go there for the purpose of occasional refreshment, but in which they pass their time? There is not a district in this county where the magistrates would not immediately suppress such a house. . . .

Do you not know that there are some called "Flash-houses," solely used by thieves and prostitutes? I do not know that there are; and if I did, I would as far as the law enables me, immediately suppress them.

Is it not an established known fact in the Police office, that there are houses, such as have been described, which are frequented by thieves, and people of the worst description; and to which resort the police officers go just as regularly as a gentleman goes to his preserve, in his manor, to find game? If I say the officers look to those places, it implies that those places exist; but I believe they do not exist upon system. . . . There is no feeling in Bow-street to nurse such places, either in the magistrates or officers.

Do not the police officers frequent those houses, knowing them to be the assemblage of thieves? They go into them, to seek for thieves whom they know are likely to associate at a particular place. A man discharged at the Old Bailey, yesterday, for a robbery, would go the same night to the place where he was last taken into custody; probably to see his old associates, and to receive their congratulations, or, perhaps, if he is distressed, for a little money; or he will go there to be treated by his friends; and, I fear, more commonly in furtherance of his former crimes.

Is there not a sort of understanding uniformly kept up between the police officer and persons of that description, thieves, at houses of this kind, so that when they want them, they know where to find them? They may keep up an understanding with the master of such a house, to say, "Let me know if Bill such a one drops in here, for I *want* him;" that is their cant expression.

Is it not a matter of notoriety, that they sit drinking at the same table, and are considered as boon companions, till just that moment arrives when they are to be seized? I do not much understand their art; but I think one mode of it would be, if they wanted to know the offences of one offender, as applicable to the particular object in view, they would be very glad to get themselves into company with another who was likely to be in his confidence; but it is a part of the mystery, or of the art, or of the policy, which I can neither understand nor explain. . . .

Has any plan ever struck you as feasible, by which that disgrace to London, to its police, and its morals, the crowds of women, some in a state of intoxication, infesting the streets and annoying the passengers during the best part of the night, could be prevented? It would be ten times worse if the police officers and watchmen did not take them up or drive them away, as they do at present; that might be done certainly more universally than it is, but the gaols would be be filled without hope of reforming them, to a degree that would not be expedient. The punishment by law is long imprisonment (for corporal punishment of another kind with women, is out of the question) and the instant they came out they must be committed again; for this degraded condition has no resource, even to friends or employment. There is a woman who for ten years past has been much the greater portion of the time in prison, but is always in the streets the moment she is out; and the same is the case of some beggars, but these are more easily restrained.

Do you not think that some means might be found, by which the outrageous nuisances might be put an end to, which prevent women of another description from walking through the streets without the protection of men? These insults are visited with such severity by the magistrates whenever they are brought before them, that I do not think they exist in any very great degree at this time; such insults are now unfrequent.

Do you not know that amongst the great capitals of the Continent, Paris in particular, no such evil as exists in the streets of London is to be found; that it is an *honour* peculiar to Great Britain? I think a severity of police similar to that in the countries alluded to, would suppress the evil here; but the lenity of the English law does not allow it to be carried to the full extent that it is in those countries; besides, this class of women in France are not in the use of spiritous liquors.

Do you not think that the employment of a more efficient race of watchmen, and at higher salaries, would be productive of much benefit in that respect? I think the mode of watching might be improved, but at an expense that would be grievous to those who pay the parish rates.

Do you think that the police of the metropolis would be under better management if the parish watchmen were placed under the superintendence of the police? I have not the least doubt that a system of watching at greater expense might be established under the police, with better effect than the parish watch, as now provided, furnishes....

Are you not of opinion, that by more effective men being employed, the number might be reduced? I do not think the number should be reduced, and any increase of their qualifications would be attended with an expense little to the satisfaction of those who pay it, or are benefited by it: I have sometimes thought, if you could get the lower description of housekeepers to engage in the watch, the one during the first part of the night, and the other towards the morning, it would double the number of watchmen in the dangerous part of the night, by their crossing each other in going to duty and returning home, and would increase the respectability of the watch; but such people would not go out for less than half-a-crown for the half night, and that is an expense which would not be satisfactory to those who have to pay it; I suppose the number of watchmen in the metropolis is as one to about seventy or eighty houses.

That is generally an old man? Yes, and he is dosing in his watch-box in the interval between crying the hours and when he is moving; men cannot walk for ten hours together; a thief will watch him to one corner of the street, while the intended depredation is perpetrated round another corner, and the lantern he carries shows where he is at a great distance. . . .

310. Instructions for associations to preserve the peace of the West Riding, 1 Aug. 1812

(Fitzwilliam MSS.)

The Luddite disturbances in the West Riding (1812) brought home the difficulty of keeping the peace in the absence of a regular and adequate police force. Voluntary associations of the local inhabitants were formed in several districts to watch for signs of disturbance and to co-operate with the military.

The Associations, which have been formed in the disturbed parts of the West Riding, should aim, rather at the prevention of future, than at the detection of past, outrages. Their exertions, in this respect, may be of essential service to their country. Each Association should sub-divide itself into a number of companies, one of which should be upon watch every night, and the number of companies should be such, that each individual need not be called upon to watch oftener than once a week. In those Associations, which are numerous, the calls upon each individual, will not be so frequent. The Associations must be voluntary and gratuitous, on the part of each individual, as it is chiefly by the exertion, good will, and zeal of every well-disposed man, that the persons and property of themselves, and the neighbourhood, can be protected.

It will be necessary that such part of the Association, as is on guard, should be armed. Arms may, in many cases, be supplied by the Association themselves, if each associator, who possesses a weapon fit for the purpose, will lend it to those who have none, on the night they themselves are not on guard. The provision of arms, there-fore, may, in this case, be supplied without any expense. When a sufficient number of arms cannot be supplied, in this mode, by the Association itself, a very small expense will provide the requisite number. It will be advisable, that a guard-room shall be provided, in some convenient part of each township, in which an association is formed, where the associators may occasionally retire. The hire of this room (which will probably be trifling) will be legally provided for, without putting the individuals to expense.

The associators themselves will be best acquainted with the mode in which their proceedings should be conducted, and with the objects towards which their attention should be directed–but there is no inhabitant, whose security and comfort, will not be materially promoted by their exertions.

311. Colonel Fletcher to Henry Hobhouse, 30 April 1819
(Public Record Office, Home Office, 42/186.)

This Bolton magistrate sends to the Under-Secretary of State for Home Affairs an account of the money he has spent between 4 June 1818 and 28 April 1819 in payments to secret agents. George Philips's speech (9 Feb. 1818) is in *Parliamentary Debates*, XXXVII, 222.

Mr. C. and his agents	£71
Mr. W. and his agents	122 – 11 – 3
L.F. and his agent B.	34 – 17 – 0
Postages and various expenses	6 – 1 – 0
	234 – 9 – 3
Bill for the prosecution of Harwood & others at the last January Sessions at Salford, for a riot & assault on Waddington (A.B.)	116 – 13 – 2
	£351 – 2 – 5

This *A.B.*, so often mentioned in my communications, has ever since March 1817, and particularly since the speech of Mr. Philips in Parliament, exposing him as a spy, been continually persecuted by the disaffected of our town. His journeymen weavers from whose services he and his family had their principal support, were so intimidated as to leave his service. His windows had been several times broken at midnight and his life threatened, particularly on the occasion that led to the indictments in January last, when both he and his family were exposed to extreme danger. He called upon me for protection, and I gave directions to prefer the indictment, on which his persecutors were convicted, and I humbly hope his Lordship will approve of the proceeding.

312. Letters from Henry Hobhouse to J. F. Foster, of Manchester, 1826

(Public Record Office, Home Office, 79/4.)

The employment of spies was continued whilst Peel was Home Secretary (1822–1827; 1828–1830). Sir John Byng commanded the troops in the Northern District.

17 July: Mr. Peel has desired me to ask you whether you have at your command any means of acquiring private intelligence of what is going on among the disaffected in Manchester and its neighbourhood. It is manifest that they are availing themselves of the present distresses to throw the country into confusion. And it is therefore become very important to ascertain what they are about. I am aware that something has passed on this subject between yourself and Sir John Byng. But lest you should feel yourself cramped on the score of expense, Mr. Peel desires me to say that he will ensure your reimbursement. At the same time it is necessary to put you on your guard against a *lavish* expenditure, because it tends to defeat its purpose; and also against having communication with any man who fans the flame or attends a meeting with any real object except that of defeating the designs of the disaffected.

21 July: I have to thank you for your favour of Tuesday evening, which is very satisfactory to Mr. Peel. He however desires me to say that whenever you can establish a check, the character of the person with whom you communicate is of less importance. And as to the ulterior use of such a person, speaking from experience of above fourteen years, during the greater part of which I have had occasion to consider such subjects, I can say that it so seldom happens that one, who has given previous intelligence, can be used as a witness with justice, with prudence and with effect, that it is not worth while to be nice in selecting a man with that view.

21 July: Mr. Peel has desired me to send you in strict confidence the enclosed papers containing accounts given by a person known to Colonel Fletcher of Bolton, by whom they have been transmitted to me. The man has Mr. Fletcher's confidence, but the internal evidence leads Mr. Peel to suspect that the narratives, if not fabricated, which he scarcely thinks likely, are greatly exaggerated. He therefore wishes that you would consider them attentively and return them with your remarks, how far your information corroborates or negatives any of the facts stated, and your opinion upon the whole matter. . . .

313. Peel on the Metropolitan Police

(a) Peel to Henry Hobhouse, 12 Dec. 1828.

(C. S. Parker, *Sir Robert Peel*, II, pp. 39–41, 111–113, 115; *Wellington Despatches, Correspondence & Memoranda*, V (1873), pp. 606–608; VI (1877), p. 287.)

Peel's creation of the Metropolitan Police Force (10 Geo. IV, c. 44) in 1829 was the great landmark in the history of modern police organization.

I have under my consideration at present very extensive changes in the Police of the metropolis.

You perhaps have read the Police Report of last Session. I am now employing Gregson in drawing up a Bill to give effect to the recommendations of the Report, so far as they concern the constitution of the nightly watch.

My plan is shortly this – to appoint some authority which shall take charge of the night police of the metropolis, connecting the force employed by night with the existing police establishments now under the Home Office and Bow Street; the authority which has charge of the police establishments, horse patrol, day patrol, night patrol, to act under the immediate superintendence of the Home Office, and in daily communication with it.

I propose that charge of the night police should be taken gradually. I mean that my system of police should be substituted for the parochial system, not *per saltum*, but by degrees.

I will first organise a force, which I will not call by the name of 'watchmen', which shall be sufficient to take charge of a district surrounding Charing Cross, composed, we will say, of four or five parishes. It shall extend on the City side as far as Temple Bar and the boundary of the City on that side, having the river as far as Westminster Bridge as the limit on another side. When it is notified to the parishes that comprise this district that this force is ready to act, and prepared to take charge of the district, the functions of the parochial watch in each of the districts shall terminate, and no rates be thereafter leviable on that account.

In the same way, as a little experience shall enable us to manage a more numerous force of nightly police, I propose to signify to other parishes from time to time that the police will take charge of them. Their present watch will continue to act until such signification be made, and will cease when it is made.

The present amount of money issued from the public funds for maintaining horse patrol, foot patrol, magistrates &c. shall continue to be issued; but the surplus that may be requisite to maintain the night police, or to improve and extend the existing patrols, shall be levied from the district within which that night police may act. A Police Rate will be levied instead of the Watch Rate. . . .

Now the out-parishes – such places as Brentford, Twickenham, Isleworth, Hounslow, and so forth – in all which the police at present is scandalous, will feel, and very justly, that if the new police system succeeds for London, it will injure them, by driving a fresh stock of thieves from the heart of the metropolis into the environs, and it will be a great object to me, as well as to them, to devise some mode of improving their police. If I undertook the immediate charge my force would be too large, the machine would be too cumbrous and complicated to be well managed by one authority. How, therefore, shall I proceed to provide for these out-parishes?

My notion is to take power for the Secretary of State to consolidate parishes bordering on the metropolis into a district for police purposes, to appoint Commissioners of Police, two for instance, resident in each parish within the district, who shall have the general superintendence of the district police. . . .

(b) *Peel to Wellington, 11 May 1829:* . . . Just conceive the state of . . . one parish, in which there are *eighteen* different local boards for the management of the watch, each acting without concert with the other! . . . Think of the state of Brentford and Deptford with no sort of police by night! . . .

My Bill enables the Secretary of State to abolish gradually the existing watch establishments [and] to substitute in their room a police force that shall act by night and day, under the control of two magistrates, who will be executive officers, and be relieved from the ordinary duties of justices, such as attending at Quarter Sessions, transacting parish business, &c. There is power to place the present Government establishments of police, the horse and foot patrols, under their superintendence.

I propose to substitute the new police gradually for the old one, not to attempt too much at first; to begin perhaps with 10 or 15 parishes in the centre of the City of Westminster, and gradually to extend the police district. The present watch and the present watch rate are to continue until the Secretary of State notifies to a parish that he is ready to undertake the superintendence of it. From that time the present watch and the watch rate are to cease.

I defray the expense by a rate in the parishes that are actually included within the new police, the new rate to be paid when the present rate ceases. The new rate is to be collected exactly like the poor rate, the same property to be assessed to each. The maximum of the new police rate is 8d. in the pound. . . .

Pray pass the Bill through this Session, for you cannot think what trouble it has given me.

(c) *Peel to Wellington, 5 Nov. 1829:* I am very glad indeed to hear that you think well of the Police. It has given me from first to last more trouble than anything I ever undertook. But the men are gaining a knowledge of their duties so rapidly that I am very sanguine of the ultimate result.

I want to teach people that liberty does not consist in having your house robbed by organised gangs of thieves, and in leaving the principal streets of London in the nightly possession of drunken women and vagabonds.

The chief danger of the failure of the new system will be, if it is made a job, if gentlemen's servants and so forth are placed in the higher offices. I must frame regulations to guard against this as effectually as I can.

C. PRISONS

314. Report from the Committee of the House of Commons on the state of the gaols of the City of London, &c., 1814

(Cobbett's *Parliamentary Debates*, XXVII, 748–759.)

Your Committee find, the gaol of Newgate, as at present regulated, is able conveniently to hold 110 debtors, and 317 criminal prisoners; and it is the opinion of the surgeon, that when the whole number exceeds 500, great danger of infectious disorder is to be apprehended. On April 5th, it contained 160 debtors and 326 criminals, and in January last the whole number amounted to 822.

That part of the prison which is appropriated to debtors, is divided into two yards; one for men, and one for women. Upon that for the men are three buildings, called the Master's Side, the Cabin Side, and the Common Side: the latter is for the poorest description of debtors; and for admission into the two former, a fee of three shillings is paid; and the prisoners in them share in none of the charities, but have the advantage of living in better society. The rooms are generally about 15 feet wide, and from 23 to 36 feet in length, and contain in each of them, day and night, from ten to fifteen men, when the prison is not crowded; but double that number have been occasionally placed in them. One room is, in the day-time, appropriated to work: and when your Committee visited the prison, they found there some persons industriously employed. For the government of the debtors, the keeper names six persons, and one of them is elected by his fellow-prisoners to hold the office of steward of the prison. In the same manner, in each ward, he names three persons, one of whom is, by the inhabitants of that ward, chosen to be their steward. It is the business of the steward of the prison to preserve order, to see the allowances weighed, and, assisted by three auditors, freely chosen by the prisoners, to examine the poor-box, and to superintend the receipt and distribution of charities; in return for which, he receives small gratuities, and an additional allowance of provisions; and similar to his, in their subordinate departments, are the duties of the stewards of the separate wards. These, and other regulations for the preservation of order, and management of the debtors fund, have been approved of by the aldermen and judges.

Misconduct, in any prisoner, is punished by removal to what is called the Disorderly Ward, which is locked up one hour sooner than the others; and, if that punishment be not sufficient, by confinement in a cell. The doors are every morning opened at eight o'clock; and, with the exception of four hours on Sunday, visitors are indiscriminately admitted from nine in the morning till nine at night, when they depart, sometimes to the amount of two hundred.

Wine and beer are sold at the bar of the prison, at the same price as in the public houses, and no one within the gaol is entitled to any profit on their sale. The quantity which each prisoner is allowed to purchase is no otherwise limited than that he shall not have, at one time, more than one bottle of wine, or one quart of ale; a regulation which little tends to preserve sobriety and order. The act of parliament against the introduction of spirituous liquors is conspicuously hung up, and all pains are taken, though sometimes ineffectually, to see that it is enforced.

No bedding is provided: the poorer description of prisoners sleep on the boards, between two rugs given by the city; those who can afford it hire beds at sixpence the night, from persons who carry on this traffic with the prison. The allowance of food to debtors is fourteen ounces of bread a day, and eight stone of meat in every week, divided amongst all; but as this quantity never varies with the numbers in aid of whose subsistence it is given, it forms a very precarious addition; and the whole allowance is barely sufficient, without the assistance of their friends, to support life. The manner of distributing the bread, which is given on every alternate day, is liable to this objection, that the prisoner is tempted on the first day to eat the allowance which is meant also to support him on the second; and that a person brought to prison immediately after the hour of distribution, receives nothing for forty-eight hours, and may be six days without receiving any meat.

To the debtors, no coals or candles, no mops or pails are given: the Master's Side prisoners provide themselves with these necessaries; and those on the Common Side are able to procure them by subscription and garnish, and by means of various charities and legacies. Your Committee feel it difficult to give an opinion upon what ought to be the allowance made to debtors for their comfort and subsistence, and under what regulations it ought to be distributed. It is not fitting that the poorest should hardly be enabled, by their allowance, to exist without the assistance of their friends; and if that should be wanting, that they should be in part supported by broken meat from taverns, and other casual and uncertain charities; nor is it reasonable, by an ample and indiscriminate distribution of bedding and coals and provisions, to incur expense on behalf of those who have ability to support themselves, and by too easy a subsistence, to leave no inducement to that industry, which it ought to be the first object in every prison to encourage. It seems then that a full allowance ought not to be general; it ought only to be given to those whose necessity cannot be doubted, and who are content to live on the Common Side of the prison; those who are on the Master's Side must be presumed to be more able to provide for themselves; and even on each of these sides, different gradations may be made, the allowance diminishing as the accommodation and rooms improve. It might be made conditional too upon cleanliness, upon attendance at chapel, and other good conduct; and if a system of work were established, it might be withheld from the idle.

Some deduction might also be made from such of the prisoners as are entitled to the daily payment of sixpence from their creditors; though from the length of time for which that payment may be delayed, and the expense of obtaining it (which amounts to 1l. 6s.) it is received by few: five only of all the debtors now in Newgate are in its receipt.

Garnish is demanded from all the prisoners on their admission to prison, and fees on their discharge: the garnish is extorted by them from each other, and varies, in the different wards, from thirteen shillings to one guinea; an inability or unwillingness to pay it is punished by keeping the defaulter from the fire, by not allowing him to partake in the charities, and by other means of annoyance. It is a disgraceful and oppressive custom, and ought not to be permitted to exist. It has been abolished in all the well-regulated prisons in the country; and your Committee have it in evidence from the gaoler of Newgate, that a very small allowance as a compensation, and a positive order from the magistrates, would cure this evil at once.

From every debtor, those of the Court of Conscience excepted, a fee is due to the sheriff for his writ of liberate, amounting in Middlesex to 4s. 6d. for the first action, and 2s. 6d. for every other; in London the demand is rather higher, and beyond this he may be further imprisoned until 6s. 10d. shall have been paid to the gaoler, and 2s. to the turnkey: and your Committee indeed regret that any right should exist, by law or by custom, of exacting fees from prisoners under these or indeed any circumstances. But when the debtor's debt is paid, or when he has abandoned his property to his creditor, and, destitute of every thing but his clothes and the instruments of his trade, looks forward to his liberty, it seems unreasonable that further demands should still be made on him, and that his liberation may yet be delayed until he shall have paid this new debt, arising only out of the satisfaction of all his former debts. That these fees have not been always extorted, nor made the subject of fresh imprisonment, is only to be attributed to charitable institutions, and to the humanity of the gaoler, whose right has never been enforced against the poor and unassisted. But your Committee feel, that the character of the present gaoler is no security for the conduct of his successors, and that this power of oppression ought not to exist.

The female Debtors Side is subject to similar regulations with that of the men, but it is less crowded, and appeared perfectly clean and well managed.

The Criminal Side of Newgate contains six yards; 1st. The press yard, for prisoners under sentence of death, to which are attached fifteen cells, each about nine feet long by seven wide. By the rule of the prison, which is however much relaxed, the prisoners are locked up in their cells from two in the afternoon till nine in the morning. Two prisoners are generally, for the sake of society, and in some cases to prevent suicide, put into each cell; though it has frequently happened, from delay in making the report, that the numbers have so accumulated as to make it necessary to confine three together. They have, with the exception of those condemned for murder, the same allowance with the other prisoners, and are permitted to purchase what wine or beer they please. Their friends are allowed freely to visit them between the hours of twelve and two; and every proper attention appears to be paid them. The ordinary attends them every Tuesday and Thursday after sentence; and, after the order for execution, every day: such as are dissenters are permitted to see ministers of their own tenets; and a Roman catholic clergyman is very properly paid by the city for attending on such as are of his persuasion. On the Sunday before the execution, all the prisoners under sentence of death, and who are of the Church of England, are obliged to attend divine service; they are placed in an open pew in the centre of the chapel; and previous to an execution, a black coffin is placed on the table before them. Your Committee feel this exposure of the condemned persons to be cruel and unnecessary; and it is consequently stated to have this bad effect, that it induces many to profess dissenting tenets, to avoid the being thus held up to public view, in this last awful situation; and in general only the most hardened consent so to appear.

In consequence of the Report in 1811 of the Committee on Penitentiary Houses, some attempt has been made to separate the tried from the untried prisoners; and the yard called the Chapel Yard is appropriated to such as are charged with felony, and to such as have been convicted or are charged with misdemeanors. It is calculated to hold in five wards seventy prisoners, and contained, on April 4th, seventy-eight. Those in custody for misdemeanors sleep in a different ward from those committed on a suspicion of felony, though in the day-time they mingle in the same yard. The rooms throughout the prison are fifteen feet wide, but vary in length. On one side of them the floor is a little raised in an inclined plane, on the top of which is a beam; and on these boards the prisoners sleep, the beam serving for a pillow; no beds are given, but each prisoner has two rugs: and the allowance of room, when the prison has only such a number as can be conveniently lodged, is one foot and a half to each person; when, as has been frequently the case, nearly double the convenient number is placed in a ward, they sleep in the same crowded situation on each side of the room, the whole floor being covered, with the exception of a passage in the middle. In the classification of the different descriptions of prisoners it has been usual, and such a system is sanctioned by the legislature in the Act 24 Geo. 3, c. 54, to confine together all persons convicted of misdemeanors. In the opinion of your Committee this classi-fication is far from just. He who has committed a common assault ought not to be made the companion of the perjured or the fraudulent, and still less of those who are committed for attempts at the most abominable crimes. And in the same class with all these the libellist is also included, who is frequently a man of feeling and education, and whose crime, however dangerous and reprehensible, seldom carries with it into society that degree of disgrace which should subject the offender to be placed on a level with the more profligate criminals above alluded to. In the opinion of your Committee, this gaol, whilst the classification of crimes is so little observed, is not fit for the confinement of persons convicted of libel. Prisoners for misdemeanors are not in irons, but all the others are, except such as have deserved to be freed from them by long good behaviour; they are considered to be necessary as a mark to distinguish the prisoners from strangers. But if this intercourse with visitors were more limited, or permitted only through a grating, the irons might, with perfect safety, be dis-continued. In the middle yard are confined persons under sentence of transportation, and convicted of felony; their number in April was eighty-two: and it will conve-niently hold eighty. It is to the great delay which frequently occurs in the removal of persons under such sentences, that the crowded state of Newgate has frequently been owing. By a return to your Committee it appears, that their numbers are very seldom less than 100, and that at one time, in December last, they amounted to 236. This delay is one of the main causes of all the inconveniences felt in the prison, and very great good would at once result from the early and regular removal of the transports.

The Master's Side will contain seventy persons, but is seldom full; it has now forty-nine. Prisoners for every crime, and of every description, liable only to removal for misconduct, may be admitted to it, on the payment of 13s. 6d. and 2s. 6d. per week for the use of a bed. Their treatment differs little from that of the other prisoners, except that they partake of no charities, and are in better society. They are, as much as possible, in their rooms, placed in different classes, but all meet in the common yard. Similar regulations prevail in what is called the State Side, which is for a still better description of prisoners, and the fee for admission to which is two guineas, and a rent of 10s. 6d. for a single bed, and 7s. when two sleep in one bed. It has accommodation for forty, and contains now twenty prisoners. The women's yards, with cells and infirmary, are calculated for seventy persons: seventy-five, with fifteen children, were, on April 4th, confined in it; and in January last, 130 were, at one time, crowded together, of all ages, of all descriptions, tried and untried; and even those under sentence of death are not removed, till the order for their execution comes down. Amongst them are now two girls of thirteen, one of twelve, and one of ten years old, exposed to all the contagion of profligacy which must prevail in this part of the prison. A division is here also made for Master's Side prisoners, for admission to which a fee of 13s. 6d. is paid; but they and the others have but one common yard, which is extremely narrow and inconvenient. Amongst the women, no visitors, except in the instance of very near relations, are admitted; an intercourse between them and their friends takes place through an iron railing. Into every other part of the prison visitors are allowed to come at any hour, from nine o'clock till dusk, but may only depart at stated times. Coals, and mops and brooms, are nearly to a sufficient quantity supplied to the Criminal Side of Newgate; and the allowance of food is, in a small degree, better than that to the debtors; but it is not sufficient properly to support life, without the assistance of friends, and casual charity; and, in the opinion of your Committee, it ought to be increased. It is hard to leave in dependence on their friends, men, many of whom are committed to prison only on suspicion of crimes, taken too from their trades, and placed in a prison in which hardly any facilities for work are afforded; whilst their families are deprived of that assistance on which they have been accustomed to depend. A very small increase of allowance would perfectly support them, and at the same time render unnecessary the unlimited concourse of visitors, by which it is to be feared the order and regularity becoming a prison are much impaired. From all the criminals, with the exception only of those on the State Side, garnish is exacted, liable to the same objections as have been already stated against it; and from them too fees are due, on particular occasions, to the keeper. Every convicted felon, on his discharge, after a term of imprisonment, pays 18s. 10d. though about again to try the world, under all the disadvantages of ruined character and circumstances, and the bad habits, and sometimes bad health, contracted during a long residence in a prison. Other fees are exacted on pardons, and from persons convicted of misdemeanors; every one of which your Committee are of opinion ought to be abolished; and they are glad to find, that a resolution to that effect passed the common council in 1810, though it is not yet acted upon. Acquitted prisoners are, as by law entitled, discharged on the moment of their acquittal; frequently at a late hour, and sometimes without money, without friends, and without a habitation in London; and instances have, in consequence, been known of their being brought back again on the same day, on a fresh charge, to Newgate. Those against whom no bill is found, are discharged in the morning; and the females have received one shilling each from a private charity.

From the want of room, and the danger of permitting the use of some tools, and the difficulty of procuring work, the prisoners are but little employed; but it is the opinion of the keeper, that the best results would be derived from fitting up a yard for the purpose of work, and giving other encouragements. The increased allowance suggested by your Committee should, if such a system were well regulated, by giving only to the industrious, and the earnings be suffered to accumulate, either for the families of the prisoners during their confinement, or for their assistance upon leaving the prison.

Four lunatics are now confined in Newgate; two of them separately, but two with the other prisoners, one of whom would, but for his insanity, have been convicted of murder. This is a practice against which a resolution of the common council was passed four years ago, but which still unfortunately continues to exist; but it is hoped, that when the new Bedlam is finished, they will be all removed.

The keeper of Newgate receives a salary of 450*l*. in addition to which all the fees and rents are paid to him, and from this fund he pays the servants of the prison; above which expense an income remains to himself of from 600*l*. to 1,000*l*. a year, which is not, in the opinion of your Committee, too great for an office of such difficulties and responsibility; but they greatly object to the manner in which that salary is paid. No part of a gaoler's income ought to be exacted from his prisoners. Such an income, frequently ill paid, to a humane gaoler, leaves him also too much open to the imputation of harshness, whilst it gives to a harsh gaoler a power of oppression; it also leads to the employment of too small a number, and an inferior description of servants. The fees ought all to be abolished; and whatever rents it may be thought proper to preserve, to be accounted for, the gaoler receiving a fixed salary. Your Committee cannot leave this part of the subject without stating, that they believe Mr. Newman to be conscientiously attentive to the duties of his office, and humane in their perfor mance. The medical department is under Mr. Box, who receives a salary of 150*l*. in addition to which he is repaid by the city for any quantity of medicines he may use. There are three infirmaries; one for the male debtors; one for the male and one for the female criminals. No apartment has been set aside for sick female debtors, and one has very rarely been wanted. A man on each side is chosen by the surgeon from the best educated of the prisoners, and employed daily to go round the prison, and to examine and report all the sick, who are immediately removed to the infirmary, and liberally furnished with attendance, and every thing which can be necessary. Mr. Box states, that since his appointment in 1802, no fatal case of infectious disease has occurred. Pulmonary complaints are the most difficult of cure in this and every other gaol; but Mr. Box has not observed any disorder to be unusually prevalent. The average yearly number of deaths since 1802 has been only nine; and your Committee have every reason to be satisfied with the liberality of the city, and the attention of Mr. Box to this department. They have only one remark to make; namely, that it would be satisfactory if every prisoner committed to Newgate, before he is allowed to mingle with the other prisoners, were to undergo a medical examination. It is a precaution observed in all well-governed prisons, and seems particularly called for in one so apparently exposed to infection as Newgate.

The ordinary, Dr. Forde, receives a salary of 250*l.* and is provided with a house. He states the attendance at chapel, which is entirely voluntary, to be far from regular, and his congregation frequently inattentive and disorderly. The different classes of prisoners are all within view of each other; and before the service begins, conversations take place between the men and women, and every sort of noise prevails. The keeper himself never attends; when on every ground of giving a good example, and preserving due decorum by his authority, he ought if possible never to be absent; and but three or four of the turnkeys are present, and attempt very insufficiently to preserve order. No clerk is appointed to lead the prisoners in their responses, and much inconvenience is felt by such a congregation from the want of this guidance. The sacrament is never administered, except to the condemned. Beyond his attendance in chapel, and on those who are sentenced to death, Dr. Forde feels but few duties to be attached to his office. He knows nothing of the state of morals in the prison; he never sees any of the prisoners in private; though fourteen boys and girls, from nine to thirteen years old, were in April last in Newgate, he does not consider any attention to them a point of his duty; he never knows that any have been sick, till he gets a warning to attend their funeral; and does not go to the infirmary, for it is not in his instructions.

Most of the evils and inconveniences of Newgate have proceeded from its being in extent wholly inadequate to the purposes for which it was intended; and the attention of the common council being called to it in 1810, by a letter to them from sir Richard Phillips, a committee to enquire was appointed, which produced a valuable report and several beneficial resolutions, and among them one for the building of a new prison for the reception of debtors. This building is to receive the debtors also of Giltspur-street, the Poultry and Ludgate compters, and is in a state of much forwardness; hopes are entertained that it will be fit for the reception of prisoners in the course of a year. Newgate will then only contain such persons as have received the sentence of the law, and the commitments from the different compters and the county prison, previously to every sessions held at the Old Bailey. This will give room for that attention to the comfort, morals, and industry of the prisoners, which, in the present crowded state of the prison, is hardly practicable; for their comfort, with increased space, an increased allowance and bedding are absolutely necessary; and their moral conduct will best be improved by a minute classification of ages, sexes, and offences, and by affording every facility of employment; perhaps this last object might be forwarded by giving a room towards the street, where articles manufactured by the prisoners might be offered for sale. Many of the magistrates of the city appear, to your Committee, to be active and frequent in their visits to this and the other gaols, and reports from them appear to find a ready attention from the committee of city lands; but a still more attentive and vigilant system of inspection, by regular meetings held at the prison, would, in the opinion of your Committee, be highly beneficial. It would be useful to have books kept, in which the surgeon and gaoler might enter the occurrences in their several departments; and one in which the visiting magistrates might write their remarks, as a guide for their conduct, and that of their successors. The opinion of Mr. Howard is strongly in favour of the appointment also of one of the superintending magistrates to act solely as an inspector; and where the gaols are so numerous and extensive as in London, this opinion seems well worthy of consideration. Your Committee cannot better state his duties, than in the words of Mr. Howard:–"The inspector should make his visits once in a week, or at most in a fortnight, changing his days. He should take with him a memorandum of all the rules, and enquire into the observance or neglect of them. He should (as is done in some of our hospitals) look into every room, to see if it be clean, &c. He should speak with every prisoner, hear all complaints, and immediately correct what he finds manifestly wrong; what he doubts of he may refer to his brethren in office, at their next meeting. A good gaoler will be pleased with this scrutiny; it will do him honour and confirm him in his station. To a less worthy gaoler the examination is more needful, in order to his being reprimanded, and, if he be incorrigible, to his being discharged." . . .

315. Diary of George Agar Ellis (M.P., 1818–1831; later, Lord Dover), 13 Sept. 1816

(Northamptonshire Record Office MSS.)

We . . . went all over Newgate, which is dreadfully crowded, and the prisoners not properly classed. The infirmary was quite horrid; a moderate sized room and very hot; with twelve sick persons in it, and two dead ones. Saw the boys school. There is one boy named Leary of thirteen who has been in Newgate twenty times, and been four times under sentence of death. Also four boys, one of nine, one of eleven, one of thirteen, and one of fourteen who have been altogether in Newgate between 70 and 80 times. These all keep their women. Such a scene of youthful depravity is almost inconceivable. . . .

316. T. F. Buxton on the state of the Prisons, 1818

(T. F. Buxton, *An Inquiry whether Crime and Misery are produced or prevented by our present system of Prison Discipline* (1818), pp. 17–19.)

Sir Thomas Fowell Buxton (1786–1845), the great humanitarian, was prominent in the agitation for the abolition of the slave trade as well as in prison reform. His *Inquiry* went into five editions in a year and led to the formation of a "Society for the Improvement of Prison Discipline and for the Reformation of Juvenile Offenders". He entered Parliament in 1818 and supported Mackintosh in his attempts to reform the criminal law.

The prisoner, after his commitment is made out, is handcuffed to a file or perhaps a dozen wretched persons in a similar situation, and marched through the streets, sometimes a considerable distance, followed by a crowd of impudent and insulting boys, exposed to the gaze and to the stare of every passenger: the moment he enters prison, irons are hammered on to him; then he is cast into the midst of a compound of all that is disgusting and depraved. At night he is locked up in a narrow cell, with perhaps half a dozen of the worst thieves in London, or as many vagrants, whose rags are alive, and in actual motion with vermin: he may find himself in bed, and in bodily contact, between a robber and a murderer; or between a man with a foul disease on one side, and one with an infectious disorder on the other. He may spend his days deprived of free air and wholesome exercise. He may be prohibited from following the handicraft on which the subsistence of his family depends. He may be half-starved for want of food, and clothing and fuel. He may be compelled to mingle with the vilest of mankind, and in self-defence, to adopt their habits, their language and their sentiments; he may become a villain by actual compulsion. His health must be impaired, and may be ruined, by filth and contagion; and as for his morals, purity itself could not continue pure, if exposed for any length of time to the society with which he must associate.

His trial may be long protracted; he may be imprisoned on suspicion, and pine in jail while his family is starving out of it, without any opportunity of removing that suspicion, and this for a whole year: if acquitted, he may be dismissed from jail without a shilling in his pocket, and without the means of returning home; if convicted, beyond the sentence awarded by the law, he may be exposed to the most intolerable hardships, and these may amount to no less than the destruction of his life now, and his soul for ever. And in the violation of his rights, you equally abandon your own interest. He is instructed in no useful branch of employment by which he may earn an honest livelihood by honest labour. You have forbidden him to repent and to reflect, by withholding from him every opportunity of reflection and repentance. Seclusion from the world has been only a closer intercourse with its very worst miscreants; his mind has lain waste and barren for every weed to take root in; he is habituated to idleness, reconciled to filth, and familiarised with crime. You give him leisure, and for the employment of that leisure you give him tutors in every branch of iniquity. You have taken no pious pains to turn him from the error of his ways, and to save his soul alive. You have not cherished the latent seeds of virtue, you have not profited by the opportunity of awakening remorse for his past misconduct. His Saviour's awful name becomes, indeed, familiar to his lips, because he learns to use it, to give zest to his conversation and vigour to his execrations; but all that Saviour's office, His tenderness, and compassion, and mercy to the returning sinner, are topics of which he learns no more than the beasts which perish. In short, by the greatest possible degree of misery, you produce the greatest possible degree of wickedness; you convert an act, perhaps of indiscretion, into a settled taste and propensity to vice; receiving him, because he is too bad for society, you return him to the world impaired in health, debased in intellect, and corrupted in principles.

D. THE ADMINISTRATION AND REFORM OF THE CRIMINAL LAW

317. Number of Commitments & Convictions in England & Wales, 1811–1832

(Report of the Select Committee on Handloom Weavers, 1834: *Parliamentary Papers*, 1834, x, p. 299.)

The Home Office issued statistics for the whole country only from 1811.

YEARS	Total Commitments in England & Wales, County Assizes	No Bill found	Acquitted	Convicted	Death: Number Sentenced	Death: Executions	Transportation: For Life	Transportation: For Fourteen Years	Transportation: For Seven Years	Imprisonment: Three to Five Years	Imprisonment: Two to One Year	Imprisonment: 1 Year and above 6 months	Imprisonment: 6 Months and under	Murder: Committed	Murder: Intent to commit	Larceny: In a Dwelling-house	Larceny: From the Person	Larceny: Not otherwise described	Burglars	Breaking into a Dwelling-house	Highway Robbery
1811	5,337	940	1,234	3,163	359	45	29	34	500	4	141	381	1,523	87	29	177	194	3,689	140	53	96
1812	6,576	1,169	1,494	3,913	450	82	25	67	588	6	211	492	1,797	66	35	215	214	4,363	156	66	157
1813	7,164	1,291	1,451	4,422	593	120	50	95	622	6	229	590	1,934	87	18	235	272	4,623	287	97	119
1814	6,390	992	1,373	4,025	488	70	53	78	625	11	177	525	1,861	80	51	216	311	4,259	163	50	109
1815	7,818	1,287	1,648	4,883	496	57	38	94	826	8	229	666	2,315	61	31	222	277	5,409	204	84	128
1816	9,091	1,410	1,884	5,797	795	95	60	133	861	19	249	704	2,691	85	66	277	402	6,123	360	109	246
1817	13,932	2,198	2,678	9,056	1,187	115	103	157	1,474	26	238	1,079	4,357	80	64	283	519	9,396	627	220	276
1818	13,567	1,987	2,622	8,958	1,157	97	122	236	1,692	7	259	1,026	4,125	51	42	315	551	9,303	568	207	222
1819	14,254	2,109	2,635	9,510	1,206	108	138	219	1,723	22	317	1,054	4,454	69	41	286	646	9,653	545	211	240
1820	13,710	1,881	2,511	9,318	1,129	107	221	242	1,655	15	355	1,153	4,089	49	45	302	776	9,160	466	222	244
1821	13,115	1,826	2,502	8,788	1,020	114	155	273	1,675	11	286	1,117	3,872	71	60	223	639	8,725	467	210	311
1822	12,241	1,684	2,348	8,209	921	95	132	84	1,316	13	376	1,129	3,899	85	74	196	625	8,445	496	142	278
1823	12,263	1,579	2,480	8,204	914	54	116	78	1,327	11	324	1,074	4,040	60	63	213	550	8,477	402	170	301
1824	13,698	1,662	2,611	9,425	1,017	49	117	107	1,491	12	339	1,218	4,861	73	71	277	695	9,554	460	176	258
1825	14,437	1,685	2,788	9,964	986	50	126	129	1,419	7	365	1,193	5,408	94	57	265	835	10,087	428	150	189
1826	16,164	1,786	3,271	11,007	1,146	57	133	185	1,945	12	297	1,204	5,819	57	47	301	1,055	11,122	478	168	307
1827	17,921	1,950	3,407	12,564	1,456	79	200	293	2,232	12	296	1,433	6,251	65	82	295	1,081	12,014	572	300	381
1828	16,364	1,672	3,169	11,723	1,086	74	318	508	2,046	12	245	1,117	5,991	83	72	122	1,079	16,989	249	491	314
1829	18,675	1,820	3,614	13,261	1,311	74	399	691	2,285	7	235	1,277	6,646	47	115	119	1,138	12,628	171	781	299
1830	18,107	1,832	3,470	12,805	1,351	46	407	659	2,169	1	209	1,220	6,458	65	80	134	1,234	12,031	155	726	301
1831	19,647	2,094	3,723	13,830	1,549	52	336	638	2,340	5	226	1,311	7,012	57	104	169	1,421	12,118	152	665	573
1832	20,829	2,066	3,706	14,947	1,449	54	547	765	2,603	3	230	1,304	7,644	66	132	180	1,748	13,469	175	759	382

318. An account of fines imposed by the Great Marlborough Street magistrates, July–Sept. 1812

(Public Record Office, Home Office, 42/128.)

Comparable figures for the other London Police Offices are as follows: Queen Square, £71 6s.; Hatton Garden, £107 8s. 9d.; Whitechapel, £38 13s.; Shoreditch, £48 2s.; Union Hall, £71 12s.; Shadwell, £42 8s. The Bow Street figures are not comparable: this account combines fines and fees. In the account below, the number of defendants is given in brackets, and F=female.

	July	£	s	d
14	Bakers exposing bread for sale deficient in weight (3)	1	0	6
15	Casting night soil on pavement		5	0
17	Casting offals on pavement (F)		5	0
18	Toll gatherer exacting	1	0	0
22	Driving barrows on pavement (2)		10	0
30	Running dustman (4)	1	0	0
	Casting night soil in streets	1	0	0
	August			
11	Casting night soil in streets (2)		5	0
15	Running dustman		5	0
20	Firing squibs		10	0
24	Placing rubbish on pavement		5	0
	Driving barrow on pavement		5	0
25	Running dustman		5	0
26	Firing squibs		10	0
27	do.		10	0
	Casting night soil on pavement	1	0	0
28	Running dustmen (3)		15	0
	Nuisance on pavement		5	0
29	Running dustman (2)		10	0
	September			
1	Running dustman		5	0
3	Casting night soil in streets	1	0	0
9	Driving barrows on pavement (5)		12	6
	do. (5)	1	5	0
10	Nuisance on pavement		5	0
12	Driving barrows on pavement (2)	1	0	0
14	do.		5	0
15	do.		2	6
16	Driving truck on pavement		2	6
21	Driving barrows on pavement (2)		10	0
22	do. (4)		10	0
23	Running dustman		5	0
24	Refusing to pay tolls	1	0	0
26	Running dustman		5	0
	do.		7	0
29	Driving barrows on pavement		2	6
		18	2	6

319. R. Peel to the Rev. Sydney Smith, on secondary punishments, 24 March 1826

(C. S. Parker, *Sir Robert Peel*, I, pp. 401–402.)

We are at this moment occupied in devising the means of giving to transportation some degree of salutary terror as a punishment. Two or three years since I procured a power from the Legislature to employ convicts in hard labour in any of the colonies, and I have now three or four hundred men at work in the Bermudas.

I admit the inefficiency of transportation to Botany Bay, but the whole subject of what is called secondary punishment is full of difficulty; a difficulty arising mainly, I regret to add, from the vast harvest of transportable crime that is reaped at every Assize.

I can hardly devise anything as secondary punishment in addition to what we have at present. We have the convict ships, which at this moment hold four or five thousand convicts employed in public works. There is a limit to this, for without regular employment found for the convicts, it is worse even than transportation.

Solitary imprisonment sounds well in theory, but it has in a peculiar degree the evil that is common to all punishment, it varies in its severity according to the disposition of the culprit. It is a punishment which requires too delicate a hand in the enforcement of it to be generally available. To some intellects its consequences are indifferent, to others they are fatal.

Public exposure by labour on the highways, with badges of disgrace, and chains, and all the necessary precautions against escape, would revolt, and very naturally I think, public opinion in this country. It is the punishment adopted in some countries, but we could not bear it here.

As for long terms of imprisonment without hard labour, we have them at present, for we have the Penitentiary with room for 800 penitents. When they lived well, their lot in the winter season was thought by people outside to be rather an enviable one. We reduced their food, and from the combined effect of low but ample diet, and the depression of spirits which is the frequent attendant on the dull unvarying punishment of imprisonment for years, there arose a malignant and contagious disorder which at the time emptied the prison, either through the death or removal of its inmates.

The present occupants are therefore again living too comfortably, I fear, for penance.

The real truth is the number of convicts is too overwhelming for the means of proper and effectual punishment. I despair of any remedy but that which I wish I could hope for–a great reduction in the amount of crime.

320. Lord Auckland to Viscount Sidmouth, 25 Aug. 1812

(*British Museum Additional MSS.* 34458, f. 382.)

Having this year been Chairman of the Committee on Transportation, and having in consequence my attention much called to the subject, I yesterday visited a brig now lying in the river and prepared for the conveyance of female convicts to

Botany Bay. In answer to a question put by me as to the means of preventing improper intercourse between the sailors and the women, I was told by the master that every sailor was allowed to have one woman to cohabit with during the voyage, but that having once made his choice he was not allowed afterwards to change.

Transportation was considered by the Committee to be beneficial not inasmuch as it is a punishment for the crimes of those sent to New South Wales, or the means of their removal from this country, but as it appeared likely to be the instrument of reforming their habits; and had information of this practice been laid before the Committee, I can have no doubt that it would have been marked with the strongest reprobation as likely to lead some and to confirm others of these unfortunate women in habits of prostitution and disorder. I have therefore thought it my duty to state its existence to your Lordship, as I believe that whatever is improper in the treatment of convicts can most readily be regulated by orders from your Lordship as Secretary of State for the Home Department.

321. Excerpts from Sir Samuel Romilly's diary, 1807–1818

(*Memoirs of . . . Sir S. Romilly*, ed. by his sons, 3 vols. (1840).)

Romilly's positive achievements as a reformer of the criminal law were meagre because the politicians, still living under the shadow of the French Revolution, were hostile to almost any sort of change which seemed to threaten the security of property. After his suicide in 1818 his work was taken over by Sir James Mackintosh, but with little more success. In 1820, indeed, he carried three Bills (1 Geo. IV, caps. 115, 116, 117) abolishing the death penalty for many offences, including that of stealing 5s. from a shop; but most of them were offences which were never at that time committed. In 1819 Mackintosh had secured the appointment of a select committee on the criminal laws, whose report (No. 322) marks an important stage in the reform movement. Its wide survey of the state of the law and of public opinion respecting capital punishments exercised a strong influence on the later course and character of reform. It was not, however, until Peel, who succeeded Lord Sidmouth as Home Secretary in 1822, took up the subject, that real progress was made. He abolished the death penalty for more than a hundred offences, leaving only the more serious felonies liable to it; and he consolidated nearly the whole of the criminal law.

16 Oct. 1807: . . . I have long been struck with the gross defects which there are in our criminal law, and with the serious evils which result from our present mode of administering it. When I first went the Circuit, which is now 23 years ago, some instances of judicial injustice which I met with made a deep impression on me; and I resolved to attempt some reform of the system, if I ever should have an opportunity of doing it with any prospect of success. . . . What I have it in contemplation to do, however, compared with what should be done, is very little. It is only, in the first place, to invest criminal courts with a power of making to persons who shall have been accused of felonies, and shall have been acquitted, a compensation, to be paid out of the County rates, for the expenses they will have been put to, the loss of time they will have incurred, the imprisonment and the other evils they will have suffered. . . .

The only other object I had in view was to remove that severity in our law, which has arisen from no intention of the Legislature, but altogether from accidental circumstances; and in all the cases of felonies made capital, according to the value of the thing stolen, and where, by the depreciation of money which has since taken place, that standard of guilt has become far different from what it originally was, to re-enact the laws;

fixing the sums mentioned in them much higher, and according to the difference between the then and the present value of money. This ought long ago to have been done. As all the articles of life have been gradually for many years becoming dearer, the life of man has, in the contemplation of the Legislature, been growing cheaper and of less account. A stop ought to be put to that shameful trifling with oaths, to those pious perjuries (as Blackstone somewhere calls them) by which juries are humanely induced to find things not to be worth a tenth part of what is notoriously their value. [II, pp. 229–230.]

20 April 1808. . . . My friend Scarlett . . . had advised me not to content myself with merely raising the amount of the value of property, the stealing of which is to subject the offender to capital punishment, but to attempt at once to repeal all the Statutes which punish with death mere thefts, unaccompanied by any act of violence, or other circumstance of aggravation. This suggestion was very agreeable to me. But, as it appeared to me that I had no chance of being able to carry through the House a Bill which was to expunge at once all these laws from the Statute Book, I determined to attempt the repeal of them one by one, and to begin with the most odious of them, the Act of Queen Elizabeth [8 Eliz., c. 4] which makes it a capital offence to steal privately from the person of another. [II, p. 239.]

15 June 1808. The House went into a Committee on my Bill to repeal the Statute of Elizabeth, and a pretty long debate took place upon it. Burton, the Welsh Judge, began it. He objected to the Bill as it was framed, it being simply a repeal of the Statute of Elizabeth, leaving the offence mere larceny, punishable with only seven years' transportation. He thought that the Judges ought to have power to inflict a much severer punishment, extending to transportation for life. . . . He stated that the crime of picking pockets had become extremely common, and was increasing; and mentioned that at Chester, where he sits as Judge, he had to try for this offence a great number of boys, who seemed to be educated to this way of life. This argument, that the crime was increasing, and that therefore there ought not to be any mitigation of the severity of the law, was also much insisted on by Plumer. It appeared to me, and I stated, that these were rather arguments for, than against the Bill. What better reason can be given for altering the law, than that it is not efficacious, and that, instead of its preventing crimes, crimes are multiplied under its operation? And if an alteration there must be, what can it be but to render the punishment less severe, but more certain in its operation? To add to its severity is impossible, since we already provide the same punishment for pickpockets and for murderers. Plumer observed that the utmost punishment which the Judges could inflict under the Bill as it stood–namely, transportation for seven years–was one of the most objectionable punishments that could be inflicted; that, when transportation was resorted to, it should be for a longer period, or for life; a seven years' transportation only rendering the criminal more hardened and depraved, and turning him loose, at the end of the seven years, a man more dangerous to society than he had ever been before. Upon this I observed that if this were an accurate representation, some alteration in our punishments ought very speedily to be adopted; because, at present, three times as many offenders are transported for seven years as are transported for any longer period; and that it was an extraordinary argument for having recourse to punishments inordinately severe, that we had made a very injudicious choice of slighter punishments. . . . [II, pp. 243–245.]

4 July 1808. . . . The Bill I brought in to take away the punishment of death for the crime of privately stealing from the person, passed, with the alterations Plumer had made in it, into a law. . . . In the House of Lords it passed without opposition, and without a word being said upon it. . . . [II, p. 252.]

[20 August] . . . Dumont brought with him to Knill several MSS. of Bentham's, which he is translating and arranging, in order to publish them, as a continuation of the work of which he has already printed three volumes. One of them, a treatise on punishments, appears to me to have very extraordinary merit, and to be likely to be more popular than most of Bentham's writings, and to produce very good effects. . . . Since the work of Beccaria, nothing has appeared on the subject of criminal law, which has made any impression on the public. This work will, I think, probably make a very deep impression.[1] [II, pp. 252–253.]

9 Feb. 1810. Friday. I moved for and obtained leave to bring into the House of Commons three Bills, to repeal the Act of 10 & 11 Will. III. c. 23, 12 Ann. st. 1. c. 7, and 24 Geo. II, which punish with death the crimes of stealing privately in a shop goods of the value of 5s., and of stealing to the amount of 40s. in dwelling-houses, or on board vessels in navigable rivers. The Solicitor-General, with his usual panegyrics on the wisdom of past ages and declamations on the danger of interfering with what is already established, announced his intention of opposing the Bills after they should be brought in. [II, pp. 303–304.]

1 May 1810. . . . The Bill to repeal the Act which makes it a capital offence to steal to the amount of 40s. in a dwelling-house . . . was, however, lost by a majority of two, there being 33 against it and 31 for it. . . . [II, pp. 315–317.]

30 May 1810. Wednesday. The second reading of the Bill to abolish capital punishment for the crime of stealing privately to the amount of 5s. in a shop, came on to-day in the House of Lords. . . . It was rejected by a majority of 31 to 11, the Ministers having procured a pretty full attendance of peers, considering the advanced season of the year, to throw it out. Amongst these were no less than seven prelates . . . I rank these prelates amongst the members who were solicited to vote against the Bill, because I would rather be convinced of their servility towards Government than that, recollecting the mild doctrines of their religion, they could have come down to the House spontaneously to vote that transportation for life is not a sufficiently severe punishment for the offence of pilfering what is of 5s. value, and that nothing but the blood of the offender can afford an adequate atonement for such a transgression. . . . The argument principally relied on by those who spoke against the Bill was that innovations in criminal law were dangerous, and that the present measure was part of a system to innovate on the whole criminal code. It was said that the House should consider, not merely the Bill itself, but the speculations in criminal jurisprudence of the author of the Bill; that he had been the author of the Act, passed two years ago, to abolish the punishment of death for the crime of picking pockets; and that the consequence of abolishing that punishment had been a very great increase of the

---

[1] Published in 1811 under the title of *Théorie des Peines et des Récompenses*.

crime. So Lord Ellenborough and the Lord Chancellor took upon themselves to affirm the fact to be from information which they said they had received. But how . . . do they know that the crime has increased? All they can know is that prosecutions are much more frequent than they were before the Act passed; and this, instead of affording any argument against the Bill, proves its efficacy. It was stated, when the Bill was proposed, that the inordinate severity of the punishment appointed by law prevented those who had been robbed from prosecuting, and by that means procured complete impunity to the offenders. Take away, it was said, this most severe punishment, and you will have many more prosecutors. The punishment is taken away; many more prosecutions are preferred; and this is the very fact which these men, blinded by their gross prejudices, put forward as proof that the measure has been unsuccessful. It is, on the contrary, the strongest proof of its success. . . . [II, pp. 325–327.]

21 Feb. 1811. Leave was given me, in the House of Commons, to bring in the same three Bills as I brought in last Session. . . . [II, p. 362.]

24 May 1811. . . . In the House of Lords, three of the Bills which I had carried through the House of Commons (those relating to stealing in dwelling-houses and on vessels in navigable rivers, and privately stealing in shops) were thrown out on the opposition of Lord Ellenborough, the Lord Chancellor, Lord Redesdale and Lord Liverpool. . . . The two other Bills relating to stealing from bleaching-grounds are to be allowed to pass. [II, p. 390.]

18 March 1812. The Bill which I brought into the House of Commons to repeal the Act of Queen Elizabeth, which punishes with death soldiers and mariners who are found begging, passed the House of Lords to-day. . . . [III, p. 19.]

17 Jan. 1813. In the House of Commons I moved for leave to bring in a Bill to repeal so much of the Act of King William as punishes with death the offence of stealing privately in a shop, warehouse or stable, goods of the value of 5s.; and also for leave to bring in a Bill to alter the punishment of high treason; and another Bill to take away corruption of blood, as a consequence of attainder of treason or felony. I omitted the Bills formerly brought in to take away capital punishments in the cases of stealing in dwelling-houses and on board vessels, because those Bills had excited much more opposition than that relating to shops; and some persons had even said that they would have voted for the latter if it had not been accompanied by the two former. The alteration I proposed to make in the punishment of high treason was to omit the embowelling and quartering. . . . [III, p. 79–80.]

26 March 1813. The Bill to repeal the Act of King William making the offence of stealing privately in shops to the amount of 5s. a capital offence was read a third time in the Commons and passed. On the division, the numbers were, Ayes 72, Noes 34. . . . [III, pp. 94–95.]

2 April 1813. The Bill was thrown out in the Lords to-day upon the second reading by a majority of 26 to 15. . . . [III, p. 95.]

5 July 1815. On the motion of Lord Ellenborough, the Bill for abolishing the punishment of the pillory was rejected by the House of Lords. He admitted that it ought not to exist as a punishment in all the cases in which it may now be inflicted, but said that the subject required consideration and ought to be referred to the

Judges. . . . He talked about the antiquity of the punishment both in England an
the rest of Europe, and said that it was mentioned by Fleta, and that its antiquity
appeared from Ducange; and, as usual, declaimed against innovation. This is the
fifth Bill sent up by the Commons, in the course of the present Session, for making
very material improvements in the law, which has been rejected at the instance of
Lord Ellenborough and Lord Redesdale. The four others were: 1st, the Bill to render
the remedy by Habeas Corpus more effectual . . . 2nd, the Bill to prevent the binding
poor children apprentices at a great distance from their parishes. 3d, the Bill to make
freehold estates assets for the payment of simple contract debts. 4th, the Bill to
prohibit British subjects embarking their capital in the foreign slave trade. Except
this last, all these Bills passed the Commons without one dissentient voice. [III,
pp. 189–190.]

15 Feb. 1816. The Bill to repeal the Shoplifting Act of King William was read a
third time and passed. It would have passed, as it had done in all its former stages,
without a word being said upon it, but I took this occasion to mention that while
the Bill had been in its progress through the House, a boy of the name of George
Barrett, who was only ten years of age, had been convicted at the Old Bailey, under
the Act, and was then lying in Newgate under sentence of death. I said that I should
not have taken notice of the case of this miserable child if I had not observed that
it was stated a little more than a year ago, in the newspapers, that the Recorder of
London had declared, from the Bench at the Old Bailey, that "it was the determination of the Prince Regent, in consequence of the number of boys who have been
lately detected in committing felonies, to make an example of the next offender of
this description who should be convicted, in order to give an effectual check to these
numerous instances of depravity". I said that I hoped that this was only a threat
never meant to be carried into execution, and that the inhuman intention had never
been really entertained of executing against children who were without education,
or friends, or means of support, and who had so much to urge in extenuation of their
guilt, a law of such excessive severity that there was not, for a great many years, a
single instance of its being enforced against men of mature age.

The Attorney-General said he doubted whether the Recorder had ever used the
expressions imputed to him; and certainly no intention of executing the law against
children could possibly be entertained. . . . [III, pp. 233–235.]

27 Feb. 1818. Dined at Mr. John Smith's (the member for Nottingham). Among
the company I met there was Mrs. Fry, who has now for about a year most generously
devoted herself to the care and improvement of the female prisoners in Newgate.
She is the wife of a rich banker in the City; and it is from pure motives of humanity
and religion that she has been induced to make such a sacrifice of her time and her
comforts. By the accounts of those who knew the prison in its former state, the reforms
she has effected are the most important and complete. I learned from her some curious
facts respecting the effects produced by capital punishments. Her observations are the
more valuable, as she has had such opportunities of seeing and conversing with the
prisoners. She told me that there prevails among them a very strong and general
sense of the great injustice of punishing mere thefts and forgeries in the same manner

as murders: that it is frequently said by them, that the crimes of which they have been guilty are nothing when compared with the crimes of Government towards themselves: that they have only been thieves, but that their governors are murderers. There is an opinion, too, very prevalent among them, that those who suffer under such unjust and cruel sentences are sure of their salvation: their sufferings they have had in this life, and they will be rewarded in that which is to come. All the crimes they have committed, they say, are more than expiated by the cruel wrongs they are made to endure. She spoke of the docility she had found, and the gratitude she had experienced from the female prisoners, though they were the most profligate and abandoned of their sex. Kind treatment and regulations, though of restraint, yet obviously framed for their benefit, seem to have been alike new to them; and to have called forth, even in the most depraved, grateful and generous feelings. [III, pp. 332–333.]

322. Report from the Select Committee on the Criminal Laws, 8 July 1819

(*Parliamentary Papers*, 1819, VIII, pp. 3–16.)

Your Committee, in execution of the trust delegated to them by the House, have endeavoured strictly to confine themselves within the limits prescribed to them by the terms of their appointment. . . . They have abstained from all consideration of those capital felonies which may be said to be of a political nature. . . . To the nature and efficacy of the secondary punishments of transportation and imprisonment, they have directed no part of their enquiries. . . . With many extensive and important parts of the criminal law, such, for example, as that which regulates the trial of offenders, they are entirely satisfied, and they should not have suggested any change in these departments, even if they had been within the appointed province of this Committee. . . . They wish expressly to disclaim all doubt of the right of the Legislature to inflict the punishment of death, wherever that punishment, and that alone, seems capable of protecting the community from enormous and atrocious crimes. The object of the Committee has been to ascertain . . . whether, in the present state of the sentiments of the people of England, capital punishment in most cases of offences unattended with violence, be a necessary or even the most effectual security against the prevalence of crimes.

. . . In the 30 years from 1755 to 1784 the whole convictions for murder in London and Middlesex were 71; and in the 30 years from 1784 to 1814 they were 66. In the years 1815, 1816, and 1817, the whole convictions in London for murder were 9, while in the three preceding years they were 14. Most of the other returns relate to too short a period, or to too narrow a district to afford materials for safe conclusion, with respect to the comparative frequency of crimes at different periods.

In general however it appears that murders, and other crimes of violence and cruelty, have either diminished, or not increased; and that the deplorable increase of criminals is not of such a nature as to indicate any diminution in the humanity of the people. . . .

In considering the subject of our penal laws, your Committee will first lay before the House their observations on that part which is the least likely to give rise to difference of opinion. That many Statutes denouncing capital punishments might be safely and wisely repealed, has long been a prevalent opinion. . . . Your Committee have not attempted a complete enumeration, which much time and considerable deliberation would be required to accomplish. They selected some capital felonies, for the continuance of which they cannot anticipate any serious argument, and which seem to them to serve no purpose but that of encumbering and discrediting the Statute Book. Various considerations have combined to guide their choice; sometimes mere levity and hurry have raised an insignificant offence, or an almost indifferent act, into a capital crime; in other acts the evil has been manifestly and indeed avowedly temporary. . . . Where the punishment of death was evidently unnecessary at the time of its original establishment, and where, if it was originally justified by a temporary danger, or excused by a temporary fear, it has long been acknowledged to be altogether disproportioned to the offence, your Committee conceive themselves warranted in confidently recommending its abolition. But they have also adverted to another consideration: if in addition to the intrinsic evidence of unwarrantable severity in a law, which arises from the comparison of the act forbidden, with the punishment threatened, they find also that the law has scarcely ever been executed since its first enactment, or if it has fallen into disuse as the nation became more humane and generally enlightened, your Committee consider themselves as authorised to recommend its repeal, by long experience, and by the deliberate judgment of the whole nation. . . . Where a penal law has not been carried into effect in Middlesex for more than a century, in the counties round London for sixty years, and in the extensive district which forms the Western Circuit for fifty, it may be safely concluded that the general opinion has pronounced it to be unfit or unnecessary to continue in force. The Committee are aware, that there are cases in which it may be said, that the dread of punishment has prevented the perpetration of the crime, and where, therefore, the law appears to be inefficacious only because it has completely accomplished its purpose. Whatever speciousness may belong to this reasoning in the case of conspicuous crimes . . . it never can be plausibly applied to rare and obscure offences . . . of which it requires a more than ordinary degree of professional accuracy habitually to recollect the existence. Your committee have endeavoured to avoid all cases which seem to them to be on this ground disputable. . . .

The Statutes creating capital felonies, which the Committee have considered under this head, are reducible to two classes; the first, relate to acts either nearly so indifferent as to require no penalty, or if injurious, not of such a magnitude that they may not safely be left punishable as misdemeanors at common law. In these your Committee propose the simple repeal. They are as follows:

1. 1 & 2 Phil. & Mary, c. 4. Egyptians remaining within the kingdom one month.
2. 18 Ch. II, c. 3. Notorious thieves in Cumberland and Northumberland.
3. 9 Geo. I, c. 22.[1] Being armed and disguised in any forest, park, &c.

[1] The notorious 'Waltham Black Act'. When Mackintosh's Bill to repeal these statutes reached the Lords (1820), Eldon, strongly supported by Lords Liverpool, Bathurst and Redesdale, objected to the repeal of the capital provisions of the 'Black Act' and carried an amendment to retain them.

4. [9 Geo. I, c. 22] in any warren
5.   in any high road, open heath, common or down
6.   Unlawfully hunting, killing, or stealing deer.
7.   Robbing warrens, &c.
8.   Stealing or taking any fish out of any river or pond, &c.
9.   Hunting in H.M.'s forests or chases.
10.   Breaking down the head or mound of a fish pond.
11. 9 Geo. I, c. 28. Being disguised within the Mint.
12. 12 Geo. II, c. 29. Injuring Westminster Bridge, and other bridges by other acts.

The second class consists of those offences, which, though in the opinion of your Committee never fit to be punished with death, are yet so malignant and dangerous as to require the highest punishments except death which are known to our laws. These the Committee would make punishable either by transportation, or imprisonment with hard labour. . . .

1. 31 Eliz., c. 9. Taking away any maid, widow, or wife, &c.
2. 21 Jac. I, c. 26. Acknowledging or procuring any fine, recovery, &c.
3. 4 Geo. I, c. 2, s. 4. Helping to the recovery of stolen goods.
4. 9 Geo. I, c. 22.[1] Maliciously killing or wounding cattle.
5. 9 Geo. I, c. 22.[1] Cutting down or destroying trees growing, &c.
6. 5 Geo. II, c. 30. Bankrupts not surrendering, &c.
7. 5 Geo. II, c. 30. Concealing or embezzling.
8. 6 Geo. II, c. 37. Cutting down the bank of any river.
9. 8 Geo. II, c. 20. Destroying any fence, lock, sluice, &c.
10. 26 Geo. II, c. 23. Making a false entry in a marriage register, &c. five felonies.
11. 27 Geo. II, c. 15. Sending threatening letters.
12. 27 Geo. II, c. 19. Destroying bank, &c. Bedford Level.
13. 3 Geo. III, c. 16. Personating out-pensioners of Greenwich Hospital.
14. 22 Geo. III, c. 40. Maliciously cutting serges.
15. 24 Geo. III, c. 47. Harbouring offenders against that (Revenue) Act, when returned from transportation.

In the more disputable questions, which relate to offences of more frequent occurrence and more extensive mischief, your Committee will limit their present practical conclusions to those cases, to which the evidence before them most distinctly refers. They cannot entertain any doubt that the general principles which have been so strikingly verified and corroborated in some particular cases by that evidence, apply with equal force to many others. . . . That some offences which the law treats as arson, and more which it punishes as burglary, are not properly classed with these crimes, and ought not to be punished with death, would probably be rendered apparent by a legislative consolidation of the laws in being respecting arson and burglary. . . .

On the three capital felonies of, privately stealing in a shop to the amount of 5s.–of privately stealing in a dwelling house to the amount of 40s.–and of privately

[1] See note 1 on p. 395.

stealing from vessels in a navigable river to the amount of 40s.–the House of Commons have pronounced their opinion, by passing Bills for reducing the punishment to transportation or imprisonment.

In proposing to revive those Bills, your Committee feel a singular satisfaction that they are enabled to present to the House so considerable a body of direct evidence in support of opinions, which had hitherto chiefly rested on general reasoning, and were often alleged by their opponents to be contradicted by experience. Numerous and respectable witnesses have borne testimony, for themselves and for the classes whom they represent, that a great reluctance prevails to prosecute, to give evidence, and to convict, in the cases of the three last-mentioned offences; and that this reluctance has had the effect of producing impunity to such a degree, that it may be considered as among the temptations to the commission of crimes. Your Committee . . . forbore to desire the opinion of the present Judges. . . . It appeared unbecoming and inconvenient that those whose office it is to execute the criminal law should be called on to give an opinion whether it ought to be altered. As the Judges could not with propriety censure what they might soon be obliged to enforce, they could scarcely be considered as at liberty to deliver an unbiassed opinion. . . .

But highly as the Committee esteem and respect the Judges, it is not from them that the most accurate and satisfactory evidence of the effect of the penal law can reasonably be expected. They only see the exterior of the criminal proceedings after they are brought into a court of justice. Of the cases which never appear there, and of the causes which prevent their appearance, they can know nothing. Of the motives which influence the testimony of witnesses, they can form but a hasty and inadequate estimate. Even in the grounds of verdicts, they may often be deceived. From any opportunity of observing the influence of punishment upon those classes of men among whom malefactors are most commonly found, the Judges are, by their stations and duties, placed at a great distance.

Your Committee have sought for evidence on these subjects from those classes of men who are sufferers from larcenies, who must be prosecutors where those larcenies are brought to trial, who are the witnesses by whom such charges must be substantiated, and who are the jurors, by whose verdicts only effect can be given to the laws. On this class of persons . . . in other words, on the traders of the cities of London and Westminster, your Committee have principally relied for information. To the clerks at the offices of magistrates, and to the officers of criminal courts . . . to experienced magistrates themselves, and to the gaolers and others, who, in the performance of their duties, have constant opportunities of observing the feelings of offenders, the Committee have also directed their enquiries; their testimony has been perfectly uniform.

Mr. Shelton, who has been near forty years Clerk of Arraigns at the Old Bailey, states, that juries are anxious to reduce the value of property below its real amount, in those larcenies where capital punishment depends on value; that they are desirous of omitting those circumstances on which the capital punishment depends in constructive burglaries; and that a reluctance to convict is perceptible in forgery. . . .

Mr. Wilkinson, a merchant in London, stated a case of property to the value of

£1000 stolen from him, where he was deterred from prosecution by the capital punishment; and expressed his belief that a similar disposition prevailed among persons of the like condition and occupation with himself. . . .

Mr. Richard Martin, a member of the House, informed the Committee, that the punishment of death prevented prosecutions in Ireland for horse, cattle, and sheep stealing, for privately stealing in dwelling houses and shops, and in general for all larcenies without violence. Though the extensive estate, of which he is proprietor, be almost laid waste by sheep stealing, he has been prevented from prosecuting by the punishment of death. . . . He has no doubt that his estate would be better protected if the law were more lenient. . . .

Mr. Collins and *Mr. Crowther*, considerable and very respectable traders in Westminster, gave evidence which the Committee consider as of particular value. Mr. Collins has suffered both from larcenies and forgeries, and was restrained by the state of the penal law from bringing the offenders to justice, which he would otherwise have taken the greatest pains to do. He thinks that the laws of God do not permit life to be taken away for mere offences against property: and that among his friends, many of whom are traders in London and Westminster, he does not know a single exception from concurrence in such sentiments. *Mr. Crowther* stated, that no porter had left their establishment for twenty years for any other cause than theft; that a prosecution had taken place in one instance, and had terminated in conviction and condemnation. "The pain and anxiety," he adds, "occasioned by that event, until we obtained for him the royal mercy, none can describe but ourselves; which made us resolve never to prosecute again for a similar offence." . . . He declared, that if he received a forged bank note, he should be prevented from prosecution by the punishment of death, and that if the punishment were less than death, he should undoubtedly consider it as his absolute duty to bring the offender to justice. He believes that nine tradesmen out of ten agree with him. . . .

. . . There is no offence in which the infliction of death seems more repugnant to the strong and general and declared sense of the public, than forgery; there is no other in which there appears to prevail a greater compassion for the offender, and more horror at capital executions. . . .

Mr. Fry, a banker in London . . . explicitly stated . . . that as a banker, he should consider his property as much more secure, if the punishment of forgery were mitigated to such a degree that the law against that offence would be generally enforced; in nine cases out of ten of forgery which he has known, there has been an indisposition to prosecute. . . .

Your Committee are of opinion, that forgeries are a class of offences, respecting which it is expedient to bring together and methodize the laws now in being. That in the present state of public feeling, a reduction of the punishment in most cases of that crime, is become necessary to the execution of the laws, and consequently to the security of property and the protection of commerce. . . . Private forgeries will, in the opinion of the Committee, be sufficiently and most effectually repressed by the punishments of transportation and imprisonment. As long as the smaller notes of the Bank of England shall continue to constitute the principal part of the circulating medium of the kingdom, it may be reasonable to place them on the same footing with the metallic currency; your Committee therefore propose that the forgery of these notes may for the present remain a capital offence; that the uttering of forged bank notes shall, for the first offence, be transportation or imprisonment; but that on the second conviction, the offender shall . . . if the prosecutor shall so desire, be . . . liable to capital punishment. . . .

Your Committee will conclude by informing the House, that in pursuance of the various opinions and recommendations which they have stated above, they have instructed their Chairman early in the next session of Parliament to move for leave to bring in Bills, for the objects and purposes of which this report is intended to explain the nature and prove the fitness.

323. Debate in the House of Commons on the Bill for altering the sentence of burning women, &c., 10 May 1790

(Cobbett's *Parliamentary History*, XXVIII, 782–784.)

The Act of 1790 (30 Geo. III, c. 48) substituted hanging for burning as the sentence to be passed on women guilty of high or petty treason.

Sir Benjamin Hammet rose to make a motion relative to the sentence of burning women convicted of certain crimes. He stated that it having been his official duty to attend on the melancholy occasion of seeing the dreadful sentence put in execution, he then designed to move for leave to bring in a Bill to make some alteration, but he did not choose to venture the measure till he had consulted and received the approbation of some high authorities in the law. The judgement of burning alive, applied to women for certain crimes, was the savage remains of Norman policy, and disgraced our Statutes, as the practice did the common law. . . . At this moment a woman was in Newgate convicted of coining; but the learned Recorder had not made his Report. The Sheriff had applied to him that morning, expressing his hopes that the Bill might pass into a law. It had been proved by experience that the shocking punishment did not prevent the crime. Formerly the men were sentenced to be quartered, in addition to their other punishment, and he supposed it arose from delicacy that the women were to be burnt; but now, the sentence of quartering was not the judgement, and all for which he contended was that women should not receive a more dreadful punishment than the men, who might influence them to the commission of the crime. . . . He then moved for leave to bring in a Bill "for altering the sentence of burning women attainted and convicted of certain crimes, and substituting other punishments in lieu thereof". . . . Sir Benjamin Hammet said that one of the first law authorities in the kingdom had given it as his opinion that such a Bill was proper; he had in fact been recommended to bring in such a Bill by several of the Judges.

The motion was agreed to.

324. Debate in the House of Commons on the Pillory Abolition Bill, 22 Feb. 1816

(Cobbett's *Parliamentary Debates*, XXXII, 803–805.)

The punishment of the pillory was abolished by 56 Geo. III, c. 138 (1816), except for perjury and subornation of perjury.

Mr. M. A. Taylor rose . . . to move for leave to bring in a Bill to abolish the punishment of the pillory. . . . It was his intention to bring in the Bill in the same shape in which he had introduced it last year. . . . The main ground upon which he rested his dislike to the punishment of the pillory was, that it was a punishment which could not be measured or dealt out by a court of justice, but was apportioned solely by the caprice of the multitude. . . . He would not now enter into the reasons why he should not even wish this punishment to extend to that abominable offence which was so disgraceful to human nature, and to which it had recently been so often apportioned. He did think that such exhibitions were productive of no moral good; but, on the contrary, tended to increase the vice it was meant to suppress. . . .

Sir Robert Heron. . . . The improved and mild morality of the present times had been disadvantageous so far as it was too lenient to crimes, and had too much pity for former acquaintances and connexions. This sometimes paralyzed the arm of the law, and gave facilities for the escape of guilty persons. . . . Certain offences had of late much increased, and, he feared, owing too much to the prevailing mildness and indulgence. All who attended the Assizes must know how difficult it was to convict capitally offenders of this nature. Evidence could generally be got only by the suspicious testimony of an accomplice. Convictions were chiefly for assaults with a further intent. As to transporting these persons, it might subject others transported to punishments worse than what the law inflicted. If such crimes were effectually checked in upper life, it would have a great effect. The wretch, who stood in little fear of imprisonment, pillory or death, might perhaps be affected by the terror of perpetual disgrace and scorn.

Mr. M. A. Taylor said he was sure he could satisfy the hon. baronet in private, that there was but little hope of reform to be expected from persons addicted to this atrocious offence, under any circumstances of punishment, however severe.

Leave was given to bring in the Bill.

325. Debate in the House of Commons on the punishment of whipping females, 10 June 1817

(Hansard's *Parliamentary Debates*, XXXVI, 932.)

The public whipping of women was abolished in 1817 by 57 Geo. III, c. 75, and the whipping of women in private in 1820 by 1 Geo. IV, c. 57.

General Thornton moved for leave to bring in a Bill to abolish the public whipping of females. He had been more especially led to this by an article which had appeared in the *Inverness Journal* which stated that a woman, young and beautiful, had been whipped in the public streets–that she was in a state of intoxication, seemed quite lost to every sense of her situation, and shortly returned to her old courses. Spectacles such as this were not likely to improve the public morals. The punishment had been partially abolished in England, and he proposed to abolish it entirely by commuting the punishment for hard labour in a workhouse for a period not exceeding three months.

The motion was agreed to.

326. William Sykes to Robert Peel, 15 Sept. 1824

(Public Record Office, Home Office, 44/14.)

Gibbeting was abolished in 1834 by 4 & 5 Will. IV, c. 26.

I am sure you will overlook the intrusion of a letter from a private individual calling your notice to the longer continuance of the revolting spectacle exhibited on the bank of the Thames, and which excites feelings of disgust in the breasts of numerous voyagers to Ramsgate, Margate, France, the Netherlands, &c. &c. I allude to the scare-crow remains of the poor wretches who long since expiated by death their crimes, now hanging upon gibbets. It is said that "persecution ceases in the grave". Let these poor remains find a grave, and the remembrance of their offences pass away. I have heard many ladies anxiously inquire if the boats had passed the gibbets, and not until then would they come upon deck. I have heard seamen say "What honest man would like to have a halter held up to him in menace, and why should they (following their lawful and honest employ) have the hint thus ingeniously prolonged to them?"

. . . Tyburn, Kennington, Hounslow, Wimbledon are all freed from the sad practice: why should it be perpetuated to the disgrace and nuisance of the Port of London? The offences were not, if I remember rightly, peculiar to that Port, but merely the Admiralty jurisdiction is here held. The remains of mortality is a sad sight under any circumstances; under *such* circumstances it is revolting, disgusting, pitiable, dishonourable to the law's omnipotence, and discreditable to the administrators of the law.

Part IV
LOCAL GOVERNMENT AND POOR LAW ADMINISTRATION

Introduction

THE machinery of eighteenth-century local government survived without material alteration to the end of this period. Its focus was the parish vestry, on which custom and innumerable statutes had placed a variety of duties exercised under the general supervision of the justices of the peace. The parish was the basic unit even in the chartered boroughs, where the corporations, still unreformed and oligarchic, performed few functions beyond the regulation of fairs and markets, the control of corporation property, the administration of such charitable funds as they could lay their hands on, and the eating of dinners.[1] They recognized few responsibilities for social welfare; they were enclaves of local government only in the sense that the work of their parishes was supervised by the town magistrates and not by the county justices. From the administrative point of view, the contemporary Englishman belonged primarily to his parish. He was likely to be called upon in his turn to serve in the unpaid offices of churchwarden, constable, surveyor of the highways, or overseer of the poor: it was to the parish that he paid his rates, or turned for relief in times of distress. Local taxation in England and Wales was largely levied and spent by the parishes, who in 1813–1815 were spending not far short of $5\frac{1}{2}$ millions a year,[2] and by 1835 disposing of a sum equal to very nearly one-fifth of the national budget.

There was little uniformity, however, in the constitution or powers of the parish vestries. Some were 'open'–the affairs of the parish being in appearance democratically determined by the whole body of the ratepayers in a usually turbulent public assembly–others were 'close' or 'select' oligarchical bodies. Attempts were made from time to time to modify the powers of the vestries as new problems arose, and individual parishes occasionally sought statutory powers to pave, light and name the streets, provide a watch service, build sewers, and control nuisances. The 'close' vestry of St. George's, Hanover Square, working under a series of Acts like that of 1789,[3] thus became exceptionally efficient and a model for other authorities, not all of whom, however, could call upon the services of so large a population of disinterested and responsible ratepayers. Efforts were made in the 'Sturges-Bourne Acts' of 1818 and 1819 to improve the efficiency of the 'open' vestries by the introduction of plural voting and by permitting the delegation of certain poor-law functions to a committee, but these proved ineffective in the long run. The problems posed by the new urban industrial and residential areas were too vast for solution by piecemeal tinkering with the institutions of another age, and after 1834 much attention was to be given to experiments in the technique and organization of a more satisfactory system of local administration and central supervision.

[1] No. 327.   [2] No. 329.   [3] No. 328.

The most pressing and by far the most burdensome of the duties exercised by the parishes in this period was the relief of poverty. The alleviation of social distress was still based on the letter of Elizabethan legislation and the Act of Settlement of 1660, but the original spirit and intentions of their framers had long been abandoned. The supervision of poor law administration by the Privy Council had ended in the mid-seventeenth century, since which time the parishes had been left to care for their own poor as best they might, subject only to the loose oversight of the justices. There was little uniformity therefore in the treatment of poverty among the 15,000 separate poor law authorities of England and Wales. Where the population was small and the problem correspondingly slight–as late as 1831 there were 6,500 parishes or townships containing less than sixty families–the tendency was to resort to outdoor doles or allowances in kind, and to rely in times of extraordinary and general distress upon the benevolence of local landowners.[1] In the more crowded towns and industrialized regions many parishes had taken advantage of 'Gilbert's Act' of 1782 to combine into unions for the more economical administration of a workhouse, where segregation of the old, the sick, the children, the insane and the workshy was rarely practised, and the result tended to be the horror of the 'general mixed workhouse' described by the Webbs, who calculated that the 4,000 workhouses of England and Wales at this time housed a population of some 100,000. Parishes occasionally sought to avoid the expense of keeping so many of their inhabitants in idleness, though not in comfort, by 'farming the poor' to a contractor[2], who assumed responsibility for the financial burden and in return was allowed the labour of the poor for his notional profit, but this rarely succeeded either in improving the treatment of the inmates or in profiting the contractor to any substantial degree. Enlightened authorities, such as the overseers of St. James's, Westminster,[3] attempted to separate the conduct of the 'House of Industry' from the more general of their duties to the sick and the aged, and to provide a better fate for the parish orphans than those of other London parishes, who were still being sent in batches to the factories despite the objections of magistrates in the receiving areas and the adverse report of the parliamentary committee of 1815.[4] Attempts to render the labour of the poor profitable to the community were generally of little benefit, however, particularly when, as at Kendal in 1795, the great majority of the workhouse population consisted of the very young and the aged.[5] Nor did the strict regimen applied to the inmates produce any apparent improvement in the health or the morals of the labouring poor of England.

The main characteristic of poor law administration in this period was not, however, undue severity towards the unfortunate; rather it was misplaced humanity, leading to the wholesale pauperization of the employed rural labourer by the 'Speenhamland System', so called from the decision of the meeting of Berkshire justices and other 'discreet persons' assembled at Speenhamland, in Newbury, in May 1795 to consider the distress of the local poor.[6] High food prices due to a bad harvest and the war-time disruption of trade were there allied to a decline in the local cloth industry. It was suggested that the powers given to the justices by Elizabethan statute to fix the wages of artisans and labourers in husbandry be revived, but the economic and political ideas of the day were entirely opposed to such interference with the free operation of economic laws and the control of private property. In any case, the justices were empowered only to fix maximum, not minimum, wages. It seemed, then, that if

<hr/>

[1] See Section V, Nos. 352, 353.   [2] No. 341.   [3] No. 342.
[4] Section VI, No. 477.   [5] No. 343.   [6] No. 331.

employers would not pay a living wage in times of scarcity, their labourers must starve. As the only practicable remedy it was decided to allow labourers in employment to receive allowances from the poor rate to supplement their wages, the allowance to be determined by reference to an agreed scale and depending on the price of bread and the size of the family. The Berkshire scale was quickly adopted throughout southern England; in 1796, and again in 1800, the House of Commons refused assent to Whitbread's alternative proposals to allow the justices to fix minimum wages.[1]

As a temporary expedient, designed to avert the threat of actual famine and destitution, the 'Speenhamland System' was a success. As a long-term solution to the economic difficulties of the time its effects were disastrous. Within two years, observers began to note the beginning of wholesale pauperization;[2] there was no longer any shame attached to receipt of parish relief, and a supplement to wages was coming to be regarded by the labourer as his entitlement, by the employer as an excuse for not adjusting wage-rates in a time of inflation. As the burden of the poor rate increased, the critics of the system made themselves heard. The most sweeping was Malthus,[3] who would have done away with the poor laws altogether and applied a harsh 'workhouse test' to the destitute and improvident. George Rose,[4] however, would have preferred to abolish the workhouses, to provide small outdoor doles to the indigent, and promote a spirit of independence by encouraging such institutions as the friendly societies.

The allowance system survived the French wars—a time of general prosperity for the English farmer—to fall as perhaps the biggest single burden on rich and poor alike in the distressed times that followed. By 1817 the poor rates accounted for some £8,000,000 a year of the national expenditure, an amount too great to be borne by landowners in a country suffering from a depression in both industry and agriculture. In 1817 the Suffolk magistrates summarized forcefully the evil effects of "mixing the wages of labour with the relief of the poor",[5] while the high bailiff of Birmingham offered a despairing picture of the problem in the manufacturing districts hardest hit by post-war difficulties.[6] The slow recovery in the 1820s eased some of the financial strain, but the social evils of which the Suffolk bench had complained were again brought to the public notice by the agrarian riots which blazed across southern England in 1830 and 1831.[7] By the end of the period it was generally recognized that the poor laws, though they had saved thousands from the worst consequences of the difficult war years, had become a wasteful, expensive, unprofitable and demoralizing exercise in philanthropy. Malthus and Bentham together inspired the remedy of 1834—a drastic, at times it was to seem inhuman, surgery, which ultimately was to preserve the self-respect of the labouring population after a generation of misplaced benevolence.

BIBLIOGRAPHY

The authoritative and monumental work of S. and B. Webb, *English Local Government from the Revolution to the Municipal Corporations Act* (9 vols., 1906–1929), is indispensable. Other standard works are J. Redlich, *Local Government in England* (2 vols., 1903), P. Ashley, *English Local Government* (1905), E. Jenks, *An Outline of English Local Government* (2nd edition, revised by

[1] No. 332. [2] No. 333. [3] No. 335. [4] No. 336.
[5] No. 337. [6] Nos. 338, 339. [7] No. 340.

R. C. K. Ensor, 1907), and E. Cannan, *History of Local Rates in England* (2nd edition, 1912). Older works still useful are H. A. Merewether and A. J. Stephens, *The History of the Boroughs and Municipal Corporations of England* (3 vols., 1835), and J. Toulmin Smith, *The Parish* (1854). Contemporary accounts of the working of local government institutions are R. Burn, *The Justice of the Peace and Parish Officer* (23rd edition, 6 vols., 1821), the eighteenth-century magistrate's handbook to his duties, and *The Laws respecting Parish Matters* (1795), notes on the duties of parish officials. Examples of the work of the county justices and borough corporations may be found in the MS. Records and Order Books of Quarter Sessions and town councils in local Record Offices; printed extracts exist in *Records of the Borough of Nottingham* (vols. VII and VIII, Nottingham, 1947, 1952, covering the years 1760–1800 and 1801–1835 respectively). Valuable local studies are A. Redford and I. S. Russell, *The History of Local Government in Manchester*, vol. I (1939), covering the period to 1841, F. H. W. Sheppard, *Local Government in St. Marylebone, 1688–1835* (1958), and P. Styles, *The Development of County Administration in the late 18th and early 19th centuries, illustrated by the rolls of the Warwickshire Court of Quarter Sessions, 1773–1837* (Dugdale Society, Occasional Papers, No. 4, Oxford, 1934). Statistics of local government expenditure may be found in the *Parliamentary Papers*, 1830–1831, vol. XI, p. 205, or, in expanded form, in G. R. Porter, *The Progress of the Nation* (3 vols., 1836–1838), or J. Marshall, *A Digest of the Accounts relating to the Population, Productions, Revenues ... of the United Kingdom* (1833).

An invaluable introduction to the study of local records is W. E. Tate, *The Parish Chest* (Cambridge, 1946). The principal guides to the sources for local history are the Historical Association's *Local History Handlist* (1947), C. Gross, *A Bibliography of British Municipal History* (New York, 1897), and A. L. Humphreys, *A Handbook to County Bibliography* (1917). J. B. Williams, *Guide to the Printed Materials for English Social and Economic History* (2 vols., New York, 1926), lists the local histories published to that date and the principal modern works on Local Government.

Contemporary literature on the administration and operation of the Poor Laws is immense. The most valuable by far of the numerous surveys of the period is Sir F. M. Eden, *The State of the Poor* (3 vols., 1797: abridged edition, 1 vol., edited by A. G. L. Rogers, 1928), based on a thorough survey of the parishes of England and Wales. P. Colquhoun, *The State of Indigence* (1799), deals with the London poor, and D. Davies, *The Case of the Labourers in Husbandry Stated and Considered* (1795), uses statistics and family budgets collected from the rural parishes. See also J. Howlett, *The Insufficiency of the Causes to which the increase of the Poor and of the Poor Rates has been ascribed* (1788). The well-known criticisms of the poor law by Malthus were answered by a host of pamphleteers; especially important is G. Rose, *Observations on the Poor Laws* (1805). The state of the poor laws at the end of the period is vividly illuminated in the Report on the Administration and Practical Operation of the Poor Laws of 1834 (*Parliamentary Papers*, 1834, vols. XXVII–XXXIX) and in the short abstract, *Extracts of Information from the Reports of Assistant Commissioners on the Poor Law* (1833). Other official surveys and inquiries conducted during the period are the Reports of the Select Committees of 1817 (*Parliamentary Papers*, 1817, vol. VI), 1818 (1818, vol. V) on Scotland, and 1831 (1831, vol. VIII). Accounts of poor law expenditure from 1750 are given in *ibid.*, 1821, vol. IV, and annual reports thereafter until 1831. An independent survey was B. F. Duppa, *The Causes of the Present Condition of the Labouring Classes in the South of England* (1831).

Later works are D. Marshall, *The English Poor in the 18th Century* (1926), and G. Slater, *Poverty and the State* (1930). An important regional study is E. M. Hampson, *The Treatment of Poverty in Cambridgeshire 1597–1834* (Cambridge, 1934), and there is a short account of Oxfordshire practice in this period in C. R. Oldham, "Oxfordshire Poor Law Papers", *Economic History Review*, IV (1934), pp. 470–474, and V, pp. 87–89.

A. THE ORGANIZATION OF LOCAL GOVERNMENT

327. The work of the borough council: minutes of the Wallingford Borough Common Council, 1797–1832

(Ledger Book of the Corporation of Wallingford: Berkshire Record Office.)

25 February 1787

At this Court a Lease of a Messuage and Plot of Ground on the south side of the Mill Brook in the said Borough to Thomas Toovey of Newnham Murren Oxon. Gent for thirty one years renewable every fourteen years under the yearly Rent of seven Shillings passed the Common Seal. . . .

At this Court also a License for Catharine Clarke Executrix of John Clark deceased to assign a Cottage etc. in Saint Leonards Parish to James Banting of the said Borough Carpenter for the remainder of the Term therein passed the Common Seal.

The Expenses attending the Feast given by the Mayor on his quitting his Office being in the Opinion of this Meeting an unnecessary burthen on him & highly improper on account of the high price of Provisions and the extensive Scale upon which the Feast is conducted and being likewise injurious to the Interest of the Corporation It is earnestly recommended that in future the Mayor for the time being will confine his Invitations to the Members for the Borough, the High Steward, the Clergymen who preached the Sermon and the Corporation and that the present Mayor Edward Wells Esq will have the goodness to set the Example.

20 October 1797.

Ordered that the Mayor's Salary in future be twenty five Pounds per annum instead of Thirty Guineas.

Ordered that the Town Clerk do apply to the Court of Kings Bench for a Mandamus to compel the Grand Jury at the next Assizes for the County of Berks to receive the Bill of Indictment against Mr. James Parker for not accepting the Office of Alderman of the said Borough or for a Mandamus to compel the said James Parker to accept the Office as Counsel shall think most advisable.

10 January 1798.

Mr. James Parker having paid the Corporation the Sum of Sixty Pounds to be excused serving the Office of one of the Aldermen of the said Borough to which he was elected at A Court of Common Council held for the said Borough on the 23ᵈ July 1795 the Corporation at this Court accept the same and Order that he be excused accordingly.

22 January 1798.

At this Court Mr. Jonathan Mayne one of the eighteen Assistants of the said Borough was unanimously elected an Alderman of the said Borough in the place of

Mr. James Parker who was excused at the last Court but the said Jonathan Mayne being present declined to take upon him the said Office and paid the Fine of Fifty Pounds into the hands of the Chamberlain to be excused serving the said Office which is accepted and he is accordingly excused.

At this Court Mr. John Pickman one of the eighteen Assistants of the said Borough was elected an Alderman of the said Borough in the place of Mr. Jonathan Mayne who paid the Fine to be excused serving the Office.

26 April 1800.

Mr. Jeremiah Hambleton applied for leave to make use of the Room over the Town Hall as a School and the Corporation agreed to grant him such leave during their pleasure.

At this Meeting it was resolved that the Corporation do at their Expense prosecute all persons who shall be guilty of forestalling Ingrossing or regrating within the Borough and the Town Clerk is desired to give public Notice of this Resolution by printed Hand Bills. . . .

15 February 1813.

At this Court a Petition to both Houses of Parliament against the Claims of the Roman Catholics and praying that the Laws for securing the Religion established in this Kingdom may undergo no alteration passed the Common Seal.

Also a Petition to the House of Commons against the Bill for making a Canal out of the Wilts and Berks Canal at or near Eastcot in the Parish of Swindon in the County of Wilts to join and communicate with the Thames and Severn Canal at or near a place called Weymour Bridge in the Parish of Latton in the same County passed the Common Seal. . . .

13 February 1832.

Whereas Complaint hath been made to this Court that Mr. George Bradford one of the eighteen Assistants of the said Borough did immediately after the breaking up of the last Court of Common Council for the said Borough on the eighth day of February instant openly and intentionally disclose and proclaim and misrepresent the private proceedings and discussions of the said Court in a certain public House within the said Borough in violation of his Oath of office as a Burgess and to the great Scandal and prejudice of the Corporation

This Court therefore being fully satisfied of the truth and correctness of the said Complaint and after taking the Premises into their most serious consideration Do Adjudge him the said George Bradford to be totally unfit any longer to fill and discharge the office of an Eighteen Assistant and do therefore unanimously agree to amove and depose him from the same And he is accordingly by virtue of the power given by the Charter of this Borough for that purpose amoved and deposed from henceforth from the said office of Eighteen Assistant of the said Borough.

At this Court David Massey of Wallingford is appointed to ring the Bell at Saint Mary's Church commonly called the 9 o'clock Bell every Night throughout the Year and also to ring the Bell at 5 o'clock in the Morning each day from Lady day to Michaelmas only during the pleasure of the Corporation at a Salary of £2:10:0

payable annually at Christmas but it is expressly understood that in the event of his not discharging the Duties of the office satisfactorily that he shall at any time be removed therefrom without any Notice and (should the Corporation deem it proper) without also receiving any portion of his salary from the preceding Christmas but otherwise he is to receive a proportionate part of the Salary for the time that shall have elapsed between the time of his discharge and the preceding Christmas.

3 March 1832.

It having been the practice, on the Election of a Burgess or Alderman, for each and every such Officer to give a Dinner or Supper on the occasion and it being deemed expedient and advisable, with a view to render such offices as unobjectionable as may be that a Dinner or Supper on such occasions shall from henceforth be discontinued. It is ordered that the same be discontinued accordingly.

At this Court Mr. Thomas Greenwood (of the Market place) of the said Borough was unanimously elected one of the eighteen Assistants of the said Borough in the room of Mr. George Bradford who was at the last Court displaced and amoved from that office. . . .

Ordered that the Chamberlain do pay Charles Peers Esquire the late Recorder the long arrear of his Salary of £5-5- per Annum which is due to him.

It is ordered that the Town Clerk do make the necessary application to the Archdeacon of Berks for obtaining a Faculty for setting apart the Seats in Saint Mary's Church hitherto held by the Corporation and commonly called "the Corporation Seat" exclusively for their use.

29 September 1832.

At this Court Charles Atherton Allnatt Esquire took the Oath of Office as Mayor for the year ensuing and also the Oaths of Allegiance and Supremacy as by Law appointed and thereupon the Mace and Seals were delivered up and he proceeded to appoint his Officers as follows

Dr. James Flamank, Chamberlain, Sworn and took the Oaths of Allegiance & Supremacy; Mr. William Shaw Clarke, Mr. Holland Thomas Birkett, Bailiffs; Mr. Charles Greenwood Senr., Mr. John Marshall, Bridgemen; James Palmer, John Birch, Constables; Job Lovelock, James Button, George Crouch Wilkinson, John Clarke (Hairdresser), Tythingmen; Job Lovelock, James Button, Ale Tasters; George Crouch Wilkinson, John Clarke (Hairdresser), Victual Tasters; John Jenner, David Massey, Serjeants at Mace.

Richard Brooker is elected Beadle–Bellman–Hallkeeper and Collector of the Returns of the Market for the year ensuing.

At the same Court also the Mayor Chamberlain Bailiffs and Bridgemen upon their admission into their respective offices severally made and subscribed the Declaration prescribed by the Act of 9th George the 4th Chap 17 and the same are ordered to be filed among the Records of the said Borough.

328. The Work of the Parish

An Act for the better relief and employment of the poor of the parish of St. George, Hanover Square, within the liberty of the City of Westminster; for repairing the highways, regulating the beadles, watch, and patrol; for paving, repairing, cleansing, lighting, and removing and preventing nuisances and annoyances within several of the streets and other public passages and places within the said parish; and for other purposes relating to the said parish (29 Geo. III, c. 75, 1789).

(*Statutes at Large*, XLII, pp. 812–813.)

The parish authorities of the eighteenth and nineteenth centuries were responsible for much of the work of local government; exceptional among them for efficiency and honesty was the Select Vestry of St. George's, Hanover Square. This summary (printed as it appears in the Statute Book) of the Act of 1789 indicates the variety and extent of the powers that the parish could take for such purposes.

Three or more governors and directors may act, and make rules and orders.

One overseer to be appointed for each ward in the parish.

Power to enlarge the infirmary, and build a chapel, and purchase places for employing the poor; and to borrow money for those purposes: £10,000 at interest, and 5 per cent. yearly to be paid off. . . .

Power to hire places to employ the poor, and to keep the workhouse and other buildings in repair. . . .

Vestry may appoint surveyors of the highways.

Rate to be laid for the relief of the poor, and for repairing highways.

Vestry to appoint beadles, watchmen, and patrols. . . .

Vestry to appoint a committee for paving, cleansing, and lighting the streets. . . . Committee to cause the streets to be repaired, cleansed, and lighted, and the garden in Hanover Square to be embellished. . . . Names of streets to be put up, and houses and lamp-irons numbered. . . .

Vestry to make rates for paving, &c. Bond Street, Blenheim Street, and part of Stafford and other Streets. . . .

Rates not to exceed the highest sum raised in any year within the last six years. . . .

Places exempt from the provisions of the act for paving, cleansing, and lighting, Berkeley Square, or Grosvenor Square, paved by 6 Geo. III, c. 54 and 14 Geo. III, c. 52. Piccadilly, between Clarges Street and Hyde Park Corner, Park Lane, between Piccadilly and Hertford Street, or to Oxford Street, or parts adjoining. . . .

Carriages not to pass along Maddox Street and Mill Street, for one hour before and an hour after divine service on Sundays, Christmas Day, and Good Friday.

Scavengers not to sweep dirt, &c. within ten feet of the common sewers. . . .

No hoards to be erected without licence.

Ascertaining the hours of taking away night soil, 12 o'clock at night and 5 o'clock in the morning, from Michaelmas to Lady Day, 12 o'clock at night and 4 o'clock in the morning the other part of the year. . . .

Rates of houses let in separate apartments, &c. to be paid by owners. Rates for ambassadors' houses to be paid by the landlords. Lands, &c. to be rated for paving, according to the extent of the pavement, 6d. per square yard, per annum. Persons dissatified with the rates may apply to the vestry for relief; and if dissatisfied may appeal to the Quarter Sessions for Middlesex. . . .

Number of vestrymen to constitute a meeting, of the rector, or curate, and one churchwarden, and eight vestrymen. . . .

Commencement of the act, 1 Dec. 1789. . . .

329. Statistics of Parochial Expenditure

(J. Marshall, *A Digest of all the Accounts relating to the Population, Productions, Revenues [&c.] ... of the United Kingdom ...* I (1833), pp. 32, 38.)

The figures are for the year 1803 and the annual averages of the years 1783–1785 and 1813–1815.

COUNTIES arranged in Order of their Total Population, in 1801.	Total Population, in 1801.	PAROCHIAL EXPENDITURE, for all other purposes than Relief of the Poor.						For Maintenance of POOR.	
		Law Charges, Removals, &c.			Church, Bye Highway, County Rate, &c.			In Workhouse.	Out of Workhouse.
		1783–5. £	1803. £	1813–15. £	1783–5. £	1803. £	1813–15. £	£	£
Middlesex	818,129	4,629	18,084	23,432	8,861	111,691	163,066	224,048	125,152
Lancaster......	672,731	4,245	12,743	28,811	6,937	70,651	144,398	34,290	113,992
York, W.R. ..	563,953	3,488	11,528	20,756	3,338	81,234	108,824	25,727	160,742
Devon........	343,001	3,819	4,542	9,060	5,124	28,241	72,769	22,377	121,646
Kent........	307,624	3,961	8,888	17,113	6,454	42,070	86,969	88,269	118,239
Somerset......	273,750	4,019	5,072	9,048	4,778	21,983	51,101	18,926	102,865
Norfolk	273,371	2,894	6,031	9,548	6,317	29,854	50,364	44,967	124,766
Surrey........	269,049	3,210	8,536	11,169	8,983	37,177	60,585	75,106	58,769
Gloucester	250,803	2,230	4,370	7,544	4,219	29,036	52,050	16,318	92,727
Stafford	239,153	2,428	5,389	10,545	4,440	20,794	36,431	15,225	68,186
Essex	226,437	3,958	7,287	13,595	8,685	32,965	45,541	40,681	136,460
Southampton..	219,656	3,556	5,101	5,999	7,045	21,338	31,406	39,558	84,461
Suffolk	210,431	2,113	4,694	8,374	4,877	27,889	51,405	51,673	68,291
Lincoln	208,557	2,168	5,320	10,964	4,166	46,694	95,083	14,937	80,638
Warwick	208,190	2,880	5,599	10,658	6,125	30,129	56,886	19,822	97,531
Chester	191,751	1,931	3,171	7,891	1,556	16,766	40,642	3,235	63,394
Cornwall	188,269	1,504	3,046	4,015	2,461	13,900	25,003	3,212	51,438
Wilts.	185,107	2,501	3,682	5,705	3,530	18,800	33,404	14,747	113,889
Salop	197,639	1,624	3,136	4,415	3,111	14,510	25,082	20,806	45,941
Derby	161,142	1,946	4,025	6,493	2,048	19,554	35,014	5,389	49,071
Durham	160,861	1,052	2,720	4,834	2,171	13,262	20,795	7,125	44,841
Sussex........	159,311	2,741	5,746	9,489	4,568	21,174	30,741	47,559	132,299
Northumbld...	157,101	815	2,149	4,927	525	12,328	19,593	5,548	46,869
York, N.R.....	155,506	872	2,509	3,902	911	25,427	44,544	5,411	43,291
Nottingham ..	140,350	1,648	3,230	6,945	3,451	16,518	36,038	9,315	34,908
York, E.R.	139,433	930	2,946	4,710	335	23,493	47,227	7,667	33,721
Worcester	139,333	1,500	3,543	4,309	3,625	13,103	20,459	11,060	60,175
Northampton..	131,757	1,808	3,287	4,621	3,543	20,921	31,401	12,812	81,795
Leicester	130,081	1,596	3,895	6,400	2,742	24,137	40,370	10,775	69,136
Cumberland ..	117,230	875	2,064	3,586	315	5,512	19,663	4,935	22,669
Dorset........	115,319	1,702	2,209	3,408	3,091	11,028	16,041	12,487	52,285
Oxford	109,620	1,496	2,614	4,457	2,239	11,836	24,771	12,124	76,565
Berks.	109,215	1,622	3,610	4,205	2,640	10,863	17,954	14,405	67,589
Buckingham ..	107,444	1,742	2,623	5,820	3,680	15,233	23,271	17,201	68,950
Hertford	97,577	1,122	2,257	3,540	3,854	11,767	15,106	21,082	35,298
Cambridge....	89,346	1,045	1,588	3,530	2,662	13,093	19,901	9,974	44,510
Hereford......	89,191	1,058	1,596	3,664	1,259	12,662	18,095	4,135	42,336
Bedford	63,393	651	1,175	1,805	1,660	8,429	17,318	8,440	28,455
Monmouth....	45,582	767	1,478	1,962	1,881	4,993	10,090	1,164	17,120
Westmorld. ..	41,617	296	459	911	140	3,353	6,340	1,224	12,613
Huntingdon ..	37,568	433	1,098	1,135	1,727	5,992	9,556	3,540	20,327
Rutland	16,356	94	398	474	318	4,180	7,058	2,061	6,215
WALES	541,546	3,365	6,433	13,610	6,573	30,225	58,198	7,086	141,282
TOTAL.	8,872,980	91,996	190,072	327,585	163,511	1,034,105	1,834,523	1,016,446	3,061,447

COUNTIES arranged in order of their Total Population, in 1801.	Number of PERSONS Relieved						Number of Members in Friendly Societies, in	
	Permanently In Workhouse.		Out of Workhouse.		Relieved Occasionally.			
	1803.	1815.	1803.	1815.	1803.	1815.	1803.	1815.
Middlesex	15,186	16,279	12,185	17,956	24,765	81,433	72,741	60,579
Lancaster.........	2,719	4,412	14,448	23,096	13,175	18,753	104,776	137,655
York, West Riding .	2,534	3,179	20,149	23,163	13,961	18,387	59,558	74,005
Devon...........	2,713	3,007	18,237	19,008	9,776	11,119	31,792	48,607
Kent	6,337	8,179	9,227	14,386	15,129	19,361	12,633	15,640
Somerset	1,902	2,027	12,944	15,612	8,144	11,278	19,848	23,883
Norfolk	3,996	3,403	13,668	16,956	14,114	14,164	14,821	13,587
Surrey...........	5,268	6,366	5,173	8,468	17,167	8,087	19,199	21,805
Gloucester	1,857	1,745	11,851	13,042	10,893	11,891	19,606	24,567
Stafford	1,828	1,767	6,829	10,414	6,608	11,863	32,852	41,213
Essex	2,969	3,175	11,219	13,916	13,412	17,334	14,890	34,425
Southampton......	3,537	3,717	7,959	10,241	11,378	9,529	4,733	11,013
Suffolk	4,098	3,788	8,066	11,709	15,850	13,080	11,448	13,335
Lincoln	1,112	1,381	6,609	7,773	5,821	6,288	7,530	8,658
Warwick	1,981	2,017	10,624	12,541	6,416	7,006	17,000	26,330
Chester	273	592	7,504	8,746	7,398	9,908	14,828	19,626
Cornwall	399	576	6,415	7,489	3,581	4,967	16,736	21,390
Wilts.	1,617	1,192	12,500	14,836	11,111	13,229	11,330	15,302
Salop	1,586	3,717	5,644	7,934	5,767	8,236	19,144	23,638
Derby	462	626	4,699	6,617	4,030	7,696	22,681	22,412
Durham	746	741	7,099	8,760	2,596	4,127	11,556	13,115
Sussex	3,823	4,387	9,415	13,876	6,891	8,065	4,419	4,790
Northumberland ..	600	765	7,801	8,946	2,618	3,453	11,606	12,193
York, North Ridg..	506	644	5,643	6,231	3,183	3,527	9,718	8,885
Nottingham	965	1,131	3,467	5,000	2,450	6,056	15,202	19,149
York, East Riding..	614	815	3,991	5,574	2,074	4,633	11,248	11,371
Worcester	1,150	1,071	6,236	6,685	5,055	5,301	12,845	13,458
Northampton	1,394	965	7,314	8,552	4,800	6,526	8,062	10,150
Leicester	954	1,183	6,446	7,693	3,919	6,799	10,889	15,425
Cumberland	602	663	3,170	4,159	1,923	1,829	7,788	9,807
Dorset...........	930	1,010	5,734	7,996	4,490	6,678	3,795	5,952
Oxford	1,243	837	6,539	7,520	6,148	7,219	5,010	5,922
Berks.	1,169	1,382	5,620	8,567	8,266	9,064	2,843	3,558
Buckingham	1,260	1,271	6,505	6,917	5,392	6,750	4,079	5,917
Hertford	1,754	1,495	4,197	4,824	4,649	5,955	8,622	10,477
Cambridge	892	748	3,870	4,805	3,368	5,625	3,173	4,524
Hereford..........	303	305	4,515	5,697	3,542	4,412	2,811	2,854
Bedford	674	880	2,516	2,979	2,072	3,171	2,730	3,647
Monmouth........	133	99	1,943	2,319	1,354	1,704	3,799	7,923
Westmorland......	152	269	1,934	2,196	911	977	2,435	1,278
Huntingdon	353	368	1,588	1,906	1,322	3,071	1,740	2,470
Rutland	169	128	498	610	393	304	1,704	1,398
WALES	722	830	24,208	28,042	9,987	14,313	30,130	45,097
TOTAL	83,468	93,141	336,199	423,678	305,899	423,158	704,350	861,657

330. County and Parochial Expenditure, 1783–1832

(G. R. Porter, *The Progress of the Nation* (1851), p. 517.)

The principal objects for which provision is thus made are, the repairing of bridges, building and repairing gaols, houses of correction, shire-halls, and courts of justice; the construction and support of lunatic asylums; the expense of criminal prosecutions; the conveyance of prisoners to and from places of confinement before and after trial; the apprehending of vagrants; the expenses of coroners, of militia, of county elections, and various minor sources of expense. [Porter.]

Years.	Total Sum Assessed and levied by local authorities.	Payments thereout for other purposes than the Relief of the Poor.	Sums Expended in Law, Removals, &c.	Sums Expended for the Relief of the Poor.	Total Sums Expended.
	£.	£.	£.	£.	£.
Average of 1783–84–85	2,167,748	163,511	91,996	1,912,241	2,167,148
1803	5,348,204	1,034,105	190,072	4,077,891	5,302,070
1812–13	8,640,842	1,861,073	325,107	6,656,105	8,865,838
1813–14	8,388,974	1,881,565	332,966	6,294,584	8,511,863
1814–15	7,457,676	1,763,020	324,664	5,418,845	7,508,853
1815–16	6,934,425	1,212,918	..	5,724,506	6,937,424
1816–17	8,128,418	1,210,200	..	6,918,217	8,128,417
1817–18	9,320,440	1,430,292	..	7,890,148	9,320,440
1818–19	8,932,185	1,300,534	..	7,531,650	8,832,184
1819–20	8,719,655	1,342,658	..	7,329,594	8,672,252
1820–21	8,411,893	1,375,868	..	6,958,445	8,334,313
1821–22	7,761,441	1,336,533	..	6,358,703	7,695,236
1822–23	6,898,153	1,148,230	..	5,773,096	6,921,326
1823–24	6,833,630	1,137,598	..	5,736,898	6,874,496
1824–25	6,972,323	1,212,199	..	5,786,989	6,999,188
1825–26	6,965,051	1,246,145	..	5,928,501	7,174,646
1826–27	7,784,352	1,362,377	..	6,441,088	7,803,465
1827–28	7,715,055	1,372,433	..	6,298,000	7,670,433
1828–29	7,642,171	1,280,328	..	6,332,410	7,612,738
1829–30	8,161,281	1,322,239	..	6,829,042	8,151,281
1830–31	8,279,217	1,540,198	..	6,798,889	8,339,087
1831–32	8,622,920	1,646,493	..	7,036,968	8,683,461
1832–33	8,606,501	1,694,670	254,412	6,790,800	8,739,882

B. THE POOR LAWS AND THEIR ADMINISTRATION

331. The Speenhamland Decision, 6 May 1795

The decision of the Speenhamland meeting, subsequently adopted as an order by the Berkshire magistrates, to allow the poor rate to be used to supplement the wages of employed labourers, was the first such decision to lay down a scale of relief according to the price of bread and the size of the family. It was quickly imitated throughout southern England and by 1830 the principle had spread to every county in England and Wales except Northumberland.

(a) Advertisement in the Reading Mercury, 20 April 1795

BERKSHIRE, TO WIT,

At the General Quarter Sessions of the Peace for this County, held at Newbury on Tuesday the fourteenth instant, the Court having taken into consideration the great inequality of Labourers' Wages, and the insufficiency of the same for the necessary support of an industrious man and his family; and it being the opinion of the gentlemen assembled on the Grand Jury, that many parishes have not advanced their labourers' weekly pay in proportion to the very high price of corn and provisions, do (in pursuance of the Acts of Parliament enabling and requiring them so to do, either at the Easter Sessions, yearly, or within six weeks next after) earnestly request the attendance of the Sheriff and all the Magistrates of this County, at a Meeting intended to be held at the Pelican Inn, in Speenhamland, on Wednesday the sixth day of May next, at ten o'clock in the forenoon, for the purpose of consulting together with such discreet persons as they shall think meet; and they will then, having respect to the plenty and scarcity of the time, and other circumstances (if approved) proceed to limit, direct, and appoint the wages of day labourers. By order of the Court.

w. BUDD, Deputy Clerk of the Peace.

Newbury, April 17, 1795.

(b) Minutes of the Berkshire Justices, meeting at Speenhamland, Newbury, on 6 May 1795

(Berkshire Sessions Order Book (1791–1795), pp. 434–436.)

6th May, 1795. BERKSHIRE, to wit.

At a General Meeting of the Justices of this County, together with several discreet persons assembled by public advertisement, on Wednesday the 6th day of May 1795, at the Pelican Inn in Speenhamland (in pursuance of an order of the last Court of General Quarter Sessions) for the purpose of rating Husbandry Wages, by the day or week, if then approved of, Charles Dundas, Esq., in the Chair,[1]

RESOLVED UNANIMOUSLY,

That the present state of the Poor does require further assistance than has been generally given them.

RESOLVED,

That it is inexpedient for the Magistrates to grant that assistance by regulating the Wages of Day Labourers, according to the directions of the Statutes of the 5th Eliz.

[1] The names of nineteen others, of whom seven were clergymen, follow.

and 1st of James: But the Magistrates very earnestly recommend to the Farmers and others throughout the county, to increase the pay of their Labourers in proportion to the present Price of Provisions; and agreeable thereto, the Magistrates now present have unanimously Resolved, That they will, in their several divisions, make the following calculations and allowances for relief of all poor and industrious Men and their families, who to the satisfaction of the Justices of their Parish, shall endeavour (as far as they can) for their own support and maintenance.

That is to say,

When the Gallon Loaf of Second Flour, weighing 8 lb. 11 ozs. shall cost 1s.

Then every poor and industrious Man shall have for his own support 3s. weekly, either produced by his own or his family's labour, or an allowance from the poor rates, and for the support of his Wife and every other of his family, 1s. 6d.

When the Gallon Loaf shall cost 1s. 4d.

Then every poor and industrious Man shall have 4s. weekly for his own, and 1s. 10d. for the support of every other of his family.

And so in proportion, as the price of Bread rises or falls (that is to say) 3d. to the Man, and 1d. to every other of the family, on every 1d. which the loaf rises above 1s.

332. Debates in the House of Commons on Samuel Whitbread's Bill to regulate the wages of labourers in husbandry, 12 Feb. 1796 and 11 Feb. 1800

(Cobbett's *Parliamentary History*, XXXII, 703–715; XXXIV, 1426–1429.)

Whitbread (1758–1815), the brewer and friend of Fox, proposed to revive the wage-fixing powers given to the Justices by the Act of 1563, and to empower them to fix minimum wages and determine hours for agricultural labourers. It was rejected without a division both in 1796 and when reintroduced in 1800.

12 February 1796.

*W*hitbread–. . . . felt as much as any man how greatly it was to be desired that there should be no legislative interference in matters of this nature, and that the price of labour, like every other commodity, should be left to find its own level. From reasonings upon the subject, the result was that it always would find its level. But the deductions of reason were confuted by experience, for he appealed to the sense of the House whether the situation of the labouring poor in this country was such as any feeling or liberal mind would wish? He did not mean that the wages of the labourer were inadequate for his subsistence and comfort in times of temporary scarcity and unusual hardship; but even at the period preceding such distress, the evil had prevailed. In most parts of the country, the labourer had long been struggling with increasing misery, till the pressure had become almost too grievous to be endured, while the patience of the sufferers under their accumulated distresses had been conspicuous and exemplary. . . . He could quote the writings of Dr. Price, in which he showed that in the course of two centuries, the price of labour had not increased more than three or at most four-fold; whereas the price of meat had increased in the proportion of six or seven; and that of clothing, no less than fourteen or fifteen-fold in the same period. The poor-rates, too, had increased since the beginning of this century from £600,000, at which they were then estimated, to upwards of three millions. Nor was this prodigious increase in the poor-rates to be ascribed to the advance of population; for it was doubtful whether any such increase had taken place. At the present period the contrary seemed to be the case. By the pressure of the times, marriage was discouraged; and among the laborious classes of the community, the birth of a child, instead of being hailed as a blessing, was considered as a curse. . . . It was his wish to rescue the labouring poor from a state of slavish dependence; to enable the husbandman, who dedicated his days to incessant toil, to feed, to clothe and to lodge his family with some degree of comfort; to exempt the youth of this country from the necessity of entering into the army or the navy, and from flocking to great towns for subsistence; and to put it in the power of him who ploughed and sowed and threshed the corn, to taste of the fruits of his industry, by giving him a right to a part of the produce of his labour. . . . Here was no departure from established precedents, no introduction of unknown principles. The Statute of the 5th of Elizabeth was enacted expressly for the purpose of regulating the price of labour. This Statute was acted upon for forty years, when it was afterwards amended by a subsequent one in the reign of James I. bearing a similar title. He would not be understood as commending the principle of these Statutes; on the contrary he was of opinion that they operated as a clog to industry by permitting Justices to fix the maximum of labour. But so late as the 8th of his Majesty, Justices were empowered to regulate the wages of tailors, and even now the Lord Mayor and Council of London control those of the silk-weavers. To those who were afraid of entrusting Justices with power, he should only say that he left the power where he found it. At present they were possessed of the power to oppress the labourer; and this Bill only invested them with the additional power to redress his grievances. By fixing the minimum of the wages of labour, a comfortable subsistence was secured to industry, and at the same time greater exertions were prompted by the hope of greater reward. . . .

Pitt–. . . . The present situation of the labouring poor in this country was certainly not such as could be wished, upon any principle, either of humanity or policy. That class had of late been exposed to hardships which they all concurred in lamenting, and were equally actuated by a desire to remove. . . . But trade, industry and barter would always find their own level, and be impeded by regulations which violated their natural operation and deranged their proper effect. . . . The evil, in his opinion, originated in a great measure, in the abuses which had crept into the Poor Laws of this country, and the complicated mode of executing them. . . . The Laws of Settlement prevented the workman from going to that market where he could dispose of his industry to the greatest advantage, and the capitalist, from employing the person who was qualified to procure him the best returns for his advances. These laws had at once increased the burdens of the poor, and taken from the collective resources of the State to supply wants which their operation had occasioned, and to alleviate a poverty which they tended to perpetuate. . . . The encouragement of Friendly Societies would contribute to alleviate that immense charge with which the public was loaded in the support of the poor, and provide by savings of industry for the comfort of distress. . . . He conceived, that to promote the free circulation of labour, to remove the obstacles by which industry is prohibited from availing itself of its resources, would go far to remedy the evils, and diminish the necessity of applying for relief to the poor-rates. . . . He should wish, therefore, that an opportunity were given of restoring the original purity of the poor laws, and of removing those corruptions by which they had been obscured. . . . By the regulations proposed, either the man with a small family would have too much wages, or the man with a large family, who had done most service to his country, would have too little. So that were the minimum fixed upon the standard of a large family, it might operate as an encouragement to idleness on one part of the community; and if it were fixed on the standard of a small family, those would not enjoy the benefit of it for whose relief it was intended. What measure then could be found to supply the defect? Let us, said he, make relief in cases where there are a number of children, a matter of right and an honour, instead of a ground for opprobrium and contempt. This will make a large family a blessing and not a curse; and this will draw a proper line of distinction between those who are able to provide for themselves by their labour, and those who, after having enriched their country with a number of children, have a claim upon its assistance for their support. All this, however, he would confess, was not enough, if they did not engraft upon it resolutions to discourage relief where it was not wanted. . . . These great points of granting relief according to the number of children, preventing removals at the caprice of the parish officer, and making them subscribe to Friendly Societies, would tend, in a very great degree, to remove every complaint to which the present partial remedy could be applied. Experience had already shown how much could be done by the industry of children and the advantages of early employing them in such branches of manufactures as they are capable to execute. The extension of schools of industry was also an object of material importance. If any one would take the trouble to compute the amount of all the earnings of the children who are already educated in this manner, he would be surprised, when he came to consider the weight which their support by their own labours, took off the country, and the addition which, by the fruits of their toil, and the habits to which they were formed, was made to its internal opulence. The suggestion of these schools was originally drawn from Lord Hale and Mr. Locke, and upon such authority he had no difficulty in recommending the plan to the encouragement of the Legislature. . . . Such a plan would convert the relief granted to the poor into an encouragement to industry, instead of being, as it is by the present Poor Laws, a premium to idleness, and a school for sloth. . . . The law which prohibits giving relief where any visible property remains should be abolished. That degrading condition should be withdrawn. No temporary occasion should force a British subject to part with the last shilling of his little capital, and compel him to descend to a state of wretchedness from which he could never recover, merely that he might be entitled to a casual supply. Another mode also of materially assisting the industrious poor was the advancing of small capitals which might be repaid in two or three years while the person who repaid it would probably have made an addition to his income. . . .

Buxton–. . . The Bill did not appear likely to be of much service, for if the price of labour were to be fixed by the Justices of Peace, he feared many industrious people would be thrown out of employ, and become a burden to their respective parishes. The people he alluded to were those who, by sickness or old age, were rendered incapable of doing so much as a common labourer, and who would consequently be rejected for persons of more strength and activity. He had consulted with various well-informed farmers and gentlemen in Norfolk who unanimously concurred in opinions that the Bill would be injurious. . . .

Whitbread–. . . It has been stated as an objection to the Bill that it goes to fix the price of labour; but gentlemen do not attend to the circumstance that it does not go to determine what should be the general price of labour, but only what should be the least price of labour under particular circumstances. As to the particular case of labourers who have to provide for a number of children, the wisest thing for Government, instead of putting the relief afforded to such on the footing of a charity, supplied, perhaps, from a precarious fund, and dealt with a reluctant hand, would be at once to institute a liberal premium for the encouragement of large families. . . . [XXXII, 703–715.]

11 February 1800.

Whitbread rose to move for leave to bring in a Bill to explain and amend the Act which regulates the wages of labourers and husbandmen. When he had first the honour of making a similar motion, his proposition was assented to *nem. con.* After he had brought in his Bill, and only upon the motion for its being read a second time, the Chancellor of the Exchequer objected to the provisions of it, observing that a thorough revision of the Poor Laws was necessary; and he pledged himself to bring in a Bill for that purpose. The Bill was brought in and printed, but was never brought under the discussion of the House. All its provisions were regarded as impracticable. Finding that the right hon. gent. had given up all idea of prosecuting a measure which he formerly seemed to have so much at heart, he himself was determined to renew his attempts, and to revive his Bill. Those who knew him would not suppose that he wished the poor to be overpaid. He was well aware that in many places, especially in great manufacturing towns, those who earned more than was sufficient to provide for their families, usually squandered the surplus away in ruinous luxuries. But in every well-regulated community, artificers and labourers should be paid so as to be enabled to keep themselves and families in a comfortable situation. It was his creed with respect to the poor, that no excuse should be left them for doing wrong, and that when they offended, severity should be employed in punishing their offences. . . . In 1795 their distresses were nearly the same as they are now; and very exemplary attention was likewise then shown by the richer classes to alleviate their distresses, but, before they received that relief, the pressure under which they laboured was extreme. The farmers would not raise the price of labour: he consulted the Statute Book, but could discover nothing in it that would compel the farmers to do their duty. The Justices, he found, had no power to grant relief, but they were armed with power to oppress the poor. In virtue of the 5th Elizabeth, c. 4. the Justices had the power of regulating the maximum of labour. This was highly oppressive to the labouring poor. A law therefore appeared necessary for enabling the Justices to regulate also the minimum of labour. . . .

Pitt-. . . . The measure now proposed struck him as highly improper. It went to introduce legislative interference into that which ought to be allowed invariably to take its natural course. . . . It proposed one standard for the price of labour, without considering whether the labourer was young or old, whether sickly or robust, whether an unmarried man, or a man with a numerous family to support. The distresses of the poor would be best relieved, not by any general law, but by parochial aid administered by those who were intimately acquainted with their situation. . . .

Whitbread said he was ready to give the higher classes credit for their charity, but he thought it an alarming thing that so many of the lower classes of society were doomed to subsist on charity. Charity afflicted the mind of a good man because it took away his independence–a consideration as valuable to the labourer as to the man of high rank. . . . [XXXIV, 1426–1429.]

333. Sir Frederick Morton Eden on the state of the Poor in 1797

(Eden, *The State of the Poor*, II (1797).)

Eden's exhaustive survey of poor law administration in England and Wales illustrates the early pauperization of agricultural labourers and town artisans in the south, and the workings of the 'roundsmen' system which was particularly common in Buckinghamshire and parts of the Midlands.

Clyst St. George (Devon). . . . No labourer can, at present, maintain himself, wife, and two children, on his earnings: they have all relief from the parish, either in money, or in corn at a reduced price. Before the present war, wheaten bread, and cheese, and, about twice a week, meat, were their usual food: it is now barley bread, and no meat: they have, however, of late, made great use of potatoes. Their common earnings are 6s. a week, and liquor. An industrious healthy man, however, can earn 8s. a week, by task work, on an average, throughout the year. Labourers' children, here, are often bound out apprentices, at 8 years of age, to the farmers by the parish; a labourer, prior to the present scarcity, if his wife was healthy, could maintain two young children on his 6s. a week, and liquor, without any parochial relief. A very few years ago, labourers thought themselves disgraced by receiving aid from the parish; but this sense of shame is now totally extinguished. . . . [p. 137.]

Reading. Many of the labouring class of the community, here, possess very little economy, or foresight. It is not uncommon for a healthy young fellow, who has ample means of supporting himself, and family, by his own industry, to request his parish to pay the midwife for his first child. It very rarely happens, that a labourer supports himself, wife, and 2 children, without applying for parochial aid: weavers, who can earn 18s. a week, do not hesitate soliciting relief, if a temporary stagnation of business curtails their common receipts, and reduces them to those difficulties, which a little parsimony might have obviated. Tea is generally used here, twice a-day, by the Poor: the other part of their diet is, principally, the best wheaten bread; and, occasionally a little bacon: it is seldom sufficiently boiled, and is thought to give them the sallow complexion which is much observable here. In point of expense, their general diet as much exceeds, as, in point of nutrition, it falls short of, the north country fare, of milk, potatoes, barley bread and hasty-pudding. [p. 14.]

Winslow (Bucks.) This parish contains about 1400 acres, and 1100 inhabitants: 101 houses pay the window-tax, and, (it is supposed,) about 110 are exempted. The occupations are shop-keeping, inn-keeping, farming, lace-making, and day-labour. Labourers earn from 6s. to 7s. a week, besides breakfast; in hay-time, 7s. a week, and board; and during the corn harvest, 2 guineas a month and board. Lace-makers earn, from 8d. to 9d. a day, on an average. There seems to be here a great want of employment: most labourers are, (as it is termed,) *on the Rounds*; that is, they go to work from one house to another *round* the parish. In winter, sometimes, 40 persons are on the rounds. They are wholly paid by the parish, unless the householders choose to employ them; and, from these circumstances, labourers often become very lazy, and imperious. Children, about ten years old, are put on the rounds; and receive from the parish, from 1s. 6d. to 3s. a week. . . .

Farms are from £60 to £400 a year. About 200 acres are arable land, and cultivated with wheat, beans, and oats: the remainder of the parish is grassland. There are no commons. In 1744 a hamlet belonging to the parish, containing about 400 acres, was enclosed; and in 1766 the other part of the parish was enclosed. Upon the enclosure of the open fields, land was given in lieu of tithe. The rise of the Rates is chiefly ascribed to the enclosure of common fields; which, it is said has lessened the number of farms, and, from the conversion of arable into pasture, has much reduced the demand for labourers. An old man of the parish says, that, before the enclosures took place, land did not let for 10s. an acre, and that, when he was young, the name of roundsman was unknown in the parish. It must however be considered, that, now a great part of the labour done in the parish, is paid for, out of the Poor's Rate, in money given to roundsmen. . . .

The Poor are maintained, partly, at a work-house, and, partly, at their own houses. 16 Paupers are at present in the work-house, under the care of a Contractor, who farms them at 3s. a week each, and is likewise allowed their earnings: he received only 2s. a week before the late dearness of provisions took place. The people in the house are old women and children, and one man. Lace-making is their chief employment. [pp. 29–30.]

334. William Hale to Patrick Colquhoun, 21 Oct. 1800

(Public Record Office, Home Office, 42/52.)

For the bad harvests of 1795–1801 and their effects, see also Nos. 351–353. There were deaths from starvation in the East End of London. Colquhoun (1745–1820), the metropolitan Police Magistrate and author of several tracts on police and poor-law reform, had helped in the establishment in 1795 of a public soup-kitchen in Spitalfields.

4, Wood Street, Spitalfields: . . . Being at this time one of the overseers of this Parish, I feel it my duty to inform you of the alarming state of our numerous poor in general. As a silk manufacturer I am in some measure acquainted with the distressed circumstances of many, and from my local situation know of many families that work for me, who, although they are in full employ, the whole amount of their week's industry is not competent to purchase for themselves and children a sufficiency of the simple article of bread. But in the discharge of my parochial office I am frequently called upon to witness scenes of the most awful distress; to visit families who, to satisfy the cravings of hunger, have long ago been forced to part with their clothes and linen, and, almost expiring amidst the awful horrors of starvation, have scarcely a rag to cover their nakedness. An apothecary not far from me informing me a few weeks back of the dreadful situation of the poor, told me that in the course of his practice since last November he knows of above a hundred cases of children dying for want of food, and of about 40 grown-up people that had also fell [sic] victims to that awful calamity; and added that he could take me to scores of families that had been so long pinched with hunger, that if I was only to give them one meal's victuals, as much as they could eat, the consequences would be fatal to their lives.

Where people are for a time out of employ, or through sickness are not able to work, their situation is dreadful in the extreme. As an overseer I am frequently under the necessity of visiting such scenes of distress, and yet have not the means of giving them an adequate relief. I leave their dismal habitations with the bitter reflection that their *weekly* pittance which I had just given them, is not sufficient to purchase a competency of the single article of bread for *one day*. I am far from wishing to describe the situation of the lower class of people in Spitalfields to be worse than the poor of other parishes. To speak in general terms as to their employment &c &c they are not, and had we but a certain proportion of poor as in other parishes, we could give them a proportionable and suitable relief; but it is their number that ruins us, and which makes it totally impossible for us to give them that succour their distressed situation requires.

I was at our workhouse near the whole of yesterday. The number of our paupers in the house then was 412. It is considerably more than full. We are obliged to put them three and in some cases four in a bed. Our parochial expenses daily increase upon us, and our debt daily accumulates. The amount of debts that we owe to the mealman, butcher, &c without any present ability to pay is £1972-16-5½, and though we had made use of every means to abridge the expense, and observed the most strict economy in all the Departments, we had the additional mortification to find we were £396-17-2 worse than we were at Midsummer. Before we can now pay any tradesman a quarter's bill, we are four quarters in arrear with him, in consequence of which we in some instances begin to find it difficult to purchase the necessary articles of life without great disadvantage. . . . A great part of our poor rates are wrung from those families who, I am certain, are not able to pay. Many of them are summoned, who appeal to the Magistrate; some are excused half the sum, and others do not pay at all. Many that are respectable mechanics in this parish, and contributed to the relief of the poor, unable to bear up under the pressure of the times, have had their goods seized. Their poverty has descended into indigency, the pride of their independency is broke, and they become paupers of the parish. Under all these afflicting circumstances, the apothecary for our parish informed me yesterday that the infirmary (in the workhouse) was more than full of the sick; that they, though bad with fevers, were obliged to lay [sic] two in a bed throughout the whole place, and that for want of better accommodation and an apartment to put them in, as they got a little better many lives were lost. We have had several consultations respecting raising the poor rates still higher. Some of course would pay more; but a great proportion who now contribute a small sum, would then break up and pay nothing, and the general opinion appears to be that it would answer no good end.

Thus, Sir, I have taken the liberty to give you a brief statement of the melancholy facts which exist in our parish, Bethnal Green and Mile End, New Town, which three parishes nearly comprehend the whole of what is generally understood to be Spitalfields. . . . We see our work-house already too full without possessing the means to go in, whilst we know not where to put them; and solicitations for relief from the distressed, daily increase upon us, whilst we are utterly unable to succour their miserable wants. Our manufactories for this month past have been greatly upon the decline, and thus, without any probable appearance of the fall of the present enormous high price of provisions our prospect with the winter before us is dreadful in the extreme, and unless we have some unexpected relief that will in some measure be adequate to meet the distresses of the poor, I tremble for the consequences. . . .

335. Malthus on the Poor Laws

(T. R. Malthus, *First Essay on Population* (1798), Economic Society Reprint (1926), pp. 71–100.)

For Malthus, and his views on population, see No. 418. His view that the poor laws did more harm than good was criticized by such observers as George Rose (No. 336), but was influential at the time and had some effect on the minds of the framers of the Poor Law Amendment Act of 1834.

To remedy the frequent distresses of the common people, the poor laws of England have been instituted; but it is to be feared, that though they may have alleviated a little the intensity of individual misfortune, they have spread the general evil over a much larger surface. It is a subject often started in conversation, and mentioned always as a matter of great surprise, that notwithstanding the immense sum that is annually collected for the poor in England, there is still so much distress among them. Some think that the money must be embezzled; others that the church-wardens and overseers consume the greater part of it in dinners. All agree that some how or other it must be very ill-managed. In short the fact, that nearly three millions are collected annually for the poor, and yet that their distresses are not removed, is the subject of continual astonishment. But a man who sees a little below the surface of things, would be very much more astonished, if the fact were otherwise than it is observed to be, or even if a collection universally of eighteen shillings in the pound instead of four, were materially to alter it. I will state a case which I hope will elucidate my meaning.

Suppose, that by a subscription of the rich, the eighteen pence a day which men earn now, was made up five shillings, it might be imagined, perhaps, that they would then be able to live comfortably, and have a piece of meat every day for their dinners. But this would be a very false conclusion. The transfer of three shillings and sixpence a day to every labourer, would not increase the quantity of meat in the country. There is not at present enough for all to have a decent share. What would then be the consequence? The competition among the buyers in the market of meat, would rapidly raise the price from six pence or seven pence, to two or three shillings in the pound; and the commodity would not be divided among many more than it is at present. When an article is scarce, and cannot be distributed to all, he that can shew the most valid patent, that is, he that offers most money becomes the possessor. If we can suppose the competition among the buyers of meat to continue long enough for a greater number of cattle to be reared annually, this could only be done at the expense of the corn, which would be a very disadvantageous exchange; for it is well known that the country could not then support the same population; and when subsistence is scarce in proportion to the number of people, it is of little consequence whether the lowest members of the society possess eighteen pence or five shillings. They must at all events be reduced to live upon the hardest fare, and in the smallest quantity.

It will be said, perhaps, that the increased number of purchases in every article, would give a spur to productive industry, and that the whole produce of the island would be increased. This might in some degree be the case. But the spur that these fancied riches would give to population, would more than counterbalance it, and the increased produce would be to be divided among a more than proportionably increased number of people. All this time I am supposing that the same quantity of work would be done as before. But this would not really take place. The receipt of five shillings a day, instead of eighteen pence, would make every man fancy himself comparatively rich, and able to indulge himself in many hours or days of leisure. This would give a strong and immediate check to productive industry; and in a short time, not only the nation would be poorer, but the lower classes themselves would be much more distressed than when they received only eighteen pence a day.

A collection from the rich of eighteen shillings in the pound, even if distributed in the most judicious manner, would have a little the same effect as that resulting from the supposition I have just made; and no possible contributions or sacrifices of the rich, particularly in money, could for any time prevent the recurrence of distress among the lower members of society whoever they were. Great changes might, indeed, be made. The rich might become poor, and some of the poor rich: but a part of the society must necessarily feel a difficulty of living; and this difficulty will naturally fall on the least fortunate members. . . .

. . . Supposing the quantity of food in any country to remain the same for many years together; it is evident that this food must be divided according to the value of each man's patent, or the sum of money that he can afford to spend in this commodity so universally in request. It is a demonstrative truth therefore, that the patents of one set of men could not be increased in value, without diminishing the value of the patents of some other set of men. If the rich were to subscribe, and give five shillings a day to five hundred thousand men without retrenching their own tables, no doubt can exist, that as these men would naturally live more at their ease, and consume a greater quantity of provisions, there would be less food remaining to divide among the rest; and consequently each man's patent would be diminished in value, or the same number of pieces of silver would purchase a smaller quantity of subsistence.

An increase of population without a proportional increase of food, will evidently have the same effect in lowering the value of each man's patent. The food must necessarily be distributed in smaller quantities, and consequently a day's labour will purchase a smaller quantity of provisions. An increase in the price of provisions would arise, either from an increase of population faster than the means of subsistence; or from a different distribution of the money of the society. The food of a country that has been long occupied, if it be increasing, increases slowly and regularly, and cannot be made to answer any sudden demands; but variations in the distribution of the money of a society are not unfrequently occurring, and are undoubtedly among the causes that occasion the continual variations which we observe in the price of provisions.

The poor-laws of England tend to depress the general condition of the poor in these two ways. Their first obvious tendency is to increase population without increasing the food for its support. A poor man may marry with little or no prospect of being able to support a family in independence. They may be said therefore in some measure to create the poor which they maintain; and as the provisions of the country must, in consequence of the increased population, be distributed to every man in smaller proportions, it is evident that the labour of those who are not supported by parish assistance, will purchase a smaller quantity of provisions than before, and consequently, more of them must be driven to ask for support.

Secondly, the quantity of provisions consumed in workhouses upon a part of the society, that cannot in general be considered as the most valuable part, diminishes the shares that would otherwise belong to more industrious, and more worthy members; and thus in the same manner forces more to become dependent. If the poor in the workhouses were to live better than they now do, this new distribution of the money of the society would tend more conspicuously to depress the condition of those out of the workhouses, by occasioning a rise in the price of provisions.

Fortunately for England, a spirit of independence still remains among the peasantry. The poor-laws are strongly calculated to eradicate this spirit. They have succeeded. in part; but had they succeeded as completely as might have been expected, their pernicious tendency would not have been so long concealed.

Hard as it may appear in individual instances, dependent poverty ought to be held disgraceful. Such a stimulus seems to be absolutely necessary to promote the happiness of the great mass of mankind; and every general attempt to weaken this stimulus, however benevolent its apparent intention, will always defeat its own purpose. If men are induced to marry from a prospect of parish provision, with little or no chance of maintaining their families in independence, they are not only unjustly tempted to bring unhappiness and dependence upon themselves and children; but they are tempted, without knowing it, to injure all in the same class with themselves. A labourer who marries without being able to support a family, may in some respects be considered as an enemy to all his fellow-labourers.

I feel no doubt whatever, that the parish laws of England have contributed to raise the price of provisions, and to lower the real price of labour. They have therefore contributed to impoverish that class of people whose only possession is their labour. It is also difficult to suppose that they have not powerfully contributed to generate that carelessness, and want of frugality observable among the poor, so contrary to the disposition frequently to be remarked among petty tradesmen and small farmers. The labouring poor, to use a vulgar expression, seem always to live from hand to mouth.

Their present wants employ their whole attention, and they seldom think of the future. Even when they have an opportunity of saving they seldom exercise it; but all that is beyond their present necessities goes, generally speaking, to the ale-house. The poor-laws of England may therefore be said to diminish both the power and the will to save, among the common people, and thus to weaken one of the strongest incentives to sobriety and industry, and consequently to happiness. . . .

To remove the wants of the lower classes of society, is indeed an arduous task. The truth is, that the pressure of distress on this part of a community is an evil so deeply seated, that no human ingenuity can reach it. Were I to propose a palliative; and palliatives are all that the nature of the case will admit; it should be, in the first place, the total abolition of all the present parish-laws. This would at any rate give liberty and freedom of action to the peasantry of England, which they can hardly be said to possess at present. They would then be able to settle without interruption, wherever there was a prospect of a greater plenty of work, and a higher price for labour. The market of labour would then be free, and those obstacles removed, which as things are now, often for a considerable time prevent the price from rising according to the demand.

Secondly, Premiums might be given for turning up fresh land, and all possible encouragements held out to agriculture above manufactures, and to tillage above grazing. Every endeavour should be used to weaken and destroy all those institutions relating to corporations, apprenticeships, &c. which cause the labours of agriculture to be worse paid than the labours of trade and manufactures. For a country can never produce its proper quantity of food while these distinctions remain in favour of artizans. Such encouragements to agriculture would tend to furnish the market with an increasing quantity of healthy work, and at the same time, by augmenting the produce of the country, would raise the comparative price of labour, and ameliorate the condition of the labourer. Being now in better circumstances, and seeing no prospect of parish assistance, he would be more able, as well as more inclined, to enter into associations for providing against the sickness of himself or family.

Lastly, for cases of extreme distress, county workhouses might be established supported by rates upon the whole kingdom, and free for persons of all counties, and indeed of all nations. The fare should be hard, and those that were able obliged to work. It would be desirable, that they should not be considered as comfortable asylums in all difficulties; but merely as places where severe distress might find some alleviation. A part of these houses might be separated, or others built for a most beneficial purpose, which has not been unfrequently taken notice of, that of providing a place, where any person, whether native or foreigner, might do a day's work at all times, and receive the market price for it. Many cases would undoubtedly be left for the exertion of individual benevolence.

A plan of this kind, the preliminary of which, should be an abolition of all the present parish laws, seems to be the best calculated to increase the mass of happiness among the common people of England. To prevent the recurrence of misery, is, alas! beyond the power of man. In the vain endeavour to attain what in the nature of things is impossible, we now sacrifice not only the possible, but certain benefits. We tell the common people, that if they will submit to a code of tyrannical regulations, they shall never be in want. They do submit to these regulations. They perform their part of the contract: but we do not, nay cannot, perform ours: and thus the poor sacrifice the valuable blessing of liberty, and receive nothing that can be called an equivalent in return.

Notwithstanding then, the institution of the poor-laws in England, I think it will be allowed, that considering the state of the lower classes altogether, both in the towns and in the country, the distresses which they suffer from the want of proper and sufficient food, from hard labour and unwholesome habitations, must operate as a constant check to incipient population. . . .

336. George Rose on the Poor Laws, 1805

(*Observations on the Poor Laws and on the Management of the Poor in Great Britain* . . .
(London, 1805), 44 pp.)

Rose's pamphlet criticized the Malthusian view, and compared the English and Scottish systems of poor-law administration. Rose was Joint Secretary of the Treasury, 1783–1801, and Treasurer of the Navy, 1807–1818.

. . . The relief of the poor, so strongly recommended by religion and humanity, is no less obviously required by the plainest dictates of good policy. It is impossible that multitudes should perish or suffer from hunger (and that multitudes must suffer and perish if not in some shape relieved, seems certain) without endangering the safety and destroying the comfort of the rest of the community.

An enquiry whether our present poor laws may not be so modified and improved as to afford this relief effectually, with a moderate burden on the community, seems peculiarly incumbent on us, when the alternative for improving the condition of the poor, proposed by one of those authors[1] who has entered most deeply into the subject . . . is considered, namely, a reduction in our population, in order to increase the price of labour, by taking measures for lessening the number of marriages, at a period when . . . the number of our people are become as necessary for our defence, as for the increase of our wealth and prosperity.

The author taking it for granted, that the whole system was wrong from the beginning, proposes what he calls a gradual abolition of the poor laws, according to which he thinks the poor's rates would begin rapidly to decrease, and in no great length of time would be completely extinguished. But when it is admitted that the basis of the measure must be a rigid denial of all assistance as of right, to the most industrious of even the married poor . . . it will probably not be necessary to say much against its being hastily embraced. It appears but too obvious that even if our population were reduced, and the wages of labour increased, and if all the inducements to improvident marriages which our present poor laws can be supposed to create were removed, still many inevitable causes of poverty would remain. A man might marry with the fairest prospect of being able to maintain a family, yet by the loss of his life

[1] Malthus.

or of his health . . . his wife and children might be reduced to the most extreme distress, without a relation or a friend to succour them; by sickness, too, and by accidents, as well as by old age, friendless persons must often become incapable of earning their bread. Fluctuation in manufactures, risks attendant on trade, a variety of accidents to which a man is . . . exposed . . . must reduce many to indigence. What is to become of persons so circumstanced under a repeal of all the poor laws? We are told the hand of charity might be stretched out to them; is it certain that it would? Or if it were, would it be fair or just to throw the whole burden of such contributions on the generous, the humane, and the benevolent . . . and to allow the unfeeling, though perhaps the most wealthy inhabitants of a district, to escape entirely? . . . It should also be remembered that in the donations of private charity there is frequently a great misapplication of its bounty, and not always a good selection of its objects, arising from frauds and impositions . . . which well-regulated public charity can easily guard against. . . .

As regards Scotland . . . I am informed, from an authority on which I can confidently rely, that the poor there are supported by collections at the church doors; by certain small fees on marriages, baptisms and funerals; and by the interest of sums given or bequeathed for that purpose; and, when the above are not sufficient, by an assessment[1] laid on the parish by authority of the heritors or landholders; and the Kirk Session, that is, the Minister and Elders of the parish. The amount of this assessment, upon the whole, is (as in fact it is in England) in proportion to the actual number of poor in the parish at the time. The selection of objects to whose relief this assessment is to be applied, is likewise vested in the Kirk Session, whose ordinary functions in this respect may, if there is any reason to suspect abuse, be controlled by a meeting of the heritors. In England the selection is in the first instance in the overseers, but checked by the vestries, consisting of the inhabitants who pay the rates, with an appeal to magistrates. The imposition therefore and appropriation of this tax, in both parts of Great Britain being lodged in the hands of the very persons who are to pay it, should give the fairest chance for such imposition and appropriation being limited by the necessity of the case. But the chief distinction between England and Scotland with regard to the poor arises from the superior management in the latter,[2] where they are as effectually provided for as in the former, though at infinitely less expense, and in some degree at least to early education. There are few workhouses in Scotland (none except in a few great towns) nor is it usual to send any persons there who can find places of residence for themselves; infinite advantage is likewise derived from the constant and active attention of the clergy, who are invariably resident, and who have no interest to balance against their feelings of humanity. Another essential difference in the management of the poor in the two countries is

---

[1] Half of this is payable by the heritors, who are the proprietors of lands and houses in the parish, and the other half by the inhabitants in it.

[2] There is but too much reason to believe that in many parts of England the cultivators of the land are more solicitous to restrain the price of labour than to keep down the poor's rate; in which case the latter in fact becomes a part of the former. In Sussex, an agricultural county, the *parishioners* relieved are 23 in 100 on the population, and the rates average £1 5s. 11½d. on it; in Surrey, 13 in 100, and 13s. 3½d.; in Kent, 14 in 100, and 16s. 7¼d.; and in Hants, 15 in 100, and 16s. 3d. There is indeed no county except Wiltshire, where the proportion of parishioners relieved is so high compared with the population as in Sussex; it is there the same, but the money raised per head on the population is only 16s. 0¾d.

that in Scotland there is no power, or at least none that is commonly exercised, of removing paupers from the parish in which they have not acquired a settlement by residence, to the parish where their right of settlement is. The just apportionment of this burden between the parishes may be, though it very seldom is, I understand, a matter of legal discussion; but it does not affect the personal freedom of the pauper, who may reside where he pleases. When disputes arise concerning the settlement of particular paupers, which are not often carried to the extremity of legal proceedings, if the parish where he is resident at the time prevails, the parish found liable, might perhaps insist on his coming to reside there; but in practice, I am assured, the managers of the funds for relief of the poor in such parish, always prefer paying a compensation to the parish where he resides, from the expense of which the law has relieved it; which saves to themselves or to the public the charges of removing him; and if he is able to do a little work in aid of the public fund, it leaves him undisturbed in the exercise of such industry or occupation.[1]

From the short account here given of the Scottish laws and practice relative to the support and employment of the poor, it will be seen that contrary to the supposition too hastily adopted, of our English writers on the subject, the general principles of the system very nearly resemble those of England; the difference seems . . . to be in the *execution* of the powers which the Legislature has provided for attaining its object.

It has been sometimes said that the habits of the people of Scotland are more friendly to order and economy than those of their richer and more populous sister kingdom; but in the first place, the situation of a considerable part of Scotland is now by a rapidly progressive improvement in agriculture, manufactures and commerce, approaching to that of England: and in the next place, it is a matter of reasonable doubt whether what is sometimes argued as the *cause* is not in truth in a very considerable degree the *effect* of the different execution of the Poor Laws in the respective countries; that in the first, being in the very nature and essence of political society, much less productive of idleness and dissipation in the labouring classes of the community, than that in the second; but so little have the Scots been disposed to abolish the similar laws for provision for the poor which subsist in their own country, that of late when peculiarly unfavourable seasons, in conjunction with other unforeseen circumstances, greatly increased the number of the poor, and the necessity for their immediate support, several districts in Scotland, where that necessity was most strongly felt, resorted to the Legislature for provisions of a kind more entirely analogous to those which the law of England afforded, than those already recognised in the law of Scotland, or the practice under it, were supposed to allow. *A special Act of Parliament* was obtained in 1802 by the inhabitants of Edinburgh and the surrounding districts, for an assessment for the support of their poor; and in Glasgow and the parts of the Counties of Lanark and Renfrew in its vicinity, which in the number and in the employment of their inhabitants, are more exactly similar than any other parts

[1] In Scotland there is no law of settlement. Every man has always been at perfect liberty to settle wherever he pleased. It is, however, established that the parish where a man has resided for three years becomes *bound* to maintain him; but there is no power to remove him before the expiration of that period, in order to prevent his acquiring a settlement. Where no such residence has taken place, the burden falls upon the parish where he was born. . . .

of Scotland, to the populous manufacturing districts of England, assessments[1] are resorted to *under the authority of the common law*, differing very little in any of its circumstances from the Poor's Rate of England.

In England, the mischiefs attendant on the Poor Laws, which have been most complained of by many eminent writers on political economy, are not so much the burden of the poor as the restraint of which that has perhaps been the principal occasion. The law of settlement, as Dr. Adam Smith, with his usual wisdom and power of illustration, has observed, separated the parishes of England, as if there were a sea between them, and prevented, as mischievously as absurdly, the free transport and circulation of labour throughout the kingdom. This evil is however at least in part remedied. By the Act for encouraging Friendly Societies which I had the honour of introducing in 1793, the law of settlement was first shaken; under that, all persons who should become members of such societies were protected from being removed, till they should become actually chargeable: the effect I expected from that was produced, for in two years afterwards another Act was passed extending that provision to all persons whatever. . . . It must be the wish of every one to avoid all unnecessary restraints on the poor; which are as hurtful to the state as they are oppressive to the individuals. . . .

Another means of improving our system, which may excite our hope and animate our zeal, still remains; I mean the abolition of workhouses, by the repeal or material alteration of the 9th of George I which was the first deviation from the principle of the laws of Queen Elizabeth. If proper employment shall be found for the poor at their own homes, workhouses will, but in a few instances, be necessary: nothing of the sort will be wanted but places of retreat for such of the aged, the infirm, or infant poor, who are so utterly friendless as to have no relations or other persons who will take care of them: and even for those, cottagers will in the country often be met with who will receive and provide for them at a moderate expense, in addition to what in most instances would be earned by the paupers; whereas, from there being no means of setting the poor at work at home, the children above a certain age, and persons whose strength has to a considerable degree failed them, are in one case taken from their parents, and in the other from their children, grandchildren or relations, and forced into the workhouse, removed from the dwelling in which perhaps they were born, and separated (in instances of aged persons) for ever, from everyone dear to them, either as relations or friends; by which, misery and wretchedness is entailed on the individuals; the remaining strength left to them is lost to the public, as before observed, and a heavier expense frequently incurred for their maintenance than the allowance which the unfortunate creatures would be content to receive at home. How often this happens is well known, and has been repeatedly observed upon; it has, indeed, fallen under my own immediate observation, in a very extensive parish where the concerns of the poor are regularly attended to weekly, by as highly respectable and as worthy a set of independent men as are to be found in any part of the kingdom. If I should be asked why I do not interpose as a magistrate, and order

[1] In the year 1804 the whole sum expended for the poor in the city and suburbs of Glasgow was £6,130, of which £5,190 was raised by assessments, and £940 arose from ordinary funds in aid thereof. The population is about 80,000, the sum raised therefore is but a trifle more than 1s. 6d. per head on that number. . . .

relief for such persons at home, my answer would be that I have hitherto confined myself to remonstrances and persuasion, by which I have sometimes, though with difficulty, succeeded; thinking that it is, on the whole, more for the interest of the poor, as well as more consonant to my own feelings to avoid the other course till the last extremity.

It appears by the returns that paupers in workhouses cost about £12 3s. 6¼d.[1] each annually, throughout England, and other parishioners relieved out of workhouses about £3 3s. 7½d.[2] Where parishes therefore do not compel *all* applicants for relief to go into the workhouse, the loss to the public may be estimated at about £9 per head on the persons so shut up, creating an augmentation of the Poor's Rate to a very large amount.

The avowed policy of workhouses, in many instances, is a mixture of maintenance, and punishment by imprisonment; hoping thus, by deterring application for relief, that so few will apply as to make the heavier expense *per head* for a smaller number in the workhouse a lighter burden on the parish, than affording relief out of the house to a greater number; which can only be corrected by the interposition of magistrates under the 36th George III, ch. 23.

If it shall be thought right to provide for adding something to the earnings of persons in advanced periods of life, without shutting them up in workhouses, which I am persuaded would be as economical as humane, a more favourable attention may possibly be thought due to the Friendly Societies, the members of which have a very strong claim on the public at large: it is now ascertained that there are of these in England alone (exclusive of very numerous Societies in Scotland) upwards of 700,000 of both sexes, although the Act I had the happiness of introducing for their encourage-ment and security has not been passed more than eleven years; before which, their establishments were precarious, and their numbers comparatively small. When it is considered that these are composed chiefly of persons supporting themselves entirely by their labour, associated for the express purpose of relieving each other during sickness, out of the hard earnings of that labour in periods of their lives when they usually have strength to do so; but whose funds, arising from the very limited sums it is possible for them to spare, cannot be sufficient to enable allowances being made to members who may live to very advanced ages, in their progress to which the ability to work gradually fails; it may not in such cases be too much to expect that there should be some contribution, as of right, from the parishes, towards the maintenance of such persons. That, I believe, would be consistent with the wisest policy as well as with humanity; for if there could be secured to the laborious poor, entering into these Societies, an independent maintenance, in the event of its pleasing God to give them a length of life beyond the strength necessary for their avocations, and they could

---

[1] There is reason to believe this is much below the true average, as in many places there are persons residing in tenements erected by, or the property of, the parish, called workhouses, who do not live under the discipline of such houses; they merely reside therein, rent free, and are relieved as other paupers are out of workhouses. This may serve to explain the apparent disparity of expenditure per head on persons in workhouses in several counties, and will make the general rate of such expenditure stated in the abstract, greatly below the truth.

[2] This supposes about 2s. a head to be given to the paupers, not parishioners, who must have been chiefly vagrants.

consequently be freed from the apprehension of confinement and separation from everything dear to them in their old age, they would, to an infinitely greater extent, become members of them, and exonerate the parishes from any charge for their maintenance in sickness till that period, at which only a small proportion of them arrive. It is hardly possible for those who have not frequently conversed with persons of this description, to form an idea how much such a prospect would contribute to their happiness and comfort. . . .

337. Memorial of the Magistrates of the County of Suffolk, respecting poor rates, 1817

(Report from the Select Committee of the House of Commons on the Poor Laws:
Parliamentary Papers, 1817, VI, pp. 166–167, App. H.)

The disadvantages of the Speenhamland system quickly became apparent after 1815. In 1795–1796 the Suffolk magistrates had supported Whitbread's project of a fixed minimum wage in preference to allowances from the poor rate.

We, the undersigned magistrates of the county of Suffolk, beg leave respectfully to submit to the Committee for the Revision of the Poor Laws, the following observations. . . .

In the present alarming state of the poor rates it must be obvious to the Committee, that there must have been some very unexpected and extraordinary alteration, either in the situation of the poor or in the management of the funds for their relief, when, in no very great space of time, these rates are swelled to an amount not only unprecedented, but beyond what any actual change in the situation of the agricultural population might appear to warrant.

We are perfectly aware, that in an institution embracing such a variety of objects as the rate for the relief of the poor, the sudden and enormous increase of this assessment is not to be ascribed to any *single* cause, but to the co-operation of *many*, concurring to produce a joint effect: nor would we be understood to affirm, that what we are about to suggest is the most general, or even the principal cause of its rapid and astonishing augmentation; but we trust it will appear . . . that it is *one* amongst many others; that it has actually added very materially to the burden of the assessment; and that it is indefensible in every point of view, as being at once unjust, impolitic and cruel.

The circumstance to which we allude is a practice which has prevailed, if not generally, certainly in a considerable part of this county, of giving reduced and insufficient wages to labourers in husbandry, and sending them to the poor rate for the remainder of the sum necessary for their support. Thus, the labourer, whose family requires 18s. a week for their maintenance, receives perhaps 9s. (in some parishes not more than six) from his employer, and the remaining nine from the overseers. It will be evident . . . that a practice like this must necessarily raise the rate far beyond its usual amount; that it is thus made subsidiary to wages; and that it becomes an assessment, not so much for the relief of the poor as of their employers; a great proportion of whose agricultural labour is paid for by the public, though the immediate benefit is exclusively their own.

. . . The evil does not stop here, but accumulates and gathers strength in its progress. If the farmer can reduce his wages to 18d. or 1s. a day, he can, by the same authority, reduce them to 6d. to 3d. or to a penny, and throw his labourer upon the parish for the rest; and if this discretionary power is permitted to the farmer, we do not see how it can be withheld from the carpenter, the bricklayer, the blacksmith, or, in short, from any person exercising a trade and employing the labour of others. By which means the wages of the whole of the labouring poor will be thrown upon the rates, and this most useful and industrious class of the community will become at once eleemosynary and dependent.

We beg to remind the Committee, that if we do not follow up our conclusion to the manufacturing poor, it is because Suffolk is principally an agricultural county, and therefore we wish to confine our suggestions to what falls immediately within our own cognizance. And we also beg to state our conviction, that the situation of the farmers is not such as disables them from paying for their labour at a fair and reasonable rate of wages. If, indeed, the poor rates were levied *solely upon those who employed labourers*, the evil, though great, would be less oppressive. But when it is recollected that the small occupier, who cultivates his little farm by his own labour and that of his family; that the tradesman, the mechanic, and (where cottages are rated, or where a little land is attached to them) *even the labourer* is compelled to pay to this assessment, the hardship and partiality of this practice is most evident and striking.

In large villages and country towns, where a considerable proportion of the inhabitants are subject to the payment of the poor rate, although not occupiers of lands, the injustice of this system is also very apparent. The professional man, the annuitant, the shopkeeper, the artisan, all are taxed for the payment of labour, from which they derive no immediate benefit, and in the profits of which they have no participation.

. . . Such an appropriation of what ought to be the *poor's rate* is *unjust*.

It is also *impolitic*; for it tends to debase the industrious labourer to the class of the pauper; it habituates him to the reception of parish relief; it teaches him to look to the rate for his usual maintenance, instead of applying to it reluctantly in sickness or old age; and it saps the vital principle of industry, and obliterates the little remaining honest pride of independence.

It is *cruel*;—because of the burden of the wages of labour, the immediate profit of which is to others, is thus thrown upon that part of the community which is already borne down by the weight of public taxes, and of the necessary parochial assessments.

. . . For the evil thus detailed, the existing laws . . . furnish no relief. If the labourer, whose earnings are insufficient for his support, applies to a magistrate, the magistrate, *having no power to fix the rate of wages*, MUST, however reluctantly, ORDER relief from the poor rate; and, *as this order is final and conclusive*, the several classes before mentioned as aggrieved by this unequal assessment, are *precluded from the benefit of appeal against the overseers account*, and left without remedy against this glaring act of injustice and oppression.

. . . We hope we may be allowed to call the attention of the Committee to the necessity of putting a stop to this pernicious practice of *mixing the wages of labour with the relief of the poor*. . . . [15 signatures.]

338. Evidence of John Turner, High Bailiff of Birmingham, given before the
Select Committee of the House of Commons on the Poor Laws, 18 March
1817

(*Parliamentary Papers*, 1817, VI, pp. 102–103.)

The burden of the poor rates was at its heaviest between 1815 and 1820: 1817 and 1818 were the
worst years.

. . . For about nine years preceding the present year, the expenses of the poor of
Birmingham have been from £24,000 to £29,000 per annum, except the year 1812,
which was £34,000; the present year the expenses of the poor will amount to £50,000
to Easter next, exclusive of £5,500 that have been collected for the purposes of
[supplying] soup, clothing and coal, making a total of £55,500; the number of
persons in and out of the [work]house have of course increased in the same ratio. . . .
The amount of the whole in the house in January 1816 was 585; in January 1817,
1,152; in February 1816, 451; in February 1817, 1,177. The out poor or casual cases
in those same months, January 1816, was 2,800; January 1817, 5,000; February 1816,
2,700; February 1817, 5,300; and I am sorry to understand today, that in the present
month the out cases are 5,400. . . .

How many do you suppose is the number of paupers entirely?–21,624.

Your whole population is what?–90,000; the present weekly expenses are £1,300;
were we to have a rate per week, which usually produced £1,600 in the year 1815, it
would produce now but £1,000 therefore we are incurring a debt of about £250
per week, in addition to a debt already contracted in the course of the last nine
months, of £12,000. . . . We had hoped that as winter had subsided, and the spring
opened upon us, the improvement of the country with the return of the foreign trade,
would have relieved us from our present difficulties; but those difficulties now, instead
of decreasing, are increasing, and were the Committee to see on a Friday, the day on
which we relieve our poor, the number of persons collected together, it has more
from their numbers the appearance of riot than persons coming to receive relief; from
their numbers only I mean. The annual rental of the parish is £210,170; the annual
rental of property paying poor rates £114,665 leaving an annual rental of £95,505
not rated. Exclusive of the expenses I have taken notice of for the maintenance of
the poor, we are under expenses, such as highways, paving, lighting, and church
levies, which amount to £13,000; . . . we have 18,000 houses in Birmingham; the
average of the expenses from last Easter to the present time is 10s. 4d. in the £, but
at the rate that we are now paying it is 17s. 4d. but then out of the 3,500 houses that
contribute to the maintenance of the poor, there are now not more than 1,500, and
a little more perhaps that contribute every rate, and out of that number a great many
of our best payers are going out of the parish, shutting up their houses, so that it will
eventually fall upon a very small portion in conclusion. I wish to press upon the
minds of the Committee, I may say the awful situation we stand in, because if our
poor have not bread, I need not state what must be the result of it. . . .

339. Statement of the receipts and expenditure of the guardians and overseers of the poor at Birmingham, 28 March 1818 to 27 March 1819

(Edmonds's *Weekly Recorder and Saturday's Advertiser*, 10 July 1819.)

RECEIPTS.	£.	s.	d.
To Balance, brought from last year's account	383	14	1¼
Arrears from Old Overseers	4092	2	1½
Produce of 27 Levies	45198	5	7½
d° d° on gardens	244	8	5
Cash recd. from fathers of illegitimate children	853	12	0
„ „ „ machine in Snow Hill	135	11	4
„ „ „ relatives of paupers	164	2	1½
„ „ „ Overseers of other Parishes (a balance)	816	19	11
„ „ „ Treasurer of the County, for militia families	214	4	0
„ „ „ Key Hill Committee	186	0	0
„ „ for Labour of the Poor	297	11	5¾
„ „ „ Bones and kitchen stuff	8	13	9
„ „ from Mr. Christian, being a surplus collected for Land Tax during his office as Constable	40	0	0
„ „ Insurance from Militia (a balance)	16	3	6
	52651	8	4½

Average number of out-poor cases relieved weekly: 2959
   „   poor in the House   „   „   „   573
   „   children in the Asylum   „   „   393

EXPENDITURE

By weekly payments to out-poor, including vagrants £177–2s. and Vaccination premiums £23	22495	8	11
Flour	2698	18	0
Cheese	509	8	0
Meat and Bacon	1419	1	1
Vegetables, oatmeal and salt	617	7	0
Beer and ale	576	19	3
Milk, butter, &c.	363	13	4
Grocery, soap, candles, &c.	653	8	4
Wine, &c. for the sick, and tobacco for the aged poor	232	0	7
Coals for the workhouse, Public Office and Prison	404	5	5
Mercery, drapery, hats, &c.	2484	3	5
Shoes and leather	1123	11	9½
Surgeons' salaries, £120; drugs £418–16–7½	538	16	7½
Coffins and burials	396	8	11½
Board of Lunatics	900	0	0
Apprentice fees	59	7	6
Removals & journeys, & keep of horse, including straw	585	11	0
A new horse for parish business (removals & journeys)	22	0	0

	£.	s.	d.
Furniture and repairs of the house	815	18	4
Watchman, during the summer season	9	8	6
Housekeeping and incidental expenses	338	1	2¼
Law & Litigation, £1064–10s.; Justices' Clerks, £455–11–9	1520	1	9
Stationery, printing, advertisements, school books, &c.	394	10	8
Constables' Accounts, £1614–3–8; County Rate, £3553–14s.	5167	17	8
Governor, Matron & late House clerk's salary, with board in the House	160	17	0
Present House clerk's salary, without board	71	15	0
Cashier, vestry clerk & assistants, salaries & wages, without board	566	16	0
Overseers, Visitors of the out-poor, salary & wages	102	0	0
Man, for removals & journeys, on parish business, wages	52	0	0
Expenses of collecting foreign district and garden levy	76	19	6¼
Collectors of poor's levies, wages	648	0	0
Keeper of the machine, wages	52	0	0
George Hinchcliffe, balance of salary on leaving his situation	655	0	0
„ „ balance of account for goods	201	18	11¼
Loss in light gold	44	12	0
„ „ workhouse silver tokens	167	16	11
House Constable's wages, 8 weeks	4	16	
By loss in base silver, £2–6s.; base copper, £1–14–6.	4	0	6
By postage	19	11	11½
Workmen on Key Hill, £5–9–4; wheelbarrows, £28–13–2.	34	2	6
Re-assessments & surveying	298	0	5
Sundry persons, for copper change (a balance)	15	3	0
Lichfield Street £1 Notes, & 2s. 6d. & 5s. cards, cancelled	10	0	0
Loss in forged notes	12	1	0
Ground rent for Public Office and Prison	30	0	0
Rent of premises in Water Street	50	0	0
Window tax for Governor's apartments & Public Office	9	15	8½
Insurance from fire, Workhouse, £4–6s.; Public Office, £10.	14	6	
Gratuities to poor persons who work in the House	64	7	9¼
Repairs of the machine in Snow Hill	9	17	0
„ „ „ pass cart, wheelbarrows, &c.	20	15	8
Cleaning Public Office (two years)	20	8	0
Garden seeds & manure for parish ground	58	8	9
Amount paid to executors of Mr. Wilday	46	5	0
Expenses of erecting flour mills & wheat to grind	1362	15	4
Bonds for collectors of poor rates	18	11	3
„ „ „ „ taxes	11	14	3
Collectors' services in obtaining signatures in the Petition against Christ Church Rate Bill	12	0	0
Expenses of deputation to London to oppose the said Bill	60		
	49417	17	4½

ASYLUM EXPENSES.	£.	s.	d.
By bread and flour	1072	8	1
Cheese	134	7	9
Meat & bacon	758	9	6
Vegetables, oatmeal & salt	197	6	0
Malt & hops	78	11	0
Grocery, soap, candles, &c.	528	19	8
Milk, butter, &c.	182	2	0
Coals	117	9	6
Worsted	14	10	6
Governor & Matron's salaries, with board	55		
By balance to next year's account	97	7	0

P.S. The bedding, linen, clothing, shoes, &c. are furnished from
the Workhouse.

	52651	8	4½

340. Report of the Poor Law Commissioners on the agricultural disturbances of 1830

(Extracts from the information received by his Majesty's Commissioners as to the Administration and Operation of the Poor Laws (1833), pp. 24–27.)

The outbreak of violence, directed particularly against threshing machinery, which spread across southern England in 1830, was attributed to distress caused by low wages, and the demoralization produced by the Speenhamland system.

General Report on the Disturbed District of East Sussex

Beer-Shops: The beer-shops are considered as most mischievous. They allow of secret meetings beyond any places previously existing, being generally in obscure situations, kept by the lowest class of persons: they are receiving houses for stolen goods, and frequently brothels; they are resorted to by the most abandoned characters—poachers, smugglers, and night depredators, who pass their time in playing at cards for the expenses of the night, in raffling for game and poultry, and concocting plans for future mischief: they are never without a scout, and are not interrupted by the observation of any person of respectability; no information can be obtained from the masters, who are in the power of their guests, spirits being usually sold without licence; and not one in ten sell home-brewed beer. Similar representations are made in East Kent. A magistrate expressed his opinion that no single measure ever caused so much mischief in so short a time, in demoralizing the labourers. . . .

Rural Police: A more efficient police is a matter of the greatest importance. All classes, proprietors and occupiers, magistrates, overseers,—all require it. Concession to paupers can hardly be avoided under the present insufficient police; and the magistrates consider the calling in the military very objectionable, unless in the last extremity. As to yeomanry, there is so much distress among farmers, and consequently so much discontent, that they are unwilling to enrol themselves: those who, in the good times of farming, had horses fit for yeomanry service, now make use of a cart-horse, or go on foot.

The few who are more opulent hang back; as, from living in isolated situations, their property is completely at the mercy of their own labourers. . . .

The common constables are usually village artizans, competent perhaps to the forms of civil process, and putting down a village broil, but totally unacquainted with the business of police, and in case of great mobs, quite inefficient; they are changed every year, and are seldom willing to serve a second time.

Smuggling: Since the establishment of the preventive service, is much diminished. This diminution has had the effect of increasing the poor-rate, or, as was expressed by an overseer, who is supposed to have had formerly a very accurate acquaintance with the business, "the putting down smuggling is the ruin of the coast". The labourers of Bexhill, and of the villages proceeding eastward towards Kent, used to have plenty of work in the summer, and had no difficulty in finding employment in smuggling during the winter.

The smugglers are divided into two classes, the carriers or bearers, who receive from five shillings per night and upwards, according to the number of tubs they secure, and the batmen. The batmen, so called from the provincial term of bat, for a bludgeon, which they use, consider themselves as of a superior class: they go out in disguise, frequently with their faces blackened, and now with fire-arms; they confine their services to the protection of the others, and are paid 20s. or more per night; and many, perhaps most of them, are at the same time in the receipt of parish relief.

Large capitals have been invested in this business, particularly at Bexhill. Many of the small farmers, if they do not participate, certainly connive at these practices; those who do not directly profit by smuggling, consider that it is advantageous, as finding employ for many who otherwise would be thrown on their parishes.

The smugglers are now much more ferocious since the use of fire-arms is more constant. . . .

Beyond all doubt the practice of smuggling has been a main cause of the riots and fires in Sussex and East Kent: labourers have acquired the habit of acting in large gangs by night, and of systematic resistance to authority. High living is become essential to them, and they cannot reconcile themselves to the moderate pay of lawful industry.

Riots: The riots in the north-east parts of the Rape of Hastings commenced simultaneously on the 5th and 6th of November, 1830. The farmers observed, that their labourers all at once left their work: they were taken away by night by a systematic arrangement; no leader could be identified, but bills were run up at the public-houses in the evening, and in the morning a stranger came and paid.

The mobs generally had written forms containing their demands, they varied a little in the amount of wages, but all agreed in the amount of 'allowance' of 1s. 6d. for every child above two; that there should be no assistant-overseer; that they should be paid full wages, wet or dry; that they would pay their own rents. There were nine cases of incendiarism that winter at Battle. The mob which assembled there, on the day of the magistrates' meeting, amounted to nearly 700: all the principal magistrates of the division, nineteen in number, assembled; the arrival of a troop of horse established order. . . .

A permanent Bench of Magistrates was established at Battle, at which Mr. Cour-
thorpe presided, at their particular request, and directed by day and night the measures
which were requisite for public tranquillity.

This harassing duty continued during a month; but from that period, a certain
degree of intimidation has prevailed in this district. The assistant-overseers having
been then ill-treated by the mobs, are reluctant to make complaints for neglect of
work, lest they should become marked men and their lives rendered uncomfortable
or even unsafe. Farmers permit their labourers to receive relief, founded on a calculation of a rate of wages lower than that actually paid: they are unwilling to put themselves in collision with the labourers, and will not give an account of earnings, or if
they do, beg that their names may not be mentioned. A similar feeling prevails in
East Kent: at Westwell, the farmers are afraid to express, at vestry-meetings, their
opinions against a pauper who applies for relief, for fear their premises should be set
fire to. Two of the fires immediately followed such a resistance; one of them happened to a most respectable farmer, a kind and liberal master, and a promoter of
cottage allotments.

The allowance system is represented to be so established, that without some
legislative enactment, neither overseers, vestries, nor magistrates, can make any
effectual change; and that if local regulations were attempted, a repetition of the
outrages of 1830 may be expected. Day wages seem to be fixed at 2s. to 2s. 3d.;
which are not thought too high, were it not for the rates, but the farmers state that
the present relief, coupled with that rate of wages, is exhausting their capital. The
relief is in great measure compulsory; but it is also considered unnecessary,--for on
an accurate examination of the population, the quantity of acres and the numbers
requisite for the cultivation of the land in its present state, it is calculated that the
money expended for labour, within the Rape of Hastings, is sufficient for the maintenance of nearly the whole of the able-bodied agricultural labourers and families
without assistance from the rates. . . .

C. THE WORKHOUSES

341. Advertisement in the *Reading Mercury*, 1 July 1793

Many parishes during this period sought to lighten the burden of the poor rate by 'farming the
poor' to a contractor, who hoped to make a profit by running the workhouse as a manufactory.

To workhouse-masters and manufacturers of woollen, flax, &c. To let, at Walton-
upon-Thames, in Surrey, a manufactory in the woollen, hemp and flax line,
established in the workhouse of that parish, where the poor consist of about 60 persons,
and the buildings capable of containing a much larger number.

The vestry hereby give notice they will be ready to receive proposals in writing
sealed up, containing the lowest sum by the year (to be paid monthly by equal
payments) on Monday the 8th of July next.

The contractor must engage to carry on the present manufactory, but may establish any other he thinks proper. There are at present about 50 spinning wheels

employed out of the house, on account of the factory, and many more persons learning.

The use of the engines, tools, new erected sheds, &c. to go in the letting, *to be valued*, and the deficiency, if any, made good at the end of the term.

The stock of the factory, which will come to about £70 or £80, to be taken at a fair valuation. The poor to be humanely treated, victualled, clothed and kept constantly clean, to the satisfaction of the select vestry.

Good security will be required, and the names of the contractors to be given in with the proposals.

For further particulars, enquire of Mr. Daniel Keene at Walton; Mr. Johnston, at the Crown Inn, ditto; and in London of Mr. Lake Young, No. 54, Watling-street.

N.B. The waterman goes to and from London twice a week and coaches every day.

342. Poor Law administration in the Parish of St. James's, Westminster

(*Sketch of the State of the Children of the Poor in the year 1756, and of the present State and Management of all the Poor in the Parish of Saint James, Westminster, in January 1797* (London, 1797), 24 pp.)

An Act of 1762 empowered the Vestry of St. James's to appoint 21 gentlemen who, together with the Churchwardens and Overseers of the Poor, were to be called Governors and Directors of the Poor, and to be authorized to make Bye-laws for administering the poor law.

The first attention was paid to the children who were mouldering away in the Workhouse or with profligate and drunken parents; after much search and great difficulty, several *cottagers* on *Wimbledon Common*, fit and proper to be entrusted with the care of children, were induced to take them, and they were placed there accordingly.

THE TERMS AS UNDER:

Three shillings per week for nursing each child; and five or six being placed in one house makes the nurse a good income.

A surgeon and apothecary upon the spot superintends their health and cleanliness.

If a *sick* or *infirm* child is sent, or one *under* the *age of twelve months*, and *recovers* or *lives a year*, the nurse has one guinea given her for her care and success.

All the children are inoculated for the smallpox when deemed proper by the surgeon, and he is paid ten shillings and sixpence for each child who survives that disorder.

The nurse is likewise paid ten shillings and sixpence for every child that has it in the natural way, or is inoculated and survives, but not else.

She has five shillings, upon the like condition, for every child that recovers from the measles or hooping cough.

Besides which gratuities, the nurses are paid such extra expenses in the above or any other sickness or infirmities of the children, as the surgeon or apothecary shall advise, and such gratuity for their trouble as shall be thought reasonable.

If two children die with any nurse in a year, she is discontinued, as it seems to imply want of skill or attention, or both.

They remain at Wimbledon till six or seven years of age, according to their strength and ability, and sometimes longer in cases of sickness or infirmity.

Those who can walk are sent to school, and threepence per week paid their respective mistresses for instructing them to read and sew.

The time when these children were to be brought home was a dreadful period to the children and to the feeling mind; yet, as the expenses of their nursing, clothing and schooling in the country so very much exceeded the expense at the Workhouse great objections were made by many of the inhabitants to the expense they were put to, little schools were established at the Workhouse, and every care taken of them that the nature of the case would admit of. But many objects of profligacy being unavoidably received into the Infirmary at the Workhouse, it became necessary to separate healthy children from the diseases and infirmities incident to old age; and from the pernicious examples of vice and immorality that sometimes are visible in the best-regulated Charities.

Great difficulties and oppositions were made to forming a separate establishment for them; however, in the year 1781, the house, stables, and Riding House, late Mr. Durell's, in King Street, were purchased for £2,200. . . .

A plan for establishing a 'Parish School of Industry' on the premises was then prepared by order of the Board of Governors and Directors of the Poor, and confirmed by Vestry, and has been found effectual to this day, with very trifling alterations.

The unwearied attention that has been given this School has brought it to a state exceeding the most sanguine expectations of its patrons.

All the children are taught their duty as Christians. The girls make and mend their gowns, petticoats and all their clothes; knit their own and the boys' stockings, and make the boys' linen. They also do needlework for hire, the produce of which is hereafter stated.

Besides which, they are taught household, kitchen and laundry work. There are at this time many girls in the School who, at twelve years of age can make a shirt fit for the most respectable inhabitant to wear, and make her own gown and other clothes; wash, iron, cook, clean and scour the house, make beds, and do everything that qualifies them for good and useful servants.

The boys make their own clothes, and clothes for hire; they also mend their own and the girls' shoes; the rest are employed in heading of pins.

The girls and boys bathe alternately during the summer season.

There are 270 children in the School at this time, and there has been (till the late great number apprenticed) 305.

The whole number of children that have *died* from October 1782 are only 6. . . .

TABLE OF DIET.

	Breakfast	Dinner	Supper
Sun.	Broth, 20 children a loaf.	Meat, 6 oz. each and vegetables, 12 children a loaf, ½ a pint of beer each.	Broth, 20 children a loaf.

Mon.	Ditto	Milk porridge, 20 children a loaf.	1 oz. butter each, 12 children a loaf, $\frac{1}{2}$ pint of beer each.
Tue.	Milk porridge, 20 children a loaf.	Meat 6 oz. each, 12 children a loaf, $\frac{1}{2}$ pint of beer each.	Broth, 20 children a loaf.
Wed.	Broth, 20 children a loaf.	Rice milk, 20 children a loaf.	2 oz. cheese each, 12 children a loaf, $\frac{1}{2}$ pint of beer each.
Thur.	Milk porridge, 20 children a loaf.	Meat 6 oz. each, 12 children a loaf.	Broth, 20 children a loaf.
Frid.	Broth, 20 children a loaf.	Milk porridge, 20 children a loaf.	2 oz. cheese each, 12 children a loaf, $\frac{1}{2}$ pint of beer each.
Sat.	Milk porridge, 20 children a loaf.	Meat 6 oz. each, 12 children a loaf, $\frac{1}{2}$ pint of beer each.★	Broth, 20 children a loaf.

The diet for the poor in the workhouse is the same except that they are allowed a greater quantity of meat, bread and beer.

THE CHILDREN'S EARNINGS IN ONE YEAR.

	£	s	d						
6331 shirts made	266	3	3						
1167 shifts	50	4	2						
115 dusters and rubbers		4	11½						
1282 handkerchiefs	3	1	0½						
148 sheets, pairs	5	17	6						
69 table cloths		17	0						
112 pillow cases and marked	2	2	3						
33 stockings marked		4	11						
5 shirts repaired		2	0						
132 napkins		14	3						
4 stocks		1	0						
7 bed gowns & pockets		3	8						
24 neckcloths		2	0						
407 towels		18	9½	330	16	9½			
Ditto boys pin-heading				294	1	11½			
Ditto slop-work				15	11	11	640	10	8
Also, by girls, for the use of the house							69	6	9
By the boys at tailors' work for ditto							82	8	3
By ditto shoe-mending, for ditto							27	19	10
							820	5	6

★ Since East India rice has been brought to England and sold cheap, and meat and bread is so very dear, the dinner on Saturdays both at the Workhouse and the Parish School of Industry is baked rice puddings.

. . . The amount per head of the Board of the Officers, servants, and children for one week: 2s. 1¾d.

. . . After they attain the age of 12½ years, if strong, healthy and well-grown, and if not, at 13, 13½, or 14 years, upon the personal examination of the Governors, they are put upon the Apprentice List, and, when proper places are provided for them, they are apprenticed out.

No children are suffered to go upon liking until the master or mistress has made personal application at the Committee, and, if then approved, the proper Officer is directed to make enquiry into the character and situation in life of every such applicant, and make his report in writing to the next Board, who either agree to, or reject the application, as the person may be fit or unfit to take an apprentice; and none are placed out without such due and strict enquiry, report, and order thereupon. At the expiration of a month or 5 or 6 weeks, the master and child appear again at the Committee, and after examining the child apart as to their diet, lodging, care, instruction and habit of going to Church, they are bound apprentice if the children's accounts are satisfactory, and £2 given with each child, and a double suit of clothing of every sort, and a Covenant entered into to pay the master a further sum of 2 guineas at the expiration of three years, if he takes proper care of his apprentice; but when demanded, a strict enquiry is always made as to the master's conduct to the child, as well as his character in life.

From October 1782 to 31 December 1796, 738 children have been placed out apprentice by the Parish of St. James, and had apprentice fees with them: £1476
And there has been also 441 additional fees paid at 2 guineas each,
amounting to   926–2–0
                                                  _____
                                                  2402–2–0

The time for demanding the remainder is not yet expired.

The children attend Divine Service every morning and evening of the Sabbath Day at St. James's New Chapel and Berwick Street Chapel. Thus by unremitting exertions the children are brought up in the fear of God, in obedience to their King with due respect for their superiors, love of each other and of all mankind; in humility, in industry, in cleanliness, content and cheerfulness.

These objects effectuated, a plan was suggested for employing all the able poor in the Workhouse at some work or manufacture, whereby they may earn their maintenance; and in the year 1790 the Governors and Directors of the Poor contracted with Messrs. Gorton and Thompson, tenants to Lord Bathurst at Cuckney in Nottinghamshire, and very considerable manufacturers, that the Governors should build a workshop capable to hold 90 looms at the least, and keep the same in repair, and that Gorton and Thompson should at their sole expense build and set up that number of patent looms, and all other machinery, wheels, &c. and keep them in repair; and find all other utensils necessary, useful and proper for carrying on the business of spinning, winding and weaving, and all other works incident thereto: and also all candles and other necessaries, and bear all other expenses whatever, except the building the workshop and keeping it in repair, and to allow 2s. 6d. per week for each poor person's labour, who shall do as much work as is usually allotted to a child of 14 years of age, and whatever more work they do, to be paid for at the usual prices; and all the poor that are capable are employed therein, whilst others are employed in needlework, tailoring, shoemaking and mending, opening horsehair. picking cotton and oakum, and in the necessary business of the house.

A state of the poor in the Workhouse, and their employment for a fortnight are as follows:

		£	s	d
At needlework		32	13	12	11
Opening Horsehair★		56	2	15	8
Stripping cotton		3		6	0
Carding flocks		4	2	5	0½
Making slop work		4		13	6
Mending shoes★★		2		12	9
Weaving calico & spinning twine		55	9	4	0
		156	29	9	10½
Making shirts, &c.	17		4	16	2
Mending linen, shoes & other articles	29		1	12	2
	—	46			
		202	35	18	2½

Expense of Provisions for the Poor in the Workhouse for a fortnight.

		£	s	d
Meat			36	11	5
Bread and flour			58	5	1
Beer			19	8	6
Butter and cheese			27	11	9
Milk			13	11	3
Salt, pease and oatmeal			4	6	1
Medicated spirits			2	8	0
Fish, tripe and pastry for sick			5	16	0
Red Port for ditto			2	2	0
Porter for ditto			6	13	11
Grocery			8	13	0
Potatoes, &c.			6	6	11
Number of poor	713	189	13	11
Master & other officers	10	94	16	11½
	723			
Weekly amount per head			2	7½

★ A casual employment, and done by those who are capable of no other work.
★★ This mending shoes is for money, the other shoe-mending is for themselves.

Two clergymen officiate at the Workhouse; the one attends daily to read Prayers, and, whenever called upon, administers the Sacrament to such as express a desire to receive the same; he also attends to baptize such children as are born in the House, and to pray to the sick. The other clergyman attends every Sabbath Day to read Prayers, and preach to such of the poor as are able to be present.

Number and Age of Poor Persons in the Workhouse.

10 years (not exceeding)	51
10 to 20	61
20 to 30	90
30 to 40	79
40 to 50	79
50 to 60	128
60 to 70	129
70 to 80	76
80 to 90	18
90 to 100	2

Total   713, of which there are

Infirm	226
Infants	33
Blind	7
Lunatics and idiots	28
Sick	120
Itch and with venereal complaints	33
Nurses and their helpers	43

—490

Employed

in making & mending house linen	17
In petty offices	29
aged persons in nursing the children of others employed in the manufactory	10
employed on the house account	11

—67

employed in various works for money	156

Total number of poor in the Workhouse	713

Besides the poor maintained in the Workhouse, the old, blind and paralytic people have a weekly allowance of 1s., 1s. 6d., and some 2s. per week out of it, but none more, except their case is attended with particular circumstances of distress.

Ancient Poor to whom Weekly Allowances are made.

Weekly pensioners from	60 to 65 years	72	
	65	70	103
	70	75	63
	75	80	31
	80	85	23
	90		1
			—
			293

Children at nurse at Wimbledon upon the before-mentioned terms	169
There are also made to widowers & widows having one child out of the Workhouse which they are unable to maintain, weekly allowances of 1s. or more, according to their circumstances and abilities; and 2s. per week or more, when there are 2 children; 4s. per week when 3 children; 6s. per week when 4 children; and 2s. per week more for every other child under 7 years of age in the family; at which period, unless prevented by sickness or lameness, they are always admitted into the Parish School of Industry	146
Wives and children of militiamen	61
Ditto paid by other Parishes, but repaid by St. James's	74
Children in Parish School of Industry	270
Lunatics at Hoxton, at 7s. per week each	17
Lunatics in Bethlem Hospital	2
	—
Total number of poor	1745

. . . To those poor whose distresses arise from sickness or otherwise, the acting Overseer, after causing due enquiry to be made (to prevent imposition, which is daily attempted) relieves them according to the nature of their case and number of their family, and reports their situation to the next Board or Committee, which are held alternately every week, and who, after due consideration give such orders as appear necessary for their future relief, either in money, clothes or both. And they also direct the apothecary or surgeon to examine and afford them such assistance as they may judge necessary.

The wives and families of militiamen and substitutes are relieved according to the Directors of the Militia Laws, and under the order of the magistrates acting for the Parish. . . . There are six magistrates, who have for many years met three times a week, and assiduously attended to the Police of the Parish, and conducted gratuitously such parochial concerns as otherwise must have occasioned a heavy expense to the Parish. The magistrates are also Governors of the Poor, as are the Churchwardens and Overseers of the Poor, who continue in office two years, by which means they are perfectly acquainted with the business. . . . It has been a rule in most Parishes that the four Overseers of the Poor continue in office one year only; but it is otherwise in St. James's Parish, and two only go out of office annually, the two junior remaining the second year, as the Church Wardens do, by which method they are perfectly acquainted with the business of the poor before they take the acting part upon them.

The Workhouse and Parish School of Industry have been visited by the Earl of Winchilsea, the late Lord Bathurst, the Lord Somers, Count Rumford, Sir Archibald Edmonstone, Bart., the Dean of Lincoln, Mr. Wilberforce, Mr. Morton Pitt, Mr. Devaynes, Mr. Barclay, and many other gentlemen well acquainted with the business of the poor, who all expressed their highest approbation at the industry, cleanliness and health of the poor, particularly of the children, whose loss by death is much less than any calculation upon that subject. . . .

The frauds and depredations daily attempted by the idle and dissolute, who are an intolerable nuisance in the metropolis, evidently points out the advantages arising from a *permanency* in the Governors and Directors of the Poor, who are thereby qualified to guard against such evils, and who from experience have (in this extensive Parish, where the poor are scattered in various places) notwithstanding their zeal, found that from the want of honesty and industry in the paupers that they cannot be trusted with materials for working at home.

Abstract of General State of Poor Children under the care and management of the Governors and Directors of the Poor of the Parish of St. James's, Westminster, from the 1st of January to the 31 of December 1796.

Number of children transferred from preceding years		650
Born and received this year		565
		1215
Of whom have died in the Workhouse	56	
Ditto in the Parish School of Industry	0	
Ditto with their mothers	32	
Ditto in the country at nurse	14	
	102	
Removed and discharged	273	
Above age	6	
Apprenticed out	113	
	392	494
Left on the care of the Parish		721

N.B. Increase of children this year   72

343. Rules of Kendal Workhouse, 1797

(Sir F. M. Eden, *The State of the Poor*, III (1797), pp. 754–757.)

Eden described this workhouse as "a commodious building, in an airy situation, and kept with great neatness and propriety". Its rules are typical of the stricter and more efficient workhouses of the time.

1, Ordered, that all persons, upon their admission, deliver up such household furniture, linen, and clothes, as they are possessed of, to the master, in order to be cleaned, and made useful for the service of the house; that they be clothed, if necessary, and have their proper apartments and employments assigned them by the master; and their old clothes are to be well cleaned; and if such persons be likely to be discharged from the house, their old clothes are to be kept until they be discharged, and then delivered to them to wear, in exchange for the clothes found by the house.

2, That all who are able, and in health, shall follow the master, or whom he shall appoint, to church, every Sunday; the men, women, boys, and girls respectively two by two, and, after divine service is ended, shall return in the same decent order, without staying by the way, or loitering, on pain of losing their next meal.

3, That, if any get drunk, they are to be severely punished by the master; and that care be taken to avoid all contentions and quarrels among themselves, that there be no cursing or swearing, nor revilings or bitterness amongst them, but they are to live in love and unity together, as becomes Christians; and, by their mutual kindness, and good offices, do all they can to make one another easy and happy.

4, That no person go out of the prescribed bounds, without leave from the master or mistress, and to return in good order at the time appointed, or be denied going out for a considerable time afterwards.

5, That the master and mistress keep peace and good order in the house; and permit none to fight, quarrel, or give abusive or rude language, without punishment; nor suffer any strong liquors to be drunk, nor tobacco to be smoked, except in the working-rooms, nor tea to be used within the house unless in case of sickness.

6, That all the able Poor be kept to such work, or employment, as they are fit for, and call them to it by ring of bell, in summer, from six in the morning till seven in the evening; in winter, from seven or eight in the morning, till eight in the evening; allowing proper time for breakfast and dinner, and the children sufficient time to learn to read: and if any grown person refuse to work, such person to be kept on bread and water, in the dungeon, till he is willing to work. Children to be corrected by the master.

7, That the slothful and idle, who pretend ailments to excuse themselves from work, be properly examined; and if it appears that they have been impostors, and have made false excuses, then they shall be punished, by restricting their allowance of diet, or by confinement in the dungeon.

8, That a bell be rung every morning in summer by six, and in winter by seven o'clock, for the healthful people to rise to work, and to go to bed by nine; that the candles and fires be carefully put out at that time in every room, except where there are sick people; and no waste fires to be made.

9, That all the beds be made by those who lie in them, by turns, as soon as those that are in health rise, the rest by persons appointed, before the hour of nine in the morning; the rooms and passages to be swept before ten, and to be washed once a week, or oftener if occasion. The dishes to be washed after every meal.

10, That the children to be washed and cleaned every morning; and some proper person chosen to teach them to read, and to perform such work as may be most beneficial, and not to be permitted to play till they have finished their task.

11, That all the provisions be cleanly and well-dressed; that they breakfast about eight, dine about twelve, and sup about seven: all those who have not done their task by supper-time, to work afterwards, till finished. Care is to be taken that they sit decently at meat.

12, That care be taken to make and mend all the linen and woollen clothes; and when any person dies, to deliver his or her clothes neat and clean to the master, to be laid up in the wardrobe, and also everything else they are possessed of, for the use of the house, and an inventory thereof to be delivered at the next meeting of the trustees.

13, That if any person fall sick or lame, due care shall be taken, and proper diet be allowed.

14, That no person be allowed to smoke in bed, or in their rooms, upon pain of being put six hours in the dungeon.

15, That a book be kept, wherein the names and surnames of every grown person shall be set down, and called every Sunday evening; and if any of the said persons are missing, or any other offence be committed by any in the house, the same shall be noted, in order that the offender be examined and punished.

16, That the visitors attend at the house once a week, and examine into the management of the master and mistress; and likewise hear the complaints and grievances of the Poor, (if any,) and redress the same.

17, Persons convicted of lying, to be set on stools, in the most public place of the dining-room, while the rest are at dinner, and have papers fixed on their breasts, with these words written thereon, INFAMOUS LYAR, and shall lose that meal.

18, That all the Poor relieved in this house, shall wear the badge K.K.P. on the place appointed; and if any of them shall take the same off, they shall be put into the dungeon for four hours.

19, That care be taken to search the beds for fleas, and other vermin; that none of the materials be wasted or spoiled; that there by no defacing of walls, or breaking of windows; and that these orders be read once a week, that none may pretend ignorance.

20, That graces be said before and after meat, and the prayers read every morning and evening, immediately after breakfast and supper, either by the master, or whom he shall appoint, &c.

The number of Paupers in the work-house at present (4th April 1795) is 136; *viz.* 57 males, and 79 females: 8 are bastards.

Of these there are 38 under 10 years of age; 26 between 10 and 20; 12 between 20 and 30; 8 between 30 and 40; 15 between 40 and 50; 4 between 50 and 60; 17 between 60 and 70; 10 between 70 and 80; 6 between 80 and 90.

Their employments are various: the men are generally employed out of the house: the women spin, and weave Kendal-cottons, &c. Children are generally sent to the different manufactories; where they earn about 1s. a week each.

Part V

ECONOMIC DEVELOPMENT

Introduction

THE documents in this section survey the economic achievements that make this period the high-water mark of the Industrial and Agricultural Revolutions, a time of transition from the agrarian society of the eighteenth century, with its emphasis still on the land and its possession, to the urbanized, industrial age that made Victorian England the 'workshop of the world'. Not only was Britain embarking on a career of industrial and commercial expansion; she still had the problem, accentuated during the long French wars, of feeding a population growing at an unprecedented rate. The coincidence of these factors produced a renewal of the 'agricultural revolution' that had taken place in the early eighteenth century. The efforts of the early pioneers in farming techniques and animal husbandry had enabled mid-century Britain not only to feed her growing population, but to remain a substantial exporter of grain. G. R. Porter's statistics[1] show, for the years 1760–1769, an excess of export over import of 1,384,561 quarters of wheat and meal; only in two of the ten years was there no exportable surplus. By 1780 the picture was changing; after 1783 and until the end of the period there were no more than six years in which there was any surplus at all, and after 1789 only two. From 1790 to 1832 the excess of imports over exports totalled more than 22 million quarters, and during that time there were years of such bad harvests that, had more foreign corn been available, imports would have been greatly swollen. The restriction of trade during the years 1793–1815 also prevents Porter's figures from offering a complete picture of Britain's new needs, but even so they are impressive.

The relative lull in the progress of enclosure during the period 1780–1795 is explained by these figures and by the state of the money market. The cost of enclosure was high, and it was often difficult to raise mortgages whenever the low price of government stock meant a high interest yield, for the usury laws still forbade the exaction of a rate of interest on private loans greater than 5 per cent. The average price of corn per decade hardly changed between 1760 and 1790; 3 per cent stock did not rise above 80 till 1789. The incentive to enclose was weakened, and the means to carry it out difficult to get, during the first decade of the Younger Pitt's administration.

The war, and an accompanying run of bad summers and severe winters, soon altered the position, while the inflation after 1797 and the increasing cost and difficulty of importing foreign corn also tended to raise prices and at the same time to make capital more easily available. It became worth the farmer's while to increase his corn acreage, even to plough normally unprofitable scrub and waste. Arthur Young accused the Norfolk farmer of complacency for thirty years from 1760 to 1790,[2] but from that date he found evidence of a second revolution, stimulated by scarcity, high

[1] No. 344. [2] No. 346.

449

450 ECONOMIC DEVELOPMENT

prices, the availability of capital, and the example of such successful landlords as Thomas Coke, and marked by a renewal of large-scale enclosure and the cultivation of the commons and wastes.

Enclosure was never the essential preliminary to improvement, nor did it necessarily lead to it: it was said that "enclosure makes a good farmer better but a bad farmer worse". Unless enclosure was followed by better management, however, its expense was hardly worth while, and there was a great demand for information on farming techniques. William Marshall, one of the foremost agriculturalists of the time and with more practical experience than Arthur Young, detailed the ways in which the landlord could encourage his tenants to make better use of their land,[1] while Young wrote in praise of the large farm, encouraged large-scale capital investment, and publicized in his *Tours* and his *Annals of Agriculture* the newest improvements and hints on estate management.[2] Enclosures have at times been criticized as harmful to the interests of the poor, and Arthur Young himself on occasion pointed out the injustice that might be done. It is true that where the enclosure of arable open fields was followed by conversion to pasture, hardship and a rise in the poor rate might ensue, and that rent-paying occupiers might be forced down to the level of landless wage-labourers. But leaseholders for life, copyholders by inheritance and squatters with twenty years' occupation were treated as owners, and received allotments of land in compensation for the loss of common rights. If some of the small farms so created were uneconomic and had to be sold to a neighbouring landowner, the seller did not necessarily fall on the parish rates; some probably became prosperous tenant farmers, using the capital gained by selling their land to stock a leasehold farm under an 'improving' landlord. The effects of enclosure on other small farmers were temporarily mitigated by the prosperity of the war years, and it was not until after 1815 that the decline of the yeomanry was noticed. On the whole, enclosure, stimulated by expanding markets and the high price of corn and meat, benefited all classes, and many observers pointed out that the demand for labour on the newly enclosed farms was often increased by the extension of old and the creation of new employments, not only on the land–where work was also made more regular by the demand for hedging and ditching and other winter work–but in the villages revitalized by enclosure and offering opportunities for more carters, wheelwrights, smiths, builders, thatchers and others.[3] Modern studies have confirmed that population tended to increase in areas of new enclosure at this time. As for the cottagers and squatters, scratching a precarious existence from the wastes, the land was better used under enclosure, and the loss of their independence compensated by steady employment as wage-labourers.[4] A complicating factor was the war-time dislocation of the currency and the country's foreign trade, which raised the cost of living rather more than the increase in agricultural wages in general allowed for,[5] and the bad harvests of 1795, 1799 and 1800[6] caused acute distress to the labouring classes, alleviated only at the cost of pauperization under Speenhamland and by the philanthropy of landowners like Lord Fitzwilliam.[7] That these famine conditions were exceptional and not endemic was largely due to the agrarian revolution, without which Britain could no longer have fed her population even in time of peace.

The prosperous war years, with their high prices and abundant credit, were succeeded by an agricultural depression the more alarming for being unexpected. It

[1] No. 347. [2] No. 348. [3] No. 349. [4] No. 350.
[5] No. 413. [6] No. 351. [7] Nos. 352, 353.

began in 1813, when large-scale imports of foreign corn were resumed, and the farmer's natural response was to demand protection against overseas competition. The real reasons for his difficulties, however, lay deeper, as was recognized by Charles Western, chief spokesman of the agricultural interest in the House of Commons.[1] He maintained that the principal cause was over-production, allied to currency difficulties, the burden of the poor rates, which pressed with particular hardship on the yeoman and small occupier, and a falling market due to a general economic slackening. Though Western was a supporter of the Corn Law policy of 1815, his analysis suggested that no fiscal regulation of itself would cure the difficulty, and this was confirmed by the report of the parliamentary committee of 1821.[2] The maintenance of the Corn Laws, after 1828 in the form of a sliding scale of duties designed to stabilize the price of corn but in practice leading to speculation and violent price fluctuations, had nevertheless become the rallying cry of the landed classes and was to be so until 1846. Then the failure of English agriculture to collapse under tons of foreign corn finally proved that the Corn Laws had in fact done little or nothing for the farmer, except make him unpopular.

The chief sufferers from the post-war depression were the small yeoman farmers and the wage-earning labourers. The evidence regarding the fluctuating fortunes of the yeomanry is scattered and contradictory; generalization is inhibited by the wide variation in local conditions and land tenures. On the whole, it seems that they shared in the general prosperity of the war years, but were disadvantageously placed to weather the post-war storms and suffered particularly from the burden of the 'Speenhamland System' which allowed their wealthier competitors to shrug off part of their wages bills on to the parish at large.[3] If in some districts the yeomanry struggled on, it was at the expense of their living standards; the evidence presented to the 1833 committee of inquiry[4] suggests that their numbers, after increasing up to 1815, declined significantly and in some places startlingly in the next fifteen years. The agricultural labourer too faced a deterioration in conditions under the 'Speenhamland System', though some observers considered that housing conditions were gradually improving.[5] Nowhere in Great Britain, however, were standards so appalling as in Ireland; O'Connell's evidence before the Select Committee of 1825[6] paints a deplorable picture of the grinding poverty that remained characteristic of Irish peasant life for the greater part of the century.

Manufacturing industry was equally affected in this period by the rapid alternation of boom and slump becoming characteristic of the British economy, but partly caused by war and its aftermath. This is, however, conventionally the period of the high 'Industrial Revolution'—a quickening of pace in almost every industry, but especially in the manufacture of cotton textiles, the great proving ground of the new power machinery and archetype of the 'factory system'. Advances were less spectacular in the older-established woollen and worsted industries, but new trends were becoming apparent here also. The decline of the older centres of production in the south-west and East Anglia[7] accompanied the growing prosperity of the West Riding, but these changes were not primarily due to the introduction of power-driven machinery; indeed, the gig mill and the shearing frame were introduced earlier and more generally into the south-western counties than into the north, where the structure of the industry made large-scale innovations difficult. A tract of country round Leeds was

[1] No. 354. [2] No. 355. [3] See Part IV, No. 337. [4] No. 356.
[5] Nos. 358, 359. [6] No. 360. [7] Nos. 361, 362.

now assuming the appearance of an industrial area,[1] but as the Report of the 1806 Committee on the Woollen Manufacture of England[2] pointed out, the 'domestic' system of manufacture was still characteristic of this region, dominated by the small, independent masters and tied together by the cloth halls where their product was marketed. The concern of the Yorkshire masters and workmen lest the factory system should displace them had promoted the setting-up of this committee; its report, though affirming its faith in the virtues and continued stability of this type of organization, was a disappointment to those who had hoped for legislative restrictions to preserve it, for it insisted on the now accepted principle that economic activities and the employment of capital ought not to be subject to artificial regulations. The recommendation that obsolete statutes against machinery, for whose revival agitation had been in progress, should be repealed, was, however, an encouragement to the introduction of the shearing frame; the result was, in 1812, the spread to the West Riding of the 'Luddite' disorders which had originated among the framework knitters of Nottinghamshire–though not, in their case, as a protest against machinery, but against certain trade practices by the employers.[3]

It was in the cotton industry that the factory system and the new power-driven machinery were rapidly changing the face of the countryside and the lives of the people of South Lancashire and Cheshire. These two counties together had 49 cotton factories in 1787, over 800, of which 792 were regularly at work, less than half a century later.[4] By 1835 the cotton industry was giving employment to nearly a quarter of a million people in the factories alone, three-quarters of them in these two counties. The invention of the power loom by the Rev. Edmund Cartwright, its improvement by men of greater practical experience, and its adoption by the manufacturers from the opening years of the century[5] quickly brought cotton to the forefront of British industry and produced profound effects on the lives not only of the population of the cotton districts but of the whole nation. That these effects were in general beneficial tends to be obscured in this period by the fate of the handloom weavers, survivors of a dying trade, for whose desperate plight in the 1820s a parliamentary committee could suggest no other remedy than emigration.[6]

The Midlands, too, prospered. The ultimate effect of the Industrial Revolution was to make Britain predominantly an engineering and textile-manufacturing country; the development of the iron and metal trades is almost as spectacular, and fully as important in this period, therefore, as that of the cotton industry.[7] The invention that made this possible was Cort's 'puddling and rolling' process, discovered in 1783, which allowed iron ore to be smelted with coked coal to make wrought iron. The consequent expansion of the industry at home[8] was accompanied by a steep decline in imports of ore; indeed, large surpluses were available for export.[9]

This was the primary cause of an equally remarkable expansion in coal-mining, particularly in Northumberland and Durham, the most productive of the British coalfields by reason of its ready access to river and sea transport; in 1830 it was still the major source of supply to London and southern and eastern England.[10] The industry's activity was further promoted by the invention of the Davy safety lamp, which enabled deeper and more dangerous seams to be worked, and by the improvement of the steam engine for drainage, ventilation and winding.[11] This coalfield, dominated by the 'Hostmen' of Newcastle whose cartel monopolized the London

---

[1] No. 363.   [2] No. 364.   [3] Nos. 375–377.   [4] No. 365.   [5] No. 367.   [6] No. 368.
[7] Nos. 370, 371.   [8] No. 372.   [9] No. 388D.   [10] See map on p. 529.   [11] No. 374.

coal trade,[1] was giving employment in 1829 to over 20,000 pit workers; shipments of coal from Newcastle and Sunderland were almost doubled, from 1,956,674 to 3,489,775 tons, between 1801 and 1828.[2]

Water transport remained the chief means of carriage of bulky industrial goods. Road communications were being steadily improved by Telford and Macadam, who introduced scientific principles into road making.[3] The turnpike trusts which now controlled most of the main arteries of the British Isles enabled John Palmer's flying coaches to cover the country with a network of passenger communications[4] which was helping to break down the localized life of the eighteenth century. For the transport of bulky commodities, however, even the improved roads remained inadequate and canal building accelerated in the 1790s, keeping pace with the general rate of industrial development. This is above all the canal age; Rennie calculated that in 1839 Great Britain had 2,236 miles of improved river navigation, costing £6,269,000, and 2,477 miles of canals, costing £24,406,389 to build, and most of the work was done during this period.

The last decade of the period foreshadowed the railway age. The collieries had long had their railroads as feeders to the canal or river network; the marriage of the iron way to the steam engine after the experiments of Trevithick, Blenkinsop, Hedley and Stephenson quickly opened up fabulous possibilities which an age quick to seize upon 'improvement' at once recognized. The Stockton and Darlington line was opened in 1825, the Liverpool and Manchester[5] in 1830; many others were already in process of construction.[6] To some onlookers, like Creevey,[7] there was 'something damnable' in this presage of the passing of the old, comfortable, unhurried England; within a generation the 'flying coaches' were rotting in their yards, and many canals becoming reedy backwaters.

England was necessarily becoming the foremost commercial as well as industrial country in the world. The statistics[8] show a startling expansion, particularly when the difficulties of a protracted continental war are taken into account (the deflationary finance and falling prices of the post-war period are not reflected in the tables of 'official values', since these remained constant). In general, the value of manufactures exported was nearly trebled between 1801 and 1832, while the cost of retained imports had less than doubled. Particularly striking are the figures for imports of raw cotton and exports of piece goods, which show an eightfold and a tenfold increase respectively from 1798 to 1830, and for the expanding production of iron. Only by such means as these was Great Britain able to finance the French wars and to feed her rising population; in the quarter-century after 1815 the rate of increase of industrial production further accelerated to reach its maximum for the whole pre-1914 period. This increase in overseas trade promoted a similar expansion in the shipbuilding industry and shipping trades.

These developments made the restrictive regulations of the old 'mercantilist' economy increasingly inappropriate. The demand for 'free trade' accordingly arose–a demand not created by Adam Smith's reasonings, important though they were, nor promoted by statesmen on theoretical grounds, but formulated as the expression of the self-confidence of British merchants and manufacturers in the technical and commercial superiority of their country. Confidence that the superior quality, quantity and cheapness of British goods would enable them to beat foreign rivals out of

[1] No. 373.   [2] No. 388E.   [3] No. 381.   [4] No. 380.
[5] No. 386.   [6] No. 385.   [7] No. 387.   [8] No. 388A–G.

the market on equal terms came gradually to the manufacturers, who had opposed Pitt's Irish commercial scheme in 1785, and accepted the 'Eden' treaty of 1786 with France not as doctrinaries but because it granted overwhelmingly favourable opportunities for British industries to dominate the French home market, while maintaining some of the restrictions and prohibitions which protected the more vulnerable of the British industries. Pitt justified the treaty[1] on grounds that Adam Smith would have approved, but it was joyfully received in England because of its one-sidedness. It lasted, however, only until 1793, and during the war the old regulations remained in force. Not until 1820 did an important body of merchants engaged in foreign trade put before the government the uncompromising case for an international 'division of labour'[2] and a parliamentary committee recommend the adoption of principles that were to govern English trading policies for the rest of the century.[3] Whilst Huskisson was President of the Board of Trade, the Navigation Acts,[4] the Ark of the Covenant of the old system, were modified; his tenure of office rather than Pitt's premiership marks the real beginning of the Free Trade movement.

The increase in the national wealth is also indicated by the assessments to the income and property taxes and the yield of the legacy duty.[5] The national income and expenditure figures[6] show a similar increase in the revenue-raising powers of the State, even allowing for exceptionally severe war-time taxation, and, after 1815, for currency readjustments. This increased wealth enabled the financial strain of the French wars to be met, and supported an unprecedented burden of debt.[7] The fiscal and financial reforms introduced by Pitt in the early years of his first ministry greatly improved the efficiency of the revenue collecting and spending departments, but his financing of the war was less successful, largely because of over-optimistic miscalculation of its probable length, and not until 1798 was the income tax introduced in order to meet the principle that the war should be financed, as far as possible, from current income. Even so, posterity was burdened by a vast increase in the National Debt. Pitt's speech introducing the income tax[8] is also interesting for its calculation of the national wealth, though his figures in some respects were later proved wildly wrong: his estimate of cultivated acreage, for example, was out by millions of acres. Nevertheless, the attempt illustrates the increasing preoccupation with statistical data that was becoming characteristic of the age.

War-time conditions also had a profound effect on the currency and the banking system. The stoppage of cash payments by the Bank of England in the crisis of 1797[9] began a process of mild inflation that at first stimulated production, but whose less favourable effects were later felt by the landed classes and the poor. The phenomena of inflation and credit control were not yet widely understood, and the situation created much alarm. The matter was placed in perspective by the famous 'Bullion Report' of 1810,[10] extracts from which have been chosen in order to illustrate the attitude of the more enlightened economists and politicians. The influence of the report was extensive and profound, though its principal recommendation–a return to the gold standard–had to be postponed until after the war, when the proposals of a further committee were adopted;[11] in 1821 the gold currency was restored.

These unusual financial conditions together with the greatly increased demand for capital, promoted a striking extension of the banking system, which was still remarkably ill-suited to the needs of a commercial and industrial community. The Bank of

[1] No. 389.   [2] No. 390.   [3] No. 391.   [4] No. 392.   [5] Nos. 393–395.   [6] Nos. 396, 398, 400.
[7] Nos. 397, 399.   [8] No. 401.   [9] No. 402.   [10] No. 403.   [11] No. 404.

England's monopoly of joint-stock banking and its reluctance to seek powers to open country branches meant that the provincial merchant and manufacturer were compelled to rely on local resources for the raising of capital and the other banking services essential to their business. Such men sometimes themselves became bankers; the Gurneys, the Barings, the Lloyds, among others, began as offshoots of local industry or commerce. These establishments[1] often lacked both an adequate reserve –the law restricted the permitted number of partners to six–and experience in the techniques of successful management. Recurrent crises were partly caused by their rashness and insecurity, and this was particularly the case with the crisis of 1825–1826,[2] when they provided over-lavish funds for the promotion and financing of joint-stock companies. The resultant crash caused the government to intervene;[3] it was decided to permit the establishment of joint-stock banks outside a 65-mile radius of London, the Bank being compensated by certain restrictions on the note-issues of new banks.[4] That the Act filled a great need is apparent from the number of joint-stock banks formed in the provinces between 1826 and 1832.[5] It also marks the beginning of the evolution of the modern banking system in England; it was on similar lines that the legislation of the 'forties was to be based.

A last group of documents offers some indication of the evidence on which an estimate of wage-rates and price-levels at this time may be founded.[6] The construction of indices and the drawing of general conclusions from such evidence is controversial, nor do the figures reflect either under-employment, which at times could substantially reduce the apparent wages of both piece and time workers, or such supplements to wages as tied cottages and allowances in kind to farm labourers, or such industrial practices as truck, which survived several attempts at its abolition during this period. Only fragmentary information as to prices can here be given: but other documents help to complete the picture by indicating, for example, the average prices of wheat per year throughout the period,[7] the cost of food, clothing and housing for the labouring classes[8] and wage-rates in the textile industry[9] and in the Birmingham metal trades,[10] while information on living conditions may be found scattered throughout the volume.

BIBLIOGRAPHY

I. BIBLIOGRAPHIES

The standard and most exhaustive work is J. B. Williams, *Guide to the Printed Materials for English Social and Economic History, 1750–1850* (2 vols., New York, 1926), which lists the contemporary material and secondary works published down to 1926. Thereafter the annual bibliographies of works on the economic history of Great Britain and Ireland, published since 1927 in the *Economic History Review*, should be consulted. Short select bibliographies are H. L. Beales and G. D. H. Cole, "A Select List of Books on Economic and Social History, 1700–1850", in *Journal of Adult Education*, vol. I (1927), Eileen Power, *The Industrial Revolution, 1750–1850* (Economic History Society's Bibliographies, No. I (1927)), and T. S. Ashton, "The Industrial Revolution: Studies in Bibliography, No. III" in *Economic History Review*, vol. V (1934–1935).

---

[1] Nos. 405, 406. [2] No. 407. [3] No. 408. [4] No. 409. [5] No. 410.
[6] Nos. 411–414. [7] No. 344. [8] No. 357, 358. [9] No. 361. [10] No. 371.

Bibliographies on individual topics include J. F. and W. Rees, "A Select Bibliography of the Economic History of Wales" in *Economic History Review*, vol. II (1947–1948), M. S. Aslin, *The Library Catalogue of Printed Books on Agriculture (1471–1840)* (1940), G. E. Fussell, "Agriculture from Young to Cobbett" (Studies in Bibliography, No. V) in *Economic History Review*, vol. VI (1936), and J. Thirsk, "The Content and Sources of English Agrarian History after 1500" in *Agricultural History Review*, vol. III (1955).

II. PRIMARY SOURCES

There is a mass of contemporary literature on economic subjects and several collections of statistics of varying reliability and usefulness were made during the period. Most of these were based on official statistics from the *Parliamentary Papers* and journals of the two Houses, whose indexes are the student's best guide. The Reports of Committees in the *Parliamentary Papers* are full of information on economic conditions and social problems: among the most valuable may be mentioned reports on the state of Agriculture (1821, vol. IX) and on Waste Lands, 1795–1800 (1st Series, vol. IX), on the state of Ireland (with much information on the peasantry) (1825, vols. VII–IX, 1826, vol. V, 1831–1832, vol. XVI). On industry, see the reports on Manufactures, Commerce and Shipping (1833, vol. VI), on the Coal Trade (1800, 1st Series, vol. X, and 1830, vol. VIII), on the Woollen Manufacture of England (1806, vol. III), on the Framework Knitters (1812, vol. II, and 1819, vol. V), on Luddism (the Committee of Secrecy) (1812, vol. II), on the Handloom Weavers (1834, vol. X) and on Emigration (with much evidence as to social distress and the standard of living) (1826, vol. IV, and 1826–1827, vol. V). On overseas trade, see the reports on the Foreign Trade of the Country (1820, vol. II) and the series of reports on particular branches of trade, 1820–1824, on the affairs of the East India Company (1830, vols. V and VI, 1831, vols. V and VI, and 1831–1832, vols. IX–XIV), on the Commercial State of the West India Colonies (1807, vol. III, and 1831–1832, vol. XX), on the Extinction of Slavery (1831–1832, vol. XX), and on the Colony of New South Wales (1822, vol. XX, and 1823, vol. X). On Communications, there is a series of reports on the Highways of the Kingdom–see particularly 1819, vol. V–and on Finance and the Currency consult the reports on the Stoppage of Cash Payments (1797, 1st Series, vol. XI) (reprinted in 1826, vol. III), the "Bullion Report" of 1810 (vol. III) and on the Resumption of Cash Payments (1819, vol. III). On Banking, see the Committee of Secrecy on the Privileges of the Bank of England (1826, vol. XIX) and on the Bank's Charter (1831–1832, vol. VI). The best guide to the *Parliamentary Papers* for this period is *Hansard's Catalogue and Breviate of Parliamentary Papers, 1694–1834*, edited by P. and G. Ford (Oxford, 1953).

Contemporary collections of statistical and other material include the official *Tables of the Revenue, Population and Commerce of the United Kingdom* (1820) (known as "Porter's tables"), G. R. Porter's indispensable *The Progress of the Nation* (3 vols., 1836–1838, revised edition, 1 vol., 1851) and a series of privately made collections throughout the period: G. Chalmers, *An Estimate of the Comparative Strength of Great Britain since the Revolution* (1782), sets the scene at the opening of the period, and is followed by D. Macpherson, *Annals of Commerce, Manufactures, Fisheries and Navigation* (4 vols., 1805), P. Colquhoun, *A Treatise on the Wealth, Power, and Resources of the British Empire* (1814, revised edition, 1815), J. Lowe, *The Present State of England in regard to Agriculture, Trade and Finance* (1822, 1823), J. Powell, *Statistical Illustrations . . . of the British Empire* (compiled for the London Statistical Society) (1825, 3rd edition, 1827), J. Marshall, *A Digest of all the Accounts relating to the Population, Productions, Revenues . . . of the United Kingdom* (1833) (a useful compilation but at times confusingly arranged and inaccurately printed), J. R. McCulloch, *A Dictionary of Commerce and Commercial Navigation* (1832, new edition, revised by H. G. Reid, 1880), the same author's *Descriptive and Statistical Account of the British Empire* (2 vols., 1837, and later editions) and T. Hopkins's collection, *Great Britain for the last Forty Years* (1834). For Scotland, Sir J. Sinclair's *Statistical Account of Scotland* (21 vols., Edinburgh, 1791–1799) is a classic. The historian of wages and prices must consult the work of

J. E. Thorold Rogers, *A History of Agriculture and Prices in England* [1259–1793] (7 vols., Oxford, 1866–1902) and his *Six Centuries of Work and Wages* (1884). Other later compilations include W. Smart, *Economic Annals of the Nineteenth Century* (2 vols., 1910–1917) (based on extracts, chiefly from *Hansard* and the *Annual Register*, on the period 1800–1830), and W. Page, *Commerce and Industry* (2 vols., 1919) (vol. II is entirely devoted to statistics, not always, however, accurately compiled). A useful article is T. S. Ashton, "Some Statistics of the Industrial Revolution in Britain", *Transactions of the Manchester Statistical Society*, 1947–1948.

Among the multitude of descriptive contemporary accounts may be mentioned the well-known *Tours of England and Wales* by Arthur Young, William Cobbett's *Rural Rides* and *Political Register*, J. Aikin's classic, *Description of the Country from Thirty to Forty Miles round Manchester* (1795), F. de la Rochefoucauld, *A Frenchman in England, 1784*, edited by J. Marchand, translated by S. C. Roberts (Cambridge, 1933), Charles, Baron Dupin, *The Commercial Power of Great Britain* (2 vols. and atlas, 1825), and other sources listed below.

On the economic ideas of the period, see particularly E. Cannan's edition of Adam Smith's *Wealth of Nations* (2 vols., 1950) and the Royal Economic Society's new editions of *The Works and Correspondence of David Ricardo*, edited by P. Sraffa and M. H. Dobb (10 vols., 1951–1955), and *Jeremy Bentham's Economic Writings*, edited by W. Stark (3 vols., 1952–1954). Indispensable is E. Cannan, *A History of the Theories of Production and Distribution in English Political Economy from 1776 to 1848* (1917).

III. GENERAL

The standard economic histories of this period are W. Cunningham, *The Growth of English Industry and Commerce* (3 vols., 6th edition, Cambridge, 1921, 1 vol., reprinted 1908 as *The Industrial Revolution*), P. Mantoux, *The Industrial Revolution in the Eighteenth Century* (revised English edition, 1947), L. C. A. Knowles, *The Industrial and Commercial Revolutions in Great Britain* (1927), whose thesis should be compared with that of J. L. and B. Hammond, *The Rise of Modern Industry* (1925), and Sir John Clapham's monumental *Economic History of Modern Britain*, vol. I (Cambridge, 1930). The latest addition is the valuable T. S. Ashton, *An Economic History of England: the Eighteenth Century* (1955). The best shorter introductions are W. H. B. Court, *A Concise Economic History of Britain from 1750* (Cambridge, 1954), T. S. Ashton, *The Industrial Revolution, 1760–1830* (Home University Library, 1948), and A. Redford, *The Economic History of England, 1760–1860* (1931). Useful surveys are C. R. Fay, *Life and Labour in the Nineteenth Century* (1920), and *Great Britain from Adam Smith to the Present Day* (Cambridge, 1928), and E. Lipson, *The Growth of English Society* (1949). A most valuable general study is A. D. Gayer, W. W. Rostow and A. Schwartz, *The Growth and Fluctuations of the British Economy, 1750–1850* (1953), reviewed by T. S. Ashton, "Economic Fluctuations 1790–1850", *Economic History Review*, 2nd Series, vol. VII (1955) and by R. C. O. Matthews, "The Trade Cycle in Britain, 1790–1850" (*Oxford Economic Papers*, New Series, vol. VI, 1954). Also of a general nature are M. Dobb, *Studies in the Development of Capitalism* (1946), essays in *Capitalism and the Historians*, edited by F. A. von Hayek (1954), and W. Woodruff, "Capitalism and the Historians: A Contribution to the Discussion of the Industrial Revolution in England" in *Journal of Economic History*, vol. XVI (1956). See also H. Hamilton, *The Industrial Revolution in Scotland* (1932), J. F. Grant, *The Economic History of Scotland* (1934), A. H. Dodd, *The Industrial Revolution in North Wales* (1933), and J. D. Chambers, *The Vale of Trent, 1670–1800: a Regional Survey of Economic Change* (Economic History Review Supplement, No. III, Cambridge, 1956).

IV. AGRICULTURE

The principal contemporary sources consist of the *Parliamentary Papers* listed above, the Reports of the Board of Agriculture's Surveyors on the Agriculture of the various counties of England (most counties having two reports), 1794–1817, and the Reviews of these reports by districts (1808–1817) by William Marshall, one of the most acute and knowledgeable observers of the day. Marshall also produced his own reports on *The Rural Economy of Norfolk* (1787),

Yorkshire (1788), *Gloucestershire* (1789), *the Midland Counties* (1790), *the West of England* (1796), and *the Southern Counties* (1798), each in 2 vols., and his *Landed Property of England* (1804) was one of the leading treatises on Estate Management. The Board of Agriculture also published a valuable *General Report on Enclosures* (1808) which studied the effects of enclosures of various sorts, and *The Agricultural States of the Kingdom, in February, March and April 1816*, which incorporated the replies of landowners all over the country to a circular letter from the Board.

Arthur Young's writings are of great value, particularly his various *Tours*, printed in the *Annals of Agriculture* (Bury St. Edmunds, 46 vols., 1784–1815), those for this period being most conveniently studied in the London School of Economics Reprints, No. 14 (1932). J. C. Loudon, *An Encyclopaedia of Agriculture* (1825), contains much information on contemporary practices, as do William Cobbett's *Rural Rides*, 3 vols., edited by G. D. H and M. Cole (1930), and Arthur Young's *Autobiography* (1898).

There is no satisfactory secondary history of English agriculture at this time. The standard work, R. E. Prothero (Lord Ernle), *English Farming, Past and Present* (revised edition, 1936), needs to be supplemented by information contained in a large number of later books and articles, many based on research into local practices and problems. The best local study is J. D. Chambers, *Nottinghamshire in the Eighteenth Century* (1932). Others are N. S. B. and E. C. Gras, *The Economic and Social History of an English Village* [Crawley, Hants], *909–1923* (1930), A. G. Ruston and D. Whitney, *Hooton Pagnell* (1934); N. Riches, *The Agricultural Revolution in Norfolk* (North Carolina, 1937), and R. A. C. Parker, "Coke of Norfolk and the Agrarian Revolution" in *Economic History Review*, 2nd Series, vol. VIII (1955), correct the older view in A. M. W. Stirling, *Coke of Norfolk and His Friends* (2 vols., 1912); see also A. M. Lambert, "The Agriculture of Oxfordshire at the end of the Eighteenth Century" in *Agricultural History* vol. XXIX (1955), W. E. Minchinton, "Agriculture in Dorset during the Napoleonic Wars" in *Dorset Nat. Hist. Arch. Soc.*, vol. LXXVII (1955), O. Wilkinson, *The Agricultural Revolution in the East Riding of Yorkshire* (York, 1956), D. Spring, "A Great Agricultural Estate: Netherby under Sir James Graham, 1820–1845" in *Agricultural History*, vol. XXIX (1955).

The enclosure movement is studied in E. C. K. Gonner, *Common Land and Enclosure* (1912), W. H. R. Curtler, *The Enclosure and Redistribution of our Land* (Oxford, 1920), G. Salter, *The English Peasantry and the Enclosure of Common Fields* (1907), V. M. Lavrovsky, *Parliamentary Enclosures of Common Lands in England in the late 18th and the early 19th Centuries* (Moscow, 1940), "The Expropriation of the English Peasantry in the Eighteenth Century" in *Economic History Review*, 2nd Series, vol. IX (1956), and "Parliamentary Enclosures in the County of Suffolk, 1797–1814", *ibid.*, vol. VII (1937), W. E. Tate, *Parliamentary Land Enclosures in the County of Nottingham during the Eighteenth and Nineteenth Centuries* (Thoroton Society, Record Series, vol. V (Nottingham, 1935)), H. G. Hunt, "The Chronology of Parliamentary Enclosure in Leicestershire" in *Economic History Review*, 2nd Series, vol. X (1957), W. E. Tate, "The Cost of Parliamentary Enclosure in England (with special reference to the County of Oxford)", *ibid.*, 2nd Series, vol. V (1952–1953), M. W. Beresford, "Commissioners of Enclosure", *ibid.*, vol. XVI (1946). J. D. Chambers, "Enclosure and the Labour Supply in the Industrial Revolution", *ibid.*, 2nd Series, vol. V (1953), disposes of the legend that enclosure drove the rural population into the factory towns.

The history of the rural population is studied in A. H. Johnson, *The Disappearance of the Small Landowner* (Oxford, 1909), E. Davies, "The Small Landowner, 1780–1832, in the light of the Land Tax Assessments", *Economic History Review*, vol. I (1927), H. Levy, *Large and Small Holdings* (English trans., Cambridge, 1911), and F. M. L. Thompson, "The End of a Great Estate" (on the 1st and 2nd dukes of Buckingham), *Economic History Review*, 2nd Series, vol. VIII (1955), together with a comment, D. Spring, "English Landownership in the Nineteenth Century: a critical note", *ibid.*, 2nd Series, vol. IX (1957). For the labouring classes, see W. H. Hasbach, *A History of the English Agricultural Labourer* (1908), G. E. Fussell, *The English Rural Labourer* (1949), G. E. and K. R. Fussell, *The English Countryman: His Life and Work 1500–1900* (1955), G. E. Fussell and C. Goodman, "The Housing of the Rural Population in the

Eighteenth Century", *Economic History*, vol. II (1930), G. E. Fussell, "The Change in Farm Labourers' Diet during two Centuries", *Economic History*, vol. II (1927), L. M. Marshall, 'The Rural Population of Bedfordshire, 1671–1921" (*Bedfordshire History Record Society*, vol. 16, 1934), N. Gash, "Rural Unemployment, 1815–34", *Economic History Review*, vol. VI (1935), K. H. Connell, "Land and Population in Ireland, 1780–1845", *ibid.*, 2nd Series, vol. II (1949), and M. H. Leigh, "The Crofting Problem 1780–1883", *Scottish Journal of Agriculture*, vol. XII (1929).

For agricultural methods, see W. F. Galpin, *The Grain Supply of England during the Napoleonic Period* (New York, 1925), and a large number of valuable works by G. E. Fussell, the most important for this period being: "Four Centuries of Cheshire Farming Systems, 1500–1900", *Transactions of the Lancashire and Cheshire Historical Society*, vol. CVI (1954), *The Farmer's Tools, 1500–1900* (1952); "Animal Husbandry in Eighteenth Century England", *Agricultural History*, vols. III (1929) and XI (1937); and, with C. Goodman, "The Eighteenth Century Traffic in Livestock" and "The Eighteenth Century Traffic in Milk Products" in *Economic History*, vol. III (1934–1937), and "Eighteenth Century Estimates of British Sheep and Wool Production" in *Agricultural History*, vol. IV (1930). See also Sir W. Ashley, *The Bread of our Forefathers* (Oxford, 1928), Sir J. C. Drummond and A. C. Wilbraham, *The Englishman's Food* (1939), and R. N. Salaman, *The History and Social Influence of the Potato* (Cambridge, 1949), a valuable and wide ranging study. The standard work on the Corn Laws is D. G. Barnes, *History of the English Corn Laws* (1930); see also C. R. Fay, *The Corn Laws and Social England* (1932), "The Significance of the Corn Laws in English History" in *Economic History Review*, vol. I (1928), and "Price Control and the Corn Averages under the Corn Laws" in *Economic History*, vol. I (1925–1926). On the post-Napoleonic War period, see L. P. Adams, *Agricultural Depression and Farm Relief in England, 1813–52* (1932).

V. INDUSTRY

The Oxford *History of Technology*, vol. IV, *The Industrial Revolution, c. 1750 to 1850*, edited by C. Singer, E. J. Holmyard, A. R. Hall, and T. I. Williams (Oxford, 1957) describes, with a wealth of illustrations, the developments of the period.

The concept of the 'Industrial Revolution' is examined in H. L. Beales, *The Industrial Revolution* (1928); N. S. B. Gras, *Industrial Evolution* (1930); G. N. Clark, *The Idea of the Industrial Revolution* (1953); and J. U. Nef, "The Industrial Revolution Reconsidered" in *Journal of Economic History*, vol. II (1942). Other books and articles on the general industrial developments of the period include A. D. Innes, *England's Industrial Development* (1912), A. P. Usher's classic *History of Mechanical Inventions* (new edition, Oxford, 1954) and his *Introduction to the Industrial History of England* (1921), W. Bowden, *Industrial Society in England towards the end of the Eighteenth Century* (1925), G. Unwin, "The Transition to the Factory System" in *English Historical Review*, vol. XXXVII (1922), and W. H. Hutt, "The Factory System of the Early Nineteenth Century" in *Economica*, vol. VI (1926). W. G. Hoffman, *British Industry 1700–1950* (translated by W. O. Henderson and W. H. Chaloner, Oxford, 1955), attempts a quantitative analysis (compare J. F. Wright, "An Index of the Output of British Industry since 1700", *Journal of Economic History*, vol. XVI (1956)).

On business and industrial organization, see R. B. Westerfield, *Middlemen in English Business* (1915), C. Wilson, "The Entrepreneur in the Industrial Revolution in Britain" in *Explor. Entrepren. Hist.*, vol. VII (1954), B. C. Hunt, *The Development of the Business Corporation in England, 1800–67* (Havard, 1936), and B. F. Hoselitz, "Entrepreneurship and Capital Formation in France and Britain since 1700" in *Capital Formation and Economic Growth*, edited by M. Abramowitz (Princeton, 1955). Amongst biographies of prominent industrialists should be mentioned S. Smiles's *Industrial Biography* (1863, new edition, 1905), *Lives of the Engineers* (1861–1862, 1905) and *Lives of Boulton and Watt* (1865).

A most valuable local study is W. H. B. Court, *The Rise of the Midland Industries, 1600–1838* (Oxford, 1938): others are A. H. John, *The Industrial Development of South Wales, 1750–1850* (Cardiff, 1950), W. H. Chaloner, *The Social and Economic Development of Crewe, 1780–1823*

(Manchester, 1950), T. C. Barker and J. R. Harris, *A Merseyside Town in the Industrial Revolution: St. Helen's, 1750–1900* (Liverpool, 1954), S. Middlebrook, *Newcastle-on-Tyne: its Growth and Achievement* (Newcastle, 1950), J. Rowe, *Cornwall in the Age of the Industrial Revolution* (Liverpool, 1953), and G. H. Tupling, *The Economic Development of Rossendale* (1927). Other general studies are I. Grubb, *Quakerism and Industry before 1800* (1930), A. Raistrick, *Quakers in Science and Industry* (1950), and I. Pinchbeck, *Women Workers and the Industrial Revolution* (1930). British influence on continental development is studied in W. O. Henderson, *Britain and Industrial Europe, 1750–1870* (Liverpool, 1954).

The standard authorities on the woollen and worsted industries are E. Lipson, *History of the Woollen and Worsted Industries* (1921) (which deals chiefly with the pre-Industrial Revolution period); J. Burnley, *History of Wool and Wool-Combing* (1889); J. James, *History of the Worsted Manufacture in England* (1857); J. H. Clapham, *The Woollen and Worsted Industries* (1907); and W. Hirst, *History of the Woollen Trade for the last Sixty Years* (Leeds, 1844), with an account of the introduction, by the author, of the new machinery into the West Riding. H. Heaton's *Yorkshire Woollen and Worsted Industries* (Oxford, 1920) stops at the Industrial Revolution. Works on a smaller scale include J. H. Clapham, "The Transference of the Worsted Industry from East Anglia to the West Riding" in *Economic Journal*, vol. xx (1910); H. Heaton, "Benjamin Gott and the Industrial Revolution in Yorkshire" in *Economic History Review*, vol. iii (1931), and "Benjamin Gott and the Anglo-American Cloth Trade" in *Journal of Economic and Business History*, vol. ii (1929–1930); W. G. Hoskins, *Industry, Trade and People in Exeter, 1688–1800, with special reference to the Serge Industry* (Manchester, 1935); and E. A. L. Moir, "'The Gentlemen Clothiers': A Study of the Organization of the Gloucestershire Cloth Industry, 1750–1835" in *Gloucestershire Studies*, edited by H. P. R. Finberg (Leicester, 1957). Contemporary documents are printed in *The Witney Blanket Industry*, edited by A. Plummer (1934) (from the records of the blanket weavers) and *The Leeds Woollen Industry*, edited by W. B. Crump (Thoresby Society, Leeds, 1931). For a summary of an unpublished thesis by J. Morris, "The West of England Woollen Industry 1750–1840", see *Bulletin of the Institute of Historical Research*, vol. xiii (1935–1936).

The authorities on the cotton industry are G. W. Daniels, *The Early English Cotton Industry* (Manchester, 1920), and S. J. Chapman, *The Lancashire Cotton Industry* (Manchester, 1904). E. Baines, *History of the Cotton Manufacture of Great Britain* (1835), is still valuable, and there is a model study by G. W. Daniels, A. Hulme and G. Taylor, *Samuel Oldknow and the Arkwrights* (Manchester, 1924). R. Burn, *Statistics of the Cotton Trade* (1847), has many valuable tables, and the best contemporary account of the mechanization of the industry is W. Radcliffe, *Origin of the New System of Manufacture, commonly called "Power Loom Weaving"* (Stockport, 1828, 2nd edition, 1840). Specialized studies on this period are A. Redford, *Manchester Merchants and Foreign Trade, 1794–1858* (Manchester, 1934); G. W. Daniels, "The Effect of the Napoleonic War on the Cotton Trade" in *Manchester Statistical Society Transactions* (1915–1916), and "The Cotton Trade at the Close of the Napoleonic War", *ibid.* (1917–1918); A. J. Taylor, "Concentration and Specialisation in the Lancashire Cotton Industry, 1825–50" in *Economic History Review*, 2nd Series, vol. i (1948); W. H. Chaloner, "Robert Owen, Peter Drinkwater and the early Factory System in Manchester, 1788–1800" in *Bulletin of the John Rylands Library*, vol. xxxvii (1955); P. J. Thomas, "The Beginnings of Calico Printing in England", *English Historical Review*, vol. xxxix (1924).

On the linen industry, see C. Gill, *The Rise of the Irish Linen Industry* (1925), and W. Carter, *Linen: the Story of an Irish Industry* (3rd edition, Belfast, 1954).

For the silk industry, see Sir Frank Warner, *The Silk Industry of the United Kingdom* (1921); G. B. Hertz, "The English Silk Industry in the Eighteenth Century" in *English Historical Review*, vol. xxiv (1909); and W. M. Jordan, "The Silk Industry in London, 1760–1830" (Thesis summary, *Bulletin of the Institute of Historical Research*, vol. x, 1932–1933). J. H. Clapham is authoritative on "The Spitalfields Acts" in *Economic Journal*, vol. xxvi (1916).

The lace and hosiery trades are best studied in the classic by W. Felkin, *A History of the Machine Wrought Hosiery and Lace Manufactures* (1867); see also E. G. Nelson, "The Putting-out

System in the English Framework Knitting Industry" in *Journal of Economic and Business History*, vol. II (1929–1930). F. Peel, *The Risings of the Luddites* (2nd edition, 1888) is standard.

The standard work on the iron and steel industries is T. S. Ashton, *Iron and Steel in the Industrial Revolution* (Manchester, 1924). H. Scrivenor, *A Comprehensive History of the Iron Trade* (1841), has much valuable first-hand information and many statistics, and J. S. Jeans, *The Iron Trade of Great Britain* (1906), is valuable. Histories of individual firms include A. Raistrick, *A Dynasty of Ironfounders: the Derbys of Coalbrookdale* (1953); E. Roll, *An Early Experiment in Industrial Organization* (1930) (the firm of Boulton and Watt); J. E. Cule, "Finance and Industry in the Eighteenth Century: the firm of Boulton and Watt" in *Economic History*, vol. IV (1940); A. Birch, "Carron Company 1784–1822; the Profits of Industry during the Industrial Revolution" in *Explor. Entrepren. Hist.*, vol. VIII (1955); J. P. Addis, *The Crawshay Dynasty* (Cardiff, 1957); and *The Walker Family, Iron Founders and Lead Manufacturers, 1741–1793*, edited by A. H. John (1951). See also C. Wilkins, *History of the Iron and Steel Trades of South Wales* (1903); W. E. Minchinton, *The British Tinplate Industry* (Oxford, 1957); and H. G. Roepke, *Movements of the British Iron and Steel Industry 1720–1951* (Urbana, Illinois, 1956). The best biography of *Matthew Boulton* is by H. W. Dickinson (Cambridge, 1937); see the same author's *Short History of the Steam Engine* (Cambridge, 1939); *James Watt* (Cambridge, 1936); and, with Rhys Jenkins, *James Watt and the Steam Engine* (1927). There is another life of *James Watt* by T. H. Marshall (1925). Also valuable is J. Lord, *Capital and Steam Power 1750–1800* (1923). On the engineering industry, see A. P. M. Fleming and H. J. Brocklehurst, *A History of Engineering* (1925), and T. S. Ashton, *An Eighteenth Century Industrialist* [Peter Stubs of Warrington, filemaker] (Manchester, 1939), and "The Domestic System in the Early Lancashire Tool Trade" in *Economic History*, vol. I (1926). The best work on the cutlery industry is G. I. H. Lloyd, *The Cutlery Trades* (1913).

The authorities on the coal industry are T. S. Ashton and J. Sykes, *The Coal Industry of the Eighteenth Century* (Manchester, 1929), and R. L. Galloway, *History of Coal Mining in Great Britain* (1882) and *Annals of Coal Mining and the Coal Trade* (2 vols., 1889). Two useful local studies are G. Rimmer, "Middleton Colliery, near Leeds (1770–1830)" in *Yorkshire Bulletin of Economic and Social Research*, vol. VII (1955), and S. M. Hardy, "The Development of Coal Mining in a North Derbyshire Village, 1635–1860" in *University of Birmingham Historical Journal*, vol. V (1956). On the coal trade, see P. M. Sweezy, *Monopoly and Competition in the English Coal Trade 1550–1850* (Harvard, 1938). On tin and lead mining, see G. R. Lewis, *The Stannaries* (Boston, Mass., 1908) (standard); A. K. Hamilton Jenkin, *The Cornish Miner* (1927); and J. W. Gough, *The Mines of Mendip* (1930).

On the potteries, see E. Meteyard, *The Life of Josiah Wedgwood* (2 vols., 1865–1866) (uncritical); J. C. Wedgwood, *Staffordshire Pottery and its History* (1913); and W. Burton, *Josiah Wedgwood and His Pottery* (1922). More recent work includes V. W. Bladon, "The Potteries in the Industrial Revolution", *Economic History*, vol. I (1926–1929); R. M. Hower, "The Wedgwoods" in *Journal of Economic and Business History*, vol. IV (1932); and J. Thomas, "The Pottery Industry and the Industrial Revolution", *Economic History*, vol. III (1937). The important but rather neglected chemical industries are studied by A. and N. Clow, *The Chemical Revolution* (1952) and "Vitriol in the Industrial Revolution", *Economic History Review*, vol. XV (1945). For the building industry, see A. K. Cairncross and B. Weber, "Fluctuations in Building in Great Britain, 1785–1849" in *Economic History Review*, 2nd Series, vol. IX (1956).

On Communications, the most comprehensive treatment is by E. A. Pratt, *A History of Inland Transportation and Communications in England* (1912). W. T. Jackman, *The Development of Transportation in Modern England* (2 vols., Cambridge, 1916), is also valuable. On the roads, see S. and B. Webb, *The Story of the King's Highway* (1913); J. W. Gregory, *The Story of the Road* (1931); and C. G. Harper, *Stage Coach and Mail in Days of Yore* (2 vols., 1903). J. L. Macadam's *Remarks on the Present System of Road Making* (Bristol, 1816) was most influential in its day. Biographies are R. Devereux, *John Loudon Macadam* (Oxford, 1936); L. T. C. Rolt, *Thomas Telford* (1958); and Sir Alexander Gibb, *The Story of Telford* (1935). The introduction of the 'flying coach' is dealt with in C. R. Clear, *John Palmer, Mail Coach Pioneer* (1955): see also

H. Robinson, *The British Post Office* (Princeton, 1948), and J. C. Hemmeon, *The History of the British Post Office* (Cambridge, Mass., 1912). On the canal system, U. A. Forbes and W. H. R. Ashford, *Our Waterways* (1906), is still standard, but may be supplemented by C. Hadfield, *The Canals of Southern England* (1955), "The Thames Navigation and the Canals, 1770–1830", *Economic History Review*, vol. xiv (1944), and G. G. Hopkinson, "The Development of Inland Navigation in South Yorkshire and North Derbyshire 1697–1850" in *Trans. Hunter. Arch. Soc.*, vol. vii (1956). See C. Hadfield, "Sources for the History of British Canals", *Journal of Transport History*, vol. ii (1955). Two contemporary accounts are J. Phillips, *A General History of Inland Navigation* (various editions, 1792–1803), an account of all the canals completed by those dates, and J. Priestley, *Historical Account of the navigable rivers, canals, and railways, throughout Great Britain* (1831). There is a voluminous literature on railway history: see C. R. Clinker, "Sources of Railway History" in *Amateur Historian*, vol. i (1952–1953). Among the best accounts for this period are A. G. Lewin, *Early British Railways* [1801–1844] (1925); C. F. D. Marshall, *A History of British Railways down to the year 1830* (Oxford, 1938) and *Early British Locomotives* (1939); H. Ellis, *British Railway History*, vol. i [1830–1876] (1954); E. Cleveland-Stevens, *English Railways, their Development and their relation to the State* (1915); and J. G. H. Warren, *A Century of Locomotive Building, by Robert Stephenson and Co. 1823–1923* (Newcastle-on-Tyne, 1923). A contemporary account of great value, by a friend of Stephenson, is N. Wood, *Practical Treatise on Railroads* (editions 1825, 1832, 1838).

The shipping services are studied in C. Jones, *British Merchant Shipping* (1922); A. P. Usher, "The Growth of English Shipping 1572–1922" in *Quarterly Journal of Economics*, vol. xlii (1928); and J. Cresswell, "English Shipping at the end of the Eighteenth Century" in *Mariners' Mirror*, vol. xxv (1939). On Lloyd's, see F. Martin, *The History of Lloyd's and of Marine Insurance in Great Britain* (1876), and C. Wright and C. E. Fayle, *History of Lloyd's* (1928).

VI. OVERSEAS TRADE

Contemporary or later collections of statistics illustrating the growth and variety of foreign trade in this period are listed above.

As regards secondary works, the most important general surveys are L. Levi, *History of British Commerce, and of the Economic Progress of the Nation, 1763–1870* (1872), and A. L. Bowley, *England's Foreign Trade in the Nineteenth Century* (1905). The free-trade movement is surveyed in S. Buxton, *Finance and Politics, An Historical Study, 1783–1885* (2 vols., 1888), and R. L. Schuyler, *The Fall of the Old Colonial System: A Study in British Free Trade, 1770–1870* (Oxford, 1945). The economic policies of the eighteen-twenties are studied in A. Brady, *William Huskisson and Liberal Reform* (Oxford, 1928). The standard work on the navigation laws is L. A. Harper, *The English Navigation Laws* (New York, 1939); J. H. Clapham, "The last years of the Navigation Acts", *English Historical Review*, vol. xxv (1910), should also be consulted. There is an article by W. O. Henderson, "The Anglo-French Commercial Treaty of 1786" in *Economic History Review*, 2nd Series, vol. x (1957). On the trade of the war years, 1793–1815, see E. F. Hecksher, *The Continental System* (Oxford, 1922) (the standard work); A. M. Imlah, "British Terms of Trade, 1798–1813" in *Journal of Economic History*, vol. ix (1950); and *The Trade Winds–A Study of British Overseas Trade during the French Wars 1793–1815*, edited by C. N. Parkinson (1948). For the post-war situation, see J. S. Nicholson, *Trade after the Napoleonic Wars* (reprinted in his *War Finance* (1917)).

Amongst the numerous studies of trades to particular regions in this period the following should be noted: J. B. Williams, "The Development of British Trade with West Africa, 1750–1850" in *Political Science Quarterly*, vol. l (1935); N. S. Buck, *The Development of the Organization of the Anglo-American Trade, 1800–1850* (Yale, 1925); J. H. Rose, "British West Indian Commerce as a Factor in the Napoleonic War", *Cambridge Historical Journal*, vol. iii (1929); S. G. Checkland, "Finance for the West Indies, 1780–1815", *Economic History Review*, 2nd Series, vol. x (1958); D. B. Goebel, "British Trade to the Spanish Colonies, 1796–1823", *American Historical Review*, vol. xliii (1938); F. P. Robinson, *The Trade of the East India Company from 1709 to 1813* (Cambridge, 1912); H. B. Morse, *Chronicles of the East India Company trading to China, 1635–1834* (5 vols., Oxford, 1926–1929); C. N. Parkinson, *Trade in the Eastern Seas 1793–1813* (Cambridge, 1937); A. C. Wood, *History of the Levant Company* (1935); H. S. K. Kent, "The Anglo-Norwegian Timber Trade in the Eighteenth Century", *Economic History Review*, 2nd Series, vol. VIII (1956); A. B. W. Chapman "Commercial Relations of England and Portugal 1487–1807", *Transactions of the Royal Historical Society*, 3rd Series, vol. I (1907); Sir R. Lodge, "The English Factory at Lisbon", *ibid.*, 4th Series, vol. XVI (1923). For the Slave Trade, see the bibliography to Part VIII.

For the Ports, see Sir D. J. Owen, *Origin and Development of the Ports of the United Kingdom* (1939); C. N. Parkinson, *The Rise of the Port of Liverpool* (Liverpool, 1952); R. C. Jarvis (editor), *Customs Letter-Books of the Port of Liverpool 1711–1813* (Manchester, 1954); W. G. East, "The Port of Kingston-upon-Hull in the Industrial Revolution", *Economica*, vol. XXXII (1930); J. E. Williams, "Whitehaven in the Eighteenth Century", *Economic History Review*, 2nd Series, vol. VIII (1956).

VII. PUBLIC FINANCE AND TAXATION

S. Dowell, *History of Taxation and Taxes* (4 vols., 1884), is still the standard work. A short introduction to the subject is J. P. Rees, *Short Fiscal and Financial History of England, 1815–1918* (1921). See also S. Buxton, *Finance and Politics 1760–1885* (2 vols., 1888), F. W. Hirst and J. E. Allen, *British War Budgets, 1793–1924* (1926), and W. Kennedy, *English Taxation, 1640–1799, An Essay on Policy and Opinion* (1913). Sir John Sinclair, *The History of the Public Revenue of the British Empire* (3rd edition, 1803), is still valuable. On the Irish administration, see E. J. Kiernan, *History of the Financial Administration of Ireland to 1817* (1931). The accounts of government revenue, expenditure and debt are in *Parliamentary Papers*, 1868–1869, vol. XXXV. On individual taxes, see E. R. A. Seligman, *The Income Tax* (New York, revised edition, 1914); E. Hope-Jones, *Income Tax in the Napoleonic Wars* (Cambridge, 1939); A. Farnsworth, *Addington, Author of the Modern Income Tax* (1951); W. R. Ward, *The English Land Tax in the Eighteenth Century* (1953), "The Administration of the Window and Assessed Taxes, 1696–1798", *English Historical Review*, vol. LXVII (1952), "The Office for Taxes, 1666–1798", *Bulletin of the Institute of Historical Research*, vol. XXV (1952), and "Some Eighteenth-century Civil Servants:–The English Revenue Commissioners" in *English Historical Review*, vol. LXX (1955); E. A. Hughes, *Studies in Administration and Finance 1558–1825* (Manchester, 1934) (on the salt duties); H. Hall, *History of the Customs Revenue in England to 1827* (2 vols., 1885); B. R. Leftwich, "The Later History and Administration of the Customs Revenue in England (1671–1814)", *Transactions of the Royal Historical Society*, 4th Series, vol. XIII (1930); R. D. Richards, "The Lottery in the History of English Government Finance", *Economic History*, vol. III (1934), and "The Exchequer Bill in the History of English Government Finance" (*ibid.*). Other aspects of the subject are studied in C. B. Cone, "Richard Price and Pitt's Sinking Fund of 1786", *Economic History Review*, 2nd Series, vol. IV (1951); W. Newmarch, *On the Loans raised by Mr. Pitt during the first French War, 1793–1801* (1855); E. L. Hargreaves, *The National Debt* (1930); R. G. Allen, "Studies in the National Income and Expenditure", *Economic Journal*, vol. LXIV (1954); P. Deane, "Contemporary Estimates of the National Income in the first half of the Nineteenth Century", *Economic History Review*, 2nd Series, vol. VIII (1956). The best contemporary criticism of Pitt's Sinking Fund is R. Hamilton, *An Inquiry concerning the Rise and Progress of the National Debt* (Edinburgh, 1813, 3rd enlarged edition, London, 1818).

On the Currency, the most important of the numerous contemporary pamphlets are H. Thornton, *An Enquiry into the Nature and Effects of the Paper Credit of Great Britain* (1802; edited by F. A. von Hayek, 1939); D. Ricardo, *The High Price of Bullion a Proof of the Depreciation of Bank Notes* (1809; 4th edition, 1811); and W. Huskisson, *The Question concerning the Depreciation of our Currency stated and examined* (1810) (an explanation for the layman of the report of the 'Bullion Committee' of 1810, by a member). The 1810 report is reprinted, with an introduction, in E. Cannan, *The Paper Pound of 1797–1821* (1919); F. W. Fetter, "The Editions of the Bullion Report", *Economica*, New Series, vol. XXII (1955), merely lists the various editions. Later works on the topic include E. W. Kemmerer, *Money* (New York, 1935) (Chap. XI, "The Paper Money Standard in England, 1797–1821"); R. G. Hawtrey, *Currency and Credit* (1919) (Chap. XVI, "The Bank Restriction of 1797"); E. V. Morgan, "Some Aspects of the Bank Restriction Period 1797–1821", *Economic History*, vol. III (1939); A. Cunningham, *British Credit in the Last Napoleonic War* (Cambridge, 1910); N. J. Silberling, "The Financial and Monetary Policy of Great Britain during the Napoleonic Wars" in *Quarterly Journal of Economics*, vol. XXXVIII (1924); and R. G. Hawtrey, "British Banking and Finance 1793–1931" in *European Civilisation*, edited by E. Eyre, vol. V (Oxford, 1937). For Ireland, see *The Irish Pound, 1797–1826*, edited by F. W. Fetter (a reprint of the report of the 1804 committee). General works are Sir C. W. C. Oman, *The Coinage of England* (Oxford, 1931), and the valuable study by A. E. Feaveryear, *The Pound Sterling: A History of English Money* (1931).

The authorities on the banking system at this time are J. H. Clapham, *The Bank of England* (2 vols., Cambridge, 1944); A. M. Andreades, *History of the Bank of England 1640–1903* (2nd edition, 1924); S. E. Thomas, *The Rise and Growth of Joint-Stock Banking*, vol. I [Britain to 1860] (1934); and on the country banks, the definitive work of L. S. Pressnell, *Country Banking in the Industrial Revolution* (Oxford, 1956), should be consulted. Other works are W. M. Acres, *The Bank of England from Within, 1694–1900* (2 vols., 1931); E. V. Morgan, *The Theory and Practice of Central Banking, 1797–1913* (Cambridge, 1943); E. Coppieters, *English Bank Note Circulation, 1694–1954* (Louvain, 1955); and J. G. van Dillen, *History of the Principal Public Banks* (1934). Useful articles are S. E. Thomas, "The First English Provincial Banks", *Economic History*, vol. III (1934); L. S. Pressnell, "Public Monies and the Development of English Banking", *Economic History Review*, 2nd Series, vol. V (1952–1953); T. S. Ashton, "The Bill of Exchange and Private Banks in Lancashire, 1790–1830", *Economic History Review*, vol. XV (1945); and I. Bowen, "Banking Controversies in 1825", *Economic History*, vol. III (1938). F. G. Hilton Price, *A Handbook of London Bankers* (1890–1891 edition), lists all the known London banking houses, changes of partnerships, etc., during the period, and contemporary guides are J. W. Gilbart, *A Practical Treatise on Banking* (1827) and *History, Principles and Practice of Banking* (1834, revised edition, 1907). A useful general survey is W. R. Bisshop, *Rise of the London Money Market, 1640–1826* (1910), and on the insurance companies, see F. B. Relton, *Account of the Fire Insurance Companies* (1893). W. T. C. King, *History of the London Discount Market* (1936), deals with the commercial crisis of 1825–1826 and the early joint-stock banks.

VIII. WAGES AND PRICES

Contemporary information is scattered and often unreliable as a general guide to conditions. The principal collections of information are T. Tooke, *A History of Prices, and of the State of the Circulation, from 1793 to 1837* (2 vols., 1838) (the first 2 vols. of the later edition of the *History of Prices* by Tooke and Newmarch); and Arthur Young's *Enquiry into the Progressive Value of Money in England* (1812), and *Enquiry into the Rise of Prices in Europe during the last 25 Years* (1815). The later compilations by J. E. Thorold Rogers, *Six Centuries of Work and Wages* (2 vols., 1884) and *A History of Agriculture and Prices in England* [1259–1793] (7 vols., Oxford, 1866–1902) are being superseded by Sir W. Beveridge and others, *Prices and Wages in England from the 12th to the 19th Century* (vol. I, 1939). Much contemporary information is also scattered through Eden's *State of the Poor* (1797), the Reports of the Board of Agriculture on the various counties during the French wars, the *Annals of Agriculture*, and the *Parliamentary Papers*–see, for example, the Report of the Committee of the House of Lords on the State of the Poor Laws, 1830–1831 (*Parliamentary Papers*, 1831, vol. VIII). G. R. Porter, *The Progress of the Nation*, vol. II (1838) also has representative tables. The contemporary collections of wage data are listed by Hopkinson and A. L. Bowley in *Economic Review* (Oct. 1898). The standard secondary works dealing with the interpretation of this data are E. W. Gilboy, *Wages in Eighteenth Century England* (Cambridge, Mass., 1934), and A. L. Bowley, *Wages in the United Kingdom in the Nineteenth*

Century (Cambridge, 1900). An index of industrial wages is printed in G. H. Wood, "The Course of Average Wages between 1790 and 1860" in *Economic Journal*, vol. IX (1899). There is also information on wages in E. H. Phelps Brown and S. V. Hopkins, "Seven Centuries of Building Wages", *Economica*, New Series, vol. XXII (1955); G. Houston, "Farm Wages in Central Scotland from 1814 to 1870", *Journal of the Royal Statistical Society*, vol. CXVIII (1955); and M. Gray, "Economic Welfare and Money Incomes in the Highlands, 1750–1850", *Scottish Journal of Political Economy*, vol. II (1955). R. S. Tucker in *Journal of the American Statistical Association*, vol. XXXI, calculates the real wages of various London artisans, 1729–1935.

Information on prices is to be found in N. J. Silberling, "British Prices and Business Cycles, 1779–1850" in *Review of Economic Statistics*, preliminary vol. V, supplement no. 2 (1923), and the 'cost of living' is discussed in T. S. Ashton, "Changes in Standards of Comfort in Eighteenth Century England" in *Proceedings of the British Academy* (1955). The conventional interpretation of Ashton, Clapham and others that living standards for the working population were gradually and generally rising through this period is summarized in T. S. Ashton, "The Standard of Life of the Workers in England, 1790–1830" in *The Tasks of Economic History* (supplement IX of the *Journal of Economic History*, 1949), but is challenged by E. J. Hobsbawm, "The British Standard of Living, 1790–1850" in *Economic History Review*, 2nd Series, vol. X (1957), who returns in some respects to the general thesis of J. L. and B. Hammond in "The Industrial Revolution and Discontent", *Economic History Review*, vol. II (1936) and *The Growth of Common Enjoyment* (1933) that the post-war period was a time of depressed living standards for a large part of the working class. E. M. Gilboy, "Demand as a Factor in the Industrial Revolution" in *Facts and Factors in Economic History, Articles by former students of E. F. Gay* (1932), should also be consulted. On the 'truck' system, see G. W. Hilton, "The Truck Act of 1831", *Economic History Review*, 2nd Series, vol. X (1957).

A. AGRICULTURE

(a) AGRICULTURAL IMPROVEMENT AND ENCLOSURE

344. Table of the number of Enclosure Bills passed by Parliament, the annual excess of imports or of exports of wheat and meal, and the average price of wheat in England, 1760–1832

(G. R. Porter, *The Progress of the Nation*, I (1836), pp. 155–156.)

Years.	Number of Inclosure Bills.	Excess of Export over Import. Quarters of Wheat and Meal	Excess of Import over Export. Quarters of Wheat and Meal	Average Price of Wheat in England. London Gazette.	
				s.	d.
1760–9	385	1,384,561		45	10
1770–9	660		431,566	45	0
1780	45	220,144	. .	35	8
1781	25	. .	56,845	44	8
1782	15	64,457	. .	47	10
1783	18	. .	532,240	52	8
1784	15	. .	127,659	48	10
1785	23	21,822	. .	51	10
1786	25	154,003	. .	38	10
1787	22	61,197	. .	41	2
1788	34	. .	65,739	45	0
1789	24	27,353	. .	51	2
	246		233,502	45	9
1790	26	. .	191,665	53	2
1791	} 38	. .	398,430	47	2
1792		277,861	. .	41	9
1793	46	. .	413,529	47	10
1794	42	. .	172,854	50	8
1795	39	. .	294,954	72	11
1796	75	. .	854,521	76	3
1797	86	. .	407,242	52	2
1798	52	. .	336,939	50	4
1799	65	. .	423,823	66	11
	469		3,216,096	55	11

Years.	Number of Inclosure Bills.	Excess of Export over Import. Quarters of Wheat and Meal.	Excess of Import over Export. Quarters of Wheat and Meal.	Average Price of Wheat in England. London Gazette.	
				s.	d.
1800	63	. .	1,242,507	110	5
1801	80	. .	1,396,359	115	11
1802	122	. .	498,359	67	9
1803	96	. .	297,145	57	1
1804	104	. .	398,067	60	5
1805	52	. .	842,879	87	1
1806	71	. .	280,776	76	9
1807	76	. .	379,833	73	1
1808	91	13,116	. .	78	11
1809	92	. .	424,709	94	5
	847		5,747,518	82	2
1810	122	. .	1,491,341	103	3
1811	107	. .	238,366	92	5
1812	133	. .	244,385	122	8
1813	119	. .	425,559	106	6
1814	120	. .	681,333	72	1
1815	81	. .	. .	63	8
1816	47	. .	225,263	76	2
1817	34	. .	1,020,949	94	0
1818	46	. .	1,593,518	83	8
1819	44	. .	122,133	72	3
	853		6,042,847	88	8
1820	40	. .	34,274	65	10
1821	25	. .	2	54	5
1822	13	. .	. .	43	3
1823	9	. .	12,137	51	9
1824	12	. .	15,777	62	0
1825	24	. .	525,231	66	6
1826	20	. .	315,892	56	11
1827	22	. .	572,733	56	9
1828	16	. .	842,050	60	5
1829	24	. .	1,364,220	66	3
	205		3,682,316	58	5
1830	21	. .	1,701,885	64	3
1831	9	. .	1,491,631	66	4
1832	12	. .	325,435	58	8
	42		3,518,951	63	1

345. Calculation of the acreage of cultivated, uncultivated, and unprofitable land in the United Kingdom, 1827

(G. R. Porter, *The Progress of the Nation*, I (1836), p. 177.)

The figures are from a report drawn up, largely on the basis of personal observation, by William Couling, a witness before the Select Committee on Emigration in 1827. The full report, giving the figures for the separate counties of the United Kingdom, is in Porter, pp. 173–177.

	Cultivated.	Uncultivated.	Unprofitable.	Summary.
England	25,632,000	3,454,000	3,256,400	32,342,400
Wales	3,117,000	530,000	1,105,000	4,752,000
Scotland	5,265,000	5,950,000	8,523,930	19,738,930
Ireland	12,125,280	4,900,000	2,416,664	19,441,944
British Islands . . .	383,690	166,000	569,469	1,119,159
	46,522,970	15,000,000	15,871,463	77,394,433

	Arable and Gardens.	Meadows, Pastures, and Marshes.	Wastes capable of Improvement.	Annual Value of Wastes in their present state.	Incapable of Improvement.	Summary.
	Statute Acres.	Statute Acres.	Statute Acres.	Sterling Pounds.	Statute Acres.	Statute Acres.
England . .	10,252,800	15,379,200	3,454,000	1,700,000	3,256,400	32,342,400
Wales . . .	890,570	2,226,430	530,000	200,000	1,105,000	4,752,000
Scotland . .	2,493,950	2,771,050	5,950,000	1,680,000	8,523,930	19,738,930
Ireland. . .	5,389,040	6,736,240	4,900,000	1,395,000	2,416,664	19,441,944
British Islands .	109,630	274,060	166,000	25,000	569,469	1,119,159
	19,135,990	27,386,980	15,000,000	5,000,000	15,871,463	77,394,433

346. Arthur Young on the new wave of agricultural improvement

(*General View of the Agriculture of the County of Norfolk* (1804), pp. 31–32.)

In respect to their husbandry, the farming mind in this county has undergone two pretty considerable revolutions. For 30 years, from 1730 to 1760, the great improvements in the north western part of the county took place, and which rendered the county in general famous. For the next 30 years, to about 1790, I think they nearly stood still; they *reposed upon their laurels.* About that period a second revolution was working: they seemed then to awaken to new ideas: an experimental spirit began to spread, much owing, it is said, to the introduction of drilling; and as so new a practice set men to thinking, it is not unlikely: nothing can be done till men think, and they certainly had not thought for 30 years preceding. About that time also, Mr. Coke (who has done more for the husbandry of this county than any man since the turnip Lord Townshend, or any other man in the county), began his sheep-shearing meetings. These causes combined (for what I know, the former sprung partly from the latter) to raise a spirit which has not subsided. The scarcities, and consequent high prices, brought immense sums into the county, and enabled farmers to exert themselves with uncommon vigour. Experiments in drilling shewed that farmers might step out of the common road, without any danger of a gaol. South Down sheep came in about the same time. Folding was by many gradually given up. These new practices operated upon the farming mind; ideas took a larger range; a disposition was established, that would not readily reject a proposal merely because it was new–the sleep of so many countries. Every thing is to be expected from this spirit. Irrigation is gaining ground, in spite of the dreams that have been ventured against it. And if the men who occupy, or rather disgrace so large a part of the light sand district, by steadily adhering to those *good old maxims* which have preserved it so long in a desert state, shall once imbibe a portion of this ardour, we shall see new plants introduced, and new practices pursued, to carry the county in general to the perfection of which its husbandry is capable. . . .

347. Marshall's "Practical Remarks on Executing the Improvements of Farm Lands"

(W. Marshall, *On the Landed Property of England* (1804), pp. 301–305.)

William Marshall (1745–1818), agriculturalist and writer, best known for his *General Survey . . . of the Rural Economy of England*, published in 12 vols. between 1787 and 1798, was in some respects a superior observer to Arthur Young. His *Landed Property of England* was a practical treatise on estate management.

The first step toward the execution of every improvement is to ascertain its reality; by calculating the advantages to arise from it, and estimating the expense of carrying it into effect. If the former, taken in their full extent, do not exceed the latter, the proposed alteration cannot, in a private view, be considered as an improvement.

The next point to be ascertained is the practicability, under the given circumstances of a case, of executing the plan under consideration.

There are three things essential to the due execution of an improvement. 1. An undertaker; or a person of skill, leisure, and activity, to direct the undertaking. 2. Men and animals with which to prosecute the work. 3. Money, or other means of answering the required expenditure. A deficiency, in any one of these, may, by frustrating a well planned work, after its commencement, be the cause, not only of its failure, but of time, money, and credit being lost.

Let us therefore take a view of the different means, whereby a man of landed property may execute the higher improvements of farm lands.

There are various methods by which he may promote the permanent improvement of his estate: namely,

By granting long leases to tenants; letting them find the requisites of improvement, and take the advantages, during their terms.

By granting shorter leases to tenants; with a covenant of remuneration, for the remainder of such improvements as they have made, at the time of quitting.

By granting leases, at a low rent, for the first years of the term, – to give the tenants time, and ability, to improve at their own expense.

By advancing money to tenants at will, or, which is the same, making allowances of rent, for specified improvements, to be executed by them; under the inspection and control of the manager: they paying interest for the money advanced, or allowed.

By employing workmen, on tenanted farms; the tenants in like manner paying interest on the money expended. The proper interest, in ordinary cases, is six percent; thus estimating the value of the improvement, at sixteen years purchase.

By taking farm lands into hand; making the required improvements; and letting them, at an advanced rent, in their improved state.

And, lastly, by improving the minds of his tenants. By infusing among them a spirit for improvement.

This is to be done, by a proprietor, or by the manager, of an estate, who has a knowledge of rural affairs, and who possesses the goodwill and confidence of its tenantry, in various ways.

By personal attention, only, much is to be done. By reviewing an estate, once or twice a year; – by conversing with each tenant in looking over his farm; – and by duly noticing the instances of good management which rise to the eye, and condemning those which are bad; – vanity and fear, two powerful stimulants of the human mind, will be roused, – and an emulation be created among superior managers; while shame will scarcely fail to bring up the more deserving of the inferior ranks. If, after repeated exhortations, an irreclaimable sloven be discharged, as such, and his farm given to another, professedly for his superior qualifications as a husbandman, an alarm will presently be spread over the estate, and none, but those who deserve to be discharged, will long remain in the field of bad management.

Even by conversation, well directed, something may be done. If, instead of collecting tenants to the audit, as sheep to the shearing, and sending them away, as sheep that are shorn; – or if, on the contrary, instead of providing for them a sump- tuous entertainment, and committing them to their fate, in a state of intoxication; – a repast, suited to their condition and habits of life, were set before them; – and if, after this, the conversation were to be bent towards agriculture, by distributing presents to superior managers, specifying the particulars of excellence, for which the rewards or acknowledgments were severally bestowed; – a spirit of emulation could not fail to take place, among the higher classes; while the minds of the lower order of tenants, and of the whole, would be stimulated and improved, by the conversation.

By encouraging leading men, in different parts of a large estate, – men who are looked up to, by ordinary tenants; – by holding out these as patterns to the rest; – by furnishing them with the means of improving their breeds of stock; by supplying them with superior varieties of crops, and with implements of improved constructions. And, in recluse and backward districts, much may be done by tempting good hus- bandmen, and expert workmen, from districts of a kindred nature, but under a better system of cultivation, to settle upon an estate.

By an experimental farm, to try new breeds of stock, new crops, new implements, new operations, and new plans of management: such as ordinary tenants ought not to attempt,–before they have seen them tried.

To this important end, let the demesne lands of a large estate, or a sufficient portion of them, be appropriated to a nursery of improvements, for the use of the estate; to be professedly held out as such, and be constantly open to the tenants; more particularly to the exemplary practitioners, the leading men of the estate, just mentioned; who, alone, can introduce improvements among the lower classes of an ignorant and prejudiced tenantry. It is in vain for a proprietor to attempt it. On the contrary, the attempt seldom fails to alarm, disgust, and prevent the growth of spontaneous improvements.

Under the present plan of demesne farming, the tenants see expensive works going forward, which they know they cannot copy, and hear of extraordinary profits, by particular articles, which they are certain cannot be obtained, by any regular course of business. They therefore conclude that the whole is mere deception, to gain a pretext for raising the rents of their farms, above their value. Whereas, if the demesne lands were held out, as trial grounds, for their immediate benefit, and conducted, as such, in a manner intelligible to them, they would not fail to visit them.

Instead of large proprietors attempting to rival the meanest of their tenants, in farming for pecuniary profit, which, on a fair calculation, they rarely, if ever, obtain, let their views in agriculture be professedly, and effectually, directed toward the pecuniary advantages of their tenants: for from these, only, their own can arise,–in any degree that is entitled to the attentions of men of fortune. Instead of boasting of the price of a bullock, or the produce of a field, let it be the pride of him, who possesses an extent of landed property, to speak of the flourishing condition of his estates at large,–the number of superior managers that he can count upon them,–and the value of the improvements which he has been the happy mean of diffusing among them.

Leave it to professional men, to yeomanry and the higher class of tenants, to carry on the improvements, and incorporate them with established practices,–to prosecute pecuniary agriculture in a superior manner,–and set examples to inferior tenantry. This is strictly their province; and their highest and best view in life. It has been through this order of men, chiefly or wholly, that valuable improvements in agriculture have been brought into practice, and rendered of general use.

The possessor of an extent of territory has higher objects to view, and a more elevated station to fill. As a superior member of society, it may be said, he has still higher views than those of aggrandizing his own income. But how can a man of fortune fill what may well be termed his legitimate station in life, with higher advantage to his country, than by promoting the prosperity of his share of its territory; by rendering not one field, or one farm, but every farm upon it, productive? This is, indeed, being faithfully at his post. And it is a good office in society which is the more incumbent upon him, as no other man on earth can of right perform it;–valuable as it is to the public.

348. Arthur Young's *Tours in England and Wales*

(*London School of Economics Reprints*, XIV, pp. 65–66, 92–94, 109–111, 203–205.)

(*a*) *Tour to Woodbridge, &c., July 1784*

July 23, crossed Sampford hundred to Woolverston; I had a great inclination to be informed of the management in this part of the county, not having seen it before. . . . The management is exceedingly masterly; the soil dry and sandy, all arable, except here and there a meadow in a bottom, and so few of them that some farmers have not a single acre, but their cultivation makes amends for the deficiency. Their course is, 1 turnips, 2 barley, 3 clover, 4 wheat. I was pleased with finding that all the dung they can raise is spread on their turnip land, in which respect some of the best farmers in Norfolk and Suffolk are in a great error in giving it to the wheat. They know so well the importance of this application of manure, that they buy large quantities at Maningtree from London, which cost 12s. a five-horse load at the quay, and 20s. by the time it is on the land. Each load three tons. Kentish chalk also is purchased at the same price, at 7s. a load, with which they form composts. They feed the turnips on the land with bullocks and sheep. Plough three or four times for barley; generally three clean earths and a *rove* (half ploughing) and get of that grain four quarters on an average; the clover supports all the stock of the farm, and when it fails they are distressed; but make up as well as they can, by keeping the last year's unploughed.

Sometimes on their poorer soils they sow trefoil and ray-grass, in which case the course is, 1 turnips, 2 barley, 3 trefoil, 4 pease dibbled, 5 barley; which is most admirable management, and calculated to keep the land always clean.

Wheat yields, on a medium, 2½ qrs. an acre. They are much troubled with smutty wheat; have also a great deal burnt; and in some years much mildew; they attribute the latter entirely to honeydews, but burnt wheat to blights, in which they are certainly mistaken. . . .

[Leiston.] Farms here are very large; up to 300, 400 and £500 a-year. The common course of crops is, 1 turnips, 2 barley, 3 clover, 4 wheat; and they cannot have a better for husbandry that is carried on upon a large scale.

Cabbages in the field for cattle have been cultivated by several farmers for more than 20 years; it declined eight or ten years ago, but of late has increased again; they have up to 10 and 15 acres a man. Plant them in rows from two to three feet asunder, and hand-hoe enough to keep them clean; they give them to all sorts of cattle; but when cows eat them, the butter is as bad as from turnips. They reckon an acre much more valuable than the best turnips.

Patches of hemp through all this country.

Leave Leiston. . . . View the abbey, which shews in its ruins the grandeur it once possessed; the farmer who lives at it, assured me, no manure he has tried is better than the mortar rubbish of the walls. Crossing a bridge in a marsh, enter the farm of Mr. Robinson, tenant to Sir Gerard Vanneck. It is extremely large, and the rent £700 a year, the road passes through it for three miles, and it extends very much to both right and left. Here are three of the greatest farms in the county contiguous, Mr. Robinson's, Mr. Howlett's, and Mr. Sparke's, their rent together is above £2,000 a year. Crossed Mr. Howlett's, tenant to Sir John Blois, for a considerable distance, who appears to carry on his business with admirable spirit. His fields are very large, from 100 to 130 acres each, and were now covered with as fine corn as ever I beheld, without a weed to be seen. I passed through one of oats, which I should not guess at less than eight or nine quarters an acre; and viewed barley that must yield five or six at least; and wheat to four and four and a half: a glorious spectacle! such crops when covering so large an extent of land. His course of crops has been 1 clay on the old waste, or new clover and rye-grass lays, and dibbles in pease on one ploughing; 2 wheat; 3 turnips, 4 barley or oats, 5 clover and ray-grass for three years; which is admirable husbandry. In claying, his exertions have been considerable: and he uses for it (as do all his neighbours) three-wheeled one-horse carts only, which, from experience, he finds the most profitable method of moving manure, whatever the distance. He has had 30 of these carts at work at a time.

He has tried a second claying, nine or ten years after the first, and found it to answer perfectly well.

Came next to Mr. Sparke's farm, Sir John Rouss, the landlord, who is famous for the great quantity of stock he keeps on a corn farm. Last winter he fattened 130 oxen, and 70 score of Wiltshire wethers. He uses great quantities of oil-cake, and in a manner not common, for he gives the cake one day and turnips the other, alternately. All through this country they carry off half the crop of turnips, and feed the other half on the land. . . .

[Stonham Aspal.] Mr. Toosey has been some years a very attentive practiser of Mr. Bakewell's cattle-husbandry. His farm consists of 70 acres, in very compleat management, as may be easily collected from the quantity of cattle it supports; *viz.* 25 sheep, 8 horses and colts, 3 working oxen, 4 cows, 1 bull, 16 beasts, heifers, and steers, in the succession system, bred and sold fat steers, or with a calf if heifers; all which cattle are kept by 50 acres of grass, of which 12 are mown for hay: from 5 to 12 of cabbages, 8 of straw. But he buys, as every good husbandman should, as much straw and stubble as he can.

His cattle are of Bakewell's breed, which is, in one word, giving them sufficient praise: the bull which he calls *Twopenny* from that of Bakewell's, of which I gave an account in my *Eastern Tour*, is, in every respect, a very fine one, particularly in the breadth and straitness of his back, the barrel carcass, and the short leg. He leaps cows at half a guinea, at which rate many have been brought to him, which shews that there is some taste in this country for breeding. The cows and other cattle whole bred, for Mr. Toosey bought cows and heifers of Mr. Bakewell as well as Twopenny, are of a very perfect mould. In tying up all his cattle, Mr. Toosey copies Bakewell's system; they are all tied up to straw, or hay and cabbages; littered well, and cleaned twice a day; the dung piled up against the sheds, and the urine, every drop of which is saved, thrown regularly on it. The water from the eaves of the building is all conveyed away, that it may not dilute the urine, an attention that cannot be too much commended. The sheep are equally well made with the cattle; some few he sells for the breed, but gets from 30s. to £3 for two year old wethers from the butchers.

A practice in which this gentleman is perfectly original, is that of stall-feeding his

sheep in winter; he does it exactly in the same manner as with oxen, having racks
and mangers provided for the purpose. It is only experience that can decide on the
project; perhaps an animal so well defended against the cold by his fleece should
never be kept hot: it must be essential, in executing this plan, to have the sheds as
open as possible, and to allow a good distance from sheep to sheep.

Upon occasion of straw and stubble being scarce, Mr. Toosey bedded all his cattle
with sand, and found that, with a small addition of litter, it did very well; he left it
off merely because of the expense of carriage, as he had three miles to go for it. The
heaps of dung, just mentioned, are moved to the compost heap several times in a year,
as by frequent stirring he can rot it in three months; it is then mixed with earth and
chalk. This system I conceive to be erroneous—that the oftener dung is moved, the
more of its virtue is lost; that a slow fermentation reduces dung to that mucilaginous
state in which it should be used, with much less loss than an accelerated fermentation,
which, from frequent stirrings, carries off so much of the volatile alkali, that the
remaining mass is robbed of its richest qualities. In general, however, Mr. Toosey,
by buying straw, &c., bringing chalk seven miles, raising a large quantity of dung,
and saving all the urine, keeps his farm in most rich order, and secures very large
crops. It requires two men in winter to take care of the above cattle, move the dung,
and bring cabbages, but they have leisure time, which is employed in chalk cart. . . .

(b) A Month's Tour to Northamptonshire, Leicestershire, &c. (1791)

19 July 1791. Taking the road from Cambridge to St. Neot's, view for six or seven
miles the worst husbandry I hope in Great Britain. All in the fallow system, and the
loss of time, and the expense submitted to, without the common benefit, these fallows
are overrun with thistles, and the dung being spread over them forms an odd mixture
of black and green that would do well enough for a meadow, but is villainous in
tillage. Some divisions of these fallows have not yet been broken up since reaping the
last year's crops. Bid the current of national improvement roll back three centuries,
and we may imagine a period of ignorance adequate to the exhibition of such exertions! To what corner of the three kingdoms—to what beggarly village must we go
to find in any branch of manufacture such sloth—such ignorance—such backwardness
—such determined resolution to stand still, while every other part of the world is at
least moving?—It is in the *agriculture* of the kingdom alone that such a spectacle is to be
sought. There seems somewhat of a coincidence between the state of cultivation
within sight of the venerable spires of Cambridge, and the utter neglect of agriculture
in the establishments of that University.

They are ploughing here with poor implements, drawn by two horses at length,
and conducted by a driver. The crops of wheat pretty good; all others bad.

At Knapwell there is a parliamentary inclosure, and such wretched husbandry in
it, that I cannot well understand for what they inclosed relative to management; rent
is the only explanation, which has risen from 5s. tythed, to 10s. or 11s. free. They
sow hay seeds and clover, but little comes except raygrass and thistles; soil a strong
loam, and some clay. Thence to St. Neot's, and all the way from Cambridge, must be
classed amongst the ugliest countries in England. The lands mostly open field, at 6s.

an acre. The management very bad, much strong clay, and some fallows not yet ploughed; the course,

1. Fallow, ploughed thrice; breaking up 7s. 6d. Two stirrings, each 3s. with 4 horses and a driver.

2. Wheat, produce 14 or 15 bush. per acre short of statute measure.

3. Oats or beans.

About St. Neot's a vast improvement by an inclosure, which took place 16 years ago, which makes the country much more beautiful, and has been a great benefit to the community. A gentleman of the town however complained, as I rode thither with him, that, notwithstanding the productiveness of the soil was certainly greater, yet that the poor were ill-treated by having about half a rood given them in lieu of a *cow keep*, the inclosure of which land costing more than they could afford, they sold the lots at £5; the money was drank out at the ale-house, and the men, spoiled by the habit, came, with their families, to the parish; by which means poor rates had risen from 2s. 6d. to 3s. and 3s. 6d. But pray, Sir, have not rates arisen equally in other parishes, where no inclosure has taken place? Admitted. And what can be the good of commons, which would not prevent poor rates coming to such a height? Better modes of giving the poor a share might easily, and have been, as in other cases, adopted.

349. The effect of enclosure upon population

(T. Brown, *General View of the Agriculture of the County of Derby* (1794), p. 35.)

Those who have urged the impolicy of inclosures, from the idea that they depopulate, must have taken up the matter on very superficial grounds. Ask any man if the planting, preserving, and rearing of hedges is not attended with much expense; and if, even after they are reared, whether the cutting and scouring, and keeping them up, does not require much attention and increase of labour? The dressing and keeping an inclosed field in a proper state of cultivation and improvement, is certainly equal to what is done in the common fields. In a word, I think no man will contend for a moment, that to cultivate and improve land after it is inclosed, requires less labour than it did in the common field state; nor that men will do more labour in a day than was formerly done. If my position be right, it will follow, that the number of hands employed cannot be diminished. I know there are places where common arable fields have been inclosed, laid down in pasture, and neglected; less ploughing done, and perhaps fewer labourers employed, after the inclosure; but this very rarely happens, for wherever inclosures are turned to the most advantage, I will contend they require an increase of capital, attention, and labour; and consequently that the number of labouring hands are not diminished. So far as my experience goes, inclosure in the first instance requires an increase of capital to be employed in agriculture; this capital renders the product of the land more abundant, and this abundance requires more hands to be employed. By the facility with which abundant produce is managed on inclosed lands, the additional capital employed makes its returns, so that there are more hands required, and more produce carried to market.

350. Sir F. M. Eden on enclosure and the cottagers

(The State of the Poor, I, Preface, pp. xviii–xx.)

. . . The advantages which cottagers and poor people derive from commons and wastes, are rather apparent than real: instead of sticking regularly to any such labour, as might enable them to purchase good fuel, they waste their time, either like the old woman in Otway's Orphan, in picking up a few dry sticks, or in grubbing up, on some bleak moor, a little furze, or heath. Their starved pig or two, together with a few wandering goslings, besides involving them in perpetual altercations with their neighbours, and almost driving and compelling them to become trespassers, are dearly paid for, by the care and time, and bought food, which are necessary to rear them. Add to this, that as commons, and wastes, however small their value may be in their present state, are undoubtedly the property, not of cottagers, but of the land-owners; these latter, by the present wretched system, are thus made to maintain their poor, in a way the most costly to themselves, and the least beneficial to the poor. There are thousands and thousands of acres in the kingdom, now the sorry pastures of geese, hogs, asses, half-grown horses, and half-starved cattle, which want but to be enclosed and taken care of, to be as rich, and as valuable, as any lands now in tillage. In whatever way, then, it may seem fit to the legislature, to make those cottagers some amends for the loss, or supposed loss, they may sustain, by the reclaiming of wastes, it must necessarily be better for them, than their present precarious, disputable, and expensive advantages, obtained, if at all, by an ill-judged connivance, or indulgence, of the owners of land; and, by an heedless sacrifice of property, of which no one takes any account, and for which, of course, no one thanks them. . . .

(b) THE VICISSITUDES OF AGRICULTURE, 1783–1832

351. Examination of Arthur Young before the Committee on the Assize and Making of Bread, 1800

(Parliamentary Papers, 1st Series, IX, pp. 76–77.)

Have you any information respecting the produce and quality of the last crop of wheat?–I have had letters from most parts of the country, the purport of which are, that the deficiency of the crop generally amounts to one-third; but from various persons I had second and third communications correcting their former statements as they advanced in threshing, which makes the deficiency still greater, in some cases amounting to half . . . of an average produce. . . .

How many bushels do you allow per acre, in your computation of an average crop?–Something between 22 and 24.

Have you any information respecting the last crop of barley, oats and rye?–The produce of barley and oats deficient perhaps one-fourth or one-fifth in point of quantity; in some places the crops worse, but varying considerably; in other places the crop equal to an average one in quantity, but, in point of quality, miserably bad. . . .

Do you not believe, when the price of wheat is high, one-third of the inhabitants recur to barley or oaten bread, including those who make it their habitual food?–I do not conceive the proportion to be so great; what it would be without parochial assistance, is another thing; but I am informed, throughout a great part of the kingdom, the general assistance given to the poor is by money, bread, or flour, all three being almost equally an encouragement to the consumption of wheat. And I beg leave to add a very important consideration, that vast sums have for two months past been expended throughout the kingdom, and are at present expending, in a manner that tends strongly to bring on a great increase of the present scarcity: I personally know many parishes, being country villages and not towns, that expend in this manner from £40 to £70 per month additional to their common rates. The common way is to sell wheat at reduced prices.

Can you suggest any means of economizing the expenditure of wheat?–I think the present scarcity so truly alarming, that no economy whatever, upon the mode of consuming wheat, will answer the exigency of the moment. In Suffolk attempts have been made, and are now making in some parishes, to mix barely and rye with wheat, and to make a browner sort of wheaten bread; but the distress of the poor is great, notwithstanding every effort of this sort. . . . And I have had information from several hard-working people, that while eating brown bread of their own making, they have not been able to labour with that force and heartiness which they have found to result from the finer sorts. . . . Something much more effectual than this is absolutely necessary; and I venture to propose as an opinion, that nothing short of stopping the consumption of oats by horses, or importing rice to a very great amount, or extending the use of soup almost generally, will be equal to the demand occasioned by the scarcity. . . .

I beg to mention a circumstance respecting the soup: I made a copper full of soup every day; and, in order to try the effect of the leanest meat that could be procured, I killed ten of the very leanest sheep there were in a flock of 500; and that effect was exceeding good. To each copper, containing 30 gallons, I put one sheep of from 25 lbs. to 30 lbs. a peck of potatoes, half a peck of onions, a peck of carrots, a peck of turnips, half a peck of pease, 6 pounds of rice, and it made most excellent soup, which the poor relished exceedingly, and the outsetters of the parish, who lived five miles off, came for it very readily; from which I conclude that one very great resource for the kingdom at present is the establishment of soup shops, or perhaps rather to enforce all parochial assistance whatever to the poor, universally, to exclude the consumption of wheat; which, if general, would do more to alleviate the present scarcity than all Assizes of Bread that can be devised.

Do you not conceive, that if the lower orders of people could be induced to diminish their consumption of bread, and would learn to make soups to fill up that deficiency, upon the most economical plan, that they would feed themselves for much less than they are at present in the habit of doing, and with much more wholesome food?–I am clearly of that opinion: but when I see that class of the people, better instructed than the poor are at present, supplying them in country villages with the produce of wheat only; when I see so gross an absurdity in their superiors, I doubt it will be found very difficult without the aid of Parliament, to enforce any such excellent a consumption as that of soup; and I am well convinced, that if proper measures were taken to prevent parochial assistance in wheat and money, substituting rice, soup, and oat-flour, and potatoes, if to be had, would have a very great effect indeed in remedying all the evils of the present situation. . . .

352. Letters from W. Hastings to Earl Fitzwilliam, 1800

(Fitzwilliam MSS.)

Hastings was Fitzwilliam's agent for his Malton estates in Yorkshire.

1 Jan. 1800:

I am happy to inform your Lordship that at the meetings held on Monday and yesterday it was finally determined to adopt your Lordship's recommendation of relieving the poor of this place &c with soup and bread three times a week and a handsome collection was made in the town yesterday for that purpose amounting in the whole to £125 already received exclusive of the subscription of some of the inhabitants who were from home but who I have no doubt will join in the subscription on their return. Towards this sum I have on behalf of your Lordship subscribed £25 which after the handsome manner in which the generality of the principal inhabitants came forward I thought was as little as could put down for your Lordship and which I trust your Lordship will not think more than enough. The committee being put to some difficulties respecting a proper place for the making and distributing the soup I made them an offer on your Lordships behalf of the *brewing vessels at the lodge* which are in an *outbuilding a distance from the house* and can for the present *be spared without any inconvenience.* Of which they have accepted and beg leave to thank your Lordship both for the use of them and your Lordships subscription. . . .

8 Jan. 1800:

I received your lordships favour of the 3rd instant and am glad your Lordship approves of what I have done with respect to the Lodge as a soup shop which I am happy in informing your Lordship is I think now *completely established.* Monday was the first day of our delivery, when we distributed 460 quarts of soup and as many penny loaves to the poor of New Malton. . . . We made our soup according to a receipt procured from Bradford, which, though it was good *strong soup,* it did not altogether please the people, being either from the *newness of all the vessels,* or, from some *other cause* not *fully ascertained,* an unpleasant *colour.* We therefore in making to-day's soup both altered the ingredients and varied the process in the making and we are all of one opinion that we have improved on the Bradford soup (though at some considerable expense) and has produced *a very good pleasant looking soup and what is much approved of by the persons for whose relief it is intended.* We have this day supplied the Old Malton poor from the same shop and has distributed to them alone 120 quarts of soup and bread accordingly making in the whole about 500 quarts (the demand in New Malton being rather reduced) for this day's distribution which according to our estimate (or allowance) of a pint a head (children included) is a relief to 1000 persons in the two towns that are most necessitous. Our plan is to take for every quart of soup *one penny* but we give them a *full pennyworth* of good wholesome household bread *along with it.* . . .

353. Earl Fitzwilliam to J. Cleaver, of Malton, 24 Dec. 1800

(Fitzwilliam MSS.)

Fitzwilliam's opposition to the supply of wheat at below the market price to the poor of Malton resulted in the substitution of a supply of salt fish and potatoes. At the general election of 1807 the cry of the town against Fitzwilliam's interest was 'Salt fish and taties'.

I have received a letter from Mr. Hastings with an account of the proceedings of a meeting at Malton, among which I find that the committee appointed has determined, "That it has power from time to time to purchase such quantities of wheat and barley as it shall think fit, for the purpose of mixing the same two-thirds barley, and one-third wheat, and to sell the same either in flour or bread to the poor at such price, as that not more than 2s. per bushel should be lost thereby, and so as the quantity sold to each family should in no case exceed his Majesty's proclamations."

Against such proceedings and against any resolution of that tendency, I beg you to enter my protest, for the following reasons,

1st. Because it is in direct contradiction to the spirit of the resolutions of a former meeting, upon the ground of which I subscribed.

2d. Because, by its operation in raising the price of grain, it will be injurious to the public and in the greatest degree cruel and oppressive to the class of people immediately above those who receive the benefit of such relief.

3dly. Because by the non-consumption of such articles of food as may be increased, and by the consumption of the ordinary articles, which cannot be increased, it tends to convert the inconveniences of scarcity into the horrors of famine.

4thly. Because it counteracts the spirit of and militates against the actual provisions of an Act of Parliament, passed after the most solemn investigation into the necessities of the juncture, and upon the most mature deliberation of the nature of the remedy alone applicable to the occasion.

354. Speech in the House of Commons by C. C. Western on the distressed state of agriculture, 7 March 1816

(The Pamphleteer, VII, pp. 504–514.)

Charles Callis Western (1767–1844), later Baron Western, country gentleman and agriculturalist, was the chief spokesman of the agricultural interest in the House of Commons. A lifelong advocate of protection for the farmer, he was one of the leading promoters of the Corn Bill of 1815.

. . . Between two and three years ago agriculture was in a flourishing and prosperous state, and yet, within the short period which has since elapsed, thousands have been already ruined, and destruction seems to impend over the property of all those whose capital is engaged in the cultivation of the soil. From what causes, I say, can such events have arisen? Are they the effects of excessive taxation, of the enormous amount of the national debt? Are they the consequences of our extensive paper circulation, which now appears to have been in a great measure withdrawn? Are they occasioned by the pressure of the tithe, or the severe burden of the poor rate?—Is it from any, or from all of these causes, that the evil has originated? I have no hesitation in saying, that it is not to one or two, but to a combination of all these causes, we must attribute our distress. Our national debt and our taxes have been carried to an extent unknown, I believe, to any other country in the universe: our paper currency has been carried also to an extent quite unexampled, and, I believe, will be found to have created a principal source of our misfortune. The poor rates have been singularly oppressive; tithes, also, have been felt in proportion as larger capital has been required to cultivate the land. Yet, in spite of all these burdens, up to the middle of 1813, agriculture did sustain them, and, under the weight of their united pressure, contributed to make most rapid advances. How then are we to account for such a change? There are those, I know, who attribute it to the return of peace, but I do not entertain that opinion. The loss of the war demand, no doubt, has had an effect, but this, I should think, is counteracted by the cutting off the foreign supply of grain under the Act of last Session; besides, by referring to the account upon the table, we shall see that the great fall in the price of corn took place prior to the possible anticipation of the return of peace. In the early part of January 1813 the price of wheat was as high as 120s. per quarter; in November it was as low as 75s. or 76s. . . . At this latter period, no confidence or expectation of returning peace could have influenced the market; and, therefore, to that cause the fall of price cannot be at all attributed. It is also to be observed, that the very year after the return of peace in 1782, the price of grain rose 2 or 3 shillings, and upon an average of 5 years compared with the last 5 years of the American war, 5s. per quarter. . . . These circumstances concurring, induce me to believe that the return of peace has had very little influence upon the rapid fall of the markets for grain. I return then to a consideration of all the other circumstances before-mentioned, and will endeavour to trace their operation from that which appears to me to have been the primary cause, though, no doubt, effects immediately following have operated as causes more powerful, perhaps, than that which was the original. The first and obvious cause, I say, has been a redundant supply in the markets, a supply considerably beyond the demand, and that created chiefly by the produce of our own agriculture. The importation of foreign corn has, no doubt, in some degree, contributed to the creation of that redundance; but as it did not exceed in the last two years the average amount of the last ten, it is evident that the surplus now existing is chiefly ascribable to the extension of our own growth.

Permit me, Sir, here to call to the recollection of the House the effect of a small surplus or deficit of supply above or below the demand of the market. It is perfectly well known that if there is a small deficiency of supply, the price will rise in a ratio far beyond any proportion of such deficiency; the effect indeed is almost incalculable: so likewise on a surplus of supply beyond demand, the price will fall in a ratio exceeding almost tenfold the amount of such surplus. Corn, being an article of prime necessity, is peculiarly liable to such variation; upon a deficit of supply the price is further advanced by alarm; and upon a surplus, it is further diminished by the difficulty the growers have in contracting the amount of their growth, compared to the means which other manufacturers possess of limiting the amount of their manufactures.

I have drawn the attention of the House to these considerations, in order to show that it is not necessary the surplus should be so large as might at first appear to be requisite, to occasion that primary depression of the price of grain which I attribute to it. I am aware, that so fixed has been the opinion for many years of our inability to grow enough for our own consumption, that it will still be difficult to convince many people that we have actually created a supply beyond our demand. I have indeed always maintained that it was easily practicable so to do; that we had abundant means for the purpose, and that from lands wholly uncultivated, as well as from those which, notwithstanding our improved agriculture, were yet very miserably farmed, we might extract resources for more than double the amount of our present population. The quantity of corn imported I have always considered as very trifling, when compared with the amount of our aggregate consumption, though it may operate very powerfully to depress a market already filled, especially as the extent of what might be drawn from foreign countries cannot be ascertained. The average import of the last twelve years has not exceeded a million of quarters of all sorts of grain. In 1811 and 1812 we exported more than we imported; and though a large proportion was sent out of the kingdom for the supply of our own subjects, yet we had at that time a great many foreigners and prisoners within the kingdom. Let the House also recollect what vast imports have been drawn from Ireland, and the quantity of wheat and other grain that has been furnished within these few years to this metropolis from Scotland, from whence formerly none was ever received. In short, throughout all parts of the Empire, during the last 20 years, agriculture has certainly advanced with rapid strides. The full effect of all our improvements has just been completely realized; and two or three good harvests from this extended and improved agriculture, together with continued import, and demand reduced, have occasioned such a surplus in the market, as very obviously accounts for the first depression of the price. The farmers soon became alarmed, and began to experience distress. Their alarm was increased by the rejection of the Corn Bills of 1813 and 1814, and by the apparent determination of the public to resist any measure of that sort, and likewise by an opinion generally entertained, that the peace would necessarily restore the low prices which existed prior to the war. They felt also conscious of their own want of resources, and that they should be soon hurried into the market, and compelled to take any price that was offered. It has been, I know, universally believed by the public, that farmers had acquired large fortunes in the course of the last 10 years: a more erroneous opinion, however, never was formed, and so the result has proved. It has been said, that the prices of grain have been so enormously high, that the farmers must have realized great fortunes. Now, Sir, I deny in the first place, that prices have been enormously high, compared with the advanced charges of every kind to which agriculture has been liable,–nay, I am surprised they have not been much higher. In the years of scarcity indeed, the prices were very high; but upon an average of ten years they have not been so. Compare the prices of a period some time back with the average price of the last ten years, take the amount of taxation in each period, and I think the House will see that I am fully warranted in making this statement. The average price of wheat during ten years prior to the commencement of the war in 1792, was 47s. per quarter, and the average charge of taxes and loans, fifteen millions per annum. The average price of wheat during ten years ending with 1812, that is, excluding the two years of scarcity, and the two last years of low price, was 88s. per quarter; the amount of taxes and loans seventy-five millions per annum. Here then we find the amount of taxation in effect quintupled, whilst the price of corn has not doubled; in addition to which, the proportional amount of the circulating medium has in the last period immensely increased.

I say that, considering all these circumstances, combined with the vast increase of burthens to which agriculture is exclusively liable, we shall find that we are not only not entitled to call the price of the last ten years enormously high, but we must rather be surprised that it has not risen to a far greater extent. Thus then, though agriculture has advanced rapidly, yet the profits have not been large; and such has been the enterprising spirit of late years, which farmers have evinced equally with all other classes of society, that their earnings have been immediately devoted to further improvements, and their capitals have been sunk in the amelioration of their lands, which in a thousand instances will now turn out to have been irrecoverably thrown away. As to the extravagance with which they have been charged, it is mere prejudice to ascribe to them a greater portion of it than is equally attributable to other members of the community. The truth is, as fast as they could realize or borrow money, they employed it in the purchase or improvement of land; and the facilities of obtaining credit in late years have universally stimulated this practice. In this situation, can we be surprised at their alarm and their distress? The price continued to fall till their property diminished one-half, and their creditors press for the repayment of advances, which they now begin to consider no longer safe. In this state of things confidence is universally shaken, and away goes an immense proportion of the circulating medium of the country banks, which in fact was founded upon the value of the products of the land. Here then we begin to feel the consequences of a loss of that circulating medium, which before had been so abundant; and it is impossible to calculate what may be the extent of the evils that may arise from the rapid withdrawing so extensive a quantity of currency, with which the country banks, by issue of their notes, and by other means, furnished to the demand of the public. I am far from denying the advantages of a paper currency, more especially when kept within limits, by the power of the holder to demand payment in specie. Unlimited as it has been, I attribute very much to its operation the vast extension of our commercial, manufacturing, and agricultural productions. A paper currency, or circulating medium, is in fact a credit currency, which has the effect of converting a dormant capital into a state of immediate activity; whilst at the same time, by its increasing abundance, it enhances the prices of all articles produced. I believe all writers upon political economy have agreed, that an increasing amount of circulating medium, together with the consequent advance of price of all commodities, has been uniformly beneficial to the industrious class of the community. These effects have been strongly felt by the increasing amount of this credit circulation of late years, whilst at the same time the power it has afforded of employing capital, has multiplied all the products of industry in a very rapid degree. To exemplify its effects, take the case of an enterprising farmer, for instance; let us suppose him, with a limited capital, in the occupation of an extensive farm; at the end of harvest he sees his yards and barns loaded with the fruits of an abundant season, he is anxious to make improvements in a variety of ways, but has not the means of so doing till his crops can be brought to market; instead of waiting that event, the facilities of credit in late years have enabled him at once to command a sum on the security of this corn, and thus he is enabled, with a rapidity unknown in former times, to improve those sources of production which keep continually multiplying as they advance, till at length they have overgrown the demand. Other manufactures, I believe, have increased from the same cause, and in the same proportion; so that, in fact, they have also overloaded the market. The demand for all commodities, and the home and foreign markets, are completely overdone. It is true that the war demand, in the first instance, gave the first moving spring to the production of corn and all other articles; the consequence of the war likewise, by giving us more complete possession of the home and foreign markets, has powerfully operated, and then followed the magical effects of this extensive credit circulation which I have endeavoured to describe. The period is now come, when we are to experience the evil attendant upon such a system, the extent of which it is impossible to estimate. If an abundant credit circulation is productive of the advantages above stated, it must be admitted likewise that it is attended with great danger under any circumstances of national difficulty or alarm. If any large class of the opulent part of the people fall into distress, calamities must ensue, to which we otherwise should not be so much exposed; and we cannot be surprised, that under the pressure which the owners and occupiers of land at present sustain, difficulties unparalleled should have arisen. . . .

There is one other cause to which I also attribute in part the progresive fall in the price of grain, though, like some other causes, it has been an effect in the first instance; and that is, diminished consumption, in consequence of diminished earnings of the laborious classes. However fast the price of provisions has fallen, the earnings of labour have recently fallen faster still; so that those who live by the labour of their hands cannot command so much of the comforts of life as when they were nearly double the price which they now are. Thus we may go on, unless a change speedily takes place, in a course of progressive impoverishment, the consequence of progressively diminishing consumption. . . .

(c) THE CORN LAWS

355. Report from the Select Committee of the House of Commons on the depressed state of agriculture, 1821

(*Parliamentary Debates*, New Series, v, App. lxix–cii.)

... By the salutary law of 1806, a free interchange in grain of every description was established between Great Britain and Ireland; and ... the trade in foreign corn is altogether governed by the provisions of the Acts of 54 and 55 George III, by which were, for the first time, enacted,

1st, a constantly free exportation from the United Kingdom, without reference to price, or without such exportation being either encouraged by any bounty, or restrained by any duty whatsoever.

2ndly, an absolute prohibition against the introduction of every description of foreign grain, meal or flour, into the consumption of the United Kingdom, when the average prices, ascertained according to the mode established by former Acts, are below certain specified rates.

3rdly, an unlimited freedom of importation from all parts of the world, without any duty whatever, when the prices are above those specified rates.

... At the present price of corn, the returns to the occupier of an arable farm, after allowing for the interest of his investment, are by no means adequate to the charges and outgoings, of which a considerable proportion can be paid only out of the capitals, and not from the profits of the tenantry.

... A large proportion of the increase of the rent which has taken place within the last twenty years, is owing to the capitals which have been permanently vested in improvements, partly by the owners and in part by the tenants of the soil; by the judicious application of which capitals, in many instances great tracts of land, theretofore waste, or comparatively of little value, have been brought into productive cultivation.

A further proportion of the increase of rent is, unquestionably, to be ascribed to the diminished value of our currency during a great part of the period when this rise took place. ... The restoration of that currency will necessarily lead, as existing engagements lapse, to new arrangements between landlord and tenant. ...

In the present year, the price of corn has been further depressed by the general abundance and good quality of the last harvest, in all articles of grain and pulse. ... Several of the witnesses examined, have stated their belief that the prices of grain have further been depressed, in the present year, by the very large importations of foreign corn which took place before the ports were closed in the month of February 1819; but looking to the very high prices, and to the constant and brisk demand which prevailed in our markets so long as the ports continued open in 1817 and 1818, it may be inferred that the greatest part of those importations was necessary, and was disposed of during those years, to supply the daily wants of our consumption, and that it is therefore only in a remote degree that the present prices can be influenced by the occurrences of that period.

... The growth of wheat has been greatly extended and improved of late years in all parts of the United Kingdom, but principally in Ireland, since the year 1807.

. . . In the years 1804 and 1814 a depression of prices – principally caused by abundant harvests and a great extension of tillage, excited by the extraordinary high prices of antecedent years – appears to have produced a temporary pressure and uneasiness among the owners and occupiers of land, and a corresponding difficulty in the payment of rents and the letting of farms, in some degree similar to the apprehensions and embarrassments which now prevail. . . .

Many commodities of general and extensive demand, the staple productions of other countries, such as corn, cotton, rice and tobacco in the U.S.A.; sugar and rum in the West Indies; tallow, flax, hemp, timber, iron, wool and corn on the continent of Europe, appear to have fallen in price, in some instances more, and scarcely in any less, in proportion to the prices of those articles prior to 1816, than the fall in the price of grain in this country. . . . It would seem that the influence of that general derangement which the convulsions of the last thirty years have produced in all the relations of commerce, in the application of capital, and in the demand for labour, is not yet spent and exhausted. . . .

It is impossible to have watched with any degree of attention the state and condition of agriculture, manufactures and trade, under the influence of this depression in the prices of so many articles of general consumption, without being convinced that it has been attended with severe loss to several classes by whose capitals those articles have been either raised, or held for sale and distribution, to supply the wants of society; but as far as depression of price has been produced by redundant production, which, at this moment, appears to be one of the causes operating to lower the price of corn both in this and other countries, it admits of no adequate remedy, except that which must arise from the progressive adjustment of the supply to the demand, either by the diminution of the one, or the increase of the other, or more probably, by the combined operation of both.

In the article of corn, however, the price . . . fluctuates more than that of any other commodity of extensive consumption, in proportion to any excess or deficiency in the supply. . . .

The annual produce of corn, the growth of the United Kingdom, is, upon an average crop, about equal to our present annual consumption. . . . With such an average crop, the present import prices, below which foreign corn is by law altogether excluded, are fully sufficient, more especially since the change in the value of our money, to secure to the British grower the complete monopoly of the home market. . . .

Upon this subject of a remunerative price, so far as relates to this country, your Committee apprehend that much misconception prevails. . . . It is obvious that what was deemed a remunerative price in 1815 under one state of things, may be more or less than a remunerative price in 1821 under a very different state of things. The sum of 80s. may represent a different value now from what it did then, and assuming rent to remain the same, the expense of seed, labour, and all other outgoings may have been materially diminished; but, making ample allowance for these grounds of variation, it would by no means be an impossible case that, in the ordinary acceptation of these words 'remunerative price', 80s. at this time may not be more, or even so much 'remunerative' as that sum was held to be in 1815. . . . If the country should require for its annual consumption one-fifth, for example, more of corn than was sufficient in 1815, this increased demand would require an extended tillage. Lands which, in 1815, would not have paid for cultivation, would be applied to the raising of corn, and it would be very possible that upon those lands paying no rent, and notwithstanding the increased value of money and diminished expense of production, corn could not be raised for 80s. a quarter. In this supposition, therefore, if it should be the policy of the State to preserve the monopoly of the home market to the home grower, it would be necessary to raise the scale of import price above 80s. a quarter; but then inasmuch as the cost of raising corn on all lands, upon which it was before produced with profit, would not be augmented, that profit would be proportionally increased for the benefit, first of the tenant, during the remainder of his engagement, and afterwards of the landlord, from the period of its termination; and, after a new engagement, 80s. would no more be a remunerative price upon the richest land, paying the highest rent, than it would upon the poorest, paying no rent at all.

If therefore the population of the country and its power of consumption should continue to increase, it would be necessary, in order to preserve in efficacy the principle and system of our corn law, from time to time to advance the import prices, even though all the charges of producing corn should remain the same.

The change in the value of our money is, virtually, such an advance; and the result of every such advance, supposing prices not to undergo a corresponding rise in other countries, must be to expose this country to greater and more grievous fluctuations in price, and the business of a farmer to greater uncertainty and hazard, according to the alternations of good or bad seasons. . . .

The ruinously low prices of agricultural produce at this moment cannot be ascribed to any deficiency in the protecting power of the law. Protection cannot be carried further than monopoly. This monopoly the British grower has enjoyed for the produce of the two last harvests; the ports (with the exception of the ill-timed and unnecessary importation of oats during six weeks of the last summer) having been uninterruptedly shut against all foreign import for nearly thirty months. . . .

To prohibit the foreign supply altogether, so long as from the casualty of seasons we are subject to years of deficient or damaged produce, has at all times been felt to be impossible. But, since the year 1815 we have had recourse to an absolute prohibition up to a certain price, and an unlimited competition beyond that price.

This system is certainly liable to sudden alterations, of which the effect may be at one time to reduce prices already low, lower than they would probably have been under a state of free trade, and at another, unnecessarily to enhance prices already high; to aggravate the evils of scarcity, and to render more severe the depression of prices from abundance. On the one hand, it deceives the grower with the false hope of a monopoly, and by its occasional interruption, may lead to consequences which deprive him of the benefits of that monopoly, when most wanted; on the other hand, it holds out to the country the prospect of an occasional free trade, but so regulated and desultory as to baffle the calculations and unsettle the transactions, both of the grower and the dealer at home; to deprive the consumer of most of the benefits of such a trade, and to involve the merchant in more than the ordinary risks of mercantile speculation. It exposes the markets of the country, either to be occasionally over-whelmed with an inundation of foreign corn, altogether disproportionate to its wants, or, in the event of any considerable deficiency in our own harvest, it creates a sudden competition on the continent, by the effect of which, the prices there are rapidly and unnecessarily raised against ourselves. But the inconvenient operation of the present corn law, which appears to be less the consequence of the quantity of foreign grain brought into this country, upon an average of years, than of the manner in which that grain is introduced, is not confined to great fluctuations in price, and consequent embarrassment both to the grower and the consumer; for the occasional prohibition of import has also a direct tendency to contract the extent of our commercial dealings with other States, and to excite in the rulers of those States a spirit of permanent exclusion against the productions or manufactures of this country and its colonies. . . .

Until that period [1815] positive prohibition was unknown to our corn laws, and importation was never permitted without the payment of some duty. The amount of that duty, it is true, when grain was above certain prices . . . was very little more than nominal; at prices somewhat lower, it was very moderate; and it was only when the prices had fallen, and remained for some time below that second stage in the scale, that any duty sufficiently high to check the importation attached, but subject to that duty the trade still continued to be free. The scale, for instance, by which importation was regulated in the article of wheat, up to the year 1815, was as follows: When the average price was at or above 66s., duty on importation 6d. a quarter; between 66s. and 63s., duty on importation 2s. 6d.; below 63s., duty 24s. 3d. The latter duty . . . operated generally as a prohibition during the short periods that it was payable.

This was the principle of our corn law, as far as relates to importation, ever since the year 1773, although the scale at which the different rates of duty commenced had more than once been raised. Its practical operation appears to have been as follows:—That from the year 1773 to the year 1814—during which period the total imports of corn have greatly exceeded the total exports, the former amounting to 30,430,189 quarters, and the latter to 5,801,440 quarters—the ports have been constantly open and the trade free, upon the payment of a duty merely nominal, with the exception of a few short intervals when the high duty was demandable—that from the year 1773 to the year 1792 (with the exception of the years of the American war, in which freights and insurance might be somewhat increased) the only advantage of protection, which the British grower had over the foreigner, was in the amount of this nominal duty, together with the ordinary expense of peace freights and other charges of conveyance in bringing the foreign grain to market—and that from the year 1792 to 1814, that protection continued the same, so far as related to the duty, but was, in fact, considerably enhanced by the high rates of charge incident to the late war, and particularly by the peculiar circumstances of the continent, during the last ten years of that war. It is also to be remarked that, up to the year 1806, the trade in corn with Ireland was under restriction; and that, since the operation of the wise law passed in that year, the importation of grain from that part of the United Kingdom, free from any charge or duty, has amounted, up to the 5th of January last, to 12,304,730 quarters, whereas the whole import from Ireland in 32 years, between 1773 and 1806, was only 7,534,202 quarters. . . .

[The Committee suggests to Parliament] . . . whether a trade in corn, constantly open to all nations of the world, and subject only to such a fixed duty as might compensate to the grower the loss of that encouragement which he received during the late war from the obstacles thrown in the way of free importation, and thereby protect the capitals now vested in agriculture from an unequal competition in the home market—is not, as a permanent system, preferable to that state of law by which the corn trade is now regulated. It would be indispensable for the just execution of this principle, that such duty should be calculated fairly to countervail the difference of expense, including the ordinary rate of profit, at which corn, in the present state of this country, can be grown and brought to market within the United Kingdom, compared with the expense, including also the ordinary rate of profit, of producing it in any of those countries from whence our principal supplies of foreign corn have usually been drawn, joined to the ordinary charges of conveying it from thence to our markets. . . .

Your Committee have abstained from urging, in favour of an open intercourse in foreign corn, those general principles of freedom of trade which are now universally acknowledged to be sound and true, in reference to the commerce of nations. If it be for the wisdom of the House, on the one hand, to endeavour to revert to those principles as far as practicable, in this and in all other cases; on the other, it is also for its prudence and its justice to take care, in that application, to spare vested interests, to deal tenderly with those obstacles to improvement which the long existence of a vicious and artificial system too often creates, and sometimes even to modify and limit that principle, in reference to considerations of general policy connected with the institutions, or the safety of the State. Looking to the possible contingencies of war, your Committee are not insensible to the importance of securing the country from a state of dependence upon other and possibly hostile countries for the subsistence of its population;—looking to the institutions of the country, in their several bearings and influence in the practice of our Constitution, they are still more anxious to preserve to the landed interest the weight, station and ascendancy which it has enjoyed so long and used so beneficially. . . .

The year 1773 was, in fact, the commencement of a great change in the practical operation, if not in the avowed policy of our corn laws. From that date, the aggregate balance of our imports of grain, taken upon a series of years, began to exceed the balance of our exports. . . . If the quantity of wheat, the growth of Great Britain, was truly estimated, as it was estimated in 1773, at four millions of quarters, and if it cannot now be stated so low as at double that amount, it is evident that the change of system has been attended with no defalcation of produce. If, since that year, the number of cattle and sheep has been vastly augmented, their breeds improved, and, by those improvements, their size and aptness to fatten, and in sheep their fleeces greatly increased; if, by this augmentation of live stock, a greater quantity of manure has been produced; if all the most important but expensive meliorations of modern husbandry have been introduced; if scientific drainages have been undertaken, and extensive wastes enclosed, to augment the produce of the land–it cannot be said that there has been a want of encouragement to invest large and adequate capitals in this branch of national industry.

If, from agriculture, your Committee look to the permanent improvements which have been made to the country itself within the same period, the bridges which have been built, the roads which have been formed, the rivers which have been rendered navigable, the canals which have been completed, the harbours which have been made and improved, the docks which have been created–not by the public revenue but by the capitals and enterprize of individuals; if they look, at the same time, to the unexampled growth of manufactures and commerce–in the contemplation of this augmentation of internal wealth, which defies all illustration from comparison with any former portion of our history, or of the history of any other State –your Committee may entertain a doubt . . . whether the only solid foundation of the flourishing state of agriculture is not laid in abstaining, as much as possible, from interference, either by protection or prohibition, with the application of capital, in any branch of industry–whether all fears for the decline of agriculture, either from temporary vicissitudes to which all speculations are liable, or from the extension of other pursuits of general industry, are not, in a great degree, imaginary–whether commerce can expand, manufactures thrive, and great public works be undertaken, without furnishing to the skill and labour which the capitals thus employed put in motion, increased means of paying for the productions of the land. . . .

So far as the present depression in the markets of agricultural produce is the effect of abundance from our own growth, the inconvenience arises from a cause which no legislative provision can alleviate; so far as it is the result of the increased value of our money, it is not one peculiar to the farmer, but which has been and still is experienced by many other classes of society. That result, however, is the more severely felt by the tenant, in consequence of its coincidence with an overstocked market, especially if he be farming with a borrowed capital and under the engagements of a lease; and it has hitherto been further aggravated by the comparative slowness with which prices generally, and particularly the price of labour, accommodate themselves to a change in the value of money. . . .

(d) THE RURAL POPULATION

356. The State of the Yeomanry, 1797–1833

The first extract is from E. Hasted, *The History of Kent* (1797), I, p. 300; the second from Arthur Young, *General View of the Agriculture of . . . Essex* (1813), pp. 39–40; the remainder from the Report of the Select Committee on Agriculture, 1833 (*Parliamentary Papers*, 1833, v). The general picture given by the 1833 committee's investigations is of prosperity for the yeoman farmer during the French wars, and hard times and a decline in numbers after 1815. The picture varied, however, from county to county.

(a) *Kent, 1797.* The yeomanry, which in most other parts of the kingdom is confined to the common people only . . . is extended much higher in Kent; for it here likewise comprehends the principal farmers and landholders, who, either from their education or intercourse of life, are not esteemed by the gentry of equal rank with themselves; and yet, in point of wealth and possessions, they are frequently superior to many of them, who, though they write themselves Yeomen, yet are usually and very properly styled Gentlemen-Farmers; for besides the largeness of their holdings, which are from £400 to £1200 per annum, they have, in general, good estates and freeholds of their own, and some, even to the amount of what they hire. And as to their hospitality and expense of living, it is in general much superior to that of their landlords.

Below these are the common yeomanry, on whom those above-mentioned look down, as of a rank much inferior to themselves, though if there is any distinction between them, it must have been in the luxury of the times, and the accumulation of farms, that have given them this superiority.

The common yeomen appear in the honest homely garb of their profession, such as their forefathers wore, and mostly content themselves with the hiring of a single farm, and the addition of their own little estate, for they are in general possessed of some. Their manners and behaviour correspond with their dress, they are just and civil in their dealings and behaviour, and enjoy the domestic happiness of their own homes. But these *yeomen* or *franklyns*, the most useful and profitable set of men that this kingdom has in it, become fewer every year, and if luxury and the monopoly of farms increase, as they have within these few years past, they will be very soon extirpated, not only from this county, but from the kingdom in general.

(*b*) *Essex, 1813.* If by estates, are meant possessions in landed property, they are, in this county, in point of size and extent, almost infinitely various: from one, five, and ten pounds a year, to ten, and even twenty, thousand; and, although there may be a few considerable and extensive estates in the hands of the nobility, or of some very wealthy private individuals, yet, perhaps, there never was a greater proportion of small and moderate-sized farms, the property of mere farmers, who retain them in their own immediate occupation, than at present. Such has been the flourishing state of agriculture for twenty or thirty years past, that scarcely an estate is sold, if divided into lots of forty or fifty to two or three hundred a year, but is purchased by farmers, who can certainly afford to give for them more than almost any other persons, as they turn them to the highest advantage by their own cultivation, and hence arises a fair prospect of landed property gradually returning to a situation of similar possession to what it was 100, or 150 years ago, when our inferior gentry resided upon their estates in the country, and, by their generous hospitality, diffused comfort and cheerfulness around them. . . .

(*c*) *Cheshire, 1833: Evidence of Joseph Lee.*

Have you many yeomen in Cheshire, men living on small estates of their own?–Not many, they are generally belonging to gentlemen of large property. . . .

What is their condition?–Those that have been provident are pretty well off; where they have been living, which I am sorry is the case with a great many, beyond their means, they are in a very bad state; their property is nearly gone.

You think they were led into habits of expense by high prices, which have not been laid aside when prices fell?–Yes, the high prices from 1810 to 1814; the prices being excessive led the farmers into an extravagant way of living, which they were very unwilling to give up; and they have been spending a great deal more than they ought to have done.

If a yeoman, tempted by the high prices of the war, had borrowed money to improve his little property, what would be the condition of that man with the price falling, the debt remaining, and his own habits remaining the same?–Entire ruin.

Do you know any cases of that kind?–. . . I know several. A great many farmers got a considerable sum of money, and were mad to lay it out in land, conceiving that the best mode of disposing of it; they purchased at very high prices, land at 40 years' purchase, in some instances, and borrowed probably half the money, and soon after the produce sold for so much less than it had done; they had the interest to pay upon the money they had borrowed, and were in such difficulties they were obliged to sell their properties for what they could get.

Have those properties been bought by large proprietors or small?–Very little by small proprietors; they have been generally taken by some gentleman who had an adjoining estate.

The effect of the ruin of small proprietors has been to reduce the number of landowners, not to increase it?–Just so.

You do not think that subdivisions have taken place equivalent to the disappearance of those small estates?–No; I think there are fewer yeomen, even of small property in the county, than I can remember there has been. [p. 272.]

(d) Cumberland and Westmorland, 1833: Evidence of William Blamire.

Throughout the counties of Cumberland and Westmorland is there not a large body of yeomanry who have inherited small properties from father to son for ages?– A very considerable number. Property is more subdivided there than I suppose in any other part of the Kingdom. . . .

What is the condition of these men now, as compared with their condition at the end of the war?–The number has considerably diminished, and the situation of those who are still in existence is considerably worse than it was; there are very few of them whose properties are altogether unencumbered.

Has their number been much diminished lately?–Their number is constantly diminishing; small estates are constantly being thrown upon the market, and often bought by wealthier classes.

As those small estates are brought to market do small proprietors step in and buy them, or are they absorbed into large properties?–Frequently absorbed into large properties, but occasionally bought by men who have realised money in trade or in large farms, and who are withdrawing their capital from large farms and investing it in the purchase of landed property.

Is not the reluctance very great on the part of the yeoman before he consents to part with his little hereditary property?–So great that he is often induced to cling to it longer than it is prudent to do so; he is paying interest for money borrowed upon it, which is pressing more severely upon him than any rent could do.

Have you reason to believe that since 1815 a greater change has taken place in the proprietors of small farms than in any antecedent period of much longer duration?–I believe that to be the case, from what I have heard and seen. . . .

Knowing the character of the men in whose circumstances that change has taken place, can you state whether it has arisen from any important alteration in their habit of living, or any extravagance, or any diminished industry?–Generally speaking, not; but the parties have had large families, and they have, from a miscalculation of their real situation, been induced to leave to their children larger fortunes than they ought to have done, and to saddle the oldest son with the payment of a sum of money which it was impossible he could provide for. That has been the case to a very great degree, particularly where the lands so devised were lands of inferior quality. I know some remarkable instances where parents have left a provision for younger children out of estates which have not been sold during the continuance of high prices, and which have fallen so much within their calculations as to leave to the eldest son hardly anything. . . . There is no difference in their mode of living; they are quite as frugal, and often more so, and their situation is often worse. . . .

Up to the war was there any tendency to lead to a decrease of this yeomanry?–They remained up to the war pretty stationary, and properties had continued long in their families.

Do you think that they have been an increasing or a decreasing class?–A decreasing class for a great number of years; the best proof of that is that there is scarcely any estate to be met with that does not consist of a great many smaller properties united in one. . . .

What has become of the yeomen who have sold their estates?–Many have become servants and gone into other employment. [pp. 309–325.]

(e) Kent, 1833: Evidence of William Taylor.

Is Kent celebrated for yeomen being small proprietors?–Yes; I should say more than any other county that I was ever in.

Are there as many as there were 20 or 30 years ago?–I should think there is not a great deal of difference in that.

They have not been driven to sell their estates?–No, but the work in these small estates is generally done by the man himself and his family, and that is the way that they have held together; he lives nearly as a workman, and has nothing to pay for labour. . . . I do not think that they live so well as they did. . . .

A great many have sold their estates?–Yes.

Who have brought them, other small proprietors?–No, I should say they generally are bought by some one who has an estate adjoining.

The number, therefore, must have diminished in that way?–Yes, but not to any considerable amount. [p. 295.]

357. Sir F. M. Eden on the condition of the Agricultural Labourer

(Sir F. M. Eden, *The State of the Poor*, I (1797), pp. 531–532, 554–558.)

It is not to be expected that milk should ever form a considerable part of the diet of labourers in the South of England, until the practice of keeping cows becomes more general among cottagers than it is at present. In many parts of the island, however, considerable difficulties will occur, in attempting to introduce this custom. In the vicinity of large towns, the value of grass land is much too high to enable labourers to rent it to advantage: and in other districts, where there is hardly any thing but arable land, and the maintenance of a cow depends on straw, turnips, cabbages, or purchased hay, the system of cow-keeping is much too operose for a labourer to engage in. A garden, however, will prove of infinite benefit to a labourer in almost every situation, but more especially in arable countries, where he would find it difficult to procure sufficient pasture to maintain a cow both in summer and winter; and where, although he might be able to cultivate a few acres of arable land for winter food for his cow, he would not always be able to procure hay, for summer food, from the farmers.

I am, however, persuaded, that, even in London, where milk is extremely dear, (now 3½d. the quart,) poor householders might occasionally use it to considerable advantage. A small quantity of it, judiciously applied, would render many dishes tender and delicate, which, from their toughness, and the drought which they occasion, are not only unpalatable, but expensive. A labouring man, in the metropolis, who thinks he cannot afford milk, and therefore obliges his family to drink their tea in a very crude state, by way of economy, buys himself half a pound of fat bacon, (at 10d. or 1s. the pound,) for dinner. This creates such a thirst, that he is fain to allay it with no inconsiderable quantity of porter. As for salt fish, (an article of diet which seems to be peculiarly suited to the poorer inhabitant of a great commercial city,) it seems now going very generally into disuse; and is little eaten, except on particular occasions. This is not to be wondered at; for, in the common way that it is cooked, salt fish is hard, dry, and unsavoury. A sauce is absolutely essential to render it palatable: but eggs and butter, which are the usual appendages to this dish, are much too expensive for the greater part of the labouring classes. . . .

The diversity is not greater between the labourers in the North and South of England, with respect to the manner in which their food is prepared, than with regard to the modes they adopt of supplying themselves with clothing. In the midland and southern counties, the labourer, in general, purchases a very considerable portion, if not the whole of his clothes, from the shop-keeper. In the vicinity of the metropolis, working-people seldom buy new clothes: they content themselves with a cast-off coat, which may be usually purchased for about 5s. and second-hand waistcoats and breeches. Their wives seldom make up any article of dress, except making and mending clothes for the children. In the North, on the contrary, almost every article of dress worn by farmers, mechanics, and labourers, is manufactured at home, shoes and hats excepted: that is, the linen thread is spun from the lint, and the yarn from the wool, and sent to the weaver's and dyer's: so that almost every family has its web of linen cloth annually, and often one of woollen also, which is either dyed for coats, or made into flannel, &c. Sometimes black and white wool are mixed; and the cloth which is made from them receives no dye: it is provincially called kelt. Although broad cloth, purchased in the shops, begins now to be worn by opulent farmers, and others, on Sundays; yet there are many respectable persons, at this day, who never wore a bought pair of stockings, coat, nor waistcoat, in their lives: and, within these twenty years, a coat bought at a shop was considered as a mark of extravagance and pride, if the buyer was not possessed of an independent fortune. There are, however, many labourers so poor, that they cannot even afford to purchase the raw material necessary to spin thread or yarn at home; as it is some time before a home manufacture can be rendered fit for use. It is generally acknowledged, that articles of clothing can be purchased in the shops at a much lower price, than those who make them at home can afford to sell them for; but that, in the wearing, those manufactured by private families are very superior both in warmth and durability. . . .

The following short account of the prices of a few home-made articles in Cumberland, will, I trust, prove not unacceptable to the reader.

The usual price of a hat worn by labourers is about 2s. 6d.: a coat purchased, (4 yards,) costs about 2s. 6d. a yard: a waistcoat takes a yard and a half: a pair of leather breeches costs 3s. 6d.: labourers sometimes wear breeches of flannel or coloured cloth. A tailor charges 5s. for making a whole suit. A linen shirt takes 3¼ yards, at 17d. a yard: this is strong, and wears well. About 11 oz. of wool, at 8d. the pound, will make a pair of stockings. They are almost invariably spun and knit at home.

Women's dress generally consists of a black stuff hat, of the price of 1s. 8d.: a linen bed-gown, (stamped with blue,) mostly of the home manufacture; this usually costs in the shops about 5s. 6d.: a cotton or linen neck-cloth, price about 1s. 6d.: two petticoats of flannel, the upper one dyed blue; value of the two about 11s. 6d.: coarse woollen stockings, home manufacture, value about 1s. 8d: linen shift, home manufacture, 2½ yards, at 1s. 5d. the yard. Women generally wear stays, or rather bodice, of various prices. Their gowns are sometimes made of woollen stuff; 6 yards, at 1s. 6d. the yard. The women, however, generally wear black silk hats, and cotton gowns, on Sundays and holidays.

The following are the prices of clothes, as sold in a slop-shop in the neighbourhood of London:

Men,–a good foul-weather coat, (will last very well two years,) 13s. 0d.; a common waistcoat 6s. 6d.; a pair of stout breeches, (one year), 3s. 9d.; stockings, the pair 1s. 10d.; a dowlas shirt 4s. 6d.; a pair of strong shoes 7s. 0d.; a hat, (will last three years) 2s. 6d.

Women,–a common stuff gown 6s. 6d.; Linsey-woolsey petticoat 4s. 6d.; a shift 3s. 8d.; a pair of shoes 3s. 9d.; coarse apron 1s. 0d.; check apron 2s. 0d.; a pair of stockings 1s. 6d.; a hat, the cheapest sort, (will last two years) 1s. 8d.; coloured neck-handkerchief 1s. 0d.; a common cap 0s. 10d.; cheapest kind of cloak, (will last two years) 4s. 6d.; pair of stays, (will last six years) 6s. 0d.

358. R. W. Dickson on housing conditions in Lancashire

(General View of the Agriculture of Lancashire (1815), pp. 103–107.)

The cottages of the county of Lancaster may be said to be principally of two kinds, such as accommodate the poor farming peasant and such as are constructed for the purpose of the artificer and mechanical labourer. Those of the former description are not by any means so deficient in number or accommodation as in many other districts, there being few properties of any considerable extent without some of them. On the eastern side, and most of the more northern parts of the county, they are in general roomy, well built with some sort of stone, and covered with slate, or sometimes with thatch. This is also the case in some places on the western border, as about Ormskirk, Wigan, Bolton, Chorley, &c: in others they are constructed occasionally with bricks and tiles, or slated, but a more ancient, though much less durable method, which is still not unfrequently had recourse to in the tract from below Leyland to some distance beyond Garstang, and throughout most of the Fylde district, is that of forming them on wattled stud-work with a composition of well-wrought loamy clay and cut straw, or what is locally termed *clat and clay*.

The covering material in these instances is almost invariably thatch prepared from wheaten straw. . . . These cottages have seldom more than a divided ground floor, which with their brown sombre colour, gives them a mean hovel-like appearance far from agreeable, and affords but little accommodation. . . .

The cottages intended for carrying on different sorts of trades and employments, are for the most part built of stone or brick, though there are some of clay occasionally met with in particular situations. Near towns and large manufacturing concerns, they are frequently erected in groups of two, four, or six together, and sometimes in long ranges containing a much greater number. For the sake of convenience, they have mostly a situation as contiguous as possible to the works, and in some instances are provided with a small portion of garden ground. These dwellings are commonly erected by building speculators, and where the rents are paid, are calculated to afford an interest of from 15 to 20, or 25 *per cent*. Many are likewise built by gentlemen of landed property; and some by the weekly contributions of the labourers themselves, who form a kind of building society. There are several societies of this nature at Chorley and the neighbouring towns. The rents are usually from £4 or £5 to £10 or £12 per annum, or more, according to the accommodation which they afford. Farther in the county they are generally detached, and have in many cases some extent of land attached to them. These sorts of cottage-houses are now become so prevalent in many situations, as to throw a most dreadful and oppressive burden on the parishes or townships to which they belong, and unless some effectual check be speedily devised, must inevitably involve them in considerable distress, if not ruin; particularly in times when the manufacturing spirit of the country is depressed by war or other political causes. These cottages being in some cases large, for the convenience of the occupiers, with separate apartments for the different apparatus requisite in carrying on their trades and employments, readily afford them settlements; and in other instances the lands which are annexed to them have the same effect. These vary from one or two to eight or ten acres. By this easy means numerous labourers of this class, with their families of course acquire settlements when the trade and manufactures of the district are going on with vigour, who afterwards, on any change of a depressing nature taking place, become heavily chargeable to the parishes; as such labourers have very rarely, either the disposition or habit of saving any thing for times of future scarcity, during such flourishing periods: nor are they in general capable of turning themselves to other sorts of labour, as many other workmen can do; they are consequently compelled either to become soldiers and leave their families, or to apply to the parishes for relief.

The case is still worse where they have lands connected with such cottages, as the whole is nearly lost. This is strikingly shown by the uncultivated and slovenly state in which such lands are almost invariably found. Men of this stamp are quite unfit for the management of land; and besides, they have neither the capital nor knowledge necessary for rendering land productive and beneficial. Whatever they perform about it, is commonly done in the worst and most irregular manner, and they seldom attend at all to any sort of improvements. If the lands are under grass, they are usually overrun with weeds; and if in tillage, mostly left without manure or any proper cultivation. In short, it appears to me from a pretty full examination of the subject, that in this district, nothing can be more prejudicial to the interests of the landed proprietors, or more injurious to the community, than the practice of annexing lands as small farms to cottages designed for weaving and other mechanical labourers. All they seem capable of rendering useful to themselves, is a small portion of ground for raising garden vegetables and potatoes. Their rents are constantly paid from the loom or some other employment, and they seldom care any thing about the land, except for the little convenience it affords them by its natural produce, of keeping a few half-starved animals. Eight or ten customary acres often does little more than support a cow and horse in an indifferent manner.

359. The *Quarterly Review* on rural housing, 1825 (xxxii, pp. 194–195)

. . . It is not many years ago that the cottages in the country had no flooring but that which nature furnished, and that a composition of lime and sand was beheld by the neighbours of him who enjoyed such a refinement, as a luxury to be envied. The mud walls were rarely covered with any coat of plastering; there was no ceiling under the straw roof, and when any chamber was in the house, it was accessible only by a ladder or by a post with notches indented to receive the foot in climbing to it. The doors and windows did not close sufficiently to exclude the rain or the snow, and in wet weather puddles were scattered over the inequalities in the mud floor. It is now rare in the country to see a cottage without a brick or stone or wood floor, without stairs to its chambers, without plastering on the walls, and without doors and windows tolerably weather-tight. The furniture and domestic utensils are increased and improved with the houses. The paucity and the homeliness which appeared forty or fifty years ago present to the recollection of those who can remember the state of that day, a striking contrast with the comparative abundance and convenience which are now exhibited. Instead of straw beds, and a single rug for a covering, are substituted feather or flock beds, several blankets, sheets, and often a cotton quilt. Chairs and tables occupy the place of benches and joint stools. Wooden trenchers have given way to earthenware plates and dishes, and to the iron pot is now commonly added the gridiron, frying-pan, and saucepans. . . .

The clothing of our poor has advanced with the progress of their other enjoyments. The linsey-woolsey garments which formerly served as a harbour for dirt, both to males and females, have been thrown aside, and their place occupied by others more flexible and oftener renewed. This may be the cause in part of the immense increase in the quantity of soap for which the duty is paid. Within the last forty years it has gradually increased from thirty-five to ninety-five million pounds. . . .

360. Daniel O'Connell on the state of the Irish peasantry, 1825

(Report from the Select Committee on the State of Ireland, 1825; *Parliamentary Papers*, 1825, VIII, pp. 48–53.)

O'Connell pointed out that the counties with which he was best acquainted were Clare, Limerick, Kerry, and Cork, where he had gone the circuit for many years.

. . . The state of the lower orders, in my observation, is such that it is astonishing to me how they preserve health, and above all, how they preserve cheerfulness, under the total privation of anything like comfort, and the existence of a state of things that the inferior animals would scarcely endure, and which they do not endure in this country. . . .

The houses are not even called houses, and they ought not to be; they are called cabins, they are built of mud, and covered with thatch partly, and partly with a surface which they call scraws, and any continuance of rain necessarily comes in. I have observed at night, however, that there is this advantage in their being built so there, that where they have firing, the entire house warms, and it is like a stove, and it produces almost the effect of a vapour bath upon the inhabitants. . . .

. . . [They have] nothing that can deserve the name of furniture; it is a luxury to have a box to put anything into; it is a luxury to have what they call a dresser for laying a plate upon, or anything of that kind; they may have, they generally have little beyond an iron cast metal-pot, a milk tub which they call a keeler, over which they put a wicker basket, in order to throw the potatoes, water and all, into the basket that the water should run into this keeler; that is frequently the extent of their furniture.

With regard to their bedding, what does that consist of?–Nothing but straw and very few blankets in the mountain districts; by the sea they are better off and more comfortable; they fish occasionally.

Are they without bedsteads?–In general without bedsteads; the entire family sleep in the same compartment; they call it a room; there is some division between it and the part where the fire is; they separate the sexes by very slight partitions, and yet I do not believe, and indeed I am convinced, that that species of promiscuous lying amongst each other, does not induce . . . immorality between persons closely related, such a thing is not heard of. . . .

Have they blankets put over the straw sufficient to cover them?–In general not.

Do they sleep in their clothes?–In the county of Kerry they seldom sleep in their clothes, they are better off in the remoter parts of it with respect to blankets; so in the remoter districts of the county of Cork; but I have reason to believe that in Limerick, and in a portion of Clare, and in parts of the county of Cork, they sleep in their clothes; I know that near Dublin they sleep in their clothes, and that upon recent investigation, within 8 or 10 miles of Dublin, out of 14 or 15 families, there were only two found in which there was a blanket. . . . Neither men nor women do in general wear shoes and stockings, it is dress and luxury.

Have they sufficient clothes, in case of being wet, to change?–Speaking of it as a general rule, they have no clothes to change; they have none but what they wear at the moment; of course, in the various grades of poverty and its shades, there are differences, but I speak of the general state of the Irish labouring peasantry.

With respect to their food, of what does it consists?–Except on the coast, of potatoes and water during the greater part of the year; potatoes and sour milk during another portion; they use some salt with their potatoes when they have nothing but water; on the sea coast they get fish, the children repair to the shore, and the women, and they get shell fish of various kinds, and indeed various kinds of fish.

Do they suffer any inconvenience in that season of the year which takes place between the going out of the old potatoes and the coming in of the new?–Almost always great distress, aggravated by the difficulties with respect to tithes. The Irish Acts enable the peasant to hold a kind of battle with the tithe owner upon everything but potatoes; with other things he can serve a notice to draw, but with potatoes it is not so; there is no Statute provision respecting the potato, and then if the peasant begins to dig his potatoes he is completely at the mercy of the tithe owner; and it is right to say that he is in general not very harshly dealt with where the clergyman has the tithes himself; but when they are in the hands of laymen, and frequently persons of the same persuasion with himself, [he] is very badly dealt with; if he begins to dig he has no mode afterwards of defending himself against the demand. . . .

Have they the means of purchasing potatoes during that season, if their own stock is exhausted?–Money is an article that the Irish peasant knows excessively little of; he has not the means.

Is there no employment sufficient to afford the means of acquiring money for cases of difficulty?–Certainly not; I do not believe there is in the world a peasantry more ready to accept small wages for employment than the Irish peasant.

Is there anything like a demand for constant employment for the labouring class?–There is not, according to my knowledge and experience, even anything that could be called an occasional demand; that is, the demand is so small that it scarcely deserves the name, it is rather an accidental demand than even occasional.

Could you give the Committee any idea of the proportion of the people that are without employment?–To attempt it numerically is matter of conjecture, but there certainly is not one out of twenty employed; that is, there is nothing like constant work for that number.

What is the customary wages for a man's labour when employed, independently of considerations of rent?–I cannot say that, except in the remote district of the county of Kerry, where I take it to be when there is employment, 6d. a day without any meal, and 4d. a day with . . . I believe during 1822 they cheerfully worked at 2d. a day without victuals, being paid in money.

Under these circumstances of a want of employment, how do the people contrive to provide themselves with food?–Every man cultivates the food of his own family, potatoes, and land becomes absolutely necessary therefore for every Irish peasant, and he cultivate[s] that food, and he makes the rent in general (I am and have been speaking of the poorer class of peasantry) by feeding the pig as well as his own family upon the same food; and if it be not wrong to call it so, at the same table, upon the same spot with that pig, he makes the rent, besides any chance he gets of daily labour.

Is there generally a facility of acquiring land?—Great difficulty: the lower class of tenantry, the mere peasant, it is painful to look for rent from, and he is supposed to injure the farm, and he does to a certain extent, and he has no capital to reinstate it, and they find therefore great difficulty in getting land, a difficulty increasing with the number of the population. . . .

How does the peasant pay his rent who takes land by the year?—The lowest class of peasant pays it by the price of his pig and his labour, whatever chance of labour he has; the better class than that pay the rent by the produce of butter; in the mountain districts of oats, in the district something better than that [sic]; in the remote parts of the county of Cork they pay the rent by the produce of barley, and in the richer parts, the better farmers by the produce of wheat; by the produce I mean the money produced. . . .

Have circumstances occurred, within your knowledge, of hardship, in respect of distraining for rent?—Very many. . . . It is a general grievance, very much aggravated by the necessity of sub-lettings; there are frequently six and seven between the proprietor of the fee and the actual occupier; and whenever any two of those happen to differ in the state of their accounts, the man who claims more than the other has paid, or is willing to pay, settles the dispute by distraining the actual occupier; and that occurs, in many instances, where the occupier has paid his own rent to his own landlord.

Then every superior tenant of the sub-tenant's has a right of distress over the actual occupier?—Unquestionably.

Have cases come to your knowledge, of hardship arising from that?—The greatest cruelty and oppression, and it is attended with this additional oppression: a recent Statute, which was passed about the year 1817, for the first time, enabled the landlords to distrain growing crops in Ireland. My own opinion is that that Statute has contributed extremely to the disturbances in the south, because in all those cases of sub-letting, it gave to every one of those individuals the power of distraining the growing crop, that growing crop being the subsistence for the family of the peasant. . . . The worst of the crimes of the South I attribute a great deal to the effect of that Act of Parliament. . . .

Have instances of grievance occurred to you, and hardship, arising out of the practice of bringing ejectments for rent?—Yes; the stamp duties, with respect to the tenure of land, of course are paid by the tenant; and with respect to a peasant, the amount of stamp duty would be more money than he could possibly command; the consequence of which is, that he deals in general upon parole, or upon a contract, written upon unstamped paper. The effect of that is, that it gives the landlord a constant power of breaking through the contract, without any remedy. Not even a civil bill action will lie for a breach of the contract, because it requires that it should be stamped before it can be produced; the consequence of which is that every species of landlords have the means of bringing ejectments, and turning the tenants out. Before the civil bill ejectment was allowed by Act of Parliament, a landlord was cautious of bringing an ejectment, for even if defence was not made, it would cost him £14 or £15, at the cheapest, to turn out a tenant; but the civil bill ejectment has very much increased the power of lower landlords, for by means of that he can turn out his tenant for a few shillings. . . . The Acts of Parliament passed since the peace, giving to Irish landlords increased facilities of ejectment and distress, have necessarily very much increased the tendency to disturbance in Ireland. . . .

Have those laws produced this effect by being made use of by the upper class of landlords?—Yes; they have been used by the upper classes of Irish gentry in the south. The resident gentry were in general very much involved in debt, and could not contrive to get their living; they were pressed themselves, and without making any further apology for them, they certainly used their tenants quite as severely as any one peasant did another. There were of course many exceptions; I do not mean to speak of it as an universal proposition at all. . . .

Have many tenants of late been turned off the lands, in the part of Ireland you are acquainted with?—Within the last 8 or 10 years, many tenants have been turned off the land.

Is that habit increasing amongst landlords of clearing their farms?—I think it is at a stand; the depreciation of prices made the tenants so unpunctual in paying that many landlords have endeavoured to clear the farms of them altogether, and to hold them in their own hands, sometimes feeding cattle upon them; in general they make cattle dairies, but on the fattening lands there have not been occupying tenants for some years.

What becomes of the families that are turned off, how do they contrive to exist?— They exist among the wretched class of labourers, or they go about begging; the man goes to England or some remote parts of Ireland to get labour, and the wife and children go begging during the autumn of the year. . . .

B. INDUSTRY AND COMMUNICATIONS

(a) THE TEXTILE INDUSTRIES

361. Sir Frederick Morton Eden on the woollen industry in East Anglia and the South-West

(The State of the Poor, II (1797), pp. 477–479, and 643–644; III, p. 796.)

Norwich. . . . A cotton manufactory was established here about 7 years ago; but the staple manufactures of Norwich are camblets, and other worsted stuffs, of various denominations. It is probable, that more hands without the city, than within it, are employed in the manufactures; for, in 1771, Arthur Young calculated the number of looms in and near Norwich, at 12,000; and, allowing 6 persons to a loom, reckoned the number of people employed in this manufacture to be 72,000, and the amount of the stuffs sent annually from Norwich to exceed a million sterling.

The Norwich trade has for some years been in a declining state, which is ascribed to the following causes: to the prevalent taste for wearing cottons, which has necessarily lessened the consumption of stuffs; the low wages of the weavers and spinners, who are, in a considerable degree at the mercy of the manufacturers, and are not supposed to receive better pay than they did 20 years ago; and, lastly, to the war, which has put a stop to the exportation of stuffs to France, Flanders, and Holland, and from the high price of insurance, much reduced the trade to other countries. The merchants and manufacturers are now overstocked with goods; and the weavers are, consequently, very ill supplied with work, and, what is worse, are obliged to work up the worst materials. While business was brisk, an industrious weaver might earn £1. 1s. a week, from fine work; and from coarser work, 12s. a week. The average earnings of weavers, at present, are thought not to exceed 7s. or 8s. a week. Women weavers earn from 5s. to 6s. a week. Females, however, are principally employed in spinning, reeling, winding, &c. in which they earn from 2s. to 4s. a week. Children, in spinning, winding, &c. earn about 2s. a week. Of late, the wages, both of women and children, have been very low; but business, since the beginning of this month, has been rather brisk, from a notion that peace is not very distant.

Frome (Somerset). The extent of this parish is estimated at 6 miles by 3½ miles. From an enumeration taken in 1785, it was found to contain 1684 houses, and 8105 persons; it is supposed that the number had increased before the present war; above 800 men, from this place, have entered H.M.'s service. Among the inhabitants, are 220 weavers; 146 sheermen; 141 scribblers; 230 labourers; 55 farmers; 47 clothiers; 39 attornies, clergymen, and other gentlemen; and 183 widows. . . . Sheermen earn from 15s. to 20s. a week; scribblers, about 12s.; and weavers, about 20s. a week. Women and children are employed in the manufactories, either in picking wool, in burling or dressing cloth, and attending the machines, &c. Women have 8d. a day at present; children of 7 or 8 years of age, earn 2s. 6d. a week, for attending the machines: common labourers receive from 16d. to 18d. the day; but when work is done by the piece, which is usually the case here, they can earn from 2s. to 2s. 6d. a day. The manufactures of this place are, cloths of the following denominations; superfine, of

Spanish wool; super and best super, of English wool; and kerseymeres. The present war has taken off a number of hands; but has not lessened the demand for cloths, except in the instance of kerseymeres, which were chiefly sent to France: that branch of manufacture is now almost ruined: last year, there was a great demand for broad cloths. To the introduction of machines, a few years ago, some persons ascribe the great increase of the poor's rates here; by others, it is imputed to the great number of soldiers and militia-men's families, who are chargeable at present. This town is very ancient, and has been the seat of the woollen manufacture for several centuries; yet, the external appearance of the town does not indicate that wealth which is usually attendant on commerce: the houses are very different from the elegant dwellings that are to be found in the Yorkshire manufacturing towns, or their neighbourhood; the streets are narrow, unpaved, and dirty. In this town there are 36 ale-houses; which, a gentleman of credibility supposes, dispose of about 6700 hogsheads of strong beer annually.

Seend (Wiltshire). As the chapelry [of Seend] consists almost entirely of dairy farms, and consequently affords very little employment in husbandry, except during the hay-harvest, the labouring poor are very dependent on the neighbouring towns, where the cloth manufacture is carried on; but, unfortunately, since the introduction of machinery, which lately took place, hand-spinning has fallen into disuse, and for these two reasons: the clothier no longer depends on the poor for the yarn which they formerly spun for him at their own homes, as he finds that 50 persons, (to speak within compass,) with the help of machines, will do as much work as 500 without them; and the poor, from the great reduction in the price of spinning, scarcely have the heart to earn the little that is obtained by it. For what they used to receive 1s. and 1s. 2d. the pound for spinning, before the application of machinery, they now are allowed only 5d.; so that a woman, in a good state of health and not incumbered with a family, can only earn 2s. 6d. a week, which is at the rate of one pound of spinning-work the day, and is the utmost that can be done: but if she has a family, she cannot earn more than 2d. a day, or 1s. a week; or spin more than 2 pounds and a half in a week: the consequence is, that their maintenance must chiefly depend on the exertions of the man, (whose wages have not increased in proportion to this defalcation from the woman's earnings,) and, therefore, the present dear times are very severely felt by all families, and even by single women, who depend solely upon spinning for their support.

362. Evidence of William Stark before the Select Committee of the House of Lords on the coal trade, 1830

(*House of Lords Sessional Papers*, No. 12 of 1830, pp. 139–141.)

Stark was a cloth dyer and dresser from Norwich.

How is your city supplied with coals?–Principally from Newcastle, by Yarmouth. . . .

What is the present price of the Newcastle coal at Norwich per chaldron . . .?–I think about 38s. or 39s. . . .

Do you find any difficulties in carrying on your manufacture in consequence of that high price . . .?–We have lost a very large proportion of manufacture in consequence of the high price of coals; formerly all the yarn used in Norwich was spun in Norwich and its neighbourhood; since the erection of machinery, they have taken all the spinning from Norwich, and hundreds of families are now unemployed that were employed in that department; many suggestions have been made as to forming establishments for spinning; not many attempts certainly; but I believe if the price of coals were less, the yarn would be spun by machinery in Norwich, as well as in the north. . . . We consider the duties on coals very hard, for our great competitors have no duty to pay; our coals must be dearer than theirs on account of the immense freight and other charges. . . .

Supposing the coal duty to be removed, would that make such a difference in the price as would enable you to resume the spinning, which you say has left the place for Yorkshire?–I do not known that it would altogether, but it would materially contribute to it. The wool is principally sent from Norfolk; it is spun in Yorkshire, and brought back in the form of yarn, of course there is the carriage twice to pay, I believe from the nearest calculation I can make, that it is about equal to what we should pay for coals necessary to be used in spinning. . . .

Does the price of coals affect you in your dyeing?–Very much so; and at this time we are losing part of the dyeing business in consequence. Goods that have been manufactured in Norwich for many centuries are now leaving Norwich, to be dyed in Yorkshire, because they can be dyed at a much cheaper rate, which we attribute solely to the coals, for the labour is as cheap, and the drugs we can purchase, of course, as cheap as they can in Yorkshire.

Are there a considerable proportion of persons out of employ at present in Norwich?–I believe not less, in all departments connected with the manufactories, than 4 or 5,000 persons. . . . The manufactures of Norwich are principally confined to two or three articles, camlets, bombazeens, and plaids; those are the staple manufactures of the place, and of course yarn is used for all; and . . . we are suffering materially in consequence of those persons in Yorkshire taking a large portion of the Worsted trade.

363. J. Aikin on the West Riding textile industry

(*A Description of the Country from thirty to forty miles round Manchester* (1795), pp. 573–574.)

The whole number of master broad-cloth manufacturers in the West Riding of Yorkshire is about 3240. The mixed cloth manufacturers reside partly in the villages belonging to the parish of Leeds; but chiefly at Morley, Guildersome, Adwalton, Driglington, Pudsey, Farsley, Calverly, Eccleshall, Idle, Baildon, Yeadon, Guisely, Rawdon, and Horsforth, in or bordering upon the vale of Aire, chiefly west of Leeds; and at Batley, Dewsbury, Ossett, Horbury, and Kirkburton, west of Wakefield, in or near the vale of Calder. Not a single manufacturer is to be found more than one mile east, or two north, of Leeds; nor are there many in the town of Leeds, and those only in the outskirts.

The white cloth is manufactured chiefly at Alverthorpe, Ossett, Kirkheaton, Dewsbury, Batley, Birstal, Hopton, Mirfield, Archet, Clackheaton, Littletown, Bowling, and Shipley; a tract of country forming an oblique belt across the hills that separate the vale of Calder from the vale of Aire, beginning about a mile west of Wakefield, leaving Huddersfield and Bradford a little to the left, terminating at Shipley on the Aire, and not coming within less than about six miles of Leeds on the right. The districts of the white and coloured cloth manufactory are generally distinct, but are a little intermixed at the south-east and north-west extremities.

The cloths are sold in their respective halls rough as they come from the fulling mills. They are finished by the merchants, who employ dressers, dyers, &c., for that purpose; these, with drysalters, shopkeepers, and the different kind of handicraftsmen common to every town, compose the bulk of the inhabitants of Leeds. The dispersed state of the manufacturers in villages and single houses over the whole face of the country, is highly favourable to their morals and happiness. They are generally men of small capitals, and often annex a small farm to their other business; great numbers of the rest have a field or two to support a horse and a cow, and are for the most part blessed with the comforts, without the superfluities, of life.

364. Report from the Committee on the state of the woollen manufacture of England, 1806

(Journals of the House of Commons, LXI, 696–703.)

The attempt to introduce cloth-dressing machines into parts of the west country at the beginning of the nineteenth century provoked a demand by the cloth workers for the enforcement of several old, unrepealed, but generally disregarded laws which placed restraints on the manufacturers of cloth. After a parliamentary inquiry in 1803 these laws were temporarily suspended; the Committee of 1806 was appointed to report on the whole question, and recommended the repeal of most of the restrictions, including those clauses of the Statute of Apprentices (1563) which enforced apprenticeship in the cloth industry. The apprenticeship laws were repealed in 1813. The Committee describes the organization of the woollen industry at this time.

It is with no small satisfaction that your Committee find themselves able at the outset of their report to inform the House, that the attention of Parliament has not been called to the woollen manufacture in consequence of any decay in its prosperity; on the contrary, it is an acknowledged fact, that it has been gradually increasing in almost all the various parts of England in which it is carried on; in some of them very rapidly; till at length, while our home consumption has of course been increasing with the growing population and wealth of our country, our exports of woollen goods have reached to the immense amount of £6,000,000 official, or near £9,000,000 real value. . . .

The rapid and prodigious increase of late years in the manufactures and commerce of this country is universally known, as well as the effects of that increase on our revenue and national strength; and in considering the immediate causes of that augmentation, it will appear that, under the favour of Providence, it is principally to be ascribed to the general spirit of enterprise and industry among a free and enlightened people, left to the unrestrained exercise of their talents in the employment of a vast capital; pushing to the utmost the principle of the division of labour; calling in all the resources of scientific research and mechanical ingenuity; and, finally, availing themselves of all the benefits to be derived from visiting foreign countries, not only for forming new, and confirming old commercial connections, but for obtaining a personal knowledge of the wants, the taste, the habits, the discoveries and improvements, the productions and fabrics of other civilized nations, and, by thus bringing home facts and suggestions, perfecting our existing manufactures, and adding new ones to our domestic stock; opening at the same time new markets for the product of our manufacturing and commercial industry, and qualifying ourselves for supplying them. It is by these means alone, and, above all, your committee must repeat it, by the effect of machinery in improving the quality and cheapening the fabrication of our various articles of export, that with a continually accumulating weight of taxes, and with all the necessaries and comforts of life gradually increasing in price, the effects of which on the wages of labour could not but be very consider-able, our commerce and manufactures have been also increasing in such a degree as to surpass the most sanguine calculations of the ablest political writers who had speculated on the improvements of a future age. . . .

There are three different modes of carrying on the woollen manufacture; that of the master clothier of the west of England, the factory, and, the domestic system.

In all the western counties as well as in the north, there are factories, but the master clothier of the west of England buys his wool from the importer, if it be foreign, or in the fleece, or of the woolstapler, if it be of domestic growth; after which, in all the different processes through which it passes, he is under the necessity of employing as many distinct classes of persons; sometimes working in their own houses, sometimes in those of the master clothier, but none of them going out of their proper line. Each class of workmen, however, acquires great skill in performing its particular operation, and hence may have arisen the acknowledged excellence, and, till of late, superiority, of the cloths of the west of England. It is however a remarkable fact, of which your committee has been assured by one of its own members, that previously to the introduction of machinery, it was very common, and it is said sometimes to happen at this day, for the north countryman to come into the west of England, and, in the clothing districts of that part of the kingdom, to purchase his wool, which he carries home; where, having worked it up into cloth, he brings it back again, and sells it in its native district. This is supposed to arise from the northern clothier being at liberty to work himself, and employ his own family and others, in any way which his interest or convenience may suggest.

In the factory system, the master manufacturers, who sometimes possess a very great capital, employ in one or more buildings or factories, under their own or their superintendant's inspection, a number of workmen, more or fewer according to the extent of their trade. This system, it is obvious, admits in practice of local variations. But both in the system of the west of England clothier, and in the factory system, the work, generally speaking, is done by persons who have no property in the goods they manufacture, for in this consists the essential distinction between the two former systems, and the domestic.

In the last-mentioned, or domestic system, which is that of Yorkshire, the manufacture is conducted by a multitude of master manufacturers, generally possessing a very small, and scarcely ever any great extent of capital. They buy the wool of the dealer; and, in their own houses, assisted by their wives and children, and from two or three to six or seven journeymen, they dye it (when dyeing is necessary) and through all the different stages work it up into undressed cloth.

Various processes however, the chief of which were formerly done by hand, under the manufacturer's own roof, are now performed by machinery, in public mills, as they are called, which work for hire. There are several such mills near every manufacturing village, so that the manufacturer, with little inconvenience or loss of time, carries thither his goods, and fetches them back again when the process is completed. When it has attained to the state of undressed cloth, he carries it on the market-day to a public hall or market, where the merchants repair to purchase.

Several thousands of these small master manufacturers attend the market of Leeds, where there are three halls for the exposure and sale of their cloths: and there are other similar halls, where the same system of selling in public market prevails, at Bradford, Halifax, and Huddersfield. The halls consist of long walks or galleries, throughout the whole length of which the master manufacturers stand in a double row, each behind his own little division or stand, as it is termed, on which his goods are exposed to sale. In the interval between these rows the merchants pass along, and make their purchases. At the end of an hour, on the ringing of a bell, the market closes, and such cloths as have been purchased are carried home to the merchants' houses; such goods as remain unsold continuing in the halls till they find a purchaser at some ensuing market. It should however be remarked, that a practice has also obtained of late years, of merchants giving out samples to some manufacturer whom they approve, which goods are brought to the merchant directly, without ever coming into the halls. These however, no less than the others, are manufactured by him in his own family. The greater merchants have their working-room, or, as it is termed, their shop, in which their workmen, or, as they are termed, croppers, all work together. The goods which, as it has been already stated, are bought in the undressed state, here undergo various processes, till, being completely finished, they are sent away for the use of the consumer, either in the home or the foreign market; the merchants sending them abroad directly without the intervention of any other factor. Sometimes again the goods are dressed at a stated rate by dressers, who take them in for that purpose.

The greater part of the domestic clothiers live in villages and detached houses, covering the whole face of a district of from 20 to 30 miles in length, and from 12 to 15 in breadth. Coal abounds throughout the whole of it; and a great proportion of the manufacturers occupy a little land, from 3 to 12 or 15 acres each. They often likewise keep a horse, to carry their cloth to the fulling mill and the market.

Though the system which has been just described be that which has been generally established in the West Riding of Yorkshire, yet there have long been a few factories in the neighbourhood of Halifax and Huddersfield; and four or five more, one however of which has been since discontinued, have been set on foot not many years ago in the neighbourhood of Leeds. These have for some time been objects of great jealousy to the domestic clothiers. The most serious apprehensions have been stated, by witnesses who have given their evidence before your committee in behalf of the domestic manufacturers, lest the factory system should gradually root out the domestic; and lest the independent little master manufacturer, who works on his own account, should sink into a journeyman working for hire. It is for the purpose of counteracting this supposed tendency of the factory system to increase, that a numerous class of petitioners wish, instead of repealing, to amend and enforce the Act of Philip and Mary, for restricting the number of looms to be worked in any one tenement; and with a similar view they wish to retain in force the 5th of Elizabeth, which enacts the system of apprenticeships. . . .

Your committee cannot wonder that the domestic clothiers of Yorkshire are warmly attached to their accustomed mode of carrying on the manufacture: It is not merely that they are *accustomed* to it—it obviously possesses many eminent advantages seldom found in a great manufacture.

It is one peculiar recommendation of the domestic system of manufacture, that, as it has been expressly stated to your committee, a young man of good character can always obtain credit for as much wool as will enable him to set up as a little master manufacturer, and the public mills, which are now established in all parts of the clothing district, and which work for hire at an easy rate, enable him to command the use of very expensive and complicated machines, the construction and necessary repairs of which would require a considerable capital. Thus, instances not unfrequently occur, wherein men rise from low beginnings, if not to excessive wealth, yet to a situation of comfort and independence.

It is another advantage of the domestic system of manufacture, and an advantage which is obviously not confined to the individuals who are engaged in it, but which, as well as other parts of this system, extends its benefits to the landholder, that any sudden stoppage of a foreign market, any failure of a great house, or any other of those adverse shocks to which our foreign trade especially is liable, in its present extended state, has not the effect of throwing a great number of workmen out of employ, as it often does, when the stroke falls on the capital of a single individual. In the domestic system, the loss is spread over a large superficies; it affects the whole body of the manufacturers; and, though each little master be a sufferer, yet few, if any, feel the blow so severely as to be altogether ruined. Moreover, it appears in evidence, that in such cases as these, they seldom turn off any of their standing set of journeymen, but keep them at work in hopes of better times.

On the whole, your committee feel no little satisfaction in bearing their testimony to the merits of the domestic system of manufacture; to the facilities it affords to men of steadiness and industry to establish themselves as little master manufacturers, and maintain their families in comfort by their own industry and frugality; and to the encouragement which it thus holds out to domestic habits and virtues. Neither can they omit to notice its favourable tendencies on the health and morals of a large and important class of the community.

But while your committee thus freely recognize the merits and value of the domestic system, they at the same time feel it their duty to declare it as their decided opinion, that the apprehensions entertained of its being rooted out by the factory system, are, at present at least, wholly without foundation.

For, happily, the merchant no less than the domestic manufacturer, finds his interest and convenience promoted by the domestic system – While it continues, he is able to carry on his trade with far less capital than if he were to be the manufacturer of his own cloth. Large sums must then be irrecoverably invested in extensive buildings and costly machinery; and, which perhaps is a consideration of even still more force, he must submit to the constant trouble and solicitude of watching over a numerous body of workmen. He might then often incur the expense of manufacturing articles, which, from some disappointment in the market, must either be kept on hand, or be sold to a loss. As it is, he can agree with his customer, at home or abroad, for any quantity of goods; and whether on a long expected or a sudden demand, he can repair at once to the market, and most probably purchase to the precise extent of his known wants; or, if the market happen not to furnish what he wishes to purchase, he can give out his sample, and have his order executed immediately.

While these and various other considerations, which might be stated, interest the merchant, as well as the manufacturer, in the continuance of the domestic system; and when it is remembered that this mode of conducting the trade greatly multiplies the merchants, by enabling men to carry on business with a comparatively small capital, your committee cannot participate in the apprehensions which are entertained by the domestic clothiers. In fact, there are many merchants, of very large capitals and of the highest credit, who for several generations have gone on purchasing in the halls, and some of this very description of persons state to your committee, that they not only had no thoughts of setting up factories themselves, but that they believed many of those who had established them were not greatly attached to that system, but only persisted in it because their buildings and machinery must otherwise lie a dead weight upon their hands. Under these circumstances, the lively fears, of the decline of the domestic, and the general establishment of the factory system, may reasonably excite surprize. It may have been in part occasioned by the decrease of the master manufacturers in the immediate neighbourhood of the large towns, especially in two or three populous hamlets adjoining to Leeds, whence they have migrated to a greater distance in the country, where they might enjoy a little land, and other conveniences and comforts. It may have strengthened the impression, that, as your committee have already stated, three or four factories have, within no very long period of time, been established in Leeds, or its vicinity.

But your committee are happy in being able to adduce one irrefragable fact, in corroboration of the sentiments they have already expressed on this question. This is, that the quantity of cloth manufactured by the domestic system has increased immensely of late years, not only in itself but as compared with the quantity made in factories.

Several factories, it has been observed, had long been established near Halifax and Huddersfield, but the principal progress of the factory system, and that which chiefly created the alarm, is stated to have been, within about the last fourteen years, in the town and neighbourhood of Leeds. Your committee succeeded in their endeavours to discover the quantity of cloth annually manufactured in all these factories, and it was found not to exceed 8,000 pieces. According to the provisions of the Acts commonly called the Stamping Acts, 11 Geo. II. and 5 and 6 Geo. III. returns are made every Easter to the Justices at Pontefract Session, of the quantity of cloth which has been made in the preceding year; the account being kept at the fulling mills by officers appointed for that purpose. These returns your committee carefully examined for the last 14 years, and find that in the year 1792, being by far the greatest year of export then known, there were manufactured 190,332 pieces of broad, and 150,666 pieces of narrow cloth: Yet the quantity of cloth manufactured in 1805 was 300,237 pieces broad and 165,847 pieces of narrow cloth, giving an increase, in favour of 1805, of 109,905 pieces broad, and 15,181 pieces narrow; from which increase deducting the cloth manufactured in factories, there remains an increase of about 100,000 broad, and 15,181 narrow pieces, to be placed to the account of the domestic system. The comparatively small quantity of cloth manufactured by the factories will excite less surprize, when it is considered that they are better adapted to the manufacturing of fancy goods, of which immense quantities and great varieties have been invented and sold, chiefly for a foreign market, of late years. . . .

On the whole, your committee do not wonder that the domestic clothiers are warmly attached to their peculiar system. This is a predilection in which the committee participate; but at the same time they must declare, that they see at present no solid ground for the alarm which has gone forth, lest the halls should be deserted, and the generality of merchants should set up factories. Your Committee, however, must not withhold the declaration, that if any such disposition had been perceived, it must have been their less pleasing duty to state, that it would by no means have followed, that it was a disposition to be counteracted by positive law.

The right of every man to employ the capital he inherits, or has acquired, according to his own discretion, without molestation or obstruction, so long as he does not infringe on the rights or property of others, is one of those privileges which the free and happy constitution of this country has long accustomed every Briton to consider as his birthright; and it cannot therefore be necessary for your committee to enlarge on its value, or to illustrate its effects. These would be indubitably confirmed by an appeal to our own commercial prosperity, no less than by the history of other trading nations, in which it has been ever found, that commerce and manufactures have flourished in free, and declined in despotic countries. But . . . your committee have the satisfaction of seeing, that the apprehensions entertained of factories are not only vicious in principle, but that they are practically erroneous; to such a degree, that even the very opposite dispositions might be reasonably entertained; nor would it be difficult to prove, that the factories, to a certain extent at least, and in the present day, seem absolutely necessary to the well-being of the domestic system; supplying those very particulars wherein the domestic system must be acknowledged to be inherently defective: for, it is obvious, that the little master manufacturers cannot afford, like the man who possesses considerable capital, to try the experiments which are requisite, and incur the risks, and even losses, which almost always occur, in inventing and perfecting new articles of manufacture, or in carrying to a state of greater perfection articles already established. He cannot learn, by personal inspection, the wants and habits; the arts, manufactures, and improvements of foreign countries; diligence, economy, and prudence are the requisites of his character, not invention, taste, and enterprize; nor would he be warranted in hazarding the loss of any part of his small capital: he walks in a sure road as long as he treads in the beaten track; but he must not deviate into the paths of speculation. The owner of a factory, on the contrary, being commonly possessed of a large capital, and having all his workmen employed under his own immediate superintendance, may make experiments, hazard speculation, invent shorter or better modes of performing old processes, may intro- duce new articles, and improve and perfect old ones, thus giving the range to his taste and fancy, and, thereby alone, enabling our manufacturers to stand the competition with their commercial rivals in other countries. Meanwhile, as is well worthy of remark (and experience abundantly warrants the assertion) many of these new fabrics and inventions, when their success is once established, become general among the whole body of manufacturers: the domestic manufacturers themselves thus benefiting, in the end, from those very factories which had been at first the objects of their jealousy. The history of almost all our other manufactures, in which great improve- ments have been made of late years, in some cases at an immense expense, and after numbers of unsuccessful experiments, strikingly illustrates and enforces the above remarks. It is besides an acknowledged fact, that the owners of factories are often among the most extensive purchasers at the halls, where they buy from the domestic clothier the established articles of manufacture, or are able at once to answer a great and sudden order; while, at home, and under their own superintendance, they make their fancy goods, and any articles of a newer, more costly, or more delicate quality, to which they are enabled by the domestic system to apply a much larger proportion of their capital. Thus, the two systems, instead of rivalling, are mutual aids to each other; each supplying the other's defects, and promoting the other's prosperity. . . .

The Cotton Industry

365. Number of Cotton Factories in Great Britain, 1787 and 1835

(R. Burn, *Statistics of the Cotton Trade* (1847), p. 26.)

	1787	1835				Total
		At work	Empty	Males Females Employed		
Berkshire . . .	2	—	—	—	—	—
Cheshire	8	109	7	15,516	15,996	31,512
Cumberland . . .	—	13	—	626	1,032	1,658
Derbyshire . . .	22	93	3	4,705	6,880	11,585
Durham	—	1	—	9	24	33
Lancashire . . .	41	683	32	60,151	62,264	122,415
Leicestershire . . .	—	6	—	325	267	592
Middlesex . . .	—	7	—	217	133	350
Nottinghamshire . .	17	20	—	481	1,242	1,723
Staffordshire . . .	—	13	—	749	1,299	2,048
Westmorland . .	5	—	—	—	—	—
Yorkshire . . .	11	126	—	5,487	5,724	11,211
Rest of England . .	6	—	—	—	—	—
Total England . .	119	1,071	42	88,266	94,861	183,127
Isle of Man . . .	1	—	—	—	—	—
Wales	4	5	—	452	699	1,151
Scotland	19	159	—	10,529	22,051	32,580
Total Great Britain .	143	1,235	42	99,247	117,611	216,858
Ireland	—	28	—	1,639	2,672	4,311
Total . . .	143	1,263	42	100,886	120,283	221,169

366. Description of Robert Peel's cotton mills at Bury, 1795

(J. Aikin, *A Description of the Country from thirty to forty miles round Manchester* (1795), pp. 268–269.

The town and neighbourhood of Bury have been highly benefited by the establishment of the very capital manufacturing and printing works belonging to the company of which that very respectable gentleman, Robert Peel, Esq., Member of Parliament for Tamworth, is the head. The principal of these works are situated on the side of the Irwell, from which they have large reservoirs of water. There is likewise a separate reservoir supplied by a spring of fine clear water, which is used for the washing of goods when the river is muddied by floods. The articles here made and printed are chiefly the finest kinds of the cotton manufactory, and they are in high request both at Manchester and London. The printing is performed in the most improved methods, both by wooden blocks and copper rollers, and the execution and colours are some of the very best of the Lancashire fabric. The premises occupy a large portion of ground, and cottages have been built for the accommodation of the workmen, which form streets, and give the appearance of a village. Ingenious artists are employed in drawing patterns, and cutting and engraving them on wood and copper, and many women and children in mixing and pencilling the colours, &c. The company has several other extensive works in the neighbourhood, as well on the Irwell as on the Roch. Some of these are confined to the carding, slubbing, and spinning of cotton; others to washing the cottons with water wheels, which go round with great velocity, but can be stopped in an instant for taking out and putting in the goods. Boiling and bleaching the goods are performed at other works. In short, the extensiveness of the whole concern is such as to find constant employ for most of the inhabitants of Bury and its neighbourhood, of both sexes and all ages, and notwithstanding their great number, they have never wanted work in the most unfavourable times. The peculiar healthiness of the people employed may be imputed partly to the judicious and humane regulations put in practice by Mr. Peel, and partly to the salubrity of the air and climate. At a short distance from Bury and the works is a large well-built house, called Chamber-hall, in which Mr. Peel himself resides, and in an adjoining meadow is a cottage or nursery for his young family. The whole is fitted up in a style of neatness and elegance, and surrounded with ornamental grounds and rising plantations.

367. R. Guest on the cotton industry

(*A compendious history of the Cotton manufacture* (1823).)

Richard Guest was one of the first historians of the cotton industry. His book was written principally to assert the claim of Thomas Highs to be the inventor of both the spinning Jenny and the water frame. The Rev. Edmund Cartwright (1743–1823), a younger brother of Major John Cartwright, the parliamentary reformer, describes, in an account supplied by him to an early edition of *Encyclopaedia Britannica*, how he came to invent the first effective power loom for weaving wide cloth. The gradual application of the invention, which met much resistance from the cloth workers and needed many improvements before it could be generally adopted, is described in the second extract. By the time that it came into wide use, Cartwright's patents had expired; he was accordingly granted £10,000 by Parliament in 1809. He also invented a wool-combing machine in 1789.

(a) *Cartwright's account of his invention of the power-loom.*

Happening to be at Matlock, in the summer of 1784, I fell in company with some gentlemen of Manchester, when the conversation turned on Arkwright's spinning machinery. One of the company observed, that as soon as Arkwright's patent expired, so many mills would be erected, and so much cotton spun, that hands never could be found to weave it. To this observation I replied that Arkwright must then set his wits to work to invent a weaving mill. This brought on a conversation on the subject, in which the Manchester gentlemen unanimously agreed that the thing was impracticable; in defence of their opinion, they adduced arguments which I certainly was incompetent to answer or even to comprehend, being totally ignorant of the subject, having never at that time seen a person weave. I controverted, however, the impracticability of the thing, by remarking that there had lately been exhibited in London, an automaton figure, which played at chess. Now you will not assert, gentlemen, said I, that it is more difficult to construct a machine that shall weave, than one which shall make all the variety of moves which are required in that complicated game.

Some little time afterwards, a particular circumstance recalling this conversation to my mind, it struck me, that, as in plain weaving, according to the conception I then had of the business, there could only be three movements, which were to follow each other in succession, there would be little difficulty in producing and repeating them. Full of these ideas, I immediately employed a carpenter and smith to carry them into effect. As soon as the machine was finished, I got a weaver to put in the warp, which was of such materials as sail cloth is usually made of. To my great delight, a piece of cloth, such as it was, was the produce.

As I had never before turned my thoughts to anything mechanical, either in theory or practice, nor had ever seen a loom at work, or knew any thing of its construction, you will readily suppose that my first loom must have been a most rude piece of machinery.

The warp was placed perpendicularly, the reed fell with a force of at least half an hundred weight, and the springs which threw the shuttle were strong enough to have thrown a Congreve rocket. In short, it required the strength of two powerful men to work the machine at a slow rate, and only for a short time. Conceiving in my great simplicity, that I had accomplished all that was required, I then secured what I thought a most valuable property, by a patent, 4 April, 1785. This being done, I then condescended to see how other people wove; and you will guess my astonishment, when I compared their easy modes of operation with mine. Availing myself, however, of what I then saw, I made a loom in its general principles, nearly as they are now made. But it was not till the year 1787, that I completed my invention, when I took out my last weaving patent, August 1st of that year. [pp. 44–45.]

(b) *The Adoption and spread of power-loom weaving.*

About 1790, Mr. Grimshaw, of Manchester, under a licence from Mr. Cartwright, erected a weaving factory turned by a steam engine. The great loss of time experienced in dressing the warp, which was done in small portions as it unrolled from the beam, and other difficulties arising from the quality of the yarn then spun, were in this instance formidable obstacles to success; the factory, however, was burnt down before it could be fully ascertained whether the experiment would succeed or not, and for many years no further attempts were made in Lancashire to weave by steam.

Mr. Austin, of Glasgow, invented a similar loom, in 1789, which he still further improved in 1798, and a building to contain 200 of these looms was erected by Mr. Monteith, of Pollockshaws, in 1800.

In the year 1803, Mr. Thomas Johnson, of Bradbury, in Cheshire, invented the dressing frame. Before this invention the warp was dressed in the loom in small portions as it unrolled from the beam, the loom ceasing to work during the operation. Mr. Johnson's machine dresses the whole warp at once; when dressed the warp is placed in the loom which now works without intermission. A factory for steam looms was built in Manchester, in 1806. Soon afterwards two others were erected at Stockport, and about 1809, a fourth was completed in Westhoughton. In these renewed attempts to weave by steam, considerable improvements were made in the structure of the looms, in the mode of warping, and in preparing the weft for the shuttle. With these improvements, aided by others in the art of spinning, which enabled the spinners to make yarn much superior to that made in 1790, and assisted by Johnson's machine, which is peculiarly adapted for the dressing of warps for steam looms, the experiment succeeded. Before the invention of the dressing frame, one weaver was required to each steam loom, at present a boy or girl, 14 or 15 years of age, can manage two steam looms, and with their help can weave three and a half times as much cloth as the best hand weaver. The best hand weavers seldom produce a piece of uniform evenness; indeed, it is next to impossible for them to do so, because a weaker or stronger blow with the lathe immediately alters the thickness of the cloth, and after an interruption of some hours, the most experienced weaver finds it difficult to recommence with a blow of precisely the same force as the one with which he left off. In steam looms, the lathe gives a steady, certain blow, and when once regulated by the engineer, moves with the greatest precision from the beginning to the end of the piece. Cloth made by these looms, when seen by those manufacturers who employ hand weavers, at once excites admiration and a consciousness that their own workmen cannot equal it. The increasing number of steam looms is a certain proof of their superiority over the hand looms. In 1818, there were in Manchester, Stockport, Middleton, Hyde, Stayley Bridge, and their vicinities, 14 factories, containing about 2,000 looms. In 1821, there were in the same neighbourhoods 32 factories, containing 5,732 looms. Since 1821, their number has still farther increased, and there are at present not less than 10,000 steam looms at work in Great Britain.

It is a curious circumstance, that, when the cotton manufacture was in its infancy, all the operations, from the dressing of the raw material to its being finally turned out in the state of cloth, were completed under the roof of the weaver's cottage. The course of improved manufacture which followed, was to spin the yarn in factories and to weave it in cottages. At the present time, when the manufacture has attained a mature growth, all the operations, with vastly increased means and more complex contrivances, are again performed in a single building. The weaver's cottage with its rude apparatus of peg warping, hand cards, hand wheels, and imperfect looms, was the steam loom factory in miniature. Those vast brick edifices in the vicinity of all the great manufacturing towns in the south of Lancashire, towering to the height of 70 or 80 feet, which strike the attention and excite the curiosity of the traveller, now perform labours which formerly employed whole villages. In the steam loom factories, the cotton is carded, roved, spun, and woven into cloth, and the same quantum of labour is now performed in one of these structures which formerly occupied the industry of an entire district.

A very good hand weaver, a man 25 or 30 years of age, will weave 2 pieces of nine-eighths shirting per week, each 24 yards long, and containing 105 shoots of weft in an inch, the reed of the cloth being a 44, Bolton count, and the warp and weft 40 hanks to the pound. A steam-loom weaver, 15 years of age, will in the same time weave

7 similar pieces. A steam loom factory containing 200 looms, with the assistance of 100 persons under 20 years of age, and of 25 men, will weave 700 pieces per week, of the length and quality before described. To manufacture 100 similar pieces per week by the hand, it would be necessary to employ at least 125 looms, because many of the weavers are females, and have cooking, washing, cleaning and various other duties to perform; others of them are children, and consequently unable to weave as much as the men. It requires a man of mature age and a very good weaver to weave 2 of the pieces in a week, and there is also an allowance to be made for sickness and other incidents. Thus, 875 hand looms would be required to produce the 700 pieces per week; and reckoning the weavers, with their children, and the aged and infirm belonging to them, at $2\frac{1}{2}$ to each loom, it may very safely be said, that the work done in a steam factory containing 200 looms, would, if done by hand weavers, find employment and support for a population of more than 2,000 persons.

The steam looms are chiefly employed in weaving printing cloth and shirtings; but they also weave thicksets, fancy cords, dimities, cambrics and quiltings, together with silks, worsteds and fine woollen or broad cloth. Invention is progressive, every improvement that is made is the foundation of another, and as the attention of hundreds of skilful mechanics and manufacturers is now turned to the improvement of the steam looms, it is probable that its application will become as general, and its efficiency as great, in weaving, as the jenny, water frame and mule, are in spinning, and that it will, in this country at least, entirely supersede the hand loom. [pp. 46–48.]

(c) *The commercial traveller.*

About 1750 there arose a second rate class of merchants, called fustian masters; these resided in the country and employed the neighbouring weavers. . . .

The master attended the weekly market at Manchester, and sold his pieces in the grey to the merchant, who afterwards dyed and finished them. Instead of travelling with their goods on pack-horses, the merchants or their travellers now rode from town to town, carrying with them patterns or samples, and on their return home the goods sold during the journey were forwarded by the carriers' waggons.

This practice, far more commodious than the rude and inconvenient mode of carrying their merchandize from town to town, has become general, not only in this, but in every other business; and it may now be asserted, that the whole of the internal wholesale trade of England is carried on by commercial travellers–they pervade every town, village and hamlet in the kingdom, carrying their samples and patterns, and taking orders from the retail tradesmen, and afterwards forwarding the goods by waggons, or canal barges, to their destination;–they form more than one-half of the immense number of persons who are constantly travelling through the country in all directions, and are the principal support of our inns, the neatness and comfort of which are so much celebrated throughout Europe. The commercial travellers are in a great measure the causes of this neatness and comfort, for they soon find out the best houses of entertainment; and, being gregarious, the news is readily communicated, and the best houses of course become more frequented: a circumstance which excites emulation among the innkeepers. These travellers are a body of men exhibiting intelligence and acuteness, combined in many instances, with self-conceit and the superficial information acquired by reading newspapers. [pp. 10–11.]

(d) *The social effects of industrialization in Lancashire.*

The progress of the cotton manufacture introduced great changes in the manners and habits of the people [of Lancashire]. The operative workmen being thrown together in great numbers, had their faculties sharpened and improved by constant communication. Conversation wandered over a variety of topics not before essayed; the questions of peace and war, which interested them importantly, inasmuch as they might produce a rise or fall of wages, became highly interesting, and this brought them into the vast field of politics and discussions on the character of their Government, and the men who composed it. They took a greater interest in the defeats and victories of their country's arms, and from being only a few degrees above their cattle in the scale of intellect, they became Political Citizens.

To these changes the establishing of Sunday Schools has very much contributed; they have been a great means of forwarding this wonderful alteration. Before their institution the lower orders were extremely illiterate; very few of them could read, and still fewer could write, and when one of them learned to read, write and cast accounts, those acquirements elevated him to a superior rank. His clerkly skill exempted him from manual labour, and as a shopman, book-keeper or town's officer –perchance in the higher dignity of parish clerk or schoolmaster–he rose a step above his original situation in life.

The labourers and operative workmen were formerly sunk in the depths of ignorance; they seldom formed an opinion of their own, and were content to believe everything their superiors told them. Sunday Schools have greatly assisted in dispelling this thick cloud of ignorance, they have taught the mass of the people to read, and the countless publications dispersed over the country, in monthly portions or numbers, at 6d. 9d. or 1s. per number, have taught them to reason and think for themselves. During the last 40 years the mind of the labouring class (taking them as a body) has been progressively improving, and within the last 20, has made an advance of centuries, and is still advancing with accelerated rapidity.

The facility with which the weavers changed their masters, the constant effort to find out and obtain the largest remuneration for their labour, the excitement to ingenuity which the higher wages for fine manufactures and skilful workmanship produced, and a conviction that they depended mainly on their own exertions, produced in them that invaluable feeling, a spirit of freedom and independence, and that guarantee for good conduct and improvement of manners, a consciousness of the value of character and of their own weight and importance.

The practical truth of these remarks must be obvious to every one who has served on the jury at Lancaster, and compared the bright, penetrating, shrewd and intelligent jurors from the south of the county, with the stupidity and utter ignorance of those from its northern parts; and to every one who witnessed the fervour and enthusiasm with which the people in the manufacturing districts flew to arms, in 1803, to defend their firesides against a foreign invader. What crowding to drills; what ardour and alacrity to learn the use of arms there then was, and how much stronger and more rapid the feeling of independence, both national and individual, is found to be among a highly-civilized dense manufacturing population, than among a scattered half-informed peasantry!

The amusements of the people have changed with their character. The athletic exercises of quoits, wrestling, football, prison-bars, and shooting with the long-bow are become obsolete and almost forgotten; and it is to be regretted that the present pursuits of pleasures of the labouring class are of a more effeminate cast.—They are now pigeon-fanciers, canary-breeders and tulip-growers. The field sports, too, have assumed a less hardy and enterprising character. Instead of the squire with his merry harriers and a score or two of ruddy, broad-chested yeomen, scouring the fields on foot heedless of thorn or briar, and scorning to turn aside for copse or ditch, we now see half a dozen fustian masters and shopkeepers with three or four greyhounds and as many beagles, attacking the poor hare with such a superiority, both as respects scent and fleetness, as to give her no chance of escape, and pouncing upon their game like poachers, rather than pursuing it with the fairness and hardiness of hunters. [pp. 37–39.]

368. Second Report of the Select Committee on Emigration from the United Kingdom, 1827

(Parliamentary Papers, 1826–1827, v, pp. 3–7.)

The report illustrates the desperate plight of the hand-loom cotton weavers in the eighteen-twenties. For examples of their wage-rates at this time, see No. 411.

. . . In addition to those ordinary causes, which in many parts of the United Kingdom appear to have led to a superabundant population, or rather to a disproportion between the demand and the supply of labour, an important change has been wrought, and is still in gradual but certain progress, in the condition of some of the manufacturing districts, by the transition from hand-loom to power-loom weaving. For some time the advance in the cotton trade was so rapid as nearly, if not altogether to absorb in the more productive system, the hands thus thrown out of employment. But difficulties arising from a temporary check in trade shortly fell upon the weavers with the double pressure of these two combined causes, a diminished demand for the produce of their industry, and an increased facility of production.

Your Committee are fully sensible that, to a certain extent, these disastrous consequences to a portion of the community must follow upon every new invention by which human labour is abridged: and that it is more especially the interest of a commercial country, far from discouraging, to afford every protection to such inventions: and while your Committee lay down this doctrine in its fullest extent, they feel themselves bound to add that those who in the present instance are the chief sufferers appear to manifest juster ideas and a more ready acquiescence in this general principle than could have been expected from their situation in life, and from the personal feelings with which their view of the case must be mixed up. But . . . two circumstances . . . appear to distinguish this special case from those of ordinary occurrence. Independently of the extent of the change, the time at which it has taken place, with reference to their peculiar branch of trade, is for the weavers most unfortunate; and most, if not all, the ordinary channels of labour are in such a state of repletion that it is difficult for them to transfer their industry elsewhere.

Though the state of distress bordering upon actual famine which these causes have produced in districts extensively concerned in the cotton trade is so notorious as hardly to require pressing upon the House, your Committee have had it confirmed by the strongest and fullest evidence. These districts appear to embrace in England a large portion of the county of Lancaster, together with parts of Cheshire, of the West Riding of Yorkshire, and of Cumberland; and in Scotland principally, so far as the evidence . . . has gone, the counties of Renfrew and Lanark. In mitigation of this extensive distress sums to a very large amount have been raised . . . and have mainly tended to preserve those districts from the immediate horrors of famine and from the possible evils of riot and disturbance. But your Committee deem it their duty not to conceal from the House that, notwithstanding the temporary aid thus afforded, the long continued pressure of the lowest class upon the poor rates . . . has extended the distress to the ranks immediately above; and that not only the local funds appear in many instances nearly exhausted, but the lower order of rate payers . . . are become themselves dependent upon casual or parochial assistance.

Under these circumstances, the Manufacturers' Relief Committee . . . agreeing with your Committee in opinion that there is little hope that any revival of trade can bring back the employment of the distressed hand-loom weavers, and that the fulness of the other branches of labour renders it difficult for them to transfer their industry; aware also, that temporary aid . . . can only produce temporary benefit . . . [and] satisfied of the efficiency and permanence of the benefit to be afforded by emigration, they have signified their readiness to contribute in furtherance of these objects the sum of £25,000 . . . provided the farther sum of £50,000 can be obtained from other sources.

Your Committee . . . are satisfied . . . that the sum of £75,000 if raised, will be sufficient to remove, provision and locate in the North American colonies above 1,200 families, amounting to between six and seven thousand souls. . . .

In the districts above alluded to, and more especially in Lancashire, there appears to be among the hand-loom weavers two classes almost wholly distinct from each other: the one, who though they take in work in their own houses or cellars, are congregated in the large manufacturing towns; and the other, scattered in small hamlets or single houses, in various directions throughout the manufacturing country. It is to the situation of this latter class, though both are in a state extremely deplorable, that your Committee would chiefly wish to direct the attention of the House. It appears that persons of this description for many years past have been occupiers of small farms of a few acres, which they have held at high rents; and combining the business of a hand-loom weaver with that of a working farmer, have assisted to raise the rent of their land from the profits of their loom. Upon this class it is that the distresses of the times have fallen with peculiar hardship. While the decline of their manufacturing business has utterly disabled them from supplying those rents which were due from them as agriculturalists, they have found themselves called upon to give support, as liable to the rates, to those of their fellow weavers who were engaged in manufacture alone: and a remnant of honest pride and shame has prevented many of those in the extremest distress from applying for parish relief: while others, being from their remote situation, less immediately under the eyes of the regular authorities, have lingered on, till found accidentally, as has been proved in evidence, in the last stages of misery and disease. Your Committee cannot but observe, that while the greater destitution of this latter class points them out as requiring more immediate attention, their partly agricultural habits render them more eligible for the particular kind of relief contemplated by your Committee; and your Committee cannot but express a hope that the hand-loom weavers in general, and this class in particular, will receive from Parliament that attention and favour to which their sufferings and their patience amply entitle them. . . .

Under these impressions your Committee . . . strongly recommend the grant of £50,000 from the national funds, in furtherance of an immediate emigration from the manufacturing districts.[1] . . .

Your Committee cannot however conclude . . . without expressing their deep conviction, that whatever may be the immediate and urgent demands from other quarters, it is vain to hope for any permanent and extensive advantage from any system of emigration which does not primarily apply to *Ireland*; whose population, unless some other outlet be opened to them, must shortly fill up every vacuum created in England or in Scotland, and reduce the labouring classes to a uniform state of degradation and misery. . . .

369. The development of the linen industry, 1800–1832

(G. R. Porter, *The Progress of the Nation*, I (1836), pp. 266–267.)

It was not until quite the end of the last century that flax spinning-mills were first erected in the north of England and in Scotland. Before that time the operation of spinning was altogether performed by women in their own dwellings. Up to 1814 the yarn spun in mills was sold to weavers or to dealers who acted as middle men between the spinners and weavers; but at the date last mentioned some spinners became also manufacturers of linen. It was at a still more recent period that power-weaving was applied to the making of linen fabrics in England and Scotland, and up to the present moment flax-spinning machinery has not been established in Ireland upon a scale sufficiently large to supply the looms of that country, to which considerable quantities of linen yarn are sent from the spinning-mills of Yorkshire.

In Scotland, this branch of manufacture was comparatively small before the peace in 1815. The town and neighbourhood of Dundee has been the scene of a most remarkable increase in the linen manufacture since the time first mentioned. In 1814, the quantity of flax imported into that town for use in the manufactories did not

[1] A return, printed in *Parliamentary Papers*, 1830, XXIX, p. 435, states the total number of persons who emigrated from the United Kingdom from 1821 to 1829 inclusive to be: emigrants to the North American colonies 99,394; to the British West Indies 13,072; to the Cape of Good Hope 1,575; and to Australia 7,693.

exceed 3,000 tons, but in the year which ended 31st May, 1831, the import was more than 15,000 tons, besides upwards of 3,000 tons of hemp. The continued progress of the manufacture in this district is shown by the fact that, in the year ending 31st May, 1833, the imports had further increased to 18,777 tons of flax, and 3,380 tons of hemp. The quantity of linen, sailcloth, and bagging, into which this material was made, and which was shipped from Dundee in the same year, amounted to 60,000,000 yards, being probably equal to the entire shipments made from the whole of Ireland.

(b) THE INDUSTRIES OF THE MIDLANDS

370. Staffordshire

(W. Pitt, *General View of the Agriculture of the county of Stafford* (1794), pp. 159–165.)

The manufactures of Staffordshire are very considerable, and comprehend a variety of articles, particularly hardware, nails, toys, japanned goods, and potter's ware; also productions in cotton, silk, leather, woollen, linen, and many other articles.

The manufacture of hardware is carried on in the fourth part of the county to a great extent; and Wolverhampton, and its neighbouring populous villages produce locks of every kind, and of the very best quality: and this may be termed the staple manufacture of this town. Buckles are also manufactured here, and a great number of hands employed upon that article. In some particulars of steel-toys, especially watch-chains, they have long been famous for exceeding every other place, and still stand unrivalled: but this manufacture in particular, and the others in general, have suffered much by the war, orders having been wanting and remittances precarious. The manufacture of edge-tools, files, augers, and japanned goods here is considerably extensive, as well as that of a great many other articles.

The staple manufacture of Walsall may be said to be shoe-buckles and chapes, in which a great number of hands are employed, and some good fortunes have been made. Also this town and neighbourhood, particularly Bloxwich, is famous for the manufacture of saddlers' ironmongery, such as bridle-bits, stirrups, spurs, &c. These are sold to the saddlers ironmongers at Walsall, and form the basis of a considerable traffic, carried on to great advantage, and by them circulated to every part of the kingdom. . . .

The manufacture of nails in Staffordshire is very extensive, employing many thousands of hands in some of the most populous country parishes, particularly Sedgeley, Rowley, Westbromwich, Smethwich, Wombourne, Pelsall, the Foreign of Walsall, and many other places. A great number of women and children, as well as men, are employed in making the finer and lighter sorts, which they do equally well. The manufactures of Mr. Bolton at Handsworth are in this county, and very considerable, employing many hundreds of hands, chiefly, I believe, in various kinds of toys, and in the machinery for steam engines. Bilstone furnishes a variety of plated, lackered, japanned, and even enamelled goods. Wednesbury I believe, does something in the gun trade. Tobacco and snuff-boxes of iron or steel, and finished in various ways, are got up at Darlaston, Willenhall, and in their neighbourhood. Most of these manufactures have suffered more or less by the war; though I understand, the trades of nails and saddlers ironmongery are pretty good; buckles and locks indifferent; and the steel-toy trade almost annihilated. These manufactures suffered a similar, or perhaps greater depression in the American war; but were extremely and uniformly flourishing during the peace, from the conclusion of the American war to the commencement of the present. This is a sufficient proof that their flourishing state is consistent only with a state of peace.

The manufacture of potter's ware in the north of the county is very extensive and important, the value of the manufactured article being, as it were, a creation of the manufacturer, from a raw material of no value.

The potteries consist of a number of scattered villages, occupying an extent of about ten miles; and may contain about twenty thousand inhabitants, including those who depend upon them for employment and subsistence. They have not been so flourishing since the war.

Stafford, the county town, has a very considerable manufacture of shoes, both for home consumption and exportation; and the tanning and other different branches of the leather trade, and also the manufacture of hats, are carried on upon a large scale in many other towns in the county.

The cotton manufactures of this county are not inconsiderable; those of Mr. Arkwright at Rocester, and elsewhere near the Dove, are upon a large scale and employ a great number of hands; and those of Messrs. Peele and Wilkes, at Fazely and Tamworth, are very considerable; besides which there are extensive cotton works at Burton and Tutbury. This manufacture has a great tendency to promote our national industry, by finding employment suitable to both sexes in early youth, and thus initiating them in early habits of industry. The country is much obliged to those gentlemen by whose exertions and perseverance this manufacture has been introduced and established.

Leek has a considerable manufacture in the silk and mohair way, the manufactured goods from which are, sewing-silks, twist, buttons, ribbons, silk-serrets, shawls and silk-handkerchiefs. In these manufactures . . . are employed about two thousand inhabitants of the town, and one thousand of the adjacent country. In this trade some good fortunes have been made, and it has been very flourishing; but the check on paper credit, which in a great measure hurt the confidence of all connections, diminished the trade here: and the war must in some degree have damped the demand for it abroad: yet the trade is now in a flourishing state, and considerably better than it was some months ago.

Cheadle and Teyn have a considerable manufacture of tape, which finds employment for the industry of its inhabitants.

The woollen manufactory within this county is not very considerable, and a large proportion of the raw wool grown therein is sold into the clothing and stocking coun tries; yet there are wool-combers in most of the towns, and some which push a considerable busi ness; and a good deal of woollen cloth is got up in the country by private families, though in less quantity than formerly.

There is no considerable public manufacture of linen, but a good deal of hurden, hempen, and flaxen cloth got up in private families; a great many people resident in the country being now, and having long been, in the habit of growing a patch of hemp and flax, which is generally manufactured within the county.

Of the population of Staffordshire, I suppose one-third are supported by agricultural or other professions or employments thereon depending, and two-thirds by manufactures, commerce, and mines. . . .

The extent of the iron trade in all its varieties, wrought and unwrought, for agricultural and other internal purposes, and for home consumption and exportation, under its innumerable shapes and forms, is now so very great, as to rival even that of the great staple, wool; and to make the superiority of the latter somewhat questionable; and from the abundance of iron ore and fuel with which this country abounds, the trade, particularly so far as relates to the production of the metal, is capable of being much extended; and there can be little doubt of the possibility that this country will wholly supply itself with that article. . . .

371. Arthur Young on the industrial development of Birmingham, 1791

(*Tours in England and Wales*: London School of Economics Reprints, xiv, pp. 255-258.)

The capital improvement wrought since I was here before is the canal to Oxford, Coventry, Wolverhampton, &c.; the port, as it may be called, or double canal head in the town crowded with coal barges is a noble spectacle, with that prodigious animation, which the immense trade of this place could alone give. I looked around me with amazement at the change effected in twelve years; so great that this place may now probably be reckoned, with justice, the first manufacturing town in the world. From this port and these quays you may now go by water to Hull, Liverpool, Bristol, Oxford (130 miles) and London. The cut was opened through the coal mines to Wolverhampton in 1769. In 1783, into the new mines of Wednesbury, and to the junction with the Coventry canal, at Faseley, near Tamworth. From Birmingham to the Staffordshire canal is 22 miles, and to Faseley 15. In the 22 miles from hence to Wolverhampton only three locks; but down to Faseley there are 44 locks; not one rivulet to supply water, and only 30 acres of reservoirs, the water coming out of the earth. At Ocher hills they have a powerful steam engine for throwing back the waste water: and in the whole extent one that cost £4,000; another of £3,000; another of £2,500, another of £1,200; and yet another building that will cost £3,500. The first-mentioned works at the charge of £200 for six months. The old and new cuts were executed at the expense of about £250,000; one mile where it is open to the depth of 44 feet £30,000 for sinking only 18 feet lower than the original level. There are 13 locks between the port and Deritan, 8 feet 2 inches wide, and the boats 7 feet; to pass the 13 takes only two hours. Coals, before these canals were made, were 6d per cwt. at Birmingham, now 4½d. The consumption is about 200,000 tons a year, which exhausts about 20 or 22 acres; it employs 40 boats, each 20 tons a day for the six summer months, besides 15 to 20 boats to Oxford, a new supply since the new cut.

In the Wednesbury mines the coal is 10 yards thick, and in some even to 12 and 14, a thing elsewhere almost unheard of: a cubical yard they reckon a ton. Shares in the navigation, which were at first done at 140 per cent are now at 1040. I was assured that shares in the Aire and Calder navigation are yet higher, even 100 per cent per ann.

These immense works, which wear so animated a face of business, correspond well with the prodigious increase of the town, which I viewed to good advantage from the top of the new church of St. Paul: it is now a very great city indeed; and it was abundantly curious to have it pointed out to me the parts added since I was here. They form the greatest part of the town, and carry in their countenance undoubted marks of their modern date. In 1768 the population was under 30,000; now the common calculation is 70,000, but more accurate calculation extend it to 80,000, which I am told is the number assigned by Dr. Priestley. In the last 10 years above 4,000 new houses have been built: and the increase is at present going on much more rapidly, for I was told that the number this year is not less than 700.

The earnings of the workmen in the manufacture are various, but in general very high: a boy of 10 or 12 years, 2s. 6d. to 3s. a week; a woman from 4s. to 10s. a week, average about 6s.; men from 10s. to 25s. a week, and some much higher; colliers earn yet more. These are immense wages, when it is considered that the whole family is sure of constant steady employment; indeed they are so great that I am inclined to think labour higher at Birmingham than in any other place in Europe: a most curious circumstance for the politician to reflect on, and which shews of how little effect to manufactures is cheap labour, for here is the most flourishing fabric that was perhaps ever known, paying the highest rates of labour. Such an instance ought to correct those common notions that have been retailed from hand to hand a thousand times, that cheap provisions are necessary for the good of manufactures, because cheap provisions suppose cheap labour, which is a combination founded in ignorance and error. Provisions at Birmingham are at the same rate as everywhere else in England, for it is remarkable that the level of price at present is very general, except the division of the east and west of the kingdom for corn; but while Birmingham and Norwich eat their provisions at nearly the same price (with allowance that the former is much the more quick, ready and active market) the price of labour is at least 150 per cent higher in one of those places than the other.

372. The production of pig-iron in Great Britain, 1788–1806

(From H. Scrivenor, *A Comprehensive History of the Iron Trade* (1841), pp. 85–87, 97.)

The 1806 figures were compiled from a statement presented by a deputation from the Ironmasters of Great Britain to the House of Commons Committee on the proposed duty on pig-iron in 1806. Of the 222 coke furnaces there numbered, 60 were out of blast. It was claimed that the capital employed in the industry was £500,000, and that it gave employment to 200,000 persons.

	1788				1806		
	Charcoal furnaces		Coke furnaces		Coke furnaces		
	Number	Total made in each county (tons per annum)	Number	Total made in each county (tons per annum)	No. of works	No. of furnaces	Total made in each county (tons per annum)
Cheshire . .	—	—	1	600	—	—	—
Cumberland .	1	300	1	700	4	4	1,491
Derbyshire . .	1	300	7	4,200	11	18	10,329
Gloucestershire .	4	2,600	—	—	2	3	1,629
Lancashire . .	3	2,100	—	—	3	4	2,500
Leicestershire .	—	—	—	—	1	1*	—
Shropshire . .	3	1,800	21	23,100	19	42	54,966
Staffordshire .	—	—	6	4,500	25	42	49,460
Sussex . .	2	300	—	—	—	—	—
Westmorland .	1	400	—	—	—	—	—
Yorkshire . .	1	600	6	4,500	14	27	26,671
Total in England	16	8,400	42	37,600	79	141	147,046
South Wales (including Monmouthshire)	7	4,300	8	8,200	28	50	78,045
North Wales .	1	400	—	—	3	4	2,075
Scotland . .	2	1,400	6	5,600	12	27	23,240
Total in Great Britain . .	26	14,500	56	51,400	122	222	250,406
1806 Total old charcoal furnaces still in use in different counties					11	11	7,800
Total production in 1806					133	233	258,206

* Out of blast.

(c) THE COAL INDUSTRY

373. The Newcastle 'Vend', 1800

(Report from the Committee appointed to enquire into the State of the Coal Trade . . .
1800, *Parliamentary Papers*, 1st Series, x, pp. 640–641.)

. . . The manner in which the trade was conducted on the rivers Tyne and Wear, and in the ports of Newcastle and Sunderland, was the first object of your committee's examination.

It appears from the evidence, that the coal mines are either carried on by the owners of the land in which they are situated, or by adventurers, to whom leases are granted for that purpose. The mines vary in the qualities of their produce, in their local situations, and in their depth. The latter differences, however, apply chiefly to the mines of different qualities as those of the same or nearly the same quality are found to vary little from each other in these circumstances, or in the expense of working.

. . . It is true the price of labour and materials of mining have advanced, but that advance seems to them to bear by no means an adequate proportion to the gradually increased price demanded by the coal owner since the year 1792.

When the winnings of coals are completed, and the pits prepared for the supply, it appears that a contract is entered into with the fitter, who is in the nature of a factor, to whom a settled commission is given for negotiating the sale of coals, conveying them to the ship and guaranteeing the debt from the ship owner, who is the purchaser. There are other small charges for loading the coals on board the ships from the keels or boats, which are borne by the ship owner.

The coals being put on board, the fitter obtains a cocket at the custom house for the ship to sail, and a certificate of loading the coals by him, specifying the price paid for them, and the colliery from which they were drawn. It is part of the business of the fitters to keep different lists in their offices of the kinds of coal they have to dispose of, for the inspection of the owner or master of every ship arriving in the port, who is at liberty to place the name of his ship on any of them, and entitled to receive a loading of the coal he has chosen, in the turn in which his ship stands on the list.

These regulations appear well adapted to insure to the market a regular supply of coals, independently of natural causes of interruption; and your committee only regret that the beneficent intentions of parliament in framing them appear to have been in some measure frustrated, by a compact that has subsisted for some years among the coal owners in the north, under the denomination of "The Limitation of Vends."

It is necessary for your committee to observe, that, previous to the compact directly pointed at, an agreement is stated to have taken place in the year 1771. Meetings were called in consequence of alleged irregularities, to which the coal trade was at that time subject. The result of such meetings produced a determination to fix the prices of coal, which appear to have been settled in the ratio of the supposed value from twelve to fifteen shillings the Newcastle chaldron, and the agreement seems to have been common alike to the Tyne and to the Wear.

About the year 1786, or 1787, a particular species of compact was resorted to, which, with temporary interruptions, your committee believe to have existed ever since. Its avowed object was to apply a remedy to a heavy depression in the price of certain kinds of coal, and to avert the danger connected with it, of the abandonment of several collieries.

This compact seems, with occasional alterations in its conditions, affecting particular pits, to have been annually renewed, and though suspended since the 1st of January 1800, the interruption has arisen from a disagreement of the parties concerned on the terms of its renewal, and is by no means to be deemed a final dereliction of the measure.

As far as respects the river Tyne, the regulations of the compact apply to the quantity to be supplied by each colliery, at a price fixed in a manner similar to the previous agreement. Its arrangement is settled in the following manner: the coal owners and coal workers meet, and take an account of the whole vend of coals for the preceding year; they add to this a large imaginary quantity, and divide the whole among the different collieries, proportioning the allotment of each to its respective powers; this is called "The Basis."

When the vend of the year subsequent to this regulation is afterwards ascertained, the aggregate of it is also divided and distributed amongst the collieries in proportion to the allotted basis. The object of the arrangement is, to give a right to each colliery to furnish, if possible, a certain proportion of the general yearly sale; and where any colliery falls short of this proportion, the collieries which exceed, are bound to make a compensation for the deficiency, at a certain rate per chaldron.

As the sum paid in compensation does not amount to the profit of the excess, to prevent any mines from transgressing too much their allotted limit, and the influx into the market becoming too large, the respective proportions of each is settled, by a superintending committee, at the beginning of every month, for the month following, according to the vend of the previous one, and to the existing circumstances of the market.

Various instances are stated of ships subjected to detention at Newcastle, by waiting for the best coals, owing in part to the greater demand for coals of that description, but an additional reason assigned is, that when the appointed vend of the coals they were to receive happened to be exhausted, no more could be supplied till the commencement of the ensuing month; and detentions of this kind as your committee have reason to believe, frequently occurred up to the period when the agreement was last suspended.

The regulation in force upon the Wear, differs in some respects from that above described upon the Tyne. The same distribution of vend amongst the coal owners, is not found to obtain under the same restriction; the compact is a general one between all the collieries of the Wear and those of the Tyne, by which the whole of the estimated vend on both rivers being divided, three parts are to be supplied by the latter, and two by the former.

The purpose of these regulations was answered, the evils to which they were avowedly directed were remedied, the depression of price complained of was removed, and the dangers apprehended to the inferior collieries effectually averted: but your committee feel it their duty to observe, that the agreement itself in the first instance, and the detention of ships which has been the consequence of it, appear (each by delaying and limiting the supply) to have contributed to the augmented price of coal so severely felt by the consumers in London. This opinion your committee are the more confirmed in, by the accounts of the import of coals since the suspension of the agreement, by which it appears that the import has largely exceeded that of the corresponding period of any preceding year: and they are induced to express their apprehensions, that a power arising from mutual compact, which enables the coal owners to provide in general for the interest of the collieries, may at any time enable them to enhance the price of an article of such necessity, to the oppression and danger of the public. . . .

374. Evidence of J. Buddle before the Select Committee of the House of Lords on the state of the coal trade, 1829

(*Parliamentary Papers*, 1830, VIII, pp. 28-54.)

Buddle was an experienced colliery viewer, and secretary to the Coal Trade Committee of Newcastle.

Have you a general knowledge of all the collieries upon the Tyne and Wear?–Yes. . . .

What is the deepest pit you know?–The deepest pit I am acquainted with as a working pit is 180 fathoms of shaft; but they frequently go deeper by inclined planes under ground.

What is the shallowest?–The shallowest pit that I know of is 23 fathoms, and of very inferior coal.

Can you state generally what is the extent of the expense incurred in sinking a single pit?–I have known, in several cases, upwards of £30,000; that includes the machinery requisite for sinking that pit, that is, the steam engine and all its apparatus; that is merely getting to the coal, and it might be called more properly a winning charge than a working charge. . . . Perhaps no stronger proof of the great risk can be adduced, than that it is a property that cannot be insured, either against fire, water, or any other accident. We have never been able to effect an insurance on a coal work.

Have you any idea of the capital employed in the coal district?–Yes, I think I have, more particularly on the Tyne, where I have had more professional business, and have been more generally employed in valuations. . . . I should think that the aggregate capital employed by the coal owners on the river Tyne must amount to about a million and a half, exclusive of craft in the river. Some of them are owners of the craft; many of them hire keels or barges. . . .

Have you made any calculation on that vested in collieries on the river Wear?–Only by approximation. . . . I should think from 6 to 700,000. . . .

Have you any . . . calculation of the number of men and ships employed on the two rivers . . .?–. . . The returns from the Tyne are [from] official documents; from the Wear . . . it is by an approximate calculation. The number of persons employed

THE COALFIELDS OF ENGLAND AND WALES AND THE AREAS NORMALLY
SUPPLIED BY THEM IN 1830
(From a map in the Report of the Select Committee on the State of the Coal Trade,
1830; *Parliamentary Papers*, 1830, VIII.)

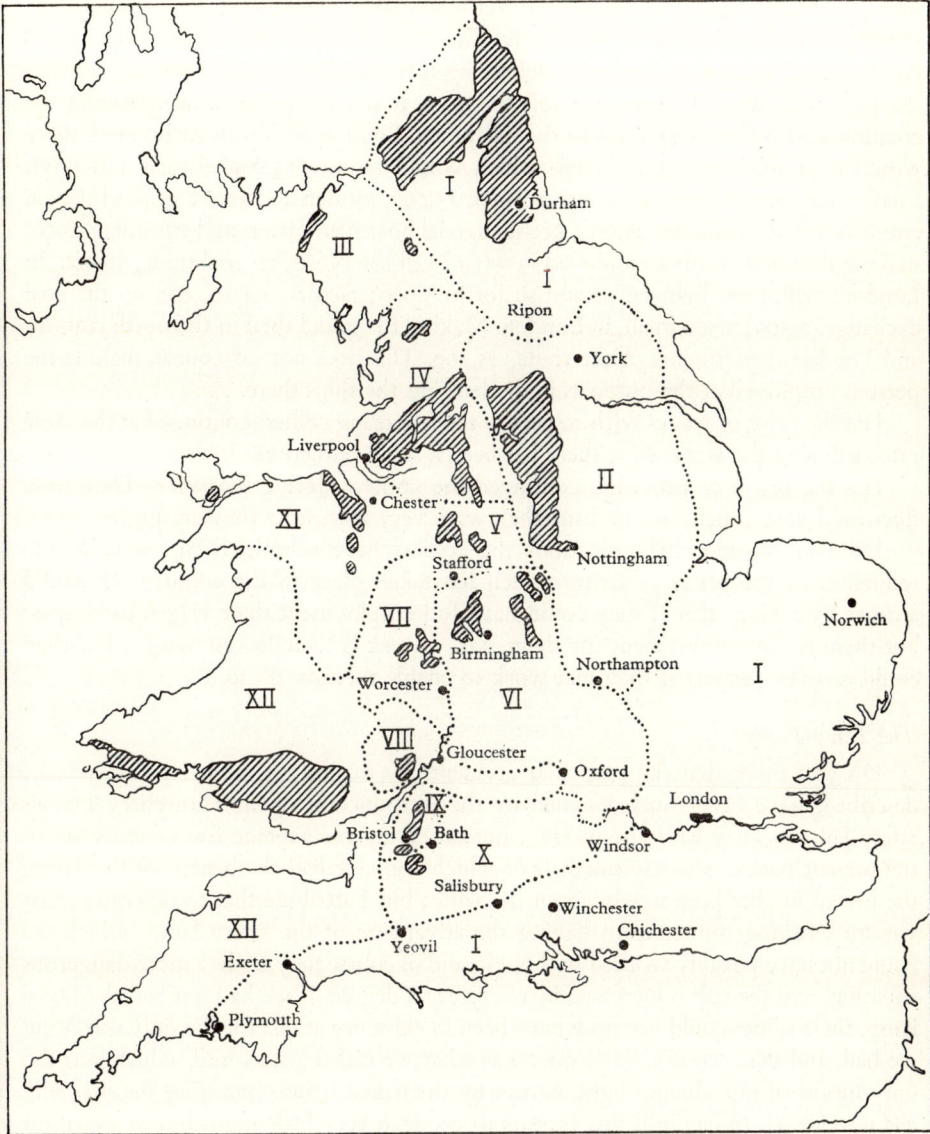

Coalfields, and areas supplied

I   *Northumberland and Durham*
II   *Yorkshire, Nottinghamshire and Derbyshire*
III *Whitehaven*
IV *Lancashire*
V   *North Staffordshire or Pottery*
VI *South Staffordshire, or Dudley and Warwick-shire*

VII *Shropshire, including Coalbrookdale and Plain of Shrewsbury*
VIII *Forest of Dean*
IX   *South Gloucestershire or Bristol*
X   *Somerset*
XI   *North Wales or Flintshire*
XII *South Wales*

under ground on the Tyne, are, men 4,937, boys 3,554, together 8,491; above ground, men 2,745, boys 718, making 3,463; making the total . . . 11,954, which in round numbers I call 12,000, because I am pretty sure there were some omissions in the returns. On the river Wear, I conceive there are 9,000 employed, making 21,000 employed in digging the coal and delivering it to the ships on the two rivers. From the best calculations I have been able to make, it would appear, that averaging the coasting vessels that carry coals to the size of 220 London chaldrons each vessel, there would be 1,400 vessels employed, which would require 15,000 seamen and boys. I have made a summary; there are, seamen 15,000, pitmen and above ground people employed at the collieries 21,000, keelmen, coal boatmen, casters and trimmers 2,000, making the total number employed in what I call the Northern coal trade, 38,000. In London, whippers, lightermen and so forth, 5,000; factors, agents, &c. on the coal exchange, 2,500; 7,500 in all, in London. Making the grand total in the north country and London departments of the trade, 45,500. This does not, of course, include the persons employed at the outports in discharging the ships there. . . .

Has the price of wages with respect to the labouring colliers continued at the same rate as during the war?–No; there has been a small reduction.

Has the prices of provision continued the same as during the war?–They have fluctuated very much; at one time they were very low, now they are higher again.

Do you consider the reductions the colliers have submitted to, equal to the reduction of the prices of living which has taken place in the country?–I would answer by saying, that if they could have full employment their wages are ample: but there is not employment for them, 14s. a week is their lowest wages; but they could earn 5s. per day if they had work to enable them to do so. . . .

The Davy Lamp

Do you think that the particular accidents by explosions, which you have . . . described, have been much lessened by the introduction of Sir Humphrey Davy's safety lamp?–They have, I conceive; but on taking the average for 34 years, up to the present period, scarcely one half of which we have had the benefit of this lamp, the loss of life has been nearly about the same; but I attribute that to this cause, that we are working mines, from having the advantage of the safety lamp, which we could not have possibly worked without it, and of course they are in a more dangerous situation, and the risk is increased in a very great degree. If we had not had the Davy lamp, these mines could not now have been in existence at all; for the only substitute we had, and that was not a safe one, was what we called a steel mill, which was the only means of introducing light, except by the naked flame, (*producing the steel mill, and working it*). In daylight this appears to produce very little light, but in a coal pit I have frequently been obliged to write by this light, before the invention of the Davy lamp: but the defect of this light is, that it is not secure from explosion at a certain mixture. . . . They were completely superseded by the Davy lamp. This (*producing it*) is the Davy lamp of the simplest construction; it costs only about 5 or 6 shillings. A steel mill is very hard work; we were obliged to have two persons to relieve each other; and this was introduced in its room: . . . this introduced quite a new era in coal mining, as many collieries are now in existence, and old collieries have been reopened, producing the best coals, which must have lain dormant but for the introduction of the Davy lamp.

(d) THE LUDDITES

375. The declaration of the framework knitters, 1 Jan. 1812

(Public Record Office, Home Office, 42/119.)

The Luddite riots of 1811-1812 began in Nottinghamshire, where the hosiery workers objected, not to the use of new machinery but to certain trade practices by the employers. The Yorkshire riots (Nos. 376 and 377), on the other hand, were directed chiefly against the introduction of cloth-dressing machinery.

BY THE FRAMEWORK KNITTERS.

A Declaration.

Whereas by the charter granted by our late sovereign Lord Charles II by the Grace of God King of Great Britain France and Ireland, the framework knitters are empowered to break and destroy all frames and engines that fabricate articles in a fraudulent and deceitful manner and to destroy all framework knitters' goods whatsoever that are so made and whereas a number of deceitful unprincipled and intriguing persons did attain an Act to be passed in the 28th year of our present sovereign Lord George III whereby it was enacted that persons entering by force into any house shop or place to break or destroy frames should be adjudged guilty of felony and as we are fully convinced that such Act was obtained in the most fraudulent interested and electioneering manner and that the honourable the Parliament of Great Britain was deceived as to the motives and intentions of the persons who obtained such Act we therefore the framework knitters do hereby declare the aforesaid Act to be null and void to all intents and purposes whatsoever as by the passing of this Act villainous and imposing persons are enabled to make fraudulent and deceitful manufactures to the discredit and utter ruin of our trade. And whereas we declare that the aforementioned Charter is as much in force as though no such Act had been passed. . . . And we do hereby declare to all hosiers lace manufacturers and proprietors of frames that we will break and destroy all manner of frames whatsoever that make the following spurious articles and all frames whatsoever that do not pay the regular prices heretofore agreed to [by] the masters and workmen—All print net frames making single press and frames not working by the rack and rent and not paying the price regulated in 1810: warp frames working single yarn or two coarse hole—not working by the rack, not paying the rent and prices regulated in 1809—whereas all plain silk frames not making work according to the gage—frames not marking the work according to quality, whereas all frames of whatsoever description the workmen of whom are not paid in the current coin of the realm will invariably be destroyed. . . .

Given under my hand this first day of January 1812.
God protect the Trade.

Ned Lud's Office
Sherwood Forest.

376. Earl Fitzwilliam to Viscount Sidmouth, 25 July 1812

(Fitzwilliam MSS.)

Fitzwilliam, Lord Lieutenant of the West Riding, reports to the Home Secretary on the supposed disaffection of the people.

. . . Having yesterday had occasion to converse with different persons, I have the satisfaction of reporting that I am very confident the country is not in that alarming state it has been supposed to be. That there is combinations for mischievous purposes, there can be no doubt: most recent events corroborate that belief–the sweeping off *every* gun at Clifton proves a system of enquiry, and means of information: the manner in which the business was done, proves also a great degree of tactic in execution: but it goes no further than in the execution of robbery: it shews no symptom of preparation for resisting men in arms, military bodies–the very means they seem desirous of obtaining, that is *guns*, will never render them formidable against firelocks –moreover, the reports of nocturnal training and drilling, when one comes to close quarters on the subject, and to enquire for evidence of fact, dwindles down to nothing; they are the offspring of fear, quite imaginary, and mere invention.

I do not mean to say, that parties of Luddites have not been met travelling from place to place, and perhaps marshalled in some degree of order, but that there is no evidence whatever, that any one person has yet established the fact of their having been assembled and drilling in a military way–as far as negative evidence can go, I think, the contrary seems established.

Nevertheless combination indisputably exists, very formidable to property and persons: most probably entered into originally for the destruction of that species of property, machinery in manufacture, and afterwards directed against the persons of the proprietors of that species of property as one means of its destruction, through the medium of intimidation. This is a very serious evil, and one, to which we must direct all our attention, the best mode of meeting it I believe to be, by anti-combination, if I may so express myself i.e. by associations, as recommended by Mr. Ryder[1]–this system has not been sufficiently pursued: in great towns it has been, with complete effect, but the lesser ones have not felt the ability of establishing the system, and moreover have not always recognized the necessity–they don't give credit to the danger, till they feel the evil. It is in the contemplation of the Lieutenancy to go out by committees into the different districts, in the hopes of spiriting up the people to put themselves into this sort of defensive array–more can hardly be done.

I took the liberty of recommending to your Lordship the case of Mr. Cartwright, who three months ago defended his mills with such laudable resolution: it would be a very acceptable thing in this country, if this man was noticed by Government, in the way the letter I put into your Lordship's hand pointing out, or in any other, that can be found for him [*sic.*]: he is a man of ability, activity, and would be an useful servant to the public in many situations. His present circumstances are grievous to him: his property the object of daily destruction, his person the butt of assassination. He is anxious to remove from such a situation. What the danger of assassination is your

[1] See No. 310.

Lordship will readily collect from the readiness with which this abominable banditti fires on every occasion. Though no resistance was made to them at Clifton, though every inhabitant yielded instant obedience to the demand of his gun, they fired into several houses. Again a party of them passing lately late at night through a village, upon a man saying they were Luddites, instantly a ball was fired at his head–your Lordship has just now before you the sad case of Hinchliffe–his murder attempted most premeditatedly, for having presumed to mention an attempt to swear him in as a Luddite. Depositions having been made to the fact, and particulars sworn to, it is hoped by the Lieutenancy that Government will offer a reward for the apprehension of the parties, but one of the two originally present having run away before the pistol was fired, it is also hoped, a pardon will be offered to the accomplice.

377. Information of a Barnsley Weaver on the Luddites, 1812

(*Fitzwilliam MSS.*)

West Riding of Yorkshire: The Information of Thomas Broughton of Barnsley, Weaver, taken before...two of H.M. Justices of the Peace in and for the said Riding this 26th day of August 1812.

. . . That about the 12th or 13th of June last the informant went to the house of Richard Howell at the old engine near Barnsley, to ask for some money he owed him . . . Howell asked the informant if he could like to see a Luddite, because he could shew him one; the informant said he could not then, but he would call the next night. The night after, Howell called upon the informant, and had with him a paper on which the oath was written; Howell and the informant went out together, and the former requested the latter to take the oath; he read it over to him, and the informant repeated it, but said he would not kiss the Book upon it, as he had taken an oath of a contrary nature. Since that time John Eadon of Barnsley, a weaver, and Craven Cookson of the same place, weaver, applied to and prevailed with the informant to be upon the secret committee, and that a fortnight ago last Sunday the oath was administered to the informant, in a lane leading from Barnsley to Dodworth, by the said Craven Cookson, and John Eadon was also in company:–it was in the forenoon: –the form of the oath is set forth in the annexed paper marked A in the hand writing of the informant and by him signed. That at the time the oath was so administered by Cookson and Eadon to the informant, they explained to him that his duty as a secret committee man, would be to attend all meetings when warned, or called upon, to collect money subscribed by the Luddites to defray the expenses of the delegates and secret committee when required, and to go when sent to collect information and carry on correspondence with other committees. The committee with whom this informant acted were the said Eadon and Cookson and William Thompson and Stephen Ritchinman both of Barnsley weavers, who were appointed to act as a secret committee for Barnsley. The informant further saith that it is also the business of the secret committee to twist in new members. That there are about 200 persons twisted in, in Barnsley, among whom, the informant particularised John Baxter, Commercial Inn, James Brown, publican, George Watson, linen manufacturer, Henry Tyne, hatter, Richard and —— Bottom, gardener. That the informant knows a great many other Luddites by sight, but not by name. That the committee at Barnsley, do not admit Irishmen to be twisted in, for fear that they should betray the secret. The delegates (as the informant has been informed by the committee) from Leeds to Sheffield, and from Sheffield to Leeds, pass and repass weekly, but neither of those committees had any intercourse or correspondence with the Barnsley committee till about a week ago, when the informant opened a correspondence with Leeds for Barnsley, through the medium of Mr. Whittle, pattern maker at Leeds. That last Monday morning at Barnsley, he heard a person, whose name he does not know, but whom he understood to come from Sheffield, declare to Joseph Isaacs, that there were 8000 men nearly complete in arms, in and about Sheffield, and would be in a few days, and therefore they did not mind the soldiers–though they once thought the South Devon were good fellows, but now they thought them worse than the Huzzars. That since he has been upon the secret committee, the informant has been told by his fellow committee men, that delegates had been at Barnsley, from Manchester, and Stockport, (but he was not present), whose business it was, to collect numbers, and other information. That one Haigh now in York Castle for administering unlawful oaths, told the informant that there were 450 Luddites twisted in, at Holmfirth; the greater part of the neighbourhood of Huddersfield, and a great number at Halifax, and that they met there as Dissenters under the cloak of religion, and also 7,000 or 8,000 in Leeds. The informant saith that a very great number of Luddites are *local militia men*. That the Luddites have in view ultimately to overturn the system of government, by revolutionising the country. That certain delegates at Ashton under Lyne, on the 4th of August inst. told the informant that the first measure to be adopted in bringing about a revolution, would be to send parties to the different houses of the members of both Houses of Parliament, and destroy them, and then the people in London belonging to that Society, would seize upon the Government. That the committee at Barnsley, and the informant for himself, thinks, and believes, that in case a revolution should take place, Sir Francis Burdett and Major Cartwright would join them. That James Haigh of Dukinfield, near Ashton, told the informant that there were persons of property concerned in the disturbances who did not actively appear, but who wrote orders and had them put under the doors of delegates. That voluntary contributions are collected from those who are twisted in from 1d. per head, to 1/- a week; and that the informant has received from the committee at Barnsley 10s. 10d. for going journies. That the Luddites at Barnsley have no arms, but believe when a rupture takes place, that they can seize the arms of the military unawares, *viz.* before they have time to collect them. . . .

A. [The Luddite Oath.]
I A.B. of my own free will and accord do hereby promise, and swear that I will never reveal any of the names of any one of this secret committee, under the penalty of being sent out of this world by the first brother that may meet me, I furthermore do swear, that I will pursue with unceasing vengeance any traitor or traitors, should there any arise should he fly to the verge of ——. I furthermore do swear that I will be sober and faithful in all my dealings with all my brothers, and if ever I declare

them, my name to be blotted out from the list of society, and never to be remembered, but with contempt and abhorrence. So help me God to keep this my oath inviolate. Signed Thomas Broughton.

B. Sign.

You must raise your right hand over your right eye if there be another Luddite in company he will raise his left hand over his left eye–then you must raise the forefinger of your right hand to the right side of your mouth–the other will raise the little finger of his left hand to the left side of his mouth and will say What are you? The answer, Determined–he will say, What for? Your answer, Free Liberty–then he will converse with you and tell you anything he knows. . . .

(e) THE RESTRICTIONS ON THE EMIGRATION OF ARTISANS AND THE EXPORT OF MACHINERY

378. Resolutions of the Select Committee of the House of Commons on Artisans and Machinery, 21 May 1824

(Hansard's *Parliamentary Debates*, New Series, XI, 813–814.)

Joseph Hume, the chairman of the committee, had secured its appointment ostensibly to inquire into the laws which, in the interests of the British manufacturer, forbade the emigration of skilled artisans and the exportation of machinery. In fact, the ultimate purpose was to promote the repeal of the Combination laws. The committee's inquiry was managed by Hume and Francis Place, the author of its report, which consisted merely of a series of resolutions. Those referring to the Combination laws are in No. 488.

Artisans:–

1. That it appears, by the evidence before this Committee, that notwithstanding the laws enacted to prevent the seduction of artisans to go abroad, many able and intelligent artisans have gone abroad to reside, and to exercise their respective arts in foreign countries; and that it is extremely difficult, if not impossible, in this country, by any mode of executing the present laws, or by any new law, to prevent artisans who may be so determined, from going out of the country.

2. That although the penalties which the laws inflict on artisans who disobey them, are not distinctly understood by the workmen, yet an unfavourable opinion is generally entertained by them, of the partial and oppressive operation of these laws, as preventing them from taking their labour and art to the best market, whilst all other classes of the community are permitted to go abroad, and to take their capital with them, whenever they think proper.

3. That it appears also by evidence that many British artisans residing abroad have been prevented from returning home, from an erroneous opinion that they have, by going abroad, violated the laws of their country, and consequently incurred penalties under them.

4. That, in the opinion of this Committee, it is both unjust and impolitic to continue these laws; they therefore recommend their entire repeal, and that artisans may be at liberty to go abroad and to return home, whenever they may be so disposed in the same manner as other classes of the community now go and return.

Machinery.

That the Committee have examined evidence respecting the export of machinery, which will be found in the Appendix: but they are of opinion that further inquiry, and a more complete investigation should take place before this important subject can be satisfactorily decided on; and they therefore recommend that the consideration of this important question should be resumed in the next session of Parliament. That the Chairman be instructed to prepare Bills, to carry the objects of the above resolutions into effect, and to ask leave of the House to present the same.

379. Debate in the House of Commons on the exportation of machinery 6 Dec. 1826

(Hansard's *Parliamentary Debates*, New Series, XVI, 291–298.)

Mr. Hume . . . Every man was now allowed to export the produce of his industry to where he could find a purchaser, except the unfortunate maker of machines. . . . If the exportation of machinery were to be prohibited, artisans would export themselves to an extent to prove highly injurious to the country. The effect of the law, as it now stood, was to encourage the emigration of our most useful machinists. No apprehension could be entertained of foreigners being enabled to rival us in manufactures by obtaining our machinery, for it was in large works that required the use of machinery, in which our supplies of coal and iron, our canals and our large capital, gave us the advantage over foreign manufacturers. In works that required little combinations of capital, and only the application of small machines, foreigners might rival us. . . . The law, as it now stood, was so contrary to good policy that it could not be carried into effect; and it accordingly operated solely as a bounty upon the smuggling of machinery out of the kingdom. . . .

Mr. Huskisson [President of the Board of Trade] appealed to the hon. member whether a question of such vast importance could with propriety be discussed at a period when thousands of manufacturers were either out of employ, or but partially employed. He assured the hon. member that if a Bill were to be introduced which had for its object the abolition of every restriction upon the exportation of machinery, it would be productive of serious alarm in the manufacturing districts, and would give rise to the presentation of numerous petitions from all parts of the country to that House. . . . It had been generally agreed that some alteration in the law respecting the exportation of machinery should take place; and the question having been agitated some time ago, a regulation was made, giving to the Board of Trade a discretion as to the kinds of machinery which might or might not be exported. The discretion thus vested in the Board of Trade was of a most disagreeable and unpleasant nature. It was, moreover, liable to this objection, that in whatever way the Board of Trade decided, the party refused the right of exportation conceived himself injured and wrongly dealt by. Upon this ground alone he felt the necessity of establishing some fixed and settled principle of exportation and prohibition of all articles of machinery. He had himself endeavoured to lay down a rule by which the discretion vested in the Board of Trade should be regulated; and that principle was–that where machinery was of great bulk, and contained a great quantity of the raw material, no objection should be made to exportation, as he considered that no injury could be done to the country by it. But where machinery was of modern construction, and depended mainly upon the ingenuity and excellence of the mechanism, and where the raw material used was trifling, then the exportation of such machinery was prohibited. It was a notorious fact that many manufacturing establishments were at this moment standing still, under the expectation of obtaining machinery from this country. Under such circumstances then, and particularly in the present state of the manufacturing interests, he implored the hon. member not to agitate the question at this period. . . .

(f) COMMUNICATIONS

(a) *Road Transport*

380. Mileage of turnpike roads in Great Britain, 1829

(G. R. Porter, *The Progress of the Nation* (1851), p. 292.)

The figures are taken from official returns.

ENGLAND.

	Miles.		Miles.		Miles.
Bedfordshire	238	Herefordshire	553	Rutlandshire	18
Berkshire	319	Hertfordshire	170	Shropshire	988
Buckinghamshire	165	Huntingdonshire	146	Somersetshire	746
Cambridgeshire	278	Kent	586	Staffordshire	630
Cheshire	349	Lancashire	631	Suffolk	279
Cornwall	318	Leicestershire	445	Surrey	281
Cumberland	215	Lincolnshire	538	Sussex	623
Derbyshire	574	Middlesex	158	Warwickshire	477
Devonshire	782	Monmouthshire	315	Westmorland	284
Dorsetshire	347	Norfolk	271	Wiltshire	768
Durham	359	Northamptonshire	358	Worcestershire	565
Essex	249	Northumberland	479	Yorkshire	1,448
Gloucestershire	840	Nottinghamshire	302		
Hampshire	810	Oxfordshire	342	Total	18,244

WALES.

	Miles.		Miles.		Miles.
Anglesea	25	Denbighshire	165	Pembrokeshire	173
Brecknockshire	169	Flintshire	85	Radnorshire	250
Cardiganshire	250	Glamorganshire	355		
Carmarthenshire	319	Merionethshire	261	Total	2,631
Carnarvonshire	129	Montgomeryshire	450		

SCOTLAND.

	Miles.		Miles.		Miles.
Aberdeenshire	232	Forfarshire	131	Renfrewshire	195
Ayrshire	486	Haddingtonshire	120	Roxburghshire	193
Banffshire	123	Kincardineshire	96	Selkirkshire	23
Berwickshire	126	Kirkcudbright	216	Stirlingshire	158
Clackmannanshire	71	Lanarkshire	374	Wigtonshire	51
Dumbartonshire	57	Linlithgowshire	117		
Dumfriesshire	251	Nairnshire	9	Total	3,666
Edinburghshire	273	Peeblesshire	113		
Elginshire	26	Perthshire	225		

381. Macadam's "Remarks on the present System of Road Making"

(Fourth edition (London, 1821), pp. 10–11, 46–54.)

John Loudon Macadam (1756–1836) developed his theories on road building at Falmouth and after 1815 as Surveyor-General of the Bristol Roads. His *Present System of Road Making*, published in 1820, ran to five editions by 1822 and was his most influential work. In 1827 he became General Surveyor of Roads, and 'macadamized' roads rapidly became common throughout the country, so making possible the era of the 'flying coaches' of the twenties and thirties.

Flint makes an excellent road if due attention be paid to the size; but from want of that attention, many of the flint roads are rough, loose and expensive.

Limestone, when properly prepared and applied, makes a smooth, solid road, and becomes consolidated sooner than any other material; but from its nature is not the most lasting.

Whinstone is the most durable of all materials, and whenever it is well and judiciously applied, the roads are comparatively good and cheap.

The pebbles of Shropshire and Staffordshire are of a hard substance, and only require a prudent application to be made good road materials.

On the other hand the Scottish roads, made of the very best materials, which are abundant and cheap in every part of that country, are the most loose, rough and expensive roads in the United Kingdom, owing to the unskilful use of the material.

The *formation* of roads is defective in most parts of the country; in particular the roads round London are made high in the middle, in the form of a roof, by which means a carriage goes upon a dangerous slope, unless kept on the very centre of the road.

These roads are repaired by throwing a large quantity of unprepared gravel in the middle, and trusting that, by its never consolidating, it will in due time move towards the sides.

When a road has been originally well made, it will be easily repaired. Such a road can never become rough or loose, though it will gradually wear thin and weak, in proportion to the use to which it is exposed; the amendment will then be made by the addition of a quantity of materials prepared as at first. As there will be no expense on such road, between the first making and each subsequent repair, except the necessary attention to the waterways, and to accidental injuries, the funds will be no longer burdened with the unceasing expenditure at present experienced from continual efforts at repairing, without amendment of the roads.

. . . It is of great consequence to consider of the means of constructing the roads of the kingdom in such a manner as shall prevent their being in future affected by any change of weather or season.

The roads can never be rendered thus perfectly secure until the following principles be fully understood, admitted and acted upon: namely, that it is the native soil which really supports the weight of traffic: that while it is preserved in a dry state, it will carry any weight without sinking, and that it does in fact carry the road and the carriages also; that this native soil must previously be made quite dry, and a covering impenetrable to rain must then be placed over it, to preserve it in that dry state; that the thickness of a road should only be regulated by the quantity of material necessary to form such impervious covering, and never by any reference to its *own* power of carrying weight.

The erroneous opinion so long acted upon and so tenaciously adhered to, that by placing a large quantity of stone under the roads, a remedy will be found for the sinking into wet clay, or other soft soils, or in other words, that a road may be made sufficiently strong, *artificially*, to carry heavy carriages, though the sub-soil be in a wet state, and by such means to avert the inconveniences of the natural soil receiving water from rain or other causes, has produced most of the defects of the roads of Great Britain. . . .

It is well known to every skilful and observant road-maker, that if strata of stone of various sizes be placed as a road, the largest stones will constantly work up by the shaking and pressure of the traffic, and that the only mode of keeping the stones of a road from motion, is to use materials of a uniform size from the bottom. In roads made upon large stones as a foundation, the perpetual motion, or change of the position of the materials, keeps open many apertures through which the water passes. . . .

The practice common in England, and universal in Scotland on the formation of a new road is to dig a trench below the surface of the ground adjoining, and in this trench to deposit a quantity of large stones; after this, a second quantity of stone, broken smaller, generally to about seven or eight pounds weight. . . . That which is properly called the road, is then placed on the bottoming, by putting large quantities of broken stone or gravel, generally a foot or eighteen inches thick, at once upon it.

Were the materials of which the road itself is composed, properly selected, prepared and laid, some of the inconveniences of this system might be avoided; but in the careless way in which this service is generally performed, the road is as open as a sieve to receive water; which penetrates through the whole mass, is received and retained in the trench, whence the road is liable to give way in all changes of weather.

The first operation in making a road should be the reverse of digging a trench. The road should not be sunk below, but rather raised above the ordinary level of the adjacent ground; care should at any rate be taken that there be a sufficient fall to take off the water, so that it should always be some inches below the level of the ground upon which the road is intended to be placed: this must be done, either by making drains to lower ground, or if that be not practicable, from the nature of the country, then the soil upon which the road is proposed to be laid must be raised by addition, so as to be some inches above the level of the water.

Having secured the soil from *under* water, the road-maker is next to secure it from rain water, by a solid road, made of clean, dry stone, or flint, so selected, prepared, and laid, as to be perfectly impervious to water: and this cannot be effected, unless the greatest care be taken, that no earth, clay, chalk or other matter that will hold or conduct water, be mixed with the broken stone, which must be so prepared and laid as to unite by its own angles into a firm, compact, impenetrable body.

The thickness of such road is immaterial, as to its strength for carrying weight; this object is already obtained by providing a dry surface, over which the road is to be placed as a covering or roof, to preserve it in that state: experience having shown that if water passes through a road and fill the native soil, the road, whatever may be its thickness, loses its support and goes to pieces. . . .

Improvement of roads, upon the principle I have endeavoured to explain, has been rapidly extended during the last four years. It has been carried into effect, on various roads, and with every variety of material, in seventeen different counties. These roads being so constructed as to exclude water, consequently none of them broke up during the late severe winter; there was no interruption to travelling, nor any additional expense by the Post Office in conveying the mails over them to the extent of upwards of one thousand miles of road. . . .

The unnecessary expense attending the making of new roads in the manner hitherto practised, is one great cause of the present heavy debt upon the road trusts of the kingdom. The principal part of the large sums originally borrowed, have been sunk in the useless, and in my opinion, mischievous preparation of a foundation. This debt presses heavily on the funds of all the roads in England, and in many cases absorbs almost their whole revenue in payment of interest. In Scotland this pressure is still more heavily felt: indeed it is not of uncommon occurrence in that country for creditors to lose both principal and interest of their loans to roads. . . .

(b) *Canals*

382. Account of the Inland Navigation to and from Liverpool, 1786–1788

(J. Aikin, *A Description of the Country from thirty to forty miles round Manchester* (1795), p. 370.)

On the Lancashire end of the Leeds canal there are employed between Liverpool and Wigan 89 boats, of 35 to 40 tons burthen each; which brought to Liverpool

	in the years	1786	1787	1788
Coals	tons	91,249	98,248	109,202
Flags, slates and millstones	do.	3,994	2,561	3,613
Merchandize	do.	347	393	405
Oak timber	feet	17,403	17,986	13,589

Took from thence,	in the years	1786	1787	1788
Merchandize	tons	3,836	4,610	4,257
Limestone and bricks	do.	2,245	2,064	1,429
Lime and manure	do.	10,213	11,129	12,224
Pine timber	feet	160,766	193,706	153,006

Between Liverpool and the river Douglas 36 boats are employed, which brought				
Coals	tons	16,724	22,592	20,706
and took back				
Limestone	do.	4,589	6,164	5,921

The tonnage of the vessels employed on the Sankey canal, the business of which is divided between Liverpool, Northwich, and Warrington, amounted to	tons	74,289	98,356	115,828

Between Liverpool on the river Mersey, and Northwich and Winsford on the Weaver, 110 vessels are employed in carrying timber, salt, coals, and merchandize to the amount of 164,000 tons annually.

Between Liverpool and Manchester there are employed, on the old navigation, 25 boats of 55 tons each, which make generally 3 trips every 2 Spring tides; or, upon an average, allowing for delays from bad weathers, 36 trips each in a year.

There are also on the Duke of Bridgewater's canal, which communicates with the Staffordshire canal, 42 boats employed of 50 tons each, which make on an average 3 trips to Liverpool every 14 days: 10 boats will be added to this part of the navigation in the summer.

383. Canal transport in Nottinghamshire

(R. Lowe, *General View of the Agriculture of the county of Nottingham* (1794), pp. 51–52.)

There is a great trade carried on in this county by water, by means of the river Trent, and the different canals. By the Trent are carried downwards, lead, copper, coals, and salt, from Cheshire, cheese, Staffordshire ware, corn, &c.; upwards, Raff or Norway timber, hemp, flax, iron, groceries, malt, corn, flints from Northfleet, near Gravesend, for the Staffordshire potteries.

By the canal from Chesterfield–to Worksop and Retford, and to the Trent at Stockwith–downwards, coal, lead, sleety stone, lime and lime-stone, chirt-stone, for the glass manufactories, coarse earthen ware, cast metal goods and pig metal, oak timber and bark, and sail cloth. Upwards, Fir timber and deals, grain, malt and flour, groceries, bar iron, and Cumberland ore, wines, spirits, and porter, hemp and flax, cotton-wool and yarn, Westmorland slate, and various sorts of small package. Upwards and downwards, bricks, tiles, hops, and candlewicks: other articles, however, bear but a small proportion to the coal, downwards; and the corn, groceries, foreign timber, and iron, upwards. . . .

384. Price of Canal Stock

(*The Scotsman*, 14 Jan. 1824)

The table is a complete copy of Wetenhall's list of the number of shares in the principal canal, bridge, and road companies in England, the dividend on each share, and its selling price.

No. of Shares.	Shares of	Annual div.			CANALS.	Price per Share.	
	£	£	s.	d.		£	s.
221	—	—			Aberdare, ...	25	0
350	100	—			Andover, ...	5	0
1482	113	—			Ashby-de-la-Zouch, . .	17	0
1766¼	98	5	0	0	Ashton and Oldham, . .	135	0
720	160	10	0	0	Barnsley, . . .	212	0
1260	100	—			Basingstoke, ...	5	5
£50,000	10	—			Do. Bonds, ...	40 pr cet	
4000	17	12	10	0	Birmingham, ...	315	0
477	250	5	0	0	Bolton and Bury, . . .	112	0
958	150	5	0	0	Brecknock and Abergavny, .	100	0
1600	50	6	0	0	Carlisle, ...	—	
100	—	5	0	0	Chelmer and Blackwater, .	93	0
1500	100	8	0	0	Chesterfield, ...	110	0
500	100	44	0	0	Coventry, ...	1100	0
1851	50	—			Crinan, ...	3	3
1545	100	—			Croydon, ...	3	3
600	110	6	0	0	Derby, ...	140	0
2060¾	100	3	0	0	Dudley, ...	60	0
3575¾	133	3	0	0	Ellesmere and Chester, . .	63	0
231	—	58	0	0	Erewash, ...	1000	0
	173	8	0	0	Glamorganshire, . . .	264	0
11,800	100	10	0	0	Grand Junction . . .	265	0
1500	100	—			Grand Surrey	49	0
£50,000	100	5	0	0	Do. Loan	103	0
2259½	100	—			Grand Union	18	0
3096	79	—			Grand Western . . .	5	0
749	150	8	0	0	Grantham	160	0
6238	—	—			Huddersfield . . .	21	0
25,322	40	0	17	0	Kennet and Avon . . .	22	0
11,699½	47	1	0	0	Lancaster	27	5
2879¾	100	12	0	0	Leeds & Liverpool . . .	380	0
18¾	80	9	12	0	Do. (New)	290	0
545	140	14	0	0	Leicester	325	0
1802	—	4	0	0	Do. & Northam. Union .	79	0
70	143	170	0	0	Loughborough . . .	4000	0
250	100	11	0	0	Melton Mowbray . . .	230	0
500	—	35	0	0	Mersey and Irwell . . .	800	0
2409	100	8	10	0	Monmouthshire . . .	175	0
£43,526	100	—			Do. Debentures . . .	100	0
700	100	—			Montgomeryshire . . .	72	0
247	107	13	0	0	Neath	330	0
500	150	12	0	0	Nottingham	240	0
522	100	3	0	0	Oakham	44	0

No. of Shares	Shares of	Annual div.				Price per Share	
	£	£	s.	d.		£	s.
1770	100	32	0	0	Oxford	750	0
2400	78	4	0	0	Peak Forest	88	0
2520	50	—			Portsmouth & Arundel . .	24	0
12,294	40	—			Regent's	40	0
5631	85	3	0	0	Rochdale	92	0
500	125	9	0	0	Shrewsbury	170	0
500	100	7	0	0	Shropshire	130	0
—	—				Sleaford	5	0
771	100	9	0	0	Somerset Coal . . .	135	0
700	—	40	0	0	Staff. & Worcestershire . .	800	0
300	145	10	10	0	Stourbridge	210	0
3647	—	—			Stratford on Avon . .	20	0
533	—	10	0	0	Swansea	190	0
350	100	—			Tavistock	150	0
2670	—	—			Thames and Medway . .	22	0
	100	—			Thames & Severn . . .	15	0
[sic]	1600	0	10	0	Ditto (new)	27	0
1300	—	75	0	0	Trent & Mersey or G. T. .	2150	0
1000 ⎱ 1000½ ⎰	—	11	0	0	Warwick & Birming. . .	240	0
980	—	10	10	0	Warwick & Napton . .	215	0
905	110	1	0	0	Wey and Arun . . .	—	
14,200	—	—			Wilts and Berks . . .	6	2
126	105	5	0	0	Wisbeach	50	0
6000	—	—			Worcester & Birming. . .	86	0
800	—	6	0	0	Wyrley & Essington . .	140	0
					BRIDGES.		
7355	100	—			Southwark	18	0
3000	100	7½ pr ct.			Southwark, new . . .	55	0
3000	100	1	0	0	Vauxhall (all paid) . . .	30	0
£78,578	100	5	0	0	Do. Bonds	103	0
5000	100	—			Waterloo . . . paid	5	0
5000	60	8	0	0	Do. old Ann. . . paid	32	0
5000	40	7	0	0	Do. new do. . . paid	29	0
					DOCKS.		
2209	147	1	9	4	Bristol	41	0
2600 & ⎱ 1065½ ⎰	100	0	10	0	Commercial	80	0
—	—				Ditto Bonds	108	0
£450,000	—	8	0	0	East-India	145	0
£16,000	100	—			East Country	26	0
£3,114,000	—	4	10	0	London	118¼	0
£1,200,000	—	10	0	0	West-India	220	0
					ROADS.		
1066	50	1	0	0	Archway and Kentish Town,	—	
300	100	2	10	0	Barking, ...	11	0
1000	100	5	0	0	Commercial, ...	50	0
492	100	1	19	0	Dover-street, 70 pd. . .	39	0
2393	50	—			Highgate Archway, . .	—	

No. of Shares	Shares of	Annual div.		Price per Share
	£	£ s. d.	IRON RAILWAYS.	£ s.
1000	65	1 0 0	Croydon, Merstham, . .	13 0
553	50	2 10 0	Monmouth, ...	44 0
3762	50	1 12 0	Severn and Wye, . . .	33 0
640	70	—	Stockton and Darlington, .	10 0
			WATER-WORKS.	
3800	100	5 0 0	East London, ...	124 0
4500	50	2 10 0	Grand Junction, . . .	64 10
1945	100	1 10 0	Kent, ...	36 0
6486	100	—	Manchester and Salford, .	22 23 [sic]
1500	50	—	Ports. and Farlington, . .	4 0
300	50	1 10 0	Do. New, ...	24 0
860	50	—	Portsea Island, ...	5 0
800	100	—	South London, . . .	40 0
7540	100	2 10 0	West Middlesex, . . .	68 10

(c) Railways

385. Railway Acts passed by Parliament, 1801–1832

(G. R. Porter, *The Progress of the Nation*, II (1838), pp. 63–64.)

Most of these railways were designed for horse-drawn traffic, sometimes with fixed steam engines to supplement horse traction on gradients. The most notable of those designed for steam locomotive traction were the Stockton and Darlington, the Liverpool and Manchester, and the Leeds and Selby lines.

Date of Act.	Name of Railway.	Places between which it passes.	Length in Miles.	Cost of Construction.
				£.
1801	Surrey	Wandsworth and Croydon . .	9	60,000
1802	Carmarthenshire . .	Llanelly and Llanfihangel, Aber-bythick	16	35,000
	Sirhowey	Newport and Sirhowey Furnaces (Monmouthshire) . . .	11	45,000
1803	Croydon, Merstham, and Godstone . . .	Croydon and Reigate—a branch to Godstone	15¾	90,000
1804	Oystermouth . . .	Swansea and Oystermouth—branch to Morriston . . .	6	12,000
1808	Kilmarnock . . .	Kilmarnock and Troon . .	9¾	40,000
1809	Forest of Dean . . .	Newnham and Churchway Engine	7½	125,000
	Severn and Wye . .	Lidbrook and Newern, and branches	26	110,000
1810	Monmouth	Howler, Slade, and Monmouth .	..	22,000
1811	Berwick and Kelso . .	Spittal and Kelso		
	Hay	Brecon and Parton Cross . .	24	50,000
	Llanfihangel . . .	Abergavenny and Llanfihangel Crucorney	6½	20,000

Date of Act.	Name of Railway.	Places between which it passes.	Length in Miles.	Cost of Construction.
				£.
1812	Grosmont	Llanfihangel Crucorney and Llangua Bridge	7	13,000
	Penrhynmaur . . .	Penrhynmaur Coalworks and Llanbedgroch	7	10,000
1814	Mamhilad	Mamhilad and Usk Bridge . .	5	6,000
1815	Gloucester & Cheltenham	Gloucester and Cheltenham .	9	50,000
1817	Mansfield and Pinxton .	Mansfield and Alfreton . .	8¼	32,800
1818	Kington	Parton Cross and Kington . .	14	23,000
1819	Plymouth and Dartmoor .	Plymouth and Lydford . .	30	35,000
1821	Stratford and Moreton .	Stratford-upon-Avon and Moreton-in-Marsh	18½	50,000
1823	Stockton and Darlington .	Stockton and Witton Park Colliery (thro' Darlington) . .	40	250,000
1824	Redruth and Chaswater .	Redruth and Point Quay, and branches	14½	22,500
	Monkland & Kirkintilloch	Palace Craig & Kirkintilloch .	10¾	25,000
1825	Rumney	Abertyswg and Sirhowey Railway	21¾	47,100
	West Lothian . . .	Ryall and Shotts	23	40,700
	Cromford and High Peak	Cromford and Whaley Bridge .	34	164,000
	Nanttle	Nanttle Pool and Caernarvon .	..	20,000
	Portland	Portland Stone Quarries and Portland Castle	2	5,000
	Duffryn Llynvi . . .	Llangoneyd and Perth Cawl .	16¾	60,000
1826	Ballochney . . .	Airdrie and Ballochney . .	5¾	18,425
	Dulais	Aber Dulais and Cwm Dulais .	8¾	10,000
	Dundee and Newtyle .	Dundee and Newtyle . . .	11	50,000
	Edinburgh and Dalkeith .	Edinburgh and Newbattle Abbey	17¼	125,000
	Garnkirk and Glasgow .	Gartsberrie Bridge & Glasgow .	8¼	40,000
	Heck and Wentbridge .	Heckbridge and Wentbridge .	7½	18,900
	Liverpool & Manchester .	Liverpool and Manchester . .	31	1,195,156
1827	Canterbury & Whitstable.	Canterbury and Whitstable .	6¼	47,000
	Johnstone and Ardrossan .	Johnstone and Ardrossan . .	22½	95,600
1828	Bristol & Gloucestershire .	Bristol and Coalpit Heath . .	9	45,000
	Bolton and Leigh . .	Bolton and Liverpool and Manchester Railway . . .	9	69,000
	Bridgend	Bridgend and Cefn Gribbwr .	4½	6,000
	Llanelly	. . . . .	..	..
	Clarence	Samphire Beacon and Sim Pasture, and branches . . .	45½	200,000
1829	Warrington and Newton	Warrington and Newton, on Liverpool and Manchester Railway	6¼	53,000
	Wishaw and Coltness .	Cambusnethan Parish and Old Monkland	..	60,000
1830	Leeds and Selby. .	Leeds and Selby . . .	20	210,000
	Leicester & Swannington .	Leicester and Swannington . .	15¾	90,000
1831	Dublin and Kingstown .	Dublin and Kingstown . .	5⅔	237,000

386. Prospectus of the Liverpool and Manchester Railroad Company, 1824

(T. Baines, *History of . . . Liverpool* (1852), pp. 601–603.)

The line was opened to traffic in 1830. The route originally proposed, through Bootle, Croxteth, Knowsley, Leigh and Salford, had to be abandoned owing to the opposition of Lords Sefton and Derby and other neighbouring landowners, and the line was diverted via Rainhill and carried by viaduct across the Sankey valley. The expenses thus incurred for bridges, tunnels and cuttings nearly doubled the estimated cost of £400,000, but the income to the promoters also greatly exceeded their calculations and the company quickly made a handsome profit.

LIVERPOOL AND MANCHESTER RAILROAD COMPANY

PROSPECTUS

The Committee of the Liverpool and Manchester Railroad Company think it right to state, concisely, the grounds upon which they rest their claims to public encouragement and support.

The importance, to a commercial state, of a safe and cheap mode of transit for merchandise, from one part of the country to another, will be readily acknowledged. This was the plea, upon the first introduction of canals: it was for the public advantage; and although the new mode of conveyance interfered with existing and inferior modes, and was opposed to the feelings and prejudices of landholders, the great principle of the public good prevailed, and experience has justified the decision.

It is upon the same principle that railroads are now proposed to be established; as a means of conveyance manifestly superior to existing modes: possessing, moreover, this recommendation, in addition to what could have been claimed in favour of canals, namely, that the railroad scheme holds out to the public not only a cheaper, but far more expeditious conveyance than any yet established. . . .

In deciding upon the proposed route, the committee have been anxious, at considerable inconvenience and expense, to select a line which may not only be eligible, . . . but may be as little objectionable as possible, with reference to individual and local interest.

The ground has been surveyed by eminent engineers, and the estimated expense of a railroad, upon the most improved construction, including the charge for locomotive engines to be employed on the line, and other contingencies, is £400,000, –which sum it is proposed to raise in 4,000 shares of £100 each.

The total quantity of merchandise passing between Liverpool and Manchester is estimated, by the lowest computation, at 1,000 tons per day. The bulk of this merchandise is transported either by the Duke of Bridgewater's Canal, or the 'Mersey and Irwell Navigation'. By both of these conveyances goods must pass up the river Mersey, a distance of 16 or 18 miles, subject to serious delays from contrary winds, and not unfrequently, to actual loss or damage from tempestuous weather. The average length of passage, by these conveyances, including the customary detention on the wharfs, may be taken at 36 hours. . . . The average charge upon merchandise for the last 14 years has been about 15s. per ton.

By the projected railroad, the transit of merchandise between Liverpool and Manchester will be effected in four or five hours, and the charge to the merchant will be reduced at least one-third. Here, then, will be accomplished an immense pecuniary saving to the public, over and above what is perhaps still more important, the *economy of time*. . . . It will afford a stimulus to the productive industry of the country; it will give a new impulse to the powers of accumulation, the value and importance of which can be fully understood only by those who are aware how seriously commerce may be impeded by petty restrictions, and how commercial enterprise is encouraged and promoted by an adherence to the principles of fair competition and free trade.

The committee are aware that it will not immediately be understood by the public how the proprietors of a railroad, requiring an invested capital of £400,000 can afford to carry goods at so great a reduction upon the charge of the present water companies. . . . It is not that the water companies have not been able to carry goods on more reasonable terms, but that, strong in the enjoyment of their monopoly, they have not thought proper to do so. . . . IT IS COMPETITION THAT IS WANTED. . . .

But it is not altogether on account of the exorbitant charges of the water-carriers that a railroad is desirable. The present canal establishments are inadequate to . . . the regular and punctual conveyance of goods at all periods and seasons. In summer time there is frequently a deficiency of water, obliging boats to go only half-loaded . . . while, in winter, they are sometimes locked up with frosts, for weeks together. . . . There is still another ground of objection to the present system of carriage by canals, namely, the pilferage, an evil for which there is seldom adequate redress . . . whereas, a conveyance by railway, effected in a few hours, and where every delay must be accounted for, may be expected to possess much of the publicity and consequent safety of the king's highways.

In addition to the transport of goods between Liverpool and Manchester, an important branch of revenue may be expected to result to the proprietors of the projected road, from the conveyance of coals from the rich mines in the vicinity of St. Helens. . . . These coals at present pass along the Sankey Canal, and down the Mersey to Liverpool, a distance of about 30 miles. By the railway the distance will be shortened one-half, and the charge for transit very materially reduced.

Amongst the widely-diffused benefits to be expected from the proposed railroad, must especially be enumerated, no inconsiderable advancement in the commercial prosperity of Ireland. The latent energies of that country, her capabilities as a manufacturing power, will be developed by being brought into easy contact and communication with the manufacturing districts of this kingdom; while every article of her agricultural industry will experience an increased demand, from the cheapness and facility with which it will be introduced into the populous counties of Lancaster and York. . . .

In the present state of trade and of commercial enterprise, dispatch is no less essential than economy. Merchandise is frequently brought across the Atlantic from New York to Liverpool in 21 days; while, owing to the various causes of delay above enumerated, goods have in some instances been longer on their passage from Liverpool to Manchester. . . .

The immediate and prominent advantages to be anticipated from the proposed railroad are, increased facilities to the general operations of commerce, arising out of that punctuality and dispatch which will attend the transit of merchandise between

Liverpool and Manchester, as well as an immense pecuniary saving to the trading community. But the inhabitants at large of these populous towns will reap their full share of direct and immediate benefit. Coals will be brought to market in greater plenty, and at a reduced price; and farming produce, of various kinds, will find its way from greater distances, and at more reasonable rates. To the landholders, also, in the vicinity of the line, the railroad offers important advantages in extensive markets for their mineral and agricultural produce, as well as in a facility of obtaining lime and manure at a cheap rate in return. Moreover, as a cheap and expeditious means of conveyance for travellers, the railway holds out the fair prospect of a public accommodation, the magnitude and importance of which cannot be immediately ascertained.

The committee do not think it necessary to dwell upon probable and contingent sources of revenue to the proprietors, and of benefit to the community; but it is impossible entirely to overlook the tendency of increased economy and dispatch to extend the commercial intercourse, not only upon the immediate line of road, but diverging in ramifications to the north and the south, and especially towards the rich and populous town of Bolton; a short branch line being sufficient to bring that extensive manufacturing district into rapid and direct communication with this port. . . .

Charles Lawrence, Chairman.

Liverpool, 29th October, 1824.

387. Thomas Creevey to Miss Ord, 14 Nov. 1829

(The Creevey Papers, ed. Sir Herbert Maxwell, II, pp. 203–204.)

Thomas Creevey (1768–1838), the Whig diarist and politician. His 'lark' took place on a section of the Liverpool–Manchester line, which was not opened to traffic until September 1830.

. . . Today we have had a *lark* of a very high order. Lady Wilton sent over yesterday from Knowsley to say that the loco motive machine was to be upon the railway at such a place at 12 o'clock for the Knowsley party to ride in if they liked, and inviting this house to be of the party. So of course we were at our post in 3 carriages and some horsemen at the hour appointed. I had the satisfaction, for I can't call it *pleasure*, of taking a trip of five miles in it, which we did in just a quarter of an hour–that is, 20 miles an hour. As accuracy upon this subject was my great object, I held my watch in my hand at starting, and all the time; and as it has a second hand, I knew I could not be deceived; and so it turned out there was not the difference of a second between the coachee or conductor and myself. But observe, during these five miles, the machine was occasionally made to put itself out or *go it*; and then we went at the rate of 23 miles an hour, and just with the same ease as to motion or absence of friction as the other reduced pace. But the quickest motion is to me *frightful*: it is really flying, and it is impossible to divest yourself of the notion of instant death to all upon the least accident happening. It gave me a headache which has not left me yet. [Lord] Sefton is convinced that some damnable thing must come of it; but he and I seem more struck with such apprehension than others. . . . The smoke is very inconsiderable indeed, but sparks of fire are abroad in some quantity: one burnt Miss de Ros's cheek, another a hole in Lady Maria's silk pelisse, and a third a hole in some one else's gown. Altogether I am extremely glad indeed to have seen this miracle, and to have travelled in it. Had I thought worse of it than I do, I should have had the curiosity to try it; but, having done so, I am quite satisfied with my *first* achievement being my *last*.

387A. The *Quarterly Review* on the projected Liverpool and Manchester Railway, March 1825

. . . As to those persons who speculate on making railways general throughout the kingdom, and superseding all the canals, all the waggons, mail and stage-coaches, post-chaises, and, in short, every other mode of conveyance by land and by water, we deem them and their visionary schemes unworthy of notice. . . . The gross exaggerations of the powers of the locomotive steam-engine, or, to speak in plain English, the *steam-carriage*, may delude for a time, but must end in the mortification of those concerned. . . . We find a countryman of Mr. Telford writing thus: 'We shall be carried at the rate of 400 miles a day, with all the ease we now enjoy in a steam-boat, but without the annoyance of sea-sickness, or the danger of being burned or drowned.' It is certainly some consolation to those who are to be whirled at the rate of 18 or 20 miles an hour, by means of a high pressure engine, to be told that they are in no danger of being seasick while on shore; that they are not to be scalded to death nor drowned by the bursting of the boiler; and that they need not mind being shot by the scattered fragments or dashed in pieces by the flying off, or the breaking of a wheel. But with all these assurances we should as soon expect the people of Woolwich to suffer themselves to be fired off upon one of Congreve's *ricochet* rockets as trust themselves to the mercy of such a machine, going at such a rate. . . . [pp. 361–362.]

C. OVERSEAS TRADE

(a) STATISTICS

388A. Foreign and colonial trade of the United Kingdom, 1801–1832

(G. R. Porter, *The Progress of the Nation*, II (1838), p. 98.)

Years.	OFFICIAL VALUE.			Real or declared Value of British and Irish Produce and Manufactures exported.
	Imports of Foreign and Colonial Merchandise.	Exports of Foreign and Colonial Merchandise.	Exports of British and Irish Produce and Manufactures.	
	£.	£.	£.	£.
1801	31,786,262	10,336,966	24,927,684	39,730,659
1802	29,826,210	12,677,431	25,632,549	45,102,330
1803	26,622,696	8,032,643	20,467,531	36,127,787
1804	27,819,552	8,938,741	22,687,309	37,135,746
1805	28,561,270	7,643,120	23,376,941	38,077,144
1806	26,899,658	7,717,555	25,861,879	40,874,983
1807	26,734,425	7,624,312	23,391,214	37,245,877
1808	26,795,540	5,776,775	24,611,215	37,275,102
1809	31,750,557	12,750,358	33,542,274	47,371,393
1810	39,301,612	9,357,435	34,061,901	48,438,680
1811	26,510,186	6,117,720	22,681,400	32,890,712
1812	26,163,431	9,533,065	29,508,508	41,716,964
1813	Records destroyed by fire.			
1814	33,755,264	19,365,981	34,207,253	45,494,219
1815	32,987,396	15,748,554	42,875,996	51,603,028
1816	27,431,604	13,480,780	35,717,070	41,657,873
1817	30,834,299	10,292,684	40,111,427	41,761,132
1818	36,885,182	10,859,817	42,700,521	46,603,249
1819	30,776,810	9,904,813	33,534,176	35,208,321
1820	32,438,650	10,555,912	38,395,625	36,424,652
1821	30,792,760	10,629,689	40,831,744	36,659,630
1822	30,500,094	9,227,589	44,236,533	36,968,964
1823	35,798,707	8,603,904	43,804,372	35,458,048
1824	37,552,935	10,204,785	48,735,551	38,396,300
1825	44,137,482	9,169,494	47,166,020	38,877,388
1826	37,686,113	10,076,286	40,965,735	31,536,723
1827	44,887,774	9,830,728	52,219,280	37,181,335
1828	45,028,805	9,946,545	52,797,455	36,812,756
1829	43,981,317	10,622,402	56,213,041	35,842,623
1830	46,245,241	8,550,437	61,140,864	38,271,597
1831	49,713,889	10,745,071	60,683,933	37,164,372
1832	44,586,741	11,044,869	65,026,702	36,450,594

388B. Distribution of exports from the United Kingdom, 1805–1811 and 1814–1832 (declared values)

(Porter, II (1838), p. 102.)

Years.	Northern Europe.	Southern Europe.	Africa.	Asia.	Un. States of America.	Brit. N. Am. Colonies & W. Indies.	Foreign West Indies.	Central and Sn. America (incl. Brazil.)	America, excl. of the Un. States.	Total.
	£	£	£	£	£	£	£	£	£	£
1805	13,625,676		756,060	2,904,584	11,011,409				7,771,418	36,069,147
1806	11,363,635		1,163,744	2,937,895	12,389,488				10,877,968	38,732,730
1807	9,002,237		765,468	3,359,226	11,846,513				10,439,423	35,412,867
1808	9,016,033		633,125	3,524,823	5,241,739				16,591,871	35,007,591
1809	15,849,449		804,452	2,867,832	7,258,500				18,014,219	44,794,452
1810	15,627,806		595,031	2,977,366	10,920,752				15,640,166	45,761,121
1811	12,834,680		336,742	2,941,194	1,841,253				11,939,680	29,893,549
1814	14,113,775	12,755,816	372,212	2,340,417	8,129	11,429,452	1,791,167	2,683,151		45,494,119
1815	11,971,692	8,764,552	333,842	2,931,935	13,255,374	10,687,551	1,156,875	2,531,150		51,632,971
1816	11,359,086	7,284,469	351,674	3,071,197	9,556,577	7,016,410	860,948	2,147,497		41,657,858
1817	11,408,083	7,685,491	406,359	3,725,386	6,930,359	7,405,516	1,279,781	2,651,337		41,492,312
1818	11,809,243	7,630,139	390,586	3,876,677	9,451,009	7,789,780	1,169,609	3,995,757		46,112,800
1819	9,895,397	6,895,255	316,294	2,715,018	4,929,815	6,861,314	892,306	2,376,328		34,881,727
1820	11,289,891	7,139,612	393,298	3,810,290	3,875,286	5,756,864	939,781	2,921,300		36,126,322
1821	9,044,155	6,859,287	482,117	4,277,790	6,214,875	5,461,863	1,050,778	2,942,237		36,333,102
1822	8,327,576	8,273,986	384,944	3,984,796	6,865,262	4,778,721	868,040	3,166,714		36,650,039
1823	8,055,638	6,801,490	507,328	3,941,448	5,464,874	5,311,757	1,073,914	4,218,893		36,375,342
1824	7,691,357	8,077,583	417,741	3,692,404	6,090,394	5,779,033	1,171,221	5,572,579		38,422,312
1825	8,547,781	6,098,577	401,588	3,622,981	7,018,934	5,847,287	907,988	6,425,715		38,870,851
1826	7,822,776	6,070,494	295,768	4,322,240	4,659,018	4,601,072	570,409	3,194,947		31,536,724
1827	8,533,263	5,945,701	671,488	4,799,452	7,018,272	4,980,572	907,309	4,004,319		36,860,376
1828	8,243,082	5,532,788	716,926	4,802,408	5,810,315	4,980,748	818,056	4,929,005		36,483,328
1829	8,346,118	6,199,356	828,729	4,231,350	4,823,415	5,193,808	969,885	4,929,966		35,522,627
1830	8,376,751	7,233,887	905,220	4,455,392	6,132,346	4,695,581	939,822	5,188,562		37,927,561
1831	7,317,870	6,232,570	803,392	4,105,444	9,053,583	4,671,276	1,039,634	3,615,969		36,839,738
1832	9,897,057	5,686,949	880,753	4,235,483	5,468,272	4,515,533	1,176,804	4,272,247		36,133,098

388c. Imports of raw cotton and exports of cotton manufactures and yarn, 1798–1830

(J. Marshall, *A Digest of all the Accounts relating to the Population, Productions, Revenues ... &c. ... of the United Kingdom*, II (1833), p. 112.)

| | | *lbs. Weight of COTTON WOOL.* | Official Value EXPORTED. | | Declared Value EXPORTED | |
| | | | | | | |
Years	IMPORTED.	Retained for Spinning.	Piece Goods. £	Yarns. £	Piece Goods. £	Yarns. £
1798	31,737,655	31,136,516	3,572,217	30,271		
9	43,046,639	42,201,968	5,593,407	204,602		
1800	55,630,390	51,213,780	5,406,501	447,556		
1	55,675,079	53,814,207	6,606,368	444,441		
2	60,239,080	56,508,600	7,195,900	428,605	No account	
3	53,427,501	51,866,448	6,442,037	639,404	kept.	
4	61,316,962	60,813,791	7,834,564	902,208		
5	59,649,549	58,845,306	8,619,990	914,475		
6	57,982,263	57,330,396	9,753,824	736,225		
7	74,786,461	72,609,518	9,708,046	601,719		
8	43,263,400	41,618,533	12,503,918	472,078		
9	91,701,923	87,350,818	18,425,614	1,020,352		
1810	134,805,596	126,018,487	17,892,519	1,053,475		
11	91,008,874	89,732,007	11,529,551	483,598		
12	61,568,673	59,827,761	15,723,225	794,465		
13						
14	58,887,183	52,604,646	16,535,528	1,119,850	17,393,796	2,907,277
15	98,790,698	92,010,306	21,480,792	808,853	19,124,061	1,781,077
16	93,685,105	86,580,051	16,183,975	1,380,486	13,072,758	2,707,385
17	124,803,057	116,647,615	20,133,966	1,125,258	14,178,021	2,131,629
18	177,178,438	172,018,985	21,292,354	1,296,776	16,643,579	2,554,059
19	149,467,129	132,844,160	16,696,539	1,585,753	12,388,833	2,707,612
1820	149,322,869	141,912,267	20,509,926	2,022,153	13,843,567	2,940,328
1	130,196,651	113,890,759	21,642,936	1,898,679	13,786,952	2,305,830
2	140,914,740	120,694,636	24,559,272	2,351,771	14,534,253	2,700,437
3	188,572,418	177,032,888	24,119,359	2,425,411	13,751,415	2,625,947
4	147,099,446	131,201,368	27,171,556	2,984,345	15,240,006	3,135,496
5	226,052,134	205,934,408	26,597,575	2,897,706	15,046,902	3,206,729
6	174,706,610	150,231,690	21,445,743	3,748,527	10,522,407	3,491,268
7	268,752,495	250,618,325	29,203,138	3,979,760	13,956,826	3,541,568
8	225,713,403	208,316,627	28,981,575	4,485,842	13,545,638	3,594,946
9	221,118,645	190,829,866	31,810,474	5,458,958	13,420,544	3,974,039
1830	263,961,452	255,426,476	35,661,381	5,656,460	15,294,943	4,133,741

388D. Imports of foreign and exports of British bar iron, 1786–1828

(Marshall, *op. cit.*, II, p. 33.)

| Years | Tons of FOREIGN IRON. | | | Tons of British Bar Iron, EXPORTED |
	Imported	Re-exported	Retained for Home Consumption	
1786	48,565	—	—	
7	46,749	—	—	
8	51,497	—	—	
9	51,043	—	—	
1790	49,241	4,493	44,748	
1	57,185	6,895	50,290	
2	57,694	9,184	48,510	332
3	58,963	4,574	54,389	180
4	42,480	5,411	37,069	104
5	49,527	4,136	45,391	220
6	53,278	7,640	45,638	408
7	36,961	6,384	30,577	1,316
8	51,929	4,781	47,148	1,889
9	48,332	6,885	41,447	2,675
1800	38,363	5,099	33,264	2,845
1	33,401	4,057	29,344	3,001
2	52,909	6,720	46,189	5,459
3	43,470	3,616	39,854	3,575
4	22,528	3,619	18,909	6,065
5	27,253	4,212	23,041	6,595
6	32,128	4,717	27,411	8,124
7	23,738	6,537	17,201	10,863
8	21,000	6,622	14,378	16,196
9	24,480	8,603	15,877	—
1810	20,184	11,368	8,816	—
11	27,956	8,104	19,852	—
12	17,429	9,959	7,470	23,810
13	—	—	—	—
14	21,909	10,275	11,634	22,636
15	21,379	14,018	7,361	24,708
16	8,490	8,624	—	26,552
17	10,139	4,057	6,082	38,931
18	16,603	4,977	11,626	48,068
19	13,969	3,909	10,060	27,225
1820	9,869	3,628	6,241	42,434
1	10,155	4,002	6,153	39,308
2	12,769	3,993	8,776	39,039
3	13,457	3,333	10,124	40,627
4	14,246	4,037	10,209	30,329
5	23,182	6,705	16,477	30,449
6	12,953	2,262	10,691	39,193
7	18,478	3,454	15,024	51,576
8	15,051	2,991	12,060	57,313

388E. Coal shipped from Newcastle and from Sunderland, 1801–1832

(Porter, I, pp. 338–339.)

Years.	NEWCASTLE		SUNDERLAND	
	Coastwise.	To Foreign Parts.	Coastwise.	To Foreign Parts.
	Tons.	Tons.	Tons.	Tons.
1801	1,198,308	133,562	612,197	12,607
1802	1,310,393	116,600	808,449	82,694
1803	1,338,613	117,458	792,207	26,942
1804	1,536,812	139,360	793,812	11,029
1805	1,464,991	131,366	830,263	15,782
1806	1,558,934	123,710	811,618	7,424
1807	1,404,367	76,674	775,987	11,331
1808	1,640,681	42,402	923,850	5,455
1809	1,428,610	36,143	858,944	2,579
1810	1,643,977	45,733	982,388	5,086
1811	1,678,401	47,528	876,996	4,583
1812	1,671,177	66,210	897,964	8,343
1813	1,548,087	39,116	919,947	4,715
1814	1,720,250	84,763	989,090	29,228
1815	1,723,054	112,450	895,443	45,021
1816	1,797,100	116,025	1,027,371	42,215
1817	1,650,889	137,262	964,250	30,811
1818	1,780,458	126,521	1,038,245	41,973
1819	1,695,965	105,297	1,002,893	40,995
1820	2,004,759	118,788	1,102,327	38,227
1821	1,834,650	127,457	1,050,443	38,624
1822	1,736,171	143,365	1,051,840	43,509
1823	1,958,109	121,391	1,317,385	41,198
1824	1,822,148	129,966	1,301,645	42,082
1825	1,820,626	136,266	1,382,759	41,157
1826	2,099,867	165,943	1,455,988	38,419
1827	1,811,924	173,355	1,387,109	39,625
1828	1,921,467	157,211	1,350,354	60,743
1829	1,956,829	163,380	. . .	. . .
1830	2,167,355	197,308	. . .	. . .
1831	2,097,617	161,247	. . .	. . .
1832	1,809,412	197,337	. . .	. . .

(Porter, II, pp. 174-175.)

(Excluding the trade with Ireland and the coasting trade.)

	INWARDS						OUTWARDS					
	British		Foreign		Total		British		Foreign		Total	
Years.	Ships.	Tons.	Ships.	Tons.	Ships.	Tons.	Ships.	Tons.	Ships.	Tons.	Ships.	Tons.
1801	4,987	922,594	5,497	780,155	10,484	1,702,749	..	..	..	..	..	..
1802	7,806	1,333,005	3,728	480,251	11,534	1,813,256	7,471	1,177,224	3,332	457,580	10,803	1,634,804
1803	6,264	1,115,702	4,254	638,104	10,518	1,753,806	5,523	959,787	3,672	574,420	9,195	1,525,207
1804	4,865	904,932	4,271	607,299	9,136	1,512,231	4,983	906,007	4,093	587,849	9,076	1,493,856
1805	5,167	953,250	4,517	691,883	9,684	1,645,133	5,319	971,496	3,932	605,821	9,251	1,577,317
1806	5,211	904,367	3,793	612,904	9,004	1,517,271	5,219	899,574	3,459	568,170	8,678	1,467,744
1807	..	..	4,087	680,144	..	..	..	..	3,846	631,910	..	..
1808	..	..	1,926	283,657	..	..	..	..	1,892	282,145	..	..
1809	5,615	938,675	4,922	759,287	10,537	1,697,962	5,488	950,565	4,530	699,750	10,018	1,650,315
1810	5,154	896,001	6,876	1,176,243	12,030	2,072,244	3,969	860,632	6,641	1,138,527	10,610	1,999,159
1811	..	..	3,216	687,180	..	..	..	..	..	..	..	..
1814	8,975	1,290,248	5,286	599,287	14,261	1,889,535	8,620	1,271,952	4,622	602,941	13,242	1,874,893
1815	8,880	1,372,108	5,314	746,085	14,194	2,119,093	8,892	1,398,688	4,701	751,377	13,593	2,150,065
1816	9,744	1,415,723	3,116	379,465	12,860	1,795,188	9,044	1,340,277	2,579	399,160	11,623	1,739,437
1817	11,255	1,625,121	3,396	445,011	14,651	2,070,132	10,713	1,558,336	2,905	440,622	13,618	1,998,958
1818	13,006	1,886,394	6,238	762,457	19,244	2,648,851	11,445	1,715,488	5,399	734,649	16,844	2,450,137
1819	11,974	1,809,128	4,215	542,684	16,189	2,351,812	10,250	1,562,332	3,795	556,511	14,045	2,118,843
1820	11,285	1,668,660	3,472	447,611	14,757	2,115,671	10,102	1,549,508	2,969	433,328	13,071	1,982,836
1821	10,810	1,599,274	3,261	396,256	14,071	1,995,530	9,797	1,488,644	2,626	383,786	12,423	1,872,430
1822	11,087	1,664,186	3,389	469,151	14,476	2,133,337	10,023	1,539,260	2,843	457,542	12,866	1,996,802
1823	11,271	1,740,859	4,069	582,996	15,340	2,323,855	9,666	1,546,976	3,437	563,571	13,103	2,110,547
1824	11,733	1,797,320	5,653	759,441	17,386	2,556,761	10,157	1,657,533	5,026	746,707	15,083	2,404,240
1825	13,516	2,144,598	6,968	958,132	20,484	3,102,730	10,848	1,793,994	6,075	905,520	16,923	2,699,514
1826	12,473	1,950,630	5,729	694,116	18,202	2,644,746	10,844	1,737,425	5,410	692,440	16,254	2,429,865
1827	13,133	2,086,898	6,046	751,864	19,179	2,839,762	11,481	1,887,682	5,714	767,821	17,195	2,655,503
1828	13,436	2,094,357	4,955	634,620	18,391	2,728,977	12,248	2,006,397	4,405	608,118	16,653	2,614,515
1829	13,659	2,184,525	5,218	710,303	18,877	2,894,828	12,636	2,063,179	5,094	730,250	17,730	2,793,429
1830	13,548	2,180,042	5,359	758,828	18,907	2,938,870	12,747	2,102,147	5,158	758,368	17,905	2,860,515
1831	14,488	2,367,322	6,085	874,605	20,573	3,241,927	13,791	2,300,731	5,927	896,051	19,718	3,196,782
1832	13,372	2,185,980	4,546	639,979	17,918	2,825,959	13,292	2,229,269	4,391	651,223	17,683	2,880,492

388G. Vessels belonging to the United Kingdom and its dependencies

(Porter, II, pp. 171 and 46.)

Years.	United Kingdom, and Possessions in Europe.		Colonies.		Total.	
	Ships.	Tons.	Ships.	Tons.	Ships.	Tons.
1803	18,068	1,986,076	2,825	181,787	20,893	2,167,863
1804	18,870	2,077,061	2,904	191,509	21,774	2,268,570
1805	19,027	2,092,489	3,024	190,953	22,051	2,283,442
1806	19,315	2,079,914	2,867	183,800	22,182	2,263,714
1807	19,373	2,096,827	2,917	184,794	22,290	2,281,621
1808	19,580	2,130,396	3,066	194,423	22,646	2,324,819
1809	19,882	2,167,221	3,188	201,247	23,070	2,368,468
1810	20,253	2,210,661	3,450	215,383	23,703	2,426,044
1811	20,478	2,247,322	3,628	227,452	24,106	2,474,774
1814	21,550	2,414,170	2,868	202,795	24,418	9,616,965
1815	21,869	2,447,831	2,991	203,445	24,860	2,681,276
1816	22,026	2,504,290	3,775	279,643	25,801	2,783,933
1817	21,775	2,421,354	3,571	243,632	25,346	2,664,986
1818	22,024	2,452,608	3,483	221,860	25,507	2,674,468
1819	21,997	2,451,597	3,485	214,799	25,482	2,666,396
1820	21,969	2,439,029	3,405	209,564	25,374	2,648,593
1821	21,652	2,355,853	3,384	204,350	25,036	2,560,203
1822	21,238	2,315,403	3,404	203,641	24,642	2,519,044
1823	21,042	2,302,867	3,500	203,893	24,542	2,506,760
1824	21,280	2,348,314	3,496	211,273	24,776	2,559,587
1825	20,701	2,328,807	3,579	214,875	24,280	2,553,682
1826	20,968	2,411,461	3,657	224,183	24,625	2,635,644
†1827	19,524	2,181,138	3,675	279,362	23,199	2,460,500
1828	19,646	2,193,300	4,449	324,891	24,095	2,518,191
1829	19,110	2,199,959	4,343	317,041	23,453	2,517,000
1830	19,174	2,201,592	4,547	330,227	23,721	2,531,819
1831	19,450	2,224,356	4,792	357,608	24,242	2,581,964
1832	19,664	2,261,860	4,771	356,208	24,435	2,618,068

STEAM VESSELS

Years.	United Kingdom.		Guernsey, &c.		B. Plantations.		Total.	
	V.	Tons.	V.	Tons.	V.	Tons.	V.	Tons.
1814	1	69	..	..	1	387	2	456
1815	8	638	..	..	2	995	10	1633
1816	12	947	..	..	3	1665	15	2612
1817	14	1039	..	..	5	2911	19	3950
1818	19	2332	..	..	8	4109	27	6441
1819	24	2548	..	..	8	4109	32	6657
1820	34	3018	..	..	9	4225	43	7243
1821	59	6051	..	..	10	4483	69	10,534
1822	85	8457	..	..	11	4668	96	13,125
1823	101	10,361	..	..	10	3792	111	14,153
1824	114	11,733	2	214	10	3792	126	15,739
1825	151	15,764	2	214	15	4309	168	20,287
1826	228	24,186	2	214	18	4558	248	28,958
1827	253	27,318	2	214	20	4958	275	32,490
1828	272	28,010	2	214	19	3808	293	32,032
1829	287	29,501	2	214	15	2568	304	32,283
1830	295	30,009	3	330	17	3105	315	33,444
1831	320	32,262	4	433	23	4750	347	37,445
1832	348	35,238	4	474	28	5957	380	41,669

† A new Registry Act (6 Geo. IV, c. 110) came into operation this year; previously to that time many vessels which had been lost from time to time were still continued in the registry, no evidence of their loss having been produced.

(b) THE FREE TRADE MOVEMENT

389. Pitt's speech in the House of Commons on the Commercial Treaty with France, 12 Feb. 1787

(Debrett's *Parliamentary Register*, XXI, pp. 168–176.)

The Anglo-French Commercial Treaty of 1786 did not establish complete free trade between the two countries; they merely agreed to certain tariff revisions, in particular the lowering of English duties on French wines, brandy, oils and vinegar and the mutual lowering of duties on manufactured goods. England, however, maintained her prohibition of French silks. Fox and his party attacked the treaty on the grounds that England should have no connexion with her 'natural enemy', but in fact the terms were so decidedly in favour of the British manufacturers that the French Revolutionary Government later denounced the treaty.

It would be necessary for the Committee to take into their consideration the relative state of the two kingdoms. . . . It was a fact generally admitted, that France had the advantage in the gift of soil and climate, and in the amount of her natural produce. That, on the contrary, Great Britain was, on her part, as confessedly superior in her manufactures and artificial productions. Undoubtedly, in point of natural produce, France had greatly the advantage in this treaty. Her wines, brandies, oils, and vinegars, particularly the two former articles, were matters of such important value in her produce, as greatly and completely to destroy all idea of reciprocity as to natural produce–we perhaps having nothing of that kind to put in competition, but simply the article of beer. But on the contrary, was it not a fact as demonstrably clear, that Britain, in its turn, possessed some manufactures exclusively her own, and that in others she had so completely the advantage of her neighbour, as to put competition to defiance? This then was the relative condition, and this the precise ground on which it was imagined that a valuable correspondence and connection between the two might be established. Having each its own and distinct staple–having each that the other wanted; and not clashing in the great and leading lines of their respective riches, they were like two great traders in different branches, they might enter into a traffic which would prove mutually beneficial to them. Granting that a large quantity of their natural produce would be brought into this country, would any man say, that we should not send more cottons by the direct course now settled, than by the circuitous passages formerly used–more of our woollens than while restricted in their importation to particular ports, and burdened under heavy duties? Would not more of our earthenware, and other articles, which, under all the disadvantages that they formerly suffered, still, from their intrinsic superiority, force their way regularly into France, now be sent thither; and would not the aggregate of our manufactures be greatly and eminently benefited in going to this market loaded only with duties from twelve to ten, and in one instance with only five per cent.? . . . A market of so many millions of people–a market so near and prompt–a market of expeditious and certain return–of necessary and extensive consumption, thus added to the manufactures and commerce of Britain, was an object which we ought to look up to with eager and satisfied ambition. To procure this, we certainly ought not to scruple to give liberal conditions. We ought not to hesitate, because this which must be so greatly advantageous to us must also have its benefit for them. It was a great boon procured on easy terms, and as such we ought to view it. . . .

We had agreed by this treaty to take from France, on small duties, the luxuries of her soil, which however the refinements of ourselves had converted into necessaries. The wines of France were already so much in the possession of our markets, that with all the high duties paid by us, they found their way to our tables. Was it then a serious injury to admit these luxuries on easier terms? The admission of them would not supplant the wines of Portugal, nor of Spain, but would supplant only an useless and pernicious manufacture in this country. . . .

. . . The next was brandy. . . . The reduction of the duties would have a material effect on the contraband in this article; it was certain that the legal importation bore no proportion to the quantity clandestinely imported–for the legal importation of brandy was no more than 600,000 gallons, and the supposed amount of the smuggled, at the most rational and best-founded estimate, was between three and four hundred thousand gallons. Seeing then that this article had taken such complete possession of the taste of the nation, it might be right to procure to the state a greater advantage from the article than heretofore, and to crush the contraband by legalizing the market.

The oil and vinegar of France were comparatively small objects, but, like the former, they were luxuries which had taken the shape of necessaries, and which we could suffer nothing from accepting on easy terms. These were the natural produce of France to be admitted under this treaty. Their next inquiry should be to see if France had any manufactures peculiar to herself, or in which she so greatly excelled as to give us alarm on account of the treaty, viewing it in that aspect. Cambric . . . was an article in which our competition with France had ceased, and there was no injury in granting an easy importation to that which we would have at any rate. In no other article was there anything very formidable in the rivalry of France. Glass would not be imported to any amount. In particular kinds of lace, indeed, they might have the advantage, but none which they would not enjoy independent of the treaty; and the clamours about millinery were vague and unmeaning, when, in addition to all these benefits we included the richness of the country with which we were to trade; its superior population of 20 millions to 8, and of course a proportionate consumption, together with its vicinity to us, and the advantages of quick and regular returns, who could hesitate for a moment to applaud the system, and look forward with ardour and impatience to its speedy ratification? The possession of so extensive and safe a market must improve our commerce, while the duties transferred from the hands of smugglers to their proper channel, would benefit our revenue–the two sources of British opulence and British power.

Viewing the relative circumstances of the two countries then in this way, he saw no objection to the principle of the exchange of their respective commodities. He saw no objection to this, because he perceived and felt that our superiority in the tariff was manifest. The excellence of our manufactures was unrivalled, and in the operation must give the balance to England. . . .

The effect of this treaty on our revenue . . . would almost exceed credibility, though it would cause an average reduction of £50 per cent. in every article in our book of rates; on French wines the reduction would be £10,000 per annum; on Portugal wines, £170,000 should the Methuen treaty be continued; and, on brandy, a reduction of £20,000. The surrender of revenue for great commercial purposes was a policy by no means unknown in the history of Great Britain, but here we enjoyed the extraordinary advantage of having them returned to us in a threefold rate, by extending and legalizing the importation of the articles. . . .

Considering the treaty in its political view, he should not hesitate to contend against the too frequently advanced doctrine, that France was, and must be, the unalterable enemy of Britain. His mind revolted from this position as monstrous and impossible. To suppose that any nation could be unalterably the enemy of another, was weak and childish. It had neither its foundation in the experience of nations nor in the history of man. It was a libel on the constitution of political societies, and supposed the existence of diabolical malice in the original frame of man. But these absurd tenets were taken up and propagated. . . . Men reasoned as if this treaty was not only to extinguish all jealousy from our bosoms, but also completely to annihilate our means of defence; as if by the treaty we gave up so much of our army, so much of our marine; as if our commerce was to be abridged, our navigation to be lessened, our colonies to be cut off or to be rendered defenceless, and as if all the functions of the state were to be sunk in apathy. What ground was there for this train of reasoning? Did the treaty suppose that the interval of peace between the two countries would be so totally unemployed by us as to disable us from meeting France in the moment of war with our accustomed strength? Did it not much rather, by opening new sources of wealth, speak this forcible language; that the interval of peace, as it would enrich the nation, would also prove the means of enabling her to combat her enemy with more effect when the day of hostility should come. It did more than this; by promoting habits of friendly intercourse, and of mutual benefit, while it invigorated the resources of Britain, it made it less likely that she should have occasion to call forth those resources. It certainly had at least the happy tendency to make the two nations enter into more intimate communion with one another, to enter into the same views even of taste and manners; and while they were mutually benefited by the connection, and endeared to one another by the result of the common benefits, it gave a better chance for the preservation of harmony between them, while so far from weakening, it strengthened their sinews for war. . . .

390. The petition of the merchants of London, respecting commercial restrictions. (Presented to Parliament, 8 May 1820.)

(Hansard's *Parliamentary Debates*, New Series, 1, 179–182.)

That foreign commerce is eminently conducive to the wealth and prosperity of the country, by enabling it to import the commodities for the production of which the soil, climate, capital and industry of other countries are best calculated, and to export in payment those articles for which its own situation is better adapted; that freedom from restraint is calculated to give the utmost extension to foreign trade, and the best direction to the capital and industry of the country; that the maxim of buying in the cheapest market and selling in the dearest, which regulates every merchant in his individual dealings, is strictly applicable, as the best rule for the trade of the whole nation; that a policy, founded on these principles, would render the commerce of the world an interchange of mutual advantages, and diffuse an increase of wealth and enjoyments among the inhabitants of each State; that, unfortunately, a policy, the very reverse of this, has been, and is more or less adopted and acted upon by the Government of this and of every other country; each trying to exclude the productions of other countries, with the specious and well-meant design of encouraging its own productions; thus inflicting on the bulk of its subjects, who are consumers, the necessity of submitting to privations in the quantity or quality of commodities, and thus rendering, what ought to be the source of mutual benefit and of harmony among States, a constantly recurring occasion of jealousy and hostility; that the prevailing prejudices in favour of the protective or restrictive system may be traced to the erroneous supposition that every importation of foreign commodities occasions a diminution or discouragement of our own productions to the same extent; whereas it may be clearly shown that although the particular description of production which could not stand against unrestrained foreign competition would be discouraged; yet, as no importation could be continued for any length of time without a corresponding exportation, direct or indirect, there would be an encouragement for the purpose of that exportation of some other production to which our situation might be better suited, thus affording at least an equal, and probably a greater, and certainly a more beneficial employment to our own capital and labour; that of the numerous protective and prohibitory duties of our commercial code, it may be proved that while all operate as a very heavy tax on the community at large, very few are of any ultimate benefit to the classes in whose favour they were originally instituted, and none to the extent of the loss occasioned by them to other classes; that among the other evils of the restrictive or protective system, not the least is that the artificial protection of one branch of industry, or source of protection against foreign competition, is set up as a ground of claim by other branches for similar protection, so that if the reasoning upon which these restrictive or prohibitory regulations are founded, were followed out consistently, it would not stop short of excluding us from all foreign commerce whatsoever; and the same train of argument, which with corresponding prohibitions and protective duties should exclude us from foreign trade, might be brought forward to justify the re-enactment of restrictions upon the interchange of productions (unconnected with public revenue) among the kingdoms composing the union, or among the counties of the same kingdom; that an investigation of the effects of the restrictive system at this time is peculiarly called for, as it may, in the opinion of the petitioners, lead to a strong presumption that the distress which now so generally prevails, is considerably aggravated by that system; and that some relief may be obtained by the earliest practicable removal of such of the restraints as may be shown to be most injurious to the capital and industry of the community, and to be attended with no compensating benefit to the public revenue; that a declaration against the anti-commercial principles of our restrictive system is of the more importance at the present juncture, inasmuch as in several instances of recent occurrence the merchants and manufacturers in foreign States have assailed their respective Governments with applications for further protective or prohibitory duties and regulations, urging the example and authority of this country, against which they are almost exclusively directed, as a sanction for the policy of such measures; and certainly, if the reasoning upon which our restrictions have been defended is worth anything, it will apply in behalf of the regulations of foreign States against us; they insist upon our superiority in capital and machinery, as we do upon their comparative exemption from taxation, and with equal foundation; that nothing would more tend to counteract the commercial hostility of foreign States than the adoption of a more enlightened and more conciliatory policy on the part of this country; that although as a matter of mere diplomacy it may sometimes answer to hold out the removal of particular prohibitions or high duties, as depending upon corresponding concessions by other States in our favour, it does not follow that we should maintain our restrictions in cases where the desired concessions on their part cannot be obtained; our restrictions would not be the less prejudicial to our own capital and industry because other Governments persisted in preserving impolitic regulations; that, upon the whole, the most liberal would prove to be the most politic course on such occasions; that, independent of the direct benefit to be derived by this country on every occasion of such concession or relaxation, a great incidental object would be gained by the recognition of a sound principle or standard, to which all subsequent arrangements might be referred, and by the salutary influence which a promulgation of such just views, by the Legislature and by the nation at large, could not fail to have on the policy of other States; that in thus declaring, as the petitioners do, their conviction of the impolicy and injustice of the restrictive system, and in desiring every practicable relaxation of it, they have in view only such parts of it as are not connected, or are only subordinately so, with the public revenue; as long as the necessity for the present amount of revenue subsists, the petitioners cannot expect so important a branch of it as the customs to be given up, nor to be materially diminished, unless some substitute less objectionable be suggested; but it is against every restrictive regulation of trade not essential to the revenue, against all duties merely protective from foreign competition, and against the excess of such duties as are partly for the purpose of revenue and partly for that of protection, that the prayer of the present petition is respectfully submitted to the wisdom of Parliament; the petitioners therefore humbly pray that the House will be pleased to take the subject into consideration, and to adopt such measures as may be calculated to give greater freedom to foreign commerce, and thereby to increase the resources of the State.

391. Report from the Select Committee of the House of Commons on the means of maintaining and improving the foreign trade of the country, 18 July 1820

(Hansard's *Parliamentary Debates*, New Series, v, App. cxxx–cxliv.)

The committee suggested certain relaxations in the Navigation laws (see No. 392). More important than its specific recommendations, however, was its declaration of the general principles on which the commercial system should in future be based.

It has appeared to your Committee, that the means of attaining the object to which their consideration has been directed . . . consisted less in affording any additional legislative protection or encouragement to the commerce of the United Kingdom with foreign States, than in relieving it from a variety of restrictions which the policy of a former period imposed upon it; and which, whether expedient or otherwise at the time when they were enacted, having ceased to be necessary for the purposes which originally recommended them, tend to embarrass its operations and impede its extension and prosperity. Your Committee are satisfied that the skill, enterprize, and capital of British merchants and manufacturers require only an open and equal field for exertion; and that the most valuable boon that can be conferred on them is as unlimited a freedom from all interference as may be compatible with what is due to private vested interests that have grown up under the existing system, and those more important considerations with which the safety and political power of the country are intimately connected.

. . . Your Committee . . . are anxious to call the observation of the House to the excessive accumulation and complexity of the laws under which the commerce of the country is regulated. . . . These laws, passed at different periods, and many of them arising out of temporary circumstances, amount . . . to upwards of 2,000; of which no less than 1,100 were in force in the year 1815, and many additions have been since made. After such a statement it will not appear extraordinary that it should be matter of complaint to the British merchant, that so far from the course in which he is to guide his transactions being plain and simple; so far from being able to undertake his operations, and to avail himself of favourable openings as they arise, with promptitude and confidence, he is frequently reduced to the necessity of resorting to the services of professional advisers, to ascertain what he may venture to do and what he must avoid, before he is able to embark in his commercial adventures with the assurance of being secure from the consequences of an infringement of the law. . . . Perhaps no service more valuable could be rendered to the trade of the Empire . . . than an accurate revision of this vast and confused mass of legislation, and the establishment of some certain, simple and consistent principles, to which all the regulations of commerce might be referred, and under which the transactions of merchants . . . might be conducted with facility, with safety, and with confidence.

The commercial restrictions to which the intercourse of the United Kingdom with foreign States is subjected, may be classed under three heads; first, those intended for the improvement of its navigation, and the support of its naval power; secondly, those which arise out of the necessity of drawing from commerce, in common with other resources, a proportion of the public revenue; and, lastly, those necessary to the protection afforded to various branches of our domestic industry, for the purpose of securing to them the internal supply of the country and the export to its several colonies.

. . . Whatever may have been the principles which dictated, or the political benefits that have accrued to the country from the . . . Navigation law and Statute of Frauds; it can scarcely be denied, that they have a tendency to cramp the operations of commerce, and to impede the growth of that opulence which may arise from foreign trade. . . . A just respect for the political wisdom from which the enactment of the navigation laws originated, and a sense of the great national advantages derived from them in their effects on the maritime greatness and power of the kingdom, have rendered them objects of attachment and veneration to every British subject. Nor can your Committee suppose that any suggestions they may offer, can lead to a suspicion of their being disposed to recommend an abandonment of the policy from which they emanated; or to advise, in favour of the extension of commerce, a remission of that protecting vigilance under which the shipping and navigation of the kingdom have so eminently grown and flourished. The only question which on this subject they have entertained is whether the advantages hitherto enjoyed by our shipping might not be compatible with increased facilities afforded to trade, and its relief from some of the restrictions which the provisions of these laws impose upon it. They are convinced, that every restriction on the freedom of commerce is in itself an evil, to be justified only by some adequate political expediency; and that every facility that can be extended to it is a benefit to the public interest, as leading . . . to the certain consequence of laying open new means of exertion to mercantile ingenuity and enterprize and disclosing to commerce new sources of eventual advantage, far beyond the power of human foresight distinctly to appreciate. . . .

The time when monopolies could be successfully supported, or would be patiently endured, either in respect to subjects against subjects, or particular countries against the rest of the world, seems to have passed away. Commerce, to continue undisturbed and secure, must be, as it was intended to be, a source of reciprocal amity between nations, and an interchange of productions, to promote the industry, the wealth, and the happiness of mankind. If it be true that different degrees of advantage will be reaped from it according to the natural and political circumstances, the skill and the industry of different countries, it is true also that whatever be the advantages so acquired, though they may excite emulation and enterprize, can rouse none of those sentiments of animosity, or that spirit of angry retaliation, naturally excited by them, when attributed to prohibitions and restrictions jealously enacted and severely maintained.

Your Committee are however sensible that at once to abandon the prohibitory system would be of all things the most visionary and dangerous: it has long subsisted; it is the law not only of this kingdom, but of the rest of the European world; and any sudden departure from it is forbidden by every consideration of prudence, safety, and justice. No such sudden change is in the contemplation of your Committee, nor indeed the adoption of any change without the utmost circumspection and caution.

But they still feel that a principle of gradual and prospective approximation to a sounder system as the standard of all future commercial regulations, may be wisely and beneficially recommended, no less with a view to the interests of the country, than to the situation of surrounding nations. Upon them the policy of Great Britain has rarely been without its influence. The principles recognized and acted upon by her may powerfully operate in aiding the general progress towards the establishment of a liberal and enlightened system of national intercourse throughout the world, as they have too long done in supporting one of a contrary character, by furnishing the example and justification of various measures of commercial exclusion and restriction. To measures of this nature her pre-eminence and prosperity have been unjustly ascribed. It is not to prohibitions and protections we are indebted for our commercial greatness and maritime power; these, like every public blessing we enjoy, are the effects of the free principles of the happy constitution under which we live, which, by protecting individual liberty and the security of property, by holding out the most splendid rewards to successful industry and merit, has, in every path of human exertion, excited the efforts, encouraged the genius, and called into action all the powers of an aspiring, enlightened, and enterprizing people.

392. Huskisson on the relaxation of the navigation laws (13 May 1826)

(Hansard's *Parliamentary Debates*, New Series, xv, 1144–1187.)

. . . The great charter of the navigation system of this country is the Act of the twelfth of Charles II. The different modes which that Act provided for the encouragement of shipping, may be arranged under the five following heads:

First, the fisheries. The ocean is a common field, alike open to all the people of the earth. Its productions belong to no particular nation. It was, therefore, our interest to take care that so much of those productions as might be wanted for the consumption of Great Britain, should be exclusively procured by British industry, and imported in British ships. . . . In this part of our navigation system, no alteration whatever has been made; nor do I believe that any will ever be contemplated.

The second object . . . was to give to the shipping of this country employment in what is called the coasting trade. When those laws were first passed, that trade was confined to England only, but, since we have become legislatively united with Scotland and with Ireland, it has embraced the whole of the British islands. . . . The law in this respect, remains unchanged, and will remain unchanged so long as we have a desire to maintain a great commercial marine.

The third object of our navigation system was the European trade. The rule laid down . . . was that the ships of the other states of Europe were to be at liberty to bring, from any port in Europe, any article of European production, with the exception of certain articles, since known in trade by the name of 'enumerated articles'. They amount in number to 28, and include those commodities which, being of the most bulky nature, employ the greatest quantity of shipping. With respect to these 'enumerated articles' the exception was this–that they should not be brought to our ports in any other than British ships, or ships of the country in which they were produced, proceeding directly from such country to this. . . . The regulations of that period were not framed merely for the preservation and encouragement of our own commerce, but also to weaken the powerful marine of Holland. Guided by this policy our ancestors applied more severe measures towards the Dutch than they thought necessary towards any other nation. In this spirit it was that they prohibited the importation, generally, of the productions of the other countries of Europe from Holland, instead of confining that prohibition to the 28 enumerated articles.

The fourth object . . . was to regulate our commerce with Asia, Africa and America. . . . No article, the produce of either of those three quarters of the globe, should be allowed to be brought into an English port, except in a British ship.

The fifth and last part of the system . . . related to our colonies. The principle on which we acted towards those colonies was strictly to confine them, in all matters of trade, to an intercourse with the mother country. They were not allowed to dispose of any of their produce otherwise than by sending it in British vessels to this country. They were equally restricted from receiving any articles necessary for their consumption, except from this country, and in British bottoms. . . .

The peace with America [1783] gave the first great blow to the navigation system of this country. There had now arisen an independent state in the New World. . . . That part of the system which provided that none of the productions of Asia, Africa or America should be imported into England except in British vessels, could no longer be adhered to.

. . . By that system [i.e. adopted by Congress in 1787] a heavy blow was aimed at the navigation of this country. It was resolved that all foreign ships trading to America should pay half a dollar–which was afterwards raised to a dollar–per ton duty, beyond what was paid by national ships. And further, that goods imported in foreign vessels should pay a duty of ten per cent over and above what was demandable on the same description of goods imported in American vessels.

This system–in the adoption of which, the Americans had, in a considerable degree, followed the example of their English ancestors–was likely to become seriously prejudicial to the commerce and navigation of this country. . . . This country found it necessary to adopt the system of reciprocity, on which, since the year 1815, the commercial intercourse between the two countries has been placed; namely, equality of all charges upon the ships belonging to either country in the ports of the other, and a like equality of duty upon all articles the production of the one country, imported into the other, whether such importation be made in the ships of the one or the other. . . .

At the latter period [1815], peace being restored, and with it, the independence of the states which had been incorporated with France, the commerce of the world began to revert to its ancient channels. The nations of Europe whose flags had, for so long a series of years, disappeared from the ocean, were now naturally anxious that their own trade should be carried on in their own ships. This gave a check to the shipping of the United States, which was also felt by the shipping of this country.

Perhaps in a greater degree by our own shipping, in consequence of the restitution of several extensive and valuable colonies which we had captured and held during the war.

Besides this material circumstance, there were others . . . which had a natural and inevitable tendency to interfere with, and diminish the employment for shipping in this country.

The first . . . is the abolition of the slave trade. . . . The arguments in opposition to the measure were grounded chiefly on the danger with which it threatened the shipping interests of the country. The necessity of kidnapping cargoes of slaves on the coast of Africa was at that time, as coolly defended, on the score of encouragement to our marine, as the taking of cod-fish on the banks of Newfoundland could be at the present day. That traffic was however abolished in 1806 [sic]; and happy I am that the interest of humanity and the honour of the English name were from that year no longer sacrificed to the plea of the shipping interest; though I may, I think, fairly adduce the abolition of the slave trade as having taken away one source of employment.

After the general pacification of Europe, but before we dismantled our fleet, we insisted on the powers of Barbary desisting from the practices of maritime warfare carried on by cruisers under their flags, in the Mediterranean. These corsairs were constantly taking prisoners either for the sake of ransom or for the purpose of carrying them into slavery. . . . Since the bombardment of Algiers, the flag of every petty state bordering on that sea, floats in equal security with our own. I am not accurately informed what was the quantity of British shipping employed in the carrying and coasting trade of those states before this change, but I have heard it stated . . . that from 8,000 to 10,000 British seamen, and from 700 to 800 British vessels, were engaged in that commerce. Consequently, to that extent has the employment for British ships been diminished in the Mediterranean.

. . . With the termination of hostilities there was necessarily a diminished demand for ships in the public service. The greatest proportion of those which had been taken up as hired transports were discharged. . . . The diminution is not less than 1226 vessels, amounting to 270,382 tons.

In the next place we had to sell out of the king's service a number of vessels which were no longer wanted in the navy. . . . His majesty's government have set free, to compete with the commercial marine of the country, 1559 vessels, amounting in tonnage to 363,912 tons; a quantity nearly equal to one-fourth of the whole shipping of the country, as it stood in the year 1793. . . .

In consequence of the restoration of peace, the demand for shipping . . . was much diminished, and the rates of freight were considerably lowered after the year 1815. This gave rise to great complaints on the part of the shipping interest. In the hope of finding some remedy for their difficulties, the House, in the year 1820, appointed a select committee to inquire into the state of our foreign commerce. . . . One change recommended by that committee, in the navigation laws was to the following effect–that whereas certain goods . . .–enumerated articles–could only be imported in British ships or in the ships of the country in Europe of which they were the produce, and directly from that country, it was the opinion of the committee that the law ought to be so far relaxed as to allow the importation of these articles in the ships of any country into which they had been previously imported.

The recommendation of the committee was adopted by the legislature. That this relaxation has been beneficial to our commerce and navigation is now, I believe, placed beyond all doubt. . . .

Another alteration in our navigation system has since been adopted, which certainly ought not to have been so long delayed. This alteration consists in putting the trade between Great Britain and Ireland upon the footing of a coasting trade. Every gentleman must, I think, see that, from the time at least of the union of the two countries, it was desirable that their interest and commercial system should be identified as much as possible. From that period it was absurd to consider the commercial intercourse with Ireland as a part of our foreign trade, and to subject the shipping employed in it to the restrictive regulations and higher charges of that trade.

. . . The revolutions which have occurred in the political state of the world, in our time, rendered other changes indispensable. There has grown up over the whole continent of America, a situation of affairs similar to that which the United States presented after their separation from the mother country. This change, from a colonial to an independent existence, necessarily draws after it, in each particular case, the application of the new rule which . . . unavoidably grew out of the independence of the United States.

The first application of that rule occurred in respect to Brazil. From the moment when in 1808 the house of Braganza transferred the seat of empire to Brazil, that country virtually ceased to be a colony. Great Britain had no choice but to apply the European principles to the commerce and navigation of Brazil, though out of Europe, and to admit Portuguese shipping–and, since the separation of Portugal and Brazil, Brazilian shipping–coming from that country into our ports, upon the same footing as the ships of any other independent nation.

This principle has been extended, from time to time, as new states have risen up in America. . . . We have disarmed all suspicion as to our commercial pretensions by frankly declaring that we sought no exclusive advantages for British ships or British trade, and that the principle of our intercourse with the new states, as with the old states, of the world, would be that of a fair and equal reciprocity.

This brings me to the *gravamen* of the charge made against his Majesty's government–namely, the step taken by them, in furtherance of this principle, by the introduction of a law, enabling the crown, with the advice of the Privy Council, to remit all discriminating duties on the goods and shipping of such countries, as may agree to impose no higher charges or duties upon British ships, and the goods imported therein, than upon their own ships, and the like goods imported in such ships.

If the system of discriminating duties for the encouragement of shipping were a secret known to this country alone; if a similar system were not, or could not be, put in force in every country, I should not be standing here to vindicate the measure to which I have just referred. . . . So long as, in fact, no independent trading community existed out of Europe, and so long as the old governments of Europe looked upon these matters ... as little deserving their attention, and were content, either from ignorance or indifference, not to thwart our system, it would have been wrong to disturb any part of it. But is this the present state of the world? Did not the United States of America, in the first instance, for the purpose of raising to themselves a great commercial marine, and of counteracting our navigation laws, adopt, in their utmost rigour, the rules of those laws, and carry, even further than we had ever done, in respect to foreign ships, this principle of discriminating duties against our shipping? Can we shut our eyes to the fact that other nations have followed, or are following, their example? Do we not see them, one after the other, taking a leaf out of our own book? Is not every government in Europe, if possessed of sea-ports, now using its utmost endeavours to force a trade, and to raise up for itself a commercial marine? Have we not boasted of our navigation laws till we have taught other nations to believe (however erroneous that belief) that they are almost the only requisite, or at least, the *sine quâ non* of commercial wealth and of maritime power? . . .

It would be worse than idle, it would be dangerous, to dissemble to ourselves the great changes which have been wrought since the establishment of American independence, in the views and sentiments of Europe upon all matters connected with commerce and navigation. . . .

In this altered state of the world it became our duty seriously to inquire whether a system of commercial hostility, of which the ultimate tendency is mutual prohibition—whether a system of high discriminating duties upon foreign ships, with the moral certainty of seeing those duties fully retaliated upon our own shipping in the ports of foreign countries—was a contest in which England was likely to gain and out of which, if persevered in, she was likely to come with dignity or advantage? . . . In the long run, this war of discriminating duties, if persevered in on both sides, must operate most to the injury of the country which, at the time of entering upon it, possesses the greatest mercantile marine. How can it be otherwise? What are these discriminating duties but a tax upon commerce and navigation? Will not the heaviest share of that tax fall, therefore, upon those who have the greatest amount of shipping and of trade? . . .

. . . His Majesty's Government have thought it more prudent and more dignified to enter into amicable arrangements with other powers, founded on the basis of mutual interest, and entire reciprocity of advantages, rather than embark in a contest of commercial hostility and reciprocal exclusion—a system, at best, of doubtful benefit to the shipping interest. . . . We entered upon an amicable negotiation with the Prussian government, upon the principle of our treaty with the United States, that of abolishing, on both sides, all discriminating duties on the ships and goods of the respective countries in the ports of the other.

Having concluded an arrangement with Prussia upon this basis, we soon found it necessary to do the same with some other of the northern states. Similar conventions were accordingly entered into with Denmark and Sweden. Reciprocity is the foundation of all those conventions. . . .

A few observations on our commercial policy with regard to our colonies abroad, will bring me, I hope, to the conclusion of this important investigation. The former colonial system of this country was simply this, that our possessions abroad should receive all their supplies from hence in British shipping, and they were prohibited from trading directly with any other country. But, so early as the year 1783 – the year in which we recognized the independence of the United States of America – it occurred to the government at home that it might be somewhat hard to require of the West India colonies to draw all their supplies from the mother country. . . . Orders-in-council, allowing those colonies to trade directly with the United States of America in British shipping, were passed, from time to time, as occasions required, and the ministers as often came down to Parliament for bills of indemnity for having so far violated the plantation laws.

In process of time, however, the government of the United States, jealous of a trade in which British shipping alone was employed, said to this country: "If you want the productions of our country for the use of your colonies, and will not allow us to send them in our ships, we will entirely prohibit the exportation to your colonies, in British shipping, of those articles of which your colonies stand in need". They did so. . . . After a suspension of intercourse had continued for some time, Parliament, in the year 1822, passed an Act by which American ships were allowed to trade, directly, between the United States and our colonies, in the West Indies and North America.

Now let me ask, was it politic, was it altogether consistent with impartiality and our friendly relations with the north of Europe, to grant to the shipping of the United States, first in the trade between them and this country, by the treaty of 1815; and secondly, in the trade, by this act regularly legalized, between those states and our colonies, privileges which we continued to deny to the shipping of Prussia, of Denmark, of Sweden, of Hamburg, and of other trading communities of Europe? Upon what principle of fairness, upon what principle of sound policy were we to continue this preference exclusively to a power, towards which, God knows, I entertain no feeling of hostility – far from it – but, when I am speaking of that nation in a British House of Commons, it is not improper to say, that in matters of navigation and naval power, there exists towards us, a spirit of rivalry in the United States; a spirit of which I do not complain, but which should incline every Englishman to doubt the wisdom of any measure tending to encourage the growth of the commercial marine of America, by giving to it privileges greater than are permitted to the shipping of other states. . . .

Considering, therefore, the act of 1822, and the changes which had taken place in the colonial system of other powers, it appeared to me that the time was arrived when upon every sound principle it would be right to extend to the foreign shipping of Europe, the same privilege of trading with our colonies in the New World, which had been granted to the shipping of America; and also to give a greater facility, and extension, to the intercourse between foreign countries and our colonies generally – strictly confining, however, to British shipping only, all trade between this country and the colonies, and all inter-colonial trade between the different foreign possessions of the British Empire.

Whether we look to the interests of our commerce, which are also the interests of our navigation—whether we look to the separate interests of the colonies, or to the general interests of the parent country—or whether we consider the changes which have recently taken place, especially in the New World—all these considerations appear to me to concur in support of the measures to which I have referred, and the enlarged views of policy upon which they are founded.

Shipping, like other branches of business in this country, is liable to fluctuation. There may be great excitement at one period, and great depression at another. Last year, for instance, the demand far exceeded the means of the British shipowners to supply it. The price of freight for foreign adventures was, in consequence, so much raised as to become a very serious injury and interruption to other branches of navigation, more especially to our coasting trade. Yet, such was the unbridled rage for speculation which then prevailed, that our tonnage could not keep pace with it, and foreign vessels were taken up in every port of Europe, not from a preference, but because British ships could not be procured. This is not the proper occasion to inquire into the origin of the almost universal mania which appears to have seized upon merchants and manufacturers, not of this country only, but, more or less, upon those of other countries, during the last year. It is now too generally seen and admitted, even by those who were most infected by that mania, that their speculations were carried on without reference to the habitual scale of our consumption, or to the rapid accumulation of goods, or to any of those circumstances which, in their calmer moments, direct the operations of commercial men. When prices had risen, in the first instance from natural causes perhaps, speculation soon forced a further and more rapid rise, and the only inference, for a time, among buyers, seems to have been that it would continue progressive and almost indefinite.

Connecting this rage for speculation with the employment of shipping, the House will be surprised to hear in what a degree the quantity of bulky articles from foreign countries, and from our possessions in North America, in the last year, exceeded the importations of former years. In the year 1822, the total importation of timber from foreign countries was 140,715 loads—in 1825 it amounted to not less than 301,548 loads.

	In 1822	In 1825
Of flax	607,143 cwts.	1,042,956 cwts.
tallow	805,238 ,,	1,164,029 ,,
wool	19,048,879 lbs.	43,700,553 lbs.
linseed	1,411,137 bushels	2,876,571 bushels

. . . . The result of all this overtrading of last year . . . is the depression which now prevails, the interruption of commercial credit, the great diminution of employment for manufacturing labour in this country, and the general derangement of business in the countries with which our principal interchange of commodities is carried on.

. . . The severe distress under which the country now labours, is attributed in some quarters to the changes which have recently taken place in our navigation system and in our commercial policy. If any hon. members entertain that opinion, all that I ask of them is to come forward, and point out distinctly to the House the specific changes to which they ascribe these consequences. It is for them to show, if they can, by evidence or by argument, the connexion of cause and effect between those changes and the difficulties in which the country is now, unhappily, involved. . . .

D. PUBLIC FINANCE, CURRENCY AND THE BANKING SYSTEM

(a) THE NATIONAL WEALTH

393. Estimated annual value of property assessed to the Property Tax in the year ended 5 April 1814

(J. Marshall, *Digest of all the Accounts relating to the Population, Productions, Revenues* .. *&c.* .... *of the United Kingdom*, II (1833), p. 30.)

The table is taken from *Parliamentary Papers*, 1814–15, x, the totals reduced to the nearest £. The figures do not add therefore to the corrected amounts shown in every case.

COUNTIES	Lands £	Houses £	Tithes £	Manors £	Fines £	Quarries £	Mines £	Iron Works £	General Profits £	TOTAL £
Middlesex	381,571	2,699,476	20,511	1,345	100	—	—	8,406	—	3,111,410
LONDON	—	935,965	16,510	—	—	—	—	—	—	952,476
Westminster	2,320	1,232,980	—	—	11,865	—	—	—	—	1,247,165
York	3,364,820	825,636	119,268	812	476	4,250	38,914	22,722	1,923	4,378,822
Lancaster	1,354,443	1,415,890	55,408	1,556	160	7,161	59,580	59,021	613	2,953,833
Somerset	1,482,674	656,697	95,099	271	10,479	603	20,183	952	549	2,267,507
Lincoln	1,801,338	144,134	60,493	3,500	2,620	82	—	6,089	—	2,018,256
Devon	1,316,867	387,147	128,525	45	10	13,266	8,206	11,402	—	1,865,468
Kent	933,938	515,706	151,196	43	5,534	10	—	2,446	—	1,608,873
Surrey	430,618	1,024,525	52,638	2,369	—	262	—	500	130	1,511,042
Essex	1,068,706	250,372	169,565	11,218	48	25	—	4,972	543	1,505,450
Norfolk	1,058,642	251,599	150,790	9,333	4,013	—	—	—	—	1,479,377
Gloucester	938,464	266,172	56,622	421	973	1,274	6,392	3,432	778	1,274,530
Northumberland	930,496	188,591	65,342	—	3	2,557	44,090	13,458	1,423	1,245,961
Wilts	943,442	138,741	96,686	—	40	136	—	1,164	3,090	1,183,299
Warwick	792,863	284,625	26,485	228	39	—	250	74,832	—	1,179,323

Southampton	687,006	337,575	126,204	1,177	11,139		214	8,734	936	1,172,986
Stafford	828,953	237,088	38,761	456	1,320	555	42,191	6,546		1,155,871
Chester	788,644	211,035	54,267	482	3,050	688	11,813	14,095	44	1,084,120
Suffolk	813,080	150,928	122,129	7,837	240	140		2,690		1,097,044
Salop	785,673	136,754	85,900	4,064	165	736	14,499	11,895	693	1,040,380
Leicester	774,366	116,346	14,947	121		918	950	42	528	908,200
Northampton	811,272	78,150	17,626	108	249	434		80		907,920
Cornwall	612,370	118,564	67,481	313	7,530	2,341	69,019	6,627	1,397	885,643
Sussex	594,179	165,268	108,457	3,348	1,633	27		778	83	873,774
Derby	681,139	93,928	19,290	144		987	21,435	20,611	11,643	849,177
Worcester	583,669	145,652	40,552	373		70	297	3,852		774,465
Durham	558,997	101,904	28,326	120	28,827	1,338	49,043	222	335	768,778
Oxford	557,967	104,513	37,642	3	47,839			68		748,367
Nottingham	580,839	119,462	15,371	4		11	3,489	322	1,468	719,498
Berks	489,562	134,633	66,038	221	3,700			3,200	3,129	698,822
Dorset	545,074	86,619	57,157	965	1,300	1,476		1,546	1,477	697,266
Cambridge	526,592	61,815	38,755	1,399	35,128				345	665,167
Cumberland	507,198	89,224	14,056	1,596		2,843	42,501	954		658,718
Bucks	525,219	82,134	30,119	607	5,289					643,369
Hereford	495,105	54,873	53,801						4,386	603,779
Hertford	375,089	113,358	47,779	3,322		58		3,617	59	547,612
Bedford	312,650	32,294	14,307	74				126		359,511
Huntingdon	258,965	30,122	10,327	1,160				1,184		301,749
Monmouth	214,175	40,836	15,933	6,255	130		6,517	2,731	105	286,577
Westmorland	241,437	28,793	5,845	1,297	10	441	1,456	451		279,836
Rutland	105,839	5,340	4,862					30		116,072
Total, England	31,058,264	14,095,464	2,406,075	66,570	183,913	42,690	441,039	299,802	35,679	48,627,495
Wales	1,758,489	195,425	177,598	1,678		1,380	54,871	24,725		2,216,169
Scotland	4,849,593	1,243,609	14		9,574	21,528	59,525	55,221	46,319	6,285,383
Total	37,666,346	15,534,498	2,583,687	68,248	193,487	65,598	555,435	379,748	81,998	57,129,047

394. The Legacy Duty, 1824

(J. Marshall, *A Digest of all the Accounts relating to the Population, Productions, Revenues . . . of the United Kingdom*, Part II (1833), p. 176.)

The Number of *Administrators* to the Personal Property of *Demises*, and the Value of the Property Administered to within the Province of Canterbury in 1824 (totals corrected).

Scale as ℔ Act, 55 Geo. III, c. 184.		Rate of Duty		No. of Administrators un. Probate	Mean amount sworn to under Probate £	Amount of Duty on same £	No. of Lttrs of Administ.	Mean amount sworn to under Lttrs. of Admstrt. £	Amount of Duty on do. £
		Probates	Letters of Administration						
£20	£50	—	10/0	—	—	—	406	10,200	203
50	100	10/0	£1	1,160	58,000	580	441	24,000	441
100	200	£2	3	501	75,000	1,002	457	70,000	1,371
200	300	5	8	203	50,000	2,015	93	23,900	744
300	450	8	11	558	200,000	4,464	112	45,000	1,232
450	600	11	15	497	249,000	5,467	68	34,000	1,020
600	800	15	22	499	349,000	7,485	57	40,000	1,254
800	1,000	22	30	391	350,000	8,602	85	77,000	2,550
1,000	1,500	30	45	640	810,000	19,200	149	200,000	6,705
1,500	2,000	40	60	418	750,000	16,720	39	70,000	2,340
2,000	3,000	50	75	516	1,280,000	25,800	79	190,000	5,925
3,000	4,000	60	90	387	1,355,000	23,220	5	18,000	477
4,000	5,000	80	120	243	1,095,000	19,440	21	90,000	2,520
5,000	6,000	100	150	142	770,000	14,200	25	138,000	3,750
6,000	7,000	120	180	139	900,000	16,680	14	91,000	2,520
7,000	8,000	140	210	107	800,000	14,980	13	97,000	2,730
8,000	9,000	160	240	74	630,000	11,840	6	51,000	1,440
9,000	10,000	180	270	84	800,000	15,120	4	38,000	1,080
10,000	12,000	200	300	127	139,700	25,400	13	143,000	3,900
12,000	14,000	220	330	71	920,000	15,620	8	104,000	2,640
14,000	16,000	250	375	54	814,000	13,500	4	60,000	1,500
16,000	18,000	280	420	48	820,000	13,440	2	34,000	840
18,000	20,000	310	465	50	950,000	15,500	1	19,000	465
20,000	25,000	350	525	77	1,800,000	26,950	3	67,000	1,575
25,000	30,000	400	600	53	1,460,000	21,200	5	137,000	3,000
30,000	35,000	450	675	32	1,080,000	14,400	2	65,000	1,350
35,000	40,000	525	785	38	1,450,000	19,950	3	112,000	2,355
40,000	45,000	600	900	22	935,000	13,200	1	42,500	900
45,000	50,000	675	1,010	19	903,000	12,825	1	47,500	1,010
50,000	60,000	750	1,125	39	2,200,000	29,250	2	110,000	2,250
60,000	70,000	900	1,350	17	1,145,000	15,300	1	65,000	1,350
70,000	80,000	1,050	1,575	12	900,000	12,600			
80,000	90,000	1,200	1,800	7	595,000	8,400			
90,000	100,000	1,350	2,025	8	760,000	10,300			
100,000	120,000	1,500	2,250	8	780,000	12,000	1	110,000	2,250
120,000	140,000	1,800	2,700	5	650,000	9,000			
140,000	160,000	2,100	3,150	5	750,000	10,500			
160,000	180,000	2,400	3,600	3	510,000	7,200			
180,000	200,000	2,700	4,050	3	380,000	5,400	1	190,000	4,050
200,000	250,000	3,000	4,500	2	675,000	9,000			
250,000	300,000	3,750	5,625	1	275,000	3,750	2,122	2,613,100	67,737
300,000	350,000	4,400	6,750	1	350,000	5,250			
350,000	400,000	5,250	7,870						
400,000	500,000	6,000	9,000	1	488,888	6,888			
500,000	600,000	7,500	11,255						
600,000	700,000	9,000	13,500	7,262	32,251,588	444,638			
700,000	800,000	18,500	15,750						
800,000	900,000	12,000	18,000						
900,000	1,000,000	13,500	20,250						
1,000,000 & upwards		15,000	22,500						

(left margin bracket: *and under*)

The Total amount of Personal Property passed under Probate, and Letters of Administration in all Great Britain in the Year 1824, was £46,435,066 and the Proportion on which Legacy Duty was charged at the rates specified below £35,806,480

	Town £	Country £	TOTAL. £
Legacy Duty on Bequests.			
To Children or their Descendants........at 1 ℔ Cent.	115,674	63,718	179,392
„ Brothers & Sisters, or their Descendants 3 „	201,708	139,439	341,147
„ do. do., of Father & Mother, or do. 5 „	33,929	34,169	68,098
„ do. do., of Grand Parents, or do. 6 „	9,138	5,622	14,760
„ Strangers.......................... 10 „	297,836	117,624	415,460
TOTAL Legacy Duty, exclusive of Arrears, prior to 5th April 1805.			
	658,285	360,572	1,018,857

395. Amount of capital subject to the Legacy Duty, 1797–1832

(G. R. Porter, *The Progress of the Nation*, II (1838), pp. 314–315.)

The figures illustrate the increase in the national wealth during the period.

Years.	Total Capital subject to Duty in each Year. £.	Years.	Total Capital subject to Duty in each Year. £.	Years.	Total Capital subject to Duty in each Year. £.
1797	1,116,180	1809	16,395,582	1821	33,023,060
1798	2,504,812	1810	14,301,564	1822	34,922,682
1799	2,939,365	1811	14,757,420	1823	32,735,674
1800	4,122,111	1812	16,622,585	1824	35,852,824
1801	3,541,931	1813	20,118,508	1825	34,801,851
1802	4,107,514	1814	27,299,806	1826	31,024,593
1803	5,109,655	1815	28,200,994	1827	34,058,313
1804	5,301,533	1816	24,073,456	1828	39,099,523
1805	4,450,984	1817	33,118,281	1829	39,667,277
1806	7,039,031	1818	30,178,613	1830	31,219,324
1807	9,515,724	1819	29,411,662	1831	39,532,397
1808	10,238,077	1820	31,245,274	1832	43,334,508

(b) PUBLIC FINANCE

396. Public Income and Expenditure, 1783–1832

(*Parliamentary Papers*, 1868–1869, xxxv, 1, pp. 432–433, and ii, pp. 148–149.)

The totals to 1801 inclusive are net accounts for Great Britain only, and from 1802 gross accounts for the United Kingdom. Years marked † were years of war.

Period Year to 10 Oct.	Total net Income	Money raised by Creation of Debt	Total Receipts including Balances	Interest and Management of the Public Debt	Civil Government	Army, Navy, Ordnance and War Expenditure	Total Expenditure	Applied to Reduction of Debt
1784	13,214,053	18,137,500	35,428,374	8,678,330	1,804,636	13,761,793	24,244,759	6,846,436
1785	15,526,646	16,595,413	36,459,238	9,229,055	1,811,994	14,791,008	25,832,057	5,640,761
1786	15,245,603	7,345,431	27,577,454	9,480,513	2,014,341	5,482,889	16,977,743	6,839,509
1787	16,453,327	9,944,277	30,157,806	9,291,768	2,014,262	4,178,415	15,484,445	11,301,142
1788	16,779,396	9,489,503	29,641,118	9,407,196	2,022,791	4,907,700	16,337,687	9,385,213
1789	16,669,147	9,973,589	30,560,954	9,425,370	2,145,738	4,447,223	16,018,331	10,384,237
1790	17,013,724	8,934,599	30,106,709	9,370,278	2,203,607	5,224,525	16,798,410	9,411,057
1791	18,505,663	10,494,921	32,897,826	9,429,629	2,387,326	6,178,618	17,995,573	10,628,496
1792	18,607,164	8,525,656	31,706,577	9,310,117	2,065,916	5,577,363	16,953,396	10,600,052
1793†	18,131,343	12,440,183	35,118,155	9,149,280	2,336,838	8,136,410	19,662,528	8,759,601
1794†	18,732,241	22,955,107	46,822,213	9,796,761	2,072,741	16,836,610	28,706,112	14,005,034
1795†	19,053,388	32,534,598	55,695,053	10,470,052	2,252,646	26,272,960	38,995,658	11,241,778
1796†	19,391,135	35,575,347	59,613,599	11,602,448	2,515,518	28,234,014	42,371,980	10,051,094
1797†	21,380,407	53,080,769	81,653,201	13,593,967	3,027,661	41,027,624	57,049,252	13,040,592
1798†	25,945,500	37,022,937	74,340,216	16,029,132	2,678,641	28,714,072	47,421,845	14,713,052
1799†	31,783,084	43,567,879	86,163,816	16,856,091	2,680,599	27,882,409	47,419,099	29,306,319
Quarter to 5 Jan. 1800†	9,674,033	9,757,146	26,668,878	3,387,121	537,275	8,458,515	12,382,911	5,403,106
Year to 5 Jan. 1801†	31,585,274	46,491,146	87,354,843	16,749,311	2,574,349	31,667,239	50,990,899	25,368,009

Period Year to 5 Jan.	Total Gross Income	Money raised by Creation of Debt	Total Receipts including Balances	Interest and Management of the Public Debt	Civil Government	Army, Navy, Ordnance and War Expenditure	Total Expenditure	Applied to Reduction of Debt
1802†	39,086,074	60,977,647	109,111,838	19,851,552	7,948,617	37,651,596	65,451,765	34,164,471
1803	41,168,024	44,645,102	95,131,538	20,407,873	9,072,087	25,290,914	54,770,874	29,536,431
1804†	42,441,655	32,441,654	85,860,862	20,692,136	7,448,969	24,856,865	52,997,970	23,692,662
1805†	50,206,138	34,750,608	94,324,004	20,678,563	7,819,726	34,312,157	62,810,446	21,013,111
1806†	55,031,403	53,008,651	118,829,918	22,256,840	7,878,389	41,247,835	71,383,064	36,304,685
1807†	60,084,106	52,852,602	124,098,149	23,242,655	7,499,024	42,126,259	72,867,938	40,025,553
1808†	64,843,042	50,396,654	126,472,173	23,749,596	8,497,529	41,021,747	73,268,872	39,852,173
1809	68,173,918	61,682,454	143,165,272	23,078,931	8,226,990	46,710,210	78,016,131	49,879,042
1810	69,169,788	60,382,346	144,686,747	24,198,986	8,811,011	48,520,231	81,530,228	48,327,575
1811	72,998,308	59,326,421	146,977,302	24,430,221	8,977,437	48,208,187	81,615,846	51,417,842
1812	71,039,934	68,604,377	152,458,910	24,578,312	9,111,246	53,592,699	87,282,257	49,970,951
1813	70,336,591	83,698,697	169,840,128	26,413,570	9,555,940	58,834,552	94,804,062	58,149,046
1814	74,686,242	107,451,379	197,020,965	27,293,977	9,669,084	74,180,385	111,143,446	69,059,231
1815†	77,887,336	92,934,267	187,693,734	30,004,659	10,439,282	72,473,101	112,917,042	59,013,967
1816†	79,101,126	97,932,505	192,734,384	32,219,344	10,768,336	56,468,866	99,456,546	77,318,265
1817	69,265,851	60,935,085	146,157,728	32,893,603	10,270,293	28,180,560	71,344,456	61,068,012
1818	57,600,698	61,485,764	132,865,859	31,457,814	9,566,231	17,702,297	58,726,342	63,333,590
1819	59,509,469	79,203,736	149,228,614	31,284,748	10,577,580	15,705,405	57,567,733	80,420,417
1820	58,073,316	63,143,923	132,135,313	31,062,603	9,780,301	16,678,158	57,521,062	60,552,931
1821	59,892,314	83,822,731	157,466,883	32,022,426	9,688,311	16,717,730	58,428,467	90,660,717
1822	61,611,769	82,330,377	152,027,578	31,901,579	9,896,612	16,629,730	58,427,921	86,404,297
1823	59,870,330	86,473,356	155,157,265	31,351,925	9,909,291	15,231,892	56,493,108	89,685,713
1824	58,624,587	57,058,457	124,486,501	30,030,998	9,919,550	14,352,640	54,303,188	59,700,553
1825	59,763,050	47,929,686	118,008,188	30,205,268	10,096,880	15,155,453	55,457,601	51,626,306
1826	57,801,049	44,172,463	112,502,214	29,238,042	9,857,921	15,002,303	54,098,266	51,229,690
1827	55,308,305	60,092,927	121,733,638	29,219,917	10,153,685	16,710,558	56,084,160	58,586,449
1828	54,778,197	58,623,280	119,856,669	29,443,461	10,290,859	16,208,552	55,942,872	58,025,121
1829	56,604,577	58,590,210	120,678,815	29,300,052	8,963,022	15,199,985	53,463,059	60,922,856
1830	55,368,474	53,977,197	115,378,686	29,146,212	9,380,965	15,182,387	53,709,564	55,744,640
1831	54,518,098	52,256,505	112,580,818	29,236,058	8,795,240	13,914,677	51,945,975	54,043,170
1832	50,626,723	49,127,102	106,324,604	28,331,316	8,761,836	14,379,096	51,472,248	50,409,310
1833	51,164,262	50,313,818	105,823,151	28,323,752	8,461,279	13,805,026	50,590,057	49,656,394

397. The National Debt, 1783–1832

(From *Parliamentary Papers*, 1868–1869, XXXV, II, pp. 304–309.)

Year	Total debt of the United Kingdom, funded and unfunded	Year	Total debt of the United Kingdom, funded and unfunded
1784	243,063,145	1809	654,461,311
1785	245,586,470	1810	662,193,856
1786	245,466,855	1811	678,200,436
1787	244,279,225	1812	706,254,587
1788	243,637,416	1813	788,093,781
1789	242,752,911	1814	813,140,176
1790	242,461,580	1815	861,039,049
1791	241,675,999	1816	845,968,483
1792	239,663,421	1817	839,382,145
1793	247,874,434	1818	840,582,664
1794	263,322,655	1819	836,530,982
1795	321,462,679	1820	834,900,960
1796	363,898,894	1821	827,984,498
1797	388,960,590	1822	835,207,294
1798	427,525,902	1823	827,480,164
1799	442,324,377	1824	819,023,672
1800	470,894,280	1825	809,831,468
1801	517,511,871	1826	808,826,590
1802	537,653,008	1827	805,098,942
1803	547,732,796	1828	800,032,289
1804	571,131,318	1829	796,799,532
1805	599,869,847	1830	784,803,997
1806	621,096,683	1831	782,716,684
1807	633,806,412	1832	781,457,599
1808	643,545,783	1833	779,730,379

398. Statement of the amount received into the Exchequer from Customs and Excise Duties, Stamps, Taxes and Postages of letters, in each Year, from 1801 to 1832.

(G. R. Porter, *The Progress of the Nation*, II (1838), p. 321.)

Years.	Customs and Excise.	Stamps.	Taxes.	Post-Office.	Total.	Population.*
	£.	£.	£.	£.	£.	
1801	19,330,867	3,049,844	8,857,134	843,976	33,081,821	16,338,102*
1802	23,524,702	3,194,354	9,063,130	972,547	35,754,733	16,559,064
1803	27,537,953	3,346,110	5,705,618	915,370	37,505,051	16,780,026
1804	31,612,842	3,670,849	8,900,839	952,894	45,137,424	17,000,987
1805	33,993,947	4,340,381	10,045,591	1,127,451	49,507,370	17,221,949
1806	35,947,535	4,609,693	11,813,027	1,151,376	53,521,631	17,442,911
1807	36,504,655	4,795,747	16,274,590	1,150,717	58,726,020	17,663,872
1808	37,074,168	5,069,371	18,044,941	1,143,600	61,332,080	17,884,834
1809	36,008,365	5,694,417	20,023,394	1,213,050	62,939,226	18,105,796
1810	38,300,069	5,899,372	20,406,428	1,333,538	65,939,407	18,326,758
1811	37,466,568	5,703,913	19,819,722	1,352,538	64,342,741	18,547,720*
1812	36,285,388	5,705,869	19,787,522	1,400,385	63,179,164	18,812,294
1813	38,281,158	6,013,120	21,400,394	1,494,615	67,189,287	19,076,868
1814	40,560,412	6,247,369	21,763,410	1,532,153	70,103,344	19,341,441
1815	41,759,340	6,373,667	21,618,123	1,621,385	71,372,515	19,606,015
1816	34,282,320	6,472,169	19,080,345	1,498,000	61,332,834	19,870,589
1817	32,741,687	6,861,169	10,002,749	1,395,231	51,000,836	20,135,163
1818	36,380,302	6,904,560	8,331,781	1,385,154	53,001,797	20,399,736
1819	35,766,301	6,666,712	7,855,246	1,528,538	51,816,797	20,664,310
1820	37,767,112	6,562,253	7,803,004	1,448,077	53,580,446	20,928,884
1821	38,765,814	6,513,599	7,814,690	1,383,538	54,477,641	21,193,458*
1822	37,947,025	6,632,546	7,218,844	1,428,231	53,226,646	21,504,784
1823	36,841,590	6,801,950	6,206,927	1,462,692	51,313,159	21,816,110
1824	38,095,781	7,244,042	4,922,070	1,520,615	51,782,508	22,127,436
1825	37,546,011	7,447,924	4,990,961	1,595,461	51,580,357	22,438,762
1826	36,452,731	6,702,350	4,702,744	1,570,000	49,427,825	22,750,089
1827	36,333,112	6,811,226	4,768,273	1,463,000	49,375,611	23,061,415
1828	37,995,094	7,107,950	4,849,303	1,508,000	51,460,347	23,372,741
1829	36,751,851	7,101,304	4,896,567	1,481,000	50,230,722	23,684,067
1830	36,184,707	7,058,121	5,013,405	1,466,012	49,722,245	23,995,393
1831	32,819,296	6,947,829	4,864,343	1,530,206	46,161,674	24,306,719*
1832	33,406,029	6,951,843	4,943,967	1,461,000	46,762,839	24,671,320

* The numbers to which an asterisk is affixed are those obtained from actual enumeration. Those assigned to other years before 1831 are obtained by dividing into equal portions the difference of numbers ascertained by the several enumerations. In 1832 an addition of 1½ per cent. is made.

399. Statement of the amount of loans and subsidies to foreign states during the wars of 1793–1814

(G. R. Porter, *The Progress of the Nation*, II (1838), pp. 335–338.)

	£.	£.		£.	£.
1793			**1801**		
Hanover	492,650		Portugal	200,114	
Hesse Cassel . . .	190,623		Sardinia	40,000	
Sardinia	150,000		Hesse Cassel . . .	100,000	
		833,273	Germany	150,000	
1794			German Princes . .	200,000	
Prussia . . .	1,226,495				690,114
Sardinia . . .	200,000		**1802**		
Hesse Cassel . .	437,105		Hesse Cassel . . .	33,451	
Hesse Darmstadt .	102,073		Sardinia . . .	52,000	
Baden	25,196		Russia	200,000	
Hanover . . .	559,376				285,451
		2,550,245	**1803**		
1795			Hanover	117,628	
Germany, Imperial Loan			Russia	63,000	
(35 Geo. III., c. 93.) .	4,600,000		Portugal	31,647	
Baden	1,794				212,275
Brunswick . . .	97,722		**1804**		
Hesse Cassel . .	317,492		Sweden	20,119	
Hesse Darmstadt .	79,605		Hesse Cassel . . .	83,304	
Hanover	478,348				103,423
Sardinia . . .	150,000		**1805**		
		5,724,961	Hanover	..	35,341
1796					
Hesse Darmstadt . .	20,076		**1806**		
Brunswick . . .	12,794		Hanover	76,865	
		32,870	Hesse Cassel . . .	18,982	
1797			Germany	500,000	
Hesse Darmstadt . .	57,015				595,847
Brunswick . . .	7,571		**1807**		
Germany, Imperial Loan			Hanover	19,899	
(37 Geo. III., c. 59) .	1,620,000		Russia	614,183	
		1,684,586	Hesse Cassel . .	45,000	
1798			Prussia	180,000	
Brunswick . . .	7,000				859,082
Portugal	120,013		**1808**		
		127,013	Spain	1,497,873	
1799			Sweden	1,100,000	
Prince of Orange . .	20,000		Sicily	300,000	
Hesse Darmstadt . .	4,812				2,897,873
Russia	825,000		**1809**		
		849,812	Spain	529,039	
1800			Portugal	600,000	
Germany	1,066,666		Sweden	300,000	
German Princes . .	500,000		Sicily	300,000	
Bavaria	501,017		Austria	850,000	
Russia	545,494				2,579,039
		2,613,177			

1810	£.	£.		£.	£.
Hesse Cassel . .	45,150		Russian Sufferers .	200,000	
Spain. . . .	402,875		Prussia . .	650,040	
Portugal . . .	1,237,518		Prince of Orange .	200,000	
Sicily. . . .	425,000		Austria . . .	500,000	
		2,110,543	Morocco . . .	14,419	
1811					6,786,022
Spain. . . .	220,690		1814		
Portugal . . .	1,832,168		Spain. . . .	450,000	
Sicily. . . .	275,000		Portugal . . .	1,500,000	
Portuguese Sufferers	39,555		Sicily. . . .	316,667	
		2,367,413	Sweden . . .	800,000	
1812			Russia . . .	2,169,982	
Spain. . . .	1,000,000		Prussia . . .	1,319,129	
Portugal . . .	2,167,832		Austria . . .	1,064,882	
Portuguese Sufferers	60,445		France (advanced to		
Sicily. . . .	400,000		Louis XVIII. to en-		
Sweden . . .	278,292		able him to return		
Morocco . . .	1,952		to France) . .	200,000	
		3,908,521	Hanover . . .	500,000	
1813			Denmark . . .	121,918	
Spain. . . .	1,000,000				8,442,578
Portugal . . .	1,644,063				
Sicily. . . .	600,000				
Sweden . . .	1,320,000				46,289,459
Russia . . .	657,500				

The direct payments made under the form of loans and subsidies did not form the whole of the contributions made by this country to its allies. Owing to the complicated form in which the public accounts were then rendered to Parliament, it would be a difficult task to unravel the whole of these transactions. It will perhaps afford a sufficient indication of the extent to which our support of the common cause was carried to state the value of the arms, clothing, and other stores that were furnished to our allies in the year 1814, and which were all in addition to the subsidies as detailed in the foregoing statement.

	£.
Austria–Arms and Clothing	410,751
France–Arms sent to the South of France	31,932
Hanover–Arms and Clothing	239,879
Holland–Ditto	267,759
Oldenburg–Clothing	10,008
Prussia–Arms	11,042
Russia–Provisions and Stores	385,491
Spain–Stores	136,338
Miscellaneous–Arms and Clothing supplied to various foreign Corps	88,845
	£1,582,045

400. Assessment and yield of the Income Tax

(J. Marshall, *A Digest of all the Accounts relating to the Population, Productions, Resources . . . &c. . . . of the United Kingdom*, II (1833), p. 27.)

Account No. I shows the number of persons assessed to the income tax in each class of income from £60 to £5,000 and over per year in the year ending 5 April 1801; Account No. II the gross receipt of the income, property, and land and assessed taxes yearly, 1798–1829 (totals corrected).

	ACCOUNT No. I.				ACCOUNT No. II.				
Rate of Income per annum. £	Number Assessed	Amount of Assessment £	Proportion of Income	Amount of Income £	Years	Income £	Property £	Land and Assessed Taxes £	Total Nett £
From 60 to 65	54,321	3,162,861	a 120th.	26,357	1798	823,286		4,608,144	5,561,309
65 „ 70	14,728	1,006,543	95 „	10,595	9	2,672,065		5,031,755	8,781,360
70 „ 75	23,913	1,617,892	70 „	23,113	1800	4,888,216		5,051,939	9,035,290
75 „ 80	9,321	666,792	65 „	10,259	1	6,011,628		4,893,456	9,857,134
80 „ 85	19,639	1,517,454	60 „	25,291	2	3,470,338		5,535,349	8,063,130
85 „ 90	7,302	611,377	55 „	11,116	3	424,322	16,918	6,178,932	5,705,618
90 „ 95	11,205	972,935	50 „	19,459	4	90,174	3,578,890	6,317,450	8,900,839
95 „ 100	7,335	689,551	45 „	15,323	5	50,472	4,496,142	6,527,980	10,045,591
100 „ 105	24,031	2,316,653	40 „	57,916	6	17,300	6,145,260	6,721,544	11,813,027
105 „ 110	4,925	499,845	38 „	13,154	7	26,665	10,131,344	7,357,756	16,274,901
110 „ 115	6,136	653,653	36 „	18,157	8	15,427	11,398,135	8,079,499	18,044,941
115 „ 120	4,083	457,687	34 „	13,461	9	26,801	12,386,913	9,063,716	20,023,394
120 „ 125	8,582	981,371	32 „	30,668	1810	11,789	13,492,215	8,311,640	20,406,428
125 „ 130	4,365	534,874	30 „	17,829	11	14,541	13,707,218	7,572,721	19,819,722
130 „ 135	5,760	723,812	28 „	25,850	12	8,274	13,628,454	7,677,204	19,787,522
135 „ 140	3,646	481,043	26 „	18,502	13	1,621	14,889,445	8,101,968	21,400,394
140 „ 145	5,784	776,873	24 „	32,370	14	1,208	15,109,803	8,207,511	21,763,410
145 „ 150	3,069	434,024	22 „	19,728	15	314	15,227,500	7,911,938	21,618,124
150 „ 155	9,203	1,305,703	20 „	65,285	16	—	12,276,871	7,562,411	19,080,345
155 „ 160	2,184	328,903	19 „	17,311	17	335	2,568,654	8,074,259	10,002,749
160 „ 165	3,761	576,183	18 „	32,010	18	31	658,338	8,271,990	8,331,781
165 „ 170	2,082	330,840	17 „	19,461	19	27	183,134	8,279,930	7,855,246
170 „ 175	3,647	598,582	16 „	37,411	1820	25	57,043	8,355,322	7,803,004
175 „ 180	2,035	344,627	15 „	22,975	1	24	44,376	8,205,033	7,814,690
180 „ 185	3,758	645,405	14 „	46,100	2	741	97,809	7,659,456	7,218,844
185 „ 190	1,884	337,404	13 „	25,954	3	—	27,897	6,811,650	6,206,927
190 „ 195	2,680	497,835	12 „	41,486	4	1,600	4,591	5,475,075	4,922,070
195 „ 200	2,320	454,321	11 „	41,302	5	—	4,062	5,178,950	1,990,961
200 „ 500	42,694	12,239,081	10 „	1,223,908	6	—	200	5,029,829	4,702,744
500 „ 1000	14,762	9,498,471	—	949,847	7	—	9,218	5,082,860	4,768,273
1000 „ 2000	6,927	9,041,154	—	904,115	8	—	800	5,169,074	4,849,303
2000 „ 5000	3,657	10,402,750	—	1,040,275	9	—	59	5,212,511	4,896,567
5000 & all abo.	1,020	9,970,395	—	997,039					
Estimate of 3 Districts in SCOTLAND, not returned in Classes.		74,676,894		5,857,826					
under £200		2,291,933		79,508					
£200 to 500		1,036,005		41,434					
500 to 1000		637,351		32,156					
1000 to 2000		375,997		30,608					
2000 to 5000		418,127		35,018					
5000 & all abo.		528,716		33,467					
Estimated		371,040		19,768					
TOTAL *Gt. Brit.*	320,659	80,337,063		6,129,785					

401. Pitt's speech introducing the Income Tax, 3 Dec. 1798

(Cobbett's *Parliamentary History*, XXXIV, 1–20.)

The trebling in 1797 of the assessment to the 'Assessed Taxes'–duties on certain luxuries, such as horses, servants, hair-powder and windows–had failed to produce the estimated revenue and had proved liable to evasion. Pitt was therefore driven to propose a graduated income tax in order to meet the unprecedentedly heavy burden of war expenditure.

... Before I proceed to submit ... the very important matters which form the subject of this day's consideration, I conceive it necessary to state the amount of the total services of the present year, and of the ways and means applicable to those services. The total sum voted for the ... navy and transport services amounts to £13,642,000, being the same sum, within a very small amount, as was granted last session. The next head of expense is the army, the estimates of which amounted to £8,840,000. The extraordinaries to be incurred in 1798 were stated at £3,200,000. There was also a vote of credit for one million, applicable to unforeseen expenses. This vote of credit will cover all the extraordinary expenses to the end of the year. But with respect to the vote of credit for this year, one million will be wanted to discharge that amount issued in exchequer bills. Under the article, then, of army expenditure, there remain the extraordinary services of the year 1799, which I may put at two millions. Thus the total amount under the head of army will be £8,840,000 including the one million ... and two millions. ... Under the head of ordnance services there has been voted £1,570,000. The above sums, with the addition of the miscellaneous services swell the total of the supply to £29,272,000.

Towards raising this supply the same resources will be applicable as are applicable at all periods, whether of peace or of war. The land and malt have always been taken at £2,750,000. There remains the lottery, £200,000, and the growing produce of the consolidated fund, which I take at £1,500,000. In addition to this, a tax was laid in the last session upon ... exports and imports. ... That duty I estimate at £1,700,000. The above articles form a total of £6,150,000. The remainder must be raised either by a tax within the year, in the same manner as the assessed tax bill of last year, or by a loan. The sum to be provided for is upwards of 23 millions. ... In the debates upon the subject of the assessed taxes last session two fundamental principles were established as the rule by which we should be guided in providing for the supplies for the service of the year. These were, first, to reduce the total amount to be at present raised by a loan; and next, as far as it was not reducible, to reduce it to such a limit that no more loan should be raised than a temporary tax should defray within a limited time. In the first place, the tax acceded to by the House last session was for the purpose of providing for the supplies of the year; and in the next place, for the purpose of extinguishing the loan raised in that year. From the modifications, however, which that measure underwent, the produce was considerably diminished. Other means, indeed, were adopted to remedy the deficiency thus occasioned. The voluntary and cheerful efforts which, so honourably to the country, came in aid of the deficit of the assessed taxes, and the produce of the exports and imports beyond the estimate, brought the amount of the sums raised to that at which they had been calculated. The different articles were estimated at $7\frac{1}{2}$ millions, and this sum is fully covered by the actual receipt under the different heads. The produce of the assessed taxes, under all the modifications, and all the tricks and evasions, is yet four millions. I had taken it at four and a half. . . . This deficiency is supplied by the excess on the head of the voluntary contributions. Instead of £1,500,000 the voluntary contributions already exceed 2 millions; and the sum of 7½ millions for which credit was taken, has been effective to the public service.

Satisfactory as it must be to review the circumstances to which we owe these advantages, and the benefits which the mode of raising the supplies to a considerable extent adopted last session has produced, it is unnecessary for me to state that, however the principle may deserve our approbation, it is much to be desired that its effects should be more extensive, and its application more efficient. . . . The wishes and the interest of individuals, I am sure, must unite in demanding a more comprehensive, a more equal, and a more vigorous application of a principle, the rare advantages of which we have been able to ascertain, if we have not yet been so fortunate as to enjoy. Last session those who acknowledged the importance of the principle of raising a considerable part of the supplies within the year, confined their objections to the proportion fixed upon the scale of the assessed taxes, as unequal in its application and liable to great evasion in practice. Though not insensible of the weight of the objection, I then felt it my duty, convinced as I was of the immense advantages of the system, to adopt some visible criterion by which to estimate and to regulate the extent of contribution, if it was not possible to devise means of embracing fully every class of property and every source of contribution. I felt it materially important to follow some durable, some apparent and sensible criterion, by which to apportion the burden. At the same time I felt that although the assessed taxes furnished the most comprehensive and efficient scale of contribution, there necessarily must be much income, much wealth, great means, which were not included in its application. It now appears that not by any error in the calculation of our resources, not by any exaggeration of our wealth, but by the general facility of modification, by the anxiety to render the measure as little oppressive as possible, a defalcation has arisen which ought not to have taken place. Yet, under the disadvantage and imperfections of an unequal and inadequate scale of application, the effects of the measure have tended to confirm our estimates of its benefits, and to encourage us to persevere in its principle. . . . Our leading principle should be to guard against all evasion, to endeavour by a fair and strict application to realize that full tenth, which it was the original purpose of the measure of the assessed taxes to obtain, and to extend this as far as possible in every direction. . . . If, then, the Committee assent to this principle, . . . they will perceive the necessity of obtaining a more specific statement of income than the loose scale of modification which, under the former measure, permitted such fraud and evasion. . . .

For this purpose it is my intention to propose, that the presumption founded upon the assessed taxes shall be laid aside, and that a general tax shall be imposed upon all the leading branches of income. . . . I trust that all who value the national honour and the national safety will co-operate in . . . obtaining by an efficient and comprehensive tax upon real ability, every advantage which flourishing and invigorated resources can confer upon national efforts. . . .

It is my intention to propose, that no income under £60 a year shall be called upon to contribute, and that the scale of modification up to £200 a year, as in the assessed taxes, shall be introduced with restriction. The quota which will then be called for ought to amount to a full tenth of the contributor's income. The mode proposed of obtaining this contribution differs from that pursued in the assessed taxes, as instead of trebling their amount, the statement of income is to proceed from the party himself. In doing this it is not proposed that income shall be distinctly laid open, but it shall only be declared that the assessment is beyond the proportion of a tenth of the income. . . . When doubts are entertained that a false statement has been given, it shall be competent for the commissioners to call for a specification of income. . . .

The next consideration is one liable to more difficulty and doubt . . . but in which we are still not without lights to guide us–I mean as to the probable amount of a tax of this kind . . . I shall proceed to state what is the first great object of income. I mean the property derived from land. . . . Examinations state the cultivated land of the country to amount to little less than 40 millions of acres. Any attempt to state what is the average value of these 40 millions of acres must be extremely uncertain. Many persons most conversant on the subject believe the average value to be 15s. per acre. I shall however take it at no more than 12s. 6d. I will put the average value at 25 millions a year. . . . It will be proper to propose a reduction for all under £60 a year, and . . . the scale of income from £60 to £200 a year, and rising from a 120th part to a tenth. I mean on this account to assume a deduction of one fifth, and to state the taxable property at only 20 millions.

. . . The value of the income from land which belongs to the tenant I take at 19 millions; the income to the landlord at 25 millions. Instead of deducting only one fifth, as I have suggested with respect to the landlord, I shall propose with respect to the tenant to deduct two-thirds, leaving 5 millions as the taxable property of the tenants. The next income arising from land, is . . . what is received from tithes. This is an income enjoyed, either by lay impropriators or by the clergy. . . . I estimate the value of them to be 5 millions . . . [with] a reduction of one fifth. . . . Another species of property is that which arises from mines, and from shares in canals . . . [and] the sale of timber. I take all these three . . . at 3 millions. Another species of rent is that received for houses. . . . I shall . . . take the rent of houses at no more than 6 millions. . . . The profits gained by the professors of the law . . . are estimated at one million and a half. . . . Allowing, besides, for all the branches of the medical professions, I conceive that 2 millions is a very small sum as the amount of incomes arising from the professions.

The next head of income related to the profits of retail trade. . . . The reduction I shall propose to take at one-eighth of the nett sum of the profits of the trade of Great Britain, after which there will remain a sum of £5,000,000 applicable to . . . tax. There will then remain another article of taxation, which is the income spent in this country by persons who derive it from other parts of the world; and unquestionably all who reside in this kingdom . . . cannot be dissatisfied at contributing to their own support and protection. Of this description, the only persons I shall think it necessary to estimate are those whose incomes arise from . . . property in Ireland, and who reside in this country, and persons owning estates in the West Indies, or receiving the interest of mortgages on estates in that part of the world. With respect to those persons whose incomes arise from Ireland, I believe it is the generally received opinion, that the property of persons of this description amounted to at least £1,000,000 a considerable time since, and now, from the increase of rents, it may reasonably be estimated far beyond that sum. With respect to the incomes of estates in the West Indies, the total amount cannot be estimated at less than £7,000,000 sterling. . . . From that are to be deducted the amount of the exports carried out, and the charge of cultivating the estates in the West Indies; after which deduction I estimate the . . . income . . . at 4 millions. . . .

The next description of property is the income of persons not in trade. Under this head will be included annuities of all kinds, public and private mortgages, and income arising from money lent upon securities under various denominations. At the same time . . . in estimating the general rental of the land of England I have taken it with all its burdens, and consequently have included the mortgages. . . . In respect therefore of this description of property I do not now make any distinct estimate. . . . I include . . . the public annuitants in the view of the proposed tax. . . . The rental of the public annuitants may be estimated at £15,000,000; but . . . there will of course be admitted the same exemptions to all annuitants who have less than £60 a year, and the same modifications to all who possess from £60 to £200 a year. At the same time it is to be considered that these exemptions and modifications are only to apply to those individuals whose whole income amounts to less than £200 a year. If persons possess incomes from various sources, they are to be calculated in the aggregate. . . . I therefore state the total income from the public funds at £12,000,000 a year.

There now remain the other great sources of trade [sic] to the inhabitants of this country; the produce of trade, foreign and domestic: and this branch of income is, in its nature, more difficult of estimate than any other. We have however lights and aids by which we may come to a knowledge of a material part at least of this source of national wealth, I mean the produce of our foreign trade. The capital employed in this way is certainly not less than £80,000,000 sterling. Assuming this as the capital, the next question is, what ought we to take as the profit to all the description of persons employed in carrying on this branch of our trade? In estimating this, we must necessarily include in our view, not merely the merchant who exports, but all the orders and descriptions of persons from the manufacturer upwards who are in any way connected with our export trade. Under this head come in the profits of broker-age, wharfage, and carriage with all the other contributory trades connected with foreign commerce; and I am sure I make a moderate calculation when I estimate the profits upon the capital of £80,000,000 at 15%. I take, therefore, £12,000,000 as the income of all the persons connected with the foreign trade of this kingdom.

There now remains that which more than any other branch of our income baffles the power of scrutiny, and affords even very limited grounds for conjecture: I mean the profits arising from domestic trade and manufacture. Here the many descriptions of persons whose skill and industry are the source of income in all the progress of our arts and manufactures . . . serve to make calculation almost impossible from their variety and extent. Even here, however, we have some means of forming an idea. Of the general capital of £80,000,000 employed in the foreign trade, it has been pretty accurately determined, that about £30,000,000 are destined and employed in the export of the leading manufactures of England. I am sure, then, that the Committee will go along with me in saying that the amount of the capital . . . employed in internal trade must be four times the amount of our export of British manufactures. . . . . I cannot take it at less than £120,000,000, and upon this capital I estimate the gain at no more than 15%, making a sum of £18,000,000 per annum of income. There is one other description of income which, though it embraces a vast variety of individuals, is reducible to none of the former heads, but comes naturally to be included in the article of domestic trade; I mean artisans, architects, brewers, distillers, builders, brickmakers, masons, carpenters, and all that innumerable class of persons who, by their skill in their professions, draw their incomes from the general prosperity of the country. . . . I am sure . . . I understate it when I take it at £10,000,000 per annum. I thus estimate the whole amount of our internal manufactures and trade at £28,000,000 a year. . . .

I make the whole annual rental and profits, after making the deductions which I think reasonable, £102,000,000 sterling. . . . Upon this sum a tax of 10% is likely to produce £10,000,000 a year. . . .

(c) THE CURRENCY AND THE BANKING SYSTEM

402. Third report of the Committee of Secrecy of the House of Commons, on the affairs of the Bank, 21 April 1797

(Cobbett's *Parliamentary History*, XXXIII, 441–449.)

. . . Your Committee find, that the cash and bullion in the Bank having been considerably reduced between the month of June 1795 and the 21st of February 1797, were on that day in so low a state, as to induce the Directors of the Bank to lay before the Chancellor of the Exchequer the precise amount, together with their apprehensions of its being still farther reduced, in order that he might take such measures as might be thought most adviseable for the public interest.

It appears . . . that between that day and the 26th of February, the drain on the Bank for cash increased in a still more rapid and alarming proportion; and . . . that there was strong reason to apprehend that the Bank might, in the course of a few days . . . be totally disabled from continuing its payments in cash in the ordinary course of its business . . . that there was no reason to suppose that the drain would on the . . . following days be in the least diminished, but rather that it would have been considerably augmented; that no means were suggested by the Directors of the Bank for preventing the danger which was apprehended, nor did any such occur to them at the time, or have since been suggested to this Committee; and it therefore appears to your Committee that no measure could then have been taken which could have prevented such danger, other than the suspension of payments in cash. . . .

The alarm of invasion which, when an immediate attack was first apprehended in Ireland, had occasioned some extraordinary demand for cash on the Bank of England in the months of December and January last, began in February to produce similar effects in the North of England. Your Committee find, that in consequence of this apprehension the farmers suddenly brought the produce of their lands to sale, and carried the notes of the country banks, which they had collected by these and other means, into those banks for payment; that this unusual and sudden demand for cash reduced the several banks at Newcastle to the necessity of suspending their payments in specie, and of availing themselves of all the means in their power of procuring a speedy supply of cash from the metropolis; that the effects of this demand on the Newcastle banks, and of their suspension of payments in cash, soon spread over various parts of the country, from whence similar applications were consequently made to the metropolis for cash; that the alarm, thus diffused, not only occasioned an increased demand for cash in the country, but probably a disposition in many to hoard what was thus obtained; that this call on the metropolis, through whatever channels, directly affected the Bank of England as the great repository of cash, and was in the course of still farther operation upon it, when stopped by the Minute of Council of the 26th of February.

Your committee further observe that, as the Directors of the Bank had, previous to the actual existence of the alarm, lessened the amount of their discounts, so as to have reduced them, by the 25th of February, one-fourth of the sum at which they stood at the beginning of the present year, and as the restriction of the accommodation afforded by them to individuals produced a similar decrease in the amount of discounts by private bankers, the joint effect of this diminished accommodation to the public, at a time when ... circumstances ... seemed to require an increase of it, must necessarily have been an additional embarrassment in commercial and pecuniary transactions, tending to increase the demand for the cash on the Bank. ...

In investigating the more remote causes which might have operated ... to increase the effect of the alarm ... your Committee have collected a great variety of statements and opinions. ...

... The balance of trade in favour of this country has, during the war, very greatly increased, so as in each of the years 1793, 1794, 1795, and 1796, to have amounted upon an average to about £6,500,000, creating a balance on the whole of about 26 millions, notwithstanding ... the great importation of corn, occasioned by the extraordinary scarcity which lately prevailed. ...

From a review of the course of exchange, particularly with Hamburg ... it appears that in the month of May 1795, the course of exchange with Hamburg was reduced to such a rate as ... rendered the export of bullion from this country a profitable traffic. That it so continued till March 1796 ... and towards the end of February last rose so high as to be favourable to the import of bullion. ...

Your Committee have next adverted to the situation of the country at the commencement of the war, in order more correctly to estimate the effects of the war on the general state of cash and bullion within the kingdom. It appears that the embarrassments which arose early in the year 1793 are to be attributed to temporary causes ... particularly the want of a circulating medium, produced by the discredit of a great quantity of country bank notes; and that from the circumstance of the distress being relieved by the loan of exchequer bills, all of which were duly repaid, there was not a deficiency of cash at that time in the kingdom. It further appears that although in the beginning of the year 1793 the cash and bullion in the Bank were reduced very much below their ordinary amount, yet the quantity of foreign gold purchased by the Bank in . . . 1793 very greatly exceeded the quantities purchased in the three preceding years . . . so that long before the close of the year the quantity of their cash and bullion was raised to an amount much above what has been deemed necessary for their ordinary purposes. . . . It also appears, that . . . the cash and bullion in the Bank increased early in the year 1794. . . .

Your Committee have next proceeded to inquire what causes, since the close of the year 1792, may have contributed to draw cash and bullion out of the country, or prevent the influx of them into it. The first that have occurred to the Committee are the expenses incident to the war, and other expenses abroad. . . . It appears that the amount of those expenditures is about £32,810,977, of which sum about £15,700,000 appears to have been expended in Europe. . . .

Your Committee have obtained accurate information of the remittances made for loans and advances to the Emperor. . . . Part of the loan of £4,600,000 negotiated in 1794 and 1795 was remitted in bullion, part of it in gold to the amount of about £150,000, consisting principally of Louis d'ors, and the remainder, about £1,043,000, in silver, chiefly Spanish dollars. It appears that the greatest part of this bullion was purchased of the Bank . . . that the rest . . . was remitted in bills of exchange; and that the advances made by Government to the Emperor and other foreign princes in 1796 and 1797 were entirely remitted by bills of exchange, no part having been remitted in cash or bullion. . . . It further appears . . . that the quantity of gold coined at the Mint during . . . 1793, 1794, 1795, and 1796, amount[ed] to upwards of six millions sterling. . . .

In addition to these causes of actual expense, your Committee think proper to advert to various circumstances which may contribute either to the delay of the due return of commercial dealings, or require enlarged means of circulation in the country. Of this nature are, the habit of the British merchant to give longer credit to the foreign merchant than he receives in return; the change of the course of trade since the war, and the opening of new accounts with new customers; the circuitous remittance of money from various parts, in consequence of interruptions in the means of direct communication. . . . To these are to be added the increase of domestic commerce, the increase of manufactures for home consumption, the general spirit of internal improvement in agriculture, and in the formation of canals and other public works . . . the increased price of freight, shipping, insurance, demurrage, and a variety of other articles, generally affecting the trade of the country . . . the advanced price of labour, and of all the necessaries of life, and almost every kind of commodity. Added to all these circumstances, the operations and expenses of the war may be supposed to require a greater quantity of circulating medium. . . .

. . . The general effect of the low price of the public funds, and the great profit to be made by purchasing floating Government securities, seems to have been to invest in various Government securities large sums of money before employed as part of the active capital of the country. . . . The advances made by the Bank to Government have also been stated, and particularly by the Governor and Directors of the Bank, as having materially contributed to their present embarrassment. . . .

403. Report of the Select Committee of the House of Commons on the high price of gold bullion, 1810

(Cobbett's *Parliamentary Debates*, XVII, App. ccii–cclxiii.)

The Act of 1797 which threw the country off the gold standard by making the Bank of England's notes inconvertible was intended to be only a temporary measure, but it was periodically renewed until 1819. This famous report, which was inspired largely by Ricardo's tract, "The High Price of Bullion a Proof of the Depreciation of Banknotes", was composed by Huskisson (then out of office), Francis Horner, the Whig economist, and Henry Thornton, the banker. The report threw the blame for the depreciated currency on the Bank Directors, who had failed (inevitably, no doubt) to keep its note issues within bounds; but the committee's chief recommendation–a speedy return to convertibility–was really impracticable so long as inflationary war conditions continued.

Since the suspension of cash payments in 1797 . . . it is certain that, even if gold is still our measure of value and standard of prices, it has been exposed to a new cause of variation, from the possible excess of that paper which is not convertible into gold at will; and the limit of this new variation is as indefinite as the excess to which that paper may be issued. It may indeed be doubted whether, since the new system of Bank of England payments has been fully established, gold has in truth continued to be our measure of value: and whether we have any other standard prices than that circulating medium, issued primarily by the Bank of England and in a secondary manner by the country Banks, the variations of which in relative value may be as indefinite as the possible excess of that circulating medium. But whether our present measure of value, and standard of prices, be this paper currency thus variable in its relative value, or continues still to be gold, but gold rendered more variable than it was before in consequence of being interchangeable for a paper currency which is not at will convertible into gold, it is, in either case, most desirable for the public that our circulating medium should again be conformed, as speedily as circumstances will permit, to its real and legal standard, gold bullion. . . .

It is due, however, in justice to the present Directors of the Bank of England, to remind the House that the suspension of their cash payments, though it appears in some degree to have originated in a mistaken view taken by the Bank of the peculiar difficulties of that time, was not a measure sought for by the Bank, but imposed upon it by the Legislature for what were held to be urgent reasons of State policy and public expediency. . . .

Under the former system, when the Bank was bound to answer its notes in specie upon demand, the state of the foreign exchanges and the price of gold did most materially influence its conduct in the issue of those notes, though it was not the practice of the Directors systematically to watch either the one or the other. So long as gold was demandable for their paper, they were speedily apprised of a depression of the exchange and a rise in the price of gold, by a run upon them for that article. If at any time they incautiously exceeded the proper limit of their advances and issues, the paper was quickly brought back to them by those who were tempted to profit by the market price of gold or by the rate of exchange. In this manner the evil soon cured itself. The Directors of the Bank having their apprehensions excited by the reduction of their stock of gold, and being able to replace their loss only by reiterated purchases of bullion at a very losing price, naturally contracted their issues of paper, and thus gave to the remaining paper, as well as to the coin for which it was inter-changeable, an increased value, while the clandestine exportation either of the coin, or the gold produced from it, combined in improving the state of the exchange, and in producing a corresponding diminution of the difference between the market price and Mint price of gold, or of paper convertible into gold. . . .

It was a necessary consequence of the suspension of cash payments to exempt the Bank from that drain of gold which, in former times, was sure to result from an unfavourable exchange and a high price of bullion. And the Directors, released from all fears of such a drain, and no longer feeling any inconvenience from such a state of things, have not been prompted to restore the exchanges and the price of gold to their proper level by a reduction of their advances and issues. The Directors, in former times, did not perhaps perceive and acknowledge the principle more distinctly than those of the present day, but they felt the inconvenience and obeyed its impulse; which practically established a check and limitation to the issue of paper. In the present times the inconvenience is not felt, and the check, accordingly, is no longer in force. But your Committee beg leave to report it to the House as their most clear opinion, that so long as the suspension of cash payments is permitted to subsist, the price of gold bullion and the general course of exchange with foreign countries, taken for any considerable period of time, form the best general criterion from which any inference can be drawn, as to the sufficiency or excess of paper currency in circulation; and that the Bank of England cannot safely regulate the amount of its issues without having reference to the criterion presented by these two circumstances. And upon a review of all the facts and reasonings which have already been stated, your Committee are further of opinion that, although the commercial state of this country, and the political state of the Continent, may have had some influence on the high price of gold bullion and the unfavourable course of exchange with foreign countries, this price, and this depreciation, are also to be ascribed to the want of a permanent check, and a sufficient limitation of the paper currency in this country. . . .

The suspension of cash payments has had the effect of committing into the hands of the Directors of the Bank of England, to be exercised by their sole discretion, the important charge of supplying the country with that quantity of circulating medium which is exactly proportioned to the wants and occasions of the public. . . . That is a trust which it is unreasonable to expect that the Directors of the Bank of England should ever be able to discharge. The most detailed knowledge of the actual trade of the country, combined with the profound science in all the principles of money and circulation, would not enable any man or set of men to adjust, and keep always adjusted, the right proportion of circulating medium in a country to the wants of trade. When the currency consists entirely of the precious metals, or of paper conver-tible at will into the precious metals, the natural process of commerce, by establishing exchanges among all the different countries of the world, adjusts, in every particular country, the proportion of circulating medium to its actual occasions, according to that supply of the precious metals which the mines furnish to the general market of the world. The proportion, which is thus adjusted and maintained by the natural operation of commerce, cannot be adjusted by any human wisdom or skill. If the natural system of currency and circulation be abandoned, and a discretionary issue of paper money substituted in its stead, it is vain to think that any rules can be devised for the exact exercise of such a discretion, though some cautions may be pointed out to check and control its consequences, such as are indicated by the effect of an excessive issue upon exchanges and the price of gold. The Directors of the Bank of England, in the judgment of your Committee, have exercised the new and extraordinary discretion reposed in them since 1797, with an integrity and a regard to the public interest, according to their conceptions of it, and indeed a degree of forbearance in turning it less to the profit of the Bank than it would easily have admitted of, that merit the continuance of that confidence which the public has so long and so justly felt in the integrity with which its affairs are directed, as well as in the unshaken stability and ample funds of that great establishment. That their recent policy involves great practical errors, which it is of the utmost public importance to correct, your Committee are fully convinced; but those errors are less to be imputed to the Bank Directors, than to be stated as the effect of a new system, of which, however it originated, or was rendered necessary as a temporary expedient, it might have been well if Parliament had sooner taken into view all the consequences. When your Committee consider that this discretionary power of supplying the kingdom with circulating medium, has been exercised under an opinion that the paper could not be issued to excess if advanced in discounts to merchants in good bills payable at stated periods, and likewise under an opinion that neither the price of bullion nor the course of exchanges need be adverted to, as affording any indication with respect to the sufficiency or excess of such paper, your Committee cannot hesitate to say that these opinions of the Bank must be regarded as in a great measure the operative cause of the continuance of the present state of things. . . .

. . . So long as the cash payments of the Bank are suspended, the whole paper of the country bankers is a superstructure raised upon the foundation of the paper of the Bank of England. The same check which the convertibility into specie, under a better system, provides against the excess of any part of the paper circulation, is, during the present system, provided against an excess of country Bank paper by its convertibility into Bank of England paper. If an excess of paper be issued in a country district while the London circulation does not exceed its due proportion, there will be a local rise of prices in that country district, but prices in London will remain as before. Those who have the country paper in their hands will prefer buying in London where things are cheaper, and will therefore return that country paper upon the banker who issued it, and will demand from him Bank of England notes or bills upon London; and thus the excess of country paper being continually returned upon the issuers for Bank of England paper, the quantity of the latter necessarily and effectually limits the quantity of the former. . . . If the Bank of England paper itself should at any time, during the suspension of cash payments, be issued to excess, a corresponding excess may be issued of country Bank paper, which will not be checked; the foundation being enlarged, the superstructure admits of a proportionate extension. And thus, under such a system, the excess of Bank of England paper will produce its effect upon prices not merely in the ratio of its own increase, but in a much higher proportion.

It has not been in the power of your Committee to obtain such information as might enable them to state with anything like accuracy, the amount of country Bank paper in circulation. But they are led to infer from all the evidence they have been able to procure on this subject, not only that a great number of new country Banks has been established within these last two years, but also that the amount of issues of those which are of an older standing has in general been very considerably increased: whilst on the other hand, the high state of mercantile and public credit, the proportionate facility of converting at short notice all public and commercial securities into Bank of England paper, joined to the preference generally given within the limits of its own circulation to the paper of a well-established country Bank over that of the Bank of England, have probably not rendered it necessary for them to keep any large permanent deposits of Bank of England paper in their hands. And it seems reasonable to believe that the total amount of the unproductive stock of all the country Banks, consisting of specie and Bank of England paper, is much less at this period, under a circulation vastly increased in extent, than it was before the restriction of 1797. The temptation to establish country Banks and issue promissory notes has therefore greatly increased. . . .

Upon a review of all the facts and reasonings which have been submitted to the consideration of your Committee in the course of their inquiry, they have formed an opinion . . . that there is at present an excess in the paper circulation of this country, of which the most unequivocal symptom is the very high price of bullion, and next to that, the low state of the continental exchanges; that this excess is to be ascribed to the want of sufficient check and control in the issues of paper from the Bank of England; and originally, to the suspension of cash payments, which removed the natural and true control. For upon a general view of the subject, your Committee are of opinion that no safe, certain and constantly adequate provision against an excess of paper currency, either occasional or permanent, can be found, except in the convertibility of all such paper into specie. Your Committee cannot, therefore, but see reason to regret that the suspension of cash payments, which, in the most favourable light in which it can be viewed, was only a temporary measure, has been continued so long; and particularly, that by the manner in which the present continuing Act is framed, the character should have been given to it of a permanent war measure.

Your Committee conceive that it would be superfluous to point out in detail the disadvantages which must result to the country from any such general excess of currency as lowers its relative value. The effect of such an augmentation of prices upon all money transactions for time; the unavoidable injury suffered by annuitants, and by creditors of every description, both private and public; the unintended advantage gained by Government and all other debtors, are consequences too obvious to require proof, and too repugnant to justice to be left without remedy. By far the most important portion of this effect appears to your Committee to be that which is communicated to the wages of common country labour, the rate of which, it is well known, adapts itself more slowly to the changes which happen in the value of money, than the price of any other species of labour or commodity. And it is enough for your Committee to allude to some classes of the public servants, whose pay, if once raised in consequence of a depreciation of money, cannot so conveniently be reduced again to its former rate, even after money shall have recovered its value. . . .

Your Committee therefore, having very anxiously and deliberately considered this subject, report it . . . as their opinion that the system of the circulating medium of this country ought to be brought back, with as much speed as is compatible with a wise and necessary caution, to the original principle of cash payments at the option of the holder of Bank paper. . . .

The particular mode of gradually effecting the resumption of cash payments ought therefore . . . to be left in a great measure to the discretion of the Bank, and Parliament ought to do little more than to fix, definitely, the time at which cash payments are to become as before compulsory. . . . Your Committee would suggest that the restriction on cash payments cannot safely be removed at an earlier period than two years from the present time; but your Committee are of opinion that early provision ought to be made by Parliament for terminating, by the end of that period, the operation of the several Statutes which have imposed and continued that restriction. . . . Even if peace should intervene, two years should be given to the Bank for resuming its payments; but . . . even if the war should be prolonged, cash payments should be resumed by the end of that period. . . .

It will be convenient also for the Chartered Banks of Ireland and Scotland, and all the country Banks, that they should not be compelled to pay in specie until some time after the resumption of payments in cash by the Bank of England; but that they should continue for a short period upon their present footing, of being liable to pay their own notes on demand in Bank of England paper.

404. Second report of the Committee of Secrecy of the House of Commons, on the expediency of the Bank resuming cash payments, 6 May 1819

(Hansard's *Parliamentary Debates*, XL, 152–178.)

The device of a temporary gold bullion standard instead of an immediate restoration of cash payments was taken from Ricardo's tract, "Proposals for an Economical and Secure Currency" (1816). The Bank of England in 1819 did not possess enough gold to supply the country with a gold currency, but it did have enough to meet the requirements of merchants who needed bullion to make gold payments abroad. In May 1821 the Bank, having by that time bought a sufficient quantity of gold, voluntarily anticipated the date when cash payments should be completely restored, and another Act was passed to enable it to do so from 1 May of that year. Thus, after a period of twenty-four years, England again possessed a gold currency. The report was largely the work of Peel, the chairman of the committee. In 1811, in company with Vansittart's majority, he had voted for the absurd proposition that banknotes had not depreciated in value. Subsequently he read the Bullion Report and was converted to a more sensible view. It was the first of his three great political recantations.

[*The Committee's proposals.*]

. . . They propose, that after the 1st May 1821, the Bank shall be liable to deliver a quantity of gold, not less than 60 ounces, of standard fineness, to be first assayed and stamped at H.M.'s Mint, at the established Mint price of £3 17s. 10½d. per oz. in exchange for such an amount of notes presented to them as shall represent, at that rate, the value of the gold demanded.

That this liability of the Bank to deliver gold in exchange for their notes shall continue for not less than two nor more than three years, from the 1st May 1821; and that at the end of that period, cash payments shall be resumed.

That on a day to be fixed by Parliament, not later than the 1st February 1820, the Bank shall be required to deliver gold, of standard fineness, assayed and stamped as before-mentioned, in exchange for their notes (an amount of not less than 60 ounces of gold being demanded) at £4 1s. per oz., that being nearly the market price of standard gold in bars on an average of the last three months.

That on or before the 1st October 1820, the Bank shall pay their notes in gold of standard fineness, at the rate of £3 19s. 6d.; and on or before the 1st May 1821, as before-mentioned, at the ancient standard rate of £3 17s. 10½d.

. . . By requiring the Bank to pay, after the 1st May 1821, a given quantity of notes in standard gold, at the Mint price, a security against fluctuation in the value of the paper currency will be provided, of the same nature with that which payments in specie afforded previously to the Restriction Act. If the issues of the Bank shall at any time exceed the amount to which they must be limited, in order to maintain their value on a par with gold, the Bank will be subjected to an immediate demand for gold, and will naturally have recourse, as before the restriction, to the contraction of the issues of their paper.

The chief recommendation of this plan . . . is that it will enable the Bank to pay their notes in gold at a much earlier period than they could pay them in the present gold currency. There cannot, while this plan is acted on, be any demand for gold for the purposes of internal circulation; and whatever quantity it would be necessary to provide, with the view of replacing the small notes at present in circulation, may therefore be dispensed with. . . .

They do not express any preference for the system of bullion payments over that of payments in specie abstractedly; nor are they prepared to recommend them as a permanent substitute; but they consider them the best means of facilitating and ensuring the resumption of payments in specie with the least public inconvenience. They are of opinion that, when once the ancient standard of value in this country has been re-established, the great impediments to a return to our former system will have been overcome; and it will be in the power of the Bank, or of individuals, by taking advantage of a favourable state of exchange, to increase the supply of the precious metals in this country, to any extent to which they are likely to be required. . . .

405. The numbers of country banks in England and Wales, 1784–1832

(L. S. Pressnell, *Country Banking in the Industrial Revolution* (1956), p. 11.)

This table was compiled from various sources: the 1784 figures (which are for England only) from *Bailey's British Directory* for 1784, those for 1793 and 1797 from evidence presented to the Committee of Secrecy on the Bank in 1797, the [*c.*] 1794 total from *The Universal British Directory* (*c.* 1791–1797) and those for 1796 and 1798 from contemporary printed lists. After 1800 the figures given in the *Post Office London Directories* are compared with official statistics, derived from the issue of licences to all note-issuing bankers under the Act of 1808, and published in *Parliamentary Papers*, 1819, III and 1843, LII. The difficulties in making a precise estimate of the actual number of country banks at any time in their existence are discussed in Pressnell, *op. cit.*, pp. 8–11. The figures do, however, give a sufficient general picture of the remarkable growth of country banking during this period.

	No. of banks, excluding branches		Official statistics	Post Office London Directory		Official statistics	Post Office London Directory
1784	119	1800	—	370	1817	585	577
		1801	—	383	1818	576	596
1793	280	1802	—	397	1819	587	595
		1803	—	410	1820	—	606
c. 1794	272	1804	—	414	1821	521	609
		1805	—	438	1822	526	623
1796	301	1806	—	478	1823	547	641
		1807	—	515	1824	547	660
1797	230	1808	—	573	1825	544	684
		1809	755	631	1826	554	597
1798	312	1810	783	654	1827	465	600
		1811	741	656	1828	456	615
		1812	739	646	1829	460	640
		1813	761	660	1830	439	628
		1814	733	657	1831	436	616
		1815	699	626	1832	424	607
		1816	643	575			

406. The value and denominations of private bank-notes on which stamp duties were paid, Oct. 1804 to Jan. 1826

(L. S. Pressnell, *Country Banking in the Industrial Revolution* (1956), p. 188.)

These figures are compiled from official statistics published in 1810, 1819, 1821 and 1826. They are defective in certain respects (see the discussion of this problem in Pressnell, pp. 180–189), but no more complete or reliable figures exist from which a more accurate picture of the circulation of the notes of country banks at this time may be drawn.

Year ending 11 October	Values (£ millions)			Numbers (millions)	
	Notes for £2. 2s. or less	Notes for more than £2. 2s.	Value of all notes stamped	£2. 2s. or less	Above £2. 2s.
1805	3·2	7·5	10·7	3·2	1·2
1806	3·3	7·6	10·8	3·2	1·2
1807	2·4	3·9	6·3	2·3	0·6
1808	2·1	6·0	8·1	2·0	0·9
1809	6·2	8·4	14·6	6·1	1·3
1810	3·7	6·1	9·8	3·5	1·0
1811	2·8	6·3	9·1	2·7	0·8
1812	3·0	6·9	9·9	3·0	1·1
1813	4·0	7·8	11·8	3·9	1·2
1814	4·2	5·8	9·9	4·1	0·9
1815	2·9	4·3	7·2	2·8	0·7
1816	2·2	4·1	6·3	2·2	0·6
1817	3·1	5·9	8·9	3·0	0·9
1818	4·0	7·9	11·9	4·0	1·1
1819	2·2	3·8	6·0	2·2	0·6
1820	1·7	1·8	3·5	1·6	0·3
1821	2·1	1·9	4·0	2·0	0·3
1822	2·0	2·2	4·2	2·0	0·4
1823	2·1	3·6	4·7	2·1	0·4
1824	2·4	3·7	6·1	2·4	0·6
1825	3·2	5·6	8·8	3·1	0·8
Quarter beginning 11 Oct. 1825	0·7	1·2	1·9	0·7	0·2

407. Table of the number of joint-stock companies formed before 1824 and then in existence

(H. English, *A Complete View of the Joint-Stock Companies formed during the Years 1824 and 1825* . . . (London, 1827).)

. . . The appendix annexed affords an ample proof of the advantages to be derived from Joint Stock Associations, where the object is legitimate, and when carried into effect by honourable means. When we consider that to them the country is indebted for an advance of no less a sum than £34,065,936:13s.:6d. outlaid in the formation of canals, docks, bridges, roads, &c. and to which we are also indebted for numerous insurance associations from which so much benefit has been derived, as well as those useful associations for the supply of water, gas, &c. no comment is necessary to prove their utility, and the policy of encouraging such modes of investment of capital, by the passing of an act for their better regulation and management. . . . [p. 33.]

Summary of Joint Stock Companies formed before 1824 and then existing:

	Company	Capital			Amount paid			No. of shares
		£	s	d	£	s	d	
63	Canals	12,202,096	0	0	12,202,096	0	0	175,374
7	Docks	6,164,590	12	0	6,164,590	12	0	57,582¼
25	Assurance	20,488,948	0	0	6,548,948	0	0	399,841
16	Water Works	2,973,170	0	0	2,973,170	0	0	39,760
4	Bridges	2,452,017	2	8	1,952,017	2	8	31,731
27	Gas	1,630,700	0	0	1,215,300	0	0	35,194
7	Roads	494,964	18	10	479,814	18	10	7,472
7	Miscellaneous	1,530,000	0	0	1,530,000	0	0	17,580
156		47,936,486	13	6	34,065,936	13	6	764,534¼

Summary of Companies formed in 1824–5 and existing in 1827:

		Capital	Amount paid	Present value	Amount liable to be called	No. of shares
44	Mining Companies	26,776,000	5,455,100	2,927,350	21,320,900	358,700
20	Gas Companies	9,061,000	2,162,000	1,504,625	6,899,000	152,140
14	Insurance Companies	28,120,000	2,247,000	1,606,000	25,873,000	545,000
49	Miscellaneous	38,824,600	5,321,850	3,265,975	33,502,750	562,500
127		102,781,600	15,185,950	9,303,950	87,595,650	1,618,340

Summary of Companies formed in 1824–5 and since abandoned:

		Capital	Amount paid	No. of shares
16	Mining Companies	5,585,000	400,900	98,200
9	Investment do.	8,550,000	746,000	78,500
20	Canal Rail Road &c.	19,135,000	393,375	246,000
30	Steam Navigation	2,927,500	79,900	35,650
43	Miscellaneous	20,409,000	799,500	390,250
118	Companies	56,606,500	2,419,675	848,600

[The pamphlet lists a further 379 companies which were projected during the wave of speculation of 1824–1825, but of whose actual formation no precise information was available. These 379 companies had a nominal capital of £212,785,000, divided into 3,494,380 shares.]

408. Memorandum by the Prime Minister and the Chancellor of the Exchequer on the banking system, 13 Jan. 1826

(*British Museum Additional MSS.* 38371, ff. 96–105.)

The memorandum was sent to the Governor and Deputy Governor of the Bank of England, for the consideration of the Court of Directors. The reply, which rejected the Government's suggestions, was dispatched on the 20th. [*Ibid., f.* 106.]

Speculation and over-production in the early 1820s had brought on a great commercial crisis in 1825, which was aggravated by unsound banking methods. In England, though not in Scotland, joint-stock banks were illegal; consequently the provincial banks, numbering several hundreds, were controlled by private individuals, and, often enough, badly managed. Their cash reserves were frequently too low, their note issues excessive when trade was booming; and the fact that the law did not allow them to have more than six partners did not tend to increase their stability. Scores of country banks had to close their doors in 1825–1826, and the Government saw that the time had come to overhaul the whole banking system of the country. It shrank, however, from the obvious remedy–compelling the country banks to keep an adequate gold reserve, proportionate to their note issues–because the proprietors were a powerful body of men with considerable parliamentary influence. What was done was to forbid them to issue notes of smaller denomination than £5. The Act was made inapplicable to Scotland. Another Act limited the privileges of the Bank of England, in that the country banks were now allowed to have more than six partners, and they might be organized on a joint-stock basis. The Bank of England, in return, was given a new privilege: any other bank, having more than six partners, which should establish itself, or a branch of itself, in London or within a 65-mile radius of London, should forfeit its right to issue its own banknotes.

The panic in the money market having subsided and the pecuniary transactions of the country having reverted to their accustomed course, it becomes important to lose no time in considering, whether any measures can be adopted to prevent the recurrence in future of such evils as we have recently experienced.

However much the recent distress may have been aggravated in the judgement of some by incidental circumstances and particular measures, there can be no doubt that the principal source of it is to be found in the rash spirit of speculation which has pervaded the country for some time, supported, fostered and encouraged by the country banks.

The remedy therefore for this evil in future, must be found in an improvement in the circulation of country paper–and the first measure which has suggested itself to most of those who have considered the subject, is a recurrence to a gold circulation throughout the country, as well as in the metropolis and its neighbourhood, by a repeal of the Act which permits country banks to issue £1 and £2 notes until the year 1833, and by the immediate enactment of a prohibition of any such issues, at the expiration of two or three years from the present period.

It appears to us to be quite clear that such a measure would be productive of much good; and it would operate as some check upon the spirit of speculation and upon the issues of country banks; and whilst on the one hand it would diminish the pressure upon the Bank and the metropolis incident to an unfavourable state of the exchanges, by spreading it over a wider surface; on the other hand, it would cause such pressure to be earlier felt, and thereby insure an earlier and more general adoption of the precautionary measures necessary for counteracting the inconveniences incident to an export of the precious metals.

But though a recurrence to a gold circulation in the country for the reasons already stated, might be productive of some good, it would by no means go to the root of the evil. We have abundant proof of the truth of this position in the events which took place in the spring of 1793, when a convulsion occurred in the money transactions and circulation of the country, more extensive than that which we have recently experienced. At that period nearly 100 country banks were obliged to stop payment, and Parliament was induced to grant an issue of exchequer bills to relieve the distress. Yet in the year 1793, there were no £1 or £2 notes in circulation in England, either by country banks or by the Bank of England.

We have a further proof of the truth of what has been advanced, in the experience of Scotland, which has escaped all the convulsions which have occurred in the money market of England for the last thirty five years, though Scotland, during the whole of that time has had a circulation of £1 notes, and the small pecuniary transactions of that part of the United Kingdom have been carried on exclusively by the means of such notes.

The issue of small notes, though it be an aggravation, cannot therefore be the sole or even the main cause of the evil in England. The failures which have occurred in England unaccompanied as they have been by the same occurences in Scotland, tend to prove that there must have been an unsolid and delusive system of banking in one part of Great Britain, and a solid and substantial one in the other.

It would be entirely at variance with our deliberate opinion, not to do full justice to the Bank of England, as the great centre of circulation and commercial credit. We believe that much of the prosperity of the country for the last century is to be ascribed to the general wisdom, justice and fairness of the dealings of the Bank–and we further think that during a great part of that time, it may have been *in itself*, and *by itself*, fully equal to all the important duties and operations confided to it. But the progress of the country during the last 30 or 40 years in every branch of industry,–in agriculture, manufactures, commerce and navigation, has been so rapid and extensive, as to make it no reflection upon the Bank of England to say that *the instrument*, which *by itself*, was fully adequate to former transactions, is no longer sufficient, without new aids, to meet the demands of the present times.

We have to a considerable degree the proof of this position in the very establishment of so many country banks. Within the memory of many living, and even of
some of those now engaged in public affairs, there were no country banks, except in
a few of the great commercial towns. The money transactions of the country were
carried on by supplies of coin and bank notes from London. The extent of the business
of the country, and the improvement made from time to time in the mode of conducting our increased commercial transactions, founded on pecuniary credit, rendered
such a system no longer adequate, and country banks must have arisen, as in fact they
did arise, from the increased wealth and *new wants* of the country. The matter of
regret is not that country banks have been suffered to exist, but that they have been
suffered so long to exist without control or limitation, or without the adoption of
provisions calculated to counteract the evils, resulting from their improvidence or excess.

It would be vain to suppose that we could now, by any Act of the Legislature,
extinguish the existing country banks, even if it were desirable; but it may be within
our power gradually at least to establish a sound system of banking throughout the
country; and if such a system can be formed, there can be little doubt that it would
ultimately extinguish and absorb all that is objectionable and dangerous in the present
banking establishments.

There appear to be two modes of attaining this object. First. That the Bank of
England should establish branches of its own body in different parts of the country.
Secondly. That the Bank of England should give up its exclusive privilege as to the
number of partners engaged in banking, except within a certain distance from the
metropolis.

It has always appeared to us that it would have been very desirable that the Bank
should have tried the first of these plans—that of establishing branch banks, upon a
limited scale. But we are not insensible to the difficulties which would have attended
such an experiment, and we are quite satisfied that it would be impossible for the
Bank, under present circumstances, to carry into execution such a system to the extent
necessary for providing for the wants of the country.

There remains therefore only the other plan,—the surrender by the Bank of their
exclusive privilege as to the number of partners beyond a certain distance from the
metropolis. The effect of such a measure would be the gradual establishment of extensive and respectable banks in different parts of the country. Some perhaps with
charters from the Crown under certain qualifications, and some without.

Here we have again the advantage of the experience of Scotland.

In England there are said to be between eight and nine hundred country banks,
and it is no exaggeration to suppose that a great proportion of them have not been
conducted with a due attention to those precautions which are necessary for the safety
of all banking establishments even where their property is most ample. When such
banks stop, their creditors may ultimately be paid the whole of their demands, but
the delay and shock to credit may in the mean time involve them in the same difficulty,
and is always attended with the greatest injury and suffering in the districts where
such stoppages occur. It this be the case where the solidity of that bank is unquestionable, what must it be when, as too often happens, they rest on no solid foundation.

In Scotland, there are not more than 30 banks, and these banks have stood firm amidst all the convulsions in the money market in England, and amidst all the distresses to which the manufacturing and agricultural interests in Scotland, as well as in England, have occasionally been subject. Banks of this description, must necessarily be conducted upon the general, understood and approved principles of banking. Individuals are from the nature of the institutions, precluded from speculating in the manner in which persons engaged in country, and even in London banks, speculate in England. If the concerns of the country could be carried on without any other Bank than the Bank of England, there might be some reason for not interfering with their exclusive privilege, but the effect of the Law at present is to permit every description of banking *except* that which is *solid* and *secure*.

Let the Bank of England reflect on the dangers to which it has been recently subject, and let its directors and proprietors then say, whether for their own interest such an improvement as is suggested in the banking system, is not desirable and even necessary. The Bank of England may perhaps propose, as they did upon a former occasion, the extension of the term of their exclusive privilege as to the metropolis and its neighbourhood beyond the year 1833, as the price of concession. It would be very much to be regretted that they should require any such condition.

It is clear that in point of security they would gain by the concession proposed to them, inasmuch as their own safety is now necessarily endangered by all such convulsions in the country circulation as we have lately and formerly witnessed. In point of profit, would they lose any thing by it for which they are entitled to demand compensation? It is notorious that at the present time their notes circulate in no part of England beyond the metropolis and its neighbourhood, except in Lancashire; and perhaps for that district some special provision might be made. But as it is the interest, so it has been and ever will be the endeavour, of the country bankers to keep the Bank of England notes out of circulation in those parts of the Kingdom where their own circulation prevails. In this they must always be successful, whilst public credit continues in its ordinary state, and the exchanges not unfavorable to this country. The consequences are, that in such times, the Bank of England becomes in a manner the sole depository for gold,–and in times of an opposite tendency, the sole resort for obtaining it:–that at one period their legitimate profit is curtailed by an accumulation of treasure beyond what would be required by a due attention to their own and private safety as a banking establishment, and at another period, they are exposed to demands which endanger that safety, and baffle all the ordinary calculations of foresight and prudence.

If then the Bank of England has no country circulation, except in the country above named, the only question for them to consider, is, whether on the ground of profit as well as security to themselves, the existing country circulation shall or shall not be improved.

With respect to the extension of the term of their exclusive privileges in the metropolis and its neighbourhood, it is obvious from what passed before, that Parliament will never agree to it. Such privileges are out of fashion, and what expectation can the bank, under present circumstances, entertain that theirs will be renewed. But there is no reason why the Bank of England should look at this consequence with dismay. They will remain a chartered corporation for carrying on the business of banking. In that character they will, we trust, always continue to be the sole bankers of the state; and with these advantages, so long as they conduct their affairs wisely and prudently, they always must be the great centre of banking and circulation. Theirs is the only establishment at which the dividends due to the public creditor can by law be paid. It is to be hoped therefore that the Bank will make no difficulty, in giving up their exclusive privileges in respect to the number of partners engaged in banking, as to any district – miles from the metropolis.

Should the Bank be disposed to consent to a measure of this nature, in time to enable the government to announce such a concession at the opening of Parliament, it would afford great facilities to the arrangement which they may have to propose for insuring the stability of private credit, in which the support of public credit and the maintenance of public prosperity, are so materially and closely involved.

409. Lord Liverpool's speech in the House of Lords on the Bank Charter Amendment Bill, 17 Feb. 1826

(Hansard's *Parliamentary Debates*, New Series, XIV, pp. 450–466.)

... Some persons attributed all the evils [of over-trading] to speculation, while others attributed them all to the currency.... The speculations in trade had been the origin of the evil; the spirit of gambling carried into every branch of trade had been the beginning, but it could not have been so extensive if it had not been aided by the state of the currency.... Up to the month of August, and even up to September 1824, the state of the exchanges was in our favour; but then they took an unfavourable turn. On this indication the Bank should have decreased its issues; but it had not – it had increased those issues. It must, however, be said in fairness towards the Bank, that they soon saw their error, for so early as March 1825 they perceived the necessity of drawing in, and between the months of February and May a reduction in their issues had taken place to the amount of £1,300,000, while from May to August the diminution was £700,000 more; and, by the month of November 1825 the Bank had contracted its issues to the amount of £3,500,000. ...

In the years 1821, 1822 and 1823 the country bank circulation continued, as far as that could be known from the number of stamps issued (which he admitted might not be exactly correct) on the average, to be somewhat more than £4,000,000. ... In 1824 the number issued had been increased from four to six millions; in 1825 it had been further increased from six to eight millions. ... Whatever reduction of the paper circulation was effected by the Bank of England, was more than made up by the issues of the country banks.

Having established this fact he would ask their Lordships if it was too much for him to say that the spirit of adventure and speculation, the gambling in joint-stock companies and mining associations, in loans, and the other extravagant projects which he had before alluded to, had been fomented and encouraged by the facilities afforded by the over-issues of the country banks; and that the failure of these speculations, necessarily involving that of those who had afforded them accommodation, was one of the main causes of the distress of the country? For where did the distress begin? The first failure which took place was that of a great house in the West of England. The second, that of a London banking house, connected with not less than 40 of the country banks. The third great stoppage was that of a large banking establishment in Yorkshire. Thus, therefore, although the run was not altogether confined to the country banks, and it was impossible when once the panic had diffused itself abroad that it should be so, still it would, he believed, be acknowledged that the run was mostly upon the country banks, and that when it extended itself to London, it fell with the greatest fury upon the establishments most connected with the country bank circulation. . . .

H.M.'s Government had suggested two remedies; one having for its object the gradual withdrawing of the £1 and £2 notes out of circulation; and the second, that which it had become his duty to propose that evening for their Lordships' adoption. . . . He could not deny that the withdrawing the £1 and £2 notes, in order to [sic] the substitution of a metallic currency, would operate as a considerable check on the supply of circulation which trade might require. . . . Let any one of your Lordships reflect upon the consequences produced . . . by the failure of a great bank in a country town, which bank had been supposed to be perfectly solvent; and, be it remembered that no less than 70 or 80 of these banks had suspended payment during the late panic. Only let the House conceive for a moment to what a lamentable situation the poor inhabitants of that town must have been reduced by such an event! All that they had been able to save from their hard earnings for years past were probably lodged in that bank; and even the very last payment of wages which they had received had been made in these worthless bits of paper; and, consequently, many of them were seen hawking them about for sale, and offering them for 5s. in the pound, to enable them to purchase the common necessaries for the support of life. Now that was a situation of things which never could take place in a country in which a metallic currency alone existed. . . . The measure, however, which he had to propose on this subject, he granted, was but a half-measure. And why was it so? Because their Lordships would recollect, they had the chartered rights of the Bank of England to contend with. . . . What was the system in existence at present? Why, the most rotten, the most insecure, the very worst in every respect that could possibly be conceived. Any petty tradesman, any grocer or cheesemonger, however destitute of property, might set up a bank in any place; whilst a joint-stock company, however large their capital, or a number of individuals, exceeding six, however respectable and wealthy they might be, were precluded from so doing by the present system. . . .

They [the Bank of England] had . . . consented to allow the restriction as to the number of partners in country banks to be removed, and so far one difficulty was removed. In return for this, the Bank might derive the consolation that they would have an opportunity of gratifying the desire, if they experienced it, of establishing branch banks throughout the country. Indeed he believed they had a right to do so at present; and he confessed he was most anxious that they should make the experiment. But he trusted that, if they did not think it prudent to make the experiment themselves, they would not suffer the people to wait until the year 1833, exposed to the consequences of the present system, but set the public free by allowing the Crown to grant charters to country banks. He believed it would not in any respect injure them, but, on the contrary, while it would be attended with the greatest advantages to the country at large, it would be beneficial also, in its consequences, to the Bank itself. . . .

After the 5th of April 1829 the issue of £1 and £2 notes was to cease altogether. It was originally intended that the circulation of the £1 and £2 notes of the Bank of England should be put upon the same footing as those of the country banks; but, upon consideration, it had been deemed advisable to allow the notes of the Bank of England to be stamped until the 10th of October next, instead of ceasing forthwith, like the country bank notes. With respect to Scotland and Ireland, it was intended ultimately to place them on precisely the same footing with England, although it had not been considered expedient to do so immediately. Upon the best consideration it was thought advisable to wait a year or two after the time limited for England, before the change took place in Ireland; while in Scotland it was intended that it should take place from the year 1829, when the change would take place in this country. . . .

410. Number of joint-stock banks established in the United Kingdom, 1826–1832

(G. R. Porter, *The Progress of the Nation*, II (1838), p. 218.)

The creation of joint-stock banks was legalized by the Act 7 Geo. IV, c. 46.

Date of Establishment.	Name of Bank.	Number of Places in which its Business is carried on.	Number of Partners.
	ENGLAND.		
June 1826 .	Bristol Old Bank	1	8
October 1826 .	Lancaster Banking Company	3	127
,,	Stuckey's Banking Company (Bristol) . .	23	34
March 1827 .	Norfolk and Norwich Joint-Stock Banking Company	9	26
June 1827 .	Huddersfield Banking Company . . .	3	335
July 1827 .	Bradford Banking Company	1	173
Nov. 1827 .	Leith Banking Company	1	9
March 1829 .	Bank of Manchester	4	552
,,	Cumberland Union Banking Company . .	6	52
May 1829 .	Whitehaven Joint-Stock Banking Company .	2	236
August 1829 .	Leicestershire Banking Company . . .	4	101
Sept. 1829 .	Birmingham Banking Company . . .	1	311
Nov. 1829 .	Halifax Joint-Stock Banking Company . .	1	178
,,	Manchester and Liverpool District Bank . .	23	1054
March 1830 .	York City and County Banking Company .	7	267
April 1831 .	Bank of Liverpool	1	441
June 1831 .	Gloucestershire Banking Company . . .	13	265
,,	Sheffield Banking Company	2	225
Sept. 1831 .	Knaresborough and Claro Banking Company.	11	160
Dec. 1831 .	Darlington District Joint-Stock Banking Company	16	247
,,	Devon & Cornwall Banking Company . .	12	146
,,	Stamford and Spalding Joint-Stock Banking Company	13	85
,,	Wolverhampton and Staffordshire Banking Company	1	238
Jan. 1832 .	Barnsley Banking Company	1	118
August 1832 .	Bank of Birmingham	1	227
Oct. 1832 .	Wakefield Banking Company	1	192
Nov. 1832 .	Leeds Banking Company	1	451
,,	North of England Joint-Stock Banking Company	9	571
Dec. 1832 .	Liverpool Commercial Banking Company .	1	263
,,	Mirfield and Huddersfield Banking Company	3	263
	IRELAND.		
Dec. 1824 .	Northern Banking Company	10	208
,,	Hibernian Joint-Stock Banking Company .	1	225
August 1825 .	Provincial Bank of Ireland	33	644
,, 1826 .	Belfast Banking Company	10	292

E. WAGES AND PRICES

411. Weekly wages of artisans, etc., in various parts of the Kingdom, 1800–1832

(G. R. Porter, *The Progress of the Nation*, II (1838), pp. 251–254.)

Years.	Carpenters. Greenwich Hospital.	Manchester.	Londonderry.	Glasgow.	Arbroath.	Bricklayers. Greenwich Hospital.	Manchester.	Glasgow.	Masons. Greenwich Hospital.	Manchester.	Londonderry.	Glasgow.	Arbroath.
	s. d.	s.	s.	s.	s.	s. d.	s. d.	s.	s. d.	s.	s. d.	s.	s. d.
1800	18 0	..	..	..	..	18 0	..	..	17 0	..	..	..	..
1805	27 0	..	..	..	..	29 0	..	..	30 0	..	..	..	..
1806	27 0	..	..	..	..	29 0	..	..	30 0	..	..	..	..
1807	30 0	..	..	..	..	28 0	..	..	30 0	..	..	..	..
1808	30 0	..	..	..	..	30 0	..	..	30 0	..	..	..	..
1809	32 0	..	..	..	..	30 6	..	..	30 6	..	..	..	..
1810	34 0	25	..	18	..	31 0	22 6	17	31 6	22	..	17	..
1811	33 0	25	..	18	..	32 6	22 6	17	34 6	22	..	17	..
1812	33 0	25	..	18	..	32 6	22 6	17	34 6	22	..	18	12 8½
1813	33 0	25	..	18	..	32 6	22 6	17	34 6	22	..	18	12 7½
1814	33 0	25	..	18	..	32 6	22 6	17	34 6	22	..	18	11 6¾
1815	33 0	25	..	18	..	30 6	22 6	17	34 6	22	..	18	10 0½
1816	31 0	25	..	18	..	30 6	22 6	17	31 6	22	..	18	9 3
1817	31 0	25	..	18	..	30 6	22 6	17	31 6	22	..	20	9 0
1818	31 0	25	..	18	14	30 6	22 6	17	31 6	22	..	19	11 4
1819	31 6	25	..	14	14	30 6	22 6	16	31 6	22	..	15	9 0
1820	31 6	25	..	..	14	30 6	22 6	..	31 6	22	..	..	9 3
1821	31 6	25	20	..	14	30 6	22 6	..	31 6	24	20 0	..	10 0
1822	31 6	26	20	..	14	30 0	25 0	..	30 0	26	20 0	..	9 10
1823	30 0	22	19	..	14	29 0	21 0	..	30 0	22	19 0	..	12 7
1824	30 0	22	19	..	14	29 0	21 0	..	30 0	22	19 0	..	14 0
1825	30 0	24	19	..	17	29 0	24 0	..	30 0	24	19 0	..	14 1½
1826	34 6	..	18	..	15	29 0	..	..	33 0	..	18 0	..	10 3½
1827	34 6	..	18	..	12	29 0	..	..	33 0	..	18 0	..	10 3½
1828	34 0	..	17	..	12	28 6	..	..	32 6	..	17 0	..	10 3½
1829	34 0	..	17	..	12	28 6	..	..	32 6	..	17 0	..	10 3½
1830	33 0	..	17	..	12	28 6	..	..	32 0	..	17 0	..	10 3½
1831	32 6	..	16	14	12	28 6	..	15	31 6	..	16 0	14	10 3½
1832	32 6	24	16	..	12	28 6	17 0	..	31 6	18	16 0	..	10 3½

Years	Plumbers		Tailors				Shoemakers				Hand-loom Weavers		
	Greenwich Hospital.	Glasgow.	Manchester.	Londonderry.	Glasgow.	Arbroath.	Manchester.	Londonderry.	Glasgow.	Arbroath.	Manchester.	Glasgow.	Arbroath.
	s. d.	s. d.	s. d.	s. d.	s.	s.	s.	s. d.	s.		s. d.	s. d.	s. d.
1800	19 6	..	..	..	..	..	..	..	..		..	13 1	..
1805	27 0	..	..	..	..	..	..	..	..		..	15 4	..
1806	27 0	..	..	..	..	..	..	..	..		..	17 8	..
1807	27 0	..	..	..	..	..	..	..	..		..	15 6	..
1808	27 0	..	..	..	..	..	..	..	..		..	13 2	..
1809	31 6	..	..	..	..	..	..	..	..		..	11 9	..
1810	34 6	22 6	18 6	..	19	..	16	..	15		16 3	11 6	..
1811	34 6	22 6	18 6	..	19	..	16	..	15		12 6	7 6	..
1812	34 6	22 6	18 6	..	19	15	16	..	15		13 0	9 9	16 0
1813	34 6	22 6	18 6	..	19	15	16	..	15		12 6	12 1½	16 0
1814	34 6	22 6	18 6	..	19	15	16	..	15		15 7	13 0	16 0
1815	34 6	22 6	21 6	..	19	15	16	..	15		13 2	11 6	14 0
1816	32 6	22 6	21 6	..	21	15	16	..	15		13 2	5 6	12 0
1817	34 6	22 6	21 6	..	21	15	16	..	15		9 6	5 9	12 0
1818	34 6	22 6	18 6	..	20	15	16	..	15		9 6	6 6	12 0
1819	34 6	22 6	18 6	..	20	15	16	..	15		9 6	5 0	12 0
1820	34 6	..	18 6	..	..	15	16	..	..		11 0	..	12 0
1821	34 6	..	18 6	20 0	..	15	18	15 0	..		11 0	..	13 6
1822	33 0	..	18 6	18 0	..	15	18	15 0	..		11 0	..	14 0
1823	33 0	..	21 0	18 0	..	15	16	14 0	..		6 6	..	13 0
1824	33 0	..	21 0	18 0	..	15	16	14 0	..		6 6	..	13 0
1825	33 0	..	21 0	18 0	..	16	16	14 0	..		6 6	..	13 0
1826	34 6	..	..	18 0	..	15	..	14 0	..		..	..	12 0
1827	34 6	..	..	16 0	..	15	..	13 0	..		..	..	12 0
1828	34 0	..	..	16 0	..	15	..	13 0	..		..	..	12 0
1829	32 6	..	..	16 0	..	15	..	12 0	..		..	..	12 0
1830	33 0	..	..	16 0	..	15	..	12 0	..		..	..	12 6
1831	33 0	21 6	..	15 6	20	15	..	12 0	15		..	6 0	12 0
1832	33 0	..	18 0	15 6	..	15	15	12 0	..		9 0	..	12 0

(Arbroath Shoemakers column: throughout the period from 1812 to 1833. From 10s. to 12s.)

Years.	Hand-loom Weavers.				Spinners.		Wool Combers.		Stocking Makers.	Seamen's Wages.	
	Forfarshire.	Bolton.	Barrowford, Lancashire.	Oldham.	Manchester, Young Women.	Manchester, Men.	Bradford.	Leicester.	Leicester.	American Trade. Per Month.	Baltic Trade. Per Month.
	s. d.	s. d.	s. d.	s. d.	s. d.	s. d.	s. d.	s. d.	s. d.	s.	s. d.
1800	..	25 0	..	..	..	..	..	..	..	..	..
1805	..	25 0	..	..	10 1½	..	..	..	..	..	..
1806	..	22 0	..	..	..	..	..	..	..	..	..
1807	..	18 0	..	..	..	..	..	..	..	..	..
1808	..	15 0	..	..	7 5½	..	..	..	..	..	..
1809	..	16 0	..	..	..	..	..	..	..	..	..
1810	14 0	19 6	..	..	..	..	..	..	..	..	..
1811	11 0	14 0	..	..	..	..	..	..	..	..	..
1812	10 0	14 0	..	..	..	..	..	..	..	..	..
1813	8 0	15 0	..	..	9 6	..	..	..	..	..	..
1814	12 0	24 0	26 0	13 9	..	..	..	..	..	..	..
1815	13 0	14 0	17 1	11 9	..	..	..	..	..	..	..
1816	7 0	12 0	13 5	9 0	..	..	..	..	..	..	..
1817	6 0	9 0	12 1	6 6	..	..	..	..	..	55	60 0
1818	8 0	9 0	14 5	8 9	10 5	..	..	20 0	..	55	55 0
1819	7 0	9 6	12 6	10 0	..	..	..	18 0	12 9	55	55 0
1820	7 0	9 0	11 8	9 0	..	..	..	18 0	12 9	50	55 0
1821	9 0	8 6	12 7	8 6	..	..	..	18 0	11 6½	50	55 0
1822	9 0	8 6	10 2	9 0	..	..	..	18 0	10 6	50	52 6
1823	9 0	8 6	9 4	9 6	9 3½	26 7	17 5	18 0	9 5½	55	55 0
1824	10 6	8 6	8 6	9 6	..	24 2	17 5	18 0	8 9¾	60	60 0
1825	11 6	8 6	8 6	8 9	..	29 8	17 5	21 0	11 6½	..	..
1826	5 0	7 0	5 3	6 6	..	..	15 8½	16 0	8 9¾	60	65 0
1827	5 6	6 6	6 6	6 6	..	26 1	15 8½	16 6	8 3	55	60 0
1828	7 6	6 0	6 6	7 0	9 1	27 4	14 2	18 0	8 3	55	57 6
1829	7 6	5 6	4 8	6 0	..	28 11	12 0½	16 0	8 3	55	60 0
1830	6 0	5 6	6 0	5 0	..	28 6	12 0½	14 0	7 8½	50	55 0
1831	6 6	5 6	6 7	5 0	..	30 2	12 0½	14 0	7 8½	55	60 0
1832	6 0	5 6	5 4	4 6	..	27 0	12 0½	14 0	7 8½	60	60 0

Years.	Seamen's Wages.	Labourers.					Compositors.			Printers	Average Price of Wheat in England
	Coal Trade to London, per Voyage.	Glasgow.	Manchester.	Londonderry.	Bradford.	Bedfont, Middlesex.	Compositors, Book-work. Lond.	Compositors. Mng. Papers. London.	Compositors, Evng. Papers. London.	Printers. Londonderry.	
	s. d.	s. d.	s. d.	s. d.	s.	s. d.	s.	s.	s. d.	s.	s. d.
1800	..	..	..	..	..	..	33	40	37 0	..	110 5
1805	..	..	..	..	..	..	33	40	37 0	..	87 1
1806	..	..	..	..	..	..	33	40	37 0	..	76 9
1807	..	..	..	..	..	..	33	40	37 0	..	73 1
1808	..	..	..	..	..	..	33	40	37 0	..	78 11
1809	..	..	..	..	..	..	33	42	38 6	..	94 5
1810	..	11 0	15 0	..	..	..	33	48	43 6	..	103 3
1811	..	11 0	15 0	..	..	18 0	36	48	43 6	..	92 5
1812	..	11 0	15 0	..	..	18 0	36	48	43 6	..	122 8
1813	..	11 0	15 0	..	..	18 0	36	48	43 6	..	106 6
1814	..	11 0	15 0	..	..	15 0	36	48	43 6	..	72 1
1815	..	11 0	15 0	..	..	15 0	36	48	43 6	..	63 8
1816	..	11 0	15 0	..	..	15 0	36	48	43 6	..	76 2
1817	65 0	11 0	15 0	..	..	15 0	36	48	43 6	..	94 0
1818	63 0	9 0	15 0	..	..	15 0	36	48	43 6	..	83 8
1819	66 0	7 6	15 0	..	..	12 0	36	48	43 6	..	72 3
1820	65 0	..	13 6	..	..	12 0	36	48	43 6	..	65 10
1821	64 0	..	15 0	10 0	..	10 6	36	48	43 6	..	54 5
1822	63 9	..	15 0	10 0	..	10 0	36	48	43 6	..	43 3
1823	70 0	..	13 0	10 0	..	12 0	36	48	43 6	21	51 9
1824	71 8	..	13 0	9 0	16	12 0	36	48	43 6	21	62 0
1825	89 2	..	14 0	9 0	..	12 0	36	48	43 6	21	66 6
1826	90 0	..	..	9 0	15	12 0	36	48	43 6	21	56 11
1827	82 6	..	..	9 0	16	12 0	36	48	43 6	21	56 9
1828	70 0	..	..	9 0	15	12 0	36	48	43 6	21	60 5
1829	70 0	..	..	8 0	15	12 0	36	48	43 6	21	66 3
1830	70 0	..	..	8 0	15	12 0	36	48	43 6	21	64 3
1831	70 0	9 0	..	8 0	15	..	36	48	43 6	21	66 4
1832	65 0	..	..	8 0	15	..	36	48	43 6	21	58 8

412. Accounts of the prices of provisions and necessaries at Greenwich Hospital, 1795–1830

(Report of the Committee of the House of Lords on the State of the Poor Laws, 1830–1831, *Parliamentary Papers*, 1831, VIII, pp. 368–371.)

Specimen years have been selected.

			1795.	1800.	1805.	1810.	1815.	1825.	1830.
			£. s. d.	£. s. d.	£. s. d.	£. s. d.	£. s. d.	£. s. d.	£. s. d.
PROVISIONS.	Flour	per sack	2 19 –	4 13 $3\frac{1}{4}$	3 18 $3\frac{3}{4}$	4 10 $6\frac{1}{2}$	3 – $-\frac{1}{2}$	2 12 $4\frac{1}{4}$	2 14 11
	Bread	per lb.	– – $2\frac{159}{360}$	– – $3\frac{1}{4}\frac{48}{360}$	– – $2\frac{3}{4}\frac{67}{360}$	– – $3\frac{299}{360}$	– – $2\frac{270}{360}$	– – $1\frac{3}{4}\frac{209}{360}$	– – $1\frac{3}{4}\frac{332}{360}$
	Meat	per cwt.	2 2 8	3 3 9	3 1 8	3 13 –	3 9 $7\frac{1}{2}$	2 19 $6\frac{1}{2}$	2 3 6
	Peas	per bushel	– 9 $9\frac{1}{2}$	– 12 $8\frac{1}{4}$	– 7 $8\frac{1}{2}$	– 9 $4\frac{3}{4}$	– 6 $7\frac{1}{4}$	Split Peas. – 11 –	– 8 –
	Oatmeal	per bushel	– 6 $-\frac{1}{2}$	– 17 $-\frac{1}{2}$	– 12 –	– 11 $7\frac{1}{2}$	– 9 9	– 17 6	– 16 11
	Salt	per bushel	– 5 8	– 14 –	– 19 $1\frac{1}{2}$	– 19 9	– 19 9	– 2 10	– 1 8
	Butter	per lb.	– – $8\frac{1}{4}$	– – 11	– – $11\frac{3}{4}$	– 1 $1\frac{1}{4}$	– 1 2	– – $10\frac{1}{4}$	– – $6\frac{1}{2}$
	Cheese	per lb.	– – $5\frac{1}{4}$	– – $6\frac{1}{4}$	– – $7\frac{1}{4}$	– – 8	– – 8	– – $5\frac{1}{4}$	– – 4
	Malt	per quarter	2 7 $8\frac{3}{4}$	4 4 $1\frac{3}{4}$	4 5 7	4 5 $1\frac{3}{4}$	3 9 6	3 11 $10\frac{1}{4}$	2 16 $1\frac{1}{4}$
	Hops, per cwt.	bags	4 4 –	16 7 $1\frac{1}{4}$	No Supply.	7 3 –	9 2 –	20 10 –	No Receipt.
	—	pockets	4 4 –	17 5 $-\frac{3}{4}$	– – –	8 4 –	9 15 – 10 18 –	23 – –	– – –
	Beer	per barrel	– 10 $4\frac{1}{2}$	1 – $4\frac{1}{4}$	– 17 $9\frac{1}{2}$	– 17 10	– 15 $4\frac{3}{4}$	– 16 $6\frac{1}{4}$	Not ascertained.
NECESSARIES.	Suits of clothes		2 – $1\frac{3}{4}$	1 19 $-\frac{1}{2}$	2 2 $11\frac{1}{2}$	2 2 $-\frac{1}{2}$	2 7 10	2 – $8\frac{1}{2}$	1 18 $6\frac{3}{4}$
	Stockings	per pair	– 1 6	– 1 6	– 2 2	– 2 2	– 3 3	– 2 $1\frac{1}{2}$	– 1 $6\frac{1}{2}$
	Linen for shirts, $\frac{7}{8}$ths	per yard	– – $11\frac{1}{2}$	– 1 $3\frac{1}{4}$	– 1 $4\frac{3}{4}$	– 1 $4\frac{1}{2}$	– 1 4	– 1 –	– – 8
	Hats	each	– 2 6	– 2 6	– 3 3	– 3 3	– 3 –	– 3 –	– 3 –
	Shoes	per pair	– 4 –	– 5 8	– 5 3	– 5 6	– 4 7	– 4 6	– 3 6
	Suits of Bedding, (viz. Bed, Bolster, Pillow, three Blankets, one Coverlet)		2 8 –	2 8 –	2 15 1	2 16 4	3 7 $7\frac{1}{2}$	2 19 $10\frac{1}{2}$	1 17 $10\frac{3}{4}$
	Sea coal	per chaldron	1 19 9	2 11 7	2 11 $8\frac{3}{4}$	3 – 8	2 15 7	2 3 2	1 12 11
	Candles	per doz. lbs.	– 9 $1\frac{3}{4}$	– 11 $5\frac{1}{4}$	– 10 $8\frac{1}{2}$	– 11 $2\frac{1}{2}$	– 11 $7\frac{1}{4}$	– 6 –	– 5 $3\frac{1}{2}$
	Mops	each	– 1 3	– 1 3	– 1 5	– 1 5	– 2 6	– 1 $2\frac{1}{4}$	– – $10\frac{1}{2}$

413. Agricultural wages and the Cost of Living

(J. H. Clapham, *Economic History of Modern Britain*, I, p. 128.)

------ *General Course of English Agricultural Wages* (after Bowley). N.B. Information as to wages is fairly ample for the periods 1780–1794 and 1823 *sqq.*: the curve for the intervening period is less certain.

―――― *Working-class cost of living Index* (after Silberling).

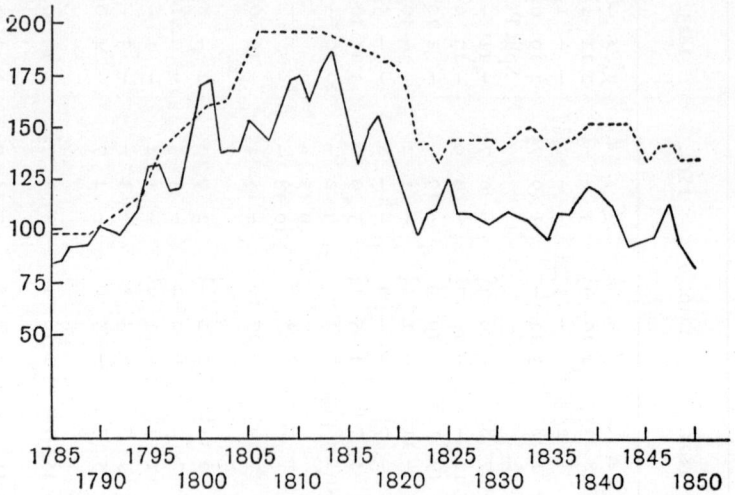

414. The general course of industrial wages, 1790–1840

(J. H. Clapham, *Economic History of Modern Britain*, I, p. 561.)

The curve (after Wood, *Economic Journal*, 1899) is based on figures from twenty-four towns or coalfields and over thirty industries. The wages of 1840 are taken as 100.

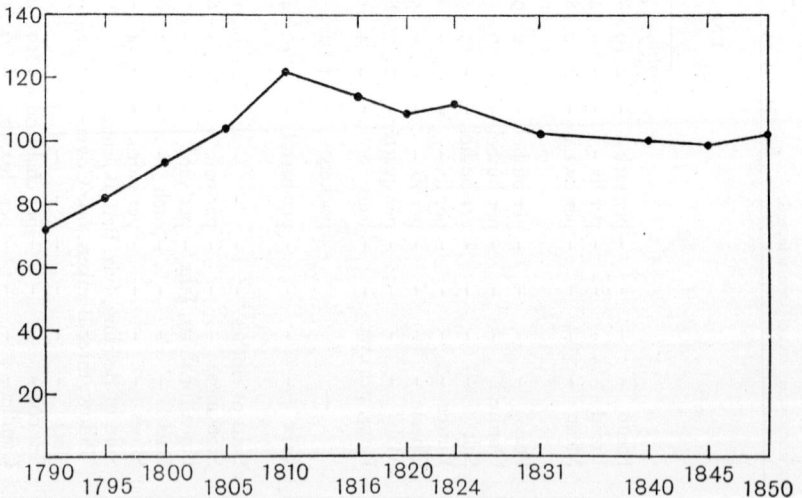

Part VI

SOCIAL AND RELIGIOUS LIFE

Introduction

PART V has shown that this was a time of remarkable economic growth, marked by a rapid increase in industrial and agricultural production, a substantial rise in exports, especially of manufactured goods, and an increase in the national wealth. Contemporaries were the more puzzled that there was no immediate and equivalent rise in the standard of life for the great majority of the population. This is explained partly by the strain of the French wars of the period, whose expense swallowed up much of the financial gain accruing from economic expansion by imposing the direct burden of financing military and naval operations, increasing freight charges and the cost of imports, diverting investment into unproductive channels, and contributing to inflation. At the same time a series of bad harvests helped to raise the price of the basic foods. The general result was to produce a fall in real wages and to delay the general improvement of living standards until after the end of the period. Yet the wars do not explain everything. There were certain basic factors which tended to hold down living standards; the chief of these were the unprecedented rise in the population,[1] which reached its maximum rate of increase in this period, and the continuance of bad medical and social conditions.

Improvements in hygiene and in medical knowledge, particularly in midwifery and child care, were the principal factors operating to increase the expectation of life[2] towards the end of the eighteenth century; Jenner's discovery of the vaccination process[3] now began to conquer the scourge of the smallpox that was responsible for the greater part of the appalling infant mortality of the day, and the work of such philanthropists as John Howard was publicizing improvements in the hospitals.[4] Yet medical science was still rudimentary, and could not yet produce better living conditions; indeed, by increasing the population to the limit of the country's resources it may have helped to worsen them. The increased national wealth was no more than sufficient to keep pace with the demands of a swollen population and to stave off general destitution. This was the background to the despair of Malthusianism.[5] The contention that however prosperous the nation, population will always press on the borders of subsistence, was so plausible, particularly when supported by a specious mathematical proof, that it provided a justification for the helplessness felt by an age always ready to discern the hand of the Almighty in the imposition of the *status quo*.

In other ways this was an age of spiritual revival. The lethargy long regarded as the prime characteristic of the Anglican Church and the sects in the eighteenth century could not long survive the shocks of industrialization and the Wesleyan revival. The evangelical movement was now penetrating the Established Church, though it influenced the laity more than the clergy; its greatest and most influential tract was the

[1] No. 415.   [2] No. 416.   [3] No. 417.   [4] No. 419.   [5] No. 418.

work of Wilberforce, whose *Practical View*[1] enjoyed a tremendous vogue, but in 1808 the *Christian Observer* calculated that less than one in ten, perhaps only one in twenty, of the clergy could be said to be evangelicals, despite the efforts of the group to find benefices for its devotees by purchasing advowsons and influencing ministers.[2] 'The Saints', as they were nicknamed by an unsympathetic generation, were still disliked as 'Methodistical' or 'pharisaical', and 'enthusiasm' was still regarded with distaste by the leaders of Church and State. The first evangelical bishop, Ryder of Gloucester, was promoted only in 1815, and then after bitter opposition–and he had the advantage of a brother in the Cabinet. As late as 1828 a High Church divine deplored the spread of evangelicalism, "creeping like a mist over the whole surface of the country, and bearing with it all the properties of a noxious fog".

The Church was also fighting a losing battle against popular feeling. Throughout the eighteenth century the Church of England had closely identified itself, not only with the secular power of the State, but with the social system of the age. Its bishops were translated for political rather than spiritual reasons, and they were almost invariably chosen from the families or the tutors of the aristocracy. The lower clergy, with their pretensions to gentility, were identified with the squire rather than with their parishioners at large, reaped the unpopularity necessarily attached to tithe-beneficiaries in an agricultural society, and when, as not infrequently happened, they served as justices of the peace, they tended to identify the Church with savage justice and repressive politics. The presence of two clergymen among the 'Peterloo' magistrates typified the Church's connexion with the established order.

Clerical abuses therefore received full attention from contemporary reformers. In 1798 the evangelicals began prosecutions for non-residence under a Reformation statute, and as a result an Act of Parliament in 1803 attempted to regulate the practice by laying down severe penalties for non-residence but establishing exemptions in certain cases, and demanding annual returns from 1805. These returns illustrate the extent of the evil; in 1807 it was calculated that, of 7,167 livings with stipends over £150 per annum–the generally accepted borderline between poverty and comfort in the clergy–over half were non-resident, a substantial proportion being benefices where residence was properly attached to the cure; of those under £150, 2,438 out of 3,997 were non-residentiary in 1808.[3]

This was not the only problem facing the Church. It was losing its hold on the people also because its churches and parishes were becoming ill-adapted to the distribution of population. In the teeming parishes of the East End and the new industrial towns there was accommodation for Anglican worship only for a small proportion of the labouring classes.[4] It seemed, as Lord Harrowby said in 1810, that the country was "tending towards that most alarming of all situations, in which the religion of the Established Church would not be the religion of the majority of the people". Parliament therefore embarked, under the guidance of Liverpool, a minister particularly conscientious in the discharge of his ecclesiastical duties, upon a programme of church building under the Additional Churches Act of 1818.[5] During the next fourteen years, 188 churches and chapels were built with accommodation for over a quarter of a million worshippers, half of them in free seats.

A more responsible attitude was becoming apparent, too, in the administration of ecclesiastical patronage. Wilberforce and the evangelicals pressed on ministers the necessity of looking chiefly or solely to spiritual qualities in ecclesiastical promotions,[6]

[1] No. 420.   [2] No. 421.   [3] No. 422.   [4] No. 425.   [5] No. 426.   [6] No. 427.

and Perceval[1] and Liverpool[2] did their best to dissociate Church patronage from political jobbery. So conscientious was Liverpool in this respect that he refused a bishopric to Gerald Wellesley, a member of the greatest family in England, on the grounds that, though an innocent party, he was separated from his wife.[3] In the lower ranks of the Church only a small minority of benefices was in the gift of the Crown, and these were correspondingly much coveted.[4] The wishes of private patrons, however, determined the majority of appointments, and the sale and purchase of advowsons was a regular and highly respectable traffic.[5]

It was perhaps in its patronage of the Bible and Missionary societies that the age showed most clearly the influence of evangelicalism. The creations of the movement itself, the Church Missionary Society (1801) and the British and Foreign Bible Society (1804)[6] were at first regarded with suspicion, and some members of the Church of England feared that to distribute the Bible without the Anglican Prayer Book would endanger the Establishment. Vansittart's answer to Dr. Marsh, the most vociferous of these critics, was a plea for a deeper understanding of the religious needs of the time.[7] Public response proved him right; by 1821 the Bible Society had become the principal beneficiary of charitable donations in London, only the Anglican S.P.C.K. rivalling the amount of its receipts.[8] Through such agencies as these the early nineteenth century was to establish its reputation as one of the great ages of English missionary endeavour at home and overseas.

The dissenting sects in this period were better able to adapt themselves to social changes. They were unhampered in the building of chapels and meeting-houses by out-dated parish boundaries or old traditions, and were able to raise funds from wealthy supporters for the extension of their activities. Particularly noteworthy was the expansion of the Methodist movement. Despite Wesley's efforts to restrain the separatist wing of his following,[9] the Methodists severed their connexion with the Church of England soon after his death in 1791.[10] Henceforth Methodism seemed to zealous churchmen to be the great rival of the Establishment, and in a sense they were right, for it gathered up the masses left untouched by the less adaptable Anglican body. A calculation of 1824 placed the number of Methodist circuits in England and Wales at 296, with over 200,000 members and an estimated attendance at services of six times as many–a total amounting to 15 per cent of the population.[11]

Together with the membership of the numerous other Nonconformist churches, this substantial proportion of the people was still denied full civil rights under the Test and Corporation Acts, which laid upon office holders in central and local government the duty of qualification by taking the Anglican communion.[12] Though in practice the annual Acts of Indemnity remitted the penalties of non-observance, it was felt to be increasingly inappropriate that the religious tests should be applied at all, at any rate to Protestants. The progress of the movement for repeal, publicized by its most influential tract, Samuel Heywood's *The Right of Protestant Dissenters*,[13] was temporarily arrested by the French Revolution and the tendency to identify Dissent, and especially Unitarianism, with revolutionary Jacobinism, for the leaders of the Dissenters were educated men, with little respect for the political system that penalized them for their opinions, and standing foremost in many of the reform agitations of the time. The more liberal attitude which grew after 1820 revived their hopes of success,

[1] No. 428. [2] No. 429. [3] Nos. 430, 431. [4] Nos. 432–435. [5] Nos. 436, 437.
[6] No. 441. [7] No. 442. [8] No. 444. [9] No. 445. [10] No. 446.
[11] No. 449. [12] No. 450. [13] No. 451.

and in 1828, despite the opposition of George IV and his government, repeal was carried.[1] Jews[2] and Atheists were, however excluded from the relaxation of the law by the form of the oath prescribed for office-holders, which required them to swear "on the true faith of a Christian", and Catholics by the Oath of Supremacy and the declaration against transubstantiation.

The movement for Catholic Emancipation developed against the troubled background of Ireland. The armed Volunteers had extorted some economic concessions and the grant of legislative and judicial independence; the Catholic disabilities now stood out the more as a badge of her inferiority. In 1793 again, England's difficulty was Ireland's opportunity; faced with the hostility of revolutionary France, the English offered a measure of Catholic relief,[3] whose principal effect was to allow Irish Catholics to vote at parliamentary elections and to hold subordinate offices in the kingdom on taking an oath of allegiance. They were still, however, excluded from both Houses of Parliament; the Irish Legislature was dominated by the Protestant absentee landlords of England and their clients, as was the Irish group in the Westminster Parliament after 1801.[4]

Further than this neither George III nor the majority of his ministers was prepared to go.[5] They viewed the exclusion of the Catholics not as a measure of religious persecution but as a political necessity. The papist was considered to have a divided allegiance, and was excluded for the safety of the Protestant Establishment and of the political system identified since 1688 with its preservation. George IV shared his father's prejudices and obstinacy, but lacked his resolution, and during his reign opinion among the Tories began to move in favour of concession, with the result that four relief motions passed the Commons between 1821 and 1828. In 1828 the remaining obstacle–the resistance of the king and the peers–was overcome by the threat of revolution in Ireland. Peel's exhaustive and judicious assessment of the situation in his three memoranda of 1829[6] illustrates the difficulties which faced Wellington and himself in overcoming the resistance of the king and in making the measure palatable to their own following; they also show, however, that the main consideration in Peel's mind was to reach a permanent solution satisfactory to both sides. In this statesmanlike manner he arrived at the second of his three great political recantations. The Catholic Relief Act of 1829[7] did not solve the Irish problem, nor did it sweep away all religious tests from English life, but it marks a significant advance in national political maturity.

This is also an important period in the history of popular education. There was little change in the character or administration of the older universities or the English public schools, where the excessive classical bias of which Sydney Smith complained[8] remained characteristic of the curriculum. Smith exaggerated the defects of the classical education–he was one of its products, as were almost all the great men of the day–but it was true that the rapidly developing technical society of the early nineteenth century was poorly catered for, and its leaders poorly qualified, in the older institutions of learning. The Scottish universities[9] had long maintained a tradition of 'modern' studies, and Scots were as a result pre-eminent in political economy, philosophy, and other 'advanced' departments of study; it was, significantly, a Scot –the poet Thomas Campbell–who placed before the public in 1825 the project of a new English university in London, which should be free from religious tests or sectarian bias, and should teach a variety of subjects from the classics through philo-

---

[1] Nos. 453–455.   [2] No. 460.   [3] No. 456.   [4] See Part II, No. 208.   [5] No. 457.
[6] No. 458.   [7] No. 459.   [8] No. 461.   [9] No. 464.

sophy, history and modern languages to medicine, law and engineering.[1] The tone of the new foundation was Utilitarian, as befitted the men–Brougham, Bentham, Place–who took up Campbell's plan and brought it to fruition in the opening of University College in 1828. "Mr. Brougham's godless College in Gower Street" was soon joined by King's College, founded on an Anglican basis, and the two were linked in 1836 as the first constituent colleges of the new London University.

The Dissenting Academies[2] did not long survive the opening of these new institutions. The most famous of them, like Warrington under Dr. Priestley, had provided a valuable supplement to higher education facilities in the previous century, when the English universities gave degrees only to Anglicans and taught only classics and mathematics. They still offered a wide education, though at times tinged by over-emphasis on sectarian theology, but they were now tending to become restricted to training candidates for the ministry in the Nonconformist churches.

Popular education was provided by a hierarchy of schools, from the endowed grammar and public schools that gave a mainly classical education to the sons of rich and of poor,[3] through the private day and boarding schools of every kind to the Sunday, charity and dame schools that were the resort of the poorest classes. The statistics for 1819[4] show the extent of this provision in England, Wales and Scotland; they show that it was in the unendowed day schools that the greater part of the population was given such education as it could get. There were still many who argued that education was not to be scattered too generously or recklessly among the ignorant. While the classics broadened the mind and refined the judgment of the future leaders of the nation, and the sons of commercial or professional men might need mathematical and literary techniques, all that education would give to the poor was a feeling of discontent with their inevitable lot. The idea that if the poor were taught to read they would read Tom Paine and that if they learned to write they would spread sedition died hard in a society that had known the fear of the mob. But the chief obstacle by this time to the provision of universal education was rather the argument that education for the poor was simply a wasteful and unnecessary luxury; it was not so much that the poor might become disaffected, though the fear was still present, as that they were better occupied in useful labour. Evangelicals like Hannah More[5] cared deeply for popular education, seeing in Bible reading a safeguard not only against 'Romish superstition' but also against the pernicious doctrines of 'modern philosophers'–as others saw in it a use for idle hands that might otherwise find satanic employment in someone else's turnip fields[6]–but they could see no benefit in teaching the poor to write.

The most important development in this field in the early nineteenth century is the achievement of Lancaster and Bell, whose 'monitorial system' was an application to the educational process of those techniques of mass-production now proving so profitable elsewhere.[7] Lancaster's school in the Borough Road quickly became one of the showplaces of London, and in 1807 he founded the Lancasterian, later renamed the British and Foreign School Society, to assume responsibility for running the school, collecting subscriptions, and extending the system. His plea for a non-sectarian approach to education was anathema to Anglicans of the stamp of Mrs. Trimmer, and fear that the masses might be taught doctrines contrary to those of the Established Church led in 1811 to the foundation of the National Society, whose schools, though

---

[1] No. 463.   [2] No. 465.   [3] Nos. 466, 467.   [4] No. 468.
[5] No. 469.   [6] No. 470.   [7] No. 471.

tracing their ancestry to Bell, an Anglican clergyman, and not to the Quaker Lancaster, were in fact indistinguishable from the Lancasterian except that they taught the catechism. Neither society sought or received aid from the State, and the proposals of Whitbread in 1807[1] and Brougham in 1820 that England should imitate the Scottish system of parochial schools maintained by local rates were shipwrecked by religious animosity. Dissenters feared that State schools would be Anglican schools; Anglicans were not prepared to tolerate anything else. The societies were therefore by the end of the period established as the principal agencies of mass education, and though the teaching under the monitorial system obviously lacked almost everything worthy of the name, it caught the imagination of an age obsessed by the achievements of the Industrial Revolution[2] – Brougham hailed it as "the steam engine of the moral world". As long as the alternative to monitorial teaching was no education at all, England's debt to Lancaster and Bell must be accounted a substantial one. Important too was the work of such propagandists as Henry Brougham, and in the 1820s of such pioneers of adult education as Dr. Birkbeck and his "Mechanics Institutes"[3] and Brougham's "Society for the Diffusion of Useful Knowledge", with its cheap editions of educational works.[4] By such means self-help and the desire for improvement were promoted to national virtues.

There were still many children whom no system of day-school education could reach – the young factory and other workers whose early labours excluded them from full-time education. Much was being done for them by the Sunday School movement promoted by Raikes in Gloucestershire in the 'eighties and taken up by the churches and lay philanthropists like the More sisters in Cheddar.[5] The early Factory Acts too were in some respects the first national Education Acts, but their main purpose was to alleviate the mental, physical and moral conditions under which the youngest victims of industrialization worked. The cotton mills were singled out for statutory regulation, not because they imposed a harsher discipline or a more exhausting labour upon young children, dreadful though the disclosures of witnesses before successive parliamentary committees were, but because in large factories the evil was more readily apparent, and the enforcement of restrictive regulations was easier. The most powerful obstacle to humanitarian efforts was the *laissez-faire* economics of the day; the more enlightened of the mill-owners themselves – Peel and Owen in particular – were among the leading agitators for reform. But it is significant that the first success was registered on behalf of one class of children to whom *laissez-faire* and freedom of contract were obviously inappropriate – the pauper apprentices who were virtually sold by the London parishes to the remote factories of the north. The first Factory Act (1802)[6] laid down regulations for their treatment, but it applied only to textile mills, and the parliamentary committee of 1815[7] found ample evidence of abuses still remaining in their treatment elsewhere. The Act was largely ineffective as a cure for the greater evil of child employment itself, for manufacturers were soon able to replace their apprentices by 'free' children, whose parents sent them voluntarily to the mills. To cure this evil was a longer task, to which men of the calibre of Peel, Owen and Ashley devoted themselves. Owen, a manufacturer himself, proved that shorter hours of labour and greater care for the health and comfort of his workpeople did not in fact ruin the mill-owner,[8] but there were many who refused to be convinced, and subsequent Acts (1819[9] and 1831[10]) to regulate the labour of all children

---

[1] No. 472.   [2] No. 473.   [3] No. 474.   [4] No. 475.   [5] No. 469.
[6] No. 476.   [7] No. 477.   [8] Nos. 478, 479.   [9] No. 480.   [10] No. 482.

in textile factories produced little effect. Oastler's campaign against the horrors of 'Yorkshire Slavery'[1] stirred public opinion to support Ashley and the other reformers who secured, in the 1833 Act, the first salaried government inspectorate and thus succeeded in obtaining at last an effective measure of regulation, though no one as yet dared to interfere directly with the hours or conditions of adult labour.

The adult worker was much at the mercy of his employer. The Industrial Revolution had largely completed the divorce of the immediate interests of master and servant in industry, and contemporary ideas of 'freedom of contract' limited the protection the worker could claim from outside. Attempts to combine in unions to achieve equality of bargaining power with the employers were equally frowned on as destructive of the rights of property and injurious to the general interests of society. It was for this reason as much as from fear of Jacobinism that the Combination Acts of 1799 and 1800[2] laid further restraint on trade unions. A succession of eighteenth-century Acts had laid penalties on unions in particular trades, and any combination had always been liable to prosecution as a conspiracy at common law. All that the new legislation did was to provide an alternative method of suppression. It did not put an end to trade unions altogether, and many societies maintained an unbroken and sometimes open existence. Their failure to strike deeper roots during the years 1800–1824 is due not to the legislation of 1800 but to difficulties and inexperience in the factories and workshops.

The demand for greater freedom to combine which intensified after the post-war depression of 1815–1820 was supported in some ways by the ideas of *laissez-faire*: there were those who, like Place himself, believed that if the worker had the freedom to combine he would not need to use it. The story of the tactics of Hume and Place in securing the repeal in 1824[3] not only of the 1800 Act but of every other statute forbidding combination, and even of the common law of conspiracy as applied to unions as well, is a familiar one. The consequence was such an outbreak of strikes and disorder that the government contemplated the re-imposition of the former restraints. However under the influence of Hume and Place the Report of the 1825 Committee[4] was moderate and statesmanlike, and the Act of 1825,[5] though denying the unions the full legal protection for which they agitated in years to come, proved to be a landmark in the history of the working-class movement. That it did not succeed in granting freedom to combine where employers were united and powerful enough to prevent it is illustrated by the activities of the Stockport mill-owners in 1831.[6]

The last group of documents in this section illustrates developments in other fields of working-class self-help. The Co-operative movement of the twentieth century owes little beyond the name to the schemes worked out by such pioneers as Owen,[7] King[8] and Lovett,[9] who thought that the aim of co-operation should be the replacement of capitalistic control by a kind of guild socialism. The government was generally willing to assist whenever the lower classes were trying to help themselves; thus protection and encouragement were given to the friendly societies, which were seen as an antidote to pauperization in hard times and an incentive to personal independence[10], and to the savings banks[11] – both largely owing to the efforts of George Rose.[12] The extent to which these institutions offered the means of security to the working classes is indicated by Sir Frederick Morton Eden's account of typical friendly societies

[1] No. 483. [2] Nos. 485–487. [3] No. 488. [4] No. 490.
[5] No. 491. [6] No. 492. [7] No. 478. [8] No. 493.
[9] No. 494. [10] No. 495. [11] No. 497. [12] No. 498.

at the turn of the century[1] and by the analysis of the depositors in a typical savings bank in 1820.[2] In such ways the 'proletariat' of the Industrial Revolution was already beginning to seek respectability and independence.

BIBLIOGRAPHY

I. PRIMARY SOURCES

The principal *Parliamentary Papers* which throw light on social conditions are the Reports on the Employment of Children in Factories (1816, vol. III; 1831–1832, vol. XV), on the Combination Laws (1825, vol. IV), on the Laws respecting Friendly Societies (1825, vol. IV; 1826–1827, vol. III), on Madhouses (1814, vol. IV; 1816, vol. VI), on the Water Supply of the Metropolis (1828, vol. XIX), on the Education of the Lower Orders (a series, 1816–1818), on the Observance of the Sabbath (presenting a vivid picture of London life) (1831–1832, vol. VII), and the Poor Law series of Reports of 1834, and, indeed, information is scattered throughout the whole of the Papers. Other contemporary sources are listed under the appropriate sub-heading below.

II. POPULATION AND PUBLIC HEALTH

The primary information on the size and distribution of the population in the official Census returns for 1801, 1811, 1821 and 1831 should be studied in conjunction with John Rickman's Prefaces to the Census reports and the later interpretations of G. T. Griffith, *Population Problems of the Age of Malthus* (Cambridge, 1926); E. C. K. Gonner, "The Population of England in the Eighteenth Century", *Journal of the Royal Statistical Society*, vol. LXXVI (1913); T. H. Marshall, "The Population Problem during the Industrial Revolution", *Economic History*, vol. I (1926–1929), and "The Population of England and Wales from the Industrial Revolution to the World War" (Historical Revisions, No. III), *Economic History Review*, vol. V (1935); H. J. Habbakuk, "The English Population in the Eighteenth Century", *Economic History Review*, 2nd Series, vol. VI (1953); B. Hammond, "Urban Death Rates in the early Nineteenth Century", *Economic History*, vol. I (1928); J. S. Blackmore and F. C. Mellonie, "Family Endowment and the Birth Rate in the Early Years of the Nineteenth Century", *ibid.*; and T. McKeown and R. G. Brown, "Medical Evidence related to English Population changes in the Eighteenth Century", *Population Studies*, vol. IX (1955). On the movement of population the standard authority is A. Redford, *Labour Migration in England, 1800–1850* (Manchester, 1926).

On Scotland and Ireland, see D. F. Macdonald, *Scotland's Shifting Population, 1750–1850* (1937); K. H. Connell, *The Population of Ireland, 1750–1845* (Oxford, 1950), and the same author's "Some unsettled problems in English and Irish Population History" in *Irish Historical Studies*, vol. VII (1950–1951). Also valuable is B. M. Kerr, "Irish Seasonal Migration to Great Britain, 1800–1838", *ibid.*, vol. III (1944).

Still of value is W. Farr, *Vital Statistics* (1885) (a collection of essays, edited by N. A. Humphrey).

Contemporary thought on population was dominated by Malthus and his critics. The argument of the *First Essay on Population* (1798) was greatly modified in the 1803 and subsequent editions, but nevertheless was extensively criticized. A full list of contemporary replies to Malthus may be found in J. B. Williams, *Guide to the Printed Materials for English Economic and Social History*, I, pp. 213–216. The most important are W. Hazlitt, *A Reply to the Essay on Population* (1807), and the anonymous *Remarks on a late publication entitled 'Essay on the Principle of Population'* (1803). Modern discussions on Malthusianism include J. Bonar, *Malthus and His Work* (1924); H. A. Boner, *Hungry Generations: the Nineteenth Century Case against Malthusianism* (New York, 1955); M. C. Buer, "The Historical Setting of the Malthusian Controversy" in

[1] No. 496.   [2] No. 499.

London Essays in Economics in honour of Edwin Cannan (1927); and R. B. Simons, "T. R. Malthus on British Society" in Journal of the History of Ideas, vol. XVI (1955).

Contemporary works illuminating the problem of public health and the death rate include several by physicians–P. Gaskell, The Manufacturing Population of England, its Moral, Social and Physical Conditions (1833); Sir J. P. Kay-Shuttleworth, The Moral and Physical Condition of the Working Classes employed in the Cotton Manufacture in Manchester (1832); R. Willan, Reports on the Diseases in London (1801); and T. Bateman, Reports on the Diseases of London (1819). The Lancet began publication in 1823. The state of the hospitals in Great Britain is studied in John Howard, An Account of the Principal Lazarettos in Europe (1789; 2nd edition, 1791), and information on death-rates and causes of mortality, including the famous 'Carlisle tables' collected by Dr. Heysham, is printed in J. Milne, A Treatise on the Value of Annuities (2 vols., 1815). The most comprehensive modern work on the public health of the period is M. C. Buer, Health, Wealth and Population in the Early Days of the Industrial Revolution (1926), with a valuable bibliography. See also A. Jephson, The Sanitary Evolution of London (1907); A. Chaplin, Medicine in England during the reign of George III (1919); B. Hamilton, "The Medical Professions in the Eighteenth Century", Economic History Review, 2nd Series, vol. III (1951); and F. G. Parsons, The History of St. Thomas's Hospital (3 vols., 1932–1936). There is much information in M. D. George, London Life in the Eighteenth Century (1925), and there is a historical survey in H. W. Dickinson, The Water Supply of Greater London (1954).

III. THE CHURCH AND DISSENT

The only comprehensive treatment of religious affairs is J. Stoughton, History of Religion in England, vols. 6–8 (1901), though religious ideas are dealt with in L. Stephen, History of English Thought in the Eighteenth Century (2 vols., 1876), and J. M. Creed and J. S. Boyes Smith, Religious Thought in the Eighteenth Century (Cambridge, 1934)–an anthology of contemporary writings.

(a) THE CHURCH OF ENGLAND

There are many useful articles in the Dictionary of Church History, edited by S. L. Ollard, G. Crosse and M. F. Bond (3rd edition, 1948). The best modern account, N. Sykes, Church and State in England in the Eighteenth Century (Cambridge, 1934), deals mainly with the first half of the century and for this period older works must still be consulted, principally C. J. Abbey and J. H. Overton, The English Church in the Eighteenth Century (2 vols., 1887); J. H. Overton, The English Church in the Nineteenth Century [1800–1833] (1894); H. O. Wakeman, An Introduction to the History of the Church of England (8th revised edition, 1914); and the volumes on this period in Stephens and Hunt's History of the English Church by J. H. Overton and F. Relton, The English Church from the Accession of George I to the end of the Eighteenth Century (1906), and F. W. Cornish, The English Church in the Nineteenth Century (2 vols., 1910). Also useful is C. J. Abbey, The English Church and its Bishops, 1700–1800 (2 vols., 1887). There are selections illustrating the conduct of services, religious practice and literature, the lives of the clergy, etc., in W. K. L. Clarke, Eighteenth Century Piety (1944), and J. Wickham Legge, English Church Life from the Restoration to the Tractarian Movement (1914).

J. Le Neve, Fasti Ecclesiae Anglicanae, edited by T. D. Hardy (3 vols., Oxford, 1854), lists the dignitaries of the Church, whose lives may be studied in W. F. Hook, Lives of the Archbishops of Canterbury (12 vols., 1860–1876); A. W. Rowden, Primates of the Four Georges (1916). Sir J. Stephen, Essays in Ecclesiastical Biography, vol. II (1849), has accounts of Wilberforce and the 'Clapham Sect'. Lives of prominent Churchmen and Divines include Bishop Watson's autobiography, Anecdotes of the Life of Richard Watson (2 vols., 1818); A. Chalmers, The Works and Life of William Paley (5 vols., 1819); A. Blomfield, A Memoir of Charles James Blomfield, Bishop of London (2 vols., 1863), Life and Correspondence of Richard Whateley, edited by E. J. Whateley (2 vols., 1866), Life and Correspondence of John Foster, edited by J. E. Ryland (2 vols., 1846); and W. Carus, Memoirs of Charles Simeon (1847). For the lower clergy, see the famous J. Woodforde, Diary of a Country Parson, edited by J. Beresford (5 vols., 1926–1931), the less well-known Diary *of the Rev. William Jones, 1771–1821*, edited by O. F. Christie (1929); *Diary of Benjamin Newton, Rector of Wath, 1816–1818*, edited by C. P. Fendall and E. A. Crutchley (Cambridge, 1933); and J. Skinner, *Journal of a Somerset Rector* (1772–1839), edited by H. Coombes and H. N. Box (1930). A. T. Hart, *The Eighteenth Century Parson* (Shrewsbury, 1955), is directed mainly to the 'general reader'.

The history of the evangelical movement may be approached through G. W. E. Russell, *A Short History of the Evangelical Movement* (1915); J. H. Overton, *The Evangelical Revival in the Eighteenth Century* (1886); and G. R. Balleine, *A History of the Evangelical Party in the Church of England* (1911). A useful short account is W. L. Mathieson, *English Church Reform, 1815–1840* (1923). See also R. A. Knox, *Enthusiasm* (Oxford, 1950); J. S. Reynolds, *The Evangelicals of Oxford, 1735–1871* (Oxford, 1953); and, on the teachings of the Church, V. F. Storr, *The Development of English Theology in the Nineteenth Century* (2 vols., 1910). The most important contemporary works produced by the evangelicals are W. Wilberforce, *A Practical View of the Prevailing Religious Systems of Professed Christians . . . contrasted with Real Christianity* (1797), and J. B. Sumner, *The Evidence of Christianity derived from its Nature and Reception* (1824). On the High Church movement, see J. Keble, *The Christian Year* (1st edition anonymous, 1827, 2 vols.; with notes and introduction by W. Lock, 1905).

On the religious societies, see E. Stock, *History of the Church Missionary Society* (3 vols., 1899); W. O. Allen and E. McClure, *Two Hundred Years: The History of the S.P.C.K.* (1898); and W. Canton, *History of the British and Foreign Bible Society* (5 vols., 1904–1910).

(b) NONCONFORMITY

General. The standard general history is H. W. Clark, *History of English Nonconformity*, vol. II [1660–1900] (1913), which should be read with E. D. Bebb, *Nonconformity and Social and Economic Life, 1660–1800* (1935), and A. H. Lincoln, *Some Political and Social Ideas of English Dissent 1763–1800* (Cambridge, 1938). For the histories of particular sects, see the *Proceedings* of the Wesley Historical Society (Burnley and London, 1898–1934), the *Transactions* of the Congregational Historical Society (1901+), the Baptist Historical Society (1908+) and the Unitarian Historical Society (1916+), *The Methodist Magazine* and *The Baptist Quarterly*. The various denominations have issued bibliographies.

The Methodists have a well-documented history in this period, the time of their separation from the Church in the generation following the death of their founder. The standard edition of John Wesley's *Journal* is edited by N. Curnock (8 vols., 1909–1916), of his letters, 1721–1791, edited by J. Telford (1931), and, of many lives, perhaps the best are R. Southey, *The Life of Wesley* (2 vols., 1820); L. Tyerman, *Life and Times of the Rev. John Wesley* (3 vols., 1870–1871), and, for his later life, J. S. Simon, *Wesley: the Last Phase* (1931). See also the same author's *John Wesley and the Religious Societies* (1921); M. Piette, *John Wesley in the Evolution of Protestantism* (1937); and E. J. S. Simpson, *Wesley and the Church of England* (1934). The standard history of the movement is *A New History of Methodism*, edited by W. J. Townsend, H. B. Workman and G. Eayres (2 vols., 1909), but the older G. Smith, *History of Wesleyan Methodism* (1857, 4th edition, 1864), is still useful. On this period particularly, see W. J. Warner, *The Methodist Movement in the Industrial Revolution* (1930); E. R. Taylor, *Methodism and Politics* (1935); R. F. Wearmouth, *Methodism and the Working-class Movements of England, 1800–1850* (1937;) and M. Edwards, "The Social and Political Influence of Methodism in the Napoleonic Period" (Thesis summary, *Bulletin of the Institute of Historical Research*, vol. XIII, 1934).

The Presbyterians. The standard works are A. H. Drysdale, *History of the Presbyterians in England* (1889), and O. M. Griffiths, *Religion and Learning: A Study in English Presbyterian Thought* (Cambridge, 1935).

The Congregationalists. Standard is R. W. Dale, *History of English Congregationalism* (1907). See also J. Waddington, *Congregational History* (5 vols., 1869–1880).

The Baptists. See W. T. Whitley, *A History of British Baptists* (1923), and A. C. Underwood, *A History of the English Baptists* (1947).

The Unitarians. See H. McLachlan, *The Unitarian Movement in the Religious Life of England, 1700–1900* (1934), and *The Methodist Unitarian Movement* (Manchester, 1919); R. V. Holt, *The Unitarian Contribution to Social Progress in England* (1938); and W. Lloyd, *Story of Protestant Dissent and English Unitarians* (1899). There are lives of the great men of the movement at this time by A. Holt, *Life of Joseph Priestley* (1931), and R. Thomas, *Richard Price* (1924).

The Quakers. The standard E. Russell, *History of Quakerism* (1942), may be supplemented for this period by R. M. Jones, *The Later Periods of Quakerism* (the period 1725–1900) (2 vols., 1921), and T. A. Clarkson, *A Portraiture of Quakerism* (1806).

On the Churches in Scotland, Wales and Ireland, see W. L. Mathieson, *Church and Reform in Scotland* (1797–1854) (1916); E. Griffith, *The Presbyterian Church of Wales, 1735–1905*; T. Rees, *History of Protestant Nonconformity in Wales* (2nd edition, 1883), and *History of the Church of Ireland*, edited by W. A. Philipps (3 vols., 1933–1934).

The Roman Catholics. The works of B. Ward, *The Dawn of the Catholic Revival in England, 1781–1803* (2 vols., 1909), and *The Eve of Catholic Emancipation* [1800–1830] (3 vols., 1911–1912) offer the most thorough treatment of this period. See also P. Hughes, *The Catholic Question, 1688–1829* (1929), and articles in *The Catholic Encyclopaedia* (15 vols., 1907–1914). The writings and sermons of the Rev. Sydney Smith, in the 1801 (2 vols.) edition of the *Sermons*, and *Letters on the Subject of the Catholics from Peter Plymley to his brother Abraham* (11th edition, 1808), are indispensable for a study of the contemporary attitude. For the opponents of emancipation, see G. F. A. Best, "The Protestant Constitution and its Supporters, 1800–1829" in *Transactions of the Royal Historical Society*, 5th Series, vol. VIII (1958).

The Jews. A. M. Hyamson, *History of the Jews in Great Britain* (2nd edition, 1928), is standard. See also his *The Sephardim of England* (1951).

Rationalism. Standard is A. W. Benn, *History of English Rationalism in the Nineteenth Century* (2 vols., 1906), and equally indispensable is W. Lecky, *History of the Rise and Influence of the Spirit of Rationalism in Europe* (2 vols., 3rd edition, 1866).

IV. EDUCATION

The best bibliographical guide is to be found in the *Cambridge Bibliography of English Literature*, vols. II (1660–1800), III (1800–1900) and V (Supplement). There are also lists in J. B. Williams, *Guide to the Printed Materials*.

Contemporary views and theories on education are to be found in scores of books and pamphlets. Particularly important are: W. Paley, *The Principles of Moral and Political Philosophy* (1785), and *Reasons for Contentment addressed to the Labouring Part of the British Public* (1793); Jeremy Bentham's *Chrestomathia*, in the Bowring edition of the *Works*, vol. VIII (1843); S. Parr, *A Discourse on Education* (n.d.); Paine's *Rights of Man* (1791–1792) and Godwin's *Enquiry concerning Political Justice* (2 vols., 1793); Mary Wollstonecraft, *A Vindication of the Rights of Woman* (1792), and Hannah More, *Strictures on the Modern System of Female Education* (2 vols., 1799); Maria and Richard Edgeworth, *Practical Education* (2 vols., 1798), and R. L. Edgeworth's *Essays on Professional Education* (1809) (see A. Paterson, *The Edgeworths* (1914)); Sarah Trimmer's works, including *Reflections upon the Education of Children in Charity Schools* (1792) and *The Oeconomy of Charity* (on the Sunday schools) (1787, enlarged edition, 2 vols., 1801). The Owenite system is described by R. Owen, *A New View of Society* (1813) and R. D. Owen, *Outlines of the New System of Education at New Lanark* (Glasgow, 1824). Henry Brougham's *Practical Observations on the Education of the People* (1825) surveys the state of popular education at that date from a practical point of view. Most influential of all, however, were Lancaster and Bell; their systems are described in Joseph Lancaster's *Improvements in Education* (1803), *The British System of Education* (1810) and *An Account of the Progress of Joseph Lancaster's Plan* (1809). Among his many critics was Sarah Trimmer, *A Comparative View of the New Plan of Education* (1805), objecting to the non-sectarian basis of Lancaster's plan. Bell's Anglican system is described by its founder in *An Experiment in Education made at the Male Asylum in Madras* (1797) and more fully in *The Madras School* (1808). The two are compared in D. Salmon, *The Practical Parts of Lancaster's 'Improvements' and Bell's Experiment* (Cambridge, 1932), and there is a 3-vol. *Life of the Rev. Andrew Bell* by R. and C. C. Southey (1844). The work of Pestalozzi, which attracted much attention at the time but was widely influential only later, may be studied in J. A. Green, *The Educational Ideas of Pestalozzi* (1905), *Pestalozzi's Educational Writings* (1912), and *The Life and Work of Pestalozzi* (1913). The lives of other educationalists of note are illuminated by A. Gregory, *Robert Raikes. A History of the Origin of Sunday Schools* (1880); R. K. Birkbeck, *W. J. Birkbeck: Life and Letters* (Oxford, 1922); and Leslie Stephen's *The English Utilitarians* (3 vols., 1900). For Hannah More, see the General Bibliography.

Other contemporary information may be found in the *Parliamentary Papers*, particularly the 12 vols. devoted to Brougham's Select Committee on the Education of the Lower Orders, 1816–1818, and the 44 vols. between 1818 and 1842, embracing the work of the Royal Commission to inquire concerning Charities for the Education of the Poor. There is scattered information in the Report of the Select Committee on the State of Children employed in Manufactories (1816, vol. III). The annual reports of the various educational societies – the National Society, the British and Foreign School Society, the Sunday School Society (1787–1789, 1797, 1799), the S.P.C.K., etc. – are also valuable.

The best general histories of English education are J. W. Adamson, *English Education 1789–1902* (Cambridge, 1930), his *Outline of English Education, 1760–1902* (reprinted from *Cambridge History of English Literature*, vol. XIV (1928)); R. L. Archer, *Secondary Education in the Nineteenth Century* (Cambridge, 1921); and F. Smith, *A History of English Elementary Education, 1760–1902* (1931). A good short introduction is H. C. Barnard, *A Short History of English Education, 1760–1944* (1947, revised edition, 1952); and other useful works are C. Birchenough, *History of Elementary Education in England and Wales from 1800* (1914, 3rd edition, 1938); R. D. Roberts, *Education in the Nineteenth Century* (Cambridge, 1901); S. J. Curtis, *History of Education in Great Britain* (1948, revised edition, 1953); and A. E. Dobbs, *Education and Social Movements, 1700–1850* (1919).

The history of the older universities during this period is unremarkable: both D. A. Winstanley in *The University of Cambridge in the Eighteenth Century* (Cambridge, 1922) and *Unreformed Cambridge* (Cambridge, 1935) and W. R. Ward, *Georgian Oxford: University Politics in the Eighteenth Century* (1958), concentrate on the politics of the universities; Oxford is studied in C. E. Malet, *History of the University of Oxford*, vol. III, *Modern Oxford* (1927). The movement in the eighteen-twenties which brought about the foundation of the London colleges should be studied in H. H. Bellot, *University College, London, 1826–1926* (1929); F. J. C. Hearnshaw, *Centenary History of King's College, London* (1929); and T. Campbell's article "Suggestions respecting the Plan of an University in London", *New Monthly Magazine*, vol. XIII (1825). Information on this, as also on the Lancasterian schools, mechanics institutes, and the Benthamite ideas, may be found in the Place MSS. (British Museum Additional MSS. 27823–27824). See also A. I. Tillyard, *History of University Reform from 1800* (Cambridge, 1913).

The Dissenting Academies should be studied in I. Parker, *Dissenting Academies in England* (Cambridge, 1914), and H. McLachlan, *English Education under the Test Acts: Nonconformist Academies, 1662–1820* (1931).

For histories of individual schools, see the lists in the Cambridge Bibliography. The printed Registers of the Universities, Inns of Court, Colleges and Schools of Great Britain and Ireland are listed by M. Johnstone in *Bulletin of the Institute of Historical Research* (3 parts), vol. IX (1931–1932). There is a contemporary account of Rugby School, 1788–1794, in J. Forster, *Walter Savage Landor* (2 vols., 1869), and of Christ's Hospital, 1782–1790, in S. T. Coleridge, *Biographica Literaria* (1817). See also E. C. Mack, *Public Schools and British Opinion*, vol. I [1780–1860] (New York, 1938).

On the education of the lower classes, see, in addition to the works mentioned above, the authoritative M. G. Jones, *The Charity School Movement* (Cambridge, 1938); H. B. Binns *et al.*, *A Century of Education, being the Centenary History of the British and Foreign School Society* (1908);

R. K. Webb, *The British Working Class Reader, 1790–1848: Literacy and Social Tension* (1955); S. E. Maltby, *Manchester and the Movement for National Elementary Education, 1800–1870* (Manchester, 1918); M. Tylecote, *The Mechanics Institutes of Lancashire and Yorkshire before 1851* (Manchester, 1957); H. M. Pollard, *Pioneers of Popular Education, 1760–1850* (1956); and J. H. Wellard, "The State of Reading among the Working Classes of England during the first half of the Nineteenth Century" in *Library Quarterly*, vol. v (1935). For Scotland, see J. Kerr, *Scottish Education* (1910). A useful and informative study of the teaching profession in the elementary schools from 1800 is A. Tropp, *The School Teachers* (1958).

V. FACTORY LEGISLATION

See the comprehensive treatment of the Factory Acts in B. L. Hutchins and A. Harrison, *A History of Factory Legislation* (1903, 3rd edition, 1926). Vol. I of S. Kydd ('Alfred'), *History of the Factory Movement* (1857), deals with the period 1802–1832 and is based on Parliamentary Debates, official records and contemporary correspondence. The latest work is N. W. Thomas, *The Early Factory Legislation* (1951). See also Robert Owen's influential *Observations on the effect of the Manufacturing System* (1818), the reports of various committees in the *Parliamentary Papers*, and the following secondary works: C. Driver, *Tory Radical: the Life of Richard Oastler* (Oxford, 1946); F. Collier, "Workers in a Lancashire Factory at the beginning of the Nineteenth Century" [the factory of Messrs. Peel, Yates and Peel at Bury] in *Manchester School*, vol. VIII (1936); and G. L. Phillips and A. L. Cole, *England's Climbing Boys* (Harvard, 1949).

VI. TRADE UNIONS

The standard work is still S. and B. Webb, *History of Trade Unionism* (1894, new editions 1902, 1911, revised edition (without bibliography), 1920). See also G. D. H. Cole, *Short History of the British Working Class Movement*, vol. I (1789–1848) (1925), and the accompanying G. D. H. Cole and A. W. Filson, *British Working Class Movements: Select Documents, 1789–1875* (1951); G. D. H. Cole and R. W. Postgate, *The Common People, 1746–1938* (1938), contains much information on a variety of topics. R. Y. Hedges and A. Winterbotham, *A Legal History of Trade Unionism* (1930), is indispensable for its account of the legal status of the unions through their history. R. M. Rayner, *The Story of Trade Unionism* (1929), is slight on this period. On the combination laws and their operation, see two articles by M. D. George, "The Combination Laws Reconsidered", *Economic History*, vol. I (1927), and "The Combination Laws" (revisions in Economic History, No. IV), *Economic History Review*, vol. VI (1936). *The Early English Trade Unions*, edited by A. Aspinall (1949), is a collection of documents from the Home Office papers, illustrating the history of trade unionism during the operation of the combination laws of 1799–1824. The repeal of the combination laws is studied in G. Wallas, *Life of Francis Place* (1898, new edition, 1918). On this period, see also J. L. Gray, "The Law of Combinations in Scotland", *Economica*, vol. VIII (1928); H. Hamilton, "Combination in the West of Scotland Coal Trade, 1790–1817", *Economic History*, vol. II (1930); T. K. Derry, "The Repeal of the Apprenticeship Clauses of the Statute of Apprentices", *Economic History Review*, vol. III (1931); and A. Temple Patterson, "Luddism, Hampden Clubs and Trade Unions in Leicestershire, 1816–1817" in *English Historical Review*, vol. LXIII (1947). On the later part of the period, see G. D. H. Cole, *Attempts at General Union: A Study in British Trade Union History, 1818–34* (1953). For the histories of unions in particular trades, see the following: R. W. Postgate, *The Builders' History* (1923); E. Howe (editor), *The London Compositor: Documents relating to Wages, Working Conditions, and Customs of the London Printing Trade, 1785–1900* (Bibliographical Society Pub., 1947); W. Kiddier, *The Old Trade Union, from unprinted records of the Brushmakers* (1930); M. D. George, "The London Coal-heavers: Attempts to regulate Waterside Labour in the Eighteenth and Nineteenth Centuries", *Economic History*, vol. I (1927); E. Welbourne, *The*

Miners' Unions of Northumberland and Durham (Cambridge, 1923); S. and B. Webb, *The Story of the Durham Miners, 1662–1921* (1921); N. Edwards, *History of the South Wales Miners* (1926); R. P. Arnot, *A History of the Scottish Miners from the Earliest Times* (1955); W. H. Warburton, *The History of Trade Union Organisation, the North Staffordshire Potteries* (1931).

The Co-operative movement. The standard authority is G. J. Holyoake, *The History of Co-operation in England* (revised edition, 2 vols., 1906). See also the later work of B. Potter, *The Co-operative Movement in Great Britain* (1930), and C. R. Fay, *Co-operation at Home and Abroad* (new edition, 2 vols., Cambridge, 1936). William Lovett's autobiography, *The Life and Struggles of William Lovett* (1876, reprint 2 vols., 1920), includes his recollections of his early life in the movement, but the chief figure is that of Robert Owen and his influential book, *A New View of Society* (1813–1814, 2nd edition, 1816). The literature on his life and influence is listed in *A Bibliography of Robert Owen, the Socialist, 1771–1858* (National Library of Wales, Aberystwyth, 1914). The early Socialist movement may be studied in such sources as *The Memoirs of Henry Hunt* (3 vols., 1820–1822); W. Hodgson, *The Commonwealth of Reason* (1795); T. Spence, *The Constitution of a Perfect Commonwealth* (1798); T. Hodgskin, *Labour defended against the claims of Capital* (1825, 1831), and in any of the numerous editions of Thomas Paine, *The Rights of Man*. Secondary histories are M. Beer, *History of British Socialism* [vol. 1 to 1834] (2 vols., 1919–1920); W. Sombart, *Socialism and the Socialist Movement in the Nineteenth Century*, translated by M. Epstein (1909); and T. Kirkup, *A History of Socialism* (1892, reprinted 1920). Various works of T. Spence, William Ogilvie and Paine are reprinted in *The Pioneers of Land Reform*, edited by M. Beer (1920).

Friendly Societies. See Sir F. M. Eden, *Observations on Friendly Societies* (1801). His *State of the Poor* (3 vols., 1797) contains much information on individual societies.

Savings Banks. The standard works are H. O. Horne, *A History of Savings Banks* (Oxford, 1947), and W. Lewins, *A History of Banks for Savings in Great Britain and Ireland* (1866). George Rose's pamphlet, *Observations on Banks for Savings* (1816, 4th enlarged edition, 1817), is important.

A. POPULATION AND PUBLIC HEALTH

THE CENSUS

415A. Comparative population, 1801–1831

(*Parliamentary Papers*, 1833, XXXVI, p. 1.)

For the population of the separate counties of England in 1801, see No. 329, and in 1811, No. 468.

	1801	Increase per cent	1811	Increase per cent	1821	Increase per cent	1831
England . . .	8,331,434	14⅔	9,551,888	17⅞	11,261,437	16	13,091,005
Wales . . .	541,546	13	611,788	17	717,438	12	806,182
Scotland . . .	1,599,068	14	1,805,688	16	2,093,456	13	2,365,114
Army, Navy, &c. .	470,598	—	640,500	—	319,300	—	277,017
Total . .	10,942,646	15¼	12,609,864	14	14,391,631	15	16,539,318

415B. The age structure of the population in 1821

(*Parliamentary Papers*, 1822, XV, p. 543)

The total number of persons in Great Britain (not including the Army, Navy, and Seamen in registered vessels) was . . . 14,072,331 . . . and the number of persons whose ages were returned was . . . 12,487,377 . . . whence it appears that the ages of one-ninth part of the persons therein enumerated have not been obtained. . . .

	Under 5 years	5 to 10	10 to 15	15 to 20	20 to 30	30 to 40	40 to 50	50 to 60	60 to 70	70 to 80	80 to 90	90 to 100	100 & upwards	Total
MALES	929,535	819,156	718,796	604,905	893,425	694,769	565,024	402,218	273,818	135,009	34,964	2,873	100	6,074,592
FEMALES	908,400	804,030	678,613	643,875	1,084,050	773,887	597,968	425,678	301,052	147,946	43,049	4,046	191	6,412,785

415C. Occupations in 1831

(Parliamentary Papers, 1833, xxxvii, pp. 1042-1043, 1044-1051.)

	PERSONS.			AGRICULTURE.			Employed in Manufacture, or in making Manufacturing Machinery.	Employed in Retail Trade, or in Handicraft as Masters or Workmen.	Capitalists, Bankers, Professional and other Educated Men.	Labourers employed in Labour not Agricultural.	Other Males 20 Years of Age (except Servants).	Male Servants.		Female Servants.
	Males.	Females.	Total of Persons.	Occupiers employing Labourers.	Occupiers not employing Labourers.	Labourers employed in Agriculture.						20 Years of Age.	Under 20 Years.	
ENGLAND .	6,376,627	6,714,378	13,091,005	141,460	94,883	744,407	314,106	964,177	179,983	500,950	189,389	70,629	30,777	518,705
WALES .	394,563	411,619	806,182	19,728	19,966	55,468	6,218	43,226	5,204	31,571	11,180	2,145	1,179	42,274
SCOTLAND	1,114,816	1,250,298	2,365,114	25,887	53,966	87,292	83,993	152,464	29,203	76,191	34,930	5,895	2,599	109,512
ARMY, NAVY, MARINES, and SEAMEN, in registered Vessels	277,017	—	277,017	—	—	—	—	—	—	—	—	—	—	—
TOTALS .	8,163,023	8,376,295	16,539,318	187,075	168,815	887,167	404,317	1,159,867	214,390	608,712	235,499	78,669	34,555	670,491

415D. Males (twenty years of age) employed in retail trade or in handicraft, as masters or workmen (totals under 5,000 omitted)

Shoe and Boot-maker or mender	133,248
Carpenter	103,247
Tailor, Breeches-maker	74,054
Publican, Hotel or Innkeeper, Retailer of Beer	61,231
Blacksmith, Horse-shoes	58,142
Mason or Waller	49,155
Shopkeeper, { Dealer in sundry necessary articles, such as are sold in a village shop. }	38,150
Butcher, Flesher	35,218
Bricklayer	29,593
Baker, Gingerbread, fancy	27,942
Grocer, Greengrocer	22,147
Cabinet-maker	21,774
Miller	19,796
Wheelwright (Cart, Ploughwright)	19,550
Sawyer	19,181
Carrier, Carter	18,859
Housepainter	15,653
Boat-builder, Shipwright	13,884
Linen-draper	13,601
Cooper	13,246
Glazier, Plumber	11,999
Huckster, Hawker, Pedlar, Duffer	10,881
Hatter and Hosier	10,858
Coach-owner, Driver, Grooms, &c.	10,514
Brick-maker	9,864
Plasterer	9,683
Whitesmith	9,543
Clock and Watch-maker	8,892
Barber, or Hairdresser, Hair-dealer	8,449
Printer	8,342
Dyer	7,867
Maltster	6,979
Saddler	6,964
Brassworker, Tinker	6,851
Rope-maker	6,596
Currier	6,012
Turner	5,902
Ironfounder	5,882
Milkman, Cowkeeper	5,795
Brewer	5,765

Coal Merchant, Fuel   5,713
Tanner   5,549
Chemist and Druggist   5,423
Coachmaker   5,397
Jeweller   5,231
Tinman   5,211
Builder   5,204

416. The expectation of life

(Parliamentary Papers, 1825, IV, Appx. B.1, pp. 125–126.)

Report of the Select Committee of the House of Commons on the laws respecting Friendly Societies, 1825.

(*a*) The figures for the early eighteenth century, calculated from observations on the nominees of the Tontine of 1695; (*b*) the 1825 figures, compiled from the records of the nominees of the life and other annuities granted by the authority of Parliament since 1785; (*c*) the comparable figures for 1953 (from *Whittaker's Almanac*, 1957 edition).

Mean duration of life to be expected by:

Age	Early 18th century		c. 1824		1953	
	Male	*Female*	*Male*	*Female*	*Male*	*Female*
0	37·6	—	50·1	55·5	67·3	72·4
5	39·0	42·4	48·9	54·2	64·7	69·5
10	35·7	40·4	45·5	51·0	59·8	64·6
15	32·0	37·3	41·7	47·1	55·0	59·7
20	29·3	34·2	38·3	43·9	50·2	54·8
25	27·9	31·6	35·9	40·8	45·5	50·0
30	26·2	28·9	33·1	37·5	40·7	45·2
35	24·1	26·3	30·1	34·3	36·0	40·5
40	21·7	23·6	27·0	31·1	31·4	35·8
45	19·1	20·6	23·7	27·8	26·8	31·2
50	16·8	17·7	20·3	24·3	22·5	26·8
55	14·5	15·4	17·1	20·7	18·6	22·5
60	11·6	13·2	14·3	17·3	15·0	18·5
65	9·2	10·2	11·6	14·0	11·9	14·7
70	7·1	7·7	9·2	10·9	9·2	11·3
75	5·6	5·5	7·1	8·4	6·9	8·3
80	4·9	3·7	4·9	6·5	5·1	6·0
85	3·5	3·8	3·1	4·8	3·7	4·1

417. Vaccination

(G. R. Porter, *The Progress of the Nation* (1851), pp. 38–39.)

Statement of the total average mortality and the average mortality arising from the small-pox, within the weekly bills of mortality, at different periods.

Period	Total average mortality	Average mortality from small-pox	Proportion of deaths from small-pox in each 1000 deaths	Year of Census	Population within the bills of mortality
1701–10	21,110	1,372	65	—	—
1721–30	27,361	2,257	82	—	—
1741–50	26,060	2,002	77	—	—
1751–60	20,849	1,957	94	—	—
1770–79	21,591	2,204	102	—	—
1780–89	19,517	1,712	88	—	—
1790–99	19,177	1,768	92	—	—
1800–09	18,891	1,374	73	1801	746,953
1810–19	19,061	833	43	1811	855,626
1820–29	20,680	715	35	1821	1,011,951
1830–36	24,356	610	25	1831	1,180,075

The introduction of vaccination as a substitute for variolous inoculation is an improvement which properly belongs to the present century. The discovery . . . was made in 1798, but although the attention of the medical world was immediately excited in the most intense degree to the subject, it required several years of experience before the value of the discovery was fully recognized by medical practitioners, and before the public were sufficiently weaned from their previous prejudices, to avail themselves to any extent of the blessing. It was not until 1808, 10 years after the first introduction of the vaccine practice, that the medical officers of the Small Pox Hospital in London ceased to inoculate out-patients for the small-pox; and so slowly did the perfect conviction of the value of the substitute make its way in their minds, that it was not until June, 1822 . . . that the practice of inoculating was discontinued within . . . that hospital.

418. Malthus on population

(T. R. Malthus, *First Essay on Population* (1798): Economic Society Reprint (1926), pp. 11–38.)

For Malthus's views on the poor laws, see No. 335.

. . . I think I may fairly make two postulata. First, That food is necessary to the existence of man. Secondly, That the passion between the sexes is necessary, and will remain nearly in its present state.

These two laws ever since we have had any knowledge of mankind, appear to have been fixed laws of our nature; and, as we have not hitherto seen any alteration in them, we have no right to conclude that they will ever cease to be what they now are, without an immediate act of power in that Being who first arranged the system of the universe; and for the advantage of his creatures, still executes, according to fixed laws, all its various operations. . . .

. . . Assuming then, my postulata as granted, I say, that the power of population is indefinitely greater than the power in the earth to produce subsistence for man. Population, when unchecked, increases in a geometrical ratio. Subsistence increases only in an arithmetical ratio. A slight acquaintance with numbers will shew the immensity of the first power in comparison of the second. By that law of our nature which makes food necessary to the life of man, the effects of these two unequal powers must be kept equal. This implies a strong and constantly operating check on population from the difficulty of subsistence. This difficulty must fall some where; and must necessarily be severely felt by a large portion of mankind.

Through the animal and vegetable kingdoms, nature has scattered the seeds of life abroad with the most profuse and liberal hand. She has been comparatively sparing in the room, and the nourishment necessary to rear them. The germs of existence contained in this spot of earth, with ample food, and ample room to expand in, would fill millions of worlds in the course of a few thousand years. Necessity, that imperious all pervading law of nature, restrains them within the prescribed bounds. The race of plants, and the race of animals shrink under this great restrictive law. And the race of man cannot, by any efforts of reason, escape from it. Among plants and animals its effects are waste of seed, sickness, and premature death. Among mankind, misery and vice. The former, misery, is an absolutely necessary consequence of it. Vice is a highly probable consequence, and we therefore see it abundantly prevail; but it ought not, perhaps, to be called an absolutely necessary consequence. The ordeal of virtue is to resist all temptation to evil.

This natural inequality of the two powers of population, and of production in the earth, and that great law of our nature which must constantly keep their effects equal, form the great difficulty that to me appears insurmountable in the way to the perfectibility of society. All other arguments are of slight and subordinate consideration in comparison of this. I see no way by which man can escape from the weight of this law which pervades all animated nature. No fancied equality, no agrarian regulations in their utmost extent, could remove the pressure of it even for a single century. And it appears, therefore, to be decisive against the possible existence of a society, all the members of which, should live in ease, happiness, and comparative leisure; and feel no anxiety about providing the means of subsistence for themselves and families.

Consequently, if the premises are just, the argument is conclusive against the perfectibility of the mass of mankind. . . .

. . . I said that population, when unchecked, increased in a geometrical ratio; and subsistence for man in an arithmetical ratio. Let us examine whether this position be just. I think it will be allowed, that no state has hitherto existed (at least that we have any account of) where the manners were so pure and simple, and the means of subsistence so abundant, that no check whatever has existed to early marriages; among the lower classes, from a fear of not providing well for their families; or among the higher classes, from a fear of lowering their condition in life. Consequently in no state that we have yet known, has the power of population been left to exert itself with perfect freedom.

Whether the law of marriage be instituted, or not, the dictate of nature and virtue, seems to be an early attachment to one woman. Supposing a liberty of changing in the case of an unfortunate choice, this liberty would not affect population till it arose to a height greatly vicious; and we are now supposing the existence of a society where vice is scarcely known. In a state therefore of great equality and virtue, where pure and simple manners prevailed, and where the means of subsistence were so abundant, that no part of the society could have any fears about providing amply for a family, the power of population being left to exert itself unchecked, the increase of the human species would evidently be much greater than any increase that has been hitherto known.

In the United States of America, where the means of subsistence have been more ample, the manners of the people more pure, and consequently the checks to early marriages fewer, than in any of the modern states of Europe, the population has been found to double itself in twenty-five years.

This ratio of increase, though short of the utmost power of population, yet as the result of actual experience, we will take as our rule; and say, that population, when unchecked, goes on doubling itself every twenty-five years, or increases in a geometrical ratio.

Let us now take any spot of earth, this Island for instance, and see in what ratio the subsistence it affords can be supposed to increase. We will begin with it under its present state of cultivation. If I allow that by the best possible policy, by breaking up more land, and by great encouragements to agriculture, the produce of this Island may be doubled in the first twenty-five years, I think it will be allowing as much as any person can well demand. In the next 25 years, it is impossible to suppose that the produce could be quadrupled. It would be contrary to all our knowledge of the qualities of land. The very utmost that we can conceive is, that the increase in the second 25 years might equal the present produce. Let us then take this for our rule, though certainly far beyond the truth; and allow that by great exertion, the whole produce of the Island might be increased every 25 years, by a quantity of subsistence equal to what it at present produces. The most enthusiastic speculator cannot suppose a greater increase than this. In a few centuries it would make every acre of land in the Island like a garden. Yet this ratio of increase is evidently arithmetical. It may be fairly said, therefore, that the means of subsistence increase in an arithmetical ratio.

Let us now bring the effects of these two ratios together. The population of the Island is computed to be about seven millions; and we will suppose the present produce equal to the support of such a number. In the first 25 years the population would be fourteen millions; and the food being also doubled, the means of subsistence would be equal to this increase. In the next 25 years the population would be 28 millions; and the means of subsistence only equal to the support of 21 millions. In the next period, the population would be 56 millions, and the means of subsistence just sufficient for half that number. And at the conclusion of the first century the population would be 112 millions, and the means of subsistence only equal to the support of 35 millions; which would leave a population of 77 millions totally unprovided for. . . .

Taking the population of the world at any number, 1,000 millions, for instance, the human species would increase in the ratio of–1, 2, 4, 8, 16, 32, 64, 128, 256, 512, &c. and subsistence as–1, 2, 3, 4, 5, 6, 7, 8, 9, 10, &c. In two centuries and a quarter, the population would be to the means of subsistence as 512 to 10: in three centuries as 4096 to 13; and in 2,000 years the difference would be almost incalculable, though the produce in that time would have increased to an immense extent.

No limits whatever are placed to the productions of the earth; they may increase for ever and be greater than any assignable quantity; yet still the power of population being a power of a superior order, the increase of the human species can only be kept commensurate to the increase of the means of subsistence, by the constant operation of the strong law of necessity acting as a check upon the greater power.

The effects of this check remain now to be considered. . . . We will suppose the means of subsistence in any country just equal to the easy support of its inhabitants. The constant effort towards population, which is found to act even in the most vicious societies, increases the number of people before the means of subsistence are increased. The food therefore which before supported seven millions, must now be divided among seven millions and a half or eight millions. The poor consequently must live much worse, and many of them be reduced to severe distress. The number of labourers also being above the proportion of the work in the market, the price of labour must tend toward a decrease; while the price of provisions would at the same time tend to rise. The labourer therefore must work harder to earn the same as he did before. During this season of distress, the discouragements to marriage, and the difficulty of rearing a family are so great, that population is at a stand. In the mean time the cheapness of labour, the plenty of labourers, and the necessity of an increased industry amongst them, encourage cultivators to employ more labour upon their land; to turn up fresh soil, and to manure and improve more completely what is already in tillage; till ultimately the means of subsistence become in the same proportion to the population as at the period from which we set out. The situation of the labourer being then again tolerably comfortable, the restraints to population are in some degree loosened; and the same retrograde and progressive movements with respect to happiness are repeated.

This sort of oscillation will not be remarked by superficial observers; and it may be difficult even for the most penetrating mind to calculate its periods. Yet that in all old states some such vibration does exist; though from various transverse causes, in a much less marked, and in a much more irregular manner than I have described it, no reflecting man who considers the subject deeply can well doubt. . . .

. . . That population cannot increase without the means of subsistence, is a proposition so evident, that it needs no illustration. That population does invariably increase, where there are the means of subsistence, the history of every people that have ever existed will abundantly prove. And, that the superior power of population cannot be checked, without producing misery or vice, the ample portion of these too bitter ingredients in the cup of human life, and the continuance of the physical causes that seem to have produced them, bear too convincing a testimony. . . .

419. John Howard's account of the London hospitals in 1788

(*An Account of the Principal Lazarettos in Europe* (1789), pp. 131–141.)

The London Hospital in Whitechapel Road.

This spacious building is for the reception and relief of sick and wounded seamen &c. It consists of 18 wards; but now 7 only are occupied. . . . The wards in general are 20 feet wide, and 12 high, and each contains about 18 beds, which have no testers. . . . The passages, which are 8 feet wide, are dark. There are no cisterns for water: the vaults are often offensive. In this, and our other hospitals, medical and chirurgical patients are together. Here the middle floor is occupied by the women, and the lower and upper floors by the men. Would it not be better if the men were on one side of the house, and the women on the other? I could wish that there were two wards appropriated to Jew patients, as they must almost starve, on their scanty allowance of bread and beer, with only 2½d. a day. . . . In a dirty room in the cellar there is a cold and a hot bath, which seem to be seldom used. The wards were not dirty, but the house has not been whitewashed for some years; nor has it, within or without, the appearance of neatness. Patients are generously admitted without any fee or reward to nurses &c nor is any security required for the expense of burial or removal; but for parish poor and soldiers, 4d. per day must be paid for their subsistence. All accidents, whether recommended or not, are received at any hour of the day or night. Here is a large chapel, in which divine service is performed twice every Sunday; and prayers are read three days in the week.

The patients' diet I disapprove of; as, their *common diet* is 8 oz. of meat *every* day for dinner; and for supper, broth 6 days in the week. *No vegetables*, and only 12 oz. of bread a day. The *middle diet* is 4 oz. of meat every day for dinner; and for supper, a pint of broth or panado. *No vegetables*, and *only* 8 oz. of bread. The breakfast for every day, of those patients that are on *common* diet, is one pint of milk pottage or water-gruel. Those on the *middle* diet, one pint of panado or water-gruel. The drink of the former is three pints of beer in summer and one quart in winter. Of the latter one pint of beer every day. Sept. 15th 1788, Patients 120. By a letter received lately, I am informed that the committee are exerting themselves, and making several improvements in this hospital.

St. Bartholomew's Hospital in Smithfield.

The wards of this hospital, which are 3 sides of a spacious quadrangle, are on the ground floor and 3 stories above. The wards . . . were clean and not offensive, except the men's 4 foul wards, which are on the uppermost storey, and had not one window open. The 2 foul wards for women were clean and fresh. The wards are lofty, 22 feet wide, and in each were about 15 beds. The bedsteads are wood, and their testers, though lofty, are a harbour for dust and lumber. The beds were not crowded, and the wards were quiet. The staircases are wide; the landing places spacious; and the windows were open. The diet of the patients is nearly the same as in the London Hospital. . . . To each ward there is a sister and a nurse; the former has a room adjoining, but no window into her ward. Fees are taken for the admission of patients: for clean patients 2s. *viz.* 1s. for the sister, 6d. to the nurse, 6d. to the beadle; for foul patients £1. 5s. 8d., *viz.* 5s. for flannels, 18s. 8d. for 2 month's subsistence at 4d. per day: 2s. ward dues. Every patient must deposit 17s. 6d. for a burial fee, or a house-keeper give security; except in case of sudden accidents. Sept. 19th 1788, Patients 428.

The Middlesex Hospital in Marylebone.

This hospital . . . consists of 16 wards, of which only 4 are occupied, the funds being very low. The rooms are close and dirty, except one. . . . The bedsteads and wooden testers are old: the house wants whitewashing, and the whole has an air of poverty. . . . Sept. 16th 1788, Patients 70.

St. Thomas's Hospital in Southwark.

Some of the wards in this hospital are only 18 feet wide: the bedsteads are iron and very properly detached from the walls: there are no testers, but semicircular irons for the curtains in winter. The wards were fresh and clean, except the 3 foul wards, in which were 53 men and 27 women: these were very offensive and had not a window open. There were no water closets. The bread was excellent. . . . I am sorry to find such great quantities of beer brought from public houses into this and other hospitals. Here and at Guy's, the patients easily get out, there being no proper atten-tion to the gates, so that the adjoining gin-shops often prevent the efficacy of medicine and diet. Sept 17th 1788, Patients 440.

Guy's Hospital in Southwark.

. . . The wards in this hospital are in general too low: the height of some is only 9½ feet. In several of the old wards (each containing about 30 beds) the beds and testers are wood, and infested with bugs. In the new wards, which were clean and fresh, are iron bedsteads and hair beds. . . . The window at the upper end of each of these wards opens from the ceiling to the floor. . . . The water closets in the new wards are on the *best* construction, and *not* in the least *offensive*; for by opening the door, water is turned into them. . . . Here are excellent baths, in clean and neat rooms. . . . Sept. 17th 1788, Patients 304.

The Westminster Hospital in James's Street.

. . . For the relief of the sick and needy from all parts; with an establishment for incurables. . . . The beds parallel and close to the walls, with wooden testers . . . the walls dirty. . . . Sept. 24th 1788, Patients 71, and 14 incurables.

St. George's Hospital for sick and lame at Hyde Park Corner.

. . . Here are three large, and three small wards for men; and the same number for women: the lower wards are for accidents. The wards . . . are too close . . . all the windows being shut. . . . A good garden. . . . Sept. 22nd 1788, Patients 150.

The British Lying-in Hospital, in Brownlow Street, for the reception of Married Women.

Here are 6 wards, and in each 6 beds. The wards were clean and quiet: provision good: kitchen and pantry clean. This is a good institution, and proper attention is paid to the patients; who continue here 3 weeks after they are delivered. . . . Here *female* pupils are instructed in the art of midwifery, and after residing 4 or 6 months, receive certificates of their ability to practise. . . . Women delivered and discharged from 31 Dec 1786 to 31 Dec 1787, 550. Died 7. Total 557.

The City of London Lying-in Hospital in the City Road, for Married Women.

Here are 8 wards . . . 6 only are occupied, each containing 8 beds. The wards and beds were clean. . . . Sept. 23rd 1788, Women 36.

The Lock Hospital near Hyde Park Corner, for the relief of venereal patients only.

Here are 3 wards for men and 3 for women. . . . Sept. 22nd 1788, men 36, women 28.

Bethlem Hospital in Moorfields, for the care of lunatics, and the reception of incurables.

The committee room and apartments for the stewards &c. are in the centre; and in long galleries and wings on either side, are the rooms for the patients. The size of these rooms is 12 feet by 8 feet 10 inches, and 12 feet 10 inches high. . . . On the 4 floors there are about 270 rooms: these were quite clean and not offensive, though the house is old and wants whitewashing. . . . The patients communicate with one another from the top to the bottom of the house, so that there is no separation of the calm and quiet from the noisy and turbulent, except those who are chained in their cells. To each side of the house there is only one vault: very offensive. . . .

There are sitting rooms with fireplaces properly guarded with iron–a cold bath and airing grounds for each sex–*no chapel*–bread allowance to patients 1 lb. a day. . . . Visitors are admitted by a governor's ticket, only on Mondays and Wednesdays, between the hours of 10 and 12. Sept. 26th 1788, men 133, women 139.

St. Luke's Hospital for Lunatics in Old Street Road.

This spacious building was first occupied on new year's day 1786. . . . Here are on each of the three floors, three long galleries and wings. . . . In each gallery there are 32 cells . . . very clean and not offensive. . . . Two sitting rooms in each gallery, one for the quiet, the other for the turbulent; but I could wish that the noisy and turbulent were in a separate part of the house. . . . Sept. 25 1788, men 54, women 108.

I shall beg leave to subjoin a few general observations concerning defects in the London Hospitals. . . .

The securities and fees required at admission into many of the hospitals bear hard upon the poor, and absolutely exclude many of those who have the greatest occasion for charitable relief. The nurses' fees in particular open a door to many impositions. The visits of Governors are too often only a matter of form, the visitor hurrying out of an offensive room, and readily acquiescing in the reports of nurses etc. Hence I apprehend, many instances of neglect in surgeons and their dressers, as well as other officers, go unnoticed. I have never found any clergyman administering consolation to the sick; and prayers are usually attended by very few. Whitewashing the wards is seldom or never practised; and *injurious* prejudices against washing floors, and admitting fresh air, are suffered to operate. Bathing, either hot or cold, is scarcely ever used; I suppose, because it would give trouble to the attendants. There are no convalescent wards or sitting rooms, so that patients are often turned out very unfit for work, or the common mode of living. The admission of great quantities of beer for the patients from ale-houses, by alleged, or pretended orders from the faculty, is a great and growing evil. Every *proper* article of diet should be provided by the hospital, and *no other*, on any account, be admitted. It is a pity that for want of these circumstances, such noble institutions should be rendered of much less public utility, than was intended by their generous founders and supporters.

B. THE CHURCH AND NONCONFORMITY

(a) THE STATE OF THE CHURCH OF ENGLAND

420. William Wilberforce on the Evangelical Movement

(Wilberforce, *Practical View of the Prevailing Religious System of Professed Christians in the Higher and Middle Classes in this Country, contrasted with Real Christianity*, pp. 196, 198, 218, 220, 221, 256–257.)

. . . It is not difficult to anticipate the effects likely to be produced on *vital* religion, both in the clergy and the laity, by such a state of external prosperity as has been assigned to them respectively. And these effects would be infallibly furthered, where the country in question should enjoy a free constitution of government. We formerly had occasion to quote the remark of an accurate observer of the stage of human life, that a much looser system of morals commonly prevails in the higher than in the middling and lower orders of society. Now, in every country, of which the middling classes are daily growing in wealth and consequence, by the success of their commercial speculations; and, most of all, in a country having such a constitution as our own, where the acquisition of riches is the possession also of rank and power; with the comforts and refinements, the vices also of the higher orders are continually descending, and a mischievous uniformity of sentiments and manners and morals gradually diffuses itself throughout the whole community. The multiplication of great cities also, and, above all, the habit, ever increasing with the increasing wealth of the country, of frequenting a splendid and luxurious metropolis, would powerfully tend to accelerate the discontinuance of the religious habits of a purer age, and to accomplish the substitution of a more relaxed morality. And it must be confessed that the commercial spirit, much as we are indebted to it, is not naturally favourable to the maintenance of the religious principle in a vigorous and lively state.

In times like these, therefore, the strict precepts and self-denying habits of Christianity naturally slide into disuse; and even among the better sort of Christians, are likely to be softened, so far at least as to be rendered less abhorrent from the general disposition to relaxation and indulgence. . . .

Everywhere we may actually trace the effects of increasing wealth and luxury, in banishing one by one the habits, and new modelling the phraseology, of stricter times; and in diffusing throughout the middle ranks those relaxed morals and dissipated manners which were formerly confined to the higher classes of society. We meet, indeed, with more refinement, and more generally with those amiable courtesies which are its proper fruits: those vices also have become less frequent, which naturally infest the darkness of a ruder and less polished age, and which recede on the approach of light and civilisation. . . . But with these grossnesses, religion, on the other hand, has also declined; God is forgotten. . . . Improving in almost every other branch of knowledge, we have become less and less acquainted with Christianity. The preceding chapters have pointed out, among those who believe themselves to be orthodox

Christians, a deplorable ignorance of the religion they profess, an utter forgetfulness of the peculiar doctrines by which it is characterised, a disposition to regard it as a mere system of ethics. . . .

. . . The distemper of which, as a community, we are sick, should be considered rather as a moral than a political malady. How much has this been forgotten by the disputants of modern times! And accordingly, how transient may be expected to be the good effects of the best of their publications! We should endeavour to tread back our steps. Every effort should be used to raise the depressed tone of public morals. This is a duty particularly incumbent on all who are in the higher walks of life; and it is impossible not to acknowledge the obligations which in this respect we owe as a nation to those exalted characters whom God in his undeserved mercy to us still suffers to continue on the throne, and who set to their subjects a pattern of decency and moderation rarely seen in their elevated station. . . .

Let them in their several stations encourage virtue and discountenance vice in others. Let them enforce the laws by which the wisdom of our forefathers has guarded against the grosser infractions of morals; and congratulate themselves, that in a leading situation on the bench of justice there is placed a man,[1] who, to his honour be it spoken, is well disposed to assist their efforts. Let them favour and take part in any plans which may be formed for the advancement of morality. Above all things, let them endeavour to instruct and improve the rising generation; that, if it be possible, an antidote may be provided for the malignity of that venom which is storing up in a neighbouring country. This has long been to my mind the most formidable feature of the present state of things in France, where, it is to be feared, a brood of moral vipers, as it were, is now hatching, which, when they shall have attained to their mischievous maturity, will go forth to poison the world. But fruitless will be all attempts to sustain, much more to revive, the fainting cause of morals, unless you can in some degree restore the prevalence of Evangelical Christianity. . . . By all, therefore, who are studious of their country's welfare, more particularly by all who desire to support our ecclesiastical establishment, every effort should be used to revive the Christianity of our better days. The attempt should especially be made in the case of the pastors of the Church, whose situation must render the principles which they hold a matter of supereminent importance. . . .

The duty of encouraging vital religion in the Church particularly devolves on all who have the disposal of ecclesiastical preferment, and more especially on the dignitaries of the sacred order. Some of these have already sounded the alarm; justly censuring the practice of suffering Christianity to degenerate into a mere system of ethics, and recommending more attention to the peculiar doctrines of our religion. In our schools, in our universities, let the study be encouraged of the writings of those venerable divines who flourished in the purer times of Christianity. Let even a considerable proficiency in their writings be required of candidates for ordination. Let our churches no longer witness that unseemly discordance which has too much prevailed between the prayers which precede, and the sermon which follows.

. . . We bear upon us but too plainly the marks of a declining empire. . . . It

---

[1] Lord Kenyon, Lord Chief Justice.

would be an instance in myself of that very false shame which I have condemned in others, if I were not boldly to avow my firm persuasion that *to the decline of religion and morality our national difficulties must both directly and indirectly be chiefly ascribed: and that my only solid hopes for the well-being of my country depend not so much on her fleets and armies, not so much on the wisdom of her rulers or the spirit of her people, as on the persuasion that she still contains many who, in a degenerate age, love and obey the Gospel of Christ.* . . .

421. Lord Liverpool to the bishop of Bristol, 19 March 1821

(*British Museum Additional MSS.* 38289, f. 117.)

. . . I had a long correspondence with Mr. Wilberforce . . . some months ago. He & his friends are very desirous of pushing a proportion of the Evangelical preachers into the higher situations of the Church. Now who are the Evangelical clergy? If by this description those are meant who are strictly attentive to all their duties, & who think it right to abstain from those worldly amusements & occupations w.ch are of a problematical nature, & who adopt such a course without ostentation or affected peculiarity, I feel all the merit of such characters, & the advantage they afford to the Establishment. But I confess I cannot approve of those who seem desirous of marking themselves as forming a distinct sect, tho' belonging to the Church, I give many of them full credit for their zeal, & believe that good may sometimes arise from their enthusiasm, but I have often found them to be wholly deficient in the qualities of simplicity & humility w.ch in my judgment ought particularly to characterize the Christian Minister. At the same time I think nothing can be so unwise as any persecution of them or any measures w.ch tend to force them to become Dissenters when they are desirous of remaining a part of the Church & submitting to its ordinances & jurisdiction. . . .

422. Non-resident clergy, 1807

(Substance of the Speech of the Earl of Harrowby delivered in the House of Lords, June 18, 1810, upon a clause in the Appropriation Act for granting the sum of £100,000 for the relief of the Poorer Clergy. (London, 1811), 31 pp.)

	On Livings under £150 per ann.	On Livings above £150 per ann.
EXEMPTIONS.		
Residence on other Benefices	684	1113
Official Chaplains	11	31
Chaplains to privileged individuals	5	46
Ecclesiastical, Cathedral & Collegiate Officers	116	224
Officers in the Royal Chapels of St. James's & Whitehall		1
Reader in His Majesty's Private Chapel at Windsor		2
Preachers & Readers in the Inns of Court or at the Rolls	2	6
Public Officers & Tutors, Oxford & Cambridge Universities	24	69
Resident Fellows in Oxford and Cambridge	23	3
Provost of Eton, Warden of Winchester, Fellows of both	1	10
Schoolmasters and Ushers of Eton, Westminster & Winchester	6	3
Students residing in Oxford & Cambridge under 30 yrs. of age		21
Exemptions not notified	13	72
Livings held by Bishops	3	20
Exempt	888	1621
LICENCES.		
Infirmity of Incumbent or family	131	349
Want or unfitness of Parsonage House	435	511
Residence in a mansion within the parish belonging to Incumbent or relative	33	119
Incumbents possessing small livings licensed to Curacies	121	133
Schoolmasters or ushers of endowed schools	79	84
Master or preacher of hospitals	6	8
Endowed preacher or lecturer	6	23
Licensed preachers in proprietary chapels	4	9
Librarians of the British Museum, Sion College, & Trustees of Lord Crewe's Charity	1	4
Incumbents residing in the neighbourhood, & performing the duties of their Parishes	247	229
Unenumerated cases within the Archbishop's Dioceses		3
Unenumerated cases confirmed by the Archbishop	4	35
Licensed	1067	1507
Absence without licence or exemption	466	376
Dilapidated churches	12	20
Sinecures & dignities not requiring residence	5	158
	483	554
Totals of the above	2438	3682
Miscellaneous, *i.e.* for other reasons than those specified in the preceding classes	201	431
	2639	4113

AN ABSTRACT OF RETURNS RESPECTING RESIDENCE & NON-RESIDENCE
for the year ending 25 March 1808.

DIOCESES	Total Benefices and Dignities	Residents	Non-Residents	Miscel-laneous[1]	Livings under £150 p. ann. Total	Non-Residents	Licensed Places of Worship
St. Asaph	160	43	106	11	42	20	233
Bangor	137	48	83	6	58	30	177
Bath & Wells	478	146	271	61	136	106	433
Bristol	286	143	130	13	86	46	46
Canterbury	349	132	205	12	87	65	131
Carlisle	134	81	52	1	88	31	120
Chester	592	324	238	30	377	161	648
Chichester	306	104	184	18	77	59	213
St. David's	507	115	392	0	344	278	—
Durham	194	81	106	7	76	49	260
Ely	154	57	97	0	64	45	84
Exeter	606	231	301	74	154	78	518
Gloucester	284	98	184	2	89	62	238
Hereford	374	112	211	51	137	103	71
Llandaff	205	34	164	7	147	119	20
Lich. & Cov.	642	266	348	28	287	175	210
Lincoln	1315	411	840	64	541	378	1537
London	631	323	286	22	83	40	417
Norwich	1145	305	813	27	272	222	1061
Oxford	212	68	138	6	93	69	81
Peterborough	315	152	147	16	77	45	210
Rochester	107	54	51	2	3	3	134
Salisbury	483	138	249	96	118	69	474
Winchester	401	173	179	49	82	34	510
Worcester	238	94	140	4	69	5;	152
York	909	679	205	25	410	98	2067
TOTALS	11,164	4412	6120	632	3997	2438	10,154*

* This is exclusive of 2,006 which have been licensed at the Sessions, and which cannot be arranged under the respective Dioceses.

[1] Includes doubtful cases, vacancies, etc., and cases not specified in the Act.

	Licences for places of worship not of the Church of England.			Licences to Preachers not of the Church of England.
	In Bishops' Registers	At Quarter Sessions	Total	At Quarter Sessions
1760–1766	387	284	671	80
1767–1773	391	193	584	38
1774–1780	652	246	898	179
1781–1787	665	213	878	379
1788–1794	1486	386	1872	610
1795–1801	3185	392	3577	1318
1802–1808	3288	292	3680	1068
	10,154	2006	12,160	3672

423. The Rev. Sydney Smith on the poverty of curates (1808)

(Works, 1848 ed., I, pp. 252–254.)

The poverty of curates has long been a favourite theme with novelists, sentimental tourists, and elegiac poets. But, notwithstanding the known accuracy of this class of philosophers, we cannot help suspecting that there is a good deal of misconception in the popular estimate of the amount of the evil.

A very great proportion of all the curacies in England are filled with men to whom the emolument is a matter of subordinate importance. They are filled by young gentlemen who have recently left college, who of course are able to subsist as they had subsisted for seven years before, and who are glad to have an opportunity, on any terms, of acquiring a practical familiarity with the duties of their profession. They move away from them to higher situations as vacancies occur; and make way for a new race of ecclesiastical apprentices. To those men, the smallness of the appointment is a grievance of no very great magnitude; nor is it fair, with relation to them, to represent the ecclesiastical order as degraded by the indigence to which some of its members are condemned. With regard, again, to those who take curacies merely as a means of subsistence, and with the prospect of remaining permanently in that situation, it is certain that by far the greater part of them are persons born in a very humble rank in society, and accustomed to no greater opulence than that of an ordinary curate. There are scarcely any of those persons who have taken a Degree in an University, and not very many who have resided there at all. Now, the son of a small Welsh farmer, who works hard every day for less than £40 a year, has no great reason to complain of degradation or disappointment, if he get from £50 to £100 for a moderate portion of labour one day in seven. The situation, accordingly, is looked upon by these people as extremely eligible; and there is a great competition for curacies, even as they are now provided. The amount of the evil, then, as to the curates themselves, cannot be considered as very enormous, when there are so few who either actually feel, or are entitled to feel, much discontent on the subject. The late regulations about residence, too, by diminishing the total number of curates, will obviously throw that office chiefly into the hands of the well-educated and comparatively independent young men, who seek for the situation rather for practice than profit, and do not complain of the want of emolument.

Still we admit it to be an evil, that the resident clergyman of a parish should not be enabled to hold a respectable rank in society from the regular emoluments of his office. But it is an evil which does not exist exclusively among curates; and which, wherever it exists, we are afraid is irremediable, without the destruction of the Episcopal Church or the augmentation of its patrimony. More than one half of the livings in England are under £80 a year; and the whole income of the Church, including that of the bishops, if thrown into a common fund, would not afford above £180 for each living. Unless Mr. Perceval,[1] therefore, will raise an additional million or two for the Church, there *must* be poor curates,–and poor rectors also; and unless he is to reduce the Episcopal hierarchy to the republican equality of our Presbyterian model, he must submit to very considerable inequalities in the distribution of this inadequate provision. . . .

424. Charles Lloyd (bishop of Oxford) to Robert Peel, 13 March 1828

(British Museum Additional MSS. 40343, f. 210.)

. . . Sir J. Newport appears by last night's paper to have talked extraordinary nonsense about curates. The fact is that instead of £75 being the sum that a bishop is ordered to assign to curates, it is on the contrary the *maximum* of pay which he is permitted to allot to any incumbents before the year 1813. And as to the promotion of curates by bishops, I know nothing of *Ireland*–but out of 10,000 livings in *England,* 7500 are in the hands of *lay* patrons; and is the bishop only to be bound to provide for curates, while the lay patron is to put in his own relations? In matter of fact, I have no doubt that 99 incumbents out of a hundred who receive preferments from English bishops, have been curates before they became vicars and rectors. I know no distinction in the Church of England between curates and beneficed clergymen–the curates in general are the younger men and beginners in their profession. . . .

425. Mrs. Trimmer on the necessity for free seating accommodation for the poor in Anglican churches

(The Oeconomy of Charity, II, pp. 220–233.)

It cannot but be matter of infinite concern to the friends of our Church Establishment, to observe the great neglect of its public offices by the common people of London, and the generality of towns and villages in other parts of the Kingdom. This unhappy alienation is imputable to various causes, amongst which must be reckoned

---

[1] Chancellor of the Exchequer.

in the metropolis and other populous places, the little provision that is made for *seating the poor* in the Churches and Chapels of their respective parishes. This certainly furnishes them with a plausible and indeed an undeniable excuse for staying away from public worship; and it is the occasion of many others joining the congregations of schismatics, or following ignorant itinerant preachers, the declared enemies of the Church of England and its ministers. . . .

It will be of little use to persuade the poor to go to their proper places of worship if, when they do so, they either find the doors shut against their entrance, or no accommodation for them as a part of the congregation; and where the pews are let for the emolument of private individuals (as is the case in many chapels) the first circumstance, I am told, frequently occurs; whilst very few parish churches in the metropolis, whatever room there may be in the *locked-up pews*, furnish seats for the poor; though it may be presumed, from the present state of religion among the lower orders, that most of the parish churches in the City, at least (where those sacred edifices abound) are capable of accommodating all the poor who would go to them, were the respective parishioners to keep to their own parish churches–a good old custom, which it would be a happiness to see restored!

In churches which have wide aisles, no farther preparation would be necessary for the poor than to furnish benches, with or without desks, and matted forms to kneel upon; but the benches should have backs, because the sitting upright, without something to lean against occasionally, is a painful posture not only to the aged but to many others who are accustomed to various kinds of labour. But few of the London churches have aisles sufficiently wide to admit such benches, without crowding the people who pass along them to their pews; and where there is not sufficient room for the poor in the aisles, galleries should be provided.

At the West End of the town, the parishes are so extensive that there certainly is not room enough in the churches for the numerous inhabitants, even of the higher orders; of course, a very small part of the poor can find places in them; and admission into the chapels, where popular preachers draw fashionable and crowded audiences, and high prices are paid for seats, is entirely out of the question; therefore till *charity* shall supply the deficiency of places of public worship for the poor, belonging to the Establishment, in cities and large towns, it is to be feared they will pursue their present courses–many will follow their daily occupations; and profaneness will be heard in the streets on the Sabbath day; whilst those who are religiously disposed will flock to Methodist Meetings. It is therefore most devoutly to be wished that *Free Chapels* may be built in convenient situations for the poor of London and Westminster, upon the plan of the *Free Church at Bath*. . . .

No circumstance in the annals of the present times is more to be lamented as detrimental to the cause of religion, than the great estrangement which has taken place between the lower orders of people and their parochial ministers, who are frequently totally unknown to each other. Yet, when we consider how large many of the parishes in London and Westminster are, and how scattered the wretched abodes of the poorer inhabitants, together with the various means employed to alienate the minds of the common people from the ministers of the Established Church, it must appear to be out of the power of the parochial clergy in London and Westminster to make acquaintance with all their poor parishioners. . . . But how easy would the task of the parochial minister become, by having his flock divided . . . into *separate congregations*, under assistants, acting in strict conformity to the doctrines of the Church, and subject to his immediate inspection! . . . There is no doubt but that there may be found in every parish zealous members of the Church, of both sexes, who would readily join with the clergy in conducting any plan likely to counteract the mistaken zeal of those who depreciate the sacred order. . . .

426. Debate in the House of Lords on the New Churches Bill, 15 May 1818

(Hansard's *Parliamentary Debates*, XXXVIII, 709–721.)

The 12th Report of the Commissioners appointed under the provisions of the Act of 1818 for the building of additional churches in populous parishes, shows how much had then (1832) been accomplished: "In their last Report, H.M.'s Commissioners stated, that 168 churches and chapels had been at that time completed; in which accommodation had been provided for 231,367 persons, including 128,082 free seats to be appropriated to the use of the poor.

They have now to state, that 20 churches and chapels have since been completed. . . . In these 20 churches and chapels accommodation has been provided for 26,361 persons, including 14,039 free seats. . . . Thus, on the whole, 188 churches and chapels have now been completed, and therein a total provision has been made for 257,728 persons, including 142,121 free seats. . . . 19 churches and chapels are building . . . [and] plans have been approved for 8 other churches and chapels. . . .

The Exchequer Bills which have been issued to this day [24 July 1832], amount to £1,440,000."
(*Parliamentary Papers*, 1831–1832, XXIII, p. 309.)

*L*ord Liverpool . . . felt he was proposing the most important measure he had ever submitted to their Lordships' consideration. It had been his intention to bring forward a measure of this nature long ago, but various circumstances in the situation of the country had caused delay. . . . It would, in its results, have the most beneficial effects on the religion, morality, and general instruction of the country. . . . Provision ought to be made for the accommodation in churches of one in every three, or one in every four of the population. . . . To supply accommodation for the metropolis, it was proposed to build additional churches in different parishes–in Marylebone 5; in Pancras 4; in St. Leonard's, Shoreditch 4; in St. Matthew's, Bethnal Green, 4; in Lambeth 3; other parishes, which he need not enumerate, would have corresponding additions. In the country, the supply would be in a similar proportion to the present deficiency. Manchester, it was thought, would require an addition of 7 churches; Sheffield 4, Stockport 3; Birmingham 3 or 4, and so on. The measure brought from the Commons which was to authorise this provision, embraced three objects. The first was a grant of £1,000,000 towards the expense of building churches; its second object was to authorise subscriptions in aid of the grant; and the third, to appoint commissioners for carrying the Act into execution. The sum proposed to be voted by Parliament, he was convinced, would, with due care and attention, do a great deal towards the accomplishment of the object of the Bill. It was estimated that it would afford the means of building about 100 churches without any aid from subscriptions. But that the addition to be derived from the latter source would be very considerable he could not doubt, when he recollected what had been done by Liverpool, where no less than 6 churches had been built by subscription. . . . It might not unreasonably be expected that, with the aid of the subscriptions, from 150 to 200 churches would be built. . . . The vast increase of the population of the country within these twenty years . . . had taken place chiefly in great manufacturing towns; and, with all the advantages the country had derived from the extraordinary extension of its manufactures, it was impossible for their Lordships to conceal from themselves this fact— that great masses of human beings could not be brought together in the manner in which they were situated in these towns, without being exposed to vicious habits and to corrupting influences, dangerous to the public security as well as to private morality. In the manufacturing districts a great want was felt of churches, which their Lordships were most imperiously called upon to supply. . . . It was impossible to look fairly at this measure without considering what was the situation of those persons who dissented from the Establishment. Their Lordships must be aware that Dissenters had in their power to build places of worship in any number. . . . It was evident, then, that the Establishment laboured under a disadvantage in that respect, for in building places of worship for the Church of England, reference must be had to the rights of property and to the discipline of the Church. . . . He had always been of opinion that the benefits of instruction ought to be extended to all classes of H.M.'s subjects, and he always viewed with satisfaction the subscriptions entered into and measures adopted for that object: but then their Lordships must perceive in this an additional inducement to direct the education which was thus diffused into a proper course. It was their duty to take care that those who received the benefits of education should not be obliged to resort to dissenting places of worship by finding the doors of the church shut against them. By building additional churches, the Establishment and the Dissenters would be placed on a fair and equal footing. . . .

Lord Holland . . . thought that a Church so rich in endowment as the Church of England, ought to contribute to its own support and increase. . . . The noble Earl had insisted that the Church should be put on an equal footing with the Dissenters, and a pretty manner the present was of putting her on an equal footing. It was no other than saying, "You gentlemen, who pay for yourselves, who pay for your own chapels and your own clergy, in addition to paying tithes to ours, shall also contribute to the erection of those churches in which you have no interest whatever". He (Lord Holland) did not say that they ought not to contribute, but he thought it most invidious in the noble Earl to affirm under all these circumstances that they enjoyed advantages beyond the Established Church. He agreed, however, that the situation of the country did call for a Bill of this nature. . . .

Lord Harrowby. . . . If the advantages now proposed were not afforded the Church, the general education of children that was taking place would have no other effect than that of turning them into Dissenters. . . .

Lord Lansdowne thought the measure most indispensable. While the State preserved an established religion, it was their duty to hold out to all the means of performing the duties of that religion. . . .

(b) ECCLESIASTICAL PATRONAGE

The higher clergy

427. William Wilberforce to William Pitt, 1 Aug. 1797

(Public Record Office, *Chatham Papers*, 189.)

. . . My dear P, let me intreat you, as I see another Bishop is dead, to consider well whom you appoint. I am persuaded that if the clergy could be brought to know and to do their duty, both the religious and civil state of this country would receive a principle of new life. *I call God to witness* that for several years I never named anyone to you for Church preferment whom I did not believe, all things considered, the best man for the situation. . . .

428. The marquess of Ely to Spencer Perceval, 7 Jan. 1810

(National Library of Ireland, *Richmond MSS.* 66/888.)

Lord Ely wished his brother, the bishop of Killaloe, to be translated to Elphin. Richmond was Lord Lieutenant of Ireland, 1807–1813; Perceval was Chancellor of the Exchequer, 1807–1812, and Prime Minister, 1809–1812; Richard Ryder succeeded Lord Liverpool as Home Secretary at the beginning of November 1809. The letter shows that in 1809 it was no longer possible to purchase a bishopric, even in Ireland, with parliamentary votes.

. . . I have this day for the first time learned from the Duke of Richmond that the plan of his Administration is to be a total neglect of parliamentary influence in his ecclesiastical arrangements . . . I have at an expense of many thousand pounds returned two members to support you in Parliament, in the place of two decidedly hostile, and I cannot help saying it would have been but fair to have informed me at first that the only object I had in view was not to be obtained. . . . As I am pressed by the Government here to attend the meeting of Parliament, I send this over by a confidential messenger who will return with your answer, whereby I shall be enabled to regulate my future conduct.

[*Perceval's reply, 11 Jan.*]

. . . With respect to the determination of Government not to advance to the bench, either of the law or of the church, any persons on the mere ground of parliamentary interest, I do not now perfectly recollect at what period I first heard of it. It was, however, in the first instance from Lord Liverpool, after my coming into my present offices; and upon Mr. Ryder succeeding to Lord Liverpool the Duke of Richmond wrote to Mr. Ryder stating to him that such had been the determination of himself and Lord Liverpool, adding that he hoped the same determination would be adhered to on our part. To Mr. Ryder and myself nothing could be more acceptable than such a determination, the propriety and merit of which at all times and under any circumstances, but most especially at the present time, considering the state of the Protestant Church in Ireland, could not fail to be felt; and we therefore did not hesitate to assure the Duke of Richmond that he might depend on our support and concurrence in carrying it into execution.

I am sure I have now stated to your Lordship enough to shew how entirely you have yourself put it out of my power by your letter to interfere in favour of the Bishop of Killaloe. It is no longer a question upon the merits and pretensions of his Lordship as compared with those of any other competitors ... but the question, after your Lordship's letter, is whether I should endeavour to interfere with his Grace in consequence of your Lordship's urging me to do so in a tone which I am sure your Lordship must wish me to understand as a plain intimation from your Lordship that if you do not succeed in this application, H.M.'s Government at this time must not expect your Lordship's parliamentary support. .... However strong my wishes might have been in favour of any arrangement which might be satisfactory to your Lordship, this circumstance alone would have been completely sufficient to prevent my interference upon this occasion. The Duke of Richmond, I am confident, would refuse, and refuse most indignantly and most justly, to have anything further to do with a Government which had so completely disappointed the expectation which we had given him, of supporting him upon a point so important to the interest of Ireland and the character of his Grace's Administration.

Independent of this consideration ... I would rather be driven from my post tomorrow than purchase my continuance in it by breaking through so wise and proper a determination, upon such an intimation as I understand to be conveyed by your Lordship's letter. .... (f. 889.)

429. Lord Liverpool to Earl Talbot, 19 Sept. 1819

(*British Museum Additional MSS.* 38279, f. 323.)

Talbot was Lord Lieutenant of Ireland, 1817–1821.

... It is an invariable rule with me when I receive applications for Church preferment in Ireland to say that all I can do is to refer them to you for inquiry and consideration.

I believe that as to the Church patronage in England no Minister has ever paid more attention to merit or so little to political objects, as myself. But it is impossible where pretensions are nearly equal, wholly to set aside all other considerations.

The aristocracy of the country will naturally expect to have some share in the patronage of the Church, and it is desirable even for the sake of the Church itself that this should be the case. The man of learning and talents who is made a bishop is of more consequence as such when he finds at his side a man of rank and family holding perhaps a bishopric inferior in rank and importance to his own. It is of great consequence, however, that the proportion of men of rank raised to the bench should not be too large. In England there is no ground for complaint on this head. I cannot quite say as much of the distribution of patronage heretofore in Ireland. If, however, individuals of rank and connection are to be promoted, it cannot be expected that friends should not be preferred to foes–but I quite agree that no person, whoever he may be, should be promoted in the Church unless he possesses decided claims from his clerical character.

430. Lord Liverpool to Lord Wellesley, 19 Aug. 1826

(*British Museum Additional MSS.* 37304, ff. 177–178.)

This correspondence illustrates the extreme scrupulousness which guided the Prime Minister in the distribution of his ecclesiastical patronage, which he always looked on as to be exercised only under a sense of most solemn responsibility. On this occasion he resisted a request made by his Cabinet colleague, the duke of Wellington, and the duke's brother, the Lord Lieutenant of Ireland. The rest of the correspondence is in Yonge's *Liverpool*, III, pp. 383–395.

Your letter of the 15th inst. on the subject of the vacancy on the Irish Episcopal Bench was forwarded to me . . . I perfectly recollect all that passed between us at Bath respecting your brother, and I feel, I can assure you, deeply for the unavoidable embarrassment of your situation, but you must have misunderstood me if you supposed me to have said that I thought that any *probable* circumstances would *do away* the objection to promoting him to the *Bench*. I believe I quoted to you, upon the occasion, a passage from St. Paul's Epistles, and I now request you to refer to it. You will find it in the seven first verses of St. Paul's Epistle to Timothy, and I allude to it, as well for the reasonableness of the injunction, as for the authority which belongs to it.

I can indeed not conceive that any person standing in the relation in which your brother unfortunately stands towards his wife, ought to be made a Bishop, but this relation is certainly aggravated in the eyes of the world (however unjustly) by his never having sued for a divorce, by which *his* conduct as well as *hers* would have been fully before the world, and his abstinence in this respect is set down to motives which may be wholly untrue, but which cannot operate otherwise than injuriously to his former life.

It is impossible to reflect on this subject without adverting to the peculiar situation of the Church in Ireland. We live in an age of controversy as to religion and religious establishments. The Established Church in Ireland is from various circumstances exposed to severe criticism and obloquy beyond that perhaps of any other Church Establishment in Europe. It is surely therefore the duty of those who have to distribute its patronage to be more than usually cautious as to the character and conduct of those who are to receive its honours and rewards.

I have the less scruple in giving you thus openly and decidedly my opinion because I should be most sorry for *your sake* that this promotion should take place.

It would of course be principally, I may say almost exclusively ascribed to you, and you would subject yourself to the unmerited reproach of an indifference to the Established Church, or of doing that for a brother which you would not do for any other individual. . . .

It would give the greatest pleasure to be able to add to your brother's income in an unexceptional way, but I really think his elevation to the Bench of Bishops would be neither for his interest nor for yours, and that it would prove a most inconvenient if not fatal measure to that Establishment which it is one of our first duties to support and uphold.

431. The duke of Wellington to Lord Wellesley, 20 Aug. 1826

(*British Museum Additional MSS.* 37304, ff. 181–185.)

... I am very happy that you have written to Lord Liverpool to suggest to him that Gerald should be appointed the Bishop of Cloyne. In truth I never thought there was much reason for laying Gerald aside. His fault was occasioned by kindness and good nature to his children, who were much attached to their mother, and whose feelings he was unwilling to shock by exposing her conduct in a Court of Justice; and he certainly wrote a letter forgiving former misconduct, which would have been produced in evidence if he had brought forward the last instance of misconduct of which she was guilty when living with him.

I was aware however, and informed Gerald of the advantage which this benevolent world in which we live would take of the whole of his conduct in these transactions, and which in fact Lord Liverpool has taken. Lord Liverpool supposes certainly without any foundation that Gerald had been guilty of something which would have given Lady Emily means of recriminating; and the world would have said so, if any extraordinary favour had been conferred upon Gerald in a short period after his separation from her. But eight years have elapsed since these events occurred. Gerald has in the meantime carried into execution strictly his determination to allow none of his children to communicate with her, notwithstanding her threats and the repeated efforts she has made to see them; and not a word has ever been whispered which would tend in any manner to cast a shade upon Gerald's character.

I have every reason to believe that he is highly respected by his numerous parishioners and by the clergy in general; several of the latter, particularly of the higher clergy, have spoken to me about him, and have expressed their regret that he had not been promoted.

I must say then that it is rather hard to refuse to promote a man in his profession stated to be professionally deserving of promotion, and who has certainly acquired by his conduct universal respect and regard, only because it may by possibility be suspected that he did not proceed to extremities with his adulterous wife eight years ago, because she might have recriminated!!! This injustice is really to be found only in a country governed as ours is by the Gentlemen of the Press! ...

Having in a manner acquiesced in Lord Liverpool's laying Gerald aside so far as this, that I had told Gerald before he finally determined upon his course in regard to Lady Emily, what would probably be the result, and had not objected to Lord Liverpool taking the ground which he did take, I applied to Lord Liverpool for some provision for Gerald in the Church, next to the Bench of Bishops; and I named particularly the Deaneries of St. Paul and of Durham. Lord Liverpool answered that these particular dignities were considered by the Church in the same light as Bishoprics, and he would not propose Gerald for either of them any more than he would for a Bishopric. The former then became vacant, and he gave it to the Bishop of Landaff; and having become vacant a second time, he has given it to Dr. Sumner, Bishop of Landaff, whom he refused the King four years ago to appoint a Canon of Windsor, and risked the existence of his Government upon that refusal. The Deanery of

Durham afterwards became vacant, and this preferment deemed by the Church the same as a Bishopric, and which he would not give to Gerald, on account of *his suspicions* of his misconduct, he gave to Dr. Hall, the Dean of Christ Church, who I really believe is the most infamous fellow that ever disgraced the Church!!! and who is behaving as ill at Durham as he did at Christ Church.

In the meantime he offered Gerald a Living in Yorkshire in performance of his promise to me that he would provide for him in the Church, which Living Gerald was under the necessity of declining to accept, as he could not reside in it, and the income was not sufficient to pay the expense of taking possession and of paying a curate.

It would not do Gerald any good for me to quarrel with Lord Liverpool about this promotion, nor indeed would I under any circumstances quarrel about any personal matter. But I cannot talk to Lord Liverpool without letting him know what I think of his conduct, and I don't think it would be advisable that I should originate the conversation. In the meantime I am abused everywhere and particularly by my own family, because Gerald is not promoted! . . .

The lower clergy

432. The marchioness of Stafford to William Pitt, 13 Feb. 1787

(Public Record Office, *Chatham Papers*, 180.)

Lord Gower's mother was Lady Louisa Egerton, daughter of the duke of Bridgewater. Lord Gower's father (the marquess of Stafford) had a son, Lord Granville Leveson-Gower, afterwards Earl Granville, by his second wife.

I am thoroughly ashamed to trouble you with a solicitation, but it is in behalf of a person whom I am very desirous to serve. His name is Woodhouse. He had the care of Lord Gower's education several years, and my son is now entirely under his tuition, which makes me doubly anxious to procure him preferment. There are so many Egertons in the Church that I cannot get a good living from the Duke of Bridgewater, and my Lord has none but small ones in his gift, and he says that you so lately behaved most kindly in preferring Mr. Vernon that he cannot make another application now. I therefore write without his knowledge to beg of you to think of Mr. Woodhouse when it is in your power to give him a good living or a prebendary. . . .

433. Rev. D. Rhudde to William Pitt, 15 June 1791

(Public Record Office, *Chatham Papers*, 170.)

East Bergholt, Suffolk. Reports being in circulation, that some smaller Church preferments, are likely soon to fall into your hands, not usually in H.M.'s disposal, I beg leave to solicit something, rather of station than emolument.

As I have not had the honor of any personal introduction to you, I presume to state my pretensions to the favour I ask. I am of forty years standing in the University of Cambridge, where I have taken a D.D. degree—was originally preferred by Archbishop Cornwallis to two Livings in Kent, which I resigned on the offer of more valuable appointments in Suffolk, from a private gentleman whose education I superintended, and with whom I travelled. I have the honor to be one of H.M.'s Chaplains, and, exclusive of my Livings, have a considerable independent fortune, in virtue of which, am an elector in Westminster, a freeholder in the several counties of Middlesex, Suffolk, Herts., and Bucks., and have a vote besides at the Bank and India House. My influence thro' life has been uniformly devoted to the support of Government, and in the late very strongly contested election for this county, more than two-thirds of my parishioners acted with me, in opposition to Sir Gerrard Vanneck.

I am well aware, Sir, that this mode of application is not what is usually pursued. It may perhaps be singular, but it is not therefore, I hope, necessarily improper. If however this address, instead of conciliating regard, should unfortunately offend, I beseech you to forget that it has been made; assuring yourself at the same time, that it will never be repeated; as I am too independent in mind and circumstances, to wish to owe to importunity, what could be only acceptable, when conferred on more liberal principles.

With the utmost zeal and attachment, I have the honour [etc.]

434. Lord Chancellor Eldon to William Adam, 2 Nov. 1824

(Blair Adam MSS.)

Adam, who had been Attorney-General to the Prince of Wales, was now Lord Chief Commissioner of the Scottish Jury Court.

I cannot dispose of the living you mention as you wish. Many and numerous are the young clergymen who have been desirous to make that very desirable living a marriage portion to offer to a young lady. Numerous and many are the parents of young ladies, who have been desirous to offer it to young clergymen as a portion with their daughters. Infinitely numerous and many are the old clerical labourers in the vineyard, whose wives have blessed them with ten, twelve, fourteen, children and who have applied for it, as support for a numerous family.

But, my dear Adam, I cannot give portions to lovers, nor support those who have felt the miseries as well as the blessings of gratified love, however ardently I wish so to do. *The old*, very *old* claims upon me are very, very many, remaining unsatisfied, where expectations have been unavoidably excited—and there are some who have claims upon me, which tho' not old but are of such a nature that to them I cannot refuse an early attention. In my 74th year I have no time to lose, and in the 23d of my Chancellorship, I cannot act so unworthily as to postpone attention to these claims. It is in the nature of things that that attention must be speedily, if it is ever to be usefully, given.

435. The Rev. John Smith to Robert Peel, 15 June 1825

(*British Museum Additional MSS.* 40379, f. 326.)

The writer, who died in 1870, became rector of Baldock, Herts., in 1832.

Barham, Harting, Norfolk. Although I have not the honour of being personally known to you, yet I venture to address you on a subject which, as the representative of a distinguished seat of learning, will I trust receive your favourable consideration. I am, Sir, the decipherer of the *Pepys' Diary*, which is just published, and to the circumstances connected with that work, it is my wish to draw your attention. In the year 1819 when I was a student at Cambridge, I commenced the task of deciphering the Diary, (although when I began I did not know a tittle of the *secret characters* in which it is written) and after three years' hard labour I succeeded in completely making out the whole, being above 3000 pages closely written in short-hand, and nearly 10,000 when transcribed by me. My whole remuneration for this immense labour, (to say nothing of the difficulties of the work) was an inconsiderable sum of money, my principal hope resting on the reputation it may give me. The Diary as it now appears embraces but a small portion of my labours, the most interesting parts only being selected. The proof of my abilities and industry being now before the world, I beg leave Sir, humbly to approach you on grounds, which I hope will be allowed to plead my apology in thus addressing you. I have been given to understand that my most gracious Sovereign having some time since heard of the work in question, has expressed a great anxiety to see it, H.M. being particularly interested in every thing relating to the House of Stuart and the eventful times in which they reigned. For this reason it is that I most anxiously entreat you Sir, as a principal Minister of the Crown, to represent to the Sovereign the labours of one of his most dutiful subjects in *bringing to light* a national work which illustrates so interesting a period of English history.

I am, Sir, the Curate of this obscure country parish, without a friend or a patron, and on the small stipend it yields me, I have to maintain a wife, her orphan sister, and an only son, and having merely sufficient to keep us from starving, I trust that you, Sir, who have risen by your merit, will excuse my anxiety (after the literary specimen I have produced) in wishing to rise a little in the scale of society.

Should my appeal prove successful and a small favour be bestowed upon me, I shall for ever feel grateful, and endeavour to prove myself worthy of it, by immediately commencing a vast work I have projected (for which the materials in a forward state are immensely abundant) and which would occupy ten years of diligent exertion, I mean that great desideratum in literature, the *Athenæ Cantabrigienses*, which several eminent men think me competent to undertake.

I have, Sir, thus related a simple narrative of my labours, and relying with confidence on your well-known friendship to the children of literature and science, I need only add that I am a native of Lancashire, and can produce the most honourable testimonials to my character and abilities.

436. Robert Peel's Memorandum, 28 March 1827

(*British Museum Additional MSS.* 40607, f. 71.)

Peel's brother (1798–1875) later became dean of Worcester.

On the 24th March 1827, I, the Right Hon. Robert Peel, Secretary of State for the Home Department, concluded a negotiation for the purchase from Wyrley Birch, Esq., of the advowson of the Living of Handsworth in the county of Warwick. I paid on that day the sum of £5,000, and signed a bond . . . for the payment of the additional sum of £12,000 within the period of 18 months, without interest.

I bequeath this property, that is to say the advowson of Handsworth and all the rights appertaining to it, in as full a manner as I possess them, to my brother, the Rev. John Peel and his heirs. . . .

437. Advertisements in *John Bull*, 25 May and 14 September 1828

25 May:

CLERICAL.–Mr. WALLIS begs to state that he may be daily consulted as to CURACIES and occasional duty, upon the purchase, sale, exchange, and value of preferment. MS. sermons, warranted original, orthodox, and of superior composition, supplied. No. 44, Regent Circus, Piccadilly. All letters must be post paid.

14 Sept.:

TO THE CLERGY.–Messrs. SAINSBURY and CO. are directed to dispose of the under-stated very DESIRABLE LIVINGS. It is now unnecessary, after the extensive patronage they have for so many years received, for Messrs. S. and Co. to re-state more of the terms on which clerical business, in all its departments, is transacted at their establishment, than that THEY make no charge whatever, unless for business actually completed, conformable to a printed scale which may be obtained gratis at their offices, No. 35, Red Lion Square.

The ADVOWSON and IMMEDIATE NEXT PRESENTATION to a RECTORY of about £400 per annum, situated within 50 miles of London.

The ADVOWSON or the NEXT PRESENTATION to a very desirable RECTORY, situated about 20 miles from London; very good house, income about £600 per annum: incumbent 72. . . .

A CURACY, about 60 miles from London, with a good house and 20 acres of good land in lieu of tithes. To a highly respectable applicant, their client would not object giving a title for orders–in fact, such an applicant would be best approved of, and a personal interview preferred to a written communication.

EXCHANGES.

Messrs. SAINSBURY and CO. have several LIVINGS and CURACIES which they are instructed to negociate for the exchange; and they will be happy to receive the particulars of others that any of their clients or the clergy at large may wish to effect an exchange of. They also beg to state for the information of those who have not yet honoured them with their instructions, that a prominent feature in their system of doing clerical business is, all instructions received, and information given by them, are considered as strictly confidential. All unpaid letters refused. Office hours from 10 until 4 o'clock.

No. 35, Red Lion Square, London, Sept. 1828.

(c) BIBLE AND MISSIONARY SOCIETIES

438. Mrs. Trimmer on the Society for Promoting Christian Knowledge
(*The Oeconomy of Charity*, II, pp. 263–267)

About the latter end of the year 1698 a few gentlemen formed themselves into a *voluntary Society* for the purpose of promoting the real and practical knowledge of true religion, by such methods as appeared to them, from time to time, conducive to this end; and their plan has been to promote and encourage the erecting of *Charity Schools* in all parts of the kingdom, and to disperse, both at home and in foreign parts, *Bibles, Common Prayer Books*, and various other *religious books* and *tracts*. This Society also contributes to the support of several missionaries in the *East Indies*, and one in the *Scilly Islands*.

There are at present upwards of 2,000 subscribing and corresponding members in Great Britain and foreign parts, many of them ladies: more than 200 members were chosen in the course of last year. The usual subscription is *one guinea*. All the members are furnished with the books and tracts upon the Society's catalogue on very low terms, which catalogue is inserted in a book, containing an account of the proceedings of the Society, with the anniversary sermon sent annually to each member.

A person desirous of becoming a member, must be recommended by two of the members, according to a prescribed form, "*As being well affected to the King and his Government, and to the Church of England as by law established*," &c.

The receipts of the Society for the last year, including legacies and the interest of money in the funds, amounted to nearly £11,000, and the following is an abstract of the number of books and tracts sent to the members last year.

Bibles 5,890; New Testaments and Psalters 8,873; Common Prayers 10,058; Other bound books 17,435; Small tracts 89,739. In all 131,995.

... It is a very great benefit to *Charity Schools* to be supplied with books upon the easy terms of the Society; and those charitable persons who are desirous of doing good amongst the adult poor by supplying them with religious books and tracts, find it very satisfactory to have their judgment directed in the choice of those which are good and proper. Not even the smallest tract is admitted upon the catalogue without being read and examined by seven members of the Society, after which it must be ballotted for at the public board. Happy would it be for the poor were every book designed for them, subject to the like scrutiny! ...

439. W. Wilberforce to the Marquess Wellesley, 5 Aug. 1811
(*Wilberforce Correspondence*, II, pp. 214–215.)

... The London Missionary Society ... is a very numerous body, which was formed about twelve to fifteen years ago (speaking from loose recollection) and has sent missionaries to the different islands in the South Seas and to various other parts. It is supported by the voluntary subscriptions of persons of all the various religious denominations in this country, and once in every year there is a meeting, commonly in May, when, for several days together, sermons are preached and collections made; persons coming in great numbers from all parts of England to attend. The influence of the Society is therefore on the whole very considerable. From all I have heard, I am inclined to believe that their missionaries have been more respectable (Dr. Vander-kemp, Mr. Kicherer, &c.) and their success greater, at the Cape and in its vicinity, than in any other quarter. I know not whether you ever happened to read Barrow's account of the Cape, 2 vols. 4to.; the accounts which it gives of the cruel treatment of the Hottentots, by the Boors, strongly confirming Mr. Read's narrative. I have also seen, I am nearly sure, in the same work, a striking confirmation of all which Mr. Read states concerning the hatred felt by the Boors towards the missionaries for their kindness to the Hottentots, of whom also Barrow, by the way, speaks in very high terms. The Boors were once planning a scheme for exterminating an entire settlement of the Moravian missionaries, and it was only the day before the assassina- tions were to have taken place that the plot was discovered and prevented. . . .

440. Sir Stamford Raffles to Wilberforce, 23 Oct. 1817

(Wilberforce Correspondence, II, p. 386.)

. . . On the subject of missions I can have no hesitation in recommending attention to the Eastern islands. Nothing of the kind has yet found its way to Sumatra and Borneo, two of the largest islands in the world, and containing a population of many millions. It is said that when the people of Celebes embraced Mahometanism, the Portuguese offered the Bible at the same time. A council was appointed by the Sovereign to report which of the religions was the best. Those of the council inclined to Mahometan- ism suggested that it was the best because it had arrived first, and God Almighty, they said, would never have allowed error to come before truth—and the argument, however specious, prevailed. Now the Mahometans are making converts daily. Nothing is so common among the islands as crusades against the infidels—all who do not embrace Mahometanism are made slaves—considered as fair booty. May not therefore the spread of the Gospel go hand in hand with the abolition of the slave trade in those countries? . . .

441. British and Foreign Bible Society

(Advertisement in The Pamphleteer, *VI (1815), pp. 278–279.)*

A Society having been formed with the above designation, it has been judged expedient to submit to the public a brief statement of the reasons which exist for such a Society, of the specific object which it embraces, and of the principles by which its operations will be directed.

The *reasons*, which call for such an institution chiefly refer to the prevalence of ignorance, superstition and idolatry over so large a portion of the world; the limited

nature of the respectable Societies now in existence; and their acknowledged insufficiency to supply the demand for Bibles in the United Kingdoms and foreign countries;
and the recent attempts which have been made on the part of infidelity to discredit
the evidence, vilify the character, and destroy the influence of Christianity.

The exclusive *object* of this Society is to diffuse the knowledge of the holy scriptures, by circulating them in the different languages spoken throughout Great Britain
and Ireland; and also, according to the extent of its funds, by promoting the printing
of them in foreign languages, and the distribution of them in foreign countries.

The *principles*, upon which this undertaking will be conducted, are as comprehensive as the nature of the object suggests that they should be. In the execution of the
plan, it is proposed to embrace the common support of Christians at large; and to
invite the concurrence of persons of every description, who profess to regard the
scriptures as the proper standard of faith.

It may be necessary to add, in soliciting the countenance of the public, that in
consequence of the enlarged means of instruction which the lower classes in this
country have enjoyed of late years, a desire of perusing the scriptures has considerably
increased among them; and also that in Wales, Ireland, Switzerland, Germany,
Denmark, and other parts of the world, bibles are greatly wanted, and in some, are
sought for with an eagerness which, but for authentic assurances to that effect, would
scarcely be credited.

The committee, in the instructions given them at the first general meeting, were
charged with procuring for the society suitable patronage, both foreign and British.
Accordingly, at the meeting, held 1st May, 1805, or first annual meeting, we find the
following honorable and highly distinguished characters placed at the head of the
society, *viz.*, *President*, The Right Honorable John Lord Teignmouth; *Vice-Presidents*,
Right Rev. Lord Bishop of London, Right Rev. Lord Bishop of Durham, Right Rev.
Lord Bishop of Exeter, Right Rev. Lord Bishop of St. David's, Sir William Pepperell,
Bart., Vice-Admiral Gambier, William Wilberforce, Esq., M.P.

442. Nicholas Vansittart's second letter to the Rev. Dr. Marsh, occasioned by his inquiry into the consequences of neglecting to give the prayer book with the Bible, 23 March 1812

(*The Pamphleteer*, 1, pp. 159–183.)

A few weeks later, Vansittart became Chancellor of the Exchequer.

. . . To the disregard of the Liturgy, which you suppose to have been produced by
the Bible Society, if real, the Reports of the Society for promoting Christian Knowledge must bear conclusive evidence. We shall, in that case, find, that during the
growth of the Bible Society, the demand for Prayer Books for distribution has been
gradually lessening. But what is the fact? The number of Prayer Books delivered by
the Society for promoting Christian Knowledge, to its members on an average of
the three years immediately previous to the institution of the Bible Society (*viz.*
1802-3-4) was 13,546; the average of the last three years was 19,815, being an *increase*

of more than one-half. I am informed also that the ordinary sale of Prayer Books has greatly increased in the same period. . . .

The Bible Society has afforded the means of preaching the Gospel in 54 languages. . . . That these exertions can be injurious to the Church of England I cannot think so meanly of the Church as to admit. It would be with the deepest regret that I should discover that the prosperity of the Church of England was incompatible with the establishment of the universal Church of Christ; because the inevitable result of such a discovery would be a conviction that the Church of England was not (as I have always thought it) a genuine and distinguished portion of that true Church. And you concur so far in the same opinion as to be willing to permit the existence of the Bible Society, and even to allow Dissenters to belong to it, provided its operations are exclusively directed abroad.

I am not surprised that you should resort to this suggestion, which has, indeed, from the first formation of the Society, been the proposal of its *enemies*; but you must not expect its *friends* to acquiesce in a proposition which would inevitably occasion its destruction. . . .

There never was a time when the Legislature more carefully guarded, or more liberally promoted, the interests of the Church. In the greatest pressure of public exertion, when it would appear hardly justifiable to add anything to the expenditure of the nation for any purpose which did not arise out of the immediate exigency of the times, grants of unexampled liberality have been made for the support of the national religion.

This would of itself go far towards proving, what I think further observation will confirm, that there is among us a growing attachment to religion. To no other cause can I attribute the rapid growth of the Bible Society, which again, by a reciprocal action of the most beneficial kind, powerfully contributes to strengthen and extend this attachment.

Yet I will own that there are possible cases in which I think danger may arise to the Church–one of them would be if the *abuses* of the Church should be confounded with its *interests*. The spirit of the age is liberally attentive to all fair claims; but it is an inquisitive and scrutinizing age, and many circumstances which formerly attracted little notice, are now drawn into full light. The Returns of the non-resident clergy, for instance, are now annually printed. If the friends of the Church, instead of taking the lead in a mild reform of abuses, contend obstinately for their protection, and treat every man as an enemy who aims at reform, they will certainly be overpowered at last, and the corrective applied by those who will apply it with no sparing hand.

The voice of the public is now *with* the Church–it may, by a pertinacious resistance to reasonable expectations, be turned *against* her. . . . After all that ingenuity and subtlety can do, the public opinion must at last be decided by the plain reason of plain men. With such, the appeal is always to fact and experience. They will not believe it to be an offence to carry home to the habitations of the poor and ignorant that Bible *alone*, which is daily read in the Church, as *alone* containing the *words of everlasting life*. They will not believe the members of the Bible Society to be bad Churchmen (with whatever dexterity you may prove that they must be so) while they perform, both in the Church and in society, the offices of good men and good Christians. . . .

To say that either the Church or the State is free from danger, would, in times like the present, be an empty and presumptuous boast. The earthquake by which so many churches and so many States have been shattered into ruin, still continues to heave the ground; and it appears evident that these dreadful convulsions of the moral and political world are, by the unseen councils of Providence, directed to bring about some great renovation in the religious state of man. . . .

Amidst public difficulty and private embarrassment I see the hand of Charity extended to every species of distress, with an extent of bounty not only unknown to former times, but which would have been incredible to them. I see everywhere new institutions forming; yet old establishments supported; and let it be remembered that in these noble works, which I trust will rise in remembrance before God on behalf of this nation, the Dissenters claim their full share with the Church of England. I see the ships of Britain no longer tearing the natives of Africa from their parent soil, but carrying to them the arts of civilised life, and the blessings of the Gospel. I see the Church of England surrounded and assisted by differing, but respectful and no longer hostile sects, extending the light of truth to the remotest regions of the earth. . . .

443. Debate in the House of Lords, 18 March 1828, on the Society for the Propagation of the Gospel

(Hansard's *Parliamentary Debates*, New Series, XVIII, 1161–1170.)

Lord King . . . The Society for the Propagation of the Gospel was incorporated in 1701, and had existed for more than a century, upon voluntary subscriptions and donations. In 1813 or 1814 first began grants of money from the public to the Society. From that time they had gone on gradually increasing, until they had reached the sum of £16,180, as appeared from the estimates of the present year. . . . Their Lordships had all heard of this Society, but very few knew the purposes for which it was originally formed. The object of it at the time it was first incorporated was to form a Society for the purpose of providing learned and orthodox clergymen for the administration of God's word and sacraments in the North American colonies, where, for the lack of spirit, the King's subjects were abandoned to infidelity, atheism, popery, superstition and idolatry. In those colonies, the great majority of the inhabitants were not of the Church of England, but Presbyterians, Baptists and other persuasions, yet the funds of the Society derived from the public were solely devoted to the maintenance of Church of England clergymen. . . . This . . . was not a fair distribution of the funds. Was it proper that money should be taken from the public for the maintenance of an Establishment which did not suit the population of the country? . . . In 1792 or 1793, when the Bill for settling Canada passed the Parliament, one-tenth part of the lands were set apart for the maintenance of the Protestant clergy. An attempt had lately been made exclusively to appropriate that grant to the benefit of the episcopal clergy. That attempt had been resisted, and he hoped successfully, for a more narrow interpretation could not be given to that law, than by appropriating exclusively to the Church of England that which was given for the maintenance of the Protestant clergy of all denominations, whether Episcopal, Presbyterian, Baptist or any other persuasion. The Church of England Establishment, he was sorry to say, when carried out across the Atlantic, exported with it the original sins which beset it in this country; namely, a useless expense, pluralities, and non-residence. . . . The real question to consider was, whether the Society did or did not mismanage the funds it received from the public. . . .

Lord Bathurst said there was no ground for the imputations which had been cast upon the Society. . . . He could bear witness to its zeal, probity and discretion. The service of North America constituted but a small part of its duties. The Society held an extensive correspondence with all parts of the world. . . .

Lord Calthorpe . . . There were a hundred millions of individuals who had claims upon this country, and when this was considered, the House might form some idea of the immense field of labour on which the religious Societies had entered. . . . As far as he was acquainted with the measures taken for the mitigation of that deplorable state of ignorance in which the Indian Empire was plunged, they were highly valuable. Their prejudices were not insulted wantonly, but the pure spirit of Christianity was insinuated in a way the most likely to conciliate and improve. . . . He could not regard the exertions of this Society in any other light than as indispensable preliminaries to those civil immunities and advantages which it was the duty as well as the interest of this country to bestow upon her colonial possessions. . . .

444. Receipts of the principal religious charities in London, for the year ending Lady Day, 1821

(*The Scotsman,* 21 July, 1821.)

	£
British and Foreign Bible Society	89,154
Society for Promoting Christian Knowledge, about	53,100
Church Missionary Society	31,200
London Missionary Society	26,174
Methodist Missionary Society, about	22,500
Baptist Missionary Society	13,200
Society for propagating the Gospel, about	13,000
Society for the conversion of the Jews	10,789
National Society for Education, about	8,000
Religious Tract Society	7,561
Hibernian Society	7,049
Moravian Missions, about	5,000
Naval and Military Bible Society	2,348
British and Foreign School Society	2,034
Prayer Book and Homily Society	1,993
	293,102

(d) DISSENT

445. Extracts from John Wesley's Journal, 1783–1789

('Everyman' edition, vol. IV.)

Sun. 19 [Jan. 1783.] I preached at St. Thomas's church in the afternoon, and at St. Swithin's in the evening. The tide is now turned, so that I have more invitations to preach in churches than I can accept of. [p. 248.]

Fri. 21 [Jan. 1783.] At our yearly meeting for that purpose, we examined our yearly accounts, and found the money received (just answering the expense) was upwards of £3,000 a year. But that is nothing to me. What I receive of it yearly is neither more nor less than £30. [p. 248.]

Sun. 4 [April 1783.] There was an ordination at St. Patrick's [Dublin]. I admired the solemnity with which the Archbishop went through the service. But the vacant faces of the ordained showed how little they were affected thereby. In the evening multitudes met to renew their covenant with God. But here was no vacant face to be seen. For God was in the midst and manifested himself to many, particularly to a daughter of good William Pennington. [pp. 251–252.]

Tues. 29 [July 1783.] Our Conference began, at which two important points were considered: first the case of Birstal House, and secondly, the state of Kingswood School, [Bristol]. . . . With regard to the latter, we all agreed that either the school should cease, or the rules of it be particularly observed; particularly, that the children should never play, and that a master should be always present with them. [p. 265.]

Mon. 15 [March 1784.] Leaving Bristol, after preaching at five in the evening, I preached at Stroud, where to my surprise, I found the morning preaching was given up, as also in the neighbouring places. If this be the case while I am alive, what must it be when I am gone? Give up this, and Methodism too will degenerate into a mere sect; only distinguished by some opinions and modes of worship. [p. 274.]

Sun. 20 [June 1784. Scarborough.] The new Vicar showed plainly why he refused those who desired the liberty for me to preach in his church. A keener sermon I never heard. So all I have done to persuade the people to attend the church is over turned at once! And all who preach thus will drive the Methodists from the church, in spite of all I can do. . . . [p. 288.]

Tues. 2 [Jan. 1787.] I went over to Deptford, but it seemed, I was got into a den of lions. Most of the leading men of the Society were mad for separating from the Church. I endeavoured to reason with them, but in vain; they had neither sense nor even good manners left. At length, after meeting the whole Society, I told them, "If you are resolved, you may have your service in church-hours, but remember, from that time, you will see my face no more." This struck deep; and from that hour I have heard no more of separating from the Church. [p. 366.]

Sun. 12 [April 1789.] Being Easter-day, we had a solemn assembly indeed. . . . Afterwards I met the Society [at Dublin,] and explained to them at large, the original design of the Methodists, viz., not to be a distinct party, but to stir up all parties, Christians or heathens, to worship God in spirit and in truth; but the Church of

England in particular, to which they belonged from the beginning. With this view I have uniformly gone on for fifty years, never varying from the doctrine of the Church at all, nor from her discipline, of choice, but of necessity. So, in a course of years, necessity was laid upon me. . . . 1. to preach in the open air; 2. to pray extempore; 3. to form societies; 4. to accept the assistance of lay preachers. . . . [p. 464.]

446. Thomas Thompson to Wilberforce, Hull, 18 July 1791

(Wilberforce Correspondence, I, pp. 81-83.)

The enclosed letter is from Mr. Joseph Benson, a preacher among the Methodists at Birmingham. I know Mr. Benson well, and I know him to be a pious man, a man of very considerable abilities and of real learning. The fact undoubtedly is, that at this moment many thousands of the Methodists in different parts of the three kingdoms, are deliberating whether they shall become Dissenters, or continue in connection with the Church of England. I wish most sincerely that by some means they may be prevented from separating from the Church; and as I know you are acquainted with some of the bishops, you may probably think it worth while to mention the matter to them. I believe the Methodists (I mean those only, at the head of whom was the late Rev. J. Wesley) are far more numerous than any sect of Dissenters in England, and should they dissent, the opposition to the Church and the present civil Government will be greatly strengthened. I hope the bishops may think it necessary to do something, although I doubt whether the plan Mr. Benson proposes can be adopted. The Dissenters lose no opportunity to spread their sentiments, both religious and civil, and labour in every possible way to increase their numbers; and I wish the bishops may be roused to counteract them, and to see the danger which threatens the Establishment.

I proposed to the Methodists here, which was unanimously agreed to, to print and send to all the Methodist societies in the nation, a letter declaring our determination to abide in connection with the Church of England, and recommending it to all the Methodists to do the same, and I hope it may have done good. But still there is some weight in what is alleged in answer to our letter. "At Hull your Ministers in the Church are men of exemplary piety, but we have none such in our town or neighbourhood." . . .

447. Robert Southey to Wilberforce, 3 Jan. 1818

(Wilberforce Correspondence, II, pp. 389-390.)

Southey's *Life of Wesley* was published in 1820.

. . . I should be most glad to receive from you any information or hints respecting Wesley. I consider him as the most influential mind of the last century–the man who will have produced the greatest effects, centuries, or perhaps millenniums hence, if the present race of men should continue so long. The early excesses of Methodism I can account and allow for; I admire his tolerant and truly Catholic spirit; and I accord so far with his opinions, as they are expressed in his latter years, that where he goes beyond me in his belief, I feel a conviction it is because I have not yet advanced far enough. For instance, I am as deeply and fully persuaded as he was, that the spirits of the departed are sometimes permitted to manifest themselves. There is a body of evidence upon this subject which it is impossible for me to disbelieve; besides it is good that it should be so, and this with me (in such matters) is sufficient reason for concluding that it is probable–but it is also probable upon the strictest reasoning. But I do not believe in witchcraft, and very much doubt the reality of demoniacal possession. Even, however, if both were admitted, the absurd stories which he credits impeach his judgment, and consequently weaken the force of his authority when he is right. . . . Even now, after all the Methodists have done, and all they have caused the Church to do, there is no part of Christendom where the state of religion of the populace is so utterly neglected. The field is left fallow, and then we wonder to find that a more active spirit has been sowing tares! . . .

448. Address of the Conference, to the Methodist societies in Great Britain, 7 Aug. 1819

(A 3-page pamphlet.)

Dearly Beloved brethren–In pursuance of a Resolution passed at our present meeting that an Address from the Conference to the Societies in Great Britain shall annually be written and printed, we now affectionately solicit your attention. . . .

We rejoice to state to you, that the increase in our Societies during the past year, including Ireland, is 6905. . . .

We deeply sympathise with those of you, dear Brethren, who, from the pressure of the times, and the suspension of an active commerce, are, in common with thousands of your countrymen, involved in various and deep afflictions. . . . As many of you to whom this measure of national suffering has been appointed reside in places where attempts are making by "unreasonable and wicked men" to render the privations of the poor the instruments of their own designs against the peace and the government of our beloved country, we are affectionately anxious to guard all of you against being led astray from your civil and religious duties by their dangerous artifices. Remember you are Christians, and are called by your profession to exemplify the power and influence of religion by your patience in suffering, and by "living peaceably with all men". Remember that you belong to a Religious Society which has, from the beginning, explicitly recognised as high and essential parts of Christian duty, to "Fear God and honour the King; to submit to magistrates for conscience' sake, and not to speak evil of dignities". You are surrounded with persons to whom these duties are the objects of contempt and ridicule: show your regard for them because they are the doctrines of your Saviour. . . .

Whilst this period of suffering continues, we affectionately and earnestly exhort the more opulent members of our Societies and congregations, to afford as ample a relief as possible to their brethren in distress. This, we are sure, *"they are forward to do"*. . . .

We are happy to find that the numerous institutions among us for the spread of the Gospel abroad, for the relief of the sick and poor at home, and for the education of the children of the poor, continue to meet, notwithstanding the pressure of public affairs, with an encouragement so liberal. The supply of the Fund for foreign Missions has exceeded all former years; and to all who love the Saviour, and the Cause for which He died, the general prosperity of our Missions will equally excite their gratitude to God, and lead them anew to pledge their exertions for the support of a Cause so sacred and animating. The extension of true religion at home will not be less their care, and the object of their liberality and prayers. Among other institutions for this purpose are our Sunday Schools; and we rejoice in their number, the zeal with which they are conducted, the sacrifices of so many of our young people who act as teachers, and the benefits which are constantly resulting from them. . . .

With regard to the financial affairs of the Connexion, it is with great satisfaction that we have to announce the success which has attended the measure recommended by the Conference of last year for the relief of distressed Chapels. The monies raised for the Chapel Fund were found, at the meeting of the Committee appointed for its disbursement, very nearly equal to the claims for deficient interest of monies borrowed on the chapels regularly recommended from the different districts. It is therefore now established; and we state it with peculiar pleasure, that if this Fund be as liberally supported as from the importance of its objects our friends will, we trust, feel it ought to be supported, the difficulties which have arisen from cases of distressed chapels, and the anxieties which were in some places in consequence created, may be entirely removed by united local exertion, and the aid of the Fund, and the Connexion be completely rescued from this branch of its embarrassments. . . .

The general finances of the Connexion continue to press heavily upon us, although we hail with great confidence the prospect of surmounting every difficulty. In those measures of retrenchment which necessity has forced, many circuits, and many of the preachers, have suffered by returning to the Circuits the proportion of deficiencies determined by the rule of the last Conference, and by our inability to comply with the reasonable demands of many of our Brethren. These measures have been very painful, but our finances are in a state of general improvement. . . .

Signed in behalf and by order of the Conference.

Jonathan Crowther, President.
Jabez Bunting, Secretary.

Bristol, August 7, 1819.

449. Advertisement in *The Scotsman*, 4 Aug. 1824

METHODISTS.

The following view of the numbers of Members in the Methodist Connexion in England and Wales, with the proportion they bear to the population of each County, is extracted from Mr Haigh's Map of "The Methodists' Circuits," published in the present year :–

	Population.	Circuits.	Members.	One in
Berkshire	131,977	5	1,233	111
Bedford	83,716	4	1,790	47
Buckingham	134,068	3	993	134
Cambridge	121,909	3	1,223	99
Cornwall	257,437	11	12,891	27
Cumberland	156,124	5	2,459	63
Cheshire	270,098	6	5,809	46
Devon	439,040	13	4,524	94
Dorset	144,499	4	1,450	99
Durham	207,673	7	6,039	34
Derby	213,333	9	6,148	34
Essex	289,424	4	1,478	189
Gloucester	335,843	7	4,744	70
Hampshire	282,203	4	1,976	170
Herts	129,714	0	0	0
Hereford	103,231	3	858	120
Huntingdon	48,771	2	680	71
Kent	426,016	13	6,505	64
Leicester	174,571	6	4,330	40
Lincoln	283,058	16	11,640	24
Lancaster	1,052,859	22	20,776	50
Middlesex	1,144,531	3	7,542	152
Monmouth	71,333	3	886	82
Nottingham	186,873	5	4,680	40
Northampton	162,483	6	2,412	67
Norfolk	344,368	9	5,315	64
Northumberland	198,965	5	3,035	65
Oxford	134,327	4	1,880	71
Rutland	18,487	0	0	0
Sussex	232,927	4	1,100	211
Surrey	398,658	1	1,600	249
Suffolk	270,542	5	1,725	151
Somerset	355,314	10	5,735	62
Stafford	341,824	10	9,903	35
Shropshire	206,266	5	2,633	78
Wiltshire	222,157	5	1,941	115
Westmorland	51,359	1	424	121
Worcester	184,424	5	1,980	93
Warwick	274,392	2	1,935	130
York	1,175,251	48	50,976	23
Wales	717,108	18	8,634	83
Total . .	11,977,663	296	211,887	56

The above numbers, it must be observed, are actually joined in connexion, exclusive of the eight thousand additional members, and it is estimated that the Methodist Congregations contain six times as many individuals as there are members upon their Class Papers.

(e) THE TEST AND CORPORATION ACTS, AND CATHOLIC EMANCIPATION

450. Francis Russell to Lord Hawkesbury, 23 Oct. 1786

(British Museum Additional MSS. 38220, f. 203.)

Hawkesbury had just been appointed Chancellor of the Duchy of Lancaster. Russell was employed in the Duchy office.

Under the several Acts of 25 Charles II, Ch. 2, and 1 George I, Ch. 13, Stat. 2^d, every person taking any kind of office or authority from the King is obliged to take the Holy Sacrament in a parish church on a Sunday, to be proved by the oaths of two witnesses and also the oaths of supremacy and allegiance either in one of the four courts at Westminster or at the Quarter Sessions of the Peace. The time for taking the sacrament is limited to three months after admission to office. That for taking the oath and subscribing the declaration is by 9 George II, c. 26 enlarged to six months.

Lord Clarendon received the sacrament at Watford and took the oaths at the Quarter Sessions for Hertfordshire. By a clause in the Act of 25 Charles II I observe that peers may take the oaths in Parliament whilst sitting, and in the intervals they may take them in Chancery.

St. Martin's Church is the place where officers in general qualify for offices, and a person attends there with all the proper forms of certificates and stamps every Sunday. . . .

451. Excerpts from Samuel Heywood's pamphlet, "The right of Protestant Dissenters to a Compleat Toleration, asserted" (London, 1787, 228 pp.)

Samuel Heywood (1753–1828) was a friend of Charles Fox, and a Unitarian. His pamphlet is said to have converted Dr. Parr, who described it as the only good book produced by the Dissenters.

. . . Protected by that law [the Toleration Act of 1689] the Dissenters have for nearly 100 years quietly submitted to a separation from the Church, and have expected only a toleration of their religious opinions.

During that period a great change has taken place in their opinions, with regard both to the doctrines and discipline of the Church; and there is not now to be found among them a single person, who either wishes for a comprehension, or believes it to be practicable. In fact persecution and resistance to their just requests are the most successful means for keeping up their numbers; for since they have been allowed the public exercise of their religion their numbers have much diminished; and some of their best friends dread their success in the present application, lest it should make their declension still more rapid. They are now become so few in number, that, taking them as one aggregate body, the Episcopalians form so large a majority that their *right* to be the Established Church cannot be disputed. The Dissenters do not consider a form of religion, of which bishops make a part, as sinful; but, believing that Christ has not imposed upon his followers any form of Church discipline, they think that it depends on the civil Government of the country to determine to which it shall give the preference. . . .

The experience of more than 120 years has sufficiently shewn that the opinions of the Dissenters are not dangerous to the Established Church in England, and they may appeal to that as a proof infinitely more strong than the most powerful speculative arguments. . . . [pp. 118–120.]

. . . The religious as well as the political system benefits by a little variety of opinion and by an opposition of characters; and the many able defences of natural and revealed religion, and the many excellent moral writings proceeding from the Dissenters, are a proof that the Dissenters have also afforded a positive advantage to the Church by confirming that grand *basis* on which the Church is ultimately built. Their writings also have, in the opinion of many of the clergy, helped to liberalize the Church itself; which if there had been no sects existing, would probably have retained many of those absurd tenets which prevailed in it a century ago. The greater strictness of education among the stricter sectaries is another advantage arising from sects, and hence chiefly it is that manufactures and commerce have been found to prosper so much in the hands of sectaries all over the world where they have not been too severely treated; and hence likewise the riches of these sectaries, and as a consequence of their riches and softened manners, their frequent reunion in a few generations, with the Establishment of the country where they are found. But such is the propensity of mankind to variety of opinions, that were there no sects now among us, they would soon start up out of the Church itself, of which certain respectable favourers of Socinianism have furnished a signal example; and persecution is not only a bad measure in itself for preventing it, but it is too late in the day for it to be practicable to use it.

But putting these arguments out of the question, it has been found in all countries, and been felt by none more forcibly than by England, that lenient measures are among those best calculated to diminish the number of Nonconformists. It is an approved maxim in religious politics that by taking away the distinctions which separate them from the Establishment, they are most likely to be joined to it. They exist best as a body, under persecution; and the instant they are suffered to form one mass indiscriminately with the rest of the people, they cease to be formidable. Deprive them of that zeal which leads martyrs to the stake, and they lose much of the power to resist the allurements of the world. . . . The most grievous oppression under which the Dissenters now labour is their exclusion from offices except upon terms which many of them cannot conscientiously conform to; and this mark of reproach is the chief circumstance which distinguishes them from their fellow citizens. Rapid as we know the decrease of the numbers of the Dissenters to have been since the Revolution, some even of their own body are of opinion that if they had been restored at that period to *all* their civil rights, it must have been much greater; and there are many among them who dread removal of the sacramental test as the most fatal circumstance that can happen to their interest. . . . [pp. 185–187.]

. . . The situation of public affairs may inspire the Protestant Dissenters with the most sanguine hopes of success. The Church is in no danger from papists or sectaries of any kind; there is now no formidable Pretender to the crown, and the nation is in profound tranquillity both at home and abroad. The heavy taxes under which the kingdom groans, and the deranged state of the finances, have engaged the principal attention of the Minister; and it cannot therefore have escaped his notice that the most certain mode of increasing the national wealth is to increase its population. . . .

The Monarch who now fills the throne, descended from a house deservedly dear to the friends of civil and religious liberty, has inherited the tolerant spirit of his ancestors, and has avowed himself an enemy to persecution in every shape. In his reign the Ministers of the Crown have, with unexampled liberality, granted an Establishment to the Roman Catholic religion in Quebec, and restored the Protestant Dissenters of Ireland to their rights as citizens, and given other testimonies of their liberality. . . .

The Protestant Dissenters may press upon the recollection of the Legislature the long trial that has been made of their principles, and the uniform proofs they have given ever since the Revolution of their attachment to the Constitution. . . . But they must not rely too much on the justice of their cause, their personal merits or their sufferings–and yet if arguments of that nature could ever have weight with any Minister, they ought to operate powerfully with the present one. When at the conclusion of the last Parliament, an attempt was made in the opinion of many, to destroy the independence of the three branches of the Legislature, and one of them had endeavoured to influence the deliberations of another, the best friends of the liberties of Britain were alarmed for the safety of the Constitution, and while the House of Commons was struggling against this dangerous innovation, the King thought proper to dissolve the Parliament. At the following election a general frenzy ran through great part of the kingdom. The Dissenters, catching the contagion, shook hands with Jacobites and High Churchmen, and, forgetting those principles which had endeared them to their country, ranged themselves under the banners of prerogative against a House of Commons who professed to support the rights of the people. Their exertions, however misplaced, were attended with success, and the present Administration was brought with triumph into power. This desertion of their principles may justly be a cause of reproach to the Dissenters from their fellow subjects, but it enhances the obligations of the present Minister to them, and gives them a right to expect his assistance in return. A few weeks will shew how far a sense of gratitude is impressed on his mind, though obligations conferred by the sacrifice of principle are not generally the best repaid.

But the Dissenters ought to bear in mind that their success does not entirely depend upon the inclinations of the Minister. It is true that he can carry votes to try the most problematical experiments by vast majorities; yet this apparently powerful Minister has been frequently left in a minority, and though *pledged* by the most solemn ties *as a Minister and as a man, boldly and honestly*, to carry a reform of Parliament, was unable to compass it. And the son of the high-spirited Chatham has continued to hold his place although the majority of the Cabinet Ministers opposed that measure, and the Secretary of the Treasury voted against it. I will not pretend to say by what power his good intentions towards the reform of Parliament were frustrated, but if he did his utmost both as a Minister and as a man there can be no doubt that the opposing power existed somewhere. . . . [pp. 201–206.]

452. George III to William Pitt, 29 March 1787

(Public Record Office, *Chatham Papers*, 103.)

The mode of rejecting the very improper motion for altering the Test and Corporation Acts is such as every friend to good order must feel rejoiced [*sic*]; I am so clear of its being so destructive a measure to any solidity in Government, that however suspicious that many members of Parliament do not sufficiently examine the tendency of great political questions, yet I did not suppose that 98 persons could have been found there, willing to support so ill-advised a proposition, which too avowedly points out that the former indulgences (which I thought right) the Dissenters have obtained, and which ought to have made them rest quiet, has encouraged them now to want power. I hope this check will prevent its being ever again agitated, but should it, my coronation oath as well as my conviction of the temper ever shown by the Church of England will oblige me in the most public manner to shew it my discountenance.

453. Lord Ellenborough's diary, 25 and 27 Feb. 1828

(Ellenborough's *Political Diary, 1828–30*, I, pp. 39–43.)

25th. . . . Cabinet at 3. Decided that the repeal of the Test and Corporation Acts should be opposed by the Government on the ground that there was no practical inconvenience, that the thing worked well, and that it was unwise to change the relative position of persons who went on so well together. Huskisson, others, and I said we must object to the repeal, not only on that ground, but as prejudicing the Catholic question. This was assented to. The Duke cautioning us as Ministers not to urge the union of Catholics and Dissenters with the view of forcing the measure upon Parliament. . . .

27th. The Committee for considering the repeal of that part of the Corporation and Test Acts which imposes the Sacramental Test, was carried against Government last night by a majority of 44. The numbers being 193 and 237. It was clear from the beginning of the evening that Government would be in a minority and even as it was many of their friends voted very reluctantly with them. The debate was dull. . . .

. . . Cabinet dinner at Lord Bathurst's. After dinner we talked of the course to be pursued as to the Test and Corporation Acts. Nothing was decided. . . .

454. Debate in the House of Commons on the repeal of the Test and Corporation Acts, 26 Feb. 1828

(Hansard's *Parliamentary Debates*, New Series, XVIII, 676–781.)

Lord John Russell . . . So great has been the improvement in knowledge and liberality, particularly among the middle classes, that the successors of those who most warmly opposed the motion of 1790 are, in 1828, its most zealous supporters. . . . The powerful antagonist of Mr. Fox, in 1790, Mr. Pitt, as is now well known, did in a few years after his opposition to the measure, completely change his mind on the subject, and express a wish that the Test and Corporation Acts should be repealed. He saw, as every man of enlarged and enlightened mind must have seen, that all things around him were changed since the passing of those Acts; that the religious questions which had been the subject of the world's debate at the time of their enactment had given place to divisions purely political; that the dispute for power no longer lay between Catholic, Lutheran and Calvinist, but between the adherents of despotism, representative monarchy, and democracy; that he could only defend the Constitution by rallying round it the victims of an extinct quarrel, and calling on men of different religious opinions to defend the same form of political government. . . .

It is said . . . "After all, the grievances of which you complain are only theoretical–they no longer exist in practice–Dissenters are not in fact kept out of office". . . . If the case be so, that is not a sufficient argument in support of these Acts. Statutes imposing penalties and restrictions on men on account of religious belief can be justified on no other ground than that of necessity. When that ground is taken away, the Acts remain exposed in all their naked deformity of principle, and that principle is religious persecution. But it is not a fact that no practical grievance is suffered by the Dissenters. Indeed the fact is far otherwise–the real practical grievance is a great deal more than the legal grievances which appear on the face of the Statute. Though it be true that by later Statutes indemnity was given to those who omitted to qualify, yet that indemnity was given on the ground that the omission was occasioned by ignorance, absence, or unavoidable accident. Those words evidently do not apply to those persons who had omitted to qualify from grounds of religious scruple. The situation in which the Dissenters at present stand is evidently considered one of practical grievance by the best and ablest defender of the Acts, I mean Lord North, who said, speaking of those Dissenters who took advantage of the indemnity, "This sort of mental fraud did not recommend these persons to the indulgence of the Legislature; it was an evasion and an abuse of an Act of Parliament". With such a declaration as this staring them in the face, how can it be expected that men whose nice scruples are the cause of their dissent will submit to the stigma–will render themselves liable to the imputation–of acting fraudulently, in order to obtain offices and emoluments which the Church would allow them to obtain in no other way? That they will not do so, I know for a fact. A great portion of the Dissenters say among themselves, "We will not accept of office on these conditions; if we cannot hold office without the degradation of being liable to an imputation which we scorn, we will refrain from office and emolument altogether". What is the consequence? The State is deprived of the service of men who would be amongst her bravest defenders in military achievement, and the most illustrious of her servants in civil capacity. . . .

Not only this; it should also be recollected that it is in the power of any Corporation, actuated by bigotry or personal animosity, to carry the Corporation Act into effect against Dissenters. I have in my possession a statement of cases which have occurred in the course of the last few years, in which persons who had a minority of votes in elections for Corporation offices have been declared duly elected, because a previous notice had been given that the individuals who had the majorities could not act from being Dissenters. If there are so many cases of this kind that appear in the records of a court of law, how many other cases must there be in which the Dissenters will not come forward to expose themselves to the risk of such an objection? More than this: persons admitted to office ought, under the Test Act, to produce their certificates. Dissenters do not like to expose themselves to the chance of those certificates being demanded. Rather than that, they will consent to forego office. The consequence is, that not one-tenth part of the Dissenters who ought, in proportion to their numbers, at present hold office. . . .

I am aware, whilst I am proving that these Acts operate to the exclusion of Dissenters, I am only confirming many persons in the belief that it is necessary to continue them. I allude to those persons who use the argument of the security of the Church, and who think that in proportion as the number of Dissenters excluded is large, it is so much the better for the Church, that the Establishment is so much the safer. I however cannot admit that the security of the Church is founded on any such exclusion. I think with Bishop Kennet, and I believe the security of the Establishment consists in its moderation, its fair temper, and in its decent worship being conformable to the wishes, sentiments, and consciences of the majority of the people; and if it were not so–if it were not agreeable to the people–can it be imagined that any Test, any exclusive laws, will save the Church, and prevent its being destroyed by the overwhelming mass of its enemies? . . .

Mr. Secretary Peel . . . I am not prepared, I confess, to argue that this question is essentially interwoven with the protection of the Church of England. I do not think that the two are so connected that the Church of England must fall if the Test and Corporation Acts are repealed. . . . Is there that great practical grievance, that insult resulting to the Dissenters from these Acts, which calls upon the House to repeal them? . . . So great is my respect for that large and respectable body denominated Protestant Dissenters, that if I could be satisfied that they really labour under such grievances as have been described, I should be very strongly induced to vote for the repeal of the Acts complained of. But I do not think that the great body of Dissenters look at them, together with the Indemnity Act, as so great an evil as hon. gentlemen have described. . . .

Under the existing system, there has, perhaps, been less of religious difference in England, for the last forty years, than in the same extent of time at any period of our history. Now, that fact, which an hon. member has treated as a reason for repealing the laws complained of, seems to me quite as capable of being made an argument the other way. . . . And it is not at all clear to me, that the Dissenters would gain what they expect by the repeal of these Acts. If they excite suspicion and dislike, will they not, as far as the alteration goes, do mischief? The fact is, that the existing law merely gives a nominal predominance to the Protestant Established Church. A predominance of some sort will be admitted, on all hands, to be necessary, and the present is as slight a one as can well be imagined. . . . All the intercourse between the Dissenters and the members of the Established Church has been marked, of late years, by the most perfect cordiality; and I regret that any chance should be hazarded, by which it is possible that that temperate and candid feeling should be weakened. . . .

455. The repeal of the Test and Corporation Acts, 1828

(Statutes at Large, LXXXII, pp. 22–25.)

An Act [9 Geo. IV, c. 17] for repealing so much of several Acts as imposes the necessity of receiving the sacrament of the Lord's Supper as a qualification for certain offices and employments. [9 May 1828.]

[Recites the Acts 13 Car. II, st. 2, c. 1, 25 Car. II, c. 2, and 16 Geo. II, c. 30] . . . and whereas it is expedient that so much of the said several Acts of Parliament as imposes the necessity of taking the sacrament of the Lord's Supper according to the rites or usage of the Church of England, for the purposes therein respectively mentioned, should be repealed; be it therefore enacted . . . that so much and such parts of the said several Acts . . . as require the person or persons in the said Acts respectively described to take or receive the sacrament . . . for the several purposes therein expressed . . . or as impose upon any such person or persons any penalty, forfeiture, incapacity, or disability whatsoever for or by reason of any neglect or omission to take or receive the said sacrament . . . are hereby repealed.

II. And whereas the Protestant Episcopal Church of England and Ireland, . . . and the Protestant Presbyterian Church of Scotland, and the doctrines, discipline, and government thereof, are by the laws of this realm severally established, permanently and inviolably: and whereas it is just and fitting, that on the repeal of such parts of the said Acts as impose the necessity of taking the sacrament of the Lord's Supper according to the rites or usage of the Church of England, as a qualification for office, a declaration to the following effect should be substituted in lieu thereof; be it therefore enacted, that every person who shall hereafter be placed, elected or chosen in or to the office of Mayor, Alderman, Recorder, Bailiff, Town Clerk or common councilman, or in or to any office of Magistracy, or . . . employment relating to the government of any city, corporation, borough, or Cinque Port within England and Wales . . . shall, within one calendar month . . . make and subscribe the declaration following:

> "I, A.B. do solemnly and sincerely, in the presence of God, profess, testify, and declare, upon the true faith of a Christian, that I will never exercise any power, authority, or influence which I may possess by virtue of the office of —— to injure or weaken the Protestant Church as it is by law established in England, or to disturb the said Church, or the bishops and clergy of the said Church, in the possession of any rights or privileges to which such Church, or the said bishops and clergy, are or may be by law entitled."

III. [The declaration to be made in the presence of two magistrates.]

IV. [In case of neglect to make the declaration, the election to be void.]

V. [Persons admitted to any office, which heretofore required the taking of the sacrament shall make the declaration within six months, or the appointment shall be void.]

VI. [Such persons to make the declaration in the Court of Chancery, or King's Bench, or at the Quarter Sessions.]

VII. [Naval officers below the rank of Rear-Admiral, military officers below the rank of Major-General, or of Colonel in the Militia, Commissioners of Customs, Excise, Stamps, and Taxes, and all officers concerned in the collection, management and receipt of the revenues, are not to be required to make the declaration.]

VIII. [Persons now in possession of any office which heretofore required the taking of the sacrament, and who have not done so, confirmed in possession, and indemnified from penalties.]

456. The Irish Catholic Relief Act, 1793 (33 Geo. III. c. 21) (Ireland)

(Statutes at Large, passed in the parliaments held in Ireland, XVI, pp. 685–692.)

An Act for the relief of his Majesty's popish, or Roman Catholic subjects of Ireland.

Whereas various Acts of Parliament have been passed, imposing on H.M.'s subjects professing the popish or Roman Catholic religion, many restraints and disabilities, to which other subjects of this realm are not liable; and from the peaceable and loyal demeanour of H.M.'s popish or Roman Catholic subjects, it is fit that such restraints and disabilities shall be discontinued: be it therefore enacted . . . that H.M.'s subjects being papists, or persons professing the . . . Roman Catholic religion, or married to papists, or persons professing the . . . Roman Catholic religion, or educating any of their children in that religion, shall not be liable or subject to any penalties, forfeitures, disabilities, or incapacities, or to any laws for the limitation, charging, or discovering of their estates and property, real or personal, or touching the acquiring of property, or securities affecting property, save such as H.M.'s subjects of the Protestant religion are liable and subject to; and that such parts of all oaths as are required to be taken by persons in order to qualify themselves for voting at elections of members to serve in Parliament; and also such parts of all oaths required to be taken by persons voting at elections . . . as import to deny that the person taking the same is a papist or married to a papist, or educates his children in the popish religion, shall not hereafter be required to be taken by any voter . . .; and that it shall not be necessary, in order to entitle a papist, or person professing the . . . Roman Catholic religion to vote at an election . . . that he should at, or previous to his voting, take the oaths of allegiance and abjuration. . . .

II. . . . All papists . . . who may claim to have a right of voting for members to serve in Parliament, or of voting for magistrates in any city, town-corporate, or borough, within this kingdom be hereby required to perform all qualifications, registries, and other requisites, which are now required of H.M.'s Protestant subjects, in like cases, by any law or laws now of force in this kingdom, save and except such oaths and parts of oaths as are herein before excepted.

III. . . . Nothing herein before contained shall extend . . . to repeal, or alter any law or Act of Parliament now in force, by which certain qualifications are required to be performed by persons enjoying any offices or places of trust under H.M., his heirs and successors, other than as hereinafter is enacted.

IV. . . . Nothing herein contained, shall extend . . . to give papists . . . a right to vote at any parish vestry, for levying of money to rebuild or repair any parish church, or respecting the demising or disposal of the income of any estate belonging to any church or parish, or for the salary of the parish clerk, or at the election of any church-warden.

VI. . . . Nothing herein contained, shall extend to authorize any papist . . . to have or keep in his hands or possession, any arms, armour, ammunition, or any warlike stores, sword-blades, barrels, locks, or stocks of guns, or fire arms [except papists, possessing freehold estate of £100 per annum, or personal estate of £1000 or up-wards; papists possessing freehold estate of from £10 to £100 per annum, or personal estate of from £300 to £1000, excepted if they take the oath of allegiance prescribed in 13 and 14 Geo. III, c. 35 (Ireland)].

VII. . . . It shall and may be lawful for papists . . . to hold, exercise, and enjoy all civil and military offices, or places of trust or profit under H.M. . . . in this kingdom; and to hold or take Degrees, or any Professorship in, or be Masters, or Fellows of any College, to be hereafter founded in this kingdom, provided that such college shall be a member of the university of Dublin, and shall not be founded exclusively for the education of papists . . . nor consist exclusively of Masters, Fellows, or other persons . . . professing the . . . Roman Catholic religion, or to hold any office or place of trust in, and to be a member of any lay-body corporate [except Trinity College Dublin] . . . without taking . . . the oaths of allegiance, supremacy, or abjuration, or making . . . the declaration required to be taken, . . . to enable any person to hold and enjoy any of such places, and without receiving the sacrament of the Lord's Supper, according to the rights and ceremonies of the Church of Ireland, any law, statutes, or bye-law of any corporation to the contrary notwithstanding; provided that every such person shall take and subscribe the oath appointed by the said Act . . . and also the oath and declaration following, that is to say,

I A.B. do hereby declare, that I do profess the Roman Catholic religion. I A.B. do swear, that I do abjure, condemn, and detest, as unchristian and impious, the principle that it is lawful to murder, destroy, or any ways injure any person whatsoever, for, or under the pretence of being an heretic; and I do declare solemnly before God, that I believe, that no act in itself unjust, immoral, or wicked, can ever be justified or excused by, or under pretence or colour, that it was done either for the good of the Church, or in obedience to any ecclesiastical power whatsoever. I also declare, that it is not an article of the Catholic faith, neither am I thereby required to believe or profess that the Pope is infallible, or that I am bound to obey any order in its own nature immoral, though the Pope or any ecclesiastical power should issue or direct such order, but on the contrary, I hold that it would be sinful in me to pay any respect or obedience thereto; I further declare, that I do not believe that any sin whatsoever, committed by me, can be forgiven at the mere will of any Pope, or of any priest, or of any person or persons whatsoever; but that sincere sorrow for past sins, a firm and sincere resolution to avoid future guilt, and to atone to God, are previous and indis-pensable requisites to establish a well-founded expectation of forgiveness; and that any person who receives absolution without these previous requisites, so far from obtaining thereby any remission of his sins, incurs the additional guilt of violating a sacrament; and I do swear that I will defend to the utmost of my power, the settlement and arrangement of property in this country as established by the laws now in being; I do hereby disclaim, disavow, and solemnly abjure any intention to subvert the present Church Establishment, for the purpose of substituting a Catholic Establishment in its stead; and I do solemnly swear that I will not exercise any privilege to which I am or may become entitled, to disturb and weaken the Protestant religion and Protestant Government in this kingdom.

So help me God.

VIII. [Papists may be elected Professors of Medicine upon the foundation of Sir Patrick Dunn.]

IX. . . . Nothing herein contained shall extend . . . to enable any person to sit or vote in either House of Parliament, or to hold, exercise, or enjoy the office of Lord Lieutenant, Lord Deputy, or other Chief Governor or Governors of this kingdom, Lord High Chancellor or Keeper, or Commissioner of the Great Seal of this kingdom, Lord High Treasurer, Chancellor of the Exchequer, Chief Justice of the Court of King's-Bench, or Common Pleas, Lord Chief Baron of the Court of Exchequer, Justice of the Court of King's-Bench or Common Pleas, or Baron of the Court of Exchequer, Judge of the High Court of Admiralty, Master or Keeper of the Rolls, Secretary of State, Keeper of the Privy Seal, Vice-Treasurer, or Deputy Vice-Treasurer, Teller and Cashier of the Exchequer, or Auditor-General, Lieutenant or Governor, or Custos Rotulorum of Counties, Secretary to the Lord Lieutenant, Lord Deputy, or other Chief Governor or Governors of this kingdom, member of H.M.'s most honourable Privy Council, Prime Serjeant, Attorney-General, Solicitor-General, second and third Serjeants-at-law, or King's Counsel, Masters in Chancery, Provost, or Fellow of the College of the holy and undivided Trinity of Queen Elizabeth, near Dublin; Postmaster-General, Master and Lieutenant-General of H.M.'s Ordnance, Commander-in-Chief of H.M.'s Forces, Generals on the Staff, and Sheriffs and Sub-Sheriffs of any County in this kingdom; or any office contrary to the rules, order and directions made and established by the Lord-Lieutenant and Council, in pursuance of the Act [17 and 18 Car. II] . . . unless he shall have taken, made, and subscribed the oaths and declaration, and performed the several requisites which by any law heretofore made, and now of force, are required to enable any person to sit or vote, or to hold, exercise and enjoy the said offices respectively.

X. . . . Nothing in this Act contained, shall enable any papist . . . to exercise any right of presentation to any ecclesiastical benefice whatsoever.

XI. . . . No papist . . . shall be liable to, or subject to any penalty for not attending divine service on the sabbath day, called Sunday, in his or her parish church.

XII. . . . Nothing herein contained, shall be construed to extend to authorize any popish priest, or reputed popish priest, to celebrate marriage between Protestant and Protestant, or between any person who hath been, or professed himself or herself to be a Protestant at any time within twelve months before such celebration of marriage, and a papist, unless such Protestant and papist shall have been first married by a clergyman of the Protestant religion; and that every popish priest, or reputed popish priest, who shall celebrate any marriage between two Protestants, or between any such Protestant and papist, unless such Protestant and papist shall have been first married by a clergyman of the Protestant religion, shall forfeit . . . £500 . . . upon conviction thereof.

XIII. . . . From and after 1 June, 1793, it shall not be necessary for any person upon taking any of the Degrees usually conferred by the . . . University [of Dublin] to make or subscribe any declaration, or to take any oath, save the oaths of allegiance and abjuration. . . .

XIV. [This Act not to apply to any papist until he shall have taken the oath and declaration herein prescribed and the oath appointed by 13 and 14 Geo. III, c. 35 (Ireland).]

XV. [Names of persons taking the oaths and declaration to be enrolled, the rolls to be transmitted yearly to the Rolls office; Masters of Rolls may give certificates to such persons.]

XVI. [From and after 1 April 1793, no papist shall be capable of voting in a parliamentary election until he has produced a certificate of his having taken the said oaths and declaration.]

457. George III to Pitt, 24 Jan. 1799, 8.56 a.m.

(Public Record Office, *Chatham Papers*, 104.)

. . . I cannot help . . . expressing to Mr. Pitt some surprize at having seen in a letter from Lord Castlereagh to the Duke of Portland on Monday an idea of an established stipend by the authority of Government for the Catholic clergy of Ireland. I am certain any encouragement to such an idea must give real offence to the Established Church in Ireland, as well as to the true friends of our Constitution; for it is certainly creating a second Church Establishment, which could not but be highly injurious. The tolerating Dissenters is fair; but the trying to perpetuate a separation in religious opinions by providing for the support of their clergy as an Establishment is certainly going far beyond the bounds of justice or policy.

458. Extracts from Sir Robert Peel's *Memoirs*

[Beginning of January 1829.] I now feared that the difficulties were almost insuperable.

There was the declared opinion of the King–the declared opinion of the House of Lords–the declared opinion of the Church–unfavourable to the measures we were disposed to recommend.

What I chiefly apprehended was this–that the King, hearing the result of the Duke's conference with the Bishops, would make some public and formal declaration of his resolution to maintain, as a matter of conscience and religious obligation, the excluding laws; and would thus take a position in reference to the Catholic Question similar to that in which his father had stood, which it might be almost impossible for H.M., however urgent the necessity, hereafter to abandon.

Up to this period I had cherished the hope that the Duke of Wellington might be enabled to overcome the difficulties which were opposed to his undertaking, and that I might be allowed to retire from office, and in a private station to lend every assistance in my power during the progress of the contemplated measures through Parliament. I had proposed my retirement from office much more from a sincere belief that by the sacrifice of office my co-operation with the Duke of Wellington would be the more effectual, than from any other consideration. All that had passed since my letter to the Duke of the 11th of August 1828 had confirmed the impression on my mind that the whole state of Ireland must be considered by the Cabinet—that the Catholic Question must be adjusted without further delay; and, above all, I felt convinced that any insuperable impediment suddenly interposed in the way of that adjustment—such, for instance, as a fixed and publicly-declared resolution of hostility on the part of the Sovereign—would be most injurious to the public welfare, and might preclude the hope of any future settlement—peaceful settlement at least—of the question at issue between Great Britain and Ireland. I could not but perceive, in the course of my constant intercourse with him, that the Duke of Wellington began to despair of success. It had been his constant desire to consult my wishes as to the retirement from office, and to avail himself of the offer of my zealous and cordial co-operation in a private capacity. He well knew that there would be nothing in the resignation of office half so painful to my feelings as the separation from him at a period of serious difficulty. From the moment of his appointment to the chief place in the Government not a day had passed without the most unreserved communication personally or in writing—not a point had arisen on which (as my correspondence with the Duke will amply testify) there had not been the most complete and cordial concurrence of opinion.

The period was at hand, on account of the near approach of the meeting of Parliament, when a formal proposal must be made to the King in respect to the position of his Government and the consideration of the state of Ireland. I was firmly convinced that if the Duke of Wellington should fail in procuring the King's consent to the proposal so to be submitted to H.M., no other public man could succeed in procuring that assent, and in prevailing over the opposition to be encountered in the House of Lords. It may perhaps have been thought by some that the high and established character of Earl Grey—his great abilities and great political experience—would have enabled him to surmount these various difficulties. In addition to those high qualifications, Earl Grey had the advantage of having been the strenuous and consistent advocate of the Roman Catholic cause—the advantage also of having stood aloof from the Administrations of Mr. Canning and Lord Ripon, and of having strong claims on the esteem and respect of all parties, without being fettered by the trammels of any. I had, however, the strongest reasons for the conviction that Lord Grey could not have succeeded in an undertaking which, in the supposed case of his accession to power, would have been abandoned as hopeless by the Duke of Wellington, and abandoned on the ground that the Sovereign would not adopt the advice of his servants in respect of the consideration of the Catholic Question.

Being convinced that the Catholic Question must be settled, and without delay—

being resolved that no act of mine should obstruct or retard its settlement–impressed with the strongest feelings of attachment to the Duke of Wellington–of admiration of his upright conduct and intentions as Prime Minister–of deep interest in the success of an undertaking on which he had entered from the purest motives and the highest sense of public duty–I determined not to insist upon retirement from office, but to make to the Duke the voluntary offer of that official co-operation, should he consider it indispensable, which he scrupled, from the influence of kind and considerate feelings, to require from me [I pp. 278–281].

Peel's Memorandum, 12 January 1829.

The time is come when, in my opinion, H.M.'s Government ought to be constituted in such a manner as may enable it to consider the state of Ireland and every matter connected with it, upon the same principles on which the Government can consider every other question of national policy.

I think that the Roman Catholic question can no longer remain what is called an open question, but that some definite course must be taken with respect to it by H.M.'s servants in their collective capacity.

It is not consistent with the character of the Government–with the proper exercise of authority in Ireland–nor with the permanent interests of the Protestant Establishments–that the Roman Catholic question should continue to be thrown loose upon the country–the King's Ministers maintaining neutrality, and expressing no opinion in common upon the subject.

Experience must have convinced us that neither a divided Government in Ireland, nor a Government in that country united in opinion, but acting under a divided Government in this, can administer the law with that vigour and authority which are requisite in the present condition of Irish affairs.

With respect to discussions in Parliament, I consider the present position of the Administration untenable.

Supposing it to maintain the same relation to the Catholic Question in which it has hitherto stood, it must pursue one or other of two courses at the meeting of Parliament.

It must either remain inactive with respect to Irish affairs, or it must propose measures of restriction and control unaccompanied by the expectation of any measure of concession.

To remain altogether inactive–to have no measures to propose–no opinion in common to pronounce in regard to the state of Ireland–is surely impossible.

Can the other course be taken? Can restraints be imposed or additional power be exacted for the Government, with an avowal that nothing else is in contemplation?

I will not inquire whether the Government, constituted as it at present is, would consent to the adoption of this course, because I think little doubt can be entertained that, if adopted, it would fail, and that the result of failure would be mischievous in the extreme.

It is needless to refer, in proof of the probability of its failure, to more than to one fact, namely, that in the last Session of Parliament the House of Commons decided by a majority of six votes that the Catholic Question ought to be taken into consideration with a view to its adjustment.

Is it probable that mere measures of coercion would be carried through all their several stages, in the face of an actual majority that had decided in favour of another principle of proceeding? It is true that in 1825 the House of Commons passed the Bill intended for the suppression of the Roman Catholic Association; but they followed up that Bill, in the course of the same Session, by another, which passed the House of Commons, for the complete removal of the disabilities of the Roman Catholics.

I come therefore to my first conclusion–a conclusion to which I apprehend most other persons are come–that matters cannot remain as they are–that the position of the Government with respect to the Catholic Question and to Ireland must be altered.

What course shall be adopted in lieu of that which it is proposed to abandon? I answer, in the first place, that the Government must be so constituted as to be enabled to pronounce, in its collective capacity, an opinion of some kind or other in reference to Irish affairs and to every question connected with them. I say more, that I see no advantage in the formation of a Government which should offer an opposition to the Catholic claims merely on grounds of temporary expediency, or which should grant some few additional privileges to the Roman Catholics, without looking into other questions which connect themselves with the discussion of the main question. The more I consider the subject the more I am satisfied that a Government ought to make its choice between two courses of action, either to offer united and unqualified resistance to the grant of further privileges to the Roman Catholics, or to undertake to consider without delay the whole state of Ireland, and to attempt to make some satisfactory adjustment on the various points which are involved in what is called the Catholic Question.

If it be admitted that such are the alternatives, it remains to be considered which of the two it is most practicable or most expedient to adopt. Can the first be adopted? Can a Government be formed on the principle of unqualified resistance, which shall be composed of persons of sufficient ability and experience in public life to fill with credit the high offices of the State, and which can command such a majority of the House of Commons as shall enable it to maintain the principle on which it is founded, and to transact the public business?

I think it must be granted that the failure of such a Government–either through its sudden dissolution or its inability to conduct public business on account of its weakness in the House of Commons–would have a prejudicial effect generally, and particularly in reference to the Catholic Question. It would surely render some settlement of the question in the way of concession unavoidable, and would in all probability materially diminish the chances of a safe and satisfactory settlement. No man can therefore honestly advise the formation of an exclusive Protestant Government, unless he believes that it can maintain its ground, and can conduct with credit and success the general administration of the country. The present state of the House of Commons appears to me an insuperable obstacle, if there were no other, to the successful issue of this experiment.

It may not be immaterial to look back to the proceedings of the House of

Commons on the Catholic Question for some time past. Since the year 1807 there have been five Parliaments—a General Election having taken place in each of the following years—1807, 1812, 1818, 1820 and 1826. In the course of each of those five Parliaments, with one exception, the House of Commons has come to a decision in favour of a consideration of the Catholic Question. The exception was in the case of the House of Commons elected in 1818, but that House negatived the consideration by a majority of only two voices, the numbers being 243 against, and 241 for consideration.

In the course of the period to which I have above referred there were no doubt various decisions adverse to consideration; but the fact is as I state it—that the House of Commons, in four out of the last five Parliaments, did on some occasion pronounce an opinion in favour of an attempt to settle the question.

The House of Commons elected in 1820 (the one preceding the present) twice sent up Bills to the Lords removing the disabilities of the Roman Catholics. The present House of Commons decided in the year 1827 against the question by a majority of four voices, the number being 276 to 272; but in the last Session of Parliament their decision was in favour of the question by a majority of 272 to 266. I am not aware that any changes have taken place calculated materially to affect the relative numbers of the present House of Commons; and I do not conceive it possible that a Government formed expressly upon a principle adverse to the opinion of 272 members of the House of Commons could conduct with vigour and advantage the public business.

It may be said, 'Dissolve the Parliament'—but immediate Dissolution is impossible. The supplies of the year must be voted—and a trial of strength, and such a trial as would probably decide the fate of a Government, would be inevitable. Even, however, if immediate Dissolution could take place, the state of the representation in Ireland, and the effect of a General Election in that country, would demand serious attention. In the course of last Session 93 members for Ireland voted on the Catholic Question. The relative numbers were, 61 in favour of the question, 32 against it. Of the 64 members for Irish counties, 61 voted—45 in favour of, 16 against the question. We may lament the existence of such a preponderance in the Irish representation, but in the case we are discussing, what would be our remedy? What would be the effect on that representation, supposing an exclusive Protestant Government to be formed, and a Dissolution of Parliament to take place, the constituent body in Ireland remaining the same? I assume that that body would remain the same, because I do not consider it possible that an alteration in the elective franchise of Ireland could be made previously to a Dissolution of Parliament in the case which I am now supposing—that of the formation of an exclusive Protestant Government. The effect, I apprehend, would be increased excitement in Ireland—a confirmation of the influence of the priesthood over the 40-shilling freeholders—the further exclusion of members in the Protestant interest, and of moderate and reasonable advocates of the Roman Catholics, and the return of persons neither connected with nor representing the landed aristocracy or property of the country, but selected purely for their ultra-devotion to Roman Catholic interests.

Now I cannot too strongly express my opinion that, supposing the effect of a

Dissolution should be materially to strengthen the hands of a Protestant Government by the returns from Great Britain, that circumstance would not be a sufficient compensation for the evil of an Irish representative body such as I have supposed. You might on important occasions overbear that representation by a majority in Parliament, but depend upon it that intolerable evils would still remain. The local Government of Ireland would be weakened in a most material degree by having opposed to it a vast majority of the constituent and representative body of the country. The Parliamentary business would be impeded by the addition to the House of Commons of 50 or 60 members, whose only chance of maintaining their influence would be unremitting attendance in the House, and violent and vexatious opposition to the progress of public business. The very circumstance of severing altogether the connection between the constituent body of Ireland and the natural aristocracy of the country would be a great, perhaps an irreparable misfortune. For these reasons, and firmly believing that an attempt to form an exclusive Protestant Government on a principle which must at once compel the dissolution of the present Government, would be ultimately injurious, and injurious above all to the Protestant interest, I cannot advise it.

I am thus conduced by the course of reasoning which I have pursued to the following conclusions:–That the time is come when the Catholic Question ought not longer to remain an open question. That the Government of this country, be it in whose hands it may, ought to take some definite and decisive course with respect to that question and to Irish affairs generally. That a Government has the choice of two courses of proceeding, either resistance to concession on permanent grounds, or a deliberate consideration of the whole state of Ireland–every question bearing upon the condition of this country being included in its view.

I have assigned the reasons for which I consider the former of those courses unadvisable. I will not shrink therefore from expressing my opinion in favour of the course which appears to me, under the circumstances of the present time, to present the least of difficulty and danger.

In this Memorandum I have hitherto chiefly dwelt upon the state of the House of Commons with reference to the Catholic Question, and the difficulties which it presents to the Government. I will not, however, deny that there are other considerations which incline me to think that the attempt to settle that question should be made. I pretend to no new lights upon the subject, and I attach their full weight to the powerful arguments which are opposed to concession. But the practical evils of the present state of things are very great and I fear increasing–and increasing in a direction unfavourable to that interest which I wish to uphold.

First–there is the evil of continued division between two branches of the Legislature on a great constitutional question.

Secondly–the power of the Roman Catholics is unduly increased by the House of Commons repeatedly pronouncing an opinion in their favour. There are many points in regard to the Roman Catholic religion and Roman Catholic proceedings in Ireland, on which Protestant opinion would be united, or at least predominant, if it were not for the difference which exists as to the civil incapacities.

Thirdly–in the course of the last autumn, out of a regular infantry force in the United Kingdom, amounting to about 30,000 men, 25,000 men were stationed either in Ireland or on the west coast of England with a view to the maintenance of tranquillity in Ireland–this country being at peace with the whole world.

Fourthly–though I have not the slightest apprehension of the result of civil commotion–though I believe it could be put down at once–yet I think the necessity of being constantly prepared for it while the Government is divided, and the two Houses of Parliament are divided, on the Catholic question, is a much worse evil than its actual occurrence.

Fifthly–the state of political excitement in Ireland will soon render it almost impracticable to administer justice in cases in which political or religious considerations are involved. Trial by jury will not be a just or a safe tribunal, and, above all, not just nor safe in cases where the Government is a party.

These are practical and growing evils, for which I see no sufficient remedy if the present state of things is to continue; and the actual pressure is so great as fully to warrant, in my opinion, a recourse to other measures. My advice therefore to H.M. will be, not to grant the Catholic claims, or any part of them, precipitately and unadvisedly, but in the first instance to remove the barrier which prevents the consideration of the Catholic Question by the Cabinet–to permit his confidential servants to consider it in all its relations, on the same principles on which they consider any other great question of public policy, in the hope that some plan of adjustment can be proposed, on the authority and responsibility of a Government likely to command the assent of Parliament, and to unite in its support a powerful weight of Protestant opinion, from a conviction that it is a settlement equitable towards the Roman Catholics, and safe as it concerns the Protestant Establishment [I, pp. 284–294].

Peel's Memorandum, 17 January 1829.

The three leading considerations involved in what is called the Catholic Question are these:–

1st. The extent to which civil incapacities shall be removed, and the manner of removing them.

2nd. The regulation and restriction of the elective franchise.

3rd. The relation in which the Roman Catholic religion shall stand in future towards the State.

Under the last head I include all questions relating to intercourse with the See of Rome–the exercise of any spiritual authority–and the appointment to any spiritual office, either of prelacy or priesthood, or the control over such appointment. . . .

It is of course notorious that the state of the Roman Catholics of England materially differs from that of the Irish Roman Catholics in respect to civil privileges; but I take for granted that whatever concessions are made to the Irish will in an equal degree be extended to the English–that they will be put on the same footing.

The principle of the law in respect to the Roman Catholics of Scotland differs from that of the laws which apply to the English and Irish Catholics respectively. The latter are disqualified as a consequence of their refusal to take certain oaths, and are disqualified solely on that account. In Scotland the exclusion of the Roman Catholic is, as to certain privileges at least, direct. He is disqualified by name as a Roman Catholic; and not consequentially, because he refuses certain oaths.

As to seats in Parliament, the exclusion of the Scottish Roman Catholics is positive and direct; and the exclusion forms part of the Act of Union between England and Scotland. . . . In my opinion, no distinction ought to be made in the case of the Scotch Roman Catholic. The Act of Union with Scotland ought not to be a bar to his participation in whatever privileges are granted to the Roman Catholics of other parts of the Empire.

As to the extent to which the civil incapacities should be removed, my impression is that there is no intermediate step between the line drawn by the Irish Act of 1793, and the general repeal of civil incapacities. I do not mean to say that there ought to be no single office excepted, or no restrictions upon the exercise of certain functions appertaining to certain offices: but I think the broad principle to be maintained should be equality of civil privilege; that that should be the rule, and that the exceptions from it should rest on special grounds.

The removal of incapacity will confer power, at least the eligibility to power, derived from two different, perhaps two opposite sources—the Crown on the one hand, and Constituent Bodies of the people on the other. Office in the service of the Crown must be derived chiefly from the Crown; but Corporate office and seats the House of Commons are dependent, not upon the will of the Crown, but upon that of certain portions of the people. To exclude from Corporate office or from Parliament would, so far as Ireland is concerned, leave the adjustment of the question incomplete.

If you remove those exclusions, and thus open every avenue to that description of power which is derived from the people, or from other authorities than the Crown, would it be expedient to limit the prerogative and the means of influence of the Crown by restricting the capacity of the Roman Catholic for that species of favour, distinction, or power which the Crown can confer? Would it not be dangerous to the State, if the Crown could neither employ nor influence those on whom popular favour had conferred real authority? Would it not invert constitutional relations to make the people the fountain of honour and of power and the Crown the bar to them?

It may, however, be expedient to except from the general rule of complete admissibility the offices which were excepted in the Bills brought in by Mr. Grattan, Mr. Plunket, and Sir Francis Burdett. The offices excepted were these:—All offices belonging to the Established Church. Offices in the Ecclesiastical Courts of Judicature. Offices in the Universities, or Schools of Ecclesiastical foundation. Offices of Lord Chancellor in England and Ireland, and of Lord Lieutenant of Ireland.

Roman Catholics were not to have the right of presentation to benefices; and if a Roman Catholic was appointed to an office which had the right of presentation to ecclesiastical benefices, the King might appoint a Protestant Commissioner to exercise *pro tempore* that right of presentation.

With the above exceptions, or others resting on the same principle, the removal of civil incapacity ought in my opinion to be general and complete.

Secondly. As to the mode of relieving the Roman Catholic from his present disabilities.

The obstacle to the admission of the Roman Catholics in England and Ireland to Parliament and certain high civil offices is to be found in the Oath of Supremacy, and the Declaration against Transubstantiation. The Declaration against Transubstantiation ought, I think, to be absolutely repealed, excepting indeed that it must continue to be taken by the King or Queen previous to Coronation.

It will be much better for every purpose positively to enact that certain offices shall not be held by Roman Catholics than to retain the Declaration against Transubstantiation, with the view of excluding them through its instrumentality.

The remaining obstacle is the Oath of Supremacy. I wish that oath could be retained in its present form, and that the Roman Catholic could be persuaded to take it in the sense in which I believe it to have been originally meant to be taken.

In the Bill brought in by Mr. Plunket in 1821, it was originally proposed to retain without any alteration the present Oath of Supremacy, and to require the Roman Catholic to take that oath as a condition of his holding office; there being inserted in the Bill a legislative interpretation of the oath, importing that those who might take the oath should be understood to declare nothing more than that they denied to any foreign Prince any jurisdiction, temporal or spiritual, that could conflict with their duty of full and undivided allegiance. The Bill was, however, afterwards altered in this respect; and an oath was proposed for the Roman Catholics, differing from the present Oath of Supremacy. The legislative interpretation was abandoned, and the Roman Catholic was called on to take an oath which denied to any foreign Prince in express terms any superiority, ecclesiastical or spiritual, that could conflict with his allegiance to the King.

I have already observed that I wish it were possible to retain the present Oath of Supremacy to be taken in common by Protestant and Roman Catholic; at the same time I think even an alteration of the oath is preferable to a legislative interpretation of it. I doubt whether any other expedient will be found less open to objection than that which I am now about to suggest.

Repeal the Declaration against Transubstantiation and the worship of the Virgin Mary. Leave the Oath of Supremacy, which is of great antiquity, to be taken in its present form by all Protestants, and by Roman Catholics who choose to take it. Retain the Oath of Allegiance, and (for the present at least) the Oath of Abjuration; to be taken by Protestant and Roman Catholic in common.

It will remain to be considered what test of civil allegiance shall be administered to the Roman Catholic. I advise one which shall be a purely civil test, but by which the Roman Catholic shall be compelled to abjure any principles or opinions that are dangerous to the State [I, pp. 300–305].

459. The Roman Catholic Relief Act, 1829 (10 Geo. IV, c. 7.)

(Statutes at Large, LXXXIII, pp. 49–59.)

Whereas by various Acts of Parliament certain restraints and disabilities are imposed on the Roman Catholic subjects of H.M., to which other subjects of H.M. are not liable; and whereas it is expedient that such restraints and disabilities shall be from henceforth discontinued; and whereas by various Acts certain oaths and declarations, commonly called the declaration against transubstantiation, and the declaration against transubstantiation and the invocation of Saints and the sacrifice of the Mass, as practised in the Church of Rome, are or may be required to be taken, made, and subscribed by the subjects of H.M., as qualifications for sitting and voting in parliament, and for the enjoyment of certain offices, franchises, and civil rights: be it enacted ... that ... all such parts of the said Acts as require the said declarations, as a qualification for sitting and voting in Parliament, or for the exercise or enjoyment of any office, franchise or civil right ... are (save as hereinafter provided and excepted) hereby repealed.

II. ... From and after the commencement of this Act it shall be lawful for any person professing the Roman Catholic religion, being a Peer, or who shall after the commencement[1] of this Act be returned as a member of the House of Commons, to sit and vote in either House of Parliament respectively, being in all other respects duly qualified to sit and vote therein, upon taking and subscribing the following oath, instead of the oaths of allegiance, supremacy and abjuration.

"I A.B. do sincerely promise and swear, that I will be faithful and bear true allegiance to H.M. King George IV, and will defend him to the utmost of my power against all conspiracies and attempts whatever, which shall be made against his person, crown, or dignity; and I will do my utmost endeavour to disclose and make known to H.M., his heirs and successors, all treasons and traitorous conspiracies which may be formed against him or them: and I do faithfully promise to maintain, support, and defend, to the utmost of my power, the succession of the Crown, which succession ... is and stands limited to the Princess Sophia, Electress of Hanover, and the heirs of her body, being Protestants; hereby utterly renouncing and abjuring any obedience or allegiance unto any other person claiming or pretending a right to the Crown of this realm: and I do further declare, that it is not an article of my faith, and that I do renounce, reject, and abjure the opinion, that Princes excommunicated or deprived by the Pope, or any other authority of the See of Rome, may be deposed or murdered by their subjects, or by any person whatsoever: and I do declare, that I do not believe that the Pope of Rome, or any other foreign Prince, prelate, person, State, or potentate, hath or ought to have any temporal or civil jurisdiction, power, superiority, or pre-eminence, directly or indirectly, within this realm. I do swear, that I will defend to the utmost of my power the settlement of property within this realm, as established

[1] These restrictive words gave great offence to Catholic Ireland by excluding from the House of Commons the newly elected member for County Clare. Some members wished to introduce an amendment to the Bill to make the new oath applicable to O'Connell, but he would not allow them to jeopardize the success of the measure by so doing. On 15 May he claimed his seat, but the Speaker would not permit him to take the new oath, and ruled that the Act was not applicable to a member elected before it became law.

by the laws: and I do hereby disclaim, disavow, and solemnly abjure any intention
to subvert the present Church Establishment, as settled by law within this realm: and
I do solemnly swear, that I never will exercise any privilege to which I am or may
become entitled, to disturb or weaken the Protestant religion or Protestant Government in the United Kingdom: and I do solemnly, in the presence of God, profess,
testify, and declare, that I do make this declaration, and every part thereof, in the plain
and ordinary sense of the words of this oath, without any evasion, equivocation, or
mental reservation whatsoever. So help me God."
III. [The name of the Sovereign for the time being to be used in the oath.]
IV. [No Roman Catholic to be capable of sitting or voting in Parliament until he has
taken the oath.]
V. [Roman Catholics may vote at elections, and be elected, upon taking the oath.]
VI. [Oaths to be administered in the same manner as former oaths.]
VII. [Persons administering the oath at elections to take an oath duly to administer
this.]
VIII. [Roman Catholics may elect and be elected Members for Scotland.]
IX. [No Roman Catholic priest to sit in the House of Commons, under the penalties
of the act of 1801 (41 Geo. III, c. 63).]
X. . . . It shall be lawful for any of H.M.'s subjects professing the Roman Catholic
religion to hold, exercise, and enjoy all civil and military offices and places of trust or
profit under H.M., his heirs or successors, and to exercise any other franchise or civil
right, except as hereinafter excepted, upon taking . . . the oath hereinbefore
appointed. . . .
XI. [Roman Catholics not to be exempted from taking any other oaths or declarations
required for admission to such offices, &c.]
XII. . . . Nothing herein contained shall extend . . . to enable any person or persons
professing the Roman Catholic religion to hold or exercise the office of Guardians
and Justices of the United Kingdom, or of Regent of the United Kingdom, under
whatever name, style, or title such office may be constituted; nor to enable any person,
otherwise than as he is now by law enabled, to hold or enjoy the office of Lord High
Chancellor, Lord Keeper or Lord Commissioner of the Great Seal of Great Britain
or Ireland; or the office of Lord Lieutenant, or Lord Deputy, or other Chief Governor
or Governors of Ireland; or H.M.'s High Commissioners to the General Assembly of
the Church of Scotland.
XIV. . . . It shall be lawful for any . . . Roman Catholic . . . to be a member of any lay
body corporate, and to hold any civil office or place of trust or profit therein, and to
do any corporate act, or vote in any corporate election or other proceeding upon
taking . . . the oath hereby appointed. . . .
XV. [Roman Catholic members of Corporations not to vote at the appointment of
any person to any ecclesiastical benefice in the gift of such Corporation.]
XVI. [The Act not to extend to offices &c., in the Established Churches of England,
Ireland or Scotland, or in their ecclesiastical courts, nor to offices &c., in the Universities and schools; nor to interfere with any local statute or rule excluding Roman
Catholics from admission to any University or school, or to any University degree;

nor to enable any Roman Catholics to exercise any right of presentation to any ecclesiastical benefice.]

XVII. [Where any Roman Catholic is appointed to any office to which the right of presentation to any benefice is attached, such right to devolve upon the Archibishop of Canterbury.]

XVIII. [No Roman Catholic to advise the Crown in the appointment to offices in the established church.]

[XIX–XXIII. Lay down the time and manner for taking oaths, penalties for acting without taking the oath, and that no other oaths are necessary to be taken by Roman Catholics except those required of other subjects.]

XXIV. [Roman Catholics not to assume the name, style or title of Archbishop, Bishop or Dean: Penalty £100.]

XXV. [Persons holding judicial or civil office not to attend with insignia of office at any place of worship, other than the Established Church: penalty £100.]

XXVI. [Roman Catholic priests not to officiate at worship except in Catholic Churches or private houses.]

XXVIII. And whereas Jesuits, and members of other religious orders, communities, or Societies of the Church of Rome, bound by monastic or religious vows, are resident within the United Kingdom; and it is expedient to make provision for the gradual suppression and final prohibition of the same therein; be it therefore enacted, that every Jesuit, and every member of any other religious Order . . . who at the time of the commencement of this Act shall be within the United Kingdom, shall, within six calendar months . . . deliver to the Clerk of the Peace of the county or place where such person shall reside . . . a notice . . . which . . . such Clerk of the Peace . . . shall preserve . . . and shall forthwith transmit a copy . . . to the Chief Secretary of the Lord Lieutenant . . . of Ireland, if such person shall reside in Ireland, or if in Great Britain, to one of H.M.'s Principal Secretaries of State. . . .

XXIX. [Jesuits, &c., entering the realm after the commencement of this Act to be banished for life.]

XXX. [Natural born subjects, being Jesuits, &c., may return to the Kingdom, and be registered.]

XXXI. [Any one Secretary of State, being a Protestant, may grant written permission to any Jesuit, &c., to enter the Kingdom and to stay not longer than six months, and may at any time revoke this licence.]

XXXIII. [Any Jesuit, &c., admitting any person in the United Kingdom to membership of any such religious Order to be deemed guilty of a misdemeanour.]

XXXIV. [Any person admitted a member of a religious Order as aforesaid to be banished for life.]

XXXVII. Provided . . . that nothing herein contained shall extend . . . to affect any religious Order, community, or establishment consisting of females bound by religious or monastic vows.

460. Debate in the House of Commons on the Jews, 5 April 1830

(Hansard's *Parliamentary Debates*, New Series, XXIII, 1287–1336.)

The new oath prescribed by the Roman Catholic Relief Act of 1829 for members of either House of Parliament was available only to Roman Catholics. Others had still to take the three oaths of allegiance, supremacy and abjuration, and the oath of abjuration, which concluded with the words "on the true faith of a Christian", could not be taken by a Jew. He would not vacate his seat by refusal to take the oath in these terms, but he would be unable to sit and vote in the House of Commons except under a penalty of £500 a day. An Act of 1858 substituted a single oath for these three, and dispensed with the use of the words "on the true faith of a Christian".

Mr. R. Grant . . . The Sacramental Test, imposed by the Corporation and Test Acts . . . excluded them [the Jews] as, previously to the Session before last it did Protestant Dissenters, from various rights and privileges. Well, the House was pleased to remove this restriction, but it was replaced by a test not to be applied subsequently, as the former was, but previously; and, worst of all, the Acts of Indemnity were at an end. Passing those Acts annually, relieved the Jews as well as the Dissenters from the consequences of not having taken the oaths. The new Act compelled a man to swear "upon the faith of a Christian". . . . They could not hold any office, civil or military; they could not be schoolmasters or ushers; they could not be serjeants-at-law, barristers, solicitors, pleaders, conveyancers, attorneys or clerks; they could not be members of Parliament, nor could they vote for return of members, if anybody chose to enforce the oath; and, finally, they were excluded from all Corporation offices. Some doubts, too, had been started if the Statute *de Judaismo* was not still in force, excluding them from the right of holding or transferring lands, and leaving their religious worship without protection. . . . In Exeter, Norwich and other parts of the kingdom, Jews might engage in all trades, and enjoy the common privileges of citizens; but he regretted to state that in the great metropolis of the commercial world, they were subjected to restrictions of the most onerous nature. They could not obtain the freedom of the City. They could not exercise a retail trade –regulations which, to the great mass of the members of the communion, were the most galling and the most oppressive. The Jews, in short, were nearly on the same footing as the Roman Catholics were last year; but the difference was in favour of the previous situation of the Roman Catholics, and against the Jews. . . .

The number of the Jews in the metropolis amounted to about 20,000. Accounts differed much respecting the number of them in the empire, but they might be estimated at from 30 to 40,000. This calculation would embrace all the United Kingdom. . . . The effect of catholic emancipation had been to aggravate the evils under which they suffered. He could mention one case in which it had been peculiarly oppressive, in which a young man, prepared to be called to the bar, was disqualified by the effects of that very Act of Toleration which had conferred such inestimable blessings upon others. . . . The Jews affirmed that, by paying taxes, they contributed to the support of the State, and that by their wealth they added to its opulence; and in return they called upon the House for that which hitherto the Legislature had denied them–an admission to the rights and privileges of the British Constitution. . . . The House might put them upon the same footing with the Roman Catholics since the passing of the Act. . . . He moved for "leave to bring in a Bill to repeal the civil disabilities affecting British-born subjects professing the Jewish religion".

Sir R. Inglis . . . defied his hon. friend, who seemed to have ransacked all history, to produce a single instance in which any but Christians had been admitted to political power. . . . He maintained that the Jews were aliens, not in the technical and legal sense, when Lord Coke called them 'aliens and perpetual enemies', but in the popular sense of the word: they were aliens because their country and their interests were not merely different, but hostile to our own. The Jews of London had more sympathy with the Jews resident in Berlin or Vienna than with the Christians among whom they resided. . . . While we were at war with France, the Jews of London had furnished Napoleon with a loan to enable him to carry on the most determined hostility. . . . He had always held that the grant or refusal of civil rights was a mere matter of discretion, to be decided by expediency and not upon abstract right; and therefore, until better arguments were advanced, he should resist the admission of Jews, on the point of expediency. It might be urged that the number was so small as to disarm apprehension; but he said with Mr. Burke, that a small number might make up for its want of weight by its activity, and produce the greatest public events. . . . The Jews might get into the House of Commons, and use that power for their own selfish and unnational purposes. They were not a sect, but to this day they called themselves a people; and they might avail themselves of their political influence for objects connected with their own aggrandisement. . . . An hon. friend of his had said that he knew of four who were ready to enter the House at once: considering that there were in the United Kingdom, at the utmost, 40,000 Jews, and that about every 40,000 Christians had only one representative, this number was considerably above their fair proportion. The command of capital would enable the Jews to obtain seats, and the introduction of a Jew ought to be considered direct evidence of bribery, for it was out of the question to suppose that they would ever obtain the unbought suffrages of the people. A Jew member would carry on his forehead the evidence of the mode by which he obtained admission; and certain he was that within seven years after the entrance of the first Jew, Parliamentary Reform would be carried. . . .

Mr. Macaulay . . . Even those most opposed to the present measure cannot deny that the Jews have borne their deprivations long in silence, and are now complaining with mildness and decency. As a contrast to this, the Roman Catholics were always described as an insinuating, restless, cunning, watchful sect, ever on the search how they might increase their power and the number of their sect, pressing for converts in every possible way, and only withheld by the want of power from following up their ancient persecutions. But the sect with which we now have to deal are even more prone to monopolise their religion than the others are to propagating the Catholic faith. Never has such a thing been heard of as an attempt on the part of the Jews to gain proselytes. . . . My hon. friend . . . allows them to have property, and in these times property is power, mighty and overwhelming power–he allows them to have knowledge, and knowledge is no less power. Then why is all this power poisoned by intolerance? Why is the Jew to have the power of a principal over his clerk–of a master over his servant–of a landlord over his tenant? Why is he to have all this, which is power, and yet to be deprived of the fair and natural consequences of this power? . . . As things now stand, a Jew may be the richest man in England–he may possess the whole of London–his interest may be the means of raising this party or depressing that–of making East India Directors, or sending members into Parliament–the influence of a Jew may be of the first consequence in a war which shall be the means of shaking all Europe to its centre. His power may come into play in assisting or retarding the greatest plans of the greatest Princes; and yet, with all this confessed, acknowledged, undenied, my hon. friend would have them deprived of power! . . . As to the matter of right, if the word 'legal' is to be attached to it, I am bound to acknowledge that the Jews have no legal right to power; but in the same way, 300 years ago, they had no legal right to be in England; and 600 years ago they had no right to the teeth in their heads: but if it is the moral right we are to look at, I say that on every principle of moral obligation, I hold that the Jew has a right to political power. Every man has a right to all that may conduce to his pleasure if it does not inflict pain on anyone else. This is one of the broadest maxims of human nature, and I cannot therefore see how its supporters can be fairly called upon to defend it–the *onus probandi* lies, not on the advocates of freedom, but on the advocates of restraint. Let my hon. friend show that there is some danger–some injury to the State, likely to arise from the admission of the Jews, and then will be the time to call upon us to answer the case that he has made out. Till such an argument, however, is fully made out, I shall contend for the moral right of the Jews. That they wish to have access to the privilege of sitting in Parliament has already been shown; it now remains to show that some harm is calculated to result from that admission. Unless this is shown, the refusal is neither more nor less than persecution. . . . The infliction of any penalties on account of religious opinions, and on account of religious opinions alone, is generally understood as coming within the meaning of the term, for all the purposes of political argument. It is as much persecution in principle as an *auto da fé*; the only difference is in degree. . . .

Mr. *Harrison Batley:* . . . It had been calculated–and he believed upon very sufficient *data*–that in the event of such a measure as the present being carried into effect, 25 Jews would obtain seats in the Commons' House of Parliament, and a few of the leading men amongst them would soon obtain as much influence there as they had already possessed over the 3% Consols. For his own part, he could never consent to anyone taking his seat in that House who did not believe in the Christian religion.

Sir *James Mackintosh:* . . . The Jews . . . were subservient because they were openly despised; the moral defects of their character arose from the oppression they had been subject to. What was the remedy? To revive their regard for the esteem of other men, to awaken their sympathies with their fellow-creatures, to give them the same interests, to teach them the same lessons, to make them prize the privileges and distinctions which other men struggle to obtain; and to accomplish these objects they must be released from their present degradation, and must be treated like their fellow-subjects. This should be the first step to reclaim them–the first means to restore the character of the Jews. . . . He was far from believing that they deserved all the odium heaped on them by popular prejudices, and he should content himself with asserting that the present depravity of some part of the Jews was one of the strongest arguments which could be urged in favour of the measure. . . . They were composed of two, or rather they contained two classes—one was extremely poor and degraded, engaged in the lowest occupations, shut out from the pale of society by the tyranny of ages, and destitute of any regard to character. They were reduced to a state of hereditary depravity, and for them emancipation was necessary to restore them to their situation in society. That was the only remedy which could relieve them from the moral malady with which they were afflicted. On the other hand, there was a large body of Jews, merchants of great credit, possessing vast wealth, engaged in extensive schemes of industry, and filling a high and respectable station in society. They were engaged in transactions with every State in Europe. He would say, with respect to them, that they deserved emancipation. The lower class of Jews could only be reclaimed, and the higher only placed in the stations they deserved to occupy, by the same measure....

The Chancellor of the Exchequer . . . opposed their claims, however, on grounds of expediency, as they were connected with the honest prejudices of the people, which ought to be respected, as they had arisen out of reverence for their own sacred religion. It was a question for the Parliament, worthy of its grave consideration, whether it would not be likely, by altering the oaths and the principles of admitting people into Parliament year after year, to run some risk of affronting the religious feelings of the people of this country. These feelings might be called prejudices, but they were honest prejudices, and the House might find in that a motive for respecting them. . . . There was this difference between the Jews and the Catholics—that the Catholics had shed their blood for us—they had fought our battles both by sea and land . . . and there was a good reason why we should not make enemies of those who had served us, and who amounted to seven million people. But the Jews had not fought our battles—they had not served in our armies and navy, and they did not amount, it was stated by a writer of their own nation, to more than 27,000 persons. . . .

The Solicitor-General: . . . The Jews . . . had a peculiar character stamped on them by their own institutions, they were severed by them from all other people, they could not form a component part of any society in which they might be mingled: and as our laws had not made them Jews, they could not make them Englishmen. They married not with Christians, and entered not into any of those relations with the rest of the community which constituted family ties, and were the real bonds of society. . . . Would hon. members be ready to associate with Jews on that familiar footing which would be necessary if they were in office? He believed not; and he therefore, for one, would not allow the law to say they were worthy of those privileges which the common sense of the community at large, and the general feelings even of those who advocated their cause would in practice deny them. . . .

The House then divided—for the Motion 115; against it 97: majority 18.

Mr. Grant then brought in the Bill, which was read a first time.

C. EDUCATION

461. The Rev. Sydney Smith on English education

(*Works*, I (1848 ed.), pp. 351–361.)

This essay was published in the *Edinburgh Review* (1809) as a review of R. L. Edgeworth's *Professional Education.*

. . . That vast advantages . . . may be derived from classical learning, there can be no doubt. The advantages which are derived from classical learning by the English manner of teaching, involve another and a very different question; and we will venture to say, that there never was a more complete instance in any country of such extravagant and overacted attachment to any branch of knowledge, as that which obtains in this country with regard to classical knowledge. A young Englishman goes to school at six or seven years old; and he remains in a course of education till 23 or 24 years of age. In all that time, his sole and exclusive occupation is learning Latin and Greek:[1] he has scarcely a notion that there is any other kind of excellence; and the great system of facts with which he is the most perfectly acquainted, are the intrigues of the heathen Gods: with whom Pan slept? with whom Jupiter?–whom Apollo ravished? These facts the English youth get by heart the moment they quit the nursery; and are most sedulously and industriously instructed in them till the best and most active part of life is passed away. Now, this long career of classical learning, we may, if we please, denominate a foundation; but it is a foundation so far above ground, that there is absolutely no room to put any thing upon it. If you occupy a man with one thing till he is 24 years of age, you have exhausted all his leisure time: he is called into the world and compelled to act; or is surrounded with pleasures, and thinks and reads no more. If you have neglected to put other things in him, they will never get in afterwards;–if you have fed him only with words, he will remain a narrow and limited being to the end of his existence. . . .

. . . The picture which a young Englishman, addicted to the pursuit of knowledge, draws–his *beau ideal*, of human nature–his top and consummation of man's powers–is a knowledge of the Greek language. His object is not to reason, to imagine, or to invent; but to conjugate, decline, and derive. The situations of imaginary glory which he draws for himself, are the detection of an anapæst in the wrong place, or the restoration of a dative case which Cranzius had passed over, and the never-dying Ernesti failed to observe. If a young classic of this kind were to meet the greatest chemist or the greatest mechanician, or the most profound political economist of his time, in company with the greatest Greek scholar, would the slightest comparison between them ever come across his mind?–would he ever dream that such men as Adam Smith and Lavoisier were equal in dignity of understanding to, or of the same utility as, Bentley and Heyne? We are inclined to think, that the feeling excited would be a good deal like that which was expressed by Dr. George about the praises of the

[1] Unless he goes to the University of Cambridge; and then classics occupy him entirely for about ten years; and divide him with mathematics for four or five more.

great King of Prussia, who entertained considerable doubts whether the King, with all his victories, knew how to conjugate a Greek verb in $\mu\iota$. . . .

The English clergy, in whose hands education entirely rests, bring up the first young men of the country as if they were all to keep grammar schools in little country towns; and a nobleman, upon whose knowledge and liberality the honour and welfare of his country may depend, is diligently worried, for half his life, with the small pedantry of longs and shorts. There is a timid and absurd apprehension, on the part of ecclesiastical tutors, of letting out the minds of youth upon difficult and important subjects. They fancy that mental exertion must end in religious scepticism; and, to preserve the principles of their pupils, they confine them to the safe and elegant imbecility of classical learning. A genuine Oxford tutor would shudder to hear his young men disputing upon moral and political truth, forming and pulling down theories, and indulging in all the boldness of youthful discussion. He would augur nothing from it, but impiety to God, and treason to kings. And yet, who vilifies both more than the holy poltroon who carefully averts from them the searching eye of reason, and who knows no better method of teaching the highest duties, than by extirpating the finest qualities and habits of the mind? If our religion is a fable, the sooner it is exploded the better. If our government is bad, it should be amended. But we have no doubt of the truth of the one, or of the excellence of the other; and are convinced that both will be placed on a firmer basis, in proportion as the minds of men are more trained to the investigation of truth. At present, we act with the minds of our young men, as the Dutch did with their exuberant spices. An infinite quantity of talent is annually destroyed in the Universities of England by the miserable jealousy and littleness of ecclesiastical instructors. It is in vain to say we have produced great men under this system. We have produced great men under all systems. Every Englishman must pass half his life in learning Latin and Greek; and classical learning is supposed to have produced the talents which it has not been able to extinguish. It is scarcely possible to prevent great men from rising up under any system of education, however bad. Teach men dæmonology or astrology, and you will still have a certain portion of original genius, in spite of these or any other branches of ignorance and folly. . . .

In those who were destined for the Church, we would undoubtedly encourage classical learning, more than in any other body of men; but if we had to do with a young man going out into public life, we would exhort him to contemn, or at least not to affect, the reputation of a great scholar, but to educate himself for the offices of civil life. He should learn what the Constitution of his country really was,—how it had grown into its present state,—the perils that had threatened it,—the malignity that had attacked it,—the courage that had fought for it, and the wisdom that had made it great. We would bring strongly before his mind the characters of those Englishmen who have been the steady friends of the public happiness; and, by their examples, would breathe into him a pure public taste, which should keep him un-tainted in all the vicissitudes of political fortune. We would teach him to burst through the well paid, and the pernicious cant of indiscriminate loyalty; and to know his Sovereign only as he discharged those duties, and displayed those qualities, for which the blood and the treasure of his people are confided to his hands. We should deem it of the utmost importance, that his attention was directed to the true principles of legislation,–what effect laws can produce upon opinions, and opinions upon laws, –what subjects are fit for legislative interference, and when men may be left to the management of their own interests. The mischief occasioned by bad laws, and the perplexity which arises from numerous laws,–the causes of national wealth,–the relations of foreign trade,–the encouragement of manufactures and agriculture,– the fictitious wealth occasioned by paper credit,–the laws of population,–the manage- ment of poverty and mendicity,–the use and abuse of monopoly,–the theory of taxation,–the consequences of the public debt. These are some of the subjects, and some of the branches of civil education to which we would turn the minds of future Judges, future Senators, and future noblemen. After the first period of life had been given up to the cultivation of the classics, and the reasoning powers were now begin- ning to evolve themselves, these are some of the propensities in study which we would endeavour to inspire. Great knowledge at such a period of life, we could not convey; but we might fix a decided taste for its acquisition, and a strong disposition to respect it in others. The formation of some great scholars we should certainly prevent, and hinder many from learning what, in a few years, they would necessarily forget; but this loss would be well repaid,–if we could show the future rulers of the country that thought and labour which it requires to make a nation happy,–or if we could inspire them with that love of public virtue, which, after religion, we most solemnly believe to be the brightest ornament of the mind of man. . . .

462. W. Wilberforce to W. Gray, 31 Dec. 1830

(*Private Papers of William Wilberforce*, ed. Wilberforce, p. 157.)

It is curious to observe the effects of the Oxford system in producing on the minds of young men a strong propensity to what may be termed Tory principles. From myself and the general tenour of our family and social circle, it might have been supposed that my children, though averse to party, would be inclined to adopt Liberal or, so far as would be consistent with party, Whig principles, but all my three Oxonians are strong friends to High Church-and-King doctrines. The effects I myself have witnessed would certainly induce me, had I to decide on the University to which any young protégé of mine should go, were he by natural temper or any other causes too prone to excess on the Tory side, I should decidedly send him to Cambridge, Trinity; were the opposite the case he should be fixed at Oriel, Oxford.

463. Statement by the council of the University of London, explanatory of the nature and objects of the Institution

(London (1827), pp. 7–13.)

The project of a metropolitan university was revived in the early eighteen-twenties by the poet Thomas Campbell (1777–1844) and taken up by Henry Brougham and an influential group of politicians and utilitarians. The scheme was launched in June 1825: the university was to be a joint-stock company with a capital of not less than £150,000 and not more than £300,000 in shares of £100, paying a dividend of 4 per cent. The university–now University College–was opened in Gower Street in October 1828. The 'Statement' of its purpose and organization was drafted by the first warden, Leonard Horner, and revised by J. S. Mill and W. Tooke, two members of the council. The university did not confer degrees until 1836, when University College and the Anglican foundation of King's College (opened 1831) became the constituent bodies of a new London University.

1. *Of the necessity which existed for the foundation of another University in England.*

It has long been a subject of regret, that a very large proportion of the youth of England, whose future professional occupations are such as to render an University education most desirable, have, owing to various causes, been deprived of that most important benefit. Oxford is, by its statutes, accessible to those only who belong to the Established Church; and although Cambridge has so far relaxed the strictness of its rules that Dissenters, while deprived of the privilege of obtaining degrees, may still receive their education there, that University is, practically, scarcely less exclusive than Oxford on the score of religion. Another, and a very serious cause of exclusion, is the very great expense incurred at those Universities: an evil, it is true, not arising from University fees or the payments for instruction,–for these are extremely moderate,–but partly from College charges, and still more from expensive habits of living among the undergraduates, which have been increasing year after year, which the authorities in both places have hitherto been unable to check, and which are in some respects the unavoidable consequence of the youth living separate from their parents. Although the regulations of the Universities do not lead to or warrant such an expense, the fashion of the place has fixed the scale of living; and while many parents are thus put to very great inconvenience, others find it impossible to give their sons the advantage of an University education. But were the obstacles on the score of religion and expense entirely removed, it would be impossible for the existing establishments to receive all the applications for admission; for even now, both Universities are overcrowded; and in the case of the Colleges of highest reputation at Oxford, application must be made some years before a young man is ready to enter, in order to secure his admission.

When it is considered, therefore, how great must be the number and the opulence of those who do not belong to the Established Church, and how large a portion of the people of England consists of persons in easy yet moderate circumstances, there cannot be a doubt that the best interests of the country urgently demand the establishment of an institution where an enlightened education may be obtained at a reasonable charge, and where persons of every religious persuasion may be freely admitted.

It is also to be remembered that a professional course of study in Law or Medicine does not avowedly rank among the leading objects of education at Oxford and Cambridge; and independently of that circumstance, there are local advantages in the metropolis for connecting the theoretical with the practical parts of these branches of knowledge, which cannot be equally enjoyed in any provincial situation. The consequence of this is, that only a very limited proportion of the members of those learned professions in England, especially the medical, receive even their general education at an University.

It has been stated that about 100 only of all the physicians now practising in England have been educated at Oxford and Cambridge, while there are more than 300 licentiates of the College of Physicians, besides as many hundreds of country practitioners, who have never been candidates for the privilege of the licentiate. There are now 6,000 members of the College of Surgeons, not 6 of whom, it has been stated, have graduated at our Universities.

In the higher branch of the law a very considerable proportion have graduated at Oxford and Cambridge; but among those who belong to that most important branch of the profession, the Attorneys, of whom there are not less than 8,000 in England, it is believed that scarcely one in a thousand has had the benefit of an University education. There is another description of persons to whom it is surely desirable to give all the advantages of a liberal education; the gentlemen who hold places in the offices of Government; but who are also unable to avail themselves of the opportunities which Oxford and Cambridge afford for that purpose, because they usually enter such offices at or below the age of the youngest undergraduates of those Universities.

If the great changes which have taken place in England since the foundation of the Universities of Oxford and Cambridge, with respect to population, wealth, and above all the general diffusion of education, have rendered the establishment of another University a matter of urgent necessity, London appears to be the situation where it can be most advantageously placed. It is indeed a matter of surprise that a city which has for ages been so populous and renowned, should have existed so long without such an institution. According to the most accurate data, there are in London not less than 5,000 young men from the age of 16 to 21, the children of persons who can easily defray the expense of an education conducted as it is proposed to be in this University. The capital is the resort of the most celebrated persons of every description; and among others, of those most eminent in the cultivation of the arts, the sciences, and letters. Thus the greatest genius and skill become available to the purposes of education in all the branches of knowledge. The capital is the most convenient situation for all those young men who would be sent from the provinces for education, on account of the greater probability of their finding connexions interested in their welfare, and greater facilities for adopting a style of living suited to their circumstances. An University so established is also very likely to form a great attraction to young men in the colonies, and in those foreign countries where science and learning are still under trammels from political causes. At the desire of some persons high in authority in one of the liberated governments of South America, inquiry has been made whether an arrangement could be entered into for the reception of about 100 young men at the University of London from that country; and that such an arrangement is practicable there can be no doubt. Were those who are to be the future legislators, governors, and leading men in the various classes of society of those countries, educated under the liberal and enlightened system of England, and accustomed, during the early years of life, to see around them the happiness and security which flow from our free institutions, it would be difficult to estimate too highly the extension that might thus be given to the moral influence of this country over the destinies of the New World.

2. *Of the various branches of knowledge which are to be taught in the University of London.*

These may be arranged under 3 heads. First, those subjects which constitute the essential parts of a liberal education; secondly, those which may be considered more in the light of ornamental accomplishment; and thirdly, those which belong to professional education.

Of the subjects which may be comprehended under the first division, it is intended that there shall be a Professor in each of the following branches: the Roman language, literature, and antiquities; the Greek language, literature, and antiquities; the French language and literature; the English language and literature; elementary mathematics; higher mathematics; natural philosophy and astronomy; logic and the philosophy of the human mind; moral and political philosophy; history, ancient and modern; political economy; chemistry.

In the second division of subjects there will be Professors of Italian literature; Spanish literature; German and Northern literature; Oriental literature; more particularly Hindostanee, Persian and Hebrew; geology and mineralogy; botany; zoology.

In the third division of subjects there will be Professors of jurisprudence, including the law of nations; English law; Roman law.

As for the profession of medicine, the following subjects will be taught: anatomy and physiology; morbid and comparative anatomy; surgery; nature and treatment of diseases; midwifery, and the diseases of women and children; materia medica and pharmacy; chemistry; botany and vegetable physiology; medical jurisprudence.

While in an hospital connected with the University, opportunities will be given for clinical lectures and practice.

There are also to be Professors on engineering and the application of mechanical philosophy to the Arts, and on the application of chemistry to the Arts.

One great and important branch–Theology–yet remains; and it is necessary to explain why that is not provided for.

The Universities of Oxford and Cambridge supply ample opportunities for the education of the clergy of the Established Church. It is a fundamental principle of the University of London, that it shall be open to persons of all religious denominations; and it was manifestly impossible to provide a course of professional education for the ministers of religion of those congregations who do not belong to the Established Church. It was equally impossible to institute any theological lectures for the instruction of lay students of different religious persuasions, which would not have been liable to grave objections; still less was it practicable to introduce any religious observances that could be generally complied with. In the Universities of Oxford and Cambridge, the students ... are placed in Colleges ... where it is necessary that religious instruction should be provided. In the case of the University of London, none of the students will reside within the walls; they will live in the houses of their parents or guardians; and those who come from a distance will live in houses selected by their friends, with such precautions for the safety of their morals and of their religious opinions as will naturally be adopted on the occasion. A plan is in contemplation ... by which those students who come from a distance may be boarded in houses where they will be under the guidance of persons of their own religious opinions, and where they will be subjected to rules of discipline for the protection of their morals. The religious education of the pupils, therefore, will be left to domestic superintendance....

The Council had many long and anxious deliberations upon this subject, which they felt to be of paramount importance; but they found it impossible to unite the principle of free admission to persons of all religious denominations with any plan of theological instruction, or any form of religious discipline; and they were thus compelled by necessity to leave this great and primary object of education, which they deem far too important for compromise, to the direction and superintendance of the natural guardians of the pupils.

3. *Of the different courses of study.*

... There will be two classes of students. The first class will consist of those who shall enter as *Members of the University*, intending to follow the regular course of academical instruction, whether for general or professional education. The second class will consist of *Occasional Students*; of those persons who, being already engaged in a profession, may still have leisure to improve their education by allotting a portion of each day to attendance on certain lectures. ...

The University year will consist of 9 months; the months of August, September, and October being the long vacation.... The hours of instruction will be from 8 in the morning to 4 in the afternoon.... On Saturday all lectures will be concluded by noon; and there will be short vacations at Christmas and Easter. ...

An Hospital capable of containing a sufficient number of patients to afford opportunities of clinical practice ... will be provided, as being an essential requisite of a medical school; and a connexion will be formed with some Dispensary at a convenient distance. ...

464. Advertisement in the *Morning Chronicle*, 26 Oct. 1809

The curriculum of the Scottish universities was wider than that of Oxford and Cambridge, and admission was not restricted, as it was in England, to members of the Established Church. The Scottish universities were organized on the Professorial, not the Tutorial, basis, and the professors were remunerated by fees levied on the students.

UNIVERSITY OF ST. ANDREWS

The Rev. JAMES HUNTER, L.L.D., Professor of Logic and Rhetoric in this University, who has been in the practice of receiving a few young men as BOARDERS, or DOMESTIC PUPILS, has at present ROOM for TWO more. All the ordinary branches of learning, including Latin, Greek, French, Mathematics, Logic, Ethics, Natural Philosophy and History, are taught by eminent Professors in a course of seven months, extending from November till May. Young men attending the University have access to a great public library. And there is in the place a respectable congregation in communion with the Church of England, under a regular clergyman of that Church. Mr. Hunter's pupils may either reside with him during the vacation or not, as they think proper. His terms, which will vary from one to two hundred pounds a year, according to the age of the pupil and the extent of the accommodation required, may be learned along with any other particulars, addressed to him at St. Andrews, N.B.

465. Prospectus of the New Academical Institution, Hackney, 24 April 1787

(Printed pamphlet.)

The Dissenting academies provided a higher education in which 'modern' subjects were extensively represented.

The committee for establishing the New Academical Institution among Protestant Dissenters, for the education of ministers and youth, have now the pleasure to inform the public, that the spacious and eligible house, which they have purchased in the parish of Hackney, will be opened for the reception of students, on the 29th day of September next. The situation of this house is recommended by a variety of local conveniences and advantages; and the committee will assiduously avail themselves of every circumstance that may be conducive to the health, moral conduct, and literary improvement of the young gentlemen, who shall be entrusted to their care. They beg leave to add, that it is a fundamental principle of this institution, that it will be open to persons of all denominations, who will be encouraged in forming their religious sentiments without restriction or imposition.

The course of education will be comprehensive and liberal, and adapted to youth in general, whether they are intended for civil or commercial life, or for any of the learned professions. This course will include the Latin, Greek, and Hebrew languages, Greek and Roman antiquities, ancient and modern geography, universal grammar, rhetoric and composition, chronology, history, civil and ecclesiastical, the principles of law and government, the several branches of mathematics, astronomy, natural and experimental philosophy and chemistry, logic, metaphysics and ethics, the evidences of religion, natural and revealed, theology, Jewish antiquities, and critical lectures on the scriptures.

The gentlemen who have engaged to conduct this plan of education, are, the Rev. Richard Price, D.D., F.R.S., Rev. Andrew Kippis, D.D., F.R.S. and S.A., Rev. Abraham Rees, D.D., F.R.S., Rev. Hugh Worthington, Rev. George Cadogan Morgan, Rev. John Kiddle.

The students will be instructed in the practice of elocution, by a person appointed for that purpose.

The usual course for young gentlemen not intended for the ministry, will be completed in three years: and with respect to those who shall continue longer in college, a proper plan of education will be pursued.

The commons will be provided by the committee; and the students will be under the more immediate direction and government of Dr. Rees, who will reside in a house contiguous to the main building, and of Mr. Kiddle, who will live in the college with the students.

The terms for each session, commencing on the third Monday in September, and closing on the first day of July, are 60 guineas, which will include apartments, board, and education. Students on the foundation will be provided for in these respects without expense: and the committee will encourage young persons intended for the ministry, whose friends are willing to defray the charges of their board and education, by a considerable abatement in the above terms.

It is scarcely necessary to observe, that the situation of this institution affords opportunity of obtaining the best means of instruction in French and other modern languages, drawing, &c., at a separate expense.

No divinity students will be admitted under the age of 16 years; nor any lay students under the age of 15 years, nor above the age of 18 years: and it is expected, that all students be well recommended both as to conduct and qualifications. . . .

466. Sixth-form examination paper in modern history at Harrow School, Nov. 1829

(A printed Paper preserved with the Palmerston MSS. at Broadlands.)

1. Who are the principal authorities for universal chronology?
2. Enumerate the various corrections which the solar year has undergone.
3. State the different modes of computing the year among the ancient Greeks, the Romans, the Jews, the Franks, the French, and the English.
4. Give an account of the Diocletian era, the mundane era of Constantinople, mundane era of modern Jews, Spanish era, era of Hegira, and Dionysian or Christian era.
5. Give the original site of the Vandals, Goths, Franks, Saxons, and Huns.
6. State the original sources from which we derive our knowledge of events from the reign of Nerva to that of Justinian.
7. Give an outline of the history of the Franks from their passage of the Rhine to the treaty of Verdun, with dates.
8. The conquests of the Visigoths and Vandals, with the ultimate fate of their monarchies, with dates.
9. When did the Romans abandon Britain? When and by whom was Christianity introduced into this country? What was the origin of the common law of England?
10. Draw a parallel between the characters of Alfred and Charlemagne.

467. Samuel Bamford's recollections of Manchester Free Grammar School

(*Early Days*, ed. H. Dunckley (1893), pp. 80-82.)

Samuel Bamford (1788-1872), the radical weaver and poet from Middleton, Lancashire, describes a typical grammar school at the opening of the nineteenth century.

. . . After a time I was sent to the Free Grammar School, with the almost forlorn hope that at a place of such high repute something would be done, or would accidentally occur, to awaken my dormant faculties, if faculties at all for the acquirement of book knowledge I had. The house apothecary, who could assume a most polished address, undertook to introduce me to the respected master of the lower school, at

this venerable and useful institution. All the rules and customs of such occasions the
old gentleman would, of course, be careful to observe. He first, therefore, took me
to a confectioner's shop in Smithy Door, where, having purchased a couple of pounds
of the best gingerbread, he toddled, and I after him, across the churchyard and down
Long Mill Gate, to the school; and having gained admittance, he respectfully presented
me to the master, with a request, on behalf of my father, that he would be so kind
as to afford me the benefit of his instruction. The master, receiving us courteously,
asked what were my present requirements, also my name, age, and place of residence,
which latter replies he entered in a book; and my conductor, depositing the gingerbread in a parcel on the table, together with a shilling, bowed and withdrew, leaving
me abashed and confused amid the gaze and observation of the scholars, which I did
not expect would be much in my favour, as I was weakly and ill-looking enough, and
the more so from wearing a white linen cap, which tied under my chin. On a sign
from the master a boy approached, and, taking me with one hand and the packet of
gingerbread with the other, he led me to his class, which was that of the spellers, into
which I was joyfully received. The boy who led me hither, and who was the head
one of his class, now went round and delivered to each boy of the class sitting in his
place a cake of the gingerbread, and continued so doing until the whole I had brought
was distributed. This was a very acceptable introduction to the boys; it was the
invariable custom of the lower school, and was always productive of a friendly
greeting towards the fresh comer; for my part, in five minutes I had a score or two
of new acquaintance, asking questions, giving me information, and ready to lend me
a helping hand in anything, especially so long as my gingerbread was sweet in their
mouths. Such was my introduction to, and thus I became the lowest scholar in the
lowest class of, the Free Grammar School.

My present instructor was a gentleman of probably 30 years of age, well-formed,
above the middle height, with his powdered hair turned back from his free open
countenance, and his face somewhat coloured by irruptions. His dress was such as
became his station, that of a curate of the Church. His coat, vest, and breeches were
of fine black cloth, the latter article of dress being held below the knee by a brace of
small silver buckles, his stockings were dark grey speckled, his shoes were also fastened
with silver buckles, and his cravat and linen were neatly adjusted, and very white.
Thus did the Reverend John Gaskell appear on that well-remembered morning when
he took me under his care; such was also his general mode of dress on other ordinary
occasions. The school was a large room of an oblong form, extending north and
south, and well lighted by large windows. At the northern end was a fireplace, with
a red cheerful fire glowing in the grate. The master's custom was to sit in an armed
chair, with his right towards the fire and his left arm resting on a square oaken table,
on which lay a newspaper or two, a magazine or other publication, a couple of canes
with the ends split, and a medley of boy's playthings, such as tops, whips, marbles,
apple-scrapers, nut-crackers, dragon banding, and such like articles. The scholars were
divided into six classes, namely, accidence, or introduction to Latin, higher Bible,
middle Bible, lower Bible, Testament, and spelling classes: the accidence class sat
opposite the master's face, and the higher Bible one was at his back. Each class sat on

a strong oaken bench, backed by a panel of the same, placed against the wall, with a narrow desk in front, so that all sat around the school in regular gradation. The spellers only had not a desk, they sat on forms outside the desk of the higher Bible class, they being considered as children amongst the boys. The boys of each class were placed according to their proficiency, and the first and second boys of the class exercised considerable authority over the others. The school hours were from 7 to 8.30 at morning, from 9.30 to 12 at noon, and from 2 till 5 afternoon. The master was seldom more than 5 minutes beyond the time, and on coming in, he first pulled off his hat, and his extra coat or handkerchief, if he brought such; he would then probably give his hands a warming at the fire, stamp the wet from his shoes, and turning his back to the pleasant warmth, he would take a survey of the muster already arrived. Every boy who now entered the school was bound to go up to the table and present his shoulders for a correction, and they in general got off with a slight cut or two of the cane, except frequent defaulters, and those were hit more severely, being often sent to their class writhing, to the amusement of their more orderly comrades. The mustering and flogging being over, the classes were severally called up, arranged round the table, and went through their lessons, the boy who in spelling or reading could readiest make out a word when those above him were at fault, moving up to their places, and thus the quickest spellers and readers were always towards the upper end of their class. When a boy had been at the head of his class some time, and especially if he happened to have some acquaintance amongst those of the next class above him, and they wished to have him amongst them, their head boy would take him by the hand, and leading him to the master, would say, "If you please, sir, must— (mentioning the surname) go into my class?" when a brief intimation, as a nod, a "yes", or "no", would decide the application, and the parties withdrew either elated with success or abashed by failure.

468. Number of children educated, free or as fee-payers, in the endowed and unendowed day schools of England in 1819

(*Parliamentary Papers*, 1820, XII, pp. 342–355.)

These tables were calculated from the returns called for by the Select Committee of 1818 (see No. 473). The totals for counties for which the returns were incomplete were calculated as averages.

COUNTIES	POPULA-TION, 1811.	POOR, 1815.	NUMBER OF CHILDREN Taught in the ENDOWED SCHOOLS.		NUMBER OF CHILDREN Taught in the UNENDOWED DAY SCHOOLS.	
			Free.	Pay.	Free.	Pay.
Bedford . . .	70,213	6,707	2,058	8	529	1,788
Berks . . .	118,277	17,535	2,110	195	3,814	4,154
Buckingham . .	117,650	14,822	1,615	156	2,295	3,425
Cambridge . . .	100,509	10,667	2,037	126	1,369	6,100
Chester . . .	227,031	17,944	2,683	784	3,180	6,214
Cornwall . . .	218,236	12,298	1,252	140	2,966	9,942
Cumberland . .	133,744	6,651	2,347	1,358	2,791	6,991
Derby . . .	185,487	12,938	2,792	1,033	2,936	8,218
Devon . . .	383,308	32,153	5,617	452	9,179	15,385
Dorset . . .	124,693	13,910	1,091	86	3,436	5,311
Durham . . .	177,964	13,460	2,211	968	2,569	12,443
Essex . . .	248,920	32,625	5,063	303	5,608	6,649
Gloucester . .	285,115	25,008	3,808	133	4,929	5,898
Hereford . .	93,455	9,990	1,693	204	2,116	1,695
Hertford . . .	108,857	11,379	1,616	39	3,049	3,331
Huntingdon . .	42,208	4,925	991	49	1,056	1,437
Kent . . .	373,095	43,004	7,103	371	9,746	11,858
Lancaster . .	828,309	38,692	10,519	1,909	6,994	19,211
Leicester . . .	150,419	14,434	2,804	158	1,839	4,948
Lincoln . . .	237,891	16,162	4,957	532	4,020	10,849
Middlesex . .	953,076	118,255	15,649	481	16,547	6,742
Monmouth . .	62,127	3,988	468	30	1,168	1,962
Norfolk . . .	291,947	31,267	3,010	713	5,100	11,595
Northampton .	141,353	15,692	3,932	318	2,807	4,160
Northumberland . .	172,161	12,826	1,577	665	2,543	11,216
Nottingham . .	162,900	11,345	2,349	303	2,181	8,241
Oxford . . .	119,190	15,032	2,265	107	2,337	3,519
Rutland . . .	16,380	1,055	269	74	607	790
Salop . . .	194,281	18,448	3,727	390	4,195	5,472
Somerset . . .	303,180	27,243	2,768	261	4,496	8,984
Southampton .	246,108	22,932	3,155	272	8,281	7,595
Stafford . . .	294,500	22,063	5,087	699	4,003	9,193
Suffolk . . .	234,211	26,215	2,981	521	4,497	8,551
Surrey . . .	321,537	23,036	6,174	42	6,348	6,619
Sussex . . .	190,083	25,310	1,997	530	6,882	8,625
Warwick . . .	228,735	20,207	4,907	293	2,706	7,053
Westmorland . .	45,922	3,212	2,347	892	48	2,759
Wilts . . .	193,818	25,830	2,308	196	2,267	5,920
Worcester . .	160,546	12,440	3,921	83	2,095	3,649
York, East Riding .	167,353	10,955	2,580	609	2,423	9,676
York, North Riding .	165,506	10,009	2,763	1,007	3,630	9,817
York, West Riding .	653,315	40,585	7,351	1,991	8,482	22,800
GRAND TOTAL .	9,543,610	853,249	145,952	19,481	168,064	310,785

Totals for England, Wales and Scotland

	Parochial Schools			Endowed Schools			Unendowed Day Schools			Sunday Schools	
	No. of Schools	No. of Children	Total Revenues	No. of Schools	No. of Children	Total Revenues	Dames Schools	Total Schools	No. of Children	No. of Schools	No. of Children
England				4,167	165,433	£300,525	3,102	14,282	478,849	5,162	452,817
Wales				209	7,625	£5,817	73	572	22,976	301	24,408
Scotland	942	54,161	£20,611	212	10,177	£13,679	257	2,479	112,187	807	53,449

469. Hannah More to the bishop of Bath and Wells, (Cowslip Green) 1801

(*Letters of Hannah More*, pp. 179–188.)

... When I settled in this country thirteen years ago, I found the poor in many of the villages in a deplorable state of ignorance and vice. There were, I think, no Sunday schools in the whole district, except one in my own parish, which had been established by our respectable rector, and another in the adjoining parish of Churchill. This drew me to the more neglected villages, whose distance made it very laborious. Not one school there did I ever attempt to establish without the hearty concurrence of the clergyman of the parish. My plan of instruction is extremely simple and limited. They learn, on week-days, such coarse works as may fit them for servants. I allow of no writing for the poor. My object is not to make fanatics but to train up the lower classes in habits of industry and piety. I knew no way of teaching morals but by teaching principles; or of inculcating Christian principles without imparting a good knowledge of scripture. I own I have laboured this point diligently. My sisters and I always teach them ourselves every Sunday, except during our absence in the winter. By being out about thirteen hours, we have generally contrived to visit two schools the same day, and to carry them to their respective churches. When we had more schools we commonly visited them on a Sunday. The only books we use in teaching are two little tracts, called 'Questions for the Mendip Schools' (to be had of Hatchard.) 'The Church Catechism' (these are framed, and half a dozen hung up in the room.) The Catechism, broken into short questions, spelling books, Psalter, Common Prayer, Testament, Bible. The little ones repeat 'Watts's Hymns.' The Collect is learned every Sunday. They generally learn the Sermon on the Mount, with many other chapters and psalms. Finding that what the children learned at school they commonly lost at home by the profaneness and ignorance of their parents, it occurred to me in some of the larger parishes to invite the latter to come at six on the Sunday evening, for an hour, to the school, together with the elder scholars. A plain printed sermon and a printed prayer is read to them, and a psalm is sung. I am not bribed by my taste, for, unluckily, I do not delight in music, but observing that singing is a help to devotion in others, I thought it right to allow the practice.

For many years I have given away annually nearly 200 Bibles, Common Prayer Books, and Testaments. To teach the poor to read without providing them with *safe* books, has always appeared to me an improper measure, and this consideration induced me to enter upon the laborious undertaking of the Cheap Repository Tracts.

In some parishes where the poor are numerous, such as Cheddar, and the distressed mining villages of Shipham and Rowbarrow, I have instituted, with considerable expense to myself, friendly benefit societies for poor women, which have proved a great relief to the sick and lying-in, especially in the late seasons of scarcity. . . .

I need not inform your lordship why the illiterate, when they become religious, are more liable to enthusiasm than the better-informed. They have also a coarse way of expressing their religious sentiments, which often appears to be enthusiasm, when it is only vulgarity or quaintness. But I am persuaded your lordship will allow that this does not furnish a reason why the poor should be left destitute of religious instruction. That the knowledge of the Bible should lay men more open to the delusions of fanaticism on the one hand, or of Jacobinism on the other, appears so unlikely, that I should have thought the probability lay all on the other side.

I do not vindicate enthusiasm, I dread it. But can the possibility that a few should become enthusiasts be justly pleaded as an argument for giving them *all* up to actual vice and barbarism? . . .

470. James McPhail to Lord Hawkesbury, 14 Feb. 1796

(*British Museum Additional MSS.* 38231, f. 15.)

Pitt proposed (unavailingly) in 1796 that children whose parents were in receipt of poor relief should be compelled to attend 'Schools of Industry'–establishments where they could be taught a trade, and where the sale of the products of their labour might pay the school's expenses. Many such schools were opened about this time.

. . . Mr. Pitt in his speech recommends the institution of national schools of industry; & my reason for writing this is to suggest that great utility which I conceive would also arise from the establishment of schools of morality–for I may safely say there are not one in 20 of the lower class which attend public worship–but instead of that we too often find many of them on the Sabbath day frequenting the ale-house & pilfering from the fences, hedges, turnip fields, &c. There are, to be sure, laws to punish for these things, but I apprehend it is best to endeavour to prevent than to punish. A great many of your Lordship's turnips were stolen last year, & I find it a difficult task this year to prevent them from a like disaster.

471. Joseph Lancaster's 'Improvements in Education'

(*Improvements in Education, as it respects the industrious classes of the community,* 2nd ed. 1803.)

Joseph Lancaster (1778–1838), the Quaker educationalist, took over a school in the Borough Road, Southwark, in 1801 and offered free education to children whose parents could not afford fees. Lack of funds to pay teachers caused him to devise his 'monitorial system' of instruction–a method independently developed by the Rev. Andrew Bell (1753–1832) at the Madras Male Orphan Asylum and published by him in England in 1797. The 'Madras system', however, attracted little attention until Lancaster's 'Improvements' appeared in 1803, after which time the system caught the public imagination as a cheap way of providing a rudimentary education for the poor. The Royal Lancasterian (later renamed the British and Foreign School Society) and the National Societies, formed in 1808 and 1811 respectively, on the principles of Lancaster and of Bell, the former providing a non-sectarian, the latter an Anglican education, were by 1832 responsible for most of the elementary education available to the English poor.

I. *An introductory account of the state of those schools in which the children of mechanics, &c. are generally educated.*

INITIATORY SCHOOLS. These are a description of schools that abound in every poor neighbourhood about London; they are frequented by boys and girls, indiscriminately, few of them above 7 years of age: the mistress is frequently the wife of some mechanic, induced to undertake this task, from a desire to increase a scanty income, or to add to her domestic comforts. The subjects of tuition are comprised in reading and needlework. The number of children that attend a school of this class is very fluctuating, and seldom exceeds 30; their pay very uncertain. Disorder, noise, &c. seem more the characteristic of these schools, than the improvement of the little ones who attend them. . . .

It is of peculiar importance to the poor, that these schools should be better regulated, as many children of that class have no education but what they obtain in them, and that at an early age, when totally unfit for other employ; . . . many poor children never obtain a second opportunity. Frequently their parents . . . must place them out to work as soon as they are fit for it, and then farewell to school, to which some would never have been sent, had they been fit for anything else. . . .

SECOND CLASS OF SCHOOLS. The masters of these are often the refuse of superior schools, and too often of society at large. The pay and number of scholars are alike low and fluctuating; of course there is little encouragement for steady men, either to engage, or continue in this line; it being impossible to keep school, defray its expenses, and do the children regular justice, without a regular income. Eventually, many schools, respectable in better times, are abandoned to men of any character, who use as much chicane to fill their pockets, as the most despicable pettifogger. Writing books, &c. scribbled through; whole pages filled with scrawls, to hasten the demand for fresh books. These schools are chiefly attended by the children of artificers, &c. whose pay fluctuates with their employ; and is sometimes withheld by bad principle. . . . It is to be regretted, that some especial Act of the Legislature has not effectually secured the pay of the teachers of youth. . . .

The complaint of bad pay, and difficulty in obtaining it, is almost generally reiterated through every department of education. It operates powerfully to depress and discourage the energy of the teacher's mind; in particular, when (as is commonly the case) much of that part of the business of the school, which is merely mechanical, falls on the master's shoulders; it becomes, indeed, laborious, with the addition of a poor consolation, that, it is worse paid for than any other employ in London.

When a man settles himself to this line as an employ, his prospects are often bounded for life. A merchant may extend his dealings, a tradesman may increase his customers, but the teacher's income depends solely upon the number of his scholars. If he is a just man, he ought not to exceed a certain number, without assistance in tuition of some kind. Here then is the *ne plus ultra* of his expectations. . . . It is not much to be wondered at, if these discouraging circumstances often produce deviations from strict rectitude. . . . The drunkenness of a schoolmaster is almost proverbial. Those who mean well are not able to do so: poverty prevents it; and the number of teachers, who are men of liberal minds, are few; yet, not being sensible of the incalculable advantages arising from system and order, it is no wonder if it is at a very low ebb among them. . . . The want of system and order is almost uniform in every class of schools within the reach of the poor. . . .

At a moderate calculation, among a million of persons inhabiting the metropolis, there are, at least, 25,000 children who attend these schools, and cost their parents as many pounds sterling, per annum. What a noble fund for education would this be, if properly employed. And how lamentable a thing it is, that a very large portion of it should be wasted, from irregularity in the parents, or want of judgment in the master. . . .

II. *Hints respecting the formation of a Society for improving the state, and facilitating the means of education among the industrious classes of the community.*

It appears, from the preceding accounts, that reformation in these schools is absolutely necessary; it remains to consider the means best suited to that end. . . .

I am sometimes sorry to hear sensible, intelligent men, talk of reformation in this respect by a compulsive law. Coercion of any kind grates upon our very hearing, and is the most disgusting, uncouth word in the British vocabulary. . . . I am . . . decided in the opinion, that teachers of any spirit will not bear attempts to cudgel them into reformation, however respectably sanctioned. . . .

A Society for this purpose should be established on general Christian principles. . . . Let the friends of youth, among every denomination of Christians, . . . laying aside all religious differences in opinion, . . . pursue two grand objects:—the promotion of good morals; and the instruction of youth in useful learning, adapted to their respective situations. . . . We have many Societies, whose benevolent exertions contribute much to the public good; but among them, I know of none, except the Sunday School establishment, which operates, in a general way, to instruct the poor, and improve their morals; and that, from the short time the children attend school, is but limited in its effects. Indeed, it is not to be wondered at, that no general plan of this kind has been adopted; there are few things in which it would appear, at first sight, that the different religious interests of the sectarians would clash more: and so they must, if a plan of this kind is eagerly pursued by one or more parties, with a view to increase proselytes, or make it a vehicle to convey their favourite tenets. It has been generally conceived, that if any particular sect obtained the principal care in a national system of education, that party would soon be likely to possess the greatest power and influence in the state. Fear that the clergy should aggrandize themselves too much has produced opposition from Dissenters to any proposal of the kind; on the other hand, the clergy have opposed any thing of this nature which might originate with Dissenters, locally or generally, fearing an increase of the dissenting influence. . . . Many thousands of youth have been deprived of the benefit of education thereby, their morals ruined, and talents irretrievably lost to society, for want of cultivation; while two parties have been idly contending who should bestow it. . . .

The principal evils attendant on the usual mode of education among the poor, are, first, improper and immoral persons having youth under their care: secondly, the poverty often distinguishing many teachers of this class, and the consequent want of that respect from parents, which contributes materially to support the master's authority: thirdly, what is of equal magnitude, the uncertainty, not only the poor, but persons in circumstances rather superior, are under, as to the character of the teacher they send their children to . . . : fourthly, the bad accommodations common school rooms afford to the poor children who attend them; many of whom suffer materially in health, by the confinement in places, that, in summer, may be compared to a baker's oven; in winter, to the peak of Derby: fifthly, the almost total want of system, and a proper stimulus to action in the minds of teachers and scholars: sixthly, the diversity of methods of teaching used in different schools. . . . The object of the society proposed, should be to remedy these, and other attendant evils. . . .

The first object of the proposed Society should be, to provide suitable masters and mistresses for any schools they might choose to establish, and to encourage such persons who have schools of their own, to do their duty by the Society's (respectable) patronage, which, properly bestowed, and avowed publicly, would (with its attendant benefits) be very valuable, and conduce much to the credit of the teachers possessing it: so, on the other hand, it would tend to expel immoral and wicked teachers from the profession, as such must ever remain destitute of its protection. . . .

I do not think it a commendable thing for any body of men to infringe the rights of individuals; therefore, it would not be proper for a society to dictate to teachers, having schools of their own, how, or what, they should teach. I conceive any person, whose moral character and abilities were likely to make him serviceable to the rising generation, should be an object of the Society's protection, let his denomination of religion be what it may; and let him pursue whatever methods, of religious or other instruction, his sincere and best intentions may dictate. I am an advocate for kind treatment on the part of the proposed Society, and flatter myself, that the good sense of persons engaged in the education of youth, would induce them to try, or adopt, such measures as the Society might recommend, if the advantage was obvious, and practice easy; and this too, without being cudgelled into obedience. . . .

It is very poor encouragement for a man, having a family, to pass laboriously away the prime of his days, with the cheerless expectation of ending them in a work-house or prison. To remedy this, a Friendly Society might be formed, composed of persons who were teachers, under the patronage of the Society . . . and its funds might be formed into a very respectable stock by the addition of public donations . . . to defray the expense of sickness and funerals; and, perhaps, a liberal and honourable support for old age. In addition to this, a fund might be established for the occasional relief of deserving teachers in distress. . . .

We daily witness the beneficial effect produced to the community by the institution of premiums, held out to encourage the inventions of ingenious mechanics. As the human mind is nearly the same in every class, . . . it is rational to suppose, that similar encouragement would produce a similar, if not superior effect among the teachers of youth. . . .

It might be proper that the Society should publish in the newspapers, the list of prizes, &c. with the names and dwellings of the persons who obtain them: . . . recommending him and his school to the respect and patronage of the public. . . .

The institution of a public library, containing books on education, would be well adapted for the information of teachers, many of whom are not able to purchase expensive publications on those subjects. . . .

An additional object would be worthy the Society's notice; to enforce, as much as possible, the regular attendance of the children at school. . . . Premiums might be instituted, at the public expense, for boys whose improvement in learning should merit it. . . .

PART III

Some account of the rise and progress of an institution for improving the plan, and facilitating the means, of attaining primary education amongst the industrious classes of the community, established in the Borough Road, Southwark: wherein 300 children are educated, and trained to habits conducive to the welfare of society.

. . . The Institution, which a benevolent Providence has been pleased to make me the happy instrument of bringing into usefulness, was begun in the year 1798. The intention was, to afford children of mechanics, &c. instruction in reading, writing, and arithmetic, at about half the usual price. As soon as the Institution became known it was well attended by scholars, whose number soon exceeded 80. In this situation, as master of the school, I have continued to this time. . . .

From this time the internal organisation of the school was gradually and materially altered for the better. The public reputation of it also increased, to such a degree, that more than 200 scholars were admitted in about eight months. . . .

My school is attended by 300 scholars. The *whole* system of tuition is almost entirely conducted by boys. . . . The school is divided into classes, to each of these a lad is appointed as monitor: he is responsible for the morals, improvement, good order, and cleanliness of the whole class. It is his duty to make a daily, weekly, and monthly report of progress, specifying the number of lessons performed, boys present, absent, &c. &c. As we naturally expect the boys who teach others to read, to leave school when their education is complete, and do not wish that they should neglect their own improvement in other studies, they are instructed to train other lads as assistants, who, in future, may supply their place, and in the meantime leave them to improve in other branches of learning. To be a monitor is coveted by the whole school, it being an office at once honourable and productive of emolument. . . .

This system of tuition is mutually for the advantage of the lads who teach, and those who are taught; by it the path of learning is strewed with flowers; for the monitors have rewards attached to the proper discharge of their respective duties. . . .

. . . It is now time to give some account of our improved methods of tuition. . . . The method of spelling seems to be the most excellent, it being entirely an addition to the regular course of studies, without interfering with, or deranging them in the least. It commands attention, gratifies the active disposition of youth, and is an excellent introduction and auxiliary to writing. It supersedes, in a great measure, the use of books in tuition, while (to speak moderately) it doubles the actual improvement of the children. It is as simple an operation as can well be conceived.–Thus, supply 20 boys with slates and pencil, and pronounce any word for them to write, suppose it is the word 'ab-so-lu-ti-on;' they are obliged to listen with attention, to catch the sound of every letter as it falls from their teacher's lips; again, they have to retrace the idea of every letter, and the pronounciation of the word, as they write it on the slates. . . .

Now these 20 boys, if they were at a common school, would each have a book, and, one at a time, would read or spell to their teacher, while the other 19 were looking at their books, or about them, as they pleased; or, if their eyes are rivetted on their books, by terror and coercion, can we be sure that the attention of their minds is engaged as appearance seems to speak it is. On the contrary, when they have slates, the 20th boy may read to the teacher, while the other 19 are spelling words on the slate, instead of sitting idle. The class, by this means, will spell, write, and read at the same instant of time. In addition to this, the same trouble which teaches 20, will suffice to teach 60 or 100, by employing some of the senior boys to inspect the slates of the others, they not omitting to spell the word themselves, and on a signal given by them to the principal teacher, that the work is finished by all the boys they overlook, he is informed when to dictate another to the class. This experiment has been repeatedly practised by 112 and 128 boys at once; and judicious persons, good judges on the subject of education, who were present, were convinced that the same trouble was sufficient to teach 200 boys, or more, on the same plan.

But if the individual advantage derived from this method in tuition is great, what must the aggregate be? If 20 boys spell 200 words each, the same number spelt by 60 boys must produce a great increase of total. Each boy can spell 100 words in a morning: if 100 scholars do this 200 mornings yearly, the following will be the total of their efforts towards improvement:

$$100 \text{ words}$$
$$\underline{200 \text{ mornings}}$$
$$20{,}000 \text{ words each boy per ann.}$$
$$\underline{100 \text{ boys}}$$
$$2{,}000{,}000 \text{ total words spelt by 100 boys per ann.} \ldots$$

. . . This is entirely an addition to their other studies, without the least additional trouble on the part of the teacher, in tuition; without any extra time of attendance being requisite from the scholar; without deranging or impeding his attention to other studies; at least doubling his efforts towards proficiency, and possessing these advantages . . . it effectually commands quietness, by commanding attention; and as certainly prevents idleness, by actively employing every boy in the class at the same instant of time. . . .

In education nothing can be more important than economy of time, even when we have a reasonable prospect of a good portion of it at our disposal, but it is most peculiarly necessary in primary schools, and in the instruction of the poor: cases wherein the pupil seldom has too much on his hands; and very often a fine genius or noble talents are lost to the state, and to mankind, from the want of it. If we wish to do the best for the welfare of youth, and to promote their interest through life, it will be well for us to study economy of their precious time. . . .

The books made use of in this school, as reading lessons, are the Bible, Testament, Turner's Introduction to the Arts and Sciences, Trimmer's Introduction to the Knowledge of Nature and Reading the Scriptures, Martinet's Catechism of Nature, and Watts's Hymns for Children.

I ought not to close my account, without acknowledging the obligation I lie under to Dr. Bell, of the Male Asylum at Madras, who so nobly gave up his time and liberal salary, that he might perfect that Institution which flourished greatly under his fostering care. He published a tract, in 1798, entitled, 'An Experiment on Education, made at the Male Asylum at Madras, suggesting a System whereby a School or Family may teach itself, under the Superintendence of the Master, or Parent'. *Cadell and Davies, Strand*, price 1s. From this publication I have adopted several useful *hints*; I beg leave to recommend it to the attentive perusal of the friends of education and of youth. . . . Dr. Bell had 200 boys, who instructed themselves, made their own pens, ruled their books, and did all that labour in school which, among a great number, is light; but resting on the shoulders of the well-meaning and honest, though unwise teacher, often proves too much for his health, and embitters, or perhaps costs him his life. I much regret that I was not acquainted with the beauty of his system, till somewhat advanced in my plan; if I had known it, it would have saved me much trouble, and some retrograde movements. . . .

472. Debates in the House of Commons and the House of Lords on Whitbread's Parochial Schools Bill, 13 July and 11 Aug. 1807

(Cobbett's *Parliamentary Debates*, IX, 798–806, 1174–1178.)

Whitbread's Bill, which was only part of a scheme to reform the whole of the poor laws, would have established a school in every parish, to be maintained by the rates, on the Scottish model. It was rejected in the Lords, largely because of the objections of the bishops and Anglican clergy.

House of Commons, 13 July:

Davies Giddy . . . However specious in theory the project might be of giving education to the labouring classes of the poor, it would, in effect, be found to be prejudicial to their morals and happiness; it would teach them to despise their lot in life, instead of making them good servants in agriculture and other laborious employments to which their rank in society had destined them; instead of teaching them subordination it would render them factious and refractory, as was evident in the manufacturing counties; it would enable them to read seditious pamphlets, vicious books, and publications against Christianity; it would render them insolent to their superiors; and in a few years the result would be that the Legislature would find it necessary to direct the strong arm of power towards them, and to furnish the executive magistrates with much more vigorous laws than were now in force. Besides, if the Bill were to pass into a law, it would go to burden the country with a most enormous and incalculable expense, and to load the industrious orders of society with still heavier imposts. . . .

Mr. Morris . . . agreed that the establishment of a system so universal must entail upon the country an incalculable expense, at least 2s. in the pound upon the poor's rates; and he thought that as a national system of education, the expense should rather be paid out of the Consolidated Fund than by a local assessment upon parishes. In Scotland . . . the public charge upon the country was but £6,000 a year for allowances to schoolmasters for the poor, while the remainder was made up by charges upon the landlord and tenant or by voluntary subscription; while in England a single charitable society for propagating Gospel knowledge expended £4,000 a year, being two-thirds of the whole public charge in Scotland. . . .

Mr. Rose . . . had no doubt that the poor ought to be taught to read; as to writing, he had some doubt, because those who had learnt to write well, were not willing to abide at the plough, but looked to a situation in some counting house. . . .

Mr. Whitbread . . . All the lower orders had an education of some sort, good or bad. It had been said that it might be as well to teach them to play on the fiddle or to be skilful boxers. This practice of boxing, by-the-bye, as a mode of settling differences, he thought ought not to be discouraged, because it was much better than the stiletto. But a fiddler or boxer would not be the worse for being able to write and read. At St. Giles's there was an education: children were taught to pick pockets and to go on from one degree of dexterity in wickedness to another, till they came to the gallows; and most of the unhappy creatures who perished there were such as were unable to read or write. . . . He denied that the people, if generally educated, would be averse to continue at the plough. On the contrary, the ground would be better tilled, masters better served, &c. The hon. gent. then replied to the argument about their reading political pamphlets. When a riotous mob was assembled, it was called an illiterate mob. If one man had knowledge, he would have a much better chance of leading a thousand ignorant creatures to mischief than if they were all so far informed as to read what might appear on both sides of the question. . . . It was said that the effect of the Bill would be to impose an additional rate of a shilling in the pound. He answered, no. It was said, it would do away charities. It would do no such thing. His aim was to provide schools and schoolmasters where they were wanted; where they were not, the magistrates would have the power to suspend the operation of the law. The business was committed to the magistrates, who were the most proper persons to carry the Act into execution. The system of magistracy had defects; but in what other country was there a body so excellent? . . .

The Chancellor of the Exchequer [Spencer Perceval] . . . feared . . . that the kind of education here proposed, though it might give learning, would not contribute much to diffuse industry, religion or morality. He feared a general legislative establishment would injure and destroy the voluntary establishments for public education now existing. . . . The education proposed would disqualify the persons possessing it from the most necessary and useful description of labour. The Quakers were mentioned as a class universally educated. The example strengthened his argument, for he never knew of an agricultural Quaker. He wished the Bill to be made as perfect as possible, though he did not think it advisable ultimately to adopt it, and without a prospect of ultimate adoption it would perhaps be useless labour to improve the plan.

House of Lords, 11 August:

The Lord Chancellor [Eldon] opposed the Bill in its present shape, though he was by no means unfriendly to the principle of diffusing instruction as generally and as widely as possible. . . . It tended to a departure from the great principle of instruction in this country, by taking it in a great measure out of the superintendence and control of the clergy. . . . He never would agree to any [Bill] that left matters of this nature to be judged of and decided by the majority of the inhabitants of a parish. . . .

The Archbishop of Canterbury trusted he should not be considered hostile to the principle of diffusing instruction among the poor, although he should oppose the further progress of this measure. . . . The provisions of the Bill left little or no control to the minister in his parish. This would go to subvert the first principles of education in this country, which had hitherto been, and he trusted would continue to be, under the control and auspices of the Establishment, and their Lordships would feel how dangerous it might be to innovate in such matters. . . .

Earl Stanhope . . . Was it reasonable or just to say that the children of Catholics, Presbyterians, Quakers and all the other innumerable sects of dissenters from the Established Church in this country, were to be debarred all sources of public education, supported by public benevolence, unless they were to become converts to our established religion? Would the Right Rev. prelate contend that because the Catholic religion was the established one in Canada, no poor Protestants should be educated there unless he was allowed to be brought up as a Catholic? . . . He could not see that its [the Bill's] purpose had anything to do with sects of religion. It was merely to teach its objects spelling, reading, writing and arithmetic for purposes useful in life; and in a manufacturing country like this, when so much of excellence in our productions depended on a clear understanding and some degree of mathematical and mechanical knowledge, which it was impossible to attain without first receiving the rudiments and foundation this Bill proposed, the superiority of workmen with some education, over those who had none, must be sensibly felt by all the great manufacturers in the country. . . .

473. Report from the Select Committee on the Education of the Lower Orders, 3 June 1818

(Hansard's *Parliamentary Debates*, XXXVIII, 1207–1212.)

Henry Brougham was chairman of this important committee, and he also secured a further inquiry into the state and misappropriation of charitable funds for popular education. In 1820 he introduced what was to have been the resulting legislation—a parish schools Bill, to set up a school in each parish to be maintained from the rates, from parental contributions, and from the educational charities. He hoped to win the support of the Anglicans, who had wrecked Whitbread's Bill in 1807, by giving the Church control over the schools, but the Bill had then to be dropped owing to the fierce opposition of Protestant Dissenters and Roman Catholics.

Your Committee rejoice in being able to state, that since their first appointment in 1816, when they examined the state of the Metropolis, there is every reason to believe that the exertions of charitable individuals and public bodies have increased, notwithstanding the severe pressure of the times; and that a great augmentation has taken place in the means provided for the instruction of the poor in that quarter. They are happy in being able to add, that the discussion excited by the first Report, and the arguments urged in the Committee to various patrons of charities who were examined as witnesses, have had the salutary effect of improving the administration of those institutions and inculcating the importance of rather bestowing their funds in merely educating a larger number, than in giving both instruction and other assistance to a more confined number of children. As the management of those excellent establishments is necessarily placed beyond the control of the Legislature, it is only by the effects of such candid discussions that improvements in them can be effected.

Since the inquiries of your Committee have been extended to the whole island, they have had reason to conclude that the means of educating the poor are steadily increasing in all considerable towns as well as in the metropolis. A circular letter has been addressed to all the clergy in England, Scotland and Wales, requiring answers to queries. It is impossible to bestow too much commendation upon the alacrity shown by those reverend persons in complying with this requisition, and the honest zeal which they displayed to promote the great object of universal education, is truly worthy of the pastors of the people, and the teachers of that gospel which was preached to the poor. . . .

It appears clearly from the returns, as well as from other sources, that a very great deficiency exists in the means of educating the poor, wherever the population is thin and scattered over country districts. The efforts of individuals combined in Societies are almost wholly confined to populous places.

Another point to which it is material to direct the attention of Parliament, regards the two opposite principles, of founding schools for children of all sorts, and for those only who belong to the Established Church. Where the means exist of erecting two schools, one upon each principle, education is not checked by the exclusive plan being adopted in one of them, because the other may comprehend the children of sectaries. In places where only one school can be supported, it is manifest that any regulations which exclude Dissenters, deprive the poor of that body of all means of education.

Your Committee, however, have the greatest satisfaction in observing that in many schools where the national system is adopted, an increasing degree of liberality prevails, and that the Church Catechism is only taught, and attendance at the established place of public worship only required, of those whose parents belong to the Establishment; due assurance being obtained that the children of sectaries shall learn the principles and attend the ordinances of religion, according to the doctrines and forms to which their families are attached.

It is with equal pleasure that your Committee have found reason to conclude that the Roman Catholic poor are anxious to avail themselves of those Protestant schools established in their neighbourhood, in which no catechism is taught; and they indulge a hope that the clergy of that persuasion may offer no discouragement to their attendance, more especially as they appear, in one instance, to have contributed to the support of schools, provided that no catechism was taught, and no religious observances exacted. It is contrary to the doctrine as well as discipline of the Romish

Church, to allow any Protestant to interfere with those matters, and consequently it is impossible for Romanists to send their children to any school where they form part of the plan.

Your Committee are happy in being able to state that in all the returns, and in all the other information laid before them, there is the most unquestionable evidence that the anxiety of the poor for education continues not only unabated, but daily increasing; that it extends to every part of the country, and is to be found equally prevalent in those smaller towns and country districts, where no means of gratifying it are provided by the charitable efforts of the richer classes.

In humbly suggesting what is fit to be done for promoting universal education, your Committee do not hesitate to state that two different plans are advisable, adapted to the opposite circumstances of the town and country districts. Wherever the efforts of individuals can support the requisite number of schools, it would be unnecessary and injurious to interpose any parliamentary assistance. But your Committee have clearly ascertained that in many places private subscriptions could be raised to meet the yearly expenses of a school, while the original cost of the undertaking, occasioned chiefly by the erection and purchase of the school-house, prevents it from being attempted.

Your Committee conceive that a sum of money might be well employed in supplying this first want, leaving the charity of individuals to furnish the annual school provision requisite for continuing the school, and possibly for repaying the advance. . . .

In the numerous districts where no aid from private exertions can be expected, and where the poor are manifestly without adequate means of instruction, your Committee are persuaded that nothing can supply the deficiency but the adoption, under certain material modifications, of the parish school system, so usefully established in the northern part of the island, ever since the latter part of the seventeenth century, and upon which many important details will be found in the Appendix.

The modifications will be dictated principally by the necessity of attending to the distinction, already pointed out, between districts where private charity may be expected to furnish the means of education, and those where no such resource can be looked to. . . . It may be fair and expedient to assist the parishes where no school-houses are erected, with the means of providing them, so as only to throw upon the inhabitants the burthen of paying the schoolmaster's salary, which ought certainly not to exceed £24 a year. It appears to your Committee that a sufficient supply of schoolmasters may be procured for this sum, allowing them the benefits of taking scholars, who can afford to pay, and permitting them of course to occupy their leisure hours in other pursuits. The expense attending this invaluable system in Scotland is found to be so very trifling that it is never made the subject of complaint by any of the landholders.

Your Committee forbear to inquire minutely in what manner this system ought to be connected with the Church Establishment. That such a connexion ought to be formed appears manifest; it is dictated by a regard to the prosperity and stability of both systems, and in Scotland the two are mutually connected together. But a difficulty arises in England, which is not to be found there. The great body of the Dissenters from the Scottish Church differ little, if at all, in doctrine from the Establishment; they are separated only by certain opinions of a political rather than a religious nature, respecting the right of patronage, and by some shades of distinction as to Church discipline; so that they may conscientiously send their children to parish schools connected with the Establishment and teaching its catechism. In England the case is widely different. . . . To place the choice of the schoolmaster in the parish vestry, subject to the approbation of the parson, and the visitation of the diocesan; but to provide that the children of sectarians shall not be compelled to learn any catechism or attend any church, other than those of their parents, seems to your Committee the safest path by which the Legislature can hope to obtain the desirable objects of security to the Establishment on the one hand, and justice to the Dissenters on the other.

The more extended inquiries of your Committee this Session have amply confirmed the opinion which a more limited investigation had led them to form two years ago, upon the neglect and abuse of charitable funds connected with education. . . . Although in many cases those large funds appear to have been misapplied through ignorance, or mismanaged through carelessness, yet . . . some instances of abuse have presented themselves, of such a nature as would have led them to recommend at an earlier period of the Session, the institution of proceedings for more promptly checking misappropriations, both in the particular cases, and by the force of a salutary example. From the investigations of the Commission about to be issued under the authority of an Act of Parliament, much advantage may be expected; and though it would not become your Committee to anticipate the measures which the wisdom of the Legislature may adopt in consequence of those inquiries, with a view to provide a speedy and cheaper remedy for the evil than the ordinary tribunals of the country afford; yet your Committee cannot avoid hoping that the mere report and publication of the existing abuses will have a material effect in leading the parties concerned, to correct them, and that even the apprehension of the inquiry about to be instituted may in the mean time produce a similar effect. . . .

474. Henry Brougham on the Mechanics Institutes

(*Practical Observations upon the Education of the People* . . . (1825), pp. 17–32.)

Brougham's *Practical Observations* went through twenty editions in a year. Its outcome was the formation of the Society for the Diffusion of Useful Knowledge (see No. 475) in the same year.

. . . It is now fit that we advert to the progress that has already been made in establishing this system of instruction. Its commencement was the work of Dr. Birkbeck, to whom the people of this island owe a debt of gratitude, the extent of which it would not be easy, perhaps in the present age not possible, to describe . . . Dr. Birkbeck, before he settled in London, where he has since reached the highest station in the medical profession, resided for some time in Glasgow as Professor in the Anderson College; and about the year 1800, he announced a course of lectures on Natural Philosophy, and its application to the Arts, for the instruction of mechanics. But a few at the first availed themselves of this advantage; by degrees, however, the extraordinary perspicuity of the teacher's method, the judicious selection of his experiments, and the natural attractions of the subject, to men whose lives were spent in directing or witnessing operations, of which the principles were now first unfolded to them, proved successful in diffusing a general taste for the study; and when he left Glasgow two or three years afterwards, about 700 eagerly and constantly attended the class....

... [In] 1821 Edinburgh adopted the plan with some variations. ...

The complete success of Dr. Birkbeck's plan both at Glasgow originally, and afterwards in a place abounding far less with artisans, very naturally suggested the idea of giving its principles a more general diffusion, by the only means which seem in this country calculated for universally recommending any scheme–its adoption in London. An Address was published by Messrs. Robertson and Hodgkin, in the Mechanics Magazine, October 1823; and the call was answered promptly by Dr. Birkbeck himself, and other friends of education, as well as by the master mechanics and workmen of the metropolis. A meeting was held in November; the Mechanics Institution was formed; a subscription opened; and a set of regulations adopted. Of these by far the most important and one which in common, I believe, with all my colleagues, I consider to be altogether essential, provides that the committee of management shall be chosen by the whole students, and consist of at least two-thirds working men. The plan was so speedily carried into execution, that in January Dr. Birkbeck, our president, most appropriately opened the Institution with an introductory address to many hundred workmen, crowding from great distances in the worst season and after the toils of the day were over, to slake that thirst of knowledge which forms the most glorious characteristic of the age. . . . In the course of the year, lectures were delivered by Mr. Phillips on chemistry, Mr. Dotchin on geometry, Dr. Birkbeck on hydrostatics, Mr. Cooper on the application of chemistry to the Arts,[1] Mr. Newton on Astronomy, and Mr. Black on the French language, to great and increasing numbers of workmen. About a thousand now belong to the Institution, and pay 20s. a year. Temporary accommodation has hitherto been provided at the chapel in Monkwell-street, formerly Dr. Lindsay's. . . . But extensive premises have been procured in Southampton Buildings, for the permanent seat of the Institution; and the foundation has been laid there of a spacious lecture-room, and other suitable apartments for the library and apparatus. The sum required for these buildings exceeds £3,000; and it has been generously advanced by Dr. Birkbeck. Others have made presents of money, books, and apparatus; and £1,000 [has been given by] . . . Sir Francis Burdett. . . .

The proceedings in London gave a great and general impulse to the friends of education in the country, and the town of Newcastle-upon-Tyne was the first to profit by it. An Institution for the instruction of mechanics by books, lectures, and scientific meetings, was established in March, 1824. . . . [Others were shortly afterwards founded in] Kendal, . . . Carlisle, . . . Hawick, . . . Haddington, . . . Alnwick, . . . Manchester, . . . Leeds. . . .

The Institutions which I have hitherto mentioned are formed avowedly for

[1] *i.e.* technology.

lectures as well as for reading, and most of them have already been able to establish lectures. Some are by their plan confined to reading, and have not hitherto contemplated any further instruction; but they may easily make the step. That of Liverpool deserves the first notice, as being earliest in point of time. . . .

There are other Mechanics Institutions respecting which I have not the details. . . . It should seem that a little exertion alone is wanting to introduce the system universally; and this is the moment beyond all doubt, best fitted for the attempt, when wages are good, and the aspect of things peaceful. . . .

I rejoice to think that it is not necessary to close these observations by combating objections to the diffusion of science among the working classes, arising from considerations of a political nature. Happily the time is past and gone when bigots could persuade mankind that the lights of philosophy were to be extinguished as dangerous to religion; and when tyrants could proscribe the instructors of the people as enemies to their power. It is preposterous to imagine that the enlargement of our acquaintance with the laws which regulate the universe, can dispose to unbelief. It may be a cure for superstition—for intolerance it will be the most certain cure; but a pure and true religion has nothing to fear from the greatest expansion which the understanding can receive by the study either of matter or of mind. The more widely science is diffused, the better will the Author of all things be known. . . .

To the Upper Classes of society, then, I would say, that the question no longer is whether or not the people shall be instructed—for that has been determined long ago, and the decision is irreversible—but whether they shall be well or ill taught—half informed or as thoroughly as their circumstances permit and their wants require. Let no one be afraid of the bulk of the community becoming too accomplished for their superiors. . . . The worst consequence that can follow to their superiors will be, that to deserve being called their *betters*, they too must devote themselves more to the pursuit of solid and refined learning; the present public seminaries must be enlarged; and some of the greater cities of the kingdom, especially the metropolis, must not be left destitute of the regular means within themselves of scientific education. . . .

475. The Society for the Diffusion of Useful Knowledge

(*Edinburgh Review* (Oct. 1829), pp. 181–193.)

. . . The great objects of the Society are to furnish the means of instruction to those who are desirous of acquiring it, and to excite the desire of those who are indifferent about it. A vast proportion of the community are now sufficiently educated to be able to read, but of these there are great numbers who can hardly be said to derive much benefit from this power. They read but little, and what they read is of little use to them. This arises, in some, from want of time and money; in others, from want of inclination; in not a few, from both causes. Many of the poor are anxious for books of useful learning, but they cannot afford to buy them; or, when they have made a shift to procure them, they find them too abstruse for their understanding, in the limited time they have to bestow on their perusal. Many, in easy circumstances, have money and time at their command, but want books in which they can learn branches of useful knowledge without the help of a teacher. But many are also to be found, both in the wealthier and the poorer classes, whose minds are listless, or engrossed with other pursuits, occupied with business, enervated by indolent habits–and who regard the effort of gaining knowledge as a toil, the pain of which is inadequately recompensed by the acquisition. To supply what is wanted by all these portions of the community, has been the purpose of the Society's operations.

The Library of Useful Knowledge is intended to furnish treatises on every branch of science and history, at the lowest possible price, and suited to every reader's capacity; from him who is ignorant of the first elements of science, to him who would reach its greatest heights. Sixty of these treatises have now been published: among these are nine containing the History of Greece, which, with the Chronology and Index, is sold in a five shilling volume, containing as much matter as is usually contained in three volumes at four-and-twenty shillings. Another volume, containing one half of Natural Philosophy, is also now completed, and only two or three treatises are wanting to finish the second volume, which will complete the whole of Natural Philosophy. It is stated in the Yearly Report that popular introductions to the subjects of astronomy, mechanics and optics, are preparing, for the purpose of teaching as much of these sciences as can be communicated to persons wholly un-acquainted with the mathematics. And, in the meantime, the truly admirable Glossary and explanation of scientific terms, which has been published to the first volume of Natural Philosophy, of itself almost supplies this desideratum as to two of the three subjects. . . .

Supposing the remaining parts of physical and mathematical science to require sixty more treatises, while their applications to the arts occupy [an]other sixty, and 120 are given to the other sciences, and ten to history, the whole Library, consisting of 400 treatises, and containing matter equal to that of forty common octavo volumes, will be sold for ten pounds; or for eleven guineas, including an Atlas of sixty maps; while complete works on each separate branch of knowledge may be obtained for four or five shillings; and upon subdivisions of these branches, for a shilling or even sixpence.

There will also be a gradation in the treatises upon subjects of difficulty, so that readers of every class, in respect of previous acquirements, may be suited; and those who have all to learn, may teach themselves, provided they can only read. . . . It is certain that if you make anything, valuable in itself, cheap, you increase the demand for it; and as the difficulties of acquiring knowledge are another impediment in the way of indolent persons, whatever lessens these, will encourage them to think of learning; so that, by making science at once cheap and easy, a considerable stimulus is given to the desire of attaining it.

This, however, we are well aware, is not sufficient encouragement for the love of useful information; and accordingly, the *Library of Entertaining Knowledge* has been instituted, for the purpose of turning to some account the reading of that large class, in every rank of the community, who are not averse to all reading, but will consent only to read what is amusing. So large a portion of important information may be conveyed in this shape, that the greatest benefit is to be expected from this Library. Since we last mentioned it, there have been published five parts; that is, a second on Menageries; two on Vegetable Substances used in the Arts, comprising timber-trees and fruits; one upon the Pursuit of Knowledge in difficult circumstances, including Anecdotes of self-taught men; and one upon Insect Architecture, a subject of the most curious and interesting nature, full of science, and yet as amusing as a novel. These works are illustrated with a profusion of the most beautiful cuts. It is not wonderful that the circulation should be extensive; it is said to be twenty thousand monthly. The price is two shillings a part, or four for a volume of above 400 pages—some of the volumes containing above seventy cuts. . . .

We hear in some quarters a charge made against the labours of the Society, originating, as it appears to us, in great want of reflection. The condition, it is said, of the working classes in this country is so wretched, that knowledge is the last thing they require. They are ground down by want and misery of every kind; they have no heart to improve their minds; let them first be better lodged, clothed and fed; and when you have provided for these necessaries, it is time to think of furnishing them with the luxury of learning.

To this we make answer, first, that the Society does not profess to confine its labours to the working classes. Its publications are adapted to all ranks of the community; and as it must be well aware that improvement always begins at the higher, and descends from thence to the humbler classes, so its efforts, in all probability, are likely to be more effectual at first with the upper and the middle, than with the lower ranks. . . . But we should give a sufficient answer to the remark we have cited, were we to say that the distresses of the working classes, which are unhappily severe almost beyond all former experience, afford no reason against providing for their better education. No association of individuals, however zealous in their benevolent intentions, can pretend to relieve those prevailing distresses. But is this any reason for neglecting the good work which individuals, combined like the members of the Society, have it in their power to perform? . . .

D. FACTORY LEGISLATION

(a) THE FACTORY CHILDREN

476. The Health and Morals of Apprentices Act, 1802 (42 Geo. III, c. 73)

(Statutes at Large, LV, pp. 632–637.)

Sir Robert Peel the elder, himself a cotton manufacturer (see No. 479), was the promoter of this, the first attempt at governmental regulation of conditions of employment in factories. The measure applied only to 'parish apprentices' in textile mills. Peel remarked of the Bill in the debate of 2 June 1802: "He confessed that it did not go to the extent that might be wished; but it was advisable to do as much good as could be done in the present instance, without venturing on anything like hazardous innovation. The great and first object he had in view in bringing in this Bill was to promote the religious and moral education of the children. . . . Without a measure like the present, no gentleman of weight in the country could visit those mills, even though fever raged in them, or other kinds of misery and distress: so that there were no hopes without it of introducing into them any system of wholesome regulations. . . ."

An Act for the preservation of the Health and Morals of Apprentices and others, employed in cotton and other mills, and cotton and other factories.

Whereas it hath of late become a practice in cotton and woollen mills, and . . . factories, to employ a great number of male and female apprentices, and other persons, in the same building; in consequence of which certain regulations are become necessary to preserve the health and morals of such apprentices and other persons; be it therefore enacted . . . that from and after 2 December, 1802, all such mills and factories within Great Britain and Ireland, wherein 3 or more apprentices, or 20 or more other persons, shall at any time be employed, shall be subject to the several rules and regulations contained in this Act. . . .

II. . . . That all . . . rooms and apartments in or belonging to any such mill or factory shall, twice at least in every year, be well and sufficiently washed with quick lime and water over every part of the walls and ceiling thereof; and that due care and attention shall be paid . . . to provide a sufficient number of windows and openings in such rooms . . . to ensure a proper supply of fresh air. . . .

III. . . . That every . . . master or mistress shall constantly supply every apprentice . . . with two whole and complete suits of clothing, with suitable linen, stockings, hats and shoes; one new complete suit being delivered to such apprentice once at least in every year.

IV. . . . That no apprentice . . . shall be employed or compelled to work for more than 12 hours in any one day, (reckoning from 6 of the clock in the morning to 9 of the clock at night), exclusive of the time that may be occupied . . . in eating the necessary meals: provided always, that from and after 1 June 1803, no apprentice shall be employed . . . between the hours of 9 . . . at night and 6 . . . in the morning.

V. [In factories where not less than 1,000 and not more than 1,500 spindles are constantly used, apprentices may be employed in the night until 25 June, 1804.]

VI. . . . That every such apprentice shall be instructed, in some part of every working day, for the first 4 years at least of his or her apprenticeship . . . in the usual hours of work, in reading, writing, and arithmetic, or either [*sic*] of them, according to the age and abilities of such apprentice, by some discreet and proper person, to be provided and paid by the master or mistress of such apprentice, in some room or place in such mill or factory to be set apart for that purpose. . . .

VII. [Sleeping apartments of male and female apprentices to be kept distinct, and not more than two to sleep in one bed.]

VIII. [Apprentices to be instructed, for at least one hour every Sunday, in the principles of the Christian religion, by some proper person to be provided and paid by the master. In England and Wales, apprentices whose parents are members of the Church of England to be examined at least once a year by the rector, vicar or curate of the parish in which the factory stands, and to be prepared for confirmation between the ages of 14 and 18. Similar regulations for Scotland. Apprentices to be sent to Church at least once a month, and on every other Sunday divine service to be held in the factory.]

IX. . . . That the justices of the peace . . . shall . . . yearly at their annual Midsummer sessions . . . appoint two persons, not interested in, or in any way connected with, any such mills or factories, to be visitors of such mills or factories . . . one of whom shall be a justice of the peace . . . and the other shall be a clergyman of the Established Church of England or Scotland. . . . And the said visitors, or either of them, shall have full power and authority . . . to enter into and inspect any such mill or factory, at any time of the day . . . and . . . shall report . . . to the quarter sessions of the peace, the state and condition of such mills and factories, and of the apprentices therein, and whether the same are or are not conducted and regulated according to the directions of this Act. . . .

X. [In case of infectious diseases prevailing in any factory, the visitors may require the master to call in medical assistance, and may require medical reports; the expenses to be borne by the master.]

XI. [Any person opposing or molesting the visitors to be fined between £5 and £10.]

XII. [Copies of this Act to be hung up in two conspicuous places in the factory.]

XIII. . . . That every master or mistress . . . who shall wilfully act contrary to or offend against any of the provisions of this Act, shall for such offence, (except where otherwise directed), forfeit and pay any sum not exceeding £5 and not less than 40s. . . . provided always, that all informations for offences against this Act, shall be laid within one calendar month after the offence committed. . . .

477. Report from the committee on Parish Apprentices, 11 April 1815

(Hansard's *Parliamentary Debates*, xxx, 533–541.)

. . . It would have been obviously an impracticable task to have attempted to ascertain the number of parish apprentices bound, from various parts of England, to a distance from their parents; and the Committee being therefore under the necessity of limiting their enquiry to those points which were capable of being ascertained, conceived that the parishes, which are comprehended in the Bills of Mortality, would afford a tolerable criterion to enable a judgment to be formed, as to the comparative number of parish apprentices bound near home and at a distance, and as to the advantages or disadvantages resulting from the latter plan.

This was the more practicable, as by the Act passed in the 2nd and 7th years of his present Majesty, some humane regulations were made in the management of parish apprentices in those parishes; and by the latter Act, in certain of those parishes, namely, the 17 parishes without the walls of London, the 23 in Middlesex and Surrey, being within the Bills of Mortality, and the liberty of the Tower of London, and the 10 parishes within the liberty and city of Westminster, a list of poor children bound apprentices was directed to be delivered annually from each parish to the clerk of the company of Parish-clerks, to be bound up and deposited with that company. To those lists your Committee have had access, an abstract having been made by the clerk of the Committee; and it appears from them that the whole number of apprentices bound, from the beginning of the year 1802 to the end of the year 1811, from these parishes amounts to 5,815; being 3,446 males, and 2,369 females. Of these were bound to trades, watermen, the sea-service, and to household employment, 2,428 males, and 1,361 females, in all 3,789; fifteen of whom were bound under 8 years of age, 493 between 8 and 11 years, 483 between 11 and 12, 1,656 between 12 and 14, and 1,102 between 14 and 18. Though not immediately applicable to the subject of enquiry, it may not be altogether irrelevant to mention, that of this gross number of children amounting to 3,789, there were bound to the sea-service to watermen, lightermen, and fishermen, 484; to household employments, 528; and to various trades and professions, 2,772: the remaining children amounting to 2,026, being 1,018 males, and 1008 females, were bound to persons in the country; of these 58 were under 8 years of age, 1008 between 8 and 11, 316 between 11 and 12, 435 between 12 and 14, and 207 between 14 and 18, besides two children whose ages are not mentioned in the returns from their parishes.

Before they enter on the subject of what has become of these children, your Committee beg leave to observe, that from all the parishes within the City of London, only 11 apprentices have been sent to masters at a distance in the country;–that of the 5 parishes in Southwark, only one (St. George's) has sent any considerable numbers;–that in Westminster, the parish of St. Anne, has not sent any since the year 1802; those of St. Margaret and St. John, since the year 1803; and the largest and populous parish of St. Pancras has discontinued the practice since the year 1806. From those of Newington, Shadwell, Islington, and several others, no children have at any time been sent.

The Committee directed precepts to be sent to the various persons in the country to whom the parish apprentices, to the amount of 2,026, were bound, directing them to make returns, stating what had become of them, to the best of their knowledge. These returns have in general been complied with, but in some instances have not, owing probably to the bankruptcy or discontinuance in business of the parties to whom these children were apprenticed; and in some cases the information required has been furnished by the overseer of the poor, to whom the charge of assigning the apprentices devolved on the failure of the master.

The general classification may be made as follows: now serving under indenture

644; served their time, and now in the same employ 108; served, and settled else-where 99; dead 80; enlisted in the army or navy 86; quitted their service, chiefly run away 166; not bound to the person mentioned in the return kept by the company of Parish-clerks 58; sent back to their friends 57; transferred to tradesmen in different parts of the kingdom 246; incapable of service 18; not accounted for or mentioned 5; in parish workhouses 26; not satisfactorily or intelligibly accounted for by the persons to whom they were bound, or by the overseers where the masters have become bankrupt 433. [Total] 2026.

. . . Of the children bound in ten years, the following is the proportion of the different trades and employments: silk throwsters 118; silk manufacturers 26; flax dressers 21; flax spinners 58; flax manufacturers 88; sail-cloth manufacturers 8; woollen manufacturers 24; worsted spinners 2; worsted manufacturers 146; carpet weavers 2; framework knitters 9; earthenware manufacturers 3; cotton spinners 353; cotton weavers 67; cotton manufacturers 771; cotton twist manufacturers 7; calico weavers 198; fustian manufacturers 71; cotton candlewick makers 24; manufacturers (supposed to be cotton) 28; [total], 2026.

It appears by the returns from the metropolis, that the children bound to manu-facturers in the country have generally been apprenticed on the same day, in numbers of from 5 or 6 to 40 or 50. They have not unfrequently been taken back to their parents, and sometimes after having been bound have been assigned to another master. In the parish of Bermondsey, out of 25 apprenticed to manufacturers, 16, it is said, did not go, but no reason is given for it; and in several instances, after the children have been taken into the country, they have been returned to the parish, in conse-quence of the surgeon having pronounced them unsound. It appears also, that of the whole number of parish apprentices included in the above returns, no less a proportion than $\frac{3}{4}$ have been bound to masters connected with the cotton manufacture. Most of the remarks, therefore which they conceive it their duty to make, will be more directly applicable to that branch of employment, though many of their general observations, as to the impolicy of removing children to a considerable distance from their parents, as well as from those whose duty it is to see that they are properly taken care of and treated, are equally applicable to all professions. . . .

In the populous districts of England, whether that population is caused by manu-facturers or by other employments, the same causes which produce it provide support for the inhabitants of all ages, by various occupations adapted to their means. Thus in manufacturing districts, the children are early taught to gain their subsistence by the different branches of those manufactures. In districts where collieries and other mines abound, they are accustomed almost from their infancy to employments under ground, which tend to train and inure them to the occupation of their ancestors; but in London the lower class of the population is not of that nature, but is composed of many different descriptions consisting of servants in and out of place, tradesmen, artisans, labourers, widows, and beggars, who being frequently destitute of the means of providing for themselves, are dependent on their parishes for relief, which is seldom bestowed without the parish claiming the exclusive right of disposing, at their pleasure, of all the children of the person claiming relief. The system of apprenticeship is therefore resorted to of necessity, and with a view of getting rid of the burden of supporting so many individuals; and as it is probably carried to a greater extent there than any where else, for the reasons here stated, your Committee has been enabled to form an opinion, without the necessity of referring to any other part of the kingdom, whether it could be discontinued, without taking away from the parishes the means of disposing of their poor children. It certainly does appear to your Committee, that this purpose might be attained, without the violation of humanity, in separating children forcibly and conveying them to a distance from their parents, whether those parents be deserving or undeserving . . . It can hardly be a matter of doubt, that apprentices, to the number of 200, which is the yearly number bound on the average of 10 years before mentioned, might, with the most trifling possible exertion on the part of the parish officers, be annually bound to trades and domestic employments, within such a distance as to admit of occasional intercourse with a parent, and (what is perhaps of more consequence) the superintendence of the officers of the parish by which they were bound. That this is not attended with much difficulty seems evident, from the fact that many parishes have never followed the practice of binding their poor children to a distance, though quite as numerous as those in which this practice has prevailed; and that some parishes which had begun it, have long discontinued it.

In making these observations, your Committee beg to be understood as not extending them to the sea service, in favour of which they make a special reservation, on account of considerations of the highest political importance connected with the maritime interests of the country. They therefore carefully abstain from recommending any interference with the law as it now stands, which admits of binding parish apprentices to the King's or merchants' naval service.

The system of binding parish apprentices, in the manner in which they are usually bound, to a distance from their parents and relations, and from those parish officers whose duty it is to attend to their moral and physical state, is indeed highly objectionable; but the details and the consequences are very little known, except to those persons to whom professional employment, local situation, or accident, may have afforded the means of inquiry and information on the subject. There are, without doubt, instances of masters, who in some degree compensate to children for the estrangement which frequently takes place at a very early age from their parents, and from the nurses and women to whom they are accustomed in the Workhouses of London, and who pay due and proper attention to the health, education, and moral and religious conduct of their apprentices; but these exceptions to the too general rule, by no means shake the opinion of your Committee as to the general impolicy of such a system.

The consideration of the inconvenience and expense brought on parishes, by binding apprentices from a distance, is of no weight, when compared with the more important one of the inhumanity of the practice: but it must not be kept out of sight, that the magistrates of the West Riding of Yorkshire, or of Lancashire, who are of all others the most conversant with the subject, may in vain pass resolutions, as they have done, declaring the impolicy of binding parish apprentices in the manner in which they are usually bound, and attempting to make regulations with a view to their better treatment, if these wholesome regulations can be entirely done away by the act of two magistrates for Middlesex or Surrey, who can, without any notice or previous intimation defeat these humane objects, by binding scores or even hundreds of children to manufacturers in a distant county, and thus increase the very evil which it has been endeavoured to check or prevent. Indeed in so slovenly and careless a manner is this duty frequently performed, and with so little attention to the condition of the children bound, that in frequent instances the magistrates have put their signatures to indentures not executed by the parties. . . .

Your Committee forbear to enter into many details connected with the subject of apprenticeship of the poor, which, though in the highest degree interesting, and worthy of the attention of the House, are yet in some measure foreign to the immediate object of the enquiry. They cannot, however, avoid mentioning the very early age at which many of these children are bound apprentices. The evils of the system of these distant removals, at all times severe, and aggravating the miseries of poverty, are yet felt more acutely and with a greater degree of aggravation, in the case of children of 6 or 7 years of age, who are removed from the care of their parents and relations at that tender time of life; and are in many cases prematurely subjected to a laborious employment, frequently very injurious to their health; and generally highly so to their morals, and from which they cannot hope to be set free under a period of 14 or 15 years, as, with the exception of two parishes only in the metropolis, they invariably are bound to the age of 21 years.

Without entering more at large into the enquiry, your Committee submit, that enough has been shown to call the attention of the House to the practicability of finding employment for parish apprentices, within a certain distance from their own homes, without the necessity of having recourse to a practice so much at variance with humanity.

478. Evidence of Robert Owen before the Select Committee on the state of children employed in Manufactories, 1816

(*Parliamentary Papers*, 1816, III, 235, pp. 20–22.)

Owen took over the New Lanark cotton mills from his father-in-law, David Dale, in 1800, and proceeded to develop his schemes for establishing a new type of social organization, based on the Community settlement and the Co-operative principle. His schools marked in many respects a great advance on the limited and mechanical teachings of the 'monitorial' schools which were then being so widely established (see No. 471). His views on the limitation of the hours to be worked by children were unusual for the time; a more orthodox view is represented in the subsequent extract.

. . . I am principal proprietor and sole acting partner of the establishment at New Lanark, in Scotland.

How many persons, young and old, are immediately supported by the New Lanark manufactory and establishment?–About 2,300. . . .

To how many out of that number do you give employment?–. . . Upon the average about 16 or 17 hundred.

The remainder of the 2,300 are the wives and children?–Children too young, and persons too old, of the same families; some of the wives are employed. . . .

At what age do you take children into your mills?–At 10 and upwards.

What are your regular hours of labour per day, exclusive of meal times?–$10\frac{3}{4}$ hours.

What time do you allow for meals?–$\frac{3}{4}$ of an hour for dinner, and $\frac{1}{2}$ an hour for breakfast.

Then your full time of work per day is 12 hours?–Yes.

Why do you not employ children at an earlier age?–Because I consider it would be injurious to the children, and not beneficial to the proprietors. . . . 17 years ago, a number of individuals, with myself, purchased the New Lanark establishment from the late Mr. Dale of Glasgow: at that period I found there were 500 children, who had been taken from poor-houses, chiefly in Edinburgh, and these children were generally from the age of 5 and 6, to 7 and 8; they were so taken because Mr. Dale could not, I learned afterwards, obtain them at a more advanced period of life; if he did not take them at those ages, he could not obtain them at all. The hours of work at that time were 13, inclusive of meal times, and an hour and a half was allowed for meals. I very soon discovered that, although those children were extremely well fed, well clothed, well lodged, and very great care taken of them when out of the mills, their growth and their minds were materially injured by being employed at those ages within the cotton mills for $11\frac{1}{2}$ hours per day. It is true that those children, in consequence of being so well fed and clothed and lodged, looked fresh, and to a superficial observer, healthy in their countenances; yet their limbs were very generally deformed, their growth was stunted, and, although one of the best schoolmasters upon the old plan was engaged to instruct those children regularly every night, in general they made but a very slow progress, even in learning the common alphabet. Those appearances strongly impressed themselves upon my mind to proceed solely from the number of hours they were employed . . . because in every other respect, they were as well taken care of . . . as any children could be. . . . Therefore, as soon as I had it in my power, I adopted regulations to put an end to a system which appeared to me to be so injurious. . . .

Do you think the age of 10 to be the best period for the admission of children into full and constant employment for 10 or 11 hours per day, within woollen, cotton, or other mills or manufactories?–I do not.

What other period would you recommend for this admission to full work?–12 years. . . . For the 2 years preceding, to be partially instructed; to be instructed one half the day, and the other half to be initiated into the manufactories by parties employing two sets of children. . . . Had the works been entirely my own, I should have acted upon that principle some time ago, but being connected with other gentlemen, I deem it necessary in practice not to deviate so much from the common regulations of the country. . . .

Do you think $10\frac{3}{4}$ hours a day the proper time for children to be employed in manufactories?–I do not.

What time would you recommend?–About 10 hours of actual employment, or, at the most, $10\frac{1}{2}$.

Do you think, if such an arrangement were made in regard to the number of hours, the manufacturers would suffer any loss in consequence?–My conviction is, that no party would suffer in consequence of it . . . either with reference to the home or the foreign trade. . . . I have found . . . that there has been a very sensible difference in the general health and spirit of the whole mass of the population so employed. . . .

Do you give instruction to any part of your population?–Yes . . . to the children from 3 years old, upwards; and to every other part of the population that choose to receive it. . . . There is a preparatory school, into which all the children, from the age of 3 to 6, are admitted at the option of the parents; there is a second school, in which all the children of the population, from 6 to 10, are admitted; and if any of the parents, from being more easy in their circumstances, and setting a higher value upon instruction, wish to continue their children at school for one, two, three, or four years longer, they are at liberty to do so; they are never asked to take the children from the school to the works. . . . The schools are supported immediately at the expense of the establishment; they are indeed literally and truly supported by the people themselves. . . .

New Lanark was a new settlement formed by Mr. Dale; the part of the country in which these works were erected was very thinly inhabited; and the Scottish peasantry generally were disinclined to work in cotton mills; it was necessary that great efforts should therefore be made to collect a new population in such a situation, and such population was collected before the usual and customary means for conveniently supplying a population with food were formed, the work people were therefore obliged to buy their food and other articles at a very high price, and under many great disadvantages; to counterbalance this inconvenience, a store was opened at the establishment, into which provisions of the best quality, and clothes of the most useful kind, were introduced, to be sold . . . at a price sufficient to cover prime-cost and charges, and to cover the accidents of such a business, it being understood . . . that whatever profits arose from this establishment, those profits should be employed for the general benefit of the work people themselves; and these school establishments have been supported, as well as other things, by the surplus profits. . . .

When these schools were opened, it was not considered sufficient that attention should be paid merely to instructing the children in what are called the common rudiments of learning, that is, in reading, writing, arithmetic, and the girls also in sewing, but it was deemed of much greater importance, that attention should be given by the masters to form the moral habits of the children, and their dispositions; and in consequence, the moral habits of the children have been improved in such a manner that from the 1st of January last to the time I left the establishment, about a week ago, out of two hundred and about twenty children, who are in school in the day, and three hundred and eighty or ninety, who are in school at night, there has not been occasion to punish one single individual; and as the school is arranged upon such principles as are calculated to give the children a good deal of exercise and some amusement, the children are more willing and more desirous of attending the school . . . than of going to their ordinary play. . . . In consequence of the individuals observing that real attention is given to their comforts and to their improvements, they are willing to work at much lower wages at that establishment, than at others at no great distance, which are esteemed to be upon the best plans in the country, with all the newest improvements. . . .

Do you think that the regulations which are in force at New Lanark, would apply to a large populous manufacturing town, where the inhabitants are not utterly dependent upon a manufactory?–The same principles, I conceive, may be applied, under different modifications, to any situation, where there are few or many.

What employment could be found for the children of the poor, in those situations, till 10 years of age?–It does not appear to me that it is necessary for children to be employed under 10 years of age, in any regular work.

If you did not employ them in any regular work, what would you do with them?–Instruct them, and give them exercise.

Would not there be a danger of their acquiring, by that time, vicious habits, for want of regular occupation?–My own experience leads me to say that I have found quite the reverse, that their habits have been good in proportion to the extent of their instruction. . . . If the children are not to be instructed, they had better be employed in any occupation that should keep them out of mischief. . . .

Examination of G. A. Lee, partner in a cotton-spinning factory at Manchester.

How many persons do you employ in your factory?–At present 937.

Will you state the number of each age?–Under ten years of age, 11; from ten to twelve, 121; from twelve to fourteen, 109; from fourteen to sixteen, 101; above sixteen, 595; in all 937.

What is the least age among the eleven under ten years of age?–There are none under 9 years of age.

Are all whom you employ free labourers? They are all at full liberty to leave when they please.

What are the hours of work?–From 6 in the morning to 8 in the evening, allowing 40 minutes for dinner, and 20 minutes grace for coming in, making 13 hours work for 5 days, and 11 hours work for Saturday, in all 76 hours per week, or 12 hours and 40 minutes per day, in which is included the time of breakfast and tea; which for the most part is taken in the mill.

Do you upon any occasions work longer and shorter periods?–Sometimes on account of accidents and stoppages, but principally for the convenience of the people, who prefer occasional holidays, especially at Whitsuntide, for 5 days, when a great number avail themselves of the opportunity and season to visit their friends and relations in the country from whence they come; and all enjoy the fair and the races. . . .

Then the mill works occasionally more hours per day, to make good this deficiency?–It does.

How much longer?–An hour over per day. . . . [pp. 339–340.]

You have been present during the greater part of the examinations that have taken place upon this subject?–I have.

In consequence of those examinations have you taken any steps to diminish the hours of labour in your manufactory, as stated in a paper before the committee?–None whatever.

Is the Committee then to understand that the evidence which you have heard in this room has made no such impression upon your mind as to induce you to ameliorate the condition of the children employed by you, by diminishing the hours of labour?–I have no intention to make any alteration whatever, not thinking it would improve the condition of the people, all circumstances considered.

The Committee is then to understand that unless any legislative provision takes place to compel you to diminish the hours of labour, you have no intention, voluntarily, to do so?–I have no intention to alter the average hours of labour; if I could make them more regular I would, and will.

Do you mean, by making them more regular, that it is your intention to refrain from causing the children to work additional hours in consequence of the occasional holidays that take place?–I do not; I mean in that case that they should take less holidays, and not diminish the time of work.

You mean to say then, that you will diminish the number of holidays, but that those holidays which you do give you will still repay yourself for by the extra labour?– Precisely so.

Then the Committee is to understand that the evidence which has appeared relative to children working extra hours in order to repay the proprietors for holidays, has made no impression on your mind so as to alter your plans?–None whatever. [p. 359.]

479. Debates in the House of Commons on the Factory Bill, 19 and 23 Feb. and 27 April 1818

(*Parliamentary Debates*, XXXVII, 559–566, 581–588; XXXVIII, 342–371.)

19 February:

Sir Robert Peel–. . . About 15 years ago he had brought in a Bill for the Regulation of Apprentices in Cotton Manufactories. At that time they were the description of persons most employed in those manufactures. He himself had 1000 of them. . . . Since that time, however, the business had been much extended. Manufactories were established in large towns, and the proprietors availed themselves of all the poor population of those towns. In Manchester alone 20,000 persons were employed in the cotton manufactories, and in the whole of England about three times that number. . . . It was notorious that children of a very tender age were dragged from their beds some hours before daylight, and confined in the factories not less than 15 hours; and it was also notoriously the opinion of the faculty that no children of 8 or 9 years of age could bear that degree of hardship with impunity to their health and constitution. It had been urged by the humane that there might be two sets of young labourers for one set of adults. He was afraid this would produce more harm than good. The better way would be to shorten the time of working for adults as well as for children, and to prevent the introduction of the latter at a very early age. . . . The children . . . were prevented from growing to their full size. In consequence, Manchester, which used to furnished numerous recruits for the army, was now wholly unproductive in that respect. . . .

Lord Lascelles–. . . The individuals who were the objects of the hon. gentleman's proposition were free labourers. This excited his jealousy; for, were the principle of interference with free labourers once admitted, it was difficult to say how far it might not be carried. . . .

Mr. Philips strongly objected to the adoption of any measure of this description, and denied that the employment of children in the cotton factories operated, as had been described, to stint their growth, impair their comfort, or scatter disease amongst them. . . . Small factories were often ill-ventilated, and from that circumstance the health of a person might suffer more in 6 hours in one of these factories than in 15 hours in a factory which was well ventilated and properly constructed in other respects. But how could this be cured by any Bill? The small factories generally went to ruin, and that was the cure for the evil. From the Returns made to the House, out of 31,117, the number of persons employed in these Returns, 1717, or 5½% were of the age of 10 and under, 13,203 from 10 to 18, and 16,197 of the age of 18 and upwards. Out of 27,827 persons, there were 1830 only who could not read. . . .

Mr. Finlay . . . warned the House against entertaining any measure which went, like the present, to interfere with a manufacture of such vital importance. . . . It employed more people than all the other manufactures of the country taken together. The exports from it exceeded 20 millions a year, and what was exported was not equal to what the home consumption was. . . . The Bill should extend to the linen and woollen manufactories, as the hours of confinement were in them equally long. . . .

23 February:

Sir Robert Peel–. . . He could not think that little children, who had not a will of their own, could be called free labourers. They were either under the control of a master or a parent. . . . In the Bill brought in in 1815, the age at which children might be employed was fixed at 10. He now proposed the age of 9 years, and that the powers of the Act should terminate when the child reached the age of 16, and could be considered a free agent. He therefore now recommended that children employed in cotton factories should, from 9 to 16, be under the protection of Parliament, and before 9 that they should not be admitted; that they should be employed in working 11 hours, which with 1½ hours for meals, made in the whole 12½ hours. . . . He knew that the iniquitous practice of working children at a time when their masters were in bed too often took place. He was ashamed to own that he had himself been concerned where that proceeding had been suffered. . . . It was his wish to have no night-work at all in the factories. . . .

27 April:

Sir Robert Peel–. . . believed that the number of master manufacturers who supported the Bill was greater than that of those who opposed it, and that many of them were even anxious that its provisions should be extended to adults. . . .

Lord Stanley–. . . The result of such a regulation must inevitably be that the children would cease to be employed, and that their parents would lose the value of their labour, while the children were consigned to unprofitable idleness. . . . Children employed in cotton factories were not put to business at an earlier age, or kept longer to labour than in many branches. . . . Water-gilding was very pernicious to those employed in it, yet it was not under the operation of any legislative restriction. The plate glass business was allowed to be highly insalubrious. Children, however, were employed in it, though exposed to violent heats and draughts of air. Glass-cutting also was unhealthy. The work was carried on in damp places; people of tender age were employed in it, but yet, in none of these cases did the Legislature think it necessary to interfere. Was the weaving trade less unwholesome than the cotton? And were not children put to it at as early an age, and kept as long at work? The weaver was pent up in a long, close, confined cabin, and often obliged to work upon a damp floor. Working people were exposed to the vicissitudes of excessive heat and cold, to damps of every kind, and to every species of bodily infirmity in the coal and lead mines, and yet nobody ever called for such legislative enactments in the management of those concerns. . . . One consequence of this Bill would be to create disunion between children and their parents. . . .

J. Smith–. . . The important allegation in the petition of the workmen of Mr. Owen had not been contradicted, viz. that in the shorter time of work they were able to spin quite as much cotton as when they laboured a greater number of hours in the day. In Mr. Owen's factory at New Lanark, the people did as much in 10½ hours as was done by any other factory in 15. The reason was, that knowing they were not required to work beyond their strength, they went about it with more cheerfulness and alacrity. . . .

Mr. Robinson–. . . The circumstance that few persons were seen in the manu-factories over 40 years of age was a proof that their strength had been wasted before they arrived at maturity. If the Bill went directly to interfere in the labour of adults, he thought it would be objectionable; but it would be going too far to say that by protecting the children the adults might be incidentally interfered with and that therefore the children should be left as they were. That would be establishing the position that there was no possible case, however strong it might be, where inter-ference could be justified. . . .

480. The Factory Act of 1819 (59 Geo. III, c. 66).

(*Statutes at Large*, LXXIII, pp. 418–419.)

An Act to make further provisions for the regulation of cotton mills and factories, and for the better preservation of the health of young persons employed therein. [2 July 1819.]

. . . Whereas it is expedient that some further provision should be made for the regulation of mills, manufactories and buildings, employed in the preparation and spinning of cotton wool: be it therefore enacted . . . that from and after 1 January 1820, no child shall be employed in any description of work for the spinning of cotton wool into yarn, or in any previous preparation of such wool, until he or she shall have attained the full age of 9 years.

II. . . . No person, being under the age of 16 years, shall be employed . . . for more than 12 hours in any one day, exclusive of the necessary time for meals; such 12 hours to be between the hours of 5 o'clock in the morning and 9 o'clock in the evening.

III. . . . There shall be allowed to every such person . . . not less than half an hour to breakfast, and not less than one full hour for dinner . . . between the hours of 11 o'clock in the forenoon and 2 o'clock in the afternoon.

IV. [Time lost in water-driven mills by reason of the want or excess of a due supply of water, may be made up at the rate of one additional hour per day.]

V. [Ceilings and interior walls to be lime-washed twice a year.]

VI. [A copy of abstract of the Act to be hung up in every factory.]

VII. [Masters breaking the law to be fined not less than £10 and not more than £20, at the discretion of the justices. Informations for offences to be laid within three months of the offence.]

481. Report on the Cotton Mills in the Parish of Bolton, 1823

(Public Record Office, Home Office, 44/14.)

Occupiers	No. of hands employed	No. under 9 years of age	No. of hrs. exclusive of meal hours	Time allowed for meals	How often and when whitewashed	Abstract of the Act hung up in the Mills
Assignees of J. Carlile[1]	320	8	12	1 hr. at dinner time	9 mths. since	In one of the rooms
John & George Jones[2]	40	2	12½	do.	3 mths. ago	Now hung up in this Mill
Edward & Wm. Bolling. New Mill & Coronation Mill[3]	520	27	12	do.	6 mths. ago	Hung up in the pay room
Edward & Wm. Bolling. Spring Garden Mill[4]	87	9	12	do.	6 mths. ago	none
Edward & Wm. Bolling. Bridge Street Mill[5]	150	1	12	do.	Last Whitsuntide	none
Edward & Wm. Bolling. Knott Mill[6]	81	5	12	do.	8 mths. ago	none
Ormrod & Hardcastle. Royal George Mill[7]	275	3	12	do.	12 mths. ago	hung up
Ormrod & Hardcastle. Royal Sovereign Mill[8]	341	1	12	do.	12 mths.	hung up
Ormrod & Hardcastle. Taylorfield Mill[9]	200	—	12	do.	6 mths. ago	hung up
Thomas Wingfield.[10]	200	—	12	do.	3 mths.	none

[1] This factory is clean & well-ventilated; there is no night work. The mill is not stopped at breakfast-time, but the workpeople are allowed ½ hr. to eat their breakfast in the mill. They begin working at 6 a.m. & leave off at 7 p.m., including dinner hour.

[2] They work at this mill from 6 a.m. till 7.30 p.m. including 1 hr. for dinner. The mill is not stopped at breakfast-time. It is clean & well-ventilated.

[3] At these mills they work from 6 a.m to 7 p.m. including 1 hr. for dinner. The 3rd. story in the Coronation Mill very hot. Both mills are clean & have good ventilations. The workpeople eat their breakfast in the mill.

[4] This mill is clean & well-ventilated. The hours of working are the same as at the last-mentioned factories.

[5] This mill is clean & well-ventilated. The hours of working are the same as at Messrs. Bolling's other mills.

[6] The hours of working at this mill are the same as at Messrs. Bolling's other mills. It is clean and well-ventilated.

[7] In summer they begin working at this mill at 6 a.m. & leave off at 7 p.m., including 1 hr. for dinner, & in winter from 7 a.m. till 8 p.m., including dinner hour. This mill is well-ventilated, the rooms are lofty, but want whitewashing.

[8] The hours at this mill are the same as at the last-mentioned one. The rooms are lofty and well-ventilated, but want whitewashing.

[9] This mill is rather dirty but well-ventilated. The hours are the same as at Ormrod & Hardcastle's other mills.

[10] At this mill they work from 6 a.m. till 7 p.m. including dinner hour. It is clean & well-ventilated.

Occupiers	No. of hands employed	No. under 9 years of age	No. of hrs. exclusive of meal hours	Time allowed for meals	How often and when whitewashed	Abstract of the Act hung up in the Mills
Simon Hilton occupies the 3 first stories; Messrs. Wood & Greenwood the other part of the mill.[1]	81	3	12	do.	3 first rooms above a year ago The other part 6 mths. ago	none
Balshaw, Marsh & Co. Makinson's Factory[2]	155	—	12	do.	partly this summer	hung up
Thos. Gregory[3]	50	—	12	do.	1 year ago	none
John Lum[4]	300	1	12	do.	5 mths. ago	hung up
John Thomason[5]	150	2	13	do.	12 mths. ago	none
Roger Holland & Co.[6]	320	3	12	do.	*	none
Abraham Haigh[7]	85	6	12	do.	partially whitewashed this summer	hung up
Jacob Greenhalgh[8]	25	3	12	do.	8 mths. ago	none
Thomas Cullen[9]	114	—	12	do.	12 mths. ago	hung up
J. Chadwick & brother[10]	135	—	11	1 hr. for dinner; ½ hr. for breakfast; ½ hr. for tea	6 mths. ago	none

* The carding rooms have been whitewashed this year, but not the other parts of the mill.

[1] This mill is altogether very dirty but particularly the 3 first rooms occupied by Simon Hilton. The hours of working are the same as at the last-mentioned factory. The ventilation not good.

[2] The hours at this mill are the same as at the above-mentioned factories. Some of the rooms want whitewashing. This mill is well-ventilated. The heat is greater than at any of the others, the thermometer being as high as 80.

[3] This mill is undergoing repairs and is in a dirty state. The hours of working are the same as at the other mills.

[4] This mill is well-ventilated and very clean. The hours of working are from 6 a.m. till 7 p.m., including dinner hours.

[5] They begin working in this mill at 6 a.m. and leave off at 8 p.m., including 1 hr. for dinner. Some of the men who live near the mill are allowed to go out to breakfast but the mill is not stopped. This mill is very dirty. The ventilation is not good.

[6] The hours of working at this mill are in summer from 5.30 a.m. to 6.30 p.m. including 1 hr. for dinner. In winter they begin at 6 a.m. and leave off at 7 p.m. including dinner hr. This mill is clean and well-ventilated.

[7] In this mill the hours of working are from 6 a.m. till 7 p.m. including 1 hr. for dinner. It is clean and well-ventilated.

[8] This mill undergoing repairs and consequently in a very rough and dirty state. The hours of working are from 6 a.m. till 7 p.m., including dinner hour.

[9] This mill wants whitewashing but is well-ventilated. The hours of working are the same as at the last-mentioned one.

[10] This mill is very clean and well-ventilated. The workpeople are allowed ¼ hr. for breakfast, 1 hr. for dinner and ½ hr. at tea-time. They generally work till 8 p.m.

Occupiers	No. of hands employed	No. under 9 years of age	No, of hrs. exclusive of meal hours	Time allowed for meals	How often and when whitewashed	Abstract of the Act hung up in the Mills
J. & Edward Ashworth[1]	135	—	12	1 hr. for dinner; ½ hr. for breakfast	4 mths. ago	none
Wm. Gray[2]	75	—	11½	do.	partly this yr.	none
J. & T. Hope[3]	30	—	12	1 hr. for dinner	2 mths. ago	hung up
Andrew Todd[4]	87	—	12	½ hr. for breakfast 1 hr. for dinner	10 mths. ago	hung up
Samuel Horrocks[5]	100	—	11½	do.	1 mth. ago	hung up
J. & J. Bridge[6]	36	—	12	1 hr. for dinner	Not since the present occupiers came	none
Henry Whitfield[7]	27	—	12	do.	12 mths. ago	none

In all the above-mentioned mills there are no apprentices employed. In 15 mills out of 28 there is more or less number of children under 9 years of age employed, but the masters say this is contrary to their directions, as these children are engaged and paid by the journeymen spinners themselves. In the whole 28 mills there are only three that are stopped during breakfast. In all the others the workpeople eat their breakfast as they work. All the mills are stopped during one hour at dinner. It does not appear that any of the mills have been whitewashed during the year but they generally promise to whitewash again before Christmas.

Only 14 out of 28 mills have the Act of Parliament or Regulations hung up, and there is not more than one copy in most of those that have it so hung up, whereas it appears to us, the undersigned, there should be one affixed in every room. The average heat of the factories from the inspection that has taken place is from 60° to 80° of the thermometer. With two or three exceptions the hours of working are 12 hours per day, exclusive of meals. Mill No. 2, the working hours are 12½ and in No. 15, 13 hours, exclusive of such meals.

29 October   R. Fletcher

    1823   H. Richardson

   [1] This mill is clean and well-ventilated. The hours of working are the same as at the other mills except when fetching up time for want or excess of water. They never fetch up more than 1 hr. per day.

   [2] The hours of working in this mill are from 6 a.m. till 7 p.m., including 1½ hrs. for meals. This mill is undergoing repairs and will be whitewashed before Christmas.

   [3] This mill is clean. The ventilation is not good. They begin working at 7 a.m. and leave off at 8 p.m., including 1 hr. for dinner.

   [4] This mill is rather dirty but very well ventilated. They begin working at 6 a.m. and leave off at 7.30 p.m., allowing 1½ hrs. for meals.

   [5] This mill is in excellent condition, very clean and well-ventilated. The appearance of the workpeople at this mill is much healthier than at the other mills. They begin working at 6 a.m. and leave off at 7 p.m. including meal hours, except when fetching up lost time, but they never exceed more than ½ hr. per day.

   [6] This mill is very dirty, the ventilation not good. The present occupiers have not been there three months. The hours of working are the same as at the generality of the other mills.

   [7] This mill is rather dirty but well-ventilated. They work from 6 a.m. till 7 or 8 p.m., including dinner hour, just as they want to fetch up lost time, never exceeding 1 hr. per day.

482. The Factory Act of 1831 (1 and 2 William IV, c. 39)

(*Statutes of the United Kingdom*, 1 and 2 Wm. IV (1831), pp. 248–252.)

An Act to repeal the laws relating to apprentices and other young persons employed in cotton factories and in cotton mills, and to make further provisions in lieu thereof. [15 October 1831.]

... Be it ... enacted ... that from ... the 1st day of November 1831 the said recited Acts [*i.e.* 59 Geo. III, c. 66; 60 Geo. III, c. 5; 6 Geo. IV, c. 63; 10 Geo. IV, c. 51; 10 Geo. IV, c. 63] shall be ... repealed.

II. And whereas it has of late become a practice in cotton mills and cotton factories to employ a great number of young persons of both sexes late at night, and in many instances all night; and certain regulations have become necessary to preserve the health and morals of such persons; be it therefore further enacted, that from and after 1 Nov. 1831 no person under 21 years of age shall be allowed to work in the night, (that is to say,) between the hours of 8.30 in the evening and 5.30 in the morning, in any of the cotton manufactories of the United Kingdom, where steam or water power is used to propel or work the machinery used in such mills or factories.

III. ... That no person under the age of 18 years shall be employed in any such mill or factory, in any description of work whatsoever, in the twisting, spinning, carding, or weaving of cotton, or in any way preparing or manufacturing that material, or in cleaning any machinery or mill work, more than 12 hours on any one day, or more than 9 hours on a Saturday.

IV. ... That there shall be allowed to every such person, in the course of every day, not less than 1½ hour for meals.

V–VII. [Owners of water-powered factories may order the working of extra hours, within defined limits, to make up time lost by want of or interference with the supply of water, breakdown of the driving machinery, &c.]

VIII. ... That in cotton mills or factories no child shall be employed in any description of work until ... the age of 9 years.

IX. [Masters not to be liable to penalties for employing or over-working children of the protected ages, in cases where their parents or guardians have given certificates of their being of the proper ages required by this Act, or where the person concerned has certified himself to be 21 years old. Persons giving such certificates liable to penalties for each offence, not exceeding £5.]

X. ... That no Justice of the Peace, being also a proprietor or occupier of any such mill ... or the father, son, or brother of any such proprietor or occupier, shall act as a Justice of the Peace under this Act.

XI. [All ceilings and interior walls of such factories to be limewashed once a year.]

XVII. [Occupiers of every such factory to keep a correct account of the time worked each day, for the inspection of the Justice whenever required.]

XXI. [Occupiers, managers, and foremen acting contrary to any of the provisions of this act liable to a fine of not less than £10 nor more than £20 for each offence: half the fine to be given to the prosecutor, half for the benefit of the poor in the parish where the offence was committed.]

483. Evidence of Richard Oastler on 'Yorkshire Slavery'

(Report from the Committee on the Bill to regulate the labour of children in the mills and factories . . . 1832: *Parliamentary Papers*, 1831–1832, xv, pp. 454–455.)

Has your mind been latterly directed to the consideration of the condition of the children and young persons engaged in the mills and factories of this country, with a view to affording them permanent legislative relief?–It has. . . . The immediate circumstance which led my attention to the facts, was a communication made to me by a very opulent spinner that it was the regular custom, to work children in factories 13 hours a day, and only allow them half an hour for dinner; that that was the regular custom, and that in many factories they were worked considerably more. I had previously observed a difference in the working classes of the West Riding of the county of York, I mean in the clothing districts. I had observed an amazing difference from what they are now, in comparison of what they were when I was a youth; but I must say that my attention had not been particularly called to the subject of the factory system, until I had that fact communicated to me. . . . I resolved from that moment that I would dedicate every power of body and mind to this object, until these poor children were relieved from that excessive labour; and from that moment, which was the 29th of September 1830, I have never ceased to use every legal means, which I had it in my power to use, for the purpose of emancipating these innocent slaves. The very day on which the fact was communicated to me, I addressed a letter to the public, in the "Leeds Mercury", upon the subject. I have since that had many opponents to contend against; but not one single fact which I have communicated has ever been contradicted, or ever can be. . . . I have refrained from exposing the worst parts of the system, for they are so gross that I dare not publish them. The demoralizing effects of the system are as bad, I know it, as the demoralizing effects of slavery in the West Indies. I know that there are instances and scenes of the grossest prostitution amongst the poor creatures who are the victims of the system, and in some cases are the objects of the cruelty and rapacity and sensuality of their masters. These things I never dared to publish, but the cruelties which are inflicted personally upon the little children not to mention the immensely long hours which they are subject to work, are such as I am very sure would disgrace a West Indian plantation. On one occasion I was very singularly placed; I was in the company of a West India slave master and three Bradford spinners; they brought the two systems into fair comparison, and the spinners were obliged to be silent when the slave-owner said, "Well, I have always thought myself disgraced by being the owner of black slaves, but we never, in the West Indies thought it was possible for any human being to be so cruel as to require a child of 9 years old to work $12\frac{1}{2}$ hours a day; and that, you acknowledge, is your regular practice." I have seen little boys and girls of 10 years old, one I have in my eye particularly now, whose forehead has been cut open by the thong; whose cheeks and lips have been laid open, and whose back has been almost covered with black stripes; and the only crime that that little boy, who was 10 years and 3 months old, had committed, was that he retched three cardings, which are three pieces of woollen yarn, about three inches each long. The same boy told me that he had been frequently knocked down with the billy-roller, and that on one occasion, he had been hung up by a rope round the body, and almost frightened to death; but I am sure it is unnecessary for me to say anything more upon the bodily sufferings that these poor creatures are subject to. I have seen their bodies almost broken down, so that they could not walk without assistance, when they have been 17 or 18 years of age. I know many cases of poor young creatures who have worked in factories, and who have been worn down by the system at the age of 16 and 17, and who, after living all their lives in this slavery, are kept in poor-houses, not by the masters for whom they have worked, as would be the case if they were negro slaves, but by other people who have reaped no advantage from their labour. These are the particular facts which I wish to state; and one which I would also call the attention of the Committee to, is the domestic system of manufacture which obtained in the West Riding of Yorkshire, when I was a boy; it was the custom for the children at that time, to mix learning their trades with other instruction and with amusement, and they learned their trades or their occupations, not by being put into places, to stop there from morning to night, but by having a little work to do, and then some time for instruction, and they were generally under the immediate care of their parents; the villages about Leeds and Huddersfield were occupied by respectable little clothiers, who could manufacture a piece of cloth or two in the week, or three or four or five pieces, and always had their family at home: and they could at that time make a good profit by what they sold; there were filial affection and parental feeling, and not over-labour; but that race of manufacturers has been almost completely destroyed; there are scarcely any of the old-fashioned domestic manufacturers left, and the villages are composed of one or two or in some cases of three or four, mill-owners, and the rest, poor creatures who are reduced and ground down to want, and in general are compelled to live upon the labour of their little ones; it is almost the general system for the little children in these manufacturing villages to know nothing of their parents at all excepting that in a morning very early, at 5 o'clock, very often before 4, they are awakened by a human being that they are told is their father, and are pulled out of bed (I have heard many a score of them give an account of it) when they are almost asleep, and lesser children are absolutely carried on the backs of the older children asleep to the mill, and they see no more of their parents, generally speaking, till they go home at night, and are sent to bed. Now that system must necessarily prevent the growth of filial affection. It destroys the happiness in the cottage family, and leads both parents and children not to regard each other in the way that Providence designed they should. . . . With regard to the fathers, I have heard many of them declare that it is such a pain to them to think that they are kept by their little children, and that their little children are subjected to so many inconveniences that they scarcely know how to bear their lives; and I have heard many of them declare that they would much rather be transported than be compelled to submit to it. I have heard mothers, more than on 10 or 11 occasions, absolutely say that they would rather that their lives were ended than that they should live to be subjected to such misery. The general effect of the system is this, and they know it, to place a bonus upon crimes; because their little children, and their parents too, know that if they only commit theft and break the laws, they will be taken up and put into the House of Correction, and there they will not have to work more than 6 or 7 hours a day. Such being the general state of things in the manufacturer's cottage, I think we need not be surprised at the present discontented, nay, one might almost say the disaffected state of the working classes. I think that arises from no other circumstance but that complete inversion of the law of nature making the little children into slaves to work for their fathers and mothers, and leaving their fathers destitute in the streets to mourn over their sorrows; I believe that is the foundation of the disaffection and unpleasantness of the present age. . . . [pp. 454–455.]

(b) THE CHIMNEY SWEEPERS

484. Report from the Committee of the House of Commons on the petitions against the employment of boys in sweeping chimneys, 23 June 1817

(*Parliamentary Papers*, 1817, VI, p. 171.)

Your Committee have felt it their duty, in the first place, to inquire into the laws that at present regulate the trade of chimney-sweeping; and they find, that in the year 1788 an Act of Parliament (28 Geo. III, chap. 48) was passed, entitled, "An Act for the better regulation of chimney-sweepers and their Apprentices." . . . This Act, though it has in some respects fulfilled the intention of the Legislature, yet your Committee have heard in evidence before them, that its principal enacting clause, *viz.*, the regulating the age at which apprentices shall be taken, is constantly evaded; and they are decidedly of opinion, that the various and complicated miseries to which the unfortunate children are exposed, cannot be relieved by regulations. The 28th of Geo. III enacts, That no person shall employ any boy, in the nature of an apprentice or servant, under the age of 8 years; yet your Committee have been informed, that infants of the early ages of 4, 5 and 6 years, have been employed, it being the practice for parents to sell their children to this trade, understating their age; besides, this clause is not considered by the master chimney-sweepers as prohibiting their employment of their own children; and instances have been adduced before your Committee, that have satisfied them that such cases are by no means unfrequent. Your Committee have also heard, from one of the master chimney-sweepers, that it is the custom of the trade to take the parent's word for the age of the apprentice–that no other evidence is asked for–that he never heard of its being the practice of the masters to get a certificate of the age, and he was ignorant that the Act of Parliament required it. Your Committee refer generally to the evidence for proofs of the cruelties that are practised, and of the ill-usage, and the peculiar hardships that are the lot of the wretched children who are employed in this trade. It is in evidence that they are stolen from their parents, and inveigled out of workhouses; that in order to conquer the natural repugnance of the infants to ascend the narrow and dangerous chimneys, to clean which their labour is required, blows are used; that pins are forced into their feet by the boy that follows them up the chimney, in order to compel them to ascend it; and that lighted straw has been applied for that purpose; that the children are subject to sores and bruises, and wounds and burns on their thighs, knees, and elbows; and that it will require many months before the extremities of the elbows and knees become sufficiently hard to resist the excoriations to which they are at first subject; and that one of the masters being asked if those boys are employed in sweeping chimneys during the soreness of those parts, he answered, "It depends upon the sort of master they have got. Some are obliged to put them to work sooner than others; you must keep them a little at it even during the sores, or they will never learn their business." Your Committee are informed that the deformity of the spine, legs, arms, &c. of these boys, proceeds generally if not wholly, from the circumstance of their being obliged to ascend chimneys at an age when their bones are in a soft and growing state; but likewise, by their being compelled to carry bags of soot and cloths, the weight of which sometimes exceed 20 or 30 pounds, not including the soot, the burden of which they also occasionally bear for a great length of distance and time; the knees and ankle joints become deformed, in the first instance, from the position they are obliged to put them in, in order to support themselves, not only while climbing up the chimney, but more particularly so whilst coming down, when they rest solely on the lower extremities, the arms being used for scraping and sweeping down the soot. Your Committee refer generally to the observation of every one as to the stinted growth, the deformed state of body, the look of wretchedness and disease which characterizes this unfortunate class; but it is in evidence before them, that there is a formidable complaint which chimney-sweepers in particular are liable to; from which circumstance, by way of distinction, it is called the Chimney-sweeper's Cancer. Mr. Wright, a surgeon, informed your Committee, that whilst he was attending Guy's and St. Bartholomew's Hospitals, he had several cases under his care, some of which were operated on; but in general they are apt to let them go too far before they apply for relief. . . . But it is not only the early and hard labour, the spare diet, wretched lodging, and harsh treatment, which is the lot of these children, but in general they are kept almost entirely destitute of education and moral or religious instruction; they form a sort of class by themselves, and from their work being done early in the day, they are turned into the streets to pass their time in idleness and depravity: thus they become an easy prey to those whose occupation it is to delude the ignorant and entrap the unwary; and if their constitution is strong enough to resist the diseases and deformities which are the consequences of their trade, and that they should grow so much in stature as no longer to be useful in it, they are cast upon the world without any means of obtaining a livelihood, with no habits of industry, or rather, what too frequently happens, with confirmed habits of idleness and vice. . . . Your Committee have endeavoured to learn the number of persons who may be considered as engaged in the trade within the bills of mortality: they have learnt that the total number of master chimney sweepers might be estimated at 200, who had among them 500 apprentices; that not above 20 of those masters were reputable tradesmen in easy circumstances, who appeared generally to conform to the provisions of the Act, and which 20 had, upon an average, from four to five apprentices each; that about 90 were of an inferior class of master chimney-sweepers, who had, upon an average, 3 apprentices each, and who were extremely negligent of their health, their morals, and their education; and that about 90, the remainder of the 200 masters, were a class of chimney-sweepers recently journeymen, who took up the trade because they had no other resource–who picked up boys as they could–who lodged them with themselves in huts, sheds, and cellars, in the outskirts of the town, occasionally wandering into the villages round: and that in these two classes, being in the proportion of 180 to 20, the miseries of the trade were principally to be found. It is in evidence before your Committee, that at Hadleigh, Barnet, Uxbridge, and Windsor, female children have been employed.

Your Committee observe, that in general among the most respectable part of the trade, the apprentices are of the age prescribed by the Act, *viz.* from 8 to 14; but even among the most respectable it is the constant practice to borrow the younger boys from one another, for the purpose of sweeping what are called the narrow flues. No accurate account could be obtained of the ages of the apprentices of the other classes; but they had the youngest children, who either were their own, or engaged as apprentices; and who, in many instances, it was ascertained, were much below the prescribed age; thus, the youngest and most delicate children are in the service of the worst class of masters, and employed exclusively to clean flues, which, from their peculiar construction, cannot be swept without great personal hazard. . . .

Having thus shortly detailed the leading facts of the evidence which has been given before them, of the miseries which the unfortunate class of beings who are sold to this trade experience, your Committee have with great anxiety examined various persons, as to the possibility of performing by the aid of machinery what is now done by the labour of the climbing boys: the result of their inquiries is, that though there may be some difference of opinion as to the extent to which machinery is here applicable, yet the lowest calculation of practical and experienced persons, master chimney-sweepers themselves, who have been brought up in the trade, establishes the fact, that of the chimneys in the metropolis three-fourths may be as well, as cleanly, and as cheaply swept by mechanical means as by the present method; and the remaining part being, on the very greatest calculation, one-fourth of the whole number, with alterations that may easily and cheaply be made, can be swept also without the employment of the climbing boy. Mr. Bevans, an architect much conversant with buildings in the Metropolis, has no doubt that 95 out of 100 can be swept by the machines that are at present in use; and he has also no doubt that, supposing there was to be a legislative enactment that no chimney should be swept by the means of climbing boys, that easy substitutes could be found that would sweep every chimney that now exists. He adds, that though there may be difficulties in cleaning an horizontal flue, from the quantity of soot, yet it is equally bad for the boys as for the machine; because the boy, as he comes down, has an accumulation of soot about him, which stops up the circulation of air necessary to support life. So that it is evident, in all those chimneys where, under their present construction, the machine cannot be used, the hazard of loss of life to the boy who sweeps them, is most imminent.

Some of these flues are stated not to be above 7 inches square; and one of the witnesses, who relates this fact to the Committee, informs them, that he himself had been often in hazard of his life; and that he has frequently swept a long narrow flue in Goldsmith's Hall, in which he was shut up 6 hours before his work was finished. Upon a review then of the evidence of the evils necessarily belonging to this trade, as well as of the remedies which have been suggested, first, in the substitution of mechanical means, thus superseding the necessity of employing children in this painful and degrading trade; and, secondly, in allowing the system to continue in the main as it is, with only those amendments to the existing law, that may attempt to remedy the present practice;—your Committee are decidedly of opinion, that no parliamentary regulations can attain this desirable end; that as long as master chimney-sweepers are permitted to employ climbing boys, the natural result of that permission will be the continuance of those miseries which the Legislature has sought, but which it has failed to put an end to; they therefore recommend, that the use of climbing boys should be prohibited altogether; and that the age at which the apprenticeship should commence should be extended from 8 to 14, putting this trade upon the same footing as others which take apprentices at that age; and, finally, your Committee have come to the following resolution:

Resolved, That the Chairman be directed to move for leave to bring in a Bill for preventing the further use of climbing boys in sweeping of chimneys.

E. TRADE UNIONS, CO-OPERATIVE SOCIETIES, FRIENDLY SOCIETIES AND SAVINGS BANKS

(a) TRADE UNIONS

485. Debates in the House of Commons on the Combination Bill of 1799

(Debrett's *Parliamentary Register*, vols. LIII–LIV.)

8 April: Sir John Anderson brought up a Report of a Select Committee, to whom the Petition of the master millwrights was referred. The substance of the Report was that there existed among the journeymen millwrights, within certain districts in and about the metropolis, a combination which was dangerous to the public, and which the masters had not sufficient power to repress.

The Report being read, Sir John Anderson moved "That leave be given to bring in a Bill to prevent unlawful combination of workmen employed in the millwright business, and to enable the magistrates to regulate their wages within certain limits."

Mr. Wilberforce said he did not object to the principle of this motion, for it appeared to him to be a very worthy one; but he rose for the purpose of submitting to the House whether it might not be advisable to extend the principle of this motion, and make it general against combinations of all workmen. These combinations he regarded as a general disease in our society; and for which, he thought, the remedy should be general; so as not only to cure the complaint for the present, but to preclude its return. He thought the worthy mover of this subject deserved praise for what he was doing, as far as the measure went; but if it was enlarged, and made general against combinations, he should be better satisfied with it, and then it would be a measure that might be of great service to society.

Mr. Speaker said that the suggestion of the hon. member who spoke last could not be carried into effect, because the order on the motion could not be more than commensurate to the petition on which the Report of the Committee was founded, and that petition only prayed that a Bill might be brought in to prevent combinations amongst workmen in the trade of millwrights. But it would be competent to the hon. member himself, or any other, to make what motion he pleased for enlarging the provision of this Bill. . . . [LIII, pp. 323–324.]

10 June: On the motion for the third reading of the Bill for preventing combinations among the working millwrights,

Sir Francis Burdett opposed the principle of the Bill. He thought the existing laws sufficient for every fair and reasonable purpose the framers of the Bill could have in view, and believed that there was seldom a combination of the kind complained of, without a great grievance to provoke it. He quoted Dr. Adam Smith in support of his opinions, and maintained that it was the wise policy of every well-regulated State to leave trade of every kind to find its own level. . . . [LIII, p. 687.]

17 June: Mr. Chancellor Pitt said it was his intention to endeavour to provide a remedy to an evil of very considerable magnitude; he meant that of unlawful combination among workmen in general–a practice which had become much too general, and was likely, if not checked, to produce very serious mischief. He could not state particularly the nature of the Bill which he intended to move for leave to bring in; but it would be modelled in some respect on that of the Bill for regulating the conduct of the paper manufacturers. . . . He then moved that leave be given to bring in a Bill to prevent unlawful combinations of workmen.–Granted. [LIV, p. 22.]

26 June: Mr. Hobhouse . . . should not go over the ground which he had trodden on a former night, when he supported his hon. friend's (Sir F. Burdett's) motion for postponing the Millwrights' Combination Bill for three months. He had then shown the evil consequences of legislative interference in regulating the price of provisions, or the price of wages, which might be considered as the property of the industrious. He had at that time, also, observed that combinations among workmen were more easily broken than combinations among masters, because it could not be long before their finances were exhausted, and then they must apply for employ. . . . The common law punishment (fine and imprisonment) would be fully adequate to the offence, if . . . the Attorney General had carried into effect the intention he had announced of bringing in a Bill to render trials for misdemeanours more speedy. Workmen, charged with conspiring to raise their wages might now put off their trials for six months, or longer; if the learned gentleman had adopted his proposed means of defeating such delay, nothing more would now be wanting. Since, therefore, resort might be had to so obvious and so good a remedy, he (Mr. Hobhouse) could not consent to a Bill which rendered the trial by jury useless (a trial gradually losing ground in the country) and gave the power entirely into the hands of the magistrates. . . . He thought that more than one magistrate should be required upon such trials. There was scarcely a single manufacture in the country in which the masters were not guilty of combinations; yet an attempt to make them liable to a commitment to the House of Correction, on conviction before one Justice of the Peace, would be deemed monstrous. . . . He should, therefore, move, that instead of the words "before one or more magistrates" be inserted "two or more magistrates".

This motion, after some opposition from Mr. Buxton, Mr. Ellison and Mr. Solicitor-General, and a reply from Mr. Hobhouse, was rejected without a division. . . . [LIV, pp. 65–66.]

486. Debates in the House of Commons on the Combination Bill, 13 and 30 June, 1800

(Parliamentary Register, LVII, pp. 110–111, 218–224.)

13 June:

*T*he Lord Mayor of London presented a petition from the journeymen and work-men residing in and about the cities of London and Westminster; setting forth that, during the last Session, an Act passed to prevent unlawful combination of workmen; and that it is therein declared illegal directly or indirectly to attempt to prevail upon any journeyman or workman to quit the service in which he is employed; and that the said Act, by the use of such uncertain terms, and others of the same nature, has created new crimes of boundless extent, to which are affixed fines, forfeitures, and imprisonment; and that, amongst the crimes created by the said Act, the breach of a private contract, by refusing to work when hired, is enumerated as one, and made punishable by discretionary imprisonment for any time not exceeding three months, to the confounding of all distinction between public and private injuries; and that, in many instances, the crimes created by the said Act are such as will encourage wilful perjury in witnesses, from the great difficulty of its being discovered, and will of course expose the petitioners to numberless false accusations, at the pleasure of any malicious prosecutor; and that by the said Act offenders are deprived of a trial by jury, and made subject to the decision of a single magistrate, which, from the securities required upon an appeal, and the expense of prosecuting it, will in effect be always final, the Act having expressly declared it illegal, under heavy penalties, to subscribe any sum for the support of such expenses; and that no *certiorari* to remove any proceedings under the Act is allowed; and that the same magistrate, who has thus the uncontrolled power over offenders, within the Act, will, in many cases, be enabled to fix the rate of wages of journeymen and workmen, and, upon their refusal to work for such wages (however inadequate to their labour) may licence masters to employ in their respective trades all persons indiscriminately, to the detriment of those trades, and to the utter destruction of the workmen who have served regular apprenticeships therein; and that offenders within the said Act are compellable to answer questions upon oath, notwithstanding the several penalties (consisting of fines, forfeitures and imprisonment) to which in consequence they may become liable, and for the discharge from which penalties the Act has made no sufficient provision; and that, in many parts of the said Act, the law is materially changed, to the great injury of all journeymen and workmen; and that, if it be not repealed, it will hereafter be dangerous for the petitioners to converse with one another, or even with their own families; and that its immediate tendency is to excite distrust and jealousy between their masters and them, and to destroy the trades and manufactures it purports to protect; and therefore praying that the said Act may be repealed, or that the House will give such other relief as it shall think fit.

30 June:

Colonel Gascoyne moved the Order of the Day for the House to resolve itself into a Committee on the Petitions of the journeymen workmen. . . .

Mr. Sheridan said . . . that the Bill of last Session . . . although intended to alter essentially the law of the land, was precipitated, he might say, in a most indecent manner, and as quickly as the forms of Parliament would allow; so that the parties whom it principally affected, so far from finding it possible to be heard by counsel against the Bill, had not even time to present petitions against it. A few indeed, in the immediate vicinity of London, were heard by counsel on the last day that it was before the House of Lords; but it was a Bill which interested, not merely a few people in the vicinity of London, but a very large and numerous part of the labouring and industrious community. He certainly felt himself much to blame in not having attended to give his opposition to that Bill, which he understood passed without any, except with a few words from an honourable friend of his who was most constant in his attendance. . . . He wished it to be repealed altogether, because he thought that no explanations or amendments could possibly rid it of its offensive nature. . . . There was one consolation to encourage its repeal, that as it had never been pretended, as an excuse for its introduction, that there were no laws to prevent and punish unlawful combinations, and as the Preamble of the Act itself sets forth that it is to explain and amend former Acts, its repeal will not be the means of letting the subject loose from the restraints of law, but will merely restore things to their former state, and give operation to laws which experience had proved to be perfectly adequate to the purposes for which they were intended.

Mr. Chancellor Pitt . . . Far from objecting to a summary method of trial, he was confident that the workmen must approve of it, as it saved them infinite time, trouble and expense. The Bill might want some literal corrections . . . but he deprecated the idea of repealing it, or destroying its efficacy by explanations and amendments. The principle of it was good, and it ought by all means to be strengthened and confirmed. . . .

487. The Combination Act of 1800 (39 and 40 Geo. III, c. 106)

(*Statutes at Large*, LIII, pp. 847–862.)

An Act to repeal an Act, passed in the last Session of Parliament, intitulated, " An Act to prevent Unlawful Combinations of Workmen"; and to substitute other provisions in lieu thereof.

Whereas it is expedient to explain and amend an Act [39 Geo. III, c. 81] . . . to prevent unlawful combinations of workmen . . . be it enacted . . . that from . . . the passing of this Act, the said Act shall be repealed; and that all contracts, covenants and agreements whatsoever . . . at any time . . . heretofore made . . . between any journeymen manufacturers or other persons . . . for obtaining an advance of wages of them or any of them, or any other journeymen manufacturers or workmen, or other persons in any manufacture, trade or business, or for lessening or altering their or any of their usual hours or time of working, or for decreasing the quantity of work (save and except any contract made or to be made between any master and his journeyman or manufacturer, for or on account of the work or service of such journeyman or manufacturer with whom such contract may be made), or for preventing or hindering any person or persons from employing whomsoever he, she, or they shall think proper to employ . . . or for controlling or anyway affecting any person or persons carrying on any manufacture, trade or business, in the conduct or management thereof, shall be . . . illegal, null and void. . . .

II. . . . No journeyman, workman or other person shall at any time after the passing of this Act make or enter into, or be concerned in the making of or entering into any such contract, covenant or agreement, in writing or not in writing . . . and every . . . workman . . . who, after the passing of this Act, shall be guilty of any of the said offences, being thereof lawfully convicted, upon his own confession, or the oath or oaths of one or more credible witness or witnesses, before any two Justices of the Peace . . . within three calendar months next after the offence shall have been committed, shall, by order of such Justices, be committed to and confined in the common gaol, within his or their jurisdiction, for any time not exceeding 3 calendar months, or at the discretion of such Justices shall be committed to some House of Correction within the same jurisdiction, there to remain and to be kept to hard labour for any time not exceeding 2 calendar months.

III. . . . Every . . . workman . . . who shall at any time after the passing of this Act enter into any combination to obtain an advance of wages, or to lessen or alter the hours or duration of the time of working, or to decrease the quantity of work, or for any other purpose contrary to this Act, or who shall, by giving money, or by persuasion, solicitation or intimidation, or any other means, wilfully and maliciously endeavour to prevent any unhired or unemployed journeyman or workman, or other person, in any manufacture, trade or business, or any other person wanting employment in such manufacture, trade or business, from hiring himself to any manufacturer or tradesman, or person conducting any manufacture, trade or business, or who shall, for the purpose of obtaining an advance of wages, or for any other purpose contrary to the provisions of this Act, wilfully and maliciously decoy, persuade, solicit, intimidate, influence or prevail, or attempt or endeavour to prevail, on any journeyman or workman, or other person hired or employed, or to be hired or employed in any such manufacture, trade or business, to quit or leave his work, service or employment, or who shall wilfully and maliciously hinder or prevent any manufacturer or tradesman, or other person, from employing in his or her manufacture, trade or business, such journeymen, workmen and other persons as he or she shall think proper, or who, being hired or employed, shall, without any just or reasonable cause, refuse to work with any other journeyman or workman employed or hired to work therein, and who shall be lawfully convicted of any of the said offences, upon his own confession, or the oath or oaths of one or more credible witness or witnesses, before any two Justices of the Peace for the county, . . . or place where such offence shall be committed, within 3 calendar months . . . shall, by order of such Justices, be committed to . . . gaol for any time not exceeding 3 calendar months; or otherwise be committed to some House of Correction . . . for any time not exceeding 2 calendar months.

IV. And for the more effectual suppression of all combinations amongst journeymen, workmen and other persons employed in any manufacture, trade or business, be it further enacted, that all and every persons and person whomsoever (whether employed in any such manufacture, trade or business, or not) who shall attend any meeting had or held for the purpose of making or entering into any contract, covenant or agreement, by this Act declared to be illegal, or of entering into, supporting, maintaining, continuing, or carrying on any combination for any purpose by this Act declared to be illegal, or who shall summons, give notice to, call upon, persuade, entice, solicit, or by intimidation, or any other means, endeavour to induce any journeyman, workman, or other person, employed in any manufacture, trade or business, to attend any such meeting, or who shall collect, demand, ask, or receive any sum of money from any such journeyman, workman, or other person, for any of the purposes aforesaid, or who shall persuade, entice, solicit, or by intimidation, or any other means, endeavour to induce any such journeyman, workman or other person to enter into or be concerned in any such combination, or who shall pay any sum of money, or make or enter into any subscription or contribution, for or towards the support or encouragement of any such illegal meeting or combination, and who shall be lawfully convicted of any of the said offences, upon his own confession, or the oath or oaths of one or more credible witness or witnesses, before any two Justices of the Peace . . . within 3 calendar months . . . shall . . . be committed to and confined in the common gaol . . . for any time not exceeding 3 calendar months, or otherwise be committed to some House of Correction . . . for any time not exceeding 2 calendar months.

V. [No person shall contribute for any expenses incurred for acting contrary to this Act, or towards the support of any person to induce him not to work, on penalty not exceeding £10, and any person collecting money for such purposes, shall forfeit, not exceeding £5. Offences shall be determined in a summary way before two Justices, who shall fix the penalty, and if not paid, shall cause it to be levied by distress, and if not to be had, shall commit the offender to the common gaol or House of Correction.]

VI. [Sums contributed as subscriptions towards any of the purposes prohibited by this Act to be forfeited.]

VII, VIII. [Concerning the recovery of such contribution money.]

IX. [Offenders may be compelled to give evidence and shall be indemnified from prosecution for any matter relative to their testimony.]

X, XI. [Justices may summon offenders and witnesses and may commit them for non-appearance or refusal to testify.]

XII. [Form of convictions.]

XIII. [Convictions to be transmitted to the next General or Quarter Sessions to be filed, and if appeal be made the Justices shall then proceed to hear it.]

XIV. [Act not to abridge powers now given by law to Justices touching combinations of manufacturers, &c.]

XV. [Act not to empower manufacturers to employ workmen contrary to the provisions now in force for regulating the conduct of any particular manufacture, without licence from a Justice, who may grant the same, whenever the ordinary course of the manufacture is obstructed.]

XVI. [No master in the trade in which any offence is charged to have been committed, shall act as a Justice under this Act.]

XVII. [All contracts between masters or other persons, for reducing the wages of workmen or for altering the usual hours of working, or increasing the quantity of work, shall be void, and masters convicted thereof shall forfeit £20.]

XVIII. And whereas it will be a great convenience and advantage to masters and workmen engaged in manufactures, that a cheap and summary mode be established for settling all disputes that may arise between them respecting wages and work; be it further enacted . . . that, from and after 1 August . . . 1800, in all cases that shall or may arise within . . . England, where the masters and workmen cannot agree respecting the price or prices to be paid for work actually done in any manufacture, or any injury or damage done or alleged to have been done by the workmen to the work, or respecting any delay or supposed delay on the part of the workmen in finishing the work, or the not finishing such work in a good and workman-like manner, or accord-ing to any contract; and in all cases of dispute or difference, touching any contract or agreement for work or wages between masters and workmen in any trade or manufacture, which cannot be otherwise mutually adjusted and settled by and between them, it shall and may be, and it is hereby declared to be lawful for such masters and workmen between whom such dispute or difference shall arise . . . or either of them, to demand and have an arbitration or reference of such matter or matters in dispute; and each of them is hereby authorised and empowered forthwith to nominate and appoint an arbitrator . . . to arbitrate and determine such matter or matters in dispute as aforesaid by writing, subscribed by him in the presence of and attested by one witness . . . and to deliver the same personally to the other party . . . and to require the other party to name an arbitrator in like manner within two days after such reference to arbitration shall have been so demanded; and such arbitrators so appointed . . . are hereby authorised and required to . . . examine upon oath the parties and their witnesses . . . and forthwith to proceed to hear and determine the complaints of the parties, and the matter or matters in dispute between them; and the award to be made by such arbitrators within the time herein-after limited, shall in all cases be final and conclusive between the parties; but in case such arbitrators so appointed shall not agree to decide such matter or matters in dispute, so to be referred to them as aforesaid, and shall not make and sign their award within the space of three days after the signing of the submission to their award by both parties, that then it shall be lawful for the parties or either of them to require such arbitrators forthwith and without delay to go before and attend upon one of his Majesty's Justices of the Peace acting in and for the county . . . or place where such dispute shall happen and be referred, and state to such Justice the points in difference between them . . . which points . . . the said Justice shall . . . hear and determine, and for that purpose . . . examine the parties and their witnesses upon oath, if he shall think fit. . . .

XIX. [The parties may extend the time limited for making an award.]

XXII. [If either party shall not perform what is directed by the award, he may be committed.]

XXIII. [Any person convicted under this Act may appeal to the General or Quarter Sessions, whose decision shall be final.]

488. Resolutions of the Select Committee of the House of Commons on the Combination Laws, 21 May 1824

(Hansard's *Parliamentary Debates*, New Series, XI, 811–813.)

For this committee, which was appointed to inquire into the laws respecting the emigration of artisans, the export of machinery, and combinations of workmen, see No. 378. The resolutions were drafted by Francis Place and formed the basis of the repealing Act of 1824, which was smuggled through Parliament without either Government or employers, apparently, being aware of what was being done.

1. That it appears, by the evidence before the Committee, that combinations of workmen have taken place in England, Scotland and Ireland, often to a great extent, to raise and keep up their wages, to regulate their hours of working, and to impose

restrictions on the masters, respecting apprentices or others whom they might think proper to employ; and that, at the time the evidence was taken, combinations were in existence, attended with strikes or suspension of work; and that the laws have not hitherto been effectual to prevent such combinations.

2. That serious breaches of the peace and acts of violence, with strikes of the workmen, often for very long periods, have taken place, in consequence of, and arising out of the combinations of workmen, and been attended with loss to both the masters and the workmen, and with considerable inconvenience and injury to the community.

3. That the masters have often united and combined to lower the rates of their workmen's wages, as well as to resist a demand for an increase, and to regulate their hours of working; and sometimes to discharge their workmen who would not consent to the conditions offered to them; which have been followed by suspension of work, riotous proceedings, and acts of violence.

4. That prosecutions have frequently been carried on, under the Statute and the Common Law against the workmen, and many of them have suffered different periods of imprisonment for combining and conspiring to raise their wages, or to resist their reduction, and to regulate their hours of working.

5. That several instances have been stated to the Committee, of prosecutions against masters for combining to lower wages and to regulate the hours of working; but no instance has been adduced of any master having been punished for that offence.

6. That the laws have not only not been efficient to prevent combinations either of masters or workmen, but, on the contrary, have, in the opinion of many of both parties, had a tendency to produce mutual irritation and distrust, and to give a violent character to the combinations, and to render them highly dangerous to the peace of the community.

7. That it is the opinion of this Committee that masters and workmen should be freed from such restrictions as regard the rate of wages and the hours of working, and be left at perfect liberty to make such agreements as they may mutually think proper.

8. That, therefore, the Statute Laws that interfere in these particulars between masters and workmen, should be repealed; and also that the common law, under which a peaceable meeting of masters or workmen may be prosecuted as a conspiracy, should be altered.

9. That the Committee regret to find from the evidence, that societies, legally enrolled as benefit societies, have been frequently made the cloak, under which funds have been raised for the support of combinations and strikes, attended with acts of violence and intimidation; and without recommending any specific course, they wish to call the attention of the House to the frequent perversion of these institutions from their avowed and legitimate objects.

10. That the practice of settling disputes by arbitration between masters and workmen, has been attended with good effects; and it is desirable that the laws which direct and regulate arbitration, should be consolidated, amended, and made applicable to all trades.

11. That it is absolutely necessary, when repealing the Combination Laws, to

enact such a law as may efficiently, and by summary process, punish either workmen or masters who, by threats, intimidation or acts of violence, should interfere with that perfect freedom which ought to be allowed to each party, of employing his labour or capital in the manner he may deem most advantageous.

489. Debate in the House of Commons on the Combination Laws, 29 March 1825

(Hansard's *Parliamentary Debates*, New Series, XII, 1288–1314.)

Mr. Huskisson . . . [The Act of 1824] commenced by a motion introduced by an hon. gentleman on the opposite side of the House, who pointed out the hardships to which, under the then subsisting laws, journeymen and others were liable. . . . A Committee was accordingly granted . . . consisting of about 50 members; and it, undoubtedly, examined a vast variety of evidence. . . . The result of those labours was–not that a Report was made to that House (which, as he thought, would have been the most desirable course) stating the grounds upon which the Committee had come to the determination of recommending the introduction of their Bill, and thereby affording to the public, and in a more especial manner to Parliament, the necessary information as to the motives which induced them to recommend such a change of the existing law; but that the Committee adopted, finally, a string of resolutions which involved no such statement whatever. . . . He was himself a member of that Committee, and perhaps he ought to mention that circumstance with considerable regret, owing to the fact of numerous other avocations of an official nature, in which he was all that time extremely busied, having prevented him from paying that degree of attention to the business of the Committee, which he could have wished to do. . . . They had equally precluded him, when the Bill in question was brought in, from considering it with all the attention and care, in its various stages, that it deserved to be considered with. And he might go further and express his regret that those of its enactments which were of a legal nature, had not, possibly, been discussed with all the technical knowledge which might have been beneficially applied to them by those hon. and learned friends of his of whose professional learning, in ordinary cases, Government had the benefit.

The consequence of all this had been that some of the provisions of the Bill, which afterwards passed into an Act, were of a very extraordinary nature. Not only did the Bill repeal all former Statutes relative to combinations and conspiracies of workmen, but it even provided that no proceedings should be had at common law, on account of any such combination, meeting, conspiracy, or uniting together of journeymen, &c, for, in fact, almost any purpose; and thus, by one clause, it went to preclude the possibility of applying any legal remedy to a state of things which might become, and which had since become, a great public evil. . . . The Bill itself . . . repealing 30 or 40 Acts of Parliament, and in this singular manner putting aside the common law altogether, was brought into the House at a late period of the Session; passed through its first stage, subsequent to the first reading, on Wednesday, the 2nd of June, and on Saturday the 5th of June, only four days after the second reading, and in the same week, was read a third time and passed, without any discussion. . . .

To . . . the Secretary of State for the Home Department numerous reports had been forwarded, detailing acts of outrage and violence on the part of workmen combined against employers, of the most disgraceful character. . . . Those reports . . . manifested, in all those classes of workmen who had misconceived the real object of the Legislature in the late Act, a disposition to combine against the masters, and a tendency to proceedings destructive of the property and business of the latter, which, if permitted to remain unchecked, must terminate in producing the greatest mischiefs to the country. . . .

Mr. Hume . . . was satisfied . . . that many classes had gone further beyond their own interest or the interest of the community, than could possibly be permitted. But it did happen that, since the passing of the Act, employment had been increasing; workmen had been more in demand, and these causes had tended to the mischief complained of. . . . He was sorry to say that the Union societies in Dublin had been productive of the greatest evil. Many persons had actually been murdered. . . . In Dublin, if the curriers were offended with their masters, they applied to the carpenters, and marked out the objects of their censure; if the carpenters were offended with theirs, they applied to the shoemakers or any other trade; and then the unhappy individual who was afterwards assaulted, could not, if he survived, bring any of the offenders to justice, for they were all unknown to him. . . . His objection to the Combination Law generally was that it punished the whole of the operative class for the offence of a few of its members. He admitted that the men had acted with extreme impropriety, but . . . in some cases the conduct of the masters was worse than that of the men. . . .

Mr. Secretary Peel . . . In the course of the three last years no less than ten lives had been lost in consequence of these combinations [in Dublin], and not one of the persons connected with these murders had been brought to justice. . . . He was glad to observe the unanimity which prevailed in the House, respecting the impropriety of combinations of all kinds. . . .

Mr. Huskisson . . . It was really as the friend, not as the enemy, of the workmen, as well as of the masters, that he proposed this inquiry. He considered this to be a question entirely disconnected with party feeling. . . .

490. Report of the Select Committee of the House of Commons on Combination Laws, 1825

(Parliamentary Papers, 1825, IV, p. 499.)

. . . The first object of your Committee was to ascertain the actual state of the country in respect to combinations existing among the working and manufacturing classes; and for this purpose they inspected various communications laid before them by . . . the Home department, and the President of the Committee of trade. From these it appeared that, in almost every part of the United Kingdom in which large bodies of men are collected for the purpose of carrying on any craft or manufacture, combination exists in a more or less objectionable form, and has been the subject of complaint and representation. . . .

Among the cases they have examined are those of the coopers, the seamen in the

Tyne and the Wear, the papermakers, the shipwrights at Bristol, at Shields, and in the river Thames; the coachmakers in Dublin, the workmen in some of the collieries in Scotland. They have also enquired into the cases of the cotton spinners and the trades in Ireland. . . . In these cases it appears either that the Associations had commenced since the passing of the Act of the last Session, or that having previously existed, had taken a more open and avowed character. That they vary considerably in extent, consisting in some instances of only a few hundred individuals, while in others they comprehend many thousands; that they are constituted with the utmost regularity, having their Presidents, Secretaries, Committees, and printed Regulations, by which they are ostensibly governed. The superintendence of the business of these Associations is generally assigned to a Committee periodically elected, by the direction of which they appear to be governed in their discussions with their masters, and in respect to the circumstances under which the labour of the whole body was to be continued or withdrawn. . . .

Their objects appear to be in most instances the regulation of wages, combined with the assumption, in certain particulars, of a power of dictation in the conduct of the business in which they are engaged; the effect of which, if submitted to, would be totally to subvert the independence of the masters, and deprive them of all means of resistance to the further demands of their workmen, of whatever nature those demands might eventually be. . . .

It will be seen that in their general construction these societies are nearly similar; their objects, although in most cases connected with the rise or maintenance of wages, usually extend to conditions affecting the conduct of the business or manufacture in which the members . . . are occupied, particularly the number and description of apprentices or persons to be engaged, and the exclusive employment of persons connected with the society. The resources on which they depend are derived from general contributions, form at once a bond of connexion, and supply powerful means of carrying into effect their purposes by the application of them to the support of such individuals as, in maintaining the common cause against the masters, may be deprived of employment, and require assistance. As, in all contests carried on by a combination of the workmen, it is indispensable to success to deprive the masters of the power of substituting other workmen for those who may be dismissed or withdrawn from their service, every effort is necessarily directed to draw or retain as large a portion of workmen within the circle of combination as possible; to effect this, every art of seduction and persuasion, every application of threat, insult, intimidation and outrage, is, as circumstances require, put in practice. . . .

In the collection of funds, in the imposition of fines, in the attempts to limit the employment of apprentices, to regulate the conduct of manufacture as well as in the means used of extending their influence over workmen, and carrying on measures against the legitimate authority of the masters, is to be found, in the opinion of your Committee, the necessity of some further legislative provision, if not to check the progress of the Association, to confine its operation to those objects alone which are essential to the protection of both the workman and the master, and may be secured without impairing the freedom of either, or endangering the public tranquillity. . . .

The first object of the Act in question [*i.e.* that of 1824], was the repeal of all the statutes which were in force against Combination, at the period of its enactment. In the wisdom of this repeal . . . your Committee fully coincide; and . . . so far from recommending the re-enactment of them, they should deem it a measure of objectionable severity towards the workmen. . . .

The alterations your Committee propose, although not departing from what they believe to have been the intention of the Act of the last Session, so far pervade the whole of the remainder of it, that they think it expedient to recommend, in the first instance, its total repeal, with a view of re-enacting such parts of it as it may be advisable to retain, and comprehending all that relates to Combination . . . in a single act.

The effect of this repeal would be to restore the operation of the common law in those particular instances in which it is suspended. . . . Your Committee, however . . . are of opinion that an exception should be made to its operation, in favour of meetings and consultations amongst either masters or workmen, the object of which is peaceably to consult upon the rate of wages . . . and to agree to co-operate with each other in endeavouring to raise or lower it, or to settle the hours of labour; an exception, they trust, which while it gives to . . . masters and workmen the ample means of maintaining their respective interests, will not afford any support to the assumption of power or dictation in either party to the prejudice of the other, least of all that assumption of control on the part of the workmen in the conduct of any business or manufacture which is utterly incompatible with the necessary authority of the master, at whose risk, and by whose capital, it is to be carried on. . . .

Your Committee feel it essential to the regard which is due to the free exercise of individual judgment, to propose that the resolutions of any such association should be allowed to bind only parties actually present, or personally consenting. . . .

This is all the freedom in respect to Combination, that seems essential for any beneficial purpose; and your Committee are of opinion, that all Combination beyond this should be at the risk of the parties, and open as heretofore, to the animadversion of the common law. . . .

Your Committee . . . recommend that every precaution should be taken, to ensure a safe and free option to those who, from whatever motive, may have no inclination to take part in such associations. . . . To this your Committee attach the highest importance, as being indispensably necessary, not less to the real interests of the working classes, than to the public peace. . . .

These are the alterations of the law to which, on the best view they can take of the nature of the Combinations now existing in the country, the Committee think it expedient to confine their recommendations, in the hope that it may have the effect of restraining the operation of those Associations to the objects which they have above described. In doing this, however, they are most desirous that their impression of the importance of imposing such a restraint on the system of Combination . . . should not be measured by the lenity with which they recommend it should in the first instance be treated. The danger arising from it, unless cautiously restrained, appears to your Committee to be of the most formidable character, and to affect equally the individual interests of those immediately concerned, the interests of the public, and the internal tranquillity of the country. If the spirit of dictation now manifested be suffered to prevail among the working classes, if the application of capital is to be controlled, and the principle of free labour totally subverted, every part of the process of manufacture and trade subjected to the judgment of committees, and every improvement by machinery or otherwise admitted or rejected at their discretion; the necessary consequence must be, that capital will be withdrawn or transported, the source of every branch of our industry gradually cut off, and the whole labouring population of the country consigned to the distress and misery, which it is the tendency of the ill advised Combinations . . . rapidly and inevitably to produce. Against such a state of things, should it be continued . . . it will become the duty of Parliament to look for effectual remedies . . . as . . . the necessary defence of the commerce and navigation, the capitalists and consumers of the country. . . . If, however, on the one hand, your Committee cannot but anticipate the fatal results the working classes are bringing upon themselves . . . on the other, they derive hope from their confidence in the good sense and good dispositions of by far the greatest proportion of those who, mistaking their own interest . . . are now enrolled amongst the members of these combinations. They are sanguine in believing . . . their good sense . . . will prevail, and they require only to understand their danger to seek the means of avoiding it. The recommendations contained in this report, if carried into effect by the Legislature and firmly executed by the magistracy, will, as your Committee trust, afford those means, by giving protection to all who wish to emancipate themselves from any association into which they have been reluctantly forced. . . . By availing themselves of these, they will not only recover the exercise of their own free will, in disposing of their labour . . . but at the same time restore to the various branches of our national industry that liberty by which they have so long flourished, equally to the advantage of every class dependent upon them, and to the strength, the security, and happiness of the Empire.

491. The Combination Act, 1825 (6 Geo. IV, c. 129)

(*Statutes at Large*, LXXIX, pp. 1066–1078.)

An Act to repeal the Laws relating to the Combinations of Workmen, and to make other provisions in lieu thereof.

Whereas an Act was passed in the last session of Parliament, entitled *An Act to repeal the laws relative to the Combination of Workmen* . . . and whereas the provisions of the said Act have not been found effectual: and whereas such combinations are injurious to trade and commerce, dangerous to the tranquillity of the country, and especially prejudicial to the interests of all who are concerned in them . . . be it therefore enacted . . . that . . . the said . . . Act . . . shall be . . . repealed.

II. [Recites 33 Acts relating to Combinations, to be wholly or partially repealed; all other enactments on the subject to be repealed.]

III. . . . From and after the passing of this Act, if any person shall by violence to the person or property, or by threats or intimidation, or by molesting or in any way obstructing another, force or endeavour to force any journeyman, manufacturer, workman or other person hired or employed in any manufacture, trade, or business, to depart from his . . . employment . . . or to return his work before the same shall be finished, or prevent or endeavour to prevent any journeyman, manufacturer, workman or other person . . . from hiring himself to, or from accepting work or employment from any person or persons; or if any person shall use . . . violence to the person or property of another, or threats or intimidation, or shall molest or in any way obstruct another for the purpose of forcing or inducing such person to belong to any club or association, or to contribute to any common fund, or to pay any fine or penalty, or on account of his not belonging to any particular club or association, or not having contributed or having refused to contribute to any common fund, or to pay any fine or penalty, or on account of his not having complied or of his refusing to comply with any rules, orders, resolutions or regulations made to obtain an advance or to reduce the rate of wages, or to lessen or alter the hours of working, or to decrease or alter the quantity of work, or to regulate the mode of carrying on any manufacture, trade, or business, or the management thereof; or if any person shall by violence to the person or property . . . or by threats or intimidation, or by molesting or in any way obstructing another, force or endeavour to force any manufacturer or person carrying on any trade or business, to make any alteration in his mode of regulating, managing, conducting or carrying on such manufacture, trade, or business, or to limit the number of his apprentices, or the number or description of his journeymen, workmen, or servants; every person so offending or aiding, abetting, or assisting therein, being convicted . . . shall be imprisoned only, or . . . may be imprisoned and kept to hard labour, for any time not exceeding three calendar months.

IV. . . . This Act shall not . . . subject any persons to punishment, who shall meet together for the sole purpose of consulting upon and determining the rate of wages or prices, which the persons present . . . shall require or demand for his or their work, or the hours or time for which he or they shall work . . . or who shall enter into any agreement, verbal or written, among themselves, for the purpose of fixing the rate of wages or prices which the parties . . . shall require or demand for his or their work, or the hours . . . for which he or they will work, in any manufacture, trade, or business; . . . persons so meeting . . . or entering into any such agreement . . . shall not be liable to any prosecution . . . any Law or Statute to the contrary notwithstanding.

V. . . . This Act shall not . . . subject any persons to punishment who shall meet together for the sole purpose of consulting upon and determining the rate of wages or prices which . . . any of them shall pay to his or their journeymen, workmen or servants . . . or the hours or time of working . . . or who shall enter into any agreement . . . for the purpose of fixing the rate of wages or prices. . . .

VI. [Offenders compelled to give evidence.]

VII. . . . Be it further enacted, that on complaint and information on oath before any one or more Justice or Justices of the Peace, of any offence having been committed against this Act, within his or their respective jurisdictions, and within six calendar months before such complaint or information shall be made, such Justice or Justices are hereby authorized and required to summon the person or persons charged . . . to appear before any two such Justices. . . . Such Justices shall . . . make enquiry touching the matters complained of, and . . . upon confession by the party, or proof by one or more credible witness or witnesses upon oath, . . . convict or acquit. . . .

[VIII. Power to summon witnesses.

IX–X. Form of convictions.

XI. Proceedings under this Act in Scotland.

XII. Appeal may be made to Quarter Sessions.]

XIII. . . . No Justice of the Peace, being also a master in the particular trade or manufacturer, in or concerning which any offence is charged to have been committed under this Act, shall act as such Justice under this Act.

492. Evidence of William Longston before the Committee on the Bill to regulate the labour of children in the mills and factories of the United Kingdom, 1832

(Parliamentary Papers, 1831–1832, xv, pp. 428–430.)

Do the operatives [in cotton mills] connive at the violations of the laws which have been enacted for their own express protection ?–Yes, almost universally. . . . If they do not connive, they must be brought forward as witnesses against the masters; but, being brought forward as a witness against the master, if the person be a voluntary witness, it is ten to one if they can obtain employment anywhere in the district where they are known, and where their name could be sent, so that their persons could be in anywise identified; I think this explanation will show and prove that employment would be exceedingly improbable for them anywhere, as employers would never deem themselves safe where they had in employ one who had been a voluntary witness against them. . . . I saw an instance of it, perhaps four or five months ago; a manufacturer in the town of Stockport was brought before the magistrates for overworking children, and the decision was in the manufacturer's favour . . . I think it was one of the cases wherein the manufacturer really was wronged; the decision, however, was in his favour; but the persons who came as witnesses against him I saw in the streets afterwards, and they told me that they could not get employment.

Neither with their actual master nor with any other person?–Nowhere; they told me they had applied at various places, but that their having become witnesses, occasioned them to be refused employment wherever they applied.

Then you presume that there is a combination among the masters, to exclude from work those individuals who give information upon the infraction of the law ?–I am not aware that there is any combination, I have judged it rather to be a tacit consent, or a general practice, than a combination.

Perhaps you have known of instances, since you speak so fully upon this subject, in which employers have dictated terms to the employed, which interfere with their rights as workmen?–Yes, I have known a great many instances of that kind. . . . There was a contention between the employers and the employed at Stockport, in the beginning of 1829, about wages; and of this contest a strike was the consequence; and the masters of Hyde thought proper to interfere, and that interference it may be necessary to give in their own words, as published and placarded. They say–

"We, the undersigned Spinners and Power-loom manufacturers of Hyde, Staley Bridge, Dukinfield, and the neighbourhood, Having observed with regret the self-inflicted and continuing distress of the operatives of Stockport, instigated by evil-designing persons to turn out against their masters, and being informed that this distress is prolonged by assistance being rendered by our work-people to the turn-outs in that town, do hereby agree to abate ten per cent every fortnight from the wages of such of our piece-work hands who shall refuse to sign a declaration, that they will not remain or become members of any combination, interfering with the free exercise of individual labour; or directly or indirectly contribute to the support of any turn-outs, on pain of forfeiting a fortnight's wages, should they be found so doing."

. . . Immediately afterwards, as is seen by that placard on the walls of Stockport, a written requirement, called an agreement, was offered by the masters for the operatives to sign, which was a *sine qua non* of employment; the operatives were to sign the following words, or not be employed; and thousands of them did so, and were obliged to do so.

[*The following document was then put in, and read:*]

"We, the undersigned, agree with Messrs. —— that we will work for them on the following terms:

"We declare that we do not belong to the society called the 'Union', or any other society for the support of turn-outs, or which has for its object any interference with the rules laid down for the government of mills or manufactories.

"We agree with our said masters, that we will not become members of, or be connected with, any such society, while we remain in our present employ.

"That we will not, directly, or indirectly, subscribe or contribute to any such society, or to any turn-out hands whatsoever.

"That we will give a fortnight's notice previous to leaving our employ; and we will observe all the other rules of this mill, and all special agreements that we may enter into with our masters.

"And if we are discovered to act contrary to the above agreement, each of us so offending will forfeit a sum equal to a fortnight's wages; and our masters shall have power to deduct the same from our wages, or discharge us from their employ without any notice, at their own option."

I may observe, that by the wording of this document, they say they would not directly or indirectly support any turn-out hands whatsoever; that they were liable to the penalty here announced, in case they supported a son, or even gave any thing, directly or indirectly, to a starving daughter or other relative. . . .

(b) CO-OPERATIVE SOCIETIES

493. Dr. William King to Henry Brougham, Brighton, 12 Dec. 1828

(T. W. Mercer, *Dr. William King and the Co-operator, 1828–1830*, pp. 119–121.)

A number of persons, chiefly of the working class, having read several works on the subject of co-operation, conceived the possibility of reducing it to practice in some shape or other. They accordingly formed themselves into a society; and met once a week for reading and conversation on the subject; they also began a weekly subscription of 1d. The members who joined were considerable—at one time upwards of 170; but, as happens in such cases, many were lukewarm and indifferent, and the numbers fluctuated. Those who remained began at once an evident improvement in their minds. When the subscription amounted to £5, it was invested in groceries, which were retailed to the members. Business kept increasing. The first week the amount sold was half-a-crown; it is now about £38. The profit is about 10 per cent; so that a return of £20 a week pays all expenses, besides which the members have a large room to meet in and work in. About six months ago, the society took a lease of 28 acres of land, about nine miles from Brighton, which they cultivate as a garden and nursery out of their surplus capital. They employ on the garden, out of 75 members, four and sometimes five men, with their own capital. They pay the men at the garden 14s. a week, the ordinary rate of wages in the county being 10s., and of parish labourers 6s. The men are also allowed rent and vegetables. They take their meals together. One man is married and his wife is housekeeper.

The principle of the society is—the value of labour. The operation is by means of a common capital. An individual capital is an impossibility to the workman, but a common capital not. The advantage of the plan is that of mutual insurance; but there is an advantage beyond, *viz.*, that the workman will thus get the whole produce of his labour to himself; and if he chooses to work harder or longer, he will benefit in proportion. If it is possible for men to work for themselves, many advantages will arise. The other day they wanted a certain quantity of land planted before the winter. Thirteen members went from Brighton early in the morning, gave a day's work, performed the task, and returned home at night. The man who formerly had the land, when he came to market, allowed himself 10s. to spend. The man who now comes to market for the society is contented with 1s. extra wages. Thus these men are in a fair way to accumulate capital enough to find all the members with constant employment; and, of course, the capital will not stop there, other societies are springing up. Those at Worthing and Findon are proceeding as prosperously as ours, only on a smaller scale. If co-operation be at once proved practicable the working classes will soon see their interest in adopting it. If this goes on, it will draw labour from the market, raise wages, and so operate upon pauperism and crime. All this is pounds, shillings and pence; but another most important feature remains. The members see immediately the value of knowledge. They employ their leisure time in reading and mutual instruction. They have appointed one of their members librarian and schoolmaster; he teaches every evening. Even their discussions involve both practice and theory, and are of a most improving nature. Their feelings are of an enlarged, liberal and charitable description. They have no disputes, and feel towards mankind at large as brethren. The *élite* of the society were members of the Mechanics' Institution, and my pupils, and their minds were no doubt prepared there for this Society. It is a happy consummation.

In conclusion, I beg to propose to your great and philanthropic mind the question as to how such societies may be affected by the present state of the law; or how far future laws may be so framed as to operate favourably to them. At the same time, they ask nothing from any one but to be let alone, and nothing from the law but protection. As I have had the opportunity of watching every step of this society, I consider their case proved; but others at a distance will want further experience. If the case is proved, I consider it due to you, sir, as a legislator, philosopher, and the friend of man, to lay it before you. This society will afford you additional motives for completing the Library of Useful Knowledge–the great forerunner of human improvement.

494. William Lovett's Autobiography

(*The Life and Struggles of William Lovett* (1876), pp. 40–46.)

Lovett (1800–1877), described by Holyoake as "the greatest radical secretary of the working class", was one of the founders in 1836 of the London Working Men's Association and took a prominent part in the Chartist agitation. He became Secretary of the British Association for Promoting Co-operative Knowledge in 1830. His autobiography was written between 1840 and 1874.

. . . I was induced to join the First London Co-operative Trading Association; a society first established in the premises of the Co-operative Society, Red Lion Square, and subsequently removed to Jerusalem Passage, Clerkenwell. I think it was about the close of the year 1828 that the first of those trading associations was established at Brighton, by a person of the name of Bryan, and its success was such that between four and five hundred similar associations were very soon established in different parts of the country. The members of those societies subscribed a small weekly sum for the raising of a common fund, with which they opened a general store, containing such articles of food, clothing, books, &c. as were most in request among working men, the profits of which were added to the common stock. As their funds increased, some of them employed their members, such as shoemakers, tailors and other domestic trades: paying them journeymen's wages, and adding the profits to their funds. Many of them were also enabled by these means to raise sufficient capital to commence manufactures on a small scale, such as broadcloths, silk, linen, and worsted goods, shoes, hats, cutlery, furniture, &c. Some few months after I had given up my shop in May's Buildings, I was induced to accept the situation of store-keeper to the 'First London Association' . . . I was sanguine that those associations formed the first step towards the social independence of the labouring classes . . . I was induced to believe that the gradual accumulation of capital by these means would enable the working classes to form themselves into joint-stock associations of labour, by which (with industry, skill and knowledge) they might ultimately have the trade, manufactures and commerce of the country in their own hands. But I failed to perceive that the great majority of them lacked the self sacrifices and economy necessary for procuring capital, the discrimination to place the right men in the right position for managing, the plodding industry, skill and knowledge necessary for successful management, the moral disposition to labour earnestly for the general good, and the brotherly fellowship and confidence in one another for making their association effective. . . .

As our association was the first formed in London, it was looked up to for information and advice from all parts of the country. This, entailing much labour, led to the formation of another society entitled, 'The British Association for Promoting Co-operative Knowledge'. As, also, several of those societies had commenced manufactures on a small scale, they were anxious for some depot or place in London where their productions might be deposited for sale to the public, or for exchange with one another. This desire induced the British Association to take a large house in 19, Greville Street, Hatton Garden, the first floor of which was fitted up as a co-operative bazaar, the lower portion being occupied by our First London Association. . . .

Those societies, from the establishment of which so much had been expected, were, however, in the course of three or four years mostly all broken up, and with them the British Association. The chief, or at least the most prominent causes of their failure were religious differences, the want of legal security, and the dislike which the women had to confine their dealings to one shop. The question of *religion* was not productive of much dissension until Mr. Owen's return from America, when his 'Sunday Morning Lectures' excited the alarm of the religious portion of their members, and caused great numbers to secede from them. The want of *legal security* was also the cause of failure, as they could not obtain the ordinary legal redress when their officers or servants robbed or defrauded them, the magistrates refusing to interfere on the ground of their not being legalized, or *enrolled societies*. The prejudice of the members' wives against their stores was no doubt another cause of failure. Whether it was their love of shopping, or their dislike that their husbands should be made acquainted with the exact extent of their dealings, which were booked against them, I know not, but certain it was that they often left the unadulterated and genuine article in search of that which was often questionable. When Mr. Owen first came over from America he looked somewhat coolly on those 'Trading Associations', and very candidly declared that their mere buying and selling formed no part of his grand 'co-operative scheme'; but when he found that great numbers among them were disposed to entertain many of his views, he took them more in favour, and ultimately took an active part among them. . . .

I was one of those who, at one time, was favourably impressed with many of Mr. Owen's views, and more especially with those of a *community of property*. This notion has a peculiar attraction for the plodding, toiling, ill-remunerated sons and daughters of labour. The idea of all the powers of machinery, of all the arts and inventions of men, being applied for the benefit of all in common, to the lightening of their toil and the increase of their comforts, is one the most captivating to those who accept the idea without investigation. The prospect of having spacious halls, gardens, libraries and museums at their command; of having light alternate labour in field or factory; of seeing their children educated, provided and cared for at the public expense; of having no fear or care of poverty themselves; nor for wife, children or friends they might leave behind them; is one of the most cheering and consolatory to an enthusiastic mind. I was one who accepted this grand idea of machinery working for the benefit of all, without considering that those powers and inventions have been chiefly called forth, and industriously and efficiently applied by the stimulus *our industrial system has afforded*, and that the benefits to the originators and successful workers of them–though large in some instances–have been few and trifling, compared to the benefits *which the millions now enjoy from their general application*. Those great results, too, have hitherto been realised by the hope of wealth, fame or station, *keeping up man's energies to the tension point*. But who can foresee what human beings may become when the *individualism* in their nature is checked by education, and endeavoured to be crushed out of them by the mandate of a majority. . . . Of what advantage the splendour and enjoyment of all art and nature *if man has no choice of enjoyment?* And what to him would be spacious halls and luxurious apartments, and all the promised blessings of a community, if he must rise, work, dress, occupy and enjoy, not as he himself desires, *but as the fiat of the majority wills it?* . . . But we shall be told of the perfect and wise arrangements that are so to perfect human character, that no man 'shall ever need to be blamed for his conduct', nor men ever have occasion to make their fellows 'responsible for their actions'. Unfortunately, the great obstacle to the realisation of this perfect state of things is, that the perfect and wise arrangements are to depend *on imperfect men and women*. . . . But though mature reflection has caused me to have lost faith in 'a *Community of Property*', I have not lost faith in the great benefits that may yet be realised by a wise and judicious system of *Co-operation in the Production of Wealth*. The former I believe to be unjust, unnatural, and despotic in its tendency, a sacrificing of the intellectual energies and moral virtues of the few, to the indolence, ignorance and despotism of the many. The latter I believe to be in accordance with wisdom and justice, an arrangement by which small means and united efforts may yet be made the instruments for upraising the multitude in knowledge, prosperity, and freedom. I am satisfied, however, that much good resulted from the formation of those co-operative trading associations, notwithstanding their failure. Their being able to purchase pure and unadulterated articles of food; their manufacturing and exchanging with one another various articles which they were induced to make up in their leisure hours, or when out of employment; the mental and moral improvement derived from their various meetings and discussions, were among the advantages that resulted from them. . . .

(c) THE FRIENDLY SOCIETIES

495. Earl Fitzwilliam to Joseph Becket, 25 Dec. 1792
(Fitzwilliam MSS.)

My sentiments respecting the propriety of securing under the authority of Parliament the property of the sick clubs and of rendering it easy to be recovered remain the same they were last year: they were founded upon a full consideration of the subject, and nothing has occurred to me to make me change the opinion I had formed of the utility of these institutions, and therefore that measures should be taken to secure the interests of their members. I really view them with the greatest partiality and admiration: I consider them as pregnant with essential good: they elevate the sentiment by inspiring a spirit of provident industry: they teach the moral lesson of reciprocal benefit by insuring its practice–as much as I am a friend to the poor law, and consider it as the ornament and glory of our constitution, as that, which reduces all ranks of people into one general mass by creating a community of interests between the rich and the poor, for by its operation and effects, the possessions of the rich become virtually the patrimony of the poor, the affluence of the one, the comfort of the other: nevertheless though its benefits should never be niggardly dealt out by the rich, but on the contrary, liberally dispensed, still for many reasons they ought to be reluctantly required by the poor, but principally because such relief always produces the bad effects of lowering the person relieved in his own estimation, and by doing so, of damping the powers and energy both of his mind and body. It is not so with relief obtained from sick clubs: the person who applies, demands but his own, he demands nothing but that deposit made by his own industry and exertion in the day of health and activity against the hour of sickness and inability. He receives it as such with pride and dignity. I see therefore with pride and satisfaction the spirit of my countrymen rising superior to a dependence on a constrained assistance, and with magnanimity providing for themselves: to assist them in doing so, I need scarcely add will be a great pleasure to me and if they think my services worth having, they may command them. . . .

496. Sir F. M. Eden on the Friendly Societies

(*The State of the Poor*, I (1797), pp. 620–621; III, p. 889.)

State of a Friendly Society of Petty Shopkeepers, (in a Parish in the Suburbs of the Metropolis,) instituted in the year 1789
To consist of 61 members

Terms of Admission

	s.	d.		£.	s.	d.
The first month - - -	10	6	The fourth month- - -	0	16	0
The second month - -	12	0	The fifth month - - -	0	18	0
The third month - -	14	0	Ever afterwards to continue	1	1	0

The subscription to be 5s. per quarter; each person to receive, when sick, 10s. 6d. per week, if able to assist themselves; if a nurse is required, 16s. per week: if superannuated, £10. per annum; if there be two, £10. each; if three, £7 each; if four, or more, on the superannuated list, the sum of £21, to be divided equally among them.

If any free member, not on the superannuated list, shall die, the sum of £10 to be allowed for his funeral; and the sum of £5. at the decease of his lawful wife. If a superannuated member dies, the sum of £3. to be allowed for his funeral. No member can be free unless he has belonged to the Club 12 months.

Years	No. of Members	Greatest No. of Sick	Fewest No. of Sick	Deaths	Allowances to sick	Subscriptions, Fines, Interest, etc.	State of the Fund
1789	—	No Allowance made the first year					£89 14 0
1790	60 & 61	4	3	3	£24 4 7	£60 5 0	112 8 7
1791	61	2	1	1	15 5 0	64 12 6	161 15 7
1792	60 & 61	4	2	3	31 8 2	64 3 0	170 14 5
1793	61	6	1	2	38 17 8	66 14 6	196 11 3
1794	60 & 61	3	1	3	27 1 8	68 1 0	221 10 7
1795	60 & 61	4	1	4	28 10 6	69 16 0	239 18 1

State of a Benefit Society of Journeymen Shoemakers, Tailors, &c
(in a Parish near the Tower,) instituted in the year 1780
To consist of 80 members, under the following regulations:

Subscriptions.–Entrance, 2s. 6d.; monthly payment, 1s. 3d.: when the stock is under £20. the box to be declared shut; and 1d. per week extra to be paid to support the sick; and 1s. by each member on the half-yearly night.

Benefits–Sick.–To the sick, when the stock is above £20., 7s. per week; when under £20., 4s. per week.

Superannuated.–A member, after being six months on the box, to be declared superannuated; and to receive 4s. per week for six months more: after that, if unable to work, to receive 2s. 6d. per week for life, or till recovered.

Death.– A member's funeral £7. and his wife or nominee £5. If the member is superannuated, only £3. for his funeral

Years	No. of Members	Greatest No. of Sick	Fewest No. of Sick	Deaths	Payments to Sick, Funerals &c.	Subscriptions, Fines, Interest &c.	State of Fund
1780	35·42	No Allowance to be paid the first Year.					£29 0 0
1781	42·51	4	1	2	£27 17 9	£39 12 7½	40 14 10½
1782	54·56	6	2	3	54 16 6	53 7 8	39 6 0
1783	53·57	6	3	5	70 14 8½	58 9 3½	27 0 7
1784	57·59	7	2	4	58 12 4	63 4 6	31 12 9
1785	58·60	5	1	5	60 7 3	66 12 4½	37 17 10½
1786	61·58	6	3	6	58 18 8	65 9 0½	42 8 2
1787	60·56	7	1	2	60 18 8½	62 19 7½	45 9 0¾
1788	55·59	7	1	5	59 16 8	56 0 9	52 13 1¾
1789	56·58	5	0	1	26 13 11½	60 7 11½	86 7 1¾
1790	60·62	7	2	3	43 16 10	61 9 6	103 19 9¾
1791	63·61	6	1	4	55 19 3	67 14 10	115 15 4¾
1792	63·64	6	3	3	76 19 10	62 5 7	101 1 1¾
1793	61·64	7	1	3	51 17 3½	62 17 9	112 1 7¼
1794	64·62	6	2	6	72 19 6	70 8 5	109 10 6¼
1795	62·58	6	3	6	81 16 10	55 14 6	83 8 2¼

(d) SAVINGS BANKS

497. Number of Savings Banks in each county, with the number of depositors and amount of deposits, 1830

(J. Marshall, *A Digest of all the Accounts relating to the Population, Productions, Resources ... &c. ... of the United Kingdom*, I (1833), p. 9.)

COUNTIES arranged in order o Total Population in 1831.	Total No. of Families in 1831.	No. of Banks, 1830.	Number of Depositors in Savings Banks in Nov. 1830				
			Of Individuals.	Friendly Societies.	Charitable Societies.	Total No. of Account.	Total Amount of Deposits. £
1 Middlesex	314,039	28	66,988	114	153	67,205	1,853,894
2 Lancaster..............	260,025	24	26,147	374	159	26,680	965,144
3 York, West Riding	198,646	17	15,426	298	99	15,861	492,104
4 Devon.................	101,911	4	26,564	378	138	27,080	965,643
5 Surrey................	109,077	19	13,389	76	38	13,503	393,511
6 Kent..................	97,142	21	16,885	171	100	17,156	556,719
7 Stafford	83,593	15	7,387	172	53	7,612	264,173
8 Somerset..............	84,571	9	12,141	170	70	12,381	563,414
9 Norfolk	84,232	10	6,168	69	18	6,255	198,554
10 Gloucester	83,446	12	13,660	185	77	13,922	563,524
11 Warwick..............	72,357	6	6,266	59	55	6,380	184,589
12 Chester...............	64,955	10	7,647	104	2	7,753	321,846
13 Lincoln...............	65,903	17	7,017	74	46	7,137	225,630
14 Essex.................	65,319	15	8,157	163	90	8,410	301,545
15 Southampton..........	64,652	11	7,860	104	53	8,017	318,516
16 Cornwall..............	59,816	8	5,513	93	14	5,620	249,874
17 Suffolk...............	61,533	12	5,371	114	37	5,522	190,567
18 Sussex................	52,716	12	8,506	51	42	8,600	276,793
19 Durham..............	54,736	10	4,578	54	22	4,654	158,298
20 Wilts	51,659	10	6,612	76	45	6,733	266,076
21 Derby................	48,320	6	5,513	123	21	5,657	220,182
22 Nottingham	47,117	6	7,725	256	15	7,996	242,752
23 Salop	46,427	13	9,234	111	26	9,371	391,964
24 Northumberland	48,364	5	6,987	90	19	7,096	307,772
25 Worcester	45,512	8	6,953	74	45	7,072	265,997
26 Leicester	42,142	5	3,366	58	27	3,451	100,601
27 York, North Riding....	40,760	10	5,677	21	12	5,704	197,411
28 Northampton..........	39,163	3	4,845	44	34	4,923	177,577
29 Cumberland	34,820	6	4,016	22	21	4,059	131,913
30 York, East Riding......	36,960	3	5,939	40	9	5,987	220,665
31 Dorset................	33,614	9	5,526	58	35	5,619	250,370
32 Oxford................	31,770	5	5,201	46	36	5,283	157,606
33 Buckingham	31,849	4	1,857	26	14	1,897	60,911
34 Berks	31,081	10	7,138	67	49	7,254	260,639
35 Cambridge............	30,210	2	1,678	46	22	1,746	69,799
36 Hertford..............	29,250	5	3,177	80	90	3,347	166,726
37 Hereford..............	23,565	4	3,892	14	15	3,921	130,712
38 Monmouth............	19,911	4	1,232	32	10	1,274	38,870
39 Bedford	20,016	3	1,765	38	22	1,825	69,661
40 Westmorland	10,984	1	674	3	—	677	24,041
41 Huntingdon	11,278	1	747	30	25	802	26,394
42 City of York & Ainsty..	7,704	1	2,974	16	16	3,006	119,874
43 Rutland	4,191	—	—	—	—	—	—
Totals { ENGLAND.... WALES	2,745,336	384	367,812 10,303	4,117 161	1,787 39	374,448 10,494	13,085,255 340,721
England and Wales....			378,115	4,278	1,826	384,942	13,425,976

Marshall's figures and (uncorrected) totals may be regarded as only approximate.

498. Debate in the House of Commons on the Savings Banks Bill, 2 April 1816

(Cobbett's *Parliamentary Debates*, XXXIII, 841–844.)

Mr. Rose . . . Many persons were not aware of the great advantages which have resulted from establishments of that sort in different parts of the country. They tended, in a remarkable and most beneficial manner, to encourage among the common people of all descriptions, a desire of saving from the earnings of their labour and industry, wherewith to secure them from the sudden reverses of misfortune. It had frequently been remarked that hitherto the most ingenious men employed in different trades, were addicted to idleness and dissipation, because they had no means of depositing that portion of their earnings which they thus squandered away. . . . There were instances where artificers earned from 30 to 40, 50, 60 and even 70s. a week, and yet, in any case of illness or sudden distress, they were forced to resort to the parish for support. It would, perhaps, be said that the plan of Savings Banks might do very well for artificers, in large cities and towns, and for domestic servants, but that they would be of very little use in the country, for those who were employed in agricultural labour. In reply to that, he need only refer to what had been done by the Savings Banks established at Bath, Edinburgh, and other places. . . . Early marriages had often been deprecated, among the poor, because they only tended to produce families without the means of maintaining them: but by this system, so small a sum as one shilling a week being put by, a man, when he attained the age of thirty, might establish himself and his family comfortably in a cottage of his own. In the capital, however, an artificer was better able to lay by 20s. a week than a day labourer in the country was able to lay by one. As a proof of the good results of these Banks, he would mention to the House that in the place which he represented, a labouring man who never earned more than 10s. a week, had, by depositing a certain portion of his earnings, accumulated no less than £100 by the time he was 33 years of age. He had received a letter also yesterday, informing him that a similar establishment had taken place in the town of Hertford, and that in the course of one day no less a sum than £197 had been deposited. He mentioned those circumstances, to induce gentlemen to exert themselves. . . . He alluded more particularly to gentlemen who were at the head of manufacturing districts. They would find an eager disposition on the part of the people to avail themselves of such opportunities to save. The moral good to be expected from the diffusion of those Banks, was great and obvious. They would gradually tend to revive in the lower classes that decent spirit of independence, now almost extinct, which shrinks from accepting parochial relief. The poor man would learn to regard his own industry and labour as the source whence he was to derive temporary aid in the hour of sickness, or permanent support when the approaches of age should unfit him from active exertions. Together with those feelings of honourable confidence in their own means of subsistence, would be allied many domestic virtues, and they who now idly and profligately looked only to the parish for relief, would progressively become better men and better subjects. They would regard their little property, the accumulation of their own industrious labour, with conscious pride and satisfaction, and scorn to be dependent upon the parish for that support which they could provide themselves.

He had hitherto argued the matter as applicable only to the poor: but it had its claims also upon the rich, for the poor-rates of the country would diminish in proportion as there were fewer persons to claim them. . . . With respect to the object of the Bill, it would at least propose to grant the same as had been granted to the Friendly Societies. . . .

Mr. *Thompson* expressed his warmest approbation of the proposed measure of the right hon. gentleman. He thought it was calculated to do as much service to the poor, as a former measure of the same right hon. gentleman for legalising Benefit Societies. They had been of great use in many parts of the country, and though in some cases abused, he believed, yet he had never known any instances, and he lived in a place where there were not less than 50 or 60 of them. With respect to Savings Banks, he knew that in Yorkshire there was a great desire to establish them, but they were a little afraid of doing so, from their apparent complexity. . . . He was sure that in many of the manufacturing districts the workmen might save 10s. a week out of their earnings, which would be a comfortable resource for themselves and their families. . . .

The *Chancellor of the Exchequer* . . . particularly hailed the institution of Savings Banks as a place where the rich and the poor met together, and mutually combined in promoting, under Divine protection, their natural rights. There, forgetful of those petty distinctions which temporary circumstances had created, they met as brethren, each to do his duty to his neighbour. . . .

Mr. *Rose* . . . stated that the members of the Benefit Societies had increased to 700,000 in England, and 60,000 in Ireland. . . .

499. The Hertfordshire Savings Bank, 1820

(*British Museum Additional MSS.* 38284, ff. 128–129.)

The following statistics are abstracted from the report for the year 1820. The bank had then been in existence for four years.

		Withdrawn
Deposits in 1st year	£3994 – 3 – 3	£193 – 9 – 3
2nd year	14451 –11 – 8	1388 –15 – 2
3rd year	18200 –15 – 7	4383 –17 – 1
4th year	15061 –10 – 1	6836 – 1 –10
	51708 – 0 – 7	12802 – 3 – 4

No. of depositors at close of 1st year	2nd yr.	3rd yr.	4th year.
356	752	1251	1615

Depositors classified.

	1820			1819	
271 labourers	£6461 – 7 – 0	186	£4646 – 0 – 7	
151 men-servants	3698 – 3 – 0	99	3293 – 8 – 6	
368 maid-servants	6945 – 0 – 6	219	4735 –19 – 6	
99 journeymen	2823 –15 –11	65	1805 –19 – 6	
35 Benefit Clubs	3858 –10 –11	25	2817 –16 – 0	
353 minors	3995 –15 – 6	254	2983 – 4 – 0	
63 in trust	2142 – 4 – 9	31	1752 – 6 – 9	
81 tradesmen	3222 – 8 – 7	68	3999 – 4 – 3	
30 widows	1448 – 1 – 1			
14 Sunday Banks	311 – 8 – 9	13		
129 persons not classed	3491 – 2 –11			
	38398 – 8 –11			
Benefaction account	138 – 5 –10			
	38536 –14 – 9			

Amount of Deposits in year 27 March 1819–25 March 1820: £15,061 –10 – 1.
No. of individual Depositors, 1662.

196	not exceeding	5s.
149	between 5s. and	10s.
248	10s.	£1
552	£1	5
217	5	10
152	10	20
106	20	50
42	50	100

Part VII

THE EMPIRE

Introduction

THE war of American independence created new problems for the remaining British colonies in North America. By depriving Canada of the vast territories to the south and west of the Great Lakes, bounded by the Ohio and Mississippi rivers, the peace treaty seriously impeded the fur traders of Montreal; and it created a new situation by bringing thousands of 'United Empire loyalists' into Canada from the United States. Some of them settled in the Maritime Provinces of Nova Scotia, New Brunswick, Prince Edward Island and Newfoundland, others near the Great Lakes, where they laid the foundations of the later province of Ontario and began to agitate for those representative institutions to which they had been accustomed in their old homes. The existence of two distinct communities, strong in their national self-consciousness and deeply divided by religion and legal systems, pointed to the division of the Province of Quebec. The French-Canadians were attached to their own civil law, the English to theirs, and it was felt that two systems of law regulating trade, property and inheritance could not be satisfactorily administered in a single province. Moreover, the granting of representative institutions would necessitate two Legislatures, otherwise religious and nationalist disputes in a single assembly could hardly be avoided. Pitt's Canada Act of 1791[1] therefore divided the huge province of Quebec into the English-Canadian province of Upper Canada and the French-Canadian province of Lower Canada, or Quebec, each with an executive consisting of a lieutenant-governor and a nominated council, and a bi-cameral Legislature consisting of a popularly elected assembly and a nominated Legislative council; and English civil law was introduced into Upper Canada. But the assemblies had no control over the executives, which were appointed by and responsible to the authorities at home: hence the demand for constitutional reform during the next forty years, and the rejection of that demand led to the famous 'rebellions' of 1837. The Imperial Government, ignorant of the state of public opinion in the two Canadas, proposed to solve some of these constitutional conflicts by reuniting the provinces in 1822, but the strength of the opposition to the Bill resulted in its withdrawal. The French-Canadians rightly feared that reunion would mean the destruction of the privileged position which the Act of 1791 had given them, and the Anglicizing of their province.[2]

The loss of the American colonies meant that some 500 English convicts could no longer be transported every year across the Atlantic to work on the southern plantations; and only a limited number could be accommodated on the overcrowded and insanitary hulks moored in the Thames. It was this problem of disposing of the criminal population that caused the Home Office to establish a convict settlement in Australia;[3] but Botany Bay, which had been discovered by Captain Cook in 1770,

---

[1] Nos. 515–516.   [2] Nos. 517–518.   [3] Nos. 500–504.

was never put to the purpose with which its name came to be associated, a much more commodious harbour, Port Jackson, which Captain Phillip renamed Sydney, being immediately discovered a few miles farther north. At first the British Government did not assume sovereignty over the whole continent, but only over that portion of it which lay between the east coast and the 135th degree of longitude (about one-half of Australia); formal possession of the rest was taken as new settlements were established on the southern, western and northern coasts during the next thirty years. Pitt's government was also anxious to get rid of another class of undesirables at home—the paupers, but the war with France which quickly followed the successful establishment of New South Wales seriously interfered with the free flow of both convicts and redundant poor. Few English people, in any case, wished to seek new homes in a colony governed like a jail, where, for the most part, the only free settlers were retired soldiers and ex-convicts. As late as 1828 the white population numbered less than 37,000, consisting of nearly 16,000 prisoners, about 7,500 liberated prisoners, nearly 9,000 native born and nearly 5,000 free immigrants. By that time explorers, penetrating into the interior after traversing the precipitous Blue Mountains, discovered that the country was highly suitable for sheep farming; these discoveries made it impossible that New South Wales should remain a mere convict settlement, but it was not until transportation was abolished in New South Wales (1840) that free emigration became popular.

Western Australia was founded in 1829 as a capitalist speculation sanctioned by the Wellington ministry.[1] Convicts were to be excluded. Captain Stirling, a Scotsman, was appointed Governor without a salary, but with a grant of 100,000 acres. An Act of Parliament (10 George IV, c. 22) gave formal recognition to the new colony. The Swan River Settlement was the first of a series of experiments in colonization which led to the occupation of the other coastal areas.

The Australian settlements were in a real sense the creation of British sea power. Without maritime supremacy their security would have been seriously threatened by Napoleon. Nelson's crowning victory at Trafalgar, followed by the second occupation of the Cape (1806) and the seizure of Mauritius four years later, gave security to these distant possessions; and the power and prestige of Great Britain in the post-war years were such that she was able to pursue her colonizing activities unchallenged by any rival.

Although there was a chronic labour shortage in the early days of Australian settlement no one thought of introducing slavery. English opinion would hardly have tolerated it, and it would in any case have been inappropriate to the character of the colony. Slavery then existed on a small scale both in Bengal (in defiance of a government decree) and on the island of Penang (with government approval), and also at the Cape, which had been conquered from the Dutch in 1795 and retaken in 1806; but it was mainly a West Indian institution.[2] In England itself slavery disappeared after Mansfield's famous judgment in the Somersett case (1772), though the law could not touch a foreign ship carrying slaves, when in an English port. At the end of the eighteenth century, English traders carried some 300,000 slaves across the Atlantic in eleven years, and sold them for £15,000,000. That public opinion tolerated this inhuman traffic on so vast a scale was due to the strength of vested interests entrenched in both Houses of Parliament, to the unfavourable influence of the French Revolution (the National Assembly's decree of 1791 which liberated slaves in the French islands

[1] No. 505.   [2] No. 506.

resulting in terrible risings against the planters), and to the belief held by men like Admiral Rodney, that, to a great naval and commercial nation the slave trade was an indispensable instrument of policy, encouraging the growth of the mercantile marine as a training ground for the navy and a source of national wealth.[1] In spite of eloquent speeches from Pitt, Fox, Burke and Wilberforce, the four greatest men in the House of Commons, the abolitionist cause made little progress because against it were arrayed the king, several Cabinet ministers, and majorities in both Houses. Sir William Dolben's Bill (1788) to limit the number of slaves which could be carried in each ship in proportion to its tonnage, and to make some provision for their health and comfort during the crossing, was the only positive achievement before the French Revolution worsened the prospects of the abolitionists; and during the ensuing war Pitt refused to forbid the revival of the slave trade with the conquered French and Dutch colonies. Fox and the Whigs were successful in 1806–1807 where Pitt had failed, because of the increasingly powerful support of public opinion, and because, in spite of the opposition of two Cabinet ministers, they were able to throw practically the whole weight of government into the scale on Wilberforce's side.[2] Had the trade not then been made illegal, the arguments used in its favour by the merchants of Liverpool and Bristol would soon have been powerfully reinforced by the mill-owners of Lancashire, who were becoming dependent for an ever-increasing quantity of slave-produced raw cotton on the southern plantations of the United States. After 1807 Tories like Lord Liverpool, Eldon, Castlereagh and Wellington, who had been some of the strongest opponents of Wilberforce, had the strongest motives for urging other European governments to forgo the profits of a trade which England had renounced, and, at the Vienna Congress, Castlereagh did all that was humanly possible to bribe or coerce the slave-trading states to overcome their resistance.

Slavery itself had yet to be abolished. Wilberforce was now too old to assume the leadership of this new crusade, and Fowell Buxton took his place in the 1820s. The campaign in the House of Commons effectively began in 1823 with Buxton's motion in favour of gradual abolition.[3] Canning's alternative resolutions for an amelioration in the condition of the slaves were reluctantly accepted by the abolitionists as an immediately attainable object, but the obstructionist tactics of the indignant planters rendered the government's policy ineffective. By 1830, however, English public opinion was firmly resolved to put an end to slavery,[4] and nothing but the protracted struggle for the Reform Bill postponed the final issue until the meeting of the first Reformed Parliament. By that time the West Indies had passed the zenith of their prosperity: some of the causes of the decline are referred to in the Report of the Select Committee of the House of Commons in document No. 514.

In 1815 the Imperial Government was considering the idea of affording "some degree of encouragement" to people willing to emigrate to Canada, but, by the beginning of 1818, it had discontinued the practice of providing free passages and 'issuing rations' after arrival. It was then receiving advice from Lord Charles Somerset, the Governor of the Cape of Good Hope (which was twice captured during the war and retained in 1814[5]) to establish a fairly compact settlement on the eastern border of the Cape province, to act as a buffer between the Boer farmers and the ravaging Kaffirs. In 1819 Parliament made a grant of approximately £50,000 to finance the venture,[6] and several thousand emigrants were sent out a year later, not, primarily, with the idea of diminishing the surplus population at home, but for the military purpose in the

[1] No. 507.   [2] Nos. 509–510.   [3] No. 512.   [4] No. 513.   [5] No. 570.   [6] No. 530A.

governor's mind. The settlers were expected to devote themselves to tillage and were consequently promised only 100 acres apiece; they failed to prosper until they were allowed to become pastoralists with much larger holdings. And from the first they were forbidden to use slave labour. Lord Charles Somerset was one of Wellington's retired generals by whom the British Empire was run, and until 1825 he ruled the colony as an autocrat, without having to share his responsibility to the Crown even with an executive council. In view of the endless trouble which the home government was having with the West Indian legislatures in persuading them to ameliorate the condition of the slaves, the Colonial Office was not at all anxious to set up similar representative institutions in another colony with a slave population of perhaps 30,000, and the new settlers could hardly expect such concessions until slavery had been abolished.

The view that a trading company, when placed under the direction and control of a committee of the privy council, was capable of governing a great empire, was embodied in Pitt's India Act of 1784,[1] and held the field until after the Mutiny. He hoped that an extension of the trade with India would go some way to compensate for the loss of the American colonies, but further annexations of territory and the making of alliances with the 'country powers' were deprecated. Events during the ensuing wars with France showed how unworkable was this policy of non-intervention; the Indian princes tended to interpret it as a confession of weakness, and renewed French intrigues at their courts compelled Lord Wellesley to embark on new defensive wars which resulted in vast territorial annexations. He was recalled before he was allowed to complete the destruction of the military power of the Marathas, and it was left to Lord Moira, later marquess of Hastings, to accomplish this task (1817–1818). The instructions which he received from Canning, the President of the India Board of Control,[2] show that in this, as in all other respects, Canning was a true disciple of Pitt. The First Burmese War (1824–1826) was forced on Hastings's successor, the Canningite Lord Amherst, and King Bagyidaw (1819–1837) was punished for unprovoked aggression by the loss of Assam and the maritime provinces of Arakan and Tenasserim.

The East India Company had already become a territorial power on that, the eastern side of the Bay of Bengal. In 1786 Penang, the first of the Straits Settlements, was occupied, for political and commercial reasons;[3] the Dutch possessions in the East Indies conquered during the Revolutionary and Napoleonic wars were restored at the peace, but Sir Stamford Raffles, Lieutenant-Governor of Java during the brief period of British occupation, was determined to "destroy the spell of Dutch monopoly" in those distant waters, and the acquisition of Singapore from the Sultan of Johore was his great achievement.[4]

The remaining documents in this sub-section are devoted to an examination of the British achievements in the sphere of law and administration[5]–achievements which, together with the abolition of the slave trade and of slavery, fill some of the few wholly virtuous pages in the history of imperialism–and provide some fascinating glimpses into the minds of the great Indian proconsuls about the future of that empire which they had done so much to create.[6]

[1] Nos. 519–520.   [2] No. 521.   [3] No. 529.   [4] No. 530.   [5] Nos. 522–524, 527.   [6] No. 528.

BIBLIOGRAPHY

GENERAL WORKS

The Cambridge History of the British Empire (7 vols., Cambridge, 1929–1940) is the standard work and has extensive bibliographies. See also, H. E. Egerton's *Short History of British Colonial Policy* (1932); J. A. Williamson's *Short History of British Expansion*, vol. II, 1945 edition; V. Harlow and F. Madden, *British Colonial Developments, 1774–1834: Select Documents* (Oxford, 1953); V. T. Harlow, *Founding of the Second British Empire, 1763–1793* (vol. I, 1952).

AUSTRALASIA

MANUSCRIPTS

(Supplementing the lists in *The Cambridge History of the British Empire*.)

Papers of George Prideaux Harris relating to the settlement of Tasmania, 1803–1812 (British Museum Additional MSS. 45156–7); Journal of the Surgeon of the *Lady Penrhyn*, one of the vessels sent to establish the first penal settlement at Botany Bay [1787–1789] (British Museum Additional MSS. 47966); Charles Sturt's Journal and Correspondence relating to exploration in Australia, 1828–1829, 1829–1830 (Bodleian, MS. Austral. S., 4–8).

PERIODICALS

Proceedings of the Church Missionary Society (1801+); Annual Reports of the Society for the Propagation of the Gospel (1704+); Annual Reports of the Wesleyan Methodist Missionary Society (1804+); Transactions of the London Missionary Society (1795–1815) (4 vols.); Quarterly Chronicle of the London Missionary Society (1815–1833); Missionary Magazine and Chronicle (1837–1866), becoming the Chronicle of the London Missionary Society (1867+); Royal Australian Historical Society: Journal and Proceedings (Sydney, 1901+); Historical Studies: Australia and New Zealand (1940+).

OTHER WORKS

Historical Records of Australia, Series I, III and IV (Sydney, 1914+); *Historical Records of New South Wales, 1762–1811*, edited by F. M. Bladen (7 vols., Sydney, 1893–1901); J. S. Battye, *Western Australia* (Oxford, 1924); J. I. Brooks, *International Rivalry in the Pacific Islands, 1800–75* (Cambridge, 1941); S. J. Butlin, *Foundations of the Australian Monetary System, 1788–1851* (Melbourne, 1953); C. M. H. Clarke, *Select Documents in Australian History, 1788–1850* (Sydney, 1950); T. Dunbabin, *The Making of Australasia* (1922); B. Fitzpatrick, *British Imperialism and Australia, 1783–1833* (1939); Forsyth, *Governor Arthur's Convict System in Van Diemen's Land, 1824–36* (1935); R. W. Giblin, *The Early History of Tasmania* (1928); R. L. Jack, *Northmost Australia* (1921); W. Lockerby, *Journal in the Fijian Islands, 1808–9*, edited by Sir E. im Thurn and L. C. Wharton (1925); G. Mackaness, *Admiral Arthur Phillip, founder of New South Wales, 1738–1814* (Sydney, 1937); R. B. Madgwick, *Immigration into Eastern Australia, 1788–1851* (1937); A. C. V. Melbourne, *Early Constitutional Development in Australia: New South Wales, 1788–1856* (Oxford, 1934); W. P. Morrell, *New Zealand* (1935); W. S. Hill-Reid, *John Grant's Journal: A Convict's Story, 1803–11* (1957); S. H. Roberts, *History of Australian Land Settlement, 1788–1920* (1925); E. Scott (editor), *Australian Discovery* (2 vols., 1929); E. Shann, *An Economic History of Australia* (Cambridge, 1930); G. A. Wood, *The Discovery of Australia* (1922).

CANADA

Reports of the Canadian Archives, published at Ottawa as Sessional Papers by the Dominion (in progress). [Lists of MSS. received, and the text or a summary of a number of the documents.]

A. G. Bradley, *The United Empire Loyalists* (1932); H. I. Cowan, *British Emigration to British North America, 1783–1837* (1928); G. M. Craig, *Early Travellers in Upper Canada, 1791–1867*

(Toronto, 1956); D. G. Creighton, *The Commercial Empire of the St. Lawrence, 1760–1850* (Oxford, 1938); A. G. Doughty and D. A. McArthur, *Documents relating to the Constitutional History of Canada, 1791–1818* (Ottawa, 1914); A. Dunham, *Political Unrest in Upper Canada, 1815–1836* (1927); H. E. Egerton and W. L. Grant, *Canadian Constitutional Development, shown by selected Speeches and Despatches* (1907); R. H. Fleming, *Minutes of Council, Northern Department of Rupert's Land, 1821–31* (Hudson's Bay Record Society, 1940); G. S. Graham, *British Policy and Canada, 1774–91* (1931); F. W. Howay, *Journal of Captain J. Colnett aboard the 'Argonaut', 1789–91* (Toronto, 1940); H. A. Innis, *The Fur Trade in Canada: An Introduction to Canadian Economic History* (Yale, 1930); H. A. Innis and A. R. M. Lower, *Select Documents in Canadian Economic History, 1783–1885* (Toronto, 1933); W. P. M. Kennedy, *Statutes, Treaties and Documents of the Canadian Constitution, 1713–1929* (Oxford, 1930 edition); C. P. Lucas, *A History of Canada, 1763–1812* (Oxford, 1909); N. Macdonald, *Canada, 1763–1841* (1939); *Duncan McGillivray's Journal*, edited by A. S. Morton (Toronto, 1929); A. H. McLintock, *The Establishment of Constitutional Government in Newfoundland, 1783–1832* (1941); F. Merk (editor), *Fur Trade and Empire* [The Journal of George Simpson] (Oxford, 1932); E. E. Rich, *Letters of John McLoughlin from Fort Vancouver to the Governor and Committee, 1825–38* (Hudson's Bay Record Society, 1941), *Moose Fort Journals, 1783–5* (1954), and *Black's Rocky Mountain Journal, 1824* (1955); W. Wood, *Select British Documents of the Canadian War of 1812* (3 vols., Toronto, 1920–1928); E. C. Wright, *The Loyalists of New Brunswick* (Fredericton, 1955).

SOUTH AFRICA

C. G. Botha, *The Public Archives of South Africa, 1652–1910* (Cape Town, 1929) [Guide to the records of the Provincial Governments of the Union].

Sir G. Cory, *The Rise of South Africa* (5 vols., 1910–1930; vol. VI, Cape Town, 1940); I. E. Edwards, *The 1820 Settlers in South Africa* (1934), and *Towards Emancipation* (University of Wales, 1943); G. W. Eybers, *Select Constitutional Documents illustrating South African History, 1795–1910* (1918); D. Fairbridge (editor), *Lady Anne Barnard at the Cape of Good Hope, 1797–1802* (Oxford, 1924); U. Long (editor), *Chronicle of Jeremiah Goldswain, Albany Settler of 1820* (Capetown, 1946); W. M. Macmillan, *The Cape Colour Question. A Historical Survey* (1927), and *Bantu, Boer and Briton* (1929); G. M. Theal, *Records of Cape Colony* (26 vols., 1897–1905); E. A. Walker, *History of South Africa* (1947 edition).

WEST AFRICA

Sir A. Burns, *History of Nigeria* (1948 edition); J. M. Gray, *A History of the Gambia* (Cambridge, 1940); E. C. Martin, *The British West African Settlements, 1750–1821* (1927); W. E. F. Ward, *A History of the Gold Coast* (1948); W. H. Claridge, *History of the Gold Coast and Ashanti* (1915); J. J. Crooks, *Records relating to the Gold Coast Settlements, 1750–1874* (Dublin, 1923).

THE WEST INDIES AND THE SLAVE TRADE

F. Armitage, *The Free Port System in the British West Indies, 1776–1822* (1953); S. Clarkson, *History of the Rise, Progress and Accomplishment of the Abolition of the African Slave Trade* (1839); R. Coupland, *The British Anti-Slavery Movement* (1933); A. Mackenzie-Grieve, *The Last Years of the English Slave Trade: Liverpool, 1750–1807* (1941); F. J. Klingberg, *The Anti-Slavery Movement in England* (Yale, 1926); E. C. P. Lascelles, *Granville Sharp and the Freedom of Slaves in England* (Oxford, 1928); M. G. Lewis, *Journal of a West India Proprietor, 1815–17*, edited by M. Wilson (1929); R. Pares, *A West India Fortune* (1950); L. Penson, *The Colonial Agents of the British West Indies* (1924); L. J. Ragatz, *The Fall of the Planter Class in the British Caribbean, 1763–1833* (New York, 1929); E. Williams, *Documents on British West Indian History, 1807–33* (Port of Spain, 1951).

INDIA AND THE FAR EAST

For an account of the 48,000 volumes of the records of the East India Company, which Grant Duff described as probably the best historical materials in the world, see Sir William

Foster's *Guide to the India Office Records, 1600–1858* (1919). See also *A Handbook to the Records of the Government of India in the Imperial Record Department in Calcutta, 1748–1859* (Calcutta, 1925). Among the many journals devoted to the study of Indian history are *Bengal, Past and Present*, the *Journal of Indian History*, the *Asiatic Annual Register*, and the *Asiatic Journal*.

GENERAL WORKS

The *Cambridge History of India*, vol. v (Cambridge, 1929), which is also vol. iv of *The Cambridge History of the British Empire*, is the best modern survey, with an ample bibliography. See also E. Thompson and G. T. Garratt, *The Rise and Fulfilment of British Rule in India* (1934); R. C. Majumdar, H. C. Raychaudhuri and K. Datta, *An Advanced History of India* (1946); H. Dodwell (editor), *The Cambridge Shorter History of India* (Cambridge, 1934); R. Muir, *The Making of British India, 1757–1858* (Manchester, 1915); Sir Courtenay Ilbert, *The Government of India* (Oxford, 1922); R. Coupland, *India: A Re-statement* (Oxford, 1945); C. H. Philips, *The East India Company, 1784–1834* (Manchester, 1940), and his *India* (1948); H. Furber, *John Company at Work: a study of European Expansion in India in the late Eighteenth Century* (Harvard, 1948); D. G. E. Hall, *Burma* (1950), *A History of South-East Asia* (1955); G. E. Harvey, *History of Burma* (1925), and *British Rule in Burma, 1824–1942* (1946); H. L. Hoskins, *British Routes to India* (1928).

OTHER WORKS

Memoirs of William Hickey, 1749–1809, edited by A. Spencer (4 vols., 1909–1925); G. W. Forrest, *Selections from the State Papers of . . . Cornwallis* (2 vols., Oxford, 1926); A. Aspinall, *Lord Cornwallis in Bengal* (Manchester, 1931); H. Furber (editor), *The Private Record of an Indian Governor-Generalship, 1793–8: the Correspondence of Sir John Shore with Henry Dundas* (Harvard, 1933); Lord Teignmouth, *Life and Correspondence of John, Lord Teignmouth* (2 vols., 1843); Sir John Malcolm, *Political History of India, 1784–1823* (2 vols., 1826); G. F. Grand, *Narrative of the Life of a Gentleman long resident in India* (Calcutta, 1910 edition); *The Second and Fifth Reports of the Select Committee of the House of Commons on East Indian Affairs* (1810–1812); W. S. Seton-Karr, *Selections from the Calcutta Gazettes* (3 vols., 1864–1865); J. C. Sinha, *Economic Annals of Bengal* (1927); *Correspondence of David Scott, Director and Chairman of the East India Company, 1787–1805*, edited by C. H. Philips (2 vols., Camden 3rd Series, 1951); S. Weitzman, *Warren Hastings and Philip Francis* (Manchester, 1929); P. E. Roberts, *India under Wellesley* (1929); *Wellesley Despatches*, edited by M. Martin (5 vols., 1836); R. Coupland, *Raffles* (Oxford, 1946 edition); Lady Raffles, *Memoir of . . . Raffles* (1909); C. D. Cowan, *Early Penang and the rise of Singapore, 1805–32* (Singapore, 1951); D. G. E. Hall, *Europe and Burma, A Study of European Relations with Burma to 1886* (Oxford, 1945), and *Symes' Journal of His Embassy to Ava in 1802* (1955); L. A. Mills, *British Malaya, 1824–67* (Singapore, 1925), and *Ceylon under British Rule 1795–1932* (1933); D. A. Owen, *British Opium Policy in China and India* (Oxford, 1934); H. B. Morse, *Chronicles of the East India Company trading to China, 1635–1834* (4 vols., Oxford, 1926); C. N. Parkinson, *Trade in the Eastern Seas, 1793–1813* (Cambridge, 1937); R. B. Ramsbottom, *Studies in the Land Revenue of Bengal, 1769–1787* (Oxford, 1926); E. Thompson, *The Making of the Indian Princes* (Oxford, 1943); W. H. Wilson, *Narrative of the Burmese War, 1824–6* (1852); G. W. Forrest, *Official Writings of Mountstuart Elphinstone* (1884); A. T. Ritchie and R. Evans, *Lord Amherst* (Oxford, 1894), and *Lord Amherst and the British Advance eastwards to Burma* (Oxford, 1909); J. W. Kaye, *Life and Correspondence of Lord Metcalfe* (2 vols., London, 1858); E. B. Impey (editor), *Memoirs of Sir Elijah Impey* (1846); *Lives* of Mountstuart Elphinstone by J. S. Cotton (Oxford, 1892) and T. E. Colebrooke (2 vols., 1884); H. T. Prinsep, *History of the Political and Military Transactions in India during the Administration of . . . Lord Hastings, 1813–23* (2 vols., 1825); V. Blacker, *Memoir of the Operations of the British Army in India during the Maratha War, 1817–19* (1821); *Lives* of Sir Thomas Munro by Sir A. J. Arbuthnot (1881), G. R. Gleig (3 vols., 1831), and J. Bradshaw (Oxford, 1894); S. J. Owen, *A Selection from the Despatches . . . of Lord Wellesley* (Oxford, 1877); K. Ingham, *Reformers in India, 1793–1833* (Cambridge, 1956) [missionary activity]; P. Woodruff, *The Men who ruled India*, vol. i (1953).

A. THE FIRST SETTLEMENTS IN AUSTRALIA

500. Lord Sydney to the Lords Commissioners of the Treasury, 18 Aug. 1786, on the decision to establish a convict settlement at Botany Bay

(*Historical Records of New South Wales*, I, Part 2, pp. 14-19.)

Lord Sydney was Home Secretary.

The several gaols and places for the confinement of felons in this kingdom being in so crowded a state that the greatest danger is to be apprehended, not only from their escape, but from infectious distempers, which may hourly be expected to break out amongst them, his Majesty, desirous of preventing by every possible means the ill consequences which might happen from either of these causes, has been pleased to signify to me his royal commands that measures should immediately be pursued for sending out of this kingdom such of the convicts as are under sentence or order of transportation.

The Nautilus, sloop, which, upon the recommendation of a Committee of the House of Commons, had been sent to explore the southern coast of Africa, in order to find out an eligible situation for the reception of the said convicts, where from their industry they might soon be likely to obtain means of subsistence, having lately returned, and it appearing by the report of her officers that the several parts of the coast which they examined . . . are sandy and barren, and from other causes unfit for a settlement of that description, H.M. has thought it advisable to fix upon Botany Bay . . . which, according to the accounts given by the late Captain Cook, as well as the representations of persons who accompanied him during his last voyage, and who have been consulted upon the subject, is looked upon as a place likely to answer the above purposes.

I am, therefore, commanded to signify to your Lordships H.M.'s pleasure that you do forthwith take such measures as may be necessary for providing a proper number of vessels for the conveyance of 750 convicts to Botany Bay, together with such provisions, necessaries, and implements for agriculture as may be necessary for their use after arrival. . . .

According to the best opinions that can be obtained, it is supposed that a quantity of provisions equal to two years' consumption should be provided. . . .

In the meantime, I have only to recommend it to your Lordships to cause every possible expedition to be used in preparing the shipping for the reception of the said convicts, and for transporting the supplies of provisions and necessaries for their use to the place of their destination.

[Enclosure]

Heads of a plan for effectually disposing of convicts, and rendering their transportation reciprocally beneficial both to themselves and to the state, by the establishment of a colony in New South Wales, a country which, by the fertility and salubrity of the climate, connected with the remoteness of its situation (from whence it is hardly possible for persons to return without permission), seems peculiarly adapted to answer the views of Government with respect to the providing a remedy for the evils likely to result from the late alarming and numerous increase of felons in this country, and more particularly in the metropolis.

It is proposed that a ship of war of a proper class, with a part of her guns mounted, and a sufficient number of men on board for her navigation, and a tender of about 200 tons burthen . . . should be got ready as soon as possible to serve as an escort to the convict ships, and for other purposes hereinafter mentioned.

That, in addition to their crews, they should take on board two companies of marines to form a military establishment on shore (not only for the protection of the settlement, if requisite, against the natives, but for the preservation of good order), together with an assortment of stores, utensils, and implements, necessary for erecting habitations and for agriculture, and such quantities of provisions as may be proper for the use of the crews.

As many of the marines as possible should be artificers, such as carpenters, sawyers, smiths, potters (if possible), and some husbandmen. To have a chaplain on board, with a surgeon, and one mate at least; the former to remain at the settlement.

That these vessels should touch at the Cape of Good Hope . . . for any seed that may be requisite to be taken . . . and for such livestock as they can possibly contain. . . .

That Government should immediately provide a certain number of ships . . . to receive on board at least seven or eight hundred convicts, and that one of them should be properly fitted for the accommodation of the women, to prevent their intercourse with the men.

That these ships should take on board as much provisions as they can possibly stow, or at least a sufficient quantity for two years' consumption; supposing one year to be issued at whole allowance, and the other year's provisions at half allowance, which will last two years longer, by which time, it is presumed, the colony, with the livestock and grain which may be raised by a common industry on the part of the new settlers, will be fully sufficient for their maintenance and support.

That, in addition to the crews of the ships appointed to contain the convicts, a company of marines should be divided between them, to be employed as guards . . . and for the protection of the crew. . . .

That each of the ships should have on board at least two surgeon's mates, to attend to the wants of the sick, and should be supplied with a proper assortment of medicines and instruments and that two of them should remain with the settlement.

After the arrival of the ships . . . the ship of war and tender may be employed in obtaining livestock from the Cape, or from the Molucca Islands . . . or the tender, if it should be thought most advisable, may be employed in conveying to the new settlement a further number of women from the Friendly Islands, New Caledonia, &c., which are contiguous thereto, and from whence any number may be procured without difficulty; and without a sufficient proportion of that sex it is well known that it would be impossible to preserve the settlement from gross irregularities and disorders. . . .

. . . Considerable advantage will arise from the cultivation of the New Zealand hemp or flax-plant in the new intended settlement, the supply of which would be of great consequence to us as a naval power, as our manufacturers are of opinion that canvas made of it would be superior in strength and beauty to any canvas made of the European material, and that a cable of the circumference of ten inches made from the former would be superior in strength to one of eighteen inches made of the latter. . . .

Most of the Asiatic productions may also without doubt be cultivated in the new settlement, and in a few years may render our recourse to our European neighbours for those productions unnecessary.

It may also be proper to attend to the possibility of procuring from New Zealand any quantity of masts and ship timber for the use of our fleets in India. . . .

Staff establishment for the Settlement at New South Wales:–

	Yearly salary		
	£	s	d
The Naval Commander to be appointed Governor or Superintendent-General	500	0	0
The Commanding Officer of the Marines to be appointed Lieut.-Gov. or Dept. Superintendent	250	0	0
The Commissary of Stores and Provisions, for himself and assistants . . .	200	0	0
Pay of a Surgeon £182. 10. 0			
Ditto of two mates 182. 10. 0			
	365	0	0
Chaplain	182	10	0
	1,497	10	0

501. An account of the expedition to Botany Bay, 7 Nov. 1787 (unsigned)

(Alnwick MSS.)

The first convoy, consisting of H.M.S. *Sirius* and six transports carrying over 700 convicts, including more than 150 women, sailed from England in April 1787 and arrived in January 1788.

Cape of Good Hope: When I recollect the kind concern you were so good to express for the success of our expedition, I cannot deny myself the pleasure of informing you that hitherto it has been prosperous & flattering almost beyond hope. We arrived in this port on the 13th of last month, after an excellent passage of little more than five weeks from Rio de Janiero; and should no unforeseen difficulty arise, shall sail for Botany Bay in two days from the date of my letter. To stock our intended Settlement we take from here black cattle, horses, sheep, hogs, goats, poultry of all kinds, and grain for sowing, so that should our last stage prove as fortunate in point of weather and dispatch as those we have passed, I see no room to doubt that the plains of New South Wales will in a few years hence afford, not only to their new possessors, but to their original lords, many of the comforts which arise from the happy arts of cultivation & society. I mention this, to obviate an objection, which the unreflecting humanity of some with you, led them to adopt. These good folks were fearful, that mischiefs alone will arise to the natives of New Holland from our communication with them. I own myself of a different opinion, and though not extravagant enough to suppose that an European connection will be altogether unattended by evil, yet, I think, more beneficial than bad consequences must spring from a mutual intercourse to a people whose whole dependence for subsistence is the precarious product of the chase & the sea. . . . Curiosity is no doubt awakened to learn how the unfortunate wretches on whose account our expedition was principally form'd, behave. Let me do them justice, & indeed I do no more, when I tell you, that half the number of soldiers would occasion twice the trouble we experience from the whole of the convicts. The turbulent & desperate spirit of resistance which threatened so many unhappy effects in the outset, is nearly subsided & habits of submission & acquiescence substituted in the stead. A better proof of this cannot be given than by saying that in the last three months I have found it necessary to exert a power, which Governor Phillip has lodged in my hands, of inflicting corporal punishment, on three persons only, and in their cases the force of example, rather than the enormity of the offences, prompted me to have recourse to measures of severity. I cannot quit this subject without informing you that Cable, his wife, & child (the Norwich prisoners) are well; as indeed the whole fleet is, surprizingly so, both marines & convicts. Of the former, we have not lost one; and of the other, only 21, since we left England: a number, which I will venture to pronounce, incredibly small, considering the variety of climates we have passed thro', and the usual consequences of long confinement. Had the wisdom & munificence of Government furnished us with all the preventives of disease generally allow'd on voyages of this nature, I think even a part of those who are no more would have been now alive. Why they did not, it neither becomes me to ask, nor pass my opinion upon.

In every part we have touched at, in our route, the most friendly & pleasing marks of regard have been shewn to us. The Spaniards, & Portuguese, at Teneriffe, & the Brazils, seemed bent on supplying our wants, and contributing to the success of our enterprize. Nor have the Dutch been less civil & attentive. To the Governor (Mynheer Van Graafe) & Colonel Gordon, the Commandant of the troops, we are particularly indebted. The ill grounded apprehension, that the High & Mighty States were inimical to the formation of our projected Settlement, had led many of us to believe that impediments would have been thrown in our way *here*; but so far from it, every assistance has been rendered us by the *people in power*. Perhaps, indeed, (tho' the suspicion is not a very generous one) the ticklish situation in which the Hollanders stand at present, may have been of service to us; for news of the disturbances which convulse the Republic, had reached this place a few days before we arrived, and seems to occasion much speculation among all ranks of men.

Were it in my power, I would give you some information of what are to be our proceedings on arriving at Botany, but I pretend not to the affectation of any insight whatever, except the result of conjecture; and with that I shall not presume to trouble you: all that I know, is, that Captain Campbell's Company, & the one I am to command, are to be the first landed, for the purpose of making matters in some shape secure. . . .

502. Governor Phillip to Lord Sydney, Sydney Cove, New South Wales, 15 May 1788

(*Records of New South Wales*, First Series, II, 121–136.)

[After describing the landfall at Botany Bay on 18 January] . . . I began to examine the bay as soon as we anchored, and found, that though extensive, it did not afford shelter to ships from the easterly winds; the greater part of the bay being so shoal that ships of even a moderate draught of water are obliged to anchor with the entrance to the bay open, and are exposed to a heavy sea that rolls in when it blows hard from the eastward.

Several small runs of fresh water were found in different parts of the bay, but I did not see any situation to which there was not some very strong objection. The small creek that is in the northern part of the bay runs a considerable way into the country, but it had only water for a boat. . . .

The best situation that offered was near Point Sutherland, where there was a small run of good water; but the ground near it, as well as a considerable part of the higher ground, was spongy, and the ships could not approach this part of the bay.

Several good situations offered for a small number of people, but none that appeared calculated for our numbers. . . . I judged it advisable to examine Port Jackson. . . . We got into Port Jackson early in the afternoon, and had the satisfaction of finding the finest harbour in the world, in which a thousand sail of the line may ride in the most perfect security. . . .

The different coves were examined with all possible expedition. I fixed on the one that had the best spring of water, and in which the ships can anchor so close to the shore that at a very small expense quays may be made at which the largest ships may unload. This cove, which I honoured with the name of Sydney, is about a quarter of a mile across at the entrance, and half a mile in length. . . .

The clearing the ground for the people and for erecting storehouses was begun as soon as the ships got round, a labour of which it will be hardly possible to give your Lordship a just idea.

The necks of land that form the different coves, and near the water for some distance, are in general so rocky that it is surprising such large trees should find sufficient nourishment, but the soil between the rocks is good, and the summits of the rocks, as well as the whole country round us, with few exceptions, are covered with trees, most of which are so large that the removing them off the ground after they are cut down is the greatest part of the labour; and the convicts, naturally indolent, having none to attend them but overseers drawn from amongst themselves, and who fear to exert any authority, makes this work go on very slowly.

Your Lordship will permit me to observe that our situation though so very different from what might be expected, is nevertheless the best that offered. My instructions did not permit me to detain the transports a sufficient length of time, to examine the coast to any considerable distance, it was absolutely necessary to be certain of a sufficient quantity of fresh water, in a situation that was healthy, and which the ships might approach within a reasonable distance for the conveniency of landing the stores and provisions, and I am fully persuaded that we should never have succeeded had it been attempted to move them only one mile from where they were landed. . . .

Some land that is near, and where the trees stand at a considerable distance from each other, will, as soon as convicts can be spared, be cultivated by the officers for raising a little corn for their stock; and this I have endeavoured to promote as much as possible, for I fear the consequences if a ship should be lost in her passage out with provisions.

As there are only 12 convicts who are carpenters, as many as could be procured from the ships have been hired to work on the hospital and storehouses. The people were healthy when landed, but the scurvy has, for some time, appeared amongst them, and now rages in a most extraordinary manner. Only 16 carpenters could be hired from the ships, and several of the convict carpenters were sick. It was now the middle of February; the rains began to fall very heavy, and pointed out the necessity of hutting the people; convicts were therefore appointed to assist the detachment in this work. . . .

The Charlotte, Scarborough, and Lady Penrhyn, transports, were cleared of all their stores and discharged from Government employ the 24th and 25th March, and left at liberty to proceed to China when they judged proper. The other ships remain till storehouses can be finished.

Your Lordship will not be surprized that I have been under the necessity of assembling a criminal court. Six men were condemned to death. One, who was the head of the gang, was executed the same day; the others I reprieved. They are to be exiled from the settlement, and when the season permits, I intend they shall be landed near the South Cape, where, by their forming connexions with the natives, some benefit may accrue to the public. These men had frequently robbed the stores and the other convicts. The one who suffered and two others were condemned for robbing the stores of provisions the very day they received a week's provisions, and at which time their allowance, as settled by the Navy Board, was the same as the soldiers, spirits excepted; the others for robbing a tent, and for stealing provisions from other convicts.

The great labour in clearing the ground will not permit more than 8 acres to be sown this year with wheat and barley. At the same time the immense number of ants and field-mice will render our crops very uncertain.

Part of the livestock brought from the Cape [of Good Hope], small as it was, has been lost, and our resource in fish is also uncertain. Some days great quantities are caught, but never sufficient to save any part of the provisions; and at times fish are scarce.

Your Lordship will, I presume see the necessity of a regular supply of provisions for 4 or 5 years, and of clothing, shoes, and frocks in the greatest proportion. The necessary implements for husbandry and for clearing the ground brought out will with difficulty be made to serve the time that is necessary for sending out a fresh supply.

The labour of the convicts shall be, as is directed, for the public stock, but it is necessary to permit a part of the convicts to work for the officers, who, in our present situation, would otherwise find it impossible to clear a sufficient quantity of ground to raise what is absolutely necessary to support the little stock they have. . . .

The very small proportion of females makes the sending out an additional number absolutely necessary, for I am certain your Lordship will think that to send for women from the Islands, in our present situation, would answer no other purpose than that of bringing them to pine away in misery. . . .

With respect to the natives, it was my determination from my first landing that nothing less than the most absolute necessity should ever make me fire upon them, and though persevering in this resolution has at times been rather difficult, I have hitherto been so fortunate that it never has been necessary. M. Lapérouse,[1] while at Botany Bay, . . . was obliged to fire on them, in consequence of which, with the bad behaviour of some of the transports' boats and some convicts, the natives have lately avoided us, but proper measures are taken to regain their confidence. . . .

When I first landed in Botany Bay the natives appeared on the beach, and were easily persuaded to receive what was offered them, and though they came armed, very readily returned the confidence I placed in them, by going to them alone and unarmed, most of them laying down their spears when desired; and while the ships remained in Botany Bay no dispute happened between our people and the natives. They were all naked, but seemed fond of ornaments, putting the beads or red baize that were given them round their heads or necks. . . .

It is not possible to determine with any accuracy the number of natives, but I think that in Botany Bay, Port Jackson, Broken Bay, and the intermediate coast they cannot be less than 1,500. . . .

503. Letter from a woman convict in Australia, Port Jackson, 14 Nov. 1788
(Berrow's Worcester Journal, 4 June 1789.)

I take the first opportunity that has been given us, to acquaint you with our disconsolate situation in this solitary waste of the creation. Our passage, you may have heard by the first ships, was tolerably favourable; but the inconveniences since suffered for want of shelter, bedding &c. are not to be imagined by any stranger. However, we have now two streets, if four rows of the most miserable huts you can possibly conceive of, deserve that name: windows they have none, as from the Governor's house, &c. now nearly finished, no glass could be spared; so that lattices of twigs are made by our people to supply their places. At the extremity of the lines, where, since our arrival, the dead are buried there is a place called the church-yard, but we hear as soon as a sufficient quantity of bricks can be made, a church is to be built, and named St. Philip, after the Governor. Notwithstanding all our presents, the savages continue to do us all the injury they can, which makes the soldiers' duty very hard, and much disaffection among the officers. I know not how many of our people have been killed. As for the distresses of the women, they are past description, as they are deprived of tea and other things they were indulged in, in the voyage, by the seamen: and as they are all totally unprovided with clothes, those who have young children are quite wretched. Besides this, though a number of marriages have taken place, several women who became pregnant on the voyage, and are since left by their

[1] The French explorer, whose expedition Phillip encountered on arrival in Australia.

partners, who have returned to England, are not likely even here to form any fresh connections. We are comforted with the hopes of a supply of tea from China, and flattered with getting riches when the settlement is complete, and the hemp which the place produces is brought to perfection. Our kangaroo cats are like mutton, but much leaner; and here is a kind of chickweed so much in taste like our spinage, that no difference can be discerned. Something like ground ivy is used for tea; but a scarcity of salt and sugar makes our best meals insipid. The separation of several of us to an uninhabited island was like a second transportation. In short, everyone is so taken up with their own misfortunes, that they have no pity to bestow upon others. All our letters are examined by an officer; but a friend takes this for me privately. The ships sail tonight.

504. Report from the Select Committee of the House of Commons on Transportation, 1812
(*Parliamentary Papers*, 1812, II, p. 575.)

This committee was appointed in consequence of criticisms of the transportation system by Romilly and Bentham. The system, declared the report, "isi n a train entirely to answer the ends proposed by its establishment".

The principal settlement on the eastern coast of New South Wales, was formed in 1788. . . . Of the total number [of inhabitants] 10,454, 5,513 are men, 2,220 women, and 2,721 children. Of these, from $\frac{1}{4}$ to $\frac{1}{3}$ are convicts. . . . The troops are about 1,100 in number, and the remainder are free persons. . . . The colony has for some years . . . been able wholly to supply itself with corn; but . . . it is still necessary to continue, to a certain extent, the importation of salted provisions. The soil and climate are described to be extremely fine, healthy, and productive; diseases, with the exception of such as arise from intemperance or accident, are little known. . . .

The currency of the colony consists principally of Government paper and copper money, but from its scarcity, many of the transactions which in other countries would be accomplished by money, are here carried on by barter; thus the labourer is not paid in money but in kind: he demands from his employer such articles as he is most in need of, and they are delivered to him at the prices which they bear in the market. At times indeed wheat and cattle have in the Courts of Justice been considered as legal tender in the payment of debts. . . . The exportations of the colony have hitherto principally consisted of oil, seal-skins, coals and wool. . . . The trade in skins and coals is the most thriving. . . . The stock of sheep is not yet sufficiently large to make wool an article of large exportation. . . . Woollen manufactories, potteries, and breweries have been established, but not with any great success. . . .

The greatest difficulties to which the Government has been subject, has arisen in its attempts to regulate the supply of spirituous liquors. Their importation used to be limited by licences granted by the Governor: on the arrival of a cargo, he fixed the price at which it was to be sold, and distributed it at this price, which was generally very low, to the persons highest in authority in the settlement. The liquors were afterwards paid away by them as wages to their labourers, or retailed at a very advanced rate to . . . the inhabitants . . .; and the eagerness for spirituous liquors has been so great in the colony, that the gains made in this traffic have been enormous. The temptations too to smuggling and illicit distillation are so great, and their facilities in that thinly inhabited country so numerous, that all attempts to check a clandestine supply have proved in vain. . . .

Many settlers have been sent out from this country by Government, to whom grants of land, sometimes to a large amount, have been made; and in many instances their want of capital, of character, and agricultural knowledge, have exposed them to difficulties. . . . Your Committee are glad to learn that greater precautions are now taken in the selection of these persons than appears formerly to have been the case. . . .

Though the religious feeling in the colony appears to have been weak, . . . churches have been built . . . and . . . clergymen have been appointed, with a sufficient provision from Government. . . . No restraint is imposed on those professing a different religion, and Roman Catholic clergymen have been allowed to perform the rites of their Church. . . . The education of youth appears by no means to be neglected, though the want of proper masters has been much felt. . . .

When the hulks are full up to their establishment, and the convicted offenders in the different counties are beginning to accumulate, a vessel is taken up for the purpose of conveying a part of them to New South Wales. A selection is in the first instance made of all the male convicts under the age of 50, who are sentenced to transportation for life and for 14 years; and the number is filled up with such from amongst those sentenced to transportation for 7 years, as are the most unruly in the hulks, or are convicted of the most atrocious crimes; with respect to female convicts, it has been customary to send, without any exception, all whose state of health will admit of it and whose age does not exceed 45 years.

The Irish convicts have generally been sent with less selection than those from England; and this has arisen from the want of hulks, and other means of confining and employing them, which are here often substituted for transportation. . . .

The evidence of Mr. McLeay distinctly and satisfactorily explains the manner in which they are transported. An order is received from the Treasury at the Transport Office, to take up vessels for New South Wales. They are advertised for, and the lowest tender accepted. Clothing and provisions for the support of the convicts during the voyage, and nine months afterwards, are sent from the Victualling Office, and medicines . . . from Apothecaries Hall. . . . The owner of the vessel provides a surgeon. . . . He is instructed to keep a diary not only of the illness on board, but of the number of convicts admitted on deck; of the scraping the decks, cleaning the berths, and general treatment of the transports. . . . He is paid a gratuity of 10s. 6d. for every convict landed in New South Wales. The instructions to the master are equally satisfactory. . . . If the conduct of the master appears to have been satisfactory, he receives a gratuity of £50. . . . About 200 men or women are generally embarked on board one ship, with a guard of 30 men and an officer. . . . However bad the treatment of the convicts on board the vessels may formerly have been, the present system appears . . . to be unobjectionable. . . . From the year 1795 to 1801, of 3,833 convicts embarked, 385 died on board . . . but since 1801, of 2,398 embarked, 52 only have died on the passage. . . . The only further observation your Committee have to make on this part of the subject is, one of regret that no arrangement whatever is made for the performance of divine service during this six months' voyage; that this, which is the heaviest part of their punishment, is also the least likely to produce reformation. ... Upon the arrival of a transport [in New South Wales], general orders are issued for returns of the number of men wanted, with the land held in cultivation by each settler. The trade, age, character, and capacity of the convicts are, as far as possible, investigated; the artificers are in general reserved for the service of Government, and as many of the others as may be wanted. Persons who have been in a higher situation of life, have tickets of leave given to them, by which they have liberty to provide for themselves, and are exempt from all compulsory labour; similar tickets are given to men unused to active employment, as goldsmiths and others; the remainder are distributed among the settlers as servants and labourers. The convicts in the service of Government, are divided into gangs. ... They work from six in the morning till three in the afternoon, and the remainder of the day is allowed to them, to be spent either in amusement or in profitable labour for themselves. They are clothed, fed, and for the most part lodged by Government; and though in the early periods of the colony, inconvenience and distress may have arisen from the irregularity of supply from this country, latterly the food and clothing have been good, and, generally speaking, in sufficient abundance. Should the convicts misconduct themselves ... the ... magistrate ... may order a punishment of 25 lashes; a regular Bench ... of three may order as many as 300. ... Another mode of correction ... is to sentence the culprit to work for a certain number of days in the gaol gang ... at some public work in irons, from six in the morning to six at night, and no hours are allowed to him for profit or amusement. The convicts distributed amongst the settlers, are clothed, supported, and lodged by them; they work either by the task or for the same number of hours as the Government convicts. ... The master has no power over them of corporal punishment. ...

In the distribution of female convicts great abuses have formerly prevailed; they were indiscriminately given to such of the inhabitants as demanded them, and were in general received rather as prostitutes than as servants; and so far from being induced to reform themselves, the disgraceful manner in which they were disposed of, operated as an encouragement to general depravity of manners. Upon the arrival of Governor Bligh, two thirds of the children annually born within the colony were illegitimate. Marriages have latterly become more frequent ... and Governor Macquarie is directing his endeavours, ... "to keep the female convicts separate till they can be properly distributed among the inhabitants, in such manner as they may best derive the advantages of industry and good character." He further states ... that the situation of the colony requires that as many male convicts as possible should be sent thither, the prosperity of the country depending on their numbers; whilst, on the contrary, female convicts are as great a drawback as the others are beneficial. To this observation your Committee feel they cannot accede: they are aware that the women sent out are of the most abandoned description, and that in many instances they are likely to whet and to encourage the vices of the men, whilst but a small proportion will make any step towards reformation; but yet, with all their vices, such women as these were the mothers of a great part of the inhabitants now existing in the colony, and from this stock only can a reasonable hope be held out of rapid increase to the population. . . . Let it be remembered, too, how much misery and vice are likely to prevail in a society in which the women bear no proportion to the men; in the colony at present, the number of men compared to that of women, is as two to one; to this, in great measure, the prevalence of prostitution is reasonably to be attributed. . . .

The supply of women to the colony must, however, be materially diminished by the proposed system of employing convicts in penitentiary houses; and your Committee think this an additional reason for affording increased facilities to the wives of male convicts . . . to accompany or follow their husbands to New South Wales. This permission is now seldom granted, and that only to the wives of men transported for life or for 14 years. . . .

At the expiration of the time to which the convicts have been sentenced, their freedom is at once obtained, and they are at liberty either to return to this country, or to settle in New South Wales; should the latter be their choice, a grant is made to the unmarried, of 40 acres of land, and to the married, of something more for the wife and each child: tools and stock (which they are not allowed to alienate) are also given to them, and for 18 months they are victualled from the Government stores. In this manner, they have an opportunity of establishing themselves in independence, and by proper conduct to regain a respectable place in society; and such instances, your Committee are glad to learn, are not unfrequent. . . .

The same advantages . . . are given to those who have been pardoned or emancipated by the Governor. . . .

No difficulty appears to exist among the major part of the men who do not wish to remain in the colony, of finding means to return to this country. All but the aged and infirm easily find employment on board the ships visiting New South Wales, and are allowed to work their passage home; but such facility is not afforded to the women; they have no possible method of leaving the colony but by prostituting themselves on board the ships whose masters may chuse to receive them. . . . To those who shrink from these means . . . transportation for 7 years is converted into banishment for life. . . .

505. Advertisement in the *Inverness Courier*, 23 Sept. 1829

EMIGRATION TO WESTERN AUSTRALIA.

———

HIS MAJESTY'S GOVERNMENT having made arrangements for
locating a New Colony on the
SWAN RIVER, WESTERN AUSTRALIA,

NOTICE IS HEREBY GIVEN to such small Capitalists, Mechanics, Agricultural Labourers, &c. &c. who may be desirous to go out as Settlers, that they will receive a FREE GRANT OF LAND FROM THE CROWN, in the order of their Arrival in the Colony, in the manner following :–

For every Man...............200 Acres of fine Pasture Land.
For every Woman...........200 Ditto..........Ditto.
For Children above 10..........200 Ditto..........Ditto.
For Ditto....9 and under 10....120 Ditto..........Ditto.
For Ditto....6 and under 9 .... 80 Ditto..........Ditto.
For Ditto....3 and under 6 .... 40 Ditto..........Ditto.
And over and above, for every £3 in Money, 40 Acres more.

Every Person must be able to pay the Passage Money for
himself and Family, as follows:-

Passage for a Man...........................£25.
Ditto....for Man and Wife....................£45.
Ditto....for Children under 15, Average........£12.

Passengers will be found in every Thing during the Voyage except Bedding.

———

SWAN RIVER is situated in a delightful and congenial Climate, on the Western Coast of Australia, in Latitude 32° South, Ninety Days Sail from England, and the Country consists of many million Acres of fine Pasture, intersected with Navigable Rivers, and averaging Ten Trees upon an Acre. The Soil is capable of producing any Crops, and the Colony will be situated in the midst of the India and China Markets. A new Town is projected, and the Government will be administered by Capt. STIRLING of the Royal Navy, as Lieut. Governor, who has already proceeded thither, together with several Hundred Settlers and their Families.

Mechanics and Agricultural Labourers of good character, may engage themselves before setting out, with a Gentleman of the highest respectability and fortune, who will give them a house to live in, free of Cost, and will protect them in case of Sickness or Infirmity; he will also furnish them with all necessaries and provisions from his own Store, at first Cost, on condition that they work for him three Days in every Week (if in Health), for which he will pay-

To a MECHANIC....................Three Shillings per Day.
To an AGRICULTURAL LABOURER......Two Shillings and Sixpence per Day.
To CHILDREN capable of Work.......One Shilling and Sixpence per Day.
And to some.....................Two Shillings per Day. The remaining three Days they may also work for the same Gentleman, if they please, at the same Rate, or for themselves if they find it more to their advantage.

Government Pensioners may receive their Pensions in the Colony.

It is not intended to send out any Convicts.

No Land will be given away after next year, and will be Sold to Settlers who wish to go out after that time, so that the present advantages are only for those who avail themselves of this opportunity.

Three fine Ships are now loading in the London Docks, and for farther information, Application must be made by those who wish to engage themselves, and for a passage to the Colony, to Mr JOHN HINDE, 33, Great Winchester Street, London; Or to Mr MERCER, Writer, Oban.

September 1, 1829.

———

Prices of Stock at Hobart Town, Van Diemen's Land, on the 19th January, 1829.

EXCELLENT SHEEP....Two to Three Shillings each.
CATTLE............Ten to Fifteen Shillings each.

☞ The Settlement at Swan River is a Free Port for Fifteen Years.

ALL LETTERS MUST BE POST PAID.

To Farmers of good character, willing to cultivate a proportion of the land belonging to the Gentleman formerly mentioned, superior advantages will be offered, which will be explained on personal application to either of the Agents above named. £20 per annum, besides board and lodging free, and a per centage on the net produce of the farm, will be given to such, besides having the farm stocked to them.

B. THE SLAVE TRADE, AND THE WEST INDIES

506. Clarkson on the Slave Trade

(T. Clarkson, *History of the Abolition of the Slave Trade*, 1 (1808), pp. 282–289.)

In 1787 Granville Sharp and other Quakers founded a committee for procuring evidence on the slave trade; it became the Abolitionist Society.

... The committee, finding that their meetings began to be approved by many, and that the cause under their care was likely to spread, and foreseeing also the necessity there would soon be of making themselves known as a public body throughout the kingdom, thought it right that they should assume some title, which should be a permanent one, and which should be expressive of their future views. This gave occasion to them to reconsider the object for which they had associated, and to fix and define it in such a manner that there should be no misunderstanding about it in the public mind. In looking into the subject, it appeared to them that there were two evils, quite distinct from each other, which it might become their duty to endeavour to remove. The first was the evil of the slave-trade, in consequence of which many thousand persons were every year fraudulently and forcibly taken from their country, their relations, and friends, and from all that they esteemed valuable in life. The second was the evil of slavery itself, in consequence of which the same persons were forced into a situation, where they were deprived of the rights of men, where they were obliged to linger out their days subject to excessive labour and cruel punishments, and where their children were to inherit the same hard lot. Now the question was, which of the two evils the committee should select as that to which they should direct their attention with a view of the removal of it; or whether, with the same view, it should direct its attention to both of them.

It appeared soon to be the sense of the committee, that to aim at the removal of both would be to aim at too much, and that by doing this we might lose all. The question then was, which of the two they were to take as their object. Now in considering this question it appeared that it did not matter where they began, or which of them they took, as far as the end to be produced was the thing desired. For, first, if the slave-trade should be really abolished, the bad usage of the slaves in the colonies, that is, the hard part of their slavery, if not the slavery itself, would fall. For, the planters and others being unable to procure more slaves from the coast of Africa, it would follow directly, whenever this great event should take place, that they must treat those better, whom they might then have. They must render marriage honourable among them. They must establish the union of one man with one wife. They must give the pregnant women more indulgences. They must pay more attention to the rearing of their offspring. They must work and punish the adults with less rigour. Now it was to be apprehended that they could not do these things without seeing the political advantages which would arise to themselves from so doing; and that, reasoning upon this, they might be induced to go on to give them greater indulgences, rights, and privileges in time. But how would every such successive improvement of their condition operate, but to bring them nearer to the state of freemen? In the same manner it was contended that the better treatment of the slaves in the colonies, or that the emancipation of them there, when fit for it, would of itself lay the foundation for the abolition of the slave-trade. For, if the slaves were kindly treated, that is, if marriage were encouraged among them; if the infants who should be born were brought up with care; if the sick were properly attended to; if the young and the adult were well fed and properly clothed, and not over worked, and not worn down by the weight of severe punishments, they would necessarily increase, and this on an extensive scale. But if the planters were thus to get their labourers from the births on their own estates, then the slave-trade would in time be no longer necessary to them, and it would die away as an useless and a noxious plant. Thus it was of no consequence, which of the two evils the committee were to select as the object for their labours; for, as far as the end in view only was concerned, that the same end would be produced in either case.

But in looking further into this question, it seemed to make a material difference which of the two they selected, as far as they had in view the due execution of any laws, which might be made respecting them, and their own prospect of success in the undertaking. For, by aiming at the abolition of the slave-trade, they were laying the axe at the very root. By doing this, and this only, they would not incur the objection that they were meddling with the property of the planters, and letting loose an irritated race of beings, who, in consequence of all the vices and infirmities which a state of slavery entails upon those who undergo it, were unfit for their freedom. By asking the Government of the country to do this, and this only, they were asking for that which it had an indisputable right to do; namely, to regulate or abolish any of its branches of commerce; whereas it was doubtful, whether it could interfere with the management of the internal affairs of the colonies, or whether this was not wholly the province of the Legislatures established there. By asking the Government, again, to do this and this only, they were asking what it could really enforce. It could station its ships of war, and command its custom-houses, so as to carry any Act of this kind into effect. But it could not ensure that an Act to be observed in the heart of the islands should be enforced. To this it was added, that if the committee were to fix upon the annihilation of slavery as the object for their labours, the slave-trade would not fall so speedily as it would by a positive law for the abolition; because, though the increase from the births might soon supply all the estates now in cultivation with labourers, yet new plantations might be opened from time to time in different islands, so that no period could be fixed upon, when it could be said that it would cease.

Impressed by these arguments, the committee were clearly of opinion, that they should define their object to be the abolition of the slave-trade, and not of the slavery which sprung from it. Hence from this time, and in allusion to the month when this discussion took place, they styled themselves in their different advertisements, and reports, though they were first associated in the month of May, "The Committee instituted in June 1787, for effecting the Abolition of the Slave-trade." Thus, at the very outset, they took a ground which was for ever tenable. Thus they were enabled also to answer the objection, which was afterwards so constantly and so industriously circulated against them, that they were going to emancipate the slaves. And I have no doubt that this wise decision contributed greatly to their success; for I am persuaded that, if they had adopted the other object, they could not for years to come, if ever, have succeeded in their attempt. . . .

507. Debates in the House of Commons on the slave trade, 12 and 21 May 1789

(Cobbett's *Parliamentary History*, XXVIII, 41–101.)

Although Wilberforce was powerfully supported by Pitt, Fox and Burke, the opponents of abolition succeeded in postponing further discussion until the next session. On the other hand, Dolben's temporary Act of 1788 was renewed, with amendments.

12 May: Wilberforce . . . A report has been made by H.M.'s Privy Council, which, I trust, every gentleman has read, and which ascertains the slave trade to be just such in practice as we know, from theory, it must be. What should we suppose must naturally be the consequence of our carrying on a slave trade with Africa? With a country vast in its extent, not utterly barbarous, but civilized in a very small degree? Does any one suppose a slave trade would help their civilization? Is it not plain, that she must suffer from it? That civilization must be checked; that her barbarous manners must be made more barbarous; and that the happiness of her millions of inhabitants must be prejudiced with her intercourse with Britain? Does not every one see that a slave trade, carried on around her coasts, must carry violence and desolation to her very centre? That in a Continent just emerging from barbarism, if a trade in men is established, if her men are all converted into goods, and become commodities that can be bartered, it follows, they must be subject to ravage just as goods are; and this, too, at a period of civilization, when there is no protecting Legislature to defend this their only sort of property, in the same manner as the rights of property are maintained by the Legislature of every civilized country. We see then, in the nature of things, how easily the practices of Africa are to be accounted for. Her Kings are never compelled to war, that we can hear of, by public principles, by national glory, still less by the love of their people. In Europe it is the extension of commerce, the maintenance of national honour, or some great public object, that is ever the motive to war with every Monarch; but, in Africa, it is the personal avarice and sensuality, of their Kings; these two vices . . . we stimulate in all these African Princes, and we depend upon these vices for the very maintenance of the slave trade. Does the King of Barbessin want brandy? He has only to send his troops, in the night time, to burn and desolate a village; the captives will serve as commodities, that may be bartered with the British trader. . . .

   Having disposed now of the first part of this subject, I must speak of the transit of the slaves in the West Indies. This I confess, in my own opinion, is the most wretched part of the whole subject. So much misery condensed in so little room, is more than the human imagination had ever before conceived. . . Let any one imagine to himself 6 or 700 of these wretches chained two and two, surrounded with every object that is nauseous and disgusting, diseased, and struggling under every kind of wretchedness! How can we bear to think of such a scene as this? One would think it had been determined to heap upon them all the varieties of bodily pain, for the purpose of blunting the feelings of the mind; and yet, in this very point (to show the power of human prejudice) the situation of the slaves has been described by Mr. Norris, one of the Liverpool delegates, in a manner which, I am sure will convince the House how interest can draw a film over the eyes, so thick, that total blindness could do no more. . . . "Their apartments," says Mr. Norris, "are fitted up as much for their advantage as circumstances will admit. The right ankle of one, indeed, is connected with the left ankle of another by a small iron fetter, and if they are turbulent, by another on their wrists. They have several meals a day; some of their own country provisions, with the best sauces of African cookery; and by way of variety, another meal of pulse, &c. according to European taste. After breakfast they have water to wash themselves, while their apartments are perfumed with frankincense and lime-juice. Before dinner, they are amused after the manner of their country. The song and dance are promoted," and, as if the whole was really a scene of pleasure and dissipation it is added, that games of chance are furnished. "The men play and sing, while the women and girls make fanciful ornaments with beads, which they are plentifully supplied with." . . . What will the House think when, by the concurring testimony of other witnesses, the true history is laid open? The slaves who are sometimes described as rejoicing at their captivity, are so wrung with misery at leaving their country, that it is the constant practice to set sail in the night, lest they should be sensible of their departure. The pulse which Mr. Norris talks of are horse beans; and the scantiness, both of water and provision, was suggested by the very Legislature of Jamaica in the report of their committee, to be a subject that called for the interference of Parliament. Mr. Norris talks of frankincense and lime juice; when the surgeons tell you the slaves are stowed so close, that there is not room to tread among them: and when you have it in evidence from Sir George Yonge, that even in a ship which wanted 200 of her complement, the stench was intolerable. The song and the dance, says Mr. Norris, are promoted. It had been more fair, perhaps, if he had explained that word promoted. The truth is, that for the sake of exercise, these miserable wretches, loaded with chains, oppressed with disease and wretchedness, are forced to dance by the terror of the lash, and sometimes by the actual use of it. . . . It may be observed, too, with respect to food, that an instrument is sometimes carried out, in order to force them to eat which is the same sort of proof how much they enjoy themselves in that instance also. As to their singing, what shall we say when we are told that their songs are songs of lamentation upon their departure which, while they sing, are always in tears, insomuch, that one captain (more humane as I should conceive him, therefore than the rest) threatened one of the women with a flogging, because the mournfulness of her song was too painful for his feelings. In order, however, not to trust too much to any sort of description, I will call the attention of the House to one species of evidence, which is absolutely infallible. Death, at least, is a sure ground of evidence, and the proportion of deaths will not only confirm, but if possible will even aggravate our suspicion of their misery in the transit. It will be found, upon an average of all the ships of which evidence has been given at the Privy Council, that exclusive of those who perish before they sail, not less than $12\frac{1}{2}$ per cent. perish in the passage. Besides these, the Jamaica report tells you, that not less than $4\frac{1}{2}$ per cent. die on shore before the day of sale, which is only a week or two from the time of landing. One third more die in the seasoning, and this in a country exactly like their own, where they are healthy and happy as some of the evidences would pretend. . . . Upon the whole, however, here is a mortality of about 50 per cent. and this among negroes who are not bought unless quite healthy at first, and unless (as the phrase is with cattle) they are sound in wind and limb. How then can the House refuse its belief to the multiplied testimonies before the Privy Council, of the savage treatment of the negroes in the middle passage? Nay, indeed, what need is there of any evidence? The number of deaths speaks for itself, and makes all such inquiry superfluous. As soon as ever I had arrived thus far in my investigation of the slave trade, I confess to you, sir, so enormous, so dreadful, so irremediable did its wickedness appear that my own mind was completely made up for the abolition. A trade founded in iniquity, and carried on as this was, must be abolished, let the policy be what it might,—let the consequences be what they would, I from this time determined that I would never rest till I had effected its abolition . . . it is true, indeed, my mind was harassed beyond measure; for when West-India planters and merchants retorted it upon me that it was the British Parliament had authorized this trade; when they said to me, "It is your Acts of Parliament, it is your encouragement, it is faith in your laws, in your protection, that has tempted us into this trade, and has now made it necessary for us," it became difficult, indeed, what to answer. If the ruin of the West-Indies threatened us on the one hand, while this load of wickedness pressed upon us on the other, the alternative, indeed, was awful. It naturally suggested itself to me, how strange it was that Providence, however mysterious in its ways, should so have constituted the world as to make one part of it depend for its existence on the depopulation and devastation of another. I could not therefore help distrusting the arguments of those who insisted that the plundering of Africa was necessary for the cultivation of the West-Indies. I could not believe that the same Being who forbids rapine and bloodshed, had made rapine, and bloodshed necessary to the well-being of any part of His universe. . . .

I hope now to prove by authentic evidence that, in truth, the West Indies have nothing to fear from the total and immediate abolition of the slave trade: . . . Let us ask then what are the causes of the mortality in the West Indies:–In the first place, the disproportion of sexes; an evil which, when the slave trade is abolished, must in the course of nature cure itself. In the second place, the disorders contracted in the middle passage. . . . A third cause of deaths in the West Indies is excessive labour joined with improper food. I mean not to blame the West Indians, for this evil springs from the very nature of things. In this country the work is fairly paid for and distributed among our labourers, according to the reasonableness of things; and if a trader or manufacturer finds his profits decrease, he retrenches his own expenses, he lessens the number of his hands, and every branch of trade finds its proper level. In the West Indies the whole number of slaves remains with the same master. Is the master pinched in his profits?–the slave allowance is pinched in consequence; for as charity begins at home, the usual gratification of the master will never be given up so long as there is a possibility of making the retrenchment from the allowance of the slaves. There is therefore a constant tendency to the very minimum with respect to slaves' allowance; and if in any one hard year the slaves get through upon a reduced allowance . . . this becomes a precedent upon other occasions; nor is the gradual destruction of the slave a consideration sufficient to counteract the immediate advantage and profit that is got by their hard usage. Here then we perceive again how the argument of interest fails also with respect to the treatment of slaves in the West Indies. . . .

Another cause of the mortality of slaves is the dreadful dissoluteness of their manners. Here it might be said that self-interest must induce the planters to wish for some order and decency around their families; but in this case also, it is slavery itself that is the mischief. Slaves, considered as cattle, left without instruction, without any institution of marriage, so depressed as to have no means almost of civilization, will undoubtedly be dissolute; and, until attempts are made to raise them a little above their present situation, this source of mortality will remain. . . .

It is now to be remarked that all these causes of mortality among the slaves do undoubtedly admit of a remedy, and it is the abolition of the slave trade that will serve as this remedy. When the manager shall know that a fresh importation is not to be had from Africa, and that he cannot retrieve the deaths he occasions by any new purchases, humanity must be introduced; an improvement in the system of treating them will thus infallibly be effected, an assiduous care of their health and of their morals, marriage institutions, and many other things, as yet little thought of, will take place; because they will be absolutely necessary. Births will thus increase naturally; instead of fresh accessions of the same negroes from Africa, each generation will then improve upon the former, and thus will the West Indies themselves eventually profit by the abolition of the slave trade. But, Sir, I will show by experience already had, how the multiplication of slaves depends upon their good treatment. All sides agree that slaves are much better treated now than they were thirty years ago in the West Indies, and that there is every day a growing improvement. I will show, therefore, by authentic documents, how their numbers have increased (or rather how the decrease has lessened) in the same proportion as the treatment has improved. There were in Jamaica, in the year 1761, 147,000 slaves; in the year 1787, there were 256,000; in all this period of 26 years, 165,000 were imported, which would be upon an average 2150 per annum, there being, on an average of the whole 26 years, 1 1-15th per cent. yearly diminution of the number of slaves on the island. In fact, however, I find that the diminution in the first period, when they were the worst used, was 2¼ per cent; in the next 7 years it was 1 per cent.; and the average of the last period is 3-5ths per cent. It should also be observed, that there has lately been, on account of the war, a much more than ordinary diminution, which was the case also in the former war, besides that 15,000 have been destroyed by the late famine and hurricanes. Upon these premises I ground a conclusion, that in Jamaica there is at this time an actual increase of population among the slaves begun. It may fairly be presumed, that since the year 1782 this has been the case, and that the births by this time exceed the deaths by about 1000 or 1100 per annum. . . . In the island of Barbadoes the case is nearly the same as at Jamaica. In St. Christopher's, there are 9600 females, and 10,300 males; so that an increase by birth, if the treatment is tolerable, may fairly be expected. In Dominica . . . there is a natural increase, though it is yet inconsiderable. . . . In Nevis there are absolutely five women to four men. In Antigua, the epidemical disorders have lately cut off 1-4th or 1-5th of the negroes; but this cannot be expected to return, especially when the grand cause of epidemical disorders is removed. In Bermudas and the Bahamas there is an actual increase. In Montserrat there is much the same decrease as there has been in Jamaica, which is to be accounted for by the emigrations from that island. . . . But, allowing even the number of negroes to be deficient, still there are many other resources to be had–the waste of labour which now prevails–the introduction of the plough and other machinery–the division of work, which in free and civilised countries is the grand source of wealth–the reduction of the number of negro servants, of whom not less than from 20 to 40 are kept in ordinary families–All these I touch upon merely as hints, to show that the West Indies are not bereaved of all the means of cultivating their estates, as some persons have feared. But, Sir, even if these suppositions are all false and idle, if every one of these succedanea should fail, I still do maintain that the West India planters can and will indemnify themselves by the increased price of their produce in our market; a principle which is so clear, that in questions of taxation, or any other question of policy, this sort of argument would undoubtedly be admitted. I say, therefore, that the West Indians who contend against the abolition, are nonsuited in every part of the argument. . . .

The next subject which I shall touch upon, is, the influence of the slave trade upon our marine: and instead of being a benefit to our sailors as some have ignorantly argued I do assert it is their grave. The evidence upon the point is clear; for, by the indefatigable industry and public spirit of Mr. Clarkson, the muster rolls of all the slave ships have been collected and compared with those of other trades; and it appears in the result that more sailors die in one year in the slave trade, than die in two years in all our other trades put together. It appears by the muster roll to 88 slave ships which sailed from Liverpool in 1787, that the original crews consisted of 3170 sailors–of these only 1428 returned: 642 died or were lost, and 1100 were discharged on the voyage or deserted either in Africa or the West Indies. . . .

There is one other argument, in my opinion a very weak and absurd one, which many persons, however, have much dwelt upon, I mean, that, if we relinquish the slave trade, France will take it up. If the slave trade be such as I have described it . . . we cannot wish a greater mischief to France than that she should adopt it. For the sake of France, however, and for the sake of humanity, I trust, nay, I am sure, she will not. France is too enlightened a nation to begin pushing a scandalous as well as ruinous traffic at the very time when England sees her folly and resolves to give it up. It is clearly no argument whatever against the wickedness of the trade, that France will adopt it: for those who argue thus may argue equally that we may rob, murder, and commit any crime which any one else would have committed if we did not. The truth is, that, by our example, we shall produce the contrary effect. If we refuse the abolition, we shall lie, therefore, under the twofold guilt of knowingly persisting in this wicked trade ourselves, and, as far as we can, of inducing France to do the same. Let us, therefore, lead the way; let this enlightened country take precedence in this noble cause, and we shall soon find that France is not backward to follow, nay, per-haps, to accompany our steps. If they should be mad enough to adopt it, they will have every disadvantage to cope with. They must buy the negroes much dearer than we; the manufactures they sell, must probably be ours; an expensive floating factory, ruinous to the health of sailors, which we have hitherto maintained, must be set up; and, after all, the trade can serve only as a sort of Gibraltar, upon which they may spend their strength, while the productive branches of their commerce must in proportion be neglected and starved. . . .

When we consider the vastness of the continent of Africa; when we reflect how all other countries have for some centuries past been advancing in happiness and civilization; when we think how in this same period all improvement in Africa has been defeated by her intercourse with Britain; when we reflect it is we ourselves that have degraded them to that wretched brutishness and barbarity which we now plead as the justification of our guilt; how the slave trade has enslaved their minds, blackened their character, and sunk them so low in the scale of animal beings, that some think the very apes are of a higher class, and fancy the ourang-outang has given them the go-by. What a mortification must we feel at having so long neglected to think of our guilt, or to attempt any reparation! It seems, indeed, as if we had deter-mined to forbear from all interference until the measure of our folly and wickedness was so full and complete: until the impolicy which eventually belongs to vice, was become so plain and glaring, that not an individual in the country should refuse to join in the abolition; it seems as if we had waited until the persons most interested should be tired out with the folly and nefariousness of the trade, and should unite in petitioning against it. . . .

I trust, therefore, I have shown, that upon every ground, the total abolition ought to take place. I have urged many things which are not my own leading motives for proposing it, since I have wished to show every description of gentlemen, and particularly the West-India planters, who deserve every attention, that the abolition is politic upon their own principles also. Policy, however, Sir, is not my principle, and I am not ashamed to say it. There is a principle above every thing that is political; and when I reflect on the command which says, "Thou shalt do no murder," believing the authority to be divine, how can I dare to set up any reasonings of my own against it? And, Sir, when we think of eternity, and of the future consequences of all human conduct, what is there in this life that should make any man contradict the dictates of his conscience, the principles of justice, the laws of religion, and of God. Sir, the nature and all the circumstances of this trade are now laid open to us; we can no longer plead ignorance, we cannot evade it, it is now an object placed before us, we cannot pass it; we may spurn it, we may kick it out of our way, but we cannot turn aside so as to avoid seeing it; for it is brought now so directly before our eyes, that this House must decide, and must justify to all the world, and to their own consciences, the rectitude of the grounds and principles of their decision. . . .

Alderman Newnham said, that though he wished as well to the cause of humanity as any man, yet, as a representative of the City of London, he could not give his consent to a proposition which, if carried, would fill the City with men suffering as much as the poor Africans. He conceived, that if wise regulations were applied to the slave trade, so as to cure it of the many abuses that he had no doubt prevailed in it, it might be made a source of revenue and material commercial advantage. If it were abolished altogether, he was persuaded it would render the City of London one scene of bankruptcy and ruin. Standing in the situation that he did in that House, he must suppress his feelings, and act upon motives of prudence. He therefore cautioned gentlemen not rashly and precipitately to put an end to a trade, so essentially advantageous as a branch of our national commerce.

Lord Penrhyn rose again, merely to prevent the Committee from going away with an idea that sugar could be cheaply cultivated by freemen. No such thing was practicable. It had been tried, and tried in vain. Notwithstanding the reveries, therefore, of the hon. mover, that speculation must be abandoned. There were mortgages in the West India Islands to the amount of seventy millions; the fact therefore was, if they passed the vote of abolition, they actually struck at seventy millions of property, they ruined the colonies, and by destroying an essential nursery for seamen, gave up the dominion of the sea at a single stroke.

21 May:

Mr. Cruger was for the Speaker's leaving the Chair, because it would give the House an opportunity of refuting what were, on a former day, considered as misrepresentations. As to the show of benevolence, and the motives that actuated gentlemen, he hoped and wished to be among the foremost in the cause of humanity, and in opposition to every species of oppression; but he thought, at the same time, if the House was determined at all hazards to carry these propositions, it would become the justice of the nation to repair such losses as might be sustained by the merchants and planters from the abolition of the trade, otherwise gentlemen might be justly considered as liberal, or even ostentatious, in their sacrifice to the cause of humanity at the expense of others. As the honour would be national, whatever losses might arise from it should not fall on a particular class of individuals, but be national also. In that case they must think of raising a fund of at least 60 or 70 millions sterling. . . . He had also heard of emancipating all the slaves in the West-India islands. Was that a part of the project? He was well persuaded that whoever offered any thing in favour of the slave trade, or engaged in it, had invincible prejudices to encounter. The people had been taught to associate every thing cruel and oppressive with the idea of the trade; but, from his own knowledge, and the evidence which would be laid before the House, he could venture to pronounce the picture over-charged. At any rate, however, as it was a trade which had been so long sanctioned by the laws of this country, and the practice of every civilized nation, those who had engaged in it, on the faith of public protection, would have a fair claim to public compensation. The planters, indeed, might be reimbursed, but the merchants stood little chance of retribution. . . .

508. George Canning to his uncle, the Rev. William Leigh, 31 May 1799
(Harewood MSS.)

Canning was now a Commissioner of the Board of Control.

. . . We are working hard, convassing for proxies night and day, to carry the two Slave Bills now in the House of Lords, and I think we shall succeed, though not without difficulty. It is very extraordinary with what diabolical zeal and spirit persons not in the smallest degree interested in the trade nor connected with the West Indies, exert themselves in favour of the slave trade; some from pure love of cruelty; some from a pretended or foolish dread of innovation in general; and others, because being a question on which no party influence was exerted, they thought it a fine opportunity to shew their independence by voting against a measure for which Pitt was personally anxious. All these causes together had conspired to collect such a body of Peers in opposition to the two Bills,[1] that Lord Grenville would have been beaten four to one if he had risked a division upon the second reading, and what is most provoking is that Lord Westmorland, a member of the Cabinet, had put himself at the head of the opposition, in league with the Duke of Clarence; and half the Peers who constantly vote with Government, were to be found in Lord Westmorland's train. This outrageous conduct has however produced or hastened the effect which for two years past I have been constantly desiring and endeavouring to produce, that of convincing Pitt that nothing is to be done in the business without making it in a great degree a Government question. The consequence of this conviction is a determination to bring on some Bill (founded chiefly on the points which my Address[2] would have comprised) to settle the question–not by total and immediate abolition (for against *that* people have been suffered to pledge themselves too much) but for the next-best measure that can be devised, limitation and regulation of the trade in

[1] Thornton's 'poor harmless' Bill for exempting that part of the African coast bordering on the Sierra Leone establishment from the slave trade, and a Bill to regulate the 'middle passage'.

[2] Canning had given notice of a motion for an address to the king "to state our persuasion that the experiment of keeping up the black population in the islands (the consequence of which must be the cessation of the slave trade) could never be fairly tried until the annual *importation* should be limited to the amount of the annual *decrease*".

a way that will necessarily lead to its termination – and to bring this on either himself or Dundas, with *Government authority*. The more immediate effect is as I have before stated, a vigorous resolution to carry the two Bills now in the House of Lords, by canvassing every individual Peer as for a question which it is made *a point* to carry. Too many have pledged themselves too far against them; but of them some may be converted and more persuaded to stay away, and many will be brought down who never thought of giving a vote upon the subject, so that in the end we may do. Lord Grenville is very earnest in the good cause. . . .

509. Richard Ryder to his brother Lord Harrowby, 27 Feb. 1807

(Harrowby MSS.)

On 23 February the Slave Trade Abolition Bill was read a second time in the Commons by 283 to 16. It received the royal assent on 25 March.

. . . I have not been in the House since the debate on the Slave Trade, when I paired off to avoid the very late hours. Nobody expected this great question would have been carried with so high a hand. I cannot but rejoice at it; but unless one is to suppose that a *sudden* and complete revolution has taken place in the public mind without any new assigned or assignable cause upon this subject, and that not confined to one but extended to both Houses of Parliament, it is to one who holds my opinion both disgusting and alarming to observe that the present Administration can do so much more than Pitt could accomplish in the plenitude of his power. I call it alarming because there is no knowing to what length or to what subjects this reluctant acquiescence (for reluctant it has been) to the will of Government may be carried in future. No one is more surprised than Wilberforce himself. He attributes it to the immediate interposition of Providence. . . .

510. An Act for the Abolition of the Slave Trade (47 Geo. III, c. 36)

(Statutes at Large, LXI, pp. 140–148.)

Whereas the two Houses of Parliament did, by their Resolutions of the 10th and 24th days of June 1806 severally resolve, upon certain grounds therein mentioned, that they would, with all practicable expedition, take effectual measures for the abolition of the *African* slave trade, in such manner and at such period as might be deemed advisable: and whereas it is fit . . . that the same should be forthwith abolished and prohibited . . . be it therefore enacted . . . that from and after the 1st day of May 1807, the *African* slave trade, and all manner of dealing and trading in the purchase, sale, barter or transfer of slaves, or of persons intended to be sold, transferred, used or dealt with as slaves, practised or carried on in, at, to or from any part of the coast or countries of *Africa*, shall be . . . utterly abolished, prohibited and declared to be unlawful; and also that all . . . manner of dealing, either by way of purchase, sale, barter or transfer, or by means of any other contract or agreement whatever, relating to any slaves, or to any persons intended to be used . . . as slaves, for the purpose of such slaves or persons being removed or transported either immediately or by transshipment at sea or otherwise, directly or indirectly from *Africa*, or from any island, country, territory or place whatever, in the *West Indies*, or in any part of *America*, not being in the dominion, possession or occupation of H.M., to any other island . . . or place whatever, is hereby . . . utterly abolished . . . and declared to be unlawful; and if any of H.M.'s subjects, or any person or persons resident within this United Kingdom, or any of the islands, colonies, dominions or territories thereto belonging, or in H.M.'s occupation or possession, shall from . . . the day aforesaid, deal or trade in, purchase, sell, barter or transfer, or contract or agree for the dealing or trading in . . . any slave . . . he or they so offending shall forfeit . . . for every such offence . . . £100 . . . for each . . . slave so purchased . . . the one moiety thereof to the use of H.M. . . . and the other moiety to the use of any person who shall inform, sue and prosecute for the same.

[II. Vessels fitted out in this Kingdom, colonies &c. for carrying on the slave trade shall be forfeited.

III. Persons prohibited from carrying as slaves inhabitants of Africa, the West Indies or America, from one place or another, or being concerned in receiving them, &c. Vessels employed in such removal, &c. to be forfeited, as also the property in the slaves. Owners to forfeit £100 for each slave.

IV. Subjects of Africa, &c. unlawfully carried away and imported into any British colony &c. as slaves, shall be forfeited to H.M.

V. Insurances on transactions concerning the slave trade unlawful: penalty, £100 and treble the amount of the premium.

VI. Act not to affect the trading in slaves exported from Africa in vessels cleared out from Great Britain on or before 1 May 1807, and landed in the West Indies by 1 March 1808.

VII. Slaves on foreign ships taken as prizes of war or seized as forfeitures, shall be condemned as prize, or forfeited to the King and freed from slavery, and may be enlisted in the armed forces or bound apprentices for 14 years.

VIII. Bounties to be paid to the captors of such slaves.]

511. Resolutions of a Select Committee of the House of Commons, 13 July 1830

(*Parliamentary Papers*, 1830, x, pp. 3–4.)

Granville Sharp, the Quaker philanthropist, who did more than any other individual to put an end to the curse of slavery in England (winning a verdict in the famous Somersett case in 1772), conceived the idea of establishing a colony of liberated slaves on the West African coast. In 1787 the first shipload sailed for Sierra Leone, and the St. George's Company was formed in 1789 to manage the new settlement. The company failed to prosper, and it was wound up in 1808.

Resolved, 1. That it is the opinion of this Committee, that the evidence respecting the comparative healthiness of Sierra Leone and other settlements on the west coast of Africa is very contradictory, owing to the different periods and seasons to which the evidence relates; but the whole of the coast may be considered as generally unhealthy and dangerous to European constitutions, and in some years to a very great degree; that it is, therefore, desirable to reduce the Europeans employed on shore on that coast, in the naval, military and civil departments, to the smallest number possible, and, in such establishments as must be kept up, to substitute black people.

Resolved, 2. That it is the opinion of this Committee that the management of the settlement of Sierra Leone has not, hitherto, been productive of advantages to the extent which were anticipated, either to the liberated Africans located there, or towards effecting an intercourse with the interior of Africa to promote its civilisation, although the expenditure by Government for that purpose has, for many years, been very large; but a better system has of late been adopted which, if persevered in, with the modification herein suggested, will secure the advantages that can fairly be expected from the maintenance of that settlement. . . .

Resolved, 4. That it is the opinion of this Committee that although it may be desirable to retain the settlement of Sierra Leone for the purposes of trade, and to protect the blacks already located there, yet it appears to this Committee that those objects may be attained at a very small expense, and that the greater part of the present establishments may be gradually and safely withdrawn. . . .

512. Debate in the House of Commons on T. F. Buxton's Motion for the Abolition of Slavery, 15 May 1823

(Hansard's *Parliamentary Debates*, New Series, IX, 256–360.)

T. Fowell Buxton . . . Of British subjects, there are one million living in personal slavery. . . . A Committee of this House sat some thirty years ago, took evidence on this subject, and, what was unusual then, published it to the world. . . . In the year 1787 a very feeble attempt was made to abate the horrors of the middle passage –to admit a little more air into the suffocating and pestilent holds of the slave-ships. The alarm was instantly taken. The cry of the West Indians, as we have heard it tonight, was the cry of that day. An insurrection of all the blacks–the massacre of all the whites–was to be the inevitable consequence. . . . The Bill passed, however; and, somehow or other, the prediction was not verified. About the same year, my hon. friend [Wilberforce] commenced that career with which his name will always be coupled; and which he brought to a glorious termination twenty years afterwards. . . .

The object at which we aim is the extinction of slavery . . . in nothing less than the whole of the British dominions; not, however, the rapid termination of that state–not the sudden emancipation of the negro–but such preparatory steps, such measures of precaution as, by slow degrees and in a course of years, first fitting and qualifying the slave for the enjoyment of freedom, shall gently conduct us to the annihilation of slavery. . . . If I succeed to the fullest extent of my desires, confessedly sanguine, no man will be able to say, I even shall be unable to predict, that at such a time, or in such a year, slavery will be abolished. In point of fact, it will never be abolished: it will never be destroyed. It will subside; it will decline; it will expire; it will, as it were, burn itself down into its socket and go out. We are far from meaning to attempt to cut down slavery in the full maturity of its vigour. We rather shall leave it gently to decay–slowly, silently, almost imperceptibly, to die away and to be forgotten.

Now, see the operation of our principle. We say–no more slaves shall be made; no more children shall be enslaved. . . . In 20 or 30 years' time, all the young, the vigorous, and those rising into life, will be free; and the slaves will be those who have passed the meridian of their days–who are declining into age–the aged and the decrepid. . . . A few years further . . . and slavery will be no more. . . . Just in this way slavery has gone out and expired in New York. Thirty years ago, New York was what is called a slave-State; that is, a proportion of its labourers were slaves. . . . The principle which I now advocate was applied; and–without rebellion, without convulsion, without a single riot, without anything that deserves the name of inconvenience–slavery has gone out in the State of New York. The same thing has been done in Philadelphia, New Jersey and several other of the United States. . . . Every American from that part of the country is ready to acknowledge that the worst of all curses has fled away. . . .

There are other parts of the world where the same principle is now in action. . . . It is in full operation at this moment in Ceylon, and has been so since 1816. . . . The same thing occurred at Bencoolen under the administration of Sir Stamford Raffles. The same at St. Helena . . . Sir Hudson Lowe gave the death-blow to slavery at St. Helena. . . . It is a crime to enslave a man: and, is it no crime to enslave a child? . . . Slave-trading and slavery (for they are but two parts of the same act) are the greatest crime that any nation ever committed: and when that day comes which shall disclose all secrets and unveil all guilt, the broadest and blackest of all will be that, the first part of which is slave-trading, and the last part slavery; and no nation under heaven has ever been so deeply tainted with both the one and the other as we have been. . . .

Now for the existing slaves. . . . Slaves, I fear, they must too generally continue; but slaves, under a description of servitude considerably mitigated. . . . Alas, Sir! the slave is not ripe for liberty. The bitterest reproach that can be uttered against the system of slavery, that it debases the man, that it enfeebles his powers, that it changes his character, that it expels all which is naturally good; this, its bitterest reproach, must be its protection. We are foiled by the very wickedness of the system. We are obliged to argue in a most vicious circle. We make the man worthless, and because he is worthless we retain him as a slave. We make him a brute, and then allege his brutality the valid reason for withholding his rights.

I will now take the liberty of reading a short extract of a letter which, on the 11th of last April I addressed to my hon. friend opposite, in order to put Lord Bathurst and H.M.'s Government, in full possession of our views and intentions:–

'The subject divides itself into two: the condition of the existing slaves, and the condition of their children. With regard to the former, I wish the following improvements:–

'1. That the slave should be attached to the island, and, under modifications, to the soil.

'2. That they cease to be chattels in the eye of the law.

'3. That their testimony may be received, *quantum valeat*.

'4. That when anyone lays in his claim to the services of a negro, the *onus probandi* should rest on the claimant.

'5. That all obstructions to manumissions should be removed.

'6. That the provisions of the Spanish law (fixing by competent authority the value of the slave, and allowing him to purchase a day at a time) should be introduced.

'7. That no Governor, Judge or Attorney-General should be a slave-owner.

'8. That an effectual provision shall be made for the religious instruction of the slave.

'9. That marriage should be enforced and sanctioned.

'10. That the Sunday should be devoted by the slave to repose and religious instruction; and that other time should be allotted for the cultivation of his provision-grounds.

'11. That some (but what I cannot say) measures should be taken to restrain the authority of the master in punishing his untried slave, and that some substitute should be found for the driving system.

'These are the proposed qualifications of the existing slavery. But I am far more anxiously bent upon the extinction of slavery altogether, by rendering all the negro children, born after a certain day, free. For them it will be necessary to provide education. God grant that H.M.'s Ministers may be disposed to accomplish these objects, or to permit others to accomplish them!'

For all the blood spilt in African wars fomented by English capital–for civil war which we contrived to render interminable–for all the villages set in flames by the contending parties–for all the horrors and the terrors of these poor creatures, roused from their rest by the yells of the man-hunter whom we sent–for civilisation excluded –for the gentle arts which embellish life excluded–for honest and harmless commerce excluded–for Christianity, and all that it comprehends, expelled for two centuries from Africa–for the tens and tens of thousands of men murdered in these midnight marauds–for the tens and tens of thousands suffocated in the holds of our slave ships– for the tens and tens of thousands of emaciated beings, cast ashore in the West Indies, emaciated beings, 'refuse men' (for such was the mercantile phrase) lingering to a speedy death–for the tens and tens of thousands still more unhappy who, surviving, lived on to perpetual slavery, to the whip of the taskmaster, to ignorance, to crime, to heathen darkness–for all these we owe large and liberal atonement. And I do thank God we still have it in our power to make some compensation. We have it in our power to sweeten a little the bitterness of captivity–to give the slaves of the West Indies something to render life more endurable–to give them something like justice and protection–to interpose a jury between the negro and the brutality of his master's servant–to declare that the slave shall not be torn from the cottage he has built, from the children he has reared, from the female whom he loves–above all, for that is effectual compensation, we may give him the truths of the Christian religion, which, as yet, we have withheld.

For his children there is a wider range of recompense. We may strip them of every vestige of servitude; and, by taking upon ourselves, for a season, the whole burden of their maintenance, education and religious instruction, we may raise them into a happy, contented, enlightened free peasantry . . . I move,

'That the state of slavery is repugnant to the principles of the British Constitution and of the Christian religion, and that it ought to be gradually abolished throughout the British colonies, with as much expedition as may be found consistent with a due regard to the well-being of the parties concerned.'

Mr. Canning: . . . In all former discussions, in all former votes against the slave trade, it cannot surely be forgotten that the ulterior purpose of emancipation was studiously disclaimed. I have myself frequently joined in that disclaimer on former occasions. In doing so, I certainly did not mean to advance so untenable a proposition as that it was intended to purchase the abolition of the slave trade by an indefinite continuance of slavery. . . . What I at least did mean . . . was that the two questions should be kept separate, and argued on their separate grounds; that the odium of that which we were labouring to abolish should not be brought to bear with increased intensity on that of which we were compelled to allow the continuance. Slavery, not willingly, but necessarily was allowed to continue. I do not say that it is therefore to continue indefinitely; I speak not of it as a system to be carefully preserved and cherished, but as one to be dealt with according to its own nature, and with reference to its inherent peculiarities. . . .

Looking, then, at the present condition of the West Indies, I find there a numerous black population, with a comparatively small proportion of whites. The question to be decided is, how civil rights, moral improvement, and general happiness are to be communicated to this overpowering multitude of slaves, with safety to the lives and security to the interests of the white population, our fellow-subjects and fellow-citizens. . . . Undoubtedly, the spirit of the British Constitution is, in its principle, hostile to any modification of slavery. But, as undoubtedly, the British Parliament has for ages tolerated, sanctioned, protected and even encouraged a system of colonial establishment of which it well knew slavery to be the foundation.

. . . No Christian will deny that the spirit of the Christian religion is hostile to slavery, as it is to every abuse and misuse of power: it is hostile to all deviations from rectitude, morality and justice; but if it be meant that in the Christian religion there is a special denunciation against slavery, that slavery and Christianity cannot exist together–I think the hon. gentleman himself must admit that the proposition is historically false. . . . One peculiar characteristic of the Christian dispensation . . . is that it has accommodated itself to all states of society, rather than that it has selected any particular state of society for the peculiar exercise of its influence. If it has added lustre to the sceptre of the Sovereign, it has equally been the consolation of the slave. It applies to all ranks of life, to all conditions of men; and the sufferings of this world, even to those upon whom they press most heavily, are rendered comparatively indifferent by the prospect of compensation in the world of which Christianity affords the assurance. . . . It is not true that there is that in the Christian religion which makes it impossible that it should co-exist with slavery in the world . . . I admit as fully as the hon. gentleman himself, that the spirit both of the British Constitution and of the Christian religion is in favour of a gradual extermination of this un-questioned evil; and I am ready to proceed with the hon. gentleman to all reasonable and practicable measures for that purpose.

. . . I think the House will be of my opinion that at this time of day we must consider property as the creature of law; and that, when law has sanctioned any particular species of property, we cannot legislate in this House as if we were legislating for a new world, the surface of which was totally clear from the obstruction of antecedent claims and obligations. If the hon. gentleman asks me, on the other hand, whether I maintain the inviolability of property so far as to affirm the proposition that the children of slaves must continue to be slaves for ever–I answer frankly, No. If again he asks me how I reconcile my notions of reverence for the sacredness of property with the degree of authority I am prepared to exercise for the attainment of my object, I answer with equal frankness, in accomplishing a great national object, in doing an act of national justice, I do not think it right to do it at the exclusive expense of any one class of the community. I am disposed to go gradually to work, in order to diminish both the danger to be risked and the burden to be incurred. . . . In order that the object which we have all in view may be undertaken safely and effectually, it is better that it should be left in the hands of the Executive Government.

With that view I have taken the liberty of preparing certain Resolutions, which I shall propose to substitute for those of the hon. gentleman.

. . . He asks if the present mode of working–that which is described by the term driving–the slaves, by means of a cart-whip in the hand of one who follows them, ought to be allowed. I reply, certainly not. But I go further. I tell the hon. gentleman that in raising any class of persons from a servile to a civil condition, one of the first principles of improvement is in the observance paid to the difference of sexes. I would therefore abolish, with respect to females, the use of the whip, not only as a stimulant to labour in the field: I would abolish it altogether as an instrument of punishment– thus saving the weaker sex from indecency and degradation. I should further be inclined to concur with the hon. gentleman as to the insufficiency of the time allowed to the negroes for religious and moral instruction, so long as the cultivation of his provision-ground and his marketing occupy the greater part of the Sabbath. In this point I am anxious to introduce improvement into the present system.

These are points on which I have no hesitation in agreeing with the hon. gentleman; but there are some others requiring more mature consideration in practice, although, in principle, I feel bound to say that I agree with him. I agree with him in thinking that what is now considered by custom and in point of fact, the property of the negro, ought to be secured to him by law. I agree with him in thinking that it would be beneficial if the liberty of bequest were assured to him: perhaps it might be made conditional upon marriage. I agree with him in thinking that it may perhaps be desirable to do something with regard to the admitting the evidence of negroes, but this I hold to be a much more difficult question, and one requiring more thorough deliberation than I have yet had time to give to it . . . I agree further with the hon. gentleman in thinking that . . . the process of the writ of *venditioni exponas*, by which the slaves are sold separately from the estates, ought, if possible, to be abolished.

I have mentioned these particulars as those which have most immediately attracted the attention of H.M.'s servants. I can assure the hon. gentleman and the

House that they have looked at this subject with a sincere desire to render all possible assistance to the undertaking of the hon. gentleman, and to co-operate in every practicable measure for ameliorating the condition of the negroes. . . .

There is, however, one point in the hon. gentleman's statement upon which I certainly entertain a difference of opinion: I mean, the proposal of fixing a period at which the children of slaves shall be free. I doubt . . . whether the measure . . . would produce the degree of satisfaction which he anticipates, and whether it might not produce feelings of an opposite nature. I doubt whether in its operation it would not prove at once the least efficient and the most hazardous mode of attaining his own object. . . .

I will now, with the leave of the House, read the Resolutions which I propose to submit to the House for its consideration.

1st. 'That it is expedient to adopt effectual and decisive measures for ameliorating the condition of the slave population in H.M.'s colonies.

2nd. 'That, through a determined and persevering, but at the same time judicious and temperate enforcement of such measures, this House looks forward to a progressive improvement in the character of the slave population, such as may prepare them for a participation in those civil rights and privileges which are enjoyed by other classes of H.M.'s subjects.

3rd. 'That this House is anxious for the accomplishment of this purpose at the earliest period that shall be compatible with the well-being of the slaves themselves, with the safety of the colonies, and with a fair and equitable consideration of the interests of private property.'

If the House should be inclined to adopt these resolutions I shall then follow them up with moving,

4th, 'That the said Resolutions be laid before H.M. by such members of this House as are of H.M.'s most hon. Privy Council.'

There now remains but one point which . . . I am peculiarly anxious to impress upon its [the House's] consideration—I mean the mode of execution—the manner in which the Executive Government would have to act in respect of these Resolutions, in the event of their adoption. The House is aware that over certain of the colonies in the West Indies the Crown exercises immediate power, without the intervention of any colonial Legislature. In their case the agency of the Crown, of course, will be more free and unfettered than in colonies having their own separate Government. At the same time I must declare that we have a right to expect from the colonial Legislatures a full and fair co-operation . . . I must add that any resistance which might be manifested to the express and declared wishes of Parliament, any resistance, I mean, which should partake, not of reason but of contumacy, would create a case (a case, however, which I sincerely trust will never occur) upon which H.M.'s Government would not hesitate to come down to Parliament for counsel. . . .

. . . I abjure the principle of perpetual slavery, but I am not prepared now to state in what way I would set about the accomplishment of the object . . . because my mind is not yet made up, and I am unwilling to say anything to-night which may reduce me hereafter to the necessity of qualifying any statement I may make.

F. Buxton: I am fully satisfied with the answer the right hon. gent. has been kind enough to give to my questions . . . I now beg leave to withdraw my motion. . . .
Mr. Canning's Amendment . . . was carried *nem. con.*

513. The Anti-Slavery Society's address to the Nation, 7 July 1830

(*The Scotsman*, 24 July 1830.)

George IV's death in June 1830 was necessarily followed by a general election. Especially in county constituencies the anti-slavery vote was a factor of some importance—nowhere more so than in Yorkshire, Wilberforce's old constituency. There, Brougham attributed his success in part to his efforts to put an end to the slave trade and to slavery itself.

ANTI-SLAVERY.

The following Address to the Electors and People of the United Kingdom, has just been issued by the Anti-Slavery Society.

Fellow Countrymen.–Parliament is about to be dissolved; and you will shortly be solicited for your votes by those who wish to be your Representatives in the House of Commons. Let your first question to every candidate be, are you a Proprietor of Slaves, or a West India merchant? If the answer is in the affirmative, we would recommend to you a positive refusal, unless he be one of the very few who have already proved themselves true friends to our cause; or who, being known to you as a man of probity and honour, will give you the security of his promise henceforth to support it in the House. But whoever the candidate may be, demand of him, as the condition of your support, that he will solemnly pledge himself to attend in his place whenever any measure is brought forward for the termination of Slavery by parliamentary enactments; and that he will give his vote for every measure of that kind. Unless such a pledge is given in these, or equivalent terms, and more especially so as to exclude the subterfuge of still committing the work to the Assemblies, the engagement will be of little value, or rather of none at all. Add to this right use of your own vote, the widest and most active influence you can employ with your brother electors to engage them to follow your example. Let Committees for the purpose be formed in every county, city, and borough in the United Kingdom, in which any independent suffrages are to be found; and let public meetings be called, and the exhortations of the press be employed, to extend the same salutary work; and that work, let us add, alone; avoiding all political distinctions, and inviting men of both or all parties, to unite in promoting that single object.

We cannot promise our countrymen, that by such means your generous wishes will be fully and certainly accomplished; but one end at least, and an inestimable one, you will be sure to obtain. You will deliver your own consciences from any participation in the guilt which you have used your best endeavours to restrain.

Come forward then; instruct your Representatives; give or withhold your suffrages for the next Parliament; and use your personal influence throughout the country; all in such a manner as may best promote the success of this great and sacred cause.

If you succeed, you will give a new triumph to the British Constitution, you will exalt the glory of your country, in that best point, her moral elevation, and recommend her to the favour of Heaven. You may rescue also yourselves and your posterity from severe calamities, which we firmly believe are now impending over us, notwithstanding our apparent prosperity, not only from the natural effects of our pernicious system in the Colonies, if longer persisted in, but from the just vengeance of a righteous and all-directing Providence.

If you fail, you will at least have the inestimable consolation that you have done what you could "to undo the heavy burden and to let the oppressed go free," and that the sins and calamities of your country, however pernicious in their consequences to yourselves or your children, were evils which you could not avert.

514. Report of a Select Committee of the House of Commons on the commercial state of the West India Colonies, 13 April 1832

(*Parliamentary Papers*, 1831–1832, xx, pp. 661–677.)

After pointing out that the British colonies were handicapped by higher production costs than their foreign rivals, who continued to import large numbers of slaves from West Africa (supplies cut off from the British planters since 1807), the report proceeds:

... The consequence of these events ... is, according to the West Indians, this: while the quantity of West India produce brought into the United Kingdom from the British colonies is greatly enlarged, that produce, being too plentiful for the English market, has to compete in the markets of Europe with an increased quantity of foreign produce. British colonial produce thus loses the advantage of the domestic monopoly, and its price is regulated in a great measure by the price of sugar in the European markets, supplied by the foreign colonies.

The same principles which dictated the abolition of the slave trade have led the Government of the United Kingdom to adopt, in the colonies under the immediate control of the Crown, measures for the amelioration of the condition of the slaves, some of which diminish the proportion of their labour and produce to the charge which they occasion, and add to the expenses of cultivation.

In its competition with foreign countries, the colonial produce of Great Britain is also subjected to disadvantages, occasioned by the commercial and maritime policy of the mother country. Partial attempts, counteracted in a degree by circumstances to be presently noticed, have been made of late years to relieve the colonies from the effects of the restrictive laws. They have been permitted to carry on a direct intercourse with those countries of Europe and America which, by complying with the terms prescribed, have entitled themselves to such intercourse; but the importation of goods from these foreign countries has been clogged by discriminating duties, and there has been in fact scarcely any intercourse with those countries. In respect of the United States of America, the most important either for export or import, the intercourse has been from time to time suspended, renewed and modified; and has finally been permitted under a system of protection for the North American colonies which, together with the uncertainty produced by frequent changes, renders it as yet doubtful whether, during the existence of that protection, any benefit will be derived by the

West India colonies from its renewal. And in regard to some very material articles of supply, a strict monopoly is still maintained in favour of the mother country, or of her North American possessions. . . .

Among the artificial causes alleged by the West Indians as diminishing the consumption of their produce, is the high duty imposed upon it in the mother country. Upon the main article of produce, sugar, this duty is imposed for financial purposes alone, but the article of rum is subjected to a duty made higher for the protection of the corresponding produce of the United Kingdom. This last, therefore, is one other and peculiar restriction upon the disposal of the West India produce. Still another is to be added – molasses, one of the products of the sugar cane, are excluded by law from the distilleries and public breweries of the United Kingdom. . . .

Where a burthensome regulation can be removed, it is much better to remove it than to grant a compensation. In proceeding therefore to a detailed examination of each of the alleged grievances of which the colonies complain, they will first treat of those which appear susceptible of this preferable mode of remedy. Under this description, indeed, may come all the legislative restrictions except those which have reference to slavery. . . .

The 'Commercial Restrictions' . . . are . . . said to impose an annual charge upon the West India colonies of no less than £1,392,353. This sum being apportioned to the several articles of West India produce, the charge upon sugar is stated at £1,101,000, and as the sugar imported is 3,972,387 cwts., the burthen upon each cwt. by this mode of calculation is 5s. 6¾d. If this statement be correct, the removal of the commercial restrictions would occasion a deduction of 5s. 6¾d. from the sum of 24s. 2d. alleged as the cost of bringing to market a cwt. of sugar: 18s. 7¼d. would thus be the sum to be set against the assumed price of 23s. 8d., leaving a balance of 5s. 0¾d. in favour of the planter instead of 6d. against him. . . .

Your Committee now leave those causes of distress which appear susceptible of removal or modification. They are now to advert to the other, and according to the representation of the colonists, much more operative causes, concerning which there arises no question but that of compensation.

The first of these causes is the addition made to the British sugar colonies at the peace of 1814. The extension of territory and the acquisition by the mother country of more fertile and therefore valuable possessions, cannot reasonably be admitted as giving to any part of the more ancient Empire a right to be compensated for the depreciation of its produce. In the general advantages of that acquisition, be they more or less considerable, the whole Empire, domestic and colonial, participates; and it would be as reasonable for an English landholder to complain of the effect of the corn and cattle of Ireland, admitted on the principle of the Union, as for a planter in Jamaica to urge that his produce is become cheaper since Demerara has been added to the British dominions. . . . This extension of the sugar colonies of Great Britain is in truth one of the most operative causes of existing distress.

Your Committee now advert to the point on which the greatest stress is laid by the West Indians – the abolition of the slave trade, unaccompanied by the abolition on the part of all foreign States. It is alleged that an increased charge of no less than

15s. 10d. the cwt. of sugar is thus occasioned—that is, 11s. as the greater cost of rearing slaves in our colonies than of purchasing them in the foreign colonies, and 4s. 10d. as the loss sustained by the smaller proportion of slaves effective for work. . . . Your Committee feel bound to remark that the several details are not supported by the evidence before them. . . . Having thus given their reasons for apprehending that the estimate of loss by the abolition laws is somewhat exaggerated, your Committee have no hesitation in submitting . . . their opinion, first, that some loss, and conse-quently some part of the present distress of the colonists, is occasioned by those laws; and secondly, that such loss constitutes a fair ground of claim for compensation. . . . The claim preferred on behalf of the West Indian body is not commensurate with their estimate of loss. What they solicit is, to be better enabled to compete with the foreign grower in the market of Europe. . . . They desire an additional drawback or bounty on exportation, calculated upon a duty exceeding by 6s. that which they actually pay. Your Committee cannot admit equalisation as a principle: British colonists, like all other proprietors, must sustain the effect of any advantage which other countries may enjoy, except where their relative situation is affected by British laws: and the question therefore still returns, whether the injury sustained by the colonies, under those laws, entitle them to the relief which they seek. . . . Your Committee, admitting the justice of the claim in principle, feel compelled to observe that the evidence of the amount of actual injury is not so specific and positive as to enable them to recommend to the House the adoption of any given rate of compensa-tion. In addition to the deduction which, according to their suggestion, must be made from the estimate of the West Indians, further allowance must be made for the insufficiency of the evidence as to the expenses of the foreign grower, and above all for the want of proof whether his superiority does not consist, in a greater degree than has been allowed, in those natural causes which common consent has excluded from consideration. . . .

It is not by the payment of the bounty upon sugar exported, that the planter is to be relieved; he hopes, by that bounty occasioning an increased export, and lessening his dependence upon foreign prices, to raise the price of his sugar in the home market; and in estimating the compensation to be paid by the country, the whole amount of this enhancement of price must be added to the sum actually paid as bounty. . . . A rise of price in the home market, by whatever means effected, must, as it tends to lessen consumption, operate in a precisely opposite direction to a reduction of duty. . . . Higher prices have a tendency to increase production; productiveness, and the possibility of extending production, are very unequal in different British colonies, and are greater in some of the new colonies than in the old. A bounty given in common to Dominica and to Demerara may have the effect of bringing to market from the newer acquisition an augmented quantity of sugar to compete with the more limited produce of the old possession. Upon all these considerations your Committee forbear to recommend any alteration in the existing drawback. . . .

The agitation of the slave question in Great Britain has tended to diminish the feeling of confidence of the West India proprietor in the security of his property, to check the investment of capital and to increase the difficulty of effecting sales and mortgages. It is not for your Committee . . . to suggest the means by which confidence may be restored. They trust that the importance attached to it by the colonists, as bearing heavily upon 'the commercial state of the West India colonies', will justify their allusion to this sense of insecurity, and that if its causes be beyond the control of Parliament, the House will at least deem it an additional motive for receiving favourably those other suggestions with which it is in their power to comply. . . .

C. THE CANADIAN PROVINCES

515. Debate in the House of Commons on the Quebec Government Bill, 8 April 1791

(Cobbett's *Parliamentary History*, XXIX, 105–113.)

This Act was passed to meet the new conditions created by the American Revolution. Thousands of loyalists from England's former colonies migrated to Canada and settled, some in New Brunswick, which was organized as a separate province in 1784, and others in the neighbourhood of the Great Lakes. The Act conceded their demand for those representative institutions to which they had always been accustomed, and it divided the colony of Quebec into two provinces–Lower Canada or Quebec, which was predominantly French in population, and Upper Canada or Ontario, which was predominantly English-Canadian. Each was to have its own Governor, popularly elected Assemby and a Legislative Council. Ignorant of the real strength of French-Canadian feeling, Fox wanted to swamp the French settlers in the English-speaking majority, and opposed the subdivision of the colony. Pitt was hardly more far-sighted: he hoped that the French Canadians would eventually become Anglicized after a sufficient experience of the blessings of English laws and institutions.

Mr. Fox . . . hoped that in promulgating the scheme of a new Constitution for the province of Quebec, the House would keep in their view those enlightened principles of freedom which had already made a rapid progress over a considerable portion of the globe, and were becoming every day more and more universal. As the love of liberty was gaining ground in consequence of the diffusion of literature and knowledge through the world, he thought that a Constitution should be formed for Canada as consistent as possible with the principles of freedom. This Bill, in his opinion, would not establish such a Government, and that was his chief reason for opposing it. The Bill proposed to give two Houses of Assembly in the two Provinces, one to each of them, and thus far it met with his approbation; but the number of persons of whom these Assemblies were to consist, deserved particular attention. Although it might be perfectly true that a country three or four times as large as Great Britain ought to have representatives three or four times as numerous, yet it was not fit to say that a small country should have an Assembly proportionably small. The great object in the institution of all popular Assemblies was that the people should be fully and freely represented, and that the representative body should have all the virtues and the vices incidental to such Assemblies. But when they made an Assembly to consist of 16 or 30 persons, they seemed to him to give a free Constitution in appearance, when, in fact, they withheld it. In Great Britain we had a Septennial Bill, but the goodness of it had been considered doubtful, at least, even by many of those who took a lead in the present Bill. The Right Hon. the Chancellor of the

Exchequer had himself supported a vote for the repeal of that Act. He did not now mean to discuss its merits, but a main ground on which it had been thought defensible was that a general election in this country was attended with a variety of inconveniences. That general elections in Great Britain were attended with several inconveniences could not be doubted; but when they came to a country so different in all circumstances as Canada, and where elections, for many years at least, were not likely to be attended with the consequences which they dreaded, why they should make such Assemblies not annual or triennial, but septennial, was beyond his comprehension. A Septennial Bill did not apply to many of the most respectable persons in that country; they might be persons engaged in trade, and if chosen representatives for seven years, they might not be in a situation to attend during all that period; their affairs might call them to England, or many other circumstances might arise, effectually to prevent them from attending the service of their country. But although it might be inconvenient for such persons to attend such Assembly for the term of seven years, they might be able to give their attendance for one, or even for three years, without any danger or inconvenience to their commercial concerns. By a Septennial Bill, the country of Canada might be deprived of many of the few representatives that were allowed by the Bill. If it should be said that this objection applied to Great Britain, he completely denied it, because although there were persons engaged in trade in the British House of Commons, and many of them very worthy members, yet they were comparatively few; and therefore he should think that, from the situation of Canada, annual or triennial Parliaments would be much preferable to septennial. Of the qualification of electors he felt it impossible to approve. In England, a freehold of 40s. was sufficient: £5 were necessary in Canada. Perhaps it might be said that when this was fairly considered, it would make no material difference; and this he suspected to be the case; but granting that it did not, when we were giving to the world by this Bill our notions of the principles of election, we should not hold out that the qualifications in Great Britain were lower than they ought to be. The qualifications on a house were still higher, he believed, £10. In fact he thought that the whole of this Constitution was an attempt to undermine and contradict the professed purport of the Bill, namely, the introduction of a popular Government into Canada. But although this was the case with respect to the two Assemblies, although they were to consist of so inconsiderable a number of members, the Legislative Councils in both provinces were unlimited as to numbers. They might consist of any number whatever, at the will of the Governor. Instead of being hereditary Councils, or Councils chosen by electors, as was the case in some of the colonies in the West Indies, or chosen by the King, they were compounded of the other two. As to the points of hereditary powers and hereditary honours, to say that they were good, or that they were not good, as a general proposition, was not easily maintained: but he saw nothing so good in hereditary powers and honours as to incline us to introduce them into a country where they were unknown, and by such means distinguish Canada from all the colonies in the West Indies. In countries where they made a part of the Constitution he did not think it wise to destroy them; but to give birth and life to such principles in countries where they did not exist, appeared to him to be exceedingly unwise. Nor could he account for it unless it was that Canada having been formerly a French colony, there might be an opportunity of reviving those titles of honour, the extinction of which some gentlemen so much deplored, and to revive in the west that spirit of chivalry which had fallen into disgrace in the neighbouring country. He asked, if those red and blue ribbons which had lost their lustre in the old world, were to shine forth again in the new? It seemed to him peculiarly absurd to introduce hereditary honours in America, where those artificial distinctions stunk in the nostrils of the natives. He declared he thought these powers and honours wholly unnecessary, and tending rather to make a new Constitution worse then better. If the Council were wholly hereditary he should equally object to it; it would only add to the power of the King and the Governor, for a Council so constituted would only be the tool of the Governor as the Governor himself would only be the tool and engine of the King. He did not clearly comprehend the provision which the Bill made for the Protestant clergy. By the Protestant clergy he supposed to be understood not only the clergy of the Church of England, but all descriptions of Protestants. He totally disapproved of the clause which enacts, 'That whenever the King shall make grants of lands, one-seventh part of those lands shall be appropriated to the Protestant clergy.' He declared he had two objections to these regulations, both of them, in his opinion, of great weight. In all grants of lands made in that country to Catholics (and a majority of the inhabitants were of that persuasion) one-seventh part of those grants was to be appropriated to the Protestant clergy, although they might not have any cure of souls, or any congregations to instruct. One tenth part of the produce of this country was assigned, and this, perhaps, was more than one-seventh part of the land. He wished to deprive no clergyman of his just rights, but in settling a new Constitution, and laying down new principles, to enact that the clergy should have one-seventh of all grants, he must confess, appeared to him an absurd doctrine. If they were all of the Church of England, this would not reconcile him to the measure. . . .

Of all the points of the Bill that which struck him the most forcibly was the division of the Province of Canada. It had been urged that, by such means, we could separate the English and the French inhabitants of the Province, that we could distinguish who were originally French from those of English origin. But was this to be desired? Was it not rather to be avoided? Was it agreeable to general political expediency? The most desirable circumstance was that the French and English inhabitants of Canada should unite and coalesce, as it were, into one body, and that the different distinctions of the people might be extinguished for ever. If this had been the object in view, the English laws might soon have prevailed universally throughout Canada, not from force, but from choice and conviction of their superiority. He had no doubt that on a fair trial they would be found free from all objection. The inhabitants of Canada had not the laws of France. The commercial code was never established there: they stood upon the exceedingly inconvenient custom of Paris. He wished the people of that country to adopt the English laws from choice, and not from force; and he did not think the division of the province the most likely means to bring about this desirable end. . . .

He trusted that the House would also seriously consider the particular situation of Canada. It was not to be compared to the West Indies; it was a country of a different nature; it did not consist of a few white inhabitants and a number of slaves; but it was a country of great growing population, which had increased very much, and which, he hoped, would increase much more. It was a country as capable of enjoying political freedom, in its utmost extent, as any other country on the face of the globe. This country was situated near the colonies of North America. All their animosity and bitterness on the quarrel between them and Great Britain was now over, and he believed that there were very few people among those colonies who would not be ready to admit every person belonging to this country into a participation of all their privileges, and would receive them with open arms. The Governments now estab-lished in North America were, in his opinion, the best adapted to the situation of the people who lived under them, of any of the Governments of the ancient or modern world: and when we had a colony like this, capable of freedom and capable of a great increase of population, it was material that the inhabitants should have nothing to look to among their neighbours to excite their envy. Canada must be preserved to Great Britain by the choice of its inhabitants. But it should be felt by the inhabitants that their situation was not worse than that of their neighbours. He wished the Canadians to be in such a situation as to have nothing to envy in any part of the King's dominions. But this would never be the case under a Bill which held out to them something like the shadow of the British Constitution, but denied them the substance. In a country where the principles of liberty were gaining ground, they should have a Government as agreeable to the genuine principles of freedom, as was consistent with the nature of circumstances. He did not think that the Government intended to be established by the Bill would prove such a Government, and this was his principal motive for opposing it. The Legislative Councils ought to be totally free, and repeatedly chosen, in a manner as much independent of the Governor as the nature of a colony would admit. Those, he conceived, would be the best; but if not, they should have their seats for life; be appointed by the King, consist of a limited number, and possess no hereditary honours. . . .

Mr. Pitt . . . doubted very much, according to the present state of the colony and the population in that province, whether the Assemblies could be rendered more numerous than was proposed. The House would, however, consider that there was no wish that the Assemblies should not be increased when the population of the Province increased. The Assemblies undoubtedly ought to be extended with the growing population of Canada. He believed that a very numerous representative body was in no respect desirable, and they ought always to bear some proportion to the circumstances of the country. With regard to the duration of the Assemblies, a House of Assembly for seven years would surely be better than one for a shorter period. In the other colonies the Council and Assembly were constituted in such a manner as to invest the Governor with more influence than would be given to him by the present Bill. If the Assembly was not properly constituted at first, it must be recollected that it was subject to revision. . . . As to the Legislative Council, he entirely differed from the right hon. gent. who thought it would be better if it were to be an elective Council, in the manner which had been lately established in America. He did not think it was the business of that House to discuss what was the best constitution of Government for France, for America, or for any foreign country; and this had been a reason why he had always declined making any remarks concerning the affairs of France. Whether France had chosen well for itself, or whether America had chosen well for itself, he had no difficulty in declaring that the English Constitution which we had chosen, was in its principle the best for us; better than any of those republican principles. . . . An aristocratical principle being one part of our mixed Government, he thought it proper that there should be such a Council in Canada as was provided for by the Bill, and which might answer to that part of the British Constitution which composed the other House of Parliament. With regard to the Protestant clergy, he wished to make an adequate provision for them, so that they might be supported in as respectable a situation as possible. The giving them a certain portion of land was the most eligible mode of supporting the clergy which had occurred to his mind; and as to the proportion of one-seventh, if it turned out to be too much in future, the state of the land appropriated to the clergy, like everything else provided by the Bill, was subject to a revision. At present he imagined that no man could think that one-seventh part was unreasonable; and it was to be recollected that one-seventh had almost grown into an established custom, where land had been given in commutation for tithes. One-tenth of the produce which took place in England must be confessed to be a far greater provision than one-seventh of land. As to the division of the province, it was, in a great measure the fundamental part of the Bill; and he had no scruple to declare that he considered it as the most material and essential part of it. He agreed with the right hon. gent. in thinking it extremely desirable that the inhabitants of Canada should be united, and led universally to prefer the English Constitution and the English laws. Dividing the province, he considered to be the most likely means to effect this purpose, since by so doing, the French subjects would be sensible that the British Government had no intention of forcing the English laws upon them, and therefore they would, with more facility, look at the operation and effect of those laws, compare them with the operation and effect of their own, and probably in time adopt them from conviction. This, he thought, was more likely to be the case than if the British Government were all at once to subject the whole inhabitants to the Constitution and laws of this country. Experience would teach them that the English laws were best; and he admitted that they ought to be governed to their satisfaction. If the province had not been divided there would have been only one House of Assembly; and there being two parties, if those parties had been equal, or nearly equal, in the Assembly, it would have been the source of perpetual faction: if one of the parties had been much stronger than the other, the other might justly have complained that they were oppressed. It was on that persuasion that the division of the Province was conceived to be the most likely way of attaining every desirable end.

516. The Canada Act of 1791 (31 Geo. III, c. xxxi)

Whereas an Act was passed in the fourteenth year of the reign of his present Majesty, intituled, An Act for making more effectual provision for the Government of the Province of Quebec in North America: And whereas . . . it is expedient and necessary that further provision should now be made for the good government and prosperity thereof, may it therefore . . . be enacted . . . that so much of the said Act as . . . relates to the appointment of a Council for the affairs of . . . Quebec, or to the power given . . . to the . . . Council . . . to make Ordinances for the peace, welfare and good government of the . . . Province, with the consent of H.M.'s Governor, Lieutenant Governor or Commander-in-Chief for the time being, shall be . . . repealed.

II. And whereas H.M. has been pleased to signify by his Message to both Houses of Parliament his royal intention to divide his Province of Quebec into two separate Provinces, to be called The Province of Upper Canada, and The Province of Lower Canada, be it enacted . . . that there shall be within each of the . . . Provinces respectively a Legislative Council and an Assembly . . . and that . . . H.M. . . . shall have power . . . by and with the advice and consent of the Legislative Council and Assembly . . . to make laws . . . such laws not being repugnant to this Act. . . .

III. . . . It shall . . . be lawful for H.M. . . . to authorize . . . the Governor or Lieutenant Governor . . . in each of the . . . Provinces . . . to summon to the . . . Legislative Council . . . a sufficient number of discreet and proper persons, being not fewer than seven to the Legislative Council for . . . Upper Canada, and not fewer than 15 to the Legislative Council for . . . Lower Canada; and . . . it shall . . . be lawful for H.M. . . . from time to time . . . to authorize . . . the Governor or Lieutenant Governor . . . in each . . . Province . . . to summon to the Legislative Council . . . such other person or persons as H.M. . . . shall think fit. . . .

IV. . . . No person shall be summoned to the . . . Legislative Council . . . who shall not be of the full age of 21 years and a natural born subject of H.M., or a subject . . . naturalised by Act of the British Parliament, or a subject . . . having become such by the conquest and cession of the Province of Canada.

V. . . . Every member of . . . the . . . Legislative Councils shall hold his seat . . . for . . . life. . . .

VI. [H.M. may annex to hereditary titles of honour, rank or dignity an hereditary right of being summoned to the Legislative Council.]

XII. [The Governor or Lieutenant Governor may appoint and remove the Speaker of the Legislative Council.]

XIII. . . . It shall . . . be lawful for H. M. . . . to authorise . . . the Governor . . . within the time hereinafter mentioned, and thereafter from time to time, as occasion shall require . . . to summon . . . an Assembly in . . . such Province.

XIV. . . . It shall . . . be lawful for H.M. . . . to authorise the Governor . . . [&c.] to issue a Proclamation dividing such Province into Districts or Counties or Circles, and towns or townships . . . and appointing the number of representatives to be chosen by each . . . District [&c.]. . . .

XVII. . . . The whole number of members to be chosen in . . . Upper Canada shall not be less than 16, and . . . the whole number . . . to be chosen in . . . Lower Canada shall not be less than 50.

XX. . . . The members . . . shall be chosen by the majority of votes of such persons as shall . . . be possessed . . . of lands or tenements within such District, or County, or Circle, as the case shall be, such lands being by them held in freehold or in fief or in roture . . . being of the yearly value of 40s. sterling or upwards, over and above all rents and charges payable out of . . . the same. . . . The members for the . . . towns or townships . . . shall be chosen by the majority of votes of such persons as either shall . . . be possessed . . . of a dwelling house and lot of ground . . . being held . . . as aforesaid, and being of the yearly value of £5 sterling or upwards, or, as having been resident within the said town or township for . . . twelve calendar months . . . shall . . . have paid one year's rent for the dwelling house in which they shall have so resided, at the rate of £10 sterling per annum or upwards.

XXI. No person shall be capable of being elected a member . . . of the . . . Assemblies, or of sitting or voting therein, who shall be a member of . . . the . . . Legislative Councils . . . or . . . a Minister of the Church of England, or a minister, priest, ecclesiastic or teacher, either according to the rites of the Church of Rome or under any other form . . . of religious faith. . . .

XXII. . . . No person shall be capable of voting at any election of a member to serve in such Assembly . . . or of being elected . . . who shall not be of the full age of 21 years, and a natural born subject . . . or a subject . . . naturalised by Act of the British Parliament, or a subject . . . having become such by . . . conquest. . . .

XXV–XXVI. [H.M. may authorise the Governor to fix the time and place of holding elections and of holding Sessions of Council and Assembly.]

XXVII. Provided always . . . that the . . . Legislative Council and Assembly . . . shall be called together once at the least in every twelve calendar months, and that every Assembly shall continue for four years . . . and no longer, subject nevertheless to be sooner prorogued or dissolved by the Governor. . . .

XXVIII. . . . All questions which shall arise in the . . . Legislative Councils or Assemblies . . . shall be decided by the majority of voices of such members as shall be present. . . . In all cases where the voices shall be equal, the Speaker . . . shall have a casting voice.

XXIX. [Members of the Legislative Council and Assembly to take an oath of allegiance to H.M.]

XXX. . . . Whenever any Bill which has been passed by the Legislative Council and by the . . . Assembly . . . shall be presented for H.M.'s assent, to the Governor [&c.] . . . such Governor [&c.] . . . is authorised . . . to declare, according to his discretion . . . that he assents to such Bill in H.M.'s name, or that he withholds H.M.'s assent . . . or that he reserves such Bill for the signification of H.M's pleasure thereon.

XXXI. [The Governor to transmit to the Secretary of State copies of Bills assented to.] . . . It shall . . . be lawful at any time within two years after such Bill shall have been so received by such Secretary of State, for H.M. . . . to declare his . . . disallowance of such Bill. . . .

XXXII. . . . No such Bill which shall be so reserved for the signification of H.M.'s pleasure thereon, shall have any force or authority . . . until the Governor [&c.] . . . shall signify . . . to the Legislative Council and Assembly . . . that H.M. has been pleased to assent to the same . . . and that no . . . Bill . . . reserved as aforesaid, shall have any force . . . unless H.M.'s assent thereto shall have been so signified as aforesaid, within the space of two years from the day on which such Bill shall have been presented for H.M.'s assent to the Governor [&c.]. . . .

XXXIV. And whereas by an Ordinance passed in the Province of Quebec, the Governor and Council . . . were constituted a Court of Civil Jurisdiction for hearing . . . appeals in certain cases . . . be it further enacted . . . that the Governor [&c.] . . . [and] Executive Council . . . shall be a Court of Civil Jurisdiction. . . .

XXXVI. . . . It shall . . . be lawful for H.M. . . . to authorise the Governor [&c] . . . to make, from . . . the lands of the Crown within such Provinces, such allotment and appropriation of lands for the support and maintenance of a Protestant clergy within the same, as may bear a due proportion to the amount of such lands within the same as have at any time been granted by . . . authority of H.M.; and that whenever any grant of lands . . . shall hereafter be made, by . . . authority of H.M. . . . there shall at the same time be made . . . a proportionable allotment . . . for the above-mentioned purpose, within the township or parish to which such lands so to be granted shall appertain or be annexed. . . .

XXXVII. . . . The rents . . . which may . . . arise from such lands so allotted . . . as aforesaid, shall be applicable solely to the maintenance and support of a Protestant clergy within the Province. . . .

XLVI. And whereas by an Act passed in . . . [1778], intituled, An Act for removing all doubts and apprehensions concerning taxation by the Parliament of Great Britain, in any of the Colonies, Provinces and Plantations in North America and the West Indies . . . it has been declared that the King and Parliament of Great Britain will not impose any duty, tax or assessment . . . payable in any of H.M.'s Colonies, Provinces and Plantations in North America or in the West Indies, except only such duties as it may be expedient to impose for the regulation of commerce, the net produce of such duties to be always . . . applied to . . . the use of the Colony, Province or Plantation in which the same shall be respectively levied . . . and whereas it is necessary for the general benefit of the British Empire that such power of regulation of commerce should continue to be exercised by H.M. . . . and the Parliament of Great Britain, subject nevertheless to the condition hereinbefore recited . . . be it . . . enacted . . . that nothing in this Act . . . shall extend . . . to prevent . . . the execution of any law which hath been or shall . . . be made by H.M. . . . and the Parliament of Great Britain, for establishing regulations or prohibitions, or for imposing . . . duties for the regulation of navigation . . . or . . . of . . . commerce to be carried on between . . . the said Provinces and any other part of H.M.'s dominions, or between . . . the . . . Provinces and any foreign country. . . .

XLVII. Provided always . . . that the net produce of all duties . . . so imposed shall . . . be applied to and for the use of . . . the said Provinces . . . and in such manner only as shall be directed by any law . . . which may be made by H.M. . . . by and with the advice and consent of the Legislative Council and Assembly of such Province.

L. [Between the commencement of the Act, and the first meeting of the Legislative Council and Assembly, temporary laws may be made by the Governor and his Executive Council.]

517. J. B. Robinson to Earl Bathurst on the proposed re-union of Upper and Lower Canada, April 1822

(V. Harlow and F. Madden, *British Colonial Developments, 1774–1834*, pp. 224–226.)

Robinson was Attorney-General of Upper Canada, and leader of the Government party in the Assembly.

. . . That an union of the provinces might add to their strength by producing a more perfect community of interest and feeling, by subjecting their militia to an uniform system of discipline, and by placing their means of defence against a foreign enemy more conveniently and effectually at the disposal of the Government that it might in time by the gradual operation of the natural consequences of such an union make the whole colony more completely British in their system of laws, in their education, in their feeling and in the general temper of all their public acts – that it would produce an uniform regulation of trade throughout the territory, and insure the interest of every part being made subservient to the welfare of the whole, and that it would necessarily put an end to all future difficulties about duties and drawbacks by sharing among all the enjoyment of that in which they have all an interest, are general advantages which, though some of them are rather indefinite as to the extent and uncertain as to the period in which they might be felt, might I think be rationally expected.

On the other hand I am doubtful of the prudence of disturbing the present system of things. . . . At present things are proceeding pleasantly and prosperously in Upper Canada. In Lower Canada they are not, but I do not think an union would remove in the least the difficulties existing there, and it might have the bad effect of involving the one province in the troubles of the other.

The number of representatives in Upper Canada is at present less than in the Lower Province, and would no doubt continue so for many years. The latter consists, with very few exceptions, of Canadian French, and I am apprehensive that an union of the two provinces would be regarded with such extreme jealousy and repugnance by the great body of the people in Lower Canada, that on future occasions they would even more studiously endeavour to exclude Englishmen from their Assembly, and confine their confidence to those who would sedulously guard their old system of things from innovation, and for many years I fear the people of Upper Canada would find it difficult to obtain any appropriation of revenue to purposes of public improvement within their province or to gain sufficient attention in their local interests from an Assembly of which the greater number would be unfriendly to their religion and unacquainted with their laws and jealous of their influence. If these consequences should follow they would retard the now rapidly increasing prosperity of Upper

Canada at the most critical moment . . . Upper Canada, it is true, contains at present much less population than the Lower Province, the one having been first settled by Europeans only 40 years ago, and the other more than 200, but it is well known that in extent of land capable of cultivation, in the excellence of its soil and climate, and consequent capability of production, the former possesses almost unrivalled advantages, and it would be much to be lamented that these should be prevented from developing themselves by being placed under the control of persons little acquainted with our agricultural interest, and even averse to the system of tenures and of laws under which the province has so surprisingly flourished. . . .

It perhaps deserves also to be considered how far it is politic upon national grounds to unite two colonies now distinct, thereby involving on all occasions the politics of one with those of the other, giving to them the means of making common cause in any unfortunate dissension which might arise, and rendering any disagreement a cause of irritation and of difficulty in two Governments, whereas otherwise it might but affect the tranquillity of one. . . .

I cannot even pretend to say how far an union would be agreeable to the people of Upper Canada generally. I have reason to think the majority of their present representatives are unfavourable to it, from a conviction that it would not be beneficial. . . . The French inhabitants of Lower Canada . . . are as peaceably disposed, as much inclined to submit to authority, and as loyally attached to the British Government, as any portion of H.M.'s subjects, and whatever trouble their representatives may give by refusing to make a permanent provision for the Civil List, or upon questions of revenue, or of any kind between themselves and the Executive Government, is not to be ascribed to the preponderance of French influence over the English, but to that desire which is found in all Assemblies to assert to the utmost the share of power which they think the Constitution gives them, a disposition which I think the descendants of English, Irish and Scotch will be found as likely to persevere in, as the descendants of Frenchmen. . . .

518. Louis Papineau (and others) to R. J. Wilmot, 16 Dec. 1822

(V. Harlow and F. Madden, *British Colonial Developments, 1774–1834*, pp. 231–232.)

Papineau was Speaker of the Lower Canadian Assembly, and was the leader of the Rebellion in Lower Canada in 1837. Wilmot (later, Wilmot Horton) was Under-Secretary of State for War and the Colonies.

Montreal: You may have been informed that the strongest and most declared opposition to the union of the Legislatures of Lower and Upper Canada, lately proposed in the Imperial Parliament, has been manifested throughout this province and Upper Canada. . . .

The Bill in question, say these friends of the union, being so well calculated to Anglify the country, which is to be ultimately peopled by a British race. . . .

The preposterous calumny against the Canadians of French origin, as to their supposed attachment to France, requires no other answer than what is derived from their uniform conduct during the wars, and the loyalty evinced by them on every occasion. They are not foreigners in this the land of their birth; they claim rights as

British subjects, in common with every other subject of H.M. in these colonies. These are their birth rights. And yet it was expected by the projectors of the Union Bill to deprive them of these rights which were so solemnly secured to them by the Act of the 31st of his late Majesty, after the elaborate discussions that then took place, and in conformity with the just and liberal views of the most enlightened politicians of those days.

By what they call Anglifying the country is meant the depriving the great majority of the people in this province of all that is dear to men; their laws, usages, institutions and religion. An insignificant minority wish for a change, and are desirous of ruling against every principle of justice by destroying what they call the Canadian influence, that is to say, the influence of the majority. . . . Great Britain wants no other Anglifying in this colony than that which is to be found in the loyalty and affection of its inhabitants, no other British race than that of natural born subjects, loyal and affectionate. Such are the inhabitants of both provinces. . . .

D. INDIA AND THE FAR EAST

519. Pitt's speech in the House of Commons on his India Bill, 6 July 1784

(Cobbett's *Parliamentary History*, XXIV, 1085–1100.)

The defeat of Fox's India Bill, in Dec. 1783 left Pitt free to introduce his own plans for the future government of the East India Company's possessions. His Bill, unlike Fox's, did not abolish the Directorate, but subordinated the political power it had hitherto exercised to a new Government Department, the Board of Control, which was to include the Chancellor of the Exchequer and a Secretary of State. Thus in effect the Government assumed responsibility for British India without sacrificing the knowledge and experience of the Directors. They were to retain their patronage (though in practice they found that they had to share it to an appreciable extent with Ministers, and, too, the Governor-General and members of the executive councils in all three Indian Presidencies were to be appointed by and removable by the Crown).

Mr. Chancellor Pitt rose to open his new system for the government of India. No one, he said, could be more deeply impressed than he was with the importance of the subject on which he was then going to enter: in whatever point of view he considered it, he felt that no subject could possibly be more interesting. In it were involved the prosperity and strength of this country; the happiness of the natives of those valuable territories in India which belonged to England; and finally the Constitution of England itself. India had at all times been of great consequence to this country, from the resources of opulence and strength it afforded: and that consequence had, of course, increased in proportion to the losses sustained by the dismemberment of other great possessions; by which losses, the limits of the Empire being more contracted, the remaining territories became more valuable. He was aware that nothing could be more difficult than to digest a plan which should at once confirm and enlarge the advantages derived to this country from its connexions with India; to render that connexion a blessing to the native Indians, and at the same time preserve inviolate the essence and spirit of our own Constitution from the injuries to which this connexion might eventually expose it. . . .

It had, he remarked, been ever held that commercial Companies could not govern Empires, but that was a matter of speculation, which general experience proved to be not true in practice, however universally admitted in theory. The East India Company had conducted its commerce and governed a vast Empire for years; and it was to be remembered that the East India Company was no new establishment; it rested on Charters and Acts of Parliament; those Charters ought undoubtedly to be regarded, and as far as possible, the rights exercised and enjoyed under them ought to be held sacred. . . . The measures he should propose were such as the Company agreed to. The control he had mentioned ought undoubtedly to remain where the Constitution had placed all power, in the Executive Government of the country. The management of the commerce he meant to leave with the Company. The patronage should be separate from the Executive Government, but be it given where it would, he should propose regulations that would essentially curtail and diminish it, so as to render it as little dangerous as possible. The patronage, however, he would trust with no political set of men whatever. Let it be in India, it would be free from corruption then; and when exercised under the restrictions and limitations he should propose, could, he flattered himself, be attended with no bad consequences. . . .

. . . Much would depend on the manner of administering the government in India, and that his endeavours should be directed to enforce clear and simple principles, as those from which alone a good government could arise. The first and principal object would be to take care to prevent the Government from being ambitious and bent on conquest. Propensities of that nature had already involved India in great expenses, and cost much bloodshed. These, therefore, ought most studiously to be avoided. Commerce was our object, and with a view to its extension, a pacific system should prevail, and a system of defence and conciliation. The Government there ought, therefore, in an especial manner to avoid wars, or entering into alliances likely to create wars. At the same time that he said this, he did not mean to carry the idea as far as to suggest that the British Government in India was not to pay a due regard to self-defence. . . .

520. Pitt's India Act, 1784 (24 Geo. III, c. 25)

(Statutes of the Realm, xxxiv, Part III, pp. 492–522.)

An Act for the better regulation and management of the affairs of the East India Company, and of the British possessions in India; and for establishing a Court of Judicature for the more speedy and effectual trial of persons accused of offences committed in the East Indies.

I. . . . It shall . . . be lawful . . . for the King's Majesty . . . to . . . appoint such persons, not exceeding six in number, as his Majesty shall think fit, being of his Majesty's most honourable Privy Council, of whom one of his Majesty's Principal Secretaries of State for the time being, and the Chancellor of the Exchequer for the time being, shall be two, . . . [to] be Commissioners for the Affairs of India.

II. . . . Any number, not less than three of the said Commissioners, shall form a

Board for executing the several powers which . . . shall be vested in the Commissioners aforesaid.

III. . . . The . . . Secretary of State, and, in his absence, the . . . Chancellor of the Exchequer, and, in the absence of both of them, the senior of the . . . other Commissioners, . . . shall . . . be President of the . . . Board; and the . . . Commissioners shall have . . . the superintendence and control over all the British territorial possessions in the East Indies, and over the affairs of the . . . Company. . . .

IV. [The President to have the casting vote.]

VI. The . . . Board shall be fully authorised . . . to superintend, direct and control all acts, operations, and concerns, which in any wise relate to the civil or military government or revenues of the British territorial possessions in the East Indies. . . .

XI. . . . All the members of the . . . Board shall, at all convenient times, have access to all papers and muniments of the . . . Company, and shall be furnished with such extracts or copies thereof as they shall . . . require; and . . . the Court of Directors of the . . . Company shall . . . deliver to the . . . Board copies of all Minutes . . . and . . . proceedings of all . . . Courts of Proprietors of the . . . Company, and of the . . . Court of Directors, so far as relate to the civil or military government or revenues of the British territorial possessions in the East Indies, within eight days after the holding of such . . . Courts; and also copies of all Dispatches which the . . . Directors . . . shall receive from any of their servants in the East Indies, immediately after the arrival thereof; and also copies of all letters, orders and instructions whatsoever relating to the civil or military government or revenues of the British territorial possessions in the East Indies, proposed to be . . . dispatched by the . . . Court of Directors, or any Committee of the said Directors, to any of the servants of the . . . Company in the East Indies; and . . . the . . . Court of Directors . . . shall . . . pay due obedience to . . . such orders and directions as they shall receive . . . from the . . . Board, touching the civil or military government and revenues of the British territorial possessions in the East Indies.

XII. . . . Within fourteen days after the receipt of such copies last mentioned, the . . . Board shall return the same to the . . . Court of Directors, with their approbation thereof . . . or their reasons at large for disapproving the same, together with instructions from the . . . Board . . . in respect thereto; and . . . the . . . Court of Directors shall thereupon dispatch . . . the letters, orders and instructions, so approved or amended, to their servants in India, without further delay, unless, on any representation made by the . . . Directors to the . . . Board, the . . . Board shall direct any alterations to be made . . .; and no letters, orders or instructions, until after such previous communication . . . to the . . . Board, shall at any time be sent . . . by the . . . Court of Directors to the East Indies, on any account or pretence whatsoever.

XIII. . . . Whenever the Court of Directors . . . neglect to transmit to the . . . Board their intended Dispatches on any subject within fourteen days after requisition made, it shall . . . be lawful . . . for the . . . Board to prepare and send to the Directors . . . any orders or instructions . . . concerning the civil or military government of the British territories and possessions in the East Indies; and the . . . Directors shall . . . transmit dispatches in the usual form (pursuant to the tenor of the said orders and instructions so transmitted to them) to the respective Governments and Presidencies in India, unless, on any representation made by the . . . Directors to the . . . Board, the . . . Board shall direct any alteration to be made. . . .

XIV. . . . It shall be lawful for the . . . Court of Directors to apply, by petition, to his Majesty in Council, touching such orders and instructions; and his Majesty in Council shall decide whether the same be, or be not, connected with the civil or military Government and revenues of the . . . territories and possessions in India; which decision shall be final. . . .

XV. . . . If the . . . Board shall be of opinion that the subject matter of any of their deliberations, concerning the levying of war or making of peace, or . . . negotiating with any of the native Princes or States in India, shall require secrecy, it shall . . . be lawful for the . . . Board to send secret orders . . . to the Secret Committee of the . . . Court of Directors . . . who shall thereupon, without disclosing the same, transmit their orders and Dispatches in the usual form, according to the tenor of the . . . orders and instructions of the Board, to the . . . Governments and Presidencies in India; and . . . the . . . Governments and Presidencies shall pay a faithful obedience to such orders and Dispatches, and shall return their answers to the same . . . to the Secret Committee, who shall forthwith communicate such answers to the . . . Board.

XVI. . . . The Court of Directors . . . are hereby required . . . to appoint a Secret Committee, to consist of any number of the . . . Directors not exceeding three. . . .

XVII. . . . Nothing in this Act . . . shall extend to give unto the . . . Board the power of nominating or appointing any of the servants of the . . . Company. . . .

XIX. . . . The government of the several Presidencies and settlements of Fort Saint George and Bombay shall, after the commencement of this Act, consist of a Governor or President, and three Councillors only, of whom the Commander-in-Chief in the said several settlements . . . shall be one . . . unless the Commander-in-Chief of the Company's forces in India shall happen to be present . . . and in such case the . . . Commander-in-Chief shall be one of the . . . Councillors instead of the Commander-in-Chief of such settlement. . . .

XXI. . . . In case the members present at any of the Boards or Councils of Fort William, Fort St. George, or Bombay, shall at any time be equally divided in opinion . . . the . . . Governor-General or the Governor or President . . . shall have two voices, or the casting vote.

XXII. . . . It shall . . . be lawful . . . for the King's Majesty . . . by any . . . instrument under his . . . sign-manual, countersigned by the . . . Secretary of State or for the Court of Directors, to . . . recall the present or any future Governor-General of Fort William at Bengal . . . or any other person . . . holding any office, civil or military, under the . . . Company in India . . . provided . . . that a . . . copy of every such instrument . . . within eight days after the same shall be signed by his Majesty . . . be transmitted . . . by the . . . Secretary of State unto the Chairman or Deputy Chairman . . . of the . . . Company. . . .

XXIII. . . . Whenever any vacancy . . . of the office of Governor-General or President, or of any member of the Council, shall happen in any of the Presidencies . . . the Court of Directors . . . shall proceed to . . . appoint a fit person . . . to supply such vacancy . . . from amongst their covenanted servants in India, except to the office of Governor-General, or the office of Governor or President of Fort St. George or Bombay, or of any Commander-in-Chief, to which several offices the . . . Court of Directors shall be at liberty . . . to nominate and appoint any other person. . . .

XXIV. . . . Provided . . . that the . . . Commanders-in-Chief at each of the . . . Presidencies . . . shall in no case succeed to the office of Governor-General or President of Fort William, Fort Saint George, or of Bombay, unless thereunto specially appointed by the Court of Directors of the . . . Company; but that in case of . . . vacancy . . . when no person shall be specially appointed to succeed thereunto, the Councillor next in rank to such Commander-in-Chief shall succeed to such office, and hold the same, until some other person shall be appointed thereunto by the said Court of Directors.

XXV. . . . When and so often as the Court of Directors shall not, within the space of two calendar months . . . proceed to supply the same . . . it shall be lawful for his Majesty . . . to . . . appoint by writing under his . . . royal sign-manual, such person . . . as his Majesty . . . shall think proper . . . with the same powers . . . as if he . . . had been nominated and appointed by the . . . Court of Directors. . . .

XXVIII. . . . No resignation . . . of the offices of the Governor-General, or Governor or President of any of the subordinate settlements, or Commander-in-Chief, or member of the . . . Councils of any of the . . . Presidencies in India, shall be deemed . . . to be valid . . . unless the same be made by an instrument in writing under the hand of the officer . . . resigning the same. . . .

XXIX. . . . No order or resolution of any General Court of the Proprietors of the . . . Company shall be available to revoke or rescind, or in any respect to affect, any act . . . or proceeding of the . . . Court of Directors by this Act . . . authorised to be . . . done by the . . . Court, after the same shall have been approved by the . . . Board. . . .

XXXI. . . . The Governor-General and Council of Fort William . . . shall have . . . authority to . . . control . . . the several Presidencies and Governments . . . in the East Indies . . . in all . . . transactions with the Country Powers, or the application of the revenues or forces of such Presidencies . . . in time of war, or any such other points as shall . . . be specially referred by the Court of Directors . . . to their . . . control.

XXXII. . . . Notwithstanding any doubt which may be entertained by the . . . Presidencies . . . to whom such orders or instructions shall be given . . . yet the . . . Presidencies . . . shall be bound to obey . . . in all cases whatever, except only where they shall have received positive orders . . . from the . . . Court of Directors, or from the Secret Committee . . . repugnant to the orders . . . of the . . . Governor-General and Council at the time of dispatching their orders. . . .

XXXIV. And whereas to pursue schemes of conquest and extension of dominion in India, are measures repugnant to the wish, the honour and policy of this nation; be it therefore enacted . . . that it shall not be lawful for the Governor-General and Council . . . without the express command . . . of the . . . Court of Directors, or of the Secret Committee . . . in any case (except where hostilities have actually been commenced, or preparations actually made for the commencement of hostilities against the British nation in India, or against some of the Princes or States . . . whose territories the . . . Company shall be . . . engaged by any subsisting Treaty to defend or guarantee) either to declare war or commence hostilities, or enter into any Treaty for making war, against any of the Country Princes or States in India, or any Treaty for guaranteeing the possessions of any country Princes, or States . . . and in all cases where hostilities shall be commenced or Treaty made, the . . . Governor-General and Council shall, by the most expeditious means they can devise, communicate the same unto the . . . Court of Directors, together with a full state of the information . . . upon which they shall have commenced such hostilities, or made such Treaties, and their motives and reasons for the same at large.

XXXV. . . . It shall not be lawful for the Governors or Presidents and Councillors of Fort Saint George and Bombay . . . to . . . issue any order for commencing hostilities or . . . to negotiate . . . any Treaty . . . with any Indian Prince or State (except in cases of sudden emergency or imminent danger, when it shall appear dangerous to postpone such hostilities or Treaty) unless in pursuance of express orders from the . . . Governor-General and Council . . . or from the . . . Court of Directors, or from the Secret Committee . . . and every such Treaty shall, if possible, contain a clause for subjecting the same to the ratification or rejection of the Governor-General and Council of Fort William aforesaid. . . .

XXXVI. . . . Presidents and Councillors who shall wilfully refuse to pay due obedience to such orders and instructions as they shall receive from the Governor-General and Council of Fort William . . . shall be liable to be suspended from the exercise of their . . . offices by order of the Governor-General and Council. . . .

XXXIX. . . . And whereas complaints have prevailed, that divers rajas, zemindars . . . and other native landholders . . . have been unjustly deprived of . . . their . . . lands, jurisdictions . . . and privileges, or that the tribute, rents and services required to be by them paid or performed for their . . . possessions to the . . . Company, are become grievous and oppressive; and whereas the principles of justice and the honour of this country require that such complaints should be forthwith inquired into and fully investigated, and if founded in truth effectually redressed : be it therefore enacted that the Court of Directors . . . shall . . . forthwith . . . take the said matters into their serious consideration, and . . . adopt . . . such methods for enquiring into the . . . truth of the . . . complaints . . . as they shall think best adapted for that purpose; and thereupon . . . give orders . . . to the several Governments and Presidencies in India, for effectually redressing, in such manner as shall be consistent with justice and the laws and customs of the country, all injuries and wrongs which the . . . rajas, zemindars . . . and other native landholders may have sustained . . . and for [the] settling . . . upon principles of moderation and justice, according to the laws and constitution of India, the permanent rules by which their tributes, rents and services shall be in future rendered and paid to the . . . Company. . . .

XL. . . . The Directors . . . shall take into their immediate consideration the . . . establishments, civil and military, of their . . . settlements in India, and give . . . orders . . . for every practicable retrenchment . . . and shall also require . . . full . . . and particular lists . . . of all the offices and employments on the civil establishment of the . . . Company in India, and of all the forces . . . in the pay or service of the . . . Company . . . together with the opinions of the respective Governments and Presidencies, what method or system can be adopted . . . for introducing a just and laudable economy in every branch of the . . . civil and military departments: and the Court of Directors . . . shall, as soon as may be . . . declare what offices . . . as well civil as military, will in their judgement be adequate to the support of the honour and dignity of this kingdom in the East Indies, and the safety, defence and security of the British possessions there . . . and specify . . . the rate . . . of the . . . salaries and emoluments to be hereafter allowed in respect thereof . . . and the . . . Court of Directors . . . are hereby required, within fourteen days after the commencement of every Session of Parliament, to bring before the two Houses of Parliament a perfect list of all offices, places and employments, in the civil and military establishments . . . with the salaries . . . and emoluments belonging thereto. . . .

XLI. . . . Until the . . . lists of the offices, places and employments shall have been made . . . the . . . Court of Directors shall be . . . prohibited from appointing or sending to India any new servant, civil or military, under the degrees of the . . . Councillors and Commanders-in-Chief; and after such lists shall have been perfected and established, the . . . Court of Directors shall in no wise appoint or send out any greater number of persons to be cadets or writers, or in any other capacity than will be actually necessary, in addition to the persons on the spot . . . to . . . keep up the proper complement . . . contained in the said lists. . . .

XLII. . . . From and after the commencement of this Act, all promotions . . . as well civil as military . . . under the degrees of the respective Councillors and Commanders-in-Chief, shall be made according to seniority of appointment, in a regular progressive succession. . . .

XLIII. . . . From and after the passing of this Act, no person shall be capable of . . . being appointed . . . by the Court of Directors to the East Indies, in the capacity of a writer or cadet, whose age shall be under fifteen years, or shall exceed the age of twenty-two years. . . .

XLIV. . . . All his Majesty's subjects . . . are hereby declared to be amenable to all courts of justice (both in India and Great Britain) of competent jurisdiction to try offences committed in India, for all acts . . . done . . . in any of the . . . territories of any native Prince . . . in the same manner as if the same had been done . . . within the territories directly subject to . . . the British Government in India.

XLV. . . . The demanding or receiving of any sum of money, or other valuable thing as a gift . . . by any British subject holding . . . any office under his Majesty or the . . . Company in the East Indies, shall be deemed . . . to be extortion, and shall be proceeded against and punished as such. . . .

521. George Canning to the earl of Moira, 30 Aug. 1816

(Harewood MSS.)

Canning was President of the Board of Control, 1816–1820. Moira (cr. marquess of Hastings, 1816) was Governor-General of Bengal, 1813–1823. Although he had been highly critical of Wellesley's ambitious policy of territorial annexation and subsidiary alliance, he was forced into the war with Nepal (1814–1816) by the Gurkhas' unprovoked aggression, and into a greater struggle with the Marathas (1817–1818) which ended with the destruction of their military power and the annexation of much of their territory.

In addressing your Lordship for the first time, it is a great satisfaction to me to begin our correspondence with my cordial congratulations on the termination of the Gurkha War; and to have to assure your Lordship that the Prince Regent & his ministers do full justice to the gallantry & skill with which the operations of the British Army have been conducted, and to the firmness and prudence with which your Lordship has secured and improved the results of those operations. . . .

Instead of commenting upon particular passages of your Lordship's minutes, it will be a shorter course and perhaps more satisfactory to your Lordship that I should state at once the objects of the Prince Regent's Government with respect to India.

The first of these objects in one word is peace: the next, if peace cannot be preserved altogether, is to have as little war as possible—and *that* war to arise only from causes demonstrably unavoidable, & to be terminated as soon as those causes can be removed. To this system, if we were not led by choice, we should find ourselves compelled by necessity. We are not unaware that a large and comprehensive forecast has often laid the foundations of permanent tranquillity and security in war, or in measures by which war was purposely and justifiably hazarded. We do not deny that in many cases it may be a prudent economy to draw upon existing resources, even at the certainty of immediate inconvenience, for the sake of avoiding a distant but more extended & more exhausting expenditure. And we are not insensible to the degree of truth which is to be found in the general maxims so often applied to our Indian Empire, that a Government created & fostered in it's growth by a concurrence of circumstances so extraordinary & anomalous, and holding its station in defiance of so many hostile prejudices and interests, reigning over millions to whom it bears no natural affinity, and surrounded by States which must deem its existence dangerous to their own, cannot afford to stand still at any point in its elevation, however exalted; that it must totter when it ceases to advance, and can maintain even its integrity only by perpetual progression.

But these general maxims we think are not only susceptible of modification from time & circumstances, but are encountered by other maxims which must be allowed to qualify & control them. If it be true that there is in a new power, established by conquest and maintained by opinion in a strange land, an irrepressible tendency to enlarge itself by swallowing up its neighbours, it is equally true that there is in an overgrown Empire a no less prone disposition to fall in pieces. To mark beforehand the precise boundary at which aggrandisement might stop and settle into firmness & consistency, is evidently a hopeless undertaking; nor could the attempt be made without adopting or being accused of adopting those doctrines of "natural limits" & "irresistible destinies" which have cost Europe so dear within the last quarter of a century. It is equally impossible to assign the period at which the maturity of States begins to turn to decay and dissolution.

But between conflicting generalities, it may perhaps be assumed, without rashness, that the progress of acquisition & incorporation, even if necessarily interminable, need not be absolutely incessant, that a pause may occasionally be made without danger of retrogradation. In like manner it can hardly be denied that although to lay out a little now, in order to save a great expense hereafter, be generally the best economy, there may be special circumstances under which the prospect of a greater pecuniary demand at a distant period, would not justify the endeavour to prevent it by overstraining our immediate resources. And whatever may be the attacks which we apprehend to be meditated against our safety or our peace, there may be cases in which it is advisable to trust, in some degree, to time and chance for dissipating the danger rather than to meet it by anticipation.

If there be any truth in these propositions, surely the precise occasion at which such a parsimony in pecuniary sacrifices, and such a relaxation of political & military efforts might be most excusably and most safely indulged, would be immediately after some great exertion of strength, and some signal display of resources, in a war unquestionably just, & for the punishment of a presumptuous aggression.

The strong persuasion which we feel that pacific counsels are likely to be most conducive to the well-being of our Indian Empire, is founded on a consideration of the actual state both of India itself and of Europe.

We doubt the desireableness, even if we were convinced of the practicability, of establishing the British Government as the recognized umpire of all Indian quarrels, and assuming to it with the authority & influence, the onerous duties of such a superintendence. We doubt the expediency of expanding our control so widely over the whole surface of the Indian Continent as to present to European observation one connected and universal system of British power, stretching towards China on the one hand and towards Russia on the other.

France was heretofore the single source of external danger to our Indian Establishments. That danger is for the present gone by: but the peculiar position of Russia, her half Asiatic character, her influence & authority in Persia, and the measures which she is understood to be taking for strengthening & improving that connection, the diffusion of military skill & military habits among her people, the example of Buonaparte, both in what he achieved and what he is known to have designed, all conspire to give a colour of probability to the supposition that Russia may be looking towards India, if not with any matured purpose, at least with a vague and undefined expectation that the time may come when her ambition or her interest may direct her arms that way.

An enterprise so gigantic and so hazardous will no doubt require both a favourable opportunity and a plausible pretext; but mankind are in a great measure familiarized to projects of wild extent & extravagant daring. The jealousy of our wealth (of which India is generally considered on the Continent of Europe as the main source & spring) may soon efface the remembrance of all that Europe owes to us for the employment of it.

Is it not possible that any indications of a new and stirring spirit of ambition on the part of the British Government in India, might furnish at once that stimulus which may alone be wanting to give life & motion to the half-formed intents of Russia; and might conciliate that favour to them from the rest of Europe, without which Russia might think her European interests left in hazard by so distant an expedition? May it not further be well worth considering whether, in the event of such a danger coming upon us, it would be fortunate that we should have bound ourselves by bringing all the States of Hindostan within the pale of our protection to meet the attack on the borders of the desert or on the banks of the Indus?

As to any advantage to be derived from extending the scale of our present system of Alliances with a view to general control, we have doubts of another kind. We are inclined to think that the subsidiary system has gone quite far enough. Each new State that we adopt into this system appears to lose by degrees its native strength and vitality, and a burdensome ally may frequently be a bad exchange for a troublesome perhaps but not very dangerous neighbour.

By widening more & more the circle of our adoption, we also take upon ourselves in the same proportion, a more extended responsibility for the suppression of those elements of disorder & disturbance which always have existed, perhaps (humanly speaking) always *must* exist in India, which cannot for a long series of years at least be expected to settle into habits of industry & peace. If we cannot hope entirely to extinguish the predatory hordes, (and even a complicated & costly scheme of new alliances & warlike operations could hardly be expected to have that effect, either promptly or permanently) an indefinite extension of territory and influence on our part would only bring them so much more immediately and constantly in contact with ourselves or our Allies.

I have said that necessity would dictate a pacific policy in India even if we were not inclined to it from choice. To speak quite plainly to your Lordship upon this point, we have not the means of war. If indeed, a war were to be forced upon us in Europe by any direct injury or insult the occasion itself would create the means out of the spirit & indignation of the people. But a war not absolutely unavoidable, and undertaken for purposes of remote advantage, would little suit the present state & temper of this country. If such be the feeling in England, with respect to European objects and interests, how much more with respect to India; where, in addition to all other considerations, distance of place operates like distance of time, to remove still further the objects of pursuit & proportionately to weaken their impression?

I am much mistaken if one effect of the astonishing changes of the last two years, produced as they were by causes obviously unforeseen and too extraordinary to have been taken into contemplation, has not been to discredit, in the ordinary judgment of the world, those calculations of policy which were heretofore considered as constituting the science of a statesman. I doubt whether the most sagacious plan that could be devised for securing by a new scheme of alliances, at the risk of new wars, the ascendancy of the British power in India, would be now received in Parliament with any other comment than an inquiry whether, half a dozen years ago, the frontier of Nepaul would have been noted as the quarter from which the first attack upon our power was to be apprehended.

Insuperable therefore would be the difficulties which the Government would have to encounter in recommending to the approbation and support of Parliament, a war in India, growing out of any other causes than absolute, immediate self-defence. Public opinion is pronounced upon these subjects in a way too clear to be misunderstood. The same feelings in deference to which the House of Commons was induced last year to abandon the most certain & productive source of public revenue [the income tax], would unquestionably obstruct the raising of a single shilling for the support of a war of conquest or aggrandizement.

Something indeed is stated in one of your Lordship's discussions with your Council, of the possibility of maintaining a war by the resources of India itself; but even in the course of the same argument you refer to the eventual aid of Parliament as available in case of a disappointment in the calculated amount of those resources.

We certainly are not very sanguine here in the expectation of an Indian surplus applicable to purposes of war, or to any other purposes: and your Lordship will have learned enough (long before this letter reaches you) of the disposition & temper of Parliament on all subjects of expenditure, to be satisfied that you cannot render a greater service to the East India Company than by keeping them out of the House of Commons. . . .

It appears to us that it is our interest to encourage what remain of the substantive States of India in maintaining their independence; without inquiring too narrowly (where the obligations of treaty, the *just* claims of an ally, or the *security* of our own possessions do not compel us to such inquiry) either into the means by which they obtained their power or the tenure by which they hold it. It appears that it would at least be worth the trial, whether alliances with independent States (when there is any immediate urgency for contracting alliances at all) would not answer, and better answer our purposes than either an extension of the subsidiary system, or a new system of universal confederation & control. . . .

Upon the whole your Lordship will collect from what I have taken the liberty of stating to you, that the situation of British India, after the close of the Nepalese War, appears to the Prince Regent's Government sufficiently satisfactory to make it our business rather to maintain & improve its present condition, than to attempt any extensive enlargements or any hazardous alterations. You will perceive that in our opinion no accession of territory or influence ought to be sought through war; nor any war incurred that can with honour and safety be avoided.

If your Lordship, after having given to the powers of India, in the prompt & effectual punishment of the aggression from Nepaul, a signal example of the danger of drawing down British vengeance by unjust & unprovoked attacks, shall be enabled to turn to account the internal tranquillity and security which your military successes must have ensured, at least for a time, by cultivating your existing alliances with a view to the continuance of peace, and by the diminution of your warlike establishments, you will have entitled yourself, by every claim, to the applause of your employers & of your country.

522. Lord Wellesley's speech in the House of Lords on Indian affairs, 9 April 1813

(Parliamentary Debates, xxv, 675–754.)

In 1813 the East India Company's Charter was renewed for a further period of twenty years after another searching parliamentary inquiry into its affairs. Although its spokesmen vigorously maintained that, if it lost its profits (which were dependent on its trade monopoly) its revenues would be insufficient to enable it to carry on the government of its eastern possessions, Parliament, giving way to the merchants who demanded admission to the ports of Asia as compensation for the loss of their European markets consequential on Napoleon's self-imposed continental blockade, abolished the Company's monopoly of the India trade, except in tea, but allowed the Company to retain its China monopoly (until 1833).

. . . There never was an organ of government, in the history of the world, so administered, as to demand more of estimation than that of the East India Company. There might, as the lot of all human institutions, be points of error to correct; but if their Lordships looked at the general state of our Empire in India–if they examined it on those heads on which the grandeur of an Empire rested–if they looked at the removal of all foreign influence and intrigue, and the discomfiture of all the efforts of France–at the suppression of all great internal danger in the country–at the regular consolidation of institutions and authorities by which all were brought into a common mass for the benefit of the Empire at large; if they adverted to the state of real solid peace, in which countries were now placed, that had in previous times been so constantly exposed to war and devastation (particularly the Deccan and the countries north of Mysore) where, instead of desolation and ruin, the arts of peace and agriculture now flourished, they would see that the success of the administration of the Government of the East India Company had been productive of strength, tranquillity and happiness. The situation of the natives had been meliorated and improved–the rights of property, before unknown, had been introduced and confirmed by the permanent settlement of Bengal. . . . No Government had better fulfilled its duties towards the people whom it governed, than that of India. . . . A judicial system had been established which, though not perfect, contained within it all the essentials of British justice. . . .

. . . As to the benefits of extending Christianity to the natives of the East, there was no man less willing than himself to throw a shade over so bright a prospect, but he must say that if we expected success, it must proceed from gradual and temperate proceedings, and by no means better than by combining religion with education. This measure should not appear to be recommended from the authority of the Government, because in the East, the recommendation of the Government is supposed to be almost equivalent to a mandate. He knew no better means of diffusing the Christian religion, without giving alarm to the natives, than by placing the head of the Church Establishment in India at the head of the Collegiate Establishment at Fort William, where there would always be a number of learned natives employed in instructing the pupils in the eastern languages; and by the gradual diffusion of knowledge, which would result from this intercourse between those learned natives and the dignitaries of our Church in India.

With regard to the missionaries he must say that while he was in India he never knew of any danger arising from them; neither had he heard of any impression produced by them in the way of conversion. The greater number of them were in the Danish settlements, but he never heard of any convulsions or any alarm being produced by them. Some of them, particularly Mr. Carey, were very learned men, and had been employed in the College in Bengal. He had always considered the missionaries who were in India during his time as a quiet, orderly, discreet and learned body, and he had employed many of them in the education of youth, and in translating the Scriptures into the eastern languages. He, however, had issued no order, nor given any authority for the dissemination of those translations among the natives. . . .

523. John Shore's Memorandum, 18 May 1785

(India Office Records, Bengal Revenue Consultations, 18 May 1785.)

Shore, later (1798) Baron Teignmouth, and Governor-General of Bengal (1793–1798) in succession to Lord Cornwallis (1786–1793), was a member of the Committee of Revenue at Calcutta in 1785. Like Cornwallis, whose right-hand man he became, he considered that the highest posts in the civil service and in the judiciary should be reserved for company's servants, Indians being as yet unfit for such positions of trust and responsibility.

The Supreme Court of Judicature was set up in Calcutta by Lord North's Regulating Act (1773). It was staffed by English judges; it administered English, not Indian law, and its jurisdiction extended to all 'British subjects'.

. . . To our Government they [the Indians] have little attachment, yet it is certain that in general, property has been more secure, and individuals less oppressed than under the despotism of their Nabobs. I assert this with all the confidence conviction inspires. I believe them to be as much attached to the English Government as they would be to any other, but if another Dominion could establish itself they would embrace it with indifference. The reason of this must be sought for in the consequences of a despotic authority, and by tracing them, the characters of the natives will be easily developed and understood. In them will be seen the source of timidity, adulation and deceit which prevail.

It is very obvious that within the last ten or twelve years a considerable alteration has taken place in the manners of the people. This alteration is the natural consequence of a greater degree of intimacy with Europeans than they formerly were admitted to. Those parts of our character which first drew their attention were bravery, clemency and good faith. They have since found that we are not wholly destitute of weaknesses and vices, and that Europeans, like all others, are open to temptation; the respect they entertained for us as individuals or as a nation is diminished, and they now consider themselves upon a more equal footing.

The introduction of the Supreme Court of Judicature has largely contributed to the elevation of the natives and to the depression of Europeans. This system, which was meant for the relief of the natives, has in very few respects answered that object. In many instances it has been a heavy grievance to them, and the natives themselves have found out the art of making the powers of the Court the means and instrument of forwarding their own views of interest and oppression, of eluding the power of the Government, and of weakening its authority, by engaging the two tribunals in contests with each other.

It is in vain that we search for men of enlightened understanding, deep reasoning and reflection amongst the natives. The education of the Hindus is confined to their being taught their own language. The Mahomedans are little better instructed. The acquisition of a few moral or political maxims, which in practice they neglect, is all they know of the art of government. If exceptions can be found, they are very rare. . . .

The grand object of our Government in this country should be to conciliate the minds of the natives. This may be effected by allowing them the free enjoyment of all their prejudices, and by securing to them their rights and property. The form of it should, I think, be despotic, and the natives should still be retained in those habits of submission which are natural and familiar to them. To this they will make no objection whilst they are treated with humanity and justice.

Between the head tribunal of Government and its subjects I would preserve a great and respectable distance, nor suffer the persons of the members of the State to be treated with a familiarity which induces contempt. . . .

After the character which has been drawn of the natives, it is needless to add that I think them ill calculated for these important trusts. I might appeal to the experience of every European who has had opportunities of seeing the natives in office, in support of my opinion.

. . . It is the part of a wise Government to provide against all contingencies. We ought not, therefore, to rely on the peaceable disposition of the natives, or on a supposed attachment to us, but establish such a control in all part of the country that, in case of a foreign invasion by a European Power or of the inroads of an eastern enemy, or the event of rebellion in any of our Provinces, the payment of the revenues may not be suspended, illicit correspondence or dangerous confederacies may be checked, and the contagion of rebellion stifled.

That the servants of the Company are qualified for the task I propose to allot to them, I may venture to pronounce. The collection of the revenues is in itself simple; and if it is now with particular embarrassments, they arise from the system which has been established or from other accidental causes. Common sense, a competent knowledge of the language, application and rectitude of intention are all the qualities required either for this or in the administration of justice. It is the part of the controlling power to retain every man in his duty, and prevent the abuse of authority.

An Englishman cannot descend to these little practices of oppression or extortion so familiar to the natives. His mind revolts at the idea of them, and admitting even that some are by habit, connections or necessity become depraved, there is after all in every breast a sense of honour and virtue that recoils from the low vicious arts of a native of Bengal. . . .

It is a very capital defect in this Government that no system is permanent. Those amongst the natives who have influence are the first to suggest changes, as they must gain by them, but this continual variation of system introduces distrust and diffidence of the Government amongst all classes; it prevents all inclination to improvement, and makes every man anxious to gather the profits of his hour lest a new change should deprive him of them. . . .

524. Lord Cornwallis's Minute of 11 Feb. 1793

(Second Report from the Select Committee of the House of Commons on the Affairs
of the East India Company, 1810. Appendix 9.)

... 7. Our arrangements should be calculated for all times and circumstances; we should endeavour to establish a Constitution for the country that will protect private property, and, with it, the internal prosperity of the State under the worst Administrations. ...

8. It may be urged that these ideas of justice are incompatible with our political situation in this country; that as the people become rich they will feel their power, and combine to subvert our Government. But there appears to me to be no ground for such apprehensions; for, although we hope to render our subjects the happiest people in India, I should by no means propose to admit the natives to any participation in framing Regulations. The Supreme Government will retain this power entire and uncontrolled as at present; it will always possess the means of safety within itself, as far as that safety may depend upon its being able to establish such Regulations as it may think advisable. The proposed arrangements only aim at insuring a general obedience to the Regulations which we may institute, and at the same time impose some check upon ourselves against passing such as may ultimately prove detrimental to our own interests, as well as the prosperity of the country. The natives have been accustomed to despotic rule from time immemorial, and are well acquainted with the miseries of their own tyrannic Administrations. When they have experienced the blessings of good government, there can be no doubt to which of the two they will give the preference.

9. We may therefore be assured that the happiness of the people and the prosperity of the country is the firmest basis on which we can build our political security. When the landholders find themselves in the possession of profitable estates, the merchants and manufacturers in the enjoyment of a lucrative commerce, and all descriptions of people protected in the free exercise of their religion, both the numerous race of the long-oppressed Hindus, and their oppressors the Mahomedans, will equally deprecate the change of a Government under which they have acquired, and under which alone they can hope to enjoy these inestimable advantages.

10. Impressed by these considerations, I have directed much of my attention during my residence in this country to the improvement of the administration of justice. Both the civil and criminal branches of this Department of our Government appeared to me to be of all others in the most weak and inefficient state. To their defects, combined with the practice of Government varying the assessment upon each person's estate according to an estimate of the produce made by its own officers, and taking nine-tenths for the State, I attribute the slow progress which the country has made towards improvement, and the poverty of the greater part of the landholders, the cultivators of the soil, and the manufacturers.

11. The constitution of the Criminal Courts was still more defective than that of the Civil, and consequently the most daring robberies and other enormities were daily committed throughout the Provinces. To put a stop to these disorders I recommended the establishment of the Courts of Circuit under the superintendence of

English Judges, and half-yearly gaol deliveries, and the removal of the Nizamut Adalat, or Superior Criminal Court, to Calcutta. The most happy effects have already been felt from this system; and when the Police arrangements adopted on the 7th December last shall have been carried completely into effect, there is every ground to expect that murders, robberies and other criminal offences will not be more frequent than must necessarily be expected from the vices and passions to which human nature is subject, and which, under the best regulated Governments, will always impel some individuals to commit the worst of crimes. . . .

525. Minutes of Evidence before the House of Lords on the East India Company's affairs, 5 April 1813

(Cobbett's *Parliamentary Debates*, xxv, 553–563.)

Excerpts from the evidence of Warren Hastings (Governor-General, 1774–1785).

. . . Great pains have been taken to inculcate into the public mind an opinion that the native Indians are in a state of complete moral turpitude, and live in the constant and unrestrained commission of every vice and crime that can disgrace human nature. . . . This description of them is untrue and wholly unfounded. . . . In speaking of the people, it is necessary to distinguish the Hindus, who form the great portion of the population, from the Muhammadans, who are intermixed with them, but generally live in separate communities. The former are gentle, benevolent, more susceptible of gratitude for kindness shown them, than prompted to vengeance for wrongs inflicted, and as exempt from the worst propensities of human passion as any people upon the face of the earth; they are faithful and affectionate in service, and submissive to legal authority; they are superstitious, it is true, but they do not think ill of us for not thinking as they do. Gross as the modes of their worship are, the precepts of their religion are wonderfully fitted to promote the best ends of society, its peace and good order; and even from their theology, arguments may be drawn to illustrate and support the most refined mysteries of our own. The intolerant and persecuting spirit of Muhammadanism has spared them through a course of three centuries, and even bound them into union with its own professors, without any ill consequences that I have ever heard resulting from it. I verily believe that both classes would unite in resisting any attempts, should any be made, to subvert the religion of either. . . .

It is impossible that the English character should coalesce with the natives in the same state of society. In the higher class of British subjects this effect may not be deduced; but if Europeans are admitted generally to go into the country to mix with the inhabitants, and to form establishments amongst them, the consequence must certainly and inevitably prove the ruin of the country; they will insult, plunder and oppress the natives because they can do it with impunity; no laws that can be enacted from hence can at such a distance, and under the cover of so many circumstances as will occur in that country, prevent them from committing acts of licentiousness of every kind with impunity. . . .

We must always keep up a strong standing force in that country; but so much depends for the peace of the country and the stability of the Government upon the attachment of the people, that it would be very unsafe and impolitic to trust to that security only. Our Government is not to expect that it shall always remain in a state of peace with its neighbours. I am not sure that we should wish to remain so : but in a general disaffection of the people, a state of external warfare would be liable to internal danger; in short, I do not believe that any nation upon earth is safe from the worst effects which may follow from a general discontent of its people. . . .

It was always my wish, and as far as my power extended, it was my endeavour, to explore the possibilities of extending our commercial intercourse with other countries, both bordering upon India, and remote from it, but within our commercial reach for that purpose. I at a very early period seized an incidental occasion which was offered to me, of introducing a communication with the countries of Bhutan and Thibet, and had at one time succeeded, or thought I had succeeded, so far as to afford an opening to a remote intercourse with China; the death of the Lama of Thibet, whom I had found means to employ as an agent of this design, with other circum-stances not necessary to be mentioned here, defeated that purpose, and all my hopes connected with it. I made a similar attempt to establish a commercial intercourse with Egypt, and another with Cochin China; all proved abortive. I think that a more effective Government than that which I possessed, might in this way open new channels of trade, to the great benefit of the Company and of the British nation; but it is only by the authority of the Company through their established agents, that these ends could be accomplished. . . .

I have understood that a great fermentation has arisen in the minds of the natives of India who are subject to the authority of the British Government, and that not partial, but extending to all our possessions, arising from a belief, however propagated, that there was an intention in this Government to encroach on the religious rights of the people. . . . If such apprehensions do exist, everything that the irritable minds of the people can connect with that will make an impression upon them, which they will adopt as certain assurances of it. So far only, considering the question as a political one, I may venture to express my apprehension of the consequences of such an estab-lishment at this particular season; in no other light am I permitted to view it : but I can conceive that in a proper time and season it would be advantageous to the interests of religion, and highly creditable to the Company and to the nation, if the ecclesiastical establishment in India were rendered complete in all its branches. . . .

526. Sir Thomas Munro to the marquess of Hastings, 12 Aug. 1817

(S. J. Owen, *A Selection from the Despatches, Treaties & other Papers of . . . Marquess Wellesley*, pp. 667–675.)

Munro was Governor of Madras, 1819–1827. He was out of sympathy with the policy of 'sub-sidiary alliance' which Wellesley had pursued, and he was critical of the Cornwallis system whereby Indians were excluded from all effective share in civil administration. The Pindaris, whom Munro mentions, were organized bands of robbers who, whilst protected by the Maratha princes, had ravaged the company's territories. They were destroyed in 1817.

. . . The situation of the British Government with regard to the native Powers is entirely changed within the last twenty years. It formerly brought very small armies into the field, with hardly any cavalry; and the issue of any war in which it engaged was extremely uncertain. It now brings armies into the field superior to those of the enemy, not only in infantry but also in cavalry, both in quality and number. The superiority is so great that the event of any struggle in which it may be engaged is no longer doubtful. It has only to bring forward its armies and dictate what terms it pleases, either without war, or after a short and fruitless resistance. It may however be doubted whether, after the settlement of the Pindaris it ought to avail itself of its predominant power, in order to extend the system of subsidiary alliances by stationing a force in Bhopal or in any other foreign territory. While the military power of Mysore and of the Maratha chiefs was yet in its vigour, subsidiary alliances were in some degree necessary for its safety, but that time is now past; and when, therefore, the evils which a subsidiary force entails upon every country in which it is established are considered, it appears advisable that future security against the Pindaris should be sought by their reduction, and by compelling Sindhia, for his conduct in supporting them, to cede the districts restored to him in 1805–6, rather than by stationing a subsidiary force in Bhopal. There are many weighty objections to the employment of a subsidiary force. It has a natural tendency to render the government of every country in which it exists, weak and oppressive; to extinguish all honourable spirit among the higher classes of society, and to degrade and impoverish the whole people. The usual remedy of a bad Government in India is a quiet revolution in the palace, or a violent one by rebellion, or foreign conquests. But the presence of a British force cuts off every chance of remedy, by supporting the Prince on the throne against every foreign and domestic enemy. It renders him indolent, by teaching him to trust to strangers for his security; and cruel and avaricious, by showing him that he has nothing to fear from the hatred of his subjects. Wherever the subsidiary system is introduced, unless the reigning Prince be a man of great abilities, the country will soon bear the marks of it in decaying villages and decreasing population. This has long been observed in the dominions of the Peishwa and the Nizam, and is now beginning to be seen in Mysore. . . .

A subsidiary force would be a most useful establishment if it could be directed solely to the support of our ascendancy, without nourishing all the vices of a bad Government; but this seems to be almost impossible. . . .

There is, however, another view under which the subsidiary system should be considered–I mean that of its inevitable tendency to bring every native State into which it is introduced, sooner or later, under the exclusive dominion of the British Government. It has already done this completely in the case of the Nawab of the Carnatic. It has made some progress in that of the Peishwa and the Nizam; and the whole of the territory of these Princes will, unquestionably, suffer the same fate as the Carnatic. . . . Even if the Prince himself were disposed to adhere rigidly to the alliance, there will always be some amongst his principal officers who will urge him to break it. As long as there remains in the country any highminded independence, which seeks to throw off the control of strangers, such counsellors will be found. I have a better opinion of the natives of India than to think that this spirit will ever be completely extinguished; and I can therefore have no doubt that the subsidiary system must everywhere run its full course, and destroy every Government which it undertakes to protect.

In this progress of things, the evil of a weak and oppressive Government, supported by a subsidiary alliance, will at least be removed. But even if all India could be brought under the British dominion it is very questionable whether such a change, either as it regards the natives or ourselves, ought to be desired. One effect of such a conquest would be that the Indian army, having no longer any warlike neighbours to combat, would gradually lose its military habits and discipline, and that the native troops would have leisure to feel their own strength, and, for want of other employment, to turn it against their European masters. But even if we could be secured against every internal convulsion, and could retain the country quietly in subjection, I doubt much if the condition of the people would be better than under their native Princes. The strength of the British Government enables it to put down every rebellion, to repel every foreign invasion, and to give to its subjects a degree of protection which those of no native Power enjoy. Its laws and institutions also afford them a security from domestic oppression, unknown in those States; but these advantages are dearly bought. They are purchased by the sacrifice of independence – of national character – and of whatever renders a people respectable. The natives of the British Provinces may without fear pursue their different occupations, as traders, meerassidars, or husband-men, and enjoy the fruits of their labour in tranquillity; but none of them can aspire to anything beyond this mere animal state of thriving in peace – none of them can look forward to any share in the legislation, or civil or military government of their country. It is from men who either hold, or are eligible to public office, that natives take their character: where no such men exist, there can be no energy in any other class of the community. The effect of this state of things is observable in all the British Provinces, whose inhabitants are certainly the most abject race in India. No elevation of character can be expected among men who, in the military line, cannot attain to any rank above that of subahdar, where they are as much below an ensign as an ensign is below the Commander-in-Chief, and who, in the civil line, can hope for nothing beyond some petty judicial or revenue office, in which they may, by corrupt means, make up for their slender salary.

The consequence, therefore, of the conquest of India by the British arms would be, in place of raising, to debase the whole people. There is perhaps no example of any conquest in which the natives have been so completely excluded from all share of the government of their country as in British India.

Among all the disorders of the native States, the field is open for every man to raise himself; and hence among them there is a spirit of emulation, of restless enter-prize and independence, far preferable to the servility of our Indian subjects. The existence of independent native States is also useful in drawing off the turbulent and disaffected among our native troops. Many of these men belonging to the Madras army, formerly sought service in Mysore.

If the British Government is not favourable to the improvement of the Indian character, that of its control through a subsidiary force is still less so. Its power is now so great that it has nothing to fear from any combination; and it is perfectly able to take satisfaction for any insult, without any extension of the subsidiary system being necessary. It will generally be found much more convenient to carry on war where it has not been introduced. This was the case in both the wars with Tipu Sultan. The conquest was complete, because our operations were not perplexed by any subsidiary alliance with him. The simple and direct mode of conquest from without, is more creditable both to our armies and to our national character, than that of dismemberment from within by the aid of a subsidiary force. However just the motives may be from which such force acts, yet the situation in which it is placed, renders its acting at all too like the movements of the Praetorian bands. It acts, it is true, only by the orders of its own Government, and only for public objects; but still it is always ready in the neighbourhood of the capital, to dictate terms to, or to depose the Prince whom it was stationed there to defend.

527. Lord William Bentinck's minute on the suppression of Sati, 8 Nov. 1829

(D. C. Boulger, *Life of Lord William Bentinck*, p. 96.)

In 1790 Cornwallis had removed some of the grossest defects in the Muhammadan criminal law which was administered in the Bengal courts–depriving the relatives of a murdered man of their power to pardon a murderer in return for a money payment, and abolishing the barbarous punishment of mutilation; but he had not ventured to prohibit *sati*. In 1829 Lord William Bentinck, feeling that he could no longer countenance a practice which involved the annual sacrifice of hundreds of lives of young Hindu widows, decided to make it illegal, after receiving assurances from eminent Hindu authorities that the practice had been engrafted on pure Hinduism. Thus he embarked on the new policy of attacking Indian religious and social customs which enlightened western opinion considered peculiarly obnoxious. The danger to the stability of the Empire in India involved in the new policy was believed to be of less consequence than the happiness and welfare of the Indian people.

Whether the question be to continue or to discontinue the practice of suttee, the decision is equally surrounded by an awful responsibility. To consent to the consignment year after year of hundreds of innocent victims to a cruel and untimely end when the power exists of preventing it, is a predicament which no conscience can contemplate without horror. But, on the other hand, if heretofore received opinions are to be considered of any value, to put to hazard by a contrary course the very safety of the British Empire in India, and to extinguish at once all hopes of those great improvements affecting the condition, not of hundreds and thousands, but of millions; which can only be expected from the continuance of our supremacy, is an alternative which even in the light of humanity itself may be considered as a still greater evil. It is upon this first and highest consideration alone, the good of mankind, that the tolerance of this inhuman and impious rite can in my opinion be justified on the part of the Government of a civilised nation. While the solution of this question is appalling from the unparalleled magnitude of its possible results, the considerations belonging to it are such as to make even the stoutest mind distrust its decision. . . . Prudence and self-interest would counsel me to tread in the footsteps of my predecessors. But in a case of such momentous importance to humanity and civilisation that man must be reckless of all his present and future happiness who could listen to the dictates of so wicked and selfish a policy. With the firm undoubting conviction entertained upon this question, I should be guilty of little short of the crime of multiplied murder if I could hesitate in the performance of this solemn obligation. I have been already stung with this feeling. Every day's delay adds a victim to the dreadful list, which might perhaps have been prevented by a more early submission of the present question. . . .

The first and primary object of my heart is the benefit of the Hindus. I know nothing so important to the improvement of their future condition as the establishment of a purer morality, whatever their belief, and a more just conception of the will of God. The first step to this better understanding will be dissociation of religious belief and practice from blood and murder. They will then, when no longer under this brutalising excitement, view with more calmness acknowledged truths. . . . When they shall have been convinced of the error of this first and most criminal of their customs, may it not be hoped that others, which stand in the way of their improvement, may likewise pass away, and that thus emancipated from those chains and shackles upon their minds and actions, they may no longer continue, as they have done, the slaves of every foreign conqueror, but that they may assume their first places among the great families of mankind? I disown in these remarks, or in this measure, any view whatever to conversion to our own faith. I write and feel as a legislator for the Hindus, and as I believe many enlightened Hindus think and feel.

Descending from these higher considerations, it cannot be a dishonest ambition that the Government of which I form a part should have the credit of an act which is to wash out a foul stain upon British rule, and to stay the sacrifice of humanity and justice to a doubtful expediency; and finally, as a branch of the general administration of the Empire, I may be permitted to feel deeply anxious that our course shall be in accordance with the noble example set us by the British Government at home, and that the adaptation, when practicable to the circumstances of this vast Indian population, of the same enlightened principles, may promote here as well as there the general prosperity, and may exalt the character of our nation.

528. Views of Warren Hastings, the marquess of Hastings, and Sir Thomas Munro on the future of British India

(Gleig, *Memoirs of Warren Hastings*, II, pp. 149, 275; *The Marquess of Hastings' Private Journal*, II, p. 326; Arbuthnot, *Minutes of Sir Thomas Munro*, II, pp. 326–327.)

(a) *Warren Hastings:*

The dominion exercised by the British Empire in India is fraught with many radical and incurable defects, besides those to which all human institutions are liable, arising from the distance of its scene of operations, the impossibility of furnishing it at all times with those aids which it requires from home, and the difficulty of reconciling its primary exigencies with those which in all States ought to take place of every other concern, the interests of the people who are subjected to its authority. All that the wisest institutions can effect in such a system can only be to improve the advantages of a temporary possession, and to protract that decay which sooner or later must end it. . . .

I am morally certain that the resources of this country [Bengal], in the hands of a military people and in the disposition of a consistent and undivided form of government, are both capable of vast internal improvement, and of raising that Power which possesses them to the dominion of all India (an event which I may not mention without adding that it is what I never wish to see); and I believe myself capable of improving them and of applying them to the real and substantial benefit of my own country.

(b) *The Marquess of Hastings.*

A time, not very remote, will arrive when England will, on sound principles of policy, wish to relinquish the domination which she has gradually, and unintentionally, assumed over this country, and from which she cannot, at present recede. In that hour it would be the proudest boast, and most delightful reflection, that she had used her sovereignty towards enlightening her temporary subjects so as to enable the native communities to walk alone in the paths of justice, and to maintain, with probity, towards their benefactress that commercial intercourse in which we should then find a solid interest.

(c) *Sir Thomas Munro.*

. . . There is one great question to which we should look in all our arrangements: what is to be their final result on the character of the people? Is it to be raised, or is it to be lowered? Are we to be satisfied with merely securing our power and protecting the inhabitants, leaving them to sink gradually in character lower than at present; or are we to endeavour to raise their character, and to render them worthy of filling higher situations in the management of their country, and of devising plans for its improvement? It ought undoubtedly to be our aim to raise the minds of the natives, and to take care that whenever our connection with India might cease, it did not appear that the only fruit of our dominion there had been to leave the people more abject and less able to govern themselves than when we found them. . . . Various measures might be suggested which might all probably be more or less useful; but no one appears to me so well calculated to insure success as that of endeavouring to give them a higher opinion of themselves, by placing more confidence in them, by employing them in important situations, and perhaps by rendering them eligible to almost every office under Government. It is not necessary at present to define the exact limit to which their eligibility should be carried, but there seems to be no reason why they should be excluded from any office for which they are qualified, without danger to the preservation of our own ascendancy. . . . We should look upon India, not as a temporary possession, but as one which is to be maintained permanently, until the natives shall in some future age have abandoned most of their superstitions and prejudices, and become sufficiently enlightened to frame a regular government for themselves, and to conduct and preserve it. Whenever such a time shall arrive, it will probably be best for both countries that the British control over India should be gradually withdrawn. That the desirable change contemplated may in some after age be effected in India, there is no cause to despair. Such a change was at one time in Britain itself at least as hopeless as it is here. When we reflect how much the character of nations has always been influenced by that of Governments, and that some, once the most cultivated, have sunk into barbarism, while others, formerly the rudest, have attained the highest point of civilisation, we shall see no reason to doubt that if we pursue steadily the proper measures, we shall in time so far improve the character of our Indian subjects as to enable them to govern and protect themselves.

529. The Governor-General-in-Council's letter to the Court of Directors, 19 Feb. 1787

(Imperial Record Department, Government of India.)

Penang, the first of the Straits Settlements, was founded in 1786. It lost its importance when Singapore was acquired in 1819.

... 49. In the letter of 25th March last, the late Government communicated to your Honourable Court the measures they proposed to adopt in regard to forming a settlement upon the Island of Penang in the Straits of Malacca, and on 21st August you were acquainted that Captain Light had sailed with a detachment on that service.

51. Captain Light having proceeded to Penang, took possession of it in the name of his Majesty and for the use of the English East India Company on 11 August 1786, and immediately commenced clearing the country and the construction of a small Fort for the protection of the detachment against any attempt of the Malay Powers whom he apprehended would be instigated by the Dutch or indeed by the fickleness of their own disposition to attempt to cut them off.

52. Having taken into consideration the application from Captain Light to be reinforced, and fully considered the advantages which may result from this settlement in opposition to the expense that must attend the increase of the Establishment, the very favourable accounts of the island received from Captain Light as well as from those gentlemen who had been at the place, we were induced to comply with his request, and accordingly resolved to afford him effectual support, though not quite to the extent he desired. . . .

54. Captain Roddam has been directed after landing the troops to proceed to Fort Marlborough, where he will receive on board 150 coffries for Prince of Wales Island, to be delivered to Captain Light for the purpose of clearing the country, and having performed the service he is to return back to this place from whence we propose to dispatch him for England early in August. . . .

55. We must confess it was with great reluctance we adopted measures which caused the Company an immediate increase of expense on a prospect of distant reimbursement, at a time when every fund is appropriated to answer a variety of demands, but the plan has gone too far to be hastily retracted, and the usurpations of the Dutch in those parts, added to the great increase of the Company's trade to China, rendered a settlement in the Straits of Malacca more requisite than ever.

56. The objects which we expect by this settlement are both commercial and political, to connect the Bengal and China trade, and procure a windward port during the north-east monsoon for the refreshment and repair of the King's ships in time of war. How far we may be justified in these expectations time and experience can alone determine.

57. We do not look upon the Eastern trade as a source from whence much specie can be drawn into this country, but the advantages to be expected from it for the

Company are principally by its becoming more extensively than at present a mart for the barter of opium and the productions of Bengal for tin, pepper and other commodities to be applied as funds in the Chinese markets for the purchase of tea, instead of the ruinous export of specie from this country as well as from Europe.

58. Captain Light having detailed the political situation of the Native Powers around him, requested our orders in consequence of repeated applications for assistance from the King of Quedah and other Princes who dreaded an attack from the Siamese forces. To this we peremptorily directed him to refuse compliance with the solicitations of either party, but at the same time instructed him to endeavour to cultivate the goodwill of all, declaring that the defence of the island must be his sole object. We however informed Captain Light that the King of Quedah was entitled to some pecuniary consideration for his grant of the island, which we authorised him to pay by instalments.

59. Not concurring in the propriety of granting passages to the Malay prows which Captain Light recommended in order to obtain greater commercial benefit by affording our protection against the exactions of the Dutch, we forbid it, for although we do not admit many of the exclusive privileges claimed by that nation in the eastern seas, yet in case of their being arrogated before we authorised the English colours to be hoisted, we considered it necessary to guard against their being insulted. We have however permitted Captain Light to grant passes to such vessels as belong to persons actually inhabitants of the island, who shall have taken the oaths of allegiance according to the tenets of their religion.

60. We have ordered Mr. Macdonald, an officer upon this Establishment but on service at Fort Marlborough, to proceed to Prince of Wales Island and survey the harbour. From his report we may be better enabled to judge how far this place will answer for the reception and repair of ships of war, and whether it will serve as a place of defence.

61. We have likewise directed Captain Light to transmit us particular accounts of the exports and imports of goods with the prices they bear, and such further information as may enable us to ascertain how far the settlement will answer our expectations in a commercial point of view.

62. Having this information before us, we shall be enabled to come to a final determination whether it will be prudent to continue or withdraw the settlement altogether.

63. We have authorised Captain Light to receive colonists as he may judge expedient, to allot such a portion of land to each family as circumstances would admit, and as an encouragement to trade, we have made the port free to all nations and peremptorily forbid his levying any kind of duty or tax on goods exported or imported.

64. The President and Council of Bombay have been requested to send an armed vessel of 14 guns and two armed galliots for the defence of the island and the coast of Sumatra, to be relieved annually in the month of May. We preferred this measure to that of establishing a marine at this place, as at Bombay it is done for half the expense, the vessels are much better, and the officers and men accustomed to discipline.

Besides, this distant service, if regularly relieved, will be of some benefit to your marine.

66. We cannot conclude this subject without informing you that from the general good character we have received of Captain Light we believe him to be a person peculiarly well qualified to accomplish the object of the expedition committed to his charge, as well from his knowledge of the language, customs and habits of the Malays as from the calmness of his disposition and moderation of temper. . . .

530. Sir Stamford Raffles to Colonel Addenbrooke, 10 June 1819

(V. Harlow and F. Madden, *British Colonial Developments 1774–1834*, p. 73.)

Raffles, who had been Lieutenant-Governor of Java and Governor of Bencoolen, persuaded the East India Company in 1819 to purchase Singapore from the Sultan of Johore. Addenbrooke had been Princess Charlotte's equerry.

Singapore: . . . I shall say nothing of the importance which I attach to the permanence of the position I have taken up at Singapore: it is a child of my own. But for my Malay studies I should hardly have known that such a place existed: not only the European but the Indian world was also ignorant of it. . . . If my plans are confirmed at home, it is my intention to make this my principal residence, and to devote the remaining years of my stay in the East to the advancement of a colony which, in every way in which it can be viewed, bids fair to be one of the most important, and at the same time one of the least expensive and troublesome, which we possess. Our object is not territory but trade; a great commercial emporium, and a *fulcrum*, whence we may extend our influence politically as circumstances may hereafter require. By taking immediate possession, we put a *negative* to the Dutch claim of exclusion, and at the same time revive the drooping confidence of our allies and friends. One free port in these seas must eventually destroy the spell of Dutch monopoly, and what *Malta* is in the West, that may Singapore become in the East. . . .

E. CAPE COLONY

530A. Debate in the House of Commons on emigration to the Cape of Good Hope, 12th July 1819

(*Hansard's Parliamentary Debates*, XL, 1549–1551.)

The *Chancellor of the Exchequer* said, he had to propose a grant for the purpose of enabling H.M.'s Government to assist unemployed workmen of this country in removing to one of our colonies. It had been the wish of H.M.'s Government first to try an experiment on a small scale, how far it might be possible to employ the surplus population of this country in one of our colonies, in such a manner as might be advantageous to the people removed, and beneficial to the country. From the satis-factory result of this experiment, it was, that Government were now desirous of trying the experiment on a larger scale. The colony selected was that of the Cape of Good Hope. The greater part of the persons disposed to emigrate from this country rather wished to go to the United States of North America, where Government could give them no direct encouragement, or to the British colonies of North America. But with respect to the latter, H.M.'s Government–considering the inconvenience to which these persons would be subjected on their arrival in America, had selected the Cape of Good Hope as the colony to which emigration might be most advantageously directed. From the mildness of the climate, and the fertility of the soil in some parts, a rapid and abundant return might reasonably be expected. That colony was also highly favourable to the multiplication of stock. The particular part of the colony selected was the south-eastern coast of Africa. It was at some distance from Cape Town. A small town was already built there. It was proposed to pay the expense of the passage, and at the same time to secure to the settler the means of employing his industry to advantage on his landing at the destined spot. But a small advance of money would be required from each settler before embarking, to be repaid him in necessaries at the Cape, by which means, and by the assistance given him by Govern-ment, he would have sufficient to procure him a comfortable subsistence till he got in his crops, which in that climate were of rapid growth. The Cape was suited to most of the productions both of temperate and warm climates–to the olive, the mulberry, the vine, as well as most sorts of culmiferous and leguminous plants. The persons emigrating to this settlement would soon find themselves comfortable. The right hon. gentleman concluded with moving the grant of a sum not exceeding £50,000 to be issued from time to time, for the purpose of enabling Government to assist persons disposed to settle in H.M.'s colony of the Cape of Good Hope.

Mr. *Hume* said, he was sorry Ministers had not gone farther. Parishes having able-bodied men willing to work, chargeable on them, ought to be called on to subscribe sums towards removing a part of them to this or some other settlement, where their industry might provide them with a comfortable subsistence. He thought that if men under such circumstances were unwilling to emigrate, it might even be advisable to transport them without their consent. If the parishes would but contribute the money they were forced to pay to these persons for one or two years, from the excellent climate of the Cape, and the fertility of the soil, the greatest advantages could not fail to be the result.

The *Chancellor of the Exchequer* said, it was a part of the plan that parishes should have the power of sending out persons who might be desirous of emigrating; but there ought to be nothing compulsory. When the parishes and the individuals chargeable on them were desirous, an opportunity would be afforded.

Mr. Alderman *Wood* was surprised that labourers should be removed from this country, when there was so much waste land in it that might be cultivated to advan-tage. There were about 80,000 acres of waste land, on which both corn and flax might be grown.

Mr. *Hutchinson* approved of the grant. The right hon. gentleman had said that persons wishing to settle in the colony must make a deposit in this country; he wished to ask him if such people as the distressed manufacturers and labourers of Cork, who had not the means of making any deposit, might not be exempted from this regulation? If Government would give a loan to such persons, and afford them protection till they came to the colony, there could be little doubt, from the glowing language in which the right hon. gentleman had described that country, that they would soon be able to repay the sums advanced.

Mr. *Williams* was convinced that this country possessed within itself the means of employment for all its inhabitants, and that nothing more was necessary than to cultivate those lands which at present were waste.

The motion was agreed to.

Part VIII

WARS AND FOREIGN POLICY

Introduction

ALTHOUGH England owed much to her great military commanders as well as to her naval heroes, the old dislike of a standing army[1] persisted in the post-war era, reflecting an attitude dating from the Cromwellian despotism. The parliamentary Whigs had to admit that the Second Treaty of Paris[2] (1815) could not have been enforced without the occupation of northern France by an allied army of 150,000 men, but characteristically they objected to it not only on financial grounds (though the British contingent of 30,000 was to be paid for by the Bourbons), and not only because it was calculated unnecessarily to irritate the French people, but also as requiring the maintenance of a military establishment much larger than the country had ever known in peace-time. That seemed to indicate that England was to consider herself no longer merely as a maritime nation but also as one of the great military Powers of Europe. And in 1819 the Whigs professed to believe that the Cabinet's decision to add another 10,000 men to the army in order to put an end to popular disturbance indicated a determination to "change the Government into one less free". But it was the deplorable conditions of service[3] rather than prejudice against a standing army which made it necessary to fill its ranks not only by all sorts of dubious expedients but also by hiring foreign mercenaries. The common soldiers were drawn from the lowest classes of the population, including vagrants and criminals, who were allowed to choose between enlistment and transportation.[4] In these circumstances it was almost inevitable that they were subject to the severest discipline.[5] The army, however, provided a fine career for the younger sons of the gentry who, if they had 'interest', could hope to receive their first commission whilst still at school, and gain rapid promotion. The purchase of commissions[6] had already, by 1783, become, as Palmerston said, "a permanent and standing rule of the service". Its expediency was often questioned, and its abolition, by buying up existing interests, was contemplated by the Perceval ministry (1809–1812), but rejected on grounds of expense. On the other hand, it was felt to have the merit of identifying the higher ranks of the army with the country's civil and political institutions by introducing into the commissioned ranks a large infusion of men belonging to the governing class, thus giving, as Palmerston remarked, "a tone and character to the profession at large".

Of the navy there was no such constitutional jealousy, and little parliamentary criticism of the money spent on naval defence. The navy, however, was less popular than the army with the aristocracy and the gentry, because, since commissions could not be purchased, the wealthy family had no advantage over a poorer one; and the officers were generally drawn from the upper middle class. Bad conditions of service

---

[1] No. 534. [2] No. 579. [3] Nos. 533, 535-540. [4] Nos. 531-532. [5] Nos. 538-540. [6] No. 536.

made the navy, too, unpopular with the lower ranks, and in war-time it had to be manned by means of the press gang and the lure of prize-money.[1] The astonishing thing is that the two services, partly recruited as they were from the gutter and the jail, should have proved, in the hands of men like Nelson and Wellington, such effective instruments of war. That they did so affords decisive proof of the essentially sound qualities of the English people.

Pitt evinced no desire that England, safe behind her 'moat', should become a formidable military Power. She should recover her weight in the counsels of Europe by increasing her naval strength, restoring her finances, and refraining from involving herself unnecessarily in the quarrels of her neighbours. From him, his disciples, Castlereagh, Canning and Palmerston learnt the lesson that continental entanglements should, whenever possible, be avoided, and that England should intervene only when her vital interests were threatened, and when she could do so, in Canning's phrase, "with commanding force". It is generally recognized that Pitt and Grenville clung tenaciously to neutrality in the continental war that broke out in 1792 as long as was practicable, and that they were driven to enter it principally owing to the provocative decrees of the Revolutionary Government in Paris in Nov. and Dec. 1792, and to the aggressive actions which followed–actions which, involving the conquest of the Austrian Netherlands, threatened England at what her statesmen had always considered a vital point.

No one today claims that Pitt, like his father, was a great war minister. No one denies that his war administration ended in failure. The military historians are apparently unanimous in condemning not only the methods employed to raise troops during the French wars, but also the starving of the army before 1793, the wilful refusal to take the best military advice, and the squandering of our inadequate resources on distant enterprises where success could never be decisive, instead of concentrating all available resources against France herself–in Flanders, in La Vendée, at Toulon. It was not until the much-maligned Castlereagh became Secretary for War in 1807 that a fair measure of success was achieved to place and maintain a more adequate force in the field, of which Wellesley was soon able to make such good use in the peninsula. Space has been found to illustrate only a few of the more important naval and military campaigns,[2] but other documents reveal the Whig objections to participation in the struggle,[3] and the defeatist attitude of the opposition in the last years when prospects of victory were definitely improving.[4] No. 559 is peculiarly important as showing Pitt's war aims at the virtual close of his career: aims that had been unrealizable in 1801,[5] but which his successors achieved in 1814–1815.

In the sphere of foreign affairs Pitt's peace-time record was one of only partial success. Much to his credit was his re-establishment of friendly relations with France after 1783, and the extension of trade relations between the two countries resulting from the 'Eden' Treaty of 1786. In collaboration with Prussia he prevented the French, two years later, from establishing a dominant influence in Holland, but his success in restoring the Stadholder to power and suppressing the so-called 'patriotic' party was short-lived, for the armies of Revolutionary France were soon to overwhelm the Dutch, whether 'patriots' or Orangists. In 1790 Pitt was more successful in preventing Spain from establishing a foothold on the Pacific shore of Canada, thus making possible the ultimate expansion of the Canadian people westwards to the ocean. But in 1791 English public opinion defeated his attempt to mediate between

[1] Nos. 533–547.   [2] Nos. 551–554, 560–562, 565, 567, 573.   [3] No. 548.   [4] No. 566.   [5] No. 555.

Turkey and the Eastern Powers, and his failure to save Turkey from the consequences of military defeat prevented him, in effect, from saving Poland from final partition in 1795.

The apparent lack of patriotism in the nation during the French wars has often been commented upon. In 1793 there was no such rush to the colours as the grave reverses to British arms produced in 1914,[1] yet the war was not unpopular at its outset, and had there been universal suffrage in England, Pitt's policy would undoubtedly have been endorsed by the great majority of the electorate. For many years, boards bearing the warning inscription "No Jacobins admitted here" faced the traveller entering the Manchester taverns. But in the novels of Maria Edgeworth and Jane Austen, written during the war, the fact that the country was engaged in the greatest struggle for survival that it had ever known, was not even mentioned; there was no suggestion that the young men figuring in these novels should have been in uniform. Even after the rupture of the peace of Amiens,[2] when invasion seemed imminent,[3] the government was afraid that a section of the lower orders, with nothing to lose but their lives, and believing that there would be work for them whether Bonaparte or George III was their ruler, might even welcome the French as liberators and leave the rich to fight for the defence of their property as best they could. "No change for the worse a mistaken notion", was the title of one of many pamphlets addressed to the masses by ministerial propagandists. There was no idea of rousing the people to an ardent patriotism, with the post-war prospect of "a land fit for heroes to live in". Not until the campaigns of 1812–1813, which for the first time brought prospects of deliverance from Napoleon, did the English people become really confident of victory, and begin to dread the prospect offered to them by the parliamentary Whigs of a patched-up peace. The renewal of the war after the Return from Elba was supported by an almost united nation, and Whitbread's motion in the House of Commons in favour of a negotiated peace[4] was backed by only thirty-seven votes. But after Waterloo there was no general demand for vengeance against the fallen emperor, comparable with the cry of "Hang the Kaiser!" after the 1914–1918 war.[5] Castlereagh and Wellington successfully resisted the 'prevailing idea' (favoured by the prince regent, the press and public opinion) that "we are fairly entitled to avail ourselves of the present moment to take back from France the principal conquests of Louis XIV", and, instead of imposing a Carthaginian peace, the Allies, thanks mainly to the firmness and good sense of Castlereagh and Wellington, who argued that they had been fighting not against France but against the armed doctrine of revolution, treated the French people with remarkable generosity.[6]

The peace treaties[7] amply safeguarded England's vital interests. The union of Holland and the former Austrian Netherlands, and the consequential exclusion of the French from the south of the Scheldt, ensured England's safety at one vital spot; and such overseas conquests as she chose to retain, protected her colonies and commerce.

The long interval of peace between the Great Powers after 1815 was due partly to the moderate nature of the 1815 treaty settlement, partly to the fact that they were exhausted as never before by the length and severity of the conflict, and partly to the belief, common to English and European Conservatives, that their co-operation alone could avert another revival of militant Jacobinism which would disrupt the social order everywhere. But the British Government realized that extensive continental commitments would be disapproved by the House of Commons, and the only specific

[1] No. 550.   [2] No. 555.   [3] Nos. 556–558.   [4] No. 572.   [5] No. 575.   [6] No. 579.   [7] Nos. 576, 579.

guarantees (embodied in the Quadruple Alliance Treaty of 20 Nov. 1815)[1] for which it assumed responsibility, were the minimum needed to avert another French military irruption over the Continent. Metternich and Alexander I subsequently strove to divert the objects of the Alliance and to turn a limited into an unlimited liability, by interfering in the internal affairs of other States whenever the revolutionary peril threatened the security of thrones and territories. The British Government's opposition to collective intervention was embodied in the famous Memorandum of 5 May 1820,[2] which was partially printed in 1823 (suppressed passages are enclosed within square brackets), and Castlereagh and his successor Canning agreed that the true policy of England had "always been not to interfere except in great emergencies". Two years, therefore, before Canning returned to the Foreign Office, England had practically withdrawn from the Concert of Europe. In 1823 Canning protested against the French claim to intervene in Spain to suppress the liberal revolution and restore Ferdinand VII to absolute power, but in view of the opposition of some of the more conservative members of the Cabinet, the king and Parliament to war with France, Canning had to content himself with expressing the hope that Spain would emerge triumphantly from the struggle. In this he was disappointed, but he succeeded in preventing the dispatch of a French expedition to South America to restore the rebellious Spanish colonies to the odious rule of Ferdinand VII;[3] and, staunchly supported by the Prime Minister, Canning overcame the opposition of George IV and some members of the Cabinet to the policy of recognizing the independence of the former Spanish colonies.[4]

The British Government, fearing Russian aggrandizement in south-eastern Europe, and considering that the preservation of the Ottoman Empire was necessary for the maintenance of peace,[5] had only limited sympathy with the Greeks who, in 1821, made a bid for independence. But when the Russians threatened the sultan with war as the only means of averting the extermination of the Greeks in the Morea, Canning induced the Tsar to co-operate with England and France to end the war on the basis of Greek independence, and, if need be, to coerce the sultan. The outcome of these negotiations was the Treaty of London (6 July 1827),[6] but Canning died a month later before his policy came to full fruition.

BIBLIOGRAPHY

A. WAR.

C. Aspinall-Oglander, Freshly Remembered. The Story of Thomas Graham, Lord Lynedoch (1956); John Barrow, Life and Correspondence of Admiral Sir Sidney Smith (2 vols., 1848); D. Bell, Wellington's Officers (1938); A. M. Broadley and R. G. Bartelot, Nelson's Hardy. His Life, Letters and Friends (1909); [Blakiston, of the East India Company's service] Twelve Years' Military Adventure . . . 1802–14 (2 vols., 1829); F. W. Brooks, "Naval Recruiting in Lindsey, 1795–7" (English Historical Review, 1928); B. Brownrigg, Life and Letters of Sir John Moore (Oxford, 1923); [Bunbury, Thos.] Reminiscences of a Veteran (3 vols., 1861); A. L. Burt, The United States, Great Britain and British North America: From the Revolution to . . . 1812 (Yale, 1940); G. Callender, The Story of H.M.S. Victory (1929 edition); Sir G. Lowry Cole's Memoirs, edited by M. Lowry Cole and S. Gwynn (1934); G. L. N. Collingwood, A Selection from the Public and Private Correspondence of Vice-Admiral Lord Collingwood (2 vols., 1937 edition); Life of Collingwood by G. Murray (1936); Constable's Miscellany, vols. xxvii and xxviii; Memorials

---

[1] No. 580.   [2] No. 581.   [3] No. 584.   [4] Nos. 582–583.   [5] No. 587.   [6] No. 585.

of the Late War (Edinburgh, 1828); J. S. Corbett, *The Campaign of Trafalgar* (1910); E. Costello, *The Adventures of a Soldier, or, Memoirs of* . . . (1841); General Sir Hew Dalrymple, *Memoir of his Proceedings* (1830); G. Davis, *Wellington and his Army* (Oxford, 1954); B. Dobrée and G. E. Manwaring, *The Floating Republic* (1937 edition); E. Desbrière, *The Naval Campaign of 1805: Trafalgar*, edited by C. Eastwick (2 vols., Oxford, 1933); earl of Dundonald, *Autobiography of a Seaman* (2 vols., 1860 edition); *Life of*, by J. W. Fortescue (1895) and by C. Lloyd (1947); *Sir Benjamin D'Urban's Peninsular Journal, 1808–17*, edited by I. J. Rousseau (1930); J. W. Fortescue, *History of the British Army*, vols. III–XI (1902–1923), and *The County Lieutenancies: The Army, 1803–14* (1909); Col. Sir A. Simon Frazer, *Letters . . . written during the Peninsular and Waterloo Campaigns*, edited by E. Sabine (1859); A. F. Fremantle, *Trafalgar* (1933); Admiral Lord Gambier, *Minutes of a Court Martial . . . 1809 . . . on the Trial of* (1809); C. Gill, *The Naval Mutinies of 1797* (Manchester, 1913); P. Guedalla, *The Hundred Days* (1934); B. H. Liddell Hart (editor), *Letters of Private Wheeler, 1809–28* (1951); W. H. James, *The Campaign of 1815* (1908); T. Keppel, *Life of Viscount Keppel* (2 vols., 1842); F. J. Klingberg and S. B. Hustvedt, *The Warning Drum: Broadsides of 1803* (University of California, 1944); C. F. Seymour Larpent, *Private Journal*, edited by Sir G. Larpent (2 vols., 1853 edition); Sir Henry McAnally, *The Irish Militia, 1793–1816* (Dublin, 1949); P. Mackesy, *The War in the Mediterranean, 1803–10* (1957); T. H. McGuffie, "The significance of military rank in the British Army between 1790 and 1830" (*Bulletin of the Institute of Historical Research*, Nov. 1957); A. T. Mahan, *Influence of Sea Power upon the French Revolution and Empire, 1793–1815* (2 vols., 1892); René Maine, *Trafalgar* (translated by R. Eldon and B. W. Robinson, 1957); General C. Mercer, *Journal of the Waterloo Campaign* (1927); E. Napier, *Life and Correspondence of Admiral Sir Charles Napier* (2 vols., 1862); Nelson: modern biographies or studies by A. T. Mahan (2 vols., 1899 edition), C. Wilkinson (1931), F. M. Kircheisen, translated by F. Collins (1931), Admiral Mark Kerr (1932), B. Tunstall (1933), Carola Oman (1954), O. Warner (1958); W. Dawson (editor), *The Nelson Collection at Lloyds'* (1932); D. H. O'Brien, *My Adventures during the late War, 1804–14*, edited by C. Oman (1902 edition); Sir Charles Oman, *History of the Peninsular War* [superseding Napier's History] (7 vols., Oxford, 1902–1930); H. J. Owen, *The Merioneth Volunteers during the Napoleonic Wars* (Dolgelly, 1934); C. N. Parkinson, *Life of Viscount Exmouth* (1934) and *War in the Eastern Seas, 1793–1815* (1954); Lieut. Gen. Sir Thomas Picton, *Memoirs*, by H. B. Robinson (2 vols., 1836 edition); Wm. Richardson, *A Mariner of England, 1780–1819*, edited by S. Childers (1908); E. Robson, "Purchase and Promotion in the British Army in the Eighteenth Century" (*History*, vol. XXXVI); J. H. Rose, "Napoleon and Sea-Power" (*Cambridge Historical Journal*, 1924), and *Lord Hood and the Defence of Toulon* (Cambridge, 1922); Sir J. Ross, *Memoirs and Correspondence of Admiral Lord De Saumarez* (2 vols., 1838); A. N. Ryan, "The Causes of the British Attack upon Copenhagen in 1807" (*English Historical Review*, Jan. 1953); A. L. F. Schaumann, *On the Road with Wellington*, translated by A. M. Ludovici (1925); E. H. Stuart-Jones, *An Invasion that failed: The French Expedition to Ireland, 1796* (Oxford, 1950), and *The Last Invasion of Britain* (University of Wales, 1950); Lieut.-Col. Wm. Tomkinson, *Diary of a Cavalry Officer . . . 1809–15*, edited by J. Tomkinson (1894); F. B. Tupper, *Life and Correspondence of Maj. Gen. Sir Isaac Brock* (1847 edition); S. G. P. Ward, *Wellington's Headquarters: A Study of the Administrative Problems in the Peninsula* (Oxford, 1957); *Battle of Waterloo*, by a Near Observer (1815); *Sketch of the Battle of Waterloo* by General Muffling (Brussels, 1833); C. Dalton, *The Waterloo Roll Call* (1904 edition); *Story of the Battle of Waterloo* by G. R. Gleig (1848); J. C. Ropes, *The Campaign of Waterloo* (New York, 1893); G. C. West, *Life and Letters of Admiral Cornwallis* (1928); J. R. Western, "The Volunteer Movement as an Anti-Revolutionary Force, 1793–1801" (*English Historical Review*, Oct. 1956), and "The Formation of the Scottish Militia in 1797" (*Scottish Historical Review*, 1955); G. Wrottesley, *Life of Sir John Burgoyne* (2 vols., 1873).

PUBLICATIONS OF THE NAVY RECORDS SOCIETY

Journal of Admiral James, edited by J. K. Laughton and J. Y. F. Sulivan (1896); *Letters and Papers of Admiral Sir T. B. Martin*, edited by Sir R. V. Hamilton (3 vols., 1898–1903); *The*

Blockade of Brest, 1803–5, edited by J. Leyland (2 vols., 1898–1901); *Great Sea Fights, 1794–1805*, edited by T. S. Jackson (2 vols., 1899–1900); *The Naval Miscellany*, edited by J. K. Laughton (vols. I and II, 1901–1912), vol. III edited by W. G. Perrin (1928), vol. IV edited by C. Lloyd (1952); *Nelson and the Neapolitan Jacobins*, edited by H. C. Gutteridge (1903); *Correspondence of Admiral John Markham*, edited by Sir C. Markham (1904); *Fighting Instructions, 1530–1816*, edited by J. S. Corbett (1905); *Recollections of James Anthony Gardner, R.N.*, edited by Sir R. V. Hamilton and J. K. Laughton (1906); *Letters of Lord Barham*, edited by Sir J. K. Laughton (3 vols., 1907–1911); *Naval Songs and Ballads*, edited by C. H. Firth (1908); *Signals and Instructions, 1776–1794*, edited by J. S. Corbett (1908); *Private Papers of 2nd Earl Spencer*, vols. I and II, edited by J. S. Corbett (1913–1914), vols. III and IV, edited by Sir H. W. Richmond (1924); *The Keith Papers*, vol. I, edited by W. G. Perrin (1927), vols. II and III, edited by C. Lloyd (1950–1955); *Piracy in the Levant, 1827–8*, edited by C. G. Pitcairn Jones (1934); *The Tomlinson Papers*, edited by J. G. Bullocke (1935); *Five Naval Journals, 1789–1817*, edited by H. G. Thursfield (1951); *Sir Wm. Henry Dillon's Narrative, 1790–1839*, vol. I, edited by M. A. Lewis (1951); *Letters of Lord St. Vincent*, edited by D. B. Smith (2 vols., 1922–1927); *Private Correspondence o Admiral Lord Collingwood*, edited by E. Hughes (1958).

B. FOREIGN POLICY.

The Cambridge History of British Foreign Policy (vols. II and III [1922–1923] cover the years 1783–1866) has useful bibliographies. See also: A. C. F. Beales, "Wellington and Louis Philippe, 1830" (*History*, vol. XVIII); S. T. Bindoff, *The Scheldt Question to 1839* (1945); *British Diplomatic Representatives, 1689–1789*, edited by D. B. Horn (Camden 3rd Series, vol. XLVI, 1932); *British Diplomatic Representatives, 1789–1852*, edited by S. T. Bindoff, E. F. Malcolm-Smith and C. K. Webster (*ibid.*, vol. L, 1934); *British and Foreign State Papers*, edited by Sir L. Hertslet [from 1812, 20 vols. cover this period]; O. Browning, *Despatches from Paris, 1784–90* (2 vols., Camden Society, 1909–1910); C. S. B. Buckland, *Metternich and the British Government from 1809 to 1813* (1932); *Gentz' Relations with the British Government . . . 1809–12* (1933); A. Cobban, *Ambassadors and Secret Agents* (1954); C. W. Crawley, *The Question of Greek Independence* (Cambridge, 1930); "Anglo-Russian Relations, 1815–30" (*Cambridge Historical Journal*, 1929); Count Gallatin (editor), *A great peace-maker: diary of James Gallatin* (1914); Sir George Jackson, *Diaries and Letters*, edited by Lady Jackson (2 vols., 1872), and *The Bath Archives. A Further Selection*, edited by Lady Jackson (2 vols., 1873); W. W. Kaufmann, *British Policy and the Independence of Latin America, 1804–28* (Yale, 1951); Sir R. Lodge, *Great Britain and Prussia in the Eighteenth Century* (Oxford, 1923); Philip von Neumann, *Diary, 1819–50*, edited by E. B. Chancellor (2 vols., 1928); J. M. Norris, "The Policy of the British Cabinet in the Nootka Crisis" (*English Historical Review*, 1955); W. Alison Phillips, *The Confederation of Europe* (1914); J. G. Renier, *Great Britain and the Establishment of the Kingdom of the Netherlands, 1813–15* (1930); H. H. Robbins, *Our First Ambassador to China . . . Life of Lord Macartney* (1908); J. H. Rose, "The Franco-British Commercial Treaty of 1786" (*English Historical Review*, 1908); *Select Despatches from the British Foreign Office on the Third Coalition, 1804–5* (Camden 3rd Series, vol. VII, 1904); J. B. Scott (editor), *The Armed Neutralities of 1780 and 1800* (New York, 1918); R. W. Seton-Watson, *Britain in Europe, 1789–1914* (Cambridge, 1937); A. G. Stapleton, *Intervention and Non-Intervention, or, the Foreign Policy of Great Britain, 1790–1865* (1866); A. J. P. Taylor, *The Trouble-makers: Dissent over Foreign Policy, 1792–1939* (1957); H. Temperley and L. M. Penson, *A Century of Diplomatic Blue Books, 1814–1914* (Cambridge, 1938); *Foundations of British Foreign Policy, 1792–1902* (Cambridge, 1938); Sir Adolphus Ward and G. P. Gooch (editor), *Cambridge History of British Foreign Policy, 1783–1919* (3 vols., Cambridge, 1922–1923); Sir C. K. Webster, *Select Documents on Britain and the Independence of Latin America, 1812–30* (2 vols., Oxford, 1938); *British Diplomacy, 1813–15* (1921); *The Congress of Vienna, 1814–15* (1934 edition); "Lord Palmerston at work, 1830–41" (*Politica*, 1934); "Palmerston, Metternich and the European System, 1830–41" (*Proceedings British Academy*, vol. XX); Henry Wellesley, 1st Lord Cowley, *Diary and Correspondence, 1790–1846*, edited by F. A. Wellesley (1930).

A. THE ARMY AS AN INSTRUMENT OF WAR AND POLICY

(a) RECRUITMENT

531. Henry Dundas to Lieutenant-Colonel Fuller, 17 March 1794

(Public Record Office, Home Office, 43/5/14–15.)

Dundas was then Home Secretary; Fuller, an officer of the 59th Regiment.

I have been favoured with your letter of the 12th inst. on the subject of the three culprits in the gaol of Salisbury, who you represent to be desirous of enlisting to serve in the 59th Regiment. If the Commanding Officer of that Regiment should be desirous of receiving these men, and Mr. Justice Perryn should be of opinion that it would be right to extend the King's mercy to them on the condition of their serving in the army, I have no doubt that the application in their favour would be attended to in the manner you desire.

It is necessary, however, that I should mention to you that in case these men are intended to form any part of the number of men which any officer may have engaged to raise to entitle him to additional rank, your application cannot under such circumstances be complied with.

532. The duke of Richmond to Robert Peel, 9 Nov. 1812

(*British Museum Additional MSS.* 40185, f. 80.)

Richmond was Lord Lieutenant of Ireland, 1807–1813; Peel, Irish Secretary, 1812–1818.

In the case of Farrell recommended by Lord Norbury and Baron George I think certainly his life should be spared. If the Com[mande]r of the Forces chooses to accept him as a recruit for the *60th Regiment*, under the circumstances of the case I have no objection. If Sir John [Hope] should however object to take a young lad guilty of stealing, Farrell should be transported. . . .

(b) CONDITIONS OF SERVICE

533. Sir William Fawcett (Adjutant General) to Lord Cornwallis, 3 March 1792

(Public Record Office, *Cornwallis Papers*, 30/11/270/85.)

. . . I have been labouring for above these twelve months past, to procure some relief for the poor foot-soldier serving in Great Britain, where the price of every necessary of life has risen to so exorbitant a height as to render it utterly impracticable for him (suffering, as he unavoidably must be, under heavy stoppages for necessaries) to satisfy the ordinary calls of nature or to get more than one single, scanty meal in the 24 hours.

The greatest difficulty and opposition that I met with in carrying this humane under-taking into effect, proceeded from a quarter to which, while we remain, as at present, without a Commander-in-Chief, I naturally looked chiefly up for my support. H.M., however, and I must add, his Ministers, having been made thoroughly sensible of the expediency of the measure, gave it their sanction, so that now the foot-soldier, instead of one miserable meal in the 24 hours, enjoys the benefit and comfort of three ample ones, like the rest of his fellow creatures, the salutary effects of which are already evident from the decrease of desertion in the infantry, which is reduced to almost nothing. . . .

534. Debate in the house of Commons on the provisions of barracks for the troops, 22 Feb. 1793

(Cobbett's *Parliamentary History*, XXX, 473–496.)

The old fear and dislike of a standing army, dating from the Cromwellian despotism, persisted. Fox and the Whigs would have been on surer ground had they criticized ministers for their scandalous treatment of the common soldier. Even thirty years later, little improvement had been made. Sir Henry Hardinge, Clerk of the Ordnance, said on 16 Feb. 1827: "The House [of Commons] had come to a determination to allow each soldier in barracks an iron bedstead, instead of hutting four of them, as was formerly the case, in one wooden crib. The change had been productive of the most beneficial effects on both the health and the morals of our soldiery, and had saved a vast consumption of life in those who were stationed in warm latitudes." (*Parliamentary Debates*, New Series, XVI, 562.)

M. A. Taylor . . . moved, That the uniform and persevering opposition given by our ancestors to every attempt to erect barracks in this country was founded upon a just understanding of the true principles of our free and excellent constitution; and that this opposition has been justified and supported by high political and legal authority, whose recorded opinion is, 'That in time of peace the soldier should live intermixed with the people, that no separate camp, no barracks, no inland fortresses, should be allowed; and that a circulation should be thus kept up between the army and the people, and the citizen and the soldier be intimately connected together'. [Blackstone's *Commentaries*.]

The Secretary at War– . . . The measure which had been adopted of erecting barracks was necessary to the security of the kingdom. He regretted that of late years in several instances the civil power had not been able to exercise its authority without calling in the aid of the military. . . . It was necessary therefore to have the soldiers so disposed of, that they could speedily be called together, and be ready to act with most effect. . . .

Mr. Minchin– . . . The measure . . . relieved a certain description of men from a grievous tax which, during last war, had been so very oppressive that several publicans had given up their licences. It was likewise a measure very favourable to the exact observance of discipline, for though soldiers were at stated hours obliged to retire to their quarters, yet when they were quartered in a public house, this regulation could not be enforced; for when the officers went to bed, the soldiers might take the opportunity to leave their quarters, and might be engaged in riots or mischiefs which there were no means of discovering or preventing. But this could not occur in barracks, which were equally conducive to the health and morals of the troops lodged in them.

In public houses the soldiers were continually exposed to the temptation of expending that pay which might procure them solid nourishment, for liquors equally pernicious to their constitution and morals. With respect to the utility of barracks, he referred to the example of Ireland, where they had always been in use, and where so much were their beneficial effects experienced, that those towns where they were not erected, even made application for them. . . .

Mr. Fox– . . . While Ministers and their friends were praising the Constitution and deprecating innovation, they themselves were introducing a system for the disposition of a standing army, which had been always held incompatible with the safety of public liberty, and always opposed. . . . Was there not as much reason to be afraid of barracks now as in the year 1740? Was there more cause for jealousy of a standing army, when we were menaced from abroad, and dreaded the invasion of a pretender to the throne? Yet, at that period, the two leading men, Mr. Pulteney and Mr. Pelham, one of whom supported, and the other opposed Sir Robert Walpole, both united in reprobating the system of erecting barracks as unconstitutional and inimical to the rights of the people. And they said well; for the mixing the soldiers with the people, by which they imbibed the same principles and the same sentiments, was the best security of the Constitution against the danger of a standing army. . . .

It was entirely new to say that the military was necessary to the execution of the civil power. The Constitution acknowledged no such auxiliary. For the exercise of the civil power, the means were always in force; and the very preamble to the annual Mutiny Bill, which some people considered as bombastic, expressly stated that a standing army, in time of peace, without the consent of Parliament, was against law. If magistrates neglected to call in the military when their assistance was necessary, they did not do their duty. If there were places where the existing police was insufficient, let means be tried to remedy the defect, but let it not be pleaded as a reason for keeping up a military force; for of all sorts of police, a military police was the most repugnant to the spirit and the letter of our Government, and ought to be the last that ever Parliament should adopt. It was not true that the building of barracks was acceptable to all the country. There were places where it was considered not as a benefit but a grievance. . . . He was still old-fashioned enough in his notions of government to dread a standing army, and to think that the conduct of it could not be watched with too much caution. . . .

535. Observations annexed to the Army Medical board's report of the sick of the army in Ireland, 1 Oct. 1801

(British Museum Additional MSS. 33108, ff. 76–79.)

Since the former month the effectives of the Army have increased 690, standing now at 62342, and the total number of sick has also increased 202, standing now at 3793.

Altho' a great part of the information supplied by the annexed Table has already appeared in a detailed form in preceding reports, still we are of opinion that it might serve an useful purpose to exhibit a concise and arranged view of the more important medical occurrences which have taken place in 20 regiments of English militia during their late residence in Ireland, and as a majority of these soldiers consisted of able-bodied men, in the prime of life, it seems to be a matter well worthy of serious attention to examine why, in an healthy climate, and under circumstances of living not very dissimilar from what they had been accustomed to in England, this description of troops should have suffered so severely from disease, more especially during a period of time when unexposed to the usual casualties of active military service.

The following observations are intended to throw some light on this subject.

Allowing the annual mortality of 1 in 32, as computed with the effectives, to be in a very high proportion, particularly when contrasted with that in the Irish militia, which stands so low as 1 in 79, still it is to be considered that the latter calculation was formed on home troops after a residence of five years in the Kingdom and the former has been made on natives of England, who, on an average of the whole did not any of them remain more than 300 days in Ireland.

It may be stated on evidence established by long and extensive experience, that regiments composed of English or Scotch seldom fail to suffer severely from fever and dysentery during the greater part of the first year's residence in this country. In proportion however as their stay is prolonged beyond that period, they become seasoned to the climate and gradually grow more healthy.

It is to be remarked that the English militia were generally quartered in the principal towns of Ireland, and it has been proved in the observations subjoined to former Reports, that in such stations the soldier is not only unavoidably exposed to every species of seduction but to the fatal influence of contagious disorders.

In addition to the effects occasioned by the sudden removal from a dry to a more damp atmosphere, it is to be noticed that the mode of living and the general accommodation provided for the soldier on his first landing in Ireland from Great Britain have, on a comparison, seldom been made better; granting that his mess consists of the same quantity of wholesome nutriment properly prepared, still the universal substitution of whiskey for malt liquor has invariably been attended with the worst consequences, and when we consider that our permanent and temporary barracks have been from necessity greatly overcrowded, that many of these latter buildings are unfavourably placed, badly constructed and worse ventilated, and that cleanliness has never anywhere been enforced to the extent its importance demanded, it is not surprizing that the combined effect of so many untoward and powerfully exciting causes of disease should have so frequently produced and aggravated acute and contagious complaints amongst unseasoned troops.

It may perhaps be worthy of observation to remark that a majority of the men of the English militia who were seized with acute diseases in Ireland, which terminated fatally, were supplementary recruits, in point of stamina much inferior to the older soldiers. The deaths in this class therefore could often be satisfactorily accounted for by the medical attendants, as depending in a great measure on a feeble, consumptive and impaired constitution.

In animadverting on the close connexion that subsists between health and the uniformly strict enforcement of regimental discipline we would wish to speak with respectful diffidence, more particularly as every sensible and experienced Officer has little to learn on this head. . . .

536. Circular letter respecting prices of commissions in the army, 29 Sept. 1821

(*Annual Register* (1821), Appendix to Chronicle, p. 292.)

Sir;—In pursuance of the commands of his Royal Highness the Commander-in-Chief, we have the honour to transmit for your information and guidance, the following copy of a Memorandum, which has received the sanction of H.M., relative to the increase of the prices of Commissions in the Army, together with the alterations in the differences between full and half pay.

Commissions	Prices	Difference in value between the several Commissions in succession.
ROYAL REGIMENT OF HORSE GUARDS.	£.	£.
Cornet	1,200	—
Lieutenant	1,600	400
Captain	3,500	1,900
Major	5,350	1,850
Lieutenant-Colonel	7,250	1,900
LIFE-GUARDS.		
Cornet	1,260	—
Lieutenant	1,785	525
Captain	3,500	1,715
Major	5,350	1,850
Lieutenant-Colonel	7,250	1,900
DRAGOON GUARDS AND DRAGOONS.		
Cornet	840	—
Lieutenant	1,190	350
Captain	3,225	2,085
Major	4,575	1,350
Lieutenant-Colonel	6,175	1,600
FOOT GUARDS.		
Ensign	1,200	—
Lieutenant	2,050	850
Captain, with the rank of Lieutenant-Colonel	4,800	2,750
Major, with the rank of Colonel	8,300	3,500
Lieutenant-Colonel	9,000	700
FUSILEERS AND RIFLE REGIMENTS.		
Second Lieutenant	500	—
First Lieutenant	700	—
MARCHING REGIMENTS OF FOOT.		
Ensign	453	—
Lieutenant	700	250
Captain	1,800	1,100
Major	3,200	1,400
Lieutenant-Colonel	4,500	1,300

537. The Rev. W. Powell to Robert Peel (Home Secretary), 24 July 1824

(Public Record Office, Home Office, 44/14.)

Radical propaganda pictured the lower clergy of the Established Church as 'black dragoons' forming part of the garrison distributed throughout the country to support law and order and for the security of property. This clergyman, of Abergavenny, had a high sense of his duties and responsibilities to the common soldier.

Before I reply to your communication of the 23rd inst., which I received by this evening's post, enclosing a copy of Major Middleton's letter to me of the 14th inst., I must beg most respectfully but most distinctly to disclaim the acknowledgment of any right of H.R.H. the Commander-in-Chief or of yourself as Secretary of State to interfere with, or to call me to account for the performance of any duties imposed upon me as a clergyman by the laws of the land.

Having recorded this my protest, I should feel myself unworthy of the repeated instances of kindness which I have experienced at your hands, in the course of my public duties as a magistrate, if I hesitated to state for your information, that 'John Jinks, a private of the 2nd Dragoon Guards, of this Parish, a bachelor, and Hester Volles, of this Parish, a spinster, were married in this Church by licence on the 6th day of July 1824, by me, William Powell, Vicar'.

And I conceive, Sir, that such licence having been presented to me, I had just as much right to refuse to marry the parties, as Major M. would have had to refuse to obey the orders he received from the proper military authorities to remove his troop from this place to Birmingham. Of the existence of any law forbidding a British soldier to take to himself a wife, or requiring the consent of his commanding officer to his marriage, notwithstanding he has complied with all the preliminary forms required by the Marriage Acts, I must confess my ignorance. And until the Legislature shall in its wisdom think fit to debar by express enactment the soldier, from the common privilege of his fellow subjects to enter into this sacred engagement, I shall not deem it derogatory from the 'character of a Christian clergyman' to sanction the union of those, whom neither the laws of God or those of my country have prohibited from entering into the state of matrimony. Major M., I am given to understand, has publicly declared that he cared not with how many women his troopers might form connections, provided they did not encumber him with wives, but you will probably agree with me, Sir, that as a clergyman and a magistrate, I am equally bound to take a different view of the subject, and to deprecate as a most serious evil, the exposure of the chastity of my female parishioners to the unbridled passions of a troop of dragoons.

Still, so far from holding out encouragement to what may be deemed improvident marriages, you will, in Major Middleton's letter find an instance, and that in the case of this very man, in which I hesitated in continuing the publication of his banns, with a woman who was represented to me by one of the officers, as a notorious bad character, who had followed him from Yorkshire, and by thus suspending his banns probably saved him from ruin – but I am happy to say, the woman, whom he has since married, has hitherto maintained an irreproachable character and has lived seventeen years with her present mistress.

. . . I have looked over my Marriage Register, and find that it contains only five marriages of soldiers during the fourteen months in which the troop has been quartered here. . . . It is true, I believe, that these form but a portion of the marriages which took place while the troop was quartered here. One lady, I know, followed her lover to Birmingham, whither he had been dispatched under escort, to escape her, and was there married to him. Another put out her banns at Monmouth, and her lover having obtained leave of absence for a day, returned a married man. A third trooper stole a march and was married at Aberystwyth, eight miles from this place, and a fourth at Llanelly in Breconshire. And because I did not refuse to marry a couple who presented me [with] a licence from the Vicar-General and principal official of the Bishop, I am to be accused of encouraging the soldiers to revolt against the authority of their officers, and in defiance of the well-known established rules of the army. . . .

538. Wellington's Memorandum on Military Punishments, 22 Dec. 1829

(*Wellington Despatches, Correspondence & Memoranda*, VI (1877), pp. 343–345.)

Wellington had been appointed Commander-in-Chief on the death of the duke of York in Jan. 1827. That office he resigned in Jan. 1828 on becoming Prime Minister.

. . . Drunkenness, the commonest of all offences among soldiers, so common as to be almost universal, is in the abstract the least criminal. But we know that it is the parent of every other military offence, and that if drunkenness prevails in a regiment, nothing whatever, either relating to conduct, discipline or efficiency can be relied upon. . . .

Next to drunkenness there is nothing so common as disrespect to, or striking non-commissioned officers. Who that is absent can say that this crime ought not to be punished?

. . . What does a soldier do when he is drunk? He invariably commits some outrage. In the prevention of this outrage the non-commissioned officer is assaulted. Is he to be ordered to allow of the outrage in order that the drunken man may not be tempted to commit an act of insubordination? . . .

We have been for years inculcating that the difference between a good regiment and a bad one, between a good commanding officer and a faulty one, is shown by the less or greater quantity of *punishment* in regiments under their command respectively. . . .

539. Wellington's letters referring to the conduct of British troops in the Peninsula, etc.

(Gurwood, *Selections from Wellington's Despatches* [1841].)

(a) *To the right hon. J. Villiers, Coimbra, 31 May 1809:*

I have long been of opinion that a British army could bear neither success nor failure, and I have had manifest proofs of the truth of this opinion in the first of its branches in the recent conduct of the soldiers of this army. They have plundered the country most terribly, which has given me the greatest concern. . . . They have plundered the people of bullocks, among other property, for what reason I am sure

I do not know, except it be, as I understand is their practice, to sell them to the people again. I shall be very much obliged to you if you will mention this practice to the Ministers of the Regency, and bid them to issue a Proclamation forbidding the people, in the most positive terms, to purchase anything from the soldiers of the British army. [p. 263.]

(b) *To Viscount Castlereagh, Coimbra, 31 May 1809.*

The army behave terribly ill. They are a rabble who cannot bear success any more than Sir J. Moore's army could bear failure. I am endeavouring to tame them; but, if I should not succeed, I must make an official complaint of them, and send one or two corps home in disgrace. They plunder in all directions. [p. 263.]

(c) *To Earl Bathurst, Caseda, on the river Aragon, 29 June 1813 (after the Battle of Vittoria).*

It is desirable that any reinforcements of infantry which you may send to this army may come to Santander, notwithstanding that I am very apprenhensive of the consequence of marching our vagabond soldiers through the province of Biscay, in that state of discipline in which they and their officers generally come out to us. It may be depended upon that the people of this province will shoot them as they would the French, if they should misbehave.

We started with the army in the highest order, and up to the day of the battle, nothing could get on better; but that event has, as usual, totally annihilated all order and discipline. The soldiers of the army have got among them about a million sterling in money, with the exception of about 100,000 dollars, which were got for the military chest. The night of the battle, instead of being passed in getting rest and food to prepare them for the pursuit of the following day, was passed by the soldiers in looking for plunder. The consequence was that they were incapable of marching in pursuit of the enemy, and were totally knocked up. The rain came on and increased their fatigue, and I am quite convinced that we have now out of the ranks double the amount of our loss in the battle; and that we have lost more men in the pursuit than the enemy have; and have never in any one day made more than an ordinary march.

This is the consequence of the state of discipline of the British army. We may gain the greatest victories, but we shall do no good until we shall so far alter our system as to force all ranks to perform their duty. [p. 706.]

(d) *To Earl Bathurst, Freneda, 27 January 1813.*

I am desirous, if possible, not to reduce this army in old soldiers. One soldier who has served one or two compaigns will render more service than two recently sent from England; at the same time that, probably, if the old soldiers of this army were sent to other climates, they would be found equally inefficient with the recruits sent out here. [p. 657.]

(e) *To Colonel Torrens, Lesaca, 18 July 1813.*

. . . The fact is that if discipline means habits of obedience to orders, as well as military instruction, we have but little of it in the army. Nobody ever thinks of obeying an order; and all the regulations of the Horse Guards, as well as of the War Office, and all the orders of the army applicable to this peculiar service, are so much waste paper.

It is, however, an unrivalled army for fighting, if the soldiers can only be kept in their ranks during the battle; but it wants some of those qualities which are indispensable to enable a General to bring them into the field in the order in which an army ought to be to meet an enemy, or to take all the advantage to be derived from a victory; and the cause of these defects is the want of habits of obedience and attention to orders by the inferior officers, and indeed, I might add, by all. They never attend to an order with an intention to obey it, or sufficiently to understand it, be it ever so clear, and therefore never obey it, when obedience becomes troublesome, or difficult or important. [p. 713.]

(f) *To Major-General Lambert, St. Jean de Luz, 28 November 1813.*

I beg to inform the Court Martial that a very common, and a most alarming crime in this army is that of striking and otherwise resisting, sometimes even by firing at, non-commissioned officers, and even officers, in the execution of their duty. It will not be disputed that there is no crime so fatal to the very existence of an army, and no crime which officers, sworn as the members of a General Court Martial are, should feel so anxious to punish as that of which this soldier has been guilty.

It is very unpleasant to me to be obliged to resist the inclination of the General Court Martial to save the life of this soldier; but I would wish the Court to observe that if the impunity with which this offence, clearly proved, shall have been committed, should, as is probable, occasion resistance to authority in other instances, the supposed mercy will turn out to be extreme cruelty, and will occasion the loss of some valuable men to the service. [p. 769.]

(g) *To Earl Bathurst, Joncourt, 25 June 1815 (a week after the battle of Waterloo).*

I hope we are going on well, and that what we are doing will bring matters to the earliest and best conclusion, as we are in a very bad way. We have not one quarter of the ammunition which we ought to have, on account of the deficiency of our drivers and carriages; and I really believe that, with the exception of my old Spanish infantry I have got not only the worst troops but the worst equipped army, with the worst Staff, that was ever brought together. . . . [p. 868.]

(h) *To Earl Bathurst, Paris, 23 October 1815.*

My opinion is that the best troops we have, probably the best in the world, are the British infantry, particularly the old infantry that has served in Spain. This is what we ought to keep up, and what I wish above all others to retain.

The cavalry, that which is the expensive branch of the cavalry, the horses, may be put down in peace; and, upon the renewal of war, it is more easy to recruit them, or even horses for the artillery, than it is to get together a good body of infantry. For this reason I would recommend to you not to lose your good infantry, if you can keep it; and to re-form rather the horses of your cavalry and artillery to the utmost, and all the expensive parts of your establishments. [pp. 901–902.]

540. Wellington's Memorandum on the proposed plan for altering the discipline of the army, 22 April 1829

(*Wellington Despatches, Correspondence & Memoranda*, New Series, v (1873), pp. 592–597.)

. . . Let us now consider what the British army is. It is an exotic in England, unknown to the old Constitution of the country; required, or supposed to be required, only for the defence of its foreign possessions; disliked by the inhabitants, particularly by the higher orders, some of whom never allow one of their family to serve in it. Even the common people will make an exertion to find means to purchase the discharge of a relation who may have enlisted, notwithstanding the advantages of pay, &c., which a soldier enjoys, compared with the common labourer.

In the moments of the greatest distress in the country, recruits cannot be obtained for the army. Service in the army is an advantage to none. The officers and soldiers of the army are an object of dislike and suspicion to the inhabitants while serving with their regiments, and of jealousy afterwards, and they are always ill-treated.

It was the object of Mr. Windham's Act to make the army a popular service in England, by rendering service therein profitable as well as honourable, but his measures totally failed.

Then the man who enlists into the British army is, in general, the most drunken and probably the worst man of the trade or profession to which he belongs, or of the village or town in which he lives. There is not one in a hundred of them who, when enlisted, ought not to be put in the second or degraded class of any society or body into which they may be introduced; and they can be brought to be fit for what is to be called the first class only by discipline, and the precept and example of the old soldiers of the company, who, if not themselves in that same second or degraded class, deserve to be placed there for some action or other twenty times in every week.

Then let us see how this army thus composed are employed. They are constantly, and for their lives, on service in all parts and climates of the world. They do not march out of their barracks and cantonments into the rich plains of southern Germany, of Flanders, or of France, to enjoy the best fruits of the earth; but, go where they will, they commence their service in a transport in which all this discipline, of honour, of secret remonstrances and reprimand, and the distinction and separation of classes, is impracticable.

Let us see then what the effect even of our discipline is in these situations, and consider what it would be if we were heedlessly to adopt the system of Prussia.

Let us only refer to our orderly books in the Peninsula. Let us remember the horrors committed by small detachments on their marches to join the army, notwithstanding the anxious care taken to prevent them. Let us only reflect upon the consequences of the Prussian system, or any part of it, or any relaxation in the severity of our own system, upon the conduct of our men, and the consequences of that conduct not only upon the honour of the army and the public interests but upon the safety of these very men themselves. . . .

I confess that I have always considered this desire to alter the system of discipline of the army as one of the morbid symptoms of the times. It is like the notion that thieves ought not to be punished, which has, at last, peopled London and its neighbourhood with thieves in thousands, who will now be driven forth, and, after plundering the country, will fall victims to the law.

We forget what the army is, and what it may become, if not kept in order; and how ready the people of the country are to cry out if, by accident, they should suffer by any act of its indiscipline; or if, for want of discipline, the army should fail in obtaining success, as it certainly will fail, as it always has failed, if not in a state of discipline and good order.

It is curious enough that those should be the persons who propose to relax the severity of the system who would have to answer for any act of indiscipline, or outrage, which may occur, or any failure.

I know that an army, even a British army, can be kept in order without the *infliction* of corporal punishment, probably, at all. But it is by the most rigorous system of police, equally inconsistent with the spirit of the institutions of the country, and with the satisfaction and contentment of the officers and soldiers.

I have myself kept whole divisions of the army under arms for days: no crime could then be committed. In the same manner I can have half-hourly or hourly roll calls or parades. I can confine men to barrack-yards; I can send them out to walk in a town, in squads, in charge of a non-commissioned officer; in short, I may torment them into regularity: but corporal punishment, unlimited, at least to the extent to which it exists at present, must be the foundation of that or any other system established in the British army.

I wish those who consider this subject would read over all the proceedings on Major ——'s case. He was anxious to have his battalion in good order, and no corporal punishment. But he inflicted misery and torture of every other description, and corporal punishment into the bargain; and the affair ended by the battalion firing their buttons at him when at exercise.

We may rely upon it that we cannot relax the severity of our system at all, and that we cannot even diminish the number of our corporal punishments without augmenting our preventive or police system.

Upon this point we ought to consider a little the nature of our officer, and compare him with the Prussian officer. Our officer is a gentleman. We require that he should be one, and above all that he should conduct himself as such; and most particularly in reference to the soldier, and to his intercourse with the non-commissioned officers and soldiers. Indeed we carry this principle of the gentleman, and the absence of intercourse with those under his command, so far as that, in my opinion, the duty of a subaltern officer, as done in a foreign army, is not done at all in the cavalry, or the British infantry of the line. It is done in the Guards by the sergeants. Then our gentleman officer, however admirable his conduct on a field of battle, however honourable to himself, however glorious and advantageous to his country, is but a poor creature in disciplining his company in camp, quarters, or cantonments.

The name, the character, the conduct, the family and relations, the fortune, the situation, the mental acquirements of each of the men of his company, are not the sole objects of his thoughts, as the same of his men are of the Prussian officer in the same situation, who carries into execution this same discipline in the company to which he belongs, with the men of which he lives as a companion, friend and adviser. . . .

I recommend that we should stand firm upon the establishment of our discipline as it is. If we can, let us make our officers do their duty, and see that the non-commissioned officers do theirs. But mind! this is a system of prevention. We shall thus avoid punishment in the best way, by preventing irregularity and crime. . . .

541. Wellington on the defence of the country

(*Wellington Despatches, Correspondence & Memoranda*, II (1867), pp. 381–383.)

(a) *Letter to Sir Herbert Taylor, 27 Dec. 1824.*

. . . There is nothing so necessary as to look forward to future wars, and to our early preparation for them. Our wars have always been long and ruinous in expense, because we were unable to prepare for the operations which must have brought them to a close, for years after they were commenced. But this system will no longer answer. We cannot venture upon any great augmentation of our debt; if we did we should find the payment of the interest impossible, together with the expense of our peace establishments. We must, therefore, first take great care to keep ourselves out of disputes if possible, and, above all, to keep our neighbours quiet; and next, to put our resources for war on such a footing as that we may apply them hereafter at a much earlier period of the contest than we have ever done hitherto.

Among others, it is for this reason that I am so earnest for the adoption of the proposed system for the infantry of the army; and I quite agree with you that we ought in time of peace to regulate our local force in war so highly as to be able to avail ourselves of all our resources at the earliest possible period.

I confess that I am one of those who do not much apprehend invasion. I think steam navigation has in some degree altered that question to our disadvantage, particularly at the commencement of a contest, and in relation to a *coup-de-main* upon one or other of our naval arsenals. In this view of the subject I have the officers of engineers now employed in the consideration of a plan for the security of Sheerness, which I will afterwards apply to Portsmouth and Plymouth if I should find the Government and Parliament disposed to adopt it. But I confess that I think a solid invasion of the country, with a view even to the plunder of the capital or of Woolwich, or even to take possession of, or to do more than bombard, one of our naval arsenals is out of the question.

It is not necessary to discuss this question, nor would I even hint to anybody that I entertained this opinion. I want to improve our local resources, because by these means I shall set at liberty those that are disposable, so as to be able at an earlier period of the supposed contest to bring it to a termination. But if I profess that to be my opinion I know I shall fail. I shall succeed if the object held out is the permanent security against invasion. I will not enter upon the details of the plan in No. 2 for the local force. I like it because it is founded on what exists, and it does not occasion an enormous expense which ought to be laid out elsewhere, and not at home where there is no danger. It tends to organize and prepare a great force without incurring the expense of calling it out till the moment at which it is wanted. I think that if these Constable Acts succeed in Ireland, a great deal may be done to enforce a ballot there, not for a force disposable for foreign service, because to form such a force in an island by compulsion is inconsistent with every principle of government, but to form a force for local defence, including this part of the United Kingdom. . . .

Enclosure.

The infantry of the army is composed of 110 battalions:–

Battalions of Guards	7
Battalions of the Line	103
	110

56 Depots at home; 54 Depots with the service companies either at home or abroad.

In India or on that establishment	20	of 10 companies each.
Ceylon, besides local corps	4	
Mauritius	3	
The Cape	3	
New South Wales	2	of 10 companies each
„ „ „ on passage	1	of 6 „ „
Gibraltar	6	
Malta	5	
Ionian Islands	6 or 7	
Jamaica	5	
West Indies, besides local corps	8	
North America and Bermuda	10	
In England	13	
In Ireland	19	
On passage	5 or 4	
	110	Battalions.

(b) *Wellington's Memorandum, 4 August 1827.*

. . . I have more than once endeavoured to draw the attention of the Government to the alteration which the invention and application of steam to ships has made in the probable operations of war; particularly a system of hostilities directed against naval arsenals at the commencement of a war. I never thought that steam could be applied successfully to ships of war. But vessels moved by steam can be used as transports, or to tow transports, and their use would give a certainty to the movements of an expedition having such objects in view which such expeditions have never had hitherto, and is well deserving the consideration of the Government in the discussion of all questions of military establishments and defence.

Portsmouth, Plymouth, Sheerness, Chatham and Milford Haven would not be safe from destruction at the commencement of a war unless there should be a large body of men in each. . . . [*Ibid.*, IV (1871), pp. 114–115.]

(c) THE MILITIA

542. To the Inhabitants of the County of West Lothian (undated printed hand-bill [c. 1794])

(Public Record Office, Home Office, 102/15.)

As many false and mistaken opinions appear to have been circulated respecting the Act of Parliament for raising a militia in Scotland; and as the people, deceived by these misrepresentations, have in several places opposed and hindered the execution of the said Act, therefore the following short but just and accurate account of the same is published for the general information of all concerned, respecting the true effect and meaning of the Act, the nature and extent of the service of a militia-man, the advantages he is entitled to, and the reasons of drawing the Act in the terms in which it stands.

I. The Act applies to all persons of a certain age, without distinction of rank or degree. The first peer in the land, equally as the day labourer, must either serve in person, or provide a substitute to serve for him.

II. The Act has been confined to persons between the age of 19 and 23; because at those years men are either not married, or have but few children, and can serve more conveniently than older men, who are married, and have large families. With the same view of making the burden as light as possible, *every man* is exempted who has more than two lawful children, *whatever his age may be.*

III. It is NOT TRUE that every man is to serve, whose name is set down in the parish list. It is only a proportion of them that are to serve, and probably not more than one in ten of those who are set down, if so many. The number to be raised for all Scotland is only 6,000 men; so that in landward parishes, or where there are no large towns, the parish may not have to furnish more than two or three men, and in some instances not so many. Those whose names are set down in the list of any district or parish may all of them avoid the actual service by producing the number of volunteer substitutes required from that district or parish, and subscribing among themselves (which will be a trifle among a number) the bounty money to be paid to such volunteers. A substitute must even be accepted at whatever time he is offered, and though this should not be till after the ballot, or after the men balloted have begun to serve.

IV. The men who are to serve are to be fixed by ballot, or drawing lots, in order to prevent the possibility of partiality or favour to one man before another.

V. The time of service is only during the present war and one month more; and it is very possible that there may be peace before a single man can be trained to arms under the Act, or even before the lots can be cast for fixing who are to serve.

VI. No militiaman can be carried out of Scotland under any pretence or on any account whatsoever; not even in case of insurrection or invasion. The oath which every man takes at [the] beginning to serve, bears that express limitation.

VII. No militiaman can be enlisted in any regiment. He is not allowed to enlist even if willing, and any officer or serjeant who attempts to enlist him, is punishable with severe fines.

VIII. The pay of a militiaman is the same as that of a soldier, which is now better than a shilling a day, besides clothing, lodging, coal and candle when on duty, and medicines and attendance when in bad health. The pay is constant, whether the man be sick or well (which no man has in his ordinary trade); and the day's work or duty is far lighter than any ordinary labour.

In case of being disabled by any accident, a militiaman is entitled to the Chelsea pension; and every married militiaman, who has served, has [the] right to set up in his trade in any place or burgh, without entering with the Corporation.

It would be doing injustice to the good sense and good dispositions of the people of Scotland, to believe that, when all these things are understood, there will be any further opposition to this necessary measure for the National Defence against its cruel, unprincipled and inveterate enemy, France.

England has at this moment 90,000 militia armed and fit for duty. Shall it be told that Scotland is unwilling to furnish even 6,000 towards the common cause?

In England, the militia is considered as the best and most CONSTITUTIONAL defence of their laws and LIBERTIES against all who may be disposed to encroach on them, because it places arms in the hands of the people themselves, and gradually trains the whole mass of the nation to the use of them. How should it happen that the same thing which in the other end of the island is a privilege, a security and an honour, should be reckoned an oppression and a grievance among Scotsmen?

It had long been looked upon as a slur and a reflection on this country, that we had no militia, and were thought unfit to be trusted with our own defence. When Parliament is willing to remove this disgraceful distinction between the two countries, shall it be found that Scotsmen have so much fallen off from the COURAGE and SPIRIT of their forefathers, that, even at THEIR OWN DOORS, they are afraid to act the part of MEN for the defence of all that is dear to them upon earth?

Last of all, let the people consider that it can only be known, upon a fair and impartial trial, whether the present plan of a militia is good or bad. If upon trial it shall be found objectionable, the wisdom of King and Parliament will contrive to improve it. The sure course to prevent any alteration or improvement of the Act is to engage in violent and unlawful proceedings in resistance of it: for of this you may be assured, that the Government of this great and powerful country will not allow itself to be overborne, or got the better of, by the clamour of mobs and tumults.

Be peaceable, therefore, and dutiful, and take benefit by the example of Ireland. In that kingdom also, within these few years, there was much opposition to the raising of a militia; and it is to that very militia that they now owe their security against a French invasion, and an insurrection of the friends of the French within their kingdom. We are not without some persons of that description here also, who make a business of misrepresenting everything for their own ends, not for your advantage, or out of any love to you. Beware of their arts, and disappoint them by keeping in your duty.

Observe, particularly, that, by law, all damage done by a mob, through fire-raising or otherwise, must be paid by the County, *and that every householder is liable for his share.*

Published by order of the Sheriff-Depute of West Lothian.

B. THE NAVY

(a) RECRUITMENT

543. Henry Dundas (Home Secretary) to Charles Stisted, of Ipswich, 20 Feb. 1793

(Public Record Office, Home Office, 43/4/188.)

In answer to your letter of the 18th inst. relative to the six sailors who were bound over in the month of November last to be tried for misdemeanours, I perfectly coincide in your opinion that it will be proper to allow as many of these men as choose it, to go on board the King's ships of war, and that the intended prosecutions against them may be stopped.

544. Debates in the House of Commons on the impressment of seamen, 27 May and 1 June 1814, and 13 Feb. 1827

(Hansard's *Parliamentary Debates*.)

Impressment was not specifically recognized by statute, but, having been practised from time immemorial, the lawyers recognized that it had become a part of the common law. It was not seriously challenged by the Whig Opposition during the war (when they were in office, in 1806, they made no attempt to end it), but if the press-gang captains abused their powers, the House of Commons might hear of it—as in 1814 when Whitbread denounced impressment as a means of breaking a strike of merchant seamen. A letter from Lord Hardwicke, the Lord Lieutenant of Ireland, to his brother Charles Yorke (12 March 1803), shows how the system worked in Ireland: "I wish the press of seamen may have [been] generally successful. Some seamen, I understand, are come over from Liverpool to avoid it, and no orders have been received from the Admiralty to press here, where I understand it has been seldom practised." (Add. MSS. 35702, f. 140.)

27 May 1814:

Lord A. Hamilton presented a Petition from the shipowners of the ports of the Clyde, praying that the mates of ships of 50 tons and upwards may not be subject to impressment. His Lordship wished to know from some of the gentlemen belonging to the Admiralty whether the orders of the Admiralty for impressment were *generally* given, as he understood there were complaints of much partiality being exercised with respect to different places.

Mr. *Bennet* wished to know whether the impress service was still continued on the Thames. . . .

Mr. *Finlay* contended that it would be a great object to have the practice converted into some specific law which would bear equally on all, and which all might know. The object of the Petition was to prevent the masters of vessels of 50 tons being exposed to be taken by captains of his Majesty's ships, contrary to the spirit of the practice.

Mr. *W. Dundas* said they were only protected while on board, and might, according to the practice, be taken when on shore.

Mr. *Bennet* repeated his question respecting the impress service on the Thames.

Mr. *Barham* expressed his astonishment that no answer had been given to this question. If this practice were persisted in, there would be an end to all the functions of the Commons. . . .

Mr. W. Dundas insisted that it was entirely new, in the practice of the House, to ask questions not relative to the subject of debate. The question of the hon. member (Mr. Bennet) had no relation to the Petition of the noble Lord. He (Mr. Dundas) was not to be frightened by menace or big words into giving an answer; this was a new parliamentary course. . . . He would, however, answer that the hon. gent. was perfectly misinformed. . . . [xxvii, 1030–1032.]

1 June 1814:

Mr. W. Dundas, seeing a noble Lord in his place who had asked some questions on a former evening respecting impressments, would take the opportunity of saying, with regard to the first question, that no distinction was made in the orders of the Admiralty as to the impress at different ports. As to the mates of ships, they were protected, by the order of the Admiralty, as long as they were doing their duty aboard their own ships, and they might also procure tickets of leave from the officer of the port to go on shore. On another question which he had put to him, Parliament alone could determine. . . . As to the impress on the Thames, it was true that it continued still; and it was necessary so long as hostilities continued with America; but it was so reduced that whereas it formerly used to produce from 70 to 100 men per month, in the last month only five men were pressed, three of whom the officer had been desired to impress as riotous persons. In the same month 51 persons had entered as volunteers.

Mr. Whitbread . . . That right hon. gentleman had said that three men had been impressed as riotous persons, at the desire of some other persons. Thus was this power of impress, illegal and oppressive as it was in itself, perverted from its legitimate object–thus were persons delivered, for purposes unknown, to the arbitrary power of the Admiralty. . . .

Mr. Croker . . . The execution of the impress-warrants rested with the officers of the ports only. When the impress was slack, the officers did not visit the different ships with particular diligence; and then, if sailors were idle or riotous, the master might inform the impress officers that they would do him no harm by taking such or such persons. It was a favour to a master of a merchant-ship, when the impress officers were obliged to take some men from his vessel, to allow him to choose those whom he would wish to remain. . . . [xxvii, 1038–1039.]

13 Feb. 1827:

Sir John Newport . . . He should never be convinced that, in this country, there was not a power to call a sufficient number of men into service whenever it might be necessary, without the exercise of that which he considered absolute tyranny. It has been shown, again and again, in that House and in numerous publications, that such means did exist; and he believed in his conscience, that until the tyrannous system to which he objected should be done away, it would operate as a drawback upon the desire which men would otherwise evince to enter the service. The consequence was, that they would be driven to other countries; and the experience of the late war with

America had shown the mischievous consequences of having the enemy's ships manned and fought by British seamen. . . .

Mr. Warburton was of opinion that if the question were put to the merchants and ship-owners, whether the system of impressment were injurious or otherwise, they would, one and all, protest against it. The shipping interest was materially affected by it; for what could be a greater hardship on the part of the owners, than that the men who worked their vessels should be taken out of them, after perhaps a long and hazardous voyage, on their arrival in the chops of the Channel? The whole system of impressment was degrading to the country, and destructive of that free spirit for which British seamen were distinguished. He was sure that the people of Great Britain would sooner submit to additional taxation, if no other means could be found by which the system of naval impressments might be abolished.

Sir George Clerk contended that the view which hon. members seemed to take of the system of impressment was founded on erroneous reasoning. It was only in cases of peculiar emergency that this mode of raising men for the service was resorted to. A sufficient supply of seamen could always be had, without having recourse to the system complained of; but the House should bear in mind, before it insisted too strongly on its abolition, that there were circumstances in which it might be necessary to require a fleet to be manned with extraordinary despatch; which could only be accomplished by resorting to impressment. The hon. member had talked of the hardship of taking men from merchant ships on their arrival in the Channel; but, would not the merchants have much more cause of complaint, if Government had not provided the means of defending their shipping from the enemy? It was to be hoped that the system of impressment would be so modified as to strip it of its grievances; and that the liberality which the country had displayed in bestowing pensions on those sailors who had served their country would have the effect of making the service less irksome. He thought it wrong, however, to insist too strongly on putting an end to impressment altogether, particularly when it was considered that the salvation of the country might depend on the celerity with which we could command a navy. . . .

Mr. Hume wished to state the result of the inquiries which he had made on the subject. It was generally admitted that the service of the navy was less laborious, and that the men had less labour, better food, better regulations, and more advantages, than in the merchant service. They stated that it was not the inferiority of the wages to the wages in the merchant service of which they complained, for that was compensated by pensions. Thousands of seamen had been examined, and they one and all declared that their aversion to the service arose from the discipline to which they were subjected. That such discipline was unnecessary had been proved in various cases. In the *Bulwark* of 74 there had not been a single corporal punishment inflicted for eighteen months. The seamen were dissatisfied that a commander had it in his power to order the infliction of a summary punishment which degraded the individual for ever, and that there was no redress. To impressment they did not object on an emergency. But they objected to being torn from their families by impressment, and then kept in the service for life. Whenever the urgency of the public service required it, the seamen had no objection to take their turn; but they wished for the establishment of some regulation to prevent their being detained after the emergency had ceased to exist. One great objection to impressment was the expense which it occasioned in tenders, &c.; for the moment a sailor was pressed, he became a prisoner, under a guard, and was divested of all the rights of an Englishman. He was satisfied that the number of desertions which took place during the late war, in consequence of the dissatisfaction of the seamen, counterbalanced the advantages of impressment, except on one or two emergencies. . . . He intreated those who had the power to introduce an amelioration of the system, to consider whether it would not be much better to have the fleet manned by volunteers, by men attached to the service, who might be allowed to go on shore without being guarded by officers, from fear of their desertion. . . .

Sir Byam Martin utterly denied that the naval service was unpopular. As a proof of it, the last ship that was put in commission, the Asia, of 80 guns, in three weeks obtained 370 volunteers, and in five weeks completed her complement. . . .

Sir C. Forbes said he had heard that such was the desire of the men engaged in the shipping of the East India Company to enter into his Majesty's service, that the Court of Directors had made application to the Admiralty to prevent it. . . . The condition and treatment of the sailor on board of a King's ship had of late years been considerably improved; and his Majesty's service was now looked to by seamen as most desirable. With regard to impressment the judicious application of a bounty would always ensure a supply of volunteers for the navy, without resorting to a measure which was generally condemned. Bounties were given to induce soldiers to enter the service; and why should they not also be offered as an inducement to man our fleets? . . . He was quite sure that the nation would not grudge the additional expense.

Mr. Fyler contended that impressment was not only contrary to the spirit of the British Constitution, but a disgrace and opprobrium to the British nation. [New Series, XVI, 450–456.]

(b) THE CONDITIONS OF SERVICE

545. The petitions of the Seamen to the House of Commons and to the Board of Admiralty, 18 April 1797; the Board's reply, 18th, and the Seamen's reply, 19th
(Cobbett's *Parliamentary History*, XXXIII, pp. 493–497.)

1797 was the darkest year of the war. At a time when both England and Ireland were in danger of invasion the Channel fleet at Spithead mutinied. Then followed the mutiny of the North Sea fleet at the Nore.

(a) *The Petition to the House of Commons:*

. . . We beg leave to remind your august Assembly that the Act of Parliament passed in the reign of King Charles II, wherein the wages of all seamen serving on board H.M.'s fleet was settled, passed at a time when the necessaries of life, and slops of every denomination, were at least 30% cheaper than at the present time, which enabled seamen and mariners to provide better for their families than we can now do with one half advance.

We therefore request your Hon. House will be so kind as to revise the Act before-mentioned, and make such amendments therein as will enable your petitioners and their families to live in the same comfortable manner as seamen and mariners did at that time. . . .

We profess ourselves as loyal to our Sovereign, and zealous in the defence of our country as the army and militia can be, and esteem ourselves equally entitled to H.M.'s munificence, therefore with jealousy we behold their pay augmented, and their out-pensions of Chelsea-College increased to £13 per annum, while we remain neglected, and the out-pensioners of Greenwich have only £7 per annum. . . .

(b) *The Petition to the Board of Admiralty:*

. . . The first grievance which we have to complain of is that our wages are too low and ought to be raised, that we might be the better able to support our wives and families in a manner comfortable, and whom we are in duty bound to support as far as our wages will allow, which we trust will be looked into by your Lordships and the Hon. House of Commons in Parliament assembled.

We, your petitioners, beg that your Lordships will take into consideration the grievances of which we complain, and now lay before you:

1. That our provisions be raised to the weight of 16 ounces to the pound, and of a better quality, and that our measures may be the same as those used in the commercial trade of this country.

2. That your petitioners request your honours will be pleased to observe there should be no flour served while we are in harbour, in any port whatever, under the command of the British flag; and also, that there might be granted a sufficient quantity of vegetables of such kind as may be the most plentiful in the ports to which we go; which we grievously complain, and lay under the want of.

3. That your Lordships will be pleased seriously to look into the state of the sick on board H.M.'s ships, that they may be better attended to, and that they may have the use of such necessaries as are allowed for them in time of their sickness, and that these necessaries be not on any account embezzled.

4. That your Lordships will be so kind as to look into this affair, which is no wise unreasonable, and that we may be looked upon as a number of men standing in defence of our country, and that we may in some wise have grant and opportunity to taste the sweets of liberty on shore, when in any harbour, and when we have completed the duty of our ship, after our return from sea; and that no man may encroach upon his liberty, there shall be a boundary limited, and those trespassing any farther, without a written order from the commanding officer, shall be punished according to the rules of the navy, which is a natural request, and congenial to the heart of man, and certainly to us, that you make the boast of being the guardians of the land.

5. That if any man is wounded in action, his pay be continued until he is cured and discharged; and if any ship has any real grievances to complain of, we hope your Lordships will readily redress them, as far as is in your power, to prevent any disturbances.

It is also unanimously agreed by the fleet that from this day no grievances shall be received, in order to convince the nation at large that we know when to cease to ask, as well as to begin, and that we ask nothing but what is moderate, and may be granted without detriment to the nation, or injury to the service. [*Ibid.*, 495–496.]

(c) *The Admiralty Board's Answer:*

Having taken into consideration the Petitions transmitted by your Lordship [Admiral Lord Bridport, C.-in-C. in the Channel] from the crews of H.M.'s ships under your command, and having the strongest desire to attend to all complaints of the seamen in H.M.'s navy, and to grant them every just and reasonable redress, and having considered the difference of the price of the necessaries of life, at this and at that period when the pay of seamen was established, we do hereby require and direct your Lordship to take the speediest method of communicating to the fleet:

That we have resolved to recommend it to H.M. to propose to Parliament to increase the wages of seamen in H.M.'s navy in the following proportions, *viz.*

To add four shillings per month to the wages of petty officers and able seamen; three shillings per month to the wages of ordinary seamen, and two shillings per month to the wages of landmen.

That we have resolved that seamen wounded in action shall be continued in pay until their wounds are healed, or until, being declared unserviceable, they shall receive a pension, or be received into the Royal Hospital at Greenwich, and that having a perfect confidence in the zeal, loyalty and courage of all the seamen in the fleet, so generally expressed in their Petition, and in their earnest desire of serving their country with that spirit which always so eminently distinguished British seamen, we have come to this resolution the more readily, that the seamen may have, as early as possible, an opportunity of showing their good dispositions by returning to their duty, as it may be necessary that the fleet should speedily put to sea to meet the enemy of the country.

(d) *The Seamen's Reply, Spithead, 19 April.*

We received your Lordship's answer to our Petition; and, in order to convince your Lordship and the nation in general of our moderation, beg leave to offer the following remarks to your consideration, *viz.*

That there never has existed but two orders of men in the navy–able and ordinary; therefore the distinction between ordinary and landmen is totally new. We therefore humbly propose to your Lordships that the old regulations be adhered to; that the wages of able seamen be raised to one shilling per day, and that of petty officers and the ordinary in the usual proportion; and, as a further proof of our moderation, and that we are actuated by a true spirit of benevolence towards our brethren, the marines, who are not noticed in your Lordships' answer, we humbly propose that their pay be augmented while serving on board, in the same proportion as ordinary seamen; this, we hope and trust, will be a convincing proof to your Lordships that we are not actuated by a spirit of contradiction, but that we earnestly wish to put a speedy end to the present affair. We beg leave to state to your Lordships that the pensions from Greenwich College, which we earnestly wish to be raised to £10 per annum; and in order to maintain which, we humbly propose to your Lordships that every seaman employed in the merchant service, instead of 6d per month, which they now pay, shall hereafter pay one shilling per month, which, we trust, will raise a fund fully adequate to the purpose; and as this, in time of peace, must be paid by your petitioners, we trust it will give a convincing proof of our disinterestedness and moderation. We would also recommend that this regulation be extended to the seamen in the service of the East India Company, as we know by experience that there are few sailors employed by them but what have been in the royal navy, and we have seen them with our own eyes, after sickness or other accident has disabled them, without any hope of relief or support but from their former services in the navy.

As to provisions, that they be augmented to 16 ozs. to the pound of bread and meat, cheese, butter and liquor in proportion, and of a better quality, and a sufficient quantity of vegetables, and that no flour be served with fresh beef. . . . [*Ibid.*, 498.]

546. Lieutenant James Watson, R.N., to Admiral Robert Digby, 12 June 1797

(Navy Records Society, XL (1910), pp. 293–296.)

Leith Tender, Leith Roads: . . . To lay before you the horrid scenes I have witnessed of late, where all order, discipline and subordination has been trampled under foot–scenes which I can never think upon but with abhorrence–is the cause of my troubling you at this time. . . .

On the 24th ult. I sailed, in consequence of the orders I had received, for the Nore, having 122 new raised men on board. No idea at that time existed of a disturbance being among any of H.M.'s ships there. In approaching Yarmouth Roads on the 19th, where I proposed anchoring, I observed three sail of the line, one frigate and a sloop, with red flags at the fore topmast head, which I conjectured was the signal of insurrection. I judged it most prudent to push forward, and called on board a Russian man-of-war at that time lying there, where I had my suspicions confirmed, but could not find that any thing of a similar nature was going forward at the Nore. Of consequence, I proceeded up [the] Swin, and the day after, at 5 p.m., brought the ship to anchor. . . .

Next morning, I found the fleet in the utmost disorder. I was surrounded by armed vessels, and told if I did not hoist the red flag the tender would be sunk. The contagion spread like fire among the volunteers, who, stimulated by some deserters and other villains then on board, made an attempt to take possession of the vessel, without success. Here I cannot help observing, to the honour of my own ship's company, only 29 in number, officers included, that at this time, when my existence depended on personal exertions, when, guided by the impulse of the moment, I was reduced to the necessity of throwing myself into the midst of the mutineers, they rallied round me; and so superior is the energy of a few men, when conscious of acting in a good cause, that the multitude were brought to subjection in a moment. How I felt afterwards at seeing every possibility of escaping rendered impracticable by the 5 men of war I passed in Yarmouth Roads coming fast up, all in a state of mutiny, is not easy to be described; I had no resource but to bring the ship to, in the midst of the fleet. I was dragged like a culprit before their infernal tribunal, to answer for my conduct, and every one under me summoned to give in his complaint. Fortunately, however, nothing of any kind was alleged against me; and the man himself that guides their whole proceedings, having been formerly under my directions, was obliged to give his testimony in my favour. This circumstance having afforded me some share of popularity among them, I used my utmost endeavour to turn it to the best advantage; and under pretence of speaking in my own defence, I took occasion to advert to that subject which ought to be nearest the heart of every man that loves his country, and said everything my imagination or abilities could suggest to bring them to a sense of their duty. I was ordered to desist; yet many of their delegates followed me out and declared in the strongest terms their regret at the situation to which they were reduced.

Their president and leader, Richard Parker, to whom I have before alluded, was originally put on board the tender about the beginning of last April as a volunteer, preferring that situation to remaining in prison where he had been confined for debt. He, at that time, told me a plausible story of his misfortunes, which induced me to put him in the mess with my midshipmen; about a month thereafter he was turned over on board a revenue vessel, to be conveyed to the fleet; from which vessel, he unluckily did not succeed in an attempt to drown himself. During my detention at the Nore he spent much of his time with his old messmates in the tender, through whom, and even personally, I worked upon him by every possible means; but whenever the subject was broached, his brain took fire; he seemed intoxicated with a sense of his own consequence, and uttered nothing but incoherent nonsense, which could be mistaken by nobody but a poor deluded seaman. I however succeeded in putting his popularity to some hazard, by causing him to be made completely drunk, knowing his propensity that way, and the punishment with them attendant on such an offence. In this state of inebriety, he exposed himself in an attempt before the volunteers &c. to display his powers of oratory. How far this had its effect I know not, because the supernumeraries were taken on board the Sandwich, and I had the good fortune to work out a release for my vessel, which I effected with much difficulty on the evening of the 2nd inst.

. . . I am happy in being able to say from every thing I have observed, that the great body of the seamen are averse to these proceedings; it is their having cut off all communication between the ships except through the means of the delegates, and the tyranny which they exercise, that keeps them so long together. Their jealousy sufficiently demonstrates their uneasiness; for although the construction of my vessel in point of sailing, filled with riotous new-raised men, and my people in a manner panic struck, precluded the possibility of making an escape, yet every motion was watched, and a great number of mutineers always kept on board, for fear an attempt should be made to carry off their president. . . .

547. Debate in the House of Commons on Flogging in the Navy, 9 June 1825

(Hansard's *Parliamentary Debates*, New Series, XIII, 1097–1110.)

*M*r. *Hume* . . . The cause of the unwillingness to enter the navy was the extensive power of arbitrary punishments. No man in the army was subjected to the punishment of flogging until his alleged crimes were decided upon by a court-martial.

Why were seamen deprived of that legal protection? Again, how was it to be explained that in large vessels of the navy, such as the *Bulwark* and the *Dictator*, there was no flogging for months together, while in comparatively small ships it was almost daily inflicted? . . . He believed that the only explanation was that it depended upon the arbitrary caprice of the commanding officers; without any reference to the offences of the seamen. No such capricious power was vested in the officers of the army. . . . He could not understand how Government could reconcile the continuance of such a revolting practice, with their efforts to relieve from arbitrary flogging the slaves in the West Indies. In their Order-in-Council of the 10th March 1824, directions were given to prevent a slave in Trinidad from receiving more than 25 lashes, and such lashes were not to be inflicted until 24 hours after the commission of the alleged offence. Were not our seamen worthy of being placed on an equal footing with the slaves of the West India colonies? The hon. member here read a statement referring to the arbitrary infliction of flogging, beginning from a period of 20 years past, down to the last year. It took place, in one instance, where a marine received four dozen lashes by the order of his commanding officer, Captain Cockburn, merely for his musket missing fire; and in a second instance where an old seaman of 35 years' standing, received the same number of strokes for declaring that he never witnessed so barefaced an act of cruelty as flogging the marine for such an offence. . . . It was one of his objects to limit the services of seamen, on the principle acted upon by the late Mr. Windham towards the army–to seven or ten years–protecting the seamen, who served so long, from future impressment. Indeed, that provision under his system, would be unnecessary; as impressment itself could then be dispensed with. With regard to the necessity of impressment, he would ask the gallant Admiral opposite where the necessity existed, when he found no difficulty by bounties and ordinary recruiting, to obtain the necessary supply of mariners? The rate of wages paid to the navy was not commensurate with the wages given to the other branches of the service. How was it to be expected that when the pay of the merchant service was £3 10s., and that of the navy 34s. a month, seamen would be induced to enter our ships of war voluntarily? If small pensions were given after a certain number of years' service, to our seamen to sustain them under the afflictions of premature old age, too frequently the result of a life of severe toil, it would operate as a great induce-ment. If so small sums as £7 or £10 annually were held out as a boon, it would be productive of the most beneficial effects. Even the trifling grants of the Trinity House, from 5 to 6s. a month, were received by that class of men with gratitude and satis-faction. He would give them small pensions proportionate to the period of service, and alter the present system of distributing prize-money. Was it right that a captain of a ship should receive as much prize-money as all the crew together? The officers of the navy ought not to consider prize-money as an object, but should give it up to the men. . . . As an emergency might arise, he would provide against it by having a register of seamen on the plan which was begun 150 years ago, but which was not prosecuted as it ought to have been. He would accompany that plan with a provision that no seaman should be excused from the service of his country in the navy; just as no landsman was now excused from the service of his country in the army, he being liable to be drawn as a militiaman and to serve five years. He would now move 'that leave be given to bring in a Bill to amend the 22nd of George II, ch. 33, and to make provision for the encouragement of seamen and for the better manning of his Majesty's fleet'.

Sir F. Burdett seconded the motion.

Sir G. Cockburn . . . If, while merchantmen give £3 10s. a month, sailors could be found willing to enter the King's service for 34s. a month, it was a proof that that service was not distasteful to them. But the hon. gentleman proposed a system of pensions to induce men to enter early into the navy. Pensions were granted at present. If a sailor, after 7 years' service (or before in some cases) was disabled by debility or accident, he received a pension. After a service of 14 years that pension was increased; and should he have served 21 years, and for any considerable part of that time with so much credit as to be rated as a petty officer, he became entitled to a pension of £45 a year. . . . The sailors were better off than the soldiers. The army enlisted for life; the navy never did. At the end of a certain service the sailors were paid off; and it was no great proof of the dislike of the sailors to the service that the men who were paid off were generally the first to enter again. So unfounded was this alleged dislike to the service, that the owners of merchantmen in all parts of the world had written to the Admiralty to beg that they would restrain the officers of the navy from receiving their men; and in consequence of those applications the Admiralty had written to the officers on the several stations not to receive men from the merchantmen to an extent that might distress them. . . . The hon. gentleman also wished to take from the officers of the navy the power of punishing the men without a court-martial, and in that point to assimilate the navy to the army. But the hon. gentleman forgot that when the army was in the field the commanding officer was invested with the power of arbitrary punishment; of punishment without any previous trial by a court-martial. Now, our ships were always in motion. A man-of-war frequently went round the world by herself. In such cases it would be impossible to have a court-martial; and a man who behaved ill might remain a prisoner for three years before he could be tried. Of this he was sure, that should the House take away this power from the officers, they would go far to destroy the discipline of the navy. The Admiralty had done everything they could to prevent the improper exercise of that power. . . . The Admiralty never sanctioned an excess of punishment, but always signified their approbation of those officers who managed their ships without punishments. . . . So necessary, however, was the power of inflicting punishment felt to be, even in the merchant service, that in the papers of that very day there was the report of a trial in which one of the crew of a merchantman had brought an action against his captain for punishing him, but in which the Judge had stated that he could have no doubt that every captain of a merchant vessel had a right to inflict corporal punishment on such of his crew as deserved it. Would the House take from the navy the power that was considered indispensable even to the merchant service? . . . With respect to impressment there could be no doubt that it was desirable to do without the practice as much as possible; but in some cases it was inevitable. It was true that all our seamen who had pensions were liable to be called upon in an emergency.

But the business of a seaman was like any other business. Dexterity in it required that the hand should always be kept in. The moment a declaration of war took place, it was desirable that we should have the means of sending out a fleet: and to effect this, it became necessary to lay hands on every seaman that could be found. It was quite impossible to put an end to the practice of impressment; unless the House would allow such a fleet to be maintained during peace as would enable us to go to war at any moment without disadvantage. It was impossible that we could have, at a moment's notice, 40,000 or 50,000 men without taking them from the merchant service. . . .

Sir Joseph Yorke protested that the punishment inflicted upon seamen arose solely from the necessities of the service, and that it was administered cautiously and conscientiously, and not according to passion and caprice. Punishment might be more formally inflicted by sentences of the courts of law and the regular tribunals; but it was impossible it could be inflicted with more deliberation and decorum than it was upon the quarter-deck of a man-of-war. . . . As to the crews, he did not deny but some two-thirds were good; of the remainder he would from his professional experience declare that so far from moral lectures about personal character operating upon them, they might as well talk to pigs. Some of them were as insensible as brutes and bore their floggings accordingly; indeed, they were classed as formerly the hard drinkers were—there were the five-dozen men, as there had been the five-bottle men. His firm persuasion was that the existing discipline, or at least the reserved power of inflicting it, could not be abrogated.

Sir F. Burdett . . . The alterations which he [Hume] proposed had been over and over again recommended by captains, commanders and other experienced persons. . . . At a time like the present, it very ill became that House to say that the country could not afford the means of inducing men to enter the naval service by rewarding them according to the market price of their labour, but that the Government were obliged to seize upon the services of the most important class of the community, and to compel them to a course of duty at a less rate of remuneration than that which they could obtain from private employers. At a time of profound peace like the present, was it for the House to say to those who had performed the most arduous and perilous services for the country, that they were not to enjoy the common rights of humanity; that they were still to be dragged from their families and compelled to serve by terror and punishment, when they might, like other servants of the public, be tempted to perform their duties by proper remuneration? . . . His hon. friend did not propose to do away with all punishment, he only wished that the system should be gradually ameliorated; that some control should be exerted over the passions of the officers; that some interval should take place between the offence and the trial, that there might be time for reflection; in short, he wished only that something like a military court-martial should be adopted, and that sailors should not be subject to the most degrading punishment at the whim and caprice of one individual. . . . As to the plea of the navy having a portion of wretches among them, whose principles and conduct could not be subdued without the roughest discipline, the answer was plain—they ought not to let such persons into the navy, any more than they were allowed to be in the army. For what was the effect of it but to degrade the honest, honourable, gallant men of our fleets to the low and brutalising condition of discharged felons? . . . The question was whether the seamen of England ought not to be induced to enter the national service by a prospect of advantage; whether their situation, whilst serving, ought not to be made comfortable; and whether the means ought not to be afforded them of passing their old age in ease and security? The nation was quite rich enough, and it was bad economy to do likewise. . . . They were doing nothing more or less than continuing in this country and upon its native inhabitants, that system of slavery from which they seemed so anxious to relieve the natives of Africa. . . .

Sir George Clerk . . . If the wages given in a man-of-war were to be increased from 34s. to 40s. per month, still the merchant service would have the preference, as the men in merchant ships would enjoy a greater degree of liberty than the discipline of our navy could possibly allow. . . . With respect to the retired allowances . . . the fact was that after 21 years, whether worn out, or disabled, or not, a man was entitled to a retired pension of 1s. 6d. per day; and if a petty officer, his allowance would amount to £45 a year. . . .

Mr. Sykes bore testimony to the evils occasioned by impressment. Murders, assaults and other offences were frequently caused by it. . . .

The House divided: For the motion 23; against it 45.

C. THE REVOLUTIONARY AND NAPOLEONIC WARS

548. Fox's resolutions against the war with France, 18 Feb. 1793

(Cobbett's *Parliamentary History*, xxx, 431–432.)

1. That it is not for the honour or interest of Great Britain to make war upon France on account of the internal circumstances of that country, for the purpose either of suppressing or punishing any opinions and principles, however pernicious in their tendency, which may prevail there, or of establishing among the French people any particular form of government.

2. That the particular complaints which have been stated against the conduct of the French Government are not of a nature to justify war in the first instance, without having attempted to obtain redress by negotiation.

3. That it appears to this House, that in the late negotiation between H.M.'s Ministers and the agents of the French Government, the said Ministers did not take such measures as were likely to procure redress, without a rupture, for the grievances of which they complained; and particularly that they never stated distinctly to the French Government any terms and conditions, the accession to which, on the part of France, would induce H.M. to persevere in a system of neutrality.

4. That it does not appear that the security of Europe, and the rights of independent nations, which had been stated as grounds of war against France, have been

attended to by H.M.'s Ministers in the case of Poland, in the invasion of which unhappy country, both in the last year, and more recently, the most open contempt of the Law of Nations, and the most unjustifiable spirit of aggrandisement has been manifested, without having produced, as far as appears to this House, any remonstrance from H.M.'s Ministers.

5. That it is the duty of H.M.'s Ministers, in the present crisis, to advise H.M. against entering into engagements which may prevent Great Britain from making a separate peace whenever the interests of H.M. and his people may render such a measure advisable, or which may countenance an opinion in Europe that H.M. is acting in concert with other Powers for the unjustifiable purpose of compelling the people of France to submit to a form of government not approved by that nation.

549. Wilberforce on the French Revolutionary War, 11 Dec. 1828

(*Life of Wilberforce*, by his sons, II, p. 391.)

The extraordinary optimism of Pitt and Dundas about the duration of the Revolutionary War is well known. Wilberforce here refers to it. It receives fresh illustration from a letter written by Dundas on 12 Sept. 1792. Recent events, especially the massacres of royalist suspects in the Paris prisons, had produced, he said, a very 'inconvenient' influx of refugees from France. But that inconvenience was trifling compared with what it would be when the duke of Brunswick's invading army reached Paris and restored Louis XVI. A less amiable type of refugee would in that event be pouring into England in considerable numbers—"those concerned in the late atrocious proceedings" in Paris. "The residence of so many persons, dangerous from their principles and flagitious in their conduct, would be productive of serious harm to the peace and good order of this country." Dundas proposed to summon a Cabinet meeting the following week to consider what could be done either to prevent these Jacobin miscreants from landing, or to compel them "to give security for their peaceable and inoffensive conduct". He believed that the restored Bourbon Government would demand the extradition of all those who might flee from justice and take refuge in England.

I am myself persuaded that the war with France, which lasted so many years and occasioned such an immense expense of blood and treasure, would never have taken place but from Mr. Dundas's influence with Mr. Pitt, and his persuasion that we should be able with ease and promptitude, at a small expense of money or men, to take the French West India islands, and to keep them when peace should be restored: in truth, but for Mr. Dundas's persuasion that the war would soon be over. Mr. Burke had formed a very different judgement; and when, being present with Mr. Pitt and Mr. Dundas, the latter exclaimed, 'Well, Mr. Burke, we must go to war, for it will be a very short war', Mr. Burke replied, 'You must indeed go to war, but you greatly mistake in thinking it will soon be over; it will be a very long war, and a very dangerous war, but it is unavoidable'. The British Minister had no intention whatever, at that time, of dispossessing France of any of her continental dominions, and as for conquering France, Mr. Fox himself could not more consider it as an utter impossibility than they did. They by no means shared in Mr. Burke's persuasions concerning the proper object and nature of the war.

550. Arthur Young on the defence of the country, 1797

(A. Young, *National Danger and the Means of Safety* (1797), 73 pp.)

. . . You, gentlemen, the yeomen and farmers of England, whose lands smile with cultivation, and are covered with exuberant harvests; you, whose farms are spectacles of industry, and your houses the residence of ease and comfort; what steps have you personally taken to add to the defence of the country, and to enable you with effect to say, 'This house is my castle, I will defend it; this woman is my wife, or my daughter, and I will die ere a ruffian invader shall deprive me of her'? Have you enrolled yourself in a patriotic corps? Have you arms prepared for the hour when they may be necessary, or have you, in a contemptible sloth, rested in tranquil security, and trusted all to Government, when Governments show, by a similar indolence, that nations must be defended by themselves, or they will not be defended at all? Are these times for farmers to jog contentedly to market with samples that sell at prices unheard of, that mark the wealth diffused in every quarter, wealth to tempt both foreign and domestic foes to plunder, without a thought at giving security to riches, or duration to so many blessings? Ought we not, from internal regulation, to be able to say that our navy may become the sport of tempests, our regular troops may be defeated, but England never can be overrun; for every man that has a horse is in a corps of cavalry, and her infantry is as numerous as her property is diffused. . .

To see country gentlemen engaged in all the common pleasures of peace and plenty, in their farms, their gardens, their hunting and shooting, as if danger could never be at their doors; with their tenants and neighbours in equal supineness and equal security, while the rest of Europe is devouring by a new torrent of barbarous tyranny: to see such unthinking security, with only handfuls of armed yeomanry that ought immediately to be multiplied a hundred-fold, at such a period as this, is a spectacle truly horrid and debasing. . . .

. . . When we see young, hearty and active men sacrificing perhaps a day in the week to a violent exercise, for which an expensive horse is kept, it should seem, to the eye of reason, a sure proof that such a man is, perhaps of all others in the community, the person that might be called upon for the public service in case of necessity. . . . So proper indeed, that it is with some degree of astonishment I have seen them galloping after foxes, and at the same time shunning the corps of yeomanry-cavalry that have been raised in their vicinity. . . .

I wish propriety would allow the same use to be made of fox-hunting parsons; many active corps might thus be raised. And, in justice, I ought to add that I believe many of them would (were they permitted) most readily enrol for the service of their country. If ecclesiastical propriety prevents it with men of this description, there is no obstacle to their finding substitutes: and who are more called upon for such exertions? We all know the views with which the French would come; we well understand what their fraternisation means. The Church would be one of the first objects of pillage, and the clergy murdered or driven into exile. Partial ruin might attend some classes, but these men would lose their all. Now, then, let them show a prudent foresight to prevent an evil, which they certainly will not be prepared to bear. . . .

Upon the most moderate calculation, there are a million of horses of husbandry in England. If every farmer, having ten or upwards, enrolled in the proportion of one trooper for every ten horses, it would probably amount to 50,000. . . .

The following is the first expense of equipping a trooper in the Suffolk corps of yeomanry-cavalry: Jacket, waistcoat and surtout £6 5s. od.; Breeches £1 11s. 6d.; Boots £1 5s. od.; Gloves 2s. od.; Cravat 3s. od.; Helmet £1 6s. od.; Bridle 15s. od.; Goatskin 7s. 6d.; Light-horse collar 4s. 9d.; Breast-plate, &c. 3s. 6d.; Crooper 1s. 9d.; Cartouch-box 1s. od.; Cloak-pad and straps 7s. 6d.; Half covers, with holster & surcingle 10s. 8d.; Spurs and leathers 2s. 6d. [Total] £13 6s. 8d.

Serjeant paid by Government, and his horse billeted.

Sabre, pistol, powder, &c. ditto.

As the clothes last three years, this expense is for that period; or £4 –8s. 10d. per annum; and for the succeeding three years, no more than £3 –2s. 2d. per annum.

The County-subscription pays 2s. a day for exercising, which, at twelve days per annum, adds there (improperly in my opinion) £1 –4s. per annum more.

In the above ratio of £13 –6s. 8d. ONE HUNDRED THOUSAND HORSE are equipped for three years at the expense of no more than £1,333,333, or, per annum, £444,444!!!

At so very trifling an expense might this nation establish and discipline an irresistible force: an expense which might, with great propriety, be thrown on individuals; on those inert, selfish individuals who, though all the preceding articles have hitherto been paid by subscriptions, and even that time which was taken from their fox-hunting, would not enrol in corps to which they most readily resorted for protection when their own extravagant prices of corn occasioned riots, from which they were protected by men of far different feelings. And with still more propriety on those great and opulent landholders who, through the idle argument that these corps, ESTABLISHED BY AUTHORITY OF PARLIAMENT, were not constitutional, would not subscribe to their support, and discouraged their tenants from enrolling. . . .

Of the landed interest, who could produce so enormous a force for internal defence, not one man in a thousand, of those who could, with small inconvenience, appear in the yeomanry-corps, has enrolled. . . .

When the measures of security are obvious and easy, I look with regret and amazement at the apathy of mankind, crowding to places of public amusement, and pursuing, with unconcern, all the common gaieties and pleasures of life, which ought to be flat and insipid to minds of the least energy, when unaccompanied by any effort to add to the national security. . . . Follow the higher classes through the business, the languor or the pleasures of the day, what are the new exertions, the novel measures, what the provisions of defence; what resources never recurred to before are called into action on the spur of this eventful moment? Nothing:–the morning's lounge or the morning's ride, the social dinner, the gay evening, the amusements of former periods. To the eye of anxious penetration, nothing but a stupid infatuation seems to lull every mind in indolence and apathy. Quit a scene, the business of which is nonsense, and its pleasures contemptible; hasten to your estates, forge bayonets for your fowling pieces, prepare arms of every kind, connect yourself with your neighbours, arm your tenants. . . .

551. Lieutenant J. Smith (Queen's Regiment) to his mother, 3 June 1794

(*Logs of the Great Sea Fights, 1794–1805*, I, p. 55, ed. T. Sturges Jackson. Navy Records Society, 1899.)

The 'Glorious First of June' was the first considerable naval action of the war, but the greater part of the French fleet escaped, and so did the important convoy which Howe had desired to capture.

. . . After a cruise of a fortnight the fleet again returned to look into Brest, when intelligence was gained that the French fleet had sailed to protect their convoy. This news was brought to us on the 17th May. Lord Howe immediately followed them, steering directly out for America, the course they had taken. A few days afterwards several ships were retaken by us which had been captured by them, an evident proof that we were not far from them. In this situation Lord Howe very prudently burnt the recaptured ships to the amount of 14, and a French armed brig sloop and cutter. He seems to have had very accurate intelligence, for when we were despairing of seeing them, a strange fleet was seen on the morning of the 28th, which proved to be the French. In the evening a partial action ensued between our windward ships (for they were to windward of us) and their rear, in which our ships had the good fortune to cut off and take a first rate, *Le Révolutionnaire*, formerly the *Bretagne*. It began about 8 in the evening and ceased about 10. In this the *Royal George* had no share, being in the rear and our van only engaged. On the morning of the 29th the French were still to windward. The signal was made to form the line as most convenient, and the *Royal George* was in the van. They edged down towards us, and were led with great gallantry by a beautiful 80-gun ship. At 10 the firing began, when we were amply repaid for our inactivity on the preceding night. The brunt of the action lay upon us and the *Queen* and *Invincible*, who supported us most nobly. At one time we had the fire of five ships upon us, and I may venture to say we were much distinguished. Lord Howe made the signal at one o'clock to tack and break the enemy's line, which was complied with by the *Queen, Royal George, Russell*, and *Invincible*, the *Queen* leading. But not being able from our damaged state, having run the gauntlet of their whole line, we ran astern of it and so weathered them. The *Queen Charlotte* then broke it herself in a most gallant manner, and the enemy were thrown to leeward in confusion, but they formed afresh, and, from the disabled state of the *Queen, Royal George* and other leading ships, it was not held prudent to renew the action. On Friday and until Saturday evening we were in so thick a fog that we could scarce distinguish each other, but the fog clearing up then, the enemy were seen to leeward, when Lord Howe formed the line, but very prudently deferred the engagement till next morning as it was then near sunset. On Sunday morning the 1st June the signal was made to break the enemy's line and engage them close. The *Royal George*, seeing that a French three-decker would fall to the lot of one of our seventy-fours as the line was then formed, changed stations with her, and the whole fleet bore down, the enemy lying to receive us in very good order. The *Royal George* led the rear, and first broke through the line by throwing a very heavy fire into the bows of an 80-gun ship on her starboard (right) quarter, and then completely raking the *Terrible* (the three-decker) on her larboard or left quarter. She then ran close up to the *Terrible* and engaged her for some time, but the Frenchman did not choose to stand it, and, being less damaged in her rigging, made off. The line was soon most completely broken. The *Queen Charlotte* dismasted an 80-gun ship, and so completely raked her in three broadsides that she lost 350 men killed or wounded. In short, after a most severe action, six French ships are taken totally dismasted, four sunk, and six towed away by their fleet totally dismasted. In two hours after the action began I counted seven Frenchmen with not a stick standing above their decks. Of our ships, the *Marlborough* and the *Defence* are totally dismasted, the *Royal George* nearly so, but we are now in tolerable order again; the *Queen* very much damaged and behaved most gallantly. The French fought with desperate bravery and great rascality. . . . One Frenchman fired into another who had struck; another struck, having been fired into by their own ships for striking; a third was sunk by the *Royal Sovereign*, and a fourth sank after she was in our possession. One fired into us in a rascally manner. Another fired into the *Phaeton* in an equally rascally manner, and killed five men; and another would have been blown up by her captain after surrendering if the crew had permitted it. This villainous behaviour disgraces the gallant and desperate spirit with which they fought. 180 prisoners are on board us from the *Juste*, which was so raked by the *Queen Charlotte* that they say they lost 350 killed and wounded. It could not be otherwise–their 80-gun ships had 1,000, and their first-rates 1,500 men, and we were so close to them they must have fallen by hundreds. Our loss is trifling in comparison –20 killed and 76 wounded. . . .

552. Rear-Admiral Sir Horatio Nelson, K.B., to Lord St. Vincent, 3 Aug. 1798

(*Annual Register* (1798), Appendix to Chronicle, p. 167.)

The Battle of the Nile established British naval supremacy in the Mediterranean and locked up a French army in Egypt.

Vanguard, off the mouth of the Nile: My Lord, Almighty God has blessed his Majesty's arms in the late battle, by a great victory over the fleet of the enemy, whom I attacked at sun-set on the 1st of August, off the mouth of the Nile. The enemy were moored in a strong line of battle for defending the entrance of the bay (of Shoals) flanked by numerous gunboats, four frigates, and a battery of guns and mortars on an island in their van; but nothing could withstand the squadron your Lordship did me the honour to place under my command. Their high state of discipline is well known to you, and with the judgment of the captains, together with their valour and that of the officers and men of every description, it was absolutely irresistible.

Could anything from my pen add to the characters of the captains, I would write it with pleasure, but that is impossible.

I have to regret the loss of Captain Westcott, of the *Majestic*, who was killed early in the action; but the ship was continued to be so well fought by her first lieutenant, Mr. Cuthbert, that I have given him an order to command her till your Lordship's pleasure is known.

The ships of the enemy, all but two rear ships, are nearly dismasted, and those two, with two frigates, I am sorry to say, made their escape; nor was it, I assure you, in my power to prevent them. Captain Hood most handsomely endeavoured to do it, but I had no ship in a condition to support the *Zealous*, and I was obliged to call her in.

The support and assistance I have received from Captain Berry cannot be sufficiently expressed. I was wounded in the head and obliged to be carried off the deck, but the service suffered no loss by that event. Captain Berry was fully equal to the important service then going on, and to him I must beg leave to refer you for every information relative to this victory. He will present you with the flag of the second in command, that of the Commander-in-Chief being burnt in the *L'Orient*.

Herewith I transmit you lists of the killed and wounded, and the lines of battle of ourselves and the French.

English Line of Battle.

1. *Culloden*, T. Trowbridge, Captain, 74 guns, 590 men.
2. *Theseus*, R. W. Miller, Captain, 74 guns, 590 men.
3. *Alexander*, Alex. J. Ball, Captain, 74 guns, 590 men.
4. *Vanguard*, Rear-Admiral Sir Horatio Nelson, K.B., Edward Berry, Captain, 74 guns, 595 men.
5. *Minotaur*, T. Louis, Captain, 74 guns, 640 men.
6. *Leander*, T. B. Thompson, Captain, 50 guns, 343 men.
7. *Swiftsure*, B. Hallowell, Captain, 74 guns, 590 men.
8. *Audacious*, D. Gould, Captain, 74 guns, 590 men.
9. *Defence*, John Peyton, Captain, 74 guns, 590 men.
10. *Zealous*, Samuel Hood, Captain, 74 guns, 590 men.
11. *Orion*, Sir J. Saumarez, Captain, 74 guns, 590 men.
12. *Goliah*, Thos. Foley, Captain, 74 guns, 590 men.
13. *Majestic*, Geo. B. Westcott, Captain, 74 guns, 590 men.
14. *Bellerophon*, Henry D. E. Darby, Captain, 74 guns, 590 men.
    La Mutine brig.

French Line of Battle.

1. *Le Guerrier*, 74 guns, 700 men, taken.
2. *Le Conquérant*, 74 guns, 700 men, taken.
3. *Le Spartiate*, 74 guns, 700 men, taken.
4. *L'Aquilon*, 74 guns, 700 men, taken.
5. *Le Souverain Peuple*, 74 guns, 700 men, taken.
6. *Le Franklin*, Blanquet, First Contre-Admiral, 80 guns, 800 men, taken.
7. *L'Orient*, Brueys, Admiral and Commander-in-Chief, 120 guns, 1010 men, burnt.
8. *Le Tonnant*, 80 guns, 800 men, taken.
9. *L'Heureux*, 74 guns, 700 men, taken.
10. *Le Timoléon*, 74 guns, 700 men, burnt.
11. *Le Mercure*, 74 guns, 700 men, taken.
12. *Le Guillaume Tell*, Villeneuve, Second Contre-Admiral, 80 guns, 800 men, escaped.
13. *Le Généreux*, 74 guns, 700 men, escaped.

Frigates.

14. *La Diane*, 48 guns, 300 men, escaped.
15. *La Justice*, 44 guns, 300 men, escaped.
16. *L'Artémise*, 36 guns, 250 men, burnt.
17. *La Sérieuse*, 36 guns, 250 men, dismasted and sunk.

553. The landing of French troops in Ireland, 1798

(*Annual Register* (1798), Appendix to Chronicle, p. 197.)

The Rebellion had been suppressed (the rebels were defeated at Vinegar Hill in June) when a small French force arrived at Killala. A larger one arriving at Lough Swilly in October was scattered by a British squadron.

(a) *The Duke of Portland* (*Home Secretary*) *to the Lord Mayor of London, 26 Aug. 1798.*

. . . By official accounts received this morning from the Lord-Lieutenant of Ireland, it appears that three French frigates, unaccompanied by any transports, appeared in the Bay of Killala on the evening of the 22d inst., and landed about 700 men, who immediately took possession of the town of Killala and made a small party of the Prince of Wales's Fencible Regiment, consisting of an officer and 20 men, and some yeomen, prisoners. A large force was collected from different quarters, and every necessary preparation made for attacking the enemy.

(b) *Lord Castlereagh* (*Irish Sec.*) *to Wm. Wickham, 29 Aug. 1798.*

. . . I beg leave to acquaint you . . . that early on the 27th inst. the French attacked Lieut.-General Lake in a position he had taken at Castlebar, before his forces were collected, and compelled him to retire. The Lieut.-General reports that his loss of men is not considerable, but that he was obliged to leave behind him six pieces of cannon. . . . [*Ibid.*, p. 198.]

(c) *Lord Cornwallis* (*Lord-Lieut. of Ireland & Comm.-in-Chief*) *to Portland, 8 Sept. 1798.*

When I wrote to your Grace on the 5th I had every reason to believe, from the enemy's movement to Drumahain, that it was their intention to march to the north, and it was natural to suppose that they might hope that a French force would get into some of the bays in that part of the country, without a succour of which kind every point of direction for their march seemed equally desperate.

I received, however, very early in the morning of the 7th, accounts from Lieut.-General Lake that they had turned to their right to Drumkeirn, and that he had reason to believe that it was their intention to go to Boyle or Carrick on Shannon, in consequence of which, I hastened the march of the troops under my immediate command, in order to arrive before the enemy at Carrick, and directed Major-Gen. Moore, who was at Tubercurry, to be prepared, in the event of the enemy's movement to Boyle.

On my arrival at Carrick I found that the enemy had passed the Shannon at Balintra, where they attempted to destroy the bridge, but Lieut.-Gen. Lake followed them so closely that they were not able to effect it. Under these circumstances I felt pretty confident that one more march would bring this disagreeable warfare to a conclusion; and having obtained satisfactory information that the enemy had halted for the night at Cloone, I moved with the troops at Carrick at 10 o'clock on the night of the 7th to Mohill, and directed Lieut.-Gen. Lake to proceed at the same time to Cloone, which is about three miles from Mohill, by which movement I should be able either to join with Lieut.-Gen. Lake in the attack of the enemy if they should remain at Cloone, or to intercept their retreat if they should (as it was most probable) retire on the approach of the enemy.

On my arrival at Mohill soon after daybreak I found that the enemy had begun to move towards Granard. I therefore proceeded with all possible expedition to this place, through which I was assured, on account of a broken bridge, that the enemy must pass in their way to Granard, and directed Lieut.-Gen. Lake to attack the enemy's rear and impede their march as much as possible, without bringing the whole of his corps into action. Lieut.-Gen. Lake performed this service with his usual attention and ability, and the enclosed letter[1] which I have just received from him will explain the circumstances which produced the immediate surrender of the enemy's army. . . . [*Ibid.*, p. 198.]

554. Letters from the earl of Mornington, Governor-General of Bengal, on the French threat to India, 1798–1801

(Imperial Record Department, Delhi: Miscell. Records in the Foreign Department, vol. 65.)

Pondichery and the other French settlements in India were quickly captured at the beginning of the Revolutionary War but sepoy forces built up by French officers were in the pay of the Nizam of the Deccan, and of the Marathas; and Tipu of Mysore was intriguing with the French at the Isle de France. Hostilities started in Feb. 1799, and in May Tipu was killed while defending his capital, Seringapatam. Rainier commanded a small squadron in the East Indies. The French army in Egypt was defeated by Abercromby in 1801 and forced to capitulate whilst Baird's force from India was advancing across the desert towards Cairo.

(a) *to Vice-Admiral Rainier, 13 Dec. 1798:*

. . . The great object of all our efforts in the present crisis is to prevent the success of the joint designs of Tipu Sahib and of the French. On the one hand we must endeavour to intercept all communication by sea between Tipu and the French; on the other hand it is an equally urgent duty with the same view to strengthen our army in the Carnatic to the utmost possible degree. . . .

The period of the season, the state of the French army in Egypt, and every accompanying circumstance, leave little apprehension of the approach of any considerable French force to the coast of Malabar before the month of March or April. In the meanwhile the happy revival of our alliances with the Native Powers, the destruction of the French party in the Deccan, the advanced state of our preparations for war on the coasts of Coromandel and of Malabar, and the expected arrival of large reinforcements from the Cape and from Europe, place us in a commanding situation in the peninsula of India. Being convinced of the hostile nature of Tipu's views, I am resolved to avail myself of the present favourable moment to reduce his powers of offence either by the terror or by the actual employment of our arms, for it is evident that if we suffer him to continue his preparations for war without molestation, the same pressure of danger under which we have lately suffered, will come upon us in the next season with redoubled force. A blow struck now may save crores of rupees and thousands of lives by rendering Tipu unable to avail himself of the future assistance of France whenever she may be able to renew her attempts against India. . . .

My intention is to try the effect of negotiation with the Sultan in the first instance; if that should fail, war will become inevitable. . . .

[1] See *Annual Register* (1798), App. to Chron., p. 199.

If one or two of the enemy's large frigates from Batavia were to enter the Bay of Bengal during the present monsoon, they would be superior to any opposition which I could provide by arming Indiamen or such other vessels. . . .

I entirely concur with your Excellency's opinion that the defence of the Company's possessions on the coast of Malabar and the blockade of Tipu's ports demand your first attention. I confess that I do not now see the least prospect of any attempt of the French through the Persian Gulf, and I conclude that you will exercise your discretion (justified by the actual state of circumstances) in the execution of such parts of the orders of the Lords Commissioners of the Admiralty as relate to the establishment of a cruiser on that quarter.

(b) *to Vice-Admiral Rainier, 21 Jan. 1799:*

. . . The last intelligence from Europe received overland leads me to apprehend that the French will at length make an effort (which I have long expected) to send a squadron into these seas. Although I have little doubt that the vigilance of H.M.'s Ministers will take an early opportunity of reinforcing the fleet under your Excellency's command, I feel it to be the duty of those on the spot to provide with every practicable degree of precaution against the possibility of the French becoming superior to the British fleet in India. . . .

(c) *to Vice Admiral Rainier, 9 March 1799:*

. . . The state of the French army in Egypt is still a matter of uncertainty and doubt in my mind; for although advices of the 3rd and 19th November 1798 have been received from Captain Wilson at Mocha stating Alexandria to be in possession of the Turks, and Cairo invested by their army, this favourable intelligence is not confirmed by the Dispatches from Constantinople of 8th December 1798.

I am entirely ignorant of the state of our naval force at the mouth of the Arabian Gulf, no account having yet reached me of the arrival of Commodore Blankett or of any of our ships at that station. The French papers uniformly speak of the early departure of a squadron from France destined to co-operate with Bonaparte in the Arabian or Persian Gulf.

In the meanwhile I am confident that the distribution which your Excellency has made of the force under your command is the best calculated to meet all possible contingencies. The French cannot move in India without the aid of some Native Power. Tipu is the only Native Power from which they can expect assistance, and the actual station of your ships seems to render a junction between him and the French utterly impracticable, even if the latter should be able to penetrate to the Red Sea, should prove superior to Commodore Blankett, and should overcome all the difficulties of the navigation which they must encounter before they can reach Malabar. General Harris with an army (in the opinion of the most experienced officers) the most powerful and well appointed which ever took the field in India, entered Mysore. . . .

(d) *to Vice-Admiral Sir Roger Curtis, 1 March 1801:*

. . . On the 6th ult. I received Dispatches from Mr. Secretary Dundas dated 6th October 1800, communicating H.M.'s commands to me to furnish a force for the purpose of disturbing the French establishments on the coasts of the Red Sea, and creating a diversion in favour of the combined British and Turkish armies acting in Egypt from the Mediterranean. By the same Dispatches I was apprized that an armament under the command of Sir Home Popham conveying a regiment of British troops was destined to touch at the Cape, and after having landed the regiment from England and having embarked a regiment from the garrison of the Cape, to proceed to Mocha for the purpose of joining the detachment from India, the army under the command of Sir Ralph Abercromby was expected to reach the shores of Egypt in the month of December, and it was calculated that the armament under Sir Home Popham would arrive in the Red Sea in the course of the month of February. . . .

I determined immediately to abandon every other enterprise for the important object of co-operating with the British and Turkish acting in Egypt.

Notwithstanding the late arrival of H.M.'s commands, I have been enabled to direct towards the Red Sea a much more considerable force than that which H.M.'s Ministers have supposed to be applicable from the resources of India. This force, I trust, has already proceeded from Ceylon, under the command of Major-General Baird and Colonel Wellesley; its operations will derive great advantage from those of Rear-Admiral Blankett's squadron which proceeded towards the Red Sea from Bombay on 28th December with a body of troops and with a considerable reinforcement of armed cruizers, bomb and fire vessels equipped at that port under my orders, for the purpose of carrying into effect a plan concerted between the Rear-Admiral and me. . . .

555. The Treaty of Amiens, 27 March 1802

(Cobbett's *Parliamentary History*, XXXVI, 557–564.)

The Definitive Treaty of Peace between his Britannic Majesty and the French Republic, his Catholic Majesty, the Batavian Republic: signed at Amiens the 27th day of March 1802.

His Majesty the King of the United Kingdom of Great Britain and Ireland, and the First Consul of the French Republic, in the name of the French people, being animated with an equal desire to put an end to the calamities of war, have laid the foundation of peace in the Preliminary Articles signed at London the 1st of October 1801. . . .

Art. 1. There shall be peace, friendship and good understanding between H.M. the King of the United Kingdom of Great Britain and Ireland, his heirs and successors, on the one part; and the French Republic, H.M. the King of Spain, his heirs and successors, and the Batavian Republic, on the other part. The contracting parties shall give the greatest attention to maintain, between themselves and their States, a perfect harmony, and without allowing on either side any kind of hostilities by sea or by land, to be committed for any cause or under any pretence whatsoever. They shall carefully avoid everything which might hereafter affect the union happily re-established, and they shall not afford any assistance or protection, directly or indirectly, to those who should cause prejudice to any of them.

Art. 2. All the prisoners taken on either side, as well by land as by sea, and the hostages carried away or given during the war, and to this day, shall be restored without ransom in six weeks at latest, to be computed from the day of the exchange of the ratifications of the present Treaty, and on paying the debts which they have contracted during their captivity. Each contracting party shall respectively discharge the advances which have been made by any of the contracting parties for the subsistence and maintenance of the prisoners in the country where they have been detained. For this purpose a commission shall be appointed by agreement, which shall be specially charged to ascertain and regulate the compensation which may be due to either of the contracting Powers. The time and place where the Commissioners who shall be charged with the execution of this Article, shall assemble, shall also be fixed upon by agreement; and the said Commissioners shall take into account the expenses occasioned, not only by the prisoners of the respective nations but also by the foreign troops, who, before they were made prisoners, were in the pay or at the disposal of any of the contracting parties.

Art. 3. His Britannic Majesty restores to the French Republic and her Allies, namely, his Catholic Majesty and the Batavian Republic, all the possessions and colonies which belonged to them respectively, and which had been occupied or conquered by the British forces in the course of the war, with the exception of the island of Trinidad, and the Dutch possessions in the island of Ceylon.

Art. 4. His Catholic Majesty cedes and guarantees, in full right and sovereignty, to his Britannic Majesty, the island of Trinidad.

Art. 5. The Batavian Republic cedes and guarantees, in full right and sovereignty, to his Britannic Majesty, all the possessions and establishments in the island of Ceylon, which belonged before the war to the Republic of the United Provinces or to their East India Company.

Art. 6. The Cape of Good Hope remains in full sovereignty to the Batavian Republic, as it was before the war. The ships of every description belonging to the other contracting parties shall have the right to put in there and to purchase such supplies as they may stand in need of as heretofore without paying any other duties than those to which the ships of the Batavian Republic are subjected.

Art. 7. The territories and possessions of her most Faithful Majesty are maintained in their integrity, such as they were previous to the commencement of the war. Nevertheless, the limits of French and Portuguese Guiana shall be determined by the river Arawari. . . .

Art. 8. The territories, possessions and rights of the Ottoman Porte are hereby maintained in their integrity, such as they were previous to the war.

Art. 9. The Republic of the Seven Islands is hereby acknowledged.

Art. 10. The islands of Malta, Gozo and Comino shall be restored to the Order of St. John of Jerusalem, and shall be held by it upon the same conditions on which the Order held them previous to the war, and under the following stipulations:

i. The Knights of the Order, whose langues shall continue to subsist after the exchange of the ratifications of the present Treaty, are invited to return to Malta as soon as that exchange shall have taken place. They shall there form a General Chapter and shall proceed to the election of a Grand Master, to be chosen from amongst the natives of those nations which preserve langues, if no such election shall have been already made since the exchange of the ratifications of the preliminary Articles of Peace. It is understood that an election which shall have been made subsequent to that period, shall alone be considered as valid to the exclusion of every other which shall have taken place at any time previous to the said period.

ii. The Governments of Great Britain and of the French Republic, being desirous of placing the Order of St. John and the island of Malta in a state of entire independence on each of those Powers, do agree that there shall be henceforth no English nor French langues, and that no individual belonging to either of the said Powers shall be admissible into the Order.

iii. A Maltese langue shall be established, to be supported out of the land revenues and commercial duties of the island. There shall be dignities with appointments, and an Auberge appropriated to this langue. No proofs of nobility shall be necessary for the admission of knights into the said langue. They shall be competent to hold every office, and to enjoy every privilege, in the like manner as the knights of the other langues. The municipal, revenue, civil, judicial and other offices under the government of the island, shall be filled at least in the proportion of one-half by native inhabitants of Malta, Gozo and Comino.

iv. The forces of his Britannic Majesty shall evacuate the island and its dependencies within three months after the exchange of the ratifications, or sooner if it can be done. At that period the island shall be delivered up to the Order in the state in which it now is, provided that the Grand Master, or Commissioners fully empowered, according to the Statutes of the Order, be upon the island to receive possession, and that the force to be furnished by his Sicilian Majesty, as hereafter stipulated, be arrived there.

v. The garrison of the island shall, at all times, consist at least one-half of native Maltese; and the Order shall have the liberty of recruiting for the remainder of the garrison from the natives of those countries only that shall continue to possess Langues. The native Maltese troops shall be officered by Maltese; and the supreme command of the garrison, as well as the appointment of the officers, shall be vested in the Grand Master of the Order. . . .

vi. The independence of the islands of Malta, Gozo and Comino, as well as the present arrangement, shall be under the protection and guarantee of Great Britain, France, Austria, Russia, Spain and Prussia.

vii. The perpetual neutrality of the Order, and of the island of Malta and its dependencies, is hereby declared.

viii. The ports of Malta shall be open to the commerce and navigation of all nations who shall pay equal and moderate duties. . . .

ix. The Barbary States are excepted from the provisions of the two preceding paragraphs until, by means of an arrangement to be made by the contracting parties, the system of hostility which subsists between the said Barbary States, the Order of St. John, and the Powers possessing Langues, or taking part in the formation of them, shall be terminated.

x. The Order shall be governed, both in spiritual and temporal matters by the same Statutes that were in force at the time when the Knights quitted the island, so far as the same shall not be derogated from by the present Treaty.

xi. The stipulations contained in paragraphs iii, v, vii, viii and x shall be converted into laws and perpetual Statutes of the Order, in the customary manner. And the Grand Master (or, if he should not be in the island at the time of its restitution to the Order, his representative) as well as his successors, shall be bound to make oath to observe them punctually.

xii. His Sicilian Majesty shall be invited to furnish 2,000 men, natives of his dominions, to serve as a garrison for the several fortresses upon the island. This force shall remain there for one year from the period of the restitution of the island to the Knights; after the expiration of which term, if the Order of St. John shall not, in the opinion of the guaranteeing Powers, have raised a sufficient force to garrison the island and its dependencies . . . the Neapolitan troops shall remain until they shall be relieved by another force judged to be sufficient by the said Powers.

xiii. The several Powers specified in paragraph vi, *viz.* Great Britain, France, Austria, Russia, Spain and Prussia, shall be invited to accede to the present arrangement.

Art. 11. The French forces shall evacuate the kingdom of Naples, and the Roman territory. The English forces shall, in like manner, evacuate Porto Ferrajo, and generally all the ports and islands which they may occupy in the Mediterranean or in the Adriatic.

Art. 12. The evacuations, cessions and restitutions, stipulated for by the present Treaty, except where otherwise expressly provided for, shall take place in Europe within one month, in the continent and seas of America and of Africa within three months, and in the continent and seas of Asia within six months after the ratification of the present definitive Treaty.

Art. 13. In all the cases of restitution agreed upon by the present Treaty, the fortifications shall be delivered up in the state in which they may have been at the time of the signature of the Preliminary Treaty; and all the works which shall have been constructed since the occupation shall remain untouched.

It is further agreed that in all the cases of cession stipulated, there shall be allowed to the inhabitants, of whatever condition or nation they may be, a term of three years to be computed from the notification of this present Treaty, for the purpose of disposing of their property acquired and possessed either before or during the war, in which term of three years they may have the free exercise of their religion and enjoyment of their property.

The same privilege is granted in the countries restored to all those, whether inhabitants or others, who shall have made therein any establishments whatsoever during the time when those countries were in the possession of Great Britain.

With respect to the inhabitants of the countries restored or ceded, it is agreed that none of them shall be prosecuted, disturbed or molested in their persons or properties, under any pretext, on account of their conduct or political opinions, or of their attachment to any of the contracting Powers, nor on any other account, except that of debts contracted to individuals, or on account of acts posterior to the present Treaty.

Art. 14. All sequestrations imposed by any of the parties on the funded property, revenues or debts, of whatever description, belonging to any of the contracting Powers, or to their subjects or citizens, shall be taken off immediately after the signature of this definitive Treaty. The decision of all claims brought forward by individuals, the subjects or citizens of any of the contracting Powers respectively, against individuals, subjects or citizens of any of the others, for rights, debts, property or effects whatsoever, which, according to received usages and the law of nations, ought to revive at the period of peace, shall be heard and decided before competent tribunals; and in all cases prompt and ample justice shall be administered in the countries where the claims are made.

Art. 15. The fisheries on the coast of Newfoundland, and of the adjacent islands, and of the Gulf of St. Lawrence, are replaced on the same footing on which they were previous to the war. The French fishermen, and the inhabitants of St. Pierre and Miquelon, shall have the privilege of cutting such wood as they may stand in need of, in the bays of Fortune and Despair, for the space of one year from the date of the notification of the present Treaty.

Art. 16. In order to prevent all causes of complaint and dispute which may arise on account of prizes which may have been made at sea, after the signature of the preliminary Articles, it is reciprocally agreed that the vessels and effects which may have been taken in the British Channel and in the North Sea, after the space of 12 days, to be computed from the exchange of the ratifications of the said preliminary Articles, shall be restored on each side; that the term shall be one month from the British Channel and the North Seas, as far as the Canary islands, inclusively, whether in the ocean or in the Mediterranean; two months from the said Canary islands as far as the equator; and lastly, five months in all other parts of the world, without any exception, or any more particular description of time or place.

Art. 17. The Ambassadors, Ministers and other agents of the contracting Powers shall enjoy respectively in the States of the said Powers, the same rank, privileges, prerogatives and immunities which public agents of the same class enjoyed previous to the war.

Art. 18. The branch of the House of Nassau, which was established in the Republic formerly called the Republic of the United Provinces, and now the Batavian Republic, having suffered losses there as well in private property as in consequence of the change of Constitution adopted in that country, an adequate compensation shall be procured for the said branch of the House of Nassau for the said losses.

Art. 19. The present Definitive Treaty is declared common to the Sublime Ottoman Porte, the ally of his Britannic Majesty, and the Sublime Porte shall be invited to transmit its act of accession thereto in the shortest delay possible.

Art. 20. It is agreed that the contracting parties shall, on requisitions made by them respectively, or by their Ministers or persons or officers duly authorised to make the same, deliver up to justice persons accused of crimes of murder, forgery or fraudulent bankruptcy, committed within the jurisdiction of the requiring party, provided that this shall be done only when the evidence of the criminality shall be so authenticated as that the laws of the country where the person so accused shall be found would justify his apprehension and commitment for trial, if the offence had been there committed. . . . It is understood that this Article does not regard in any manner crimes of murder, forgery or fraudulent bankruptcy, committed antecedently to the conclusion of this definitive Treaty.

Art. 21. The contracting parties promise to observe sincerely and *bona fide* all the Articles contained in the present Treaty; and they will not suffer the same to be infringed, directly or indirectly, by their respective subjects or citizens, and the said contracting parties generally and reciprocally guarantee to each other all the stipulations of the present Treaty.

Art. 22. The present Treaty shall be ratified by the contracting parties in 30 days, or sooner if possible, and the ratifications shall be exchanged in due form at Paris. . . .

Cornwallis.
Joseph Bonaparte.
J. Nicolas de Azara.
R. J. Schimmelpenninck.

Separate Article. It is agreed that the omission of some titles, which may have taken place in the present Treaty, shall not be prejudicial to the Powers or to the persons concerned. . . .

556. Charles Yorke to the Attorney and Solicitor-General, 3 Oct. 1803
(Public Record Office, Home Office, 42/73.)

Renewed French aggressions in Italy, Switzerland and Holland led to the rupture of the Peace of Amiens in May 1803, and the English people, unaided by a single ally, had to meet the invasion threat.

It being judged highly expedient at this moment that H.M.'s confidential servants should receive the information requisite, in order to their being prepared, should events require it, to receive H.M.'s pleasure relative to the proclamation of martial law, I am to desire that you will take the following points into your consideration, and report to me, with as little delay as the importance of the subject will allow of, your opinion,

1st. Under what circumstances, particularly with respect to invasion, H.M. may proclaim martial law?
2nd. What is the effect of such proclamation?
3rd. What should be the form of it?
4th. What is the consequence of disobedience to such proclamation?

557. The mayor of Leicester (H. Clark) to Charles Yorke, 21 Oct. 1803
(Public Record Office, Home Office, 42/73.)

. . . If the enemy should effect a landing with forces sufficient to maintain for a time their standard in the country, it is evident that trade would be so checked that some thousands of people in this manufacturing town must be left without employ and without provision for a single day in advance. I am aware that the overseers are bound to maintain these people, and authorised to make [*sic*] as many rates on the richer inhabitants as may be necessary for the purpose – but if the paper money which shall be received for these levies should be so depreciated that the parish officers cannot purchase with it food enough to satisfy the poor, and if scarcely any coin should be in circulation (which seems probable enough as we have hardly any now) what course must be pursued to ensure a supply of what will be so absolutely necessary? ... I think that if whilst the enemy remains in force the people of this town were to suffer from the want of bread, *a fourth of the population* would join the French standard if they had an opportunity; and, if I am not utterly mistaken in my judgement, this renders what I have troubled you with a question of high moment in policy as well as justice. ...

558. George III to the bishop of Worcester (Dr. Hurd), 30 Nov. 1803

(B. Dobrée, *Letters of George III*, p. 264.)

... We are here in daily expectation that Buonaparte will attempt his threatened invasion, but the chances against his success seem so many that it is wonderful he persists in it. I own I place that thorough dependence on the protection of Divine Providence, that I cannot help thinking the usurper is encouraged to make the trial that his ill-success may put an end to his wicked purposes. Should his troops effect a landing, I shall certainly put myself at the head of mine, and my other armed subjects, to repel them; but as it is impossible to foresee the events of such a conflict, should the enemy approach too near to Windsor, I shall think it right the Queen and my daughters should cross the Severn, and shall send them to your episcopal palace at Worcester. By this hint I do not in the least mean they shall be any inconvenience to you, and shall send a proper servant and furniture for their accommodation. Should such an event arise, I certainly would rather that what I value most in life should remain during the conflict in your diocese and under your roof, than in any other place in the island.

559. Official Communication made to the Russian Ambassador at London on 19 Jan. 1805, explanatory of the views which His Majesty and the Emperor of Russia formed for the deliverance and security of Europe

(Cobbett's *Parliamentary Debates*, XXXI, 177–182.)

The document is too long to be reproduced here *in toto*. The full version is in C. K. Webster's *British Diplomacy* (1813–15) [1921].

The result of the communications which have been made by Prince Czartoriski to his Majesty's Ambassador at St. Petersburgh, and of the confidential explanations which have been received from your Excellency, has been laid before the King; and H.M. has seen with inexpressible satisfaction the wise, dignified and generous policy which the Emperor of Russia is disposed to adopt under the present calamitous situation of Europe. H.M. is also happy to perceive that the views and sentiments of the Emperor respecting the deliverance of Europe, and providing for its future tranquillity and safety, correspond so entirely with his own. He is therefore desirous of entering into the most explicit and unreserved explanations on every point connected with this great object, and of forming the closest union of councils, and concert of measures with his Imperial Majesty, in order, by their joint influence and exertions, to insure the co-operation and assistance of other Powers of the Continent, on a scale adequate to the magnitude and importance of an undertaking, on the success of which the future safety of Europe must depend.

For this purpose, the first step must be to fix as precisely as possible the distinct objects to which such a concert is to be directed.

These, according to the explanation given of the sentiments of the Emperor, in which H.M. entirely concurs, appear to be three:

1. To rescue from the dominion of France those countries which it has subjugated since the beginning of the Revolution, and to reduce France within its former limits, as they stood before that time.

2. To make such an arrangement with respect to the territories recovered from France, as may provide for their security and happiness, and may at the same time constitute a more effectual barrier in future against encroachments on the part of France.

3. To form, at the restoration of peace, a general agreement and guarantee for the mutual protection and security of different Powers, and for re-establishing a general system of public law in Europe.

The first and second objects are stated generally, and in their broadest extent; but neither of them can be properly considered in detail without reference to the nature and extent of the means by which they may be accomplished. The first is certainly that to which, without any modification or exception, H.M.'s wishes, as well as those of the Emperor, would be preferably directed, and nothing short of it can *completely* satisfy the views which both Sovereigns form for the deliverance and security of Europe. Should it be possible to unite in concert with Great Britain and Russia, the two other great military Powers of the Continent, there seems little doubt that such a union of force would enable them to accomplish all that is proposed. But if (as there is too much reason to imagine may be the case) it should be found impossible to engage Prussia in the Confederacy, it may be doubted whether such operations could be carried on in all the quarters of Europe, as would be necessary for the success of the whole of this project.

The second point of itself involves in it many important considerations. The views and sentiments by which H.M. and the Emperor of Russia are equally animated in endeavouring to establish this concert, are pure and disinterested.

The first view, therefore, with respect to any of the countries which may be recovered from France, must be to restore, as far as possible, their ancient rights, and provide for the internal happiness of their inhabitants; but in looking at this object, they must not lose sight of the general security of Europe, on which even that separate object must principally depend.

Pursuant to this principle, there can be no question that, whenever any of these countries are capable of being restored to their former independence, and of being placed in a situation in which they can protect it, such an arrangement must be most congenial to the policy and the feelings on which this system is founded: but there will be found to be other countries among those now under the dominion of France, to which these considerations cannot apply, where either the ancient relations of the country are so completely destroyed that they cannot be restored, or where independence would be merely nominal, and alike inconsistent with security for the country itself, or for Europe; happily the larger number is of the first description. Should the arms of the Allies be successful to the full extent of expelling France from all the dominions she has acquired since the Revolution, it would certainly be the first object, as has already been stated, to re-establish the republics of the United Provinces and Switzerland, the territories of the King of Sardinia, Tuscany, Modena (under the protection of Austria) and Naples. But the territories of Genoa, of the Italian Republic, including the three Legations, Parma and Placentia; and on the other side of Europe, the Austrian Netherlands, and the States which have been detached from the German Empire on the left bank of the Rhine, evidently belong to the second class. With respect to the territories enumerated in Italy, experience has shown how little disposition existed in some, and how little means in any, to resist the aggression or influence of France. The King of Spain was certainly too much a party to the system of which so large a part of Europe has been a victim, to entitle the former interests of his family in Italy to any consideration; nor does the past conduct of Genoa, or any of the other States, give them any claim, either of justice or liberality. It is also obvious that these separate petty sovereignties would never again have any solid existence in themselves, and would only serve to weaken and impair the force which ought to be, as much as possible, concentrated in the hands of the chief Powers in Italy.

It is needless to dwell particularly on the state of the Netherlands. Events have put out of the question the restoration of them to the House of Austria; they are therefore necessarily open to new arrangements, and evidently can never exist separate and independent. Nearly the same considerations apply to the Ecclesiastical Electorates and the other territories on the left bank of the Rhine, after their being once detached from the Empire, and the former possessors of them indemnified. There appears, therefore, to be no possible objection, on the strictest principles of justice and public morality, to making such a disposition with respect to any of these territories as may be most conducive to the general interests; and there is evidently no other mode of accomplishing the great and beneficent object of re-establishing (after so much misery and bloodshed) the safety and repose of Europe on a solid and permanent basis. It is fortunate too that such a plan of arrangements as is in itself essential to the end proposed, is also likely to contribute, in the greatest degree, to secure the means by which that great end can best be promoted.

It is evidently of the utmost importance, if not absolutely indispensable for this purpose, to secure the vigorous and effectual co-operation both of Austria and Prussia; but there is little reason to hope that either of those Powers, and especially Prussia, will be brought to embark in the common cause, without the prospect of obtaining some important acquisition to compensate for its exertions. On the grounds which have been already stated, H.M. conceives that nothing could so much contribute to the general security as giving to Austria fresh means of resisting the views of France on the side of Italy, and placing Prussia in a similar situation with respect to the Low Countries; and the relative situations of the two Powers would naturally make those the quarters to which their views would respectively be directed.

In Italy, sound policy would require that the power and influence of the King of Sardinia should be augmented, and that Austria should be replaced in a situation which may enable her to afford an immediate and effectual support to his dominions, in case of their being attacked. H.M. sees with satisfaction, from the secret and confidential communications recently received through your Excellency, that the views of the Court of Vienna are perfectly conformable to this general principle, and that the extension at which she aims, might not only safely be admitted, but might even be increased, with advantage to the general interest. In other respects H.M. entirely concurs in the outline of the arrangement which he understands the Emperor of Russia to be desirous of seeing effected in this quarter. H.M. considers it as absolutely necessary for the general security that Italy should be completely rescued both from the occupation and influence of France, and that no Powers should be left within it who are not likely to enter into a general system of defence for maintaining its independence. For this purpose it is essential that the countries now composing what is called the Italian Republic should be transferred to other Powers. In distributing these territories an increase of wealth and power should undoubtedly be given to the King of Sardinia; and it seems material that his possessions, as well as the Duchy of Tuscany (which it is proposed to restore to the Grand Duke) should be brought into immediate contact, or ready communication with those of Austria. On this principle, the whole of the territories which now compose the Ligurian Republic might, it is conceived, be annexed to Piedmont.

Supposing the efforts of the Allies to have been completely successful, and the two objects already discussed to have been fully obtained, H.M. would nevertheless consider this salutary work as still imperfect if the restoration of peace were not accompanied by the most effectual measures for giving solidity and permanence to the system which shall thus have been established. Much will undoubtedly be effected for the future repose of Europe by these territorial arrangements, which will furnish a more effectual barrier than has before existed against the ambition of France. But in order to render this security as complete as possible, it seems necessary, at the period of a general pacification, to form a Treaty to which all the principal Powers of Europe should be parties, by which their respective rights and possessions, as they shall then have been established, shall be fixed and recognised; and they should all bind themselves mutually to protect and support each other against any attempt to infringe them. It should re-establish a general and comprehensive system of public law in Europe, and provide, as far as possible, for repressive future attempts to disturb the general tranquillity; and above all, for restraining any projects of aggrandisement and ambition similar to those which have produced all the calamities inflicted on Europe since the disastrous era of the French Revolution.

560. Vice-Admiral Collingwood, Commander-in-Chief off Cadiz, to the Admiralty, 22 Oct. 1805

(*Annual Register* (1805), Appendix to Chronicle, p. 140.)

Canning's moving tribute to England's greatest sailor, in a letter, dated 11 Nov. 1805, is an appropriate introduction to Collingwood's Despatch, addressed to Wm. Marsden at the Admiralty, announcing the victory at Trafalgar: ". . . Poor, dear, glorious Lord Nelson! I shook hands with him on board the *Victory* the day before he sailed—and he promised we should soon hear from him. I knew him not before that day—but, though even that short acquaintance makes one's regret a private as well as, in common with all the world, a public grief (and I have really felt as if I had lost a friend) yet would I not give up for any consideration the satisfaction of having passed those few hours in contemplating, in the very theatre of his glory, a character the most heroic that modern times have produced. It will always warm one's heart—the recollection of that day—of the admiration with which he was evidently looked-up to by all around him—of the enthusiastic patriotism which he appeared so sincerely to feel himself, and which he had the talent of communicating and making the soul and spirit of action in all who acted with him. He shewed us on the map the station that he should take, and the plan that he should pursue to draw the enemy out, and having them out, to bring them to action. He has done all and more than all. When shall we find such another?" (*Harewood MSS.*)

Euryalus, off Cape Trafalgar: The ever-to-be-lamented death of Vice-Admiral Lord Viscount Nelson, who, in the late conflict with the enemy, fell in the hour of victory, leaves to me the duty of informing my Lords Commissioners of the Admiralty, that on the 19th inst. it was communicated to the Commander-in-Chief, from the ships watching the motions of the enemy in Cadiz, that the combined fleet had put to sea. As they sailed with light winds westerly, his Lordship concluded their destination was the Mediterranean, and immediately made all sail for the Straits entrance with the British squadron, consisting of 27 ships, three of them sixty-fours, where his Lordship was informed by Captain Blackwood (whose vigilance in watching, and giving notice of the enemy's movements, has been highly meritorious) that they had not yet passed the Straits.

On Monday the 21st inst., at daylight, when Cape Trafalgar bore east by south about seven leagues, the enemy was discovered six or seven miles to the eastward, the wind about west, and very light. The Commander-in-Chief immediately made the signal for the fleet to bear up in two columns, as they formed in order of sailing: a mode of attack his Lordship had previously directed, to avoid the inconvenience and delay in forming a line of battle in the usual manner. The enemy's line consisted of 33 ships (of which 18 were French and 15 Spanish) commanded in chief by Admiral Villeneuve; the Spaniards, under the direction of Gravina, wore, with their heads to the northward, and formed their line of battle with great closeness and correctness; but as the mode of attack was unusual, so the structure of their line was new; it formed a crescent convexing to leeward, so that, in leading down to their centre, I had both their van and rear abaft the beam. Before the fire opened, every alternate ship was about a cable's length to windward of her second ahead and astern, forming a kind of double line, and appeared, when on their beam, to leave a very little interval between them, and this without crowding their ships. Admiral Villeneuve was in the *Bucentaure*, in the centre, and the *Prince of Asturias* bore Gravina's flag in the rear, but the French and Spanish ships were mixed without any apparent regard to order of national squadron.

As the mode of our attack had been previously determined on, and communicated to the Flag Officers and Captains, few signals were necessary, and none were made except to direct close order as the lines bore down. The Commander-in-Chief, in the *Victory*, led the weather-column, and the *Royal Sovereign*, which bore my flag, the lee.

The attack began at 12 o'clock, by the leading ships of the columns breaking through the enemy's line, the Commander-in-Chief about the tenth ship from the van, the second in command about the twelfth from the rear, leaving the van of the enemy unoccupied; the succeeding ships breaking through in all parts astern of their leaders, and engaging the enemy at the muzzles of their guns. The conflict was severe; the enemy's ships were fought with a gallantry highly honourable to their officers; but the attack on them was irresistible, and it pleased the Almighty Disposer of all events to grant his Majesty's arms a complete and glorious victory. About 3 p.m. many of the enemy's ships having struck their colours, their line gave way. Admiral Gravina, with 10 ships, joining their frigates to leeward, stood towards Cadiz. The five headmost ships in their van tacked, and, standing to the southward, to windward of the British line, were engaged, and the sternmost of them taken; the others went off, leaving to H.M.'s squadron 19 ships of the line, of which two are first-rates, the *Santissima Trinidada* and the *Santa Anna*, with three Flag officers, *viz*. Admiral Villeneuve the Commander-in-Chief, Don Ignatio Maria D'Aliva, Vice-Admiral, and the Spanish Rear-Admiral Don Balthazar Hidalgo Cisneros.

After such a victory it may appear unnecessary to enter into encomiums on the particular parts taken by the several commanders; the conclusion says more·on the subject than I have language to express; the spirit which animated all was the same: when all exert themselves zealously in their country's service, all deserve that their high merits should stand recorded; and never was high merit more conspicuous than in the battle I have described.

The *Achille*, a French 74, after having surrendered, by some mismanagement of the Frenchmen, took fire and blew up. Two hundred of her men were saved by the tenders.

A circumstance occurred during the action which so strongly marks the invincible spirit of British seamen when engaging the enemies of their country, that I cannot resist the pleasure I have in making it known to their Lordships. The *Temeraire* was boarded, by accident or design, by a French ship on one side and a Spaniard on the other; the contest was vigorous but in the end the combined ensigns were torn from the poop and the British hoisted in their places.

Such a battle could not be fought without sustaining a great loss of men. I have not only to lament, in common with the British navy and the British nation, in the fall of the Commander-in-Chief, the loss of a hero whose name will be immortal and his memory ever dear to his country, but my heart is rent with the most poignant grief for the death of a friend to whom, by many years' intimacy and a perfect knowledge of the virtues of his mind, which inspired ideas superior to the common race of men, I was bound by the strongest ties of affection; a grief to which even the glorious occasion in which he fell does not bring the consolation which perhaps it ought. His Lordship received a musket ball in his left breast, about the middle of the action, and sent an officer to me immediately, with his last farewell, and soon after expired. I have also to lament the loss of those excellent officers, Captains Duff of the *Mars* and Cooke of the *Bellerophon*; I have yet heard of none others. I fear the numbers that have fallen will be found very great when the returns come to me, but it having blowed a gale of wind ever since the action, I have not yet had it in my power to collect any reports from the ships. The *Royal Sovereign* having lost her masts except the tottering foremast, I called the *Euryalus* to me while the action continued, which ship lying within hail, made my signals; a service Captain Blackwood performed with great attention. After the action I shifted my flag to her, that I might more easily communicate my orders to, and collect the ships, and towed the *Royal Sovereign* out to seaward. The whole fleet were now in a very perilous situation, many dismasted, all shattered, in 13 fathoms water off the shoals of Trafalgar, and when I made the signal to prepare to anchor, few of the ships had an anchor to let go, their cables being shot, but the same good Providence which aided us through such a day preserved us in the night by the wind shifting a few points and drifting the ships off the land, except four of the captured dismasted ships which are now at anchor off Trafalgar, and I hope will ride safe until those gales are over. Having thus detailed the proceedings of the fleet on this occasion I beg to congratulate their Lordships on a victory which, I hope, will add a ray to the glory of H.M.'s crown and be attended with public benefit to our country.

The order in which the ships of the British squadron attacked the combined fleets:
Van: Victory, Temeraire, Neptune, Conqueror, Leviathan, Ajax, Orion, Agamemnon, Minotaur, Spartiate, Britannia, Africa, Euryalus, Sirius, Phoebe, Naiad, Pickle schooner, Entreprenante cutter.
Rear: Royal Sovereign, Mars, Belleisle, Tonnant, Bellerophon, Colossus, Achille, Polyphemus, Revenge, Swiftsure, Defence, Thunderer, Defiance, Prince, Dreadnought.

561. *The Times* on the Battle of Trafalgar, 7 Nov. 1805

In a *second Edition* of our Paper of yesterday, published on occasion of the most GLORIOUS, and at the same time the most *afflicting* intelligence which has ever elated or depressed the British nation, we stated briefly the important fact, that *a Russian and Prussian force* had taken possession of Hanover. This satisfactory information, completely decisive of the disposition of Prussia, has reached us in too authentic shape to admit of any doubt. . . .

The official account of the late Naval Action, which terminated in the most decisive victory that has ever been achieved by British skill and gallantry, will be found in our Paper of this day. That the triumph, great and glorious as it is, has been dearly bought, and that such was the general opinion, was powerfully evinced in the deep and universal affliction with which the news of Lord Nelson's death was received. The victory created none of those enthusiastic emotions in the public mind, which the success of our naval arms have [*sic*] in every former instance produced. There was not a man who did not think that the life of the Hero of the Nile was too great a price for the capture and destruction of 20 sail of French and Spanish men of war. No ebullitions of popular transport, no demonstrations of public joy, marked this great and important event. The honest and manly feeling of the people appeared as it should have done: they felt an inward satisfaction at the triumph of their favourite arms; they mourned with all the sincerity and poignancy of domestic grief, their HERO slain.

To the official details, we are enabled to add the following particulars respecting the death of as great an Admiral as ever wielded the naval thunder of Britain. When Lord Nelson found that by his skilful manœuvres he had placed the enemy in such a situation that they could not avoid an engagement, he displayed the utmost animation, and his usual confidence of victory. He said to Captain Hardy, and the other Officers who surrounded him on the quarter-deck, 'Now they cannot escape us, I think we shall at least make sure of 20 of them. I shall probably lose a leg, but that will be purchasing a victory cheaply.' About two hours before the close of the action, His Lordship received a wound in the shoulder from a musket-ball, which was fired from the tops of the *Santissima Trinidada*, with which ship he was closely engaged. The ball penetrated his breast, and he instantly fell; he was immediately carried below, and the surgeons pronounced the wound *mortal*. His Lordship received the intelligence with all the firmness and pious resignation to the will of Divine Providence, of which he has given such frequent and signal examples during his brilliant course of peril and of glory. He immediately sent an Officer to Admiral Collingwood, the second in command, with his instructions for continuing the action which he had so gloriously commenced, and the melancholy bequest of his last farewell.

During the short interval between his receiving his wound and his final dissolution, he remained perfectly collected, displaying in his last moments the heroism that had marked every action of his glorious life. In that trying moment, 'cut off from nature and from glory's course', all his anxiety, all his thoughts, were directed to his country and her fame.

A few minutes before he expired he sent for Captain Hardy; when the Captain came, he enquired how many of the enemy's ships had struck. The Captain replied that, as nearly as he could ascertain, 15 sail of the line had struck their colours. His Lordship then, with that fervent piety which so strongly marked his character, returned thanks to the Almighty; then turning to Captain Hardy, he said, 'I know I am dying. I could have wished to survive to breathe my last upon British ground, but the will of God be done.' In a few moments he expired!!

If ever there was a man who deserved to be 'praised, wept and honoured' by his country, it is Lord Nelson. His three great naval achievements have eclipsed the brilliancy of the most dazzling victories in the annals of English daring. If ever there was a hero who merited the honours of a public funeral, and a public mourning, it is the pious, the modest, and the gallant Nelson, the darling of the British navy, whose death has plunged a whole nation into the deepest grief; and to whose talents and bravery, even the enemy he has conquered will bear testimony.

The action appears to have been gallantly contested by the French and Spaniards. Their object in risking an encounter with such a fleet, commanded by such a man, must have been one of imperious necessity at this moment; no less, we suspect, than a bold effort to acquire a complete ascendancy in the Mediterranean. Had they succeeded in liberating that portion of the Spanish navy which is confined to the port of Carthagina by the bare apprehension of an English squadron, their united force would have amounted to upwards of 40 sail of the line. There are also some ships at Toulon, and the Rochefort squadron, with its usual success, might perhaps have also added its strength to the combined force. With such a port as Toulon to take refuge in, a fleet of this extent, under Commanders of common capacity, must have occupied a very large portion indeed of our naval strength. . . .

There was a partial illumination throughout the Metropolis last night. A general one will take place this evening.

562. The secret committee of the Court of Directors to the Governor-General-in-Council, 24 Sept. 1807

(Imperial Record Department, Government of India.)

The Russian threat to the security of India did not become a reality until the 1870s, but in 1807, when Alexander I made peace with Napoleon at Tilsit and agreed to make war against England, plans were drawn up for a joint Franco-Russian advance through Central Asia against British India.

The events which have recently taken place in the north of Europe and the conclusion of a peace between Russia and France on terms which are certainly not favourable, and may possibly be highly prejudicial to the interests of the British Empire, renders it our indispensable duty to call your early and serious attention to the defence of our Indian territories, not merely with a view to meet an attack from any of the native Powers aided by an inconsiderable body of Europeans, but to withstand the efforts of France in conjunction perhaps with Persia and even with Russia, and the invasion of Hindostan on its north-western frontier by a numerous and powerful European force.

It is impossible not to admit that they would have to encounter many difficulties and to surmount many obstacles before such a plan could be carried into effect, but however improbable its execution may appear, the character of the present ruler of France renders it by no means unlikely that the scheme will be attempted, and that every effort of force and intrigue will be employed for the attainment of his object and the destruction of British power in India.

The mission of Sir Harford Jones to the Court of Persia is the only measure in our power to adopt at the present moment for the purpose of counteracting the intrigues of France in that country, and we recommend to your consideration to omit no means of conciliation that may tend to inspire the native Powers of India, and more particularly the countries situated between the dominions of Persia and our territories in Hindostan, with a conviction that it is for their interests to unite with us in vigorously opposing an invasion of such a description. We entertain the confident expectation that the system of moderation and the sincere desire of peace which we have manifested in our intercourse with the native Powers will by this time have convinced them that their condition is not likely to be bettered by the substitution of any other European Power in India or even by the aggrandisement of any one amongst themselves. It will be very satisfactory to us to find that you have been enabled to form such connections with the countries to the westward of Lahore and also with the Sikh chieftains and other States in the Punjab, and to the westward of the Jumna as may secure their cordial co-operation in assisting any invasion on the side of Persia without departing from the system which has been adopted on our part of avoiding as much as possible any interference in their internal concerns or any other defensive engagements that might involve us in future contests. You will of course endeavour by employing native emissaries for that purpose to procure constant intelligence of the state of affairs in those countries and of the dispositions and view of their rulers. . . .

If Russia enters into the scheme and embarks a considerable force on the Caspian, proceeding from Astrakhan to Asterabad, we have been taught to believe that with the assistance and co-operation of Persia the march of an army from the Caspian to the banks of the Indus would be attended with little difficulty, and would be accomplished within a very short period. The other routes by which a European army could march either from the Black Sea or from Syria through Persia have for several years been the subject of discussion in this country, and are particularly adverted to in a letter from Lieutenant-Colonel Malcolm to the Earl of Elgin, H.M.'s Ambassador at Constantinople. . . .

We have reason to believe the amount of European force now in India or on the passage, exclusive of Ceylon, is little short of 24,000 men, and it is the intention of H.M.'s Ministers with a view to the emergency to which we have alluded, to have a large additional force disposable at any period and ready to be transported to India at the shortest notice of any preparations carrying on in France or elsewhere. They do not deem it expedient to adopt that measure in the first instance and on the mere possibility of the attempt being made, because they are unwilling either that we should incur unnecessarily such a large additional expense, or that the country should be deprived of the power of employing those troops in other quarters, if it should eventually happen that they would not be required in India. Immediate measures, however, will be taken for completing our corps of artillery to its full establishment, and if possible also for increasing the effective strength of H.M.'s regiments of infantry and our European battalions and perhaps of increasing the amount of European cavalry.

Whatever additions you may think it necessary to make to your native army for the purpose of meeting any attack on the side of Persia, we cannot help suggesting to your consideration the expediency of raising (whenever you may deem it proper to prepare for such an emergency, and that hostilities shall evidently be unavoidable) a large body of irregular horse in corps officered or at least commanded by Europeans with a view to impede the march of the enemy's army by cutting off their supplies, laying waste the country through which they must pass, and constantly harassing them in every mode and direction. We conceive that a numerous and well appointed body of light field artillery would be of essential service in such a contest, more especially as your enemy would spare no effort to be amply provided in that respect, and we have no doubt that the state of the fortifications and magazines particularly in the north-western provinces of Hindostan will not fail to engage your attention.

It may also be a fit subject for your consideration whether by the employment of gunboats or other vessels at Bombay you may not oppose a serious obstacle to a hostile army attempting to cross or navigate the Indus. . . .

563. Canning's speech in the House of Commons, 15 June 1808, on the Spanish rising

(Cobbett's *Parliamentary Debates*, XI, 889–891.)

With the Spanish rising against the French invaders, the war assumed a national character, and the British Foreign Secretary saw prospects of Europe's deliverance from Napoleon's tyranny.

. . . I declare to the House and to the country that H.M.'s Ministers see with as deep and lively an interest as my right hon. friend [Sheridan] the noble struggle which a part of the Spanish nation is now making to resist the unexampled atrocity of France, and to preserve the independence of their country; and that there exists the strongest disposition on the part of the British Government to afford every practicable aid in a contest so magnanimous. In endeavouring to afford this aid, Sir, it will never occur to us to consider that a state of war exists between Spain and Great Britain. We shall proceed upon the principle that any nation of Europe that starts up with a determination to oppose a Power which, whether professing insidious peace or declaring open war, is the common enemy of all nations, whatever may be the existing political relations of that nation with Great Britain, becomes instantly our essential ally. In that event H.M.'s Ministers will have three objects in view. The first, to direct the united efforts of the two countries against the common foe; the second, to direct those efforts in a way which shall be most beneficial to the new Ally; the third, to direct them in a manner conducive to peculiarly British interests. But, Sir, of those objects, the last will be out of the question as compared with the other two.

564. W. J. Bankes, M.P., to his grandmother, Mrs. Bankes, 22 Aug. 1811

(Kingston Hall MSS.)

. . . At Porchester we saw the French prisoners, who amount to upwards of 5000. They are wonderfully ingenious and make abundance of toys and trinkets for sale; but what struck me the most was a number who are kept apart by themselves entirely naked, and some almost starved to appearance. These I found upon enquiry are as healthy naturally as the rest, and have the same clothes and victuals allowed them, but have such a wonderful passion for gaming that they will not only stake and lose their clothes off their backs, but their food for many days to come, and will rather absolutely starve than desist. The keeper told me that these habits are so constantly allied with thieving that if he were to let out these bad ones amongst the rest, he thinks they would be torn to pieces. I saw the whole number fed: it is shocking to see how like brutes they are. . . .

565. Wellington to Earl Bathurst, 24 July 1812

(Gurwood, *Selections from Wellington's Despatches*, p. 609.)

Flores de Avila, 24th July, 1812.

My aide de camp, Captain Lord Clinton, will present to your Lordship this account of a victory which the allied troops under my command gained in a general action, fought near Salamanca on the evening of the 22nd inst., which I have been under the necessity of delaying to send till now, having been engaged ever since the action in the pursuit of the enemy's flying troops.

In my letter of the 21st, I informed your Lordship that both armies were near the Tormes; and the enemy crossed that river with the greatest part of his troops, in the afternoon, by the fords between Alba de Tormes and Huerta, and moved by their left towards the roads leading to Ciudad Rodrigo.

The allied army, with the exception of the 3rd division, and General D'Urban's cavalry, likewise crossed the Tormes in the evening by the bridge of Salamanca and the fords in the neighbourhood; and I placed the troops in a position, of which the right was upon one of the 2 heights called Dos Arapiles, and the left on the Tormes, below the ford of Sta Marta.

The 3rd division, and Brig. General D'Urban's cavalry, were left at Cabrerizos, on the right of the Tormes, as the enemy had still a large corps on the heights above Babilafuente, on the same side of the river; and I considered it not improbable that, finding our army prepared for them in the morning on the left of the Tormes, they would alter their plan, and manœuvre by the other bank.

In the course of the night of the 21st, I received intelligence, of the truth of which I could not doubt, that General Chauvel had arrived at Pollos on the 20th with the cavalry and horse artillery of the army of the North, to join Marshal Marmont; and I was quite certain that these troops would join him on the 22nd or 23rd at latest.

There was no time to be lost therefore; and I determined that, if circumstances should not permit me to attack him on the 22nd, I would move towards Ciudad Rodrigo without further loss of time, as the difference of the numbers of cavalry might have made a march of manœuvre, such as we have had for the last 4 or 5 days, very difficult, and its result doubtful.

During the night of the 21st, the enemy had taken possession of the village of Calvarassa de Arriba, and of the heights near it called N. S. de la Peña, our cavalry being in possession of Calvarassa de Abaxo; and shortly after daylight, detachments from both armies attempted to obtain possession of the more distant from our right of the 2 hills called Dos Arapiles. The enemy, however, succeeded; their detachments being the strongest, and having been concealed in the woods nearer the hill than we were; by which success they strengthened materially their own position, and had in their power increased means of annoying ours.

In the morning the light troops of the 7th division, and the 4th cacadores belonging to General Pack's brigade, were engaged with the enemy on the height called N. S. de la Peña, on which height they maintained themselves with the enemy throughout the day. The possession by the enemy, however, of the more distant of the Arapiles rendered it necessary for me to extend the right of the army *en potence* to the height behind the village of Arapiles, and to occupy that village with light infantry; and here I placed the 4th division, under the command of Lieut. General the Hon. L. Cole; and although, from the variety of the enemy's movements, it was difficult to form a satisfactory judgment of his intentions, I considered that upon the whole his objects were upon the left of the Tormes. I therefore ordered Major General the Hon. E. Pakenham, who commanded the 3rd division in the absence of Lieut. General Picton, on account of ill health, to move across the Tormes with the troops under his command, including Brig. General D'Urban's cavalry, and to place himself behind Aldea Tejada; Brig. General Bradford's brigade of Portuguese infantry, and Don Carlos de España's infantry, having been moved up likewise to the neighbourhood of Las Torres, between the 3rd and 4th divisions.

After a variety of evolutions and movements, the enemy appears to have determined upon his plan about 2 in the afternoon; and, under cover of a very heavy cannonade, which, however, did us but very little damage, he extended his left, and moved forward his troops, apparently with an intention to embrace, by the position of his troops, and by his fire, our post on that of the two Arapiles which we possessed, and from thence to attack and break our line, or, at all events, to render difficult any movement of ours to our right.

The extension of his line to his left, however, and its advance upon our right, notwithstanding that his troops still occupied very strong ground, and his position was well defended by cannon, gave me an opportunity of attacking him, for which I had long been anxious. I reinforced our right with the 5th division, under Lieut. General Leith, which I placed behind the village of Arapiles, on the right of the 4th division, and with the 6th and 7th divisions in reserve; and as soon as these troops had taken their station, I ordered Major General the Hon. E. Pakenham to move forward with the 3rd division and General D'Urban's cavalry, and 2 squadrons of the 14th light dragoons, under Lieut. Colonel Hervey, in 4 columns, to turn the enemy's left on the heights; while Brig. General Bradford's brigade, the 5th division, under Lieut. General Leith, the 4th division, under Lieut. General the Hon. L. Cole, and the cavalry, under Lieut. General Sir S. Cotton, should attack them in front, supported in reserve by the 6th division, under Major General Clinton, the 7th, under Major General Hope, and Don Carlos de España's Spanish division; and Brig. General Pack should support the left of the 4th division, by attacking that of the Dos Arapiles which the enemy held. The 1st and Light divisions occupied the ground on the left, and were in reserve.

The attack upon the enemy's left was made in the manner above described, and completely succeeded. Major General the Hon. E. Pakenham formed the 3rd division across the enemy's flank, and overthrew every thing opposed to him. The troops were supported in the most gallant style by the Portuguese cavalry, under Brig.

General D'Urban, and Lieut. Colonel Hervey's squadrons of the 14th, who success-fully defeated every attempt made by the enemy on the flank of the 3rd division. Brig. General Bradford's brigade, the 5th and 4th divisions, and the cavalry under Lieut. General Sir S. Cotton attacked the enemy in front, and drove his troops before them from one height to another, bringing forward their right, so as to acquire strength upon the enemy's flank in proportion to the advance. Brig. General Pack made a very gallant attack upon the Arapiles, in which, however, he did not succeed, excepting in diverting the attention of the enemy's corps placed upon it from the troops under the command of Lieut. General Cole in his advance.

The cavalry under Lieut. General Sir S. Cotton made a most gallant and successful charge against a body of the enemy's infantry, which they overthrew and cut to pieces. In this charge Major General Le Marchant was killed at the head of his brigade; and I have to regret the loss of a most able officer.

After the crest of the height was carried, one division of the enemy's infantry made a stand against the 4th division, which, after a severe contest, was obliged to give way, in consequence of the enemy having thrown some troops on the left of the 4th division, after the failure of Brig. General Pack's attack upon the Arapiles, and Lieut. General the Hon. L. Cole having been wounded. Marshal Sir W. Beresford, who happened to be on the spot, directed Brig. General Spry's brigade of the 5th division, which was in the second line, to change its front, and to bring its fire on the flank of the enemy's division; and, I am sorry to add that, while engaged in this service, he received a wound which I am apprehensive will deprive me of the benefit of his counsel and assistance for some time. Nearly about the same time Lieut. General Leith received a wound which unfortunately obliged him to quit the field. I ordered up the 6th division, under Major General Clinton, to relieve the 4th, and the battle was soon restored to its former success.

The enemy's right, however, reinforced by the troops which had fled from his left, and by those which had now retired from the Arapiles, still continued to resist; and I ordered the first and Light divisions, and Colonel Stubbs' Portuguese brigade of the 4th division, which was reformed, and Major General W. Anson's brigade, likewise of the 4th division, to turn the right, while the 6th division, supported by the 3rd and 5th, attacked the front. It was dark before this point was carried by the 6th division; and the enemy fled through the woods towards the Tormes. I pursued them with the 1st and Light divisions, and Major General W. Anson's brigade of the 4th division, and some squadrons of cavalry under Lieut. General Sir S. Cotton, as long as we could find any of them together, directing our march upon Huerta and the fords of the Tormes, by which the enemy had passed on their advance; but the darkness of the night was highly advantageous to the enemy, many of whom escaped under its cover who must otherwise have been in our hands. I am sorry to report that, owing to the same cause, Lieut. General Sir S. Cotton was unfortunately wounded by one of our own sentries after we had halted.

We renewed the pursuit at break of day in the morning with the same troops, and Major General Bock's and Major General Anson's brigades of cavalry, which joined during the night; and, having crossed the Tormes, we came up with the enemy's rear of cavalry and infantry near La Serna. They were immediately attacked by the 2 brigades of dragoons, and the cavalry fled, leaving the infantry to their fate. I have never witnessed a more gallant charge than was made on the enemy's infantry by the heavy brigade of the King's German Legion, under Major General Bock, which was completely successful; and the whole body of infantry, consisting of 3 battalions of the enemy's 1st division, were made prisoners. The pursuit was afterwards continued as far as Peñaranda last night, and our troops were still following the flying enemy. Their head quarters were in this town, not less than 10 leagues from the field of battle, for a few hours last night; and they are now considerably advanced on the road towards Valladolid, by Arevalo. They were joined yesterday on their retreat by the cavalry and artillery of the army of the North, which have arrived at too late a period, it is to be hoped, to be of much use to them.

It is impossible to form a conjecture of the amount of the enemy's loss in this action; but, from all reports, it is very considerable. We have taken from them 11 pieces of cannon,* several ammunition waggons, 2 eagles, and 6 colours; and 1 General, 3 Colonels, 3 Lieut. Colonels, 130 officers of inferior rank, and between 6000 and 7000 soldiers are prisoners;† and our detachments are sending in more at every moment. The number of dead on the field is very large.

I am informed that Marshal Marmont is badly wounded, and has lost one of his arms; and that 4 General Officers have been killed, and several wounded.

Such an advantage could not have been acquired without material loss on our side; but it certainly has not been of a magnitude to distress the army, or to cripple its operations. . . .

* The official returns only account for 11 pieces of cannon, but it is believed that 20 have fallen into our hands.

† The prisoners are supposed to amount to 7000; but it has not been possible to ascertain their number exactly, from the advance of the army immediately after the action was over.

566. Letters from Earl Grey to Lord Grenville on the conduct of the war, 27 Oct. and 12 Nov. 1813

(Historical MSS. Comm., Dropmore Papers, x, pp. 351–357.)

The prince regent's decision, taken in Feb. 1812, to retain his father's Tory ministers, caused a breach between him and the Whigs, most of whom, led by Grey and Grenville, went into opposition. They had become convinced of the hopelessness of carrying on the struggle against Napoleon until victory had been achieved; Grey was ready to recommend a peace which would have left the French undisputed masters of the Continent. Grenville, indeed, detested the idea of a negotiated peace, but he too favoured the withdrawal of the British army from the peninsula, where Wellington was draining away Napoleon's military strength. The regent's decision, therefore, though indefensible on personal grounds, was in the best interests of the country.

[27 Oct.] . . . I must say I agree with Holland as to the expediency of holding a pacific language, and have already expressed that opinion to him. . . . This opinion I entertain because, as you say you do, I fear more than I hope from a continuance of the present contest. Under this impression, though I feel and acknowledge that a peace with Buonaparte on the best terms that we could hope for at this moment would leave France in possession of a power most formidable to the independence of Europe, yet comparing that with the situation in which we should be placed if he were to succeed in breaking the present Confederacy (the last, certainly, if unsuccessful, that

Europe will see) I cannot hesitate as to the policy of securing ourselves, if it can be done, by any reasonable terms, against so fatal a hazard. If I were in Government, therefore, I should propose, not separately, but conjointly with our Allies, a fair offer of peace, on terms certainly far below what our security requires, infinitely below what our sanguine politicians would demand, but such as, leaving Russia, Austria and Prussia entire Powers, would together with this example of successful resistance, and the chances of Buonaparte's life, place us in a situation of ease and safety compared with the best hope we could have formed a year ago, or with the consequences which must necessarily result from the failure of this coalition. Into the grounds of my apprehension of this failure it is not necessary to enter, because you express the same fear ; I will only say that I believe the seeds of division amongst the Allies exist even now to a degree that their common danger ought to have prevented ; that the Confederacy was very near its ruin at Dresden ; that any reverse will probably dissolve it ; that a protracted war without decisive success will have the same effect ; and that there is not in France itself, on account of the pressure of the war, a stronger desire of peace than there exists in the population, and in the armies, and even in the Cabinets of the Allied Powers. . . .

But peace is unattainable! It may be so, and I certainly am not sanguine in my expectations that Buonaparte would subscribe, in a moment of calamity, to such terms as even I, with my moderate views, would consent to propose to him. I think it not improbable that he may still feel, what he expressed in 1806, that a retrograde step would be his ruin. In this opinion perhaps he is right, and I am by no means sure that the most effectual blow that could be given to his power would not be by a peace, however inadequate the terms might be to our apparent security, which would be made by him with a diminished reputation and with the acknowledgement of failure in a contest so wantonly provoked by him. But this surely is rather a reason why we should make such a peace if we can ; and I am still so incorrigible in my old opinions as to believe that even to propose a peace, which all the world and parti-cularly his own people think he ought to accept, would be attended with great advantages. . . .

I cannot agree with you in thinking that the money spent in Spain has been ineffectual in producing the better hope which now exists ; or that Buonaparte's power, which even in his present circumstances makes you fear more than you hope, would not be much more formidable to the Allies if he had to oppose to them not only the armies which he is at present obliged to maintain on the frontiers of Spain, but all the military resources which the subjugation of the Peninsula must have placed at his command. . . . I cannot say that as things have turned out, contrary certainly to my expectations, the event of the Spanish war has not been both honourable and advantageous to this country. . . .

12 November:

. . . Between the writing of my last letter and its arrival, we received accounts of the accession of Bavaria to the Confederacy, and of the victory of Leipsic : both of them evnets which, I confess, I had not allowed myself to hope. With changes of such importance new views of policy and conduct must necessarily arise, for I am not a subscriber to the strange position of Whitbread, that after a signal and decisive success we are to limit our demands to the same terms that we might have accepted when we had to calculate and to fear the chances of defeat. But moderation in success is still my motto. To that general policy you will not object. . . .

In our objects there can be no difference. You will, I am sure, give me full credit for a sincere desire that the balance of Europe should be established; nay for a disposition to make great sacrifices for that purpose. But there may be circumstances in which it would be expedient to negotiate on terms short of that full security. It will be so whenever the probabilities and the danger of failure preponderate over all reasonable hopes of success. . . . What I dread is another fatal reaction from France, or that in a protracted contest—and who can hope for the accomplishment of all our objects by a short effort?—the present Confederacy may be dissolved. Against such dangers, if reasonably to be feared, it would surely be wise and politic to guard by a negotiation, if they cannot be otherwise obviated. . . .

There is, I will confess, one part of your speech which I wish you had omitted; I allude to what you said about Holland; not because I do not feel all the interest that belongs to the situation of that country, but because I do doubt very much the possibility of our re-establishing its independence. The great advantage of the present Confederacy, in my mind, is that it has been produced rather by the feeling of the people than by the policy of the Governments which it has embraced. As the Allies advance towards France the war will assume, on their part, more of an offensive character. The views of a remoter policy, however just, are not so effective, particularly on the feelings of the people, as the pressure of immediate danger; and I much fear when you come to carry on the war beyond the limits of Germany, you will find all the causes, moral, political and military, which have contributed to your present success, in a great measure reversed. My doubts therefore of the policy of such an attempt are strong. . . . Your hopes may be greater and mine less as to the probability of reducing the power of France by a continuance of the war, but by our opinions of that probability our views of policy must be regulated, either in pressing negotiation or framing terms of peace. . . .

567. Wellington to Earl Bathurst, 21 Dec. 1813

(Gurwood, *Selections from Wellington's Despatches*, p. 776.)

St. Jean de Luz.

I have received your Lordship's letter of the 10th instant, and I beg you will assure the Russian Ambassador that there is nothing that I can do with the force under my command to forward the general interests that I will not do. I am already farther advanced on the French territory than any of the Allied Powers; and I believe I am better prepared than any of them to take advantage of any opportunities which may offer of annoying the enemy, either in consequence of my own situation, or of the operations of the armies of the Allies.

Your Lordship is acquainted, by my last dispatches, with the nature and objects of my recent operations, and with the position in which we were at their close. The enemy have since considerably weakened their force in Bayonne, and they occupy the right of the Adour as far as Dax. I cannot tell yet what force they have in Bayonne, or whether their force is so reduced as that I can attack their entrenched camp.

In military operations there are some things which cannot be done; one of these is to move troops in this country during or immediately after a violent fall of rain. I believe I shall lose many more men than I shall ever replace, by putting any troops in camp in this bad weather; but I should be guilty of an useless waste of men, if I were to attempt an operation during the violent falls of rain which we have here. Our operations, then, must necessarily be slow, but they shall not be discontinued.

In regard to the scene of the operations of the army, it is a question for the Government and not for me. By having kept in the field about 30,000 men in the Peninsula, the British Government have now, for 5 years, given employment to at least 200,000 French troops of the best Napoleon had, as it is ridiculous to suppose that either the Spaniards or Portuguese could have resisted for a moment, if the British force had been withdrawn. The armies now employed against us cannot be less than 100,000 men, indeed more, including garrisons; and I see in the French newspapers that orders have been given for the formation at Bordeaux of an army of reserve of 100,000 men. Is there any man weak enough to suppose that one third of the numbers first mentioned would be employed against the Spaniards and Portuguese, if we were withdrawn? They would, if it were still an object to Buonaparte to conquer the Peninsula. And he would succeed in his object: but it is much more likely that he would make peace with the powers of the Peninsula, and then have it in his power to turn against the allied armies the 200,000 men, of which 100,000 men are such troops as those armies have not yet had to deal with.

Another observation which I have to submit is, that, in a war in which every day offers a crisis, the result of which may affect the world for ages, the change of the scene of the operations of the British army would put that army entirely *hors de combat* for 4 months at least, even if the new scene were Holland; and they would not then be such a machine as this army is.

Your Lordship very reasonably, however, asks what objects we propose to ourselves here which are to induce Napoleon to make peace? I am now in a commanding situation on the most vulnerable frontier of France, probably the only vulnerable frontier. If I could put 20,000 Spaniards into the field, which I could do if I had money and was properly supported by the fleet, I must have the only fortress there is on this frontier, if it can be called a fortress, and that in a very short space of time. If I could put 40,000 Spaniards into the field, I should most probably have my posts on the Garonne. Does any man believe that Napoleon would not feel an army in such a position more than he would feel 30 or 40,000 British troops laying siege to one of his fortresses in Holland? If it be only the resource of men and money, of which he will be deprived, and the reputation he will lose by our being in this position, it will do ten times more to procure peace than ten armies on the side of Flanders. But, if I am right in believing that there is a strong Bourbon party in France, and that that party is the preponderating one in the South of France, what mischief must not our army do him in the position I have supposed, and what sacrifices would he not make to get rid of us!

It is the business of the Government, and not my business, to dispose of the resources of the nation; and I have no right to give an opinion on the subject. I wish, however, to impress upon your Lordship's mind, that you cannot maintain military operations in the Peninsula and in Holland with British troops; you must give up either the one or the other, as, if I am not mistaken, the British establishment is not equal to the maintenance of two armies in the field. I began last campaign with 70,000 British and Portuguese troops; and taking away from me the German troops, and adding to me what could be got from the militia, and by enabling me to bring up the Portuguese recruits, I expected this year to take the field with 80,000 men; but this is now quite out of the question. If you should form the Hanoverian army, which is in my opinion the most reasonable plan to go upon, I shall not take the field with much more than 50,000 men, unless I shall receive real and efficient assistance to bring up the Portuguese recruits; and it will then be about 55,000, or if our wounded recover well, and we have no more actions, about 60,000 men.

Then I beg you to observe that, whenever you extend your assistance to any country, unless at the same time fresh means are put in action, the service is necessarily stinted in all its branches on the old stage. I do not wish to make complaints, but if you will look at every branch of the service here now, you will find it stinted, particularly the naval branch, and those supplies which necessarily come from England. I lately sent you a return of the supply of clothing received for the Spanish army for the year 1813, from which you will see how that branch stands; and I have not heard of the arrival at Plymouth of the 25,000 suits to be lodged in store there, which will still leave a deficiency of 3000 suits for 1813; 7800 suits having lately arrived at Coruña. Nearly all the great coats are deficient. The reason of this is, that the inferior departments do not observe, that when British exertion is to be made on a new scene, the old means are not sufficient. New engines must be set at work, otherwise the service must be stinted in one or both scenes, and there must be complaints.

The different reports which I have sent your Lordship will show how we stand for want of naval means; and I beg you to take the state and condition of the ships *on the stations*, striking out those coming out and going home, which the Admiralty will insert on the 1st and 15th of every month since June last, and you will see whether or not there is reason to complain. But whatever may be the numbers employed, I complain that there are not enough, because they do not perform the service. This is certainly not the intention of the Admiralty. . . .

Your Lordship is also acquainted with the state of our financial resources. We are overwhelmed with debts, and I can scarcely stir out of my house on account of the public creditors waiting to demand payment of what is due to them. Some of the muleteers are 26 months in arrears; and only yesterday I was obliged to give them bills upon the Treasury for a part of their demands, or lose their services; which bills they will, I know, sell at a depreciated rate of exchange to the *sharks* who are waiting at Pasages, and in this town, to take advantage of the public distresses. I have reason to suspect that they became thus clamorous at the instigation of British merchants.

I draw your Lordship's attention to these facts just to show that Great Britain cannot extend her operations by British troops, or even her pecuniary or other assistance, without starving the service here, unless additional means and exertion should be used to procure what is wanted.

568. The Treaty of Chaumont, 1 March 1814

Treaty of Union, Concert and Subsidy between His Britannic Majesty and His Imperial and Royal Apostolic Majesty the Emperor of Austria.

(*British and Foreign State Papers, 1812–1814*, I, pp. 121–129.)

Treaties containing the same stipulations, *verbatim*, were concluded on the same day between Great Britain on the one hand, Prussia and Russia on the other hand. Castlereagh, the British Foreign Secretary (since 1812), was the main architect of the Grand Alliance against Napoleon, and he was mainly responsible for holding it together until the collapse of the Napoleonic Empire.

His Majesty the King of the United Kingdom of Great Britain and Ireland, His Imperial and Royal Apostolic Majesty the Emperor of Austria, King of Hungary and Bohemia, H.M. the Emperor of All the Russias, and H.M. the King of Prussia, having transmitted to the French Government proposals for concluding a General Peace, and being desirous, should France refuse the conditions therein contained, to draw closer the ties which unite them for the vigorous prosecution of a War undertaken for the salutary purpose of putting an end to the miseries of Europe, of securing its future repose, by re-establishing a just balance of Power, and being at the same time desirous, should the Almighty bless their pacific intentions, to fix the means of maintaining against every attempt the order of things which shall have been the happy consequence of their efforts, have agreed to sanction by a solemn Treaty, signed separately by each of the 4 Powers with the 3 others, this twofold engagement. . . .

Article I. The High Contracting Parties above named solemnly engage by the present Treaty, and in the event of France refusing to accede to the conditions of Peace now proposed, to apply all the means of their respective States to the vigorous prosecution of the war against that Power, and to employ them in perfect concert, in order to obtain for themselves and for Europe a General Peace, under the protection of which the rights and liberties of all nations may be established and secured.

This engagement shall in no respect affect the stipulations which the several Powers have already contracted relative to the number of troops to be kept against the enemy; and it is understood that the Courts of England, Austria, Russia and Prussia, engage by the present Treaty to keep in the field, each of them, 150,000 effective men, exclusive of garrisons, to be employed in active service against the common enemy.

II. The High Contracting Parties reciprocally engage not to negotiate separately with the common enemy, nor to sign Peace, Truce nor Convention, but with common consent. They, moreover, engage not to lay down their arms until the object of the war, mutually understood and agreed upon, shall have been attained.

III. In order to contribute in the most prompt and decisive manner to fulfil this great object, His Britannic Majesty engages to furnish a Subsidy of £5,000,000 for the service of the year 1814, to be divided in equal proportions amongst the three Powers; and his said Majesty promises moreover to arrange, before the 1st of January in each year, with their Imperial and Royal Majesties, the further succours to be furnished during the subsequent year, if (which God forbid) the War should so long continue. . . .

V. The High Contracting Powers, reserving to themselves to concert together, on the conclusion of a Peace with France, as to the means best adapted to guarantee to Europe, and to themselves reciprocally, the continuance of the Peace, have also determined to enter, without delay, into defensive engagements for the protection of their respective States in Europe against every attempt which France might make to infringe the order of things resulting from such Pacification.

VI. To effect this, they agree that in the event of one of the High Contracting Parties being threatened with an attack on the part of France, the others shall employ their most strenuous efforts to prevent it, by friendly interposition.

VII. In the case of these endeavours proving ineffectual, the High Contracting Parties promise to come to the immediate assistance of the Power attacked, each with a body of 60,000 men. . . .

XV. In order to render more effectual the defensive engagements above stipulated, by uniting for their common defence the Powers the most exposed to a French invasion, the High Contracting Parties engage to invite those Powers to accede to the present Treaty of Defensive Alliance.

XVI. The present Treaty of Defensive Alliance having for its object to maintain the equilibrium of Europe, to secure the repose and independence of its States, and to prevent the invasions which during so many years have desolated the world, the High Contracting Parties have agreed to extend the duration of it to 20 years, to take date from the day of its signature; and they reserve to themselves to concert upon its ulterior prolongation, 3 years before its expiration, should circumstances require it. . . .

569. The First Treaty of Paris, 30 May 1814

(*British and Foreign State Papers*, I (1812–1814), pp. 151–173.)

Treaties containing the same stipulations, *verbatim*, were concluded on the same day between France and Austria, Prussia and Russia.

H.M. the King of the United Kingdom of Great Britain and Ireland, and his Allies on the one part, and H.M. the King of France and of Navarre on the other part, animated by an equal desire to terminate the long agitations of Europe, and the sufferings of mankind, by a permanent Peace, founded upon a just repartition of force between its States, and containing in its stipulations the pledge of its durability; and his Britannic Majesty, together with his Allies, being unwilling to require of France, now that, replaced under the paternal government of her Kings, she offers the assurance of security and stability to Europe, the conditions and guarantees which they had with regret demanded from her former Government, their said Majesties have named Plenipotentiaries to discuss, settle and sign a Treaty of Peace and Amity. . . .

Article I. There shall be from this day forward perpetual peace and friendship between his Britannic Majesty and his Allies on the one part, and H.M. the King of France and Navarre on the other, their heirs and successors, their dominions and subjects, respectively.

The High Contracting Parties shall devote their best attention to maintain, not only between themselves, but, inasmuch as depends upon them, between all the States of Europe, that harmony and good understanding which are so necessary for their tranquillity.

II. The Kingdom of France retains its limits entire, as they existed on the 1st of January 1792. It shall further receive the increase of territory comprised within the line established by the following Article:

III. On the side of Belgium, Germany and Italy, the ancient frontiers shall be re-established as they existed the 1st of January 1792, extending from the North Sea, between Dunkirk and Nieuport, to the Mediterranean between Cannes and Nice, with the following modifications: . . .

IV. To secure the communications of the town of Geneva with other parts of the Swiss territory situated on the Lake, France consents that the road by Versoy shall be common to the two countries. . . .

V. The navigation of the Rhine, from the point where it becomes navigable unto the sea, and *vice versâ*, shall be free, so that it can be interdicted to no one; and at the future Congress, attention shall be paid to the establishment of the principles according to which the duties to be raised by the States bordering on the Rhine may be regulated, in the mode the most impartial, and the most favourable to the commerce of all nations.

The future Congress, with a view to facilitate the communication between nations, and continually to render them less strangers to each other, shall likewise examine and determine in what manner the above provisions can be extended to other rivers which, in their navigable course, separate or traverse different States.

VI. Holland, placed under the sovereignty of the House of Orange, shall receive an increase of territory. The title and exercise of that sovereignty shall not in any case belong to a Prince wearing or destined to wear a foreign Crown.

The States of Germany shall be independent, and united by a Federative Bund. Switzerland, independent, shall continue to govern herself.

Italy, beyond the limits of the countries which are to revert to Austria, shall be composed of Sovereign States.

VII. The Island of Malta and its Dependencies shall belong in full right and sovereignty to his Britannic Majesty.

VIII. His Britannic Majesty, stipulating for himself and his Allies, engages to restore to His Most Christian Majesty, within the term which shall be hereafter fixed, the colonies, fisheries, factories and establishments of every kind which were possessed by France on the 1st of January 1792, in the seas and on the Continents of America, Africa and Asia; with the exception, however, of the Islands of Tobago and St. Lucie, and of the Isle of France and its Dependencies, especially Rodrigue and Les Séchelles, which several colonies and possessions His Most Christian Majesty cedes in full right and sovereignty to His Britannic Majesty, and also the portion of St. Domingo ceded to France by the Treaty of Basle, and which His Most Christian Majesty restores in full right and sovereignty to His Catholic Majesty.

IX. His Majesty the King of Sweden and Norway, in virtue of the arrangements stipulated with the Allies, and in execution of the preceding Article, consents that the island of Guadaloupe be restored to His Most Christian Majesty, and gives up all the rights he may have acquired over that island.

X. Her Most Faithful Majesty, in virtue of the arrangements stipulated with her Allies, and in execution of the VIIIth Article, engages to restore French Guiana as it existed on the 1st of January 1792, to His Most Christian Majesty, within the term hereafter fixed.

The renewal of the dispute which existed at that period on the subject of the frontier, being the effect of this stipulation, it is agreed that that dispute shall be terminated by a friendly arrangement between the two Courts, under the mediation of His Britannic Majesty.

XI. The places and forts in those colonies and settlements, which, by virtue of the VIIIth, IXth and Xth Articles, are to be restored to His Most Christian Majesty, shall be given up in the state in which they may be at the moment of the signature of the present Treaty.

XII. His Britannic Majesty guarantees to the subjects of His Most Christian Majesty the same facilities, privileges, and protection, with respect to commerce, and the security of their persons and property within the limits of the British Sovereignty on the Continent of India, as are now, or shall be granted to the most favoured nations.

His Most Christian Majesty, on his part, having nothing more at heart than the perpetual duration of peace between the two Crowns of England and of France, and wishing to do his utmost to avoid anything which might affect their mutual good understanding, engages not to erect any fortifications in the establishments which are to be restored to him within the limits of the British sovereignty upon the Continent of India, and only to place in those establishments the number of troops necessary for the maintenance of the police.

XIII. The French right of fishery upon the Great Bank of Newfoundland, upon the coasts of the island of that name, and of the adjacent islands in the Gulf of St. Lawrence, shall be replaced upon the footing on which it stood in 1792.

XIV. Those colonies, factories and establishments which are to be restored to His Most Christian Majesty or his Allies in the Northern Seas, or in the Seas on the Continents of America and Africa, shall be given up within the 3 months, and those which are beyond the Cape of Good Hope within the 6 months which follow the ratification of the present Treaty.

XV. The High Contracting Parties having, by the IVth Article of the Convention of the 23rd of April last, reserved to themselves the right of disposing, in the present Definitive Treaty of Peace, of the Arsenals and ships of war, armed and unarmed, which may be found in the maritime places restored by the IInd Article of the said Convention, it is agreed that the said vessels and ships of war, armed and unarmed, together with the Naval Ordnance and naval stores, and all materials for building and equipment shall be divided between France and the countries where the said places are situated, in the proportion of two-thirds for France and one-third for the Power to whom the said places shall belong. . . .

Antwerp shall for the future be solely a Commercial Port.

XVI. The High Contracting Parties, desirous to bury in entire oblivion the dissensions which have agitated Europe, declare and promise that no individual, of whatever rank or condition he may be, in the countries restored and ceded by the present Treaty, shall be prosecuted, disturbed or molested in his person or property, under any pretext whatsoever, either on account of his conduct or political opinions, his attachment either to any of the Contracting Parties or to any Government which has ceased to exist, or for any other reason, except for debts contracted towards individuals, or acts posterior to the date of the present Treaty.

XVII. The native inhabitants and aliens, of whatever nation and condition they may be, in those countries which are to change Sovereigns, as well in virtue of the present Treaty as of the subsequent arrangements to which it may give rise, shall be allowed a period of six years, reckoning from the exchange of the Ratifications, for the purpose of disposing of their property, if they think fit, whether it be acquired before or during the present War, and retiring to whatever country they may choose.

XVIII. The Allied Powers, desiring to offer His Most Christian Majesty a new proof of their anxiety to arrest, as far as in them lies, the bad consequences of the disastrous epoch fortunately terminated by the present Peace, renounce all the sums which their Governments claim from France, whether on account of contracts, supplies, or any other advances whatsoever to the French Government, during the different Wars which have taken place since 1792.

His Most Christian Majesty, on his part, renounces every claim which he might bring forward against the Allied Powers on the same grounds. . . .

XIX. The French Government engages to liquidate and pay all debts it may be found to owe in countries beyond its own territory, on account of contracts, or other formal engagements between individuals, or private establishments, and the French authorities, as well for supplies, as in satisfaction of legal engagements.

XX. The High Contracting Parties, immediately after the exchange of the Ratifications of the present Treaty, shall name Commissioners to direct and superintend the execution of the whole of the stipulations contained in the XVIIIth and XIXth Articles. These Commissioners shall undertake the examination of the claims referred to in the preceding Article, the liquidation of the sums claimed, and the consideration of the manner in which the French Government may propose to pay them. . . .

XXI. The debts which in their origin were specially mortgaged upon the countries no longer belonging to France, or were contracted for the support of their internal administration, shall remain at the charge of the said countries. . . .

XXII. The French Government shall remain charged with the reimbursement of all sums paid by the subjects of the said countries into the French coffers, whether under the denomination of surety, deposit or consignment. . . .

XXVII. National domains acquired for valuable considerations by French subjects in the late Departments of Belgium, and of the left bank of the Rhine and the Alps, beyond the ancient limits of France, and which now cease to belong to her, shall be guaranteed to the purchasers. . . .

XXXII. All the Powers engaged on either side in the present War, shall, within the space of two months, send Plenipotentiaries to Vienna, for the purpose of regulating, in General Congress, the arrangements which are to complete the provisions of the present Treaty.

XXXIII. The present Treaty shall be ratified, and the Ratifications shall be exchanged within the period of 15 days, or sooner if possible.

In witness whereof, the respective Plenipotentiaries have signed and affixed to it the seals of their arms. . . .

> Castlereagh.
> Aberdeen.
> Cathcart.
> Charles Stewart, Lieut. Genl.
> Le Prince de Benevent.

Separate and Secret Articles between France and Great Britain, Austria,
Prussia and Russia.–Paris, 30 May 1814. [Extract.]

Article I. The disposal of the territories given up by His Most Christian Majesty, under the IIIrd Article of the Public Treaty, and the relations from whence a system of real and permanent balance of power in Europe is to be derived, shall be regulated at the Congress upon the principles determined upon by the Allied Powers among themselves, and according to the general provisions contained in the following Articles.

II. The possessions of His Imperial and Royal Apostolic Majesty in Italy shall be bounded by the Po, the Tessino, and the Lago Maggiore. The King of Sardinia shall return to the possession of his ancient dominions, with the exception of that part of Savoy secured to France by the IIIrd Article of the present Treaty. His Majesty shall receive an increase of territory from the State of Genoa. The Port of Genoa shall continue to be a Free Port; the Powers reserving to themselves the right of making arrangements upon this point with the King of Sardinia.

France shall acknowledge and guarantee, conjointly with the Allied Powers, and on the same footing, the political organisation which Switzerland shall adopt under the auspices of the said Allied Powers, and according to the basis already agreed upon with them.

III. The establishment of a just balance of power in Europe requiring that Holland should be so constituted as to be enabled to support her independence through her own resources, the countries comprised between the sea, the frontiers of France, such as they are defined by the present Treaty, and the Meuse, shall be given up for ever to Holland.

The frontiers upon the right bank of the Meuse shall be regulated according to the military convenience of Holland and her neighbours.

The freedom of the navigation of the Scheldt shall be established upon the same principle which has regulated the navigation of the Rhine, in the Vth Article of the present Treaty.

IV. The German territories upon the left bank of the Rhine, which have been united to France since 1792, shall contribute to the aggrandisement of Holland, and shall be further applied to compensate Prussia and other German States. . . .

Additional Articles between France and Great Britain, Paris, 30 May 1814.

Article I. His Most Christian Majesty, concurring without reserve in the sentiments of his Britannic Majesty, with respect to a description of traffic repugnant to the principles of natural justice and of the enlightened age in which we live, engages to unite all his efforts to those of his Britannic Majesty, at the approaching Congress, to induce all the Powers of Christendom to decree the abolition of the Slave Trade, so that the said Trade shall cease universally, as it shall cease definitely, under any circumstances, on the part of the French Government, in the course of 5 years; and that, during the said period, no slave merchant shall import or sell slaves, except in the colonies of the State of which he is a subject. . . .

570. Convention between Great Britain and the Netherlands, 13 Aug. 1814
(*British and Foreign State Papers, 1814–1815*, pp. 370–378.)

The United Provinces of the Netherlands, under the favour of Divine Providence, having been restored to their independence, and having been placed by the loyalty of the Dutch people and the achievements of the Allied Powers, under the Government of the Illustrious House of Orange; and his Britannic Majesty being desirous of entering into such arrangements with the Prince Sovereign of the United Netherlands concerning the colonies of the said United Netherlands, which have been conquered by his Majesty's arms during the late War, as may conduce to the prosperity of the said State, and may afford a lasting testimony of his Majesty's friendship and attachment to the family of Orange and to the Dutch nation; the said High Contracting Parties, equally animated by those sentiments of cordial goodwill and attachment to each other, have nominated for their Plenipotentiaries. . . .

Article I. His Britannic Majesty engages to restore to the Prince Sovereign of the United Netherlands, within the term which shall be hereafter fixed, the colonies, Factories and establishments which were possessed by Holland at the commencement of the late war, *viz.* on the 1st of January 1803, in the seas and on the Continent of America, Africa and Asia; with the exception of the Cape of Good Hope and the settlements of Demerara, Essequibo and Berbice, of which possessions the High Contracting Parties reserve to themselves the right to dispose by a Supplementary Convention, hereafter to be negotiated, according to their mutual interests, and especially with reference to the provisions contained in the VIth and IXth Articles of the Treaty of Peace, signed between his Britannic Majesty and His Most Christian Majesty on the 30th of May 1814.

II. His Britannic Majesty agrees to cede in full sovereignty the island of Banca, in the Eastern Seas, to the Prince Sovereign of the Netherlands, in exchange for the settlement of Cochin and its dependencies on the coast of Malabar, which is to remain in full sovereignty to his Britannic Majesty. . . .

IV. . . . His Royal Highness the Prince Sovereign . . . engages not to erect any fortifications in the establishments which are to be restored to him within the limits of the British Sovereignty upon the Continent of India, and only to place in those establishments the number of troops necessary for the maintenance of the Police.

V. Those colonies, Factories and establishments which are to be ceded to his Royal Highness the Sovereign Prince of the United Netherlands, . . . in the seas or on the Continent of America, shall be given up within 3 months, and those which are beyond the Cape of Good Hope within the 6 months which follow the ratification of the present Convention.

VIII. The Prince Sovereign of the United Netherlands, anxious to co-operate in the most effectual manner with his Majesty the King of the United Kingdom of Great Britain and Ireland, so as to bring about the total abolition of the trade in slaves on the coast of Africa, and having spontaneously issued a Decree dated the 15th of June 1814, wherein it is enjoined that no ships or vessels whatever, destined for the trade in slaves, be cleared out or equipped in any of the harbours or places of his dominions, nor admitted to the forts or possessions on the coast of Guinea, and that no inhabitants of that country shall be sold or exported as slaves–does moreover hereby engage to prohibit all his subjects, in the most effectual manner and by the most solemn laws, from taking any share whatsoever in such inhuman traffic. . . . Done at London, this 13th day of August 1814—Castlereagh, H. Fagel.

Additional Articles.

I. In order the better to provide for the defence and incorporation of the Belgic Provinces with Holland, and also to provide, in conformity to the IXth Article of the Treaty of Paris, a suitable compensation for the rights ceded by his Swedish Majesty under the said Article, which compensation, it is understood, in the event of the above Reunion, Holland should be liable to furnish, in pursuance of the above stipulations; it is hereby agreed between the High Contracting Parties that his Britannic Majesty shall take upon himself and engage to defray the following charges:

1. The payment of £1,000,000 to Sweden, in satisfaction of the claims afore-said. . . .

2. The advance of £2,000,000 to be applied, in concert with the Prince Sovereign of the Netherlands, and in aid of an equal sum to be furnished by him, towards augmenting and improving the defences of the Low Countries.

3. To bear, equally with Holland, such further charges as may be agreed upon between the said High Contracting Parties and their Allies, towards the final and satisfactory settlement of the Low Countries in union with Holland, and under the dominion of the House of Orange, not exceeding, in the whole, the sum of £3,000,000 to be defrayed by Great Britain.

In consideration, and in satisfaction of the above engagements, as taken by his Britannic Majesty, the Prince Sovereign of the Netherlands agrees to cede in full sovereignty to his Britannic Majesty, the Cape of Good Hope, and the settlements of Demerara, Essequibo, and Berbice, upon the condition, nevertheless, that the subjects of the said Sovereign Prince, being proprietors in the said colonies or settlements, shall be at liberty . . . to carry on trade between the said settlements and the territories in Europe of the said Sovereign Prince.

It is also agreed between the two High Contracting Parties that the ships of every kind belonging to Holland shall have permission to resort freely to the Cape of Good Hope for the purposes of refreshment and repairs, without being liable to other charges than such as British subjects are required to pay.

II. The small district of Bernagore, situated close to Calcutta, being requisite to the due preservation of the peace and police of that city, the Prince of Orange agrees to cede the said district to his Britannic Majesty upon a payment of such sum annually to his Royal Highness as may be considered, by Commissioners to be appointed by the respective Governments, to be just and reasonable, with reference to the profits or revenue usually derived by the Dutch Government from the same. . .

Castlereagh.

H. Fagel.

571. The Treaty of Ghent, 24 Dec. 1814 (Extracts)

(*British and Foreign State Papers, 1814–1815*, pp. 357–364.)

Article I. . . . All territory, places and possessions whatsoever, taken by either party from the other during the War, or which may be taken after the signing of this Treaty, excepting only the islands hereinafter mentioned, shall be restored without delay. . . . Such of the islands in the Bay of Passamaquoddy as are claimed by both parties shall remain in the possession of the party in whose occupation they may be at the time of the exchange of the Ratifications of this Treaty, until the decision respecting the title to the said Islands shall have been made in conformity with the IVth Article of this Treaty. . . .

IV. Whereas it was stipulated by the IInd Article in the Treaty of Peace of 1783 . . . that the boundary of the United States should comprehend all islands within 20 leagues of any part of the shores of the United States, and lying between lines to be drawn due east from the points where the aforesaid boundaries, between Nova Scotia, on the one part, and East Florida, on the other, shall respectively touch the Bay of Fundy, and the Atlantic Ocean, excepting such islands as now are, or heretofore have been, within the limits of Nova Scotia; and whereas the several islands in the Bay of Passamaquoddy, which is part of the Bay of Fundy, and the island of Grand Menan, in the said Bay of Fundy, are claimed by the United States, as being comprehended within their aforesaid boundaries, which said islands are claimed as belonging to his Britannic Majesty, as having been at the time of, and previous to the aforesaid Treaty of 1783, within the limits of the Province of Nova Scotia.

In order, therefore, finally to decide upon these claims, it is agreed that they shall be referred to two Commissioners, to be appointed in the following manner, *viz.*, one Commissioner shall be appointed by his Britannic Majesty, and one by the President of the United States, by and with the advice and consent of the Senate thereof; and the said two Commissioners so appointed shall be sworn impartially to examine and decide upon the said claims according to such evidence as shall be laid before them on the part of his Britannic Majesty and of the United States respectively.

. . . If the said Commissioners shall agree in their decision, both parties shall consider such decision as final and conclusive.

It is further agreed that in the event of the two Commissioners differing upon all or any of the matters so referred to them . . . they shall make jointly or separately a Report or Reports, as well to the Government of his Britannic Majesty as to that of the United States, stating in detail, the points on which they differ, and the grounds upon which they or either of them, have so refused, declined or omitted to act.

And his Britannic Majesty and the Government of the United States hereby agree to refer the Report or Reports . . . to some friendly Sovereign or State, to be then named for that purpose, and who shall be requested to decide on the differences which may be stated in the said Report or Reports, or upon the Report of one Commissioner, together with the grounds upon which the other Commissioner shall have refused, declined or omitted to act, as the case may be. . . . His Britannic Majesty and the Government of the United States engage to consider the decision of such friendly Sovereign or State to be final and conclusive on all the matters so referred.

V. Whereas neither that point of the Highlands lying due north from the source of the River St. Croix, and designated in the former Treaty of Peace between the two Powers, as the North-West Angle of Nova Scotia, nor the North-Westernmost head of Connecticut river, has yet been ascertained: and whereas that part of the boundary line between the dominions of the two Powers which extends from the source of the River St. Croix, directly north to the above-mentioned North-West angle of Nova Scotia, thence along the said Highlands which divide those rivers that empty themselves into the river St. Lawrence from those which fall into the Atlantic Ocean, to the North-Westernmost head of Connecticut river, thence down along the middle of that river to the 45th degree of North Latitude, thence by a line due west on said Latitude, until it strikes the river Iroquois or Cataraguy, has not yet been surveyed; it is agreed that for these several purposes two Commissioners shall be appointed, sworn and authorised to act exactly in the manner directed with respect to those mentioned in the next preceding Article, unless otherwise specified in the present Article.

. . . The said Commissioners shall have power to ascertain and determine the points above-mentioned, in conformity with the provisions of the said Treaty of Peace of 1783, and shall cause the boundary aforesaid . . . to be surveyed and marked, according to the said provisions. The said Commissioners shall make a map of the said boundary, and annex to it a Declaration . . . certifying it to be the true map of the said boundary. . . . And both parties agree to consider such map and Declaration as finally and conclusively fixing the said boundary. And in the event of the said two Commissioners differing, or both, or either of them refusing, declining or wilfully omitting to act, such Reports, Declarations, or Statements, shall be made by them, or either of them, and such reference to a friendly Sovereign or State shall be made, in all respects, as in the latter part of the IVth Article is contained. . . .

VI. Whereas, by the former Treaty of Peace, that portion of the boundary of the

United States, from the point where the 45th degree of North Latitude strikes the river Iroquois or Cataraguy to the Lake Superior, was declared to be 'along the middle of said river into Lake Ontario, through the middle of said Lake, until it strikes the communication by water between that Lake and Lake Erie, through the middle of said Lake, until it arrives at the water-communication into the Lake Huron; thence through the middle of said Lake to the water-communication between that Lake and Lake Superior'. And whereas doubts have arisen what was the middle of the said river, Lakes and Water-communications, and whether certain islands lying in the same were within the dominions of his Britannic Majesty or of the United States. In order, therefore, finally to decide these doubts, they shall be referred to two Commissioners, to be appointed, sworn and authorised to act exactly in the manner directed, with respect to those mentioned in the next preceding Article, unless otherwise specified in this present Article. . . .

. . . Both parties agree to consider such designation and decision as final and conclusive. And in the event of the said two Commissioners differing . . . such reference to a friendly Sovereign or State shall be made in all respects as in the latter part of the IVth Article is contained. . . .

VII. It is further agreed that the said two last-mentioned Commissioners . . . shall be . . . authorised . . . impartially to fix and determine, according to the true intent of the said Treaty of Peace of 1783, that part of the Boundary between the dominions of the two Powers, which extends from the Water-communication between Lake Huron and Lake Superior to the most North-Western point of the Lake of the Woods, to decide to which of the two parties the several islands lying in the Lakes, Water-communications and rivers forming the said boundary, do respectively belong, in conformity with the true intent of the said Treaty of Peace of 1783; and to cause such parts of the said Boundary, as require it, to be surveyed and marked. . . . In the event of the said two Commissioners differing . . . such Reports . . . shall be made by them, or either of them, and such reference to a friendly Sovereign or State, shall be made . . . as in the latter part of the IVth Article is contained. . . .

IX. The United States of America engage to put an end, immediately after the ratification of the present Treaty, to hostilities with all the tribes or nations of Indians with whom they may be at war at the time of such ratification; and forthwith to restore to such tribes or nations respectively, all the possessions, rights and privileges which they may have enjoyed or been entitled to in 1811, previous to such hostilities: provided always, that such tribes or nations shall agree to desist from all hostilities against the United States of America. . . .

And his Britannic Majesty engages on his part to put an end, immediately after the ratification of the present Treaty, to hostilities with all the tribes or nations of Indians with whom he may be at war at the time of such ratification; and forthwith to restore to such tribes or nations respectively, all the possessions, rights and privileges which they may have enjoyed or been entitled to in 1811, previous to such hostilities. . . .

X. Whereas the traffic in slaves in irreconcilable with the principles of humanity and justice; and whereas both his Majesty and the United States are desirous of continuing their efforts to promote its entire abolition; it is hereby agreed that both the Contracting Parties shall use their best endeavours to accomplish so desirable an object. . . .

Gambier.	Henry Goulburn.	William Adams.
John Quincy Adams.	J. A. Bayard.	H. Clay.
Jona. Russell.	Albert Gallatin.	

572. Whitbread's motion against the renewal of war with France

(*Sir Samuel Romilly's Diary*, III (28 April 1815), pp. 167–169.)

Whitbread moved, in the House of Commons, that an Address should be presented to the Regent, praying that H.R.H. would not involve the country in war on the ground of the Government of France being in the hands of any particular individual, or to that effect . . . I voted for the motion, in a minority of 72 against 273. . . . The principal arguments of those who opposed the motion, and were for making war, were—that experience had proved that there could be no security for this country as long as Bonaparte was at the head of the French Government: that his ambition was insatiable, and the destruction of this country the object nearest his heart: that no reliance could be placed on his present professions: that to conclude a peace with him was only to enable him at his leisure to make preparations to overwhelm us: that, as long as he was the ruler of France, it must be a military nation, and its relations with this country must be those of actual or suspended war, of open hostility or an armed truce: that an armed peace was a state little less mischievous to England than open war: that the expense of it would be most burdensome, if not ruinous to the country; and that such a great military peace establishment. as must be kept on foot, was wholly inconsistent with the spirit of our Constitution, and would justly excite alarms for the liberties of the nation: that, at the present moment, the Allies were all united, and were prepared for very great exertions in the common cause; but what they might be at some future period, when, having for the present suffered ourselves to be deceived into an anxious security, we should at last awake unrefreshed from our haunted and disturbed repose to a sense of our real danger; what views might have opened to their ambition in the interval, what jealousies might have arisen, what successful seductions might have been practised, what a state of incapacity to engage in immediate war any of the Allies might have fallen into, the most sagacious could not foresee: that, in these circumstances, our greatest safety seemed to be in war, and was unquestionably in co-operating with our Allies, whatever might be their determination.

To this it was answered, that it would readily be admitted that Bonaparte was not sincere in his professions of moderation; that if he had the power he would at present grasp at the same objects of unbounded ambition as he had done formerly; but that in reality he was now deprived of all power: that he now, for the first time, felt the necessity of cultivating the favour of those who were friendly to the establishment of a free Government: that without their concurrence he could not raise such an army as would set him above the control of every domestic party, and make him an object of jealousy to foreign States: that the hostility of the Allies was what could alone relieve him from these difficulties, and set him free from all restraint: that the threat of a hostile invasion, and the preparations carrying on to execute it, would make indispensable great levies of troops in France, and must necessarily invest with the command Bonaparte, as the military chief, in whose talents the nation could best confide: and that when once he was placed at the head of a great military force which he could lead to victory and conquest, he would scorn all domestic parties: that the most extraordinary expedient that ever was thought of for preventing the French from becoming a military nation was to force them reluctantly into a war: that in determining on the expediency of war, we must consider our means and our resources; and that with the present exhausted state of our resources, the most sanguine could hardly hope that we should be able to supply the expenditure necessary for carrying it on for a period of more than two years: that if peace would afford France time to recruit her strength and put herself in a formidable state of military preparation, it should be recollected that it would afford the same advantage to the Allies, who seemed to stand in still greater need of it: that if the union of the Allies was not to be depended on in time of peace, how much less could any reliance be placed on it during the various occurrences of war, which were continually opening new situations to work upon their hopes or their fears, and to seduce them from their alliance.

573. Wellington to Earl Bathurst, 19 June 1815

(Gurwood, *Selections from Wellington's Despatches*, p. 857.)

Waterloo

Buonaparte, having collected the 1st, 2nd, 3rd, 4th, and 6th corps of the French army, and the Imperial Guards, and nearly all the cavalry, on the Sambre, and between that river and the Meuse, between the 10th and 14th of the month, advanced on the 15th and attacked the Prussian posts at Thuin and Lobbes, on the Sambre, at daylight in the morning.

I did not hear of these events till in the evening of the 15th; and I immediately ordered the troops to prepare to march, and afterwards to march to their left, as soon as I had intelligence from other quarters to prove that the enemy's movement upon Charleroi was the real attack.

The enemy drove the Prussian posts from the Sambre on that day; and General Ziethen, who commanded the corps which had been at Charleroi, retired upon Fleurus; and Marshal Prince Blücher concentrated the Prussian army upon Sombref, holding the villages in front of his position of St. Amand and Ligny.

The enemy continued his march along the road from Charleroi towards Bruxelles; and, on the same evening, the 15th, attacked a brigade of the army of the Netherlands, under the Prince de Weimar, posted at Frasne, and forced it back to the farm house, on the same road, called Les Quatre Bras.

The Prince of Orange immediately reinforced this brigade with another of the same division, under General Perponcher, and, in the morning early, regained part of the ground which had been lost, so as to have the command of the communication leading from Nivelles and Bruxelles with Marshal Blücher's position.

In the mean time, I had directed the whole army to march upon Les Quatre Bras; and the 5th division, under Lieut. General Sir T. Picton, arrived at about half past 2 in the day, followed by the corps of troops under the Duke of Brunswick, and afterwards by the contingent of Nassau.

At this time the enemy commenced an attack upon Prince Blücher with his whole force, excepting the 1st and 2nd corps, and a corps of cavalry under General Kellermann, with which he attacked our post at Les Quatre Bras.

The Prussian army maintained their position with their usual gallantry and perseverance against a great disparity of numbers, as the 4th corps of their army, under General Bülow, had not joined; and I was not able to assist them as I wished, as I was attacked myself, and the troops, the cavalry in particular, which had a long distance to march, had not arrived.

We maintained our position also, and completely defeated and repulsed all the enemy's attempts to get possession of it. The enemy repeatedly attacked us with a large body of infantry and cavalry, supported by a numerous and powerful artillery. He made several charges with the cavalry upon our infantry, but all were repulsed in the steadiest manner.

In this affair, H.R.H. the Prince of Orange, the Duke of Brunswick, and Lieut. General Sir T. Picton, and Major Generals Sir. J. Kempt and Sir Denis Pack, who were engaged from the commencement of the enemy's attack, highly distinguished themselves, as well as Lieut. General C. Baron Alten, Major General Sir C. Halkett, Lieut. General Cooke, and Major Generals Maitland and Byng, as they successively arrived. The troops of the 5th division, and those of the Brunswick corps, were long and severely engaged, and conducted themselves with the utmost gallantry. I must particularly mention the 28th, 42nd, 79th, and 92nd regts., and the battalion of Hanoverians.

Our loss was great, as your Lordship will perceive by the enclosed return; and I have particularly to regret H.S.H. the Duke of Brunswick, who fell fighting gallantly at the head of his troops.

Although Marshal Blücher had maintained his position at Sombref, he still found himself much weakened by the severity of the contest in which he had been engaged, and, as the 4th corps had not arrived, he determined to fall back and to concentrate his army upon Wavre; and he marched in the night, after the action was over.

This movement of the Marshal rendered necessary a corresponding one upon my part; and I retired from the farm of Quatre Bras upon Genappe, and thence upon Waterloo, the next morning, the 17th, at 10 o'clock.

The enemy made no effort to pursue Marshal Blücher. On the contrary, a patrole which I sent to Sombref in the morning found all quiet;* and the enemy's vedettes fell back as the patrole advanced. Neither did he attempt to molest our march to the rear, although made in the middle of the day, excepting by following, with a large body of cavalry brought from his right, the cavalry under the Earl of Uxbridge.

* Lieut. Colonel the Hon. A. Gordon was sent, escorted by a squadron of the 10th hussars, to communicate with the Prussian head quarters, as to co-operation with the British army ordered to retire to the position in front of Waterloo.

This gave Lord Uxbridge an opportunity of charging them with the 1st Life Guards, upon their *débouché* from the village of Genappe, upon which occasion his Lordship has declared himself to be well satisfied with that regiment.

The position which I took up in front of Waterloo crossed the high roads from Charleroi and Nivelles, and had its right thrown back to a ravine near Merke Braine, which was occupied, and its left extended to a height above the hamlet Ter la Haye, which was likewise occupied. In front of the right centre, and near the Nivelles road, we occupied the house and gardens of Hougoumont, which covered the return of that flank; and in front of the left centre we occupied the farm of La Haye Sainte. By our left we communicated with Marshal Prince Blücher at Wavre, through Ohain; and the Marshal had promised me that, in case we should be attacked, he would support me with one or more corps, as might be necessary.

The enemy collected his army, with the exception of the 3rd corps, which had been sent to observe Marshal Blücher, on a range of heights in our front, in the course of the night of the 17th and yesterday morning, and at about 10 o'clock he commenced a furious attack upon our post at Hougoumont. I had occupied that post with a detachment from General Byng's brigade of Guards, which was in position in its rear; and it was for some time under the command of Lieut. Colonel Macdonell, and afterwards of Colonel Home; and I am happy to add, that it was maintained throughout the day with the utmost gallantry by these brave troops, notwithstanding the repeated efforts of large bodies of the enemy to obtain possession of it.

This attack upon the right of our centre was accompanied by a very heavy cannonade upon our whole line, which was destined to support the repeated attacks of cavalry and infantry, occasionally mixed, but sometimes separate, which were made upon it. In one of these the enemy carried the farm house of La Haye Sainte, as the detachment of the light battalion of the German Legion, which occupied it, had expended all its ammunition; and the enemy occupied the only communication there was with them.

The enemy repeatedly charged our infantry with his cavalry, but these attacks were uniformly unsuccessful; and they afforded opportunities to our cavalry to charge, in one of which Lord E. Somerset's brigade, consisting of the Life Guards, the Royal Horse Guards, and 1st dragoon guards, highly distinguished themselves, as did that of Major General Sir W. Ponsonby, having taken many prisoners and an eagle.

These attacks were repeated till about 7 in the evening, when the enemy made a desperate effort with cavalry and infantry, supported by the fire of artillery, to force our left centre, near the farm of La Haye Sainte, which, after a severe contest, was defeated; and, having observed that the troops retired from this attack in great confusion, and that the march of General Bülow's corps, by Frischermont, upon Planchenois and La Belle Alliance, had begun to take effect, and as I could perceive the fire of his cannon, and as Marshal Prince Blücher had joined in person with a corps of his army to the left of our line by Ohain, I determined to attack the enemy, and immediately advanced the whole line of infantry, supported by the cavalry and artillery. The attack succeeded in every point: the enemy was forced from his positions on the heights, and fled in the utmost confusion, leaving behind him, as far as I could judge, 150 pieces of cannon, with their ammunition, which fell into our hands.

I continued the pursuit till long after dark, and then discontinued it only on account of the fatigue of our troops, who had been engaged during 12 hours, and because I found myself on the same road with Marshal Blücher, who assured me of his intention to follow the enemy throughout the night. He has sent me word this morning that he had taken 60 pieces of cannon belonging to the Imperial Guard, and several carriages, baggage, &c., belonging to Buonaparte, in Genappe.

I propose to move this morning upon Nivelles, and not to discontinue my operations.

Your Lordship will observe that such a desperate action could not be fought, and such advantages could not be gained, without great loss; and I am sorry to add that ours has been immense. In Lieut. General Sir T. Picton His Majesty has sustained the loss of an officer who has frequently distinguished himself in his service; and he fell gloriously leading his division to a charge with bayonets, by which one of the most serious attacks made by the enemy on our position was repulsed. The Earl of Uxbridge, after having successfully got through this arduous day, received a wound by almost the last shot fired, which will, I am afraid, deprive His Majesty for some time of his services.

H.R.H. the Prince of Orange distinguished himself by his gallantry and conduct, till he received a wound from a musket ball through the shoulder, which obliged him to quit the field.

It gives me the greatest satisfaction to assure your Lordship that the army never, upon any occasion, conducted itself better. The division of Guards, under Lieut. General Cooke, who is severely wounded, Major General Maitland, and Major General Byng, set an example which was followed by all; and there is no officer nor description of troops that did not behave well.

I must, however, particularly mention, for His Royal Highness' approbation, Lieut. General Sir H. Clinton, Major General Adam, Lieut. General C. Baron Alten (severely wounded), Major General Sir C. Halkett (severely wounded), Colonel Ompteda, Colonel Mitchell (commanding a brigade of the 4th division), Major Generals Sir J. Kempt and Sir D. Pack, Major General Lambert, Major General Lord E. Somerset, Major General Sir W. Ponsonby, Major General Sir C. Grant, and Major General Sir H. Vivian, Major General Sir J. O. Vandeleur, and Major General Count Dornberg.

I am also particularly indebted to General Lord Hill for his assistance and conduct upon this, as upon all former occasions.

The artillery and engineer departments were conducted much to my satisfaction by Colonel Sir G. Wood and Colonel Smyth; and I had every reason to be satisfied with the conduct of the Adjutant General, Major General Barnes, who was wounded, and of the Quarter Master General, Colonel De Lancey, who was killed by a cannon shot in the middle of the action. This officer is a serious loss to His Majesty's service, and to me at this moment.

I was likewise much indebted to the assistance of Lieut. Colonel Lord FitzRoy Somerset, who was severely wounded, and of the officers composing my personal Staff, who have suffered severely in this action. Lieut. Colonel the Hon. Sir A. Gordon, who has died of his wounds, was a most promising officer, and is a serious loss to His Majesty's service.

General Krüse, of the Nassau service, likewise conducted himself much to my satisfaction; as did General Trip, commanding the heavy brigade of cavalry, and General Vanhope, commanding a brigade of infantry in the service of the King of the Netherlands.

General Pozzo di Borgo, General Baron Vincent, General Müffling, and General Alava, were in the field during the action, and rendered me every assistance in their power. Baron Vincent is wounded, but I hope not severely; and General Pozzo di Borgo received a contusion.

I should not do justice to my own feelings, or to Marshal Blücher and the Prussian army, if I did not attribute the successful result of this arduous day to the cordial and timely assistance I received from them. The operation of General Bülow upon the enemy's flank was a most decisive one; and, even if I had not found myself in a situation to make the attack which produced the final result, it would have forced the enemy to retire if his attacks should have failed, and would have prevented him from taking advantage of them if they should unfortunately have succeeded.

Since writing the above, I have received a report that Major General Sir W. Ponsonby is killed; and, in announcing this intelligence to your Lordship, I have to add the expression of my grief for the fate of an officer who had already rendered very brilliant and important services, and was an ornament to his profession.

I send with this dispatch 3 eagles, taken by the troops in this action, which Major Percy will have the honor of laying at the feet of His Royal Highness. I beg leave to recommend him to your Lordship's protection.

Return of the Killed, Wounded, and Missing of the British and Hanoverian Army under the command of Field Marshal the Duke of Wellington, K.G., in the battle fought at Quatre Bras on the 16th June, 1815.

	Officers.	Serjeants.	Rank & File.	Total loss of Officers, Non-commissioned Officers, and Rank and File.	British.	Hanoverians.	Horses.
Killed . .	29	19	302	350	316	34	19
Wounded .	126	111	2143	2380	2156	224	14
Missing . .	4	6	171	181	32	149	1

On the retreat from Quatre Bras to Waterloo, on the 17th June, 1815.

	Officers.	Serjeants.	Rank & File.	Total loss of Officers, Non-commissioned Officers, and Rank and File.	British.	Hanoverians.	Horses.
Killed . .	I	I	33	35	26	9	45
Wounded .	7	13	112	132	52	80	20
Missing . .	4	3	64	71	30	32	33

In the battle fought at Waterloo on the 18th June, 1815.

	Officers.	Serjeants.	Rank & File.	Total loss of Officers, Non-commissioned Officers, and Rank and File.	British.	Hanoverians.	Horses.
Killed . .	116	109	1822	2047	1759	288	1495
Wounded .	504	364	6148	7016	5892	1124	891
Missing . .	20	29	1574	1623	807	816	773

	Killed.	Wounded.	Missing.
Total . .	2432	9528	1875

The greater number of the men returned missing had gone to the rear with wounded officers and soldiers, and joined afterwards. The officers are supposed killed.

574. Napoleon's letter to the Prince Regent (Translation)

(This is, perhaps, the most celebrated letter in the Royal Archives at Windsor.)

Exposed to the factions which distract my country and to the enmity of the greatest Powers of Europe, I have ended my political career, and I come, like Themistocles, to throw myself upon the hospitality of the British people. I put myself under the protection of their laws, which I claim from your Royal Highness, as the most powerful, the most constant, and the most generous of my enemies.

Rochefort, 13 July 1815.

575. Lord Liverpool to Lord Castlereagh, 15 and 20 July 1815

(C. D. Yonge, Life of Lord Liverpool, II, pp. 196, 198–199.)

15 July:

. . . I am desirous of apprising you of our sentiments respecting Buonaparte. If you should succeed in getting possession of his person, and the King of France does not feel himself sufficiently strong to bring him to justice as a rebel, we are ready to take upon ourselves the custody of his person on the part of the Allied Powers, and, indeed, we should think it better that he should be assigned to us than to any other member of the confederacy. In this case, however, we should prefer that there were not Commissioners appointed on the part of the other Powers, but that the discretion should be vested entirely in ourselves; and that we should be at liberty to fix the place of his confinement either in Great Britain or at Gibraltar, Malta, St. Helena, the Cape of Good Hope, or any other colony we might think most secure.

We incline at present strongly to the opinion that the best place of custody would be at a distance from Europe, and that the Cape of Good Hope, or St. Helena would be the most proper stations for the purpose.

If, however, we are to have the severe responsibility of such a charge, it is but just that we should have the choice of the place of confinement, and a complete discretion as to the means necessary to render that confinement effectual.

20 July: ... We are all decidedly of opinion that it would not answer to confine him in this country. Very nice legal questions might arise upon the subject, which would be particularly embarrassing; but, independent of these considerations, you know enough of the feelings of people in this country not to doubt that he would become an object of curiosity immediately, and possibly of compassion in the course of a few months; and the very circumstances of his being here, or indeed anywhere else in Europe, would contribute to keep up a certain degree of ferment in France. ...

To conclude: we wish that the King of France would hang or shoot Buonaparte, as the best termination of the business; but if this is impracticable, and the Allies are desirous that we should have the custody of him, it is not unreasonable that we should be allowed to judge of the means by which that custody can be made effectual.

D. THE SETTLEMENT OF EUROPE, AND POST-WAR PROBLEMS

576. The general treaty signed in Congress at Vienna, 9 June 1815

(Cobbett's *Parliamentary Debates*, XXXII, 71–113.)

The treaty is too lengthy to be quoted in full: its provisions are summarized.

In the name of the Most Holy and Undivided Trinity.

The Powers who signed the Treaty concluded at Paris on the 30th of May 1814, having assembled at Vienna, in pursuance of the 32d Article of that Act, with the Princes and States their Allies, to complete the provisions of the said Treaty, and to add to them the arrangements rendered necessary by the state in which Europe was left at the termination of the last war, being now desirous to embrace, in one common transaction, the various results of their negotiations, for the purpose of confirming them by their reciprocal ratifications, have authorised their Plenipotentiaries to unite, in a general instrument, the regulations of superior and permanent interest, and to join to that act, as integral parts of the arrangements of Congress, the Treaties, Conventions, Declarations, Regulations, and other particular acts, as cited in the present Treaty. And the above-mentioned Powers having appointed Plenipotentiaries to the Congress, that is to say: H.M. the Emperor of Austria, King of Hungary and Bohemia, the . . . Prince de Metternich . . . and the . . . Baron de Wessenberg. . . . H.M. the King of Spain and the Indies, Don Peter Gomez Labrador. . . . H.M. the King of France and Navarre, the Sieur Charles Maurice de Talleyrand-Perigord, Prince of Talleyrand . . . the Sieur Duke d'Alberg . . . the Sieur Count Gouvernet de Latour du Pin . . . and the Sieur Alexis Count de Noailles. . . . H.M. the King of the United Kingdom of Great Britain and Ireland, . . . Viscount Castlereagh . . . the Duke . . . of Wellington, . . . the . . . Earl of Clancarty . . ., Earl Cathcart . . . and . . . Lord Stewart. . . . H.R.H. the Prince Regent of the Kingdoms of Portugal and the Brazils, the . . . Count of Palmella, . . . the Sieur Antonio de Saldanha da Gama . . . and the Sieur Don Joachim Lobo da Silveira. . . . H.M. the King of Prussia, the Prince Hardenberg . . . and the . . . Baron de Humboldt. . . . H.M. the Emperor of all the Russias, the . . . Prince de Rasoumoffsky . . ., the . . . Count de Stackelberg . . . and the . . . Count de Nesselrode. . . . H.M. the King of Sweden and Norway, the . . . Count de Lowenhielm. . . .

ARTICLE I. The Duchy of Warsaw, with the exception of the provinces and districts which are otherwise disposed of by the following Articles, is united to the Russian Empire, to which it shall be irrevocably attached by its Constitution, and be possessed by H.M. the Emperor of all the Russias, his heirs and successors in perpetuity. His Imperial Majesty reserves to himself to give to this State, enjoying a distinct Administration, the interior improvement which he shall judge proper. He shall assume with his other titles that of Czar, King of Poland, agreeably to the form established for the titles attached to his other possessions. The Poles, who are respective subjects of Russia, Austria and Prussia, shall obtain a representation, and national institutions, regulated according to the degree of political consideration, that each of the Governments to which they belong shall judge expedient and proper to grant them.

ARTICLE II. [Defines the part of the Duchy of Warsaw which Prussia shall possess under the title of the Grand Duchy of Posen.]

ARTICLE III. [The Emperor of Austria to possess] . . . the salt-mines of Wieliczka and the territory thereto belonging.

ARTICLE IV. [Defines the Galician boundary with Russia.]

ARTICLE V. [Russia cedes to Austria the districts which have been separated from Eastern Galicia in consequence of the Treaty of Vienna of 1809.]

ARTICLE VI. The town of Cracow, with its territory, is declared to be for ever a free, independent, and strictly neutral city, under the protection of Austria, Russia and Prussia.

ARTICLE VII. [Defines the territory of the free town of Cracow.]

ARTICLE VIII. . . . No military establishment shall be formed that can menace the neutrality of Cracow, or obstruct the liberty of commerce which his Imperial and Royal Apostolic Majesty grants to the town and district of Podgorze.

ARTICLE IX. [Russia, Austria and Prussia engage to respect Cracow's neutrality.]

ARTICLE X. [Matters concerning the internal affairs of Cracow.]

ARTICLE XI. A full, general, and special amnesty shall be granted in favour of all individuals, of whatever rank, sex, or condition they may be.

ARTICLE XII. In consequence of the preceding Article, no person in future shall be prosecuted or disturbed, in any manner, by reason of any participation, direct or indirect, at any time, in the political, civil or military events in Poland. All proceedings, suits or prosecutions are considered as null, the sequestrations and provisional confiscations shall be taken off, and every Act promulgated on this ground shall be of no effect.

ARTICLE XIII. From these general regulations on the subject of confiscations are excepted all those cases in which edicts or sentences, finally pronounced, have already been fully executed, and have not been annulled by subsequent events.

ARTICLE XIV. The principles established for the free navigation of rivers and canals, in the whole extent of ancient Poland, as well as for the trade to the ports, for the circulation of articles the growth and produce of the different Polish provinces, and for the commerce, relative to goods in transitu, such as they are specified in the 24th, 25th, 26th, 28th and 29th Articles of the Treaty between Austria and Russia . . . shall be invariably maintained.

ARTICLE XV. H.M. the King of Saxony renounces in perpetuity for himself and all his descendants and successors, in favour of H.M. the King of Prussia, all his right and title to the provinces, districts and territories . . . of the kingdom of Saxony, hereafter named. . . .

ARTICLE XVI. [The territory transferred from Saxony to Prussia to be distinguished by the name of the Duchy of Saxony.]

ARTICLE XVII. Austria, Russia, Great Britain and France guarantee to H.M. the King of Prussia, his descendants and successors, the possession of the countries marked out in the 15th Article, in full property and sovereignty.

ARTICLE XVIII. His Imperial and Royal Apostolic Majesty, wishing to give to the King of Prussia a fresh proof of his desire to remove every object of future discussion between their two Courts, renounces . . . his rights of sovereignty over the Margraviates of Upper and Lower Lusatia, which belonged to him as King of Bohemia, as far as these rights concern the portion of these provinces placed under the dominion of H.M. the King of Prussia, by virtue of the Treaty with H.M. the King of Saxony, concluded at Vienna on the 18th of May 1813. . . .

ARTICLE XIX. H.M. the King of Prussia and H.M. the King of Saxony . . . renounce . . . all feudal rights or pretensions which they might exercise . . . beyond the frontiers fixed by the present Treaty.

ARTICLE XX. [The inhabitants of the Saxon provinces ceded to Prussia] . . . shall be allowed to emigrate from one territory to the other, without being exempted, however, from military service. . . . They may also remove their property without being subject to any fine or drawback (*Abzugsgeld*).

ARTICLE XXI. The communities, corporations and religious establishments, and those for public instruction in the provinces ceded by . . . Saxony to Prussia . . . shall preserve their property. . . .

ARTICLE XXII. No individual domiciled in [Saxony] . . . shall be molested in his person . . . [or property for any part he may have taken in the War, terminated by the Peace of Paris, 30 May 1814.]

ARTICLES XXIII to XXV. [Prussian territorial gains specified in detail.]

ARTICLE XXVI. H.M. the King of the United Kingdom of Great Britain and Ireland, having substituted to his ancient title of Elector of the Holy Roman Empire, that of King of Hanover, and this title having been acknowledged by all the Powers of Europe, and by the Princes and free towns of Germany, the countries which have till now composed the Electorate of Brunswick-Luneburg, according as their limits have been recognised and fixed for the future, by the following Articles, shall henceforth form the Kingdom of Hanover.

ARTICLE XXVII. H.M. the King of Prussia cedes to H.M. the King of the United Kingdom of Great Britain and Ireland, King of Hanover, to be possessed by H.M. and his successors, in full property and sovereignty:

1. The principality of Hildesheim. . . . 2. The town and territory of Goslar. 3. The principality of East Friesland. . . . 4. The lower County (*Nieder Graftschaft*) of Lingen. . . .

ARTICLE XXVIII. [King of Prussia renounces certain rights in Hanoverian territory.]

ARTICLE XXIX. H.M. the King of the United Kingdom of Great Britain and Ireland, King of Hanover, cedes to H.M. the King of Prussia. . . . 1. That part of the Duchy of Lauenbourg situated upon the right bank of the Elbe. . . . 2. The bailiwick of Klötze. 3. The bailiwick of Elbingesode. 4. The villages of Rudegershagen and Gœnseteich. 5. The bailiwick of Reckeberg. . . .

ARTICLE XXX. [The Hanoverian Government agrees to undertake certain works necessary to render navigable that part of the River Ems which extends from the Prussian frontier to its mouth. Prussian ships and Prussian merchants shall not pay for navigation, for exportation or importation of merchandise, or for warehousing, any other tolls or duties than those charged upon the Hanoverian subjects.]

ARTICLE XXXI. [The Prussian and Hanoverian Governments agree to the construction of certain military roads through their respective dominions.]

ARTICLE XXXII. [Providing for the fixing of part of the frontier of Hanover.]

ARTICLE XXXIII. His Britannic Majesty, King of Hanover, in order to meet the wishes of his Prussian Majesty to procure a suitable arrondissement of territory for his Serene Highness the Duke of Oldenburg, promises to cede to him a district containing a population of 5,000 inhabitants.

ARTICLE XXXIV. His Serene Highness the Duke of Holstein-Oldenburg shall assume the title of Grand Duke of Oldenburg.

ARTICLE XXXV. Their Serene Highnesses the Dukes of Mecklenburg-Schwerin and Mecklenburg-Strelitz, shall assume the titles of Grand Dukes of Mecklenburg-Schwerin and Strelitz.

ARTICLE XXXVI. His Highness the Duke of Saxe-Weimar shall assume the title of Grand Duke of Saxe-Weimar.

ARTICLE XXXVII. [The King of Prussia to cede to the Grand Duke of Saxe-Weimar, districts bordering on the principality of Weimar, and part of the principality of Fulda.]

ARTICLE XXXVIII. [The above-mentioned districts shall be determined by a particular Convention.]

ARTICLE XXXIX. [Certain of the above-mentioned districts to be ceded within a fortnight.]

ARTICLE XL. [Further provisions respecting part of the principality of Fulda.]

ARTICLE XLI. [Further provisions respecting the principality of Fulda and the County of Hanau.]

ARTICLE XLII. [The town and territory of Wetzlar ceded to Prussia.]

ARTICLE XLIII. [Arrangements respecting certain mediatised German districts.]

ARTICLE XLIV. [The King of Bavaria to possess the Grand Duchy of Wurtzburg and the principality of Aschaffenburg.]

ARTICLE XLV. [Arrangements respecting the rights, prerogatives and maintenance of the Prince Primate.]

ARTICLE XLVI. [The city of Frankfort is declared free, and shall constitute a part of the Germanic League.]

ARTICLE XLVII. [The Grand Duke of Hesse, in exchange for the Duchy of Westphalia, ceded to the King of Prussia, to obtain certain territory on the Rhine.]

ARTICLE XLVIII. [The Landgrave of Homburg to be reinstated in his possessions of which he was deprived in consequence of the Confederation of the Rhine.]

ARTICLE XLIX. [A certain district in the ci-devant Department of the Saar to be partitioned between the Dukes of Saxe-Coburg, Oldenburg and Mecklenburg-Strelitz, the Landgrave of Hesse-Homburg, and the Count of Pappenheim.]

ARTICLES L, LI. [Further provisions respecting the above-mentioned district.]

ARTICLE LII. [The principality of Issenburg placed under the sovereignty of the Emperor of Austria.]

ARTICLE LIII. The Sovereign Princes and Free Towns of Germany, under which denomination, for the present purpose, are comprehended their Majesties the Emperor of Austria, the Kings of Prussia, of Denmark, and of the Netherlands; that is to say, the Emperor of Austria and the King of Prussia for all their possessions which anciently belonged to the German Empire, the King of Denmark for the Duchy of Holstein, and the King of the Netherlands for the Grand Duchy of Luxemburg, establish among themselves a perpetual Confederation, which shall be called 'the Germanic Confederation'.

ARTICLE LIV. The object of this Confederation is the maintenance of the external and internal safety of Germany, and of the independence and inviolability of the confederated States.

ARTICLE LV. The Members of the Confederation, as such, are equal with regard to their rights; and they all equally engage to maintain the Act which constitutes their union.

ARTICLE LVI. The affairs of the Confederation shall be confided to a Federative Diet, in which all the Members shall vote by their Plenipotentiaries, either individually or collectively, in the following manner, without prejudice to their rank [each to have one vote]:

1. Austria. 2. Prussia. 3. Bavaria. 4. Saxony. 5. Hanover. 6. Wurtemburg. 7. Baden.

8. Electoral Hesse. 9. Grand Duchy of Hesse. 10. Denmark, for Holstein. 11. The Netherlands, for Luxemburg. 12. Grand-Ducal and Ducal Houses of Saxony. 13. Brunswick and Nassau. 14. Mecklenburg-Schwerin and Strelitz. 15. Holstein-Oldenburg, Anhalt and Schwartzburg. 16. Hohenzollern, Lichtenstein, Reuss, Schaumburg, Lippe, Lippe and Waldeck. 17. The Free Towns of Lubeck, Frankfort, Bremen and Hamburg.

ARTICLE LVII. Austria shall preside at the Federative Diet. Each State of the Confederation has the right of making propositions, and the presiding State shall bring them under deliberation within a definitive time.

ARTICLE LVIII. Whenever fundamental laws are to be enacted, changes made in the fundamental laws of the Confederation, measures adopted relative to the Federative Act itself, and organic institutions or other arrangements made for the common interest, the Diet shall form itself into a General Assembly, and, in that case, the distribution of votes shall be as follows, calculated according to the respective extent of the individual States:

Austria, Prussia, Saxony, Bavaria, Hanover, Wurtemburg to have 4 votes each; Baden, Electoral Hesse, Grand Duchy of Hesse, Holstein, Luxemburg to have 3 votes each; Brunswick, Mecklenburg-Schwerin, Nassau to have 2 votes each; Saxe-Weimar, Saxe Gotha, Saxe-Coburg, Saxe-Meiningen, Saxe-Hildburghausen, Mecklenburg-Strelitz, Holstein-Oldenburg, Anhalt-Dessau, Anhalt-Bernburg, Anhalt-Kotthen, Schwartzburg-Sondershausen, Schwartzburg-Rudolstadt, Hohen-zollern-Heckingen, Lichtenstein, Hohenzollern-Sigmaringen, Waldeck, Reuss (Elder Branch), Reuss (Younger Branch), Schaumburg-Lippe, Lippe, The Free towns of Lubeck, Frankfort, Bremen, Hamburg to have one vote each. Total votes, 69.

The Diet, in deliberating on the organic laws of the Confederation, shall consider whether any collective votes ought to be granted to the ancient mediatised States of the Empire.

ARTICLE LIX. The question whether a subject is to be discussed by the General Assembly, conformably to the principles above established, shall be decided in the Ordinary Assembly by a majority of votes. The same assembly shall prepare the drafts of Resolutions which are to be proposed to the General Assembly, and shall furnish the latter with all the necessary information, either for adopting or rejecting them. The plurality of votes shall regulate the decisions, both in the Ordinary and General Assemblies, with this difference, however, that in the Ordinary Assembly, an absolute majority shall be deemed sufficient, while in the other, two-thirds of the votes shall be necessary to form the majority. When the votes are even in the Ordinary Assembly, the President shall have the casting vote; but when the Assembly is to deliberate on the acceptance or change of any of the fundamental laws, upon organic institutions, upon individual rights, or upon affairs of religion, the plurality of votes shall not be deemed sufficient, either in the Ordinary or in the General Assembly. The Diet is permanent: it may, however, when the subjects submitted to its deliberation are disposed of, adjourn for a fixed period, which shall not exceed four months. . . .

ARTICLE LX. [Respecting the order in which the members of the Confederation shall vote.]

ARTICLE LXI. The Diet shall assemble at Frankfort on the Main. Its first meeting is fixed for the 1st of September 1815.

ARTICLE LXII. The first object to be considered by the Diet after its opening, shall be the framing of the fundamental laws of the Confederation, and of its organic institutions, with respect to its exterior, military and interior relations.

ARTICLE LXIII. The States of the Confederation engage to defend not only the whole of Germany, but each individual State of the Union, in case it should be attacked, and they mutually guarantee to each other such of their possessions as are comprised in this Union. When war shall be declared by the Confederation, no member can open a separate negotiation with the enemy, nor make peace, nor conclude an armistice, without the consent of the other members. The confederated States engage, in the same manner, not to make war against each other, on any pretext, nor to pursue their differences by force of arms, but to submit them to the Diet, which will attempt a mediation by means of a Commission. If this should not succeed, and a juridical sentence becomes necessary, recourse shall be had to a well-organised Austregal Court (Austregal instanz), to the decision of which the contending parties are to submit without appeal.

ARTICLE LXIV. The Articles comprised under the title of Particular Arrangements, in the Act of the Germanic Confederation, as annexed to the present General Treaty . . . shall have the same force and validity as if they were textually inserted herein.

ARTICLE LXV. The ancient United Provinces of the Netherlands and the late Belgic provinces, both within the limits fixed by the following Article, shall form, together with the countries and territories designated in the same Article, under the sovereignty of his Royal Highness the Prince of Orange-Nassau, sovereign prince of the United Provinces, the kingdom of the Netherlands, hereditary in the order of succession already established by the Act of the Constitution of the said United Provinces. The title and the prerogatives of the royal dignity are recognised by all the Powers in the house of Orange-Nassau.

ARTICLE LXVI. [Respecting the precise boundaries of the Kingdom of the Netherlands.]

ARTICLE LXVII. That part of the old Duchy of Luxemburg which is comprised in the limits specified in the following Article, is likewise ceded to the Sovereign Prince of the United Provinces, now King of the Netherlands, to be possessed in perpetuity by him and his successors, in full property and sovereignty. The Sovereign of the Netherlands shall add to his titles that of Grand Duke of Luxemburg. . . .

ARTICLE LXVIII. [Defines the boundaries of the Grand Duchy of Luxemburg.]

ARTICLE LXIX. [Respecting the Duchy of Bouillon.]

ARTICLE LXX. H.M. the King of the Netherlands renounces in perpetuity . . . in favour of . . . the King of Prussia, the sovereign possessions which the House of Nassau-Orange held in Germany, namely, the principalities of Dillenburg, Dietz, Siegen and Hadamar, with the lordships of Beilstein. . . .

ARTICLE LXXI. [Respecting the order of succession of the two branches of the House of Nassau, to the Grand Duchy of Luxemburg].

ARTICLE LXXII. [The King of the Netherlands enters into all the rights relative to the districts detached from France by the Treaty of Paris, 30 May 1814.]

ARTICLE LXXIII. . . . The King of the Netherlands, having recognised . . . as the basis of the union of the Belgic Provinces with the United Provinces, the eight Articles contained in the document annexed to the present Treaty, the said Articles shall have the same force and validity as if they were inserted . . . in the present instrument.

ARTICLE LXXIV. The integrity of the nineteen Cantons . . . is recognised as the basis of the Helvetic system.

ARTICLE LXXV. The Vallais, the territory of Geneva, and the principality of Neufchatel, are united to Switzerland, and shall form three new Cantons. . . .

ARTICLE LXXVI. The bishopric of Basle and the city and territory of Bienne shall be united to the Helvetic Confederation, and shall form part of the Canton of Berne. . . .

ARTICLE LXXVII. [The inhabitants of Basle and Bienne shall enjoy the same political and civil rights which are enjoyed by the inhabitants of the ancient parts of the Cantons of Berne and Basle.]

ARTICLE LXXVIII. [The lordship of Razüns to be reunited to the Canton of the Grisons.]

ARTICLE LXXIX. [Respecting the customs houses on the road from Geneva into Switzerland via Versoy.]

ARTICLE LXXX. [The King of Sardinia cedes part of Savoy to Switzerland.]

ARTICLE LXXXI. Certain financial arrangements between certain of the Swiss Cantons.

ARTICLE LXXXII. [Respecting the disposal of certain funds of the Cantons of Zurich and Berne.]

ARTICLE LXXXIII. [Respecting compensation for the abolition of certain lauds, in Vaud.]

ARTICLE LXXXIV. The Declaration of the 20th March, addressed by the Allied Powers who signed the Treaty of Paris, to the Diet of the Swiss Confederation . . . is confirmed. . . .

ARTICLE LXXXV. [Defines the frontiers of the states of the King of Sardinia.]

ARTICLE LXXXVI. The states which constituted the former republic of Genoa, are united in perpetuity to those of his Majesty the King of Sardinia. . . .

ARTICLE LXXXVII. The King of Sardinia shall add to his present titles, that of Duke of Genoa.

ARTICLE LXXXVIII. [Rights and privileges of the Genoese guaranteed.]

ARTICLE LXXXIX. The countries called Imperial Fiefs, formerly united to the ancient Ligurian Republic, are definitively united to the states of his Majesty the King of Sardinia. . . .

ARTICLE XC. The right that the Powers who signed the Treaty of Paris . . . reserved to themselves by the 3rd Article of that Treaty, of fortifying such points of their States as they might judge proper for their safety, is equally reserved, without restriction, to . . . the King of Sardinia.

ARTICLE XCI. [The Act entitled 'Cession made by his Majesty the King of Sardinia to the Canton of Geneva', to be considered an integral part of this General Treaty, to which it is annexed.]

ARTICLE XCII. The provinces of Chablais and Faucigny, and the whole of the territory of Savoy to the north of Ugine, belonging to . . . the King of Sardinia, shall form a part of the neutrality of Switzerland, as it is recognised and guaranteed by the Powers. . . .

ARTICLE XCIII. In pursuance of the renunciations agreed upon by the Treaty of Paris of the 30th May 1814, the Powers who sign the present Treaty, recognise . . . the Emperor of Austria . . . as legitimate Sovereign of the provinces and territories which had been ceded, either wholly or in part, by the Treaties of Campo-Formio of 1797, of Lunéville of 1801, of Pressburg of 1805, by the additional Convention of Fontaine-bleau of 1807, and by the Treaty of Vienna of 1809:- . . . Istria, Austrian as well as heretofore Venetian, Dalmatia, the ancient Venetian isles of the Adriatic, the mouths of the Cattaro, the city of Venice, with its waters, as well as all the other provinces and districts of the formerly Venetian States of the Terra Firma, upon the left bank of the Adige, the Duchies of Milan and Mantua, the principalities of Brixen and Trente, the county of Tyrol, the Voralberg, the Austrian Frioul, the ancient Venetian Frioule, the territory of Montefalcone, the government and town of Trieste, Carniola, Upper Carinthia, Croatia on the right of the Save, Fiume, and the Hungarian *Littorale*, and the district of Castua.

ARTICLE XCIV. His Imperial and Royal Apostolic Majesty shall unite to his monarchy, to be possessed by him and his successors, in full property and sovereignty, 1. Besides the portions of the Terra-Firma in the Venetian states mentioned in the preceding Article, the other parts of those States, as well as all other territory situated between the Tessin, the Po, and the Adriatic sea. 2. The valleys of the Valtelline, of Bormio, and of Chiavenna. 3. The territories which formerly composed the Republic of Ragusa.

ARTICLE XCV. [Detailing the Austrian Emperor's frontiers in Italy.]

ARTICLE XCVI. The general principles, adopted by the Congress at Vienna, for the navigation of rivers, shall be applicable to that of the Po. Commissioners shall be named by the states bordering on rivers, within three months at latest after the termination of the Congress, to regulate all that concerns the execution of the present Article.

ARTICLE XCVII. [Relating to the establishment of the Mont-Napoleon at Milan.]

ARTICLE XCVIII. H.R.H. the Archduke Francis d'Este, his heirs and successors, shall possess, in full sovereignty, the Duchies of Modena, Reggio and Mirandola. . . .

ARTICLE XCIX. H.M. the Empress Maria Louisa shall possess, in full property and sovereignty, the duchies of Parma, Placentia, and Guastalla. . . . The reversion of these countries shall be regulated by common consent, with the Courts of Austria, Russia, France, Spain, England and Prussia; due regard being had to the rights of reversion of the House of Austria, and of his Majesty the King of Sardinia to the said countries.

ARTICLE C. His Imperial Highness the Archduke Ferdinand of Austria, is re-estab-lished . . . in the Grand Duchy of Tuscany and its dependencies. . . .

ARTICLE CI. The principality of Lucca shall be possessed in full sovereignty by her

Majesty the Infant Maria Louisa and her descendants, in the direct male line. The principality is erected into a Duchy. . . .

ARTICLE CII. The Duchy of Lucca shall revert to the Grand Duke of Tuscany. . . .

ARTICLE CIII. The Marches, with Camerino, and their dependencies, as well as the Duchy of Benevento and the principality of Ponte-Corvo, are restored to the Holy See. The Holy See shall resume possession of the Legations of Ravenna, Bologna and Ferrara. . . .

ARTICLE CIV. H.M. King Ferdinand . . . is restored to the throne of Naples, and H.M. is acknowledged by the Powers as King of the Two Sicilies.

ARTICLE CV. The Powers, recognising the justice of the claims of H.R.H. the Prince Regent of Portugal and the Brazils, upon the town of Olivença and the other territories ceded to Spain by the Treaty of Badajos of 1801, and viewing the restitution of the same as a measure necessary to insure that perfect and constant harmony between the two Kingdoms of the Peninsula, the preservation of which in all parts of Europe has been the constant object of their arrangements, formally engage to use their utmost endeavours, by amicable means, to procure the retrocession of the said territories in favour of Portugal. And the Powers declare, as far as depends upon them, that this arrangement shall take place as soon as possible.

ARTICLE CVI. [The stipulations contained in the 10th Article of the Treaty of 30 May 1814 between Portugal and France, shall be of no effect.]

ARTICLE CVII. [Portugal to restore to France part of French Guiana.]

ARTICLE CVIII. The Powers whose States are separated or crossed by the same navigable river, engage to regulate, by common consent, all that regards its navigation. For this purpose they will name Commissioners, who shall assemble, at latest, within six months after the termination of the Congress, and who shall adopt as the basis of their proceedings, the principles established by the following Articles.

ARTICLE CIX. The navigation of the rivers, along their whole course, referred to in the preceding Article, from the point where each of them becomes navigable, to its mouth, shall be entirely free, and shall not, in respect to commerce, be prohibited to anyone; it being understood that the regulations established with regard to the police of this navigation, shall be respected; as they will be framed alike for all, and as favourable as possible to the commerce of all nations.

ARTICLE CX. The system that shall be established both for the collection of the duties and for the maintenance of the police, shall be, as nearly as possible, the same along the whole course of the river; and shall also extend, unless particular circumstances prevent it, to those of its branches and junctions, which, in their navigable course, separate or traverse different States.

ARTICLE CXI. The duties on navigation shall be regulated in an uniform and settled manner, and with as little reference as possible to the different quality of the merchandise, in order that a minute examination of the cargo may be rendered unnecessary, except with a view to prevent fraud and evasion. The amount of the duties, which shall in no case exceed those now paid, shall be determined by local circumstances, which scarcely allow of a general rule in this respect. The tariff shall, however, be prepared in such a manner as to encourage commerce by facilitating navigation; for which purpose the duties established upon the Rhine, and now in force on that river, may serve as an approximating rule for its construction. The tariff once settled, no increase shall take place therein, except by the common consent of the States bordering on the rivers; nor shall the navigation be burdened with any other duties than those fixed in the regulation.

ARTICLE CXII. The offices for the collection of duties . . . shall be determined upon in the above regulation. . . .

ARTICLE CXIII. Each State bordering on the rivers is to be at the expense of keeping in good repair the towing paths which pass through its territory, and of maintaining the necessary works through the same extent in the channels of the river, in order that no obstacle may be experienced to the navigation. . . .

ARTICLE CXIV. There shall nowhere be established storehouse, port, or forced harbour-duties. Those already existing shall be preserved for such time only as the States bordering on rivers (without regard to the local interest of the place or the country where they are established) shall find them necessary or useful to navigation and commerce in general.

ARTICLE CXV. The custom-houses belonging to the States bordering on rivers shall not interfere in the duties of navigation. Regulations shall be established to prevent officers of the customs, in the exercise of their functions, throwing obstacles in the way of the navigation; but care shall be taken, by means of a strict police on the bank, to preclude every attempt of the inhabitants to smuggle goods through the medium of boatmen.

ARTICLE CXVI. Everything expressed in the preceding Articles shall be settled by a general arrangement in which there shall also be comprised whatever may need an ulterior determination. The arrangement once settled shall not be changed, but by and with the consent of all the States bordering on rivers. . . .

ARTICLE CXVII. The particular regulations relative to the navigation of the Rhine, the Necker, the Main, the Moselle, the Meuse, and the Scheldt, such as they are annexed to the present Act, shall have the same force and validity as if they were textually inserted herein.

ARTICLE CXVIII. The Treaties, Conventions, Declarations, Regulations, and other particular Acts which are annexed to the present Act, *viz.* 1. The Treaty between Russia and Austria of the 21st April (3 May) 1815. 2. The Treaty between Russia and Prussia of the 21st April (3 May) 1815. 3. The Additional Treaty relative to Cracow, between Austria, Prussia and Russia, of the 21st April (3 May) 1815. 4. The Treaty between Prussia and Saxony of the 18th May 1815. 5. The Declaration of the King of Saxony respecting the rights of the House of Schoenburg, of the 18th May 1815. 6. The Treaty between Prussia and Hanover of the 29th May 1815. 7. The Convention between Prussia and the Grand Duke of Saxe-Weimar of the 1st June 1815. 8. The Convention between Prussia and the Duke and Prince of Nassau of the 31st May 1815. 9. The Act concerning the Federative Constitution of Germany of the 8th June 1915. 10. The Treaty between the King of the Netherlands, and Prussia, England, Austria, and Russia, of the 31st May 1815. 11. The Declaration of the Powers on the Affairs of the Helvetic Confederation of the 20th March, and the Act of Accession of the Diet of the 28th May 1815. 12. The Protocol of the 29th March 1815, on the cessions made by the King of Sardinia to the Canton of Geneva. 13. The Treaty between the King of Sardinia, Austria, England, Russia, and France, of the 21st May 1815. 14. The Act entitled 'Conditions which are to serve as the bases of the Union of the States of Genoa with those of his Sardinian Majesty'. 15. The Declaration of the Powers on the Abolition of the Slave Trade, of the 8th February 1815. 16. The Regulations respecting the free navigation of Rivers. 17. The Regulation concerning the precedence of Diplomatic agents–shall be considered as integral parts of the arrangements of the Congress, and shall have throughout, the same force and validity as if they were inserted, word for word, in the General Treaty.

ARTICLE CXIX. All the Powers assembled in Congress, as well as the Princes and Free Towns, who have concurred in the arrangements specified, and in the Acts confirmed, in this General Treaty, are invited to accede to it.

ARTICLE CXX. The French language having been exclusively employed in all the copies of the present Treaty, it is declared, by the Powers who have concurred in this Act, that the use made of that language shall not be construed into a precedent for the future; every Power, therefore, reserves to itself the adoption in future negotiations and Conventions, the language it has heretofore employed in its diplomatic relations; and this Treaty shall not be cited as a precedent contrary to the established practice.

ARTICLE CXXI. The present Treaty shall be ratified, and the ratifications exchanged in six months, and by the Court of Portugal in a year, or sooner if possible.

577. The 'Holy Alliance' Treaty, 26 Sept. 1815

Convention concluded at Paris on 26 September 1815 between the Emperor of Russia, the Emperor of Austria, and the King of Prussia.

(Cobbett's *Parliamentary Debates*, XXXII, 355–357.)

Castlereagh explained the origin of this celebrated treaty, which he described as a piece of sublime mysticism and nonsense, in a letter to Lord Liverpool written from Paris on 28 Sept.: "You will receive a *lettre autographe* from the three Allied Sovereigns addressed to the Prince Regent, which I have been desired to transmit. . . . Although the Emperor of Austria is the ostensible organ, the measure has entirely originated with the Emperor of Russia, whose mind has lately taken a deeply religious tinge. Since he came to Paris he has passed a part of every evening with a Madame de Krudener, an old fanatic, who has a considerable reputation amongst the few highflyers in religion that are to be found at Paris. The first intimation I had of this extraordinary act was from the Emperor himself; and I was rather surprised to find it traced back to a conversation with which I was honoured by the Emperor when leaving Vienna. You may remember my sending home a *projet* of declaration with which I proposed the Congress should close, in which the Sovereigns were solemnly to pledge themselves in the face of the world to preserve to their people the peace they had conquered, and to treat as a common enemy whatever Power should violate it. The Emperor told me that this idea, with which he seemed much pleased at the time, had never passed from his mind, but that he thought it ought to assume a more formal shape, and one directly personal to the Sovereigns. . . ."

In the name of the Most Holy and Indivisible Trinity,

Their Majesties, the Emperor of Austria, the King of Prussia and the Emperor of Russia, having–in consequence of the great events which have marked the course of the three last years in Europe, and especially of the blessings which it has pleased

Divine Providence to shower down upon those States which place their confidence and their hope on it alone–acquired the intimate conviction of the necessity of founding the conduct to be observed by the Powers, in their reciprocal relations, upon the sublime truths which the holy religion of our Saviour teaches;

They solemnly declare that the present Act has no other object than to publish in the face of the whole world their fixed resolution, both in the administration of their respective States, and in their political relations with every other Government, to take for their sole guide the precepts of that holy religion, namely, the precepts of justice, Christian charity, and peace, which, far from being applicable only to private concerns, must have an immediate influence on the councils of princes, and guide all their steps, as being the only means of consolidating human institutions, and remedying their imperfections.

In consequence their Majesties have agreed on the following Articles:–

Article 1. Conformably to the words of the holy Scriptures, which command all men to consider each other as brethren, the three contracting monarchs will remain united by the bonds of a true and indissoluble fraternity, and considering each other as fellow-countrymen, they will, on all occasions, and in all places, lend each other aid and assistance, and regarding themselves towards their subjects and armies as fathers of families, they will lead them in the same spirit of fraternity with which they are animated, to protect religion, peace and justice.

Article 2. In consequence, the sole principle in force, whether between the said Governments, or between their subjects, shall be, that of doing each other reciprocal service, and of testifying by unalterable goodwill, the mutual affection with which they ought to be animated, to consider themselves all as members of one and the same Christian nation; the three Allied Princes looking on themselves as merely delegated by Providence to govern three branches of the one family, namely, Austria, Prussia and Russia: thus confessing that the Christian nation, of which they and their people form a part, has in reality no other Sovereign than Him to whom alone power really belongs, because in Him alone are found all the treasures of love, science, and infinite wisdom; that is to say, God, our Divine Saviour, the word of the Most High, the Word of Life. Their Majesties consequently recommend to their people, with the most tender solicitude, as the sole means of enjoying that peace which arises from a good conscience, and which alone is durable, to strengthen themselves every day more and more in the principles and exercise of the duties which the Divine Saviour has taught to mankind.

Article 3. All the Powers who shall choose solemnly to avow the sacred principles which have dictated the present Act, and shall acknowledge how important it is for the happiness of nations, too long agitated, that those truths should henceforth exercise over the destinies of mankind all the influence which belongs to them, will be received with equal ardour and affection into this Holy Alliance.

Done in triplicate, and signed at Paris the year of Grace, 1815, 14–26 September.

Francis.
Frederic William.
Alexander.

578. Lord Liverpool to Lord Castlereagh, Walmer Castle, 3 Oct. 1815

(C. D. Yonge, *Life of Lord Liverpool*, II, pp. 232-233.)

. . . It is quite impossible . . . to advise the Prince to sign the act of accession which has been transmitted to him. Such a step would be inconsistent with all the forms and principles of our Government, and would subject those who advised it to a very serious responsibility.

A Treaty is an act of State; and this Treaty (if it is of any use) is obviously meant to be so. Now nothing is more clear than that the King or Regent of Great Britain can be a party to no act of State personally; he can only be a party to it through the instrumentality of others, who are responsible for it.

The Sovereign, therefore, never signs any treaty in the first instance. He negotiates, concludes and signs by plentipotentiaries whom he empowers to do those acts. He afterwards ratifies whatever they have done, if he approves of it; but this ratification must have the Great Seal affixed to it.

If the Sovereign cannot sign a treaty personally, neither can he accede to it personally. He must therefore authorise you, or some plenipotentiary, to accede to it in his name, and on his part. But, independent of all other objections to such a course, it would be an incongruity for the Sovereign or Regent of Great Britain to accede to a treaty through a plenipotentiary which the other Sovereigns had thought proper to sign personally. We are bound to suppose that such a personal act is not inconsistent with the forms and principles of their Governments, though it is repugnant to those of ours. . . .

579. The Second Treaty of Paris, 20 Nov. 1815

(Cobbett's *Parliamentary Debates*, XXXII, 247-253.)

Definitive Treaty between France and the Allied Powers, signed at Paris, the 20th of November 1815

In the Name of the Most Holy and Undivided Trinity.

The Allied Powers having by their united efforts, and by the success of their arms, preserved France and Europe from the convulsions with which they were menaced by the late enterprise of Napoleon Buonaparte, and by the Revolutionary system reproduced in France, to promote its success; participating at present with His Most Christian Majesty in the desire to consolidate, by maintaining inviolate the royal authority, and by restoring the operation of the Constitutional Charter, the order of things which had been happily re-established in France, as also in the object of restoring between France and her neighbours those relations of reciprocal confidence and goodwill which the fatal effects of the Revolution and of the system of conquest had for so long a time disturbed: persuaded, at the same time, that this last object can only be obtained by an arrangement framed to secure to the Allies proper indemnities for the past and solid guarantees for the future, they have, in concert with H.M. the King of France, taken into consideration the means of giving effect to this arrangement; and being satisfied that the indemnity due to the Allied Powers cannot be either entirely territorial or entirely pecuniary, without prejudice to France in the one or other of her essential interests, and that it would be more fit to combine both the modes, in order to avoid the inconvenience which would result, were either resorted to separately, their Imperial and Royal majesties have adopted this basis for their present transactions; and agreeing alike as to the necessity of retaining for a fixed time in the Frontier Provinces of France, a certain number of Allied Troops, they have determined to combine their different arrangements, founded upon these bases, in a Definitive Treaty. . . .

Article I. The frontiers of France shall be the same as they were in the year 1790, save and except the modifications on one side and on the other, which are detailed in the present Article. First, on the northern frontiers, the line of demarcation shall remain as it was fixed by the Treaty of Paris, as far as opposite to Quiverain, from thence it shall follow the ancient limits of the Belgian Provinces, of the late Bishopric of Liège, and of the Duchy of Bouillon, as they existed in the year 1790, leaving the territories included (*enclavés*) within that line, of Phillippeville and Marienbourg, with the Fortresses so called, together with the whole of the Duchy of Bouillon without the frontiers of France. From Villers near Orval upon the confines of the Department des Ardennes, and of the Grand Duchy of Luxembourg as far as Perle, upon the great road leading from Thionville to Treves, the line shall remain as it was laid down by the Treaty of Paris. From Perle it shall pass by Lauensdorff, Walwich, Schardorff, Niederveiling, Pelweiler . . . to Houvre; and shall follow from thence the old limits of the district (*Pays*) of Sarrebruck, leaving Sarrelouis and the course of the Sarre, together with the places situated to the right of the line above described . . . without the limits of France. From the limits of the district of Sarrebruck the line of demarcation shall be the same which at present separates from Germany the Departments of the Moselle and of the Lower Rhine, as far as to the Lauter, which river shall from thence serve as the frontier until it falls into the Rhine. All the territory on the left bank of the Lauter, including the fortress of Landau, shall form part of Germany.

The town of Weissenbourg, however, through which that river runs, shall remain entirely to France. . . . Secondly, leaving the mouth of the Lauter, and continuing along the departments of the Lower Rhine, the Upper Rhine, the Doubs and the Jura to the Canton de Vaud, the frontiers shall remain as fixed by the Treaty of Paris. The *Thalweg* of the Rhine shall form the boundary between France and the States of Germany. . . . One half of the bridge between Strasburg and Kehl shall belong to France, and the other half to the Grand Duchy of Baden. Thirdly, in order to establish a direct communication between the Canton of Geneva and Switzerland, that part of the Pays de Gex, bounded on the east by the Lake Leman; on the south by the territory of the Canton of Geneva; on the north by that of the Canton de Vaud; on the west, by the course of the Versoix, and by a line which comprehends the communes of Collex, Bossy and Meyrin, leaving the commune of Ferney to France, shall be ceded to the Helvetic Confederacy, in order to be united to the Canton of Geneva. The line of the French custom-houses shall be placed to the west of the Jura, so that the whole of the Pays de Gex shall be without that line. Fourthly, from the frontiers of the Canton of Geneva, as far as the Mediterranean, the line of demarcation shall be that which in the year 1790 separated France from Savoy, and from the County of Nice. The relations which the Treaty of Paris of 1814 had re-established between France and the Principality of Monaco, shall cease for ever, and the same relations shall exist between that Principality and H.M. the King of Sardinia. . . .

Article II. The fortresses, places and districts which, according to the preceding Article, are no longer to form part of the French territory, shall be placed at the disposal of the Allied Powers, at the periods fixed by the ninth Article of the Military Convention annexed to the present Treaty; and H.M. the King of France renounces for himself, his heirs and successors for ever, the rights of sovereignty and property which he has hitherto exercised over the said fortresses, places and districts.

Article III. The fortifications of Huninguen having been constantly an object of uneasiness to the town of Basle, the High Contracting Parties, in order to give to the Helvetic Confederacy a new proof of their goodwill and of their solicitude for its welfare, have agreed among themselves to demolish the fortifications of Huninguen....

Article IV. The pecuniary part of the indemnity to be furnished by France to the Allied Powers is fixed at the sum of 700 millions of francs. The mode, the periods and the guarantees for the payment of this sum shall be regulated by a Special Convention, which shall have the same force and effect as if it were inserted, word for word, in the present Treaty.

Article V. The state of uneasiness and of fermentation, which after so many violent convulsions, and particularly after the last catastrophe, France must still experience, notwithstanding the paternal intentions of her King, and the advantages secured to every class of his subjects by the Constitutional Charter, requiring, for the security of the neighbouring States, certain measures of precaution and of temporary guarantee, it has been judged indispensable to occupy, during a fixed time, by a corps of Allied troops, certain military positions along the frontiers of France, under the express reserve that such occupation shall in no way prejudice the sovereignty of His Most Christian Majesty, nor the state of possession, such as it is recognised and confirmed by the present Treaty. The number of these troops shall not exceed 150,000 men. The Commander-in-Chief of this army shall be nominated by the Allied Powers. This army shall occupy the fortresses of Condé, Valenciennes, Bouchain, Cambrai, Le Quesnoy, Maubeuge, Landrecies, Avesnes, Recroy, Givet, with Charlemont, Mezières, Sedan, Montmedy, Thionville, Longwy, Bitsch, and the Tête-de-Pont of Fort Louis. As the maintenance of the army destined for this service is to be provided by France, a Special Convention shall regulate everything which may relate to that object. This Convention, which shall have the same force and effect as if it were inserted in the present Treaty, shall also regulate the relations of the Army of Occupation with the civil and military authorities of the country. The utmost extent of the duration of this military occupation is fixed at five years. It may terminate before that period if, at the end of three years, the Allied Sovereigns, after having, in concert with his Majesty the King of France, maturely examined their reciprocal situation and interests, and the progress which shall have been made in France in the re-establishment of order and tranquillity, shall agree to acknowledge that the motives which led them to that measure have ceased to exist. But whatever may be the result of this deliberation, all the fortresses and positions occupied by the Allied troops shall, at the expiration of five years, be evacuated without further delay, and given up to his Most Christian Majesty, or to his heirs and successors.

Article VI. The foreign troops not forming part of the Army of Occupation, shall evacuate the French territory within the term fixed by the 9th Article of the Military Convention annexed to the present Treaty.

Article VII. In all countries which shall change Sovereigns, as well in virtue of the present Treaty, as of the arrangements which are to be made in consequence thereof, a period of six years from the date of the exchange of the ratifications shall be allowed to the inhabitants, natives or foreigners, of whatever condition and nation they may be, to dispose of their property, if they should think fit so to do, and to retire to whatever country they may choose.

Article VIII. All the dispositions of the Treaty of Paris of the 30th of May 1814, relative to the countries ceded by that Treaty, shall equally apply to the several territories and districts ceded by the present Treaty.

Article IX. The High Contracting Parties having caused representation to be made of the different claims arising out of the non-execution of the 19th and following Articles of the Treaty of the 30th of May 1814, as well as of the Additional Articles of that Treaty signed between Great Britain and France, desiring to render more efficacious the stipulations made thereby, and having determined, by two separate Conventions, the line to be pursued on each side for that purpose, the said two Conventions, as annexed to the present Treaty, shall, in order to secure the complete execution of the above-mentioned Articles, have the same force and effect as if the same were inserted, word for word, herein.

Article X. All prisoners taken during the hostilities, as well as all hostages which may have been carried off or given, shall be restored in the shortest time possible. The same shall be the case with respect to the prisoners taken previously to the Treaty of the 30th of May 1814, and who shall not already have been restored.

Article XI. The Treaty of Paris of the 30th of May 1814, and the Final Act of the Congress of Vienna of the 9th of June 1815, are confirmed, and shall be maintained in all such of their enactments which shall not have been modified by the Articles of the present Treaty.

Article XII. The present Treaty, with the Conventions annexed thereto, shall be ratified in one Act, and the Ratifications thereof shall be exchanged in the space of two months, or sooner, if possible.

In witness whereof, the respective Plenipotentiaries have signed the same, and have affixed thereunto the seals of their arms. Done at Paris this 20th day of November 1815.

Castlereagh.   Richelieu.
Wellington.

ADDITIONAL ARTICLE.

The High Contracting Powers, sincerely desiring to give effect to the measures on which they deliberated at the Congress of Vienna, relative to the complete and universal abolition of the slave trade, and having, each in their respective dominions, prohibited without restriction their colonies and subjects from taking any part whatever in this traffic, engage to renew conjointly their efforts, with the view of securing final success to those principles which they proclaimed in the Declaration of the 4th of February 1815, and of concerting, without loss of time, through their Ministers at the Courts of London and of Paris, the most effectual measures for the entire and definitive abolition of a commerce so odious and so strongly condemned by the laws of religion and of nature.

The present Additional Article shall have the same force and effect as if it were inserted, word for word, in the Treaty signed this day. It shall be included in the ratification of the said Treaty. . . .

Castlereagh.　　　　　　　Richelieu.
Wellington.

580. Treaty of Alliance and Friendship between Great Britain, Austria, Prussia and Russia. Signed at Paris, 20 Nov. 1815

(*British and Foreign State Papers, 1815–1816*, pp. 273–280.)

The purpose of the Alliance concluded at Vienna the 25th day of March 1815, having been happily attained by the re-establishment in France of the order of things which the last criminal attempt of Napoleon Bonaparte had momentarily subverted; their Majesties the King of the United Kingdom and Ireland, the Emperor of Austria, King of Hungary and Bohemia, the Emperor of all the Russias, and the King of Prussia, considering that the repose of Europe is essentially interwoven with the confirmation of the order of things founded on the maintenance of the royal authority and of the Constitutional Charter, and wishing to employ all their means to prevent the general tranquillity (the object of the wishes of mankind and the constant end of their efforts) from being again disturbed; desirous moreover to draw closer the ties which unite them for the common interests of their people, have resolved to give to the principles solemnly laid down in the Treaties of Chaumont of the 1st of March 1814, and of Vienna of the 25th of March 1815, the application the most analogous to the present state of affairs, and to fix beforehand by a solemn Treaty the principles which they propose to follow, in order to guarantee Europe from the dangers by which she may still be menaced: for which purpose the High Contracting Parties have named, to discuss, settle and sign the conditions of this Treaty, namely. . . .

Article I. The High Contracting Parties reciprocally promise to maintain, in its force and vigour, the Treaty signed this day with His Most Christian Majesty, and to see that the stipulations of the said Treaty, as well as those of the Particular Conventions which have reference thereto, shall be strictly and faithfully executed in their fullest extent.

II. The High Contracting Parties, having engaged in the War which is just terminated, for the purpose of maintaining inviolably the arrangements settled at

Paris last year, for the safety and interest of Europe, have judged it advisable to renew the said engagements by the present Act, and to confirm them as mutually obligatory –subject to the modifications contained in the Treaty signed this day with the Plenipotentiaries of His Most Christian Majesty–and particularly those by which Napoleon Bonaparte and his family, in pursuance of the Treaty of the 11th of April 1814, have been for ever excluded from the Supreme Power in France, which exclusion the Contracting Powers bind themselves, by the present Act, to maintain in full vigour, and, should it be necessary, with the whole of their forces. And as the same revolutionary principles which upheld the last criminal usurpation might again, under other forms, convulse France, and thereby endanger the repose of other States; under these circumstances the High Contracting Parties, solemnly admitting it to be their duty to redouble their watchfulness for the tranquillity and interests of their people, engage, in case so unfortunate an event should again occur, to concert amongst themselves, and with His Most Christian Majesty, the measures which they may judge necessary to be pursued for the safety of their respective States, and for the general tranquillity of Europe.

III. The High Contracting Parties, in agreeing with His Most Christian Majesty that a line of military positions in France should be occupied by a Corps of Allied troops, during a certain number of years, had in view to secure, as far as lay in their power, the effect of the Stipulations contained in Articles I and II of the present Treaty; and, uniformly disposed to adopt every salutary measure calculated to secure the tranquillity of Europe by maintaining the order of things re-established in France, they engage that, in case the said body of troops should be attacked or menaced with an attack on the part of France, the said Powers should be again obliged to place themselves on a war establishment against that Power, in order to maintain either of the said stipulations, or to secure and support the great interests to which they relate, each of the High Contracting Parties shall furnish, without delay, according to the stipulations of the Treaty of Chaumont, and especially in pursuance of the VIIth and VIIIth Articles of this Treaty, its full contingent of 60,000 men, in addition to the forces left in France, or such part of the said contingent as the exigency of the case may require, should be put in motion.

IV. If, unfortunately, the forces stipulated in the preceding Article should be found insufficient, the High Contracting Parties will concert together, without loss of time, as to the additional number of troops to be furnished by each for the support of the common cause; and they engage to employ, in case of need, the whole of their forces, in order to bring the war to a speedy and successful termination; reserving to themselves the right to prescribe, by common consent, such conditions of peace as shall hold out to Europe a sufficient guarantee against the recurrence of a similar calamity.

V. The High Contracting Parties, having agreed to the dispositions laid down in the preceding Articles, for the purpose of securing the effect of their engagements during the period of the temporary occupation, declare, moreover, that even after the expiration of this measure, the said engagements shall still remain in full force and vigour, for the purpose of carrying into effect such measures as may be deemed necessary for the maintenance of the stipulations contained in the Articles I and II of the present Act.

VI. To facilitate and to secure the execution of the present Treaty, and to consolidate the connections which at the present moment so closely unite the four Sovereigns for the happiness of the world, the High Contracting Parties have agreed to renew their meetings at fixed periods, either under the immediate auspices of the Sovereigns themselves, or by their respective Ministers, for the purpose of consulting upon their common interests, and for the consideration of the measures which at each of those periods shall be considered the most salutary for the repose and prosperity of nations, and for the maintenance of the peace of Europe.

VII. The present Treaty shall be ratified, and the ratifications shall be exchanged within two months, or sooner, if possible.

581. Castlereagh's Confidential State Paper of 5 May 1820

(*Cambridge History of British Foreign Policy*, II, pp. 622–633.)

The events which have occurred in Spain have, as might be expected, excited, in proportion as they have developed themselves, the utmost anxiety throughout Europe. [The Russian Despatch of March the 3rd, written when the first news of the military insurrection in Andalusia had reached St. Petersburgh, invites the Allied Powers confidentially to discuss what measures they should adopt, or what attitude they should assume:

1st. In case the King's Government should be unable to suppress the revolt.

2nd. In case the King should spontaneously solicit the support of his Allies.

3rd. In case the insurrection should be protracted. The Despatch from Mr. Rose of the 31st March, referring to a later period of the insurrection, reports that the Russian Minister at Berlin, M. Alopeus, had suggested to the Prussian Government the necessity of referring the whole question of Spain to the consideration of the Allied Ministers at Paris, including the Minister of France.

Prince Hardenberg in a letter to Lord Castlereagh of the 31st ult. refers to M. Alopeus's suggestion and appears to approve of the discussion being referred to Paris. It is also understood that the language held at Paris by some of the Allied Ministers is that the moment is arrived when the sovereigns themselves should assemble, under the extraordinary provisions of the Treaty of Alliance.]

The British Cabinet upon this, as upon all other occasions, is ever ready to deliberate with those of the Allies, and will unreservedly explain itself upon this great question of common interest; but as to the form in which it may be prudent to conduct these deliberations, they conceive they cannot too early recommend that course of deliberation which will excite the least attention or alarm, or which can least provoke jealousy in the minds of the Spanish nation or Government. In this view, it appears to them advisable, studiously to avoid any reunion of the Sovereigns;–to abstain, at least in the present stage of the question, from charging any ostensible Conference with commission to deliberate on the affairs of Spain. They conceive it preferable that their intercourse should be limited to those confidential communications between the Cabinets, which are, in themselves, best adapted to approximate ideas, and to lead, as far as may be, to the adoption of common principles, rather than to hazard a discussion in a Ministerial Conference, which, from the necessarily limited powers of the individuals composing it, must ever be better fitted to execute a purpose already decided upon, than to frame a course of policy under delicate and difficult circumstances.

There seems the less motive for precipitating any step of this nature in the case immediately under consideration, as, from all the information which reaches us, there exists in Spain no order of things upon which to deliberate; nor as yet any governing authority with which foreign Powers can communicate.

The King's authority, for the moment at least, seems to be dissolved. His Majesty is represented, in the last Despatches from Madrid, as having wholly abandoned himself to the tide of events, and as conceding whatever is called for by the Provisional Junta and the Clubs.

The authority of the Provisional Government does not appear to extend beyond the two Castilles and a part of Andalusia:—distinct local authorities prevail in the various Provinces, and the King's personal safety is regarded as extremely liable to be hazarded by any step which might lay him open to the suspicion of entertaining a design to bring about a counter-revolution, whether by internal or external means.

This important subject having been referred to, and considered by, the Duke of Wellington, his Memorandum accompanies this Minute. His Grace does not hesitate, upon his intimate experience of Spanish affairs, to pronounce, that the Spanish nation is, of all the European people[s], that, which will least brook any interference from abroad: he states the many instances in which, during the last War, this distinguishing trait of national character rendered them obstinately blind to the most pressing considerations of public safety: he states the imminent danger in which the suspicion of foreign interference, and more especially of interference on the part of France, is likely to involve the King;—and he further describes the difficulties which would oppose themselves to any military operations in Spain, undertaken for the purpose of reducing, by force, the nation to submit themselves to an order of things, to be either suggested or prescribed to them from without.

Sir Henry Wellesley has, in coincidence with this opinion, reported the alarm which the intended Mission of M. de La Tour du Pin had excited at Madrid, the prejudice which, in the opinion of all the Foreign Ministers at Madrid, it was calculated to occasion to the King's interests and possible safety. He also reports the steps which it was in contemplation to have adopted, on the part of the King, to endeavour to prevent the French Minister from prosecuting his journey to Madrid, when the intelligence of the abandonment of the Mission was received from Paris.

At all events, therefore, until some Central Authority shall establish itself in Spain, all notion of operating upon her Councils seems utterly impracticable, and calculated to lead to no other possible result, than that of compromising either the King or the Allies, or probably both.

[The Emperor of Russia, in the several cases which H.I.M. has successively suggested for deliberation, is altogether silent upon the particular case which has really occurred: it may therefore be inferred that His Imperial Majesty's reasoning is not meant to be applied to that total change in the order of things previously existing in Spain, which has been effected with the avowed concurrence and under the formal sanction of the King. This change, no doubt forced by circumstances, has been regularly notified by his Majesty to all foreign Powers, and is apparently acquiesced in, if not adopted by, the great body of the nation.

In these circumstances can the other States of Europe, in prudence proceed publicly to deliberate upon the King's acts, much more to call them into question? If not, would it be wise to give advice, wholly unasked, which is very little likely to contain any suggestion for the salutary modification of the Constitution of 1812 other than such as will readily occur to those public men within the country who have good intentions, and whose influence and means of effectuating an amelioration of the Constitution are likely to be weakened rather than strengthened by an interference from abroad?]

The present state of Spain, no doubt, seriously extends the range of political agitation in Europe, but it must nevertheless be admitted that there is no portion of Europe of equal magnitude, in which such a revolution could have happened, less likely to menace other States with that direct and imminent danger, which has always been regarded, at least in this country, as alone constituting the case which would justify external interference. If the case is not such as to warrant such an interference –if we do not feel that we have at this moment either the right or the means to interfere with effect by force–if the semblance of such an interference is more likely to irritate than to overawe, and if we have proved, by experience, how little a Spanish Government, whether of King or Cortes, is disposed to listen to advice from foreign States, is it not prudent at least to pause before we assume an attitude which would seem to pledge us in the eyes of Europe to some decisive proceeding? Before we embark in such a measure, is it not expedient at least to ascertain with some degree of precision, what we really mean to do? This course of temperate and cautious policy, so befitting the occasion and the critical position in which the King is personally placed, will in no degree fetter our action, when, if ever, the case for acting shall arise.

In the mean time, as independent States, the Allied Powers may awaken, through their respective Missions at Madrid, with not less effect than would attend any joint representation, a salutary apprehension of the consequences that might be produced by any violence offered to the King's person or family, or by any hostile measures directed against the Portuguese dominions in Europe, for the protection of which Great Britain is bound by specific Treaty.

In conveying any such intimation, however, the utmost delicacy should be observed; and though it is to be presumed that the views and wishes of all the Allied Powers must be essentially the same, and that the sentiments they are likely to express cannot materially differ, it does not follow that they should speak either in their corporate character, or through any common organ–both which expedients would be calculated rather to offend than to conciliate or persuade.

There can be no doubt of the general danger which menaces more or less the stability of all existing Governments, from the principles which are afloat, and from the circumstances that so many States of Europe are now employed in the difficult task of casting anew their Governments upon the representative principle—but the notion of revising, limiting, or regulating the course of such experiments, either by foreign council or by foreign force, would be as dangerous to avow as it would be impossible to execute; and the illusion too prevalent on this subject, should not be encouraged in our intercourse with the Allies. That circumstances might arise out of such experiments in any country directly menacing to the safety of other States, cannot be denied, and against such a danger, well ascertained, the Allies may justifiably, and must in all prudence, be on their guard; but such is not the present case. Fearful as is the example which is furnished by Spain, of an army in revolt, and a monarch swearing to a Constitution which contains in its frame hardly the semblance of a monarchy, there is no ground for apprehension that Europe is likely to be speedily endangered by Spanish arms.

[The argument against any ostensible step whatever being taken by the Allies to interpose even their good offices in the affairs of Spain, and the serious difficulties that must present themselves to an armed interference under any circumstances in that country, have been so forcibly detailed in the Duke of Wellington's paper as to exhaust that part of the question.

It[1] remains to be considered what course can best be pursued by the Allies in the present critical state of Europe, in order to preserve in the utmost cordiality and vigour the bonds which at this day so happily unite the great European Powers together, and to draw from their Alliance should the moment of danger and contest arrive, the fullest extent of benefit of which it is in its nature susceptible.]

In this Alliance, as in all other human arrangements, nothing is more likely to impair, or even to destroy its real utility, than any attempt to push its duties and its obligations beyond the sphere which its original conception and understood principles will warrant. It was an union for the re-conquest and liberation of a great proportion of the Continent of Europe from the military dominion of France; and having subdued the conqueror, it took the state of possession, as established by the Peace, under the protection of the Alliance. It never was, however, intended as an union for the government of the world, or for the superintendence of the internal affairs of other States.

[It provided specifically against an infraction on the part of France of the state of possession then created; it provided against the return of the usurper or of any of his family to the throne; it further designated the revolutionary Power which had convulsed France and desolated Europe, as an object of its constant solicitude, but it was the revolutionary Power more particularly in its military character actual and existent within France against which it intended to take precautions, rather than against the democratic principles, then as now, but too generally spread throughout Europe.

In thus attempting to limit the objects of the Alliance within their legitimate boundary, it is not meant to discourage the utmost frankness of communication between the Allied Cabinets; their confidential intercourse upon all matters, however foreign to the purposes of the Alliance, is in itself a valuable expedient for keeping the

---

[1] This paragraph is scratched through in pencil.

current of sentiment in Europe as equable and as uniform as may be: it is not meant that in particular and definite cases, the Alliance may not (and especially when invited to do so by the parties interested) advantageously interpose, with due caution, in matters lying beyond the boundaries of their immediate and particular connection; but what is intended to be combated as forming any part of their duty as Allies, is the notion, but too perceptibly prevalent, that whenever any great political event shall occur, as in Spain, pregnant perhaps with future danger, it is to be regarded almost as a matter of course, that it belongs to the Allies to charge themselves collectively with the responsibility of exercising some jurisdiction concerning such possible eventual danger. One objection to this view of our duties, if there was no other, is, that unless we are prepared to support our interference with force, our judgement or advice is likely to be but rarely listened to, and would by frequent repetition soon fall into complete contempt. So long as we keep to the great and simple conservative principles of the Alliance, when the dangers therein contemplated shall be visibly realised, there is little risk of difference or of disunion amongst the Allies.

All will have a common interest: but it is far otherwise when we attempt, with the alliance, to embrace subordinate, remote and speculative cases of danger; all the Powers may indeed have an interest in averting the assumed danger, but all have not by any means a common faculty of combating it, in its more speculative shapes, nor can they all without embarrassing seriously the internal administration of their own affairs be prepared to show themselves in jealous observation of transactions which, before they have assumed a practical character, public opinion would not go along with them in counteracting.

This principle is perfectly clear and intelligible in the case of Spain. We may all agree that nothing can be more lamentable, or of more dangerous example, than the late revolt of the Spanish army. We may all agree that nothing can be more unlike a monarchical Government, or less suited to the wants and true interests of the Spanish nation, than the Constitution of the year 1812. We may also agree, with shades of difference, that the consequence of this state of things in Spain may eventually bring danger home to all our own doors, but it does not follow that we have therefore equal means of acting upon this opinion. For instance, the Emperor of Russia, from the nature of his authority, can have nothing to weigh but the physical or moral difficulties external from his own Government or dominions, which are in the way of his giving effect to his designs; if H.I.M.'s mind is settled upon these points, his action is free and his means are in his own hands. The King of Great Britain, from the nature of our Constitution, has on the contrary all his means to acquire through Parliament, and he must well know that if embarked in a War which the voice of the country does not support, the efforts of the strongest Administration which ever served the Crown would soon be unequal to the prosecution of the contest. In Russia there is but little public sentiment with regard to Spain, which can embarrass the decision of the Sovereign; in Great Britain there is a great deal, and the current of that sentiment runs strongly against the late policy of the King of Spain.

Besides, the people of this country would probably not recognise (unless Portugal was attacked) that our safety could be so far menaced by any state of things in Spain, as to warrant their Government in sending an army to that country to meddle in its internal affairs. We cannot conceal from ourselves how generally the acts of the King of Spain since his restoration have rendered his Government unpopular, and how impossible it would be to reconcile the people of England to the use of force, if such a proceeding could for a moment be thought of by the British Cabinet for the purpose of replacing power in his hands, however he might engage to qualify it. The principle upon which the British Government acted in the discussions with respect to the Colonies (*viz*, never to employ forcible means for their reduction) would equally preclude them from any intervention of such a character with regard to Old Spain. The interposition of our good offices, whether singly, or in concert with the Allied Governments, if uncalled for by any authority within Spain, even by the King himself, is by no means free from a like inconvenience as far as regards the position of the British Government at home. This species of intervention, especially when coming from five great Powers, has more or less the air of dictation and of menace, and the possibility of its being intended to be pushed to a forcible intervention is always assumed or imputed by an adverse party. The grounds of the intervention thus become unpopular, the intention of the parties is misunderstood, the public mind is agitated and perverted, and the general political situation of the Government is thereby essentially embarrassed.

This statement is only meant to prove that we ought to see somewhat clearly to what purpose of real utility our effort tends, before we embark in proceedings which can never be indifferent in their bearings upon the Government taking part in them. In this country at all times, but especially at the present conjuncture, when the whole energy of the State is required to unite reasonable men in defence of our existing institutions, and to put down the spirit of treason and disaffection which in certain of the manufacturing districts in particular, pervades the lower orders, it is of the greatest moment, that the public sentiment should not be distracted or divided by any unnecessary interference of the Government in events, passing abroad, over which they can have none, or at best very imperfect means of control. Nothing could be more injurious to the Continental Powers than to have their affairs made matter of daily discussion in our Parliament, which nevertheless must be the consequence of their precipitately mixing themselves in the affairs of other States, if we should consent to proceed *pari passu* with them in such interferences. It is not merely the temporary inconvenience produced to the British Government by being so committed, that is to be apprehended, but it is the exposing ourselves to have the public mind soured by the effects of a meddling policy, when it can tend to nothing effectual, and pledged perhaps beforehand against any exertion whatever in Continental affairs; the fatal effects of such a false step might be irreparable when the moment at which we might be indispensably called upon by duty and interest to take a part should arise.

These considerations will suggest a doubt whether that extreme degree of unanimity and supposed concurrence upon all political subjects would be either a practicable or a desirable principle of action among the Allied States, upon matters not essentially connected with the main purposes of the Alliance. If this identity is to be sought for, it can only be obtained by a proportionate degree of inaction in all the States. The position of the Ministers at Paris for instance can never be altogether uniform, unless their language upon public affairs is either of the most general description, or they agree to hold no public language whatever. The latter expedient is perhaps the most prudent, but then the unanimity of the sentiment, thus assumed to be established, will not be free from inconvenience to some of the parties, if the Cabinets of other States by their public documents assign objects to that Concert, to which, at least as described by them, the others cannot conveniently subscribe.

The fact is that we do not, and cannot feel alike upon all subjects. Our position, our institutions, the habits of thinking, and the prejudice of our people, render us essentially different. We cannot in all matters reason or feel alike; we should lose the confidence of our respective nations if we did, and the very affectation of such an impossibility would soon render the Alliance an object of odium and distrust, whereas, if we keep it within its *common sense* limits, the Representative Governments, and those which are more purely monarchical, may well find each a common interest, and a common facility in discharging their duties under the Alliance, without creating an impression that they have made a surrender of the first principles upon which their respective Governments are founded. Each Government will then retain its due faculty of independent action, always recollecting, that they have all a common refuge in the Alliance, as well as a common duty to perform, whenever such a danger shall really exist, as that against which the Alliance was specially intended to provide. There is at present very naturally a widespread apprehension of the fatal consequences to the public tranquillity of Europe, that may be expected to flow from the dangerous principles of the present day, at work more or less in every European State: consequences which no human foresight can presume to estimate. In all dangers the first calculation of prudence is to consider what we should avoid and on what we should endeavour to rely. In considering Continental Europe as divided into two great masses, the western, consisting of France and Spain, the eastern of all the other Continental States still subsisting with some limited exceptions, under the form of their ancient institutions, the great question is, what system of general and defensive policy (subject of course to special exceptions arising out of the circumstances of the particular case) ought the latter States to adopt with a view of securing themselves against those dangers, which may directly or indirectly assail them from the former. By the late proceedings at Vienna, which for all purposes of internal tranquillity bind up the various States of Germany into a single and undivided Power, a great degree of additional simplicity as well as strength has been given to this portion of Europe. By this expedient there is established on that side of Europe, instead of a multitude of dispersed States, two great bodies, Russia and Germany, of the latter of which Austria and Prussia may for purposes of internal tranquillity be regarded as component parts. In addition to these there remain but few pieces on the board to complicate the game of public safety.

In considering then how the game can best be played, the first thing that occurs for our consideration is, what good can these States hope to effect in France or Spain by their mere councils? Perhaps it would not be far from the truth to say, none whatever. When the chances of error, jealousy and national sentiment are considered, the probability of mischief would be more truly assigned to the system of constant European interference upon these volcanic masses.

Of this truth the Duke de Richelieu seems fully satisfied, as appears by the manly and earnest entreaties which he has lately addressed to certain of the Allies' Courts, that they would keep their Ministers quiet at Paris, and that abstaining themselves from all advice or interference, they would leave the French Government to combat for themselves and upon their own views of things the dangers which surround them.

What could the Allied Powers look to effect by their arms, if the supposition of an armed interference in the internal affairs of another State could be admitted? Perhaps as little, because in supposing them finally triumphant, we have the problem still to solve, how the country in which such interference had been successful was to provide for its self-government after the Allied armies shall have withdrawn, without soon becoming an equal source of danger to the tranquillity of neighbouring States; but when we consider how much danger may arise to the internal safety of the rest of Europe, by the absence of those armies which must be withdrawn to overrun the country in which the supposed interference was to take place – what may be the danger of these armies being contaminated, what may be the incumbrances to be added by such renewed exertions to the already overwhelming weight of the debts of the different States – what the local irritation which must be occasioned by pouring forth such immense armies pressing severely as they must do upon the resources of countries already agitated and inflamed – no rational statesman surely would found his prospects of security on such a calculation. He would rather be of opinion that the only necessity which could in wisdom justify such an attempt is that which, temperately considered, appears to leave to Europe no other option than that of either going to meet that danger which they cannot avoid, or having it poured in the full tide of military invasion upon their own States. The actual existence of such a danger may indeed be inferred from many circumstances short of the visible preparations for attack, but it is submitted that on this basis the conclusion should always be examined.

If this position is correctly laid down, it may be asserted that the case supposed, not only does not at present exist, but the chances of such a danger have latterly rather declined in proportion as both France and Spain are almost exclusively and deeply occupied by their own internal embarrassments. The military power in France at this day is circumscribed within those limits which are not more than competent to the necessary duties of the interior; that of Spain is upon even a more reduced scale, whilst the military establishments of all the other European States, and especially that of Russia, were never perhaps at any period of their history upon a footing of more formidable efficiency both in point of discipline and numbers. Surely, then, if these States can preserve harmony among themselves, and exercise a proper degree of vigilance with respect to their interior police, there is nothing in this state of things which should prevent them from abiding with patience and with firmness the result of the great political process to which circumstances have given existence in the States to the westward of their frontiers. They may surely permit these nations to work out by their own means, and by the lights of their own councils, that result which no doubt materially bears upon the general interests of the world, but which is more especially to decide their own particular destinies, without being led to interfere with them, at least so long as their own immediate security is not directly menaced, or until some crisis shall arise which may call for some specific, intelligible and practicable interposition on their part. The principle of one State interfering by force in the internal affairs of another, in order to enforce obedience to the governing authority, is always a question of the greatest possible moral as well as political delicacy, and it is not meant here to examine it. It is only important on the present occasion, to observe that to generalise such a principle and to think of reducing it to a system, or to impose it as an obligation, is a scheme utterly impracticable and objectionable. There is not only the physical impossibility of giving execution to such a system, but there is the moral impracticability arising from the inaptitude of particular States to recognise or to act upon it. No country having a representative system of government could act upon it—and the sooner such a doctrine shall be distinctly abjured as forming in any degree the basis of our Alliance, the better; in order that States, in calculating the means of their own security may not suffer disappointment by expecting from the Allied Powers a support which, under the special circumstances of the national institutions they cannot give: Great Britain has perhaps equal power with any other State to oppose herself to a practical and intelligible danger, capable of being brought home to the national feeling. When the territorial balance of Europe is disturbed, she can interfere with effect, but she is the last Government in Europe which can be expected, or can venture to commit herself on any question of an abstract character.

These observations are made to point attention to what is practicable and what is not. If the dreaded moral contagion should unfortunately extend itself into Germany, and if the flame of military revolt should, for example, burst forth in any of the German States, it is in vain for that State, however anxiously and sincerely we deprecate such a calamity, to turn its eyes to this country for the means of effectually suppressing such a danger. If external means are indispensable for its suppression, such State must not reckon for assistance upon Governments constituted as that of Great Britain, but it is not therefore without its resource.

The internal peace of each German State is by law placed under the protection of the army of the Empire. The duty which is imposed by the Laws of the Confederacy upon all German States to suppress, by the military power of the whole mass, insurrection within the territories of each and every, of the co-Estates, is an immense resource in itself, and ought to give to the centre of Europe a sense of security which, previous to the reunion of Vienna, was wholly wanting. The importance of preventing the Low Countries, the military barrier of Europe, from being lost, by being melted down into the general mass of French power, whether by insurrection or by conquest, might enable the British Government to act more promptly upon this, than perhaps upon any other case of an internal character that can be stated. But upon all cases we must admit ourselves to be, and our Allies should in fairness understand that we are, a Power that must take our principle of action, and our scale of acting, not merely from the expediency of the case, but from those maxims, which a system of government strongly popular and national in its character, has irresistibly imposed upon us.]

We shall be found in our place when actual danger menaces the system of Europe; but this country cannot and will not act upon abstract and speculative principles of precaution. The Alliance which exists had no such purpose in view in its original formation. It was never so explained to Parliament; if it had, most assuredly the sanction of Parliament would never have been given to it; and it would now be a breach of faith, were the Ministers of the Crown to acquiesce in a construction being put upon it, or were they to suffer themselves to be betrayed into a course of measures, inconsistent with those principles which they avowed at the time, and which they have since uniformly maintained both at home and abroad, [and which were more fully developed in a confidential Memorandum delivered in by the British Plenipotentiaries to those of the Allies, at Aix-la-Chapelle, bearing date in October 1818, to which Memorandum they now refer as more fully illustrative of their sentiments].

THE RECOGNITION OF THE INDEPENDENCE OF
SPANISH AMERICA, 1825

582. George IV's communication to the Cabinet on the Spanish American Question, 27 Jan. 1825

(Wellington Despatches, Correspondence & Memoranda, II (1867), pp. 401–402.)

The line of policy pursued by the King's Government under the King's direction at the close of the late war, which terminated under such happy circumstances, was, unanimity of co-operation with the great Continental Powers, not only for the purpose of putting an end to the then existing hostilities, but for preserving the future tranquillity and peace of Europe.

The late Lord Londonderry, in conjunction with the Duke of Wellington, so effectually accomplished this great and desirable object, that this country took a position that she had never before held.

The King supposes it will not be denied that the anarchy produced throughout the world by the French Revolution has left us a record so instructive that the councils of the British Government should never fail to be regulated by the wholesome remembrance of that terrible event.

That we should, therefore, regard with the most anxious suspicion every attempt to revive the example of British America, which ended, unhappily for Great Britain, in a separation from the mother country. France *treacherously* assisted that rebellious successful enterprise, and by *her* fatal policy, gave the first impulse to that revolution which entailed for a quarter of a century such complicated misery on the whole of Europe.

The revolutionary spirit of passed years, although lulled and suspended, is by no means extinguished; and it would be wisdom to look to the ultimate consequences which the result of our intended recognition of the independence of the South American provinces may probably produce on the evil and discontented, who are controlled, even at this moment, with difficulty by the established power of regular Governments.

Let us also look at home, and observe the dangerous attempts which the active firebrands of Ireland are at this time pursuing under the deceptive pretence of catholic emancipation.

The rebellious and organised schemes so actively afloat in that unhappy country, are only a part of the same system promoted by the same evil spirit which gave rise to the calamities of the French Revolution.

The liberalism of late adopted by the King's Government appears to the King to be a substantial part of that creed, which was hailed in the House of Commons, in those revolutionary days, when it required all the talent and firmness of the late Mr. Pitt to put it down; and the support which that great statesman received from the King's revered and excellent father, gave him the opportunity of using his great ability with such effect as enabled him successfully to resist the desolating storm.

The King has been long aware that the principles promulgated by the King's early friends were at that period the bane which threatened the destruction of our happy Constitution, and with it our internal peace and happiness; and if the King withdrew himself from his early friends for the good of the country, can the present Government suppose that the King will permit any individuals to force upon him at this time a line of policy, of which he so entirely disapproves, and which is in direct opposition to those wise principles, that the King's Government has for so many years supported, and uniformly acted upon.

The King would wish to ask Lord Liverpool whether he supposes the great abettors of this Spanish American question connected with the Opposition give their support to a recognition of the Spanish provinces, in relation to the great mercantile advantages which this measure may offer to this country, or, from their love of democracy, in opposition to a monarchical aristocracy.

The King has no difficulty in answering this question, and let the opportunity arise, the same line of conduct would be as promptly applied by these gentlemen, to the emancipation of our own colonial possessions or to any other of the remote settlements, at present under the dominion of the British Crown.

The King cannot but be aware that this, as well as every other kingdom, must have its own latent sources of wealth and power, peculiar to itself, the cultivation of which becomes essential to the maintenance of its individual prosperity; but the King desires to observe that the policy or wisdom, which is to balance the interest of kingdoms, is not to be found in Party divisions.

The King has too much reason to apprehend that the separation from our Allies, so justly and so honestly referred to by the Emperor of Austria, will very soon lead to consequences that will end in disturbing the tranquillity of Europe.

Why was the Quadruple Alliance formed? To carry into execution not only the maintenance of the Treaties of Peace connected with the settlement of Europe (just then concluded) but also for the purposes of controlling the ambition and jealousies of the great Allied Powers themselves, in relation to each other.

The Jacobins of the world (now calling themselves the Liberals) saw the peace of Europe secured by this great measure, and have therefore never ceased to vilify the principle of the Quadruple Alliance.

The late policy of Great Britain has loosened these beneficial ties by demonstrating a restless desire of self interest in direct opposition to these wise and comprehensive principles, in which the peace and general interests of Europe were bound together.

The King desires, therefore, distinctly to know from his Cabinet, individually (seriatim) whether the great principles of policy established by his Government in the years 1814, 1815 and 1818 *are or are not to be abandoned.*

The answer to this question will enable the King to satisfy himself of the steps necessary to be taken for the purpose of preventing this country from being again involved in a ruinous and disastrous war.

583. Cabinet minute, Jan. 1825

(*Ibid.*, II, pp. 402–404.)

Lord Liverpool has, in obedience to your Majesty's commands, communicated to your Majesty's confidential servants the paper which your Majesty has transmitted to him for that purpose.

Your Majesty is graciously pleased to propose at the conclusion of this paper, the following question to your confidential servants, and to desire them to submit their opinions to your Majesty individually.

'Whether the great principles of policy established by your Majesty's Government in the years 1814, 1815 and 1818 *are or are not to be abandoned.*'

Upon communicating freely with each other their respective individual opinions, your Majesty's servants have found so entire an agreement to subsist between them, as to the substance of the answer to be returned to your Majesty's question, that they humbly request your Majesty's permission to give that answer generally and collectively.

Your Majesty's servants think it their duty to remind your Majesty that a divergence of opinion between your Majesty and your Allies, as to the nature of their engagements for the maintenance of the peace of Europe, began to appear even in the negotiations of 1815; and your Majesty's Plenipotentiary upon that occasion declared to your Majesty's Allies the extent to which alone your Majesty could be a party to such engagements.

This divergence became still more apparent in the Conferences at Aix-la-Chapelle in 1818; and after several intermediate explanations, the Allied Governments still persisting in their own interpretation of the principles of those Treaties, and even in representing your Majesty as concurring in such interpretation, your Majesty found it necessary to proclaim to the world by the Circular Note of the late Lord Londonderry of the 19th of January 1821, your Majesty's dissent from that interpretation.

Your Majesty's servants feel it to be their duty therefore to state that they fully recognise the principles of policy laid down in 1814, 1815 and 1818, in the sense given to them repeatedly by your Majesty's plenipotentiaries, and specially in the Circular so issued by your Majesty's command in 1821, and in no other.

With respect to the future application of these principles, your Majesty's servants are deeply impressed with the obligation of preserving your Majesty's engagements in the sense in which they have been declared on the part of your Majesty and with the advantages which may result from maintaining the system of confidence and reciprocal communication established with your Majesty's Allies at the periods to which your Majesty refers.

Your Majesty's servants having thus answered the question which your Majesty has been pleased to propose to them, must humbly request your Majesty's permission to advert to that part of your Majesty's paper which respects the new States of Spanish America.

It was not their wish to conceal from your Majesty that there existed amongst them some difference of opinion as to the advice to be tendered to your Majesty upon this subject.

The decision of your Majesty's Cabinet was not submitted to your Majesty till after as long and as continued a deliberation as ever has been given to any great question of national policy.

Your Majesty's servants deeply regretted that your Majesty's feelings and sentiments appeared to be adverse to the opinion of a great majority of your Cabinet, and nothing but an overruling sense of duty could have induced them, under such circumstances, to press their decision upon your Majesty.

Your Majesty was graciously pleased to consent that this decision should be acted upon, and it was by your Majesty's special directions that communication was made to all the Great Powers of Europe of the decision adopted by your Majesty's Government.

Whatever difference, or shades of difference of opinion, may have hitherto existed amongst your Majesty's servants on the subject of Spanish America, they humbly submit now to your Majesty their unanimous opinion that the measures in progress respecting Spanish America are in no way inconsistent with any engagement between your Majesty and your Allies; that those measures are now irrevocable, and that the faith and honour of the country are pledged to all their necessary consequences.

Your Majesty's servants cannot conclude without assuring your Majesty that in the advice which they have humbly submitted to your Majesty upon this, and upon all former occasions, the object nearest all their hearts has been to uphold your Majesty's honour and dignity, and to promote the interests and prosperity of your people.

584. Canning's 'New World' speech in the Commons, 12 Dec. 1826

(Hansard's *Parliamentary Debates*, New Series, XVI, 395–398.)

In April 1823 a French army entered Spain to restore Ferdinand VII to absolute power (of which the revolution of 1820 had deprived him). Canning vigorously protested against French armed intervention, but in view of the hostility of George IV, some of the Cabinet ministers, and a majority of the House of Commons to war with France, Canning had to content himself with expressing a hope that Spain "would come triumphantly out of the struggle". Not until 1827 was the French army withdrawn.

. . . The House knows—the country knows—that when the French army was on the point of entering Spain, H.M.'s Government did all in their power to prevent it; that we resisted it by all means, short of war. I have just now stated some of the reasons why we did not think the entry of that army into Spain a sufficient ground for war; but there was, in addition to those which I have stated, this peculiar reason—that whatever effect a war, commenced upon the mere ground of the entry of a French army into Spain, might have, it probably would not have had the effect of getting that army out of Spain. In a war against France at that time, as at any other, you might, perhaps, have acquired military glory; you might, perhaps, have extended your colonial possessions; you might even have achieved, at great cost of blood and treasure, an honourable peace; but as to getting the French out of Spain, that would have been the one object which you almost certainly would not have accomplished. How seldom, in the whole history of the wars of Europe, has any war between two great Powers ended, in the obtaining of the exact, the identical, object for which the war was begun!

Besides, Sir, I confess I think that the effects of the French occupation of Spain have been infinitely exaggerated. I do not blame those exaggerations, because I am aware that they are to be attributed to the recollections of some of the best times of our history; that they are the echoes of sentiments which, in the days of William and of Anne, animated the debates and dictated the votes of the British Parliament. No peace was in those days thought safe for this country while the crown of Spain continued on the head of a Bourbon. But were not the apprehensions of those days greatly overstated? Has the power of Spain swallowed up the power of maritime England? Or does England still remain, after the lapse of more than a century, during which the crown of Spain has been worn by a Bourbon—niched in a nook of that same Spain, Gibraltar; an occupation which was contemporaneous with the apprehensions that I have described, and which has happily survived them?

Again, Sir, is the Spain of the present day the Spain of which the statesmen of the times of William and Anne were so much afraid? Is it indeed the nation whose puissance was expected to shake England from her sphere? No, Sir, it was quite another Spain—it was the Spain, within the limits of whose empire the sun never set—it was Spain 'with the Indies' that excited the jealousies and alarmed the imaginations of our ancestors.

But then, Sir, the balance of power! The entry of the French army into Spain disturbed that balance, and we ought to have gone to war to restore it! . . . Were there no other means than war for restoring the balance of power? Is the balance of power a fixed and unalterable standard? Or is it not a standard perpetually varying, as civilisation advances, and as new nations spring up and take their place among established political communities? The balance of power a century and a half ago was to be adjusted between France and Spain, the Netherlands, Austria and England. Some years afterwards Russia assumed her high station in European politics. Some years after that again, Prussia became not only a substantive, but a preponderating monarchy. Thus, while the balance of power continued in principle the same, the means of adjusting it became more varied and enlarged. They became enlarged, in proportion to the increased number of considerable States—in proportion, I may say, to the number of weights which might be shifted into the one or the other scale. To look to the policy of Europe in the times of William and Anne, for the purpose of regulating the balance of power in Europe at the present day, is to disregard the progress of events, and to confuse dates and facts which throw a reciprocal light upon each other.

It would be disingenuous, indeed, not to admit that the entry of the French army into Spain was in a certain sense, a disparagement–an affront to the pride–a blow to the feelings of England: and it can hardly be supposed that the Government did not sympathise on that occasion with the feelings of the people. But I deny that, questionable or censurable as the act might be, it was one which necessarily called for our direct and hostile opposition. Was nothing then to be done? Was there no other mode of resistance than by a direct attack upon France–or by a war to be undertaken on the soil of Spain? What, if the possession of Spain might be rendered harmless in rival hands–harmless as regarded us–and valueless to the possessors? Might not compensation for disparagement be obtained, and the policy of our ancestors vindicated, by means better adapted to the present time? If France occupied Spain, was it necessary, in order to avoid the consequences of that occupation, that we should blockade Cadiz? No. I looked another way–I sought materials of compensation in another hemisphere. Contemplating Spain, such as our ancestors had known her, I resolved that if France had Spain, it should not be Spain 'with the Indies'. I called the New World into existence, to redress the balance of the Old.

It is thus, Sir, that I answer the accusation brought against H.M.'s Government, of having allowed the French army to usurp and to retain the occupation of Spain. That occupation, I am quite confident, is an unpaid and unredeemed burden to France. It is a burden of which, I verily believe, France would be glad to rid herself. But they know little of the feelings of the French Government, and of the spirit of the French nation, who do not know that, worthless or burdensome as that occupation may be, the way to rivet her in it would be, by angry or intemperate representations, to make the continuance of that occupation a point of honour. . . .

585. The Treaty of London, between Great Britain, France and Russia, 6 July 1827

(British and Foreign State Papers, 1826–1827, pp. 632–639.)

Turkish misgovernment provoked a Greek revolt in 1821. In spite of intense Philhellenist feeling in England, Canning, acting on the traditional principle of non-intervention in the internal affairs of another State, refused to consider giving active assistance to the rebels, who, however, were recognized as belligerents in March 1823. When in 1824 the Sultan obtained powerful help from his vassal, Mehemet Ali, and the Greeks were threatened with annihilation, the danger arose of Russia's isolated intervention. To avert it, Canning proposed the intervention of the Powers, justifying joint intervention thus: "A contest so ferocious, leading to excesses of piracy and plunder, so intolerable to civilised Europe, justifies extraordinary intervention, and renders lawful any expedients short of positive hostility." The Treaty of London was the outcome. Three months later the Allied fleet practically annihilated the Turkish fleet in Navarino Bay. After Canning's death Wellington reversed the policy of co-operation with Russia, but ceased to control events. Russia declared war on Turkey in 1828 and dictated peace at Adrianople in 1829; and Greece achieved her independence.

H.M. the King of the United Kingdom . . . and H.M. the King of France and Navarre, and H.M. the Emperor of all the Russias, penetrated with the necessity of putting an end to the sanguinary struggle which, while it abandons the Greek

Provinces and the islands of the Archipelago to all the disorders of anarchy, daily causes fresh impediments to the commerce of the States of Europe, and gives opportunity for acts of piracy which not only expose the subjects of the high contracting parties to grievous losses, but also render necessary measures which are burdensome for their observation and suppression; [they] . . . having moreover received from the Greeks an earnest invitation to interpose their mediation with the Ottoman Porte, and . . . being animated with the desire of putting a stop to the effusion of blood, and of preventing the evils of every kind which the continuance of such a state of affairs may produce; they have resolved to combine their efforts . . . for the object of re-establishing peace between the contending parties, by means of an arrangement called for, no less by sentiments of humanity than by interests for the tranquillity of Europe. . . .

Art. I. The contracting Powers shall offer their mediation to the Ottoman Porte, with the view of effecting a reconciliation between it and the Greeks. This offer of mediation shall be made to that Power immediately after the ratification of the present Treaty, by means of a joint Declaration, signed by plenipotentiaries of the Allied Courts at Constantinople; and at the same time, a demand for an immediate armistice shall be made to the two contending parties, as a preliminary and indispensable condition to the opening of any negotiation.

II. The arrangement to be proposed to the Ottoman Porte shall rest upon the following bases: The Greeks shall hold under the Sultan as under a Lord paramount; and in consequence thereof, they shall pay to the Ottoman Empire an annual tribute, the amount of which shall be fixed, once for all, by common agreement. They shall be governed by Authorities whom they shall choose and appoint themselves, but in the nomination of whom the Porte shall have a defined right. In order to effect a complete separation between the individuals of the two nations, and to prevent the collisions which would be the inevitable consequence of so protracted a struggle, the Greeks shall become possessors of all Turkish property situated either upon the Continent, or in the islands of Greece, on condition of indemnifying the former proprietors, either by an annual sum to be added to the tribute which they shall pay to the Porte, or by some other arrangement of the same nature.

III. The details of this arrangement, as well as the limits of the territory upon the Continent, and the designation of the islands of the Archipelago to which it shall be applicable, shall be settled by a negotiation to be hereafter entered into between the High Powers and the two contracting parties.

IV. The contracting Powers engage to pursue the salutary work of the pacification of Greece, upon the bases laid down in the preceding Articles, and to furnish, without the least delay, their representatives at Constantinople with all the instructions which are required for the execution of the Treaty which they now sign.

V. The contracting Powers will not seek, in these arrangements, any augmentation of territory, any exclusive influence, or any commercial advantage for their subjects, which those of every other nation may not equally obtain.

VI. The arrangements for reconciliation and peace which shall be definitely agreed upon between the contending parties, shall be guaranteed by those of the signing

Powers who may judge it expedient or possible to contract that obligation. The operation and the effects of such guarantee shall become the subject of future stipulation between the High Powers.

VII. The present Treaty shall be ratified, and the ratifications shall be exchanged in 2 months, or sooner if possible. . . .

[Signed by Viscount Dudley, the Prince de Polignac, and Prince Lieven.]

Additional [and Secret] Article: In case the Ottoman Porte should not, within the space of one month, accept the mediation which is to be proposed to it, the high contracting parties agree upon the following measures:

I. It shall be declared to the Porte . . . that the inconveniences and evils described . . . as inseparable from the state of things which has, for six years, existed in the East, and the termination of which, by the means at the command of the . . . Porte, appears to be still distant, impose upon the high contracting parties the necessity of taking immediate measures for forming a connexion with the Greeks. It is understood that this shall be effected by establishing commercial relations with the Greeks, and by sending to and receiving from them for this purpose Consular Agents. . . .

II. If, within the said term of one month, the Porte does not accept the Armistice proposed . . . or if the Greeks refuse to carry it into execution, the . . . Powers shall declare to either of the contending parties which may be disposed to continue hostilities, or to both of them if necessary, that the said High Powers intend to exert all the means which circumstances may suggest to their prudence, for the purpose of obtaining the immediate effects of the Armistice of which they desire the execution, by preventing, as far as possible, all collision between the contending parties . . . and . . . the . . . Powers will jointly exert all their efforts to accomplish the object of such Armistice, without however taking any part in the hostilities between the two contending parties. Immediately after the signature of the present Additional Article, the . . . Powers will . . . transmit to the Admirals commanding their respective squadrons in the Levant conditional instructions in conformity to the arrangements above described.

III. Finally, if, contrary to all expectation, these measures do not prove sufficient to procure the adoption of the propositions . . . the . . . Powers will nevertheless continue to pursue the work of pacification, on the bases upon which they have agreed. . . .

586. Wellington's Memorandum on British relations with France, 14 Aug. 1830

(*Wellington Despatches, Correspondence & Memoranda*, VII (1878), pp. 162–169.)

The reactionary Charles X violated the Constitution in July 1830 by issuing ordinances which dissolved the Chamber of Deputies, changed the electoral system so as to give the landed aristocracy a virtual monopoly of political power within the Legislature, ordered new elections in September, and destroyed the liberty of the Press. Three days of civil war in Paris followed; Charles X was deposed, and Louis Philippe, duke of Orleans, was invited to become king.

I have perused with the utmost attention all that passed upon making our different arrangements and treaties with France, and it is quite clear that the existing state of affairs was not foreseen at the time, and was not provided for by any of them. . . .

There can be no doubt . . . that it is with the *legitimate and constitutional monarch* of France that our treaties were made. . . .

It is quite obvious . . . that the insurrection at Paris which occasioned the abdication was caused by the Ordonnances of the 25th July. These instruments are inconsistent with, and a violation of the *constitutional laws* which all the treaties and declarations of the Allies consider to be a part of the system recognised by them as the *constitutional and legitimate* monarchy of France. The sovereign who proclaimed these Ordonnances can claim no rights under the 2nd article of the Treaty, and the Allies have no duties to perform towards Charles X under that article.

It remains to be considered how far we are bound by our treaties to act in concert with our Allies in respect to the course which we shall pursue upon this occasion. There is no doubt that it is desirable so to act if possible. But I will first consider how far the obligations of our treaties carry us.

There can be no doubt that the resistance to the Ordonnances of King Charles X, however improper and unjustifiable the conduct of the King and his Ministers, was an arranged plan, formed and executed by the old enemies of this country and of Europe, and by the revolutionary party. What has happened is the revolution acted over again by many of the same characters, the use of the same means, the same symbols, and the adoption of nearly the same measures. . . . The measures and the course pursued are the same, and if persevered in, or rather if not changed, will certainly affect the interior of France ultimately in the same manner; or in the words of the Treaty, will 'convulse France, and thereby endanger the repose of other States'. There will be a civil or a foreign war, possibly both, if the latter should precede the former, and all Europe will be more or less involved.

In the meantime the Liberal party in every country in Europe will be in operation against the Government and under the protection of France.

These are undoubtedly the dangers upon which it was the intention of that part of the second Article of the Treaty of Paris, that the Allies should deliberate *among themselves*, as well as with His Most Christian Majesty, and upon which it would be desirable that the four Courts, parties to the Treaty, should take their course in concert.

But it must be observed that the distance between them is very great, and that much time must elapse before any real consultation or concert can take place; that the progress of events is most rapid, and that no man can calculate upon those which may occur in the six weeks, or even twice that time, which must elapse before there could be any real consultation and decision by the four Allied Courts.

In the existing state of the House of Bourbon, the Duc d'Orléans, whether as King or Regent, is the only person to whom the four Courts could look to conduct the government of France if the choice could rest with them. All may wish, and some might be disposed to stipulate that he had continued in his office of Lieutenant-General, or had assumed that of Regent, and guardian of the Duc de Bordeaux. But it cannot be denied that, whether in one office or the other, the Duc d'Orléans is the person under whose administration of the Government the best hopes of continued peace are afforded under existing circumstances.

Nobody can believe that the revolutionary evils which I have above described would not be aggravated, the authority of the Duc d'Orléans injured, and the confidence of the country in him diminished, by any declaration of the four Allied Courts against him, and by any doubt or hesitation in recognising his authority, particularly by his Majesty and the Government of this country.

The evil hanging over Europe as the consequence of the transactions of the last fortnight will come soon enough. I cannot hope that any step that we or our Allies can take will prevent it.

It is obvious that the only feeble hope we have of maintaining the peace of the world is in the moderation of the character of the Duc d'Orléans. He will endeavour to preserve peace, and he may succeed if he has strength to govern the country. But he can have strength only by the countenance, and the protection which that countenance can give him, of the Great Powers of Europe.

It appears to me, then, that good policy requires that we should recognise the Duc d'Orléans as King at an early period after notification of his authority, allowing a reasonable period for deliberation.

I think that it is expected by the Ambassadors of our Allies that we should take this course. We ought to consult with them, although we should persevere in taking the course proposed. I am convinced that none of them will object to it, and that our example will be followed by every Court in Europe. Indeed, we may be anticipated by some. . . .

587. Wellington's Memorandum on the Greek question [Nov. 1830]

(*Wellington Despatches, Correspondence & Memoranda*, VII (1878), pp. 335–344.)

The policy of the British Government has invariably been to prevent the overthrow of the Turkish Power in Europe, and the substitution for it of a Russian Power or a Power under Russian influence at Constantinople. This policy has prevailed down to a very late period indeed; and has occasioned at different periods the exercise of the influence, and at some, of the power of the Government, to reconcile the Emperor of Russia with the Porte; and in some instances, as in the years 1811, 1812, this influence was exercised in a very beneficial manner, even to the Emperor of Russia, to make peace between those two Powers.

It must here be observed that the interest which the British Government feel in the maintenance of the Turkish Power in Europe is common to the rest of the world, Russia excepted. Neither France, nor Spain, nor Portugal, nor the Netherlands, nor Austria, nor even Prussia could see without alarm the establishment at Constantinople of a Russian Power, or one under Russian influence; and in this as well as in many other respects our well understood interests are consistent with those of the rest of the world.

In the year 1821 the state of affairs in Spain and Italy, and the attention which the Allies paid to the troubles in those countries, occasioned a rebellion in Wallachia, Moldavia, and Greece against the government of the Porte. It is useless now to consider the causes of these rebellions or the measures adopted by the Porte to get the better of them. These measures were considered by the Emperor of Russia to be inconsistent with the treaties between his Government and the Porte; and the British Government again exerted its influence, as well in Russia as at the Porte, to put an end to these differences, to bring the Porte to a reasonable sense of the obligations by which the Ottoman Government was bound towards that of Russia; and to prevent hostilities between the parties, which might, in their result, have disturbed the general peace of Europe. Among these treaties is one which gives the Emperor of Russia a right of protection of the rites of the Christian religion in Greece; and it was with reason apprehended that the Emperor of Russia might avail himself of some of the causes of complaint which the Porte had undeniably given him, to carry on war against the Porte; that he would become *ipso facto* the ally and protector of the Greeks; that the war thus kindled might become general on account of the interest which other Powers would naturally feel in the result to be expected, and their jealousy of the establishment of a Greek Power in the Mediterranean under the influence and acting in the system of Russia. Under these circumstances the insurrection in Greece from its commencement excited the utmost interest throughout Europe; and particularly in the councils of this country. But this Government invariably felt an interest that the Porte might be able to re-establish its authority in Greece. We were neutral in the contest; and our neutrality was favourable to the cause of the Greeks. But that was not to be attributed to us. We were fairly and *bonâ fide* neutral, and declined to be parties to any measures which tended to coerce the Porte to come to terms with the Greeks. The following words are to be found in a Despatch from Mr. Canning, dated in the month of September 1822; and from that time forwards till the month of October 1825, when Mr. Stratford Canning was sent upon his mission to Constantinople, I assert that, notwithstanding that our active endeavours were used to induce the Porte to do justice to the Emperor of Russia, in relation to his demands regarding the Principalities of Wallachia and Moldavia, not a word was uttered to the Porte in relation to its sovereignty over the Greeks, excepting with a view to mitigate the severity of the punishment of rebels, and the extremity of violence in carrying on the war.

'Our object, in common with our Allies, has been and is, to maintain peace among nations; aware that a new war, on whatever pretext or in whatever quarter it might be kindled, might presently involve all Europe in its consequences. Our object in respect to ourselves has been to avoid all interference in the internal concerns of any nation; an interference not authorised in our case by the positive rights or obligations of treaty, nor justified as we think (except when treaty or some very special circumstances justify it) by the principles of international law'.

Between Turks and Greeks it is said 'we have neither the right to interfere nor the means of effectual interference. Whatever might be our wishes, our prejudices, our sympathies, we were bound in political justice to respect in this case that rational independence, which in case of civil commotion we should expect to be respected in our own case. Nor was it for a Christian Government, which rules in its distant possessions over a population of millions of Mahomedans, to proclaim a war of religion.'

In the discussions between Greeks and Turks '*we have not the pretence of a right to interfere*'.

In the year 1825 the late Emperor Alexander having been dissatisfied with the result of certain Conferences held at St. Petersburg with the Ministers of his Allies (which Conferences the Ambassador from this country did not attend), and of the consequent negotiations at Constantinople with the Porte, ceased to have any communication with his Allies upon the still unsettled questions between his Imperial Majesty and the Porte, which had grown out of the rebellion in Moldavia and Wallachia, and in Greece. He had before ceased to have any communication with his Majesty's Government upon those questions; and it was generally understood and apprehended in the autumn of 1825 that his Imperial Majesty was preparing to take these unsettled questions into his own hands, and to push them to all extremities with the Porte.

I have since had reason to believe, and indeed to know, that much more was apprehended from the late Emperor Alexander than his Imperial Majesty ever intended to carry into execution. But this is certain, that the Emperor abstained from all communications with his Allies; that he was communicating with the Porte alone through his own Chargé d'Affaires singly; and that his military preparations were all made for the result, and that they were of the most formidable description.

In this state of things Mr. Stratford Canning was sent on his Embassy to the Porte. The leaders of the Greeks, and I believe their agent in this country, had been in communication with his Majesty's Secretary of State, and had expressed an anxious desire that his Majesty should endeavour by his good offices to mediate their reconciliation with the Porte; and Mr. Stratford Canning was instructed to warn the Porte of the state of things in Russia, of the dangerous position in which it was placed, and to urge the Ottoman Government to listen to the terms of peace which should reach them through his Majesty's Government.

This was the state of affairs when the Alexander Emperor died in the month of December 1825, when I was sent on a mission to St. Petersburg to congratulate the present Emperor in the name of his Majesty, on his accession to the throne.

His Majesty thought proper to avail himself of the opportunity which the mission of myself to St. Petersburg afforded to endeavour to prevent those hostilities which had occasioned such apprehensions throughout Europe in the year 1825.

The present Emperor of Russia, with that respect for his lamented brother which his great actions and the uniform tenor of his life had merited, had at an early period of his reign declared his determination to carry into execution all the measures and designs of his predecessor; and it was naturally apprehended throughout Europe that the designs respecting the Government of the Porte which had occasioned so much apprehension were those which his Imperial Majesty had in view.

. . . I was ordered to inform the Government of his Imperial Majesty of the instructions given to Mr. Stratford Canning, during a period in which the Government of this country had not been in communication with the late Emperor upon his discussions with Turkey; that I was to express his Majesty's desire to concert his measures upon this subject with the Emperor of Russia, on condition however that there was to be no war, to which his Majesty could never be a party; or even a party in negotiations which were to end in war.

The Government of this country, of that day, did not admit the right of the Emperor of Russia to go to war to force a reconciliation with the Greeks, much less to force the admission of a mediation between the Porte and its revolted subjects; and I must do the Emperor Nicholas the justice to say that he was as little disposed to assert or to exercise that right as his Majesty's Government were to admit it.

'Great care must be taken not to pledge ourselves to the acceptance of it (that is, the joint mediation) without the previous consent of the Turks, lest their refusal of it should be assumed by the Emperor of Russia as a ground of offence and cause of war. A war by Russia against the Porte would be a war of ambition and conquest, and it is not with respect to a war of that nature that England could take counsel with Russia. . . .'

. . . Although his Imperial Majesty was not disposed to go to war to force the Porte to come to an arrangement with the Greeks, or to force the Porte to admit his Majesty's mediation between the Porte and its revolted subjects, there were other questions depending between his Imperial Majesty and the Porte in regard to which his Imperial Majesty was determined to have justice done to him without delay.

Some of these questions regarded the Principalities of Moldavia and Wallachia, upon examining which I was under the necessity of admitting that the Emperor was in the right and the Porte in the wrong, contrary to the previous determination of his Majesty's Government, passed certainly without seeing the documents which were laid before me.

There were other questions arising out of the Treaty of Bucharest in 1812, which up to 1826 had never been settled, and which his Imperial Majesty had determined that he would forthwith bring to a conclusion.

It was under these circumstances that the Protocol of April 1826 was negotiated. It is obvious that the object in taking up the subject at all was to prevent the peace of Europe from being disturbed.

It was found that the Emperor of Russia had two important negotiations in hand, for the termination of one of which he had named a day, after which, if the negotiations were not terminated to his satisfaction, his troops were to march. In this negotiation he was indubitably in the right. There was, behind, another negotiation to be conducted by Plenipotentiaries to be assembled within the Russian frontier; which Plenipotentiaries actually met afterwards at Akerman. Either negotiation might have led to war between Russia and the Porte, not for Russian aggrandisement but for the redress of grievances which the Porte had omitted to redress, notwithstanding the solemn promises made that they should be redressed.

A war with the Porte undertaken on any ground would undoubtedly have placed the Greek case in the hands of the Emperor of Russia. The Greeks would have become his Imperial Majesty's Allies, and he would have stipulated for them what he pleased at the termination of such war.

It was this which had created all the anxiety throughout Europe during the discussion of these Russian questions at the Porte.

The Protocol put an end to these apprehensions. It put forward reasonable terms of accommodation between the Porte and its revolted subjects; terms founded upon the actual offers of the latter made to Mr. Stratford Canning; and which were advantageous to the Porte, if it was true that the Porte was incapable of making the conquest of the Morea and the Greek provinces.

This instrument at the same time took Greece out of the chances of war. The Emperor of Russia and his Majesty were equally bound by this instrument always to consider these terms of accommodation between the Porte and its revolted subjects, as those to be pressed upon the Porte by the mediation of one or both of the Powers as opportunities might offer; and both engaged to avail themselves of every opportunity to exert their influence, whether jointly or separately, to obtain this settlement.

Thus then the probability of the disturbance of the peace of Europe was what first embarked the late Government in these negotiations respecting Greece; they were persevered in with a view to prevent that peace from being disturbed; and this instrument, the Protocol, actually succeeded in preventing the peace of Europe from being disturbed, excepting as far as was necessary for the settlement of the questions which remained unsettled between Russia and the Porte. . . .

SCOTLAND

COUNTY AND BURGH REPRESENTATION

Based on the map in E. and A. G. Porritt, *The Unreformed House of Commons*, 1909, Vol. II.

Bute and Caithness	These six counties were arranged in
Clackmannan and Kinross	pairs at the Union, each to elect a
Nairn and Cromarty	member to alternate Parliaments

The sixty-five Royal Burghs, Edinburgh excepted, were at the Union arranged in fourteen groups, as numbered, to elect the fourteen burgh members

IRELAND

COUNTY AND BOROUGH REPRESENTATION
Based on the map in E. and A. G. Porritt, *The Unreformed House of Commons*, 1909, Vol. II.
Boroughs underlined sent representatives to the United Parliament after 1800

THE ROYAL FAMILY

Augusta of Saxe-Gotha＝Frederick Lewis, Prince of Wales
(1719–1772)　(1707–1751)

(1761)
George III　＝Charlotte Sophia of Mecklenburg-Strelitz　William Henry, duke＝Maria,
(1738–1820)　(1744–1818)　of Gloucester　Countess Dowager
(1743–1805)　of Waldegrave
(1739–1807)

(1795)
(1) George IV (1762–1830)＝Caroline (1768–1821), d. of Charles William Ferdinand,
duke of Brunswick (1735–1806)

(1816)
Charlotte　＝Leopold of Saxe-Coburg-Saalfeld,
(1796–1817)　later, king of the Belgians (1790–1865)

(1791)
(2) Frederick, duke of York (1763–1827)＝Frederica (1767–1820), d. of Frederick William II
of Prussia

(1818)
(3) William IV (1765–1837)＝Adelaide of Saxe-Meiningen (1792–1849)

(1797)
(4) Charlotte (1766–1828)＝Frederick I, king of Wurtemberg (1754–1816)

(1818)
(5) Edward, duke of Kent＝Victoria of Saxe-Coburg-Saalfeld (Prince Leopold's sister)
(1767–1820)　(1786–1861)

(1840)
Queen Victoria＝Albert of Saxe-Coburg and Gotha (1819–1861)
(1819–1901)

(6) Augusta (1768–1840)

(1818)
(7) Elizabeth (1770–1840)＝Frederick of Hesse-Homburg (1769–1829)

(1815)
(8) Ernest, duke of Cumberland (1771–1851)＝Frederica of Mecklenburg-Strelitz
(king of Hanover, 1837)　(1778–1841)

(9) Augustus, duke of Sussex (1773–1843)

(1818)
(10) Adolphus, duke of Cambridge (1774–1850)＝Augusta of Hesse-Cassel (1797–1889)

(1816)
(11) Mary (1776–1857)＝William Frederick, duke of Gloucester (1776–1834)

(12) Sophia (1777–1848)

(13) Octavius (1779–1783)

(14) Alfred (1780–1782)

(15) Amelia (1783–1810)

THE ROYAL FAMILY

INDEX TO TEXTS

The figures refer to the numbered documents, not to the pages. Acts of Parliament are grouped under 'Statutes', Reports of Parliamentary Committees under 'Reports', Parliamentary Debates under 'Parliament'. Statistics and Treaties are also indexed together. Letters are indexed under both the name of the writer and that of the addressee.

ARCHBISHOP HOLGATE'S
GRAMMAR SCHOOL, YORK